An Approach to Literature

to Literature

FOURTH EDITION

Cleanth Brooks
YALE UNIVERSITY

John Thibaut Purser
SOUTHEASTERN LOUISIANA COLLEGE

Robert Penn Warren
YALE UNIVERSITY

ACKNOWLEDGMENTS

SHERWOOD ANDERSON, "I'm a Fool," from *Horses and Men.* Copyright 1923. Published by the Viking Press.

W. H. AUDEN, "Lay Your Sleeping Head," from *The Collected Poetry of W. H. Auden,* copyright © 1940 by W. H. Auden. Reprinted by permission of Random House, Inc. and Faber and Faber, Ltd.; and "Robert Frost," from *The Dyer's Hand,* copyright © 1962 by W. H. Auden, by permission of Random House, Inc.

ISAAC BABEL, "Kronkin's Prisoner," from *The Collected Stories.* Copyright 1955 by Criterion Books, Inc. By permission of the publishers.

JACQUES BARZUN, "In Favor of Capital Punishment," reprinted from *The American Scholar,* Volume 31, Number 2, Spring, 1962. Copyright © 1962 by the United Chapters of Phi Beta Kappa. By permission of the publishers.

JOHN PEALE BISHOP, "Experience of the West," from *The Southern Review,* 1946; and "Homage to Hemingway," from *The Collected Essays of John Peale Bishop.* Copyright 1948 by Charles Scribner's Sons; used by permission of the publishers.

DANIEL J. BOORSTIN, "From Hero to Celebrity," from *The Image: Or What Happened to the American Dream.* Copyright © 1961 by Daniel J. Boorstin. Reprinted by permission of Atheneum Publishers.

ROBERT BRIDGES, "A Passer-by," from *The Shorter Poems of Robert Bridges,* by permission of the Clarendon Press, Oxford.

JIM BROSNAN, "En Route to Chicago," from *The Long Season.* Copyright © 1960 by James P. Brosnan. Reprinted with the permission of Harper & Row, Publishers.

ART BUCHWALD, "Let's See Who Salutes," from *Don't Forget to Write.* Copyright © 1958, 1959 by Art Buchwald. By permission of The World Publishing Company.

JOHN CHEEVER, "O Youth and Beauty!" By permission of the author. Originally, 1954, in *The New Yorker.*

ANTON CHEKHOV, "The Lottery Ticket," from *The Wife and Other Stories,* translated by Constance Garnett, by permission of The Macmillan Company, New York, Mr. David Garnett and Chatto & Windus, London.

SIR WINSTON CHURCHILL, "The Deliverance of Dunkirk," from *Their Finest Hour.* Reprinted by permission of and arrangement with Houghton Mifflin Company, the authorized publishers.

JOHN COLLIER, "Wet Saturday." Copyright 1938 by John Collier. Reprinted by permission of Harold Matson Company, Inc. Originally appeared in *The New Yorker.*

JOSEPH CONRAD, "The Lagoon," from *Tales of Unrest,* by permission of J. M. Dent & Sons, Ltd.

STEPHEN CRANE, "An Episode of War," from *Stephen Crane: An Omnibus* edited by Robert Wooster Stallman, published 1952 by Alfred A. Knopf, Inc. By permission of Alfred A. Knopf, Inc.

WALTER DE LA MARE, "Silver," from *Collected Poems.* Copyright, 1920, by Holt, Rinehart & Winston, Inc. Copyright, 1948, by Walter de la Mare. Used by permission of the publishers.

EMILY DICKINSON, "These are the days when Birds come back"; "The Sky is low—the Clouds are mean"; "The Mountains stood in Haze"; "I could not prove the Years had feet"; " 'Hope' is the thing with feathers"; "Success is counted sweetest"; "Our journey had advanced"; "I Years had been from Home"; "Her final Summer was it"; "Because I could not stop for Death"; "I heard a Fly buzz—when I died," from *The Poems of Emily Dickinson,* edited by Thomas H. Johnson. Copyright 1951, 1955 by the President and Fellows of Harvard College. Reprinted by permission of the publishers, The Belknap Press of Harvard University Press.

RICHARD EBERHART, "I Walked Out to the Graveyard," from *Collected Poems 1930-1960.* © Richard Eberhart, 1960. Reprinted by permission of Oxford University Press, Inc. and Chatto & Windus, Ltd.

T. S. ELIOT, "Literature and the Modern World, 1935." This essay appeared in *American Prefaces* in 1935 and is used by arrangement with Mr. T. S. Eliot. "Murder in the Cathedral," from *Murder in the Cathedral,* copyright, 1935, by Harcourt, Brace & World, Inc. By permission of the publishers and Faber and Faber, Ltd. *Caution:* Professionals and amateurs are hereby warned that *Murder in the Cathedral,* being fully protected under the copyright laws of the United States of America, the British Empire, including the Dominion of Canada, and all other countries of the Copyright Union, is subject to a royalty. All rights, including professional, amateur, motion pictures, recitation, public reading, radio broadcasting and the rights of translation into foreign languages are strictly reserved. Amateurs may produce this play upon payment of a royalty of $35.00 for each performance one week be-

An Approach to Literature

 New York

APPLETON-CENTURY-CROFTS

DIVISION OF MEREDITH PUBLISHING COMPANY

fore the play is to be given to Samuel French, at 25 W. 45 St., New York 19, N. Y., or, 7623 Sunset Boulevard, Hollywood 46, Calif., or, if in Canada, to Samuel French (Canada) Ltd., 480 University Ave., Toronto, Ont.

WILLIAM FAULKNER, "Spotted Horses," by permission of Morton Goldman.

F. SCOTT FITZGERALD, "The Rich Boy," from *All the Sad Young Men;* copyright 1926 by Charles Scribner's Sons; used by permission of the publishers.

ROBERT FROST, "The Star-Splitter"; and "The Need of Being Versed in Country Things," from *New Hampshire.* Copyright, 1923, by Holt, Rinehart & Winston, Inc. Copyright, 1951, by Robert Frost. Used by permission of the publishers. "A Leaf Treader;" "To Earthward;" "Come In," from *Complete Poems of Robert Frost.* Copyright 1923 by Holt, Rinehart & Winston, Inc. Copyright 1936, 1942 by Robert Frost. Copyright renewed © 1964 by Lesley Frost Ballantine. By permission of Holt, Rinehart & Winston, Inc. "The Oven Bird," from *Mountain Interval.* Copyright 1916, 1921, by Holt, Rinehart & Winston, Inc. Copyright 1944, by Robert Frost. By permission of the publishers. "The Wood-Pile," from *North of Boston.* By permission of Holt, Rinehart & Winston, Inc.

THOMAS HARDY, "Neutral Tones;" "On an Invitation to the United States;" and "The Convergence of the Twain," from *Collected Poems.* By permission of The Macmillan Company, and by arrangement with the Hardy Estate and Collier-Macmillan, Ltd., London. "The Three Strangers," from *Wessex Tales.* By permission of Harper & Row, Publishers, the Trustees of the Hardy Estate and The Macmillan Company.

ERNEST HEMINGWAY, "In Another Country;" and "The Killers," from *Men Without Women.* Copyright 1926, 1927 by Charles Scribner's Sons; used by permission of the publishers.

A. E. HOUSMAN, "Bredon Hill;" "The True Lover;" and "The Tree of Man," from *A Shropshire Lad* (1896), by permission of The Society of Authors as the literary representative of the Estate of the late A. E. Housman, and Jonathan Cape, Ltd., publishers of A. E. Housman's *Collected Poems.*

RANDALL JARRELL, "Burning the Letters;" and "Eighth Air Force," from *Losses,* copyright, 1948, by Harcourt, Brace & World, Inc. By permission of the publishers. "Some Lines from Whitman," from *Poetry and the Age,* Vintage Edition, copyright 1953 by Randall Jarrell, by permission of Alfred A. Knopf, Inc.

JAMES JOYCE, "Araby;" and "Clay," from Dubliners, included in *The Portable James Joyce.* Copyright 1946, 1947 by The Viking Press. By permission of The Viking Press.

RUDYARD KIPLING, "Danny Deever," from *Departmental Ditties and Ballads and Barrack-Room Ballads.* Reprinted by permission of Mrs. George Bambridge, Doubleday & Company, Inc. and The Macmillan Company of Canada, Ltd.

JOSEPH WOOD KRUTCH, "On Walden Two," from *The Measure of Man,* copyright 1953, 1954 by Joseph Wood Krutch, reprinted by permission of the publishers, The Bobbs-Merrill Company, Inc.

D. H. LAWRENCE, "Love on the Farm," from *Collected Poems.* Copyright, 1929, by Jonathan Cape and Harrison Smith, Inc. Reprinted by permission of The Viking Press. "The House Dealer's Daughter," from *England My England.* Copyright 1922 by Thomas Seltzer, Inc., 1950 by Frieda Lawrence. By permission of The Viking Press.

ROBERT LOWELL, "Christmas Eve under Hooker's Statue," from *Lord Weary's Castle,* copyright, 1944, 1946, by Robert Lowell. Reprinted by permission of Harcourt, Brace & World, Inc. By permission of the publishers. "Colonel Shaw and the Massachusetts '54th," from *Life Studies,* copyright © 1956, 1959, by Robert Lowell. By permission of Farrar, Straus & Company, Inc.

ANDREW LYTLE, "Jerico, Jerico, Jerico," *The Southern Review,* 1936.

DWIGHT MACDONALD, "Ernest Hemingway," from *Against the American Grain,* copyright © by Dwight MacDonald; by permission of Random House, Inc.

ARCHIBALD MACLEISH, "You, Andrew Marvell," from *Poems, 1924-1933,* reprinted by permission of and arrangement with Houghton Mifflin Company, the authorized publishers.

THOMAS MANN, "Disorder and Early Sorrow," from *Stories of Three Decades.* By permission of Alfred A. Knopf, Inc.

EDGAR LEE MASTERS, "Lucinda Matlock," from *Spoon River Anthology.* By permission of the Estate of Edgar Lee Masters.

W. SOMERSET MAUGHAM, "The Circle," from *Collected Plays of W. Somerset Maugham, Vol. IV.* Copyright 1921 by W. Somerset Maugham. By permission of Mr. Maugham, Doubleday & Company, Inc. and William Heinemann, Ltd. Caution: Especial notice should be taken that the possession of this book without a valid contract for production first having been obtained, confers no right or license to produce the play publicly or in private for gain or charity. In its present form *The Circle* is dedicated to the reading public only, and no performance, representation, production, recitation, or public reading may be given except by special arrangement with Baker's Plays, Boston 16, Massachusetts. The royalty for presentation of *The Circle* by amateurs will be quoted upon application.

GUY DE MAUPASSANT, "La Mère Sauvage," from *The Odd Number.* By permission of Harper & Row, Publishers.

MARY MCCARTHY, "Artists in Uniform," from *On the Contrary,* by permission of Farrar, Straus & Company, Inc. Copyright 1953, 1961 by Mary McCarthy.

CHARLOTTE MEW, "The Farmer's Bride," from *The Farmer's Bride and Other Poems.* Published by Gerald Duckworth & Co., Ltd.

GEORGE MILBURN, "The Apostate," from *No More Trumpets.* Copyright 1933 by Harcourt, Brace & World, Inc.

JOSEPH MITCHELL, "Lady Olga," from *McSorley's Wonderful Saloon.* Copyright 1938, 1939, 1940, 1941, 1942, 1943, by Joseph Mitchell. By permission of the Publishers, Duell, Sloan and Pearce, Inc.

SAMUEL ELIOT MORISON, "The Young Man Washington," from *By Land and by Sea,* copyright, 1953 by Priscilla B. Morison; by permission of Alfred A. Knopf, Inc.

OGDEN NASH, "Very Like a Whale," from *Many Long Years Ago.* Copyright 1935 by Ogden Nash. By permission of Little, Brown & Co.

FRANK O'CONNOR, "Legal Aid," from *The Stories of Frank O'Connor,* copyright 1951 by Frank O'Connor, by permission of Alfred A. Knopf, Inc. Canadian rights by permission of Harold Matson Co., Inc., and A. D. Peters.

LUIGI PIRANDELLO, "The Jar," from *Better Think Twice About It.* Copyright 1934, E. P. Dutton & Co., Inc. By permission of the Estate of Luigi Pirandello.

KATHERINE ANNE PORTER, "Noon Wine," from *Pale Horse, Pale Rider,* copyright 1936, 1937, 1939 by Katherine Anne Porter. By permission of Harcourt, Brace & World, Inc.

J. F. POWERS, "The Valiant Woman," from *Prince of Darkness and Other Stories.* Copyright 1943, 1944, 1946, 1947 by J. F. Powers. By permission of Doubleday & Company, Inc.

~~~~~~~PREFACE~~

An Approach to Literature was published in 1936. That first edition was a natural outgrowth of work in the classroom. The revisions made in subsequent editions, including this fourth edition, spring from the continuing classroom experience of the editors as well as from the numerous criticisms and suggestions made by teachers who have been using this book.

In preparing this revision, we have not hesitated to discard methods that we have come to believe are limiting or to add approaches that put the work in fuller perspective. In the fiction, for example, we have adopted an entirely new method—one that we have, however, tried in the classroom. The method is to have the student move into the study of fiction with something of the same concerns, *mutatis mutandis*, with which an author moves into his writing of a story. So instead of beginning with the story as formally organized in terms of plot, etc., we begin with such key topics as "Episode and Fictional Point" or "The Tale: Feeling and Idea" or "Personality: Action and Idea." Proceeding from such a base, the student easily and naturally moves toward a comprehension of fictional structure.

We have also been concerned to relate the fiction to the other sections of the book. In treating individual stories, we have undertaken to lay the groundwork for discussing tragedy and comedy, irony and pathos, and similar concepts that have to be dealt with in the study of poetry and drama. We have been at pains, too, to select for comparative study certain stories that are related in theme, method, or tone. The relations among certain stories in the earlier groups are worthy of study, but the especially significant relations of this sort are most often found between stories in the earlier groups and those which appear without any editorial comment in the long Section VIII. For instance, "An Episode of War," by Stephen Crane, in Section I, offers excellent opportunities for comparison with "Kronkin's Prisoner," by Isaac Babel, in Section VIII. Indeed, we should like to point out as a source of fruitful exercises the use that may be made of the "pool" stories of Section VIII in conjunction with stories of the earlier sections that have been studied with editorial comment. Using the latter for contrast or comparison, the teacher may, as he likes, develop his own classroom interpretation of the stories in Section VIII.

As for the selections themselves, of the thirty-three stories and novelettes, ten are new to this book. Among the ten one finds the names of brilliant younger masters of the form such as James Purdy, John Updike, and John Cheever.

The poetry section has been carefully revised, and three new features may deserve comment. First, we have geared some of the examples of the Critical Essay (in the general division of Discursive Prose) to particular poets exhibited here at length; for instance, we represent Randall Jarrell on Walt Whitman and W. H. Auden on Robert Frost. Second, in order to indicate even more emphatically to the student that a poem need not be studied in splendid isolation but can profitably be viewed as part of a continuing, organic body of work—the outgrowth of the experience of a particular man—we have treated two poets, Keats and Frost, in considerable depth, and have tried to indicate characteristic themes and methods as a basis for whatever additional discussion of personal style and philosophy the teacher may feel moved to make. Third, we have provided, without any editorial comment, a little "selected edition" of the work of another poet, Emily Dickinson, for the student to study in the same spirit. It could provide the subject for a paper to be written on his completion of the poetry section.

The division called Discursive Prose, which includes biographical and historical writing, has, like the division of fiction, been organized in terms of a principle new to this book: the selections now range between two extremes. At one end of the scale we have essays like "Dream Children," which lie close to the frontiers of fiction and poetry; at the other, essays that are primarily analytical or argumentative. This principle has necessitated, of course, a large number of new selections. Of the twenty-six items under this general head, thirteen are new; and almost all the editorial material is new.

In making our selections we have tried to support, with new material, such older pieces as those of Arnold and Eliot, dealing with problems of our culture and civilization. We have added an essay by the eminent psychologist, B. F. Skinner, "Freedom and the Control of Men," which treats, with dramatic clarity, the problem of moral responsibility and psychological conditioning. This challenging essay serves as a backdrop for many of the other essays on values in society. We have included discussions of special problems of American life by Mary McCarthy and by Daniel Boorstin, and, with reference to the problem of capital punishment, two essays, by William Styron and Jacques Barzun, that constitute a debate. There is what amounts to a second debate provided in the two essays on Hemingway, one by John Peale Bishop (held over from the last edition) and a recent and already famous one by Dwight McDonald. There is also a more general essay, new to this book, on the appeals of fiction. Two essays that bear upon the poetry of Whitman and Frost have already been mentioned. We have retained in this section Plutarch's *Life of Antony* which provides background for Shakespeare's *Antony and Cleopatra*.

In the division of drama we have dropped one item which, by all reports, had dated badly, and have added three to make a total of seven full-scale plays. This distinguished group provides a rich spectrum of dramatic possibilities. Sophocles' *Oedipus Rex* (presented here in a brilliant translation) is not only in itself thrilling and teachable, but raises some of the most fundamental problems of tragedy. Over against it may be set three other plays which, in their several ways, are tragedies or which deal with tragic situations—*Antony and Cleopatra, Hedda Gabler,* and *Murder in the Cathedral.* Maugham's *The Circle* is a standard comedy which may serve as foil or background for the comic, ironic, and satiric elements in *The Skin of Our Teeth,* and even those in *Saint Joan, Hedda Gabler,* and *Antony and Cleopatra.*

The possibilities for comparison, contrast, and thematic relationship provided by these seven plays are many. One notes, for example, that Hedda, Cleopatra, and Joan are all "wilful women"—as also is Lady Kitty of *The Circle,* for she, too, has flouted the ordinary pattern of life. Or, to take another example, two of the plays are specifically about sainthood. Or again, *Antony and Cleopatra* and *Saint Joan* are in some sense "history plays"—and even *Hedda Gabler,* in a more oblique fashion, deals with fundamental problems of history.

It is impossible, of course, in making a careful revision, to separate the processes of rethinking and rewriting. One necessarily implies the other. As we sought to consider afresh the makeup of this book, we soon found ourselves casting a very cold eye on every line which we ourselves had previously written. This process sometimes amounted to a penitential exercise; and often it led to embarrassed rewriting as well as rethinking. But we hope that in the last twelve years we have learned something to justify the rethinking and rewriting—enough, in any case, to make this a better book. It will be more accurate if we amend the last phrase to read: "to help make this a better book." For if it is a better book, much of the credit must go to the many teachers who have used the book, who have given careful thought to its defects and virtues, and who have taken the trouble to tell us what they think.

C. B.

J. T. P.

R. P. W.

~~~CONTENTS~

DISCURSIVE PROSE

An Approach to Literature

GENERAL INTRODUCTION

Why Do People Read?

Why do people read? The usual answer to such a question is: "For information or amusement." But does this reply give a very clear answer to the further question: "Why do people read literature"?

People do read *Who's Who,* or *The Boston Cook Book,* or a *History of France* for information. But what sort of information do we find in Keats' "Ode on a Grecian Urn"? If any information at all is contained there, it is surely not the kind of information that one finds in a book of chemistry. Literature, in general, does contain much information, especially information about history, sociology, and psychology; but even the inclusion of this sort of information will hardly in itself justify our reading of literature. Such information is much more readily available elsewhere, and in a much more systematic form.

People read books and magazines, novels and stories for amusement. But the word *amusement* is very vague. Clearly there are many kinds of enjoyment. There is the enjoyment found in *Hamlet,* and that found in a western. The two kinds of enjoyment have certain elements in common, but there are important differences. The aim of this book is to indicate, little by little, some of these differences. The reading of good literature does give pleasure—a very keen pleasure—but there is no use in saying that Hamlet gives a "higher" pleasure than the western if we cannot indicate, however fumblingly, what that higher and keener pleasure is.

There is a snobbery often hidden in the statement that literature gives a "higher" pleasure—just as there is in the statement that it is "cultural" or "uplifting." Such a thing as culture exists (sometimes, one feels, in spite of its most vocal proponents), but to appeal to the "cultural effect" as an argument for reading good literature is simply a way of begging the question, unless we can arrive at some notion of what culture is and such a notion is to be arrived at late rather than early. The sceptical student will be quick to point out that the statement that other people have found literature culturally valuable is not quite the same thing as a statement of its value for him. Moreover, if the case for literature is so strong, he is apt to ask why it can't be stated simply and positively.

The case can be stated, but not briefly, for an understanding of the meaning of literature can only come through the study of literature itself. Literature, in one sense, is a product of, and a commentary on, the life process, and we can only get some sense of the meaning of experience by living through it. For the present then, let us content ourselves with a general approach to our question. A liking for literature springs from a liking for life. Literature appeals to us because it enlarges our experience of the world and of ourselves—and in literature these two kinds of enlargement are the same enlargement, for insofar as literature opens a new world for us, and a new view of the old world we have lived in, it also indicates new kinds of response to the world. To state the matter a little differently, any person with a healthy love of life wants to develop, through experience, his own possibilities. The study of literature is one of the things that can lead to the discovery of new dimensions of the self.

What Literature Is

One way to consider the value of literature is to try to determine what it is—what it characteristically tells us. To do this, we may compare the kind of telling we find in a piece of literature—in this case a poem, with the kind of telling we find in several other types of writing dealing with the same material.

Suppose that we take an incident. A man murders a girl with whom he is in love. How may the various accounts of this situation differ? What is the purpose of each of them? How do the literary accounts differ from the practical and factual accounts? Where does literature as literature begin?

Let us consider first the report that the autopsy surgeon would make on the situation; second, the indictment based on the murder; and third, the account which would appear in the daily newspaper.

From the Autopsy Surgeon's Report

Death occurred from the effects of asphyxia, cerebral anemia, and shock. The victim's hair was used for the constricting ligature. Local marks of the ligature were readily discernible: there was some abrasion and a slight ecchymosis in the skin. But I found no obvious lesions in the blood vessels of the neck.

Cyanosis of the head was very slight and there were no pronounced hemorrhages in the galea of the scalp. I should judge that very great compression was effected almost immediately, with compression of the arteries as well as of the veins, and that the superior laryngeal nerve was traumatized with the effect of throwing the victim into profound shock. . . .

The lungs revealed cyanosis, congestion, overaeration, and subpleural petechial hemorrhages. . . .

Legal Indictment

State of ———
——— County
TWENTY-FIRST JUDICIAL
   DISTRICT COURT
   THE GRAND JURORS of the State of ———, duly impanelled and sworn, in and for ——— County in the name and by the authority of the said State upon their oath, find and present:

THAT ONE John Doe late of ——— County, on the 23rd day of January in the year of Our Lord One Thousand Nine Hundred and Twenty-Four, with force and arms, in ——— County, aforesaid, and within the jurisdiction of the Twenty-First Judicial District Court of ———, for the ——— County, did unlawfully, feloniously, with malice aforethought kill and slay one Porphyria Blank by strangulation.

Contrary to the form and the Statutes of the State of ———, in such cases made and provided and against the peace and dignity of the same.

. . . .
District Attorney for the 21st
Judicial District of ———

Local Girl Found Slain by Rejected Lover

Miss Porphyria Blank, 21, daughter of Mr. and Mrs. R. J. Blank, of Barton Park, was found strangled this morning in the cottage owned by John Doe, 25, who was apprehended on the scene of the crime by officers Bailey and Hodge. Doe was found holding the body in his arms, and appeared to be in a stupor, his only reply to repeated questioning being, "I killed her because I loved her."

According to members of the Blank family, Doe had paid attentions to Miss Blank for the last several months, though it was strenuously denied that his regard for Miss Blank was returned. Miss Blank's engagement to Mr. Roger Weston was announced last month. Mr. Weston could not be reached for a statement. Mrs. Blank was prostrated by the news of her daughter's death.

The slain girl disappeared last evening at approximately eleven o'clock from a dinner party given at her parents' home in honor of the approaching wedding. The family became alarmed when it was discovered that she was not in her room, and instituted a search for her about midnight. The police, who were promptly notified, in the course of their search knocked at Mr. Doe's cottage, a building some quarter of a mile from the Blank estate, at five in the morning. Receiving no answer, they forced the door and discovered Doe sitting with the dead girl in his lap. She had apparently been strangled; Dr. A. P. Reynolds, Autopsy Surgeon for the county, stated that, from the condition of the body, death must have occurred at about midnight.

Doe, who has been charged with murder, could give no coherent account of what happened.

All three of these accounts are concerned with facts, and *only* with facts. But they are concerned with the facts as viewed from three different standpoints. The first is a scientific standpoint, the second legal, and the third journalistic. The language of each of these is different, for each of these three professions, in trying to attain the special kind of accuracy it needs in dealing with its subject, has developed a vocabulary and a form of expression of its own. The primary purpose of each of these accounts is to give information. But they are not literature.

These pieces are not literature, and were never intended to be literature; but a literary man, a writer of fiction, poems, plays, or even essays, might take one of these reports as a starting point for his own special kind of work. Assuming that a literary man should write his story, play, or poem about the situation described in these reports, what would he be trying to do? But it may be clearer to point out first what he would not be trying to do. In the first place, he would not try to give *merely* the facts—or if facts, another kind of facts, a kind which does not appear in the *practical* and *scientific* reports given above. A person anxious to arrive at the facts, a person wishing to get a résumé of the news, would not turn to a story or poem based on the incident; he would quite properly turn to his newspaper.

Moreover, almost any poem or story or play based on the incident would probably leave out facts which the man of practical interests would want to know: *e.g.*, the address of the house where the dead girl lived or a technical description of the state of the dead girl's lungs and of the bruises on her throat. In general, these factual accounts attempt to tell who was murdered and who was the murderer, and when and where and how and why. The man writing a story or poem or play will be interested in going beyond these details. He will be interested in placing the bare facts in a human context—especially in dealing with the human *why* of the story and the human meaning. This humanizing of the facts is one feature that distinguishes any literary account from the three accounts given above.

Someone may point out, however, that in saying this we are not quite fair to newspapers; that newspapers sometimes do attempt to make us feel vividly a human situation, that they do give "human interest" stories. It is true that after such a murder as we have for our subject, we should in all likelihood discover in the newspaper some feature story which would attempt to give us a sense of pathos or terror or sorrow —which would attempt to tell us how the dead girl looked, and what the murderer was thinking about, and how he could have come, out of his very love, to kill her, etc., etc.

All this is quite true. Human interest stories do appear in the newspapers, for people are not satisfied to live merely upon a diet of facts. They are hungry for color and humanity; they do want to *feel* as well as to *know*. But this only means that people, as a matter of fact, do have the sort of interest which literature attempts to satisfy—that a great many people who never actually read a poem, for instance, are interested in some of the effects which are best given by poetry. Literature, then, including poetry, is not a mysterious and strange sort of thing which can make its appeal only to a special class; on the other hand, everyone is interested in the literary account of life as well as in the practical account. The question is not then: "Is literature important to human beings generally?" But rather: "In what way does literature satisfy our needs, and how does good literature satisfy them more fully than bad?"

Let us take a typical example of a sob sister's story. The story is, in intention, literature: it tries to appeal to the same interests that literature appeals to.

The Sob Sister's Story

The dead girl, beautiful and peaceful in death, her scarlet lips slightly parted as though whispering a caress to her lover, her blue eyes gentle and unquestioning as a baby's, lay in the murderer's arms like a child who has been rocked to sleep. Her golden hair falling in profusion about her shoulders all but concealed the cruel welt of red about her throat. The murderer, clutching his still burden to him, like a mother holding an infant, appeared dazed. As the police came in, he rose to meet them, still carrying his precious burden in his arms. The officers had almost to force him to relinquish her. He could not answer questions—could merely clutch the closer to his breast all that remained of the girl he loved better than life, and mutter, "I loved her, I loved her," like a man in a dream. A few hours later when I saw him in the sordid surroundings of the 10th Precinct Station House, so different from the cozy cottage which had been the abode of a tragic love, he was still dry-eyed, though his face wore a ghastly pallor. But when I tried to question him, I became aware of the terrific strain under which he suffered, and he showed all the signs of a man on the verge of hysteria. When I tried to draw from him the motive for the pitiful tragedy, he could only reply, his pale boyish face like a mask: "I killed her, but God didn't say a word, a word."

At last he managed pitifully to say: "I killed her so that she would be mine alone for always!"

And this is the irony of fate! The very greatness of his love made him strangle her. Separated as they were by wealth, social position, and all that that implies, it was only in death that they could be united.

Who are we to pass judgment on such a love?

Compare this account with the following poem:

Porphyria's Lover

The rain set early in tonight,
  The sullen wind was soon awake,
It tore the elm-tops down for spite,
  And did its worst to vex the lake:
I listened with heart fit to break.
When glided in Porphyria; straight
  She shut the cold out and the storm,
And kneeled and made the cheerless grate
  Blaze up, and all the cottage warm;
Which done, she rose, and from her form
Withdrew the dripping cloak and shawl,
  And laid her soiled gloves by, untied
Her hat and let the damp hair fall,
  And, last, she sat down by my side
And called me. When no voice replied,
She put my arm about her waist,
  And made her smooth white shoulder bare
And all her yellow hair displaced,
  And, stooping, made my cheek lie there,
And spread, o'er all, her yellow hair,
Murmuring how she loved me—she
  Too weak, for all her heart's endeavor,
To set its struggling passion free
  From pride, and vainer ties dissever,
And give herself to me forever.
But passion sometimes would prevail,
  Nor could tonight's gay feast restrain
A sudden thought of one so pale
  For love of her, and all in vain:
So, she was come through wind and rain.
Be sure I looked up at her eyes
  Happy and proud; at last I knew
Porphyria worshipped me; surprise
  Made my heart swell, and still it grew
While I debated what to do.
That moment she was mine, mine, fair,
  Perfectly pure and good: I found
A thing to do, and all her hair
  In one long yellow string I wound
Three times her little throat around,
And strangled her. No pain felt she;
  I am quite sure she felt no pain.
As a shut bud that holds a bee,
  I warily oped her lids: again
Laughed the blue eyes without a stain.
And I untightened next the tress
  About her neck; her cheek once more

Blushed bright beneath my burning kiss:
  I propped her head up as before,
Only, this time my shoulder bore
Her head, which droops upon it still:
  The smiling rosy little head,
So glad it has its utmost will,
  That all it scorned at once is fled.
And I, its love, am gained instead!
Porphyria's love: she guessed not how
  Her darling one wish would be heard.
And thus we sit together now,
  And all night long we have not stirred,
And yet God has not said a word!

Both the sob story and this poem by Robert Browning are attempts to get at the motives and feelings of the murderer, and to make the reader respond to the pathos of the situation. Both writers are obviously trying to get inside the murderer's head and make the reader feel what the murderer was feeling, and, at the same time, to understand the original meaning of that feeling. But the methods are different.

In the first place one notices that the poet makes his treatment really dramatic by speaking in the murderer's own person. He imagines, for the purpose of the poem, that he *is* the murderer. He is therefore not bound by the mere historical facts of the situation. Now, the sob sister also is trying to get inside the murderer's personality, but her method is much more clumsy, for she has not been able to achieve an imaginative identification with the man. She has been forced to view him from the outside—not, as the writer of fiction or of poetry is able to see him, from the inside.

Looking further, suppose we compare the motive for the murder as given in the two accounts. The sob sister's treatment is much more general, and, consequently, much more crude. It is true that she tries to tell us why the act was performed, but she cannot give us the direct perception, the picture, of the moment when the man looked into Porphyria's eyes and asked himself how his happiness with her could be preserved.

The sob story account is crude because the motive as *stated* in it could be applied to a number of types of men and situations. For example, the murderer, insofar as the sob sister's account goes, might be an unusually sensitive and meditative man or he might be a man of action with uncontrollable impulses to violence; and he might have arrived at his decision after long brooding, or in the heat of a momentary fury. Her account of the motive would fit either case, and a number of other cases as well. The question is this: Does the reader understand better the man in the sob story or the man in the poem?

There is a difference, moreover, between telling the reader the motive—even between having the murderer tell the motive—and building up the whole situation which led to the act so that the reader feels it, and feels it as credible. Granting that the poem is successful to a degree in accomplishing this, how does the poet do it, and how does the sob sister fail to do it?

In the first place, the poem is better organized for building to a climax. There is the description of the weather, then of the bleakness of the room, and then of the contrast after the girl's entry into the room. All of these serve to indicate why the thought of the girl's leaving again, the return of the previous bleakness and hopelessness, could crystallize the despair into a sudden decision. How is the decision made credible to the reader? The murderer says, "I found a thing to do," in order to preserve the happiness. Here the poet is attempting to reproduce the murderer's own feelings at the time. The murderer will not call it *murder* even to himself, for he is not thinking of it as murder. He is completely obsessed by his desire to keep as it is the present moment of happiness. The statement, "I wound three times," carries further the psychology of the murderer, for it implies the methodical, calm, and apparently reasoned process of his mind. Then he says, "I am quite sure she felt no pain." This more fully indicates the detachment of the lover from ordinary considerations. The whole act, which seems so incredible on the face of it, is made credible by the poet's penetration into the psychology of the murderer. The sob sister is in possession of most of the facts: she remarks that the murderer was dry-eyed, pallid, and strained, and she quotes the speeches that might have served as a key to the understanding of the man. But the arrangement she uses is haphazard.

In the second place, because the sob sister does not have a firm grasp on the nature of the murderer, she feels the need of trying to awaken the reader's emotional response in some other way. She resorts to description that is calculated to pull the heart strings of her readers. She knows that the scene has a pathos about it; but since she has not imaginatively mastered the psychology of the murderer, she has to get her effect by setting up a superficial excitement in using highly colored description. Examination will show that the sob story has more phrases that are ordinarily thought of as being "poetical" than the poem has. For example: "Her scarlet lips parted as though whispering a caress"; "lay in the murderer's arms like a child who has been rocked to sleep"; "clutching his still burden"; "clutch the closer to his breast all that remained of the girl whom he loved better than life"; "like a man in a dream"; "cozy cottage"; "ghastly pallor"; "pitiful tragedy."

The motive of the sob writer in using such language is a literary motive; she is trying to make language convey an emotional reaction—something more than mere facts. But she has to resort to it in such a strained manner because she has only a superficial kind of fact, the historical fact of the situation, to deal with; she hasn't been able to grasp the psychological fact which the poet uses. This means that the effect of the sob story is *sentimental*.

Why is it sentimental? The really grown-up reader grasps the fact (though he may not state it to himself in so many words) that the sob sister has tried to stir his emotions without knowing exactly why they should be stirred *and* without showing exactly what emotions should be stirred. We usually think of the sentimentalist as being a "mushy" person. And so he is. He is having so much pleasure sloshing around in a warm bath of emotions that he doesn't care where the emotions come from or whether they are appropriate to the situation which is supposed to call them forth. For example, take the person who builds up around a cat or a parrot all the profound emotional life usually devoted to another person or a family. We call such a person sentimental. We say he lacks a sense of proportion and is immature. A cat is worth a certain amount of affection, but a cat is, after all, only a cat. Consequently, a really grown-up person, when he talks with a gushy sentimental person, or reads a gushy sentimental poem, far from being seriously stirred, merely feels amusement or disgust. How, for example, does such a person feel when he reads the sob sister's account?

In the paragraph before the last, it was mentioned that the sob sister expresses herself in a *strained* manner. She distrusts, quite rightly, the bare factual outline of the event; she wants to make us feel the pathos. But the only way that she knows is to overwhelm us with pitiable pictures and adjectives. She has little real imagination herself, and consequently knows nothing about leaving something to the imagination of the reader. She does not know that much of the best writing, both in poetry and prose, merely directs the imagination of the reader so that he feels that he has discovered the meaning of the experience for himself, and consequently feels it to be much richer. She does not give, as it were, the reader a map, so that he can follow his own investigation, but instead, hauls him into a sight-seeing bus—a rubber-neck bus—and shouts out to him through a megaphone what to look at and what to feel about it.

For example, the poet is treating a situation that does have a tragic (see Glossary) and ironical (see Glossary) aspect: a beautiful young girl is killed by a young man who loves her very dearly. But the poet has too much respect for the reader to feel it necessary to beat it into his head by direct statement and repetition. The sob sister, however, is constantly using words such as *pitiful* and *tragic,* and in the end must make the statement about "the irony of fate."

All of this has a bearing on the kind of language the sob sister uses. It has been said earlier that the phrases in the sob story are more like what is ordinarily thought of as "poetical" than the phrases of the poem. Why, then, aren't they really poetical? The reason why they are not can be put in three ways. First, the phrases are "false alarms." Second, they appeal to "stock responses" (see Glossary). Third, they are worn-out.

Why should one call them "false alarms"? The phrases are emphatic and exaggerated and try to appeal immediately to deep emotions. But the reader is not ready to believe in those emo-tions, unless he, like the sob sister, is a sentimentalist. The old story of the boy who cried "Wolf! Wolf!" is relevant here. People grow indifferent to false alarms, and the readers grow indifferent to highly emotive language when they find that the writer is really faking and cannot prove that his signals to deep emotional response are justified. The poet in "Porphyria's Lover" makes a much more guarded use of such language, and the result is that the poet gets a response from the reader. He has prepared for it.

It is easier to touch off the emotional responses that people have been taught they should have. No one knows this better than the advertising man, who tries to connect his product, no matter what it is, with some common feeling. One may see pictures of beautiful young girls on advertisements ranging from soup to cigarettes; or pictures of a mother and child on billboards advertising everything from automobile tires to men's overcoats. The advertising man knows that people have been taught to revere mother love, and so he tries to connect the feeling for his product with the respect in which people hold the idea of maternity. In reality, most truly grown-up people feel that such practice is a trick that vulgarizes and debases the emotion to which the advertiser appeals. Now, in the sob story the writer is trying in the same way to "sell" us on the "pity" of the situation. By her comparisons, she constantly appeals to the reader's pity for an innocent child. Now that sort of pity is not the basic emotion appropriate to the situation. It is too soft and simple, but the sob sister uses it because she believes that it is the thing to which the greatest number of people will respond most readily.

A comparison with the poem will show why this kind of pity is "too soft and simple." In the poem, the fact that the girl is unable to make up her mind to choose whom she really loves is made clear to the reader; as a matter of fact the motive for her murder turns upon this fact. Consequently, the reader's response to the poem contains a judgment on the girl as well as mere pity for her. And if one considers carefully the way in which the poet has told the story from line to line he will notice that the poet has implied a mixture of these two elements. One is made to feel pity—one is made to feel that the lover pities the girl with something of the tenderness of an adult for a child who must be protected from her own irresponsible and unworthy impulses. But this tenderness is merely implied—"little throat"—"little head," etc.—"No pain felt she," etc.—the poet does not insist on the childlike character of the girl to the extent that he turns the reader's response into mere pity. Furthermore, this attitude of tenderness is not presented as the *poet's* attitude, but as that of the lover. It is the lover's attitude toward his victim that is being developed dramatically for us. As for our total response—and that of the poet himself—that response is more massive and complicated and reflects our judgment of the whole situation: it is not a response of simple pity.

In discussing the phrases used in the sob story it was said that, in the third place, they are worn-out. Everybody has seen them many times before: Any cheap story of tragedy will have phrases like "ghastly pallor," "scarlet lips parted as though whispering a caress," "like a child who has been rocked to sleep," etc. Such worn-out phrases are called *clichés*. Such phrases at one time were original and embodied a new and vivid description. But their constant use and misuse has robbed them of any sense of freshness or originality. They no longer carry with them any conviction that they represent a real and sharp perception—that is, that the writer has carefully observed the thing he is writing about or has felt anything about it. The use of *clichés* (see Glossary), therefore, is one way the writer takes to appeal to stock responses in his readers. It is the usual method for getting the usual response, and the presence of *clichés* is one of the best indications that the writer has no actual interest in his subject but is avoiding the task of waking the reader's imagination by giving him a new and accurate perception.

For example, consider one of the typical phrases in the sob sister's description: "like a child who has been rocked to sleep." With it compare the lines from "Porphyria's Lover":

> As a shut bud that holds a bee,
> I warily oped her lids.

The first thing that strikes the reader is the freshness of the lines quoted from the poem as opposed to the stale quality of that from the sob story. That is, the first is a *cliché* and the second is not. As has been previously pointed out, the sob sister is merely trying to find an easy way to emphasize the pathos of the situation. But the poet was trying to make his comparison carry a more accurate and more particular meaning. What is the picture brought to mind by the poet's comparison? The picture is that of a person who, in an idle moment, has closed between his finger and thumb a blossom into which a bee has entered. Then he cautiously (the poet says *warily*) releases the blossom to look at the bee. He meant no harm to the bee; he was merely playing with it or teasing it. This tells us something about the murderer's mind and about his motive. To have the murderer compare his action in strangling the girl to such an innocent thing is to indicate that the murderer has lost contact with the mature world of right and wrong and of practical affairs. The fact that such a comparison could occur to the lover—and the poet enforces this point by having the whole poem told in the first person—indicates that he does not feel guilt—that he is really detached from the normal world in which we live.

We may say, then, that in his relatively short piece of writing the poet has given us more penetration into the psychology of the murderer than the writer of the sob story has. Since this penetration impresses us as successful we can more readily surrender ourselves to the emotional effect intended. Furthermore, the poet does not have to strain for his effect, for the pathos or the irony of the situation, because he has a real grasp on the underlying motivation. He can afford to suggest rather than to demand that we react in a certain way. The feeling of experience as a result of the poem is based on understanding; it is not detached from understanding and judgment. Therefore, it is not sentimental, for as we have observed, sentimentality is the enjoyment of emotion for emotion's own sake, separate from intelligence.

We have been contrasting the sob story, which is a crude and unsuccessful attempt at literature, with Browning's poem, which, though not a great poem, represents well enough within its scope what literature does. But the sob story might equally well have been contrasted with a good short story, play, or novel using the same material. Every contrast made between the sob story and the poem can be paralleled by a similar contrast between the sob story and one of the other literary types. For a successful performance in any of the other types depends on the imaginative penetration into the "meaning" of the situation. Literature gives us a picture of life—not the picture that science gives and not a picture that is actually (historically) true, but a picture that has its own kind of truth—a "truth" that includes important elements that science, from its very nature, is forced to leave out. The "truth" of literature takes the form, not of abstract statement, but of a concrete and dramatic presentation; which may allow us to experience imaginatively the "lived" meanings of a piece of life.

FORM

We have just said that a piece of literature of any type depends for success on the imaginative penetration into the material—or to put the matter another way, on the imaginative realization of the possibilities of human meaning in the material. But we have just referred, also, to the "vivid and moving form" which characterizes a successful piece of literature. And if we return to our comparison of the poem with the sob sister's story, we shall see that many of the things we commented on are as much a matter of form as of content—the choice of language, the use of simile (see Glossary), the matter of stock responses. At one point we even compared the haphazard "arrangement" of materials in the sob sister's story with the psychologically convincing progression in the poem.

A great deal of our study in this book will lead us, directly or indirectly, to the question of form; and the only way to approach the general notion of form is through the examination of individual stories, poems, essays, and plays. But at this stage we may allow ourselves one general statement: A piece of literature exists in its form. We shall be constantly concerned with the implications of this fact. *We shall be concerned not only because questions of form are in themselves important, but because without an understanding of, and feeling for, form, we can never grasp the human significance of literature.* To say this, however, is not to bind us to an empty formalism. We are, as human beings, inevitably interested in content, for content, if thought of as the stuff of human experience, is made available and is interpreted through the form, and only through the form, which the artist creates. Form, in this sense, is meaning: it involves the selection and arrangement, the ordering and emphasis, without which the raw stuff of human experience would not be comprehensible.

EXERCISE

1. It would be generally agreed that the young man who murders Porphyria is mentally unbalanced. If this is true, then what significance can the poem have for the sane reader?

2. Write the same story in your own words, putting the episode in a contemporary setting. Now try to decide what your version "means." Compare it with the poem by Browning.

~FICTION~

Introduction

What Is Fiction?

Fiction, like the essay, play, poem, sermon, or philosophical treatise, is the projection of the author's view of life. The writer has certain *ideas* about life, even though he may never bother to state them to himself: every man has a "philosophy"—or rather, every man's way of life embodies a philosophy. In addition, a man has certain *feelings* about life which are intimately connected with his ideas; in fact, ideas cannot be sharply set off from feelings. Ideas and feelings merge and blend, now in conjunction, now in opposition. In some cases, for example, a writer may not be able to relate his feelings to the ideas which he thinks are important to him, but can only express and explore them in the images of character and action which constitute fiction. The fiction, then, would represent an attempt to make the ideas and feelings consistent.

In general, a writer of fiction is different from other men only in his need (and ability) to give his ideas and feelings about life a form that permits them to be better contemplated and mastered, and perhaps communicated to other people. The preacher, the philosopher, or the essayist is likely to be more interested in his ideas than in his feelings, and tends to make a sharp distinction between them; at least, he tends to state his ideas in abstract and general terms, even though he may use concrete examples to illustrate his point. But the writer of fiction does not make abstract and general statements. He tends to embody his ideas—and feelings—in an "action" that is concretely presented. In such a presentation, ideas and feelings become inextricably blended. In creating such an image of action, the fiction writer provides for his reader a carefully selected and controlled experience, an experience in which the reader may share, and in doing so participate in the writer's ideas and feelings about life—in what may be called the writer's "vision."

The poet and the dramatist are moved by the same impulse as the writer of fiction. The difference lies not in the impulse, but in the mechanics of presentation. We know that a play is presented to an audience by action and dialogue on a stage. We know that poetry, as printed on the page, doesn't even look like prose, and we know that it strikes the ear differently, with more emphatic and more highly organized rhythms. There are other, and perhaps as important differences between fiction and the other literary forms, but for the moment we can distinguish fiction from the others by saying that it is a story told in prose, a story which is assumed to be made up. This does not mean that a writer of fiction may not use material drawn from real life: all his material must in fact come from and conform to life. But in trying to fix upon the essential nature of fiction we are concerned, not with where the writer gets his material but with what he does with it —with the pattern and meaning he gives it, with how strongly he can charge it with emotion, with how persuasively and coherently he can make it embody his view of life.

We have said that fiction, like other types of literature, springs from the writer's impulse to explore, through a forming process, his experience of life, to understand, through form, his vision of life. It may be added that the impulse that leads people to read fiction is fundamentally the same as the impulse that leads to its creation. The reader wants to enter more fully and understandingly into life, and therefore turns to the controlled images of life the writer has prepared. Fiction extends his experience of life, and at the same time feeds his fundamental curiosity about life and its meaning.

Our curiosity about life can take a number of forms. But though they are always involved with each other in the fictional work, we can separate them out for inspection. These concerns may be expressed by the questions:

1. What happens next?
2. What are the characters like?
3. Why did what happened happen?
4. What does it all mean?

SUSPENSE

If asked what kind of fiction he likes, it is probable that the average person would say that he likes a story that keeps him in suspense, a story that makes him want to know what will happen next. He likes, he says, a story with a good plot. Certain critics have tried to persuade themselves and other people that the novel or story that builds up suspense about what-happens-next is crude and not artistic. But this censure smacks of literary snobbery, for suspense is fundamental to all fiction—just as it is a fundamental part of our life experience. It is fundamental to fiction because fiction is an image of people in action, moving toward an undeclared end. That end, we presume, will fulfill the expectations aroused in the story—and our suspense springs from a perfectly natural appetite. But this appetite is not crudely simple; it is complex. It has to do not merely with the simple event (what-happens-next) but with the motives that determine the event and the final meaning of the event.

Suspense can, then, work in different ways. Curiosity about the outcome of a piece of fiction, even the simplest curiosity in what is called the "action story" (adventure or detective fiction), depends on other factors, and by *itself* cannot account for the interest one takes in such a piece of writing. Let us take the detective story, a type of fiction in which the element of plot suspense is very strong. The story is about people, after all. There are the criminal, the detective, and a number of other people. Our interest in the story, our suspense even, depends to a large degree on the way in which these people call our sympathies and antipathies into play. The story is not about X, Y, and Z, but about Archibald Donaldson, the polished and suave gentleman who commits seven murders before detection; Henry Milton, the gruff police inspector who has a softer side after all,

and who collects old china; and Isabel Ravenal, the heiress whom the inspector saves from Mr. Donaldson. X, Y, and Z must have certain personalities, and these personalities must react on each other before the reader can feel that they are people; and unless the reader, even for the moment, accepts X, Y, and Z as people, he can have no interest in the story, and the plot cannot provoke his suspense. For instance, a story is like a pin-ball game. Nobody cares, in general, whether a small metal ball falls into a hole in a polished board. We care only when some value can be attached to the fact: when we are pleased with our own skill, are concerned with beating another person, or have some money bet on the event. When we play pinball, we assign some value to placing the metal ball in a particular hole; and so we assign some value to the behavior of X, Y, and Z when we accept them as people. We like or dislike them. They violate or support our ideas about human conduct and about right and wrong. That an interest in mere plot cannot exist by itself, even in the detective story, is amply illustrated by the fact that the most successful and popular writers of detective fiction have a decided gift for characterization and can make the reader believe, for the moment anyway, in their people. Take, for instance, Conan Doyle, or Dashiell Hammett.

But the interest the reader has in the characters of a story is not the kind of interest that can be satisfied with a mere description such as would be given in a character sketch in an essay, for a story is an account of characters in action. The characters are doing something, and the reader wants to know the *why* as well as the *what* of the affair. This applies even in cases of the purest action story. For instance, there is our detective story. If the matter of the villain's motive is not explained on acceptable grounds, the reader feels cheated, and all the excitement of the unraveling of the plot and the detection of the criminal cannot fully compensate for this defect. The writer of detective fiction who makes his criminal a mere lunatic has cheated the reader by avoiding the problem of motive. The motivation of a character in a story—one of the answers to the question *why*—is of fundamental importance.

We can, however, go a step further. Characters not only act, but are acted upon. We all know that people change with time and experience. A young man growing older changes. The degree to which he influences his own development may be great or small. We know how physical weaklings have, by force of will, made themselves, as Theodore Roosevelt did, into vigorous and effective men; we also know how vigorous and effective men have been ruined by circumstances apparently beyond their control. But whatever a man becomes, we feel that what he is cannot be regarded as a new creation, or the result of accidental circumstances; we feel that his final condition bears some relation to his earlier character.

One of the factors of most constant interest in fiction is this relation of character to event. A character in a story does something to fulfil some motive, but in doing so he starts a train of action; then, this train of action has certain effects on him. At the end of the story or novel he may be a very different man from the man at the beginning. Not only his external fortunes in the world may have changed, but his internal make-up may have changed. Our curiosity about this relation of character and event and about the changes within a man gives rise to one of the most abiding forms of suspense in fiction—or, for that matter, in drama. And one of the greatest tests of a fiction writer's skill is the way in which he handles this matter of character and fate. To summarize: *character is action, and action is character.*

ACTION

We say that a piece of fiction involves "an action." We clearly mean something different from the incidental particulars of action that take place in the course of the story. We mean a significant relation, involving sequence and cause, among the various incidental parts of the action.

Let us consider an example. Looking from the window of a moving train at night we see, under a streetlamp, a man strike a woman with his fist, so that she falls to the pavement. That is a piece of action. But it is only a *piece* of action and not a fictional action, in the sense that a story or a novel possesses *an* action. We see, in a moment before the motion of the train draws us away, the expression on the two faces, and

then the descending blow, and the woman's fall. We experience a feeling of horror at the random brutality.

But when the horror passes we may begin to try to create imaginatively a full fictional action leading up to the final act of the blow. In other words, we try to explain the apparently random and meaningless nature of what we saw from the train window and try to put it into a comprehensible form, into a form that we can contemplate as a progression of events, from cause to effect. The fact of the imaginative sequence of events does not remove our first impression of horror, but it makes the event manageable. Contemplating our sequence, we may now try to relate the thing that happened to the previous notion we have had of the way the world operates; in other words, as critics are fond of putting it, we try to "interpret" life. But we try, in so far as we are artists, fiction writers, for instance, to interpret it without robbing it of its power to give a direct experience— the shock of something happening in real life. Therefore, we put our interpretation into a plot, or action, instead of into some abstract statement about life.

CONFLICT AND FICTIONAL ORDER

The central fact about a fictional action is that it arises in conflict. There may be a collision between one character and another, between a character and some element in the world about him—even the world of physical nature—or between divergent impulses and values within himself. *No conflict, no story.* For the working out of the conflict to a point of victory or defeat, acceptance or desperation, gives us the order of the story, the principle by which its stages emerge.

We ordinarily speak of those stages as the *beginning,* the *middle,* and the *end.* The beginning is the presentation of the situation in which the germ of conflict lies. The middle is the presentation of the actual process of conflict. Here there is great range, from the narrow scope of a little short story, such as William Carlos Williams' "The Use of Force" (p. 26), to the great scale of Leo Tolstoi's magnificent novel, *War and Peace.* The end gives us the summarizing event which leads to the moment of resolution and poise—the moment, too, in which the meaning implicit in the action becomes manifest.

UNITY

It is the end of the action which makes the unity of the action clear to us. The action, as we have said, is composed of various individual episodes, grouped in the stages we have discussed; but the action itself constitutes a unity.

There are various ways in which an action may be unified. One of the most obvious is the presence in the story of a single leading character whose fortunes we follow through thick and thin to the happy or unhappy conclusion. For instance, the character of Becky Sharp is what most obviously gives unity to such a novel as *Vanity Fair,* just as the presence of the boy in "I'm a Fool," by Sherwood Anderson (p. 65), is the most obvious means for establishing the unity of that story.

Mere place may contribute to the impression of unity. The setting of the bankrupt house and dreary countryside is a very important unifying element, in "The Horse Dealer's Daughter," by D. H. Lawrence (p. 114); the farm is important in the same way in "Noon Wine," by Katherine Anne Porter (p. 158). But the fictional idea or theme may sometimes be the most obvious force making for unity. Neither the character of Nick, nor the setting, contributes so much to the sense of the unity of Hemingway's "The Killers" (p. 137), as does something else: the fact of the shocking discovery of the true nature of the world. It is Nick, to be sure, who makes the discovery, but it is the drama of discovery and not Nick as such that gives the sense of unity. In "The Horse Dealer's Daughter," the reader's interest is divided between the two principal characters; it is not their eventual union with each other or their personal fate at any level that most clearly holds the story together. It is rather the deep implications, the thematic projections from the personal story, that provide the focus for the whole.

To take an extreme case, "The Gentleman from San Francisco," by Ivan Bunin (p. 143), is, in only a most limited and purely technical sense, focused on the "gentleman"; the working out of the fictional idea is what is most important, as we see clearly illustrated by the fact that the interpretive climax of the story comes well after the death of the "main character."

But in all cases the ultimate unity of an action inheres in the significance of the end of the action. We do not sense the unity unless the end resolves the forces that have been released in the course of the conflict. *In this implicit meaningfulness the action finds its fundamental unity.*

ACTION AND PLOT

Here we should turn aside to distinguish two things that are often confused: action and plot. As the student may have inferred, we think of the action of a piece of fiction as though it existed in real time, in its strictly chronological and causal sequence. Thus, we think of the action as the little "history" that is presented in the story. But a moment's reflection will show that a story need not present the individual elements of the action in what we think of as their natural historical order. The story may begin anywhere and go back and forth in time. In "Jerico, Jerico, Jerico," by Andrew Lytle (p. 230), we see a woman on her death bed, we enter her consciousness, and relive with her the various significant experiences of her past. In such a story there is a total violation of the natural historical order. In "Keela, the Outcast Indian Maiden," by Eudora Welty (p. 109), the story has two lines, dealing with two different "times," one recent, but the other out of a more remote past. Plot, then, may be defined in its simplest terms as the *significant order in which the action is presented.*

In a good piece of fiction, the order of presentation is neither accidental nor arbitrary. It does not "just happen." Nor is it chosen wilfully. The plot stands, in other words, as a natural development of a particular writer's interpretation of the action. The order, the pattern, is, in a very deep sense, the meaning of a story. The plot is not a mere convenience; it is meaning in its dynamic manifestation. It is, in itself, an index to the author's basic attitude toward life.

The full implications of that notion may not emerge immediately. They can emerge, as a matter of fact, only in the process of reading and thinking about a number of stories. But let us hang on to the notion, and in the course of our study it will, we trust, assume something of its potential of meaning.[1]

LOGIC

Let us return to our topic of the unity of an action. We have said that in the end of an action the unity becomes clear to us. Perhaps we ought to emend this to say: the unity becomes clear in the end of an action *as presented to us in the plot,* for it is in the order of actual presentation that our awareness develops. Our grasping of this unity is our grasping of the inner logic of the action as it has been made available through the plot, through all the reticences and meanderings and half-hints which the plot may have involved in its stimulation, development, and even teasing of our interest. What we grasp now in this logic is what distinguishes the fictional order from the natural order—the way in which it happens in actual life. Life comes to us in an undifferentiated texture, demanding from moment to moment that we apply our powers of logic to it if we are to survive. Fiction comes to us with an offer to lay bare the inner logic of its world.

It has been said that truth is stranger than fiction; this is but one way of saying that life sometimes appears to be more illogical than fiction. Very often in real life we see people do things for motives which we cannot understand, but a novelist whose characters behave without a motivation which we can understand does not satisfy us. This logic of fiction may take many forms and all forms may not be found in a single piece of fiction, but some kind of logic does appear in every piece of fiction that satisfies us. We may ask ourselves in reading a story whether the characters behave with a fitting degree of probability. That is one way of asking whether they are "real."

The logic of the action of a piece of fiction obviously depends on the kind of people involved and the kind of situation in which they are originally placed. The writer asks himself: "How will my character X act in this original situation?" Then he tries to answer the question by using his imagination. But X is not alone in the story, and so the writer has to ask how Y will act as soon as X has performed his first action. And then there is character Z to be considered. But something has been neglected. The instant X has performed his first action, the general situation has changed, and X, Y, and Z are living in a new world to which they have to be adapted and to which they will respond in new ways. The writer's task is to explore these combinations, and the logic of his story is the line he finds that will take him through to a conclusion. It should be quite clear that the story of X, Y, and Z, those characters being given for a start, might result in a marriage in one given set of original circumstances, and in a murder in another set of circumstances. Or if we put the characters A, B, and C in either of these two sets of circumstances, we have two new stories. For instance, if a slightly different young man were put in the place of Porphyria's lover, he might not murder Porphyria because her social position and weakness of will had ruined their love, but would set himself to become rich in order to break into that privileged circle; or would join the Socialist Party to reform the injustices of society; or would become a great scientist, not because he was ambitious to do so, but because work helped him to forget. Change the conception of the character very slightly and a new story results; a new "logic" has been discovered, a new kind of cause-and-effect, a new relation between the characters, and between the characters and the original situation. There is a new action which appears logical because we know what causes what; a good writer of fiction usually tries to make us feel that with the given circumstances and people things had to come out to his conclusion and that the piece of fiction, therefore, possesses inevitability.

We must not understand the inevitability of fiction (or drama) to be absolute, however. The elements of accident and coincidence are always present to a degree and usually to a very high degree. For all practical purposes, the fact that certain characters are in a certain situation at the beginning of a piece of fiction may generally be taken to be the result of accident or coincidence. The character X goes to Atlantic City for a vacation and meets Y. The story has started

---

[1] The view expressed here is not universally accepted. Some eminent theorists of fiction—E. M. Forster, for instance—tend to treat plot as a mere spine, a necessary inconvenience. Aristotle, by the way, did not.

with a preliminary coincidence, for there is no "inevitability" in the fact that X and Y are in Atlantic City on May 12, 1923, at ten o'clock in the morning when X meets Y. In the work of some writers the margin of accident or coincidence is very large, but even in such cases we shall find that the writer, if successful, has organized his action so that the end depends upon the beginning. The merely accidental or coincidental end never satisfies us. The writer must try to persuade the reader, and if successful does persuade him, that probability has not been violated and that the thistle has not brought forth figs. Even a very cynical writer who believes that accident governs our lives and whose fiction is based on this idea will still refrain from violating the conception he gives us of his characters; he merely tends to separate the "logic of events" from the "logic of character."

INTERPRETATION

Fiction differs from life in one other important respect: it represents an *interpretation*. A fiction writer, even if he should want to do so, could not give his reader a "slice of life." He can only give his own version, which is colored by a thousand things about his own interests, history, race, and personality. It is a platitude that no two people see a thing exactly alike. But the divergence is multiplied infinitely when we get beyond simple facts into a field where emotions and ideas come into play.

Let us recall the man's striking the woman under the streetlamp, the event seen from the moving train. A moving-picture camera might record the scene. In the film the expression on the man's face is one of the utmost savagery. But suppose that, at the same instant, another camera from another angle is recording the incident. From that angle the light from the streetlamp falls differently, and so the man's face wears an expression of horror. Which film are we to believe? The camera does not lie, but what has the camera seen? If such a difference can exist between the two film versions, a difference that really gives two separate interpretations of the event, then consider how different two reports by people on the train might be.

Let us suppose, then, that the two spectators determined to write short stories based on the incident. They must create characters; they must give those characters, the man and the woman, a history; they must define a relationship that will be fulfilled, somehow, by that last blow under the streetlamp and must explain the motivation of the characters; they must do all these things and many more to make a story. In short, they must interpret the incident. And so one of them writes a story demonstrating the curse of the Demon Rum, and another writes a story of the degradation of a good but simple man by a vain and unfaithful wife whom he, at last in horror at his own ruin, strikes down under the streetlamp on a deserted corner.

In these two hypothetical stories both writers start from the same scene as a stimulus, and the stories are worlds apart. Think, therefore, of the infinite difference possible when our two hypothetical writers do not even start from the same scene, but range over their private observations and experiences, being guided in a choice by all the subtle factors of temperament and training. A writer chooses his material in accordance with these factors, but this is another way of saying that he chooses material that he can, or thinks he can, interpret in a way congenial to his general view of life and his general set of values. For behind every piece of fiction is a special feeling about life, a special view of life, and a special set of values. All of these things enter into the interpretation.

Fiction must have a point if it is to satisfy us. Usually the writer does not go so far as to state in the course of his narrative what his point is; he is not like a preacher who tells the story merely to make a moral clear. The fiction writer ordinarily does not even make his point as schematically clear as does an essayist. In fact the point—the theme—of a story may be revealed only in the action itself, and may demand the sensitive and devoted participation of the reader for its realization. For instance, take the story "An Episode of War," by Stephen Crane (p. 29), or "Araby," by James Joyce (p. 125). The theme may, in fact, be merely an implication of the feeling evoked by a story—for, as we have said, there is no sharp line between feeling and idea; one involves the other. A story like "Araby" will indeed demand for its full realization the participation of a reader who is alert and responsive.

There are some critics—again we are tempted to call them literary snobs—who insist that for a story to "state" the theme is basically inartistic. But suppose that such a story succeeds, nevertheless, in moving us to an emotionally charged awareness of meaning in human experience. Are we to say that it is not artistic? Is, for example, "The Gentleman from San Francisco," a story that is very direct in some of its treatment of theme, inferior to a closely wrought story like "Araby," in which the meaning is implicit and never overt? We think not. We can observe that in general the direct method is most successful when the connection between theme and action is, at one level, very simple, obvious, and powerful—when the import of the whole action seems to make for a conclusion that is unavoidable and that consequently must stir an emotional response.

But the reader objects when the writer seems to be using the art of fiction for a disguise for preaching. In previous pages we have seen that the writer of fiction undertakes to express his characters in action, not in mere description; in the same way, he undertakes to express his theme through the action of these characters—not in some abstract proposition about life. When the writer falls into this error, he usually does so because he tends to make the elements of life as given in his fiction too simple by making them fit his special point of preaching. An adult reader finds it impossible to read the Pollyanna books because too much has been left out and too much has been made simple. We know that the cheerfulness of Pollyanna doesn't solve all our problems. In the second place, the reader also objects when he feels that the writer is using the art of fiction for the presentation of trivial themes. An adult reader could not be interested in fiction written to prove that the United States should not go off the gold standard, for that would be, for the purposes of fiction, a trivial theme. The problem of the gold standard is extremely important as an economic and political issue, but *as a theme* for fiction it does not involve any essential element of human nature.

BELIEF

Another question arises in connection with the idea, or theme, or values of a piece of fiction. Suppose that the idea or the values involved in a piece of fiction do not agree with those of the reader. Can he still enjoy the fiction in question? And if so, to what degree? This, again, is a very complicated question, and we cannot attempt a statement that will completely solve it. But we know from experience that the same person can enjoy the novels of Walter Scott, which are based on a romantic, simple, and chivalric idea of human conduct, and the stories of de Maupassant, which are based on an ironical and realistic view of life. Scott's heroes are very heroic and are suitably rewarded. De Maupassant has no heroes in this sense, and in his stories ironical accident plays a more important part than justice. Perhaps we can say that, insofar as the themes and values of fiction are concerned, our reading is often provisional and experimental. If the fiction is good enough—if the characters are real, the action convincing, and the idea serious—we are prepared to experience the world as the writer conceives it to be. We may say to ourselves: "Well, perhaps the world is like this after all, and we shall see." But we do demand that the writer's themes shall not be trivial and absurd. And we demand that the story presented be coherent, that it be true to the basis from which it starts, and true to the "view" of life which it professes to express.

We have concluded that the action of fiction is different from the random piece of action given us by life in that it (1) is unified and complete, (2) has a certain logic of organization, and (3) embodies an interpretation. Indeed, each of these things implies the others, for there cannot be unity in fiction without a logic of organization, for instance; or a logical organization that does not embody, to a degree at least, some interpretation. Furthermore, we have seen that the discussion of such a thing as the plot or action of a piece of fiction immediately involves the writer's conception of his characters and theme. These things, action, character, and theme, are aspects of a unity which we call the novel or story. The story or the novel gives an effect, an experience; and that experience is what we finally value in fiction.

We shall not be able to define the exact nature of that experience here. A great body of criticism has been written on this subject without results that are finally clear and satisfactory. But we may make several points that may help to an understanding.

In the first place, the experience in question is not merely the effect of the reader's effort to sympathize with a character and go through his experiences. We can easily show that this is true. We frequently hear someone say: "When I read that story I simply lived through everything with the character Jane, who was so nice, and when she died at the end I felt so bad." We may observe two very peculiar things about this statement, which we always take to be praise of a novel or story. First, the speaker has made a distinction, unconsciously perhaps, between living through things with Jane and the feeling after Jane's death. So the experience of the story is not merely the sympathetic experience shared with a character; the reader has an experience of his own which is different. Second, the speaker felt "so bad" when Jane died at the end of the book, but this feeling bad is taken to be praise of the book. The speaker is just as likely to add: "You ought to read it too." We know that the speaker does not enjoy the death of a person like Jane in real life, but we know that the speaker enjoyed feeling bad about the death of the nice Jane in the book. So what was enjoyed was not the fact of Jane's death, but a total effect of the story which involved the death of Jane. We know that people pay money for books with unhappy endings; and we also know that people do not ordinarily pay money to be tortured. The book gives something which the mere facts of the conclusion do not give.

In the second place, we know that a good book can be read over again with equal or added enjoyment. People have favorite books to which they return again and again. Why? They know the ending and so are not held by the desire to know how things will come out. They know what the characters are like, and so are not curious about them. They know what the descriptive passages present. They know what the writer's main idea is. These things might easily

be obtained in one or two careful readings. It is not a desire to satisfy any curiosity, or to gain any information, that leads them back to the story or novel. No, it is a desire to have again the experience the story or novel can give—the complicated effect that belongs to that single story or novel, and to it alone. It makes the reader feel a certain way; it gives him an emotional experience; and he knows that by coming back to this piece of fiction he can regain that experience. This experience is valuable to him as a thing in itself. We can say that the experience is the experience of the form of the piece of fiction, an appreciation of the precise way it is put together, the way the various elements—characters, setting, action, ideas, style, etc.—are interrelated and integrated. At first thought, this seems like a trivial thing, but the more closely acquainted we become with literature, or with any of the arts, say music or painting, the more we realize that the way the thing is done, and what the thing means, are scarcely to be separated. The form and the content are but aspects of the story, or the poem, picture, or musical composition.

How Is Fiction Made?

We have been discussing something of the nature of fiction in general and its relation to some of the other literary forms, but we have not discussed what might be called *the method of fiction.* It will perhaps be more instructive to try to put ourselves in the place of a writer who is setting out to compose a piece of fiction than to think of ourselves as breaking up a piece of fiction already composed. For it must always be remembered that a good piece of fiction—like the poem or drama, in addition—can better be compared to a plan that *grows* than to an object that is *made.*

It is, of course, true that the actual process that goes on in the head of a good writer as he works at a piece of fiction may be very different from time to time and from writer to writer. One may start from a fragment of a situation in which the characters are very vague, and may gradually develop them from the hints he has in the situation. Another may start from a character which has struck his imagination. Another, like Hawthorne in many of his stories, may get his start from some general idea which means a great deal to him, and the story may develop from his attempt to understand how the idea would work out in human experience. One cannot necessarily tell from the given piece of fiction how the writer got started in its creation. But despite the differences possible in the beginning of the process, it may be said that all successful fiction represents a growth rather than a *mere* construction. There are many bad pieces of fiction—the magazines are full of them—that fulfill all the rules in the textbooks for constructing stories. These pieces are bad because they are nothing more than constructions. As constructions, they are predictable. We pick up the magazine and know what kind of story or novel it will have in it. There is what might be called a *formula* of the action and characters. The writer has concerned himself with the mere construction of his story but has not concerned himself with the emotional and thematic inwardness. In such pieces of fiction there is no effect; when the reading is over, the story is over completely. The story is manufactured, as it were, and is not organic.

But all writers have to use their intelligence while creating a piece of fiction; the process of writing is a process of trial and error in the mind of the writer, all of this process being dominated by a constant awareness of the final effect he wishes to produce on the reader. To produce this effect the writer must consider adapting his means to his end. For instance, he may experiment with various ways of getting an essential bit of information over to the reader: shall he use a direct statement of summary; shall he put the information into the mouth of a character; shall he have a letter found under a carpet? In larger aspects of his work he will be concerned with the proportion to be occupied by various parts and characters and by the relation of the various parts and characters to each other and to the main intention. But he cannot make a blue print of his story as a beginning; when he is able to make a blue print, as it were, he has finished the major work on his fiction, for he has felt his way imaginatively to his end. And some writers, of course, do not finish this process until their novel or story is actually written down to the last word.

When the work is finished, if it is successful, we can say that it is organic, that its parts all contribute toward the final emotion of the story. The process of its creation was a growth, as we have said, a kind of imaginative growth; but after the story is finished we can speak of its structure, or construction, just as we speak of the structure of a plant, which likewise is the product of growth. And in both cases, that of the story and that of the plant, we feel that we appreciate more fully the mystery of the growth if we understand as well as we can the structure; that is, the function performed by the various parts and their relation to each other and to the whole.

To study some of the problems of structure let us assume that a writer of fiction is in command of the facts of the Porphyria murder, and feels that it is good material for fiction. It might appeal to him for a variety of different reasons, depending on his temperament, training, beliefs, etc. He might, as we have already pointed out, be interested first because of the paradox implied by the murderer's statement that he killed the girl because he loved her; or, for instance, he might be interested first because he saw the murder as a result of a bad social system, as Theodore Dreiser saw the murder of the girl in his *An American Tragedy*. In any case, many of the problems of method, of getting the material into shape, would remain the same. Furthermore, one writer might see the short story as the proper form, and another might see the novel as the proper form for the work to take. The choice of form would depend on a number of factors, but in either case many of the problems of method would be the same. Our purpose, therefore, shall be to define some of the problems of method that arise in writing or criticizing any piece of fiction, no matter what led the writer to choose either the subject or form.

SELECTIVITY

Let us assume, then, that our hypothetical writer, in command of the facts of the death of

Porphyria, sets out to use them as the basis of a piece of fiction. As we have already said, a given piece of fiction, in so far as it is successful, is a unity. It has, as we have also said, a logic, and therefore, a pattern in which each thing is related to the whole intention the writer has. But this unity, this logic, this pattern, does not appear in the material just as it happens, and it does not appear, usually or necessarily, in what the writer knows about the event or can imagine about it. The writer has to develop this unity and pattern for his fiction. It is easy to realize the infinite amount of material which the writer has at his disposal if he chooses to base a story on Porphyria's death. There is the whole life of Porphyria, her home surroundings, her family, how she met her lover who later kills her, what she felt and thought about him at different times, etc. And then, there is the lover, his history, surroundings, education, etc. There is a tremendous background of situation, character, and incident open to the writer. It is not necessary that he have factual information about all these things, for since he is a fiction writer he can draw on his imagination to supply him with all these things, and they are therefore potential for the story. It is probable that, if he is a serious writer, he will think a great deal along these lines and try to reconstruct for himself as completely as possible the lives of the people involved, even though he knows that he will actually use in his fiction a small amount of the material that comes to him. In one sense, then, the plot may be said to represent the principle of selectivity as applied to the action: *plot is the action as specifically envisioned.*

In selecting those items which will specifically and immediately serve to convey the story, the writer must remember that the items selected must also make the reader imaginatively aware of things that are not told. In reading a book we often feel that we know what kind of childhood a character must have had or know how the character would behave in a situation that is never actually given in the book. We feel those things because the writer has chosen the significant parts of the vast amount of material that was potential for him. His selectivity has been successful.

FOCUS

Selectivity is successful only if it represents a principle of unity, if it creates a pattern. Therefore we must consider some of the ways in which a writer may arrive at his unity and pattern. He must find, as it were, some center of gravity for the large amount of material that is to be organized—some principles that will give it shape. A writer often centers his fiction on some character, though, of course, he may treat a number of other related characters in his story or novel. In the case of Porphyria and her lover a decision must be made: whose story is it? Browning, in his poem, only tells the lover's story. But it would be quite possible to treat the whole matter with Porphyria dominant. Or one might go further and make the judge, for instance, who finally tries the murderer, the dominant character, basing the interest on some problem the trial raises in the mind of the judge.

But fiction exists in which we can scarcely say that this or that character is dominant and so provides a kind of unity. In such cases—usually novels to be sure, Tolstoi's *War and Peace* or Aldous Huxley's *Point Counterpoint,* for example—no one character is dominant, though many characters are fully presented and have independent stories of their own. But we may undertake at present a general statement about the "center of gravity" of such pieces of fiction.

That statement will mean that we must recall to mind the discussion earlier in this section of unity and theme in fiction. All fiction, by reason of the very fact that it is the product of a human mind and not a product of the infinitely complicated and often apparently accidental forces of nature and society, has a theme, even though in many cases, as has been said, the theme is only implied and not stated directly. That is, the theme may appear only in terms of the plot and character. Every story, in other words, is an interpretation of material. But theme is always present and gives any story its underlying point. In some cases, however, the total unity of the story or novel may be dictated by the theme, and in such cases the theme takes on an added importance in the construction of the piece. Then, not the presence of a dominant character, and perhaps not even complications of plot, but the reference of the various parts of the story to the theme itself binds those parts together and makes them appear as an organic expression of that theme. Both Bunin's "The Gentleman from San Francisco," and "Disorder and Early Sorrow," by Thomas Mann (p. 246), will provide us with examples of a theme working to unify very diverse and complex materials.

The writer, approaching his story, must deal, consciously or unconsciously, with the questions: "Whose story is this? What does the story mean? What is the logic of plot? How does the plot express the meaning of the story?" But fiction is a seamless garment, and such questions cannot be answered individually and in isolation. There is another question that must be answered before a single word can go down on the sheet of paper.

POINT OF VIEW

That question is: "Who tells the story?" This question of the point of view is an extremely important one, and one on which hinges the problem of the control and arrangement of the material—that is, the very nature of the plot—and to a large extent the problem of style. Let us regard some of the possibilities that may present themselves to a writer.

First, there is the first person. The writer may tell a story with an "I." That seems very simple, but the use of an "I" in fiction involves several possibilities. The narrator or speaker, the "I" of the story, may be the dominant character, the person who owns, as it were, the story; or he may be a minor character in the action; or he may be merely an observer. The first-person point of view, in general, has certain advantages and disadvantages, which a writer has to weigh against each other for the purpose of dealing with any given body of material. The "I" of a story tends to convince the reader of the truth or the reality of the events and the persons. We tend to believe first-hand reports more quickly than hearsay. This is not to say that we are "deceived" by the use of a first-person narrator. We know, of course, that the first-person narrator is a fictional invention—is not "real." But the use of this fictional first person can give an impression of casualness and intimacy that

fits the writer's intention, and it can often allow necessary comment to enter the narrative more easily and naturally than under different circumstances. Then this point of view gives an easy basis for the writer's selectivity, since whatever the "I" has not directly seen cannot logically enter the story as a "scene." Much material can naturally come in as summary, a thing that the reader tends to resent in fiction written from another point of view. In a first-person story he easily accepts such a statement as, "When I saw him three years later he was greatly changed." But such a transition and summary appears very crude and arbitrary in a story told in the third person.

Other special advantages may accrue from the first-person point of view. For instance, in "The Apostate," by George Milburn (p. 216), the first person allows an ironical effect otherwise not available: the ignorance of the narrator allows us to see above and beyond him. Or in "I'm a Fool," by Sherwood Anderson, the intimate characterization of the boy, and perhaps our sympathy for him, would not be possible if the story were not presented as directly his own in his own words.

It is usually said that opposed to the point of view of the first person is the omniscient point of view, that is, the point of view of the author who knows everything. But, quite clearly, the author, although he may know everything in his fiction, cannot tell everything; he must practice his principle of selectivity. With this limitation, however, such a writer can enter at will into the thoughts and sensations of his characters, and can present information no single character might have presented—a method impossible to the writer who employs a narrator to whose consciousness the presentation of the fiction is bound. The writer who adopts this method may remain entirely anonymous and withdrawn from his story, as do the authors of "Jerico, Jerico, Jerico," and "The Lottery Ticket." Or he may drop the impersonal attitude and address the reader familiarly, as many of the older fiction writers, such as Fielding, Hawthorne, and Thackeray, were accustomed to do. But in either case, that of Chekhov in "The Lottery Ticket" or Thackeray in *Vanity Fair,* the writer, being omniscient, has taken the privilege of entering into the consciousness of characters.

But the omniscient point of view is capable of many complicated differentiations. The writer employing such a point of view, we have said, may enter at will into the being of his characters. But since for the purposes of fiction he obviously cannot dwell in the being of all his characters at all times he must use his power according to some principle. He may work by presenting a situation in an objective way, that is, without going into the consciousness of a character, and then pick and choose critical moments to dip into the consciousness of this character and then of that one to present important fragments of their experience. Or he may work, as does Andrew Lytle in "Jerico, Jerico, Jerico," by entering only into the consciousness of one character and dwelling there for almost the entire period of the story, detaching himself only for the purpose of giving setting and dialogue. The character on whose consciousness the author chooses to exercise his powers of omniscience in such a fashion may be the dominant character, as in "Jerico, Jerico, Jerico," or it may be a character who has been chosen for the same reasons a narrator would be chosen, that is, to provide a kind of mirror for the story or to act as an interpreter.

But, again, a writer may refrain entirely from entering into the mind of any of his characters and may simply present the setting and dialogue much in the manner of a play. He may also refrain from summary, comment, and analysis, pretending that he is merely recording the scenes. This, of course, is even more like the method of drama. "The Killers," by Ernest Hemingway, illustrates this method better than any other story in this collection.

These examples do not exhaust the variations possible in fiction. Most short stories, because of the limitation of length, keep one point of view in presenting the material, but many novels shift the method from time to time, not only mixing different types of the omniscient point of view, but also varieties of the omniscient with varieties of the first-person point of view. There is no rule that binds a fiction writer to one practice. Probably the only rule to be observed is that one must not confuse the reader by capricious shifts from one point of view to another. The author must consider very carefully how a given point of view will be related to the general effect of his story or novel. For instance, the use of a narrator or even of an observer into whose mind the omniscient author could penetrate would weaken the effect of "The Gentleman from San Francisco." The author is, indeed, omniscient, and does enter the mind of this character or that, but he does not follow one character's inward responses, as does, for instance, Andrew Lytle in "Jerico, Jerico, Jerico." What Bunin, in fact, does is to adopt the tone of a summary or a history, as if he were writing about a period and a class now gone. He takes what we may call a "distance" from his material. For instance: "The class of people to which he belonged was in the habit of beginning its enjoyment of life by a trip to Europe, India, Egypt." When Bunin enters the mind of an individual he does so by approaching from this "distance," and then again withdraws to that distance. Such an effect, as well as the elaborate descriptions of the ship, for instance, would be impossible with any other point of view. Bunin writes with the care of a historian describing for our instruction a kind of life that has disappeared; this implies, of course, that he considers that kind of life already doomed to extinction because of its rottenness.

STYLE

As just remarked, the style of "The Gentleman from San Francisco" depends to a degree on the point of view the author assumes. This is, as a matter of fact, a constant consideration for both the writer and the reader of fiction. The truth of this is perfectly clear in fiction which has an actual narrator, for the style depends directly on the education, experience, temperament and skill of the character who is directly telling the story. And the author must decide whether the character is "talking" or "writing." In such cases the author has surrendered his own normal style and must, as it were, let the narrator do the talking or writing. Sherwood Anderson has beautifully succeeded in doing this in "I'm a Fool" and in many of his other stories. The reader can easily see that the vocabulary and the grammar are those of a boy raised without much education:

It was a peachey time for me, I'll say that. Sometimes now I think that boys who are raised regular in houses, and never have a fine nigger like Burt for best friend, and go to high schools and college, and never steal anything, or get drunk a little, or learn to swear from fellows who know how, or come walking up in front of a grand stand in their shirt sleeves and with dirty horsy pants on when the races are going on and the grand stand is full of people all dressed up—What's the use of talking about it? Such fellows don't know nothing at all. They've never had no opportunity.

Almost any writer would be able to use the phraseology and grammar appropriate for such a character, but comparatively few would be able to capture the movement and rhythm of the boy's speech. Anderson is able to make the style dramatically appropriate to the narrator in all these respects.

But the same principle is sometimes applied when a character is not a narrator but when the omniscient author is depending on that character to establish the point of view for his fiction. Andrew Lytle in "Jerico, Jerico, Jerico" uses the consciousness of the dying woman to establish the point of view for the story; but this use is indirect, for he does not make her a narrator and very sparingly quotes directly from her thinking. But the style is flavored here and there by phrases, constructions, and comparisons that are appropriate to the woman. For instance, "no-count," or "of a winter's night." Or:

She could not see but she could feel the heavy cluster of mahogany grapes that tumbled from the center of the head board—out of its vines curling down the sides it tumbled. How much longer would these never-picked grapes hang above her head? How much longer would she, rather, hang to the vine of this world, she who lay beneath as dry as any raisin.

Or:

She could smell her soul burning and see it. What a fire it would make below, dripping with sin, like a rag soaked in kerosene.

Though this is indirectly referred to the woman's mind and is not quoted but is written, as it were, on the author's own responsibility, the Biblical flavor of "the vine of this world"

and the homely comparisons of the raisin and the rag soaked with kerosene arise from the connection of the author's style with the point of view adopted. In all pieces of fiction the relationship between the point of view and the style is not so obvious as in "I'm a Fool" and "Jerico, Jerico, Jerico." Thus, in "The Gentleman from San Francisco" one has to search a little more carefully for the relationship; but the relationship is there, even though we are reading a translation. The subject of this relationship, as a matter of fact, is one that the reader should always consider in studying fiction. There is not always a "right" and a "wrong" to this relationship that can be stated on general grounds beforehand (except, of course, that the style must not be inappropriate to the personality of the narrator); but the reader should attempt to define whatever relationship exists and to see how it bears on the total effect of the given piece of fiction.

EXPOSITION

Just as the writer cannot set down his first word without settling the question of the point of view, so he cannot set down the first word without involving himself in the problem of exposition. As the action has its "beginning," so the plot has its *exposition*. The first line of the story may plunge us boldly and baldly into an unexplained action—say the episode seen from the window of the moving train, the man striking down the woman—but we must immediately reach into a context to make the event comprehensible. The fictional event cannot remain random and gratuitous. Every situation, even the most simple, has roots that reach back into past time. To make us aware of these roots means, ultimately, to *present the conflict on which the story is based.*

In all cases, some selective exposition is necessary, for the writer must give the reader his bearings, the information that is necessary to make the piece of fiction fully comprehensible. It can be done, especially in the short story, as simply and directly as Chekhov does it in the first sentence of "The Lottery Ticket":

Ivan Dmitritch, a middle-class man who lived with his family on an income of twelve hundred a year and was very well satisfied with his lot, sat down on the sofa after supper and began reading the newspaper.

That is all we need really to know about Ivan for the purpose of beginning the story. A few other bits of exposition are inserted after the story is moving, but they are so incidental that we make use of them without being aware that the author has given them to us. Chekhov is a master of economical exposition; that is, he has the trick of giving just what is necessary for the effect of the story in hand. We are never even told what Ivan looks like, but we find that we know. He is a nondescript sort of man, nothing very striking about him, not quite shabby in his dress and not quite clean in his person, about forty-five years of age, etc. In other words, he is the sort of person a casual observer would find hard to describe because he is so much like a horde of people of his condition and class. He is, further, a somewhat dull, unimaginative, and unambitious man, whose life, we know, has long ago fallen into an unbroken routine with no hope or desire for change or enlargement. The lottery ticket alters all this, and then by disappointing him, converts his old attitude of complacency into one of bitterness. At first glance it seems as though Chekhov has done no better by his exposition than any ordinary writer could do; but we may realize when we consider the implications of his one sentence that he has given us precisely the information we need for his story, no more, no less, so that the result is an impression of great control and artistry. Chekhov has even made his omissions of information instructive: the blanks in the exposition are blanks in the awareness the characters have of their own lives.

Sherwood Anderson employs a very different method of exposition in "I'm a Fool." The first paragraph indicates that the hero has been shaken by an experience which has just occurred and we sense that this experience will be the "story." The suspense is heightened because, at this point, the nature of the experience is only hinted at. The second paragraph starts to give some of the facts—the *when* and the *where*—but the narrator immediately turns aside to discuss the events leading up to the *when* and the *where*. This method of heightening the

suspense, which might seem mechanical in a story told by the author, here seems natural because of the character of the narrator, who himself is the hero of the story. The next paragraph, in fact, begins to define the hero's character. The narrator's account of himself as he fumbles to get at the "story" gives us the necessary exposition; that is, the exposition is dramatized in terms of the narrator's character, which is being defined also by his way of approaching the story. There is an even more complicated management of exposition in "Jerico, Jerico, Jerico," in which the presentation of the past by flashes of memory in the mind of the dying woman gives meaning to the present; but, as a matter of fact, these flashes of memory work not only as exposition but as part of the forwarding action of the story.

These three cases of exposition by no means include the possible methods open to a writer of fiction. The methods vary in detail almost from story to story and novel to novel. There is no set proportion of exposition that a piece of fiction demands; for instance, observe the difference in this respect between "The Lottery Ticket" and "Jerico, Jerico, Jerico." Nor is there a set place in a piece of fiction where the exposition should be placed. One author may deliberately delay information that another might have given as preliminary exposition, and so may build up a curiosity in the reader that will lead him forward with as much force as any suspense about the outcome of an action. Or another author may blend his exposition, bit by bit, with the general movement of his fiction so that the reader is rarely conscious of the process. Still other authors may select their material so carefully that exposition is reduced to a bare minimum, as in "The Killers," by Ernest Hemingway. In general, it may be said that in the short story, because of the limitation of length, the problem of handling exposition skillfully offers more difficulties than in the novel; but in all fiction it is a problem of the utmost importance for both writer and reader. But it is a problem that cannot be solved by itself; it can only be handled in relation to the other problems that confront the writer or reader and in relation to the final effect of the piece of fiction.

COMPLICATION: MOVEMENT

Another problem for both writer and reader is one that we might call simply the problem of *complication*. By complication we mean the evolving of the conflict that is implicit in the original situation; and this evolution is an intensification, involving the suspense of intensification. There is movement in space, and movement in time; there is a series of changes of position and a series of instants of time, and for each character involved each type of series is involved. The writer's task is to relate each series to all the others so that a unit results. We may put the matter in this way. The movement of fiction is not an even, unbroken flow, for the action, naturally, involves positions and moments more important than others. The author selects these moments for his emphasis, the "key" moments, the "focal" moments, of his story or novel. He tends to give these moments his detail work, and tends to present them directly as "scenes" with the fullness of dialogue and gesture that a dramatist would give a scene. Between these directly presented scenes there may be nothing for the reader, just as there is nothing for the spectator when the curtain is down at a play. Or between directly presented scenes there may be transitions involving narrative, summary, and comment. Or again the chief business of the fiction may be handled by the narrator: one may observe how much of "The Gentleman from San Francisco" is occupied by the omniscient narrator who provides connections between scenes, builds towards scenes, and interprets scenes. Most of "Araby" is also taken up with a narrative rather than a scenic treatment. "Jerico, Jerico, Jerico" is, however, handled with a scenic rather than a narrative method, and "The Killers," is almost exclusively scenic in treatment.

Whatever methods are used in presenting the complication, we must remember that, however sinuous and fluctuating the movement may be, the movement is always toward the moment of greatest intensity. There will be a breaking point. We are waiting for the crack.

CLIMAX: DENOUEMENT

But the focal moments of a piece of fiction, whether treated by scene or narrative, are not of equal importance, even though in some instances none of them could be omitted; that is, there is presumably a moment in which the action comes to a head. For instance, in "The Three Strangers" the climax occurs when the condemned man's brother comes to the door; in "The Gentleman from San Francisco" at the moment when the manager of the hotel will not permit the body to be carried back to the room. The climax of a story need not be the most fully developed scene, for a writer can sometimes emphasize the effect by compression rather than expansion.

There is no arbitrary way to arrive at the position of the climax in a piece of fiction, though it naturally falls toward the end. We can probably define the climax as the point where the forces of the piece of fiction reach their moment of maximum concentration; it is, in other words, the "high point" or the "big moment" of a story or novel. It is the moment toward which action is directed, but it does not have to be the end. It is merely the moment at which the end becomes for the reader most probable or, to use the common critical term, "inevitable." Further developments may, and usually do, proceed from the climax to round out a proper conclusion.

We have said that the climax of a piece of fiction is the *point where the forces reach their moment of maximum concentration*. It is the moment toward which the given piece of fiction has been built. How is it built toward this point? Usually it is said that the structure of a piece of fiction may be described as follows: A situation and a character, or characters, are presented by either direct or indirect exposition; then a complication, or a series of complications, is developed leading to the climax; the conclusion settles the complication developd in the body of the story. Some pieces of fiction, such as "La Mère Sauvage," by de Maupassant, demonstrate this structure very clearly. The basic exposition of "La Mère Sauvage" is rendered by a narrator who tells a friend the story. In the story proper the situation is fairly simple: a peasant woman grieves for her son who is away at war. The complication begins when enemy soldiers, billeted at her house, appeal to her maternal affection. The second step in the complication occurs when she receives news of her son's death. The climax comes when the soldiers, unaware of her son's death, laughingly bring her the bloody body of a rabbit which they ask her to cook. The conclusion involves the working out of her vengeance, and the little epilogue (see Glossary) concerning the blackened stone which, symbolically, returns us to the conflict in which the story originates. This part of a story which presents the resolution of the forces in conflict—which unties the tangled knot of the action—is called the *denouement*. (The word literally means *untieing*.) The denouement may be thought of as the end of the action as manifested in plot. Here, if the story is successful, we apprehend the final sense of unity in the story.

SETTING, ATMOSPHERE, AND UNITY

When we have finished a good story or novel we are aware that it has a characteristic "feel," that the world it has created carries a characteristic "atmosphere," and we are aware, too, that this feel, this atmosphere, is a component of that satisfying sense of unity which we find in the conclusion.

We can begin by thinking of the physical setting of the action. A story occurs in a particular place—or in a series of places. But places provoke feelings in us. If we are not preoccupied with something else, the sight of a dingy alley affects us very differently from the sight of a green field, a luxurious room, or a tropical jungle. Aside from the mere facts of ugliness or beauty in a scene, we have, in addition, certain associations, usually very complicated ones, built up about various places. We are depressed by the dingy alley, not only because it is ugly, but because with it we associate, perhaps not always consciously, the poverty, misery, viciousness, and struggle of human beings who are forced to live under such conditions. A scene of a tropical jungle, for instance, a scene from one of Joseph Conrad's novels, might involve an even more complicated analysis: the pleasure in the beauty of the colors and forms of vegetation, the discom-

fort of the humidity, heat, and insects, the fear of danger, etc. We may say, then, that our reaction to a place is not merely based on the way it looks, but on the potentialities of action suggested by it.

Furthermore, even though we may believe that human beings are very much alike from one place to another and that they are motivated by the same basic impulses—hate, love, avarice, pride, etc.—we are also aware of differences in the kind of life that is led from place to place. People have different social values, customs, manners, and occupations. There are some stories, therefore, that belong to certain settings, and not to others. Other pieces of fiction depend for a part of their effect on the relation of people to a place, *The Return of the Native*, by Thomas Hardy, for instance; and in such cases the presentation of setting assumes an unusual importance. But even in the more ordinary cases, the skill of the writer in giving the setting is important, because the reader, if he accepts as credible the setting of a story—if the description is so good that he really sees the things described—is prepared to take the slightly more difficult step of believing in the reality of the characters.

There is that transference of the sense of reality in scene to a sense of reality in character. But we can go further. A setting invites a certain action. We say, "This is a great place for a murder." Or, "How could anyone be unhappy here?" In such expressions we reveal that we recognize some simple correlation. In neither life nor fiction, of course, do we regularly find such simple correlations, but the human impulse to seize on them underlies all the effects and responses that deal with positive correlations as when we associate the death of an old man with a winter evening but also with the negative instances as well—the failures in simple correlations as when a child is killed by a truck on a beautiful sunlit spring morning, while the maples all about are just coming to leaf.

The working out of any principle is, of course, a matter of tact and sensitivity and experience. But let us state the bare principle: *The scene is the action.*

Some critics of fiction, without actually confusing the two terms, *setting* and *atmosphere*, perhaps make the connection between them more exclusive than can be justified by the analysis of actual pieces of fiction. There is, however, an intimate if not exclusive connection that is of considerable importance in the effect, a given story or novel makes on the reader. *Atmosphere* is a very vague term. It is, of course, a metaphor for a feeling or impression which we cannot, perhaps, readily attach to some tangible cause. We say that an old farmhouse set among large maples, on a green lawn, has "an atmosphere of peace." We say that a mountain valley with great boulders covered by lichen, and a cataract shadowed by tall cedars, has a "romantic atmosphere." What we mean is that the house, by reason of the look of quietness and by reason of a number of pleasant associations we have with the routine of the kind of life lived there, stirs a certain reaction in us which we do not attach to any single incident or object, but generally to the whole scene. Or we mean that the mountain valley, which we think has a romantic atmosphere, stirs in us a restlessness and expectation which we cannot definitely explain. In the same way we may say that the setting of a story contributes to defining its atmosphere. For instance, the description at the beginning of "The Horse Dealer's Daughter," by Lawrence, contributes to the atmosphere of the story, and the description of Egdon Heath in the early pages of *The Return of the Native,* by Hardy, gives a start to the atmosphere or feeling that surrounds the subsequent story.

But it is a mistake to say that the atmosphere of a piece of fiction depends on the setting alone. That is merely one factor that may contribute to the atmosphere. For instance, the rhythm of the sentences helps to establish the general feeling. The movement may be long and swinging, or short and clipped, strongly or weakly marked, simple or complicated, lulling or exciting, etc.; and this factor will always contribute very positively, although the reader may not be conscious of it, to the atmosphere. Or further, the kind of vocabulary and the kind of figures of speech help define the kind of atmosphere, for by these factors the writer endeavors to control the kind of associations that come to the reader's mind; and, as we have said, the atmosphere of a place or a piece of fiction derives very largely from the associations and suggestions connected with it. But atmosphere also depends on character and action. In short, we may say that the atmosphere of fiction is the pervasive, general feeling, generated by a number of factors (setting, character, action, and style) that is characteristic of a given story or novel. Every piece of successful fiction has its own special atmosphere, and it is a mistake to speak as if the term were confined to those stories or novels in which the writer depends heavily on description to maintain this feeling. That feel, that atmosphere, which we associate with a good story is really a kind of pervasive meaning, like electricity in the gathering storm. In recognizing it we sense some kind of unity between the physical and moral spheres. It is, as it were, a circumambient metaphor, the key metaphor, sometimes, of a work. The darkness of *Macbeth is* the play.

SECTION I

Episode and Fictional Point

There are many different ways to approach the study of fiction, and each way has a characteristic value. We might, for instance, begin with a complicated, highly developed story and study its various elements in relation to the meaning of the whole and the effect the whole makes upon us. But we shall begin quite differently—by taking two little narratives which scarcely seem to be stories at all, mere anecdotes (see Glossary), mere episodes, without much complication, perhaps seeming pointless at first glance.

In trying to discover what makes these little narratives fiction, a definition does not help much. But we may attempt a definition as a point of departure: fiction is a narrative, involving human beings, of some significant conflict that is resolved in such a way as to imply a comment on human values.

Someone may object here to the phrase "involving human beings," and remind us of stories about dogs and cats and so on. But we may counter by saying that always, whether in Jack London's half-dog, half-wolf hero White Fang or in Wee Willie Chipmunk, what catches our real interest is the projection of human qualities into the animal.

Or again, someone may object to our saying that the resolution of the fictional conflict always implies a comment on human values, arguing that this view smacks of the moralistic. Our appeal again must be to what catches our interest in a story. The mere collision of forces does not long engage us. We want to know what is at stake in the collision. We instinctively take sides, and in the end there is the victory or the defeat in which we imaginatively participate. Our own values have been involved in the collision and by the conclusion will be clarified or even modified.

This is true, perhaps most deeply true, when the collision on which the story is based divides our sympathies. For instance, let us recall the story of Shakespeare's play *Henry IV, Part I*, where we are "officially" on the side of Prince Hal but also admire his chief enemy and rival Hotspur, and are drawn, at the same time, to Falstaff, who represents everything contrary to the world of chivalry of Hal and Hotspur, and who, as we know, will be cast off by Hal at the end. This is a long way from the simple division into cops and robbers, hero and villain, which we find in crude fiction, but the principle is the same: the question of taking sides is raised and it is raised most acutely and deeply when the choice is difficult and when the choice sets up tensions among our own loyalties and values.

By the same token, the question of the meaning of the resolution, the kind of comment implied by a piece of fiction, is raised most acutely when the conflict is a complex one and we have not been able to take sides with automatic ease, that is, when the resolution itself comes with some difficulty and internal resistance. That resolution is most meaningful that makes us take stock of our own values and does not merely illustrate for us what we are ready beforehand to accept.

The Use of Force

WILLIAM CARLOS WILLIAMS (1883-1963)

THEY WERE new patients to me, all I had was the name, Olson. Please come down as soon as you can, my daughter is very sick.

When I arrived I was met by the mother, a big startled looking woman, very clean and apologetic who merely said, Is this the doctor? and let me in. In the back, she added. You must excuse us, doctor, we have her in the kitchen where it is warm. It is very damp here sometimes.

The child was fully dressed and sitting on her father's lap near the kitchen table. He tried to get up, but I motioned for him not to bother, took off my overcoat and started to look things over. I could see that they were all very nervous, eyeing me up and down distrustfully. As often, in such cases, they weren't telling me more than they had to, it was up to me to tell them; that's why they were spending three dollars on me.

The child was fairly eating me up with her cold, steady eyes, and no expression to her face whatever. She did not move and seemed, inwardly, quiet; an unusually attractive little thing, and as strong as a heifer in appearance. But her face was flushed, she was breathing rapidly, and I realized that she had a high fever. She had magnificent blonde hair, in profusion. One of those picture children often reproduced in advertising leaflets and the photogravure sections of the Sunday papers.

She's had a fever for three days, began the father and we don't know what it comes from. My wife has given her things, you know, like people do, but it don't do no good. And there's been a lot of sickness around. So we tho't you'd better look her over and tell us what is the matter.

As doctors often do I took a trial shot at it as a point of departure. Has she had a sore throat?

Both parents answered me together, No . . . No, she says her throat don't hurt her.

Does your throat hurt you? added the mother to the child. But the little girl's expression didn't change nor did she move her eyes from my face.

Have you looked?

I tried to, said the mother, but I couldn't see.

As it happens we had been having a number of cases of diphtheria in the school to which this child went during that month and we were all, quite apparently, thinking of that, though no one had as yet spoken of the thing.

Well, I said, suppose we take a look at the throat first. I smiled in my best professional manner and asking for the child's first name I said, come on, Mathilda, open your mouth and let's take a look at your throat.

Nothing doing.

Aw, come on, I coaxed, just open your mouth wide and let me take a look. Look, I said opening both hands wide, I haven't anything in my hands. Just open up and let me see.

Such a nice man, put in the mother. Look how kind he is to you. Come on, do what he tells you to. He won't hurt you.

At that I ground my teeth in disgust. If only they wouldn't use the word "hurt" I might be able to get somewhere. But I did not allow myself to be hurried or disturbed but speaking quietly and slowly I approached the child again.

As I moved my chair a little nearer suddenly with one catlike movement both her hands clawed instinctively for my eyes and she almost reached them too. In fact she knocked my glasses flying and they fell, though unbroken, several feet away from me on the kitchen floor.

Both the mother and father almost turned themselves inside out in embarrassment and apology. You bad girl, said the mother, taking her and shaking her by one arm. Look what you've done. The nice man . . .

For heaven's sake, I broke in. Don't call me a nice man to her. I'm here to look at her throat on the chance that she might have diphtheria and possibly die of it. But that's nothing to her. Look here, I said to the child, we're going to look at your throat. You're old enough to understand what I'm saying. Will you open it now by yourself or shall we have to open it for you?

Not a move. Even her expression hadn't changed. Her breaths however were coming faster and faster. Then the battle began. I had to do it. I had to have a throat culture for her own protection. But first I told the parents that it was entirely up to them. I explained the danger but said that I would not insist on a throat examination so long as they would take the responsibility.

If you don't do what the doctor says you'll have to go to the hospital, the mother admonished her severely.

Oh yeah? I had to smile to myself. After all, I had already fallen in love with the savage brat, the parents were contemptible to me. In the ensuing struggle they grew more and more abject, crushed, exhausted while she surely rose to magnificent heights of insane fury of effort bred of her terror of me.

The father tried his best, and he was a big man but the fact that she was his daughter, his shame at her behavior and his dread of hurting her made him release her just at the critical times when I had almost achieved success, till I wanted to kill him. But his dread also that she might have diphtheria made him tell me to go on, go on though he himself was almost fainting, while the mother moved back and forth behind us raising and lowering her hands in an agony of apprehension.

Put her in front of you on your lap, I ordered, and hold both her wrists.

But as soon as he did the child let out a scream. Don't, you're hurting me. Let go of my hands. Let them go I tell you. Then she shrieked terrifyingly, hysterically. Stop it! Stop it! You're killing me!

Do you think she can stand it, doctor! said the mother.

You get out, said the husband to his wife. Do you want her to die of diphtheria?

Come on now, hold her, I said.

Then I grasped the child's head with my left hand and tried to get the wooden tongue depressor between her teeth. She fought, with clenched teeth, desperately! But now I also had grown furious—at a child. I tried to hold myself down but I couldn't. I know how to expose a throat for inspection. And I did my best. When finally I got the wooden spatula behind the last teeth and just the point of it into the mouth cavity, she opened up for an instant but before I could see anything she came down again and gripping the wooden blade between her molars she reduced it to splinters before I could get it out again.

Aren't you ashamed, the mother yelled at her. Aren't you ashamed to act like that in front of the doctor?

Get me a smooth-handled spoon of some sort, I told the mother. We're going through with this. The child's mouth was already bleeding. Her tongue was cut and she was screaming in wild hysterical shrieks. Perhaps I should have desisted and come back in an hour or more. No doubt it would have been better. But I have seen at least two children lying dead in bed of neglect in such cases, and feeling that I must get a diagnosis now or never I went at it again. But the worst of it was that I too had got beyond reason. I could have torn the child apart in my own fury and enjoyed it. It was a pleasure to attack her. My face was burning with it.

The damned little brat must be protected against her own idiocy, one says to one's self at such times. Others must be protected against her. It is a social necessity. And all these things are true. But a blind fury, a feeling of adult shame, bred of a longing for muscular release are the operatives. One goes on to the end.

In a final unreasoning assault I overpowered the child's neck and jaws. I forced the heavy silver spoon back of her teeth and down her throat till she gagged. And there it was—both tonsils covered with membrane. She had fought valiantly to keep me from knowing her secret. She had been hiding that sore throat for three days at least and lying to her parents in order to escape just such an outcome as this.

Now truly she was furious. She had been on the defensive before but now she attacked. Tried to get off her father's lap and fly at me while tears of defeat blinded her eyes.

DISCUSSION

Our question, we recall, is to determine what gives a little narrative like this a fictional point. Does it stem from a humanly significant conflict? Is the conflict resolved or even put into such a light that things look different from the way they did at the beginning?

Naturally we see that the conflict is significant in one sense, the purely practical sense —it is important for the doctor to make the diagnosis. But the diagnosis of the child's illness is not the real—the internal—significance of the piece.

The title gives us the lead to this real significance. What is at stake in the use of force? Persuasion will not serve, and so the doctor must use force: "The damned little brat must be protected against her own idiocy . . . Others must be protected against her. It is a social necessity." At the same time the child recognizes the use of force as a fundamental affront, a violation, and so resists with all her power. Both the child and the doctor are "right." Both appeal to our sympathies. Even the doctor recognizes the child's rightness and sympathizes with her: "After all, I had already fallen in love with the savage brat." With this division of feeling, the doctor, however, must continue his effort to pry open the child's jaws.

In the end the doctor succeeds, and discovers that the child does have diphtheria. Is that the resolution, the point? No, for what we —including the doctor—learn is something about the use of force. The real point is in the unmasking of something in human nature. The use of force, even in a good cause, opens up some dark depth of our nature, a "blind fury," a will to conquest, a delight in cruelty. The doctor admits: "I could have torn the child apart in my own fury and enjoyed it. It was a pleasure to attack her." That is the terrifying revelation the story comes to. The fact that, in the end, the symptoms of the disease are revealed on the child's tonsils is not the significant fact in the resolution. It is significant only insofar as it echoes, serves as a kind of image for, the real thing revealed—that other kind of disease in our nature which the use of force defines.

EXERCISE

Read "Daddy Wolf" by James Purdy (page 219). This story is much longer than "The Use of Force," but as an episode (see Glossary) may seem, to some readers, almost as pointless. What is the point?

An Episode of War

STEPHEN CRANE (1871-1900)

THE LIEUTENANT'S rubber blanket lay on the ground, and upon it had been poured the company's supply of coffee. Corporals and other representatives of the grimy and hot-throated men who lined the breastwork had come for each squad's portion.

The lieutenant was frowning and serious at this task of division. His lips pursed as he drew with his sword various crevices in the heap until brown squares of coffee, astoundingly equal in size, appeared on the blanket. He was on the verge of a great triumph in mathematics, and the corporals were thronging forward, each to reap a little square, when suddenly the lieutenant cried out and looked quickly at a man near him as if he suspected it was a case of personal assault. The others cried out also when they saw blood upon the lieutenant's sleeve.

He had winced like a man stung, swayed dangerously, and then straightened. The sound of his hoarse breathing was plainly audible. He looked sadly, mystically, over the breastwork at the green face of a wood, where now were many little puffs of white smoke. During this moment the men about him gazed statue-like and silent, astonished and awed by this catastrophe which happened when catastrophes were not expected —when they had leisure to observe it.

As the lieutenant stared at the wood, they too swung their heads, so that for another instant all hands, still silent, contemplated the distant forest as if their minds were fixed upon the mystery of a bullet's journey.

The officer had, of course, been compelled to take his sword into his left hand. He did not hold it by the hilt. He gripped it at the middle of the blade, awkwardly. Turning his eyes from the hostile wood, he looked at the sword as he held it there, and seemed puzzled as to what to do with it, where to put it. In short, this weapon had of a sudden become a strange thing to him. He looked at it in a kind of stupefaction, as if he had been endowed with a trident, a sceptre, or a spade.

Finally he tried to sheath it. To sheath a sword held by the left hand, at the middle of the blade, in a scabbard hung at the left hip, is a feat worthy of a sawdust ring. This wounded officer engaged in a desperate struggle with the sword and the wobbling scabbard, and during the time of it he breathed like a wrestler.

But at this instant the men, the spectators, awoke from their stone-like poses and crowded forward sympathetically. The orderly-sergeant took the sword and tenderly placed it in the scabbard. At the time, he leaned nervously backward, and did not allow even his finger to brush the body of the lieutenant. A wound gives strange dignity to him who bears it. Well men shy from this new and terrible majesty. It is as if the wounded man's hand is upon the curtain which hangs before the revelations of all existence—the meaning of ants, potentates, wars, cities, sunshine, snow, a feather dropped from a bird's wing; and the power of it sheds radiance upon a bloody form, and makes the other men understand sometimes that they are little. His comrades look at him with large eyes thoughtfully. Moreover, they fear vaguely that the weight of a finger upon him might send him headlong, precipitate the tragedy, hurl him at once into the dim, gray unknown. And so the orderly-sergeant, while sheathing the sword, leaned nervously backward.

There were others who proffered assistance. One timidly presented his shoulder and asked the lieutenant if he cared to lean upon it, but the latter waved him away mournfully. He wore the look of one who knows he is the victim of a terrible disease and understands his helplessness. He again stared over the breastwork at the forest, and then turning went slowly rearward. He held his right wrist tenderly in his left hand as if the wounded arm was made of very brittle glass.

And the men in silence stared at the wood, then at the departing lieutenant—then at the wood, then at the lieutenant.

As the wounded officer passed from the line of battle, he was enabled to see many things which as a participant in the fight were unknown to him. He saw a general on a black horse gazing over the lines of blue infantry at the green woods which veiled his problems. An aide galloped furiously, dragged his horse suddenly to a halt, saluted, and presented a paper. It was, for a wonder, precisely like an historical painting.

To the rear of the general and his staff a group, composed of a bugler, two or three orderlies, and the bearer of the corps standard, all upon maniacal horses, were working like slaves to hold their ground, preserve their respectful interval, while the shells boomed in the air about them, and caused their chargers to make furious quivering leaps.

A battery, a tumultuous and shining mass, was swirling toward the right. The wild thud of hoofs, the cries of the riders shouting blame and praise, menace and encouragement, and, last, the roar of the wheels, the slant of the glistening guns, brought the lieutenant to an intent pause. The battery swept in curves that stirred the heart; it made halts as dramatic as the crash of a wave on the rocks, and when it fled onward, this aggregation of wheels, lever,

motors, had a beautiful unity, as if it were a missile. The sound of it was a war-chorus that reached into the depths of man's emotion.

The lieutenant, still holding his arm as if it were of glass, stood watching this battery until all detail of it was lost, save the figures of the riders, which rose and fell and waved lashes over the black mass.

Later, he turned his eyes toward the battle where the shooting sometimes crackled like bush-fires, sometimes sputtered with exasperating irregularity, and sometimes reverberated like the thunder. He saw the smoke rolling upward and saw crowds of men who ran and cheered, or stood and blazed away at the inscrutable distance.

He came upon some stragglers, and they told him how to find the field hospital. They described its exact location. In fact, these men, no longer having part in the battle, knew more of it than others. They told the performance of every corps, every division, the opinion of every general. The lieutenant, carrying his wounded arm rearward, looked upon them with wonder.

At the roadside a brigade was making coffee and buzzing with talk like a girls' boarding-school. Several officers came out to him and inquired concerning things of which he knew nothing. One, seeing his arm, began to scold. "Why, man, that's no way to do. You want to fix that thing." He appropriated the lieutenant and the lieutenant's wound. He cut the sleeve and laid bare the arm, every nerve of which softly fluttered under his touch. He bound his handkerchief over the wound, scolding away in the meantime. His tone allowed one to think that he was in the habit of being wounded every day. The lieutenant hung his head, feeling, in this presence, that he did not know how to be correctly wounded.

The low white tents of the hospital were grouped around an old school-house. There was here a singular commotion. In the foreground two ambulances interlocked wheels in the deep mud. The drivers were tossing the blame of it back and forth, gesticulating and berating, while from the ambulances, both crammed with wounded, there came an occasional groan. An interminable crowd of bandaged men were coming and going. Great numbers sat under the trees nursing heads or arms or legs. There was a dispute of some kind raging on the steps of the school-house. Sitting with his back against a tree a man with a face as gray as a new army blanket was serenely smoking a corn-cob pipe. The lieutenant wished to rush forward and inform him that he was dying.

A busy surgeon was passing near the lieutenant. "Good morning," he said, with a friendly smile. Then he caught sight of the lieutenant's arm and his face at once changed. "Well, let's have a look at it." He seemed possessed suddenly of a great contempt for the lieutenant. This wound evidently placed the latter on a very low social plane. The doctor cried out impatiently, "What mutton-head had tied it up that way anyhow?" The lieutenant answered, "Oh, a man."

When the wound was disclosed the doctor fingered it disdainfully. "Humph," he said. "You come along with me and I'll tend to you." His voice contained the same scorn as if he were saying, "You will have to go to jail."

The lieutenant had been very meek, but now his face flushed, and he looked into the doctor's eyes. "I guess I won't have it amputated," he said.

"Nonsense, man! Nonsense! Nonsense!" cried the doctor. "Come along, now. I won't amputate it. Come along. Don't be a baby."

"Let go of me," said the lieutenant, holding back wrathfully, his glance fixed upon the door of the old school-house, as sinister to him as the portals of death.

And this is the story of how the lieutenant lost his arm. When he reached home, his sisters, his mother, his wife, sobbed for a long time at the sight of the flat sleeve. "Oh, well," he said, standing shamefaced amid these tears, "I don't suppose it matters so much as all that."

EXERCISE

At first glance this seems a mere sketch. The plot element is slight; there seems to be no real conflict, and the resolution is vague. But is it possible to make out a case for this as fiction? In examining this possibility attempt to answer the following questions:

1. What is the function of the relatively large amount of description?

2. The author has taken pains to indicate how the wound sets the lieutenant apart from his fellows. How do men regard him? How do the officers regard him? The surgeon? Do these elements help to define a theme?

3. What elements of contrast are employed in the story?

4. What is the significance of the last line?

5. Is there any reason for Crane's refusal to give the lieutenant's name?

6. What are the implications of Crane's comparison of the actual battle to "an historical painting"?

7. Read "Kronkin's Prisoner," by Isaac Babel (p. 207), an episode in the war between the Russians and the Poles just after the Communist Revolution of 1917. Frame a set of questions which might lead to a statement of its fictional point. You may not be able to answer all your own questions, but asking the right questions about a thing is half way to an understanding and appreciation of it. Compare your questions with those framed by other students.

SECTION II

The Tale: Feeling and Idea

The pieces in this group are not simple episodes. They are rather long narratives, involving a series of events. But these narratives do not have the close organization of events and the kind of interrelation of characters we expect in the highly developed piece of fiction. The sense of being "told" is strong in the first two pieces— being "told" rather than presented in a series of dramatically developed scenes connected by narrative, or supported in the tissue of narrative, which is the characteristic method of what we regard as a "well made" short story.

These pieces are tales, or chronicles, rather than short stories, in the strict sense of that term. The first one given here is, specifically, a fairy tale. Let us ask ourselves, again, what fictional point we find. What holds such a tale together?

The Fir Tree

HANS CHRISTIAN ANDERSEN (1805-1875)

OUT IN the forest stood a pretty little Fir Tree. It had a good place; it could have sunlight, air there was in plenty, and all around grew many larger comrades—pines as well as firs. But the little Fir Tree was in such a hurry to grow. It did not care for the warm sun and the fresh air; it took no notice of the peasant children, who went about talking together, when they had come out to look for strawberries and raspberries. Often they came with a whole pot-full, or had strung berries on a straw; then they would sit down by the little Fir Tree and say, 'How pretty and small that one is!' and the Tree did not like to hear that at all.

Next year it had grown a great joint, and the following year it was longer still, for in fir trees one can always tell by the number of joints they have how many years they have been growing.

'Oh, if I were only as great a tree as the others!' sighed the little Fir, 'then I would spread my branches far around, and look out from my crown into the wide world. The birds would then build nests in my boughs, and when the wind blew I could nod just as grandly as the others yonder.'

It took no pleasure in the sunshine, in the birds, and in the red clouds that went sailing over it morning and evening.

When it was winter, and the snow lay all around, white and sparkling, a hare would often come jumping along, and spring right over the little Fir Tree. Oh! this made it so angry. But two winters went by, and when the third came the little Tree had grown so tall that the hare was obliged to run round it.

'Oh! to grow, to grow, and become old; that's the only fine thing in the world,' thought the Tree.

In the autumn woodcutters always came and felled a few of the largest trees; that happened every year, and the little Fir Tree, that was now quite well grown, shuddered with fear, for the great stately trees fell to the ground with a crash, and their branches were cut off, so that the trees looked quite naked, long, and slender—they could hardly be recognized. But then they were laid upon wagons, and horses dragged them away out of the wood. Where were they going? What destiny awaited them?

In the spring, when Swallows and the Stork came, the Tree asked them, 'Do you know where they were taken? Did you not meet them?'

The Swallows knew nothing about it, but the Stork looked thoughtful, nodded his head, and said,

'Yes, I think so. I met many new ships when I flew out of Egypt; on the ships were stately masts; I fancy that these were the trees. They smelt like fir. I can assure you they're stately—very stately.'

'Oh that I were only big enough to go over the sea! What kind of thing is this sea, and how does it look?'

'It would take too long to explain all that,' said the Stork, and he went away.

'Rejoice in thy youth,' said the Sunbeams; 'rejoice in thy fresh growth, and in the young life that is within thee.'

And the wind kissed the Tree, and the dew wept tears upon it; but the Fir Tree did not understand that.

When Christmas-time approached, quite young trees were felled, sometimes trees which were neither so old nor so large as this Fir Tree, that never rested but always wanted to go away. These young trees, which were just the most beautiful, kept all their branches; they were put upon wagons, and horses dragged them away out of the wood.

'Where are they all going?' asked the Fir Tree. 'They are not greater than I—indeed, one of them was much smaller. Why do they keep all their branches? Whither are they taken?'

'We know that! We know that!' chirped the Sparrows. 'Yonder in the town we looked in at the windows. We know where they go. Oh! they are dressed up in the greatest pomp and splendour that can be imagined. We have looked in at the windows, and have perceived that they are planted in the middle of the warm room, and adorned with the most beautiful things—gilt apples, honeycakes, playthings, and many hundreds of candles.'

'And then?' asked the Fir Tree, and trembled through all its branches. 'And then? What happens then?'

'Why, we have not seen anything more. But it was incomparable.'

'Perhaps I may be destined to tread this glorious path one day!' cried the Fir Tree rejoicingly. 'That is even better than travelling across the sea. How painfully I long for it! If it were only Christmas now! Now I am great and grown up, like the rest who were led away last year. Oh, if I were only on the carriage! If I were only in the warm room, among all the pomp and splendour! And then? Yes, then something even better will come, something far more charming, or else why should they adorn me so? There must be something grander, something greater still to come; but what? Oh! I'm suffering, I'm longing! I don't know myself what is the matter with me!'

'Rejoice in us,' said Air and Sunshine. 'Rejoice in thy fresh youth here in the woodland.'

But the Fir Tree did not rejoice at all, but it grew and grew; winter and summer it stood there, green, dark green. The people who saw it said, 'That's a handsome tree!' and at Christmas-time it was felled before any one of the others. The axe cut deep into its marrow, and the Tree fell to the ground with a sigh: it felt a pain, a sensation of faintness, and could not think

at all of happiness, for it was sad at parting from its home, from the place where it had grown up: it knew that it should never again see the dear old companions, the little bushes and flowers all around—perhaps not even the birds. The parting was not at all agreeable.

The Tree only came to itself when it was unloaded in a yard, with other trees, and heard a man say,

'This one is famous; we only want this one!'

Now two servants came in gay liveries, and carried the Fir Tree into a large beautiful saloon. All around the walls hung pictures, and by the great stove stood large Chinese vases with lions on the covers; there were rocking-chairs, silken sofas, great tables covered with picture-books, and toys worth a hundred times a hundred dollars, at least the children said so. And the Fir Tree was put into a great tub filled with sand; but no one could see that it was a tub, for it was hung round with green cloth, and stood on a large many-coloured carpet. Oh, how the Tree trembled! What was to happen now? The servants, and the young ladies also, decked it out. On one branch they hung little nets, cut out of coloured paper; every net was filled with sweetmeats; golden apples and walnuts hung down as if they grew there, and more than a hundred little candles, red, white, and blue, were fastened to the different boughs. Dolls that looked exactly like real people—the Tree had never seen such before—swung among the foliage, and high on the summit of the Tree was fixed a tinsel star. It was splendid, particularly splendid.

'This evening,' said all, 'this evening it will shine.'

'Oh,' thought the Tree, 'that it were evening already! Oh that the lights may be soon lit up! What will happen then? I wonder if trees will come out of the forest to look at me? Will the sparrows fly against the panes? Shall I grow fast here, and stand adorned in summer and winter?'

Yes, it knew all about it. But it had a regular bark-ache from mere longing, and the bark-ache is just as bad for a Tree as the headache for a person.

At last the candles were lighted. What a brilliance, what splendour! The Tree trembled so in all its branches that one of the candles set fire to a green twig, and it was really painful.

'Heaven preserve us!' cried the young ladies; and they hastily put the fire out.

Now the Tree might not even tremble. Oh, that was terrible! It was so afraid of losing any of its ornaments, and it was quite bewildered with all the brillance. And now the folding doors were thrown open, and a number of children rushed in as if they would have overturned the whole Tree; the older people followed more deliberately. The little ones stood quite silent, but only for a minute; then they shouted till the room rang: they danced gleefully round the Tree, and one present after another was plucked from it.

'What are they about?' thought the Tree. 'What's going to be done?'

And the candles burned down to the twigs, and as they burned down they were extinguished, and then the children received permission to plunder the Tree. Oh! they rushed in upon it, so that very branch cracked again: if it had not been fastened by the top and by the golden star to the ceiling, it would have fallen down.

The children danced about with their pretty toys. No one looked at the Tree except the old nursemaid, who came up and peeped among the branches, but only to see if a fig or an apple had not been forgotten.

'A story! a story!' shouted the children: and they drew a little fat man towards the Tree; and he sat down just beneath it,—'for then we shall be in the green wood,' said he, 'and the tree may have the advantage of listening to my tale. But I can only tell one. Will you hear the story of Ivede-Avede, or of Humpty-Dumpty, who fell downstairs, and still was raised up to honour and married the Princess?'

'Ivede-Avede!' cried some, 'Humpty-Dumpty!' cried others, and there was a great crying and shouting. Only the Fir Tree was quite silent, and thought, 'Shall I not be in it? shall I have nothing to do in it?' But it had been in the evening's amusement, and had done what was required of it.

And the fat man told about Humpty-Dumpty, who fell downstairs, and yet was raised to honour and married the Princess. And the children clapped their hands, and cried, 'Tell another! tell another!' for they wanted to hear about Ivede-Avede; but they only got the story of Humpty-Dumpty. The Fir Tree stood quite silent and thoughtful; never had the birds in the wood told such a story as that. Humpty-Dumpty fell downstairs, and yet came to honour and married the Princess!

'Yes, so it happens in the world!' thought the Fir Tree, and believed it must be true, because that was such a nice man who told it. 'Well, who can know? Perhaps I shall fall downstairs too, and marry a Princess!' And it looked forward with pleasure to being adorned again, the next evening, with candles and toys, gold and fruit. 'To-morrow I shall not tremble,' it thought. 'I will rejoice in all my splendour. To-morrow I shall hear the story of Humpty-Dumpty again, and, perhaps, that of Ivede-Avede too.'

And the Tree stood all night quiet and thoughtful.

In the morning the servants and the chambermaid came in.

'Now my splendour will begin afresh,' thought the Tree. But they dragged it out of the room, and upstairs to the garret, and here they put it in a dark corner where no daylight shone.

'What's the meaning of this?' thought the Tree. 'What am I to do here? What am I to get to know here?'

And he leaned against the wall, and thought, and thought. And he had time enough, for days and nights went by, and nobody came up; and when at length some one came, it was only to put some great boxes in a corner. Now the Tree stood quite hidden away, and one would think that it was quite forgotten.

'Now it's winter outside,' thought the Tree. 'The earth is hard and covered with snow, and people cannot plant me; therefore I suppose I'm to be sheltered here until spring comes. How considerate that is! How good people are! If it were only not so dark here, and so terribly solitary!—not even a little hare! It was pretty out there in the wood, when the snow lay thick and the hare sprang past; yes, even when he jumped over me, although I did not like that at the time. It is terribly lonely up here!'

'Piep! piep!' said a little Mouse, and crept forward, and then came another little one. They smelt at the Fir Tree, and then slipped among the branches.

'It's horribly cold,' said the two little Mice,

'or else it would be comfortable here. Don't you think so, you old Fir Tree?'

'I'm not old at all,' said the Fir Tree. 'There are many much older than I.'

'Where do you come from?' asked the Mice. 'And what do you know?' They were dreadfully inquisitive. 'Tell us about the most beautiful spot on earth. Have you been there? Have you been in the store-room, where cheeses lie on the shelves, and hams hang from the ceiling, where one dances on tallow candles, and goes in thin and comes out fat?'

'I don't know that!' replied the Tree; 'but I know the wood, where the sun shines, and where the birds sing.'

And then it told all about its youth.

And the little Mice had never heard anything of the kind; and they listened and said,

'What a number of things you have seen! How happy you must have been!'

'I?' said the Fir Tree; and it thought about what it had told. 'Yes, those were really quite happy times.' But then it told of the Christmas-eve, when it had been hung with sweetmeats and candles.

'Oh!' said the little Mice, 'how happy you have been, you old Fir Tree!'

'I'm not old at all,' said the Tree. 'I only came out of the wood this winter. I'm in my very best years.'

'What splendid stories you can tell!' said the little Mice.

And next night they came with four other little Mice, to hear what the Tree had to relate; and the more it said, the more clearly did it remember everything, and thought, 'Those were quite merry days! But they may come again. Humpty-Dumpty fell downstairs, and yet he married the Princess. Perhaps I may marry a Princess too!' And then the Fir Tree thought of a pretty little birch tree that grew out in the forest: for the Fir Tree, that birch was a real Princess.

'Who's Humpty-Dumpty?' asked the little Mice.

And then the Fir Tree told the whole story. It could remember every single word; and the little Mice were ready to leap to the very top of the tree with pleasure. Next night a great many more Mice came, and on Sunday two Rats even appeared; but these thought the story was not pretty, and the little Mice were sorry for that, for now they also did not like it so much as before.

'Do you only know one story?' asked the Rats.

'Only that one,' replied the Tree. 'I heard that on the happiest evening of my life; I did not think then how happy I was.'

'That's an exceedingly poor story. Don't you know any about bacon and tallow candles—a store-room story?'

'No,' said the Tree.

'Then we'd rather not hear you,' said the Rats.

And they went back to their own people. The little Mice at last stayed away also; and then the Tree sighed and said,

'It was very nice when they sat round me, the merry little Mice, and listened when I spoke to them. Now that's past too. But I shall remember to be pleased when they take me out.'

But when did that happen? Why, it was one morning that people came and rummaged in the garret: the boxes were put away, and the Tree brought out; they certainly threw it rather roughly on the floor, but a servant dragged it away at once to the stairs, where the daylight shone.

'Now life is beginning again!' thought the Tree.

It felt the fresh air and the first sunbeams, and now it was out in the courtyard. Everything passed so quickly that the Tree quite forgot to look at itself, there was so much to look at all round. The courtyard was close to a garden, and here everything was blooming; the roses hung fresh and fragrant over the little paling, the linden trees were in blossom, and the swallows cried, 'Quirre-virre-vit! my husband's come!' But it was not the Fir Tree that they meant.

'Now I shall live!' said the Tree, rejoicingly, and spread its branches far out; but, alas! they were all withered and yellow; and it lay in the corner among nettles and weeds. The tinsel star was still upon it, and shone in the bright sunshine.

In the courtyard a couple of the merry children were playing, who had danced round the tree at Christmas-time, and had rejoiced over it.

One of the youngest ran up and tore off the golden star.

'Look what is sticking to the ugly old fir tree,' said the child, and he trod upon the branches till they cracked again under his boots.

And the Tree looked at all the blooming flowers and the splendour of the garden, and then looked at itself, and wished it had remained in the dark corner of the garret; it thought of its fresh youth in the wood, of the merry Christmas-eve, and of the little Mice which had listened so pleasantly to the story of Humpty-Dumpty.

'Past! past!' said the poor Tree. 'Had I but rejoiced when I could have done so! Past! past!'

And the servant came and chopped the Tree into little pieces; a whole bundle lay there: it blazed brightly under the great brewing copper, and it sighed deeply, and each sigh was like a little shot: and the children who were at play there ran up and seated themselves at the fire, looked into it, and cried, 'Puff! puff!' But at each explosion, which was a deep sigh, the tree thought of a summer day in the woods, or of a winter night there, when the stars beamed; it thought of Christmas-eve and of Humpty-Dumpty, the only story it had ever heard or knew how to tell; and then the Tree was burned.

The boys played in the garden, and the youngest had on his breast a golden star, which the Tree had worn on its happiest evening. Now that was past, and the Tree's life was past, and the story is past too: past! past!—and that's the way with all stories.

EXERCISE

1. What is the conflict, if any, in this story? What idea emerges at the end of the story?

2. Though this is a tale intended for small children, the grown-up reader finds something here too. What is it? And is it precisely the same thing that the child finds in the story? If "The Fir Tree" were rewritten in a more sophisticated style, would it have a more powerful effect upon the mature reader or a less powerful? Is not the very fact that the story is designed for a child audience, in itself important in creating a special effect upon the grown-up reader? That is, is not the grown-up reader looking at the story, as it were, over the shoulder of the child reader? How do you think a child would respond to "The Fir Tree"? How does our response to the story differ from his? Is there some significant relation between the child's response and our own?

The Three Strangers

THOMAS HARDY (1840-1928)

AMONG THE few features of agricultural England which retain an appearance but little modified by the lapse of centuries may be reckoned the high, grassy and furzy downs, coombs, or eweleases, as they are indifferently called, that fill a large area of certain counties in the south and southwest. If any mark of human occupation is met with hereon, it usually takes the form of the solitary cottage of some shepherd.

Fifty years ago such a lonely cottage stood on such a down, and may possibly be standing there now. In spite of its loneliness, however, the spot, by actual measurement, was not more than five miles from a county-town. Yet that affected it little. Five miles of irregular upland, during the long inimical seasons, with their sleets, snows, rains, and mists, afford withdrawing space enough to isolate a Timon or a Nebuchadnezzar; much less, in fair weather, to please that less repellent tribe, the poets, philosophers, artists, and others who "conceive and meditate of pleasant things."

Some old earthen camp or barrow, some clump of trees, at least some starved fragment of ancient hedge is usually taken advantage of in the erection of these forlorn dwellings. But, in the present case, such a kind of shelter had been disregarded. Higher Crowstairs, as the house was called, stood quite detached and undefended. The only reason for its precise situation seemed to be the crossing of two footpaths at right angles hard by, which may have crossed there and thus for a good five hundred years. Hence the house was exposed to the elements on all sides. But, though the wind up here blew unmistakably when it did blow, and the rain hit hard whenever it fell, the various weathers of the winter season were not quite so formidable on the coomb as they were imagined to be by dwellers on low ground. The raw rimes were not so pernicious as in the hollows, and the frosts were scarcely so severe. When the shepherd and his family who tenanted the house were pitied for their sufferings from the exposure, they said that upon the whole they were less inconvenienced by "wuzzes and flames" (hoarses and phlegms) than when they had lived by the stream of a snug neighboring valley.

The night of March 28, 182- was precisely one of the nights that were wont to call forth these expressions of commiseration. The level rainstorm smote walls, slopes, and hedges like the clothyard shafts of Senlac and Crecy. Such sheep and outdoor animals as had no shelter stood with their buttocks to the winds; while the tails of little birds trying to roost on some scraggy thorn were blown inside-out like umbrellas. The gable-end of the cottage was stained with wet, and the eavesdroppings flapped against the wall. Yet never was commiseration for the shepherd more misplaced. For that cheerful rustic was entertaining a large party in glorification of the christening of his second girl.

The guests had arrived before the rain began to fall, and they were all now assembled in the chief or living room of the dwelling. A glance into the apartment at eight o'clock on this eventful evening would have resulted in the opinion that it was as cozy and comfortable a nook as could be wished for in boisterous weather. The calling of its inhabitant was proclaimed by a number of highly polished sheep-crooks without stems that were hung ornamentally over the fireplace, the curl of each shining crook varying from the antiquated type engraved in the patriarchal pictures of old family Bibles to the most approved fashion of the last local sheep-fair. The room was lighted by half-a-dozen candles, having wicks only a trifle smaller than the grease which enveloped them, in candlesticks that were never used but at high-days, holy-days, and family feasts. The lights were scattered about the room, two of them standing on the chimney-piece. This position of candles was in itself significant. Candles on the chimney-piece always meant a party.

On the hearth, in front of a back-brand to give substance, blazed a fire of thorns, that crackled "like the laughter of the fool."

Nineteen persons were gathered here. Of these, five women, wearing gowns of various bright hues, sat in chairs along the wall; girls shy and not shy filled the window-bench; four men, including Charley Jake the hedge-carpenter, Elijah New the parish-clerk, and John Pitcher, a neighboring dairyman, the shepherd's father-in-law, lolled in the settle; a young man and maid, who were blushing over tentative *pourparlers* on a life-companionship, sat beneath the corner-cupboard; and an elderly engaged man of fifty or upward moved restlessly about from spots where his betrothed was not to the spot where she was. Enjoyment was pretty general, and so much the more prevailed in being unhampered by conventional restrictions. Absolute confidence in each other's good opinion begat perfect ease, while the finishing stroke of manner, amounting to a truly princely serenity, was lent to the majority by the absence of any expression or trait denoting that they wished to get on in the world, enlarge their minds, or do any eclipsing thing whatever—which nowadays so generally nips the bloom and *bonhomie* of all except the two extremes of the social scale.

Shepherd Fennel had married well, his wife being a dairyman's daughter from a vale at a distance, who brought fifty guineas in her pocket —and kept them there, till they should be required for ministering to the needs of a coming family. This frugal woman had been somewhat exercised as to the character that should be given to the gathering. A sit-still party had its advantages; but an undisturbed position of ease in chairs and settles was apt to lead on the men to such an unconscionable deal of toping that they would sometimes fairly drink the house dry. A dancing-party was the alternative; but this, while avoiding the foregoing objection on the score of good drink, had a counterbalancing disadvantage in the matter of good victuals, the ravenous appetites engendered by the exercise causing immense havoc in the buttery. Shepherdess Fennel fell back upon the intermediate plan of mingling short dances with short periods of talk and singing, so as to hinder any ungovernable rage in either. But this scheme was entirely confined to her own gentle mind: the shepherd himself was in the mood to exhibit the most reckless phases of hospitality.

The fiddler was a boy of those parts, about twelve years of age, who had a wonderful dexterity in jigs and reels, though his fingers were so small and short as to necessitate a constant shifting for the high notes, from which he scrambled back to the first position with sounds not of unmixed purity of tone. At seven the shrill tweedle-dee of this youngster had begun, accompanied by a booming ground-bass from Elijah New, the parish-clerk, who had thoughtfully brought with him his favorite musical instrument, the serpent. Dancing was instantaneous, Mrs. Fennel privately enjoining the players on no account to let the dance exceed the length of a quarter of an hour.

But Elijah and the boy, in the excitement of their position, quite forgot the injunction. Moreover, Oliver Giles, a man of seventeen, one of the dancers, who was enamored of his partner, a fair girl of thirty-three rolling years, had recklessly handed a new crown-piece to the musicians, as a bribe to keep going as long as they had muscle and wind. Mrs. Fennel, seeing the steam begin to generate on the countenances of her guests, crossed over and touched the fiddler's elbow and put her hand on the serpent's mouth. But they took no notice, and fearing she might lose her character of genial hostess if she were to interfere too markedly, she retired and sat down helpless. And so the dance whizzed on with cumulative fury, the performers moving in their planet-like courses, direct and retrograde, from apogee to perigee, till the hand of the well-kicked clock at the bottom of the room had traveled over the circumference of an hour.

While these cheerful events were in course of enactment within Fennel's pastoral dwelling, an incident having considerable bearing on the party had occurred in the gloomy night without. Mrs. Fennel's concern about the growing fierceness of the dance corresponded in point of time with the ascent of a human figure to the solitary hill of Higher Crowstairs from the direction of the distant town. This personage strode on through the rain without a pause, following the little-worn path which, further on in its course, skirted the shepherd's cottage.

It was nearly the time of full moon, and on this account, though the sky was lined with a uniform sheet of dripping cloud, ordinary objects out of doors were readily visible. The sad wan light revealed the lonely pedestrian to be a man of supple frame; his gait suggested that he had somewhat passed the period of perfect and instinctive agility, though not so far as to be otherwise than rapid of motion when occasion required. At a rough guess, he might have been about forty years of age. He appeared tall, but a recruiting sergeant, or other person accustomed to the judging of men's heights by the eye, would have discerned that this was chiefly owing to his gauntness, and that he was not more than five-feet-eight or nine.

Notwithstanding the regularity of his tread, there was caution in it, as in that of one who mentally feels his way; and despite the fact that it was not a black coat nor a dark garment of any sort that he wore, there was something about him which suggested that he naturally belonged to the black-coated tribes of men. His clothes were of fustian, and his boots hobnailed, yet in his progress he showed not the mud-accustomed bearing of hobnailed and fustianed peasantry.

By the time that he had arrived abreast of the shepherd's premises the rain came down, or rather came along, with yet more determined violence. The outskirts of the little settlement partially broke the force of wind and rain, and this induced him to stand still. The most salient of the shepherd's domestic erections was an empty sty at the forward corner of his hedge-less garden, for in these latitudes the principle of masking the homelier features of your establishment by a conventional frontage was unknown. The traveler's eye was attracted to this small building by the pallid shine of the wet slates that covered it. He turned aside, and, finding it empty, stood under the pent-roof for shelter.

While he stood, the boom of the serpent within the adjacent house, and the lesser strains of the fiddler, reached the spot as an accompaniment to the surging hiss of the flying rain on the sod, its louder beating on the cabbage-leaves of the garden, on the eight or ten bee-hives just discernible by the path, and its drip-ping from the eaves into a row of buckets and pans that had been placed under the walls of the cottage. For at Higher Crowstairs, as at all such elevated domiciles, the grand difficulty of housekeeping was an insufficiency of water; and a casual rainfall was utilized by turning out, as catchers, every utensil that the house contained. Some queer stories might be told of the con-trivances for economy in suds and dishwaters that are absolutely necessitated in upland habita-tions during the droughts of summer. But at this season there were no such exigencies; a mere acceptance of what the skies bestowed was suf-ficient for an abundant store.

At last the notes of the serpent ceased and the house was silent. This cessation of activity aroused the solitary pedestrian from the reverie into which he had lapsed, and, emerging from the shed, with an apparently new intention, he walked up the path to the house-door. Ar-rived here, his first act was to kneel down on a large stone beside the row of vessels, and to drink a copious draught from one of them. Having quenched his thirst he rose and lifted his hand to knock, but paused with his eye upon the panel. Since the dark surface of the wood revealed absolutely nothing, it was evi-dent that he must be mentally looking through the door, as if he wished to measure thereby all the possibilities that a house of this sort might include, and how they might bear upon the ques-tion of his entry.

In his indecision he turned and surveyed the scene around. Not a soul was anywhere visible. The garden-path stretched downward from his feet, gleaming like the track of a snail; the roof of the little well (mostly dry), the well-cover, the top rail of the garden-gate, were varnished with the same dull liquid glaze; while, far away in the vale, a faint whiteness of more than usual extent showed that the rivers were high in the meads. Beyond all this winked a few bleared lamplights through the beating drops—lights that denoted the situation of the county-town from which he had appeared to come. The absence of all notes of life in that direction

seemed to clinch his intentions, and he knocked at the door.

Within, a desultory chat had taken the place of movement and musical sound. The hedge-carpenter was suggesting a song to the com-pany, which nobody just then was inclined to undertake, so that the knock afforded a not unwelcome diversion.

"Walk in!" said the shepherd promptly.

The latch clicked upward, and out of the night our pedestrian appeared upon the door-mat. The shepherd arose, snuffed two of the nearest candles, and turned to look at him.

Their light disclosed that the stranger was dark in complexion and not unprepossessing as to feature. His hat, which for a moment he did not remove, hung low over his eyes, without concealing that they were large, open, and deter-mined, moving with a flash rather than a glance round the room. He seemed pleased with his survey, and, baring his shaggy head, said, in a rich deep voice, "The rain is so heavy, friends, that I ask leave to come in and rest awhile."

"To be sure, stranger," said the shepherd. "And faith, you've been lucky in choosing your time, for we are having a bit of a fling for a glad cause—though, to be sure, a man could hardly wish that glad cause to happen more than once a year."

"Nor less," spoke up a woman. "For 'tis best to get your family over and done with, as soon as you can, so as to be all the earlier out of the fag o't."

"And what may be this glad cause?" asked the stranger.

"A birth and christening," said the shepherd.

The stranger hoped his host might not be made unhappy, either by too many or too few of such episodes, and being invited by a ges-ture to a pull at the mug, he readily acquiesced. His manner, which, before entering, had been so dubious, was now altogether that of a care-less and candid man.

"Late to be traipsing athwart this coomb—hey?" said the engaged man of fifty.

"Late it is, master, as you say.—I'll take a seat in the chimney-corner, if you have noth-ing to urge against it, ma'am; for I am a little moist on the side that was next the rain."

Mrs. Shepherd Fennel assented, and made

room for the self-invited comer, who, having got completely inside the chimney-corner, stretched out his legs and his arms with the expansiveness of a person quite at home.

"Yes, I am rather cracked in the vamp," he said freely, seeing that the eyes of the shepherd's wife fell upon his boots, "and I am not well fitted either. I have had some rough times lately, and have been forced to pick up what I can get in the way of wearing, but I must find a suit better fit for working-days when I reach home."

"One of hereabouts?" she inquired.

"Not quite that—further up the country."

"I thought so. And so be I; and by your tongue you come from my neighborhood."

"But you would hardly have heard of me," he said quickly. "My time would be long before yours, ma'am, you see."

This testimony to the youthfulness of his hostess had the effect of stopping her cross-examination.

"There is only one thing more wanted to make me happy," continued the new-comer. "And that is a little baccy, which I am sorry to say I am out of."

"I'll fill your pipe," said the shepherd.

"I must ask you to lend me a pipe likewise."

"A smoke, and no pipe about 'ee?"

"I have dropped it somewhere on the road."

The shepherd filled and handed him a new clay pipe, saying, as he did so, "Hand me your baccy-box—I'll fill that too, now I am about it."

The man went through the movement of searching his pockets.

"Lost that too?" said his entertainer, with some surprise.

"I am afraid so," said the man with some confusion. "Give it to me in a screw of paper." Lighting his pipe at the candle with a suction that drew the whole flame into the bowl, he re-settled himself in the corner and bent his looks upon the faint steam from his damp legs, as if he wished to say no more.

Meanwhile the general body of guests had been taking little notice of this visitor by reason of an absorbing discussion in which they were engaged with the band about a tune for the next dance. The matter being settled, they were about to stand up when an interruption came in the shape of another knock at the door.

At sound of the same the man in the chimney-corner took up the poker and began stirring the brands as if doing it thoroughly were the one aim of his existence; and a second time the shepherd said, "Walk in!" In a moment another man stood upon the straw-woven door-mat. He too was a stranger.

This individual was one of a type radically different from the first. There was more of the commonplace in his manner, and a certain jovial cosmopolitanism sat upon his features. He was several years older than the first arrival, his hair being slightly frosted, his eyebrows bristly, and his whiskers cut back from his cheeks. His face was rather full and flabby, and yet it was not altogether a face without power. A few grog-blossoms marked the neighborhood of his nose. He flung back his long drab greatcoat, revealing that beneath it he wore a suit of cinder-gray shade throughout, large heavy seals, of some metal or other that would take a polish, dangling from his fob as his only personal ornament. Shaking the water-drops from his low-crowned glazed hat, he said, "I must ask for a few minutes' shelter, comrades, or I shall be wetted to my skin before I get to Casterbridge."

"Make yourself at home, master," said the shepherd, perhaps a trifle less heartily than on the first occasion. Not that Fennel had the least tinge of niggardliness in his composition; but the room was far from large, spare chairs were not numerous, and damp companions were not altogether desirable at close quarters for the women and girls in their bright-colored gowns.

However, the second comer, after taking off his greatcoat, and hanging his hat on a nail in one of the ceiling-beams as if he had been specially invited to put it there, advanced and sat down at the table. This had been pushed so closely into the chimney-corner, to give all available room to the dancers, that its inner edge grazed the elbow of the man who had ensconced himself by the fire; and thus the two strangers were brought into close companionship. They nodded to each other by way of breaking the ice of unacquaintance, and the first stranger handed his neighbor the family mug—a huge vessel of brown ware, having its upper edge worn away like a threshold by the rub of whole generations of thirsty lips that had gone the way of all flesh, and bearing the following inscription burnt upon its rotund side in yellow letters:

THERE IS NO FUN
UNTILL I CUM

The other man, nothing loth, raised the mug to his lips, and drank on, and on, and on—till a curious blueness overspread the countenance of the shepherd's wife, who had regarded with no little surprise the first stranger's free offer to the second of what did not belong to him to dispense.

"I knew it!" said the toper to the shepherd with much satisfaction. "When I walked up your garden before coming in, and saw the hives all of a row, I said to myself, 'Where there's bees there's honey, and where there's honey there's mead.' But mead of such a truly comfortable sort as this I really didn't expect to meet in my older days." He took yet another pull at the mug, till it assumed an ominous elevation.

"Glad you enjoy it!" said the shepherd warmly.

"It is goodish mead," assented Mrs. Fennel, with an absence of enthusiasm which seemed to say that it was possible to buy praise for one's cellar at too heavy a price. "It is trouble enough to make—and really I hardly think we shall make any more. For honey sells well, and we ourselves can make shift with a drop o' small mead and metheglin for common use from the comb-washings."

"O, but you'll never have the heart!" reproachfully cried the stranger in cinder-gray, after taking up the mug a third time and setting it down empty. "I love mead, when 'tis old like this, as I love to go to church o' Sundays, or to relieve the needy any day of the week."

"Ha, ha, ha!" said the man in the chimney-corner, who, in spite of the taciturnity induced by the pipe of tobacco, could not or would not refrain from this slight testimony to his comrade's humor.

Now the old mead of those days, brewed of the purest first year or maiden honey, four pounds to the gallon—with its due complement of white of eggs, cinnamon, ginger, cloves, mace, rosemary, yeast, and processes of working, bottling and cellaring—tasted remarkably strong; but it did not taste so strong as it actually was. Hence, presently, the stranger in cinder-gray at the table, moved by its creeping influence, unbuttoned his waistcoat, threw himself back in his chair, spread his legs, and made his presence felt in various ways.

"Well, well, as I say," he resumed, "I am going to Casterbridge, and to Casterbridge I must go. I should have been almost there by this time; but the rain drove me into your dwelling, and I'm not sorry for it."

"You don't live in Casterbridge?" said the shepherd.

"Not as yet; though I shortly mean to move there."

"Going to set up in trade, perhaps?"

"No, no," said the shepherd's wife. "It is easy to see that the gentleman is rich, and don't want to work at anything."

The cinder-gray stranger paused, as if to consider whether he would accept that definition of himself. He presently rejected it by answering, "Rich is not quite the word for me, dame. I do work, and I must work. And even if I only get to Casterbridge by midnight I must begin work there at eight tomorrow morning. Yes, het or wet, blow or snow, famine or sword, my day's work tomorrow must be done."

"Poor man! Then, in spite o' seeming, you be worse off than we?" replied the shepherd's wife.

"'Tis the nature of my trade, men and maidens. 'Tis the nature of my trade more than my poverty. . . . But really and truly I must up and off, or I shan't get a lodging in the town." However, the speaker did not move, and directly added, "There's time for one more draught of friendship before I go; and I'd perform it at once if the mug were not dry."

"Here's a mug o' small," said Mrs. Fennel. "Small, we call it, though to be sure 'tis only the first wash o' the combs."

"No," said the stranger disdainfully. "I won't spoil your first kindness by partaking o' your second."

"Certainly not," broke in Fennel. "We don't increase and multiply every day, and I'll fill the mug again." He went away to the dark place under the stairs where the barrel stood. The shepherdess followed him.

"Why should you do this?" she said reproachfully, as soon as they were alone. "He's emptied it once, though it held enough for ten people; and now he's not contented wi' the small, but must needs call for more o' the strong! And a stranger unbeknown to any of us. For my part, I don't like the look o' the man at all."

"But he's in the house, my honey; and 'tis a wet night, and a christening. Daze it, what's a cup of mead more or less? There'll be plenty more next bee-burning."

"Very well—this time, then," she answered, looking wistfully at the barrel. "But what is the man's calling, and where is he one of, that he should come in and join us like this?"

"I don't know. I'll ask him again."

The catastrophe of having the mug drained dry at one pull by the stranger in cinder-gray was effectually guarded against this time by Mrs. Fennel. She poured out his allowance in a small cup, keeping the large one at a discreet distance from him. When he had tossed off his portion the shepherd renewed his inquiry about the stranger's occupation.

The latter did not immediately reply, and the man in the chimney-corner, with sudden demonstrativeness, said, "Anybody may know my trade—I'm a wheelwright."

"A very good trade for these parts," said the shepherd.

"And anybody may know mine—if they've the sense to find it out," said the stranger in cinder-gray.

"You may generally tell what a man is by his claws," observed the hedge-carpenter, looking at his own hands. "My fingers be as full of thorns as an old pincushion is of pins."

The hands of the man in the chimney-corner instinctively sought the shade, and he gazed into the fire as he resumed his pipe. The man at the table took up the hedge-carpenter's remark, and added smartly, "True; but the oddity of my trade is that, instead of setting a mark upon me, it sets a mark upon my customers."

No observation being offered by anybody in elucidation of this enigma, the shepherd's wife once more called for a song. The same obstacles presented themselves as at the former time—one had no voice, another had forgotten the first verse. The stranger at the table, whose soul had now risen to a good working temperature, relieved the difficulty by exclaiming that, to start the company, he would sing himself. Thrusting one thumb into the arm-hole of his waistcoat, he waved the other hand in the air, and, with an extemporizing gaze at the shining sheep-crooks above the mantelpiece, began:

> O my trade it is the rarest one,
> 　　　　　Simple shepherds all—
> For my customers I tie, and take them up on high,
> 　　And waft 'em to a far countree!

The room was silent when he had finished the verse—with one exception, that of the man in the chimney-corner, who, at the singer's word, "Chorus!" joined him in a deep bass voice of musical relish:

> And waft 'em to a far countree!

Oliver Giles, John Pitcher the dairyman, the parish-clerk, the engaged man of fifty, the row of young women against the wall, seemed lost in thought not of the gayest kind. The shepherd looked meditatively on the ground, the shepherdess gazed keenly at the singer, and with some suspicion; she was doubting whether this stranger were merely singing an old song from recollection, or was composing one there and then for the occasion. All were as perplexed at the obscure revelation as the guests at Belshazzar's Feast, except the man in the chimney-corner, who quietly said, "Second verse, stranger," and smoked on.

The singer thoroughly moistened himself from his lips inwards, and went on with the next stanza as requested:

> My tools are but common ones,
> 　　　　　Simple shepherds all—
> 　My tools are no sight to see:
> A little hempen string, and a post whereon to swing
> 　　Are implements enough for me!

Shepherd Fennel glanced round. There was no longer any doubt that the stranger was answering his question rhythmically. The guests one and all started back with suppressed exclamations. The young woman engaged to the man of fifty fainted half-way, and would have proceeded, but finding him wanting in alacrity for catching her she sat down trembling.

"O, he's the—!" whispered the people in the background, mentioning the name of an ominous public officer. "He's come to do it! 'Tis to be at Casterbridge jail tomorrow—the man for sheep-stealing—the poor clock-maker we heard of, who used to live away at Shottsford and had no work to do—Timothy Summers, whose family were a-starving, and so he went out of Shottsford by the high-road, and took a sheep in open daylight, defying the farmer and the farmer's wife and the farmer's lad, and every man jack among 'em. He" (and they nodded towards the stranger of the deadly trade) "is come from up the country to do it because there's not enough to do in his own county-town, and he's got the place here now our own county man's dead; he's going to live in the same cottage under the prison wall."

The stranger in cinder-gray took no notice of this whispered string of observations, but again wetted his lips. Seeing that his friend in the chimney-corner was the only one who reciprocated his joviality in any way, he held out his cup towards that appreciative comrade, who also held out his own. They clinked together, the eyes of the rest of the room hanging upon the singer's actions. He parted his lips for the third verse; but at that moment another knock was audible upon the door. This time the knock was faint and hesitating.

The company seemed scared; the shepherd looked with consternation towards the entrance, and it was with some effort that he resisted his alarmed wife's deprecatory glance, and uttered for the third time the welcoming words, "Walk in!"

The door was gently opened, and another man stood upon the mat. He, like those who had preceded him, was a stranger. This time it was a short, small personage, of fair complexion, and dressed in a decent suit of dark clothes.

"Can you tell me the way to——?" he began: when, gazing round the room to observe the nature of the company amongst whom he had fallen, his eyes lighted on the stranger in cinder-gray. It was just at the instant when the latter, who had thrown his mind into his song with such a will that he scarcely heeded the interruption, silenced all whispers and inquiries by bursting into his third verse.

> *Tomorrow is my working day,*
> > *Simple shepherds all—*
> *Tomorrow is a working day for me:*
> *For the farmer's sheep is slain, and the lad who did it ta'en,*
> > *And on his soul may God ha' merc-y!*

The stranger in the chimney-corner, waving cups with the singer so heartily that his mead splashed over on the hearth, repeated in his bass voice as before:

> *And on his soul may God ha' merc-y!*

All this time the third stranger had been standing in the doorway. Finding now that he did not come forward or go on speaking, the guests particularly regarded him. They noticed to their surprise that he stood before them the picture of abject terror—his knees trembling, his hand shaking so violently that the door-latch by which he supported himself rattled audibly: his white lips were parted, and his eyes fixed on the merry officer of justice in the middle of the room. A moment more and he had turned, closed the door, and fled.

"What a man can it be?" said the shepherd.

The rest, between the awfulness of their late discovery and the odd conduct of this third visitor, looked as if they knew not what to think, and said nothing. Instinctively they withdrew further and further from the grim gentleman in their midst, whom some of them seemed to take for the Prince of Darkness himself, till they formed a remote circle, and empty space of floor being left between them and him:

> *. . . circulus, cujus centrum diabolus.*

The room was so silent—though there were more than twenty people in it—that nothing could be heard but the patter of the rain against the window-shutters, accompanied by the occasional hiss of a stray drop that fell down the chimney into the fire, and the steady puffing of the man in the corner, who had now resumed his pipe of long clay.

The stillness was unexpectedly broken. The distant sound of a gun reverberated through the air—apparently from the direction of the county-town.

"Be jiggered!" cried the stranger who had sung the song, jumping up.

"What does that mean?" asked several.

"A prisoner escaped from the jail—that's what it means."

All listened. The sound was repeated, and none of them spoke but the man in the chimney-corner, who said quietly, "I've often been told that in this county they fire a gun at such times; but I never heard it till now."

"I wonder if it is *my* man?" murmured the personage in cinder-gray.

"Surely it is!" said the shepherd involuntarily. "And surely we've zeed him! That little man who looked in at the door by now, and quivered like a leaf when he zeed ye and heard your song!"

"His teeth chattered, and the breath went out of his body," said the dairyman.

"And his heart seemed to sink within him like a stone," said Oliver Giles.

"And he bolted as if he'd been shot at," said the hedge-carpenter.

"True—his teeth chattered, and his heart seemed to sink; and he bolted as if he'd been shot at," slowly summed up the man in the chimney-corner.

"I didn't notice it," remarked the hangman.

"We were all a-wondering what made him run off in such a fright," faltered one of the women against the wall, "and now 'tis explained!"

The firing of the alarm-gun went on at intervals, low and sullenly, and their suspicions became a certainty. The sinister gentleman in cinder-gray roused himself. "Is there a constable here?" he asked, in thick tones. "If so, let him step forward."

The engaged man of fifty stepped quavering out from the wall, his betrothed beginning to sob on the back of the chair.

"You are a sworn constable?"

"I be, sir."

"Then pursue the criminal at once, with assistance, and bring him back here. He can't have gone far."

"I will, sir, I will—when I've got my staff. I'll go home and get it, and come sharp here, and start in a body."

"Staff!—never mind your staff; the man'll be gone!"

"But I can't do nothing without my staff—can I, William, and John, and Charles Jake? No; for there's the king's royal crown a painted on en in yaller and gold, and the lion and the unicorn, so as when I raise en up and hit my prisoner, 'tis made a lawful blow thereby. I wouldn't 'tempt to take up a man without my staff—no, not I. If I hadn't the law to gie me courage, why, instead o' my taking up him he might take up me!"

"Now, I'm a king's man, myself, and can give you authority enough for this," said the formidable officer in gray. "Now then, all of ye, be ready. Have ye any lanterns?"

"Yes—have ye any lanterns?—I demand it!" said the constable.

"And the rest of you able-bodied—"

"Able-bodied men—yes—the rest of ye!" said the constable.

"Have you some good stout staves and pitchforks—"

"Staves and pitchforks—in the name o' the law! And take 'em in yer hands and go in quest, and do as we in authority tell ye!"

Thus aroused, the men prepared to give chase. The evidence was, indeed, though circumstantial, so convincing, that but little argument was needed to show the shepherd's guests that after what they had seen it would look very much like connivance if they did not instantly pursue the unhappy third stranger who could not as yet have gone more than a few hundred yards over such uneven country.

A shepherd is always well provided with lanterns; and, lighting these hastily, and with hurdle-staves in their hands, they poured out of the door, taking a direction along the crest of the hill, away from the town, the rain having fortunately a little abated.

Disturbed by the noise, or possibly by unpleasant dreams of her baptism, the child who had been christened began to cry heart-brokenly in the room overhead. These notes of grief came down through the chinks of the floor to the ears of the women below, who jumped up one by one, and seemed glad of the excuse to ascend and comfort the baby, for the incidents of the last half-hour greatly oppressed them. Thus in the space of two or three minutes the room on the ground-floor was deserted quite.

But it was not for long. Hardly had the sound of footsteps died away when a man returned round the corner of the house from the direction the pursuers had taken. Peeping in at the door, and seeing nobody there, he entered leisurely. It was the stranger of the chimney-corner, who had gone out with the rest. The motive of his return was shown by his helping himself to a cut piece of skimmer-cake that lay on a ledge beside where he had sat, and which he had apparently forgotten to take with him. He also poured out half a cup more mead from the quantity that remained, ravenously eating and drinking these as he stood. He had not finished when another figure came in just as quietly—his friend in cinder-gray.

"O—you here?" said the latter, smiling. "I thought you had gone to help in the capture." And this speaker also revealed the object of his return by looking solicitously round for the fascinating mug of old mead.

"And I thought you had gone," said the other, continuing his skimmer-cake with some effort.

"Well, on second thoughts, I felt there were enough without me," said the first confidentially, "and such a night as it is, too. Besides, 'tis the business o' the Government to take care of its criminals—not mine."

"True; so it is. And I felt as you did, that there were enough without me."

"I don't want to break my limbs running over the humps and hollows of this wild country."

"Nor I neither, between you and me."

"These shepherd-people are used to it—simple-minded souls, you know, stirred up to anything in a moment. They'll have him ready for me before morning, and no trouble to me at all."

"They'll have him, and we shall have saved ourselves all labor in the matter."

"True, true. Well, my way is to Casterbridge; and 'tis as much as my legs will do to take me that far. Going the same way?"

"No, I am sorry to say! I have to get home over there" (he nodded indefinitely to the right), "and I feel as you do, that it is quite enough for my legs to do before bedtime."

The other had by this time finished the mead in the mug, after which, shaking hands heartily at the door, and wishing each other well, they went their several ways.

In the meantime the company of pursuers had reached the end of the hog's-back elevation which dominated this part of the down. They had decided on no particular plan of action; and, finding that the man of the baleful trade was no longer in their company, they seemed quite unable to form any such plan now. They descended in all directions down the hill, and straightway several of the party fell into the snare set by Nature for all misguided midnight ramblers over this part of the cretaceous formation. The "lanchets," or flint slopes, which belted the escarpment at intervals of a dozen yards, took the less cautious ones unawares, and losing their footing on the rubbly steep they slid sharply downwards, the lanterns rolling from their hands to the bottom, and there lying on their sides till the horn was scorched through.

When they had again gathered themselves together, the shepherd, as the man who knew the country best, took the lead, and guided them round these treacherous inclines. The lanterns, which seemed rather to dazzle their eyes and warn the fugitive than to assist them in the exploration, were extinguished, due silence was observed; and in this more rational order they plunged into the vale. It was a grassy, briery, moist defile, affording some shelter to any person who had sought it; but the party perambulated it in vain, and ascended on the other side. Here they wandered apart, and after an interval closed together again to report progress. At the second time of closing in they found themselves near a lonely ash, the single tree on this part of the coomb, probably sown there by a passing bird some fifty years before. And here, standing a little to one side of the trunk, as motionless as the trunk itself, appeared the man they were in quest of, his outline being well defined against the sky beyond. The band noiselessly drew up and faced him.

"Your money or your life!" said the constable sternly to the still figure.

"No, no," whispered John Pitcher. " 'Tisn't our side ought to say that. That's the doctrine of vagabonds like him, and we be on the side of the law."

"Well, well," replied the constable impatiently; "I must say something, mustn't I? and if you had all the weight o' this undertaking upon your mind, perhaps you'd say the wrong thing too!—Prisoner at the bar, surrender, in the name of the Father—the Crown, I mane!"

The man under the tree seemed now to notice them for the first time, and, giving them no opportunity whatever for exhibiting their courage, he strolled slowly towards them. He was, indeed, the little man, the third stranger; but his trepidation had in a great measure gone.

"Well, travelers," he said, "did I hear ye speak to me?"

"You did: you've got to come and be our prisoner at once!" said the constable. "We arrest 'ee on the charge of not biding in Casterbridge jail in a decent proper manner to be hung tomorrow morning. Neighbors, do your duty, and seize the culpet!"

On hearing the charge, the man seemed enlightened, and, saying not another word, resigned himself with preternatural civility to the search-party, who, with their staves in their hands, surrounded him on all sides, and marched him back towards the shepherd's cottage.

It was eleven o'clock by the time they arrived. The light shining from the open door, a sound of men's voices within, proclaimed to them as they approached the house that some new events had arisen in their absence. On entering they discovered the shepherd's living room to be invaded by two officers from the Casterbridge jail, and a well-known magistrate who lived at the nearest county-seat, intelligence of the escape having become generally circulated.

"Gentlemen," said the constable, "I have brought back your man—not without risk and danger; but every one must do his duty! He is inside this circle of able-bodied persons, who have lent me useful aid, considering their ignorance of Crown work. Men, bring forward your prisoner!" And the third stranger was led to the light.

"Who is this?" said one of the officials.

"The man," said the constable.

"Certainly not," said the turnkey; and the first corroborated his statement.

"But how can it be otherwise?" asked the constable. "Or why was he so terrified at sight o' the singing instrument of the law who sat there?" Here he related the strange behavior of the third stranger on entering the house during the hangman's song.

"Can't understand it," said the officer coolly. "All I know is that it is not the condemned man. He's quite a different character from this one; a gauntish fellow, with dark hair and eyes, rather good-looking, and with a musical bass voice that if you heard it once you'd never mistake as long as you lived."

"Why, souls—'twas the man in the chimney-corner!"

"Hey—what?" said the magistrate, coming forward after inquiring particulars from the shepherd in the background. "Haven't you got the man after all?"

"Well, sir," said the constable, "he's the man we were in search of, that's true; and yet he's not the man we were in search of. For the man we were in search of was not the man we wanted, sir, if you understand my every-day way; for 'twas the man in the chimney-corner!"

"A pretty kettle of fish altogether!" said the magistrate. "You had better start for the other man at once."

The prisoner now spoke for the first time. The mention of the man in the chimney-corner seemed to have moved him as nothing else could do. "Sir," he said, stepping forward to the magistrate, "take no more trouble about me. The time is come when I may as well speak. I have done nothing; my crime is that the condemned man is my brother. Early this afternoon I left home at Shottsford to tramp it all the way to Casterbridge jail to bid him farewell. I was benighted, and called here to rest and ask the way. When I opened the door I saw before me the very man, my brother, that I thought to see in the condemned cell at Casterbridge. He was in this chimney-corner; and jammed close to him, so that he could not have got out if he had tried, was the executioner who'd come to take his life, singing a song about it and not knowing that it was his victim who was close by, joining in to save appearances. My brother looked a glance of agony at me, and I knew he meant, 'Don't reveal what you see; my life depends on it.' I was so terror-struck that I could hardly stand, and, not knowing what I did, I turned and hurried away."

The narrator's manner and tone had the stamp of truth, and his story made a great impression on all around. "And do you know where your brother is at the present time?" asked the magistrate.

"I do not. I have never seen him since I closed this door."

"I can testify to that, for we've been between ye ever since," said the constable.

"Where does he think to fly to?—what is his occupation?"

"He's a watch-and-clock-maker, sir."

"'A said 'a was a wheelwright—a wicked rogue," said the constable.

"The wheels of clocks and watches he meant, no doubt," said Shepherd Fennel. "I thought his hands were palish for's trade."

"Well, it appears to me that nothing can be gained by retaining this poor man in custody," said the magistrate; "your business lies with the other, unquestionably."

And so the little man was released off-hand; but he looked nothing the less sad on that account, it being beyond the power of magistrate or constable to raze out the written troubles in his brain, for they concerned another whom he regarded with more solicitude than himself. When this was done, and the man had gone his way, the night was found to be so far advanced that it was deemed useless to renew the search before the next morning.

Next day, accordingly, the quest for the clever sheep-stealer became general and keen, to all appearance at least. But the intended punishment was cruelly disproportioned to the transgression, and the sympathy of a great many country-folk in that district was strongly on the side of the fugitive. Moreover, his marvelous coolness and daring in hob-and-nobbing with the hangman, under the unprecedented circumstances of the shepherd's party, won their admiration. So that it may be questioned if all those who ostensibly made themselves so busy in exploring woods and fields and lanes were quite so thorough when it came to the private examination of their own lofts and outhouses. Stories were afloat of a mysterious figure being occasionally seen in some overgrown trackway or other, remote from turnpike roads; but when a search was instituted in any of these suspected quarters nobody was found. Thus the days and weeks passed without tidings.

In brief, the bass-voiced man of the chimney-corner was never recaptured. Some said that he went across the sea, others that he did not, but buried himself in the depths of a populous city. At any rate, the gentleman in cinder-gray never did his morning's work at Casterbridge, nor met anywhere at all, for business purposes, the genial comrade with whom he had passed an hour of relaxation in the lonely house on the coomb.

The grass has long been green on the graves of Shepherd Fennel and his frugal wife; the guests who made up the christening party have mainly followed their entertainers to the tomb; the baby in whose honor they all had met is a matron in the sere and yellow leaf. But the arrival of the three strangers at the shepherd's that night, and the details connected therewith, is a story as well known as ever in the country about Higher Crowstairs.

DISCUSSION

If the plot element in "The Three Strangers" is separated from the total story it appears to be a rather poor and mechanical contrivance. The coincidence may seem strained and the whole action, finally, rather pointless. Does Hardy's method of presentation mitigate these criticisms? Does it, in fact, give point to the story?

In the first place, Hardy does give a picture of a way of life which in itself holds some interest for the reader. The careful description of the countryside and of the cottage, the presentation of the manners and customs of the isolated community, appeal to the interest that many readers have in such details of "local color" for themselves. The main persons, the hangman and the condemned, are rendered rather fully, at least in regard to appearance and in hints of character, as in the conversation between them and in the sudden flight of the third stranger. But granting the competence of much of this treatment, the reader may still have the feeling that many of the details do not bear directly on the action, that the story is filled with much irrelevant descriptive matter, and that the general organization is very loose.

In the course of the story, we may come to see that some of this material is relevant, and that, in its special way, the organization is effective. For instance, the fact that the shepherd's cottage is located at the crossing of the paths helps to make more plausible the coincidental arrival of the several men there; or the fact that one of the strangers is without pipe and tobacco and borrows from the shepherd comes to have a real significance when we learn that he is a fugitive. Even such a detail as the fact that Shepherd Fennel's wife is proud of the quality of her mead, yet is anxious to husband it, though it does not bear a relation to the series of events unfolding here, may have a function.

We shall miss much of the point of the story if we consider that Hardy is merely taking the occasion to present some of the quaint customs of Wessex or a picture of pleasant rural simplicity. Actually, the total effect of the background and atmosphere of the story is not to emphasize the quaint peculiarities of the people, but to affirm the elemental humanity of these people, the qualities which they share with, let us say, an Irish peasant or a Tennessee mountaineer. Their world is a simple world. Their life is constantly related to the necessity for getting food and shelter, and is tied to the natural routine of the seasons. The occasion for the celebration described in the story is one of the universal human occasions for rejoicing, but even in the midst of the celebration the shepherd's wife can count the cups of mead. This emphasis on the nature of the life of these people will be seen to be integral in the story. At the very end of the story Hardy writes: "But the arrival of the three strangers at the shepherd's that night, and the details connected therewith, is a story as well known as ever in the country about Higher Crowstairs." In other words, Hardy has defined the little world where the event, which in itself may seem so bare and mechanical, came to be perpetuated in a "tale," a legend.

But what would make the event significant?

To these people, who had gathered to celebrate a birth and a christening, there enter the condemned man and the hangman, who participate in the celebration; and this accidental juxtaposition between birth and death provides the basic ironical situation of the story. But it is not merely natural death, but death decreed by society, legalistically and mechanically, for the infraction of a code which has been broken for the most "natural" of reasons—to secure food for a hungry family. In other words, the situation is a little two-fold parable (see Glossary) of the essential circumstances of the human being's condition in this world. First, the parable involves the natural unpredictability of fate, the natural association—here so accidentally and ironically arrived at—of death with life, sorrow with joy. The neighbors who have turned out to celebrate the birth find themselves, before the evening is over, hunting for the condemned man who is to be punished by death; and this fact suggests an ironical commentary concerning the kind of world into which the human being is born. Second, the parable involves a contrast between the warm, spontaneous quality of the average person when he is allowed to approach another without the restrictions and considerations which society would impose upon him, and the cold, mechanical, dehumanized quality of the codes and conventions by which society necessarily operates: even the hangman's humanity triumphs over his dehumanized and dehumanizing profession so that he can join in the spirit of the occasion. Hardy expresses a similar contrast in one of his poems, "The Man He Killed," the last stanza of which is quoted here:

> Yes: quaint and curious war is!
> You shoot a fellow down
> You'd treat if met where any bar is,
> Or help to half-a-crown.

Hardy never actually states the point in the story as he states it in the poem; none of the characters moralizes the situation as does the soldier in the poem. And undoubtedly the oddity of the coincidence itself, and the coolness of the condemned man, which makes possible his escape, help make the incident immediately memorable, but these matters alone do not account for the incident's becoming a legend. Another consideration operated: whether the shepherd folk realized it or not, the incident became a legend because it dramatized a fundamental insight into human circumstance.

If this account of the theme of the story is correct, then it will be seen that Hardy has *not been building toward* a coincidence—has not been depending upon a coincidence to solve a problem of plot and structure—but *has worked from* the coincidence as an essential part of the situation which he undertook to interpret as a story. But this does not completely answer the possible charge of implausibility which may be brought against the coincidence as such. Why is the coincidence here relatively easy to accept? The answer may lie in the particular approach which Hardy has taken to the material. He sets the situation up as a tale, a legend, an event which, presumably, really happened, and which found its way, because of its striking quality, into the consciousness of the simple world of

the shepherds to be "told" and retold. His strategy is to imply that he takes no responsibility for the events of the story but only for the imaginative reconstruction of the incident, for the presentation of the world which preserved its memory, for the interpretation which made memorable the event.

EXERCISE

We have seen the utility of the rather elaborate background in interpreting the legend itself and in giving it plausibility. But some of the details have other functions. For example, the incident of the girl's decision not to faint because her betrothed was, apparently, not prepared to catch her. The incident has a humorous quality, although it comes at the very moment when the profession of the hangman is revealed. The element of humor helps to prevent the "life-death" contrast from appearing oversolemn, stagey, and mechanical. What are the functions of various other details in the story?

Flight

JOHN STEINBECK (1902-   )

ABOUT FIFTEEN miles below Monterey, on the wild coast, the Torres family had their farm, a few sloping acres above a cliff that dropped to the brown reefs and to the hissing white waters of the ocean. Behind the farm the stone mountains stood up against the sky. The farm buildings huddled like little clinging aphids on the mountain skirts, crouched low to the ground as though the wind might blow them into the sea. The little shack, the rattling, rotting barn were gray-bitten with sea salt, beaten by the damp wind until they had taken on the color of the granite hills. Two horses, a red cow and a red calf, half a dozen pigs and a flock of lean, multi-colored chickens stocked the place. A little corn was raised on the sterile slope, and it grew short and thick under the wind, and all the cobs formed on the landward side of the stalks.

Mama Torres, a lean, dry woman with ancient eyes, had ruled the farm for ten years, ever

since her husband tripped over a stone in the field one day and fell full length on a rattlesnake. When one is bitten on the chest there is not much that can be done.

Mama Torres had three children, two undersized black ones of twelve and fourteen, Emilio and Rosy, whom Mama kept fishing on the rocks below the farm when the sea was kind and when the truant officer was in some distant part of Monterey County. And there was Pepé, the tall smiling son of nineteen, a gentle, affectionate boy, but very lazy. Pepé had a tall head, pointed at the top, and from its peak, coarse black hair grew down like a thatch all around. Over his smiling little eyes Mama cut a straight bang so he could see. Pepé had sharp Indian cheekbones and an eagle nose, but his mouth was as sweet and shapely as a girl's mouth, and his chin was fragile and chiseled. He was loose and gangling, all legs and feet and wrists, and he was very lazy. Mama thought him fine and brave, but she never told him so. She said, "Some lazy cow must have got into thy father's family, else how could I have a son like thee." And she said, "When I carried thee, a sneaking lazy coyote came out of the brush and looked at me one day. That must have made thee so."

Pepé smiled sheepishly and stabbed at the ground with his knife to keep the blade sharp and free from rust. It was his inheritance, that knife, his father's knife. The long heavy blade folded back into the black handle. There was a button on the handle. When Pepé pressed the button, the blade leaped out ready for use. The knife was with Pepé always, for it had been his father's knife.

One sunny morning when the sea below the cliff was glinting and blue and the white surf creamed on the reef, when even the stone mountains looked kindly, Mama Torres called out the door of the shack, "Pepé, I have a labor for thee."

There was no answer. Mama listened. From behind the barn she heard a burst of laughter. She lifted her full long skirt and walked in the direction of the noise.

Pepé was sitting on the ground with his back against a box. His white teeth glistened. On either side of him stood the two black ones, tense and expectant. Fifteen feet away a redwood post was set in the ground. Pepé's right hand lay limply in his lap, and in the palm the big black knife rested. The blade was closed back into the handle. Pepé looked smiling at the sky.

Suddenly Emilio cried, "Ya!"

Pepé's wrist flicked like the head of a snake. The blade seemed to fly open in mid-air, and with a thump the point dug into the redwood post, and the black handle quivered. The three burst into excited laughter. Rosy ran to the post and pulled out the knife and brought it back to Pepé. He closed the blade and settled the knife carefully in his listless palm again. He grinned self-consciously at the sky.

"Ya!"

The heavy knife lanced out and sunk into the post again. Mama moved forward like a ship and scattered the play.

"All day you do foolish things with the knife, like a toy-baby," she stormed. "Get up on thy huge feet that eat up shoes. Get up!" She took him by one loose shoulder and hoisted at him. Pepé grinned sheepishly and came half-heartedly to his feet. "Look!" Mama cried. "Big lazy, you must catch the horse and put on him thy father's saddle. You must ride to Monterey. The medicine bottle is empty. There is no salt. Go thou now, Peanut! Catch the horse."

A revolution took place in the relaxed figure of Pepé. "To Monterey, me? Alone? Si, Mama."

She scowled at him. "Do not think, big sheep, that you will buy candy. No, I will give you only enough for the medicine and the salt."

Pepé smiled. "Mama, you will put the hatband on the hat?"

She relented then. "Yes, Pepé. You may wear the hatband."

His voice grew insinuating, "And the green handkerchief, Mama?"

"Yes, if you go quickly and return with no trouble, the silk green handkerchief will go. If you make sure to take off the handkerchief when you eat so no spot may fall on it. . . ."

"Si, Mama. I will be careful. I am a man."

"Thou? A man? Thou art a peanut."

He went into the rickety barn and brought out a rope, and he walked agilely enough up the hill to catch the horse.

When he was ready and mounted before the door, mounted on his father's saddle that was so old that the oaken frame showed through torn leather in many places, then Mama brought out the round black hat with the tooled leather band, and she reached up and knotted the green silk handkerchief about his neck. Pepé's blue denim coat was much darker than his jeans, for it had been washed much less often.

Mama handed up the big medicine bottle and the silver coins. "That for the medicine," she said, "and that for the salt. That for a candle to burn for the papa. That for *dulces* for the little ones. Our friend Mrs. Rodriguez will give you dinner and maybe a bed for the night. When you go to the church say only ten Paternosters and only twenty-five Ave Marias. Oh! I know, big coyote. You would sit there flapping your mouth over Aves all day while you looked at the candles and the holy pictures. That is not good devotion to stare at the pretty things."

The black hat, covering the high pointed head and black thatched hair of Pepé, gave him dignity and age. He sat the rangy horse well. Mama thought how handsome he was, dark and lean and tall. "I would not send thee now alone, thou little one, except for the medicine," she said softly. "It is not good to have no medicine, for who knows when the toothache will come, or the sadness of the stomach. These things are."

"Adios, Mama," Pepé cried. "I will come back soon. You may send me often alone. I am a man."

"Thou art a foolish chicken."

He straightened his shoulders, flipped the reins against the horse's shoulder and rode away. He turned once and saw that they still watched him, Emilio and Rosy and Mama. Pepé grinned with pride and gladness and lifted the tough buckskin horse to a trot.

When he had dropped out of sight over a little dip in the road, Mama turned to the black ones, but she spoke to herself. "He is nearly a man now," she said. "It will be a nice thing to have a man in the house again." Her eyes sharpened on the children. "Go to the rocks now. The tide is going out. There will be abalones to be found." She put the iron hooks into their hands and saw them down the steep trail to the reefs. She brought the smooth stone *metate* to the doorway and sat grinding her corn to flour and looking occasionally at the road over which Pepé had gone. The noonday came and then the afternoon, when the little ones beat the abalones on a rock to make them tender and Mama patted the tortillas to make them thin. They ate their dinner as the red sun was plunging down toward the ocean. They sat on the doorsteps and watched the big white moon come over the mountain tops.

Mama said, "He is now at the house of our friend Mrs. Rodriguez. She will give him nice things to eat and maybe a present."

Emilio said, "Some day I too will ride to Monterey for medicine. Did Pepé come to be a man today?"

Mama said wisely, "A boy gets to be a man when a man is needed. Remember this thing. I have known boys forty years old because there was no need for a man."

Soon afterwards they retired, Mama in her big oak bed on one side of the room, Emilio and Rosy in their boxes full of straw and sheepskins on the other side of the room.

The moon went over the sky and the surf roared on the rocks. The roosters crowed the first call. The surf subsided to a whispering surge against the reef. The moon dropped toward the sea. The roosters crowed again.

The moon was near down to the water when Pepé rode on a winded horse to his home flat. His dog bounced out and circled the horse yelping with pleasure. Pepé slid off the saddle to the ground. The weathered little shack was silver in the moonlight and the square shadow of it was black to the north and east. Against the east the piling mountains were misty with light; their tops melted into the sky.

Pepé walked wearily up the three steps and into the house. It was dark inside. There was a rustle in the corner.

Mama cried out from her bed. "Who comes? Pepé, is it thou?"

"Si, Mama."

"Did you get the medicine?"

"Si, Mama."

"Well, go to sleep, then. I thought you would be sleeping at the house of Mrs. Rodriguez." Pepé stood silently in the dark room. "Why do you stand there, Pepé? Did you drink wine?"

"Si, Mama."

"Well, go to bed then and sleep out the wine."

His voice was tired and patient, but very firm. "Light the candle, Mama. I must go away into the mountains."

"What is this, Pepé? You are crazy." Mama struck a sulphur match and held the little blue burr until the flame spread up the stick. She set light to the candle on the floor beside her bed. "Now, Pepé, what is this you say?" She looked anxiously into his face.

He was changed. The fragile quality seemed to have gone from his chin. His mouth was less full than it had been, the lines of the lips were straighter, but in his eyes the greatest change had taken place. There was no laughter in them any more nor any bashfulness. They were sharp and bright and purposeful.

He told her in a tired monotone, told her everything just as it had happened. A few people came into the kitchen of Mrs. Rodriguez. There was wine to drink. Pepé drank wine. The little quarrel—the man started toward Pepé and then the knife—it went almost by itself. It flew, it darted before Pepé knew it. As he talked, Mama's face grew stern, and it seemed to grow more lean. Pepé finished. "I am a man now, Mama. The man said names to me I could not allow."

Mama nodded. "Yes, thou art a man, my poor little Pepé. Thou art a man. I have seen it coming on thee. I have watched you throwing the knife into the post, and I have been afraid." For a moment her face had softened, but now it grew stern again. "Come! We must get you ready. Go. Awaken Emilio and Rosy. Go quickly."

Pepé stepped over to the corner where his brother and sister slept among the sheepskins. He leaned down and shook them gently. "Come, Rosy! Come, Emilio! The mama says you must arise."

The little black ones sat up and rubbed their eyes in the candlelight. Mama was out of bed now, her long black skirt over her nightgown. "Emilio," she cried. "Go up and catch the other horse for Pepé. Quickly, now! Quickly." Emilio put his legs in his overalls and stumbled sleepily out the door.

"You heard no one behind you on the road?" Mama demanded.

"No, Mama. I listened carefully. No one was on the road."

Mama darted like a bird about the room. From a nail on the wall she took a canvas water bag and threw it on the floor. She stripped a blanket from her bed and rolled it into a tight tube and tied the ends with string. From a box beside the stove she lifted a flour sack half full of black stringy jerky. "Your father's black coat, Pepé. Here, put it on."

Pepé stood in the middle of the floor watching her activity. She reached behind the door and brought out the rifle, a long 38-56, worn shiny the whole length of the barrel. Pepé took it from her and held it in the crook of his elbow. Mama brought a little leather bag and counted the cartridges into his hand. "Only ten left," she warned. "You must not waste them."

Emilio put his head in the door. "'Qui 'st 'l caballo, Mama."

"Put on the saddle from the other horse. Tie on the blanket. Here, tie the jerky to the saddle horn."

Still Pepé stood silently watching his mother's frantic activity. His chin looked hard, and his sweet mouth was drawn and thin. His little eyes followed Mama about the room almost suspiciously.

Rosy asked softly, "Where goes Pepé?"

Mama's eyes were fierce. "Pepé goes on a journey. Pepé is a man now. He has a man's thing to do."

Pepé straightened his shoulders. His mouth changed until he looked very much like Mama.

At last the preparation was finished. The loaded horse stood outside the door. The water bag dripped a line of moisture down the bay shoulder.

The moonlight was being thinned by the dawn and the big white moon was near down to the sea. The family stood by the shack. Mama confronted Pepé. "Look, my son! Do not stop until it is dark again. Do not sleep even though you are tired. Take care of the horse in order that he may not stop of weariness. Remember to be careful with the bullets—there are only ten. Do not fill thy stomach with jerky or it will make thee sick. Eat a little jerky and fill thy stomach with grass. When thou comest to the high mountains, if thou seest any of the dark watching men, go not near to them nor try to speak to them. And forget not thy prayers." She put her lean hands on Pepé's shoulders, stood on her toes and kissed him formally on both cheeks, and Pepé kissed her on both cheeks. Then he went to Emilio and Rosy and kissed both of their cheeks.

Pepé turned back to Mama. He seemed to look for a little softness, a little weakness in her. His eyes were searching, but Mama's face remained fierce. "Go now," she said. "Do not wait to be caught like a chicken."

Pepé pulled himself into the saddle. "I am a man," he said.

It was the first dawn when he rode up the

hill toward the little canyon which let a trail into the mountains. Moonlight and daylight fought with each other, and the two warring qualities made it difficult to see. Before Pepé had gone a hundred yards, the outlines of his figure were misty; and long before he entered the canyon, he had become a gray, indefinite shadow.

Mama stood stiffly in front of her doorstep, and on either side of her stood Emilio and Rosy. They cast furtive glances at Mama now and then.

When the gray shape of Pepé melted into the hillside and disappeared, Mama relaxed. She began the high, whining keen of the death wail. "Our beautiful—our brave," she cried. "Our protector, our son is gone." Emilio and Rosy moaned beside her. "Our beautiful—our brave, he is gone." It was the formal wail. It rose to a high piercing whine and subsided to a moan. Mama raised it three times and then she turned and went into the house and shut the door.

Emilio and Rosy stood wondering in the dawn. They heard Mama whimpering in the house. They went out to sit on the cliff above the ocean. They touched shoulders. "When did Pepé come to be a man?" Emilio asked.

"Last night," said Rosy. "Last night in Monterey." The ocean clouds turned red with the sun that was behind the mountains.

"We will have no breakfast," said Emilio. "Mama will not want to cook." Rosy did not answer him. "Where is Pepé gone?" he asked.

Rosy looked around at him. She drew her knowledge from the quiet air. "He has gone on a journey. He will never come back."

"Is he dead? Do you think he is dead?"

Rosy looked back at the ocean again. A little steamer, drawing a line of smoke sat on the edge of the horizon. "He is not dead," Rosy explained. "Not yet."

Pepé rested the big rifle across the saddle in front of him. He let the horse walk up the hill and he didn't look back. The stony slope took on a coat of short brush so that Pepé found the entrance to a trail and entered it.

When he came to the canyon opening, he swung once in his saddle and looked back, but

the houses were swallowed in the misty light. Pepé jerked forward again. The high shoulder of the canyon closed in on him. His horse stretched out its neck and sighed and settled to the trail.

It was a well-worn path, dark soft leaf-mold earth strewn with broken pieces of sandstone. The trail rounded the shoulder of the canyon and dropped steeply into the bed of the stream. In the shallows the water ran smoothly, glinting in the first morning sun. Small round stones on the bottom were as brown as rust with sun moss. In the sand along the edges of the stream the tall, rich wild mint grew, while in the water itself the cress, old and tough, had gone to heavy seed.

The path went into the stream and emerged on the other side. The horse sloshed into the water and stopped. Pepé dropped his bridle and let the beast drink of the running water.

Soon the canyon sides became steep and the first giant sentinel redwoods guarded the trail, great round red trunks bearing foliage as green and lacy as ferns. Once Pepé was among the trees, the sun was lost. A perfumed and purple light lay in the pale green of the underbrush. Gooseberry bushes and blackberries and tall ferns lined the stream, and overhead the branches of the redwoods met and cut off the sky.

Pepé drank from the water bag, and he reached into the flour sack and brought out a black string of jerky. His white teeth gnawed at the string until the tough meat parted. He chewed slowly and drank occasionally from the water bag. His little eyes were slumberous and tired, but the muscles of his face were hard set. The earth of the trail was black now. It gave up a hollow sound under the walking hoofbeats.

The stream fell more sharply. Little waterfalls splashed on the stones. Five-fingered ferns hung over the water and dripped spray from their fingertips. Pepé rode half over in his saddle, dangling one leg loosely. He picked a bay leaf from a tree beside the way and put it into his mouth for a moment to flavor the dry jerky. He held the gun loosely across the pommel.

Suddenly he squared in his saddle, swung the horse from the trail and kicked it hurriedly up behind a big redwood tree. He pulled up the reins tight against the bit to keep the horse from whinnying. His face was intent and his nostrils quivered a little.

A hollow pounding came down the trail, and a horseman rode by, a fat man with red cheeks and a white stubble beard. His horse put down its head and blubbered at the trail when it came to the place where Pepé had turned off. "Hold up!" said the man and he pulled up his horse's head.

When the last sound of the hoofs died away, Pepé came back into the trail again. He did not relax in the saddle any more. He lifted the big rifle and swung the lever to throw a shell into the chamber, and then he let down the hammer to half cock.

The trail grew very steep. Now the redwood trees were smaller and their tops were dead, bitten dead where the wind reached them. The horse plodded on; the sun went slowly overhead and started down toward the afternoon.

Where the stream came out of a side canyon, the trail left it. Pepé dismounted and watered his horse and filled up his water bag. As soon as the trail had parted from the stream, the trees were gone and only the thick brittle sage and manzanita and chaparral edged the trail. And the soft black earth was gone, too, leaving only the light tan broken rock for the trail bed. Lizards scampered away into the brush as the horse rattled over the little stones.

Pepé turned in his saddle and looked back. He was in the open now: he could be seen from a distance. As he ascended the trail the country grew more rough and terrible and dry. The way wound about the bases of great square rocks. Little gray rabbits skittered in the brush. A bird made a monotonous high creaking. Eastward the bare rock mountaintops were pale and powder-dry under the dropping sun. The horse plodded up and up the trail toward a little V in the ridge which was the pass.

Pepé looked suspiciously back every minute or so, and his eyes sought the tops of the ridges ahead. Once, on a white barren spur, he saw a black figure for a moment, but he looked quickly away, for it was one of the dark watchers. No one knew who the watchers were, nor where they lived, but it was better to ignore them and never to show interest in them. They did not

bother one who stayed on the trail and minded his own business.

The air was parched and full of light dust blown by the breeze from the eroding mountains. Pepé drank sparingly from his bag and corked it tightly and hung it on the horn again. The trail moved up the dry shale hillside, avoiding rocks, dropping under clefts, climbing in and out of old water scars. When he arrived at the little pass he stopped and looked back for a long time. No dark watchers were to be seen now. The trail behind was empty. Only the high tops of the redwoods indicated where the stream flowed.

Pepé rode on through the pass. His little eyes were nearly closed with weariness, but his face was stern, relentless and manly. The high mountain wind coasted sighing through the pass and whistled on the edges of the big blocks of broken granite. In the air, a red-tailed hawk sailed over close to the ridge and screamed angrily. Pepé went slowly through the broken jagged pass and looked down on the other side.

The trail dropped quickly, staggering among broken rock. At the bottom of the slope there was a dark crease, thick with brush, and on the other side of the crease a little flat, in which a grove of oak trees grew. A scar of green grass cut across the flat. And behind the flat another mountain rose, desolate with dead rocks and starving little black bushes. Pepé drank from the bag again for the air was so dry that it encrusted his nostrils and burned his lips. He put the horse down the trail. The hooves slipped and struggled on the steep way, starting little stones that rolled off into the brush. The sun was gone behind the westward mountain now, but still it glowed brilliantly on the oaks and on the grassy flat. The rocks and the hillsides still sent up waves of the heat they had gathered from the day's sun.

Pepé looked up to the top of the next dry withered ridge. He saw a dark form against the sky, a man's figure standing on top of a rock, and he glanced away quickly not to appear curious. When a moment later he looked up again, the figure was gone.

Downward the trail was quickly covered. Sometimes the horse floundered for footing, sometimes set his feet and slid a little way. They came at last to the bottom where the dark chaparral was higher than Pepé's head. He held up his rifle on one side and his arm on the other to shield his face from the sharp brittle fingers of the brush.

Up and out of the crease he rode, and up a little cliff. The grassy flat was before him, and the round comfortable oaks. For a moment he studied the trail down which he had come, but there was no movement and no sound from it. Finally he rode out over the flat, to the green streak, and at the upper end of the damp he found a little spring welling out of the earth and dropping into a dug basin before it seeped out over the flat.

Pepé filled his bag first, and then he let the thirsty horse drink out of the pool. He led the horse to the clump of oaks, and in the middle of the grove, fairly protected from sight on all sides, he took off the saddle and the bridle and laid them on the ground. The horse stretched his jaws sideways and yawned. Pepé knotted the lead rope about the horse's neck and tied him to a sapling among the oaks, where he could graze in a fairly large circle.

When the horse was gnawing hungrily at the dry grass, Pepé went to the saddle and took a black string of jerky from the sack and strolled to an oak tree on the edge of the grove, from under which he could watch the trail. He sat down in the crisp dry oak leaves and automatically felt for his big black knife to cut the jerky, but he had no knife. He leaned back on his elbow and gnawed at the tough strong meat. His face was blank, but it was a man's face.

The bright evening light washed the eastern ridge, but the valley was darkening. Doves flew down from the hills to the spring, and the quail came running out of the brush and joined them, calling clearly to one another.

Out of the corner of his eye Pepé saw a shadow grow out of the bushy crease. He turned his head slowly. A big spotted wildcat was creeping toward the spring, belly to the ground, moving like thought.

Pepé cocked his rifle and edged the muzzle slowly around. Then he looked apprehensively up the trail and dropped the hammer again. From the ground beside him he picked an oak twig and threw it toward the spring. The quail flew up with a roar and the doves whistled away. The big cat stood up: for a long moment he looked at Pepé with cold yellow eyes, and then fearlessly walked back into the gulch.

The dusk gathered quickly in the deep valley. Pepé muttered his prayers, put his head down on his arm and went instantly to sleep.

The moon came up and filled the valley with cold blue light, and the wind swept rustling down from the peaks. The owls worked up and down the slopes looking for rabbits. Down in the brush of the gulch a coyote gabbled. The oak trees whispered softly in the night breeze.

Pepé started up, listening. His horse had whinnied. The moon was just slipping behind the western ridge, leaving the valley in darkness behind it. Pepé sat tensely gripping his rifle. From far up the trail he heard an answering whinny and the crash of shod hooves on the broken rock. He jumped to his feet, ran to his horse and led it under the trees. He threw on the saddle and cinched it tight for the steep trail, caught the unwilling head and forced the bit into the mouth. He felt the saddle to make sure the water bag and the sack of jerky were there. Then he mounted and turned up the hill.

It was velvet dark. The horse found the entrance to the trail where it left the flat, and started up, stumbling and slipping on the rocks. Pepé's hand rose up to his head. His hat was gone. He had left it under the oak tree.

The horse had struggled far up the trail when the first change of dawn came into the air, a steel grayness as light mixed thoroughly with dark. Gradually the sharp snaggled edge of the ridge stood out above them, rotten granite tortured and eaten by the wind of time. Pepé had dropped his reins on the horn, leaving direction to the horse. The brush grabbed at his legs in the dark until one knee of his jeans was ripped.

Gradually the light flowed down over the ridge. The starved brush and rocks stood out in the half light, strange and lonely in high perspective. Then there came warmth into the light. Pepé drew up and looked back, but he could see nothing in the darker valley below. The sky turned blue over the coming sun. In the waste of the mountainside, the poor dry brush grew only three feet high. Here and there, big outcroppings of unrotted granite stood up like moldering houses. Pepé relaxed a little. He drank from his water bag and bit off a piece of jerky. A single eagle flew over, high in the light.

Without warning Pepé's horse screamed and fell on its side. He was almost down before the rifle crash echoed up from the valley. From a hole behind the struggling shoulder, a stream of bright crimson blood pumped and stopped and pumped and stopped. The hooves threshed on the ground. Pepé lay half stunned beside the horse. He looked slowly down the hill. A piece of sage clipped off beside his head and another crash echoed up from side to side of the canyon. Pepé flung himself frantically behind a bush.

He crawled up the hill on his knees and on one hand. His right hand held the rifle up off the ground and pushed it ahead of him. He moved with the instinctive care of an animal. Rapidly he wormed his way toward one of the big outcroppings of granite on the hill above him. Where the brush was high he doubled up and ran, but where the cover was slight he wriggled forward on his stomach, pushing the rifle ahead of him. In the last little distance there was no cover at all. Pepé poised and then he darted across the space and flashed around the corner of the rock.

He leaned panting against the stone. When his breath came easier he moved along behind the big rock until he came to a narrow split that offered a thin section of vision down the hill. Pepé lay on his stomach and pushed the rifle barrel through the slit and waited.

The sun reddened the western ridges now. Already the buzzards were settling down toward the place where the horse lay. A small brown bird scratched in the dead sage leaves directly in front of the rifle muzzle. The coasting eagle flew back toward the rising sun.

Pepé saw a little movement in the brush far below. His grip tightened on the gun. A little brown doe stepped daintily out on the trail and crossed it and disappeared into the brush again. For a long time Pepé waited. Far below he could see the little flat and the oak trees and the slash of green. Suddenly his eyes flashed back at the trail again. A quarter of a mile down there had been a quick movement in the chaparral. The rifle swung over. The front sight nestled in the V of the rear sight. Pepé studied for a moment and then raised the rear sight a notch. The little movement in the brush came again. The sight settled on it. Pepé squeezed the trigger. The explosion crashed down the mountain and up the other side, and came rattling back. The whole side of the slope grew still. No more movement. And then a white streak cut into the granite of the slit and a bullet whined away and a crash sounded up from below. Pepé felt a sharp pain in his right hand. A sliver of granite was sticking out from between his first and second knuckles and the point protruded from his palm. Carefully he pulled out the sliver of stone. The wound bled evenly and gently. No vein nor artery was cut.

Pepé looked into a little dusty cave in the rock and gathered a handful of spider web, and he pressed the mass into the cut, plastering the soft web into the blood. The flow stopped almost at once.

The rifle was on the ground. Pepé picked it up, levered a new shell into the chamber. And then he slid into the brush on his stomach. Far to the right he crawled, and then up the hill, moving slowly and carefully, crawling to cover and resting and then crawling again.

In the mountains the sun is high in its arc before it penetrates the gorges. The hot face looked over the hill and brought instant heat with it. The white light beat on the rocks and reflected from them and rose up quivering from the earth again, and the rocks and bushes seemed to quiver behind the air.

Pepé crawled in the general direction of the ridge peak, zig-zagging for cover. The deep cut between his knuckles began to throb. He crawled close to a rattlesnake before he saw it, and when it raised its dry head and made a soft beginning whirr, he backed up and took another way. The quick gray lizards flashed in front of him, raising a tiny line of dust. He found another mass of spider web and pressed it against his throbbing hand.

Pepé was pushing the rifle with his left hand now. Little drops of sweat ran to the ends of his coarse black hair and rolled down his cheeks. His lips and tongue were growing thick and heavy. His lips writhed to draw saliva into his mouth. His little dark eyes were uneasy and suspicious. Once when a gray lizard paused in front of him on the parched ground and turned its head sideways he crushed it flat with a stone.

When the sun slid past noon he had not gone a mile. He crawled exhaustedly a last hundred yards to a patch of high sharp manzanita, crawled desperately, and when the patch was reached he wriggled in among the tough gnarly trunks and dropped his head on his left arm. There was little shade in the meager brush, but there was cover and safety. Pepé went to sleep as he lay and the sun beat on his back. A few little birds hopped close to him and peered and hopped away. Pepé squirmed in his sleep and he raised and dropped his wounded hand again and again.

The sun went down behind the peaks and the cool evening came, and then the dark. A coyote yelled from the hillside, Pepé started awake and looked about with misty eyes. His hand was swollen and heavy; a little thread of pain ran up the inside of his arm and settled in a pocket in his armpit. He peered about and then stood up, for the mountains were black and the moon had not yet risen. Pepé stood up in the dark. The coat of his father pressed on his arm. His tongue was swollen until it nearly filled his mouth. He wriggled out of the coat and dropped it in the brush, and then he struggled up the hill, falling over rocks and tearing his way through the brush. The rifle knocked against stones as he went. Little dry avalanches of gravel and shattered stone went whispering down the hill behind him.

After a while the old moon came up and showed the jagged ridge top ahead of him. By moonlight Pepé traveled more easily. He bent forward so that his throbbing arm hung away from his body. The journey uphill was made in dashes and rests, a frantic rush up a few yards and then a rest. The wind coasted down the slope rattling the dry stems of the bushes.

The moon was at meridian when Pepé came at last to the sharp backbone of the ridge top. On the last hundred yards of the rise no soil had clung under the wearing winds. The way was on solid rock. He clambered to the top and looked down on the other side. There was a draw like the last below him, misty with moonlight, brushed with dry struggling sage and chaparral. On the other side the hill rose up sharply and at the top the jagged rotten teeth of the mountain showed against the sky. At the bottom of the cut the brush was thick and dark.

Pepé stumbled down the hill. His throat was almost closed with thirst. At first he tried to run, but immediately he fell and rolled. After that he went more carefully. The moon was just disappearing behind the mountains when he came to the bottom. He crawled into the heavy brush feeling with his fingers for water. There was no water in the bed of the stream, only damp earth. Pepé laid his gun down and scooped up a handful of mud and put it in his mouth, and then he spluttered and scraped the earth from his tongue with his finger, for the mud drew at his mouth like a poultice. He dug a hole in the stream bed with his fingers, dug a little basin to catch water; but before it was very deep his head fell forward on the damp ground and he slept.

The dawn came and the heat of the day fell on the earth, and still Pepé slept. Late in the afternoon his head jerked up. He looked slowly around. His eyes were slits of wariness. Twenty feet away in the heavy brush a big tawny mountain lion stood looking at him. Its long thick tail waved gracefully, its ears erect with interest, not laid back dangerously. The lion squatted down on its stomach and watched him.

Pepé looked at the hole he had dug in the earth. A half inch of muddy water had collected in the bottom. He tore the sleeve from his hurt arm, with his teeth ripped out a little square, soaked it in the water and put it in his mouth. Over and over he filled the cloth and sucked it.

Still the lion sat and watched him. The evening came down but there was no movement on the hills. No birds visited the dry bottom of the cut. Pepé looked occasionally at the lion. The eyes of the yellow beast drooped as though he were about to sleep. He yawned and his long thin red tongue curled out. Suddenly his head jerked around and his nostrils quivered. His big tail lashed. He stood up and slunk like a tawny shadow into the thick brush.

A moment later Pepé heard the sound, the

faint far crash of horses' hooves on gravel. And he heard something else, a high whining yelp of a dog.

Pepé took his rifle in his left hand and he glided into the brush almost as quietly as the lion had. In the darkening evening he crouched up the hill toward the next ridge. Only when the dark came did he stand up. His energy was short. Once it was dark he fell over the rocks and slipped to his knees on the steep slope, but he moved on and on up the hill, climbing and scrabbling over the broken hillside.

When he was far up toward the top, he lay down and slept for a little while. The withered moon, shining on his face, awakened him. He stood up and moved up the hill. Fifty yards away he stopped and turned back, for he had forgotten his rifle. He walked heavily down and poked about in the brush, but he could not find his gun. At last he lay down to rest. The pocket of pain in his armpit had grown more sharp. His arm seemed to swell out and fall with every heartbeat. There was no position lying down where the heavy arm did not press against his armpit.

With the effort of a hurt beast, Pepé got up and moved again toward the top of the ridge. He held his swollen arm away from his body with his left hand. Up the steep hill he dragged himself, a few steps and a rest, and a few more steps. At last he was nearing the top. The moon showed the uneven sharp back of it against the sky.

Pepé's brain spun in a big spiral up and away from him. He slumped to the ground and lay still. The rock ridge top was only a hundred feet above him.

The moon moved over the sky. Pepé half turned on his back. His tongue tried to make words, but only a thick hissing came from between his lips.

When the dawn came, Pepé pulled himself up. His eyes were sane again. He drew his great puffed arm in front of him and looked at the angry wound. The black line ran up from his wrist to his armpit. Automatically he reached in his pocket for the big black knife, but it was not there. His eyes searched the ground. He picked up a sharp blade of stone and scraped at the wound, sawed at the proud flesh and then squeezed the green juice out in big drops. Instantly he threw back his head and whined like a dog. His whole right side shuddered at the pain, but the pain cleared his head.

In the gray light he struggled up the last slope to the ridge and crawled over and lay down behind a line of rocks. Below him lay a deep canyon exactly like the last, waterless and desolate. There was no flat, no oak trees, not even heavy brush in the bottom of it. And on the other side a sharp ridge stood up, thinly brushed with starving sage, littered with broken granite. Strewn over the hill there were giant outcroppings, and on the top the granite teeth stood out against the sky.

The new day was light now. The flame of sun came over the ridge and fell on Pepé where he lay on the ground. His coarse black hair was littered with twigs and bits of spider web. His eyes had retreated back into his head. Between his lips the tip of his black tongue showed.

He sat up and dragged his great arm into his lap and nursed it, rocking his body and moaning in his throat. He threw back his head and looked up into the pale sky. A big black bird circled nearly out of sight, and far to the left another was sailing near.

He lifted his head to listen, for a familiar sound had come to him from the valley he had climbed out of; it was the crying yelp of hounds, excited and feverish, on a trail.

Pepé bowed his head quickly. He tried to speak rapid words but only a thick hiss came from his lips. He drew a shaky cross on his breast with his left hand. It was a long struggle to get to his feet. He crawled slowly and mechanically to the top of a big rock on the ridge peak. Once there, he arose slowly, swaying to his feet, and stood erect. Far below he could see the dark brush where he had slept. He braced his feet and stood there, black against the morning sky.

There came a ripping sound at his feet. A piece of stone flew up and a bullet droned off into the next gorge. The hollow crash echoed up from below. Pepé looked down for a moment and then pulled himself straight again.

His body jarred back. His left hand fluttered helplessly toward his breast. The second crash sounded from below. Pepé swung forward and toppled from the rock. His body struck and rolled over and over, starting a little avalanche. And when at last he stopped against a bush, the avalanche slid slowly down and covered up his head.

EXERCISE

1. Clearly there is a conflict between Pepé and the unseen pursuer, and the most obvious suspense of the story is based on this. But is there another conflict? To answer this, think of the kind of world Pepé and his family live in, the values they live by.

2. It is clear that the story is, in a way, the account of the growing up of Pepé. How does this relate to the deeper conflict in the story?

3. Why is it significant that the pursuer is never seen as a person?

4. One critic has pointed out that during the flight Pepé becomes more and more identified with the natural world, that he seems to be absorbed in it. How does the author's use of the various wild creatures encountered during the flight support this notion? What other indications are there for the identification with nature? What connection does this identification have with the conflict between the two worlds?

5. Characterize the mother. What is her attitude toward Pepé's situation? How does this relate to the main idea of the story?

6. In this story Steinbeck has very vividly presented the country through which Pepé flees. Select certain details of presentation that strike you as especially vivid. Why is this important to the story?

7. What is the significance of the last paragraph of the story?

8. What is gained by keeping the sense of translated language in the dialogue between Pepé and his mother rather than rendering it in ordinary English? Compare this quality of "translation English" in the dialogue with the style of "The Fir Tree." (Remember that we observed that the style of "The Fir Tree" suggested that the story was addressed to children.) Are the effects of the style in this instance comparable?

9. Can you see any similarity of idea between this story and "The Three Strangers"?

10. Read "La Lupa," by Giovanni Verga (page 209). How does the handling of the narrative compare with that of "Flight"? What similarity is there in the backgrounds of the two stories? Can we imagine either story set in a big city? If so, what differences can you imagine? Greater complexity in social implication? Loss of the natural background? What would this imply for the development of the narrative? Of the theme? What is the fictional point—the theme—of "La Lupa"? Does it have any relation to that of "The Use of Force"?

11. In "Flight" and "La Lupa" is there as much sense of being "told" as in "The Fir Tree" and "The Three Strangers"? If not, can you relate this difference to the themes of the two stories? To the fact that the authors are aiming at a type of "interpretation" different from that which Hardy aims in "The Three Strangers"?

SECTION III

Personality: Action and Idea

We have said, in our provisional definition, that fiction is a narrative involving human beings (that even in animal stories we project human qualities and values on to White Fang or Wee Willie Chipmunk). Character is always involved in fiction, even in the story of the most simple and violent action; and sometimes character is at the very center of our interest, so much so that our interest in action seems merely an extension of our interest in character. But let us not forget that fictional character is always *character in action,* and that the character gets into action because it is caught in a situation of conflict. And, further, let us not forget that the action is humanly significant, that it ends in a shift in, or clarification of, human values.

This shift, or clarification, may be simply the fact that we discover pity or sympathy for some character that we might, in real life, ignore or pass by. Or it may be in our sudden feeling that something which, in real life, we had casually accepted is morally repugnant. Or it may be that we suddenly realize our own fate in a new way, and with a new feeling toward it—as in "The Fir Tree." That is, the shift, or clarification, may appear as a shift, or clarification, of feeling. But let us not forget, too, that feelings imply values—and imply ideas. And some stories, of course, actually state the shift in values resulting from the events recounted.

In all fiction, to come back to our general topic in this section, character implies values; character is, in one sense, an embodiment of an idea; and a character in action implies a shift in values and ideas.

Clay

JAMES JOYCE (1882-1941)

THE MATRON had given her leave to go out as soon as the women's tea was over and Maria looked forward to her evening out. The kitchen was spick and span: the cook said you could see yourself in the big copper boilers. The fire was nice and bright and on one of the side-tables were four very big barmbracks. These barmbracks seemed uncut; but if you went closer you would see that they had been cut into long thick even slices and were ready to be handed round at tea. Maria had cut them herself.

Maria was a very, very small person indeed but she had a very long nose and a very long chin. She talked a little through her nose, always soothingly: "Yes, my dear," and "No, my dear." She was always sent for when the women quarreled over their tubs and always succeeded in making peace. One day the matron had said to her:

"Maria, you are a veritable peace-maker!"

And the sub-matron and two of the Board ladies had heard the compliment. And Ginger Mooney was always saying what she wouldn't do to the dummy who had charge of the irons if it wasn't for Maria. Everyone was so fond of Maria.

The women would have their tea at six o'clock and she would be able to get away before seven. From Ballsbridge to the Pillar, twenty minutes; from the Pillar to Drumcondra, twenty minutes; and twenty minutes to buy the things. She would be there before eight. She took out her purse with the silver clasps and read again the words *A Present from Belfast*. She was very fond of that purse because Joe had

brought it to her five years before when he and Alphy had gone to Belfast on a Whit-Monday trip. In the purse were two half-crowns and some coppers. She would have five shillings clear after paying tram fare. What a nice evening they would have, all the children singing! Only she hoped that Joe wouldn't come in drunk. He was so different when he took any drink.

Often he had wanted her to go and live with them; but she would have felt herself in the way (though Joe's wife was ever so nice with her) and she had become accustomed to the life of the laundry. Joe was a good fellow. She had nursed him and Alphy too; and Joe used often say:

"Mamma is mamma but Maria is my proper mother."

After the break-up at home the boys had got her that position in the *Dublin by Lamplight* laundry, and she liked it. She used to have such a bad opinion of Protestants but now she thought they were very nice people, a little quiet and serious, but still very nice people to live with. Then she had her plants in the conservatory and she liked looking after them. She had lovely ferns and wax-plants and, whenever anyone came to visit her, she always gave the visitor one or two slips from her conservatory. There was one thing she didn't like and that was the tracts on the walls; but the matron was such a nice person to deal with, so genteel.

When the cook told her everything was ready she went into the women's room and began to pull the big bell. In a few minutes the women began to come in by twos and threes, wiping their steaming hands in their petticoats and pulling down the sleeves of their blouses over their red steaming arms. They settled down before their huge mugs which the cook and the dummy filled up with hot tea, already mixed with milk and sugar in huge tin cans. Maria superintended the distribution of the barmbrack and saw that every woman got her four slices. There was a great deal of laughing and joking during the meal. Lizzie Fleming said Maria was sure to get the ring and, though Fleming had said that for so many Hallow Eves, Maria had to laugh and say she didn't want any ring or man either; and when she laughed her gray-green eyes sparkled with disappointed shyness and the tip of her nose nearly met the tip of her chin. Then Ginger Mooney lifted up her mug of tea and proposed Maria's health while all the other women clattered with their mugs on the table, and said she was sorry she hadn't a sup of porter to drink it in. And Maria laughed again till the tip of her nose nearly met the tip of her chin and till her minute body nearly shook itself asunder because she knew that Mooney meant well though, of course, she had the notions of a common woman.

But wasn't Maria glad when the women had finished their tea and the cook and the dummy had begun to clear away the tea-things! She went into her little bedroom and, remembering that the next morning was a mass morning, changed the hand of the alarm from seven to six. Then she took off her working skirt and her house-boots and laid her best skirt out on the bed and her tiny dress-boots beside the foot of the bed. She changed her blouse too and, as she stood before the mirror, she thought of how she used to dress for mass on Sunday morning when she was a young girl; and she looked with quaint affection at the diminutive body which she had so often adorned. In spite of its years she found it a nice tidy little body.

When she got outside the streets were shining with rain and she was glad of her old brown waterproof. The tram was full and she had to sit on the little stool at the end of the car, facing all the people, with her toes barely touching the floor. She arranged in her mind all she was going to do and thought how much better it was to be independent and to have your own money in your pocket. She hoped they would have a nice evening. She was sure they would but she could not help thinking what a pity it was Alphy and Joe were not speaking. They were always falling out now but when they were boys together they used to be the best of friends: but such was life.

She got out of her tram at the Pillar and ferreted her way quickly among the crowds. She went into Downes's cake-shop but the shop was so full of people that it was a long time before she could get herself attended to. She bought a dozen of mixed penny cakes, and at last came out of the shop laden with a big bag. Then she thought what else would she buy: she wanted to buy something really nice. They would be sure to have plenty of apples and nuts. It was hard to know what to buy and all she could think of was cake. She decided to buy some plumcake but Downes's plumcake had not enough almond icing on top of it so she went over to a shop in Henry Street. Here she was a long time in suiting herself and the stylish young lady behind the counter, who was evidently a little annoyed by her, asked her was it wedding-cake she wanted to buy. That made Maria blush and smile at the young lady; but the young lady took it all very seriously and finally cut a thick slice of plumcake, parceled it up and said:

"Two-and-four, please."

She thought she would have to stand in the Drumcondra tram because none of the young men seemed to notice her but an elderly gentleman made room for her. He was a stout gentleman and he wore a brown hard hat; he had a square red face and a grayish mustache. Maria thought he was a colonel-looking gentleman and she reflected how much more polite he was than the young men who simply stared straight before them. The gentleman began to chat with her about Hallow Eve and the rainy weather. He supposed the bag was full of good things for the little ones and said it was only right that the youngsters should enjoy themselves while they were young. Maria agreed with him and favored him with demure nods and hems. He was very nice with her, and when she was getting out at the Canal Bridge she thanked him and bowed, and he bowed to her and raised his hat and smiled agreeably; and while she was going up along the terrace, bending her tiny head under the rain, she thought how easy it was to know a gentleman even when he has a drop taken.

Everybody said: *"O, here's Maria!"* when she came to Joe's house. Joe was there, having come home from business, and all the children had their Sunday dresses on. There were two big girls in from next door and games were going on. Maria gave the bag of cakes to the eldest boy, Alphy, to divide and Mrs. Donnelly said it was too good of her to bring such a big bag of cakes and made all the children say:

"Thanks, Maria."

But Maria said she had brought something special for papa and mamma, something they would be sure to like, and she began to look for her plumcake. She tried in Downes's bag and then in the pockets of her waterproof and then on the hall-stand but nowhere could she find it. Then she asked all the children had any of them eaten it—by mistake, of course—but the children all said no and looked as if they did not like to eat cakes if they were to be accused of stealing. Everybody had a solution for the mystery and Mrs. Donnelly said it was plain that Maria had left it behind her in the tram. Maria, remembering how confused the gentleman with the grayish mustache had made her, colored with shame and vexation and disappointment. At the thought of the failure of her little surprise and of the two and four-pence she had thrown away for nothing she nearly cried outright.

But Joe said it didn't matter and made her sit down by the fire. He was very nice with her. He told her all that went on in his office, repeating for her a smart answer which he had made to the manager. Maria did not understand why Joe laughed so much over the answer he had made but she said that the manager must have been a very overbearing person to deal with. Joe said he wasn't so bad when you knew how to take him, that he was a decent sort so long as you didn't rub him the wrong way. Mrs. Donnelly played the piano for the children and they danced and sang. Then the two next-door girls handed round the nuts. Nobody could find the nutcrackers and Joe was nearly getting cross over it and asked how did they expect Maria to crack

nuts without a nutcracker. But Maria said she didn't like nuts and that they weren't to bother about her. Then Joe asked would she take a bottle of stout and Mrs. Donnelly said there was port wine too in the house if she would prefer that. Maria said she would rather they didn't ask her to take anything: but Joe insisted.

So Maria let him have his way and they sat by the fire talking over old times and Maria thought she would put in a good word for Alphy. But Joe cried that God might strike him stone dead if ever he spoke a word to his brother again and Maria said she was sorry she had mentioned the matter. Mrs. Donnelly told her husband it was a great shame for him to speak that way of his own flesh and blood but Joe said that Alphy was no brother of his and there was nearly being a row on the head of it. But Joe said he would not lose his temper on account of the night it was and asked his wife to open some more stout. The two next-door girls had arranged some Hallow Eve games and soon everything was merry again. Maria was delighted to see the children so merry and Joe and his wife in such good spirits. The next-door girls put some saucers on the table and then led the children up to the table, blindfold. One got the prayer-book and the other three got the water; and when one of the next-door girls got the ring Mrs. Donnelly shook her finger at the blushing girl as much as to say: *O, I know all about it!* They insisted then on blindfolding Maria and leading her up to the table to see what she would get; and, while they were putting on the bandage, Maria laughed and laughed again till the tip of her nose nearly met the tip of her chin.

They led her up to the table amid laughing and joking and she put her hand out in the air as she was told to do. She moved her hand about here and there in the air and descended on one of the saucers. She felt a soft wet substance with her fingers and was surprised that nobody spoke or took off her bandage. There was a pause for a few seconds; and then a great deal of scuffling and whispering. Somebody said something about the garden, and at last Mrs. Donnelly said something very cross to one of the next-door girls and told her to throw it out at once: that was no play. Maria understood that it was wrong that time and so she had to do it over again: and this time she got the prayer-book.

After that Mrs. Donnelly played Miss Mc-Cloud's Reel for the children and Joe made Maria take a glass of wine. Soon they were all quite merry again and Mrs. Donnelly said Maria would enter a convent before the year was out because she had got the prayer-book. Maria had never seen Joe so nice to her as he was that night, so full of pleasant talk and reminiscences. She said they were all very good to her.

At last the children grew tired and sleepy and Joe asked Maria would she not sing some little song before she went, one of the old songs. Mrs. Donnelly said: *"Do, please, Maria!"* and so Maria had to get up and stand beside the piano. Mrs. Donnelly bade the children be quiet and listen to Maria's song. Then she played the prelude and said *"Now, Maria!"* and Maria, blushing very much, began to sing in a tiny quavering voice. She sang *I Dreamt that I Dwelt,* and when she came to the second verse she sang again:

> *I dreamt that I dwelt in marble halls*
> *With vassals and serfs at my side*
> *And of all who assembled within those walls*
> *That I was the hope and the pride.*
>
> *I had riches too great to count, could boast*
> *Of a high ancestral name,*
> *But I also dreamt, which pleased me most,*
> *That you loved me still the same.*

But no one tried to show her her mistake; and when she had ended her song Joe was very much moved. He said that there was no time like the long ago and no music for him like poor old Balfe, whatever other people might say; and his eyes filled up so much with tears that he could not find what he was looking for and in the end he had to ask his wife to tell him where the corkscrew was.

DISCUSSION

A character is always in some significant relation to place and society, and to a time. Even if a story is about a rootless wanderer, or a man in conflict with his place and time, there is a meaningful relation even in the rootlessness or conflict. For instance, in "Flight" the fact that Pepé is an outsider to society is very significant, as is the fact that he is an "insider" to the natural background, almost sinking into it, identified with it.

In "Clay," Maria is fully set in her society, that of middle-class Dublin, and her time, that of the early years of this century. Certainly the details of that life are here in abundance: the "Dublin by Lamplight Laundry," the "colonel-looking gentleman" on the Drumcondra tram, the "purse with the silver clasps" bearing the inscription *A Present from Belfast,* etc. Moreover, the story is not only filled with such details: the details are presented to the reader in the idiom and even in the rhythms of speech of a middle-class Dubliner of the time. The reader is therefore the more likely to find the story static: a mere presentation of a scene, perhaps for ironic effect, but without real plot and without drama.

Though an easy misconception to adopt, this is a misconception; for this story involves tension and conflict, however subdued they may appear, and something happens to Maria that is decisive for her life.

The story is obviously Maria's: it is her fate that is at stake. What sort of person is she? She is an ugly old maid ("a very long nose and a very long chin") who works in a laundry but is conscious of her refinement and gentility as compared with the coarser women who actually work at the tubs ("she knew that Mooney meant well though, of course, she had the notions of a common woman"). On the day described in this story she is going to visit her brother and his family as they celebrate Hallow Eve. (Some readers see Maria as the family maid who has reared the motherless boys, Joe and Alphy—not as their older sister. It seems to the editors unlikely that a family in the economic circumstances presented would have had a maid, and that the story becomes more poignant if we see Maria as the older sister, for whom Joe feels some kind of reluctant responsibility but whom his wife keeps at a distance: Joe is Joe to her but his wife is Mrs. Donnelly. But the point is of no great importance, and the story is not substantially altered, whether we take her to be Joe's sister, aunt, cousin, or former privileged family servant. What is important is that the boys whom she has reared have got her this nice job in the laundry, and that Joe's wife evidently looks with satisfaction on the prospect of Maria's entrance into a "convent before the year is out.")

What does Maria think of herself? What does she want from life? She scarcely knows, for she is hardly an introspective person, and perhaps she thinks of herself as a happy or at least well-satisfied person. But whether or not Maria knows what she wants, the author has made it possible for the reader to know. We have said that she is an unattractive old maid, but Joyce has indicated that Maria does not think that marriage is impossible for her, and, without perhaps fully realizing it, she yearns for a home.

What are some of the indications that this is true? Maria is quietly proud of being praised as a "veritable peace-maker," and that Joe used to say "Maria is my proper mother." She bridles a little when the coarse women at the laundry tease her about getting the ring—a prophecy of matrimony—at the Hallow Eve games. When she dresses for the evening she looks "with quaint affection at her diminutive body. . . . In spite of its years she found it a nice tidy little body." Later, at the cake shop, she blushes when the "stylish young lady behind the counter" makes the sarcastic comment that in view of the time she is taking she must be selecting a wedding cake. (Her sarcasm goes quite over Maria's head.)

In the tram Maria enjoys the courteous attentions which "the colonel-looking gentleman" pays to her. One judges that Maria rarely enjoys such attentions—"none of the young men seem to notice her," and she is so flustered that she forgets the plum cake for which she has shopped so carefully.

All of these hints are worked in unobtrusively enough: on one level they are merely the details of Maria's preparation for her visit. But they tell us a great deal about Maria and they render meaningful in a way in which Maria herself is unaware the song which she sings at the end of the story.

The paragraphs that deal with Maria's reception at Joe's house fill out and extend the hints about Maria's past and her present status. Joe is "very nice with her"—at least so it seems to Maria in her gratitude for the ordinary enough civilities which he accords her. The practical and competent Mrs. Donnelly, his wife, evidently keeps Maria at arm's length. The children take her for granted and are not above playing jokes upon her. (The attitude of the children is the surest indication of all of the whole family's attitude to Maria. But family pride dictates that what is allowable in her own children can hardly be tolerated in the neighbor's children: Mrs. Donnelly scolds *them* for allowing Maria to get the booby prize—the clay.)

Is it the mere chance of the game that Maria in her second chance gets the prayer book? Were the articles shifted so that Maria puts her hand upon the article considered appropriate for her? It is impossible to prove from the story that more than mere chance was involved, and it is not necessary to do so. But the child's game may involve a truer prophecy of Maria's future career than the careless reader might assume. For it is appropriate that Maria should not get the ring, and Mrs. Donnelly a little later in the evening is prepared to interpret seriously her getting the prayer book: "Maria would enter a convent before the year was out." We can take Mrs. Donnelly's comment as mere banter, but one guesses that Joe and his wife would be happy enough to see Maria enter a convent. She is evidently not going to marry. She is not getting any younger. And she will not be able to work at the laundry (where Joe and his brother had kindly got her a job) always. Were she provided for by some attachment to a religious order, Joe would be relieved of his grudging responsibility for her. If the Donnellys do have such a scheme in mind, there is every chance that it will succeed; for Maria is as plastic as the clay into which she has earlier thrust her fingers. Notice how often Joyce has suggested this plasticity: "made her sit down"—"Maria let him have his way"—"and so she had to do it over again" etc. When Mrs. Donnelly says *Do, please, Maria!* Maria "had to get up and stand beside the piano."

And what does Maria choose to sing? A song which from this singer is as ironically inappropriate as a song can be. Maria does not dwell in marble halls. She is not the hope and pride of the people assembled within *these* walls. She has neither riches nor name nor a "you" who loves her still the same. It is not necessary to assume that Maria consciously chooses this song to express her own forlorn aspirations. The song by the Irish composer, Balfe, is a prefectly natural choice. It is perhaps one of the few in Maria's meager repertory. It is not even necessary to assume that Maria herself is aware of all the ironies implicit in her singing the song. Yet in some sense the song expresses her own hidden yearning, and she loses herself for the moment in it, for she repeats the first verse unaware that she has already sung it.

The song, sung in Maria's "tiny quavering voice," and Joe's sentimental reaction to the occasion make a fitting climax to the story. We know what is going to happen to Maria, and we know that she will accept cheerfully enough what is going to happen to her, even if it is not what her inner being actually yearns for. Even for the reader who feels that we read too much into the story in supposing that Maria is actually, under the Donnellys' nudging, being pushed into the convent, the ending is adequate. For one may say to such a reader "This ending reveals sharply in one instant the essential pathos of Maria's life. We know what she wants to have and we know that she will never have it."

Joyce felt that a story should give what he called an "epiphany"—that is, a showing forth, a revelation—through some scrap of conversation or some incident, of the inner nature of a person or a situation. "Clay" is such an epiphany.

A few lines above we used the phrase the "pathos of Maria's life." The term *pathos* was used advisedly, for this is not a tragic story. Tragedy implies a struggle, a resistance of fate, a downfall springing from some action of the hero himself. Tragedy involves a much more complex attitude than does pathos. Maria cannot struggle and is not even aware of the issues. She is a pathetic but not a tragic figure. Yet pure pathos is actually to be met with quite as infrequently as tragedy; for pathos is rarely kept pure. It is usually corrupted into sentimentality.

How has Joyce kept the sense of pity pure and unsentimental? For one thing, he keeps the story objective; he does not pluck at our sleeves and urge us to pity Maria's plight. For another, he works through implication and almost without any commentary upon the situation. Perhaps most important of all, he does not show Maria as pitying *herself*. We are aware of a pathos of which the victim herself is not aware. Maria will go home this evening rather tranquil and moderately happy. That is her nature.

EXERCISE

1. In this story, the point does not lie in a changed awareness on the part of a character; it lies in our discovery of the pathos of Maria's situation. How does this fact relate to the effect of the story?

2. Read "Tomorrow and Tomorrow and So Forth," by John Updike (page 211). Our primary concern is with the character of Prosser, whom, in the person of Geoffrey Langer, we even get a glimpse of as a boy. What are his basic qualities? What does the climax of the story reveal? How fully is he aware of himself—of his own situation? What attitude does the author expect us to take to Prosser? What are we to make of the last sentence of the story?

3. Read "Jerico, Jerico, Jerico," by Andrew Lytle (page 230). Compose a set of questions on this story.

I'm a Fool

SHERWOOD ANDERSON (1876-1941)

IT WAS a hard jolt for me, one of the most bitterest I ever had to face. And it all came about through my own foolishness, too. Even yet sometimes, when I think of it, I want to cry or swear or kick myself. Perhaps, even now, after all this time, there will be a kind of satisfaction in making myself look cheap by telling of it.

It began at three o'clock one October afternoon as I sat in the grand stand at the fall trotting and pacing meet at Sandusky, Ohio.

To tell the truth, I felt a little foolish that I should be sitting in the grand stand at all. During the summer before I had left my home town with Harry Whitehead and, with a nigger named Burt, had taken a job as swipe with one of the two horses Harry was campaigning through the fall race meets that year. Mother cried and my sister Mildred, who wanted to get a job as a school teacher in our town that fall, stormed and scolded about the house all during the week before I left. They both thought it was something disgraceful that one of our family should take a place as a swipe with race horses. I've an idea Mildred thought my taking the place would stand in the way of her getting the job she'd been working so long for.

But after all I had to work, and there was no other work to be got. A big lumbering fellow of nineteen couldn't just hang around the house and I had got too big to mow people's lawns and sell newspapers. Little chaps who could get next to people's sympathies by their sizes were always getting jobs away from me. There was one fellow who kept saying to everyone who wanted a lawn mowed or a cistern cleaned, that he was saving money to work his way through college, and I used to lay awake nights thinking up ways to injure him without being found out. I kept thinking of wagons running over him and bricks falling on his head as he walked along the street. But never mind him.

I got the place with Harry and I liked Burt fine. We got along splendid together. He was a big nigger with a lazy sprawling body and soft, kind eyes, and when it came to a fight he could hit like Jack Johnson. He had Bucephalus, a big black pacing stallion that could do 2.09 or 2.10, if he had to, and I had a little gelding named Doctor Fritz that never lost a race all fall when Harry wanted him to win.

We set out from home late in July in a box car with the two horses and after that, until late November, we kept moving along to the race meets and the fairs. It was a peachey time for me, I'll say that. Sometimes now I think that boys who are raised regular in houses, and never have a fine nigger like Burt for best friend, and go to high schools and college, and never steal anything, or get drunk a little, or learn to swear from fellows who know how, or come walking up in front of a grand stand in their shirt sleeves and with dirty horsy pants on when the races are going on and the grand stand is full of people all dressed up— What's

the use of talking about it? Such fellows don't know nothing at all. They've never had no opportunity.

But I did. Burt taught me how to rub down a horse and put the bandages on after a race and steam a horse out and a lot of valuable things for any man to know. He could wrap a bandage on a horse's leg so smooth that if it had been the same color you would think it was his skin, and I guess he'd have been a big driver, too, and got to the top like Murphy and Walter Cox and the others if he hadn't been black.

Gee whizz, it was fun. You got to a county seat town, maybe say on a Saturday or Sunday, and the fair began the next Tuesday and lasted until Friday afternoon. Doctor Fritz would be, say in the 2.25 trot on Tuesday afternoon and on Thursday afternoon Bucephalus would knock 'em cold in the "free-for-all" pace. It left you a lot of time to hang around and listen to horse talk, and see Burt knock some yap cold that got too gay, and you'd find out about horses and men and pick up a lot of stuff you could use all the rest of your life, if you had some sense and salted down what you heard and felt and saw.

And then at the end of the week when the race meet was over, and Harry had run home to tend up to his livery stable business, you and Burt hitched the two horses to carts and drove slow and steady across country, to the place for the next meeting, so as to not overheat the horses, etc., etc., you know.

Gee whizz, Gosh amighty, the nice hickory-nut and beechnut and oaks and other kinds of trees along the roads, all brown and red, and the good smells, and Burt singing a song that was called Deep River, and all the country girls at the windows of houses and everything. You can stick your colleges up your nose for all me. I guess I know where I got my education.

Why, one of those little burgs of towns you come to on the way, say now on a Saturday afternoon, and Burt says, "let's lay up here." And you did.

And you took the horses to a livery stable and fed them, and you got your good clothes out of a box and put them on.

And the town was full of farmers gaping, because they could see you were race horse people, and the kids maybe never see a nigger before and was afraid and run away when the two of us walked down their main street.

And that was before prohibition and all that foolishness, and so you went into a saloon, the two of you, and all the yaps come and stood around, and there was always someone pretended he was horsy and knew things and spoke up and began asking questions, and all you did was to lie and lie all you could about what horses you had, and I said I owned them, and then some fellow said, "Will you have a drink of whiskey" and Burt knocked his eye out the way he could say, off-hand like, "Oh well, all right, I'm agreeable to a little nip. I'll split a quart with you." Gee whizz.

But that isn't what I want to tell my story about. We got home late in November and I promised mother I'd quit the race horses for good. There's a lot of things you've got to promise a mother because she don't know any better.

And so, there not being any work in our town any more than when I left there to go to the races, I went off to Sandusky and got a pretty good place taking care of horses for a man who owned a teaming and delivery and storage and coal and real estate business there. It was a pretty good place with good eats, and a day off each week, and sleeping on a cot in a big barn, and mostly just shovelling in hay and oats to a lot of big good-enough skates of horses, that couldn't have trotted a race with a toad. I wasn't dissatisfied and I could send money home.

And then, as I started to tell you, the fall races come to Sandusky and I got the day off and I went. I left the job at noon and had on my good clothes and my new brown derby hat, I'd just bought the Saturday before, and a stand-up collar.

First of all I went down-town and walked about with the dudes. I've always thought to myself, "put up a good front" and so I did it. I had forty dollars in my pocket and so I went into the West House, a big hotel, and walked up to the cigar stand. "Give me three twenty-five cent cigars," I said. There was a lot of horsemen and strangers and dressed-up people from other towns standing around in the lobby

and in the bar, and I mingled amongst them. In the bar there was a fellow with a cane and a Windsor tie on, that it made me sick to look at him. I like a man to be a man and dress up, but not to go put on that kind of airs. So I pushed him aside, kind of rough, and had me a drink of whiskey. And then he looked at me, as though he thought maybe he'd get gay, but he changed his mind and didn't say anything. And then I had another drink of whiskey, just to show him something, and went out and had a hack out to the races, all to myself, and when I got there I bought myself the best seat I could get up in the grand stand, but didn't go in for any of these boxes. That's putting on too many airs.

And so there I was, sitting up in the grand stand as gay as you please and looking down on the swipes coming out with their horses, and with their dirty horsy pants on and the horse blankets swung over their shoulders, same as I had been doing all the year before. I liked one thing about the same as the other, sitting up there and feeling grand and being down there and looking up at the yaps and feeling grander and more important, too. One thing's about as good as another, if you take it just right. I've often said that.

Well, right in front of me, in the grand stand that day, there was a fellow with a couple of girls and they was about my age. The young fellow was a nice guy all right. He was the kind maybe that goes to college and then comes to be a lawyer or maybe a newspaper editor or something like that, but he wasn't stuck on himself. There are some of that kind are all right and he was one of the ones.

He had his sister with him and another girl and the sister looked around over his shoulder, accidental at first, not intending to start anything—she wasn't that kind—and her eyes and mine happened to meet.

You know how it is. Gee, she was a peach! She had on a soft dress, kind of a blue stuff and it looked carelessly made, but was well sewed and made and everything. I knew that much. I blushed when she looked right at me and so did she. She was the nicest girl I've ever seen in my life. She wasn't stuck on herself and she could talk proper grammar without being

like a school teacher or something like that.
What I mean, is, she was O.K. I think maybe
her father was well-to-do, but not rich to make
her chesty because she was his daughter, as
some are. Maybe he owned a drug store or a dry-
goods store in their home town, or something
like that. She never told me and I never asked.

My own people are all O.K. too, when you
come to that. My grandfather was Welsh and
over in the old country, in Wales he was— But
never mind that.

The first heat of the first race come off and
the young fellow setting there with the two
girls left them and went down to make a bet.
I knew what he was up to, but he didn't talk
big and noisy and let everyone around know he
was a sport, as some do. He wasn't that kind.
Well, he come back and I heard him tell the
two girls what horse he'd bet on, and when the
heat trotted they all half got to their feet and
acted in the excited, sweaty way people do
when they've got money down on a race, and
the horse they bet on is up there pretty close
at the end, and they think maybe he'll come
on with a rush, but he never does because he
hasn't got the old juice in him, come right
down to it.

And then, pretty soon, the horses came out
for the 2.18 pace and there was a horse in it
I knew. He was a horse Bob French had in his
string but Bob didn't own him. He was a horse
owned by a Mr. Mathers down at Marietta,
Ohio.

This Mr. Mathers had a lot of money and
owned some coal mines or something and he
had a swell place out in the country, and he
was stuck on race horses, but was a Presbyterian or something, and I think more than
likely his wife was one, too, maybe a stiffer
one than himself. So he never raced his horses
hisself, and the story round the Ohio race tracks
was that when one of his horses got ready to
go to the races he turned him over to Bob French
and pretended to his wife he was sold.

So Bob had the horses and he did pretty
much as he pleased and you can't blame Bob,
at least, I never did. Sometimes he was out to
win and sometimes he wasn't. I never cared
much about that when I was swiping a horse.
What I did want to know was that my horse

had the speed and could go out in front, if you
wanted him to.

And, as I'm telling you, there was Bob in this
race with one of Mr. Mathers' horses, was named
"About Ben Ahem" or something like that, and
was fast as a streak. He was a gelding and had
a mark of 2.21, but could step in .08 or .09.

Because when Burt and I were out, as I've
told you, the year before, there was a nigger,
Burt knew, worked for Mr. Mathers and we
went out there one day when we didn't have
no race on at the Marietta Fair and our boss
Harry was gone home.

And so everyone was gone to the fair but just
this one nigger and he took us all through Mr.
Mathers' swell house and he and Burt tapped
a bottle of wine Mr. Mathers had hid in his
bedroom, back in a closet, without his wife
knowing, and he showed us this Ahem horse.
Burt was always stuck on being a driver but
didn't have much chance to get to the top,
being a nigger, and he and the other nigger
gulped the whole bottle of wine and Burt got
a little lit up.

So the nigger let Burt take this About Ben
Ahem and step him a mile in a track Mr.
Mathers had all to himself, right there on the
farm. And Mr. Mathers had one child, a daughter, kinda sick and not very good looking, and
she came home and we had to hustle and get
About Ben Ahem stuck back in the barn.

I'm only telling you to get everything
straight. At Sandusky, that afternoon I was at
the fair, this young fellow with the two girls
was fussed, being with the girls and losing his
bet. You know how a fellow is that way. One
of them was his girl and the other his sister.
I had figured that out.

"Gee whizz," I says to myself, "I'm going to
give him the dope."

He was mighty nice when I touched him on
the shoulder. He and the girls were nice to me
right from the start and clear to the end. I'm
not blaming them.

And so he leaned back and I give him the
dope on About Ben Ahem. "Don't bet a cent
on this first heat because he'll go like an oxen
hitched to a plow, but when the first heat is
over go right down and lay on your pile." That's
what I told him.

Well, I never saw a fellow treat any one sweller. There was a fat man sitting beside the little girl, that had looked at me twice by this time, and I at her, and both blushing, and what did he do but have the nerve to turn and ask the fat man to get up and change places with me so I could set with his crowd.

Gee whizz, craps amighty. There I was. What a chump I was to go and get gay up there in the West House bar, and just because that dude was standing there with a cane and that kind of a necktie on, to go and get all balled up and drink that whiskey, just to show off.

Of course she would know, me setting right beside her and letting her smell of my breath. I could have kicked myself right down out of that grand stand and all around that race track and made a faster record than most of the skates of horses they had there that year.

Because that girl wasn't any mutt of a girl. What wouldn't I have give right then for a stick of chewing gum to chew, or a lozenger, or some licorice, or most anything. I was glad I had those twenty-five cent cigars in my pocket and right away I give that fellow one and lit one myself. Then that fat man got up and we changed places and there I was, plunked right down beside her.

They introduced themselves and the fellow's best girl, he had with him, was named Miss Elinor Woodbury, and her father was a manufacturer of barrels from a place called Tiffin, Ohio. And the fellow himself was named Wilbur Wessen and his sister was Miss Lucy Wessen.

I suppose it was their having such swell names that got me off my trolley. A fellow, just because he has been a swipe with a race horse, and works taking care of horses for a man in the teaming, delivery, and storage business isn't any better or worse than any one else. I've often thought that, and said it too.

But you know how a fellow is. There's something in that kind of nice clothes, and the kind of nice eyes she had, and the way she had looked at me, awhile before, over her brother's shoulder, and me looking back at her, and both of us blushing.

I couldn't show her up for a boob, could I? I made a fool of myself, that's what I did. I said my name was Walter Mathers from Marietta, Ohio, and then I told all three of them the smashingest lie you ever heard. What I said was that my father owned the horse About Ben Ahem and that he had let him out to this Bob French for racing purposes, because our family was proud and had never gone into racing that way, in our own name, I mean. Then I had got started and they were all leaning over and listening, and Miss Lucy Wessen's eyes were shining, and I went the whole hog.

I told about our place down at Marietta, and about the big stables and the grand brick house we had on a hill, up above the Ohio River, but I knew enough not to do it in no bragging way. What I did was to start things and then let them drag the rest out of me. I acted just as reluctant to tell as I could. Our family hasn't got any barrel factory, and since I've known us, we've always been pretty poor, but not asking anything of any one at that, and my grandfather, over in Wales—but never mind that.

We set there talking like we had known each other for years and years, and I went and told them that my father had been expecting maybe this Bob French wasn't on the square, and had sent me up to Sandusky on the sly to find out what I could.

And I bluffed it through I had found out all about the 2.18 pace, in which About Ben Ahem was to start.

I said he would lose the first heat by pacing like a lame cow and then he would come back and skin 'em alive after that. And to back up what I said I took thirty dollars out of my pocket and handed it to Mr. Wilbur Wessen and asked him, would he mind, after the first heat, to go down and place it on About Ben Ahem for whatever odds he could get. What I said was that I didn't want Bob French to see me and none of the swipes.

Sure enough the first heat come off and About Ben Ahem went off his stride, up the back stretch, and looked like a wooden horse or a sick one, and come in to be last. Then this Wilbur Wessen went down to the betting place under the grand stand and there I was with the two girls, and when that Miss Woodbury was looking the other way once, Lucy Wessen kinda, with her shoulder you know, kinda touched me. Not just tucking down, I don't mean. You know how a woman can do. They get close, but not getting gay either. You know what they do. Gee whizz.

And then they give me a jolt. What they had done, when I didn't know, was to get together, and they had decided Wilbur Wessen' would bet fifty dollars, and the two girls had gone and put in ten dollars each, of their own money, too. I was sick then, but I was sicker later.

About the gelding, About Ben Ahem, and their winning their money, I wasn't worried a lot about that. It come out O.K. Ahem stepped the next three heats like a bushel of spoiled eggs going to market before they could be found out, and Wilbur Wessen had got nine to two for the money. There was something else eating at me.

Because Wilbur come back, after he had bet the money, and after that he spent most of his time talking to that Miss Woodbury, and Lucy Wessen and I was left alone together like on a desert island. Gee, if I'd only been on the square or if there had been any way of getting myself on the square. There ain't any Walter Mathers, like I said to her and them, and there hasn't ever been one, but if there was, I bet I'd go to Marietta, Ohio, and shoot him tomorrow.

There I was, big boob that I am. Pretty soon the race was over, and Wilbur had gone down and collected our money, and we had a hack down-town, and he stood us a swell supper at the West House, and a bottle of champagne beside.

And I was with that girl and she wasn't saying much, and I wasn't saying much either. One thing I know. She wasn't stuck on me because of the lie about my father being rich and all that. There's a way you know. . . . Craps amighty. There's a kind of girl, you see just once in your life, and if you don't get busy and make hay, then you're gone for good and all, and might as well go jump off a bridge. They give you a look from inside of them somewhere, and it ain't no vamping, and what it means is— you want that girl to be your wife, and you want nice things around her like flowers and swell clothes, and you want her to have the

kids you're going to have, and you want good music played and no rag time. Gee whizz.

There's a place over near Sandusky, across a kind of bay, and it's called Cedar Point. And after we had supper we went over to it in a launch, all by ourselves. Wilbur and Miss Lucy and that Miss Woodbury had to catch a ten o'clock train back to Tiffin, Ohio, because, when you're out with girls like that you can't get careless and miss any trains and stay out all night, like you can with some kinds of Janes.

And Wilbur blowed himself to the launch and it cost him fifteen cold plunks, but I wouldn't never have knew if I hadn't listened. He wasn't no tin horn kind of a sport.

Over at the Cedar Point place, we didn't stay around where there was a gang of common kind of cattle at all.

There was big dance halls and dining places for yaps, and there was a beach you would walk along and get where it was dark, and we went there.

She didn't talk hardly at all and neither did I, and I was thinking how glad I was my mother was all right, and always made us kids learn to eat with a fork at table, and not swill soup, and not be noisy and rough like a gang you see around a race track that way.

Then Wilbur and his girl went away up the beach and Lucy and I sat down in a dark place, where there was some roots of old trees, the water had washed up, and after that the time, till we had to go back in the launch and they had to catch their trains, wasn't nothing at all. It went like winking your eye.

Here's how it was. The place we were setting in was dark, like I said, and there was the roots from that old stump sticking up like arms, and there was a watery smell, and the night was like —as if you could put your hand out and feel it— so warm and soft and dark and sweet like an orange.

I most cried and I most swore and I most jumped up and danced, I was so mad and happy and sad.

When Wilbur come back from being alone with his girl, and she saw him coming, Lucy she says, "we got to go to the train now," and she was most crying too, but she never knew nothing I knew, and she couldn't be so all busted up. And then, before Wilbur and Miss Woodbury got up to where we was, she put her face up and kissed me quick and put her head up against me and she was all quivering and—Gee whizz.

Sometimes I hope I have cancer and die. I guess you know what I mean. We went in the launch across the bay to the train like that, and it was dark, too. She whispered and said it was like she and I could get out of the boat and walk on the water, and it sounded foolish, but I knew what she meant.

And then quick we were right at the depot, and there was a big gang of yaps, the kind that goes to the fairs, and crowded and milling around like cattle, and how could I tell her? "It won't be long because you'll write and I'll write to you." That's all she said.

I got a chance like a hay barn afire. A swell chance I got.

And maybe she would write me, down at Marietta that way, and the letter would come back, and stamped on the front of it by the U.S.A. "there ain't any such guy," or something like that, whatever they stamp on a letter that way.

And me trying to pass myself off for a big-bug and a swell—to her, as decent a little body as God ever made. Craps amighty—a swell chance I got!

And then the train come in, and she got on it, and Wilbur Wessen, he come and shook hands with me, and that Miss Woodbury was nice too and bowed to me, and I at her, and the train went and I busted out and cried like a kid.

Gee, I could have run after that train and made Dan Patch look like a freight train after a wreck but, socks amighty, what was the use? Did you ever see such a fool?

I'll bet you what—if I had an arm broke right now or a train had run over my foot—I wouldn't go to no doctor at all. I'd go set down and let her hurt and hurt—that's what I'd do.

I'll bet you what—if I hadn't a drunk that booze I'd a never been such a boob as to go tell such a lie—that couldn't never be made straight to a lady like her.

I wish I had that fellow right here that had on a Windsor tie and carried a cane. I'd smash him for fair. Gosh darn his eyes. He's a big fool—that's what he is.

And if I'm not another you just go find me one and I'll quit working and be a bum and give him my job. I don't care nothing for working, and earning money, and saving it for no such boob as myself.

EXERCISE

1. In "Clay" we have a character unaware of the fate which we know is impending. The character is lacking in self-knowledge. In "I'm a Fool" we have a boy brought to a poignant moment of self-knowledge. In other words, in this story, in contrast to "Clay," it is the character upon whom the effect is made—who, as it were, embodies the shift or clarification of values. What does the boy find out about himself?

2. What are the stages in the story by which the self-knowledge emerges?

3. This story is told from the point of view of the first person. Does this have a significant relation to the main idea of the story? Try to imagine the story told by the objective *omniscient narrator* (see Glossary), such as we find in "Clay." What might be the difference in effect? For one thing, what might be the difference in our sense of place and society? For another, the difference in the amount of objective exposition required? For another, the difference in sympathy with the boy?

4. Again read "Daddy Wolf," by Purdy (page 219). What is our attitude toward the main character? What is the emotional effect of the story? There are many comic elements in the story. Do they seem to contradict the attitude felt toward the main character and the emotional effect of the story? If there is such a contradiction, can you see any relation between this fact and the obvious conflict on which the story is based? What is the use of the implied listener in the story? What differences might appear if this story were not told in the first person?

5. What degree of self-awareness does the heroine have in "Jerico, Jerico, Jerico"?

6. Read "The Apostate," by George Milburn (page 216). This story, like "I'm a Fool," is told in the first person. But unlike the narrator in the former story, the "H. T." of "The Apostate" does not come to awareness. In fact, the whole point here is that "H. T." thinks he is telling one story but is actually telling another. The reader sees, as it were, over "H. T.'s" head to the truth of the situation. The effect of Maria's unawareness in "Clay" is to heighten the pathos and, at the same time, avoid sentimentality. The effect of "H. T.'s" unawareness is to play the pathos of his groping against the irony in our awareness of his self-deception. The key to the irony is, of course, the fact that he convicts himself out of

his own mouth. What is the "content" of this irony? Where does our sympathy finally lie? With the father or the son? What good qualities does the father have? How do you know? If Rotary, which is scorned by some of the boys at the fraternity, is very much like the fraternity itself, then at whose expense does the irony work in the end? Can it even be said that the pressure of the group at the fraternity house that leads the son to sneer at Rotary is exactly the same pressure that induces the father to join Rotary?

Spotted Horses

WILLIAM FAULKNER (1897-1962)

I

YES SIR. Flem Snopes has filled that whole country full of spotted horses. You can hear folks running them all day and all night, whooping and hollering, and the horses running back and forth across them little wooden bridges ever now and then kind of like thunder. Here I was this morning pretty near half way to town, with the team ambling along and me setting in the buckboard about half asleep, when all of a sudden something come swurging up outen the bushes and jumped the road clean, without touching hoof to it. It flew right over my team big as a billboard and flying through the air like a hawk. It taken me thirty minutes to stop my team and untangle the harness and the buckboard and hitch them up again.

That Flem Snopes. I be dog if he ain't a case, now. One morning about ten years ago the boys was just getting settled down on Varner's porch for a little talk and tobacco, when here come Flem out from behind the counter, with his coat off and his hair all parted, like he might have been clerking for Varner for ten years already. Folks all knowed him; it was a big family of them about five miles down the bottom. That year, at least. Share-cropping. They never stayed on any place over a year. Then they would move on to another place, with the chap or maybe the twins of that year's litter. It was a regular nest of them. But Flem. The rest of them stayed tenant farmers, moving ever year, but here come Flem one day, walking out from behind Jody Varner's counter like he owned it. And he wasn't there but a year or two before folks knowed that if him and Jody was both still in that store in ten years more it would be Jody clerking for Flem Snopes. Why, that fellow could make a nickel where it wasn't but four cents to begin with. He skun me in two trades, myself, and the fellow that can do that, I just hope he'll get rich before I do; that's all.

All right. So here Flem was, clerking at Varner's, making a nickel here and there and not telling nobody about it. No, sir. Folks never knowed when Flem got the better of somebody lessen the fellow he beat told it. He'd just set there in the store-chair, chewing his tobacco and keeping his own business to hisself, until about a week later we'd find out it was somebody else's business he was keeping to hisself —provided the fellow he trimmed was mad enough to tell it. That's Flem.

We give him ten years to own ever thing Jody Varner had. But he never waited no ten years. I reckon you-all know that gal of Uncle Billy Varner's, the youngest one; Eula. Jody's sister. Ever Sunday ever yellow-wheeled buggy and curried riding horse in that country would be hitched to Bill Varner's fence, and the young bucks setting on the porch, swarming around Eula like bees around a honey pot. One of these here kind of big, soft-looking gals that could giggle richer than plowed new-ground. Wouldn't none of them leave before the others, and so they would set there on the porch until time to go home, with some of them with nine and ten miles to ride and then get up tomorrow and go back to the field. So they would all leave together and they would ride in a clump down to the creek ford and hitch them curried horses and yellow-wheeled buggies and get out and fight one another. Then they would get in the buggies again and go on home.

Well, one day about a year ago, one of them yellow-wheeled buggies and one of them curried saddle-horses quit this country. We heard they was heading for Texas. The next day Uncle Billy and Eula and Flem come in to town in Uncle Bill's surrey, and when they come back, Flem and Eula was married. And on the next day we heard that two more of them yellow-wheeled buggies had left the country. They mought have gone to Texas, too. It's a big place.

Anyway, about a month after the wedding, Flem and Eula went to Texas, too. They was gone pretty near a year. Then one day last month, Eula come back, with a baby. We figered up, and we decided that it was as well-growed a three-months-old baby as we ever see. It can already pull up on a chair. I reckon Texas makes big men quick, being a big place. Anyway, if it keeps on like it started, it'll be chewing tobacco and voting time it's eight years old.

And so last Friday here come Flem himself. He was on a wagon with another fellow. The other fellow had one of these two-gallon hats and a ivory-handled pistol and a box of ginger snaps sticking out of his hind pocket, and tied to the tail-gate of the wagon was about two dozen of them Texas ponies, hitched to one another with barbed wire. They was colored like parrots and they was quiet as doves, and ere a one of them would kill you quick as a rattlesnake. Nere a one of them had two eyes the same color, and nere a one of them had ever see a bridle, I reckon; and when that Texas man got down offen the wagon and walked up to them to show how gentle they was, one of them cut his vest clean offen him, same as with a razor.

Flem had done already disappeared; he had went on to see his wife, I reckon, and to see if that ere baby had done gone on to the field to help Uncle Billy plow, maybe. It was the Texas man that taken the horses on to Mrs. Littlejohn's lot. He had a little trouble at first, when they come to the gate, because they hadn't never see a fence before, and when he finally got them in and taken a pair of wire cutters and unhitched them and got them into the barn and poured some shell corn into the trough, they durn nigh tore down the barn. I reckon they thought that shell corn was bugs, maybe. So he left them in the lot and he announced that the auction would begin at sunup tomorrow.

That night we was setting on Mrs. Littlejohn's porch. You-all mind the moon was nigh full that night, and we could watch them spotted varmints swirling along the fence and back and forth across the lot same as minnows in a pond. And then now and then they would all kind of huddle up against the barn and rest themselves by biting and kicking one another. We would hear a squeal, and then a set of hoofs would go Bam! against the barn, like a pistol. It sounded just like a fellow with a pistol, in a nest of cattymounts, taking his time.

II

It wasn't ere a man knowed yet if Flem owned them things or not. They just knowed one thing: that they wasn't never going to know for sho if Flem did or not, or if maybe he didn't just get on that wagon at the edge of town, for the ride or not. Even Eck Snopes didn't know, Flem's own cousin. But wasn't nobody surprised at that. We knowed that Flem would skin Eck quick as he would ere a one of us.

They was there by sunup next morning, some of them come twelve and sixteen miles, with seed-money tied up in tobacco sacks in their overalls, standing along the fence, when the Texas man come out of Mrs. Littlejohn's after breakfast and clumb onto the gate post with that ere white pistol butt sticking outen his hind pocket. He taken a new box of ginger-snaps outen his pocket and bit the end offen it like a cigar and spit out the paper, and said the auction was open. And still they was coming up in wagons and a horse- and mule-back and hitching the teams across the road and coming to the fence. Flem wasn't nowhere in sight.

But he couldn't get them started. He begun to work on Eck, because Eck holp him last night to get them into the barn and feed them that shell corn. Eck got out just in time. He come outen that barn like a chip on the crest of a busted dam of water, and clumb into the wagon just in time.

He was working on Eck when Henry Armstid come up in his wagon. Eck was saying he was skeered to bid on one of them, because he might get it, and the Texas man says, "Them ponies? Them little horses?" He clumb down offen the gate post and went toward the horses. They broke and run, and him following them, kind of chirping to them, with his hand out like he was fixing to catch a fly, until he got three or four of them cornered. Then he jumped into them, and then we couldn't see nothing for a while because of the dust. It was a big cloud of it, and them blare eyed, spotted things swoaring outen it twenty foot to a jump, in forty directions without counting up. Then the dust settled and there they was, that Texas man and the horse. He had its head twisted clean around like a owl's head. Its legs was braced and it was trembling like a new bride and groaning like a saw mill, and him holding its head wrung clean around on its neck so it was snuffing sky. "Look it over," he says, with his heels dug too and that white pistol sticking outen his pocket and his neck swole up like a spreading adder's until you could just tell what he was saying, cussing the horse and talking to us all at once: "Look him over, the fiddle headed son of fourteen fathers. Try him, buy him; you will get the best—" Then it was all dust again, and we couldn't see nothing but spotted hide and mane, and that ere Texas man's boot-heels like a couple of walnuts on two strings, and after a while that two-gallon hat come sailing out like a fat old hen crossing a fence.

When the dust settled again, he was just getting outen the far fence corner, brushing himself off. He come and got his hat and brushed it off and come and clumb onto the gate post again. He was breathing hard. The hammer-head horse was still running round and round the lot like a merry-go-round at a fair. That was when Henry Armstid come shoving up to the gate in them patched overalls and one of them dangle-armed shirts of hisn. Hadn't nobody noticed him until then. We was all watching the Texas man and the horses. Even Mrs. Littlejohn; she had done come out and built a fire under the wash-pot in her back yard, and she would stand at the fence a while and then go back into the house and come out

again with a arm full of wash and stand at the fence again. Well, here come Henry shoving up, and then we see Mrs. Armstid right behind him, in that ere faded wrapper and sunbonnet and them tennis shoes. "Git on back to that wagon," Henry says.

"Henry," she says.

"Here, boys," the Texas man says; "make room for missus to git up and see. Come on Henry," he says; "here's your chance to buy that saddle-horse missus has been wanting. What about ten dollars, Henry?"

"Henry," Mrs. Armstid says. She put her hand on Henry's arm. Henry knocked her hand down.

"Git on back to that wagon, like I told you," he says.

Mrs. Armstid never moved. She stood behind Henry, with her hands rolled into her dress, not looking at nothing. "He hain't no more despair than to buy one of them things," she says. "And us not five dollars ahead of the pore house, he hain't no more despair." It was the truth, too. They ain't never made more than a bare living offen that place of theirs, and them with four chaps and the very clothes they wears she earns by weaving by the firelight at night while Henry's asleep.

"Shut your mouth and git on back to that wagon," Henry says. "Do you want I taken a wagon stake to you here in the big road?"

Well, that Texas man taken one look at her. Then he begun on Eck again; like Henry wasn't even there. But Eck was skeered. "I can git me a snapping turtle or a water moccasin for nothing. I ain't going to buy none."

So the Texas man said he would give Eck a horse. "To start the auction, and because you holp me last night. If you'll start the bidding on the next horse," he says, "I'll give you that fiddle-head horse."

I wish you could have seen them, standing there with their seed-money in their pockets, watching that Texas man give Eck Snopes a live horse, all fixed to call him a fool if he taken it or not. Finally Eck says he'll take it. "Only I just starts the bidding," he says. "I don't have to buy the next one lessen I ain't overtopped." The Texas man said all right, and Eck bid a dollar on the next one, with

Henry Armstid standing there with his mouth already open, watching Eck and the Texas man like a mad-dog or something. "A dollar," Eck says.

The Texas man looked at Eck. His mouth was already open too, like he had started to say something and what he was going to say had up and died on him. "A dollar? You mean, *one* dollar, Eck?"

"Durn it," Eck says; "two dollars, then."

Well, sir, I wish you could a seen that Texas man. He taken out that gingersnap box and held it up and looked into it, careful, like it might have been a diamond ring in it, or a spider. Then he throwed it away and wiped his face with a bandanna. "Well," he says. "Well. Two dollars. Two dollars. Is your pulse all right, Eck?" he says. "Do you have ager-sweats at night, maybe?" he says. "Well," he says, "I got to take it. But are you boys going to stand there and see Eck get two horses at a dollar a head?"

That done it. I be dog if he wasn't nigh as smart as Flem Snopes. He hadn't no more than got the words outen his mouth before here was Henry Armstid, waving his hand. "Three dollars," Henry says. Mrs. Armstid tried to hold him again. He knocked her hand off, shoving up to the gate post.

"Mister," Mrs. Armstid says, "we got chaps in the house and not corn to feed the stock. We got five dollars I earned my chaps a-weaving after dark, and him snoring in the bed. And he hain't no more despair."

"Henry bids three dollars," the Texas man says. "Raise him a dollar, Eck, and the horse is yours."

"Henry," Mrs. Armstid says.

"Raise him, Eck," the Texas man says.

"Four dollars," Eck says.

"Five dollars," Henry says, shaking his fist. He shoved up right under the gate post. Mrs. Armstid was looking at the Texas man too.

"Mister," she says, "if you take that five dollars I earned my chaps a-weaving for one of them things, it'll be a curse onto you and yourn during all the time of man."

But it wasn't no stopping Henry. He had shoved up, waving his fist at the Texas man. He opened it; the money was in nickels and quarters, and one dollar bill that looked like a cow's cud. "Five dollars," he says. "And the man that raises it'll have to beat my head off, or I'll beat hisn."

"All right," the Texas man says. "Five dollars is bid. But don't you shake your hand at me."

III

It taken till nigh sundown before the last one was sold. He got them hotted up once and the bidding got up to seven dollars and a quarter, but most of them went around three or four dollars, him setting on the gate post and picking the horses out one at a time by mouth-word, and Mrs. Littlejohn pumping up and down at the tub and stopping and coming to the fence for a while and going back to the tub again. She had done got done too, and the wash was hung on the line in the back yard, and we could smell supper cooking. Finally they was all sold; he swapped the last two and the wagon for a buckboard.

We was all kind of tired, but Henry Armstid looked more like a mad-dog than ever. When he bought, Mrs. Armstid had went back to tne wagon, setting in it behind them two rabbit-sized, bone-pore mules, and the wagon itself looking like it would fall all to pieces soon as the mules moved. Henry hadn't even waited to pull it outen the road; it was still in the middle of the road and her setting in it, not looking at nothing, ever since this morning.

Henry was right up against the gate. He went up to the Texas man. "I bought a horse and I paid cash," Henry says. "And yet you expect me to stand around here until they are all sold before I can get my horse. I'm going to take my horse outen that lot."

The Texas man looked at Henry. He talked like he might have been asking for a cup of coffee at the table. "Take your horse," he says.

Then Henry quit looking at the Texas man. He begun to swallow, holding onto the gate. "Ain't you going to help me?" he says.

"It ain't my horse," the Texas man says.

Henry never looked at the Texas man again, he never looked at nobody. "Who'll help me catch my horse?" he says. Never nobody said nothing. "Bring the plowline," Henry says. Mrs. Armstid got outen the wagon and brought the plowline. The Texas man got down offen the post. The woman made to pass him, carrying the rope.

"Don't you go in there, missus," the Texas man says.

Henry opened the gate. He didn't look back. "Come on here," he says.

"Don't you go in there, missus," the Texas man says.

Mrs. Armstid wasn't looking at nobody, neither, with her hands across her middle, holding the rope. "I reckon I better," she says. Her and Henry went into the lot. The horses broke and run. Henry and Mrs. Armstid followed.

"Get him into the corner," Henry says. They got Henry's horse cornered finally, and Henry taken the rope, but Mrs. Armstid let the horse get out. They hemmed it up again, but Mrs. Armstid let it get out again, and Henry turned and hit her with the rope. "Why didn't you head him back?" Henry says. He hit her again. "Why didn't you?" It was about that time I looked around and see Flem Snopes standing there.

It was the Texas man that done something. He moved fast for a big man. He caught the rope before Henry could hit the third time, and Henry whirled and make like he would jump at the Texas man. But he never jumped. The Texas man went and taken Henry's arm and led him outen the lot. Mrs. Armstid come behind them and the Texas man taken some money outen his pocket and he give it into Mrs. Armstid's hand. "Get him into the wagon and take him on home," the Texas man says, like he might have been telling them he enjoyed his supper.

Then here come Flem. "What's that for Buck?" Flem says.

"Thinks he bought one of them ponies," the Texas man says. "Get him on away, missus."

But Henry wouldn't go. "Give him back that money," he says. "I bought that horse and I aim to have him if I have to shoot him."

And there was Flem, standing there with his hands in his pockets, chewing, like he had just happened to be passing.

"You take your money and I take my horse,"

Henry says. "Give it back to him," he says to Mrs. Armstid.

"You don't own no horse of mine," the Texas man says. "Get him on home, missus."

Then Henry seen Flem. "You got something to do with these horses," he says. "I bought one. Here's the money for it." He taken the bill outen Mrs. Armstid's hand. He offered it to Flem. "I bought one. Ask him. Here. Here's the money," he says, giving the bill to Flem.

When Flem taken the money, the Texas man dropped the rope he had snatched outen Henry's hand. He had done sent Eck Snopes's boy up to the store for another box of ginger-snaps, and he taken the box outen his pocket and looked into it. It was empty and he dropped it on the ground. "Mr. Snopes will have your money for you tomorrow," he says to Mrs. Armstid. "You can get it from him tomorrow. He don't own no horse. You get him into the wagon and get him on home." Mrs. Armstid went back to the wagon and got in. "Where's that ere buckboard I bought?" the Texas man says. It was after sundown then. And then Mrs. Littlejohn come out on the porch and rung the supper bell.

IV

I come on in and et supper. Mrs. Littlejohn would bring in a pan of bread or something, then she would go out to the porch a minute and come back and tell us. The Texas man had hitched his team to the buckboard he had swapped them last two horses for, and him and Flem had gone, and then she told that the rest of them that never had ropes had went back to the store with I. O. Snopes to get some ropes, and wasn't nobody at the gate but Henry Armstid, and Mrs. Armstid setting in the wagon in the road, and Eck Snopes and that boy of hisn. "I don't care how many of them fool men gets killed by them things," Mrs. Littlejohn says, "but I ain't going to let Eck Snopes take that boy into that lot again." So she went down to the gate, but she come back without the boy or Eck neither.

"It ain't no need to worry about that boy," I says. "He's charmed." He was right behind Eck last night when Eck went to help feed them. The whole drove of them jumped clean over that boy's head and never touched him.

It was Eck that touched him. Eck snatched him into the wagon and taken a rope and frailed the tar outen him.

So I had done et and went to my room and was undressing, long as I had a long trip to make next day; I was trying to sell a machine to Mrs. Bundren up past Whiteleaf; when Henry Armstid opened that gate and went in by hisself. They couldn't make him wait for the balance of them to get back with their ropes. Eck Snopes said he tried to make Henry wait, but Henry wouldn't do it. Eck said Henry walked right up to them and that when they broke, they run clean over Henry like a hay-mow breaking down. Eck said he snatched that boy of hisn out of the way just in time and that them things went through that gate like a creek flood and into the wagons and teams hitched side the road, busting wagon tongues and snapping harness like it was fishing-line, with Mrs. Armstid still setting in their wagon in the middle of it like something carved outen wood. Then they scattered, wild horses and tame mules with pieces of harness and single trees dangling offen them, both ways up and down the road.

"There goes ourn, paw!" Eck says his boy said. "There it goes, into Mrs. Littlejohn's house." Eck says it run right up the steps and into the house like a boarder late for supper. I reckon so. Anyway, I was in my room, in my underclothes, with one sock on and one sock in my hand, leaning out the window when the commotion busted out, when I heard something run into the melodeon in the hall; it sounded like a railroad engine. Then the door to my room come sailing in like when you throw a tin bucket top into the wind and I looked over my shoulder and see something that looked like a fourteen-foot pinwheel a-blaring its eyes at me. It had to blare them fast, because I was already done jumped out the window.

I reckon it was anxious, too. I reckon it hadn't never seen barbed wire or shell corn before, but I know it hadn't never seen underclothes before, or maybe it was a sewing-machine agent it hadn't never seen. Anyway, it whirled and turned to run back up the hall and outen the house, when it met Eck Snopes and that boy just coming in, carrying a rope. It swirled again

and run down the hall and out the back door just in time to meet Mrs. Littlejohn. She had just gathered up the clothes she had washed, and she was coming onto the back porch with a armful of washing in one hand and a scrubbing-board in the other, when the horse skidded up to her, trying to stop and swirl again. It never taken Mrs. Littlejohn no time a-tall.

"Git outen here, you son," she says. She hit it across the face with the scrubbing-board; that ere scrubbing-board split as neat as ere a axe could have done it, and when the horse swirled to run back up the hall, she hit it again with what was left of the scrubbing-board, not on the head this time. "And stay out," she says.

Eck and that boy was half-way down the hall by this time. I reckon that horse looked like a pinwheel to Eck too. "Git to hell outen here, Ad!" Eck says. Only there wasn't time. Eck dropped flat on his face, but the boy never moved. The boy was about a yard tall maybe, in overalls just like Eck's; that horse swoared over his head without touching a hair. I saw that, because I was just coming back up the front steps, still carrying that ere sock and still in my underclothes, when the horse come onto the porch again. It taken one look at me and swirled again and run to the end of the porch and jumped the banisters and the lot fence like a hen-hawk and lit in the lot running and went out the gate again and jumped eight or ten upside-down wagons and went on down the road. It was a full moon then. Mrs. Armstid was still setting in the wagon like she had done been carved outen wood and left there and forgot.

That horse. It ain't never missed a lick. It was going about forty miles a hour when it come to the bridge over the creek. It would have had a clear road, but it so happened that Vernon Tull was already using the bridge when it got there. He was coming back from town; he hadn't heard about the auction; him and his wife and three daughters and Mrs. Tull's aunt, all setting in chairs in the wagon bed, and all asleep, including the mules. They waked up when the horse hit the bridge one time, but Tull said the first he knew was when the mules tried to turn the wagon around in the middle of the bridge and he seen that spotted varmint run right twixt the mules and run up the wagon tongue like a squirrel. He said he just had time to hit it across the face with his whip-stock, because about that time the mules turned the wagon around on that ere one-way bridge and that horse clumb across onto the bridge again and went on, with Vernon standing up in the wagon and kicking at it.

Tull said the mules turned in the harness and clumb back into the wagon too, with Tull trying to beat them out again, with the reins wrapped around his wrist. After that he says all he seen was overturned chairs and women-folks' legs and white drawers shining in the moonlight, and his mules and that spotted horse going on up the road like a ghost.

The mules jerked Tull outen the wagon and drug him a spell on the bridge before the reins broke. They thought at first that he was dead, and while they was kneeling around him, picking the bridge splinters outen him, here come Eck and that boy, still carrying the rope. They was running and breathing a little hard. "Where'd he go?" Eck says.

V

I went back and got my pants and shirt and shoes on just in time to go and help get Henry Armstid outen the trash in the lot. I be dog if he didn't look like he was dead, with his head hanging back and his teeth showing in the moonlight, and a little rim of white under his eye-lids. We could still hear them horses, here and there; hadn't none of them got more than four—five miles away yet, not knowing the country, I reckon. So we could hear them and folks yelling now and then: "Whooey. Head him!"

We toted Henry into Mrs. Littlejohn's. She was in the hall; she hadn't put down the armful of clothes. She taken one look at us, and she laid down the busted scrubbing-board and taken up the lamp and opened a empty door. "Bring him in here," she says.

We toted him in and laid him on the bed. Mrs. Littlejohn set the lamp on the dresser, still carrying the clothes. "I'll declare, you men," she says. Our shadows was way up the wall, tiptoeing too; we could hear ourselves breath-

ing. "Better get his wife," Mrs. Littlejohn says. She went out, carrying the clothes.

"I reckon we had," Quick says. "Go get her, somebody."

"Whyn't you go?" Winterbottom says.

"Let Ernest git her," Durley says. "He lives neighbors with them."

Ernest went to fetch her. I be dog if Henry didn't look like he was dead. Mrs. Littlejohn come back, with a kettle and some towels. She went to work on Henry, and then Mrs. Armstid and Ernest come in. Mrs. Armstid come to the foot of the bed and stood there, with her hands rolled into her apron, watching what Mrs. Littlejohn was doing, I reckon.

"You men get outen the way," Mrs. Littlejohn says. "Git outside," she says. "See if you can't find something else to play with that will kill some more of you."

"Is he dead?" Winterbottom says.

"It ain't your fault if he ain't," Mrs. Littlejohn says. "Go tell Will Varner to come up here. I reckon a man ain't so different from a mule, come long come short. Except maybe a mule's got more sense."

We went to get Uncle Billy. It was a full moon. We could hear them, now and then, four miles away: "Whooey. Head him." The country was full of them, one on ever wooden bridge in the land, running across it like thunder: "Whooey. There he goes. Head him."

We hadn't got far before Henry begun to scream. I reckon Mrs. Littlejohn's water had brung him to; anyway, he wasn't dead. We went on to Uncle Billy's. The house was dark. We called to him, and after a while the window opened and Uncle Billy put his head out, peart as a peckerwood, listening. "Are they still trying to catch them durn rabbits?" he says.

He come down, with his britches on over his night-shirt and his suspenders dangling, carrying his horse-doctoring grip. "Yes, sir," he says, cocking his head like a woodpecker; "they're still a-trying."

We could hear Henry before we reached Mrs. Littlejohn's. He was going Ah-Ah-Ah. We stopped in the yard. Uncle Billy went on in. We could hear Henry. We stood in the yard, hearing them on the bridges, this-a-way and that: "Whooey. Whooey."

"Eck Snopes ought to caught hisn," Ernest says.

"Looks like he ought," Winterbottom said.

Henry was going Ah-Ah-Ah steady in the house; then he begun to scream. "Uncle Billy's started," Quick says. We looked into the hall. We could see the light where the door was. Then Mrs. Littlejohn come out.

"Will needs some help," she says. "You, Ernest. You'll do." Ernest went into the house.

"Hear them?" Quick said. "That one was on Four Mile bridge." We could hear them; it sounded like thunder a long way off; it didn't last long:

"Whooey."

We could hear Henry: "Ah-Ah-Ah-Ah-Ah."

"They are both started now," Winterbottom says. "Ernest too."

That was early in the night. Which was a good thing, because it taken a long night for folks to chase them things right and for Henry to lay there and holler, being as Uncle Billy never had none of this here chloryfoam to set Henry's leg with. So it was considerate in Flem to get them started early. And what do you reckon Flem's com-ment was?

That's right. Nothing. Because he wasn't there. Hadn't nobody see him since that Texas man left.

VI

That was Saturday night. I reckon Mrs. Armstid got home about daylight, to see about the chaps. I don't know where they thought her and Henry was. But lucky the oldest one was a gal, about twelve, big enough to take care of the little ones. Which she did for the next two days. Mrs. Armstid would nurse Henry all night and work in the kitchen for hern and Henry's keep, and in the afternoon she would drive home (it was about four miles) to see to the chaps. She would cook up a pot of victuals and leave it on the stove, and the gal would bar the house and keep the little ones quiet. I would hear Mrs. Littlejohn and Mrs. Armstid talking in the kitchen. "How are the chaps making out?" Mrs. Littlejohn says.

"All right," Mrs. Armstid says.

"Don't they git skeered at night?" Mrs. Littlejohn says.

"Ina May bars the door when I leave," Mrs. Armstid says. "She's got the axe in bed with her. I reckon she can make out."

I reckon they did. And I reckon Mrs. Armstid was waiting for Flem to come back to town; hadn't nobody seen him until this morning; to get her money the Texas man said Flem was keeping for her. Sho. I reckon she was.

Anyway, I heard Mrs. Armstid and Mrs. Littlejohn talking in the kitchen this morning while I was eating breakfast. Mrs. Littlejohn had just told Mrs. Armstid that Flem was in town. "You can ask him for that five dollars," Mrs. Littlejohn says.

"You reckon he'll give it to me?" Mrs. Armstid says.

Mrs. Littlejohn was washing dishes, washing them like a man, like they was made out of iron. "No," she says. "But asking him won't do no hurt. It might shame him. I don't reckon it will, but it might."

"If he wouldn't give it back, it ain't no use to ask," Mrs. Armstid says.

"Suit yourself," Mrs. Littlejohn says. "It's your money."

I could hear the dishes.

"Do you reckon he might give it back to me?" Mrs. Armstid says. "That Texas man said he would. He said I could get it from Mr. Snopes later."

"Then go and ask him for it," Mrs. Littlejohn says.

I could hear the dishes.

"He won't give it back to me," Mrs. Armstid says.

"All right," Mrs. Littlejohn says. "Don't ask him for it, then."

I could hear the dishes; Mrs. Armstid was helping. "You don't reckon he would, do you?" she says. Mrs. Littlejohn never said nothing. It sounded like she was throwing the dishes at one another. "Maybe I better go and talk to Henry about it," Mrs. Armstid says.

"I would," Mrs. Littlejohn says. I be dog if it didn't sound like she had two plates in her hands, beating them together. "Then Henry can buy another five-dollar horse with it. Maybe he'll buy one next time that will out and out kill him. If I thought that, I'd give you back the money, myself."

"I reckon I better talk to him first," Mrs. Armstid said. Then it sounded like Mrs. Littlejohn taken up all the dishes and throwed them at the cook-stove, and I come away.

That was this morning. I had been up to Bundren's and back, and I thought that things would have kind of settled down. So after breakfast, I went up to the store. And there was Flem, setting in the store chair and whittling, like he might not have ever moved since he come to clerk for Jody Varner. I. O. was leaning in the door, in his shirt sleeves and with his hair parted too, same as Flem was before he turned the clerking job over to I. O. It's a funny thing about them Snopes: they all looks alike, yet there ain't ere a two of them that claims brothers. They're always just cousins, like Flem and Eck and Flem and I. O. Eck was there too, squatting against the wall, him and that boy, eating cheese and crackers outen a sack; they told me that Eck hadn't been home a-tall. And that Lon Quick hadn't got back to town, even. He followed his horse clean down to Samson's Bridge, with a wagon and a camp outfit. Eck finally caught one of hisn. It run into a blind lane at Freeman's and Eck and the boy taken and tied their rope across the end of the lane, about three foot high. The horse come to the end of the lane and whirled and run back without ever stopping. Eck says it never seen the rope a-tall. He says it looked just like one of these here Christmas pinwheels. "Didn't it try to run again?" I says.

"No," Eck says, eating a bite of cheese offen his knife blade. "Just kicked some."

"Kicked some?" I says.

"It broke its neck," Eck says.

Well, they was squatting there, about six of them, talking, talking at Flem; never nobody knowed yet if Flem had ere a interest in them horses or not. So finally I come right out and asked him. "Flem's done skun all of us so much," I says, "that we're proud of him. Come on, Flem," I says, "how much did you and that Texas man make offen them horses? You can tell us. Ain't nobody here but Eck that bought one of them; the others ain't got back to town yet, and Eck's your own cousin; he'll be proud to hear, too. How much did you-all make?"

They was all whittling, not looking at Flem, making like they was studying. But you could a heard a pin drop. And I. O. He had been rubbing his back up and down on the door, but he stopped now, watching Flem like a pointing dog. Flem finished cutting the sliver offen his stick. He spit across the porch, into the road. "Twarn't none of my horses," he says.

I. O. cackled, like a hen, slapping his legs with both hands. "You boys might just as well quit trying to get ahead of Flem," he said.

Well, about that time I see Mrs. Armstid come outen Mrs. Littlejohn's gate, coming up the road. I never said nothing. I says, "Well, if a man can't take care of himself in a trade, he can't blame the man that trims him."

Flem never said nothing, trimming at the stick. He hadn't seen Mrs. Armstid. "Yes, sir," I says. "A fellow like Henry Armstid ain't got nobody but hisself to blame."

"Course he ain't," I. O. says. He ain't seen her, either. "Henry Armstid's a born fool. Always is been. If Flem hadn't a got his money, somebody else would."

We looked at Flem. He never moved. Mrs. Armstid come on up the road.

"That's right," I says. "But come to think of it, Henry never bought no horse." We looked at Flem; you could a heard a match drop. "That Texas man told her to get five dollars back from Flem next day. I reckon Flem's done already taken that money to Mrs. Littlejohn's and give it to Mrs. Armstid."

We watched Flem. I. O. quit rubbing his back against the door again. After a while Flem raised his head and spit across the porch, into the dust. I. O. cackled, just like a hen. "Ain't he a beating fellow, now?" I. O. says.

Mrs. Armstid was getting closer, so I kept on talking, watching to see if Flem would look up and see her. But he never looked up. I went on talking about Tull, about how he was going to sue Flem, and Flem setting there, whittling his stick, not saying nothing else after he said they wasn't none of his horses.

Then I. O. happened to look around. He seen Mrs. Armstid. "Pssssst!" he says. Flem looked up. "Here she comes!" I. O. says. "Go out the back. I'll tell her you done went in to town today."

But Flem never moved. He just set there,

whittling, and we watched Mrs. Armstid come up onto the porch, in that ere faded sunbonnet and wrapper and them tennis shoes that made a kind of hissing noise on the porch. She come onto the porch and stopped, her hands rolled into her dress in front, not looking at nothing.

"He said Saturday," she says, "that he wouldn't sell Henry no horse. He said I could get the money from you."

Flem looked up. The knife never stopped. It went on trimming off a sliver same as if he was watching it. "He taken that money off with him when he left," Flem says.

Mrs. Armstid never looked at nothing. We never looked at her, neither, except that boy of Eck's. He had a half-et cracker in his hand, watching her, chewing.

"He said Henry hadn't bought no horse," Mrs. Armstid says. "He said for me to get the money from you today."

"I reckon he forgot about it," Flem said. "He taken that money off with him Saturday." He whittled again. I. O. kept on rubbing his back, slow. He licked his lips. After a while the woman looked up the road, where it went on up the hill, toward the graveyard. She looked up that way for a while, with that boy of Eck's watching her and I. O. rubbing his back slow against the door. Then she turned back toward the steps.

"I reckon it's time to get dinner started," she says.

"How's Henry this morning, Mrs. Armstid?" Winterbottom says.

She looked at Winterbottom; she almost stopped. "He's resting, I thank you kindly," she says.

Flem got up, outen the chair, putting his knife away. He spit across the porch. "Wait a minute, Mrs. Armstid," he says. She stopped again. She didn't look at him. Flem went on into the store, with I. O. done quit rubbing his back now, with his head craned after Flem, and Mrs. Armstid standing there with her hands rolled into her dress, not looking at nothing. A wagon come up the road and passed; it was Freeman, on the way to town. Then Flem come out again, with I. O. still watching him. Flem had one of these little striped sacks of Jody Varner's candy; I bet he still owes Jody that

nickel, too. He put the sack into Mrs. Armstid's hand, like he would have put it into a hollow stump. He spit again across the porch. "A little sweetening for the chaps," he says.

"You're right kind," Mrs. Armstid says. She held the sack of candy in her hand, not looking at nothing. Eck's boy was watching the sack, the half-et cracker in his hand; he wasn't chewing now. He watched Mrs. Armstid roll the sack into her apron. "I reckon I better get on back and help with dinner," she says. She turned and went back across the porch. Flem set down in the chair again and opened his knife. He spit across the porch again, past Mrs. Armstid where she hadn't went down the steps yet. Then she went on, in that ere sunbonnet and wrapper all the same color, back down the road toward Mrs. Littlejohn's. You couldn't see her dress move, like a natural woman walking. She looked like a old snag still standing up and moving along on a high water. We watched her turn in at Mrs. Littlejohn's and go outen sight. Flem was whittling. I. O. begun to rub his back on the door. Then he begun to cackle, just like a durn hen.

"You boys might just as well quit trying," I. O. says. "You can't git ahead of Flem. You can't touch him. Ain't he a sight, now?"

I be dog if he ain't. If I had brung a herd of wild cattymounts into town and sold them to my neighbors and kinfolks, they would have lynched me. Yes, sir.

EXERCISE

1. Describe the character of Flem Snopes. Describe the other important persons in the story. Does this lead you to an idea of the basic conflict?

2. What is the attitude of the narrator toward Flem?

3. What is the quality of the humor? Is it subtle? Ironical? Extravagant? Satirical? Indulgent and sympathetic? Or what? How is the quality of the humor related to the society of the story? Contrast it with the humor in "Daddy Wolf."

4. Imagine this story given by the objective omniscient third-person narrator. What would be the difference in effect? How might this modify the humor? What is the narrator's evaluation of Flem? Does it differ from the evaluation any other characters have of Flem? Does it differ from your own evaluation of him?

5. Is the story merely a piece of humor—of rural high-jinks? If not, what else do we find in it, what other feelings and attitudes? Does the humor run

counter to such feelings and attitudes? If so, is this an ineptitude on the part of the author? Compare "Spotted Horses" with "Daddy Wolf" in this respect.

6. Mrs. Armstid is a pathetic figure. She has suffered real loss in the injury of her husband, and she is so poor that she cannot afford to lose the $5. Why has the author put her into the story and made her appearance the more emphatic by putting her

at the end of the story? What effect does it have upon the humor? What effect does it have upon the meaning of the story as a whole?

7. Can it be said that "Spotted Horses" might, as far as the general feel and the structure are concerned, be put in Group II? What points of similarity do you find with "The Three Strangers"?

SECTION IV

Plot: The Simple Turn

In the stories of this group there is a sudden turn of plot, a surprising reversal, which opens our eyes to a new meaning, and on which the effect of the story rests. We can see how different this emphasis on plot is from the handling of event in a story like "Clay" or "Flight" or "The Three Strangers." In those stories there may be elements of suspense, even of surprise (as in the discovery that the jolly stranger in the last story is the executioner), but the effect is primarily achieved by the gradual accumulation of detail, the delineation of a personality, the creation of a certain feeling and atmosphere. In the tale, we may say, the sequence of event is its own excuse for being—the "teller" presumably is telling what happens; he washes his hands, as it were, of the responsibility for what

happens. In fact, there is the implied defense: "It happened this way, I'm just telling it." In the more highly organized short story, the mere sequence of events does not justify the story; there is a more obvious concern with the cause-and-effect organization of events—that is, with plot: *with action as theme.*

But we must remember, of course, that the events recounted in a tale may be no more firmly grounded in fact than those in a formal short story. Both are "fictional." The air of casually telling a tale is a convention (see Glossary)—one of the many technical devices of fiction.

We must remember, too, that both the tale and the formal short story, though they differ in organization, aim at the same kind of significance.

Wet Saturday

JOHN COLLIER (1901-   )

IT WAS July. In the large, dull house they were imprisoned by the swish and the gurgle and all the hundred sounds of rain. They were in the drawing-room, behind four tall and weeping windows, in a lake of damp and faded chintz.

This house, ill-kept and unprepossessing,

was necessary to Mr. Princey, who detested his wife, his daughter, and his hulking son. His life was to walk through the village, touching his hat, not smiling. His cold pleasure was to recapture snapshot memories of the infinitely remote summers of his childhood—coming into the orangery and finding his lost wooden horse, the tunnel in the box hedge, and the little square of light at the end of it. But now all this was threatened—his austere pride of position in the village, his passionate attachment to the house—and all because Millicent, his cloddish daughter Millicent, had done this shocking and incredibly stupid thing. Mr. Princey turned from her in revulsion and spoke to his wife.

"They'd send her to a lunatic asylum," he said. "A criminal-lunatic asylum. We should have to move away. It would be impossible."

His daughter began to shake again. "I'll kill myself," she said.

"Be quiet," said Mr. Princey. "We have very little time. No time for nonsense. I intend to deal with this." He called to his son, who stood looking out of the window. "George, come here. Listen. How far did you get with your medicine before they threw you out as hopeless?"

"You know as well as I do," said George.

"Do you know enough—did they drive enough into your head for you to be able to guess what a competent doctor could tell about such a wound?"

"Well, it's a—it's a knock or blow."

"If a tile fell from the roof? Or a piece of the coping?"

"Well, guv'nor, you see, it's like this——"

"Is it possible?"

"No."

"Why not?"

"Oh, because she hit him several times."

"I can't stand it," said Mrs. Princey.

"You have got to stand it, my dear," said her husband. "And keep that hysterical note out of your voice. It might be overheard. We are talking about the weather. If he fell down the well, George, striking his head several times?"

"I really don't know, guv'nor."

"He'd have had to hit the sides several times in thirty or forty feet, and at the correct angles. No, I'm afraid not. We must go over it all again. Millicent."

"No! No!"

"Millicent, we must go over it all again. Perhaps you have forgotten something. One tiny irrelevant detail may save or ruin us. Particularly you, Millicent. You don't *want* to be put in an asylum, do you? Or be hanged? They might hang you, Millicent. You must stop that shaking. You must keep your voice quiet. We are talking of the weather. Now."

"I can't. I . . . I . . ."

"Be quiet, child. Be quiet." He put his long, cold face very near to his daughter's. He found himself horribly revolted by her. Her features were thick, her jaw heavy, her whole figure repellently powerful. "Answer me," he said. "You were in the stable?"

"Yes."

"One moment, though. Who knew you were in love with this wretched curate?"

"No one. I've never said a——"

"Don't worry," said George. "The whole god-damned village knows. They've been sniggering about it in the Plough for three years past."

"Likely enough," said Mr. Princey. "Likely enough. What filth!" He made as if to wipe something off the backs of his hands. "Well, now, we continue. You were in the stable?"

"Yes."

"You were putting the croquet set into its box?"

"Yes."

"You heard someone crossing the yard?"

"Yes."

"It was Withers?"

"Yes."

"So you called him?"

"Yes."

"Loudly? Did you call him loudly? Could anyone have heard?"

"No, Father. I'm sure not. I didn't call him. He saw me as I went to the door. He just waved his hand and came over."

"How *can* I find out from you whether there was anyone about? Whether he *could* have been seen?"

"I'm sure not, Father. I'm quite sure."

"So you both went into the stable?"

"Yes. It was raining hard."

"What did he say?"

"He said 'Hullo, Milly.' And to excuse him coming in the back way, but he'd set out to walk over to Bass Hill."

"Yes."

"And he said, passing the park, he'd seen the house and suddenly thought of me, and he thought he'd just look in for a minute, just to tell me something. He said he was so happy, he wanted me to share it. He'd heard from the Bishop he was to have the vicarage. And it wasn't only that. It meant he could marry. And he began to stutter. And I thought he meant me."

"Don't tell me what you thought. Exactly what he said. Nothing else."

"Well . . . Oh dear!"

"Don't cry. It is a luxury you cannot afford. Tell me."

"He said no. He said it wasn't me. It's Ella Brangwyn-Davies. And he was sorry. And all that. Then he went to go."

"And then?"

"I went mad. He turned his back. I had the winning post of the croquet set in my hand——"

"Did you shout or scream? I mean, as you hit him?"

"No. I'm sure I didn't."

"Did he? Come on. Tell me."

"No, Father."

"And then?"

"I threw it down. I came straight into the house. That's all. I wish I were dead!"

"And you met none of the servants. No one will go into the stable. You see, George, he probably told people he was going to Bass Hill. Certainly no one knows he came here. He might have been attacked in the woods. We must consider every detail . . . A curate, with his head battered in——"

"Don't, Father!" cried Millicent.

"Do you want to be hanged? A curate, with his head battered in, found in the woods. Who'd want to kill Withers?"

There was a tap on the door, which opened immediately. It was little Captain Smollett, who never stood on ceremony. "Who'd kill Withers?" he said. "I would, with pleasure. How d'you do, Mrs. Princey. I walked right in."

"He heard you, Father," moaned Millicent.

"My dear, we can all have our little joke," said her father. "Don't pretend to be shocked. A little theoretical curate-killing, Smollett. In these days we talk nothing but thrillers."

"Parsonicide," said Captain Smollett. "Justifiable parsonicide. Have you heard about Ella Brangwyn-Davies? I shall be laughed at."

"Why?" said Mr. Princey. "Why should you be laughed at?"

"Had a shot in that direction myself," said Smollett, with careful sang-froid. "She half said yes, too. Hadn't you heard? She told most people. Now it'll look as if I got turned down for a white rat in a dog collar."

"Too bad!" said Mr. Princey.

"Fortune of war," said the little captain.

"Sit down," said Mr. Princey. "Mother, Millicent, console Captain Smollett with your best light conversation. George and I have something to look to. We shall be back in a minute or two, Smollett. Come, George."

It was actually five minutes before Mr. Princey and his son returned.

"Excuse me, my dear," said Mr. Princey to his wife. "Smollett, would you care to see something rather interesting? Come out to the stables for a moment."

They went into the stable yard. The buildings were now unused except as odd sheds. No one ever went there. Captain Smollett entered, George followed him, Mr. Princey came last. As he closed the door he took up a gun which stood behind it. "Smollett," said he, "we have come out to shoot a rat which George heard squeaking under that tub. Now, you must listen to me very carefully or you will be shot by accident. I mean that."

Smollett looked at him. "Very well," said he. "Go on."

"A very tragic happening has taken place this afternoon," said Mr. Princey. "It will be even more tragic unless it is smoothed over."

"Oh?" said Smollett.

"You heard me ask," said Mr. Princey, "who would kill Withers. You heard Millicent make a comment, an unguarded comment."

"Well?" said Smollett. "What of it?"

"Very little," said Mr. Princey. "Unless you heard that Withers had met a violent end this very afternoon. And that, my dear Smollett, is what you are going to hear."

"Have you killed him?" cried Smollett.

"Millicent has," said Mr. Princey.

"Hell!" said Smollett.

"It *is* hell," said Mr. Princey. "You would have remembered—and guessed."

"Maybe," said Smollett. "Yes. I suppose I should."

"Therefore," said Mr. Princey, "you constitute a problem."

"Why did she kill him?" said Smollett.

"It is one of these disgusting things," said Mr. Princey. "Pitiable, too. She deluded herself that he was in love with her."

"Oh, of course," said Smollett.

"And he told her about the Brangwyn-Davies girl."

"I see," said Smollett.

"I have no wish," said Mr. Princey, "that she should be proved either a lunatic or a murderess. I could hardly live here after that."

"I suppose not," said Smollett.

"On the other hand," said Mr. Princey, *you* know about it."

"Yes," said Smollett. "I am wondering if I could keep my mouth shut. If I promised you——"

"I am wondering if I could believe you," said Mr. Princey.

"If I promised," said Smollett.

"If things went smoothly," said Mr. Princey. "But not if there was any sort of suspicion, any questioning. You would be afraid of being an accessory."

"I don't know," said Smollett.

"I do," said Mr. Princey. "What are we going to do?"

"I can't see anything else," said Smollett. "You'd never be fool enough to do me in. You can't get rid of two corpses."

"I regard it," said Mr. Princey, "as a better risk than the other. It could be an accident. Or you and Withers could both disappear. There are possibilities in that."

"Listen," said Smollett. "You can't——"

"Listen," said Mr. Princey. "There may be a way out. There *is* a way out, Smollett. You gave me the idea yourself."

"Did I?" said Smollett. "What?"

"You said you would kill Withers," said Mr. Princey. "You have a motive."

"I was joking," said Smollett.

"You are always joking," said Mr. Princey. "People think there must be something behind it. Listen, Smollett, I can't trust you, therefore you must trust me. Or I will kill you now, in the

next minute. I mean that. You can choose between dying and living."

"Go on," said Smollett.

"There is a sewer here," said Mr. Princey, speaking fast and forcefully. "That is where I am going to put Withers. No outsider knows he has come up here this afternoon. No one will ever look there for him unless you tell them. You must give me evidence that you have murdered Withers."

"Why?" said Smollett.

"So that I shall be dead sure that you will never open your lips on the matter," said Mr. Princey.

"What evidence?" said Smollett.

"George," said Mr. Princey, "hit him in the face, hard."

"Good God!" said Smollett.

"Again," said Mr. Princey. "Don't bruise your knuckles."

"Oh!" said Smollett.

"I'm sorry," said Mr. Princey. "There must be traces of a struggle between you and Withers. Then it will not be altogether safe for you to go to the police."

"Why won't you take my word?" said Smollett.

"I will when we've finished," said Mr. Princey. "George, get that croquet post. Take your handkerchief to it. As I told you. Smollett, you'll just grasp the end of this croquet post. I shall shoot you if you don't."

"Oh, hell," said Smollett. "All right."

"Pull two hairs out of his head, George," said Mr. Princey, "and remember what I told you to do with them. Now, Smollett, you take that bar and raise the big flagstone with the ring in it. Withers is in the next stall. You've got to drag him through and dump him in."

"I won't touch him," said Smollett.

"Stand back, George," said Mr. Princey, raising his gun.

"Wait a minute," cried Smollett. "Wait a minute." He did as he was told.

Mr. Princey wiped his brow. "Look here," said he. "Everything is perfectly safe. Remember, no one knows that Withers came here. Everyone thinks he walked over to Bass Hill. That's five miles of country to search. They'll never look in our sewer. Do you see how safe it is?"

"I suppose it is," said Smollett.

"Now come into the house," said Mr. Princey. "We shall never get that rat."

They went into the house. The maid was bringing tea into the drawing-room. "See, my dear," said Mr. Princey to his wife, "we went to the stable to shoot a rat and we found Captain Smollett. Don't be offended, my dear fellow."

"You must have walked up the back drive," said Mrs. Princey.

"Yes. Yes. That was it," said Smollett in some confusion.

"You've cut your lip," said George, handing him a cup of tea.

"I . . . I just knocked it."

"Shall I tell Bridget to bring some iodine?" said Mrs. Princey. The maid looked up, waiting.

"Don't trouble, please," said Smollett. "It's nothing."

"Very well, Bridget," said Mrs. Princey. "That's all."

"Smollett is very kind," said Mr. Princey. "He knows all our trouble. We can rely on him. We have his word."

"Oh, have we, Captain Smollett?" cried Mrs. Princey. "You *are* good."

"Don't worry, old fellow," Mr. Princey said. "They'll never find anything."

Pretty soon Smollett took his leave. Mrs. Princey pressed his hand very hard. Tears came into her eyes. All three of them watched him go down the drive. Then Mr. Princey spoke very earnestly to his wife for a few minutes and the two of them went upstairs and spoke still more earnestly to Millicent. Soon after, the rain having ceased, Mr. Princey took a stroll round the stable yard.

He came back and went to the telephone. "Put me through to Bass Hill police station," said he. "Quickly . . . Hullo, is that the police station? This is Mr. Princey, of Abbott's Laxton. I'm afraid something rather terrible has happened up here. Can you send someone at once?"

DISCUSSION

The structure of this little story is very simple. The exposition (see Glossary), consists in the revelation that Mr. Princey likes his house and position in the village but detests his family, that his daughter Millicent has committed a murder, and that he must save her, not because he likes her, but because he can't continue to live here if there is a scandal. The complication (see Glossary) discloses that Captain Smollett had a grudge against the curate whom Millicent had murdered, and presents the gradual involvement of Smollett to the point where he has been forced to incriminate himself as a safeguard against betraying the Princey family. With the denouement (see Glossary), Mr. Princey has succeeded in making all safe for himself. Smollett, at gun point to be sure, is now necessarily committed to the Princeys' side. A solution has been reached for the original problem—the original conflict—from which the story arises: the struggle of Mr. Princey to escape the consequences of Millicent's act. This could be the end of the story, even if a rather tame and falling-away end.

But it is not the end. We have the sharp turn in the last paragraph, when Mr. Princey calls the police. Mr. Smollett is not merely going to keep quiet about the murder: he is going to hang for it! There is, in this turn, a shock—the revelation of the completeness of Mr. Princey's cold-blooded isolation from life.

How do we react to the story? What sort of sympathies do we have or what identifications do we make? We start out committed—dramatically, at least—to the solution of Mr. Princey's problem. The reservation implied by the word "dramatically" is important. That is, this is not simply a moral question—a question of who is right and who is wrong. For instance, in Shakespeare's play *Macbeth* we have some commitment with Macbeth in his ambition that leads him to the murder of Duncan, and some commitment with him in his struggle to avoid the consequences. In "Wet Saturday," in a much more modest way, our sympathies are involved with Mr. Princey in his effort to solve his problem.

But we can go a little further. Millicent is made pathetic, perhaps in some deep, long-range way, the victim of her father's cold egotism. The curate whom she murders is made heartless and unattractive; in a way, he "deserves" his fate. As for the second victim, Captain Smollett, we are given no hint of any human qualities to make us feel for him. In fact, he walks into it, the stupe. Against him, we tend to identify ourselves with the cold ruthless cunning of Mr. Princey—for that represents one of our own potentialities, too.

The reader's general identification with Mr. Princey carries along with it a general attitude toward the events of the story. What is this attitude? What is the tone of this story? To understand "tone" in this sense, it may be useful to reflect on how the tone of one's voice may modify the meaning of what is being said—how, for instance, the word *yes* changes its meaning in a kind of spectrum from enthusiastic agreement through acceptance, warm or cool, on to a sarcastic utterance of the word which means exactly the opposite of the literal meaning of the word, the "oh yeah" of denial. Tone, then, implies the attitude of the speaker or writer toward what is said and, we may add, toward the audience.

In this connection it is significant that Collier gives a detached factual narrative. He does not aim for—in fact, he tries to suppress—emotional effects. He is treating the plot like a mechanism, with the human values kept in the background.

By implication he is saying that if you look at life with a certain cool detachment, things feel somewhat different. Think how different we should feel if the anguish of Millicent were developed. Or if, for example, Mr. Princey did have a profound feeling for his daughter and at the same time a deep moral sense. Or if he should discover in this moment a tragic revelation about himself. But no, Collier gives us the coldly mechanical working out of Mr. Princey's plan. It is a splendid plan, beautifully conceived, accurately worked out. Bravo!

The story is a very good illustration of what the French philosopher Bergson takes to be the basis of comedy—the contrast between the mechanical and the vital—Mr. Princey's plan set over against all the human issues. Comedy does not, to be sure, deny human issues; it merely gives a perspective on them, in this story a coldly ironical one. Comedy, even in this cold irony, is another way for us to learn something about ourselves.

EXERCISE

Read "Tomorrow and Tomorrow and So Forth," by John Updike (page 211). What elements do you find there that might be regarded as comic?

The Lottery Ticket

ANTON CHEKHOV (1860-1904)

IVAN DMITRITCH, a middle-class man who lived with his family on an income of twelve hundred a year and was very well satisfied with his lot, sat down on the sofa after supper and began reading the newspaper.

"I forgot to look at the newspaper today," his wife said to him as she cleared the table. "Look and see whether the list of drawings is there."

"Yes, it is," said Ivan Dmitritch; "but hasn't your ticket lapsed?"

"No; I took the interest on Tuesday."

"What is the number?"

"Series 9,499, number 26."

"All right . . . we will look . . . 9,499 and 26."

Ivan Dmitritch had no faith in lottery luck, and would not, as a rule, have consented to look at the lists of winning numbers, but now, as he had nothing else to do and as the newspaper was before his eyes, he passed his finger downwards along the column of numbers. And immediately, as though in mockery of his scepticism, no further than the second line from the top, his eye was caught by the figure 9,499! Unable to believe his eyes, he hurriedly dropped the paper on his knees without looking to see the number of the ticket, and, just as though some one had given him a douche of cold water, he felt an agreeable chill in the pit of the stomach; tingling and terrible and sweet!

"Masha, 9,499 is there!" he said in a hollow voice.

His wife looked at his astonished and panic-stricken face, and realized that he was not joking.

"9,499?" she asked, turning pale and dropping the folded tablecloth on the table.

"Yes, yes . . . it really is there!"

"And the number of the ticket?"

"Oh, yes! There's the number of the ticket too. But stay . . . wait! No, I say! Anyway, the number of our series is there! Anyway, you understand. . . ."

Looking at his wife, Ivan Dmitritch gave a broad, senseless smile, like a baby when a bright object is shown it. His wife smiled too; it was as pleasant to her as to him that he only mentioned the series, and did not try to find out the number of the winning ticket. To torment and tantalize oneself with hopes of possible fortune is so sweet, so thrilling!

"It is our series," said Ivan Dmitritch, after a long silence. "So there is a probability that we have won. It's only a probability, but there it is!"

"Well, now look!"

"Wait a little. We have plenty of time to be disappointed. It's on the second line from the top, so the prize is seventy-five thousand. That's not money, but power, capital! And in a minute I shall look at the list, and there—26! Eh? I say, what if we really have won?"

The husband and wife began laughing and staring at one another in silence. The possibility of winning bewildered them; they could not have said, could not have dreamed, what they both needed that seventy-five thousand for, what they would buy, where they would go. They thought only of the figures 9,499 and 75,000 and pictured them in their imagination, while somehow they could not think of the happiness itself which was so possible.

Ivan Dmitritch, holding the paper in his hand, walked several times from corner to corner, and only when he had recovered from the first impression began dreaming a little.

"And if we have won," he said—"why, it will be a new life, it will be a transformation! The ticket is yours, but if it were mine I should, first of all, of course, spend twenty-five thousand on real property in the shape of an estate; ten thousand on immediate expenses, new furnishing . . . travelling . . . paying debts, and so on. . . . The other forty thousand I would put in the bank and get interest on it."

"Yes, an estate, that would be nice," said his wife, sitting down and dropping her hands in her lap.

"Somewhere in the Tula or Oryol provinces. . . . In the first place we shouldn't need a summer villa, and besides, it would always bring in an income."

And pictures came crowding on his imagination, each more gracious and poetical than the last. And in all these pictures he saw himself well-fed, serene, healthy, felt warm, even hot! Here, after eating a summer soup, cold as ice, he lay on his back on the burning sand close to a stream or in the garden under a lime-tree. . . . It is hot. . . . His little boy and girl are crawling about near him, digging in the sand or catching ladybirds in the grass. He dozes sweetly, thinking of nothing, and feeling all over that he need not go to the office today, tomorrow, or the day after. Or, tired of lying still, he goes to the hayfield, or to the forest for mushrooms, or watches the peasants catching fish with a net. When the sun sets he takes a towel and soap and saunters to the bathing-shed, where he undresses at his leisure, slowly rubs his bare chest with his hands, and goes into the water. And in the water, near the opaque soapy circles, little fish flit to and fro and green water-weeds nod their heads. After bathing there is tea with cream and milk rolls. . . . In the evening a walk or *vint* with the neighbors.

"Yes, it would be nice to buy an estate," said his wife, also dreaming, and from her face it was evident that she was enchanted by her thoughts.

Ivan Dmitritch pictured to himself autumn with its rains, its cold evenings, and its St. Martin's summer. At that season he would have to take longer walks about the garden and beside the river, so as to get thoroughly chilled, and then drink a big glass of vodka and eat a salted mushroom or a soused cucumber, and then—drink another. . . . The children would come running from the kitchen-garden, bringing a carrot and a radish smelling of fresh earth. . . . And then, he would lie stretched full length on the sofa, and in leisurely fashion turn over the pages of some illustrated magazine, or, covering his face with it and unbuttoning his waistcoat, give himself up to slumber.

The St. Martin's summer is followed by cloudy, gloomy weather. It rains day and night, the bare trees weep, the wind is damp and cold. The dogs, the horss, the fowls—all are wet, depressed, downcast. There is nowhere to walk; one can't go out for days together; one has to pace up and down the room, looking despondently at the grey window. It is dreary!

Ivan Dmitritch stopped and looked at his wife.

"I should go abroad, you know, Masha," he said.

And he began thinking how nice it would be in late autumn to go abroad somewhere to the South of France . . . to Italy . . . to India!

"I should certainly go abroad too," his wife said. "But look at the number of the ticket!"

"Wait, wait! . . ."

He walked about the room and went on thinking. It occurred to him: what if his wife really did go abroad? It is pleasant to travel alone, or in the society of light, careless women who live in the present, and not such as think and talk all the journey about nothing but their children, sigh, and tremble with dismay over every farthing. Ivan Dmitritch imagined his wife in the train with a multitude of parcels, baskets, and bags; she would be sighing over something, complaining that the train made her head ache, that she had spent so much money. . . . At the stations he would continually be having to run for boiling water, bread and butter. . . . She wouldn't have dinner because of its being too dear. . . .

"She would begrudge me every farthing," he thought, with a glance at his wife. "The lottery ticket is hers, not mine! Besides, what is the use of her going abroad? What does she want there? She would shut herself up in the hotel, and not let me out of her sight . . . I know!"

And for the first time in his life his mind dwelt on the fact that his wife had grown elderly and plain, and that she was saturated through and through with the smell of cooking, while he was still young, fresh, and healthy, and might well have got married again.

"Of course, all that is silly nonsense," he thought; "but . . . why should she go abroad? What would she make of it? And yet she would go, of course. . . . I can fancy. . . . In reality it is all one to her, whether it is Naples or Klin. She would only be in my way. I should be dependent upon her. I can fancy how, like a regular woman, she will lock the money up as soon as she gets it. . . . She will look after her relations and grudge me every farthing."

Ivan Dmitritch thought of her relations. All those wretched brothers and sisters and aunts and uncles would come crawling about as soon as they heard of the winning ticket, would begin whining like beggars, and fawning upon them with oily, hypocritical smiles. Wretched, detestable people! If they were given anything, they would ask for more; while if they were refused, they would swear at them, slander them, and wish them every kind of misfortune.

Ivan Dmitritch remembered his own relations, and their faces, at which he had looked impartially in the past, struck him now as repulsive and hateful.

"They are such reptiles!" he thought.

And his wife's face, too, struck him as repulsive and hateful. Anger surged up in his heart against her, and he thought malignantly:

"She knows nothing about money, and so she is stingy. If she won it she would give me a hundred roubles, and put the rest away under lock and key."

And he looked at his wife, not with a smile now, but with hatred. She glanced at him too, and also with hatred and anger. She had her own daydreams, her own plans, her own reflections; she understood perfectly well what her husband's dreams were. She knew who would be the first to try to grab her winnings.

"It's very nice making daydreams at other people's expense!" is what her eyes expressed. "No, don't you dare!"

Her husband understood her look; hatred began stirring again in his breast, and in order to annoy his wife he glanced quickly, to spite her at the fourth page on the newspaper and read out triumphantly:

"Series 9,499, number 46! Not 26!"

Hatred and hope both disappeared at once, and it began immediately to seem to Ivan Dmitritch and his wife that their rooms were dark and small and low-pitched, that the supper they had been eating was not doing them good, but lying heavy on their stomachs, that the evenings were long and wearisome. . . .

"What the devil's the meaning of it?" said Ivan Dmitritch, beginning to be ill-humored. "Wherever one steps there are bits of paper under one's feet, crumbs, husks. The rooms are never swept! One is simply forced to go out. Damnation take my soul entirely! I shall go and hang myself on the first aspen-tree!"

EXERCISE

1. Locate the exposition, the complication, and the denouement of this story. Compare its structure with that of "Wet Saturday."

2. What is the question, problem, or conflict on which this story is based? Or can we say that it begins with one question, a fairly objective superficial one, and ends with a deep subjective one? Working from this matter of the conflict, state the theme (see Glossary) of the story.

3. In working on Exercise 2 you may find it desirable to consider the following questions: Have new facts of the past life of the husband and wife been revealed? Or has, merely, their idea of the facts been changed? Have they previously deceived themselves about their relationship, or can we say that, under the earlier circumstances, they had been sincere in their humdrum affection and mutual acceptance? Is it logical and credible that out of the dream of winning the lottery should come the change of attitude? Are we to suppose that later on, long after the events recounted in the story, the husband and wife may again find their old comfortable relationship? Do we find in the story any indication of an answer to this question? Or is the question itself relevant to the effectiveness or even to the meaning of the story?

4. This story, like "The Three Strangers," may be said to be based on a very extraordinary coincidence, an accident. Does this invalidate the story? If not, why not?

Legal Aid

FRANK O'CONNOR (1903-   )

DELIA CARTY came of a very respectable family. It was going as maid to the O'Gradys of Pouladuff that ruined her. That whole family was slightly touched. The old man, a national teacher, was hardly ever at home, and the daughters weren't much better. When they weren't away visiting, they had people visiting them, and it was nothing to Delia to come in late at night and find one of them plastered round some young fellow on the sofa.

That sort of thing isn't good for any young girl. Like mistress like maid; inside six months she was smoking, and within a year she was carrying on with one Tom Flynn, a farmer's son. Her father, a respectable, hard-working man, knew nothing about it, for he would have realized that she was no match for one of the Flynns, and even if Tom's father, Ned, had known, he would never have thought it possible that any labourer's daughter could imagine herself a match for Tom.

Not, God knows, that Tom was any great catch. He was a big uncouth galoot who was certain that lovemaking, like drink, was one of the simple pleasures his father tried to deprive him of, out of spite. He used to call at the house while the O'Gradys were away, and there would be Delia in one of Eileen O'Grady's frocks and with Eileen O'Grady's lipstick and powder on, doing the lady over the tea things in the parlour. Throwing a glance over his shoulder in case anyone might spot him, Tom would heave himself onto the sofa with his boots over the end.

"Begod, I love sofas," he would say with simple pleasure.

"Put a cushion behind you," Delia would say.

"Oh, begod," Tom would say, making himself comfortable, "if ever I have a house of my own 'tis unknown what sofas and cushions I'll have. Them teachers must get great money. What the hell do they go away at all for?"

Delia loved making the tea and handing it out like a real lady, but you couldn't catch Tom out like that.

"Ah, what do I want tay for?" he would say with a doubtful glance at the cup. "Haven't you any whisky? Ould O'Grady must have gallons of it. . . . Leave it there on the table. Why the hell don't they have proper mugs with handles a man could get a grip on? Is that taypot silver? Pity I'm not a teacher!"

It was only natural for Delia to show him the bedrooms and the dressing-tables with the three mirrors, the way you could see yourself from all sides, but Tom, his hands under his head, threw himself with incredulous delight on the low double bed and cried: "Springs! Begod, 'tis like a car!"

What the springs gave rise to was entirely the O'Gradys' fault since no one but themselves would have left a house in a lonesome part to a girl of nineteen to mind. The only surprising thing was that it lasted two years without Delia showing any signs of it. It probably took Tom that time to find the right way.

But when he did he got into a terrible state. It was hardly in him to believe that a harmless poor devil like himself whom no one ever bothered his head about could achieve such unprecedented results on one girl, but when he understood it he knew only too well what the result of it would be. His father would first beat hell out of him and then throw him out and leave the farm to his nephews. There being no hope of conciliating his father, Tom turned his attention to God, who, though supposed to share Ned Flynn's views about fellows and girls, had some nature in Him. Tom stopped seeing Delia, to persuade God that he was reforming and to show that anyway it wasn't his fault. Left alone he could be a decent, good-living young fellow, but the Carty girl was a forward, deceitful hussy who had led him on instead of putting him off the way any well-bred girl

would do. Between lipsticks, sofas, and tay in the parlour, Tom put it up to God that it was a great wonder she hadn't got him into worse trouble.

Delia had to tell her mother, and Mrs. Carty went to Father Corcoran to see could he induce Tom to marry her. Father Corcoran was a tall, testy old man who, even at the age of sixty-five, couldn't make out for the life of him what young fellows saw in girls, but if he didn't know much about lovers he knew a lot about farmers.

"Wisha, Mrs. Carty," he said crankily, "how could I get him to marry her? Wouldn't you have a bit of sense? Some little financial arrangement, maybe, so that she could leave the parish and not be a cause of scandal—I might be able to do that."

He interviewed Ned Flynn, who by this time had got Tom's version of the story and knew financial arrangements were going to be the order of the day unless he could put a stop to them. Ned was a man of over six foot with a bald brow and a smooth unlined face as though he never had a care except his general concern for the welfare of humanity which made him look so abnormally thoughtful. Even Tom's conduct hadn't brought a wrinkle to his brow.

"I don't know, father," he said, stroking his bald brow with a dieaway air, "I don't know what you could do at all."

"Wisha, Mr. Flynn," said the priest who, when it came to the pinch, had more nature than twenty Flynns, "wouldn't you do the handsome thing and let him marry her before it goes any farther?"

"I don't see how much farther it could go, father," said Ned.

"It could become a scandal."

"I'm afraid 'tis that already, father."

"And after all," said Father Corcoran, forcing himself to put in a good word for one of the unfortunate sex whose very existence was a mystery to him, "is she any worse than the rest of the girls that are going? Bad is the best of them, from what I see, and Delia is a great deal better than most."

"That's not my information at all, father," said Ned, looking like "The Heart Bowed Down."

"That's a very serious statement, Mr. Flynn," said Father Corcoran, giving him a challenging look.

"It can be proved, father," said Ned gloomily. "Of course I'm not denying the boy was foolish, but the cleverest can be caught."

"You astonish me, Mr. Flynn," said Father Corcoran who was beginning to realize that he wasn't even going to get a subscription. "Of course I can't contradict you, but 'twill cause a terrible scandal."

"I'm as sorry for that as you are, father," said Ned, "but I have my son's future to think of."

Then, of course, the fun began. Foolish to the last, the O'Gradys wanted to keep Delia on till it was pointed out to them that Mr. O'Grady would be bound to get the blame. After this, her father had to be told. Dick Carty knew exactly what became a devoted father, and he beat Delia till he had to be hauled off her by the neighbours. He was a man who loved to sit in his garden reading his paper; now he felt he owed it to himself not to be seen enjoying himself, so instead he sat over the fire and brooded. The more he brooded the angrier he became. But seeing that, with the best will in the world, he could not beat Delia every time he got angry, he turned his attention to the Flynns. Ned Flynn, that contemptible bosthoon, had slighted one of the Cartys in a parish where they had lived for hundreds of years with unblemished reputations; the Flynns, as everyone knew, being mere upstarts and outsiders without a date on their gravestones before 1850—nobodies!

He brought Delia to see Jackie Canty, the solicitor in town. Jackie was a little jenny-ass of a man with thin lips, a pointed nose, and a pince-nez that wouldn't stop in place, and he listened with grave enjoyment to the story of Delia's misconduct. "And what happened then, please?" he asked in his shrill singsong, looking at the floor and trying hard not to burst out into a giggle of delight. "The devils!" he thought. "The devils!" It was as close as Jackie was ever likely to get to the facts of life, an opportunity not to be missed.

"Anything in writing?" he sang, looking at her over the pince-nez. "Any letters? Any documents?"

"Only a couple of notes I burned," said Delia, who thought him a very queer man, and no wonder.

"Pity!" Jackie said with an admiring smile. "A smart man! Oh, a very smart man!"

"Ah, 'tisn't that at all," said Delia uncomfortably, "only he had no occasion for writing."

"Ah, Miss Carty," cried Jackie in great indignation, looking at her challengingly through the specs while his voice took on a steely ring, "a gentleman in love always finds plenty of occasion for writing. He's a smart man; your father might succeed in an action for seduction, but if 'tis defended 'twill be a dirty case."

"Mr. Canty," said her father solemnly, "I don't mind how dirty it is so long as I get justice." He stood up, a powerful man of six feet, and held up his clenched fist. "Justice is what I want," he said dramatically. "That's the sort I am. I keep myself to myself and mind my own business, but give me a cut, and I'll fight in a bag, tied up."

"Don't forget that Ned Flynn has the money, Dick," wailed Jackie.

"Mr. Canty," said Dick with a dignity verging on pathos, "you know me?"

"I do, Dick, I do."

"I'm living in this neighbourhood, man and boy, fifty years, and I owe nobody a ha-penny. If it took me ten years, breaking stones by the road, I'd pay it back, every penny."

"I know, Dick, I know," moaned Jackie. "But there's other things as well. There's your daughter's reputation. Do you know what they'll do? They'll go into court and swear someone else was the father."

"Tom could never say that," Delia cried despairingly. "The tongue would rot in his mouth."

Jackie had no patience at all with this chit of a girl, telling him his business. He sat back with a weary air, his arm over the back of his chair.

"That statement has no foundation," he said icily. "There is no record of any such thing happening a witness. If there was, the inhabitants of Ireland would have considerably less to say for themselves. You would be surprised the things respectable people will say in the witness box. Rot in their mouths indeed! Ah, dear me, no. With documents, of course, it would be different, but it is only our word against theirs. Can it be proved that you weren't knocking round with any other man at this time, Miss Carty?"

"Indeed, I was doing nothing of the sort," Delia said indignantly. "I swear to God I wasn't, Mr. Canty. I hardly spoke to a fellow the whole time, only when Tom and myself might have a row and I'd go out with Timmy Martin."

"Timmy Martin!" Canty cried dramatically pointing an accusing finger at her. "There is their man!"

"But Tom did the same with Betty Daly," cried Delia on the point of tears, "and he only did it to spite me. I swear there was nothing else in it, Mr. Canty, nor he never accused me of it."

"Mark my words," chanted Jackie with a mournful smile, "he'll make up for lost time now."

In this he showed considerably more foresight than Delia gave him credit for. After the baby was born and the action begun, Tom and his father went to town to see their solicitor, Peter Humphreys. Peter, who knew all he wanted to know about the facts of life, liked the case much less than Jackie. A crosseyed, full-blooded man who had made his money when law was about land, not love, he thought it a terrible comedown. Besides, he didn't think it nice to be listening to such things.

"And so, according to you, Timmy Martin is the father?" he asked Tom.

"Oh, I'm not swearing he is," said Tom earnestly, giving himself a heave in his chair and crossing his legs. "How the hell could I? All I am saying is that I wasn't the only one, and what's more she boasted about it. Boasted about it, begod!" he added with a look of astonishment at such female depravity.

"Before witnesses?" asked Peter, his eyes doing a double cross with hopelessness.

"As to that," replied Tom with great solemnity, looking over his shoulder for an open window he could spit through, "I couldn't swear."

"But you understood her to mean Timmy Martin?"

"I'm not accusing Timmy Martin at all," said Tom in great alarm, seeing how the processes of law were tending to involve him in a row with the Martins, who were a turbulent family with ways of getting their own back unknown to any law. "Timmy Martin is one man she used to be round with. It might be Timmy Martin or it might be someone else, or what's more," he added with the look of a man who has had a sudden revelation, "it might be more than one." He looked from Peter to his father and back again to see what effect the revelation was having, but like other revelations it didn't seem to be going down too well. "Begod," he said, giving himself another heave, "it might be any God's number. . . . But, as to that," he added cautiously, "I wouldn't like to swear."

"Nor indeed, Tom," said his solicitor with a great effort at politeness, "no one would advise you. You'll want a good counsel."

"Begod, I suppose I will," said Tom with astonished resignation before the idea that there might be people in the world bad enough to doubt his word.

There was great excitement in the village when it became known that the Flynns were having the Roarer Cooper as counsel. Even as a first-class variety turn Cooper could always command attention, and everyone knew that the rights and wrongs of the case would be relegated to their proper position while the little matter of Eileen O'Grady's best frock received the attention it deserved.

On the day of the hearing the court was crowded. Tom and his father were sitting at the back with Peter Humphreys, waiting for Cooper, while Delia and her father were talking to Jackie Canty and their own counsel, Ivers. He was a well-built young man with a high brow, black hair, and half-closed, red-tinged sleepy eyes. He talked in a bland drawl.

"You're not worrying, are you?" he asked Delia kindly. "Don't be a bit afraid. . . . I suppose there's no chance of them settling, Jackie?"

"Musha, what chance would there be?" Canty asked scoldingly. "Don't you know yourself what sort they are?"

"I'll have a word with Cooper myself," said Ivers. "Dan isn't as bad as he looks." He went to talk to a coarse-looking man in wig and gown who had just come in. To say he wasn't as bad as he looked was no great compliment. He had a face that was almost a square, with a big jaw and blue eyes in wicked little slits that made deep dents across his cheekbones.

"What about settling this case of ours, Dan?" Ivers asked gently.

Cooper didn't even return his look; apparently he was not responsive to charm.

"Did you ever know me to settle when I could fight?" he growled.

"Not when you could fight your match," Ivers said, without taking offence. "You don't consider that poor girl your match?"

"We'll soon see what sort of girl she is," replied Cooper complacently as his eyes fell on the Flynns. "Tell me," he whispered, "what did she see in my client?"

"What you saw yourself when you were her age, I suppose," said Ivers. "You don't mean there wasn't a girl in a tobacconist's shop that you thought came down from heaven with the purpose of consoling you?"

"She had nothing in writing," Cooper replied gravely. "And, unlike your client, I never saw double."

"You don't believe that yarn, do you?"

"That's one of the things I'm going to inquire into."

"I can save you the trouble. She was too fond of him."

"Hah!" snorted Cooper as though this were a good joke. "And I suppose that's why she wants the cash."

"The girl doesn't care if she never got a penny. Don't you know yourself what's behind it? A respectable father. Two respectable fathers! The trouble about marriage in this country, Dan Cooper, is that the fathers always insist on doing the coorting."

"Hah!" grunted Cooper, rather more uncertain of himself. "Show me this paragon of the female sex, Ivers."

"There in the brown hat beside Canty," said Ivers without looking round. "Come on, you old devil, and stop trying to pretend you're Buffalo Bill. It's enough going through what she had to go through. I don't want her to go through any more."

"And why in God's name do you come to me?" Cooper asked in sudden indignation. "What the hell do you take me for? A Society for Protecting Fallen Women? Why didn't the priest make him marry her?"

"When the Catholic Church can make a farmer marry a labourer's daughter the Kingdom of God will be at hand," said Ivers. "I'm surprised at you, Dan Cooper, not knowing better at your age."

"And what are the neighbours doing here if she has nothing to hide?"

"Who said she had nothing to hide?" Ivers asked lightly, throwing in his hand. "Haven't you daughters of your own? You know she played the fine lady in the O'Gradys' frocks. If 'tis any information to you she wore their jewellery as well."

"Ivers, you're a young man of great plausibility," said Cooper, "but you can spare your charm on me. I have my client's interests to consider. Did she sleep with the other fellow?"

"She did not."

"Do you believe that?"

"As I believe in my own mother."

"The faith that moves mountains," Cooper said despondently. "How much are ye asking?"

"Two hundred and fifty," replied Ivers, shaky for the first time.

"Merciful God Almighty!" moaned Cooper, turning his eyes to the ceiling. "As if any responsible Irish court would put that price on a girl's virtue. Still, it might be as well. I'll see what I can do."

He moved ponderously across the court and with two big arms outstretched like wings shepherded out the Flynns.

"Two hundred and fifty pounds?" gasped Ned, going white. "Where in God's name would I get that money?"

"My dear Mr. Flynn," Cooper said with coarse amiability, "that's only half the yearly allowance his Lordship makes the young lady that obliges him, and she's not a patch on that girl in court. After a lifetime of experience I can assure you that for two years' fornication with a fine girl like that you won't pay a penny less than five hundred."

Peter Humphreys's eyes almost grew straight with the shock of such reckless slander on a blameless judge. He didn't know what had come over the Roarer. But that wasn't the worst. When the settlement was announced and the Flynns were leaving he went up to them again.

"You can believe me when I say you did the right thing, Mr. Flynn," he said. "I never like cases involving good-looking girls. Gentlemen of his Lordship's age are terribly susceptible. But tell me, why wouldn't your son marry her now as he's about it?"

"Marry her?" echoed Ned, who hadn't yet got over the shock of having to pay two hundred and fifty pounds and costs for a little matter he could have compounded for with Father Corcoran for fifty. "A thing like that!"

"With two hundred and fifty pounds, man?" snarled Cooper. "'Tisn't every day you'll pick up a daughter-in-law with that. . . . What do you say to the girl yourself?" he asked Tom.

"Oh, begod, the girl is all right," said Tom.

Tom looked different. It was partly relief that he wouldn't have to perjure himself, partly astonishment at seeing his father so swiftly overthrown. His face said: "The world is wide."

"Ah, Mr. Flynn, Mr. Flynn," whispered Cooper scornfully, "sure you're not such a fool as to let all that good money out of the family?"

Leaving Ned gasping, he went on to where Dick Carty, aglow with pride and malice, was receiving congratulations. There were no congratulations for Delia who was standing near him. She felt a big paw on her arm and looked up to see the Roarer.

"Are you still fond of that boy?" he whispered.

"I have reason to be, haven't I?" she retorted bitterly.

"You have," he replied with no great sympathy. "The best. I got you that money so that you could marry him if you wanted to. Do you want to?"

Her eyes filled with tears as she thought of the poor broken china of an idol that was being offered her now.

"Once a fool, always a fool," she said sullenly.

"You're no fool at all, girl," he said, giving her arm an encouraging squeeze. "You might make a man of him yet. I don't know what the law in this country is coming to. Get him away

to hell out of this till I find Michael Ivers and get him to talk to your father."

The two lawyers made the match themselves at Johnny Desmond's pub, and Johnny said it was like nothing in the world so much as a mission, with the Roarer roaring and threatening hell-fire on all concerned, and Michael Ivers piping away about the joys of heaven. Johnny said it was the most instructive evening he ever had. Ivers was always recognized as a weak man so the marriage did him no great harm, but of course it was a terrible comedown for a true Roarer, and Cooper's reputation has never been the same since then.

EXERCISE

1. This story seems much more complicated than "Wet Saturday" or "The Lottery Ticket," but on inspection we may find that what seems complication is, rather, a development of detail and not a change of basic structure. What is the basic structure? Here, as in the previous stories of this group, does the story depend on a single final turn?

2. We have, clearly, an objective conflict between the two families. The issue may be put in the question, "Will Delia win her law suit?" Somewhat in the background is another question, "Will Delia get her man?" But there is another deeper and more pervasive conflict, one between the assumptions of romantic love and the views of love and sex which belong to the society portrayed in the story. How would you state this conflict?

3. This deeper, more pervasive conflict is the basis of the humor of the story. Locate examples of this sort of humorous effect. But there is another humor mingled with this. At bottom the story is about calling in legal aid to avoid payment, the whole question of payment arising in turn from the desire of the farmer to avoid the marriage of his son to the dowry-less daughter of a laborer. But, humorously enough, and ironically enough, the calling in of legal aid ends in a marriage—the trap has been sprung. How is this humor of someone trapping himself related to the pervasive conflict?

The pervasive humor here stems from the author's general attitude toward the world he depicts. His feeling, his attitude, is what comes through and dominates the story. It is what gives the plot mechanism (the "trap") its final fictional significance. For, as we have said (see p. 9), the sense of a special, personal vision of life is what, in the end, makes a story good. A good story is more than plot, character, setting, symbols, theme—or any mechanically conceived set of relations among such things. It involves such things, but involves them as unified and interpenetrating, as the embodiment of the author's special vision of life.

4. What is the tone of the story?

5. Read "O Youth and Beauty," by John Cheever (page 236). Though this story is rather long and full of detail it ends with a sharp turn, with what might be called a "trick ending" (see Glossary). Is the shooting of Cash merely a trick—a way to end the story with a shock of irony? Or does the accidental and ironical quality of the end have some relation to the meaning of the story? Can it be said of this story, as of "Legal Aid," that the world depicted here, and the author's feeling about that world is fundamental to the effect of the story? That Cash, though a well developed character of interest as an individual, is primarily significant in relation to his world?

6. How would you compare "The Apostate," by George Milburn (page 216) to "Legal Aid" and "O Youth and Beauty"?

SECTION V

Plot and Complexity of Movement

The stories in this section do not move in a more or less straight line toward the decisive turn that will mark the denouement. There is a complexity in their very conception. Our concern here is to see how such complexities are related to the basic meaning of a story.

The Jar

LUIGI PIRANDELLO (1867-1936)

THE OLIVE CROP was a bumper one that year; the trees had flowered luxuriantly the year before, and, though there had been a long spell of misty weather at the time, the fruit had set well. Lollo Zirafa had a fine plantation on his farm at Primosole. Reckoning that the five old jars of glazed earthenware which he had in his wine-cellar would not suffice to hold all the oil of that harvest, he had placed an order well beforehand at Santo Stefano Di Camastra, where they are made. His new jar was to be of greater capacity —breast-high and pot-bellied; it would be the mother-superior to the little community of five other jars.

I need scarcely say that Don Lollo Zirafa had had a dispute with the potter concerning the jar. It would indeed be hard to name any-one with whom he had not picked a quarrel: for every trifle—be it merely a stone that had fallen from his boundary wall, or a handful of straw—he would shout out to the servants to saddle his mule, so that he could hurry to the town and file a suit. He had half-ruined himself, because of the large sums he had had to spend on court fees and lawyers' bills, bringing actions against one person after another, which always ended in his having to pay the costs of both sides. People said that his legal adviser grew so tired of seeing him appear two or three times a week that he tried to reduce the frequency of his visits by making him a present of a volume which looked like a prayer-book; it contained the judicial code—the idea being that he should take the trouble to see for himself what the rights and wrongs of the case were before hurry-ing to bring a suit.

Previously, when anyone had a difference with him, they would try to make him lose his temper by shouting out: "Saddle the mule!" but now they changed it to "Go and look up your pocket-code!" Don Lollo would reply: "That I will and I'll break the lot of you, you sons of bitches!"

In course of time, the new jar, for which he had paid the goodly sum of four florins, duly arrived; until room could be found for it in the wine-cellar, it was lodged in the crushing-shed for a few days. Never had there been a finer jar. It was quite distressing to see it lodged in that foul den, which reeked of stale grape-juice and had that musty smell of places deprived of light and air.

It was now two days since the harvesting of the olives had begun and Don Lollo was almost beside himself, having to supervise not only the men who were beating down the fruit from the trees, but also a number of others who had come with mule-loads of manure to be deposited in heaps on the hillside, where he had a field in which he was going to sow beans for the next crop. He felt that it was really more than one man could manage, he was at his wits' ends whom to attend to: cursing like a trooper, he vowed he would exterminate, first this man and then that, if an olive—one single olive—was missing: he almost talked as if he had counted them, one by one, on his trees; then he would turn to the muleteers and utter the direst threats as to what would happen, if any one heap of manure were not exactly the same size as the others. A little white cap on his head, his sleeves rolled up and his shirt open at the front, he rushed here, there and everywhere; his face was a bright red and poured with sweat, his eyes glared about him wolfishly, while his hands rubbed angrily at his shaven chin, where a fresh growth of beard always sprouted the moment the razor had left it.

At the close of the third day's work, three of the farm-hands—rough fellows with dirty, brutish faces—went to the crushing-shed; they had been beating the olive trees and went to replace their ladders and poles in the shed. They stood aghast at the sight of the fine new jar in two pieces, looking for all the world as if some one had caught hold of the bulging front and cut it off with a sharp sweep of the knife.

¹ Zi' (uncle) is used as a familiar prefix.

"Oh, my God! look! look!"

"How on earth has that happened?"

"My holy aunt! When Don Lollo hears of it! The new jar! What a pity, though!"

The first of the three, more frightened than his companions, proposed to shut the door again at once and to sneak away very quietly, leaving their ladders and poles outside leaning up against the wall; but the second took him up sharply.

"That's a stupid idea! You can't try that on Don Lollo. As like as not he'd believe we broke it ourselves. No, we all stay here!"

He went out of the shed and, using his hands as a trumpet, called out:—

"Don Lollo! Oh! Don LOLLOOOOO!"

When the farmer came up and saw the damage, he fell into a towering passion. First he vented his fury on the three men. He seized one of them by the throat, pinned him against the wall, and shouted:—

"By the Virgin's blood, you'll pay for that!"

The other two sprang forward in wild excitement, fell upon Don Lollo and pulled him away. Then his mad rage turned against himself: he stamped his feet, flung his cap on the ground and slapped his cheeks, bewailing his loss with screams suited only for the death of a relation.

"The new jar! A four-florin jar! Brand new!"

Who could have broken it? Could it possibly have broken of itself? Certainly someone must have broken it, out of malice or from envy at his possession of such a beauty. But when? How? There was no sign of violence. Could it conceivably have come in a broken condition from the pottery? No, it rang like a bell on its arrival.

As soon as the farm-hands saw that their master's first outburst of rage was spent, they began to console him, saying that he should not take it so to heart, as the jar could be mended. After all, the break was not a bad one, for the front had come away all in one piece; a clever rivetter could repair it and make it as good as new. Zi' Dima Licasi ¹ was just the man for the job; he had invented a marvelous cement made of some composition which he kept a strict secret—miraculous stuff! Once it had set, you couldn't loosen it, even with a hammer. So they suggested that, if Don Lollo agreed, Zi' Dima Licasi should turn up at day-break and—as sure as eggs were eggs—the jar would be repaired and be even better than a new one.

For a long time Don Lollo turned a deaf ear to their advice—it was quite useless, there was no making good the damage—but in the end he allowed himself to be persuaded and punctually at day-break Zi' Dima Licasi arrived at Primosole, with his outfit in a basket slung on his back. He turned out to be a misshapen old man with swollen, crooked joints, like the stem of an ancient Saracen olive tree. To extract a word from him, it looked as if you would have to use a pair of forceps on his mouth.

His ungraceful figure seemed to radiate discontent or gloom, due perhaps to his disappointment that no one had so far been found willing to do justice to his merits as an inventor. For Zi' Dima Licasi had not yet patented his discovery; he wanted to make a name for it first by its successful application. Meanwhile he felt it necessary to keep a sharp lookout, for fear lest someone steal the secret of his process.

"Let me see that cement of yours," began Don Lollo in a distrustful tone, after examining him from head to foot for several minutes.

Zi' Dima declined, with a dignified shake of the head.

"You'll see its results."

"But, will it hold?"

Zi' Dima put his basket on the ground and took out from it a red bundle composed of a large cotton handkerchief, much the worse for wear, wrapped round and round something. He began to unroll it very carefully, while they stood round watching him with close attention. When at last, however, nothing came to light save a pair of spectacles with bridge and sides broken and tied up with a string, there was a general laugh. Zi' Dima took no notice, but wiped his fingers before handling the spectacles, then put them on and, with much solemnity, began his examination of the jar, which had been brought outside on to the threshing-floor. Finally he said:

"It'll hold."

"But I can't trust cement alone," Don Lollo stipulated, "I must have rivets as well."

"I'm off," Zi' Dima promptly replied, stand-

ing up and replacing his basket on his back.

Don Lollo caught hold of his arm:—

"Off? Where to? You've got no more manners than a pig! . . . Just look at this pauper putting on an air of royalty! . . . Why! you wretched fool, I've got to put oil in that jar, and don't you know that oil oozes? Yards and yards to join together, and you talk of using cement alone! I want rivets—cement and rivets. It's for me to decide."

Zi' Dima shut his eyes, closed his lips tightly and shook his head. People were all like that—they refused to give him the satisfaction of turning out a neat bit of work, performed with artistic thoroughness and proving the wonderful virtues of his cement.

"If," he said, "the jar doesn't ring as true as a bell once more . . ."

"I won't listen to a word," Don Lollo broke in. "I want rivets! I'll pay you for cement and rivets. How much will it come to?"

"If I use cement only. . . ."

"My God! what an obstinate fellow! What did I say? I told you I wanted rivets. We'll settle the terms after the work is done. I've no more time to waste on you."

And he went off to look after his men.

In a state of great indignation Zi' Dima started on the job and his temper continued to rise as he bored hole after hole in the jar and in its broken section—holes for his iron rivets. Along with the squeaking of his tool went a running accompaniment of grunts which grew steadily louder and more frequent; his fury made his eyes more piercing and bloodshot and his face became green with bile. When he had finished that first operation, he flung his borer angrily into the basket and held the detached portion up against the jar to satisfy himself that the holes were at equal distances and fitted one another; next he took his pliers and cut a length of iron wire into as many pieces as he needed rivets, and then called to one of the men who were beating the olive trees to come and help him.

"Cheer up, Zi' Dima!" said the labourer, seeing how upset the old man looked.

Zi' Dima raised his hand with a savage gesture. He opened the tin which contained the cement and held it up towards heaven, as if offering it to God, seeing that men refused to recognise its value. Then he began to spread it with his finger all round the detached portion and along the broken edge of the jar. Taking his pliers and the iron rivets he had prepared, he crept inside the open belly of the jar and instructed the farm-hand to hold the piece up, fitting it closely to the jar as he had himself done a short time previously. Before starting to put in the rivets, he spoke from inside the jar:—

"Pull! Pull! Tug at it with all your might! . . . You see it doesn't come loose. Curses on people who won't believe me! Knock it! Yes, knock it! . . . Doesn't it ring like a bell, even with me inside it? Go and tell your master that!"

"It's for the top-dog to give orders, Zi' Dima," said the man with a sigh, "and it's for the under-dog to carry them out. Put the rivets in. Put 'em in."

Zi' Dima began to pass the bits of iron through the adjacent holes, one on each side of the crack, twisting up the ends with his pliers. It took him an hour to put them all in, and he poured with sweat inside the jar. As he worked, he complained of his misfortune and the farm-hand stayed near, trying to console him.

"Now help me get out," said Zi' Dima, when all was finished.

But large though its belly was, the jar had a distinctly narrow neck—a fact which Zi' Dima had overlooked, being so absorbed in his grievance. Now, try as he would, he could not manage to squeeze his way out. Instead of helping him, the farm-hand stood idly by, convulsed with laughter. So there was poor Zi' Dima, imprisoned in the jar which he had mended and—there was no use in blinking at the fact—in a jar which would have to be broken to let him out, and this time broken for good.

Hearing the laughter and shouts, Don Lollo came rushing up. Inside the jar, Zi' Dima was spitting like an agry cat.

"Let me out," he screamed, "for God's sake! I want to get out! Be quick! Help!"

Don Lollo was quite taken aback and unable to believe his own ears.

"What? Inside there? He's rivetted himself up inside?"

Then he went up to the jar and shouted out to Zi' Dima:—

"Help you? What help do you think I can give you? You stupid old dodderer, what d'you mean by it? Why couldn't you measure it first? Come, have a try! Put an arm out . . . that's it! Now the head! Up you come! . . . No, no, gently! . . . Down again . . . Wait a bit! . . . Not that way. . . . Down, get down. . . . How on earth could you do such a thing? . . . What about my jar now? . . .

"Keep calm! Keep calm!" he recommended to all the onlookers, as if it was they who were becoming excited and not himself. . . . "My head's going round! Keep calm! This is quite a new point! Get me my mule!"

He rapped the jar with his knuckles. Yes, it really rang like a bell once again.

"Fine! Repaired as good as new . . . You wait a bit!" he said to the prisoner; then instructed his man to be off and saddle the mule. He rubbed his forehead vigorously with his fingers and continued:—

"I wonder what's the best course. That's not a jar, it's a contrivance of the devil himself . . . Keep still! Keep still!" he exclaimed, rushing up to steady the jar, in which Zi' Dima, now in a towering passion, was struggling like a wild animal in a trap.

"It's a new point, my good man, which the lawyer must settle. I can't rely on my own judgment . . . Where's that mule? Hurry up with the mule! . . . I'll go straight there and back. You must wait patiently; it's in your own interest . . . Meanwhile, keep quiet, be calm! I must look after my own rights. And, first of all, to put myself in the right, I fulfill my obligation. Here you are! I am paying you for your work, for a whole day's work. Here are five lire. Is that enough?"

"I don't want anything," shouted Zi' Dima. "I want to get out!"

"You shall get out, but meanwhile I, for my part, am paying you. There they are—five lire."

He took the money out of his waistcoat pocket and tossed it into the jar, then enquired in a tone of great concern:—

"Have you had any lunch? . . . Bread and something to eat with it, at once! . . . What! You don't want it? Well, then, throw it to the dogs! I shall have done my duty when I've given it to you."

Having ordered the food, he mounted and set out for the town. His wild gesticulations made those who saw him galloping past think that he might well be hastening to shut himself up in a lunatic asylum.

As luck would have it, he did not have to spend much time in the ante-room before being admitted to the lawyer's study; he had, however, to wait a long while before the lawyer could finish laughing, after the matter had been related to him. Annoyed at the amusement he caused, Don Lollo said irritably:—

"Excuse me, but I don't see anything to laugh at. It's all very well for your Honour, who is not the sufferer, but the jar is my property."

The lawyer, however, continued to laugh and then made him tell the story all over again, just as it happened, so that he could raise another laugh out of it.

"Inside, eh? So he'd rivetted himself inside?" And what did Don Lollo want to do? . . . "To ke . . . to ke . . . keep him there inside:—ha! ha! ha! . . . keep him there inside, so as not to lose the jar?"

"Why should I lose it?" cried Don Lollo, clenching his fists. "Why should I put up with the loss of my money, and have people laughing at me?"

"But don't you know what that's called?" said the lawyer at last. "It's called 'wrongful confinement'."

"Confinement? Well, who's confined him? He's confined himself! What fault is that of mine?"

The lawyer then explained to him that the matter gave rise to two cases: on the one hand he, Don Lollo, must straightway liberate the prisoner, if he wished to escape from being prosecuted for wrongful confinement; while, on the other hand, the rivetter would be responsible for making good the loss resulting from his lack of skill or his stupidity.

"Ah!" said Don Lollo, with a sigh of relief. "So he'll have to pay me for my jar?"

"Wait a bit," remarked the lawyer. "Not as if it were a new jar, remember!"

"Why not?"

"Because it was a broken one, badly broken, too."

"Broken! No, Sir. Not broken. It's perfectly sound now and better than it ever was—he says so himself. And if I have to break it again, I shall not be able to have it mended. The jar will be ruined, Sir!"

The lawyer assured him that that point would be taken into account and that the rivetter would have to pay the value which the jar had in its present condition.

"Therefore," he counselled, "get the man himself to give you an estimate of its value first."

"I kiss your hands," Don Lollo murmured, and hurried away.

On his return home towards evening, he found all his labourers engaged in a celebration around the inhabited jar. The watch-dogs joined in the festivities with joyous barks and capers. Zi' Dima had not only calmed down, but had even come to enjoy his curious adventure and was able to laugh at it, with the melancholy humour of the unfortunate.

Don Lollo drove them all aside and bent down to look into the jar.

"Hallo! Getting along well?"

"Splendid! An open-air life for me!" replied the man. "It's better than in my own house."

"I'm glad to hear it. Meanwhile I'd just like you to know that that jar cost me four florins when it was new. How much do you think it's worth now?"

"With me inside it?" asked Zi' Dima.

The rustics laughed.

"Silence!" shouted Don Lollo. "Either your cement is of some use or it is of no use. There is no third possibility. If it is of no use, you are a fraud. If it is of some use, the jar, in its present condition, must have a value. What is the value? I ask for your estimate."

After a space for reflection, Zi' Dima said:—

"Here is my answer: if you had let me mend it with cement only—as I wanted to do—first of all I should not have been shut up inside it and the jar would have had its original value, without any doubt. But spoilt by these rivets, which had to be done from inside, it has lost most of its value. It's worth a third of its former price, more or less."

"One-third? That's one florin, thirty-three cents."

"Maybe less, but not more than that."

"Well," said Don Lollo. "Promise me that you'll pay me one florin thirty-three cents."

"What?" asked Zi' Dima, as if he did not grasp the point.

"I will break the jar to let you out," replied Don Lollo. "And—the lawyer tells me—you are to pay me its value according to your own estimate—one florin thirty-three."

"I? Pay?" laughed Zi' Dima, "I'd sooner stay here till I rot!"

With some difficulty he managed to extract from his pocket a short and peculiarly foul pipe and lighted it, puffing out the smoke through the neck of the jar.

Don Lollo stood there scowling: the possibility that Zi' Dima would no longer be willing to leave the jar, had not been foreseen either by himself or by the lawyer. What step should he take now? He was on the point of ordering them to saddle the mule, but reflected that it was already evening.

"Oh ho!" he said. "So you want to take up your abode in my jar! I call upon all you men as witnesses to his statement. He refuses to come out, in order to escape from paying. I am quite prepared to break it. Well, as you insist on staying there, I shall take proceedings against you tomorrow for unlawful occupancy of the jar and for preventing me from my rightful use of it."

Zi' Dima blew out another puff of smoke and answered calmly:—

"No, your Honour, I don't want to prevent you at all. Do you think I am here because I like it? Let me out and I'll go away gladly enough. But as for paying, I wouldn't dream of it, your Honour."

In a sudden access of fury Don Lollo made to give a kick at the jar but stopped in time. Instead he seized it with both hands and shook it violently, uttering a hoarse growl.

"You see what fine cement it is," Zi' Dima remarked from inside.

"You rascal!" roared Don Lollo. "Whose fault is it, yours or mine? You expect me to pay for it, do you? You can starve to death inside first. We'll see who'll win."

He went away, forgetting all about the five lire which he had tossed into the jar that morning. But the first thing Zi' Dima thought of doing was to spend that money in having a festive evening, in company with the farm-hands, who had been delayed in their work by that strange accident, and had decided to spend the night at the farm, in the open air, sleeping on the threshing-floor. One of them went to a neighboring tavern to make the necessary purchases. The moon was so bright that it seemed almost day—a splendid night for their carousal.

Many hours later Don Lollo was awakened by an infernal din. Looking out from the farmhouse balcony, he could see in the moonlight what looked like a gang of devils on his threshing-floor; his men all roaring drunk, were holding hands and performing a dance round the jar, while Zi' Dima, inside it, was singing at the top of his voice.

This time Don Lollo could not restrain himself, but rushed down like a mad bull and, before they could stop him, gave the jar a push which started it rolling down the slope. It continued on its course, to the delight of the intoxicated company, until it hit an olive tree and cracked in pieces, leaving Zi' Dima the winner in the dispute.

DISCUSSION

This story, though it is primarily the story of Lollo Zirafa, is also the story of Zi' Dima and his comic plight. The interplay between these two stories defines the meaning of the whole.

"The Jar," like "Legal Aid," is the story of a trap, and like that story has an irony in the end. In fact, here are two traps. One is quite literally the jar. Zi' Dima, in his obsession with his invented cement and his grievance that he is not allowed to demonstrate its powers, seals himself up in the jar. He traps himself. But Lollo traps himself, too. He has his own obsession which cuts him off from reality, which makes it impossible for him to deal with situations in a reasonable way. And here we have the root of the comic effect of the story. We have already referred to the idea that comic effect may, in one perspective, be thought of as rooted in a contrast between a mechanical response to a situation and a response that is fluid and adaptive, that accepts, in other words, the life process. Here neither Zi' Dima nor Lollo can make the adequate response. Each is caught up in his obsession.

EXERCISE

1. How would you describe the obsession of Zi' Dima? Of Lollo? What hints are provided in the story to give us a glimpse of the character behind each obsession? What traits of character do the two men share?

2. We have said that the interplay between the story of Zi' Dima and that of Lollo defines the meaning of the whole. How would you describe this interplay? What is the meaning that is defined by this interplay—in other words, what is the theme of the story?

3. What is the tone of the story? Warmly humorous and indulgent? Ironical? Sarcastic? Coolly detached? Or what?

4. If by this time you have not read "La Lupa," by Giovanni Verga (page 209), do so now. Both "La Lupa" and "The Jar" deal with obsessed characters, and both deal with entrapment in obsession. As Zi' Dima and Lollo, in their different ways, are entrapped by the jar, so both La Lupa herself, and her son-in-law, are entrapped by their obsessing attachment for each other. Both, we may say, recognize the entrapment and are desperate to escape. The son-in-law will kill La Lupa and be freed from the sexual bondage which is torturing him. And La Lupa herself, when she sees the axe raised continues to go toward him. It is true that her feeling here may be such that, in the intensity of the obsession, the violence of death merges with the violence of love; but this feeling would not discount the other, the desire to escape, even by death, from the obsession.

One main point, however, is that a basic situation—in "The Jar" and "La Lupa" that of self-imposed entrapment—may be the ground for either comedy or tragedy. The difference would involve, of course, the seriousness of the consequences of the issues raised (Lollo's litigiousness as contrasted with La Lupa's sexual obsession), the degree of our sympathetic involvement (we feel more involvement with La Lupa than with Lollo), and the tone of the treatment.

With these comments in mind, describe the difference in tone of treatment between "The Jar" and "La Lupa." Compare "Wet Saturday" with both.

The Valiant Woman

J. F. POWERS (1917-   )

THEY HAD come to the dessert in a dinner that was a shambles. "Well, John," Father Nulty said, turning away from Mrs. Stoner and to Father Firman, long gone silent at his own table. "You've got the bishop coming for confirmations next week."

"Yes," Mrs. Stoner cut in, "and for dinner. And if he don't eat any more than he did last year—"

Father Firman, in a rare moment, faced it. "Mrs. Stoner, the bishop is not well. You know that."

"And after I fixed that fine dinner and all." Mrs. Stoner pouted in Father Nulty's direction.

"I wouldn't feel bad about it, Mrs. Stoner," Father Nulty said. "He never eats much anywhere."

"It's funny. And that new Mrs. Allers said he ate just fine when he was there," Mrs. Stoner argued, and then spit out, "but she's a damned liar!"

Father Nulty, unsettled but trying not to show it, said, "Who's Mrs. Allers?"

"She's at Holy Cross," Mrs. Stoner said.

"She's the housekeeper," Father Firman added, thinking Mrs. Stoner made it sound as though Mrs. Allers were the pastor there.

"I swear I don't know what to do about the dinner this year," Mrs. Stoner said.

Father Firman moaned. "Just do as you've always done, Mrs. Stoner."

"Huh! And have it all to throw out! Is that any way to do?"

"Is there any dessert?" Father Firman asked coldly.

Mrs. Stoner leaped up from the table and bolted into the kitchen, mumbling. She came back with a birthday cake. She plunged it in the center of the table. She found a big wooden match in her apron pocket and thrust it at Father Firman.

"I don't like this bishop," she said. "I never

did. And the way he went and cut poor Ellen Kennedy out of Father Doolin's will!"

She went back into the kitchen.

"Didn't they talk a lot of filth about Doolin and the housekeeper?" Father Nulty asked.

"I should think they did," Father Firman said. "All because he took her to the movies on Sunday night. After he died and the bishop cut her out of the will, though I hear he gives her a pension privately, they talked about the bishop."

"I don't like this bishop at all," Mrs. Stoner said, appearing with a cake knife. "Bishop Doran —there was the man!"

"We know," Father Firman said. "All man and all priest."

"He did know real estate," Father Nulty said.

Father Firman struck the match.

"Not on the chair!" Mrs. Stoner cried, too late.

Father Firman set the candle burning—it was suspiciously large and yellow, like a blessed one, but he could not be sure. They watched the fluttering flame.

"I'm forgetting the lights!" Mrs. Stoner said, and got up to turn them off. She went into the kitchen again.

The priests had a moment of silence in the candle-light.

"Happy birthday, John," Father Nulty said softly. "Is it fifty-nine you are?"

"As if you didn't know, Frank," Father Firman said, "and you the same but one."

Father Nulty smiled, the old gold of his incisors shining in the flickering light, his collar whiter in the dark, and raised his glass of water, which would have been wine or better in the bygone days, and toasted Father Firman.

"Many of 'em, John."

"Blow it out," Mrs. Stoner said, returning to the room. She waited by the light switch for Father Firman to blow out the candle.

Mrs. Stoner, who ate no desserts, began to clear the dishes into the kitchen, and the priests, finishing their cake and coffee in a hurry, went to sit in the study.

Father Nulty offered a cigar.

"John?"

"My ulcers, Frank."

"Ah, well, you're better off." Father Nulty lit the cigar and crossed his long black legs. "Fish Frawley has got him a Filipino, John. Did you hear?"

Father Firman leaned forward, interested. "He got rid of the woman he had?"

"He did. It seems she snooped."

"Snooped, eh?"

"She did. And gossiped. Fish introduced two town boys to her, said, 'Would you think these boys were my nephews?' That's all, and the next week the paper had it that his two nephews were visiting him from Erie. After that, he let her believe he was going East to see his parents, though both are dead. The paper carried the story. Fish returned and made a sermon out of it. Then he got the Filipino."

Father Firman squirmed with pleasure in his chair. "That's like Fish, Frank. He can do that." He stared at the tips of his fingers bleakly. "You could never get a Filipino to come to a place like this."

"Probably not," Father Nulty said. "Fish is pretty close to Minneapolis. Ah, say, do you remember the trick he played on us all in Marmion Hall!"

"That I'll not forget!" Father Firman's eyes remembered. "Getting up New Year's morning and finding the toilet seats all painted!"

"*Happy Circumcision!* Hah!" Father Nulty had a coughing fit.

When he had got himself together again, a mosquito came and sat on his wrist. He watched it a moment before bringing his heavy hand down. He raised his hand slowly, viewed the dead mosquito, and sent it spinning with a plunk of his middle finger.

"Only the female bites," he said.

"I didn't know that," Father Firman said.

"Ah, yes . . ."

Mrs. Stoner entered the study and sat down with some sewing—Father Firman's black socks.

She smiled pleasantly at Father Nulty. "And what do you think of the atom bomb, Father?"

"Not much," Father Nulty said.

Mrs. Stoner had stopped smiling. Father Firman yawned.

Mrs. Stoner served up another: "Did you read about this communist convert, Father?"

"He's been in the Church before," Father

Nulty said, "and so it's not a conversion, Mrs. Stoner."

"No? Well, I already got him down on my list of Monsignor's converts."

"It's better than a conversion, Mrs. Stoner, for there is more rejoicing in heaven over the return of . . . uh, he that was lost, Mrs. Stoner, is found."

"And that congresswoman, Father?"

"Yes. A convert—she."

"And Henry Ford's grandson, Father. I got him down."

"Yes, to be sure."

Father Firman yawned, this time audibly, and held his jaw.

"But he's one only by marriage, Father," Mrs. Stoner said. "I always say you got to watch those kind."

"Indeed you do, but a convert nonetheless, Mrs. Stoner. Remember, Cardinal Newman himself was one."

Mrs. Stoner was unimpressed. "I see where Henry Ford's making steering wheels out of soybeans, Father."

"I didn't see that."

"I read it in the *Reader's Digest* or some place."

"Yes, well . . ." Father Nulty rose and held his hand out to Father Firman. "John," he said. "It's been good."

"I heard Hirohito's next," Mrs. Stoner said, returning to converts.

"Let's wait and see, Mrs. Stoner," Father Nulty said.

The priests walked to the door.

"You know where I live, John."

"Yes. Come again, Frank. Good night."

Father Firman watched Father Nulty go down the walk to his car at the curb. He hooked the screen door and turned off the porch light. He hesitated at the foot of the stairs, suddenly moved to go to bed. But he went back into the study.

"Phew!" Mrs. Stoner said. "I thought he'd never go. Here it is after eight o'clock."

Father Firman sat down in his rocking chair. "I don't see him often," he said.

"I give up!" Mrs. Stoner exclaimed, flinging the holey socks upon the horsehair sofa. "I'd swear you had a nail in your shoe."

"I told you I looked."

"Well, you ought to look again. And cut your toenails, why don't you? Haven't I got enough to do?"

Father Firman scratched in his coat pocket for a pill, found one, swallowed it. He let his head sink back against the chair and closed his eyes. He could hear her moving about the room, making the preparations; and how he knew them—the fumbling in the drawer for a pencil with a point, the rip of the page from his daily calendar, and finally the leg of the card table sliding up against his leg.

He opened his eyes. She yanked the floor lamp alongside the table, setting the bead fringe tinkling on the shade, and pulled up her chair on the other side. She sat down and smiled at him for the first time that day. Now she was happy.

She swept up the cards and began to shuffle with the abandoned virtuosity of an old riverboat gambler, standing them on end, fanning them out, whirling them through her fingers, dancing them halfway up her arms, cracking the whip over them. At last they lay before him tamed into a neat deck.

"Cut?"

"Go ahead," he said. She liked to go first.

She gave him her faint, avenging smile and drew a card, cast it aside for another which he thought must be an ace from the way she clutched it face down.

She was getting all the cards, as usual, and would have been invincible if she had possessed his restraint and if her cunning had been of a higher order. He knew a few things about leading and lying back that she would never learn. Her strategy was attack, forever attack, with one baffling departure: she might sacrifice certain tricks as expendable if only she could have the last ones, the heartbreaking ones, if she could slap them down one after another, shatteringly.

She played for blood, no bones about it, but for her there was no other way; it was her nature, as it was the lion's, and for this reason he found her ferocity pardonable, more a defect of the flesh, venial, while his own trouble was all in the will, mortal. He did not sweat and pray over each card as she must, but he did keep an eye out for reneging and demanded a cut now and then just to aggravate her, and he was always secretly hoping for aces.

With one card left in her hand, the telltale trick coming next, she delayed playing it, showing him first the smile, the preview of defeat. She laid it on the table—so! She held one more trump than he had reasoned possible. Had she palmed it from somewhere? No, she would not go that far; that would not be fair, was worse than reneging, which so easily and often happened accidentally, and she believed in being fair. Besides he had been watching her.

God smote the vines with hail, the sycamore trees with frost, and offered up the flocks to the lightning—but Mrs. Stoner! What a cross Father Firman had from God in Mrs. Stoner! There were other housekeepers as bad, no doubt, walking the rectories of the world, yes, but . . . yes. He could name one and maybe two priests who were worse off. One, maybe two. Cronin. His scraggly blonde of sixty—take her, with her everlasting banging on the grand piano, the gift of the pastor; her proud talk about the goiter operation at the Mayo Brothers', also a gift; her honking the parish Buick at passing strange priests because they were all in the game together. She was worse. She was something to keep the home fires burning. Yes sir. And Cronin said she was not a bad person really, but what was he? He was quite a freak himself.

For that matter, could anyone say that Mrs. Stoner was a bad person? No. He could not say it himself, and he was no freak. She had her points, Mrs. Stoner. She was clean. And though she cooked poorly, could not play the organ, would not take up the collection in an emergency, and went to card parties, and told all—even so, she was clean. She washed everything. Sometimes her underwear hung down beneath her dress like a paratrooper's pants, but it and everything she touched was clean. She washed constantly. She was clean.

She had her other points, to be sure—her faults, you might say. She snooped—no mistake about it—but it was not snooping for snooping's sake; she had a reason. She did other things, always with a reason. She overcharged on rosaries and prayer books, but that was for the sake of the poor. She censored the pamphlet rack, but that was to prevent scandal. She pried into the baptismal and matrimonial records, but there was no other way if Father was out, and in this way she had once uncovered a bastard and flushed him out of the rectory, but that was the perverted decency of the times. She held her nose over bad marriages in the presence of the victims, but that was her sorrow and came from having her husband buried in a mine. And he had caught her telling a bewildered young couple that there was only one good reason for their wanting to enter into a mixed marriage—the child had to have a name, and that—that was what?

She hid his books, kept him from smoking, picked his friends (usually the pastors of her colleagues), bawled out people for calling after dark, had no humor, except at cards, and then it was grim, very grim, and she sat hatchet-faced every morning at Mass. But she went to Mass, which was all that kept the church from being empty some mornings. She did annoying things all day long. She said annoying things into the night. She said she had given him the best years of her life. Had she? Perhaps—for the miner had her only a year. It was too bad, sinfully bad, when he thought of it like that. But all talk of best years and life was nonsense. He had to consider the heart of the matter, the essence. The essence was that housekeepers were hard to get, harder to get than ushers, than willing workers, than organists, than secretaries—yes, harder to get than assistants or vocations.

And she was a *saver*—saved money, saved electricity, saved string, bags, sugar, saved—him. That's what she did. That's what she said she did, and she was right, in a way. In a way, she was usually right. In fact, she was always right—in a way. And you could never get a Filipino to come way out here and live. Not a young one anyway, and he had never seen an old one. Not a Filipino. They liked to dress up and live.

Should he let it drop about Fish having one, just to throw a scare into her, let her know he was doing some thinking? No. It would be a perfect cue for the one about a man needing a woman to look after him. He was not up to that again, not tonight.

Now she was doing what she liked most of all. She was making a grand slam, playing it out card for card, though it was in the bag, prolonging what would have been cut short out of mercy in gentle company. Father Firman knew the agony of losing.

She slashed down the last card, a miserable deuce trump, and did in the hapless king of hearts he had been saving.

"Skunked you!"

She was awful in victory. Here was the bitter end of their long day together, the final murderous hour in which all they wanted to say— all he wouldn't and all she couldn't—came out in the cards. Whoever won at honeymoon won the day, slept on the other's scalp, and God alone had to help the loser.

"We've been at it long enough, Mrs. Stoner," he said, seeing her assembling the cards for another round.

"Had enough, huh!"

Father Firman grumbled something.

"No?"

"Yes."

She pulled the table away and left it against the wall for the next time. She went out of the study carrying the socks, content and clucking. He closed his eyes after her and began to get under way in the rocking chair, the nightly trip to nowhere. He could hear her brewing a cup of tea in the kitchen and conversing with the cat. She made her way up the stairs, carrying the tea, followed by the cat, purring.

He waited, rocking out to sea, until she would be sure to be through in the bathroom. Then he got up and locked the front door (she looked after the back door) and loosened his collar going upstairs.

In the bathroom he mixed a glass of antiseptic, always afraid of pyorrhea, and gargled to ward off pharyngitis.

When he turned on the light in his room, the moths and beetles began to batter against the screens, the lighter insects humming. . . .

Yes, and she had the guest room. How did she come to get that? Why wasn't she in the back room, in her proper place? He knew, if he cared to remember. The screen in the back room—it let in mosquitoes, and if it didn't do that she'd love to sleep back there, Father, looking out at the steeple and the blessed cross on top, Father, if it just weren't for the screen,

Father. Very well, Mrs. Stoner, I'll get it fixed or fix it myself. Oh, could you now, Father? I could, Mrs. Stoner, and I will. In the meantime you take the guest room. Yes, Father, and thank you, Father, the house ringing with amenities then. Years ago, all that. She was a pie-faced girl then, not really a girl perhaps, but not too old to marry again. But she never had. In fact, he could not remember that she had even tried for a husband since coming to the recovery, but, of course, he could be wrong, not knowing how they went about it. God! God save us! Had she got her wires crossed and mistaken him all these years for *that? That!* Him! Suffering God! No. That was going too far. That was getting morbid. No. He must not think of that again, ever. No.

But just the same she had got the guest room and she had it yet. Well, did it matter? Nobody ever came to see him any more, nobody to stay overnight anyway, nobody to stay very long . . . not any more. He knew how they laughed at him. He had heard Frank humming all right —before he saw how serious and sad the situation was and took pity—humming, "Wedding Bells Are Breaking Up That Old Gang of Mine." But then they'd always laughed at him for something—for not being an athlete, for wearing glasses, for having kidney trouble . . . and mail coming addressed to Rev. and Mrs. Stoner.

Removing his shirt, he bent over the table to read the volume left open from last night. He read, translating easily, "Eisdem licet cum illis . . . Clerics are allowed to reside only with women about whom there can be no suspicion, either because of a natural bond (as mother, sister, aunt) or of advanced age, combined in both cases with good repute."

Last night he had read it, and many nights before, each time as though this time to find what was missing, to find what obviously was not in the paragraph, his problem considered, a way out. She was not mother, not sister, not aunt, and *advanced age* was a relative term (why, she was younger than he was) and so, eureka, she did not meet the letter of the law—but, alas, how she fulfilled the spirit! And besides it would be a slimy way of handling it after all her years of service. He could not afford to pension her off, either.

He slammed the book shut. He slapped himself fiercely on the back, missing the wily mosquito, and whirled to find it. He took a magazine and folded it into a swatter. Then he saw it—oh, the preternatural cunning of it!—poised in the beard of St. Joseph on the bookcase. He could not hit it there. He teased it away, wanting it to light on the wall, but it knew his thoughts and flew high away. He swung wildly, hoping to stun it, missed, swung back, catching St. Joseph across the neck. The statue fell to the floor and broke.

Mrs. Stoner was panting in the hall outside his door.

"What is it!"

"Mosquitoes!"

"What is it, Father? Are you hurt?"

"Mosquitoes—damn it! And only the female bites!"

Mrs. Stoner, after a moment, said, "Shame on you, Father. She needs the blood for her eggs."

He dropped the magazine and lunged at the mosquito with his bare hand.

She went back to her room, saying, "Pshaw, I thought it was burglars murdering you in your bed."

He lunged again.

DISCUSSION

This is a comic story, a humorous story. What gives it this quality? We usually say that the comic effect involves some kind of contrast, the expected in contrast with the unexpected, the pretension in contrast with the reality, a sudden upset. Let us take an example. A man slips on a banana peel and comes crashing down.

If the man is an inoffensive, ordinary fellow going quietly down the street, the situation is not nearly as funny as if he were pompous and lordly and condescending, with a top hat. The comedy, then, involves the contrast between the man's pretension and what actually happens to him. This, of course, is a very simple situation, but it may give us a way into the discussion of more complicated comedy.

What contrast do we find in "The Valiant Woman"? The basic situation is a standard one, that of the henpecked man. Man who sets up as the lord and master finds himself under

female tyranny and can vent his protest and rebellion only by killing a mosquito: "And only the female bites!" We can imagine a comic story with the main characters husband and wife, but, as we have said, that situation is a standard one and a story based on it would run the risk of being somewhat hackneyed. Here, however, the standard situation of the henpecked man receives a new twist. The situation does not involve man and wife, but a priest and his housekeeper. A priest is celibate. He is supposed to be removed from the cares and distractions of domestic life. Ideally, his thoughts and energies go into the duties of his high calling. But, in contrast to all this we find the poor Father Firman just as henpecked as the butcher or baker or candlestick maker down the street. Mrs. Stoner has him under her thumb, and writhe and twist and rebel as he may, he can never escape. Even her piety and her good works and her economies and her attentions are simply a mask for her tyranny. Poor Father Firman might as well be married to some dragon of a wife, for the situation is a kind of parody of domestic life—even to Mrs. Stoner's words that she had given the best years of her life to Father Firman, the very words of an angry or aggrieved wife.

Are we to conclude from this that when we get a contrast we automatically get a comic effect? No, that does not follow. Let us return to our example of the man who slips on the banana peel. The situation will be comic only if we don't worry sympathetically about the poor fellow's broken leg, or neck. There must be some degree of detachment from the victim of the comic situation. We must feel ourselves not too deeply involved in the possible seriousness of things. This, of course, does not depend merely on the situation but also on ourselves. A gross, insensitive person may laugh at the man falling on the banana peel where another person might run to help him up. But sometimes we are able to see the funny element even in a serious situation or in a situation set in a larger context that is serious.

This last statement leads us to a question: Is "The Valiant Woman" disrespectful to the Catholic Church and the priesthood? Only a completely humorless person would think so.

In fact, in so far as one had respect for the Church and the priesthood, the more fully he would appreciate the contrast between Father Firman's role as priest and his human condition. In other words, we are aware of the funny element in a situation that is set in a serious context, the context of the Church and the priest's function. Let us look at it this way: If we had no notion of the Church and the priesthood there would be no contrast to give comic salt to the story.

We have said that we must have some detachment in order to appreciate the comedy of a situation. We may add that for a thing to be comic, in real life or in fiction, there must be some speed, some quickness. We must grasp the situation immediately. In a story, for example, there is never the comic effect if the author belabors the point, if he systematically analyzes the situation for us. No, he must arrange things so that the significance flashes on us, out of the very texture of personality or event. Let us look at a passage of conversation from "The Valiant Woman":

Mrs. Stoner served up another: "Did you read about this communist convert, Father?"

"He's been in the Church before," Father Nulty said, "and so it's not a conversion, Mrs. Stoner."

"No? Well, I already got him down on my list of Monsignor's converts."

"It's better than a conversion, Mrs. Stoner, for there is more rejoicing in heaven over the return of . . . uh, he that was lost, Mrs. Stoner, is found."

"And that congresswoman, Father?"

"Yes. A convert—she."

"And Henry Ford's grandson, Father. I got him down."

"Yes, to be sure."

Father Firman yawned, this time audibly, and held his jaw.

"But he's one only by marriage, Father," Mrs. Stoner said. "I always say you got to watch those kind."

"Indeed you do, but a convert nonetheless, Mrs. Stoner. Remember, Cardinal Newman himself was one."

Mrs. Stoner was unimpressed. "I see where Henry Ford's making steering wheels out of soy beans, Father."

"I didn't see that."

"I read it in the *Reader's Digest* or some place."

"Yes, well . . ." Father Nulty rose and held his hand out to Father Firman. "John," he said. "It's been good."

"I hear Hirohito's next," Mrs. Stoner said, returning to converts.

We get it all—Mrs. Stoner's domination of the conversation, her churchiness, which we know does not have a shred of real piety in it, just a kind of gossipy clubbiness, her scatterbrained irrelevancy (converts to soy beans), Father Nulty's strained politeness to his friend's housekeeper, Father Firman's yawn. It all comes over directly, in a flash, without discussion or preparation.

EXERCISE

1. How would you treat this story in terms of exposition, complication, and denouement? Does it break up rather neatly into these divisions or is there a general interpenetration? What is the basic conflict?

2. Comment on the comic elements in the following passages:

(a) "I don't like this bishop at all," Mrs. Stoner said, appearing with a cake knife. "Bishop Doran—there was the man!"

"We know," Father Firman said. "All man and all priest."

"He did know real estate," Father Nulty said.

Father Firman struck the match.

"Not on the chair!" Mrs. Stoner cried, too late.

Father Firman set the candle burning—it was suspiciously large and yellow, like a blessed one, but he could not be sure. They watched the fluttering flame.

(b) She swept up the cards and began to shuffle with the abandoned virtuosity of an old river-boat gambler, standing them on end, fanning them out, whirling them through her fingers, dancing them halfway up her arms, cracking the whip over them. At last they lay before him tamed into a neat deck.

(c) He could name one or maybe two priests who were worse off. One, maybe two. Cronin. His scraggly blonde of sixty—take her, with her everlasting banging on the grand piano, the gift of the pastor; her proud talk about the goiter operation at the Mayo Brothers', also a gift; her honking the parish Buick at passing strange priests because they were all in the game together.

3. When Mrs. Stoner hears Father Firman say that he is trying to kill a mosquito, she calls back: "Shame on you, Father. She needs the blood for her eggs." What is the point of this in the story?

4. Can you locate the basic divisions of this story? What is accomplished in each?

Keela, the Outcast Indian Maiden

EUDORA WELTY (1909-   )

ONE MORNING in summertime, when all his sons and daughters were off picking plums and Little Lee Roy was all alone, sitting on the porch and only listening to the screech owls away down in the woods, he had a surprise.

First he heard white men talking. He heard two white men coming up the path from the highway. Little Lee Roy ducked his head and held his breath; then he patted all around back of him for his crutches. The chickens all came out from under the house and waited attentively on the steps.

The men came closer. It was the young man who was doing all of the talking. But when they got through the fence, Max, the older man, interrupted him. He tapped him on the arm and pointed his thumb toward Little Lee Roy. He said, "Bud? Yonder he is."

But the younger man kept straight on talking, in an explanatory voice.

"Bud?" said Max again. "Look, Bud, yonder's the only little clubfooted nigger man was ever around Cane Springs. Is he the party?"

They came nearer and nearer to Little Lee Roy and then stopped and stood there in the middle of the yard. But the young man was so excited he did not seem to realize that they had arrived anywhere. He was only about twenty years old, very sunburned. He talked constantly, making only one gesture—raising his hand stiffly and then moving it a little to one side.

"They dressed it in a red dress, and it ate chickens alive," he said. "I sold tickets and I thought it was worth a dime, honest. They gimme a piece of paper with the thing wrote off I had to say. That was easy. 'Keela, the Outcast Indian Maiden!' I call it out through a pasteboard megaphone. Then ever' time it was fixin' to eat a live chicken, I blowed the sireen out front."

"Just tell me, Bud," said Max, resting back on the heels of his perforated tan-and-white sport shoes. "Is this nigger the one? Is that him sittin' there?"

Little Lee Roy sat huddled and blinking, a smile on his face. . . . But the young man did not look his way.

"Just took the job that time. I didn't mean to—I mean, I meant to go to Port Arthur because my brother was on a boat," he said. "My name is Steve, mister. But I worked with this show selling tickets for three months, and I never would of knowed it was like that if it hadn't been for that man." He arrested his gesture.

"Yeah, what man?" said Max in a hopeless voice.

Little Lee Roy was looking from one white man to the other, excited almost beyond respectful silence. He trembled all over, and a look of amazement and sudden life came into his eyes.

"Two years ago," Steve was saying impatiently. "And we was travelin' through Texas in those ole trucks.—See, the reason nobody ever come clost to it before was they give it a iron bar this long. And tole it if anybody come near, to shake the bar good at 'em, like this. But it couldn't say nothin'. Turned out they'd tole it it couldn't say nothin' to anybody ever, so it just kind of mumbled and growled, like a animal."

"Hee! hee!" This from Little Lee Roy, softly.

"Tell me again," said Max, and just from his look you could tell that everybody knew old Max. "Somehow I can't yet it straight in my mind. Is this the boy? Is this little nigger boy the same as this Keela, the Outcast Indian Maiden?"

Up on the porch, above them, Little Lee Roy gave Max a glance full of hilarity, and then bent the other way to catch Steve's next words.

"Why, if anybody was to even come near it or even bresh their shoulder against the rope it'd growl and take on and shake its iron rod. When it would eat the live chickens it'd growl somethin' awful—you ought to heard it."

"Hee! hee!" It was a soft, almost incredulous laugh that began to escape from Little Lee Roy's tight lips, a little mew of delight.

"They'd throw it this chicken, and it would reach out an' grab it. Would sort of rub over the chicken's neck with its thumb an' press on it good, an' then it would bite its head off."

"O.K.," said Max.

"It skint back the feathers and stuff from the neck and sucked the blood. But ever'body said it was still alive." Steve drew closer to Max and fastened his light-colored, troubled eyes on his face.

"O.K."

"Then it would pull the feathers out easy and neat-like, awful fast, an' growl the whole time, kind of moan, an' then it would commence to eat all the white meat. I'd go in an' look at it. I reckon I seen it a thousand times."

"That was you, boy?" Max demanded of Little Lee Roy unexpectedly.

But Little Lee Roy could only say, "Hee! hee!" The little man at the head of the steps where the chickens sat, one on each step, and the two men facing each other below made a pyramid.

Steve stuck his hand out for silence. "They said—I mean, I said it, out front through the megaphone, I said it myself, that it wouldn't eat nothin' but only live meat. It was supposed to be a Indian woman, see, in this red dress an' stockin's. It didn't have on no shoes, so when it drug its foot ever'body could see. . . . When it come to the chicken's heart, it would eat that too, real fast, and the heart would still be jumpin'."

"Wait a second, Bud," said Max briefly. "Say, boy, is this white man here crazy?"

Little Lee Roy burst into hysterical, deprecatory giggles. He said, "Naw suh, don't think so." He tried to catch Steve's eye, seeking appreciation, crying, "Naw suh, don't think he crazy, mista."

Steve gripped Max's arm. "Wait! Wait!" he cried anxiously. "You ain't listenin'. I want to tell you about it. You didn't catch my name—Steve. You never did hear about that little nigger—all that happened to him? Lived in Cane Springs, Miss'ippi?"

"Bud," said Max, disengaging himself, "I don't hear anything. I got a juke box, see, so I don't have to listen."

"Look—I was really the one," said Steve more patiently, but nervously, as if he had been slowly breaking bad news. He walked up and down the bare-swept ground in front of Little Lee Roy's porch, along the row of princess feathers and snow-on-the-mountain. Little Lee Roy's turning head followed him. "I was the one—that's what I'm tellin' you."

"Suppose I was to listen to what every dope comes in Max's Place got to say, I'd be nuts," said Max.

"It's all me, see," said Steve. "I know that. I was the one was the cause for it goin' on an' on an' not bein' found out—such an awful thing. It was me, what I said out front through the megaphone."

He stopped still and stared at Max in despair.

"Look," said Max. He sat on the steps, and the chickens hopped off. "I know I ain't nobody but Max. I got Max's Place. I only run a place, understand, fifty yards down the highway. Liquor buried twenty feet from the premises, and no trouble yet. I ain't ever been up here before. I don't claim to been anywhere. People come to my place. Now. You're the hitchhiker. You're tellin' me, see. You claim a lot of information. If I don't get it I don't get it and I ain't complaining about it, see. But I think you're nuts, and did from the first. I only come up here with you because I figured you's crazy."

"Maybe you don't believe I remember every word of it even now," Steve was saying gently. "I think about it at night—that an' drums on the midway. You ever hear drums on the midway?" He paused and stared politely at Max and Little Lee Roy.

"Yeh," said Max.

"Don't it make you feel sad. I remember how the drums was goin' and I was yellin', 'Ladies and gents! Do not try to touch Keela, the Outcast Indian Maiden—she will only beat your brains out with her iron rod, and eat them alive!' " Steve waved his arm gently in the air, and Little Lee Roy drew back and squealed. " 'Do not go near her, ladies and gents! I'm warnin' you!' So nobody ever did. Nobody ever come near her. Until that man."

"Sure," said Max. "That fella." He shut his eyes.

"Afterwards when he come up so bold, I remembered seein' him walk up an' buy the ticket an' go in the tent. I'll never forget that man as long as I live. To me he's a sort of—well—"

"Hero," said Max.

"I wish I could remember what he looked like. Seem like he was a tallish man with a sort of white face. Seem like he had bad teeth, but I may be wrong. I remember he frowned a lot. Kept frownin'. Whenever he'd buy a ticket, why, he'd frown."

"Ever seen him since?" asked Max cautiously, still with his eyes closed. "Ever hunt him up?"

"No, never did," said Steve. Then he went on. "He'd frown an' buy a ticket ever' day we was in these two little smelly towns in Texas, sometimes three-four times a day, whether it was fixin' to eat a chicken or not."

"O.K., so he gets in the tent," said Max.

"Well, what the man finally done was, he walked right up to the little stand where it was tied up and laid his hand out open on the planks in the platform. He just laid his hand out open there and said, 'Come here,' real low and quick, that-a-way."

Steve laid his open hand on Little Lee Roy's porch and held it there, frowning in concentration.

"I get it," said Max. "He'd caught on it was a fake."

Steve straightened up. "So ever'body yelled to git away, git away," he continued, his voice rising, "because it was growlin' an' carryin' on an' shakin' its iron bar like they tole it. When I heard all that commotion—boy! I was scared."

"You didn't know it was a fake."

Steve was silent for a moment, and Little Lee Roy held his breath, for fear everything was all over.

"Look," said Steve finally, his voice trembling. "I guess I was supposed to feel bad like this, and you wasn't. I wasn't supposed to ship out on that boat from Port Arthur and all like that. This other had to happen to me—not you all. Feelin' responsible. You'll be O.K., mister, but I won't. I feel awful about it. That poor little old thing."

"Look, you got him right here," said Max quickly. "See him? Use your eyes. He's O.K., ain't he? Looks O.K. to me. It's just you. You're nuts, is all."

"You know—when that man laid out his open hand on the boards, why, it just let go the iron bar," continued Steve, "let it fall down like that—bang—and act like it didn't know what to do. Then it drug itself over to where the fella was standin' an' leaned down an' grabbed holt onto that white man's hand as tight as it could an' cried like a baby. It didn't want to hit him!"

"Hee! hee! hee!"

"No sir, it didn't want to hit him. You know what it wanted?"

Max shook his head.

"It wanted him to help it. So the man said, 'Do you wanta get out of this place, whoever you are?' An' it never answered—none of us knowed it could talk—but it just wouldn't let that man's hand a-loose. It hung on, cryin' like a baby. So the man says, 'Well, wait here till I come back.' "

"Uh-huh?" said Max.

"Went off an' come back with the sheriff. Took us all to jail. But just the man owned the show and his son got took to the pen. They said I could go free. I kep' tellin' 'em I didn't know it wouldn't hit me with the iron bar an' kep' tellin' 'em I didn't know it could tell what you was sayin' to it."

"Yeh, guess you told 'em," said Max.

"By that time I felt bad. Been feelin' bad ever since. Can't hold onto a job or stay in one place for nothin' in the world. They made it stay in jail to see if it could talk or not, and the first night it wouldn't say nothin'. Some time it cried. And they undressed it an' found out it wasn't no outcast Indian woman a-tall. It was a little clubfooted nigger man."

"Hee! hee!"

"You mean it was this boy here—yeh. It was him."

"Washed its face, and it was paint all over it made it look red. It all come off. And it could talk—as good as me or you. But they'd tole it not to, so it never did. They'd tole it if anybody was to come near it they was comin' to git it—and for it to hit 'em quick with that iron bar an' growl. So nobody ever come near it—until that man. I was yellin' outside, tellin' 'em to keep away, keep away. You could see where they'd whup it. They had to whup it some to make it eat all the chickens. It was awful dirty. They let it go back home free, to where they got it in the first place. They made them pay its ticket from Little Oil, Texas, to Cane Springs, Miss'ippi."

"You got a good memory," said Max.

"The way it *started* was," said Steve, in a wondering voice, "the show was just travelin' along in ole trucks through the country, and just seen this little deformed nigger man, sittin' on a fence, and just took it. It couldn't help it."

Little Lee Roy tossed his head back in a frenzy of amusement.

"I found it all out later. I was up on the Ferris wheel with one of the boys—got to talkin' up yonder in the peace an' quiet—an' said they just kind of happened up on it. Like a cyclone happens: it wasn't nothin' it could do. It was just took up." Steve suddenly paled through his sunburn. "An' they found out that back in Miss'ippi it had it a little bitty pair of crutches an' could just go runnin' on 'em!"

"And there they are," said Max.

Little Lee Roy held up a crutch and turned it about, and then snatched it back like a monkey.

"But if it hadn't been for that man, I wouldn't of knowed it till yet. If it wasn't for him bein' so bold. If he hadn't knowed what he was doin'."

"You remember that man this fella's talkin' about, boy?" asked Max, eying Little Lee Roy.

Little Lee Roy, in reluctance and shyness, shook his head gently.

"Naw suh, I can't say as I remembas that ve'y man, suh," he said softly, looking down where just then a sparrow alighted on his child's shoe. He added happily, as if on inspiration, "Now I remembas *this* man."

Steve did not look up, but when Max shook

with silent laughter, alarm seemed to seize him like a spasm in his side. He walked painfully over and stood in the shade for a few minutes, leaning his head on a sycamore tree.

"Seemed like that man just studied it out an' knowed it was somethin' wrong," he said presently, his voice coming more remotely than ever. "But I didn't know. I can't look at nothin' an' be sure what it is. Then afterwards I know. Then I see how it was."

"Yeh, but you're nuts," said Max affably.

"You wouldn't of knowed it either!" cried Steve in sudden boyish, defensive anger. Then he came out from under the tree and stood again almost pleadingly in the sun, facing Max where he was sitting below Little Lee Roy on the steps. "You'd of let it go on an' on when they made it do those things—just like I did."

"Bet I could tell a man from a woman and an Indian from a nigger though," said Max.

Steve scuffed the dust into little puffs with his worn shoe. The chickens scattered, alarmed at last.

Little Lee Roy looked from one man to the other radiantly, his hands pressed over his grinning gums.

Then Steve sighed, and as if he did not know what else he could do, he reached out and without any warning hit Max in the jaw with his fist. Max fell off the steps.

Little Lee Roy suddenly sat as still and dark as a statue, looking on.

"Say! Say!" cried Steve. He pulled shyly at Max where he lay on the ground, with his lips pursed up like a whistler, and then stepped back. He looked horrified. "How you feel?"

"Lousy," said Max thoughtfully. "Let me alone." He raised up on one elbow and lay there looking all around, at the cabin, at Little Lee Roy sitting cross-legged on the porch, and at Steve with his hand out. Finally he got up.

"I can't figure out how I could of ever knocked down an athaletic guy like you. I had to do it," said Steve. "But I guess you don't understand. I had to hit you. First you didn't believe me, and then it didn't bother you."

"That's all O.K., only hush," said Max, and added, "some dope is always giving me the lowdown on something, but this is the first time one of 'em ever got away with a thing like this. I got to watch out."

"I hope it don't stay black long," said Steve.

"I got to be going," said Max. But he waited. "What you want to transact with Keela? You come a long way to see him." He stared at Steve with his eyes wide open now, and interested.

"Well, I was goin' to give him some money or somethin', I guess, if I ever found him, only now I ain't got any," said Steve defiantly.

"O.K.," said Max. "Here's some change for you, boy. Just take it. Go on back in the house. Go on."

Little Lee Roy took the money speechlessly, and then fell upon his yellow crutches and hopped with miraculous rapidity away through the door. Max stared after him for a moment.

"As for you"—he brushed himself off, turned to Steve and then said, "When did you eat last?"

"Well, I'll tell you," said Steve.

"Not here," said Max. "I didn't go to ask you a question. Just follow me. We serve eats at Max's Place, and I want to play the juke box. You eat, and I'll listen to the juke box."

"Well . . ." said Steve. "But when it cools off I got to catch a ride some place."

"Today while all you all was gone, and not a soul in de house," said Little Lee Roy at the supper table that night, "two white mens come heah to de house. Wouldn't come in. But talks to me about de ole times when I use to be wid de circus—"

"Hush up, Pappy," said the children.

EXERCISE

Write an essay analyzing and interpreting this story. In studying the story it may be useful to use the following questions and topics as a kind of guide:

1. In the first two paragraphs what impression do we get of Lee Roy and of the writer's attitude toward him? Notice how the story opens almost with the simplicity of a tale told to children: "One morning in summertime . . ." Notice Lee Roy's occupation—listening to the screech owls—and the way

the subsequent events are defined as a "surprise," the notion of something pleasantly falling across the vacancy of the morning. How does the fact that the chickens come out and wait "attentively" for the arrival of the strangers relate to the general impression we get of Lee Roy?

2. In the early stages of the story, how does the writer build up suspense? That is, how are interests stimulated but not gratified?

3. In the first description of Steve how is it indicated that he is under some nervous compulsion?

4. Why has Steve come to seek out the "outcast Indian maiden"?

5. If the central fact of a story is a conflict, how would you define the conflict here? We see, of course, that it exists between Steve and Max. Why does Steve finally strike Max? And why doesn't Max, a big, strong man, defend himself? Does the fact that he doesn't defend himself indicate that he has accepted Steve's view, or has begun to understand it? Why does Max give the money to Lee Roy? And why does he ask Steve to come and have a meal?

6. What is Lee Roy's attitude during the encounter between the white men? Does he understand why Steve is here? How does the very end of the story relate to this question? From the fact that the children try to hush up their father when he begins to talk about "de ole times when I use to be wid de circus," what do we learn of Lee Roy's present attitude toward what had been a pitiful and degrading experience? Is this ending intended to make the story less serious in its impact? Or is Lee Roy's attitude a way of intensifying the pitiful aspect of the whole situation?

7. If you have read Coleridge's poem "The Ancient Mariner," how would you compare the story with the poem in regard to theme? In what sense can we say that Steve has committed a crime similar to that of the Mariner and must expiate his crime in much the same way?

8. Read "The Lagoon," by Joseph Conrad page 223). This, like "Keela," is a story within a story—that is, a story told by a character who has an actual fictional presence and a relation to the story he narrates. You have no doubt determined what is the relation of the narrator in "Keela" to the story which he narrates. What is that of the narrator in "The Lagoon"? What is the attitude of the white man who hears the story? What is his place and importance in the story? How does his role compare with that of the hearer in "Keela"? Is he there merely to provoke the story? Does he have any relation to the underlying conflict? To the theme?

SECTION VI

Theme and Method

Every story, of course, has a theme. To state the matter negatively, if a narrative means nothing it isn't a story. We have not selected stories for this group because their themes are presented more obviously than those of stories in previous groups. In fact, in some of the stories in this group, the meaning is merely hinted at. Rather we are concerned here in illustrating some of the methods by which narrative moves toward meaning. Some of the stories have what, as far as a general statement goes, might be called the same theme, for instance, "The Horse Dealer's Daughter" and "Araby." But the fact that two stories are similar in theme does not mean that they mean the same thing. The attitude toward the theme may be very different; the tone of treatment may be, for example, either comic or tragic, ironic or straightforward. The writer's vision of life, as we have said, is the special underlying fact of any story, and a theme, abstractly stated, is not the same thing as a vision of life.

The Horse Dealer's Daughter

D. H. LAWRENCE (1885-1930)

"WELL, MABEL, and what are you going to do with yourself?" asked Joe, with foolish flippancy. He felt quite safe himself. Without listening for an answer, he turned aside, worked a grain of tobacco to the tip of his tongue, and spat it out. He did not care about anything, since he felt safe himself.

The three brothers and the sister sat round the desolate breakfast table, attempting some sort of desultory consultation. The morning's post had given the final tap to the family fortune, and all was over. The dreary dining-room itself, with its heavy mahogany furniture, looked as if it were waiting to be done away with.

But the consultation amounted to nothing. There was a strange air of ineffectuality about the three men, as they sprawled at table, smoking and reflecting vaguely on their own condition. The girl was alone, a rather short, sullen-looking young woman of twenty-seven. She did not share the same life as her brothers. She would have been good-looking, save for the impassive fixity of her face, "bull-dog," as her brothers called it.

There was a confused tramping of horses' feet outside. The three men all sprawled round in their chairs to watch. Beyond the dark holly-bushes that separated the strip of lawn from the highroad, they could see a cavalcade of shire horses swinging out of their own yard, being taken for exercise. This was the last time. These were the last horses that would go through their hands. The young men watched with critical, callous look. They were all frightened at the collapse of their lives, and the sense of disaster in which they were involved left them no inner freedom.

Yet they were three fine, well-set fellows

enough. Joe, the eldest, was a man of thirty-three, broad and handsome in a hot, flushed way. His face was red, he twisted his black moustache over a thick finger, his eyes were shallow and restless. He had a sensual way of uncovering his teeth when he laughed, and his bearing was stupid. Now he watched the horses with a glazed look of helplessness in his eyes, a certain stupor of downfall.

The great draught-horses swung past. They were tied head to tail, four of them, and they heaved along to where a lane branched off from the highroad, planting their great hoofs floutingly in the fine black mud, swinging their great rounded haunches sumptuously, and trotting a few sudden steps as they were led into the lane, round the corner. Every movement showed a massive, slumbrous strength, and a stupidity which held them in subjection. The groom at the head looked back, jerking the leading rope. And the cavalcade moved out of sight up the lane, the tail of the last horse, bobbed up tight and stiff, held out taut from the swinging great haunches as they rocked behind the hedges in a motion like sleep.

Joe watched with glazed hopeless eyes. The horses were almost like his own body to him. He felt he was done for now. Luckily he was engaged to a woman as old as himself, and therefore her father, who was steward of a neighbouring estate, would provide him with a job. He would marry and go into harness. His life was over, he would be a subject animal now.

He turned uneasily aside, the retreating steps of the horses echoing in his ears. Then, with foolish restlessness, he reached for the scraps of bacon-rind from the plates, and making a faint whistling sound, flung them to the terrier that lay against the fender. He watched the dog swallow them, and waited till the creature looked into his eyes. Then a faint grin came on his face, and in a high, foolish voice he said:

"You won't get much more bacon, shall you, you little bitch?"

The dog faintly and dismally wagged its tail, then lowered its haunches, circled round, and lay down again.

There was another helpless silence at the table. Joe sprawled uneasily in his seat, not willing to go till the family conclave was dis-

solved. Fred Henry, the second brother, was erect, clean-limbed, alert. He had watched the passing of the horses with more sang-froid. If he was an animal, like Joe, he was an animal which controls, not one which is controlled. He was master of any horse, and he carried himself with a well-tempered air of mastery. But he was not master of the situations of life. He pushed his coarse brown moustache upwards, off his lip, and glanced irritably at his sister, who sat impassive and inscrutable.

"You'll go and stop with Lucy for a bit, shan't you?" he asked. The girl did not answer.

"I don't see what else you can do," persisted Fred Henry.

"Go as a skivvy," Joe interpolated laconically.

The girl did not move a muscle.

"If I was her, I should go in for training for a nurse," said Malcolm, the youngest of them all. He was the baby of the family, a young man of twenty-two, with a fresh, jaunty *museau*.

But Mabel did not take any notice of him. They had talked at her and round her for so many years, that she hardly heard them at all.

The marble clock on the mantelpiece softly chimed the half-hour, the dog rose uneasily from the hearthrug and looked at the party at the breakfast table. But still they sat on in ineffectual conclave.

"Oh, all right," said Joe suddenly, apropos of nothing. "I'll get a move on."

He pushed back his chair, straddled his knees with a downward jerk, to get them free, in horsey fashion, and went to the fire. Still he did not go out of the room; he was curious to know what the others would do or say. He began to charge his pipe, looking down at the dog and saying, in a high, affected voice:

"Going wi' me? Going wi' me are ter? Tha'rt goin' further tha that counts on just now, dost hear?"

The dog faintly wagged its tail, the man stuck out his jaw and covered his pipe with his hands, and puffed intently, losing himself in the tobacco, looking down all the while at the dog with an absent brown eye. The dog looked up at him in mournful distrust. Joe stood with his knees stuck out, in real horsey fashion.

"Have you had a letter from Lucy?" Fred Henry asked of his sister.

"Last week," came the neutral reply.

"And what does she say?"

There was no answer.

"Does she *ask* you to go and stop there?" persisted Fred Henry.

"She says I can if I like."

"Well, then, you'd better. Tell her you'll come on Monday."

This was received in silence.

"That's what you'll do then, is it?" said Fred Henry, in some exasperation.

But she made no answer. There was a silence of futility and irritation in the room. Malcolm grinned fatuously.

"You'll have to make up your mind between now and next Wednesday," said Joe loudly, "or else find yourself lodgings on the kerbstone."

The face of the young woman darkened, but she sat on immutable.

"Here's Jack Fergusson!" exclaimed Malcolm, who was looking aimlessly out of the window.

"Where?" exclaimed Joe, loudly.

"Just gone past."

"Coming in?"

Malcolm craned his neck to see the gate.

"Yes," he said.

There was a slience. Mable sat on like one condemned, at the head of the table. Then a whistle was heard from the kitchen. The dog got up and barked sharply. Joe opened the door and shouted:

"Come on."

After a moment a young man entered. He was muffled up in overcoat and a purple woollen scarf, and his tweed cap, which he did not remove, was pulled down on his head. He was of medium height, his face was rather long and pale, his eyes looked tired.

"Hello, Jack! Well, Jack!" exclaimed Malcolm and Joe. Fred Henry merely said, "Jack."

"What's doing?" asked the newcomer, evidently addressing Fred Henry.

"Same. We've got to be out by Wednesday. Got a cold?"

"I have—got it bad, too."

"Why don't you stop in?"

"*Me* stop in? When I can't stand on my legs, perhaps I shall have a chance." The young man spoke huskily. He had a slight Scotch accent.

"It's a knock-out, isn't it," said Joe, boisterously, "if a doctor goes round croaking with a cold. Looks bad for the patients, doesn't it?"

The young doctor looked at him slowly.

"Anything the matter with *you*, then?" he asked sarcastically.

"Not as I know of. Damn your eyes, I hope not. Why?"

"I thought you were very concerned about the patients, wondered if you might be one yourself."

"Damn it, no, I've never been patient to no flaming doctor, and hope I never shall be," returned Joe.

At this point Mabel rose from the table, and they all seemed to become aware of her existence. She began putting the dishes together. The young doctor looked at her, but did not address her. He had not greeted her. She went out of the room with the tray, her face impassive and unchanged.

"When are you off then, all of you?" asked the doctor.

"I'm catching the eleven-forty," replied Malcolm. "Are you goin' down wi' th' trap, Joe?"

"Yes, I've told you I'm going down wi' th' trap, haven't I?"

"We'd better be getting her in then. So long, Jack, if I don't see you before I go," said Malcolm, shaking hands.

He went out, followed by Joe, who seemed to have his tail between his legs.

"Well, this is the devil's own," exclaimed the doctor, when he was left alone with Fred Henry. "Going before Wednesday, are you?"

"That's the orders," replied the other.

"Where, to Northampton?"

"That's it."

"The devil!" exclaimed Fergusson, with quiet chagrin.

And there was silence between the two.

"All settled up, are you?" asked Fergusson.

"About."

There was another pause.

"Well, I shall miss yer, Freddy, boy," said the young doctor.

"And I shall miss thee, Jack," returned the other.

"Miss you like hell," mused the doctor.

Fred Henry turned aside. There was nothing to say. Mabel came in again, to finish clearing the table.

"What are *you* going to do, then, Miss Pervin?" asked Fergusson. "Going to your sister's, are you?"

Mabel looked at him with her steady, dangerous eyes, that always made him uncomfortable, unsettling his superficial ease.

"No," she said.

"Well, what in the name of fortune *are* you going to do? Say what you mean to do," cried Fred Henry, with futile intensity.

But she only averted her head, and continued her work. She folded the white table-cloth, and put on the chenille cloth.

"The sulkiest bitch that ever trod!" muttered her brother.

But she finished her task with perfectly impassive face, the young doctor watching her interestedly all the while. Then she went out.

Fred Henry stared after her, clenching his lips, his blue eyes fixing in sharp antagonism, as he made a grimace of sour exasperation.

"You could bray her into bits, and that's all you'd get out of her," he said in a small, narrowed tone.

The doctor smiled faintly.

"What's she *going* to do, then?" he asked.

"Strike me if *I* know!" returned the other.

There was a pause. Then the doctor stirred.

"I'll be seeing you to-night, shall I?" he said to his friend.

"Ay—where's it to be? Are we going over to Jessdale?"

"I don't know. I've got such a cold on me. I'll come round to the Moon and Stars, anyway."

"Let Lizzie and May miss their night for once, eh?"

"That's it—if I feel as I do now."

"All's one—"

The two young men went through the passage and down to the back door together. The house was large, but it was servantless now, and desolate. At the back was a small bricked house-yard, and beyond that a big square, gravelled fine and red, and having stables on two sides. Sloping, dank, winter-dark fields stretched away on the open sides.

But the stables were empty. Joseph Pervin, the father of the family, had been a man of no education, who had become a fairly large horse dealer. The stables had been full of horses, there was a great turmoil and come-and-go of horses and of dealers and grooms. Then the kitchen was full of servants. But of late things had declined. The old man had married a second time, to retrieve his fortunes. Now he was dead and everything was gone to the dogs, there was nothing but debt and threatening.

For months, Mabel had been servantless in the big house, keeping the home together in penury for her ineffectual brothers. She had kept house for ten years. But previously it was with unstinted means. Then, however brutal and coarse everything was, the sense of money had kept her proud, confident. The men might be foul-mouthed, the women in the kitchen might have bad reputations, her brothers might have illegitimate children. But so long as there was money, the girl felt herself established, and brutally proud, reserved.

No company came to the house, save dealers and coarse men. Mabel had no associates of her own sex, after her sister went away. But she did not mind. She went regularly to church, she attended to her father. And she lived in the memory of her mother, who had died when she was fourteen, and whom she had loved. She had loved her father, too, in a different way, depending upon him, and feeling secure in him, until at the age of fifty-four he married again. And then she had set hard against him. Now he had died and left them all hopelessly in debt.

She had suffered badly during the period of poverty. Nothing, however, could shake the curious sullen, animal pride that dominated each member of the family. Now, for Mabel, the end had come. Still she would not cast about her. She would follow her own way just the same. She would always hold the keys of her own situation. Mindless and persistent, she endured from day to day. Why should she think? Why should she answer anybody? It was enough that this was the end, and there was no way out. She need not pass any more darkly along the main street of the small town, avoiding every eye. She need not demean herself any more, going into the shops and buying the cheapest food. This was at an end. She thought of nobody, not even of herself. Mindless and persistent, she seemed in a sort of ecstasy to be coming nearer to her fulfilment, her own glorification, approaching her dead mother, who was glorified.

In the afternoon she took a little bag, with shears and sponge and a small scrubbing brush, and went out. It was a grey, wintry day, with saddened, dark green fields and an atmosphere blackened by the smoke of foundries not far off. She went quickly, darkly along the causeway, heeding nobody, through the town to the churchyard.

There she always felt secure, as if no one could see her, although as a matter of fact she was exposed to the stare of every one who passed along under the churchyard wall. Nevertheless, once under the shadow of the great looming church, among the graves, she felt immune from the world, reserved within the thick churchyard wall as in another country.

Carefully she clipped the grass from the grave, and arranged the pinky white, small chrysanthemums in the tin cross. When this was done, she took an empty jar from a neighbouring grave, brought water, and carefully, most scrupulously sponged the marble headstone and the coping-stone.

It gave her sincere satisfaction to do this. She felt in immediate contact with the world of her mother. She took minute pains, went through the park in a state bordering on pure happiness, as if in performing this task she came into a subtle, intimate connection with her mother. For the life she followed here in the world was far less real than the world of death she inherited from her mother.

The doctor's house was just by the church. Fergusson, being a mere hired assistant, was slave to the country-side. As he hurried now to attend to the outpatients in the surgery, glancing across the graveyard with his quick eye, he saw the girl at her task at the grave. She seemed so intent and remote, it was like looking into another world. Some mystical element was touched in him. He slowed down as he walked, watching her as if spell-bound.

She lifted her eyes, feeling him looking. Their eyes met. And each looked away again at once, each feeling, in some way, found out by the other. He lifted his cap and passed on down the road. There remained distinct in his consciousness, like a vision, the memory of her face, lifted from the tombstone in the churchyard, and looking at him with slow, large, portentous eyes. It *was* portentous, her face. It seemed to mesmerize him. There was a heavy power in her eyes which laid hold of his whole being, as if he had drunk some powerful drug. He had been feeling weak and done before. Now the life came back into him, he felt delivered from his own fretted, daily self.

He finished his duties at the surgery as quickly as might be, hastily filling up the bottle of the waiting people with cheap drugs. Then, in perpetual haste, he set off again to visit several cases in another part of his round, before teatime. At all times he preferred to walk if he could, but particularly when he was not well. He fancied the motion restored him.

The afternoon was falling. It was grey, deadened, and wintry, with a slow, moist, heavy coldness sinking in and deadening all the faculties. But why should he think or notice? He hastily climbed the hill and turned across the dark green fields, following the black cinder-track. In the distance, across a shallow dip in the country, the small town was clustered like smouldering ash, a tower, a spire, a heap of low, raw, extinct houses. And on the nearest fringe of the town, sloping into the dip, was Oldmeadow, the Pervins' house. He could see the stables and the outbuildings distinctly, as they lay towards him on the slope. Well, he would not go there many more times! Another resource would be lost to him, another place gone: the only company he cared for in the alien, ugly little town he was losing. Nothing but work, drudgery, constant hastening from dwelling to dwelling among the colliers and the iron-workers. It wore him out, but at the same time he had a craving for it. It was a stimulant to him to be in the homes of the working people, moving as it were through the innermost body of their life. His nerves were excited and gratified. He could come so near, into the very lives of the rough, inarticulate, powerfully emotional men and women. He grumbled, he said he hated the hellish hole. But as a matter of fact it excited him, the contact with the rough, strongly-feeling people was a stimulant applied direct to his nerves.

Below Oldmeadow, in the green, shallow, soddened hollow of fields, lay a square, deep pond. Roving across the landscape, the doctor's quick eye detected a figure in black passing through the gate of the field, down towards the pond. He looked again. It would be Mabel Pervin. His mind suddenly became alive and attentive.

Why was she going down there? He pulled up on the path on the slope above, and stood staring. He could just make sure of the small black figure moving in the hollow of the failing day. He seemed to see her in the midst of such obscurity, that he was like a clairvoyant, seeing rather with the mind's eye than with ordinary sight. Yet he could see her positively enough, whilst he kept his eye attentive. He felt, if he looked away from her, in the thick, ugly falling dusk, he would lose her altogether.

He followed her minutely as she moved, direct and intent, like something transmitted rather than stirring in voluntary activity, straight down the field towards the pond. There she stood on the bank for a moment. She never raised her head. Then she waded slowly into the water.

He stood motionless as the small black figure walked slowly and deliberately towards the centre of the pond, very slowly, gradually moving deeper into the motionless water, and still moving forward as the water got up to her breast. Then he could see her no more in the dusk of the dead afternoon.

"There!" he exclaimed. "Would you believe it?"

And he hastened straight down, running over the wet, soddened fields, pushing through the hedges, down into the depression of callous wintry obscurity. It took him several minutes to come to the pond. He stood on the bank, breathing heavily. He could see nothing. His eyes seemed to penetrate the dead water. Yes, perhaps that was the dark shadow of her black clothing beneath the surface of the water.

He slowly ventured into the pond. The bottom was deep, soft clay, he sank in, and the water clasped dead cold round his legs. As he stirred he could smell the cold, rotten clay that fouled up into the water. It was objectionable in his lungs. Still, repelled and yet not heeding, he moved deeper into the pond. The cold water rose over his thighs, over his loins, upon his abdomen. The lower part of his body was all sunk in the hideous cold element. And the bottom was so deeply soft and uncertain, he was afraid of pitching with his mouth underneath. He could not swim, and was afraid.

He crouched a little, spreading his hands under the water and moving them round, trying to feel for her. The dead cold pond swayed upon his chest. He moved again, a little deeper, and again, with his hands underneath, he felt all around under the water. And he touched her clothing. But it evaded his fingers. He made a desperate effort to grasp it.

And so doing he lost his balance and went under, horribly, suffocating in the foul earthy water, struggling madly for a few moments. At last, after what seemed an eternity, he got his footing, rose again into the air, and looked around. He gasped, and knew he was in the world. Then he looked at the water. She had risen near him. He grasped her clothing, and drawing her nearer, turned to take his way to land again.

He went very slowly, carefully, absorbed in the slow progress. He rose higher, climbing out of the pond. The water was now only about his legs; he was thankful, full of relief to be out of the clutches of the pond. He lifted her and staggered on to the bank, out of the horror of wet, grey clay.

He laid her down on the bank. She was quite unconscious and running with water. He made the water come from her mouth, he worked to restore her. He did not have to work very long before he could feel the breathing begin again in her; she was breathing naturally. He worked a little longer. He could feel her live beneath his hands; she was coming back. He wiped her face, wrapped her in his overcoat, looked round into the dim, dark grey world, then lifted her and staggered down the bank and across the fields.

It seemed an unthinkably long way, and his

burden so heavy he felt he would never get to the house. But at last he was in the stable-yard, and then in the house-yard. He opened the door and went into the house. In the kitchen he laid her down on the hearthrug, and called. The house was empty. But the fire was burning in the grate.

Then again he kneeled to attend to her. She was breathing regularly, her eyes were wide open and as if conscious, but there seemed something missing in her look. She was conscious in herself, but unconscious of her surroundings.

He ran upstairs, took blankets from a bed, and put them before the fire to warm. Then he removed her saturated, earthy-smelling clothing, rubbed her dry with a towel, and wrapped her naked in the blankets. Then he went into the dining-room, to look for spirits. There was a little whisky. He drank a gulp himself, and put some into her mouth.

The effect was instantaneous. She looked full into his face, as if she had been seeing him for some time, and yet had only just become conscious of him.

"Dr. Fergusson?" she said.

"What?" he answered.

He was divesting himself of his coat, intending to find some dry clothing upstairs. He could not bear the smell of the dead, clayey water, and he was mortally afraid for his own health.

"What did I do?" she asked.

"Walked into the pond," he replied. He had begun to shudder like one sick, and could hardly attend to her. Her eyes remained full on him, he seemed to be going dark in his mind, looking back at her helplessly. The shuddering became quieter in him, his life came back in him, dark and unknowing, but strong again.

"Was I out of my mind?" she asked, while her eyes were fixed on him all the time.

"Maybe, for the moment," he replied. He felt quiet, because his strength had come back. The strange fretful strain had left him.

"Am I out of my mind now?" she asked.

"Are you?" he reflected a moment. "No," he answered truthfully, "I don't see that you are." He turned his face aside. He was afraid now, because he felt dazed, and felt dimly that her power was stronger than his, in this issue.

And she continued to look at him fixedly all the time. "Can you tell me where I shall find some dry things to put on?" he asked.

"Did you dive into the pond for me?" she asked.

"No," he answered. "I walked in. But I went in overhead as well."

There was silence for a moment. He hesitated. He very much wanted to go upstairs to get into dry clothing. But there was another desire in him. And she seemed to hold him. His will seemed to have gone to sleep, and left him, standing there slack before her. But he felt warm inside himself. He did not shudder at all, though his clothes were sodden on him.

"Why did you?" she asked.

"Because I didn't want you to do such a foolish thing," he said.

"It wasn't foolish," she said, still gazing at him as she lay on the floor, with a sofa cushion under her head. "It was the right thing to do. I knew best, then."

"I'll go and shift these wet things," he said. But still he had not the power to move out of her presence, until she sent him. It was as if she had the life of his body in her hands, and he could not extricate himself. Or perhaps he did not want to.

Suddenly she sat up. Then she became aware of her own immediate condition. She felt the blankets about her, she knew her own limbs. For a moment it seemed as if her reason were going. She looked round, with wild eye, as if seeking something. He stood still with fear. She saw her clothing lying scattered.

"Who undressed me?" she asked, her eyes resting full and inevitable on his face.

"I did," he replied, "to bring you round."

For some moments she sat and gazed at him awfully, her lips parted.

"Do you love me, then?" she asked.

He only stood and stared at her, fascinated. His soul seemed to melt.

She shuffled forward on her knees, and put her arms round him, round his legs, as he stood there, pressing her breasts against his knees and thighs, clutching him with strange, convulsive certainty, pressing his thighs against her, drawing him to her face, her throat, as she looked up at him with flaring, humble eyes of transfiguration, triumphant in first possession.

"You love me," she murmured, in strange transport, yearning and triumphant and confident. "You love me. I know you love me, I know."

And she was passionately kissing his knees, through the wet clothing, passionately and indiscriminately kissing his knees, his legs, as if unaware of everything.

He looked down at the tangled wet hair, the wild, bare, animal shoulders. He was amazed, bewildered, and afraid. He had never thought of loving her. He had never wanted to love her. When he rescued her and restored her, he was a doctor, and she was a patient. He had had no single personal thought of her. Nay, this introduction of the personal element was very distasteful to him, a violation of his professional honour. It was horrible to have her there embracing his knees. It was horrible. He revolted from it, violently. And yet—and yet—he had not the power to break away.

She looked at him again, with the same supplication of powerful love, and that same transcendent, frightening light of triumph. In view of the delicate flame which seemed to come from her face like a light, he was powerless. And yet he had never intended to love her. He had never intended. And something stubborn in him could not give way.

"You love me," she repeated, in a murmur of deep, rhapsodic assurance. "You love me."

Her hands were drawing him, drawing him down to her. He was afraid, even a little horrified. For he had, really, no intention of loving her. Yet her hands were drawing him towards her. He put out his hand quickly to steady himself, and grasped her bare shoulder. A flame seemed to burn the hand that grasped her soft shoulder. He had no intention of loving her: his whole will was against his yielding. It was horrible. And yet wonderful was the touch of her shoulders, beautiful the shining of her face. Was she perhaps mad? He had a horror of yielding to her. Yet something in him ached also.

He had been staring away at the door, away from her. But his hand remained on her shoulder. She had gone suddenly very still. He looked down at her. Her eyes were now wide with fear, with doubt, the light was dying from her face, a shadow of terrible greyness was returning. He could not bear the touch of her eyes' question upon him, and the look of death behind the question.

With an inward groan he gave way, and let his heart yield towards her. A sudden gentle smile came on his face. And her eyes, which never left his face, slowly, slowly filled with tears. He watched the strange water rise in her eyes, like some slow fountain coming up. And his heart seemed to burn and melt away in his breast.

He could not bear to look at her any more. He dropped on his knees and caught her head with his arms and pressed her face against his throat. She was very still. His heart, which seemed to have broken, was burning with a kind of agony in his breast. And he felt her slow, hot tears wetting his throat. But he could not move.

He felt the hot tears wet his neck and the hollows of his neck, and he remained motionless, suspended through one of man's eternities. Only now it had become indispensable to him to have her face pressed close to him; he could never let her go again. He could never let her head go away from the close clutch of his arm. He wanted to remain like that for ever, with his heart hurting him in a pain that was also life to him. Without knowing, he was looking down on her damp, soft brown hair.

Then, as it were suddenly, he smelt the horrid stagnant smell of that water. And at the same moment she drew away from him and looked at him. Her eyes were wistful and unfathomable. He was afraid of them, and he fell to kissing her, not knowing what he was doing. He wanted her eyes not to have that terrible, wistful, unfathomable look.

When she turned her face to him again, a faint delicate flush was glowing, and there was again dawning that terrible shining of joy in her eyes, which really terrified him, and yet which he now wanted to see, because he feared the look of doubt still more.

"You love me?" she said, rather faltering.

"Yes." The word cost him a painful effort. Not because it wasn't true. But because it was too newly true, the *saying* seemed to tear open again his newly-torn heart. And he hardly wanted it to be true, even now.

She lifted her face to him, and he bent forward and kissed her on the mouth, gently, with the one kiss that is an eternal pledge. And as he kissed her his heart strained again in his breast. He never intended to love her. But now it was over. He had crossed over the gulf to her, and all that he had left behind had shrivelled and become void.

After the kiss, her eyes again slowly filled with tears. She sat still, away from him, with her face drooped aside, and her hands folded in her lap. The tears fell very slowly. There was complete silence. He too sat there motionless and silent on the hearthrug. The strange pain of his heart that was broken seemed to consume him. That he should love her? That this was love! That he should be ripped open in this way! Him, a doctor! How they would all jeer if they knew! It was agony to him to think they might know.

In the curious naked pain of the thought he looked again to her. She was sitting there drooped into a muse. He saw a tear fall, and his heart flared hot. He saw for the first time that one of her shoulders was quite uncovered, one arm bare, he could see one of her small breasts; dimly, because it had become almost dark in the room.

"Why are you crying?" he asked, in an altered voice.

She looked up at him, and behind her tears the consciousness of her situation for the first time brought a dark look of shame to her eyes.

"I'm not crying, really," she said, watching him half frightened.

He reached his hand, and softly closed it on her bare arm.

"I love you! I love you!" he said in a soft, low vibrating voice, unlike himself.

She shrank, and dropped her head. The soft, penetrating grip of his hand on her arm distressed her. She looked up at him.

"I want to go," she said. "I want to go and get you some dry things."

"Why?" he said. "I'm all right."

"But I want to go," she said. "And I want you to change your things."

He released her arm, and she wrapped herself in the blanket, looking at him rather frightened. And still she did not rise.

"Kiss me," she said wistfully.

He kissed her, but briefly, half in anger.

Then, after a second, she rose nervously, all mixed up in the blanket. He watched her in her confusion, as she tried to extricate herself and wrap herself up so that she could walk. He watched her relentlessly, as she knew. And as she went, the blanket trailing, and as he saw a glimpse of her feet and her white leg, he tried to remember her as she was when he had wrapped her in the blanket. But then he didn't want to remember, because she had been nothing to him then, and his nature revolted from remembering her as she was when she was nothing to him.

A tumbling, muffled noise from within the dark house startled him. Then he heard her voice:—"There are clothes." He rose and went to the foot of the stairs, and gathered up the garments she had thrown down. Then he came back to the fire, to rub himself down and dress. He grinned at his own appearance when he had finished.

The fire was sinking, so he put on coal. The house was now quite dark, save for the light of a street-lamp that shone in faintly from beyond the holly trees. He lit the gas with matches he found on the mantelpiece. Then he emptied the pockets of his own clothes, and threw all his wet things in a heap into the scullery. After which he gathered up her sodden clothes, gently, and put them in a separate heap on the copper-top in the scullery.

It was six o'clock on the clock. His own watch had stopped. He ought to go back to the surgery. He waited, and still she did not come down. So he went to the foot of the stairs and called:

"I shall have to go."

Almost immediately he heard her coming down. She had on her best dress of black voile, and her hair was tidy, but still damp. She looked at him—and in spite of herself, smiled.

"I don't like you in those clothes," she said.

"Do I look a sight?" he answered.

They were shy of one another.

"I'll make you some tea," she said.

"No, I must go."

"Must you?" And she looked at him again with the wide, strained, doubtful eyes. And again, from the pain of his breast, he knew how he loved her. He went and bent to kiss her, gently, passionately, with his heart's painful kiss.

"And my hair smells so horrible," she murmured in distraction. "And I'm so awful, I'm so awful! Oh, no, I'm too awful." And she broke into bitter, heart-broken sobbing. "You can't want to love me, I'm horrible."

"Don't be silly, don't be silly," he said, trying to comfort her, kissing her, holding her in his arms. "I want you, I want to marry you, we're going to be married, quickly, quickly—tomorrow if I can."

But she only sobbed terribly, and cried:

"I feel awful. I feel awful. I feel I'm horrible to you."

"No, I want you, I want you," was all he answered, blindly, with that terrible intonation which frightened her almost more than her horror lest he should *not* want her.

DISCUSSION

This story is an interpretation of love, of the paradoxical quality of love, which in its shocking and distressing destruction of the self is a kind of death, and in its awakening of new hopes and powers is a kind of birth. Since the story is primarily about the nature of love, and not about the nature of individual persons, it presents two quite diverse people being surprised into the same experience. That is, we may say that it is scarcely more the story of the horse dealer's daughter than of Dr. Fergusson. True, we approach the story through her, but at the crisis his consciousness dominates the action until the very end.

"Well, Mabel, and what are you going to do with yourself?" one of the brothers asks in the opening sentence, and that question sets the line for the story. The question of Mabel's future is the main topic of discussion, but it is a discussion into which she does not enter. It is a question that Dr. Fergusson himself repeats at the end of what we may consider the first section, or movement, of the story. But the question is more than a practical one, a question about her plans for occupation, etc.; we, the readers, know that it concerns her fundamental fate, the kind of being she will achieve.

The whole temper of the first section is one of heaviness and futility. The dining room is "dreary." The men reflect "vaguely on their own condition," each one locked within himself. They all feel the lack of "inner freedom." The horses that move past swing their haunches sumptuously and show a massive, slumbrous strength, but they are held in subjection by their own "stupidity," and they rock behind the hedges in a "motion like sleep." Mabel's face wears an "impassive fixity," and later on, after the arrival of Dr. Fergusson, she sits "like one condemned." And from the big, cheerless house, "sloping, dank, winter-dark fields" stretch away. The world of the story is a deathly, unawakened, wintry world. The awakening and regeneration of this world will constitute the action.

The second section has to do with Mabel's life in the past and her identification with the dead mother: "Mindless and persistent, she seemed in a sort of ecstasy to be coming nearer to her fulfilment, her own glorification, approaching her dead mother, who was glorified." At the graveyard she feels "immune from the world," and "the life she followed here in the world was far less real than the world of death she inherited from her mother." In one sense, this section prepares us for the attempted suicide, but in another sense it foreshadows the symbolic death through love which will lead to Mabel's "glorification." In this section, the diffuse atmosphere of unfulfilment and death that had characterized the first section is now associated with Mabel herself. But this section ends when Mabel lifts her eyes to the eyes of Dr. Fergusson, and each feels, "in some way, found out by the other."

The third section shifts into the consciousness of Dr. Fergusson. It begins with his discovery of the "heavy power in her eyes" and the reviving effect on him: "Now the life came back into him, he felt delivered from his own fretted, daily self." This, then, corresponds to the foreshadowing of Mabel's "glorification." But he is still caught in the "gray, deadened, wintry" world, so "why should he think or notice?" The only life he now has is the stimulation he gets from his contact with the "rough, inarticulate, powerfully emotional men and women" who are his poor patients. He has no life of his own. This section ends with the moment when he sees Mabel pass and feels that if he looks away from her, "in the thick, ugly falling dusk," he will "lose her altogether."

The fourth section shows Mabel entering the pond with the intention of suicide, and Dr. Fergusson's rescue. The pond is "cold," "rotten," "fouled," and "earthy," with the "horror of wet, gray clay." It is the pond of death that they both enter, symbolically the risk of the destruction of self. Perhaps, too, the pond with its repellent qualities symbolizes the aspects of sexuality that may seem "unclean." The pond remains, of course, a real pond in a real world, a pond of dirty water in which a person can really drown, but in the pattern of meaning in the story we see that it has also other significances.

The fifth section shows the consequences of the crucial decision to enter the pond, a decision made by Mabel and then by Dr. Fergusson. This is the section of the awakening, the regeneration, the "glorification." Mabel, who has more fully accepted the idea of death (she had actually intended suicide), is therefore the more ready of the two for the awakening: she had already renounced the self. Dr. Fergusson, however, had entered the pond with fear and revulsion, and even now "something stubborn in him could not give way," and even now, as she embraces him, he smells "the horrid stagnant smell of that water." But the pain he now experiences is "also life to him," and in the end he accepts that life, and the past becomes nothing: he does not even want to remember Mabel as she had been before when she "was nothing to him."

The last part of this section (or shall we call it another section?) shows their return to the ordinary world. Dr. Fergusson must go to the surgery. Mabel changes clothes. She offers to make him some tea. They are shy of each other. But in the midst of this ordinary life, their new sense of the world bursts out again with joy and terror.

Looking back over the story, we can now see how vividly the real world is presented, how strongly felt and visualized are the scenes. But we can also see how almost every detail, details that at first may seem merely descriptive and casual, are related to the main line of the story, that is, how they tend to move from description to symbolism. The details of the brooding, deathy, winter world apply also to the condition of the lovers before their awakening. The horror of the real pond applies also to an emotional experience. In other words, the story is strongly integrated: we sense meaningfulness in even the smallest details.

EXERCISE

1. After the rescue from the pond, the following sentence about Mabel appears: "She was conscious in herself, but unconscious of her surroundings." What is the significance of this in relation to the theme? A little later there is the sentence about Dr. Fergusson: "He could not bear the smell of the dead, clayey water, and he was mortally afraid for his own health." What is the significance of this?

2. What is the gain in having Dr. Fergusson discover the attempted suicide rather than in having the reader follow the process with Mabel? Do we grasp enough of Mabel's motivation to be able to leave her before the decision is made and yet not be surprised when we discover the results of the decision?

3. We have said of this story that some of the details that are quite realistic in their presentation tend to take on a symbolic (see Glossary) relation to the theme of the story, or at the least generate an atmosphere (see Glossary) that is significant for the story. Can you locate some such details?

Araby

JAMES JOYCE (1882-1941)

NORTH RICHMOND Street, being blind, was a quiet street except at the hour when the Christian Brothers' School set the boys free. An uninhabited house of two stories stood at the blind end, detached from its neighbors in a square ground. The other houses of the street, conscious of decent lives within them, gazed at one another with brown imperturbable faces.

The former tenant of our house, a priest, had died in the back drawing-room. Air, musty from having been long enclosed, hung in all the rooms, and the waste room behind the kitchen was littered with old useless papers. Among these I found a few paper-covered books, the pages of which were curled and damp: *The Abbot,* by Walter Scott, *The Devout Communicant,* and *The Memoirs of Vidocq.* I liked the last best, because its leaves were yellow. The wild garden behind the house contained a central apple tree and a few straggling bushes, under one of which I found the late tenant's rusty bicycle-pump. He had been a very charitable priest; in his will he had left all his money to institutions and the furniture of his house to his sister.

When the short days of winter came, dusk fell before we had well eaten our dinners. When we met in the street, the houses had grown sombre. The space of sky above us was the color of ever-changing violet, and towards it the lamps of the street lifted their feeble lanterns. The cold air stung us and we played till our bodies glowed. Our shouts echoed in the silent street. The career of our play brought us through the dark muddy lanes behind the houses where we ran the gauntlet of the rough tribes from the cottages, to the back doors of the dark dripping gardens where odors arose from the ashpits, to the dark odorous stables where a coachman smoothed and combed the horse or shook music from the buckled harness. When we returned to the street, if uncle was seen turning the corner, we hid in the shadow until we had seen him safely housed. Or if Mangan's sister came out on the doorstep to call her brother in to his tea, we watched her from our shadow peer up and down the street. We waited to see whether she would remain or go in, and, if she remained, we left our shadow and walked up to Mangan's steps resignedly. She was waiting for us, her figure defined by the light from the half-opened door. Her brother always teased her before he obeyed, and I stood by the railings looking at her. Her dress swung as she moved her body, and the soft rope of her hair tossed from side to side.

Every morning I lay on the floor in the front parlor watching her door. The blind was pulled down to within an inch of the sash, so that I could not be seen. When she came out on the doorstep my heart leaped. I ran to the hall, seized my books, and followed her. I kept her brown figure always in my eye, and, when we came near the point at which our ways diverged, I quickened my pace and passed her. This happened morning after morning. I had never spoken to her, except for a few casual words, and yet her name was like a summons to all my foolish blood.

Her image accompanied me even in places the most hostile to romance. On Saturday evenings, when my aunt went marketing, I had to go to carry some of the parcels. We walked through the flaring streets, jostled by drunken men and bargaining women, amid the curses of laborers, the shrill litanies of shop-boys, who stood on guard by the barrels of pigs' cheeks, the nasal chanting of street-singers, who sang a *come-all-you* about O'Donovan Rossa, or a ballad about the troubles in our native land. These noises converged in a single sensation of life for me: I imagined that I bore my chalice safely through a throng of foes. Her name sprang to my lips at moments in strange prayers and praises which I myself did not understand. My eyes were often full of tears (I could not tell why) and at times a flood from my heart seemed to pour itself out into my bosom. I thought little of the future. I did not know whether I would ever speak to her or not, or, if I spoke to her, how I could tell her of my confused adoration. But my body was like a harp, and her words and gestures were like fingers running upon the wires.

One evening I went into the back drawing-room, in which the priest had died. It was a dark rainy evening, and there was no sound in the house. Through one of the broken panes I heard the rain impinge upon the earth, the fine incessant needles of water playing in the sodden beds. Some distant lamp or lighted window gleamed below me. I was thankful that I could see so little. All my senses seemed to desire to veil themselves, and, feeling that I was about to slip from them, I pressed the palms of my hands together until they trembled, murmuring: *"O love! O love!"* many times.

At last she spoke to me. When she addressed the first words to me, I was so confused that I did not know what to answer. She asked me was I going to *Araby*. I forget whether I answered yes or no. It would be a splendid bazaar; she said she would love to go.

"And why can't you?" I asked.

While she spoke, she turned a silver bracelet round and round her wrist. She could not go, she said, because there would be a retreat that week in her convent. Her brother and two other boys were fighting for their caps, and I was alone at the railings. She held one of the spikes, bowing her head towards me. The light from the lamp opposite our door caught the white curve of her neck, lit up her hair that rested there, and, falling, lit up the hand upon the railing. It fell over one side of her dress and caught the white border of a petticoat, just visible as she stood at ease.

"It's well for you," she said.

"If I go," I said, "I will bring you something."

What innumerable follies laid waste my waking and sleeping thoughts after that evening! I wished to annihilate the tedious intervening days. I chafed against the work of school. At night in my bedroom and by day in the classroom her image came between me and the page I strove to read. The syllables of the word *Araby* were called to me through the silence in which my soul luxuriated and cast an Eastern enchantment over me. I asked for leave to go to the bazaar on Saturday night. My aunt was surprised and hoped it was not some Freemason affair. I answered few questions in class. I watched my master's face pass from amiability to sternness; he hoped I was not beginning to idle. I could not call my wandering thoughts together. I had hardly any patience with the serious work of life, which, now that it stood between me and my desire, seemed to me child's play, ugly monotonous child's play.

On Saturday morning I reminded my uncle that I wished to go to the bazaar in the evening. He was fussing at the hallstand looking for the hat-brush, and answered me curtly:

"Yes, boy, I know."

As he was in the hall, I could not go into the front parlor and lie at the window. I left the house in bad humor and walked slowly towards the school. The air was pitilessly raw, and already my heart misgave me.

When I came home to dinner, my uncle had not yet been home. Still, it was early. I sat staring at the clock for some time, and, when its ticking began to irritate me, I left the room. I mounted the staircase and gained the upper part of the house. The high cold empty gloomy rooms liberated me and I went from room to room singing. From the front window I saw my companions playing below in the street. Their cries reached me weakened and indistinct, and, leaning my forehead against the cool glass, I looked over at the dark house where she lived. I may have stood there for an hour, seeing nothing but the brown-clad figure cast by my imagination, touched discreetly by the lamplight at the curved neck, at the hand upon the railings, and at the border below the dress.

When I came downstairs again, I found Mrs. Mercer sitting at the fire. She was an old garrulous woman, a pawn-broker's widow, who collected used stamps for some pious purpose. I had to endure the gossip of the tea-table. The meal was prolonged beyond an hour, and still my uncle did not come. Mrs. Mercer stood up to go: she was sorry she couldn't wait any longer, but it was after eight o'clock and she did not like to be out late, as the night air was bad for her. When she had gone, I began to walk up and down the room, clenching my fists. My aunt said:

"I'm afraid you may put off your bazaar for this night of Our Lord."

At nine o'clock I heard my uncle's latchkey in the hall-door. I heard him talking to himself and heard the hallstand rocking when it had received the weight of his overcoat. I could interpret these signs. When he was midway through his dinner, I asked him to give me the money to go to the bazaar. He had forgotten.

"The people are in bed and after their first sleep now," he said.

I did not smile. My aunt said to him energetically:

"Can't you give him the money and let him go? You've kept him late enough as it is."

My uncle said he was very sorry he had forgotten. He said he believed in the old saying: "All work and no play makes Jack a dull boy." He asked me where I was going, and, when I had told him a second time, he asked me did I know *The Arab's Farewell to His Steed.* When I left the kitchen, he was about to recite the opening lines of the piece to my aunt.

I held a florin tightly in my hand as I strode down Buckingham Street towards the station. The sight of the streets thronged with buyers and glaring with gas recalled to me the purpose of my journey. I took my seat in a third-class carriage of a deserted train. After an intolerable delay the train moved out of the station slowly. It crept onward among ruinous houses and over the twinkling river. At Westland Row Station a crowd of people pressed to the carriage doors; but the porters moved them back, saying that it was a special train for the bazaar. I remained alone in the bare carriage. In a few minutes the train drew up beside an improvised wooden platform. I passed out on to the road and saw by the lighted dial of a clock that it was ten minutes to ten. In front of me was a

large building which displayed the magical name.

I could not find any sixpenny entrance, and, fearing that the bazaar would be closed, I passed in quickly through a turnstile, handing a shilling to a weary-looking man. I found myself in a big hall girdled at half its height by a gallery. Nearly all the stalls were closed and the greater part of the hall was in darkness. I recognized a silence like that which pervades a church after a service. I walked into the center of the bazaar timidly. A few people were gathered about the stalls which were still open. Before a curtain, over which the words *Café Chantant* were written in colored lamps, two men were counting money on a salver. I listened to the fall of the coins.

Remembering with difficulty why I had come, I went over to one of the stalls and examined porcelain vases and flowered tea-sets. At the door of the stall a young lady was talking and laughing with two young gentlemen. I remarked their English accents and listened vaguely to their conversation.

"O, I never said such a thing!"

"O, but you did!"

"O, but I didn't!"

"Didn't she say that?"

"Yes. I heard her."

"O, there's a . . . fib!"

Observing me, the young lady came over and asked me did I wish to buy anything. The tone of her voice was not encouraging; she seemed to have spoken to me out of a sense of duty. I looked humbly at the great jars that stood like eastern guards at either side of the dark entrance to the stall and murmured:

"No, thank you."

The young lady changed the position of one of the vases and went back to the two young men. They began to talk of the same subject. Once or twice the young lady glanced at me over her shoulder.

I lingered before her stall, though I knew my stay was useless, to make my interest in her wares seem the more real. Then I turned away slowly and walked down the middle of the bazaar. I allowed the two pennies to fall against the sixpence in my pocket. I heard a voice call from one end of the gallery that the light was out. The upper part of the hall was now completely dark.

Gazing up into the darkness, I saw myself as a creature driven and derided by vanity; and my eyes burned with anguish and anger.

EXERCISE

1. This story, like "The Horse Dealer's Daughter," deals with the birth of love. It also resembles, in certain ways, "I'm a Fool." Yet the story by Lawrence and that by Anderson are very different. Which elements or aspects of "Araby" make us associate it with one or the other of these stories?

2. What is the significance of the religious background of the story? For instance, consider that the building of the bazaar is like a temple.

3. The story is in the first person. How old is the narrator at the time of the telling? How old at the time of the story told? What is the significance of these facts? What is the effect, for instance, on the tone? What, if anything, is gained by the use of the first-person narrator? Can you connect the style of the story with the fact of the first-person narrator? Is this the style the narrator would have used had he told it immediately after the events of the story? Compare the story on this point with "I'm a Fool." With "Spotted Horses."

4. Can you imagine "The Horse Dealer's Daughter" told in the first person? What would be lost?

5. In discussing "Clay," we referred to Joyce's idea of a story as an "epiphany." What is the "epiphany" here? Is the story making a comment merely on the befuddlements and disappointments of puppy love? Or is the comment projected into adult experiences? Connect this question with the style and method of the first-person narration.

6. Do you see any points of similarity between "Araby" and "Clay" that might indicate that these stories are the work of the same writer?

7. Read "In Dreams Begin Responsibilities," by Delmore Schwartz (page 242). Here, in the form of a dream, the main character looks back, not on an episode of his own early youth, but on the story of his parents when they were young. What is the meaning of this story? How would you relate it to "Araby"?

La Mère Sauvage

GUY DE MAUPASSANT (1850-1893)

I HAD not been at Virelogne for fifteen years. I went back there in the autumn, to shoot with my friend Serval, who had at last rebuilt his château, which had been destroyed by the Prussians.

I loved that district very much. It is one of those corners of the world which have a sensuous charm for the eyes. You love it with a bodily love. We, whom the country seduces, we keep tender memories for certain springs, for certain woods, for certain pools, for certain hills, seen very often, and which have stirred us like joyful events. Sometimes our thoughts turn back towards a corner in a forest, or the end of a bank, or an orchard powdered with flowers, seen but a single time, on some gay day; yet remaining in our hearts like the images of certain women met in the street on a spring morning, with bright transparent dresses; and leaving in soul and body an unappeased desire which is not to be forgotten, a feeling that you have just rubbed elbows with happiness.

At Virelogne I loved the whole countryside, dotted with little woods, and crossed by brooks which flashed in the sun and looked like veins, carrying blood to the earth. You fished in them for crawfish, trout, and eels! Divine happiness! You could bathe in places, and you often found snipe among the high grass which grew along the borders of these slender watercourses.

I was walking, lightly as a goat, watching my two dogs ranging before me. Serval, a hundred metres to my right, was beating a field of lucern. I turned the thicket which forms the boundary of the wood of Sandres, and I saw a cottage in ruins.

All of a sudden, I remembered it as I had seen it the last time, in 1869, neat, covered with vines, with chickens before the door. What is sadder than a dead house, with its skeleton standing upright, bare and sinister?

I also remembered that in it, one very tiring day, the good woman had given me a glass of wine to drink, and that Serval had then told me the history of its inhabitants. The father, an old poacher, had been killed by the gendarmes. The son, whom I had once seen, was a tall, dry fellow who also passed for a ferocious destroyer of game. People called them *"les Sauvage."*

Was that a name or a nickname?

I hailed Serval. He came up with his long strides like a crane.

I asked him:

"What's become of those people?"

And he told me this story:

When war was declared, the son Sauvage, who was then thirty-three years old, enlisted, leaving his mother alone in the house. People did not pity the old woman very much because she had money; they knew it.

But she remained quite alone in that isolated dwelling so far from the village, on the edge of the wood. She was not afraid, however, being of the same strain as her menfolk; a hardy old woman, tall and thin, who laughed seldom, and with whom one never jested. The women of the fields laugh but little in any case; that is men's business, that! But they themselves have sad and narrowed hearts, leading a melancholy, gloomy life. The peasants learn a little boisterous merriment at the tavern, but their helpmates remain grave, with countenances which are always severe. The muscles of their faces have never learned the movements of the laugh.

La Mère Sauvage continued her ordinary existence in her cottage, which was soon covered by the snows. She came to the village once a week, to get bread and a little meat; then she returned into her house. As there was talk of wolves, she went out with a gun upon her back —her son's gun, rusty, and with the butt worn by the rubbing of the hand; and she was strange to see, the tall "Sauvage," a little bent, going with slow strides over the snow, the muzzle of the piece extending beyond the black headdress, which pressed close to her head and imprisoned her white hair, which no one had ever seen.

One day a Prussian force arrived. It was billeted upon the inhabitants, according to the property and resources of each. Four were al-lotted to the old woman, who was known to be rich.

They were four great boys with blond skin, with blond beards, with blue eyes, who had remained stout notwithstanding the fatigues which they had endured already, and who also, though in a conquered country, had remained kind and gentle. Alone with this aged woman, they showed themselves full of consideration, sparing her, as much as they could, all expenses and fatigue. They would be seen, all four of them, making their toilet round the well, of a morning, in their shirt-sleeves, splashing with great swishes of water, under the crude daylight of the snowy weather, their pink-white Northman's flesh, while La Mère Sauvage went and came, making ready the soup. Then they would be seen cleaning the kitchen, rubbing the tiles, splitting wood, peeling potatoes, doing up all the housework, like four good sons about their mother.

But the old woman thought always of her own, so tall and thin, with his hooked nose and his brown eyes and his heavy mustache which made a roll of black hairs upon his lip. She asked each day of each of the soldiers who were installed beside her hearth:

"Do you know where the French Marching Regiment No. 23 was sent? My boy is in it."

They answered, "No, not know, not know at all." And, understanding her pain and her uneasiness (they, who had mothers too, there at home), they rendered her a thousand little services. She loved them well, moreover, her four enemies, since the peasantry feels no patriotic hatred; that belongs to the upper class alone. The humble, those who pay the most, because they are poor, and because every new burden crushes them down; those who are killed in masses, who make the true cannon's-meat, because they are so many; those, in fine, who suffer most cruelly the atrocious miseries of war, because they are the feeblest, and offer least resistance—they hardly understand at all those bellicose ardors, that excitable sense of honor, or those pretended political combinations which in six months exhaust two nations, the conqueror with the conquered.

They said on the countryside in speaking of the Germans of La Mère Sauvage:

"There are four who have found a soft place."

Now, one morning, when the old woman was alone in the house, she perceived far off on the plain a man coming towards her dwelling. Soon she recognized him; it was the postman charged to distribute the letters. He gave her a folded paper, and she drew out of her case the spectacles which she used for sewing; then she read:

MADAME SAUVAGE,—The present letter is to tell you sad news. Your boy Victor was killed yesterday by a shell which near cut him in two. I was just by, seeing that we stood next each other in the company, and he would talk to me about you to let you know on the same day if anything happened to him.

I took his watch, which was in his pocket, to bring it back to you when the war is done.

I salute you very friendly.

CÉSAIRE RIVOT
Soldier of the 2d class, March. Reg. No. 23

The letter was dated three weeks back.

She did not cry at all. She remained motionless, so seized and stupefied that she did not even suffer as yet. She thought: "V'la Victor who is killed now." Then little by little the tears mounted to her eyes, and the sorrow caught her heart. The ideas came to her, one by one, dreadful, torturing. She would never kiss him again, her child, her big boy, never again! The gendarmes had killed the father, the Prussians had killed the son. He had been cut in two by a cannon-ball. She seemed to see the thing, the horrible thing: the head falling, the eyes open, while he chewed the corner of his big mustache as he always did in moments of anger.

What had they done with his body afterwards? If they had only let her have her boy back as they had given her back her husband —with the bullet in the middle of his forehead!

But she heard a noise of voices. It was the Prussians returning from the village. She hid her letter very quickly in her pocket, and she received them quietly, with her ordinary face, having had time to wipe her eyes.

They were laughing, all four, delighted, since they brought with them a fine rabbit— stolen, doubtless—and they made signs to the old woman that there was to be something good to eat.

She set herself to work at once to prepare breakfast; but when it came to killing the rabbit, her heart failed her. And yet it was not the first. One of the soldiers struck it down with a blow of his fist behind the ears.

The beast once dead, she separated the red body from the skin; but the sight of the blood which she was touching, and which covered her hands, of the warm blood which she felt cooling and coagulating, made her tremble from head to foot; and she kept seeing her big boy cut in two, and quite red also, like this still-palpitating animal.

She set herself at table with the Prussians, but she could not eat, not even a mouthful. They devoured the rabbit without troubling themselves about her. She looked at them askance, without speaking, ripening a thought, and with a face so impassible that they perceived nothing.

All of a sudden she said: "I don't even know your names, and here's a whole month that we've been together." They understood, not without difficulty, what she wanted, and told their names. That was not sufficient; she had them written for her on a paper, with the addresses of their families, and, resting her spectacles on her great nose, she considered that strange handwriting, then folded the sheet and put it in her pocket, on top of the letter which told her of the death of her son.

When the meal was ended, she said to the men:

"I am going to work for you."

And she began to carry up hay into the loft where they slept.

They were astonished at her taking all this trouble; she explained to them that thus they would not be so cold; and they helped her. They heaped the trusses of hay as high as the straw roof; and in that manner they made a sort of great chamber with four walls of fodder, warm and perfumed, where they should sleep splendidly.

At dinner, one of them was worried to see that La Mère Sauvage still ate nothing. She told him that she had the cramps. Then she kindled a good fire to warm herself up, and the four Germans mounted to their lodging-place by the ladder which served them every night for this purpose.

As soon as they closed the trap, the old woman removed the ladder, then opened the outside door noiselessly, and went back to look for more bundles of straw, with which she filled her kitchen. She went barefoot in the snow, so softly that no sound was heard. From time to time she listened to the sonorous and unequal snoring of the four soldiers who were fast asleep.

When she judged her preparations to be sufficient, she threw one of the bundles into the fireplace, and when it was alight she scattered it all over the others. Then she went outside again and looked.

In a few seconds the whole interior of the cottage was illumined with a violent brightness and became a dreadful brasier, a gigantic fiery furnace, whose brilliance spouted out of the narrow window and threw a glittering beam upon the snow.

Then a great cry issued from the summit of the house; it was a clamor of human shriekings, heart-rending calls of anguish and of fear. At last, the trap having fallen in, a whirlwind of fire shot up into the loft, pierced the straw roof, rose to the sky like the immense flame of a torch; and all the cottage flared.

Nothing more was heard therein but the crackling of the fire, the crackling sound of the walls, the falling of the rafters. All of a sudden the roof fell in, and the burning carcass of the dwelling hurled a great plume of sparks into the air, amid a cloud of smoke.

The country, all white, lit up by the fire, shone like a cloth of silver tinted with red.

A bell, far off, began to toll.

The old "Sauvage" remained standing before her ruined dwelling, armed with her gun, her son's gun, for fear lest one of those men might escape.

When she saw that it was ended, she threw her weapon into the brasier. A loud report rang back.

People were coming, the peasants, the Prussians.

They found the woman seated on the trunk of a tree, calm and satisfied.

A German officer, who spoke French like a son of France, demanded of her:

"Where are your soldiers?"

She extended her thin arm towards the red heap of fire which was gradually going out, and she answered with a strong voice:

"There!"

They crowded round her. The Prussian asked:

"How did it take fire?"

She said:

"It was I who set it on fire."

They did not believe her, they thought that the sudden disaster had made her crazy. So, while all pressed round and listened, she told the thing from one end to the other, from the arrival of the letter to the last cry of the men who were burned with her house. She did not forget a detail of all which she had felt, nor of all which she had done.

When she had finished, she drew two pieces of paper from her pocket, and, to distinguish them by the last glimmers of the fire, she again adjusted her spectacles; then she said, showing one: "That, that is the death of Victor." Showing the other, she added, indicating the red ruins with a bend of the head: "That, that is their names, so that you can write home." She calmly held the white sheet out to the officer, who held her by the shoulders, and she continued:

"You must write how it happened, and you must say to their mothers that it was I who did that, Victoire Simon, la Sauvage! Do not forget."

The officer shouted some orders in German. They seized her, they threw her against the walls of her house, still hot. Then twelve men drew quickly up before her, at twenty paces. She did not move. She had understood; she waited.

An order rang out, followed instantly by a long report. A belated shot went off by itself, after the others.

The old woman did not fall. She sank as though they had mowed off her legs.

The Prussian officer approached. She was almost cut in two, and in her withered hand she held her letter bathed with blood.

My friend Serval added:

"It was by way of reprisal that the Germans

destroyed the château of the district, which belonged to me."

As for me, I thought of the mothers of those four gentle fellows burned in that house; and of the atrocious heroism of that other mother shot against the wall.

And I picked up a little stone, still blackened by the flames.

EXERCISE

1. This story, like many stories by Guy de Maupassant, is ironical. From what does the irony spring? In this connection think of the relation the woman has to her own son and to the German soldiers quartered on her; of the killing of an enemy in battle and the killing of an enemy in a purely personal way as the mother does at the end. As a matter of fact, in what sense are the Germans her enemy? How do these considerations lead us to the theme of the story?

2. What does the author gain by giving a framework for the story, that is, by giving the hunt and the discovery, years after the main event, of the ruins of the house? What is the effect of the last paragraph? What is the meaning of the small blackened stone? Is it to be taken as symbolic in the sense that the pond is symbolic in "The Horse Dealer's Daughter"? Or is the significance more generalized and allusive?

In Another Country

ERNEST HEMINGWAY (1899-1961)

IN THE fall the war was always there, but we did not go to it any more. It was cold in the fall in Milan and the dark came very early. Then the electric lights came on, and it was pleasant along the streets looking in the windows. There was much game hanging outside the shops, and the snow powdered in the fur of the foxes and the wind blew their tails. The deer hung stiff and heavy and empty, and small birds blew in the wind and the wind turned their feathers. It was a cold fall and the wind came down from the mountains.

We were all at the hospital every afternoon, and there were different ways of walking across the town through the dusk to the hospital. Two of the ways were alongside canals, but they were long. Always, though, you crossed a bridge across a canal to enter the hospital. There was a choice of three bridges. On one of them a woman sold roasted chestnuts. It was warm, standing in front of her charcoal fire, and the chestnuts were warm afterward in your pocket. The hospital was very old and very beautiful, and you entered through a gate and walked across a courtyard and out a gate on the other side. There were usually funerals starting from the courtyard. Beyond the old hospital were the new brick pavilions, and there we met every afternoon and were all very polite and interested in what was the matter, and sat in the machines that were to make so much difference.

The doctor came up to the machine where I was sitting and said: "What did you like best to do before the war? Did you practice a sport?"

I said: "Yes, football."

"Good," he said. "You will be able to play football again better than ever."

My knee did not bend and the leg dropped straight from the knee to the ankle without a calf, and the machine was to bend the knee and make it move as in riding a tricycle. But it did not bend yet, and instead the machine lurched when it came to the bending part. The doctor said: "That will all pass. You are a fortunate young man. You will play football again like a champion."

In the next machine was a major who had a little hand like a baby's. He winked at me when the doctor examined his hand, which was between two leather straps that bounced up and down and flapped the stiff fingers, and said: "And will I too play football, captain-doctor?" He had been a very great fencer, and before the war the greatest fencer in Italy.

The doctor went to his office in a back room and brought a photograph which showed a hand that had been withered almost as small as the major's, before it had taken a machine course, and after was a little larger. The major held the photograph with his good hand and looked at it very carefully. "A wound?" he asked.

"An industrial accident," the doctor said.

"Very interesting, very interesting," the major said, and handed it back to the doctor.

"You have confidence?"

"No," said the major.

There were three boys who came each day who were about the same age I was. They were all three from Milan, and one of them was to be a lawyer, and one was to be a painter, and one had intended to be a soldier, and after we were finished with the machines, sometimes we walked back together to the Café Cova, which was next door to the Scala. We walked the short way through the communist quarter because we were four together. The people hated us because we were officers, and from a wine-shop someone called out, "A basso gli ufficiali!" as we passed. Another boy who walked with us sometimes and made us five wore a black silk handkerchief across his face because he had no nose then and his face was to be rebuilt. He had gone out to the front from the military academy and been wounded within an hour after he had gone into the front line for the first time. They rebuilt his face, but he came from a very old family and they could never get the nose exactly right. He went to South America and worked in a bank. But this was a long time ago, and then we did not any of us know how it was going to be afterward. We only knew then that there was always the war, but that we were not going to it any more.

We all had the same medals, except the boy with the black silk bandage across his face, and he had not been at the front long enough to get any medals. The tall boy with a very pale face who was to be a lawyer had been a lieutenant of Arditi and had three medals of the sort we each had only one of. He had lived a very long time with death and was a little detached. We were all a little detached, and there was nothing that held us together except that we met every afternoon at the hospital. Although, as we walked to the Cova through the tough part of town, walking in the dark, with light and singing coming out of the wine-shops, and sometimes having to walk into the street when the men and women would crowd together on the sidewalk so that we would have had to jostle them to get by, we felt held together by there being something that had happened that they, the people who disliked us, did not understand.

We ourselves all understood the Cova, where it was rich and warm and not too brightly lighted, and noisy and smoky at certain hours, and there were always girls at the tables and the illustrated papers on a rack on the wall. The girls at the Cova were very patriotic, and I found that the most patriotic people in Italy were the café girls—and I believe they are still patriotic.

The boys at first were very polite about my medals and asked me what I had done to get them. I showed them the papers, which were written in very beautiful language and full of *fratellanza* and *abnegazione,* but which really said, with the adjectives removed, that I had been given the medals because I was an American. After that their manner changed a little toward me, although I was their friend against outsiders. I was a friend, but I was never really one of them after they had read the citations, because it had been different with them and they had done very different things to get their medals. I had been wounded, it was true; but we all knew that being wounded, after all, was really an accident. I was never ashamed of the ribbons, though, and sometimes, after the cock-tail hour, I would imagine myself having done all the things they had done to get their medals; but walking home at night through the empty streets with the cold wind and all the shops closed, trying to keep near the street lights, I knew that I would never have done such things, and I was very much afraid to die, and often lay in bed at night by myself, afraid to die and wondering how I would be when I went back to the front again.

The three with the medals were like hunting-hawks; and I was not a hawk, although I might seem a hawk to those who had never hunted; they, the three, knew better and so we drifted apart. But I stayed good friends with the boy who had been wounded his first day at the front, because he would never know now how he would have turned out; so he could never be accepted either, and I liked him because I thought perhaps he would not have turned out to be a hawk either.

The major, who had been the great fencer, did not believe in bravery, and spent much time while we sat in the machines correcting my grammar. He had complimented me on how I spoke Italian, and we talked together very easily. One day I had said that Italian seemed such an easy language to me that I could not take a great interest in it; everything was so easy to say. "Ah, yes," the major said. "Why, then, do you not take up the use of grammar?" So we took up the use of grammar, and soon Italian was such a difficult language that I was afraid to talk to him until I had the grammar straight in my mind.

The major came very regularly to the hospital. I do not think he ever missed a day, although I am sure he did not believe in the machines. There was a time when none of us believed in the machines, and one day the major said it was all nonsense. The machines were new then and it was we who were to prove them. It was an idiotic idea, he said, "a theory, like another." I had not learned my grammar, and he said I was a stupid impossible disgrace, and he was a fool to have bothered with me. He was a small man and he sat straight up in his chair with his right hand thrust into the machine and looked straight ahead at the wall while the straps thumped up and down with his fingers in them.

"What will you do when the war is over if it is over?" he asked me. "Speak grammatically!"

"I will go to the States."

"Are you married?"

"No, but I hope to be."

"The more of a fool you are," he said. He seemed very angry. "A man must not marry."

"Why, Signor Maggiore?"

"Don't call me 'Signor Maggiore.'"

"Why must not a man marry?"

"He cannot marry. He cannot marry," he said angrily. "If he is to lose everything, he should not place himself in a position to lose that. He should not place himself in a position to lose. He should find things he cannot lose."

He spoke very angrily and bitterly, and looked straight ahead while he talked.

"But why should he necessarily lose it?"

"He'll lose it," the major said. He was looking at the wall. Then he looked down at the machine and jerked his little hand out from between the straps and slapped it hard against his thigh. "He'll lose it," he almost shouted. "Don't argue with me!" Then he called to the attendant who ran the machines. "Come and turn this damned thing off."

He went back into the other room for the light treatment and the massage. Then I heard him ask the doctor if he might use his telephone and he shut the door. When he came back into the room, I was sitting in another machine. He was wearing his cape and had his cap on, and he came directly toward my machine and put his arm on my shoulder.

"I am so sorry," he said, and patted me on the shoulder with his good hand. "I would not be rude. My wife has just died. You must forgive me."

"Oh—" I said, feeling sick for him. "I am *so* sorry."

He stood there biting his lower lip. "It is very difficult," he said. "I cannot resign myself."

He looked straight past me and out through the window. Then he began to cry. "I am utterly unable to resign myself," he said and choked. And then crying, his head up looking at nothing, carrying himself straight and soldierly, with tears on both his cheeks and biting his lips, he walked past the machines and out the door.

The doctor told me that the major's wife, who was very young and whom he had not married until he was definitely invalided out of the war, had died of pneumonia. She had been sick only a few days. No one expected her to die. The major did not come to the hospital for three days. Then he came at the usual hour, wearing a black band on the sleeve of his uniform. When he came back, there were large framed photographs around the wall, of all sorts of wounds before and after they had been cured by the machines. In front of the machine the major used were three photographs of hands like his that were completely restored. I do not know where the doctor got them. I always understood we were the first to use the machines. The photographs did not make much difference to the major because he only looked out of the window.

DISCUSSION

The student may at first be puzzled to decide what this story is about. Indeed, a first reading if it be hasty, may yield little more than some excellent description of walks through a North Italian city in the winter, followed by an incident which the narrator witnessed in an Italian hospital. The incident does not concern the narrator directly. The last paragraph is quiet and neutral in tone; the significance of the incident is not pointed up so much as deliberately played down. The student, therefore, may be pardoned for feeling that the story is almost pointless.

It is true that the American boy who tells the story has nothing in particular happen to him in the story, and it is further true that the Italian major to whom something does happen does not come into sharp focus until the story is two-thirds over. Yet "In Another Country" is a highly unified story after all; and, as we shall see, it does not lack drama.

Is it the boy's story? Or is it the major's? The answer to this question is best postponed until we have seen toward what the story is building; and once we have seen that, the answer will perhaps appear to be not so important after all. In any case, we must begin by asking what is the boy's state of mind, and what is the situation in which he finds himself; for unless we understand these things, we shall scarcely see why the major and what happens to the major make so powerful an impact upon him—and through him upon us.

The narrator is evidently a boy of keen and alert senses. The sights and sounds and smells of wartime Milan register upon him very vividly. There are, for instance, such details as "The deer hung stiff and heavy and empty, and small birds flew in the wind and the wind turned their feathers," or "The chestnuts were warm afterward in your pocket." Indeed the boy's description of what he sees and hears is so vividly factual that we may not at first realize how much

concerned he is with the problem of bravery.

He has been given a medal, but he suspects that the medal has been given him, not because he has been brave but because he is an American fighting in the Italian Army. He is not at all sure that he really would be brave under a supreme test, and therefore feels closer to the boy who "had not been at the front long enough to get any medals" than he does to the three boys whom he calls "hunting hawks." He feels that he "was never really one of them after they had read the citations"; and his isolation here is reinforced by his being in a foreign country, and by the hostility of the common people toward all officers in general.

The first half of the story, then, does much more than merely describe a place and time with its appropriate atmosphere. It suggests the peculiar alienation of the narrator, though it does this quietly, and relates his sense of alienation to his own lack of confidence in himself. On one level this prepares for his response to the attention that the major pays to him. On a deeper level, however, it points to the more special interest that the major holds for him, for the major, though he has three medals, does not believe in bravery. Moreover, the major has no confidence in the machines. He pays little attention to them; he does not discuss the war; he spends his time correcting the boy's grammar. He is dry, civil, common-sensical, and apparently even cynical.

For all of these reasons, the major's sudden outburst against marriage and his bitterness and anger evidently shock the boy as they shock us. We, no more than the boy, understand this emotional explosion so much out of character until the major comes back to apologize and to say "I would not be rude. My wife has just died. You must forgive me." The momentary outbreak, however, actually underlines the iron control with which the major habitually disciplines himself. It suggests, furthermore, in what kind of personal philosophy this discipline is rooted: the major dreads all posturing and posing; he dreads anything that would possibly suggest personal indulgence of emotion. He prefers to keep his own deeds of bravery and his own sense of loss to himself. The man who does not believe in bravery is actually the bravest man of all, though his bravery is grounded not upon hope but upon despair.

Stated in these terms, the story might seem too obviously a little tract on bravery. Hemingway, of course, has not stated it in these terms. The story has been kept as dry and factual and understated as the major's own characteristic utterance. The kind of description given in the first half of the story plays its part in corroborating this quality of feeling. It also helps to undercut any sense of the author's having sentimentalized the major's tragedy. In the last paragraph, we get, for example, a few sentences which fill out the exposition—the fact that the major's wife had been sick for only a few days and the fact that her death had been shockingly unexpected. We get also a final picture of the major: the discreet black mourning band, the machine bearing three photographs of hands that had been "completely restored," and the major himself, not noticing them but looking "out of the window."

The major in his grief had said "I am utterly unable to resign myself." But after three days he has won to a state which, if not resignation, is at least one of outward calm, and which, if despair, is surely not self-pitying despair.

At this point the student might try to answer for himself two questions raised by this last paragraph: (1) Where would the doctor have got the three photographs of hands after treatment? (2) Why does the major, though obviously not believing in the curative power of the machines, return to the machine? We may add, as a third question, the question raised earlier: is this the major's story? Or is it the boy's story —the impact of the incident upon the boy?

This story is typical of Hemingway's characteristic work. The situations and characters of Hemingway's world are usually violent. There is the hard-drinking and sexually promiscuous world of *The Sun Also Rises;* the chaotic and brutal world of war as in *A Farewell to Arms, For Whom the Bell Tolls,* many of the inserted sketches of *In Our Time,* the play *The Fifth Column,* and some of the stories; the world of sport, as in "Fifty Grand," "My Old Man," "The Undefeated," "The Snows of Kilimanjaro"; the world of crime as in "The Killers," "The Gambler, the Nun, and the Radio," and *To Have*

and To Have Not. Even when the situation of a story does not fall into one of these categories, it usually involves a desperate risk, and behind it is the shadow of ruin, physical or spiritual. As for the typical characters, they are usually tough men, experienced in the hard worlds they inhabit, and not obviously given to emotional display or sensitive shrinking, men like Rinaldi or Frederick Henry of *A Farewell to Arms,* Robert Jordan of *For Whom the Bell Tolls,* Harry Morgan of *To Have and To Have Not,* the big-game hunter of "The Snows of Kilimanjaro," the old bullfighter of "The Undefeated," or the pugilist of "Fifty Grand." Or if the typical character is not of this seasoned order, he is a very young man, or boy, first entering the violent world and learning his first adjustment to it. Both typical characters are obviously to be found in "In Another Country": the tough experienced man who knows the hard world, and the boy who is being initiated into that world.

We have said that the shadow of ruin is behind the typical Hemingway situation. The typical character faces defeat or death. But out of defeat or death the character usually manages to salvage something. And here we discover Hemingway's special interest in such situations and such characters. His heroes are not defeated except upon their own terms. They are not squealers, welchers, compromisers, or cowards, and when they confront defeat, they realize that the stance they take, the stoic endurance, the stiff upper lip, mean a kind of victory. Defeated upon their own terms, some of them hold, even in the practical defeat, an ideal of themselves, some definition of how a man should behave, formulated or unformulated, by which they have lived. They represent some notion of a code, some notion of honor, which makes a man a man, and which distinguishes him from people who merely follow their random impulses and who are, by consequence, "messy."

Most writers—one is tempted to say all good writers—have a characteristic "world" in their fiction. The "world" may be a literal place—as the "South" of Faulkner, Katherine Anne Porter, or Eudora Welty. But if it is such a place, that place will be inhabited by a special kind of character in a special kind of situation. For example, the South of Faulkner is not at all the South of Katherine Anne Porter, for the "South" of each is to some extent the projection of the author. One can push this notion further still, the world of Ernest Hemingway cannot be located on any map: it is the world defined in great part by the special kind of character in the special kind of situation that engages his imagination.

This leads to the notion that the special "world" of a writer is neither accidental nor arbitrary. The kind of world a writer knows, in the literal sense, is, of course, an accident of his birth and experience. Yet on reflection, we must modify even this statement. The world of a writer depends upon the accident of his birth, but not, in a final sense, upon the accident of his experience. For any man's experience is, within limits, a projection of himself: as his character develops in time (a development modified, of course, by accidents and limitations of experience) it rejects or accepts, flees from or seeks, certain kinds of experience. So even the world of factual experience available to a writer, including his world of observation, the world on which he must necessarily base his imaginatively projected world, is not merely accidental; it is in itself, in part at least, a creative expression of his own process of living.

Nor is the "world" of a writer arbitrary. A good writer does not deliberately, and by an act of will, select a world that he thinks would be popular among his readers. He turns, more or less instinctively, to the world that not only is available to him in the factual sense but is, we may say, *expressively available* to him—that is, *to a world that will embody and dramatize the issues that he feels significant in experience.*

To sum up this point, the special world of a writer has some aura of significance in itself. Such a world embodies significantly the conflict that underlies the specific conflicts in the individual works of fiction (or poems or plays, for that matter), and the problem of values that underlies the specific themes treated in the individual works.

EXERCISE

1. Turn to the essay "Why We Read Fiction" (page 553). How does it relate to the problem of the "world" of a writer? To the "world" a reader finds congenial and significant?

2. In the story "In Another Country," locate the paragraph beginning: "There were three boys who came each day who were about the same age I was," and ending, "We only knew then that there was always the war, but that we were not going to it any more." What is the significance of this paragraph for the story?

3. Do you find any points of similarity in either theme or treatment between this story and "The Lagoon," by Conrad (page 223)?

The Killers

ERNEST HEMINGWAY (1899-1961)

THE DOOR of Henry's lunch-room opened and two men came in. They sat down at the counter.

"What's yours?" George asked them.

"I don't know," one of the men said. "What do you want to eat, Al?"

"I don't know," said Al. "I don't know what I want to eat."

Outside it was getting dark. The street-light came on outside the window. The two men at the counter read the menu. From the other end of the counter Nick Adams watched them. He had been talking to George when they came in.

"I'll have a roast pork tenderloin with apple sauce and mashed potatoes," the first man said.

"It isn't ready yet."

"What the hell do you put it on the card for?"

"That's the dinner," George explained. "You can get that at six o'clock."

George looked at the clock on the wall behind the counter.

"It's five o'clock."

"The clock says twenty minutes past five," the second man said.

"It's twenty minutes fast."

"Oh, to hell with the clock," the first man said. "What have you got to eat?"

"I can give you any kind of sandwiches," George said. "You can have ham and eggs, bacon and eggs, liver and bacon, or a steak."

"Give me chicken croquettes with green peas and cream sauce and mashed potatoes."

"That's the dinner."

"Everything we want's the dinner, eh? That's the way you work it."

"I can give you ham and eggs, bacon and eggs, liver——"

"I'll take ham and eggs," the man called Al said. He wore a derby hat and a black overcoat buttoned across the chest. His face was small and white and he had tight lips. He wore a silk muffler and gloves.

"Give me bacon and eggs," said the other man. He was about the same size as Al. Their faces were different, but they were dressed like twins. Both wore overcoats too tight for them. They sat leaning forward, their elbows on the counter.

"Got anything to drink?" Al asked.

"Silver beer, bevo, ginger-ale," George said.

"I mean you got anything to *drink?*"

"Just those I said."

"This is a hot town," said the other. "What do they call it?"

"Summit."

"Ever hear of it?" Al asked his friend.

"No," said the friend.

"What do you do here nights?" Al asked.

"They eat the dinner," his friend said. "They all come here and eat the big dinner."

"That's right," George said.

"So you think that's right?" Al asked George.

"Sure," said George.

"You're a pretty bright boy, aren't you?"

"Sure," said George.

"Well, you're not," said the other little man. "Is he, Al?"

"He's dumb," said Al. He turned to Nick. "What's your name?"

"Adams."

"Another bright boy," Al said. "Ain't he a bright boy, Max?"

"The town's full of bright boys," Max said.

George put the two platters, one of ham and eggs, the other of bacon and eggs, on the counter. He set down two side-dishes of fried potatoes and closed the wicket into the kitchen.

"Which is yours?" he asked Al.

"Don't you remember?"

"Ham and eggs."

"Just a bright boy," Max said. He leaned forward and took the ham and eggs. Both men ate with their gloves on. George watched them eat.

"What are *you* looking at?" Max looked at George.

"Nothing."

"The hell you were. You were looking at me."

"Maybe the boy meant it for a joke, Max," Al said.

George laughed.

"*You* don't have to laugh," Max said to him. "*You* don't have to laugh at all, see?"

"All right," said George.

"So he thinks it's all right." Max turned to Al. "He thinks it's all right. That's a good one."

"Oh, he's a thinker," Al said. They went on eating.

"What's the bright boy's name down the counter?" Al asked Max.

"Hey, bright boy," Max said to Nick. "You go around on the other side of the counter with your boy friend."

"What's the idea?" Nick asked.

"There isn't any idea."

"You better go around, bright boy," Al said. Nick went around behind the counter.

"What's the idea?" George asked.

"None of your damn business," Al said. "Who's out in the kitchen?"

"The nigger."

"What do you mean the nigger?"

"The nigger that cooks."

"Tell him to come in."

"What's the idea?"

"Tell him to come in."

"Where do you think you are?"

"We know damn well where we are," the man called Max said. "Do we look silly?"

"You talk silly," Al said to him. "What the hell do you argue with this kid for? Listen," he said to George, "tell the nigger to come out here."

"What are you going to do to him?"

"Nothing. Use your head, bright boy. What would we do to a nigger?"

George opened the slit that opened back into the kitchen. "Sam," he called. "Come in here a minute."

The door to the kitchen opened and the nigger came in. "What was it?" he asked. The two men at the counter took a look at him.

"All right, nigger. You stand right there," Al said.

Sam, the nigger, standing in his apron, looked at the two men sitting at the counter. "Yes, sir," he said. Al got down from his stool.

"I'm going back to the kitchen with the nigger and bright boy," he said. "Go on back to the kitchen, nigger. You go with him, bright boy." The little man walked after Nick and Sam, the cook, back into the kitchen. The door shut after them. The man called Max sat at the counter opposite George. He didn't look at George but looked in the mirror that ran along back of the counter. Henry's had been made over from a saloon into a lunch-counter.

"Well, bright boy," Max said, looking into the mirror, "why don't you say something?"

"What's it all about?"

"Hey, Al," Max called, "bright boy wants to know what it's all about."

"Why don't you tell him?" Al's voice came from the kitchen.

"What do you think it's all about?"

"I don't know."

"What do you think?"

Max looked into the mirror all the time he was talking.

"I wouldn't say."

"Hey, Al, bright boy says he wouldn't say what he thinks it's all about."

"I can hear you, all right," Al said from the kitchen. He had propped open the slit that dishes passed through into the kitchen with a catsup bottle. "Listen, bright boy," he said from the kitchen to George. "Stand a little further along the bar. You move a little to the left, Max." He was like a photographer arranging for a group picture.

"Talk to me, bright boy," Max said. "What do you think's going to happen?"

George did not say anything.

"I'll tell you," Max said. "We're going to kill a Swede. Do you know a big Swede named Ole Andreson?"

"Yes."

"He comes here to eat every night, don't he?"

"Sometimes he comes here."

"He comes here at six o'clock, don't he?"

"If he comes."

"We know all that, bright boy," Max said. "Talk about something else. Ever go to the movies?"

"Once in a while."

"You ought to go to the movies more. The movies are fine for a bright boy like you."

"What are you going to kill Ole Andreson for? What did he ever do to you?"

"He never had a chance to do anything to us. He never even seen us."

"And he's only going to see us once," Al said from the kitchen.

"What are you going to kill him for, then?" George asked.

"We're killing him for a friend. Just to oblige a friend, bright boy."

"Shut up," said Al from the kitchen. "You talk too goddam much."

"Well, I got to keep bright boy amused. Don't I, bright boy?"

"You talk too damn much," Al said. "The nigger and my bright boy are amused by themselves. I got them tied up like a couple of girl friends in the convent."

"I suppose you were in a convent."

"You never know."

"You were in a kosher convent. That's where you were."

George looked up at the clock.

"If anybody comes in you tell them the cook is off, and if they keep after it, you tell them you'll go back and cook yourself. Do you get that, bright boy?"

"All right," George said. "What you going to do with us afterward?"

"That'll depend," Max said. "That's one of those things you never know at the time."

George looked up at the clock. It was a quarter past six. The door from the street opened. A streetcar motorman came in.

"Hello, George," he said. "Can I get supper?"

"Sam's gone out," George said. "He'll be back in about half an hour."

"I'd better go up the street," the motorman said. George looked at the clock. It was twenty minutes past six.

"That was nice, bright boy," Max said. "You're a regular little gentleman."

"He knew I'd blow his head off," Al said from the kitchen.

"No," said Max. "It ain't that. Bright boy is nice. He's a nice boy. I like him."

At six-fifty-five George said: "He's not coming."

Two other people had been in the lunchroom. Once George had gone out to the kitchen and made a ham-and-egg sandwich "to go" that a man wanted to take with him. Inside the kitchen he saw Al, his derby hat tipped back, sitting on a stool beside the wicket with the muzzle of a sawed-off shotgun resting on the ledge. Nick and the cook were back to back in the corner, a towel tied in each of their mouths. George had cooked the sandwich, wrapped it up in oiled paper, put it in a bag, brought it in, and the man had paid for it and gone out.

"Bright boy can do everything," Max said. "He can cook and everything. You'd make some girl a nice wife, bright boy."

"Yes?" George said. "Your friend, Ole Andreson, isn't going to come."

"We'll give him ten minutes," Max said.

Max watched the mirror and the clock. The hands of the clock marked seven o'clock, and then five minutes past seven.

"Come on, Al," said Max. "We'd better go. He's not coming."

"Better give him five minutes," Al said from the kitchen.

In the five minutes a man came in, and George explained that the cook was sick.

"Why the hell don't you get another cook?" the man asked. "Aren't you running a lunch-counter?" He went out.

"Come on, Al," Max said.

"What about the two bright boys and the nigger?"

"They're all right."

"You think so?"

"Sure. We're through with it."

"I don't like it," said Al. "It's sloppy. You talk too much."

"Oh, what the hell," said Max. "We got to keep amused, haven't we?"

"You talk too much, all the same," Al said. He came out from the kitchen. The cut-off barrels of the shotgun made a slight bulge under the waist of his too tight-fitting overcoat. He straightened his coat with his gloved hands.

"So long, bright boy," he said to George. "You got a lot of luck."

"That's the truth," Max said. "You ought to play the races, bright boy."

The two of them went out the door. George watched them, through the window, pass under the arc-light and cross the street. In their tight overcoats and derby hats they looked like a vaudeville team. George went back through the swinging-door into the kitchen and untied Nick and the cook.

"I don't want any more of that," said Sam, the cook. "I don't want any more of that."

Nick stood up. He had never had a towel in his mouth before.

"Say," he said. "What the hell?" He was trying to swagger it off.

"They were going to kill Ole Andreson," George said. "They were going to shoot him when he came in to eat."

"Ole Andreson?"

"Sure."

The cook felt the corners of his mouth with his thumbs.

"They all gone?" he asked.

"Yeah," said George. "They're gone now."

"I don't like it," said the cook. "I don't like any of it at all."

"Listen," George said to Nick. "You better go see Ole Andreson."

"All right."

"You better not have anything to do with it at all," Sam the cook, said. "You better stay way out of it."

"Don't go if you don't want to," George said.

"Mixing up in this ain't going to get you anywhere," the cook said. "You stay out of it."

"I'll go see him," Nick said to George. "Where does he live?"

The cook turned away.

"Little boys always know what they want to do," he said.

"He lives up at Hirsch's rooming-house," George said to Nick.

"I'll go up there."

Outside the arc-light shone through the bare branches of a tree. Nick walked up the street beside the car-tracks and turned at the next arc-light down a side-street. Three houses up the street was Hirsch's rooming-house. Nick walked up the two steps and pushed the bell. A woman came to the door.

"Is Ole Andreson here?"

"Do you want to see him?"

"Yes, if he's in."

Nick followed the woman up a flight of stairs and back to the end of a corridor. She knocked on the door.

"Who is it?"

"It's somebody to see you, Mr. Andreson," the woman said.

"It's Nick Adams."

"Come in."

Nick opened the door and went into the room. Ole Andreson was lying on the bed with all his clothes on. He had been a heavyweight prizefighter and he was too long for the bed. He lay with his head on two pillows. He did not look at Nick.

"What was it?" he asked.

"I was up at Henry's," Nick said, "and two fellows came in and tied up me and the cook, and they said they were going to kill you."

It sounded silly when he said it. Ole Andreson said nothing.

"They put us out in the kitchen," Nick went on. "They were going to shoot you when you came in to supper."

Ole Andreson looked at the wall and did not say anything.

"George thought I better come and tell you about it."

"There isn't anything I can do about it," Ole Andreson said.

"I'll tell you what they were like."

"I don't want to know what they were like," Ole Andreson said. He looked at the wall. "Thanks for coming to tell me about it."

"That's all right."

Nick looked at the big man lying on the bed.

"Don't you want me to go and see the police?"

"No," Ole Andreson said. "That wouldn't do any good."

"Isn't there something I could do?"

"No. There ain't anything to do."

"Maybe it was just a bluff."

"No. It ain't just a bluff."

Ole Andreson rolled over toward the wall.

"The only thing is," he said, talking toward the wall, "I just can't make up my mind to go out. I been in here all day."

"Couldn't you get out of town?"

"No," Ole Andreson said. "I'm through with all that running around."

He looked at the wall.

"There ain't anything to do now."

"Couldn't you fix it up some way?"

"No. I got in wrong." He talked in the same flat voice. "There ain't anything to do. After a while I'll make up my mind to go out."

"I better go back and see George," Nick said.

"So long," said Ole Andreson. He did not look toward Nick. "Thanks for coming around."

Nick went out. As he shut the door he saw Ole Andreson with all his clothes on, lying on the bed looking at the wall.

"He's been in his room all day," the landlady said downstairs. "I guess he don't feel well. I said to him: 'Mr. Andreson, you ought to go out and take a walk on a nice fall day like this,' but he didn't feel like it."

"He doesn't want to go out."

"I'm sorry he don't feel well," the woman said. "He's an awfully nice man. He was in the ring, you know."

"I know it."

"You'd never know it except from the way his face is," the woman said. They stood talking just inside the street door. "He's just as gentle."

"Well, good-night, Mrs. Hirsch," Nick said.

"I'm not Mrs. Hirsch," the woman said. "She owns the place. I just look after it for her. I'm Mrs. Bell."

"Well, good-night, Mrs. Bell," Nick said.

"Good-night," the woman said.

Nick walked up the dark street to the corner under the arc-light, and then along the car-tracks to Henry's eating-house. George was inside, back of the counter.

"Did you see Ole?"

"Yes," said Nick. "He's in his room and he won't go out."

The cook opened the door from the kitchen when he heard Nick's voice.

"I don't even listen to it," he said and shut the door.

"Did you tell him about it?" George asked.

"Sure. I told him but he knows what it's all about."

"What's he going to do?"

"Nothing."

"They'll kill him."

"I guess they will."

"He must have got mixed up in something in Chicago."

"I guess so," said Nick.

"It's a hell of a thing."

"It's an awful thing," Nick said.

They did not say anything. George reached down for a towel and wiped the counter.

"I wonder what he did?" Nick said.

"Double-crossed somebody. That's what they kill them for."

"I'm going to get out of this town," Nick said.

"Yes," said George. "That's a good thing to do."

"I can't stand to think about him waiting in the room and knowing he's going to get it. It's too damned awful."

"Well," said George, "you better not think about it."

DISCUSSION

"In Another Country" and "The Killers" are very different in certain respects, but we can readily see how they spring from the same basic attitude toward life. In fact, in any good writer there is such a basic attitude which may find expression in stories or novels which have, superficially regarded, very different themes and tones. One of the limitations of such a book as our present one is the fact that, for the most part, we deal with stories individually and cannot see how an acquaintance with the body of a writer's work may give added force and significance to the separate items. But in these two stories, at least, we can see something of the continuity characteristic of Hemingway's whole work.

EXERCISE

1. In our discussion of "In Another Country," we have said that Hemingway's stories and novels are usually about a man toughened by experience to the point where he can survive by means of a certain stoical code of bravery, or about a young man who is being initiated into the brutal world that demands such a code for those who would survive with honor. In "The Killers," the story begins with an attempt of gangsters to kill an exprize-fighter, Ole Andreson, but well before the end of the story we have lost touch with Ole. On whom is the final effect of the story made? In other words, who is the central character? Which of the two characteristic Hemingway situations does this story illustrate?

2. How is the necessary exposition given in this story? How does the author avoid breaking the complete dramatic objectivity of his method? Can you say how this objective method, which gives no comment by the author, no interpretation of situations, ideas, or feelings, is related to Hemingway's characteristic subject matter and the characteristic attitude toward that subject matter? To put it another way, is this method the method which might be used by one of Hemingway's own characters if he were writing a story?

3. Hemingway has been praised for his handling of dialogue. Can you describe his method? How does he employ devices such as rhythm and repetition to give his dialogue a sense of movement?

4. In the novel *A Farewell to Arms* the hero, who is a typical Hemingway character, says of the big, official talk of the First World War:

I was always embarrassed by the words sacred, glorious, and sacrifice and the expression in vain. We had heard them, sometimes standing in the rain almost out of earshot, so that only the shouted words came through, and had read them, on proclamations that were slapped up by billposters over other proclamations, now for a long time, and I had seen nothing sacred, and the things that were glorious had no glory and the sacrifices were like the stockyards in Chicago if nothing was done with the meat except to bury it. There were many words that you could not stand to hear and finally only the names of places had dignity. . . . Abstract words such as glory, honor, courage, or hallow were obscene beside the concrete names of villages, the numbers of roads, the names of rivers, the numbers of regiments and the dates.

How does the attitude expressed here relate to the general style of Hemingway? Is his vocabulary characterized by big or little words, by abstract or concrete words? What is his usual sentence structure like? Is it simple or complex? Is subordination generally used? Can you say how the general style of Hemingway, as you know it through these two stories, is appropriate for the attitude expressed in his work?

5. Read the two essays "Homage to Hemingway," by John Peale Bishop (page 526), and "Ernest Hemingway," by Dwight MacDonald (page 532). In what way, if any, do these essays change your view of these stories by Hemingway?

The Gentleman from San Francisco

IVAN BUNIN (1870-1953)

Translated by A. YARMOLINSKY

"Alas, Alas, that great city Babylon, that mighty city!"—
—REVELATION OF ST. JOHN

THE GENTLEMAN from San Francisco—neither at Naples nor on Capri could any one recall his name—with his wife and daughter, was on his way to Europe, where he intended to stay for two whole years, solely for the pleasure of it.

He was firmly convinced that he had a full right to a rest, enjoyment, a long comfortable trip, and what not. This conviction had a two-fold reason: first he was rich, and second, despite his fifty-eight years, he was just about to enter the stream of life's pleasures. Until now he had not really lived, but simply existed, to be sure—fairly well, yet putting off his fondest hopes for the future. He toiled unweariedly —the Chinese, whom he imported by thousands for his works, knew full well what it meant— and finally he saw that he had made much, and that he had nearly come up to the level of those whom he had once taken as a model, and he decided to catch his breath. The class of people to which he belonged was in the habit of beginning its enjoyment of life with a trip to Europe, India, Egypt. He made up his mind to do the same. Of course, it was first of all himself that he desired to reward for the years of toil, but he was also glad for his wife and daughter's sake. His wife was never distinguished by any extraordinary impressionability, but then, all elderly American women are ardent travelers. As for his daughter, a girl of marriageable age, and somewhat sickly—travel was the very thing she needed. Not to speak of the benefit to her health, do not happy meetings occur during travels? Abroad, one may chance to sit at the same table with a prince, or examine frescoes side by side with a multi-millionaire.

The itinerary the Gentleman from San Francisco planned out was an extensive one. In December and January he expected to relish the sun of southern Italy, monuments of antiquity, the tarantella, serenades of wandering minstrels, and that which at his age is felt most keenly— the love, not entirely disinterested though, of young Neapolitan girls. The Carnival days he planned to spend at Nice and Monte Carlo, which at that time of the year is the meeting-place of the choicest society, the society upon which depend all the blessings of civilization: the cut of dress suits, the stability of thrones, the declaration of wars, the prosperity of hotels. Some of these people passionately give themselves over to automobile and boat races, others to roulette, others, again, busy themselves with what is called flirtation, and others shoot pigeons, which soar so beautifully from the dovecote, hover awhile over the emerald lawn, on the background of the forget-me-not colored sea, and then suddenly hit the ground, like little white lumps. Early March he wanted to devote to Florence, and at Easter, to hear the Miserere in Paris. His plans also included Venice, Paris, bull-baiting at Seville, bathing on the British Islands, also Athens, Constantinople, Palestine, Egypt, and even Japan, of course, on the way back. . . . And at first things went very well indeed.

It was the end of November, and all the way to Gibraltar the ship sailed across seas which were either clad by icy darkness or swept by storms carrying wet snow. But there were no accidents, and the vessel did not even roll. The passengers—all people of consequence—were numerous, and the steamer, the famous *Atlantis,* resembled the most expensive European hotel with all improvements: a night refreshment-bar, Oriental baths, even a newspaper of its own. The manner of living was a most aristocratic one; passengers rose early, awakened by the shrill voice of a bugle, filling the corridors at the gloomy hour when the day broke slowly and sulkily over the grayish-green watery desert, which rolled heavily in the fog. After putting on their flannel pajamas, they took coffee, chocolate, cocoa; they seated themselves in marble baths, went through their exercises, whetting their appetites and increasing their sense of well-being, dressed for the day, and had their breakfast. Till eleven o'clock they were supposed to stroll on the deck, breathing in the chill freshness of the ocean, or they played table-tennis, or other games which arouse the appetite. At eleven o'clock a collation was served consisting of sandwiches and bouillon, after which people read their newspapers, quietly waiting for luncheon, which was more nourishing and varied than the breakfast. The next two hours were given to rest; all the decks were crowded then with steamer chairs, on which the passengers, wrapped in plaids, lay stretched, dozing lazily, or watching the cloudy sky and the foamy-fringed water hillocks flashing beyond the sides of the vessel. At five o'clock, refreshed and gay, they drank strong, fragrant tea; at seven the sound of the bugle announced a dinner of nine courses. . . . Then the Gentleman from San Francisco, rubbing his hands in an onrush of vital energy, hastened to his luxurious stateroom to dress.

In the evening, all the decks of the *Atlantis* yawned in the darkness, shone with their innumerable fiery eyes, and a multitude of servants worked with increased feverishness in the kitchens, dish-washing compartments, and wine-cellars. The ocean, which heaved about the sides of the ship, was dreadful, but no one thought of it. All had faith in the controlling power of the captain, a red-headed giant, heavy and very sleepy, who, clad in a uniform with broad golden stripes, looked like a huge idol, and but rarely emerged, for the benefit of the public, from his mysterious retreat. On the forecastle, the siren gloomily roared or screeched in a fit of mad rage, but few of the diners heard the siren: its hellish voice was covered by the sounds of an excellent string orchestra, which played ceaselessly and exquisitely in a vast hall, decorated with marble and spread with velvety carpets. The hall was flooded with torrents of light, radiated by crystal lustres and gilt chandeliers; it was filled with a throng of bejeweled ladies in low-necked dresses, of men in dinner-coats, graceful waiters, and deferential maîtres-d'hôtel. One of these—who accepted wine orders exclusively—wore a chain on his neck like some lord mayor. The evening dress, and the ideal linen, made the Gentleman from San Francisco look very young. Dry-skinned, of average height, strongly, though irregularly built, glossy with thorough washing and cleaning, and moderately animated, he sat in the golden splendor of this palace. Near him stood a bottle of amber-colored Johannisberg, and goblets of most delicate glass and of varied sizes, surmounted by a frizzled bunch of fresh hyacinths. There was something Mongolian in his yellowish face with its trimmd silvery moustache; his large teeth glimmered with gold fillings, and his strong, bald head had a dull glow, like old ivory. His wife, a big, broad and placid woman, was dressed richly, but in keeping with her age. Complicated, but light, transparent, and innocently immodest was the dress of his daughter, tall and slender, with magnificent hair gracefully combed; her breath was sweet with violet-scented tablets, and she had a number of tiny and most delicate pink pimples near her lips and between her slightly-powdered shoulder blades. . . .

The dinner lasted two whole hours, and was followed by dances in the dancing hall, while the men—the Gentleman from San Francisco among them—made their way to the refreshment bar, where negroes in red jackets and with eye-balls like shelled hard-boiled eggs, waited on them. There, with their feet on tables, smoking Havana cigars, and drinking themselves purple in the face, they settled the destinies of nations on the basis of the latest political and stock exchange news. Outside, the ocean tossed up black mountains with a thud; and the snow-storm hissed furiously in the rigging grown heavy with slush; the ship trembled in every limb, struggling with the storm and ploughing with difficulty the shifting and seething mountainous masses that threw far and high their foaming tails; the siren groaned in agony, choked by storm and fog; the watchmen in their towers froze and almost went out of their minds under the superhuman stress of attention. Like the gloomy and sultry mass of the inferno, like its last, ninth circle, was the submersed womb of the steamer, where monstrous furnaces yawned with red-hot open jaws, and emitted deep, hooting sounds, and where the stokers, stripped to the waist, and purple with reflected flames, bathed in their own dirty, acid sweat. And here, in the refreshment bar, carefree men, with their feet, encased in dancing shoes, on the table, sipped cognac and liqueurs, swam in waves of spiced smoke, and exchanged subtle remarks, while in the dancing hall everything sparkled and radiated light, warmth and joy. The couples now turned around in a waltz, now swayed in the tango; and the music, sweetly shameless and sad, persisted in its ceaseless entreaties. . . . There were many persons of note in this magnificent crowd: an ambassador, a dry, modest old man; a great millionaire, shaved, tall, of an indefinite age, who, in his old-fashioned dress-coat, looked like a prelate; also a famous Spanish writer, and an international belle, already slightly faded and of dubious morals. There was also among them a loving pair, exquisite and refined, whom everybody watched with curiosity and who did not conceal their bliss; he danced only with her, sang—with great

skill—only to her accompaniment, and they were so charming, so graceful. The captain alone knew that they had been hired by the company at a good salary to play at love, and that they had been sailing now on one, now on another steamer, for quite a long time.

In Gibraltar everybody was gladdened by the sun, and by the weather which was like early spring. A new passenger appeared aboard the *Atlantis* and aroused everybody's interest. It was the crown-prince of an Asiatic state, who traveled incognito, a small man, very nimble, though looking as if made of wood, broad-faced, narrow-eyed, in gold-rimmed glasses, somewhat disagreeable because of his long black moustache, which was sparse like that of a corpse, but otherwise—charming, plain, modest. In the Mediterranean the breath of winter was again felt. The seas were heavy and motley like a peacock's tail and the waves, stirred up by the gay gusts of the tramontane, tossed their white crests under a sparkling and perfectly clear sky. Next morning, the sky grew paler and the skyline misty. Land was near. Then Ischia and Capri came in sight, and one could descry, through an opera-glass, Naples, looking like pieces of sugar strewn at the foot of an indistinct dove-colored mass, and above them, a snow-covered chain of distant mountains. The decks were crowded, many ladies and gentlemen put on light-fur-coats; Chinese servants, bandy-legged youths—with pitch black braids down to the heels and with girlish, thick eyelashes—always quiet and speaking in a whisper, were carrying to the foot of the staircases, plaid wraps, canes, and crocodile-leather valises and hand-bags. The daughter of the Gentleman from San Francisco stood near the prince, who, by a happy chance, had been introduced to her the evening before, and feigned to be looking steadily at something far-off, which he was pointing out to her, while he was, at the same time, explaining something, saying something rapidly and quietly. He was so small that he looked like a boy among other men, and he was not handsome at all. And then there was something strange about him; his glasses, derby, and coat were most commonplace, but there was something horse-like in the hair of his sparse moustache, and the thin, tanned skin of his flat face looked as though it were somewhat stretched and varnished. But the girl listened to him, and so great was her excitement that she could hardly grasp the meaning of his words, her heart palpitated with incomprehensible rapture and with pride that he was standing and speaking with her and nobody else. Everything about him was different: his dry hands, his clean skin, under which flowed ancient kingly blood, even his light shoes and his European dress, plain, but singularly tidy—everything hid an inexplicable fascination and engendered thoughts of love. And the Gentleman from San Francisco himself, in a silk-hat, gray leggings, patent leather shoes, kept eyeing the famous beauty who was standing near him, a tall, stately blonde, with eyes painted according to the latest Parisian fashion, and a tiny, bent peeled-off pet-dog, to whom she addressed herself. And the daughter, in a kind of vague perplexity, tried not to notice him.

Like all wealthy Americans he was very liberal when traveling, and believed in the complete sincerity and goodwill of those who so painstakingly fed him, served him day and night, anticipating his slightest desire, protected him from dirt and disturbance, hauled things for him, hailed carriers, and delivered his luggage to hotels. So it was everywhere, and it had to be so at Naples. Meanwhile, Naples grew and came nearer. The musicians, with their shining brass instruments, had already formed a group on the deck, and all of a sudden deafened everybody with the triumphant sounds of a ragtime march. The giant captain, in his full uniform appeared on the bridge and like a gracious pagan idol, waved his hands to the passengers —and it seemed to the Gentleman from San Francisco, as it did to all the rest, that for him alone thundered the march, so greatly loved by proud America, and that him alone did the captain congratulate on the safe arrival. And when the *Atlantis* had finally entered the port and all its many-decked mass leaned against the quay, and the gang-plank began to rattle heavily,—what a crowd of porters, with their assistants, in caps with golden galloons, what a crowd of various boys and husky ragamuffins with pads of colored postal cards attacked the Gentleman from San Francisco, offering their

services! With kindly contempt he grinned at these beggars, and, walking towards the automobile of the hotel where the prince might stop, muttered between his teeth, now in English, now in Italian—"Go away! *Via.* . . ."

Immediately, life at Naples began to follow a set routine. Early in the morning breakfast was served in the gloomy dining-room, swept by a wet draught from the open windows looking upon a stony garden, while outside the sky was cloudy and cheerless, and a crowd of guides swarmed at the door of the vestibule. Then came the first smiles of the warm roseate sun, and from the high suspended balcony, a broad vista unfolded itself: Vesuvius, wrapped to its base in radiant morning vapors; the pearly ripple, touched to silver, of the bay, the delicate outline of Capri on the skyline; tiny asses dragging two-wheeled buggies along the soft, sticky embankment, and detachments of little soldiers marching somewhere to the tune of cheerful and defiant music.

Next on the day's program was a slow automobile ride along crowded, narrow, and damp corridors of streets, between high, many-windowed buildings. It was followed by visits to museums, lifelessly clean and lighted evenly and pleasantly, but as though with the dull light cast by snow; then to churches, cold, smelling of wax, always alike: a majestic entrance, closed by a ponderous, leather curtain, and inside—a vast, void, silence, quiet flames of seven-branched candlesticks, sending forth a red glow from where they stood at the farther end, on the bedecked altar—a lonely, old woman lost among the dark wooden benches, slippery gravestones under the feet, and somebody's "Descent from the Cross," infallibly famous. At one o'clock—luncheon, on the mountain of San-Martius, where at noon the choicest people gathered, and where the daughter of the Gentleman from San Francisco once almost fainted with joy, because it seemed to her that she saw the prince in the hall, although she had learned from the newspapers that he had temporarily left for Rome. At five o'clock it was customary to take tea at the hotel, in a smart salon, where it was far too warm because of the carpets and the blazing fireplaces; and then came dinner-time—and again did the mighty, commanding voice of the gong resound throughout the building, again did silk rustle and the mirrors reflect files of ladies in low-necked dresses ascending the staircases, and again the splendid palatial dining hall opened with broad hospitality, and again the musicians' jackets formed red patches on the estrade, and the black figures of the waiters swarmed around the maître-d'hôtel, who, with extraordinary skill, poured a thick pink soup into plates. . . . As everywhere, the dinner was the crown of the day. People dressed for it as for a wedding, and so abundant was it in food, wines, mineral waters, sweets and fruits, that about eleven o'clock in the evening chambermaids would carry to all the rooms hot-water bags.

That year, however, December did not happen to be a very propitious one. The doormen were abashed when people spoke to them about the weather, and shrugged their shoulders guiltily, mumbling that they could not recollect such a year, although, to tell the truth, that it was not the first year they mumbled those words, usually adding that "things are terrible everywhere"; that unprecedented showers and storms had broken out on the Riviera, that it was snowing in Athens, that Ætna, too, was all blocked up with snow, and glowed brightly at night, and that tourists were fleeing from Palermo to save themselves from the cold spell. . . .

That winter, the morning sun daily deceived Naples; toward noon the sky would invariably grow gray, and a light rain would begin to fall, growing thicker and duller. Then the palms at the hotel porch glistened disagreeably like wet tin, the town appeared exceptionally dirty and congested, the museums too monotonous, the cigars of the drivers in their rubber rain-coats, which flattened in the wind like wings, intolerably stinking, and the energetic flapping of their whips over their thin-necked nags—obviously false. The shoes of the signors, who cleaned the street-car tracks, were in a frightful state; the women who splashed in the mud, with black hair unprotected from the rain, were ugly and short-legged, and the humidity mingled with the foul smell of rotting fish, that came from the foaming sea, was simply disheartening. And so, early-morning quarrels began to break out between the Gentleman from San Francisco and his wife; and their daughter now grew pale and suffered from headaches, and now became animated, enthusiastic over everything, and at such times was lovely and beautiful. Beautiful were the tender, complex feelings which her meeting with the ungainly man aroused in her—the man in whose veins flowed unusual blood, for, after all, it does not matter what in particular stirs up a maiden's soul: money, or fame, or nobility of birth. . . . Everybody assured the tourists that it was quite different at Sorrento and on Capri, that lemon trees were blossoming there, that it was warmer and sunnier there, the morals purer, and the wine less adulterated. And the family from San Francisco decided to set out with all their luggage for Capri. They planned to settle down at Sorrento, but first to visit the island, tread the stones where stood Tiberius's palaces, examine the fabulous wonders of the Blue Grotto, and listen to the bagpipes of Abruzzi, who roam about the island during the whole month preceding Christmas and sing the praises of the Madonna.

On the day of departure—a very memorable day for the family from San Francisco—the sun did not appear even in the morning. A heavy winter fog covered Vesuvius down to its very base and hung like a gray curtain low over the leaden surge of the sea, hiding it completely at a distance of half a mile. Capri was completely out of sight, as though it had never existed on this earth. And the little steamboat which was making for the island tossed and pitched so fiercely that the family lay prostrated on the sofas in the miserable cabin of the little steamer, with their feet wrapped in plaids and their eyes shut because of their nausea. The older lady suffered, as she thought, most; several times she was overcome with sea-sickness, and it seemed to her then she was dying, but the chambermaid, who repeatedly brought her the basin, and who for many years, in heat and in cold, had been tossing on these waves, ever on the alert, ever kindly to all—the chambermaid only laughed. The lady's daughter was frightfully pale and kept a slice of lemon between her teeth. Not even the hope of an unexpected meeting with the prince at Sorrento, where he planned to arrive on Christmas, served to cheer her. The Gentleman from San Francisco, who was lying on his back, dressed in a large overcoat and a big cap, did not loosen his jaws throughout the voyage. His face grew dark, his moustache white, and his head ached heavily; for the last few days, because of the bad weather, he had drunk far too much in the evenings.

And the rain kept on beating against the rattling window panes, and water dripped down from them on the sofas; the howling wind attacked the masts, and sometimes, aided by a heavy sea, it laid the little steamer on its side, and then something below rolled about with a rattle.

While the steamer was anchored at Castellamare and Sorrento, the situation was more cheerful; but even here the ship rolled terribly, and the coast with all its precipices, gardens and pines, with its pink and white hotels and hazy mountains clad in curling verdure, flew up and down as if it were on swings. The rowboats hit against the sides of the steamer, the sailors and the deck passengers shouted at the top of their voices, and somewhere a baby screamed as if it were being crushed to pieces. A wet wind blew through the door, and from a wavering barge flying the flag of the Hotel Royal, an urchin kept on unwearyingly shouting "Kgoyal-al! Hotel Kgoyal-al! . . ." inviting tourists. And the Gentleman from San Francisco felt like the old man that he was, and it was with weariness and animosity that he thought of all these "Royals," "Splendids," "Excelsiors," and of all those greedy bugs, reeking with garlic, who are called Italians. Once, during a stop, having opened his eyes and half-risen from the sofa, he noticed in the shadow of the rock beach a heap of stone huts, miserable, mildewed through and through, huddled close by the water, near boats, rags, tin-boxes, and brown fishing nets, and as he remembered that this was the very Italy he had come to enjoy, he felt a great despair. . . . Finally, in twilight, the black mass of the island began to grow nearer, as though burrowed through at the base by red fires, the wind grew softer, warmer, more fragrant; from the dock-lanterns huge golden serpents flowed down the tame waves which undulated like black oil. . . .

Then, suddenly, the anchor rumbled and fell with a splash into the water, the fierce yells of the boatmen filled the air—and at once everyone's heart grew easy. The electric lights in the cabin grew more brilliant, and there came a desire to eat, drink, smoke, move. . . . Ten minutes later the family from San Francisco found themselves in a large ferry-boat; fifteen minutes later they trod the stones of the quay, and then seated themselves in a small lighted car, which, with a buzz, started to ascend the slope, while vineyard stakes, half-ruined stone fences, and wet, crooked lemon trees, in spots shielded by straw sheds, with their glimmering orange-colored fruit and thick glossy foliage, were sliding down past the open car windows. . . . After rain, the earth smells sweet in Italy, and each of her islands has a fragrance of its own.

The island of Capri was dark and damp on that evening. But for a while it grew animated and lit up, in spots, as always in the hour of the steamer's arrival. On the top of the hill, at the station of the *funiculaire,* there stood already the crowd of those whose duty it was to receive properly the Gentleman from San Francisco. The rest of the tourists hardly deserved any attention. There were a few Russians, who had settled on Capri, untidy, absent-minded people, absorbed in their bookish thoughts, spectacled, bearded, with the collars of their cloth overcoats raised. There was also a company of long-legged, long-necked, round-headed German youths in Tyrolean costume, and with linen bags on their backs, who need no one's services, are everywhere at home, and are by no means liberal in their expenses. The Gentleman from San Francisco, who kept quietly aloof from both the Russians and the Germans, was noticed at once. He and his ladies were hurriedly helped from the car, a man ran before them to show them the way, and they were again surrounded by boys and those thickset Caprean peasant women, who carry on their heads the trunks and valises of wealthy travelers. Their tiny, wooden footstools rapped against the pavement of the small square, which looked almost like an opera square, and over which an electric lantern swung in the damp wind; the gang of urchins whistled like birds and turned somersaults, and as the Gentleman from San Francisco passed among them, it all looked like a stage scene; he went first under some kind of medieval archway, beneath houses huddled close together, and then along a steep echoing lane which led to the hotel entrance, flooded with light. At the left, a palm tree raised its tuft above the flat roofs, and higher up, blue stars burned in the black sky. And again things looked as though it was in honor of the guests from San Francisco that the stony damp little town had awakened on its rocky island in the Mediterranean, that it was they who had made the owner of the hotel so happy and beaming, and that the Chinese gong, which had sounded the call to dinner through all the floors as soon as they entered the lobby, had been waiting only for them.

The owner, an elegant young man, who met the guests with a polite and exquisite bow, for a moment startled the Gentleman from San Francisco. Having caught sight of him, the Gentleman from San Francisco suddenly recollected that on the previous night, among other confused images which disturbed his sleep, he had seen this very man. His vision resembled the hotel keeper to a dot, had the same head, the same hair, shining and scrupulously combed, and wore the same frock-coat with rounded skirts. Amazed, he almost stopped for a while. But as there was not a mustard seed of what is called mysticism in his heart, his surprise subsided at once; in passing the corridor of the hotel he jestingly told his wife and daughter about this strange coincidence of dream and reality. His daughter alone glanced at him with alarm; longing suddenly compressed her heart, and such a strong feeling of solitude on this strange, dark island seized her that she almost began to cry. But, as usual, she said nothing about her feelings to her father.

A person of high dignity, Rex XVII, who had spent three entire weeks on Capri, had just left the island, and the guests from San Francisco were given the apartments he had occupied. At their disposal was put the most handsome and skillful chambermaid, a Belgian, with a figure rendered slim and firm by her corset, and with a starched cap, shaped like a small, indented crown; and they had the privilege of being served by the most well-appearing and portly footman, a black, fiery-eyed Sicilian, and by the quickest waiter, the small, stout Luigi, who was a fiend at cracking jokes and had changed many places in his life. Then the maître-d'hôtel, a Frenchman, gently rapped at the door of the American gentleman's room. He came to ask whether the gentleman and the ladies would dine, and in case they would, which he did not doubt, to report that there was to be had that day lobsters, roast beef, asparagus, pheasants, etc., etc.

The floor was still rocking under the Gentleman from San Francisco—so sea-sick had the wretched Italian steamer made him—yet, he slowly, though awkwardly, shut the window which had banged when the maître-d'hôtel entered, and which let in the smell of the distant kitchen and wet flowers in the garden, and answered with slow distinctness, that they would dine, that their table must be placed farther away from the door, in the depth of the hall, that they would have local wine and champagne, moderately dry and but slightly cooled. The maître-d'hôtel approved the words of the guest in various intonations, which all meant, however, only one thing; there is and can be no doubt that the desires of the Gentleman from San Francisco are right, and that everything would be carried out, in exact conformity with his words. At last he inclined his head and asked delicately:

"Is that all, sir?"

And having received in reply a slow "Yes," he added that today they were going to have the tarantella danced in the vestibule by Carmella and Giuseppe, known to all Italy and to "the entire world of tourists."

"I saw her on post card pictures," said the Gentleman from San Francisco in a tone of voice which expressed nothing. "And this Giuseppe, is he her husband?"

"Her cousin, sir," answered the maître-d'hôtel.

The Gentleman from San Francisco tarried a little, evidently musing on something, but said nothing, then dismissed him with a nod of his head.

Then he started making preparations, as though for a wedding: he turned on all the electric lamps, and filled the mirrors with re-flections of light and the sheen of furniture, and opened trunks; he began to shave and to wash himself, and the sound of his bell was heard every minute in the corridor, crossing with other impatient calls which came from the rooms of his wife and daughter. Luigi, in his red apron, with the ease characteristic of stout people, made funny faces at the chambermaids, who were dashing by with tile buckets in their hands, making them laugh until the tears came. He rolled head over heels to the door, and, tapping with his knuckles, asked with feigned timidity and with an obsequiousness which he knew how to render idiotic:

"Ha sonato, Signore?" (Did you ring, sir?)

And from behind the door a slow, grating, insultingly polite voice, answered:

"Yes, come in."

What did the Gentleman from San Francisco think and feel on that evening forever memorable to him? It must be said frankly: absolutely nothing exceptional. The trouble is that everything on this earth appears too simple. Even had he felt anything deep in his heart, a premonition that something was going to happen, he would have imagined that it was not going to happen so soon, at least not at once. Besides, as is usually the case just after sea-sickness is over, he was very hungry, and he anticipated with real delight the first spoonful of soup, and the first gulp of wine; therefore, he was performing the habitual process of dressing, in a state of excitement which left no time for reflection.

Having shaved and washed himself, and dexterously put in place a few false teeth, he then, standing before the mirror, moistened and vigorously plastered what was left of his thick pearly-colored hair, close to his tawny-yellow skull. Then he put on, with some effort, a tight-fitting undershirt of cream-colored silk, fitted tight to his strong, aged body with its waist swelling out because of an abundant diet; and he pulled black silk socks and patent leather dancing shoes on his dry feet with their fallen arches. Squatting down, he set right his black trousers, drawn high by means of silk suspenders, adjusted his snow-white shirt with its bulging front, put the buttons into the shining cuffs, and

began the painful process of hunting up the front button under the hard collar. The floor was still swaying under him, the tips of his fingers hurt terribly, the button at times painfully pinched the flabby skin in the depression under his Adam's apple, but he persevered, and finally, with his eyes shining from the effort, his face blue because of the narrow collar which squeezed his neck, he triumphed over the difficulties—and all exhausted, he sat down before the pier glass, his reflected image repeating itself in all the mirrors.

"It's terrible!" he muttered, lowering his strong, bald head and making no effort to understand what was terrible; then, with a careful and habitual gesture, he examined his short fingers with gouty callosities in the joints, and their large, convex, almond-colored nails, and repeated with conviction, "It's terrible!"

But here the stentorian voice of the second gong sounded throughout the house, as in a heathen temple. And having risen hurriedly, the Gentleman from San Francisco drew his tie more taut and firm around his collar and pulled together his abdomen by means of a tight waistcoat, put on a dinner-coat, set to rights the cuffs, and for the last time he examined himself in the mirror. . . . This Carmella, tawny, as a mulatto, with fiery eyes, in a dazzling dress in which orange-color predominated, must be an extraordinary dancer—it occurred to him. And cheerfully leaving his room, he walked on the carpet, to his wife's chamber, and asked in a loud tone of voice if they would be long.

"In five minutes, papa!" answered cheerfully and gaily a girlish voice. "I am combing my hair."

"Very well," said the Gentleman from San Francisco.

And thinking of her wonderful hair, streaming on her shoulders, he slowly walked down along corridors and staircases, spread with red velvet carpets, looking for the library. The servants he met hugged the walls, and he walked by as if not noticing them. An old lady, late for dinner, already bowed with years, with milk-white hair, yet bare-necked, in a light-gray silk dress, hurried at top speed, but she walked in a mincing, funny, hen-like manner, and he easily overtook her. At the glass door of the dining hall where the guests had already gathered and started eating, he stopped before the table crowded with boxes of matches and Egyptian cigarettes, took a great Manila cigar, and threw three liras on the table. On the winter veranda he glanced into the open window; a stream of soft air came to him from the darkness, the top of the old palm loomed up before him afar-off, with its boughs spread among the stars and looking gigantic, and the distant even noise of the sea reached his ear. In the library-room, snug, quiet, a German in round silver-bowed glasses and with crazy, wondering eyes stood turning the rustling pages of a newspaper. Having coldly eyed him, the Gentleman from San Francisco seated himself in a deep leather arm-chair near a lamp under a green hood, put on his pince-nez and twitching his head because of the collar which choked him, hid himself from view behind a newspaper. He glanced at a few headlines, read a few lines about the intermi-nable Balkan war, and turned over the page with an habitual gesture. Suddenly, the lines blazed up with a glassy sheen, the veins of his neck swelled, his eyes bulged out, the pince-nez fell from his nose. . . . He dashed forward, wanted to swallow air—and made a wild, rattling noise; his lower jaw dropped, dropped on his shoulder and began to shake, the shirt-front bulged out—and the whole body, writhing, the heels catching in the carpet, slowly fell to the floor in a desperate struggle with an invisible foe. . . .

Had not the German been in the library, this frightful accident would have been quickly and adroitly hushed up. The body of the Gentleman from San Francisco would have been rushed away to some far corner—and none of the guests would have known of the occurrence. But the German dashed out of the library with outcries and spread the alarm all over the house. And many rose from their meal, upsetting chairs, others growing pale, ran along the corridors to the library, and the question, asked in many languages, was heard; "What is it? What has happened?" And no one was able to answer it clearly, no one understood anything, for until this very day men still wonder most at death and most absolutely refuse to believe in it. The owner rushed from one guest to another, trying to keep back those who were running and soothe them with hasty assurances, that this was nothing, a mere trifle, a little fainting-spell by which a Gentleman from San Francisco had been over-come. But no one listened to him, many saw how the footmen and waiters tore from the gentleman his tie, collar, waistcoat, the rumpled evening coat, and even—for no visible reason—the danc-ing shoes from his black silk-covered feet. And he kept on writhing. He obstinately struggled with death, he did not want to yield to the foe that attacked him so unexpectedly and grossly. He shook his head, emitted rattling sounds like one throttled, and turned up his eye-balls like one drunk with wine. When he was hastily brought into Number Forty-three,—the smallest, worst, dampest, and coldest room at the end of the lower corridor—and stretched on the bed— his daughter came running, her hair falling over her shoulders, the skirts of her dressing-gown thrown open, with bare breasts raised by the corset. Then came his wife, big, heavy, al-most completely dressed for dinner, her mouth round with terror.

In a quarter of an hour all was again in good trim at the hotel. But the evening was irrepa-rably spoiled. Some tourists returned to the dining hall and finished their dinner, but they kept silent, and it was obvious that they took the accident as a personal insult, while the owner went from one guest to another, shrug-ging his shoulders in impotent and appropriate irritation, feeling like one innocently victim-ized, assuring everyone that he understood per-fectly well "how disagreeable this is," and giving his word that he would take all "the measures that are within his power" to do away with the trouble. Yet it was found necessary to cancel the tarantella. The unnecessary electric lamps were put out, most of the guests left for the beer hall, and it grew so quiet in the hotel that one could distinctly hear the tick-tock of the clock in the lobby, where a lonely parrot babbled something in its expressionless manner, stirring in its cage, and trying to fall asleep with its paw clutching the upper perch in a most absurd manner. The Gentleman from San Francisco lay stretched in a cheap iron bed, under coarse woolen blankets, dimly lighted by a single gas-burner fastened in the ceiling. An ice bag slid down on his wet, cold forehead. His blue, already lifeless face grew gradually cold; the hoarse, rattling noise which came from his mouth, lighted by the glimmer of the golden fillings, gradually weakened. It was not the Gentleman from San Francisco that was emitting those weird sounds; he was no more—someone else did it. His wife and daughter, the doctor, the servants were standing and watching him apathetically. Suddenly, that which they expected and feared happened. The rattling sound ceased. And slowly, slowly, in everybody's sight a pallor stole over the face of the dead man, and his features began to grow thinner and more luminous, beautiful with the beauty that he had long shunned and that became him well. . . .

The proprietor entered. "Gia é morto," whispered the doctor to him. The proprietor shrugged his shoulders indifferently. The older lady, with tears slowly running down her cheeks, approached him and said timidly that now the deceased must be taken to his room.

"O no, madam," answered the proprietor politely, but without any amiability and not in English, but in French. He was no longer interested in the trifle which the guests from San Francisco could now leave at his cash-office. "This is absolutely impossible," he said, and added in the form of an explanation that he valued this apartment highly, and if he satisfied her desire, this would become known over Capri and the tourists would begin to avoid it.

The girl, who had looked at him strangely, sat down, and with her handkerchief to her mouth, began to cry. Her mother's tears dried up at once, and her face flared up. She raised her tone, began to demand, using her own language and still unable to realize that the respect for her was absolutely gone. The proprietor, with polite dignity, cut her short: "If madam does not like the ways of this hotel, he dare not detain her." And he firmly announced that the corpse must leave the hotel that very day, at dawn, that the police had been informed, that an agent would call immediately and attend to all the necessary formalities. . . . "Is it possible to get on Capri at least a plain coffin?" madam asks. . . . Unfortunately not; by no means, and as for making one, there will be no time. It will

be necessary to arrange things some other way. . . . For instance, he gets English soda-water in big, oblong boxes. . . . The partitions could be taken out from such a box. . . .

By night, the whole hotel was asleep. A waiter opened the window in Number 43—it faced a corner of the garden where a consumptive banana tree grew in the shadow of a high stone wall set with broken glass on the top—turned out the electric light, locked the door, and went away. The deceased remained alone in the darkness. Blue stars looked down at him from the black sky, the cricket in the wall started his melancholy, carefree song. In the dimly lighted corridor two chambermaids were sitting on the window-sill, mending something. Then Luigi came in, in slippered feet, with a heap of clothes on his arm.

"Pronto?"—he asked in a stage whisper, as if greatly concerned, directing his eyes toward the terrible door, at the end of the corridor. And waving his free hand in that direction, "Partenza!" he cried out in a whisper, as if seeing off a train—and the chambermaids, choking with noiseless laughter, put their heads on each other's shoulders.

Then, stepping softly, he ran to the door, slightly rapped at it, and inclining his ear, asked most obsequiously in a subdued tone of voice:

"Ha sonato, Signore?"

And, squeezing his throat and thrusting his lower jaw forward, he answered himself in a drawling, grating, sad voice, as if from behind the door:

"Yes, come in. . . ."

At dawn, when the window panes in Number Forty-three grew white, and a damp wind rustled in the leaves of the banana tree, when the pale-blue morning sky rose and stretched over Capri, and the sun, rising from behind the distant mountains of Italy, touched into gold the pure, clearly outlined summit of Monte Solaro, when the masons, who mended the paths for the tourists on the island, went out to their work—an oblong box was brought to room Number Forty-three. Soon it grew very heavy and painfully pressed against the knees of the assistant doorman who was conveying it in a one-horse carriage along the white high-road which winded on the slopes, among stone fences and vineyards, all the way down to the seacoast. The driver, a sickly man, with red eyes, in an old short-sleeved coat and in worn-out shoes, had a drunken headache; all night long he had played dice at the eatinghouse—and he kept on flogging his vigorous little horse. According to Sicilian custom, the animal was heavily burdened with decorations: all sorts of bells tinkled on the bridle, which was ornamented with colored woolen fringes; there were bells also on the edges of the high saddle; and a bird's feather, two feet long, stuck in the trimmed crest of the horse, nodded up and down. The driver kept silence: he was depressed by his wrongheadedness and vices, by the fact that last night he had lost in gambling all the copper coins with which his pockets had been full—neither more nor less than four liras and forty centesimi. But on such a morning, when the air is so fresh, and the sea stretches near by, and the sky is serene with a morning serenity, a headache passes rapidly and one becomes carefree again. Besides, the driver was also somewhat cheered by the unexpected earnings which the Gentleman from San Francisco, who bumped his dead head against the walls of the box behind his back, had brought him. The little steamer, shaped like a great bug, which lay far down, on the tender and brilliant blue filling to the brim the Neapolitan bay, was blowing the signal of departure, and the sounds swiftly resounded all over Capri. Every bend of the island, every ridge and stone was seen as distinctly as if there were no air between heaven and earth. Near the quay the driver was overtaken by the head doorman who conducted in an auto the wife and daughter of the Gentleman from San Francisco. Their faces were pale and their eyes sunken with tears and a sleepless night. And in ten minutes the little steamer was again stirring up the water and picking its way toward Sorrento and Castellamare, carrying the American family away from Capri forever. . . . Meanwhile, peace and rest were restored on the island.

Two thousand years ago there had lived on that island a man who became utterly entangled in his own brutal and filthy actions. For some unknown reason he usurped the rule over millions of men and found himself bewildered by the absurdity of this power, while the fear that someone might kill him unawares, made him commit deeds inhuman beyond all measure. And mankind has forever retained his memory, and those who, taken together, now rule the world, as incomprehensibly and, essentially, as cruelly as he did—come from all the corners of the earth to look at the remnants of the stone house he inhabited, which stands on one of the steepest cliffs of the island. On that wonderful morning the tourists, who had come to Capri for precisely that purpose, were still asleep in the various hotels, but tiny long-eared asses under red saddles were already being led to the hotel entrances. Americans and Germans, men and women, old and young, after having arisen and breakfasted heartily, were to scramble on them, and the old beggarwomen of Capri, with sticks in their sinewy hands, were again to run after them along stony, mountainous paths, all the way up to the summit of Monte Tiberia. The dead old man from San Francisco, who had planned to keep the tourists company but who had, instead, only scared them by reminding them of death, was already shipped to Naples, and soothed by this, the travelers slept soundly, and silence reigned over the island. The stores in the little town were still closed, with the exception of the fish and greens market on the tiny square. Among the plain people who filled it, going about their business, stood idly by, as usual, Lorenzo, a tall old boatman, a carefree reveller and once a handsome man, famous all over Italy, who had many times served as a model for painters. He had brought and already sold—for a song—two big sea-crawfish, which he had caught at night and which were rustling in the apron of Don Cataldo, the cook of the hotel where the family from San Francisco had been lodged, and now Lorenzo could stand calmly until nightfall, wearing princely airs, showing off his rags, his clay pipe with its long reed mouth-piece, and his red woolen cap, tilted on one ear. Meanwhile, among the precipices of Monte Solare, down the ancient Phoenician road, cut in the rocks in the form of a gigantic staircase, two Abruzzi mountaineers were coming from Anacapri. One carried under his leather mantle a bagpipe, a large goat's skin with two pipes; the other, something in the nature of a wooden flute. They walked, and the entire country, joyous, beautiful, sunny, stretched below them; the rocky shoulders of the island, which lay at their feet, the fabulous blue in which it swam, the shining morning vapors over the sea westward, beneath the dazzling sun, and the wavering masses of Italy's mountains, both near and distant, whose beauty human word is powerless to render. . . . Midway they slowed up. Overshadowing the road stood, in a grotto of the rock wall of Monte Solare, the Holy Virgin, all radiant, bathed in the warmth and the splendor of the sun. The rust of her snow-white plaster-of-Paris vestures and queenly crown was touched into gold, and there were meekness and mercy in her eyes raised toward the heavens, toward the eternal and beatific abode of her thrice-blessed Son. They bared their heads, applied the pipes to their lips, and praises flowed on, candid and humbly-joyous, praises to the sun and the morning, to Her, the Immaculate Intercessor for all who suffer in this evil and beautiful world, and to Him who had been born of her womb in the cavern of Bethlehem, in a hut of lowly shepherds in distant Judea.

As for the body of the dead Gentleman from San Francisco, it was on its way home, to the shores of the New World, where a grave awaited it. Having undergone many humiliations and suffered much human neglect, having wandered about a week from one port warehouse to another, it finally got on that same famous ship which had brought the family, such a short while ago and with such a pomp, to the Old World. But now he was concealed from the living: in a tar-coated coffin he was lowered deep into the black hold of the steamer. And again did the ship set out on its far sea journey. At night it sailed by the island of Capri, and, for those who watched it from the islands, its lights slowly disappearing in the dark sea, it seemed infinitely sad. But there, on the vast steamer, in its lighted halls shining with brilliance and marble, a noisy dancing party was going on, as usual.

On the second and the third night there was again a ball—this time in mid-ocean, during the furious storm sweeping over the ocean, which roared like a funeral mass and rolled up mountainous seas fringed with mourning silvery foam. The Devil, who from the rocks of Gibraltar, the stony gateway of two worlds, watched the ship vanish into night and storm, could hardly distinguish from behind the snow the innumerable fiery eyes of the ship. The Devil was as huge as a cliff, but the ship was even bigger, a many-storied, many-stacked giant, created by the arrogance of the New Man with the old heart. The blizzard battered the ship's rigging and its broad-necked stacks, whitened with snow, but it remained firm, majestic—and terrible. On its uppermost deck, amidst a snowy whirlwind there loomed up in a loneliness the cozy, dimly lighted cabin, where, only half awake, the vessel's ponderous pilot reigned over its entire mass, bearing the semblance of a pagan idol. He heard the wailing moans and the furious screeching of the siren, choked by the storm, but the nearness of that which was behind the wall and which in the last account was incomprehensible to him, removed his fears. He was reassured by the thought of the large, armored cabin, which now and then was filled with mysterious rumbling sounds and with the dry creaking of blue fires, flaring up and exploding around a man with a metallic headpiece, who was eagerly catching the indistinct voices of the vessels that hailed him, hundreds of miles away. At the very bottom, in the under-water womb of the *Atlantis,* the huge masses of tanks and various other machines, their steel parts shining dully, wheezed with steam and oozed hot water and oil; here was the gigantic kitchen, heated by hellish furnaces, where the motion of the vessel was being generated; here seethed those forces terrible in their concentration which were transmitted to the keel of the vessel, and into that endless round tunnel, which was lighted by electricity, and looked like a gigantic cannon barrel, where slowly, with a punctuality and certainty that crushes the human soul, a colossal shaft was revolving in its oily nest, like a living monster stretching in its lair. As for the middle part of the *Atlantis,* its warm, luxurious cabins, dining-rooms, and halls, they radiated light and joy, were astir with a chattering smartly dressed crowd, were filled with the fragrance of fresh flowers, and resounded with a string orchestra. And again did the slender supple pair of hired lovers painfully turn and twist and at times clash convulsively amid the splendor of lights, silks, diamonds, and bare feminine shoulders: she—a sinfully modest pretty girl, with lowered eyelashes and an innocent hair-dressing, he—a tall, young man, with black hair, looking as if they were pasted, pale with powder, in most exquisite patent leather shoes, in a narrow, long-skirted dress-coat,—a beautiful man resembling a leech. And no one knew that this couple had long since been weary of torturing themselves with a feigned beatific torture under the sounds of shamefully melancholy music; nor did anyone know what lay deep, deep, beneath them, on the very bottom of the hold, in the neighborhood of the gloomy and sultry maw of the ship, that heavily struggled with the ocean, the darkness, and the storm.

DISCUSSION

At first glance "The Gentleman from San Francisco" seems a very puzzling story. The main character, the Gentleman, goes on a trip, he amuses himself with his dissipations, he dies of a stroke while staying at a fashionable hotel, his body is hurried out of the hotel, ignominiously crated in a box designed for the shipment of soda water, and sent back to America by the same liner by which he had come to Europe. This simple narrative would, as we have suggested in the Introduction (p. 12), seem merely to unfold a process and therefore scarcely deserve to be called a plot. The narrative itself is surrounded by a number of characters and episodes, most of which have little if any direct relation to the personal story of the Gentleman. What are such characters and episodes doing here? What holds the story together? What, in other words, serves the same function here that plot does in the ordinary story?

We may say that, though the Gentleman's story does provide a kind of spine for the whole, and is to be taken as the most important single element, the real principle of progression is the development of an idea, through its various complications. Here thematic organization exists with only the most tenuous connection with organization by action. We see the relation of parts to the whole only as related to the idea, not as related to the action. As for the theme, the epigraph from *Revelation* indicates that it involves pride and the fall of pride, and statements in the story, most explicitly in the comparison of the modern ruling class to the Emperor Tiberius, indicate that it involves the question of social justice. Let us turn back to the story itself and try to see how these ideas are developed.

We may start with the Gentleman himself—the proud man who is struck down in the moment of his pride. He is the central character. But we know astonishingly little about him: he is proud, he is self-indulgent, he is contemptuous of others, especially those of inferior economic and social station, he is a complete materialist without even "a mustard seed of what is called mysticism in his heart." There are only two moments when we get some hint of an inner life: when he tells his daughter the dream and when, dressing for dinner on his last night of life, he is struck by a nameless distress. We do not even know his name—"neither at Naples nor on Capri could anyone recall his name." In other words, as Bunin seems to imply, his individuality, his name, is not important. It is not important because the Gentleman as a person is not important; he is important only as a type, as a member of a class, the class who "taken together, now rule the world, as incomprehensibly and, essentially, as cruelly" as the Roman Emperor Tiberius did. This namelessness, then, points us beyond the individual to the development of an idea.

In support of this we find the method of the story. Bunin takes the tone of a historian, as it were, as if he were giving an account long afterwards of the way life had existed at a certain period. He says, for example: "The class of people to which he belonged was in the habit . . ." Furthermore, observe the great detail devoted to the life of that class, the class upon which, Bunin ironically says, "depend all the blessings of civilization: the cut of dress suits, the stability of thrones, the declaration of wars, the prosperity of hotels."

Once we have accepted the development of a theme, an idea, as the principle of organization of this story, we understand, too, the significance of many digressions involving minor characters, such as the hired lovers on the ship, the Asiatic prince and the Gentleman's daughter, the valet Luigi, the boatman Lorenzo, the cab driver, the Emperor Tiberius, the Abruzzi pipers, the hotel proprietor on Capri. A few of these characters belong to the class that rules the world, but most of them belong to the class that, in one way or another, serves the Gentleman and his kind.

We may now notice what at first glance may appear a peculiar fact in a story which has an important element of protest against social injustice: the fact that we do not have a simple arrangement of the rulers as bad and the ruled as good. The daughter of the Gentleman, though she belongs to the class of the rulers and though her notion of love has been corrupted, is yet presented with a certain sympathy: she has some sensitivity, some awareness of her isolation, as we understand from her reaction when her father tells about his dream. On the other hand, most of the class of the ruled—for example, Lorenzo, the cabman, and the valet Luigi—are presented as corrupted in one way or another. Lorenzo has been spoiled and turned into an idler and reveller by others' admiration for his picturesque good looks. The cabman is a drunkard and gambler. Luigi has been so embittered by his condition that his satiric humor appears even after the Gentleman's death. The general point here seems to be that the system spreads corruption downward as well as upward, that the stain spreads in all directions, and that injustice has persisted, as is indicated by the references to Tiberius, from the ancient to the modern world.

Let us lay aside for the moment the theme of social justice. We can see that many of the elements in the story do not seem to be accommodated to it. For instance, the various references to love, the Gentleman's relations with prostitutes, the young couple who are hired to pose as lovers on the liner, the love of the daughter for the Asiatic prince, the figure of the Virgin on the road to Monte Solare. We have here a scale from a degraded form of human love up to Divine love. In between the two extremes there are the hired lovers and the daughter. They imply the same thing: even in the corrupted world people want to believe in love, to have at least the illusion of love. The hired lovers provide a romantic atmosphere by their pretended devotion. The daughter, though she is drawn to the prince merely by social snobbery (personally he is described as very unattractive), must convert this into the emotion of love. Bunin says: "Beautiful were the tender, complex feelings which her meeting with the ungainly man aroused in her—the man in whose veins flowed unusual blood, for after all, it does not matter what in particular stirs up a maiden's soul: money, or fame, or nobility of birth." Bunin has put the matter ironically—"it does not matter." But it does matter, for all human beings have some yearning for meaning in life and some awareness of possibilities beyond the physical routines of life. For instance, we may recall the two moments when even the Gentleman exhibits, in a confused way, his sense of an inner life. So with the daughter, Bunin is implying that the human being, even when the victim of his system, when accepting the false values of money, fame, and birth, must still try to maintain the illusion of love. That is, over against the injustice of the world there is the idea of love, culminating in Divine love.

A second set of elements that does not seem to be readily accounted for by the theme of injustice centers on the ship and the captain. It is true that the ship first appears as an easily interpreted symbol for society—the Gentleman and his kind take their ease in the dining room or bar, while the stokers sweat before the furnaces and the lookouts freeze in the crow's nest. But we begin to sense that more is meant. The darkness and the storm are outside the ship, but people ignore that terror for they "trust" the captain, who is presented as a "pagan idol." We can begin now to read the symbolism. The modern world worships its "pagan idol," the technician, the scientist, the administrator, the man who has apparently conquered nature and made irrelevant any concern with the mysteries of life and death. But we see that death does strike down the Gentleman—even though "men still wonder most at death and most absolutely refuse to believe in it." The mystery of death remains despite the skills of all the pagan idols. And even the pagan idol himself who reigns over the ship would be afraid of the darkness and mystery of the sea if he did not have the comfort of the wireless. But let us notice that the wireless is put down as a mystery, a thing "in the last account incomprehensible to him," and notice that the wireless shack is described as a kind of shrine or temple: ". . . the large armored cabin, which now and then filled with mysterious rumbling sounds and with the dry creaking of blue fires . . ." So in the end the idol, the man who is supposed to know the solution to all problems and who is supposed to bring all to safety, must trust a "mystery."

Before we try to relate this idea to the theme of justice, we may look at the last paragraph of the story, the scene where the Devil leans on Gibraltar and watches the great ship disappear in the dark and storm toward America. What is the Devil doing in this story? There are several details to be observed before we frame an answer. Gibraltar is defined as the "gateway of two worlds," the Old World and the New World, Europe and America. The ship is bigger than the Devil and leaves him behind, staring after it. The ship is a "giant created by the arrogance of the New Man with the old heart."

To put these details together into a pattern, we may begin by taking the Devil as the embodiment of Evil, a quite conventional and usual equation. Then we may say that the Devil is left behind in the Old World because the New World doesn't believe in Evil. The spirit of modernism, it is sometimes said, takes it that all difficulties are merely difficulties of adjustment of one kind or another. If there is injustice in society, simply change the system. Moral problems, by such reasoning, are not really moral problems, they are problems in "conditioning." The chief concern is not with right and wrong, good and evil, but with what will work. To sum up this point, the modern spirit, which in the story is taken as characteristically American, ignores Evil; it thinks that it can solve all problems by the application of technical skills. Therefore the ship, the symbol of the achievement of the modern spirit, is "bigger" than the Devil.

Now for the second point. The ship is a "giant created by the arrogance of the New Man with the old heart." To interpret, we must say that the New Man, with all his skills has not solved the final problem, the problem of the heart. There can be no justice by merely changing systems, by tinkering machines, either literal machines or social machines. The problem is, in the end, a problem of a change of heart, a birth of moral awareness, a spiritual redemption. Systems *must* be changed, machines *must* be tinkered—but without "redemption" no final gain can be expected. With this idea, which is the central and final theme of the story, we can now see how the elements concerning love and the elements concerning the captain as idol are related to the rest of the story. Love may be taken as the redeeming power, the beneficent mystery as opposed to the terrible mystery of death. Then the captain—*i.e.,* the technician, the scientist, the administrator, the being whom all men trust—must himself finally trust a mystery. There is always the mystery of nature and man's fate (the sea outside the hull of the ship, we may say, the night, the storm), for there are always love and death; there is the mystery of the human heart.

We must not conclude this interpretation without a word of caution. We must not be too ready to read the story as an attack on the achievements of the modern spirit. We might even go so far as to say that the story is not an attack at all, but a warning, rather, against a misinterpretation of the modern spirit, an oversimplification of it. The story provides, as it were, a perspective on a problem, and not an absolute and dogmatic solution for it.

EXERCISE

1. Why are the museums visited by the Gentleman described as "lifelessly clean"? Does Bunin mean to imply that the objects in those museums never had any relation to life, or that they have now lost it? Why is there irony in the description of the interior of the churches—for instance, in the phrase, "somebody's 'Descent from the Cross,' infallibly famous"? Is this irony a sneer at either painting or religion? If not, at what is the irony directed? Contrast this with the tone adopted toward the simple pipers who honor the Virgin with their music.

2. What is the thematic significance of the hotel proprietor's change of attitude after the death of the Gentleman?

3. Why does Bunin make the Gentleman say while dressing on his last night, "It's terrible"? What does this signify psychologically? Thematically?

4. Why is the male dancer on shipboard compared, at the end of the story, to a leech?

5. Does the fact that the Gentleman is from San Francisco have any significance?

SECTION VII

Scale, Pace, and Time

Here we shall place two pieces of fiction that are very much longer than the ordinary story, one something over 20,000 words, the other something under. We shall ask ourselves how, in the light of the materials involved, we may account for the scale. In this connection, we are necessarily led to consider the relations of summary treatment of narratives to dramatically developed treatment, in other words, to consider shifts of pace in the treatment of time. Summary treatment moves swiftly over time, dramatic treatment slowly. The shift from one kind of treatment to the other is connected, of course, with the question of selectivity: on what basis does a writer summarize here and present there? And the answer to this question is finally related to the dominant interest the writer finds in his material—the interest that gives a story its thematic and emotional focus.

Noon Wine

KATHERINE ANNE PORTER (1894-   )

Time: 1896-1905
Place: Small South Texas Farm

I

THE TWO grubby small boys with tow-colored hair who were digging among the ragweed in the front yard sat back on their heels and said, "Hello," when the tall bony man with straw-colored hair turned in at their gate. He did not pause at the gate; it had swung back, conveniently half open, long ago, and was now sunk so firmly on its broken hinges no one thought of trying to close it. He did not even glance at the small boys, much less give them good-day. He just clumped down his big square dusty shoes one after the other steadily, like a man following a plow, as if he knew the place well and knew where he was going and what he would find there. Rounding the right-hand corner of the house under the row of chinaberry trees, he walked up to the side porch where Mr. Thompson was pushing a big swing churn back and forth.

Mr. Thompson was a tough weather-beaten man with stiff black hair and a week's growth of black whiskers. He was a noisy proud man who held his neck so straight his whole face stood level with his Adam's apple, and the whiskers continued down his neck and disappeared into a black thatch under his open collar. The churn rumbled and swished like the belly of a trotting horse, and Mr. Thompson seemed somehow to be driving a horse with one hand, reining it in and urging it forward; and every now and then he turned halfway around and squirted a tremendous spit of tobacco juice out over the steps. The door stones were brown and gleaming with fresh tobacco juice. Mr. Thompson had been churning quite a while and he was tired of it. He was just fetching a mouthful of juice to squirt again when the stranger came around the corner and stopped. Mr. Thompson saw a narrow-chested man with blue eyes so pale they were almost white, looking and not looking at him from a long gaunt face, under white eyebrows. Mr. Thompson judged him to be another of these Irishmen, by his long upper lip.

"Howdy do, sir," said Mr. Thompson politely, swinging his churn.

"I need work," said the man, clearly enough but with some kind of foreign accent Mr. Thompson couldn't place. It wasn't Cajun and it wasn't Nigger and it wasn't Dutch, so it had him stumped. "You need a man here?"

Mr. Thompson gave the churn a great shove and it swung back and forth several times on its own momentum. He sat on the steps, shot his quid into the grass, and said, "Set down. Maybe we can make a deal. I been kinda lookin' round for somebody. I had two niggers but they got into a cutting scrape up the creek last week, one of 'em dead now and the other in the hoosegow at Cold Springs. Neither one of 'em worth killing, come right down to it. So it looks like I'd better get somebody. Where'd you work last?"

"North Dakota," said the man, folding himself down on the other end of the steps, but not as if he were tired. He folded up and settled down as if it would be a long time before he got up again. He never had looked at Mr. Thompson, but there wasn't anything sneaking in his eye, either. He didn't seem to be looking anywhere else. His eyes sat in his head and let things pass by them. They didn't seem to be expecting to see anything worth looking at. Mr. Thompson waited a long time for the man to say something more, but he had gone into a brown study.

"North Dakota," said Mr. Thompson, trying to remember where that was. "That's a right smart distance off, seems to me."

"I can do everything on farm," said the man; "cheap. I need work."

Mr. Thompson settled himself to get down to business. "My name's Thompson, Mr. Royal Earle Thompson," he said.

"I'm Mr. Helton," said the man, "Mr. Olaf Helton." He did not move.

"Well, now," said Mr. Thompson in his most carrying voice, "I guess we'd better talk turkey."

When Mr. Thompson expected to drive a bargain he always grew very hearty and jovial. There was nothing wrong with him except that he hated like the devil to pay wages. He said so himself. "You furnish grub and a shack," he said, "and then you got to pay 'em besides. It ain't right. Besides the wear and tear on your implements," he said, "they just let everything go to rack and ruin." So he began to laugh and shout his way through the deal.

"Now, what I want to know is, how much you fixing to gouge outa me?" he brayed, slapping his knee. After he had kept it up as long as he could, he quieted down, feeling a little sheepish, and cut himself a chew. Mr. Helton was staring out somewhere between the barn and the orchard, and seemed to be sleeping with his eyes open.

"I'm good worker," said Mr. Helton as from the tomb. "I get dollar a day."

Mr. Thompson was so shocked he forgot to start laughing again at the top of his voice until it was nearly too late to do any good. "Haw, haw," he bawled. "Why, for a dollar a day I'd hire out myself. What kinda work is it where they pay you a dollar a day?"

"Wheatfields, North Dakota," said Mr. Helton, not even smiling.

Mr. Thompson stopped laughing. "Well, this ain't any wheatfield by a long shot. This is more of a dairy farm," he said, feeling apologetic. "My wife, she was set on a dairy, she seemed to like working around with cows and calves, so I humored her. But it was a mistake," he said. "I got nearly everything to do, anyhow. My wife ain't very strong. She's sick today, that's a fact. She's been porely for the last few days. We plant a little feed, and a corn patch, and there's the orchard, and a few pigs and chickens, but our main hold is the cows. Now just speakin' as one man to another, there ain't any money in it. Now I can't give you no dollar a day because ackshally I don't make that much out of it. No, sir, we get along on a lot less than a dollar a day, I'd say, if we figger up everything in the long run. Now, I paid seven dollars a month to the two niggers, three-fifty each, and grub, but what I say is, one middlin'-good white man ekals a whole passel of niggers any day in the week, so I'll give you seven dollars and you eat at the table with us, and you'll be treated like a white man, as the feller says—"

"That's all right," said Mr. Helton. "I take it."

"Well, now I guess we'll call it a deal, hey?" Mr. Thompson jumped up as if he had re-membered important business. "Now, you just take hold of that churn and give it a few swings, will you, while I ride to town on a coupla little errands. I ain't been able to leave the place all week. I guess you know what to do with butter after you get it, don't you?"

"I know," said Mr. Helton without turning his head. "I know butter business." He had a strange drawling voice, and even when he spoke only two words his voice waved slowly up and down and the emphasis was in the wrong place. Mr. Thompson wondered what kind of foreigner Mr. Helton could be.

"Now just where did you say you worked last?" he asked, as if he expected Mr. Helton to contradict himself.

"North Dakota," said Mr. Helton.

"Well, one place is good as another once you get used to it," said Mr. Thompson, amply. "You're a forriner, ain't you?"

"I'm a Swede," said Mr. Helton, beginning to swing the churn.

Mr. Thompson let forth a booming laugh, as if this was the best joke on somebody he'd ever heard. "Well, I'll be damned," he said at the top of his voice. "A Swede: well, now, I'm afraid you'll get pretty lonesome around here. I never seen any Swedes in this neck of the woods."

"That's all right," said Mr. Helton. He went on swinging the churn as if he had been working on the place for years.

"In fact, I might as well tell you, you're practically the first Swede I ever laid eyes on."

"That's all right," said Mr. Helton.

II

Mr. Thompson went into the front room where Mrs. Thompson was lying down, with the green shades drawn. She had a bowl of water by her on the table and a wet cloth over her eyes. She took the cloth off at the sound of Mr. Thompson's boots and said, "What's all the noise out there? Who is it?"

"Got a feller out there says he's a Swede, Ellie," said Mr. Thompson, "says he knows how to make butter."

"I hope it turns out to be the truth," said Mrs. Thompson. "Looks like my head never will get any better."

"Don't you worry," said Mr. Thompson. "You fret too much. Now I'm gointa ride into town and get a little order of groceries."

"Don't you linger, now, Mr. Thompson," said Mrs. Thompson. "Don't go to the hotel." She meant the saloon; the proprietor also had rooms for rent upstairs.

"Just a coupla little toddies," said Mr. Thompson, laughing loudly, "never hurt any-body."

"I never took a dram in my life," said Mrs. Thompson, "and what's more I never will."

"I wasn't talking about the womenfolks," said Mr. Thompson.

The sound of the swinging churn rocked Mrs. Thompson first into a gentle doze, then a deep drowse from which she waked suddenly knowing that the swinging had stopped a good while ago. She sat up shading her weak eyes from the flat strips of late summer sunlight be-tween the sill and the lowered shades. There she was, thank God, still alive, with supper to cook but no churning on hand, and her head still bewildered, but easy. Slowly she realized she had been hearing a new sound even in her sleep. Somebody was playing a tune on the harmonica, not merely shrilling up and down making a sickening noise, but really playing a pretty tune, merry and sad.

She went out through the kitchen, stepped off the porch, and stood facing the east, shad-ing her eyes. When her vision cleared and settled, she saw a long, pale-haired man in blue jeans sitting in the doorway of the hired man's shack, tilted back in a kitchen chair, blowing away at the harmonica with his eyes shut. Mrs. Thompson's heart fluttered and sank. Heavens, he looked lazy and worthless, he did, now. First a lot of no-count fiddling darkies and then a no-count white man. It was just like Mr. Thompson to take on that kind. She did wish he would be more considerate, and take a little trouble with his business. She wanted to believe in her husband, and there were too many times when she couldn't. She wanted to believe that tomorrow, or at least the day after, life, such a battle at best, was going to be better.

She walked past the shack without glancing aside, stepping carefully, bent at the waist because of the nagging pain in her side, and went to the springhouse, trying to harden her mind to speak very plainly to that new hired man if he had not done his work.

The milk house was only another shack of weather-beaten boards nailed together hastily years before because they needed a milk house; it was meant to be temporary, and it was; already shapeless, leaning this way and that over a perpetual cool trickle of water that fell from a little grot, almost choked with pallid ferns. No one else in the whole countryside had such a spring on his land. Mr. and Mrs. Thompson felt they had a fortune in that spring, if ever they got around to doing anything with it.

Rickety wooden shelves clung at hazard in the square around the small pool where the larger pails of milk and butter stood, fresh and sweet in the cold water. One hand supporting her flat, pained side, the other shading her eyes, Mrs. Thompson leaned over and peered into the pails. The cream had been skimmed and set aside, there was a rich roll of butter, the wooden molds and shallow pans had been scrubbed and scalded for the first time in who knows when, the barrel was full of buttermilk ready for the pigs and the weanling calves, the hard packed-dirt floor had been swept smooth. Mrs. Thompson straightened up again, smiling tenderly. She had been ready to scold him, a poor man who needed a job, who had just come there and who might not have been expected to do things properly at first. There was nothing she could do to make up for the injustice she had done him in her thoughts but to tell him how she appreciated his good clean work, finished already, in no time at all. She ventured near the door of the shack with her careful steps; Mr. Helton opened his eyes, stopped playing, and brought his chair down straight, but did not look at her, or get up. She was a little frail woman with long thick brown

hair in a braid, a suffering patient mouth and diseased eyes which cried easily. She wove her fingers into an eyeshade, thumbs on temples, and, winking her tearful lids, said with a polite little manner, "Howdy do, sir. I'm Miz Thompson, and I wanted to tell you I think you did real well in the milk house. It's always been a hard place to keep."

He said, "That's all right," in a slow voice, without moving.

Mrs. Thompson waited a moment. "That's a pretty tune you're playing. Most folks don't seem to get much music out of a harmonica."

Mr. Helton sat humped over, long legs sprawling, his spine in a bow, running his thumb over the square mouth-stops; except for his moving hand he might have been asleep. The harmonica was a big shiny new one, and Mrs. Thompson, her gaze wandering about, counted five others, all good and expensive, standing in a row on the shelf beside his cot. "He must carry them around in his jumper pocket," she thought, and noted there was not a sign of any other possession lying about. "I see you're mighty fond of music," she said. "We used to have an old accordion, and Mr. Thompson could play it right smart, but the little boys broke it up."

Mr. Helton stood up rather suddenly, the chair clattered under him, his knees straightened though his shoulders did not, and he looked at the floor as if he were listening carefully. "You know how little boys are," said Mrs. Thompson. "You'd better set them harmonicas on a high shelf or they'll be after them. They're great hands for getting into things. I try to learn 'em, but it don't do much good."

Mr. Helton, in one wide gesture of his long arms, swept his harmonicas up against his chest, and from there transferred them in a row to the ledge where the roof joined to the wall. He pushed them back almost out of sight.

"That's do, maybe," said Mrs. Thompson. "Now I wonder," she said, turning and closing her eyes helplessly against the stronger western light, "I wonder what became of them little tads. I can't keep up with them." She had a way of speaking about her children as if they were rather troublesome nephews on a prolonged visit.

"Down by the creek," said Mr. Helton, in

his hollow voice. Mrs. Thompson, pausing confusedly, decided he had answered her question. He stood in silent patience, not exactly waiting for her to go, perhaps, but pretty plainly not waiting for anything else. Mrs. Thompson was perfectly accustomed to all kinds of men full of all kinds of cranky ways. The point was, to find out just how Mr. Helton's crankiness was different from any other man's, and then get used to it, and let him feel at home. Her father had been cranky, her brothers and uncles had all been set in their ways and none of them alike; and every hired man she'd ever seen had quirks and crotchets of his own. Now here was Mr. Helton, who was a Swede, who wouldn't talk, and who played the harmonica besides.

"They'll be needing something to eat," said Mrs. Thompson in a vague friendly way, "pretty soon. Now I wonder what I ought to be thinking about for supper? Now what do you like to eat, Mr. Helton? We always have plenty of good butter and milk and cream, that's a blessing. Mr. Thompson says we ought to sell all of it, but I say my family comes first." Her little face went all out of shape in a pained blind smile.

"I eat anything," said Mr. Helton, his words wandering up and down.

He *can't* talk, for one thing, thought Mrs. Thompson; it's a shame to keep at him when he don't know the language good. She took a slow step away from the shack, looking back over her shoulder. "We usually have cornbread except on Sundays," she told him. "I suppose in your part of the country you don't get much good cornbread."

Not a word from Mr. Helton. She saw from her eye-corner that he had sat down again, looking at his harmonica, chair tilted. She hoped he would remember it was getting near milking time. As she moved away, he started playing again, the same tune.

Milking time came and went. Mrs. Thompson saw Mr. Helton going back and forth between the cow barn and the milk house. He swung along in an easy lope, shoulders bent, head hanging, the big buckets balancing like a pair of scales at the ends of his bony arms. Mr. Thompson rode in from town sitting straighter than usual, chin in, a towsack full of supplies swung behind the saddle. After a

trip to the barn, he came into the kitchen full of good will, and gave Mrs. Thompson a hearty smack on the cheek after dusting her face off with his tough whiskers. He had been to the hotel, that was plain. "Took a look around the premises, Ellie," he shouted. "That Swede sure is grinding out the labor. But he is the closest mouthed feller I ever met up with in all my days. Looks like he's scared he'll crack his jaw if he opens his front teeth."

Mrs. Thompson was stirring up a big bowl of buttermilk cornbread. "You smell like a toper, Mr. Thompson," she said with perfect dignity. "I wish you'd get one of the little boys to bring me in an extra load of firewood. I'm thinking about baking a batch of cookies tomorrow."

Mr. Thompson, all at once smelling the liquor on his own breath, sneaked out, justly rebuked, and brought in the firewood himself. Arthur and Herbert, grubby from thatched head to toes, from skin to shirt, came stamping in yelling for supper. "Go wash you faces and comb your hair," said Mrs. Thompson, automatically. They retired to the porch. Each one put his hand under the pump and wet his forelock, combed it down with his fingers, and returned at once to the kitchen, where all the fair prospects of life were centered. Mrs. Thompson set an extra plate and commanded Arthur, the eldest, eight years old, to call Mr. Helton for supper.

Arthur, without moving from the spot, bawled like a bull calf, "Saaaaaay, Helllllllton, suuuuuupper's read!" and added in a lower voice, "You big Swede!"

"Listen to me," said Mrs. Thompson, "that's no way to act. Now you go out there and ask him decent, or I'll get your daddy to give you a good licking."

Mr. Helton loomed, long and gloomy, in the doorway. "Sit right there," boomed Mr. Thompson, waving his arm. Mr. Helton swung his square shoes across the kitchen in two steps, slumped onto the bench and sat. Mr. Thompson occupied his chair at the head of the table, the two boys scrambled into place opposite Mr. Helton, and Mrs. Thompson sat at the end nearest the stove. Mrs. Thompson clasped her hands, bowed her head and said aloud hastily,

"Lord, for all these and Thy other blessings we thank Thee in Jesus' name, amen," trying to finish before Herbert's rusty little paw reached the nearest dish. Otherwise she would be duty-bound to send him away from the table, and growing children need their meals. Mr. Thompson and Arthur always waited, but Herbert, aged six, was too young to take training yet.

Mr. and Mrs. Thompson tried to engage Mr. Helton in conversation, but it was a failure. They tried first the weather, and then the crops, and then the cows, but Mr. Helton simply did not reply. Mr. Thompson then told something funny he had seen in town. It was about some of the other old grangers at the hotel, friends of his, giving beer to a goat, and the goat's subsequent behavior. Mr. Helton did not seem to hear. Mrs. Thompson laughed dutifully, but she didn't think it was very funny. She had heard it often before, though Mr. Thompson, each time he told it, pretended it had happened that self-same day. It must have happened years ago if it ever happened at all, and it had never been a story that Mrs. Thompson thought suitable for mixed company. The whole thing came of Mr. Thompson's weakness for a dram too much now and then, though he voted for local option at every election. She passed the food to Mr. Helton, who took a helping of everything, but not much, not enough to keep him up to his full powers if he expected to go on working the way he had started.

At last, he took a fair-sized piece of cornbread, wiped his plate up as clean as if it had been licked by a hound dog, stuffed his mouth full, and, still chewing, slid off the bench and started for the door.

"Good night, Mr. Helton," said Mrs. Thompson, and the other Thompsons took it up in a scattered chorus. "Good night, Mr. Helton!"

"Good night," said Mr. Helton's wavering voice grudgingly from the darkness.

"Gude not," said Arthur, imitating Mr. Helton.

"Gude not," said Herbert, the copy-cat.

"You don't do it right," said Arthur. "Now listen to me. Guuuuuude naht," and he ran a hollow scale in a luxury of successful impersonation. Herbert almost went into a fit with joy.

"Now you *stop* that," said Mrs. Thompson. "He can't help the way he talks. You ought to be ashamed of yourselves, both of you, making fun of a poor stranger like that. How'd you like to be a stranger in a strange land?"

"I'd like it," said Arthur. "I think it would be fun."

"They're both regular heathens, Ellie," said Mr. Thompson. "Just plain ignoramuses." He turned the face of awful fatherhood upon his young. "You're both going to get sent to school next year, and that'll knock some sense into you."

"I'm going to git sent to the 'formatory when I'm old enough," piped up Herbert. "That's where I'm goin'."

"Oh, you are, are you?" asked Mr. Thompson. "Who says so?"

"The Sunday School Supintendant," said Herbert, a bright boy showing off.

"You see?" said Mr. Thompson, staring at his wife. "What did I tell you?" He became a hurricane of wrath. "Get to bed, you two," he roared until his Adam's apple shuddered. "Get now before I take the hide off you!" They got, and shortly from their attic bedroom the sounds of scuffling and snorting and giggling and growling filled the house and shook the kitchen ceiling.

Mrs. Thompson held her head and said in a small uncertain voice, "It's no use picking on them when they're so young and tender. I can't stand it."

"My goodness, Ellie," said Mr. Thompson, "we've got to raise 'em. We can't just let 'em grow up hog wild."

She went on in another tone. "That Mr. Helton seems all right, even if he can't be made to talk. Wonder how he comes to be so far from home."

"Like I said, he isn't no whamper-jaw," said Mr. Thompson, "but he sure knows how to lay out the work. I guess that's the main thing around here. Country's full of fellers trampin' round looking for work."

Mrs. Thompson was gathering up the dishes. She now gathered up Mr. Thompson's plate from under his chin. "To tell you the honest truth," she remarked, "I think it's a mighty good change to have a man round the place who knows how to work and keep his mouth shut.

Means he'll keep out of our business. Not that we've got anything to hide, but it's convenient."

"That's a fact," said Mr. Thompson. "Haw, haw," he shouted suddenly. "Means you can do all the talking, huh?"

"The only thing," went on Mrs. Thompson, "is this: he don't eat hearty enough to suit me. I like to see a man set down and relish a good meal. My granma used to say it was no use putting dependence on a man who won't set down and make out his dinner. I hope it won't be that way this time."

"Tell *you* the truth, Ellie," said Mr. Thompson, picking his teeth with a fork and leaning back in the best of good humors, "I always thought your granma was a ter'ble ole fool. She'd just say the first thing that popped into her head and call it God's wisdom."

"My granma wasn't anybody's fool. Nine times out of ten she knew what she was talking about. I always say, the first thing you think is the best thing you can say."

"Well," said Mr. Thompson, going into another shout, "you're so re*ee*fined about that goat story, you just try speaking out in mixed comp'ny sometime! You just try it. S'pose you happened to be thinking about a hen and a rooster, hey? I reckon you'd shock the Babtist preacher!" He gave her a good pinch on her thin little rump. "No more meat on you than a rabbit," he said, fondly. "Now I like 'em cornfed."

Mrs. Thompson looked at him open-eyed and blushed. She could see better by lamplight. "Why, Mr. Thompson, sometimes I think you're the evilest-minded man that ever lived." She took a handful of hair on the crown of his head and gave it a good, slow pull. "That's to show you how it feels, pinching so hard when you're supposed to be playing," she said, gently.

III

In spite of his situation in life, Mr. Thompson had never been able to outgrow his deep conviction that running a dairy and chasing after chickens was woman's work. He was fond of saying that he could plow a furrow, cut sorghum, shuck corn, handle a team, build a corn crib, as well as any man. Buying and selling, too, were man's work. Twice a week he drove the spring wagon to market with the fresh butter, a few eggs, fruits in their proper season, sold them, pocketed the change, and spent it as seemed best, being careful not to dig into Mrs. Thompson's pin money.

But from the first the cows worried him, coming up regularly twice a day to be milked, standing there reproaching him with their smug female faces. Calves worried him, fighting the rope and strangling themselves until their eyes bulged, trying to get at the teat. Wrestling with a calf unmanned him, like having to change a baby's diaper. Milk worried him, coming bitter sometimes, drying up, turning sour. Hens worried him, cackling, clucking, hatching out when you least expected it and leading their broods into the barnyard where the horses could step on them; dying of roup and wryneck and getting plagues of chicken lice; laying eggs all over God's creation so that half of them were spoiled before a man could find them, in spite of a rack of nests Mrs. Thompson had set out for them in the feed room. Hens were a blasted nuisance.

Slopping hogs was hired man's work, in Mr. Thompson's opinion. Killing hogs was a job for the boss, but scraping them and cutting them up was for the hired man again; and again woman's proper work was dressing meat, smoking, pickling, and making lard and sausage. All his carefully limited fields of activity were related somehow to Mr. Thompson's feeling for the appearance of things, his own appearance in the sight of God and man. "It don't *look* right," was his final reason for not doing anything he did not wish to do.

It was his dignity and his reputation that he cared about, and there were only a few kinds of work manly enough for Mr. Thompson to undertake with his own hands. Mrs. Thompson, to whom so many forms of work would have been becoming, had simply gone down on him early. He saw, after a while, how short-sighted it had been of him to expect much from Mrs. Thompson; he had fallen in love with her delicate waist and lace-trimmed petticoats and big blue eyes, and, though all those charms had disappeared, she had in the meantime become Ellie to him, not at all the same person as Miss Ellen Bridges, popular Sunday School teacher in the Mountain City First Baptist Church, but his dear wife, Ellie, who was not strong. Deprived as he was, however, of the main support in life which a man might expect in marriage, he had almost without knowing it resigned himself to failure. Head erect, a prompt payer of taxes, yearly subscriber to the preacher's salary, land owner and father of a family, employer, a hearty good fellow among men, Mr. Thompson knew, without putting it into words, that he had been going steadily down hill. God amighty, it did look like somebody around the place might take a rake in hand now and then and clear up the clutter around the barn and the kitchen steps. The wagon shed was so full of broken-down machinery and ragged harness and old wagon wheels and battered milk pails and rotting lumber you could hardly drive in there any more. Not a soul on the place would raise a hand to it, and as for him, he had all he could do with his regular work. He would sometimes in the slack season sit for hours worrying about it, squirting tobacco on the ragweeds growing in a thicket against the wood pile, wondering what a fellow could do, handicapped as he was. He looked forward to the boys growing up soon; he was going to put them through the mill just as his own father had done with him when he was a boy; they were going to learn how to take hold and run the place right. He wasn't going to overdo it, but those two boys were going to earn their salt, or he'd know why. Great big lubbers sitting around whittling! Mr. Thompson sometimes grew quite enraged with them, when imagining their possible future, big lubbers sitting around whittling or thinking about fishing trips. Well, he'd put a stop to that, mighty damn quick.

As the seasons passed, and Mr. Helton took hold more and more, Mr. Thompson began to relax in his mind a little. There seemed to be nothing the fellow couldn't do, all in the day's work and as a matter of course. He got up at five o'clock in the morning, boiled his own coffee and fried his own bacon and was out in the cow lot before Mr. Thompson had even begun to yawn, stretch, groan, roar and thump around looking for his jeans. He milked the cows, kept the milk house, and churned the butter; rounded the hens up and somehow persuaded them to lay in the nests, not under the house and behind the haystacks; he fed them

regularly and they hatched out until you couldn't set a foot down for them. Little by little the piles of trash around the barns and house disappeared. He carried buttermilk and corn to the hogs, and curried cockleburs out of the horses' manes. He was gentle with the calves, if a little grim with the cows and hens; judging by his conduct, Mr. Helton had never heard of the difference between man's and woman's work on a farm.

In the second year, he showed Mr. Thompson the picture of a cheese press in a mail order catalogue, and said, "This is a good thing. You buy this, I make cheese." The press was bought and Mr. Helton did make cheese, and it was sold, along with the increased butter and the crates of eggs. Sometimes Mr. Thompson felt a little contemptuous of Mr. Helton's ways. It did seem kind of picayune for a man to go around picking up half a dozen ears of corn that had fallen off the wagon on the way from the field, gathering up fallen fruit to feed to the pigs, storing up old nails and stray parts of machinery, spending good time stamping a fancy pattern on the butter before it went to market. Mr. Thompson, sitting up high on the spring-wagon seat, with the decorated butter in a five-gallon lard can wrapped in wet towsack, driving to town, chirruping to the horses and snapping the reins over their backs, sometimes thought that Mr. Helton was a pretty meeching sort of fellow; but he never gave way to these feelings, he knew a good thing when he had it. It was a fact the hogs were in better shape and sold for more money. It was a fact that Mr. Thompson stopped buying feed, Mr. Helton managed the crops so well. When beef- and hog-slaughtering time came, Mr. Helton knew how to save the scraps that Mr. Thompson had thrown away, and wasn't above scraping guts and filling them with sausages that he made by his own methods. In all, Mr. Thompson had no grounds for complaint. In the third year, he raised Mr. Helton's wages, though Mr. Helton had not asked for a raise. The fourth year, when Mr. Thompson was not only out of debt but had a little cash in the bank, he raised Mr. Helton's wages again, two dollars and a half a month each time.

"The man's worth it, Ellie," said Mr.

Thompson, in a glow of self-justification for his extravagance. "He's made this place pay, and I want him to know I appreciate it."

Mr. Helton's silence, the pallor of his eyebrows and hair, his long, glum jaw and eyes that refused to see anything, even the work under his hands, had grown perfectly familiar to the Thompsons. At first, Mrs. Thompson complained a little. "It's like sitting down at the table with a disembodied spirit," she said. "You'd think he'd find something to say, sooner or later."

"Let him alone," said Mr. Thompson. "When he gets ready to talk, he'll talk."

The years passed, and Mr. Helton never got ready to talk. After his work was finished for the day, he would come up from the barn or the milk house or the chicken house, swinging his lantern, his big shoes clumping like pony hoofs on the hard path. They, sitting in the kitchen in the winter, or on the back porch in summer, would hear him drag out his wooden chair, hear the creak of it tilted back, and then for a little while he would play his single tune on one or another of his harmonicas. The harmonicas were in different keys, some lower and sweeter than the others, but the same changeless tune went on, a strange tune, with sudden turns in it, night after night, and sometimes even in the afternoons when Mr. Helton sat down to catch his breath. At first the Thompsons liked it very much, and always stopped to listen. Later there came a time when they were fairly sick of it, and began to wish to each other that he would learn a new one. At last they did not hear it any more, it was as natural as the sound of the wind rising in the evenings, or the cows lowing, or their own voices.

Mrs. Thompson pondered now and then over Mr. Helton's soul. He didn't seem to be a church-goer, and worked straight through Sunday as if it were any common day of the week. "I think we ought to invite him to go to hear Dr. Martin," she told Mr. Thompson. "It isn't very Christian of us not to ask him. He's not a forward kind of man. He'd wait to be asked."

"Let him alone," said Mr. Thompson. "The way I look at it, his religion is every man's own business. Besides, he ain't got any Sunday clothes. He wouldn't want to go to church in

them jeans and jumpers of his. I don't know what he does with his money. He certainly don't spend it foolishly."

Still, once the notion got into her head, Mrs. Thompson could not rest until she invited Mr. Helton to go to church with the family next Sunday. He was pitching hay into neat little piles in the field back of the orchard. Mrs. Thompson put on smoked glasses and a sunbonnet and walked all the way down there to speak to him. He stopped and leaned on his pitchfork, listening, and for a moment Mrs. Thompson was almost frightened at his face. The pale eyes seemed to glare past her, the eyebrows frowned, the long jaw hardened. "I got work," he said bluntly, and lifting his pitchfork he turned from her and began to toss the hay. Mrs. Thompson, her feelings hurt, walked back thinking that by now she should be used to Mr. Helton's ways, but it did seem like a man, even a foreigner, could be just a little polite when you gave him a Christian invitation. "He's not polite, that's the only thing I've got against him," she said to Mr. Thompson. "He just can't seem to behave like other people. You'd think he had a grudge against the world," she said. "I sometimes don't know what to make of it."

In the second year something had happened that made Mrs. Thompson uneasy, the kind of thing she could not put into words, hardly into thoughts, and if she had tried to explain to Mr. Thompson it would have sounded worse than it was, or not bad enough. It was that kind of queer thing that seems to be giving a warning, and yet, nearly always nothing comes of it. It was on a hot, still spring day, and Mrs. Thompson had been down to the garden patch to pull some new carrots and green onions and string beans for dinner. As she worked, sunbonnet low over her eyes, putting each kind of vegetable in a pile by itself in her basket, she noticed how neatly Mr. Helton weeded, and how rich the soil was. He had spread it all over with manure from the barns, and worked it in, in the fall, and the vegetables were coming up fine and full. She walked back under the nubbly little fig trees where the unpruned branches leaned almost to the ground, and the thick leaves made a cool screen. Mrs. Thompson was always looking for shade to save her eyes. So she, looking idly about, saw through the screen a sight that struck her as very strange. If it had been a noisy spectacle, it would have been quite natural. It was the silence that struck her. Mr. Helton was shaking Arthur by the shoulders, ferociously, his face most terribly fixed and pale. Arthur's head snapped back and forth and he had not stiffened in resistance, as he did when Mrs. Thompson tried to shake him. His eyes were rather frightened, but surprised, too, probably more surprised than anything else. Herbert stood by meekly, watching. Mr. Helton dropped Arthur, and seized Herbert, and shook him with the same methodical ferocity, the same face of hatred. Herbert's mouth crumpled as if he would cry, but he made no sound. Mr. Helton let him go, turned and strode into the shack, and the little boys ran, as if for their lives, without a word. They disappeared around the corner to the front of the house.

Mrs. Thompson took time to set her basket on the kitchen table, to push her sunbonnet back on her head and draw it forward again, to look in the stove and make certain the fire was going, before she followed the boys. They were sitting huddled together under a clump of chinaberry trees in plain sight of her bedroom window, as if it were a safe place they had discovered.

"What are you doing?" asked Mrs. Thompson.

They looked hang-dog from under their foreheads and Arthur mumbled, "Nothin'."

"Nothing now, you mean," said Mrs. Thompson, severely. "Well, I have plenty for you to do. Come right in here this minute and help me fix vegetables. This minute."

They scrambled up very eagerly and followed her close. Mrs. Thompson tried to imagine what they had been up to; she did not like the notion of Mr. Helton taking it on himself to correct her little boys, but she was afraid to ask them for reasons. They might tell her a lie, and she would have to overtake them in it, and whip them. Or she would have to pretend to believe them, and they would get in the habit of lying. Or they might tell her the truth, and it would be something she would have to whip them for. The very thought of it gave her a headache. She supposed she might ask Mr. Helton, but it was not her place to ask. She would wait and tell Mr. Thompson, and let him get at the bottom of it. While her mind ran on, she kept the little boys hopping. "Cut those carrot tops closer, Herbert, you're just being careless. Arthur, stop breaking up the beans so little. They're little enough already. Herbert, you go get an armload of wood. Arthur, you take these onions and wash them under the pump. Herbert, as soon as you're done here, you get a broom and sweep out this kitchen. Arthur, you get a shovel and take up the ashes. Stop picking your nose, Herbert. How often must I tell you? Arthur, you go look in the top drawer of my bureau, left-hand side, and bring me the vaseline for Herbert's nose. Herbert, come here to me. . . ."

They galloped through their chores, their animal spirits rose with activity, and shortly they were out in the front yard again, engaged in a wrestling match. They sprawled and fought, scrambled, clutched, rose and fell shouting, as aimlessly, noisily, monotonously as two puppies. They imitated various animals, not a human sound from them, and their dirty faces were streaked with sweat. Mrs. Thompson, sitting at her window, watched them with baffled pride and tenderness, they were so sturdy and healthy and growing so fast; but uneasily, too, with her pained little smile and the tears rolling from her eyelids that clinched themselves against the sunlight. They were so idle and careless, as if they had no future in this world, and no immortal souls to save, and oh, what had they been up to that Mr. Helton had shaken them, with his face positively dangerous?

In the evening before supper, without a word to Mr. Thompson of the curious fear the sight had caused her, she told him that Mr. Helton had shaken the little boys for some reason. He stepped out to the shack and spoke to Mr. Helton. In five minutes he was back, glaring at his young. "He says them brats been fooling with his harmonicas, Ellie, blowing in them and getting them all dirty and full of spit and they don't play good."

"Did he say all that?" asked Mrs. Thompson. "It doesn't seem possible."

"Well, that's what he meant, anyhow," said

Mr. Thompson. "He didn't say it just that way. But he acted pretty worked up about it."

"That's a shame," said Mrs. Thompson, "a perfect shame. Now we've got to do something so they'll remember they mustn't go into Mr. Helton's things."

"I'll tan their hides for them," said Mr. Thompson. "I'll take a calf rope to them if they don't look out."

"Maybe you'd better leave the whipping to me," said Mrs. Thompson. "You haven't got a light enough hand for children."

"That's just what's the matter with them now," shouted Mr. Thompson, "rotten spoiled and they'll wind up in the penitentiary. You don't half whip 'em. Just little love taps. My pa used to knock me down with a stick of stove wood or anything else that came handy."

"Well, that's not saying it's right," said Mrs. Thompson. "I don't hold with that way of raising children. It makes them run away from home. I've seen too much of it."

"I'll break every bone in 'em," said Mr. Thompson, simmering down, "if they don't mind you better and stop being so bull-headed."

"Leave the table and wash your face and hands," Mrs. Thompson commanded the boys, suddenly. They slunk out and dabbled at the pump and slunk in again, trying to make themselves small. They had learned long ago that their mother always made them wash when there was trouble ahead. They looked at their plates. Mr. Thompson opened up on them.

"Well, now, what you got to say for yourselves about going into Mr. Helton's shack and ruining his harmonicas?"

The two little boys wilted, their faces drooped into the grieved hopeless lines of children's faces when they are brought to the terrible bar of blind adult justice; their eyes telegraphed each other in panic, "Now we're really going to catch a licking"; in despair, they dropped their buttered cornbread on their plates, their hands lagged on the edge of the table.

"I ought to break your ribs," said Mr. Thompson, "and I'm a good mind to do it."

"Yes, sir," whispered Arthur, faintly.

"Yes, sir," said Herbert, his lip trembling.

"Now, papa," said Mrs. Thompson in a warning tone. The children did not glance at her. They had no faith in her good will. She had betrayed them in the first place. There was no trusting her. Now she might save them and she might not. No use depending on her.

"Well, you ought to get a good thrashing. You deserve it, don't you, Arthur?"

Arthur hung his head. "Yes, sir."

"And the next time I catch either of you hanging around Mr. Helton's shack, I'm going to take the hide off *both* of you, you hear me, Herbert?"

Herbert mumbled and choked, scattering his cornbread. "Yes, sir."

"Well, now sit up and eat your supper and not another word out of you," said Mr. Thompson, beginning on his own food. The little boys perked up somewhat and started chewing, but every time they looked around they met their parents' eyes, regarding them steadily. There was no telling when they would think of something new. The boys ate warily, trying not to be seen or heard, the cornbread sticking, the buttermilk gurgling, as it went down their gullets.

"And something else, Mr. Thompson," said Mrs. Thompson after a pause. "Tell Mr. Helton he's to come straight to us when they bother him, and not to trouble shaking them himself. Tell him we'll look after that."

"They're so mean," answered Mr. Thompson, staring at them. "It's a wonder he don't just kill 'em off and be done with it." But there was something in the tone that told Arthur and Herbert that nothing more worth worrying about was going to happen this time. Heaving deep sighs, they sat up, reaching for the food nearest them.

"Listen," said Mrs. Thompson, suddenly. The little boys stopped eating. "Mr. Helton hasn't come for his supper. Arthur, go and tell Mr. Helton he's late for supper. Tell him nice, now."

Arthur, miserably depressed, slid out of his place and made for the door, without a word.

IV

There were no miracles of fortune to be brought to pass on a small dairy farm. The Thompsons did not grow rich, but they kept out of the poor house, as Mr. Thompson was fond of saying, meaning he had got a little foothold in spite of Ellie's poor health, and unexpected weather, and strange declines in market prices, and his own mysterious handicaps which weighed him down. Mr. Helton was the hope and the prop of the family, and all the Thompsons became fond of him, or at any rate they ceased to regard him as in any way peculiar, and looked upon him, from a distance they did not know how to bridge, as a good man and a good friend. Mr. Helton went his way, worked, played his tune. Nine years passed. The boys grew up and learned to work. They could not remember the time when Ole Helton hadn't been there: a grouchy cuss, Brother Bones; Mr. Helton, the dairymaid; that Big Swede. If he had heard them, he might have been annoyed at some of the names they called him. But he did not hear them, and besides they meant no harm—or at least such harm as existed was all there, in the names; the boys referred to their father as the Old Man, or the Old Geezer, but not to his face. They lived through by main strength all the grimy, secret, oblique phases of growing up and got past the crisis safely if anyone does. Their parents could see they were good solid boys with hearts of gold in spite of their rough ways. Mr. Thompson was relieved to find that, without knowing how he had done it, he had succeeded in raising a set of boys who were not trifling whittlers. They were such good boys Mr. Thompson began to believe they were born that way, and that he had never spoken a harsh word to them in their lives, much less thrashed them. Herbert and Arthur never disputed his word.

V

Mr. Helton, his hair wet with sweat, plastered to his dripping forehead, his jumper streaked dark and light blue and clinging to his ribs, was chopping a little firewood. He chopped slowly, struck the ax into the end of the chopping log, and piled the wood up neatly. He then disappeared round the house into his shack, which shared with the wood pile a good shade from a row of mulberry trees. Mr. Thompson was lolling in a swing chair on the front porch, a place he had never liked. The chair was new, and Mrs. Thompson had wanted it on the front porch, though the side porch was the place for it, being cooler; and Mr. Thompson wanted to sit in the chair, so there he was. As soon as the new wore off of it, and Ellie's pride in it was exhausted, he would move it round to the side porch. Meantime the August heat was almost unbearable, the air so thick you could poke a hole in it. The dust was inches thick on everything, though Mr. Helton sprinkled the whole yard regularly every night. He even shot the hose upward and washed the tree tops and the roof of the house. They had laid waterpipes to the kitchen and an outside faucet. Mr. Thompson must have dozed, for he opened his eyes and shut his mouth just in time to save his face before a stranger who had driven up to the front gate. Mr. Thompson stood up, put on his hat, pulled up his jeans, and watched while the stranger tied his team, attached to a light spring wagon, to the hitching post. Mr. Thompson recognized the team and wagon. They were from a livery stable in Buda. While the stranger was opening the gate, a strong gate that Mr. Helton had built and set firmly on its hinges several years back, Mr. Thompson strolled down the path to greet him and find out what in God's world a man's business might be that would bring him out at this time of day, in all this dust and welter.

He wasn't exactly a fat man. He was more like a man who had been fat recently. His skin was baggy and his clothes were too big for him, and he somehow looked like a man who should be fat, ordinarily, but who might have just got over a spell of sickness. Mr. Thompson didn't take to his looks at all, he couldn't say why.

The stranger took off his hat. He said in a loud hearty voice, "Is this Mr. Thompson, Mr. Royal Earle Thompson?"

"That's my name," said Mr. Thompson, almost quietly, he was so taken aback by the free manner of the stranger.

"My name is Hatch," said the stranger, "Mr. Homer T. Hatch, and I've come to see you about buying a horse."

"I reckon you've been misdirected," said Mr. Thompson. "I haven't got a horse for sale. Usually if I've got anything like that to sell," he said, "I tell the neighbors and tack up a little sign on the gate."

The fat man opened his mouth and roared with joy, showing rabbit teeth brown as shoe-leather. Mr. Thompson saw nothing to laugh at, for once. The stranger shouted, "That's just an old joke of mine." He caught one of his hands in the other and shook hands with himself heartily. "I always say something like that when I'm calling on a stranger, because I've noticed that when a feller says he's come to buy something nobody takes him for a suspicious character. You see? Haw, haw, haw."

His joviality made Mr. Thompson nervous, because the expression in the man's eyes didn't match the sounds he was making. "Haw, haw," laughed Mr. Thompson obligingly, still not seeing the joke. "Well, that's all wasted on me because I never take any man for a suspicious character 'til he shows hisself to be one. Says or does something," he explained. "Until that happens, one man's as good as another, so far's *I'm* concerned."

"Well," said the stranger, suddenly very sober and sensible, "I ain't come neither to buy nor sell. Fact is, I want to see you about something that's of interest to us both. Yes, sir, I'd like to have a little talk with you, and it won't cost you a cent."

"I guess that's fair enough," said Mr. Thompson, reluctantly. "Come on around the house where there's a little shade."

They went round and seated themselves on two stumps under a chinaberry tree.

"Yes, sir, Homer T. Hatch is my name and America is my nation," said the stranger. "I reckon you must know the name? I used to have a cousin named Jameson Hatch lived up the country a ways."

"Don't think I know the name," said Mr. Thompson. "There's some Hatchers settled somewhere around Mountain City."

"Don't know the old Hatch family," cried the man in deep concern. He seemed to be pitying Mr. Thompson's ignorance. "Why, we came over from Georgia fifty years ago. Been here long yourself?"

"Just all my whole life," said Mr. Thompson, beginning to feel peevish. "And my pa and my grampap before me. Yes, sir, we've been right here all along. Anybody wants to find a Thompson knows where to look for him. My grampap immigrated in 1836."

"From Ireland, I reckon?" said the stranger.

"From Pennsylvania," said Mr. Thompson. "Now what makes you think we came from Ireland?"

The stranger opened his mouth and began to shout with merriment, and he shook hands with himself as if he hadn't met himself for a long time. "Well, what I always says is, a feller's got to come from *somewhere*, ain't he?"

While they were talking, Mr. Thompson kept glancing at the face near him. He certainly did remind Mr. Thompson of somebody, or maybe he really had seen the man himself somewhere. He couldn't just place the features. Mr. Thompson finally decided it was just that all rabbit-teethed men looked alike.

"That's right," acknowledged Mr. Thompson, rather sourly, "but what I always say is, Thompsons have been settled here for so long it don't make much difference any more *where* they come from. Now a course, this is the slack season, and we're all just laying round a little, but nevertheless we've all got our chores to do, and I don't want to hurry you, and so if you've come to see me on business maybe we'd better get down to it."

"As I said, it's not in a way, and again in a way it is," said the fat man. "Now I'm looking for a man named Helton, Mr. Olaf Eric Helton, from North Dakota, and I was told up around the country a ways that I might find him here, and I wouldn't mind having a little talk with him. No, siree, I sure wouldn't mind, if it's all the same to you."

"I never knew his middle name," said Mr. Thompson, "but Mr. Helton is right here, and been here now for going on nine years. He's a mighty steady man, and you can tell anybody I said so."

"I'm glad to hear that," said Mr. Homer T. Hatch. "I like to hear of a feller mending his ways and settling down. Now when I knew Mr. Helton he was pretty wild, yes, sir, wild is what he was, he didn't know his own mind atall. Well, now, it's going to be a great pleasure to me to meet up with an old friend and find him all settled down and doing well by hisself."

"We've all got to be young once," said Mr. Thompson. "It's like the measles, it breaks out all over you, and you're a nuisance to yourself and everybody else, but it don't last, and it usually don't leave no ill effects." He was so pleased with this notion he forgot and broke into a guffaw. The stranger folded his arms over his stomach and went into a kind of fit, roaring until he had tears in his eyes. Mr. Thompson stopped shouting and eyed the stranger uneasily. Now he liked a good laugh as well as any man, but there ought to be a little moderation. Now this feller laughed like a perfect lunatic, that was a fact. And he wasn't laughing because he really thought things were funny, either. He was laughing for reasons of his own. Mr. Thompson fell into a moody silence, and waited until Mr. Hatch settled down a little.

Mr. Hatch got out a very dirty blue cotton bandanna and wiped his eyes. "That joke just about caught me where I live," he said, almost apologetically. "Now I wish I could think up things as funny as that to say. It's a gift. It's . . ."

"If you want to speak to Mr. Helton, I'll go and round him up," said Mr. Thompson, making motions as if he might get up. "He may be in the milk house and he may be setting in his shack this time of day." It was drawing towards five o'clock. "It's right around the corner," he said.

"Oh, well, there ain't no special hurry," said Mr. Hatch. "I've been wanting to speak to him for a good long spell now and I guess a few minutes more won't make no difference. I just more wanted to locate him, like. That's all."

Mr. Thompson stopped beginning to stand up, and unbuttoned one more button of his shirt, and said, "Well, he's here, and he's this kind of man, that if he had any business with you he'd like to get it over. He don't dawdle, that's one thing you can say for him."

Mr. Hatch appeared to sulk a little at these words. He wiped his face with the bandanna and opened his mouth to speak, when round the house there came the music of Mr. Helton's harmonica. Mr. Thompson raised a finger. "There he is," said Mr. Thompson. "Now's your time."

Mr. Hatch cocked an ear towards the east side of the house and listened for a few seconds, a very strange expression on his face.

"I know that tune like I know the palm of my own hand," said Mr. Thompson, "but I never heard Mr. Helton say what it was."

"That's a kind of Scandahoovian song," said Mr. Hatch. "Where I come from they sing it a lot. In North Dakota, they sing it. It says something about starting out in the morning feeling so good you can't hardly stand it, so you drink up all your likker before noon. All the likker, y' understand, that you was saving for the noon lay-off. The words ain't much, but it's a pretty tune. It's a kind of drinking song." He sat there drooping a little, and Mr. Thompson didn't like his expression. It was a satisfied expression, but it was more like the cat that et the canary.

"So far as I know," said Mr. Thompson, "he ain't touched a drop since he's been on the place, and that's nine years this coming September. Yes, sir, nine years, so far as I know, he ain't wetted his whistle once. And that's more than I can say for myself," he said, meekly proud.

"Yes, that's a drinking song," said Mr. Hatch. "I used to play 'Little Brown Jug' on the fiddle when I was younger than I am now," he went on, "but this Helton, he just keeps it up. He just sits and plays it by himself."

"He's been playing it off and on for nine years right here on the place," said Mr. Thompson, feeling a little proprietary.

"And he was certainly singing it as well, fifteen years before that, in North Dakota," said Mr. Hatch. "He used to sit up in a straitjacket, practically, when he was in the asylum—"

"What's that you say?" said Mr. Thompson. "What's that?"

"Shucks, I didn't mean to tell you," said Mr. Hatch, a faint leer of regret in his drooping eyelids. "Shucks, that just slipped out. Funny, now I'd made up my mind I wouldn' say a word, because it would just make a lot of excitement, and what I say is, if a man has lived harmless and quiet for nine years it don't matter if he *is* loony, does it? So long's he keeps quiet and don't do nobody harm."

"You mean they had him in a straitjacket?"

asked Mr. Thompson, uneasily. "In a lunatic asylum?"

"They sure did," said Mr. Hatch. "That's right where they had him, from time to time."

"They put my Aunt Ida in one of them things in the State asylum," said Mr. Thompson. "She got vi'lent, and they put her in one of these jackets with long sleeves and tied her to an iron ring in the wall, and Aunt Ida got so wild she broke a blood vessel and when they went to look after her she was dead. I'd think one of them things was dangerous."

"Mr. Helton used to sing his drinking song when he was in a straitjacket," said Mr. Hatch. "Nothing ever bothered him, except if you tried to make him talk. That bothered him, and he'd get vi'lent, like your Aunt Ida. He'd get vi'lent and then they'd put him in the jacket and go off and leave him, and he'd lay there perfickly contented, so far's you could see, singing his song. Then one night he just disappeared. Left, you might say, just went, and nobody ever saw hide or hair of him again. And then I come along and find him here," said Mr. Hatch, "all settled down and playing the same song."

"He never acted crazy to me," said Mr. Thompson. "He always acted like a sensible man, to me. He never got married, for one thing, and he works like a horse, and I bet he's got the first cent I paid him when he landed here, and he don't drink, and he never says a word, much less swear, and he don't waste time runnin' around Saturday nights, and if he's crazy," said Mr. Thompson, "why, I think I'll go crazy myself for a change."

"Haw, ha," said Mr. Hatch, "heh, he, that's good! Ha, ha, ha, I hadn't thought of it jes like that. Yeah, that's right! Let's all go crazy and get rid of our wives and save our money, hey?" He smiled unpleasantly, showing his little rabbit teeth.

Mr. Thompson felt he was being misunderstood. He turned around and motioned toward the open window back of the honeysuckle trellis. "Let's move off down here a little," he said. "I oughta thought of that before." His visitor bothered Mr. Thompson. He had a way of taking the words out of Mr. Thompson's mouth, turning them around and mixing them up until Mr. Thompson didn't know himself what he had said. "My wife's not very strong," said Mr. Thompson. "She's been kind of invalid now goin' on fourteen years. It's mighty tough on a poor man, havin' sickness in the family. She had four operations," he said proudly, "one right after the other, but they didn't do any good. For five years handrunnin', I just turned every nickel I made over to the doctors. Upshot is, she's a mighty delicate woman."

"My old woman," said Mr. Homer T. Hatch, "had a back like a mule, yes, sir. That woman could have moved the barn with her bare hands if she'd ever took notion. I used to say, it was a good thing she didn't know her own stren'th. She's dead now, though. That kind wear out quicker than the puny ones. I never had much use for a woman always complainin'. I'd get rid of her mighty quick, yes, sir, mighty quick. It's just as you say: a dead loss, keepin' one of 'em up."

This was not at all what Mr. Thompson had heard himself say; he had been trying to explain that a wife as expensive as his was a credit to a man. "She's a mighty reasonable woman," said Mr. Thompson, feeling baffled, "but I wouldn't answer for what she'd say or do if she found out we'd had a lunatic on the place all this time." They had moved away from the window; Mr. Thompson took Mr. Hatch the front way, because if he went the back way they would have to pass Mr. Helton's shack. For some reason he didn't want the stranger to see or talk to Mr. Helton. It was strange, but that was the way Mr. Thompson felt.

Mr. Thompson sat down again, on the chopping log, offering his guest another tree stump. "Now, I mighta got upset myself at such a thing, once," said Mr. Thompson, "but now I *deefy* anything to get me lathered up." He cut himself an enormous plug of tobacco with his horn-handled pocketknife, and offered it to Mr. Hatch, who then produced his own plug and, opening a huge bowie knife with a long blade sharply whetted, cut off a large wad and put it in his mouth. They then compared plugs and both of them were astonished to see how different men's ideas of good chewing tobacco were.

"Now, for instance," said Mr. Hatch, "mine

is lighter colored. That's because, for one thing, there ain't any sweetenin' in this plug. I like it dry, natural leaf, medium strong."

"A little sweetenin' don't do no harm so far as I'm concerned," said Mr. Thompson, "but it's got to be mighty little. But with me, now, I want a strong leaf, I want it heavy-cured, as the feller says. There's a man near here, named Williams, Mr. John Morgan Williams, who chews a plug—well, sir, it's black as your hat and soft as melted tar. It fairly drips with molasses, jus' plain molasses, and it chews like licorice. Now, I don't call that a good chew."

"One man's meat," said Mr. Hatch, "is another man's poison. Now, such a chew would simply gag me. I couldn't begin to put it in my mouth."

"Well," said Mr. Thompson, a tinge of apology in his voice, "I jus' barely tasted it myself, you might say. Just took a little piece in my mouth and spit it out again."

"I'm dead sure I couldn't even get that far." said Mr. Hatch. "I like a dry natural chew without any artificial flavorin' of any kind."

Mr. Thompson began to feel that Mr. Hatch was trying to make out he had the best judgment in tobacco, and was going to keep up the argument until he proved it. He began to feel seriously annoyed with the fat man. After all, who was he and where did he come from? Who was he to go around telling other people what kind of tobacco to chew?

"Artificial flavorin'," Mr. Hatch went on, doggedly, "is jes put in to cover up a cheap leaf and make a man think he's gettin' somethin' more than he *is* gettin'. Even a little sweetenin' is a sign of cheap leaf, you can mark my words."

"I've always paid a fair price for my plug," said Mr. Thompson, stiffly. "I'm not a rich man and I don't go round settin' myself up for one, but I'll say this, when it comes to such things as tobacco, I buy the best on the market."

"Sweetenin', even a little," began Mr. Hatch, shifting his plug and squirting tobacco juice at a dry-looking little rose bush that was having a hard enough time as it was, standing all day in the blazing sun, its roots clenched in the baked earth, "is the sign of—"

"About this Mr. Helton, now," said Mr.

Thompson, determinedly, "I don't see no reason to hold it against a man because he went loony once or twice in his lifetime and so I don't expect to take no steps about it. Not a step. I've got nothin' against the man, he's always treated me fair. They's things and people," he went on, " 'nough to drive any man loony. The wonder to me is, more men don't wind up in straitjackets, the way things are going these days and times."

"That's right," said Mr. Hatch, promptly, entirely too promptly, as if he were turning Mr. Thompson's meaning back on him. "You took the words right out of my mouth. There ain't every man in a straitjacket that ought to be there. Ha, ha, you're right all right. You got the idea."

Mr. Thompson sat silent and chewed steadily and stared at a spot on the ground about six feet away and felt a slow muffled resentment climbing from somewhere deep down in him, climbing and spreading all through him. What was this fellow driving at? What was he trying to say? It wasn't so much his words, but his looks and his way of talking: that droopy look in the eye, that tone of voice, as if he was trying to mortify Mr. Thompson about something. Mr. Thompson didn't like it, but he couldn't get hold of it either. He wanted to turn around and shove the fellow off the stump, but it wouldn't look reasonable. Suppose something happened to the fellow when he fell off the stump, just for instance, if he fell on the ax and cut himself, and then someone should ask Mr. Thompson why he shoved him, and what could a man say? It would look mighty funny, it would sound mighty strange to say, Well, him and me fell out over a plug of tobacco. He might just shove him anyhow and then tell people he was a fat man not used to the heat and while he was talking he got dizzy and fell off by himself, or something like that, and it wouldn't be the truth either, because it wasn't the heat and it wasn't the tobacco. Mr. Thompson made up his mind to get the fellow off the place pretty quick, without seeming to be anxious, and watch him sharp till he was out of sight. It doesn't pay to be friendly with strangers from another part of the country. They're always up to something, or they'd stay at home where they belong.

"And they's some people," said Mr. Hatch, "would jus' as soon have a loonatic around their house as not, they can't see no difference between them and anybody else. I always say, if that's the way a man feels, don't care who he associates with, why, why, that's his business, not mine. I don't wanta have a thing to do with it. Now back home in North Dakota, we don't feel that way. I'd like to a seen anybody hiring a loonatic there, aspecially after what he done."

"I didn't understand your home was North Dakota," said Mr. Thompson. "I thought you said Georgia."

"I've got a married sister in North Dakota," said Mr. Hatch, "married a Swede, but a white man if ever I saw one. So I say *we* because we got into a little business together out that way. And it seems like home, kind of."

"What did he do," asked Mr. Thompson, feeling very uneasy again.

"Oh, nothin' to speak of," said Mr. Hatch, jovially, "jus' went loony one day in the hayfield and shoved a pitchfork right square through his brother, when they was makin' hay. They was goin' to execute him, but they found out he had went crazy with the heat, as the feller says, and so they put him in the asylum. That's all he done. Nothin' to get lathered up about, ha, ha, ha!" he said, and taking out his sharp knife he began to slice off a chew as carefully as if he were cutting cake.

"Well," said Mr. Thompson, "I don't deny that's news. Yes, sir, news. But I still say somethin' must have drove him to it. Some men make you feel like giving 'em a good killing just by lookin' at you. His brother may a been a mean ornery cuss."

"Brother was going to get married," said Mr. Hatch; "used to go courtin' his girl nights. Borrowed Mr. Helton's harmonica to give her a serenade one evenin', and lost it. Brand new harmonica."

"He thinks a heap of his harmonicas," said Mr. Thompson. "Only money he ever spends, now and then he buys hisself a new one. Must have a dozen in that shack, all kinds and sizes."

"Brother wouldn't buy him a new one," said Mr. Hatch, "so Mr. Helton just ups, as I says, and runs his pitchfork through his brother.

Now you know he musta been crazy to get all worked up over a little thing like that."

"Sounds like it," said Mr. Thompson, reluctant to agree in anything with this intrusive and disagreeable fellow. He kept thinking he couldn't remember when he had taken such a dislike to a man on first sight.

"Seems to me you'd get pretty sick of hearin' the same tune year in, year out," said Mr. Hatch.

"Well, sometimes I think it wouldn't do no harm if he learned a new one," said Mr. Thompson, "but he don't, so there's nothin' to be done about it. It's a pretty good tune, though."

"One of the Scandahoovians told me what it meant, that's how I come to know," said Mr. Hatch. "Especially that part about getting so gay you jus' go ahead and drink up all the likker you got on hand before noon. It seems like up in them Swede countries a man carries a bottle of wine around with him as a matter of course, at least that's the way I understood it. Those fellers will tell you anything, though—" He broke off and spat.

The idea of drinking any kind of liquor in this heat made Mr. Thompson dizzy. The idea of anybody feeling good on a day like this, for instance, made him tired. He felt he was really suffering from the heat. The fat man looked as if he had grown to the stump; he slumped there in his damp, dark clothes too big for him, his belly slack in his pants, his wide black felt hat pushed off his narrow forehead red with prickly heat. A bottle of good cold beer, now, would be a help, thought Mr. Thompson, remembering the four bottles sitting deep in the pool at the springhouse, and his dry tongue squirmed in his mouth. He wasn't going to offer this man anything, though, not even a drop of water. He wasn't even going to chew any more tobacco with him. He shot out his quid suddenly, and wiped his mouth on the back of his hand, and studied the head near him attentively. The man was no good, and he was there for no good, but what was he up to? Mr. Thompson made up his mind he'd give him a little more time to get his business, whatever it was, with Mr. Helton over, and then if he didn't get off the place he'd kick him off.

Mr. Hatch, as if he suspected Mr. Thompson's thoughts, turned his eyes, wicked and pig-like, on Mr. Thompson. "Fact is," he said, as if he had made up his mind about something, "I might need your help in the little matter I've got on hand, but it won't cost you any trouble. Now, this Mr. Helton here, like I tell you, he's a dangerous escaped loonatic, you might say. Now fact is, in the last twelve years or so I musta rounded up twenty-odd escaped loonatics, besides a couple of escaped convicts that I just run into by accident, like. I don't make a business of it, but if there's a reward, and there usually is a reward, of course, I get it. It amounts to a tidy little sum in the long run, but that ain't the main question. Fact is, I'm for law and order, I don't like to see law-breakers and loonatics at large. It ain't the place for them. Now I reckon you're bound to agree with me on that, aren't you?"

Mr. Thompson said, "Well, circumstances alters cases, as the feller says. Now, what I know of Mr. Helton, he ain't dangerous, as I told you." Something serious was going to happen, Mr. Thompson could see that. He stopped thinking about it. He'd just let this fellow shoot off his head and then see what could be done about it. Without thinking he got out his knife and plug and started to cut a chew, then remembered himself and put them back in his pocket.

"The law," said Mr. Hatch, "is solidly behind me. Now this Mr. Helton, he's been one of my toughest cases. He's kept my record from being practically one hundred per cent. I knew him before he went loony, and I know the fam'ly, so I undertook to help out rounding him up. Well, sir, he was gone slick as a whistle, for all we knew the man was as good as dead long while ago. Now we never might have caught up with him, but do you know what he did? Well, sir, about two weeks ago his old mother gets a letter from him, and in that letter, what do you reckon she found? Well, it was a check on that little bank in town for eight hundred and fifty dollars, just like that; the letter wasn't nothing much, just said he was sending her a few little savings, she might need something, but there it was, name, postmark, date, everything. The old woman practically lost her mind with joy. She's gettin' childish, and it

looked like she kinda forgot that her only living son killed his brother and went loony. Mr. Helton said he was getting along all right, and for her not to tell nobody. Well, natchally, she couldn't keep it to herself, with that check to cash and everything. So that's how I come to know." His feelings got the better of him. "You coulda knocked me down with a feather." He shook hands with himself and rocked, wagging his head, going "Heh, heh," in his throat. Mr. Thompson felt the corners of his mouth turning down. Why, the dirty low-down hound, sneaking around spying into other people's business like that. Collecting blood money, that's what it was! Let him talk!

"Yea, well, that musta been a surprise all right," he said, trying to hold his voice even. "I'd say a surprise."

"Well, siree," said Mr. Hatch, "the more I got to thinking about it, the more I just come to the conclusion that I'd better look into the matter a little, and so I talked to the old woman. She's pretty decrepit, now, half blind and all, but she was all for taking the first train out and going to see her son. I put it up to her square—how she was too feeble for the trip, and all. So, just as a favor to her, I told her for my expenses I'd come down and see Mr. Helton and bring her back all the news about him. She gave me a new shirt she made herself by hand, and a big Swedish kind of cake to bring to him, but I musta mislaid them along the road somewhere. It don't reely matter, though, he prob'ly ain't in any state of mind to appreciate 'em."

Mr. Thompson sat up and turning round on the log looked at Mr. Hatch and asked as quietly as he could, "And now what are you aiming to do? That's the question."

Mr. Hatch slouched up to his feet and shook himself. "Well, I come all prepared for a little scuffle," he said. "I got the handcuffs," he said, "but I don't want no violence if I can help it. I didn't want to say nothing around the countryside, making an uproar. I figured the two of us could overpower him." He reached into his big inside pocket and pulled them out. Handcuffs, for God's sake, thought Mr. Thompson. Coming round on a peaceable afternoon worrying a man, and making trouble, and fishing handcuffs out of his pocket on a decent family homestead, as if it was all in the day's work.

Mr. Thompson, his head buzzing, got up too. "Well," he said, roundly, "I want to tell you I think you've got a mighty sorry job on hand, you sure must be hard up for something to do, and now I want to give you a good piece of advice. You just drop the idea that you're going to come here and make trouble for Mr. Helton, and the quicker you drive that hired rig away from my front gate the better I'll be satisfied."

Mr. Hatch put one handcuff in his outside pocket, the other dangling down. He pulled his hat down over his eyes, and reminded Mr. Thompson of a sheriff, somehow. He didn't seem in the least nervous, and didn't take up Mr. Thompson's words. He said, "Now listen just a minute, it ain't reasonable to suppose that a man like yourself is going to stand in the way of getting an escaped loonatic back to the asylum where he belongs. Now I know it's enough to throw you off, coming sudden like this, but fact is I counted on your being a respectable man and helping me out to see that justice is done. Now a course, if you won't help, I'll have to look around for help somewheres else. It won't look very good to your neighbors that you was harbring an escaped loonatic who killed his own brother, and then you refused to give him up. It will look mighty funny."

Mr. Thompson knew almost before he heard the words that it would look funny. It would put him in a mighty awkward position. He said, "But I've been trying to tell you all along that the man ain't loony now. He's been perfectly harmless for nine years. He's—he's—"

Mr. Thompson couldn't think how to describe how it was with Mr. Helton. "Why, he's been like one of the family," he said, "the best standby a man ever had." Mr. Thompson tried to see his way out. It was a fact Mr. Helton might go loony again any minute, and now this fellow talking around the country would put Mr. Thompson in a fix. It was a terrible position. He couldn't think of any way out. "You're crazy," Mr. Thompson roared suddenly, "you're the crazy one around here, you're crazier than

he ever was! You get off this place or I'll handcuff you and turn you over to the law. You're trespassing," shouted Mr. Thompson. "Get out of here before I knock you down!"

He took a step towards the fat man, who backed off, shrinking. "Try it, try it, go ahead!" and then something happened that Mr. Thompson tried hard afterwards to piece together in his mind, and in fact it never did come straight. He saw the fat man with his long bowie knife in his hand, he saw Mr. Helton come round the corner on the run, his long jaw dropped, his arms swinging, his eyes wild. Mr. Helton came in between them, fists doubled up, then stopped short, glaring at the fat man, his big frame seemed to collapse, he trembled like a shied horse; and then the fat man drove at him, knife in one hand, handcuffs in the other. Mr. Thompson saw it coming, he saw the blade going into Mr. Helton's stomach, he knew he had the ax out of the log in his own hands, felt his arms go up over his head and bring the ax down on Mr. Hatch's head as if he were stunning a beef.

Mrs. Thompson had been listening uneasily for some time to the voices going on, one of them strange to her, but she was too tired at first to get up and come out to see what was going on. The confused shouting that rose so suddenly brought her up to her feet and out across the front porch without her slippers, hair half-braided. Shading her eyes, she saw first Mr. Helton, running all stooped over through the orchard, running like a man with dogs after him; and Mr. Thompson supporting himself on the ax handle was leaning over shaking by the shoulder a man Mrs. Thompson had never seen, who lay doubled up with the top of his head smashed and the blood running away in a greasy-looking puddle. Mr. Thompson without taking his hand from the man's shoulder, said in a thick voice, "He killed Mr. Helton, he killed him, I saw him do it. I had to knock him out," he called loudly, "but he won't come to."

Mrs. Thompson said in a faint scream, "Why, yonder goes Mr. Helton," and she pointed. Mr. Thompson pulled himself up and looked where she pointed. Mrs. Thompson sat down slowly against the side of the house and began to slide forward on her face; she felt as if she were drowning, she couldn't rise to the top somehow, and her only thought was she was glad the boys were not there, they were out, fishing at Halifax, oh, God, she was glad the boys were not there.

VI

Mr. and Mrs. Thompson drove up to their barn about sunset. Mr. Thompson handed the reins to his wife, got out to open the big door, and Mrs. Thompson guided old Jim in under the roof. The buggy was gray with dust and age, Mrs. Thompson's face was gray with dust and weariness, and Mr. Thompson's face, as he stood at the horse's head and began unhitching, was gray except for the dark blue of his freshly shaven jaws and chin, gray and blue and caved in, but patient, like a dead man's face.

Mrs. Thompson stepped down to the hard packed manure of the barn floor, and shook out her light flower-sprigged dress. She wore her smoked glasses, and her wide shady leghorn hat with the wreath of exhausted pink and blue forget-me-nots hid her forehead, fixed in a knot of distress.

The horse hung his head, raised a huge sigh and flexed his stiffened legs. Mr. Thompson's words came up muffled and hollow. "Poor ole Jim," he said, clearing his throat, "he looks pretty sunk in the ribs. I guess he's had a hard week." He lifted the harness up in one piece, slid it off and Jim walked out of the shafts halting a little. "Well, this is the last time," Mrs. Thompson said, still talking to Jim. "Now you can get a good rest."

Mrs. Thompson closed her eyes behind her smoked glasses. The last time, and high time, and they should never have gone at all. She did not need her glasses any more, now the good darkness was coming down again, but her eyes ran full of tears steadily, though she was not crying, and she felt better with the glasses, safer, hidden away behind them. She took out her handkerchief with her hands shaking as they had been shaking ever since *that day*, and blew her nose. She said, "I see the boys have lighted the lamps. I hope they've started the stove going."

She stepped along the rough path holding her thin dress and starched petticoats around her, feeling her way between the sharp small stones, leaving the barn because she could hardly bear to be near Mr. Thompson, advancing slowly towards the house because she dreaded going there. Life was all one dread, the faces of her neighbors, of her boys, of her husband, the face of the whole world, the shape of her own house in the darkness, the very smell of the grass and the trees were horrible to her. There was no place to go, only one thing to do, bear it somehow—but how? She asked herself that question often. How was she going to keep on living now? Why had she lived at all? She wished now she had died one of those times when she had been so sick, instead of living on for this.

The boys were in the kitchen; Herbert was looking at the funny pictures from last Sunday's newspapers, the Katzenjammer Kids and Happy Hooligan. His chin was in his hands and his elbows on the table, and he was really reading and looking at the pictures, but his face was unhappy. Arthur was building the fire, adding kindling a stick at a time, watching it catch and blaze. His face was heavier and darker than Herbert's, but he was a little sullen by nature; Mrs. Thompson thought, he takes things harder, too. Arthur said, "Hello, Momma," and went on with his work. Herbert swept the papers together and moved over on the bench. They were big boys—fifteen and seventeen, and Arthur as tall as his father. Mrs. Thompson sat down beside Herbert, taking off her hat. She said, "I guess you're hungry. We were late today. We went the Log Hollow road, it's rougher than ever." Her pale mouth drooped with a sad fold on either side.

"I guess you saw the Mannings, then," said Herbert.

"Yes, and the Fergusons, and the Allbrights, and that new family McClellan."

"Anybody say anything?" asked Herbert.

"Nothing much, you know how it's been all along, some of them keeps saying, yes, they know it was a clear case and a fair trial and they say how glad they are your papa came out so well, and all that, some of 'em do, anyhow, but it looks like they don't really take sides with him. I'm about wore out," she said, the tears rolling again from under her dark glasses. "I don't know what good it does, but your papa can't seem to rest unless he's telling how it happened. I don't know."

"I don't think it does any good, not a speck," said Arthur, moving away from the stove. "It just keeps the whole question stirred up in people's minds. Everybody will go round telling what he heard, and the whole thing is going to get worse mixed up than ever. It just makes matters worse. I wish you could get Papa to stop driving round the country talking like that."

"Your papa knows best," said Mrs. Thompson. "You oughtn't to criticize him. He's got enough to put up with without that."

Arthur said nothing, his jaw stubborn. Mr. Thompson came in, his eyes hollowed out and dead-looking, his thick hands gray white and seamed from washing them clean every day before he started out to see the neighbors to tell them his side of the story. He was wearing his Sunday clothes, a thick pepper-and-salt-colored suit with a black string tie.

Mrs. Thompson stood up, her head swimming. "Now you-all get out of the kitchen, it's too hot in here and I need room. I'll get us a little bite of supper, if you'll just get out and give me some room."

They went as if they were glad to go, the boys outside, Mr. Thompson into his bedroom. She heard him groaning to himself as he took off his shoes, and heard the bed creak as he lay down. Mrs. Thompson opened the icebox and felt the sweet coldness flow out of it; she had never expected to have an icebox, much less did she hope to afford to keep it filled with ice. It still seemed like a miracle, after two or three years. There was the food, cold and clean, all ready to be warmed over. She would never have had that icebox if Mr. Helton hadn't happened along one day, just by the strangest luck; so saving, and so managing, so good, thought Mrs. Thompson, her heart swelling until she feared she would faint again, standing there with the door open and leaning her head upon it. She simply could not bear to remember Mr. Helton, with his long sad face and silent ways, who had always been so quiet and harmless, who had worked so hard and helped Mr. Thompson so

much, running through the hot fields and woods, being hunted like a mad dog, everybody turning out with ropes and guns and sticks to catch and tie him. Oh, God, said Mrs. Thompson in a long dry moan, kneeling before the icebox and fumbling inside for the dishes, even if they did pile mattresses all over the jail floor and against the walls, and five men there to hold him to keep him from hurting himself any more, he was already hurt too badly, he couldn't have lived anyway. Mr. Barbee, the sheriff, told her about it. He said, well, they didn't aim to harm him but they had to catch him, he was crazy as a loon; he picked up rocks and tried to brain every man that got near him. He had two harmonicas in his jumper pocket, said the sheriff, but they fell out in the scuffle, and Mr. Helton tried to pick 'em up again, and that's when they finally got him. "They *had* to be rough, Miz Thompson, he fought like a wildcat." Yes, thought Mrs. Thompson again with the same bitterness, of course, they had to be rough. They always have to be rough. Mr. Thompson can't argue with a man and get him off the place peaceably; no, she thought, standing up and shutting the icebox, he has to kill somebody, he has to be a murderer and ruin his boys' lives and cause Mr. Helton to be killed like a mad dog.

Her thoughts stopped with a little soundless explosion, cleared and began again. The rest of Mr. Helton's harmonicas were still in the shack, his tune ran in Mrs. Thompson's head at certain times of the day. She missed it in the evenings. It seemed so strange she had never known the name of that song, nor what it meant, until after Mr. Helton was gone. Mrs. Thompson, trembling in the knees, took a drink of water at the sink and poured the red beans into the baking dish, and began to roll the pieces of chicken in flour to fry them. There was a time, she said to herself, when I thought I had neighbors and friends, there was a time when we could hold up our heads, there was a time when my husband hadn't killed a man and I could tell the truth to anybody about anything.

VII

Mr. Thompson, turning on his bed, figured

that he had done all he could, he'd just try to let the matter rest from now on. His lawyer, Mr. Burleigh, had told him right at the beginning, "Now you keep calm and collected. You've got a fine case, even if you haven't got witnesses. Your wife must sit in court, she'll be a powerful argument with the jury. You just plead not guilty and I'll do the rest. The trial is going to be a mere formality, you haven't got a thing to worry about. You'll be clean out of this before you know it." And to make talk Mr. Burleigh had got to telling about all the men he knew around the country who for one reason or another had been forced to kill somebody, always in self-defense, and there just wasn't anything to it at all. He even told about how his own father in the old days had shot and killed a man just for setting foot inside his gate when he told him not to. "Sure, I shot the scoundrel," said Mr. Burleigh's father, "in self-defense; I *told* him I'd shoot him if he set his foot in my yard, and he did, and I did." There had been bad blood between them for years, Mr. Burleigh said, and his father had waited a long time to catch the other fellow in the wrong, and when he did he certainly made the most of his opportunity.

"But Mr. Hatch, as I told you," Mr. Thompson had said, "made a pass at Mr. Helton with his bowie knife. That's why I took a hand."

"All the better," said Mr. Burleigh. "That stranger hadn't any right coming to your house on such an errand. Why, hell," said Mr. Burleigh, "that wasn't even manslaughter you committed. So now you just hold your horses and keep your shirt on. And don't say one word without I tell you."

Wasn't even manslaughter. Mr. Thompson had to cover Mr. Hatch with a piece of wagon canvas and ride to town to tell the sheriff. It had been hard on Ellie. When they got back, the sheriff and the coroner and two deputies, they found her sitting beside the road, on a low bridge over a gulley, about half a mile from the place. He had taken her up behind his saddle and got her back to the house. He had already told the sheriff that his wife had witnessed the whole business, and now he had time, getting her to her room and in bed, to tell her what to say if they asked anything.

He had left out the part about Mr. Helton being crazy all along, but it came out at the trial. By Mr. Burleigh's advice Mr. Thompson had pretended to be perfectly ignorant; Mr. Hatch hadn't said a word about that. Mr. Thompson pretended to believe that Mr. Hatch had just come looking for Mr. Helton to settle old scores, and the two members of Mr. Hatch's family who had come down to try to get Mr. Thompson convicted didn't get anywhere at all. It hadn't been much of a trial, Mr. Burleigh saw to that. He had charged a reasonable fee, and Mr. Thompson had paid him and felt grateful, but after it was over Mr. Burleigh didn't seem pleased to see him when he got to dropping into the office to talk it over, telling him things that had slipped his mind at first: trying to explain what an ornery low hound Mr. Hatch had been, anyhow. Mr. Burleigh seemed to have lost his interest; he looked sour and upset when he saw Mr. Thompson at the door. Mr. Thompson kept saying to himself that he'd got off, all right, just as Mr. Burleigh had predicted, but, but—and it was right there that Mr. Thompson's mind stuck, squirming like an angleworm on a fishhook: he had killed Mr. Hatch, and he was a murderer. That was the truth about himself that Mr. Thompson couldn't grasp, even when he said the word to himself. Why, he had not even once *thought* of killing anybody, much less Mr. Hatch, and if Mr. Helton hadn't come out so unexpectedly, hearing the row, why, then—but then, Mr. Helton had come on the run that way to help him. What he couldn't understand was what happened next. He had seen Mr. Hatch go after Mr. Helton with the knife, he had seen the point, blade up, go into Mr. Helton's stomach and slice up like you slice a hog, but when they finally caught Mr. Helton there wasn't a knife scratch on him. Mr. Thompson knew he had the ax in his own hands and felt himself lifting it, but he couldn't remember hitting Mr. Hatch. He couldn't remember it. He couldn't. He remembered only that he had been determined to stop Mr. Hatch from cutting Mr. Helton. If he was given a chance he could explain the whole matter. At the trial they hadn't let him talk. They just asked questions and he answered yes or no, and they never did get to the core of the matter. Since the trial, now, every day for a week he had washed and shaved and put on his best clothes and had taken Ellie with him to tell every neighbor he had that he never killed Mr. Hatch on purpose, and what good did it do? Nobody believed him. Even when he turned to Ellie and said, "You was there, you saw it, didn't you?" and Ellie spoke up, saying, "Yes, that's the truth. Mr. Thompson was trying to save Mr. Helton's life," and he added, "If you don't believe me, you can believe my wife. She won't lie," Mr. Thompson saw something in all their faces that disheartened him, made him feel empty and tired out. They didn't believe he was not a murderer.

Even Ellie never said anything to comfort him. He hoped she would say finally, "I remember now, Mr. Thompson, I really did come round the corner in time to see everything. It's not a lie, Mr. Thompson. Don't you worry." But as they drove together in silence, with the days still hot and dry, shortening for fall, day after day, the buggy jolting in the ruts, she said nothing; they grew to dread the sight of another house, and the people in it: all houses looked alike now, and the people—old neighbors or new —had the same expression when Mr. Thompson told them why he had come and began his story. Their eyes looked as if someone had pinched the eyeball at the back; they shriveled and the light went out of them. Some of them sat with fixed tight smiles trying to be friendly. "Yes, Mr. Thompson, we know how you must feel. It must be terrible for you, Mrs. Thompson. Yes, you know, I've about come to the point where I believe in such a thing as killing in self-defense. Why, certainly, we believe you, Mr. Thompson, why shouldn't we believe you? Didn't you have a perfectly fair and above-board trial? Well, now, natchally, Mr. Thompson, we think you done right."

Mr. Thompson was satisfied they didn't think so. Sometimes the air around him was so thick with their blame he fought and pushed with his fists, and the sweat broke out all over him, he shouted his story in a dust-choked voice, he would fairly bellow at last: "My wife, here, you know her, she was there, she saw and heard it all, if you don't believe me, ask her, she won't lie!" and Mrs. Thompson, with her hands knotted together, aching, her chin trembling, would never fail to say: "Yes, that's right, that's the truth—"

The last straw had been laid on today, Mr. Thompson decided. Tom Allbright, an old beau of Ellie's, why, he had squired Ellie around a whole summer, had come out to meet them when they drove up, and standing there bareheaded had stopped them from getting out. He had looked past them with an embarrassed frown on his face, telling them his wife's sister was there with a raft of young ones, and the house was pretty full and everything upset, or he'd ask them to come in. "We've been thinking of trying to get up to your place one of these days," said Mr. Allbright, moving away trying to look busy, "we've been mighty occupied up here of late." So they had to say, "Well, we just happened to be driving this way," and go on. "The Allbrights," said Mrs. Thompson, "always was fair-weather friends." "They look out for number one, that's a fact," said Mr. Thompson. But it was cold comfort to them both.

Finally Mrs. Thompson had given up. "Let's go home," she said. "Old Jim's tired and thirsty, and we've gone far enough."

Mr. Thompson said, "Well, while we're out this way, we might as well stop at the McClellans'." They drove in, and asked a little cotton-haired boy if his mamma and papa were at home. Mr. Thompson wanted to see them. The little boy stood gazing with his mouth open, then galloped into the house shouting, "Mommer, Popper, come out hyah. That man that kilt Mr. Hatch has come ter see yer!"

The man came out in his sock feet, with one gallus up, the other broken and dangling, and said, "Light down, Mr. Thompson, and come in. The ole woman's washing, but she'll git here." Mrs. Thompson, feeling her way, stepped down and sat in a broken rocking-chair on the porch that sagged under her feet. The woman of the house, barefooted, in a calico wrapper, sat on the edge of the porch, her fat sallow face full of curiosity. Mr. Thompson began, "Well, as I reckon you happen to know, I've had some strange troubles lately, and, as the feller says, it's not the kind of trouble that happens to a man every day in the year, and there's some things I don't want no misunderstanding about in the neighbors' minds, so—" He halted and stumbled forward, and the two listening faces took on a mean look, a greedy, despising look, a look that said plain as day, "My, you must be a purty sorry feller to come round worrying about what *we* think, *we* know you wouldn't be here if you had anybody else to turn to—my, I wouldn't lower myself that much, myself." Mr. Thompson was ashamed of himself, he was suddenly in a rage, he'd like to knock their dirty skunk heads together, the low-down white trash—but he held himself down and went on to the end. "My wife will tell you," he said, and this was the hardest place, because Ellie always without moving a muscle seemed to stiffen as if somebody had threatened to hit her; "ask my wife, she won't lie."

"It's true, I saw it—"

"Well, now," said the man, drily, scratching his ribs inside his shirt, "that sholy is too bad. Well, now, I kaint see what we've got to do with all this here, however. I kaint see no good reason for us to git mixed up in these murder matters, I shore kaint. Whichever way you look at it, it ain't none of my business. However, it's mighty nice of you-all to come around and give us the straight of it, fur we've heerd some mighty queer yarns about it, mighty queer, I golly you couldn't hardly make head ner tail of it."

"Evvybody goin' round shootin' they heads off," said the woman. "Now we don't hold with killin'; the Bible says—"

"Shet yer trap," said the man, "and keep it shet 'r I'll shet it fer yer. Now it shore looks like to me—"

"We mustn't linger," said Mrs. Thompson, unclasping her hands. "We've lingered too long now. It's getting late, and we've far to go." Mr. Thompson took the hint and followed her. The man and the woman lolled against their rickety porch poles and watched them go.

Now lying on his bed, Mr. Thompson knew the end had come. Now, this minute, lying in the bed where he had slept with Ellie for eighteen years; under this roof where he had laid the shingles when he was waiting to get married; there as he was with his whiskers already sprouting since his shave that morning; with his fingers feeling his bony chin, Mr.

Thompson felt he was a dead man. He was dead to his other life, he had got to the end of something without knowing why, and he had to make a fresh start, he did not know how. Something different was going to begin, he didn't know what. It was in some way not his business. He didn't feel he was going to have much to do with it. He got up, aching, hollow, and went out to the kitchen where Mrs. Thompson was just taking up the supper.

"Call the boys," said Mrs. Thompson. They had been down to the barn, and Arthur put out the lantern before hanging it on a nail near the door. Mr. Thompson didn't like their silence. They had hardly said a word about anything to him since that day. They seemed to avoid him, they ran the place together as if he wasn't there, and attended to everything without asking him for any advice. "What you boys been up to?" he asked, trying to be hearty. "Finishing your chores?"

"No, sir," said Arthur, "there ain't much to do. Just greasing some axles." Herbert said nothing. Mrs. Thompson bowed her head: "For these and all Thy blessings. . . . Amen," she whispered weakly, and the Thompsons sat there with their eyes down and their faces sorrowful, as if they were at a funeral.

VIII

Every time he shut his eyes, trying to sleep, Mr. Thompson's mind started up and began to run like a rabbit. It jumped from one thing to another, trying to pick up a trail here or there that would straighten out what had happened that day he killed Mr. Hatch. Try as he might, Mr. Thompson's mind would not go anywhere that it had not already been, he could not see anything but what he had seen once, and he knew that was not right. If he had not seen straight that first time, then everything about his killing Mr. Hatch was wrong from start to finish, and there was nothing more to be done about it, he might just as well give up. It still seemed to him that he had done, maybe not the right thing, but the only thing he could do, that day, but had he? *Did he have to kill Mr. Hatch?* He had never seen a man he hated more, the minute he laid eyes on him. He knew in his bones the fellow was there for trouble.

What seemed so funny now was this: Why hadn't he just told Mr. Hatch to get out before he ever even got in?

Mrs. Thompson, her arms crossed on her breast, was lying beside him, perfectly still, but she seemed awake, somehow. "Asleep, Ellie?"

After all, he might have got rid of him peaceably, or maybe he might have had to overpower him and put those handcuffs on him and turn him over to the sheriff for disturbing the peace. The most they could have done was to lock Mr. Hatch up while he cooled off for a few days, or fine him a little something. He would try to think of things he might have said to Mr. Hatch. Why, let's see, I could just have said, Now look here, Mr. Hatch, I want to talk to you as man to man. But his brain would go empty. What could he have said or done? But if he *could* have done anything else almost except kill Mr. Hatch, then nothing would have happened to Mr. Helton. Mr. Thompson hardly ever thought of Mr. Helton. His mind just skipped over him and went on. If he stopped to think about Mr. Helton he'd never in God's world get anywhere. He tried to imagine how it might all have been, this very night even, if Mr. Helton were still safe and sound out in his shack playing his tune about feeling so good in the morning, drinking up all the wine so you'd feel even better; and Mr. Hatch safe in jail somewhere, mad as hops, maybe, but out of harm's way and ready to listen to reason and to repent of his meanness, the dirty, yellow-livered hound coming around persecuting an innocent man and ruining a whole family that never harmed him! Mr. Thompson felt the veins of his forehead start up, his fists clutched as if they seized an ax handle, the sweat broke out on him, he bounded up from the bed with a yell smothered in his throat, and Ellie started up after him, crying out, "Oh, oh, don't! Don't! Don't!" as if she were having a nightmare. He stood shaking until his bones rattled in him, crying hoarsely, "Light the lamp, light the lamp, Ellie."

Instead, Mrs. Thompson gave a shrill weak scream, almost the same scream he had heard on that day she came around the house when he was standing there with the ax in his hand. He could not see her in the dark, but she was on the bed, rolling violently. He felt for her in horror, and his groping hands found her arms, up, and her own hands pulling her hair straight out from her head, her neck strained back, and the tight screams strangling her. He shouted out for Arthur, for Herbert. "Your mother!" he bawled, his voice cracking. As he held Mrs. Thompson's arms, the boys came tumbling in, Arthur with the lamp above his head. By this light Mr. Thompson saw Mrs. Thompson's eyes, wide open, staring dreadfully at him, the tears pouring. She sat up at sight of the boys, and held out one arm towards them, the hand wagging in a crazy circle, then dropped on her back again, and suddenly went limp. Arthur set the lamp on the table and turned on Mr. Thompson. "She's scared," he said, "she's scared to death." His face was in a knot of rage, his fists were doubled up, he faced his father as if he meant to strike him. Mr. Thompson's jaw fell, he was so surprised he stepped back from the bed. Herbert went to the other side. They stood on each side of Mrs. Thompson and watched Mr. Thompson as if he were a dangerous wild beast. "What did you do to her?" shouted Arthur, in a grown man's voice. "You touch her again and I'll blow your heart out!" Herbert was pale and his cheek twitched, but he was on Arthur's side; he would do what he could to help Arthur.

Mr. Thompson had no fight left in him. His knees bent as he stood, his chest collapsed. "Why, Arthur," he said, his words crumbling and his breath coming short. "She's fainted again. Get the ammonia." Arthur did not move. Herbert brought the bottle, and handed it, shrinking, to his father.

Mr. Thompson held it under Mrs. Thompson's nose. He poured a little in the palm of his hand and rubbed it on her forehead. She gasped and opened her eyes and turned her head away from him. Herbert began a doleful hopeless sniffling. "Mamma," he kept saying, "Mamma, don't die."

"I'm all right," Mrs. Thompson said. "Now don't you worry around. Now Herbert, you mustn't do that. I'm all right." She closed her eyes. Mr. Thompson began pulling on his best pants; he put on his socks and shoes. The boys sat on each side of the bed, watching Mrs.

Thompson's face. Mr. Thompson put on his shirt and coat. He said, "I reckon I'll ride over and get the doctor. Don't look like all this fainting is a good sign. Now you just keep watch until I get back." They listened, but said nothing. He said, "Don't you get any notions in your head. I never did your mother any harm in my life, on purpose." He went out, and, looking back, saw Herbert staring at him from under his brows, like a stranger. "You'll know how to look after her," said Mr. Thompson.

Mr. Thompson went through the kitchen. There he lighted the lantern, took a thin pad of scratch paper and a stub pencil from the shelf where the boys kept their schoolbooks. He swung the lantern on his arm and reached into the cupboard where he kept the guns. The shotgun was there to his hand, primed and ready, a man never knows when he may need a shotgun. He went out of the house without looking around, or looking back when he had left it, passed his barn without seeing it, and struck out to the farthest end of his fields, which ran for half a mile to the east. So many blows had been struck at Mr. Thompson and from so many directions he couldn't stop any more to find out where he was hit. He walked on, over plowed ground and over meadow, going through barbed wire fences cautiously, putting his gun through first; he could almost see in the dark, now his eyes were used to it. Finally he came to the last fence; here he sat down, back against a post, lantern at his side, and, with the pad on his knee, moistened the stub pencil and began to write:

"Before Almighty God, the great judge of all before who I am about to appear, I do hereby solemnly swear that I did not take the life of Mr. Homer T. Hatch on purpose. It was done in defense of Mr. Helton. I did not aim to hit him with the ax but only to keep him off Mr. Helton. He aimed a blow at Mr. Helton who was not looking for it. It was my belief at the time that Mr. Hatch would of taken the life of Mr. Helton if I did not interfere. I have told all this to the judge and the jury and they let me off but nobody believes it. This is the only way I can prove I am not a cold blooded murderer like everybody seems to think. If I had

been in Mr. Helton's place he would of done the same for me. I still think I done the only thing there was to do. My wife—"

Mr. Thompson stopped here to think a while. He wet the pencil point with the tip of his tongue and marked out the last two words. He sat a while blacking out the words until he had made a neat oblong patch where they had been, and started again:

"It was Mr. Homer T. Hatch who came to do wrong to a harmless man. He caused all this trouble and he deserved to die but I am sorry it was me who had to kill him."

He licked the point of his pencil again, and signed his full name carefully, folded the paper and put it in his outside pocket. Taking off his right shoe and sock, he set the butt of the shotgun along the ground with the twin barrels pointed towards his head. It was very awkward. He thought about this a little, leaning his head against the gun mouth. He was trembling and his head was drumming until he was deaf and blind, but he lay down flat on the earth on his side, drew the barrel under his chin and fumbled for the trigger with his great toe. That way he could work it.

DISCUSSION

This story, for all its length, is essentially simple. A stranger turns up as a hand on a poor Texas farm, and makes the place pay for the first time. Nine years later, another stranger appears and reveals that the hand is a murderer and a lunatic. The farmer, for reasons which he himself cannot define, kills the second stranger who would arrest the hand, and then when he finds that, first, his neighbors, and finally his family, believe him guilty, kills himself. But the story is fleshed out with considerable detail. What justifies this detail? What justifies the scale of the story?

First, we may say that the very vividness and richness provide some justification for the detail. The world of the Thompsons is set up with great completeness, and we enjoy the precision with which it is presented, the recognition of the world. We know the springhouse, the kitchen, the stumps in the yard. But more, we get the whole "feel" of the place, the sense of the kind of life lived there. Then we have the Thompsons themselves, and poor Mr. Helton. They are visualized very fully, but we realize before we have gone far into the story that all the details of their appearance begin to have some bearing on our understanding of their characters and on our feeling for them.

We first see Mr. Thompson: "He was a noisy proud man who held his neck so straight his whole face stood level with his Adam's apple, and the whiskers continued down his neck and disappeared into a black thatch under his open collar." Later, looking back, we can see that the story is the story of a noisy, proud, stiff-necked man, whose pride has constantly suffered from failures, who salves his hurt pride by harmless bluster with his children and with his refusal to do anything but proper "man's work," and who, in the end, stumbles into a situation which takes the last prop of certainty from his life. In a sense, he finally kills himself out of pride. He can't stand the moral uncertainty of his situation, the moral isolation when even his family turns against him, and he shoots himself as a way of justifying himself before the world.

So with our first glimpse of Mrs. Thompson lying down in the "front room" with the green shades down and a wet cloth over her poor weak eyes, we get a central indication of her pitiful story. The constant shading of her eyes from the light, the constant weeping, the waiting for the cool darkness, all these details lead to our conception of her inward as well as her outward being.

The same principle applies to certain episodes that at first glance seem to be unrelated to the main line of the story, for instance, the conversation between Mr. and Mrs. Thompson at the beginning of Section II, the episode of the pinch at the end of Section II, and the episode toward the end of Section III, after the boys have tampered with the Swede's harmonicas. All of these episodes establish the quality of the life lived on the Thompson place. Let us look at the second:

"Tell *you* the truth, Ellie," said Mr. Thompson, picking his teeth with a fork and leaning back in the best of good humors, "I always thought your granma was a ter'ble ole fool. She'd just say the first thing that popped into her head and call it God's wisdom."

"My granma wasn't anybody's fool. Nine times out of ten she knew what she was talking about. I always say, the first thing you think is the best thing you can say."

"Well," said Mr. Thompson, going into another shout, "You're so re*ee*fined about that goat story, you just try speaking out in mixed comp'ny sometime! You just try it. S'pose you happened to be thinking about a hen and a rooster, hey? I reckon you'd shock the Babtist preacher!" He gave her a good pinch on her thin little rump. "No more meat on you than a rabbit," he said, fondly. "Now I like 'em cornfed."

Mrs. Thompson looked at him open-eyed and blushed. She could see better by lamplight. "Why, Mr. Thompson, sometimes I think you're the evil-est-minded man that ever lived." She took a handful of hair on the crown of his head and gave it a good, slow pull. "That's to show you how it feels, pinching so hard when you're supposed to be playing," she said gently.

This little glimpse of their secret life together, Mr. Thompson's masculine, affectionate bragging and bullying and teasing, Mrs. Thompson's shy and embarrassed playfulness, comes as surprise in the middle of their drab world, a sudden brightness and warmth. Without this episode we should not get the full force of Mr. Thompson's bafflement and anger when Mr. Hatch misinterprets Mr. Thompson's talk of Mrs. Thompson's ill health and says he'd get rid of a puny wife mighty quick. And without it we would not have the same sense of pity when the terrible end comes to their life together. What seems at first glance to be a casual, incidental episode really gives the emotional charge to the conclusion: it makes us believe in Mr. and Mrs. Thompson as people.

But let us come back to the main idea of the story. We have said that the story is the story of a noisy, proud, stiff-necked man whose bluster really conceals a sense of failure, and who in the end stumbles into a situation which takes the last prop of certainty from his life. Is he innocent or guilty? He himself doesn't really know. He is sure that he had seen the stranger's knife enter the body of Mr. Helton, but then, that is proved to be a delusion. He had felt himself to be acting to protect Mr. Helton, but before the act of violence he had experienced a long building up of a mysterious anger against the stranger. Furthermore, we know that Mr. Helton has made life possible for the Thompsons and now that support is about to be snatched away. Poor Mr. Thompson is both innocent and guilty. He can't sort out the facts, the complex of motives working within himself. So he takes refuge in a lie, the lie his wife must tell. But the lie isn't enough, least of all for him, and when he finds that his own family think him a murderer he has to kill himself to prove, in his last pride, that he is innocent.

The story, then, is about the difficult definition of guilt and innocence: because Mr. Thompson had not been able to trust his own sense of innocence he had taken refuge in the lie, and the lie, in the end, kills him. We must remember, however, that it is not the abstract idea that is important here. Rather, it is the human warmth and sympathy that the writer has managed to create as the context of the idea. We see the terrible ruin of the lives of good, decent people, a ruin brought about not so much by actual faults of their own as by a striving to be good and decent. That is all the Thompsons want.

But let us come back to the point where we started, the question of scale, the justification of the elaborate detail. We have commented on the vividness and richness of the reader's pleasure in that; but the deeper justification lies in the creation of a little world, a world so fully realized that the events that come to shake it come with terrific emotional force. This story has a very complex and strongly articulated plot (a fact that in itself does something to account for the scale), but the plot is not obtruded; we are concerned, as the writer is, with the emotional complications around the facts of the plot. And this concern is the determining factor in the scale.

EXERCISE

1. "Noon Wine" is divided into eight sections. What is the point of each section?

2. The story covers nine years. Are the transitions from one time to another made arbitrarily or are they absorbed into narrative? If they are absorbed, how does the writer succeed in giving this effect?

3. Katherine Anne Porter is famous for vividness of style. Indicate bits of description of places and people and actions in "Noon Wine" that seem especially good.

4. Can you think of a reason why the writer did not use one point of view but several? Why, since she uses several, does she never give us a glimpse of things as Mr. Helton sees them? Or Mr. Hatch?

5. Can you tell how suspense is maintained in this story?

6. What qualities does this story share with "A Wife of Nashville" by Peter Taylor (page 263)? What difference in the method of handling time do you observe?

7. "La Lupa," by Verga (p. 209) is very short yet covers a long span of time. On the basis of scale and pace compare this with "Noon Wine." What are the differences of method? How do you relate them to the differences in interest the two writers find in their material? To differences in tone?

The Rich Boy

F. SCOTT FITZGERALD (1896-1940)

I

BEGIN WITH an individual, and before you know it you find that you have created a type; begin with a type, and you find that you have created —nothing. That is because we are all queer fish, queerer behind our faces and voices than we want any one to know or than we know ourselves. When I hear a man proclaiming himself an "average, honest, open fellow," I feel pretty sure that he has some definite and perhaps terrible abnormality which he has agreed to conceal —and his protestation of being average and honest and open is his way of reminding himself of his misprision.

There are no types, no plurals. There is a rich boy, and this is his and not his brothers' story. All my life I have lived among his brothers but this one has been my friend. Besides, if I wrote about his brothers I should have to begin

by attacking all the lies that the poor have told
about the rich and the rich have told about
themselves—such a wild structure they have
erected that when we pick up a book about the
rich, some instinct prepares us for unreality.
Even the intelligent and impassioned reporters
of life have made the country of the rich as unreal as fairy-land.

Let me tell you about the very rich. They
are different from you and me. They possess and
enjoy early, and it does something to them,
makes them soft where we are hard, and cynical
where we are trustful, in a way that, unless
you were born rich, it is very difficult to understand. They think, deep in their hearts, that
they are better than we are because we had to
discover the compensations and refuges of life
for ourselves. Even when they enter deep into
our world or sink below us, they still think that
they are better than we are. They are different.
The only way I can describe young Anson
Hunter is to approach him as if he were a
foreigner and cling stubbornly to my point of
view. If I accept his for a moment I am lost—I
have nothing to show but a preposterous movie.

II

Anson was the eldest of six children who
would some day divide a fortune of fifteen million dollars, and he reached the age of reason
—is it seven?—at the beginning of the century
when daring young women were already gliding
along Fifth Avenue in electric "mobiles." In
those days he and his brother had an English
governess who spoke the language very clearly
and crisply and well, so that the two boys grew
to speak as she did—their words and sentences
were all crisp and clear and not run together as
ours are. They didn't talk exactly like English
children but acquired an accent that is peculiar
to fashionable people in the city of New York.

In the summer the six children were moved
from the house on Seventy-first Street to a big
estate in northern Connecticut. It was not a
fashionable locality—Anson's father wanted to
delay as long as possible his children's knowledge of that side of life. He was a man somewhat superior to his class, which composed New
York society, and to his period, which was the
snobbish and formalized vulgarity of the Gilded

Age, and he wanted his sons to learn habits of
concentration and have sound constitutions and
grow up into right-living and successful men.
He and his wife kept an eye on them as well
as they were able until the two older boys went
away to school, but in huge establishments this
is difficult—it was much simpler in the series
of small and medium-sized houses in which my
own youth was spent—I was never far out of the
reach of my mother's voice, of the sense of her
presence, her approval or disapproval.

Anson's first sense of his superiority came to
him when he realized the half-grudging American deference that was paid to him in the Connecticut village. The parents of the boys he
played with always inquired after his father and
mother, and were vaguely excited when their own
children were asked to the Hunters' house. He
accepted this as the natural state of things, and
a sort of impatience with all groups of which he
was not the center—in money, in position, in
authority—remained with him for the rest of his
life. He disdained to struggle with other boys for
precedence—he expected it to be given him
freely, and when it wasn't he withdrew into his
family. His family was sufficient, for in the East
money is still a somewhat feudal thing, a clan-
forming thing. In the snobbish West, money
separates families to form "sets."

At eighteen, when he went to New Haven,
Anson was tall and thick-set, with a clear complexion and a healthy color from the ordered
life he had led in school. His hair was yellow
and grew in a funny way on his head, his nose
was beaked—these two things kept him from
being handsome—but he had a confident charm
and a certain brusque style, and the upper-class
men who passed him on the street knew without being told that he was a rich boy and had
gone to one of the best schools. Nevertheless,
his very superiority kept him from being a success in college—the independence was mistaken
for egotism, and the refusal to accept Yale standards with the proper awe seemed to belittle all
those who had. So, long before he graduated, he
began to shift the center of his life to New York.

He was at home in New York—there was
his own house with "the kind of servants you
can't get any more"—and his own family, of
which, because of his good humor and a cer-

tain ability to make things go, he was rapidly becoming the centre, and the débutante parties, and the correct manly world of the men's clubs, and the occasional wild spree with the gallant girls whom New Haven only knew from the fifth row. His aspirations were conventional enough—they included even the irreproachable shadow he would some day marry, but they differed from the aspirations of the majority of young men in that there was no mist over them, none of that quality which is variously known as "idealism" or "illusion." Anson accepted without reservation the world of high finance and high extravagance, of divorce and dissipation, of snobbery and of privilege. Most of our lives end as a compromise—it was as a compromise that his life began.

He and I first met in the late summer of 1917 when he was just out of Yale, and, like the rest of us, was swept up into the systematized hysteria of the war. In the blue-green uniform of the naval aviation he came down to Pensacola, where the hotel orchestras played "I'm sorry, dear," and we young officers danced with the girls. Everyone liked him, and though he ran with the drinkers and wasn't an especially good pilot, even the instructors treated him with a certain respect. He was always having long talks with them in his confident, logical voice—talks which ended by his getting himself, or, more frequently, another officer, out of some impending trouble. He was convivial, bawdy, robustly avid for pleasure, and we were all surprised when he fell in love with a conservative and rather proper girl.

Her name was Paula Legendre, a dark, serious beauty from somewhere in California. Her family kept a winter residence just outside of town, and in spite of her primness she was enormously popular; there is a large class of men whose egotism can't endure humor in a woman. But Anson wasn't that sort, and I couldn't understand the attraction of her "sincerity"—that was the thing to say about her—for his keen and somewhat sardonic mind.

Nevertheless, they fell in love—and on her terms. He no longer joined the twilight gathering at the De Sota bar, and whenever they were seen together they were engaged in a long, serious dialogue, which must have gone on several weeks. Long afterward he told me that it was not about anything in particular but was composed on both sides of immature and even meaningless statements—the emotional content that gradually came to fill it grew up not out of the words but out of its enormous seriousness. It was a sort of hypnosis. Often it was interrupted, giving way to that emasculated humor we call fun; when they were alone it was resumed again, solemn, low-keyed, and pitched so as to give each other a sense of unity in feeling and thought. They came to resent any interruptions of it, to be unresponsive to facetiousness about life, even to the mild cynicism of their contemporaries. They were only happy when the dialogue was going on, and its seriousness bathed them like the amber glow of an open fire. Toward the end there came an interruption they did not resent—it began to be interrupted by passion.

Oddly enough, Anson was as engrossed in the dialogue as she was and as profoundly affected by it, yet at the same time aware that on his side much was insincere, and on hers much was merely simple. At first, too, he despised her emotional simplicity as well, but with his love her nature deepened and blossomed, and he could despise it no longer. He felt that if he could enter into Paula's warm safe life he would be happy. The long preparation of the dialogue removed any constraint—he taught her some of what he had learned from more adventurous women, and she responded with a rapt holy intensity. One evening after a dance they agreed to marry, and he wrote a long letter about her to his mother. The next day Paula told him that she was rich, that she had a personal fortune of nearly a million dollars.

III

It was exactly as if they could say "Neither of us has anything: we shall be poor together" —just as delightful that they should be rich instead. It gave them the same communion of adventure. Yet when Anson got leave in April, and Paula and her mother accompanied him North, she was impressed with the standing of his family in New York and with the scale on which they lived. Alone with Anson for the first time in the rooms where he had played as a boy, she was filled with a comfortable emotion, as though she were preëminently safe and taken care of. The pictures of Anson in a skull cap at his first school, of Anson on horseback with the sweetheart of a mysterious forgotten summer, of Anson in a gay group of ushers and bridesmaids at a wedding, made her jealous of his life apart from her in the past, and so completely did his authoritative person seem to sum up and typify these possessions of his that she was inspired with the idea of being married immediately and returning to Pensacola as his wife.

But an immediate marriage wasn't discussed —even the engagement was to be secret until after the war. When she realized that only two days of his leave remained, her dissatisfaction crystallized in the intention of making him as unwilling to wait as she was. They were driving to the country for dinner, and she determined to force the issue that night.

Now a cousin of Paula's was staying with them at the Ritz, a severe, bitter girl who loved Paula but was somewhat jealous of her impressive engagement, and as Paula was late in dressing, the cousin, who wasn't going to the party, received Anson in the parlor of the suite.

Anson had met friends at five o'clock and drunk freely and indiscreetly with them for an hour. He left the Yale Club at a proper time, and his mother's chauffeur drove him to the Ritz, but his usual capacity was not in evidence, and the impact of the steam-heated sitting-room made him suddenly dizzy. He knew it, and he was both amused and sorry.

Paula's cousin was twenty-five, but she was exceptionally naïve, and at first failed to realize what was up. She had never met Anson before, and she was surprised when he mumbled strange information and nearly fell off his chair, but until Paula appeared it didn't occur to her that what she had taken for the odor of a dry-cleaned uniform was really whisky. But Paula understood as soon as she appeared; her only thought was to get Anson away before her mother saw him, and at the look in her eyes the cousin understood too.

When Paula and Anson descended to the limousine they found two men inside, both asleep; they were the men with whom he had been drinking at the Yale Club, and they were also going to the party. He had entirely forgotten their presence in the car. On the way to Hempstead they awoke and sang. Some of the songs were rough, and though Paula tried to reconcile herself to the fact that Anson had few verbal inhibitions, her lips tightened with shame and distaste.

Back at the hotel the cousin, confused and agitated, considered the incident, and then walked into Mrs. Legendre's bedroom, saying: "Isn't he funny?"

"Who is funny?"

"Why—Mr. Hunter. He seemed so funny."

Mrs. Legendre looked at her sharply.

"How is he funny?"

"Why, he said he was French. I didn't know he was French."

"That's absurd. You must have misunderstood." She smiled: "It was a joke."

The cousin shook her head stubbornly.

"No. He said he was brought up in France. He said he couldn't speak any English, and that's why he couldn't talk to me. And he couldn't!"

Mrs. Legendre looked away with impatience just as the cousin added thoughtfully, "Perhaps it was because he was so drunk," and walked out of the room.

This curious report was true. Anson, finding his voice thick and uncontrollable, had taken the unusual refuge of announcing that he spoke no English. Years afterward he used to tell that part of the story, and he invariably communicated the uproarious laughter which the memory aroused in him.

Five times in the next hour Mrs. Legendre tried to get Hempstead on the phone. When she succeeded, there was a ten-minute delay before she heard Paula's voice on the wire.

"Cousin Jo told me Anson was intoxicated."

"Oh, no. . . ."

"Oh, yes. Cousin Jo says he was intoxicated. He told her he was French, and fell off his chair and behaved as if he was very intoxicated. I don't want you to come home with him."

"Mother, he's all right! Please don't worry about——"

"But I do worry. I think it's dreadful. I want you to promise me not to come home with him."

"I'll take care of it, mother. . . ."

"I don't want you to come home with him."

"All right, mother. Good-by."

"Be sure now, Paula. Ask some one to bring you."

Deliberately Paula took the receiver from her ear and hung it up. Her face was flushed with helpless annoyance. Anson was stretched out asleep in a bedroom upstairs, while the dinner party below was proceeding lamely toward conclusion.

The hour's drive had sobered him somewhat —his arrival was merely hilarious—and Paula hoped that the evening was not spoiled, after all, but two imprudent cocktails before dinner completed the disaster. He talked boisterously and somewhat offensively to the party at large for fifteen minutes, and then slid silently under the table; like a man in an old print—but, unlike an old print, it was rather horrible without being at all quaint. None of the young girls present remarked upon the incident—it seemed to merit only silence. His uncle and two other men carried him upstairs, and it was just after this that Paula was called to the phone.

An hour later Anson awoke in a fog of nervous agony, through which he perceived after a moment the figure of his Uncle Robert standing by the door.

". . . I said are you better?"

"What?"

"Do you feel better, old man?"

"Terrible," said Anson.

"I'm going to try you on another Bromoseltzer. If you can hold it down, it'll do you good to sleep."

With an effort Anson slid his legs from the bed and stood up.

"I'm all right," he said dully.

"Take it easy."

"I thin' if you gave me a glassbrandy I could go downstairs."

"Oh, no——"

"Yes, that's the only thin'. I'm all right now. . . . I suppose I'm in dutch dow' there."

"They know you're a little under the weather," said his uncle deprecatingly. "But don't worry about it. Schuyler didn't even get here. He passed away in the locker-room over at the Links."

Indifferent to any opinion, except Paula's, Anson was nevertheless determined to save the débris of the evening, but when after a cold bath he made his appearance most of the party had already left. Paula got up immediately to go home.

In the limousine the old serious dialogue began. She had known that he drank, she admitted, but she had never expected anything like this—it seemed to her that perhaps they were not suited to each other, after all. Their ideas about life were too different, and so forth. When she finished speaking, Anson spoke in turn, very soberly. Then Paula said she'd have to think it over; she wouldn't decide tonight; she was not angry but she was terribly sorry. Nor would she let him come into the hotel with her, but just before she got out of the car she leaned and kissed him unhappily on the cheek.

The next afternoon Anson had a long talk with Mrs. Legendre while Paula sat listening in silence. It was agreed that Paula was to brood over the incident for a proper period and then, if mother and daughter thought it best, they would follow Anson to Pensacola. On his part he apologized with sincerity and dignity— that was all; with every card in her hand Mrs. Legendre was unable to establish any advantage over him. He made no promises, showed no humility, only delivered a few serious comments on life which brought him off with rather a moral superiority at the end. When they came South three weeks later, neither Anson in his satisfaction nor Paula in her relief at the reunion realized that the psychological moment had passed forever.

IV

He dominated and attracted her, and at the same time filled her with anxiety. Confused by his mixture of solidity and self-indulgence, of sentiment and cynicism—incongruities which her gentle mind was unable to resolve—Paula grew to think of him as two alternating personalities. When she saw him alone, or at a formal party, or with his casual inferiors, she felt a tremendous pride in his strong, attractive presence, the paternal, understanding stature of his mind. In other company she became uneasy when what had been a fine imperviousness to mere gentility showed its other face. The other face was gross, humorous, reckless of everything but pleasure. It startled her mind temporarily away from him, even led her into a short covert experiment with an old beau, but it was no use—after four months of Anson's enveloping vitality there was an anæmic pallor in all other men.

In July he was ordered abroad, and their tenderness and desire reached a crescendo. Paula considered a last-minute marriage—decided against it only because there were always cocktails on his breath now, but the parting itself made her physically ill with grief. After his departure she wrote him long letters of regret for the days of love they had missed by waiting. In August Anson's plane slipped down into the North Sea. He was pulled onto a destroyer after a night in the water and sent to hospital with pneumonia; the armistice was signed before he was finally sent home.

Then, with every opportunity given back to them, with no material obstacle to overcome, the secret weavings of their temperaments came between them, drying up their kisses and their tears, making their voices less loud to one another, muffling the intimate chatter of their hearts until the old communication was only possible by letters, from far away. One afternoon a society reporter waited for two hours in the Hunters' house for a confirmation of their engagement. Anson denied it; nevertheless an early issue carried the report as a leading paragraph—they were "constantly seen together at Southampton, Hot Springs, and Tuxedo Park." But the serious dialogue had turned a corner into a long-sustained quarrel, and the affair was almost played out. Anson got drunk flagrantly and missed an engagement with her, whereupon Paula made certain behavioristic demands. His despair was helpless before his pride and his knowledge of himself: the engagement was definitely broken.

"Dearest," said their letters now, "Dearest, Dearest, when I wake up in the middle of the night and realize that after all it was not to be, I feel that I want to die. I can't go on living any more. Perhaps when we meet this summer we may talk things over and decide differently —we were so excited and sad that day, and I don't feel that I can live all my life without you. You speak of other people. Don't you know there are no other people for me, but only you. . . ."

But as Paula drifted here and there around the East she would sometimes mention her gaieties to make him wonder. Anson was too acute to wonder. When he saw a man's name in her letters he felt more sure of her and a little disdainful—he was always superior to such things. But he still hoped that they would some day marry.

Meanwhile he plunged vigorously into all the movement and glitter of post-bellum New York, entering a brokerage house, joining half a dozen clubs, dancing late, and moving in three worlds—his own world, the world of young Yale graduates, and that section of the half-world which rests one end on Broadway. But there was always a thorough and infractible eight hours devoted to his work in Wall Street, where the combination of his influential family connection, his sharp intelligence, and his abundance of sheer physical energy brought him almost immediately forward. He had one of those invaluable minds with partitions in it; sometimes he appeared at his office refreshed by less than an hour's sleep, but such occurrences were rare. So early as 1920 his income in salary and commission exceeded twelve thousand dollars.

As the Yale tradition slipped into the past he became more and more of a popular figure among his classmates in New York, more popular than he had ever been in college. He lived in a great house, and had the means of introducing young men into other great houses. Moreover, his life already seemed secure, while theirs, for the most part, had arrived again at precarious beginnings. They commenced to turn to him for amusement and escape, and Anson responded readily, taking pleasure in helping people and arranging their affairs.

There were no men in Paula's letters now, but a note of tenderness ran through them that had not been there before. From several sources he heard that she had "a heavy beau," Lowell Thayer, a Bostonian of wealth and position, and though he was sure she still loved him, it made him uneasy to think that he might lose her, after all. Save for one unsatisfactory day she had not been in New York for almost five months, and as the rumors multiplied he became increasingly anxious to see her. In February he took his vacation and went down to Florida.

Palm Beach sprawled plump and opulent between the sparkling sapphire of Lake Worth, flawed here and there by houseboats at anchor, and the great turquoise bar of the Atlantic Ocean. The huge bulks of the Breakers and the Royal Poinciana rose as twin paunches from the bright level of the sand, and around them clustered the Dancing Glade, Bradley's House of Chance, and a dozen modistes and milliners with goods at triple prices from New York. Upon the trellissed veranda of the Breakers two hundred women stepped right, stepped left, wheeled, and slid in that then celebrated calisthenic known as the double-shuffle, while in half-time to the music two thousand bracelets clicked up and down on two hundred arms.

At the Everglades Club after dark Paula and Lowell Thayer and Anson and a casual fourth played bridge with hot cards. It seemed to Anson that her kind, serious face was wan and tired—she had been around now for four, five, years. He had known her for three.

"Two spades."

"Cigarette? . . . Oh, I beg your pardon. By me."

"By."

"I'll double three spades."

There were a dozen tables of bridge in the room, which was filling up with smoke. Anson's eyes met Paula's, held them persistently even when Thayer's glance fell between them. . . .

"What was bid?" he asked abstractedly.

Rose of Washington Square

sang the young people in the corners:

> *I'm withering there*
> *In basement air——*

The smoke banked like fog, and the opening of a door filled the room with blown swirls of ectoplasm. Little Bright Eyes streaked past the tables seeking Mr. Conan Doyle among the Englishmen who were posing as Englishmen about the lobby.

"You could cut it with a knife."

". . . cut it with a knife."

". . . a knife."

At the end of the rubber Paula suddenly got up and spoke to Anson in a tense, low voice. With scarcely a glance at Lowell Thayer, they walked out the door and descended a long flight of stone steps—in a moment they were walking hand in hand along the moonlit beach.

"Darling, darling. . . ." They embraced recklessly, passionately, in a shadow. . . . Then Paula drew back her face to let his lips say what she wanted to hear—she could feel the words forming as they kissed again. . . . Again she broke away, listening, but as he pulled her close once more she realized that he had said nothing—only *"Darling! Darling!"* in that deep, sad whisper that always made her cry. Humbly, obediently, her emotions yielded to him and the tears streamed down her face, but her heart kept on crying: "Ask me—oh, Anson, dearest, ask me!"

"Paula. . . . *Paula!*"

The words wrung her heart like hands, and Anson, feeling her tremble, knew that emotion was enough. He need say no more, commit their destinies to no practical enigma. Why should he, when he might hold her so, biding his own time, for another year—forever? He was considering them both, her more than himself. For a moment, when she said suddenly that she must go back to her hotel, he hesitated, thinking, first, "This is the moment, after all," and then: "No, let it wait—she is mine. . . ."

He had forgotten that Paula too was worn away inside with the strain of three years. Her mood passed forever in the night.

He went back to New York next morning filled with a certain restless dissatisfaction. Late in April, without warning, he received a telegram from Bar Harbor in which Paula told him that she was engaged to Lowell Thayer, and that they would be married immediately in Boston. What he never really believed could happen had happened at last.

Anson filled himself with whisky that morning, and going to the office, carried on his work without a break—rather with a fear of what would happen if he stopped. In the evening he went out as usual, saying nothing of what had occurred; he was cordial, humorous, unabstracted. But one thing he could not help—for three days, in any place, in any company, he would suddenly bend his head into his hands and cry like a child.

V

In 1922 when Anson went abroad with the junior partner to investigate some London loans, the journey intimated that he was to be taken into the firm. He was twenty-seven now, a little heavy without being definitely stout, and with a manner older than his years. Old people and young people liked him and trusted him, and mothers felt safe when their daughters were in his charge, for he had a way, when he came into a room, of putting himself on a footing with the oldest and most conservative people there. "You and I," he seemed to say, "we're solid. We understand."

He had an instinctive and rather charitable knowledge of the weaknesses of men and women, and, like a priest, it made him the more concerned for the maintenance of outward forms. It was typical of him that every Sunday morning he taught in a fashionable Episcopal Sunday school—even though a cold shower and a quick change into a cutaway coat were all that separated him from the wild night before.

After his father's death he was the practical head of his family, and, in effect, guided the destinies of the younger children. Through a complication his authority did not extend to his father's estate, which was administrated by his Uncle Robert, who was the horsy member of the family, a good-natured, hard-drinking member of that set which centers about Wheatley Hills.

Uncle Robert and his wife, Edna, had been great friends of Anson's youth, and the former was disappointed when his nephew's superiority failed to take a horsy form. He backed him for a city club which was the most difficult in America to enter—one could only join if one's family had "helped to build up New York" (or, in other words, were rich before 1880)—and when Anson, after his election, neglected it for the Yale Club, Uncle Robert gave him a little talk on the subject. But when on top of that Anson declined to enter Robert Hunter's own conservative and somewhat neglected brokerage house, his manner grew cooler. Like a primary

teacher who has taught all he knew, he slipped out of Anson's life.

There were so many friends in Anson's life —scarcely one for whom he had not done some unusual kindness and scarcely one whom he did not occasionally embarrass by his bursts of rough conversation or his habit of getting drunk whenever and however he liked. It annoyed him when any one else blundered in that regard— about his own lapses he was always humorous. Odd things happened to him and he told them with infectious laughter.

I was working in New York that spring, and I used to lunch with him at the Yale Club, which my university was sharing until the completion of our own. I had read of Paula's marriage, and one afternoon, when I asked him about her, something moved him to tell me the story. After that he frequently invited me to family dinners at his house and behaved as though there was a special relation between us, as though with his confidence a little of that consuming memory had passed into me.

I found that despite the trusting mothers, his attitude toward girls was not indiscriminately protective. It was up to the girl—if she showed an inclination toward looseness, she must take care of herself, even with him.

"Life," he would explain sometimes, "has made a cynic of me."

By life he meant Paula. Sometimes, especially when he was drinking, it became a little twisted in his mind, and he thought that she had callously thrown him over.

This "cynicism," or rather his realization that naturally fast girls were not worth sparing, led to his affair with Dolly Karger. It wasn't his only affair in those years, but it came nearest to touching him deeply, and it had a profound effect upon his attitude toward life.

Dolly was the daughter of a notorious "publicist" who had married into society. She herself grew up into the Junior League, came out at the Plaza, and went to the Assembly; and only a few old families like the Hunters could question whether or not she "belonged," for her picture was often in the papers, and she had more enviable attention than many girls who undoubtedly did. She was dark-haired, with carmine lips and a high, lovely color, which she concealed under pinkish-gray powder all through the first year out, because high color was unfashionable—Victorian-pale was the thing to be. She wore black, severe suits and stood with her hands in her pockets leaning a little forward, with a humorous restraint on her face. She danced exquisitely—better than anything she liked to dance—better than anything except making love. Since she was ten she had always been in love, and, usually, with some boy who didn't respond to her. Those who did—and there were many—bored her after a brief encounter, but for her failures she reserved the warmest spot in her heart. When she met them she would always try once more—sometimes she succeeded, more often she failed.

It never occurred to this gypsy of the unattainable that there was a certain resemblance in those who refused to love her—they shared a hard intuition that saw through to her weakness, not a weakness of emotion but a weakness of rudder. Anson perceived this when he first met her, less than a month after Paula's marriage. He was drinking rather heavily, and he pretended for a week that he was falling in love with her. Then he dropped her abruptly and forgot—immediately he took up the commanding position in her heart.

Like so many girls of that day Dolly was slackly and indiscreetly wild. The unconventionality of a slightly older generation had been simply one facet of a postwar movement to discredit obsolete manners—Dolly's was both older and shabbier, and she saw in Anson the two extremes which the emotionally shiftless woman seeks, an abandon to indulgence alternating with a protective strength. In his character she felt both the sybarite and the solid rock, and these two satisfied every need of her nature.

She felt that it was going to be difficult, but she mistook the reason—she thought that Anson and his family expected a more spectacular marriage, but she guessed immediately that her advantage lay in his tendency to drink.

They met at the large débutante dances, but as her infatuation increased they managed to be more and more together. Like most mothers, Mrs. Karger believed that Anson was exceptionally reliable, so she allowed Dolly to go with him to distant country clubs and suburban houses without inquiring closely into their activities or questioning her explanations when they came in late. At first these explanations might have been accurate, but Dolly's worldly ideas of capturing Anson were soon engulfed in the rising sweep of her emotion. Kisses in the back of taxis and motor-cars were no longer enough; they did a curious thing:

They dropped out of their world for a while and made another world just beneath it where Anson's tippling and Dolly's irregular hours would be less noticed and commented on. It was composed, this world, of varying elements—several of Anson's Yale friends and their wives, two or three young brokers and bond salesmen and a handful of unattached men, fresh from college, with money and a propensity to dissipation. What this world lacked in spaciousness and scale it made up for by allowing them a liberty that it scarcely permitted itself. Moreover, it centered around them and permitted Dolly the pleasure of a faint condescension—a pleasure which Anson, whose whole life was a condescension from the certitudes of his childhood, was unable to share.

He was not in love with her, and in the long feverish winter of their affair he frequently told her so. In the spring he was weary—he wanted to renew his life at some other source—moreover, he saw that either he must break with her now or accept the responsibility of a definite seduction. Her family's encouraging attitude precipitated his decision—one evening when Mr. Karger knocked discreetly at the library door to announce that he had left a bottle of old brandy in the dining-room, Anson felt that life was hemming him in. That night he wrote her a short letter in which he told her that he was going on his vacation, and that in view of all the circumstances they had better meet no more.

It was June. His family had closed up the house and gone to the country, so he was living temporarily at the Yale Club. I had heard about his affair with Dolly as it developed—accounts salted with humor, for he despised unstable women, and granted them no place in the social edifice in which he believed—and when he told me that night that he was definitely breaking with her I was glad. I had seen Dolly here and there, and each time with a feeling of pity at the hopelessness of her struggle, and of shame at knowing so much about her that I had no right to know. She was what is known as "a pretty little thing," but there was a certain recklessness which rather fascinated me. Her dedication to the goddess of waste would have been less obvious had she been less spirited—she would most certainly throw herself away, but I was glad when I heard that the sacrifice would not be consummated in my sight.

Anson was going to leave the letter of farewell at her house next morning. It was one of the few houses left open in the Fifth Avenue district, and he knew that the Kargers, acting upon erroneous information from Dolly, had foregone a trip abroad to give their daughter her chance. As he stepped out the door of the Yale Club into Madison Avenue the postman passed him, and he followed back inside. The first letter that caught his eye was in Dolly's hand.

He knew what it would be—a lonely and tragic monologue, full of the reproaches he knew, the invoked memories, the "I wonder if's"—all the immemorial intimacies that he had communicated to Paula Legendre in what seemed another age. Thumbing over some bills, he brought it on top again and opened it. To his surprise it was a short, somewhat formal note, which said that Dolly would be unable to go to the country with him for the week-end, because Perry Hull from Chicago had unexpectedly come to town. It added that Anson had brought this on himself: "—if I felt that you loved me as I love you I would go with you at any time, any place, but Perry is *so* nice, and he so much wants me to marry him——"

Anson smiled contemptuously—he had had experience with such decoy epistles. Moreover, he knew how Dolly had labored over this plan, probably sent for the faithful Perry and calculated the time of his arrival—even labored over the note so that it would make him jealous without driving him away. Like most compromises, it had neither force nor vitality but only a timorous despair.

Suddenly he was angry. He sat down in the lobby and read it again. Then he went to the phone, called Dolly and told her in his clear, compelling voice that he had received her note

and would call for her at five o'clock as they had previously planned. Scarcely waiting for the pretended uncertainty of her "Perhaps I can see you for an hour," he hung up the receiver and went down to his office. On the way he tore his own letter into bits and dropped it in the street.

He was not jealous—she meant nothing to him—but at her pathetic ruse everything stubborn and self-indulgent in him came to the surface. It was a presumption from a mental inferior and it could not be overlooked. If she wanted to know to whom she belonged she would see.

He was on the door-step at quarter past five. Dolly was dressed for the street, and he listened in silence to the paragraph of "I can only see you for an hour," which she had begun on the phone.

"Put on your hat, Dolly," he said, "we'll take a walk."

They strolled up Madison Avenue and over to Fifth while Anson's shirt dampened upon his portly body in the deep heat. He talked little, scolding her, making no love to her, but before they had walked six blocks she was his again, apologizing for the note, offering not to see Perry at all as an atonement, offering anything. She thought that he had come because he was beginning to love her.

"I'm hot," he said when they reached 71st Street. "This is a winter suit. If I stop by the house and change, would you mind waiting for me downstairs? I'll only be a minute."

She was happy; the intimacy of his being hot, of any physical fact about him, thrilled her. When they came to the iron-grated door and Anson took out his key she experienced a sort of delight.

Downstairs it was dark, and after he ascended in the lift Dolly raised a curtain and looked out through opaque lace at the houses over the way. She heard the lift machinery stop, and with the notion of teasing him pressed the button that brought it down. Then on what was more than an impulse she got into it and sent it up to what she guessed was his floor.

"Anson," she called, laughing a little.

"Just a minute," he answered from his bedroom . . . then after a brief delay: "Now you can come in."

He had changed and was buttoning his vest. "This is my room," he said lightly. "How do you like it?"

She caught sight of Paula's picture on the wall and stared at it in fascination, just as Paula had stared at the pictures of Anson's childish sweethearts five years before. She knew something about Paula—sometimes she tortured herself with fragments of the story.

Suddenly she came close to Anson, raising her arms. They embraced. Outside the area window a soft artificial twilight already hovered, though the sun was still bright on a back roof across the way. In half an hour the room would be quite dark. The uncalculated opportunity overwhelmed them, made them both breathless, and they clung more closely. It was eminent, inevitable. Still holding one another, they raised their heads—their eyes fell together upon Paula's picture, staring down at them from the wall.

Suddenly Anson dropped his arms, and sitting down at his desk tried the drawer with a bunch of keys.

"Like a drink?" he asked in a gruff voice.

"No, Anson."

He poured himself half a tumbler of whisky, swallowed it, and then opened the door into the hall.

"Come on," he said.

Dolly hesitated.

"Anson—I'm going to the country with you tonight, after all. You understand that, don't you?"

"Of course," he answered brusquely.

In Dolly's car they rode on to Long Island, closer in their emotions than they had ever been before. They knew what would happen—not with Paula's face to remind them that something was lacking, but when they were alone in the still, hot Long Island night they did not care.

The estate in Port Washington where they were to spend the week-end belonged to a cousin of Anson's who had married a Montana copper operator. An interminable drive began at the lodge and twisted under imported poplar saplings toward a huge, pink, Spanish house. Anson had often visited there before.

After dinner they danced at the Linx Club. About midnight Anson assured himself that his cousins would not leave before two—then he explained that Dolly was tired; he would take her home and return to the dance later. Trembling a little with excitement, they got into a borrowed car together and drove to Port Washington. As they reached the lodge he stopped and spoke to the night-watchman.

"When are you making a round, Carl?"

"Right away."

"Then you'll be here till everybody's in?"

"Yes, sir."

"All right. Listen: if any automobile, no matter whose it is, turns in at this gate, I want you to phone the house immediately." He put a five-dollar bill into Carl's hand. "Is that clear?"

"Yes, Mr. Anson." Being of the Old World, he neither winked nor smiled. Yet Dolly sat with her face turned slightly away.

Anson had a key. Once inside he poured a drink for both of them—Dolly left hers untouched—then he ascertained definitely the location of the phone, and found that it was within easy hearing distance of their rooms, both of which were on the first floor.

Five minutes later he knocked at the door of Dolly's room.

"Anson?" He went in, closing the door behind him. She was in bed, leaning up anxiously with elbows on the pillow; sitting beside her he took her in his arms.

"Anson, darling."

He didn't answer.

"Anson. . . . Anson! I love you. . . . Say you love me. Say it now—can't you say it now? Even if you don't mean it?"

He did not listen. Over her head he perceived that the picture of Paula was hanging here upon this wall.

He got up and went close to it. The frame gleamed faintly with thrice-reflected moonlight —within was a blurred shadow of a face that he saw he did not know. Almost sobbing, he turned around and stared with abomination at the little figure on the bed.

"This is all foolishness," he said thickly. "I don't know what I was thinking about. I don't love you and you'd better wait for somebody that loves you. I don't love you a bit, can't you understand?"

His voice broke, and he went hurriedly out.

Back in the salon he was pouring himself a drink with uneasy fingers, when the front door opened suddenly, and his cousin came in.

"Why, Anson, I hear Dolly's sick," she began solicitously. "I hear she's sick. . . ."

"It was nothing," he interrupted, raising his voice so that it would carry into Dolly's room. "She was a little tired. She went to bed."

For a long time afterward Anson believed that a protective God sometimes interfered in human affairs. But Dolly Karger, lying awake and staring at the ceiling, never again believed in anything at all.

VI

When Dolly married during the following autumn, Anson was in London on business. Like Paula's marriage, it was sudden, but it affected him in a different way. At first he felt that it was funny, and had an inclination to laugh when he thought of it. Later it depressed him—it made him feel old.

There was something repetitive about it—why, Paula and Dolly had belonged to different generations. He had a foretaste of the sensation of a man of forty who hears that the daughter of an old flame has married. He wired congratulations and, as was not the case with Paula, they were sincere—he had never really hoped that Paula would be happy.

When he returned to New York, he was made a partner in the firm, and, as his responsibilities increased, he had less time on his hands. The refusal of a life-insurance company to issue him a policy made such an impression on him that he stopped drinking for a year, and claimed that he felt better physically, though I think he missed the convivial recounting of those Celliniesque adventures which, in his early twenties, had played such a part of his life. But he never abandoned the Yale Club. He was a figure there, a personality, and the tendency of his class, who were now seven years out of college, to drift away to more sober haunts was checked by his presence.

His day was never too full nor his mind too weary to give any sort of aid to any one who asked it. What had been done at first through pride and superiority had become a habit and a passion. And there was always something—a younger brother in trouble at New Haven, a quarrel to be patched up between a friend and his wife, a position to be found for this man, an investment for that. But his specialty was the solving of problems for young married people. Young married people fascinated him and their apartments were almost sacred to him—he knew the story of their love-affair, advised them where to live and how, and remembered their babies' names. Toward young wives his attitude was circumspect: he never abused the trust which their husbands—strangely enough in view of his unconcealed irregularities—invariably reposed in him.

He came to take a vicarious pleasure in happy marriages, and to be inspired to an almost equally pleasant melancholy by those that went astray. Not a season passed that he did not witness the collapse of an affair that perhaps he himself had fathered. When Paula was divorced and almost immediately remarried to another Bostonian, he talked about her to me all one afternoon. He would never love any one as he had loved Paula, but he insisted that he no longer cared.

"I'll never marry," he came to say; "I've seen too much of it, and I know a happy marriage is a very rare thing. Besides, I'm too old."

But he did believe in marriage. Like all men who spring from a happy and successful marriage, he believed in it passionately—nothing he had seen would change his belief, his cynicism dissolved upon it like air. But he did really believe he was too old. At twenty-eight he began to accept with equanimity the prospect of marrying without romantic love; he resolutely chose a New York girl of his own class, pretty, intelligent, congenial, above reproach—and set about falling in love with her. The things he had said to Paula with sincerity, to other girls with grace, he could no longer say at all without smiling, or with the force necessary to convince.

"When I'm forty," he told his friends, "I'll be ripe. I'll fall for some chorus girl like the rest."

Nevertheless, he persisted in his attempt. His mother wanted to see him married, and he could now well afford it—he had a seat on the Stock Exchange, and his earned income came to twenty-five thousand a year. The idea was agreeable: when his friends—he spent most of his time with the set he and Dolly had evolved —closed themselves in behind domestic doors at night, he no longer rejoiced in his freedom. He even wondered if he should have married Dolly. Not even Paula had loved him more, and he was learning the rarity, in a single life, of encountering true emotion.

Just as this mood began to creep over him a disquieting story reached his ear. His Aunt Edna, a woman just this side of forty, was carrying on an open intrigue with a dissolute, hard-drinking young man named Cary Sloane. Every one knew of it except Anson's Uncle Robert, who for fifteen years had talked long in clubs and taken his wife for granted.

Anson heard the story again and again with increasing annoyance. Something of his old feeling for his uncle came back to him, a feeling that was more than personal, a reversion toward that family solidarity on which he had based his pride. His intuition singled out the essential point of the affair, which was that his uncle shouldn't be hurt. It was his first experiment in unsolicited meddling, but with his knowledge of Edna's character he felt that he could handle the matter better than a district judge or his uncle.

His uncle was in Hot Springs. Anson traced down the sources of the scandal so that there should be no possibility of mistake and then he called Edna and asked her to lunch with him at the Plaza next day. Something in his tone must have frightened her, for she was reluctant, but he insisted, putting off the date until she had no excuse for refusing.

She met him at the appointed time in the Plaza lobby, a lovely, faded, gray-eyed blonde in a coat of Russian sable. Five great rings, cold with diamonds and emeralds, sparkled on her slender hands. It occurred to Anson that it was his father's intelligence and not his uncle's that had earned the fur and the stones, the rich brilliance that buoyed up her passing beauty.

Though Edna scented his hostility, she was unprepared for the directness of his approach.

"Edna, I'm astonished at the way you've been acting," he said in a strong, frank voice. "At first I couldn't believe it."

"Believe what?" she demanded sharply.

"You needn't pretend with me, Edna. I'm talking about Cary Sloane. Aside from any other consideration, I didn't think you could treat Uncle Robert——"

"Now look here, Anson—" she began angrily, but his peremptory voice broke through hers:

"—and your children in such a way. You've been married eighteen years, and you're old enough to know better."

"You can't talk to me like that! You——"

"Yes, I can. Uncle Robert has always been my best friend." He was tremendously moved. He felt a real distress about his uncle, about his three young cousins.

Edna stood up, leaving her crab-flake cocktail untasted.

"This is the silliest thing——"

"Very well, if you won't listen to me I'll go to Uncle Robert and tell him the whole story— he's bound to hear it sooner or later. And afterward I'll go to old Moses Sloane."

Edna faltered back into her chair.

"Don't talk so loud," she begged him. Her eyes blurred with tears. "You have no idea how your voice carries. You might have chosen a less public place to make all these crazy accusations."

He didn't answer.

"Oh, you never liked me, I know," she went on. "You're just taking advantage of some silly gossip to try and break up the only interesting friendship I've ever had. What did I ever do to make you hate me so?"

Still Anson waited. There would be the appeal to his chivalry, then to his pity, finally to his superior sophistication—when he had shouldered his way through all these there would be admissions, and he could come to grips with her. By being silent, by being impervious, by returning constantly to his main weapon, which was his own true emotion, he bullied her into frantic despair as the luncheon hour slipped away. At two o'clock she took out a mirror and a handkerchief, shined away the marks of her tears and powdered the slight hollows where they had lain. She had agreed to meet him at her own house at five.

When he arrived she was stretched on a

chaise longue which was covered with cretonne for the summer, and the tears he had called up at luncheon seemed still to be standing in her eyes. Then he was aware of Cary Sloane's dark anxious presence upon the cold hearth.

"What's this idea of yours?" broke out Sloane immediately. "I understand you invited Edna to lunch and then threatened her on the basis of some cheap scandal."

Anson sat down.

"I have no reason to think it's only scandal."

"I hear you're going to take it to Robert Hunter, and to my father."

Anson nodded.

"Either you break it off—or I will," he said.

"What God damned business is it of yours, Hunter?"

"Don't lose your temper, Cary," said Edna nervously. "It's only a question of showing him how absurd——"

"For one thing, it's my name that's being handed around," interrupted Anson. "That's all that concerns you, Cary."

"Edna isn't a member of your family."

"She most certainly is!" His anger mounted. "Why—she owes this house and the rings on her fingers to my father's brains. When Uncle Robert married her she didn't have a penny."

They all looked at the rings as if they had a significant bearing on the situation. Edna made a gesture to take them from her hand.

"I guess they're not the only rings in the world," said Sloane.

"Oh, this is absurd," cried Edna. "Anson, will you listen to me? I've found out how the silly story started. It was a maid I discharged who went right to the Chilicheffs—all these Russians pump things out of their servants and then put a false meaning on them." She brought down her fist angrily on the table: "And after Tom lent them the limousine for a whole month when we were South last winter——"

"Do you see?" demanded Sloane eagerly. "This maid got hold of the wrong end of the thing. She knew that Edna and I were friends, and she carried it to the Chilicheffs. In Russia they assume that if a man and a woman——"

He enlarged the theme to a disquisition upon social relations in the Caucasus.

"If that's the case it better be explained to Uncle Robert," said Anson dryly, "so that when the rumors do reach him he'll know they're not true."

Adopting the method he had followed with Edna at luncheon he let them explain it all away. He knew that they were guilty and that presently they would cross the line from explanation into justification and convict themselves more definitely than he could ever do. By seven they had taken the desperate step of telling him the truth—Robert Hunter's neglect, Edna's empty life, the casual dalliance that had flamed up into passion—but like so many true stories it had the misfortune of being old, and its enfeebled body beat helplessly against the armor of Anson's will. The threat to go to Sloane's father sealed their helplessness, for the latter, a retired cotton broker out of Alabama, was a notorious fundamentalist who controlled his son by a rigid allowance and the promise that at his next vagary the allowance would stop forever.

They dined at a small French restaurant, and the discussion continued—at one time Sloane resorted to physical threats, a little later they were both imploring him to give them time. But Anson was obdurate. He saw that Edna was breaking up, and that her spirit must not be refreshed by any renewal of their passion.

At two o'clock in a small night-club on 53d Street, Edna's nerves suddenly collapsed, and she cried to go home. Sloane had been drinking heavily all evening, and he was faintly maudlin, leaning on the table and weeping a little with his face in his hands. Quickly Anson gave them his terms. Sloane was to leave town for six months, and he must be gone within forty-eight hours. When he returned there was to be no resumption of the affair, but at the end of a year Edna might, if she wished, tell Robert Hunter that she wanted a divorce and go about it in the usual way.

He paused, gaining confidence from their faces for his final word.

"Or there's another thing you can do," he said slowly, "if Edna wants to leave her children, there's nothing I can do to prevent your running off together."

"I want to go home!" cried Edna again.

"Oh, haven't you done enough to us for one day?"

Outside it was dark, save for a blurred glow from Sixth Avenue down the street. In that light those two who had been lovers looked for the last time into each other's tragic faces, realizing that between them there was not enough youth and strength to avert their eternal parting. Sloane walked suddenly off down the street and Anson tapped a dozing taxi-driver on the arm.

It was almost four; there was a patient flow of cleaning water along the ghostly pavement of Fifth Avenue, and the shadows of two night women flitted over the dark façade of St. Thomas's church. Then the desolate shrubbery of Central Park where Anson had often played as a child, and the mounting numbers, significant as names, of the marching streets. This was his city, he thought, where his name had flourished through five generations. No change could alter the permanence of its place here, for change itself was the essential substratum by which he and those of his name identified themselves with the spirit of New York. Resourcefulness and a powerful will—for his threats in weaker hands would have been less than nothing—had beaten the gathering dust from his uncle's name, from the name of his family, from even this shivering figure that sat beside him in the car.

Cary Sloane's body was found next morning on the lower shelf of a pillar of Queensboro Bridge. In the darkness and in his excitement he had thought that it was the water flowing black beneath him, but in less than a second it made no possible difference—unless he had planned to think one last thought of Edna, and call out her name as he struggled feebly in the water.

VII

Anson never blamed himself for his part in this affair—the situation which brought it about had not been of his making. But the just suffer with the unjust, and he found that his oldest and somehow his most precious friendship was over. He never knew what distorted story Edna told, but he was welcome in his uncle's house no longer.

Just before Christmas Mrs. Hunter retired to a select Episcopal heaven, and Anson became the responsible head of his family. An unmarried aunt who had lived with them for years ran the house, and attempted with helpless inefficiency to chaperone the younger girls. All the children were less self-reliant than Anson, more conventional both in their virtues and in their shortcomings. Mrs. Hunter's death had postponed the début of one daughter and the wedding of another. Also it had taken something deeply material from all of them, for with her passing the quiet, expensive superiority of the Hunters came to an end.

For one thing, the estate, considerably diminished by two inheritance taxes and soon to be divided among six children, was not a notable fortune any more. Anson saw a tendency in his youngest sisters to speak rather respectfully of families that hadn't "existed" twenty years ago. His own feeling of precedence was not echoed in them—sometimes they were conventionally snobbish, that was all. For another thing, this was the last summer they would spend on the Connecticut estate; the clamor against it was too loud: "Who wants to waste the best months of the year shut up in that dead old town?" Reluctantly he yielded—the house would go into the market in the fall, and next summer they would rent a smaller place in Westchester County. It was a step down from the expensive simplicity of his father's idea, and, while he sympathized with the revolt, it also annoyed him; during his mother's lifetime he had gone up there at least every other week-end—even in the gayest summers.

Yet he himself was part of this change, and his strong instinct for life had turned him in his twenties from the hollow obsequies of that abortive leisure class. He did not see this clearly —he still felt that there was a norm, a standard of society. But there was no norm, it was doubtful if there had ever been a true norm in New York. The few who still paid and fought to enter a particular set succeeded only to find that as a society it scarcely functioned—or, what was more alarming, that the Bohemia from which they fled sat above them at table.

At twenty-nine Anson's chief concern was his own growing loneliness. He was sure now that he would never marry. The number of weddings at which he had officiated as best man or usher was past all counting—there was a drawer at home that bulged with the official neckties of this or that wedding-party, neckties standing for romances that had not endured a year, for couples who had passed completely from his life. Scarf-pins, gold pencils, cuff-buttons, presents from a generation of grooms had passed through his jewel-box and been lost —and with every ceremony he was less and less able to imagine himself in the groom's place. Under his hearty good-will toward all those marriages there was despair about his own.

And as he neared thirty he became not a little depressed at the inroads that marriage, especially lately, had made upon his friendships. Groups of people had a disconcerting tendency to dissolve and disappear. The men from his own college—and it was upon them he had expended the most time and affection—were the most elusive of all. Most of them were drawn deep into domesticity, two were dead, one lived abroad, one was in Hollywood writing continuities for pictures that Anson went faithfully to see.

Most of them, however, were permanent commuters with an intricate family life centering around some suburban country club, and it was from these that he felt his estrangement most keenly.

In the early days of their married life they had all needed him; he gave them advice about their slim finances, he exorcised their doubts about the advisability of bringing a baby into two rooms and a bath, especially he stood for the great world outside. But now their financial troubles were in the past and the fearfully expected child had evolved into an absorbing family. They were always glad to see old Anson, but they dressed up for him and tried to impress him with their present importance, and kept their troubles to themselves. They needed him no longer.

A few weeks before his thirtieth birthday the last of his early and intimate friends was married. Anson acted in his usual rôle of best man, gave his usual silver tea-service, and went down to the usual *Homeric* to say good-by. It was a hot Friday afternoon in May, and as he walked from the pier he realized that Saturday closing had begun and he was free until Monday morning.

"Go where?" he asked himself.

The Yale Club, of course; bridge until dinner, then four or five raw cocktails in somebody's room and a pleasant confused evening. He regretted that this afternoon's groom wouldn't be along—they had always been able to cram so much into such nights: they knew how to attach women and how to get rid of them, how much consideration any girl deserved from their intelligent hedonism. A party was an adjusted thing—you took certain girls to certain places and spent just so much on their amusement; you drank a little, not much, more than you ought to drink, and at a certain time in the morning you stood up and said you were going home. You avoided college boys, sponges, future engagements, fights, sentiment, and indiscretions. That was the way it was done. All the rest was dissipation.

In the morning you were never violently sorry—you made no resolutions, but if you had overdone it and your heart was slightly out of order, you went on the wagon for a few days without saying anything about it, and waited until an accumulation of nervous boredom projected you into another party.

The lobby of the Yale Club was unpopulated. In the bar three very young alumni looked up at him, momentarily and without curiosity.

"Hello there, Oscar," he said to the bartender. "Mr. Cahill been around this afternoon?"

"Mr. Cahill's gone to New Haven."

"Oh . . . that so?"

"Gone to the ball game. Lot of men gone up."

Anson looked once again into the lobby, considered for a moment, and then walked out and over to Fifth Avenue. From the broad window of one of his clubs—one that he had scarcely visited in five years—a gray man with watery eyes stared down at him. Anson looked quickly away—that figure sitting in vacant resignation, in supercilious solitude, depressed him. He stopped and, retracing his steps, started over 47th Street toward Teak Warden's apartment. Teak and his wife had once been his most familiar friends—it was a household where he and Dolly Karger had been used to go in the days of their affair. But Teak had taken to drink, and his wife had remarked publicly that Anson was a bad influence on him. The remark reached Anson in an exaggerated form—when it was finally cleared up, the delicate spell of intimacy was broken, never to be renewed.

"Is Mr. Warden at home?" he inquired.

"They've gone to the country."

The fact unexpectedly cut at him. They were gone to the country and he hadn't known. Two years before he would have known the date, the hour, come up at the last moment for a final drink, and planned his first visit to them. Now they had gone without a word.

Anson looked at his watch and considered a week-end with his family, but the only train was a local that would jolt through the aggressive heat for three hours. And tomorrow in the country, and Sunday—he was in no mood for porch-bridge with polite undergraduates, and dancing after dinner at a rural road-house, a diminutive of gaiety which his father had estimated too well.

"Oh, no," he said to himself. . . . "No."

He was a dignified, impressive young man, rather stout now, but otherwise unmarked by dissipation. He could have been cast for a pillar of something—at times you were sure it was not society, at others nothing else—for the law, for the church. He stood for a few minutes motionless on the sidewalk in front of a 47th Street apartment-house; for almost the first time in his life he had nothing whatever to do.

Then he began to walk briskly up Fifth Avenue, as if he had just been reminded of an important engagement there. The necessity of dissimulation is one of the few characteristics that we share with dogs, and I think of Anson on that day as some well-bred specimen who had been disappointed at a familiar back door. He was going to see Nick, once a fashionable bartender in demand at all private dances, and now employed in cooling non-alcoholic champagne among the labyrinthine cellars of the Plaza Hotel.

"Nick," he said, "what's happened to everything?"

"Dead," Nick said.

"Make me a whisky sour." Anson handed a pint bottle over the counter. "Nick, the girls are different; I had a little girl in Brooklyn and she got married last week without letting me know."

"That a fact? Ha-ha-ha," responded Nick diplomatically. "Slipped it over on you."

"Absolutely," said Anson. "And I was out with her the night before."

"Ha-ha-ha," said Nick, "ha-ha-ha!"

"Do you remember the wedding, Nick, in Hot Springs where I had the waiters and the musicians singing 'God save the King'?"

"Now where was that, Mr. Hunter?" Nick concentrated doubtfully. "Seems to me that was——"

"Next time they were back for more, and I began to wonder how much I'd paid them," continued Anson.

"—seems to me that was at Mr. Trenholm's wedding."

"Don't know him," said Anson decisively. He was offended that a strange name should intrude upon his reminiscences; Nick perceived this.

"Naw—aw—" he admitted, "I ought to know that. It was one of *your* crowd—Brakins. . . . Baker——"

"Bicker Baker," said Anson responsively. "They put me in a hearse after it was over and covered me up with flowers and drove me away."

"Ha-ha-ha," said Nick. "Ha-ha-ha."

Nick's simulation of the old family servant paled presently and Anson went upstairs to the lobby. He looked around—his eyes met the glance of an unfamiliar clerk at the desk, then fell upon a flower from the morning's marriage hesitating in the mouth of a brass cuspidor. He went out and walked slowly toward the blood-red sun over Columbus Circle. Suddenly he turned around and, retracing his steps to the Plaza, immured himself in a telephone-booth.

Later he said that he tried to get me three times that afternoon, that he tried every one who might be in New York—men and girls he had not seen for years, an artist's model of his college days whose faded number was still in his address book—Central told him that even the exchange existed no longer. At length his quest roved into the country, and he held brief disappointing conversations with emphatic butlers and maids. So-and-so- was out, riding, swimming, playing golf, sailed to Europe last week. Who shall I say phoned?

It was intolerable that he should pass the evening alone—the private reckonings which one plans for a moment of leisure lose every charm when the solitude is enforced. There were always women of a sort, but the ones he knew had temporarily vanished, and to pass a New York evening in the hired company of a stranger never occurred to him—he would have considered that that was something shameful and secret, the diversion of a traveling salesman in a strange town.

Anson paid the telephone bill—the girl tried unsuccessfully to joke with him about its size —and for the second time that afternoon started to leave the Plaza and go he knew not where. Near the revolving door the figure of a woman, obviously with child, stood sideways to the light —a sheer beige cape fluttered at her shoulders when the door turned and, each time, she looked impatiently toward it as if she were weary of waiting. At the first sight of her a strong nervous thrill of familiarity went over him, but not until he was within five feet of her did he realize that it was Paula.

"Why, Anson Hunter!"

His heart turned over.

"Why, Paula——"

"Why, this is wonderful. I can't believe it, *Anson!*"

She took both his hands, and he saw in the freedom of the gesture that the memory of him had lost poignancy to her. But not to him—he felt that old mood that she evoked in him stealing over his brain, that gentleness with which he had always met her optimism as if afraid to mar its surface.

"We're at Rye for the summer. Pete had to come East on business—you know of course I'm Mrs. Peter Hagerty now—so we brought the children and took a house. You've got to come out and see us."

"Can I?" he asked directly. "When?"

"When you like. Here's Peter." The revolving door functioned, giving up a fine tall man of thirty with a tanned face and a trim mustache. His immaculate fitness made a sharp contrast with Anson's increasing bulk, which

was obvious under the faintly tight cutaway coat.

"You oughtn't to be standing," said Hagerty to his wife. "Let's sit down here." He indicated lobby chairs, but Paula hesitated.

"I've got to go right home," she said. "Anson, why don't you—why don't you come out and have dinner with us tonight? We're just getting settled, but if you can stand that——"

Hagerty confirmed the invitation cordially.

"Come out for the night."

Their car waited in front of the hotel, and Paula with a tired gesture sank back against silk cushions in the corner.

"There's so much I want to talk to you about," she said, "it seems hopeless."

"I want to hear about you."

"Well"—she smiled at Hagerty—"that would take a long time too. I have three children—by my first marriage. The oldest is five, then four, then three." She smiled again. "I didn't waste much time having them, did I?"

"Boys?"

"A boy and two girls. Then—oh, a lot of things happened, and I got a divorce in Paris a year ago and married Pete. That's all—except that I'm awfully happy."

In Rye they drove up to a large house near the Beach Club, from which there issued presently three dark, slim children who broke from an English governess and approached them with an esoteric cry. Abstractedly and with difficulty Paula took each one into her arms, a caress which they accepted stiffly, as they had evidently been told not to bump into Mummy. Even against their fresh faces Paula's skin showed scarcely any weariness—for all her physical languor she seemed younger than when he had last seen her at Palm Beach seven years ago.

At dinner she was preoccupied, and afterward, during the homage to the radio, she lay with closed eyes on the sofa, until Anson wondered if his presence at this time were not an intrusion. But at nine o'clock, when Hagerty rose and said pleasantly that he was going to leave them by themselves for a while, she began to talk slowly about herself and the past.

"My first baby," she said—"the one we call Darling, the biggest little girl—I wanted to die when I knew I was going to have her, because

Lowell was like a stranger to me. It didn't seem as though she could be my own. I wrote you a letter and tore it up. Oh, you were *so* bad to me, Anson."

It was the dialogue again, rising and falling. Anson felt a sudden quickening of memory.

"Weren't you engaged once?" she asked—"a girl named Dolly something?"

"I wasn't ever engaged. I tried to be engaged, but I never loved anybody but you, Paula."

"Oh," she said. Then after a moment: "This baby is the first one I ever really wanted. You see, I'm in love now—at last."

He didn't answer, shocked at the treachery of her remembrance. She must have seen that the "at last" bruised him, for she continued:

"I was infatuated with you, Anson—you could make me do anything you liked. But we wouldn't have been happy. I'm not smart enough for you. I don't like things to be complicated like you do." She paused. "You'll never settle down," she said.

The phrase struck at him from behind—it was an accusation that of all accusations he had never merited.

"I could settle down if women were different," he said. "If I didn't understand so much about them, if women didn't spoil you for other women, if they had only a little pride. If I could go to sleep for a while and wake up into a home that was really mine—why, that's what I'm made for, Paula, that's what women have seen in me and liked in me. It's only that I can't get through the preliminaries any more."

Hagerty came in a little before eleven; after a whisky Paula stood up and announced that she was going to bed. She went over and stood by her husband.

"Where did you go, dearest?" she demanded.

"I had a drink with Ed Saunders."

"I was worried. I thought maybe you'd run away."

She rested her head against his coat.

"He's sweet, isn't he, Anson?" she demanded.

"Absolutely," said Anson, laughing.

She raised her face to her husband.

"Well, I'm ready," she said. She turned to Anson: "Do you want to see our family gymnastic stunt?"

"Yes," he said in an interested voice.

"All right. Here we go!"

Hagerty picked her up easily in his arms.

"This is called the family acrobatic stunt," said Paula. "He carries me upstairs. Isn't it sweet of him?"

"Yes," said Anson.

Hagerty bent his head slightly until his face touched Paula's.

"And I love him," she said. "I've just been telling you, haven't I, Anson?"

"Yes," he said.

"He's the dearest thing that ever lived in this world; aren't you, darling? . . . Well, good night. Here we go. Isn't he strong?"

"Yes," Anson said.

"You'll find a pair of Pete's pajamas laid out for you. Sweet dreams—see you at breakfast."

"Yes," Anson said.

VIII

The older members of the firm insisted that Anson should go abroad for the summer. He had scarcely had a vacation in seven years, they said. He was stale and needed a change. Anson resisted.

"If I go," he declared, "I won't come back any more."

"That's absurd, old man. You'll be back in three months with all this depression gone. Fit as ever."

"No." He shook his head stubbornly. "If I stop, I won't go back to work. If I stop, that means I've given up—I'm through."

"We'll take a chance on that. Stay six months if you like—we're not afraid you'll leave us. Why, you'd be miserable if you didn't work."

They arranged his passage for him. They liked Anson—every one liked Anson—and the change that had been coming over him cast a sort of pall over the office. The enthusiasm that had invariably signaled up business, the consideration toward his equals and his inferiors, the lift of his vital presence—within the past four months his intense nervousness had melted down these qualities into the fussy pessimism of a man of forty. On every transaction in which he was involved he acted as a drag and a strain.

"If I go I'll never come back," he said.

Three days before he sailed Paula Legendre Hagerty died in childbirth. I was with him a great deal then, for we were crossing together, but for the first time in our friendship he told me not a word of how he felt, nor did I see the slightest sign of emotion. His chief preoccupation was with the fact that he was thirty years old—he would turn the conversation to the point where he could remind you of it and then fall silent, as if he assumed that the statement would start a chain of thought sufficient to itself. Like his partners, I was amazed at the change in him, and I was glad when the *Paris* moved off into the wet space between the worlds, leaving his principality behind.

"How about a drink?" he suggested.

We walked into the bar with that defiant feeling that characterizes the day of departure and ordered four Martinis. After one cocktail a change came over him—he suddenly reached across and slapped my knee with the first joviality I had seen him exhibit for months.

"Did you see that girl in the red tam?" he demanded, "the one with the high color who had the two police dogs down to bid her good-by."

"She's pretty," I agreed.

"I looked her up in the purser's office and found out that she's alone. I'm going down to see the steward in a few minutes. We'll have dinner with her tonight."

After a while he left me, and within an hour he was walking up and down the deck with her, talking to her in his strong, clear voice. Her red tam was a bright spot of color against the steel-green sea, and from time to time she looked up with a flashing bob of her head, and smiled with amusement and interest, and anticipation. At dinner we had champagne, and were very joyous—afterward Anson ran the pool with infectious gusto, and several people who had seen me with him asked me his name. He and the girl were talking and laughing together on a lounge in the bar when I went to bed.

I saw less of him on the trip than I had hoped. He wanted to arrange a foursome, but there was no one available, so I saw him only at meals. Sometimes, though, he would have a cocktail in the bar, and he told me about the girl in the red tam, and his adventures with her, making them all bizarre and amusing, as he had a way of doing, and I was glad that he was himself again, or at least the self that I knew, and with which I felt at home. I don't think he was ever happy unless some one was in love with him, responding to him like filings to a magnet, helping him to explain himself, promising him something. What it was I do not know. Perhaps they promised that there would always be women in the world who would spend their brightest, freshest, rarest hours to nurse and protect that superiority he cherished in his heart.

DISCUSSION

This novelette has something of the range and complexity of a novel. It is really what the word *novelette* is sometimes taken to imply: a little novel. In time it covers some thirty years, the period from Anson's childhood to the moment when his character is fully defined. The main element in the story is the love affair with Paula, which runs through various stages, but there is also the story of Dolly Karger, the story of Anson's interference with his aunt's love affair, and various minor episodes, such as the conversation with Nick, the barman, and the encounter with the girl on shipboard. All of this is not to say that "The Rich Boy" is necessarily better than a long story—for instance, "The Gentleman from San Francisco," which is over 10,000 words, but which is very simple in organization—or better than a simpler kind of novelette, such as "Noon Wine." It is merely to indicate a difference.

If "The Rich Boy" has this range and complexity, how does Fitzgerald manage the material so that there is no impression of mere summary? For one thing, the use of a narrator permits what we may call a foreshortening of time. If the author himself were telling the story on his own responsibility as author, with the assumption of complete knowledge of his characters and their lives, we should expect some filling out of the narrative: we should be inclined to ask, "If he knows all, why doesn't he tell more?" But when the narrator appears in the story, we recognize the limitations of his knowledge; he can tell only what he knows. This difference is purely conventional; that is, in the final analysis we understand, of course, that the author is responsible for his story and the method used to tell it, but we accept the narrator and his function in the same sense that we accept any character in the story. And his presence is a device for controlling the material and giving it the desired scale.

The presence of the narrator is, however, not the only thing that allows Fitzgerald to manage his material so that it does not give the impression of a mere summary. We notice that Section I does not really begin the action of the story. It is concerned with establishing the attitude of the narrator to his material—the attitude of the "poor" narrator to the rich boy—and through this attitude the general proposition about the rich on which the story depends:

They possess and enjoy early, and it does something to them, makes them soft where we are hard, and cynical where we are trustful, in a way that, unless you were born rich, it is very difficult to understand. They think, deep in their hearts, that they are better than we are because we had to discover the compensations and refuges of life for ourselves.

The story, then, is an analysis of Anson's life and development as an illustration of the proposition. By treating the story as an illustration, Fitzgerald (through his narrator, of course) is able to practice another kind of foreshortening: he needs to tell only what is relevant to the proposition, what significantly illustrates the proposition. This means that he can summarize or omit at will without breaking the line of interest—the interest we have in the development of the proposition. The air of detachment, of authority, of almost scientific analysis all go with the method of illustration. Fitzgerald is not trying, this air seems to imply, to make us realize the full quality of Anson's life; he is interested only in what supports the proposition, in what makes Anson a specimen. For Anson is a specimen. Even though Fitzgerald says in the second paragraph of the story that "There are no types, no plurals," his proposition in the end deals with a type, the "very rich," and Anson is presented as an example of what inherited wealth may do to human personality and character.

What is that effect on Anson Hunter? As Arthur Mizener, the biographer of Fitzgerald, puts it, the story is "primarily one of how Anson's queer, rich-boy's pride deprived him of what he wanted most, a home and an ordered life. Hating not to dominate, Anson cannot love those whom he does dominate, cannot commit himself to the human muddle as he must if he is to have the life he wants." [1] Anson must finally live by that sense of superiority which has robbed him of what he really wants. As the last lines of the story put it:

I don't think he was ever happy unless some one was in love with him, responding to him like filings to a magnet, helping him to explain himself, promising him something. What it was I do not know. Perhaps they promised that there would always be women in the world who would spend their brightest, freshest, rarest hours to nurse and protect that superiority he cherished in his heart.

EXERCISE

1. "The Rich Boy" is divided into eight sections. Study these divisions as units of the structure of the story. That is, try to answer the question, "What point is made in each section in relation to the theme behind the story?" Section I is clearly a kind of prologue. In what sense is Section VIII a kind of epilogue, a way of summing up what has already been established by the story? Can you state why Anson's rejection of Paula should come at the middle of the story (end of Section IV) and not near the end?

2. Why was Anson's day "never too full nor his mind too weary to give any sort of aid to any one who asked it"? (Section VI)

3. When Anson is talking with his uncle's wife (Section VI) about her love affair, we find the following passage: " 'Yes, I can. Uncle Robert has been my best friend.' He was tremendously moved. He felt a real distress about his uncle, about his three young cousins." Is Anson's distress to be taken as completely sincere? Or do we understand that there is some self-deception, some shallowness, in it? Argue this question.

4. Why did Anson never blame himself for his part in the death of Cary Sloane, the lover of his uncle's wife? Does the author imply that in some sense he might have properly blamed himself?

5. Toward the middle of Section VII, when Anson finds himself idle and without plans on a Friday afternoon, we read the following passage: "Anson looked once again into the lobby, considered for a moment, and then walked out and over to Fifth Avenue. From the broad window of one of his clubs—one that he had scarcely visited in five years—a gray

---

[1] *The Far Side of Paradise,* Houghton Mifflin Company, 1951, pp. 193-194.

man. with watery eyes stared down at him. Anson looked quickly away—that figure sitting in vacant resignation, in supercilious solitude, depressed him."

What is the point of this passage?

6. Read Fitzgerald's story "Winter Dreams" or his novel *The Great Gatsby*. What points of similarity do you find between these and "The Rich Boy"? How would you describe the "world" of Fitzgerald? The basic conflict in that world? Compare this conflict with that you find in "A Wife of Nashville," by Peter Taylor (page 263).

7. Read "Disorder and Early Sorrow," by Thomas Mann (page 246). This is almost as long as "The Rich Boy." But do you think of it as a novelette or as a very long story? The answer to this depends, of course, on your definition of a novelette. Do you distinguish the novelette from the story merely on the basis of length? Or is the novelette, to you, a special form, a special genre? We say "to you" because there is no generally accepted answer to this question. You must work it out for yourself. In any case, you cannot discuss questions of form abstractly. Form involves meanings. So let us look at "Disorder and Early Sorrow" in some detail.

The story is concerned with the period of wild inflation in Germany just after the First World War. It was a period in which the economic base of the middle class was nearly destroyed, and in which the whole order of pre-War values, traditions, and customs was turned topsy-turvy.

In this story, however, nothing that seems very dire is happening to the professor's family. The two adolescent children disturb their father by some of their attitudes and interests. The son, for example, thinks that he wants to be a waiter in a nightclub. But the professor is trying to be tolerant and understanding—evidently with a good deal of success. The older children feel free to bring their friends to their home, to play the "new" music, and in general to be their uninhibited selves. (And from an American standpoint, they are not terribly wild or unconventional.)

The story has to do with preparations for a party that the older children are giving, with the party itself, and with a trivial happening at the party. The baby girl Ellie takes, as children sometimes will, a fancy to one of the young men guests, doesn't want to go to bed, and bursts into a fit of childish weeping. The young man, Herr Hergesell, amiably goes up to tell her good night so that she will be comforted and go to sleep. The father watches the incident with a "singular mixture of thankfulness, embarrassment, and hatred."

Does anything really "happen" in this story? Or is the story relatively pointless? Has the author been content to give us simply a "slice of life"—a typical instance of life in Germany during the postwar inflationary period? If anything of importance does happen, it is pretty obvious that it happens within the professor's mind. (It is also obvious that this is the professor's story.) Our questions may properly begin, therefore, with a consideration of the kind of person that the professor is.

a. Is it of any importance that the professor is a history professor rather than a chemistry professor, say, or a biologist? Is it significant that the lecture that the professor is preparing for the next day concerns the growth of public debt and the effect of inflation on various countries at various periods of history? (see page 252)

b. Much is made of the professor's devotion to Ellie. Isn't he fond of his other children? What does the relationship to Ellie mean to him? Is its significance pointed up in the story?

c. In order to answer Question b we may have to answer this question: What does history mean to the professor? What is meant by the statement on page 250 that "history professors do not love history because it is something that comes to pass, but only because it is something that *has* come to pass"? How, if at all, is the professor's love for Ellie related to his love for history? The life of a little child and life transmuted into history would superficially seem to have little in common.

d. How has the little incident at the end been charged with significance? How has the professor's disturbance over the chaotic, undisciplined world which boils all around him been suggested? Be specific in your answers. How has the professor's almost jealous and fearful regard for his little girl been suggested? Is the professor quite stupid? Or is he quite sensitive and knowing? Is he aware that his clinging to the child has in it something of desperation?

e. Does the professor understand himself—his weaknesses as well as his strength? How does the measure of self-knowledge qualify the tone of the story?

SECTION VIII

Stories

The stories in this section represent a variety of topics, themes, conventions, and techniques. In our comments on stories in the earlier sections we have often referred to stories in this "pool" for purposes of comparison and clarification. But here we refrain from adding further comments and analyses. We hope, in fact, that the student will approach these stories as freshly as possible, ready to make his own explorations and evaluations.

Kronkin's Prisoner

ISAAC BABEL (1894-   )

WE WAS wiping out the Poles up Belaya Tserkov way. We was wiping them out and making a clean job of it, so that even the trees bent. I got a scratch in the morning, but managed to get about somehow. The day was getting on for evening, I remember, and I'd got away from the Brigade Commander with only five Cossacks of the proletariat to stick with me. All around there's hand to hand fighting going on, all going at one another like cats and dogs. Blood's trickling down from me and my horse. You know the sort of thing.

I and Spirka Zabuty got away together, further away from the forest, and lo and behold —a lucky break—three hundred yards off, not more, dust what may be from a Staff, or from transport wagons. If it's Staff—all right, and if it's transport wagons—better still. The kids were going about in rags, and their shirts didn't reach down to their little bottoms.

"Zabuty," says I to Spirka, "you damned so-and-so, one way and another, I call upon you as the speaker—up and doing, man! That must be their Staff lighting out."

"I don't say no," says Spirka, "only there's two of us and eight of them."

"Puff away, Spirka," I says, "anyway, I'll go and dirty their chasubles. Come along and die for a pin and the World Revolution!"

Well, we went for them. There were eight swordsmen among 'em. Two we put out of action with our rifles. The third, I see, Spirka's gone and done in. And I takes aim at a big pot, boys, with a gold watch and chain. I got him up against a farm, all over apple trees and cherries. My big pot's mount was a regular beauty, but he was fagged. Then the Pan General drops his bridle, points his Mauser at me, and makes a hole in my leg.

"All right," I thinks, "I'll get you to kick your legs up all right."

So I got busy and put two bullets in the little horse. I was sorry about the stallion. He was a little Bolshevik—a regular little Bolshevik that stallion was, all chestnut, like a copper coin, with a good brush of tail and hocks like cords. I thought to myself: I'll take it alive to Lenin. But it didn't come off: I went and did that little horse in. It plumped down all of a heap like a bride, and my big pot fell out of the saddle. He jerked to one side and turned around and made a draft in my face again. So now I've got three distinctions in action.

"Jesus," I thinks, "he's as like as not to go and kill me by mistake."

So I galloped up to him, and he'd already got his sword out, and tears were running down his cheeks—white tears, real human milk.

"I'll get the Order of the Red Banner through you," I shouts. "Hands up, as I'm alive, Your Worship!"

"I can't, Pan," the old fellow answers. "You'll do me in."

Then suddenly up comes Spirka from nowhere, all bathed in sweat and his eyes hanging from his mug by threads.

"Vasily," he shouts to me, "you'll never believe the amount I've finished off! As for that general with trimmings all over him, I wouldn't mind finishing him off too."

"Go to blazes!" I says to Zabuty, losing my temper. "The trimmings cost me blood, I can tell you!"

And I got my mare to drive the general into a shed with hay in it or something. It was quiet in there and dark and cool.

"Pan," I says, "go steady in your old age. Now hands up, for the love of Mike, and we'll have a talk together."

He puffs away with his back to the wall and wipes his forehead with his red fingers.

"I can't," he says, "you'll do me in. I'll only give up my sword to Budenny."

Go and fetch him Budenny! That's gone and torn it! I see the old guy's had his day.

"Pan," I shouts, crying and grinding my teeth, "I'll give you my proletarian word that I'm myself commander-in-chief here. You needn't go looking for trimmings on me, but I've got the title all right. Here's my title; musical entertainer and drawing-room ventriloquist from the town of Nizhni—Nizhny Novogorod on the Volga River."

And a devil in me worked me up. The general's eyes were blinking like lanterns. A red sea opened up in front of me. The offense was like putting salt in a wound, because I could see the old fellow didn't believe me. So I shut my mouth, lads, squeezed in my belly in the old way, in our way, in the Nizhni-town way, and proved to the Pole that I was a ventriloquist.

And the old chap went quite white and clutched at his heart and sat down on the ground.

"Now d'you believe Vasily the Entertainer, Commissar of the 3rd Invincible Cavalry Brigade?"

"Commissar?" he cries.

"Commissar," I says.

"Communist?" he cries.

"Communist," I says.

"In my last hour," he cries, "as I draw my last breath, tell me, Cossack friend, are you really a Communist, or are you lying?"

"I'm a Communist all right," I says.

Then my old fellow sits there on the ground and kisses some amulet or other and breaks his sword in two, while two lamps light up in his eyes—two lanterns over the dark steppe.

"Forgive me," he says, "I can't surrender to a Communist." And he shakes me by the hand. "Forgive me," says he. "And kill me like a true soldier."

This story was related to us some time ago, during a halt, and in the customary farcical manner, by Kronkin, the political commissar of the N. Cavalry Brigade, thrice Knight of the Order of the Red Banner.

"And what came of your talk with the general, Vasily?"

"Could anything come of it with a chap like that, full of his sense of honor? I bowed to him again, but he would stick to it, so then we took the papers that were on him, the queer old bird, and his Mauser and the saddle that's under me now. And then I noticed my strength's all ebbing away and a terrible sleepiness is descending upon me—well, and I couldn't be bothered with him any more. . . ."

"So the old fellow was put out of his misery?"

" 'Fraid so."

La Lupa*

GIOVANNI VERGA (1840-1922)

Translated by D. H. LAWRENCE

SHE WAS tall, and thin; but she had the firm, vigorous bosom of a grown woman, though she was no longer young. Her face was pale, as though she had the malaria always on her, and in her pallor, two great dark eyes and fresh, red lips that seemed to eat you.

In the village they called her La Lupa, because she had never had enough—of anything. The women crossed themselves when they saw her go by, alone like a roving she-dog, with that ranging, suspicious motion of a hungry wolf. She bled their sons and their husbands dry in a twinkling, with those red lips of hers, and she had merely to look at them with her great evil eyes to have them running after her skirts, even if they'd been kneeling at the altar of Saint Agrippina. Fortunately, La Lupa never entered the church, neither at Easter nor at Christmas, nor to hear Mass, nor to confess. Fra Angiolino, of Santa Maria di Jesu, who had been a true servant of God, had lost his soul because of her.

Maricchia, poor thing, was a good girl and a nice girl, and she wept in secret because she was La Lupa's daughter, and nobody would take her in marriage, although she had her marriage chest full of linen, and her piece of fertile land in the sun, as good as any other girl in the village.

Then one day La Lupa fell in love with a handsome lad who'd just come back from serving as a soldier and was cutting the hay alongside her in the closes belonging to the lawyer: but really what you'd call falling in love, feeling your body burn under your stuff bodice, and suffering, when you stared into his eyes, the thirst that you suffer in the hot hours of June, away in the burning plains. But he went on mowing quietly, with his nose bent over his swath, and he said to her: "Why, what's wrong

with you, Mrs. Pina?" —In the immense fields, where only the grasshoppers crackled into flight, when the sun beat down like lead, La Lupa gathered armful after armful together, tied sheaf after sheaf, without ever wearying, without straightening her back for a moment, without putting her lips to the flask, so that she could keep at Nanni's heels, as he mowed and mowed, and asked her from time to time: "Why, what do you want, Mrs. Pina?"

One evening she told him, while the men were dozing in the stackyard, tired from the long day, and the dogs were howling away in the vast, dark, open country: "You! I want you! Thou'rt handsome as the day, and sweet as honey to me. I want thee, lad!"

"Ah! I'd rather have your daughter, who's a filly," replied Nanni, laughing.

La Lupa clutched her hands in her hair and tore her temples, without saying a word, and went away and was seen no more in the yard. But in October she saw Nanni again, when they were getting the oil out of the olives, because he worked next her house, and the screeching of the oil press didn't let her sleep at night.

"Take the sack of olives," she said to her daughter, "and come with me."

Nanni was throwing the olives under the millstone with the shovel, in the dark chamber like a cave, where the olives were ground and pressed, and he kept shouting Ohee! to the mule, so it shouldn't stop.

"Do you want my daughter Maricchia?" Mrs. Pina asked him.

"What are you giving your daughter Maricchia?" replied Nanni.

"She has what her father left, and I'll give her my house into the bargain; it's enough for me if you'll leave me a corner in the kitchen,

* Lu Lupa means the she-wolf, and also the prostitute, the enticer.

where I can spread myself a bit of a straw mattress to sleep on."

"All right! If it's like that, we can talk about it at Christmas," said Nanni.

Nanni was all greasy and grimy with the oil and the olives set to ferment, and Maricchia didn't want him at any price; but her mother seized her by the hair, at home in front of the fireplace, and said to her between her teeth: "If thou doesn't take him, I'll lay thee out!"

La Lupa was almost ill, and the folks were saying that the devil turns hermit when he gets old. She no longer went roving round; she no longer sat in the doorway, with those eyes of one possessed. Her son-in-law, when she fixed on him those eyes of hers, would start laughing and draw out from his breast the bit of Madonna's dress,* to cross himself. Maricchia stayed at home nursing the children, and her mother went to the fields, to work with the men, just like a man, weeding, hoeing, tending the cattle, pruning the vines, whether in the northeast wind or the east winds of January, or in the hot, stifling African wind of August, when the mules let their heads hang in dead weight, and the men slept face downward under the wall, on the north side. Between vesper bell and the night bell's sound, when no good woman goes roving around, Mrs. Pina was the only soul to be seen wandering through the countryside, on the ever-burning stones of the little roads, through the parched stubble of the immense fields, which lost themselves in the sultry haze of the distance, far off, far of, toward misty Etna, where the sky weighed down upon the horizon, in the afternoon heat.

"Wake up!" said La Lupa to Nanni, who was asleep in the ditch, under the dusty hedge, with his arms around his head. "Wake up! I've brought thee some wine to cool thy throat."

Nanni opened his eyes wide like a disturbed child, half-awake, seeing her erect above him, pale, with her arrogant bosom, and her eyes black as coals, and he stretched out his hand gropingly, to keep her off.

"No! No good woman goes roving around between vespers and night," sobbed Nanni, pressing his face down again in the dry grass of the ditch bottom, away from her, clutching his hair with his hands. "Go away! Go away! Don't you come into the stackyard again!"

She did indeed go away, La Lupa, but fastening up again the coils of her superb black hair, staring straight in front of her, as she stepped over the hot stubble, with eyes black as coals.

And she came back into the stackyard time and again, and Nanni no longer said anything; and when she was late coming, in the hour between evensong and night, he went to the top of the white, deserted little road to look for her, with sweat on his forehead; and afterward, he clutched his hair in his hand and repeated the same thing every time: "Go away! Go away! Don't you come into the stackyard again!"

Maricchia wept night and day; and she glared at her mother with eyes that burned with tears and jealousy; like a young she-wolf herself now, when she saw her coming in from the fields, every time silent and pallid.

"Vile woman!" she said to her. "Vile, vile mother!"

"Be quiet!"

"Thief! Thief that you are!"

"Be quiet!"

"I'll go to the Sergeant, I will."

"Then go!"

And she did go, finally, with her child in her arms, went fearless and without shedding a tear, like a madwoman, because now she also was in love with that husband of hers, whom they'd forced her to accept, greasy and grimy from the olives set to ferment.

The Sergeant went for Nanni and threatened him with jail and the gallows. Nanni began to sob and to tear his hair; he denied nothing, he didn't try to excuse himself. —"It's the temptation," he said. "It's the temptation of hell!" and he threw himself at the feet of the Sergeant, begging to be sent to jail.

"For pity's sake, Sergeant, get me out of this hell! Have me hung, or send me to prison; but don't let me see her again, never, never!"

"No!" replied La Lupa to the Sergeant. "I

---

* When the dress of the Madonna in the church is renewed, the old dress is divided in tiny fragments among the parishioners; the fragment is sewn in a tiny heart-shaped or locket-shaped sack and worn around the neck on a cord, hidden in the breast, to ward off evil.

kept myself a corner in the kitchen, to sleep in, when I gave her my house for her dowry. The house is mine. I won't be turned out."

A little later, Nanni got a kick in the chest from a mule and was likely to die; but the parish priest wouldn't bring the Host to him, unless La Lupa left the house. La Lupa departed, and then her son-in-law could prepare himself to depart also, like a good Christian; he confessed and took the communion with such evident signs of repentance and contrition that all the neighbors and the busybodies wept round the bed of the dying man.

And better for him if he had died that time, before the devil came back to tempt him and to get a grip on his body and his soul, when he was well.

"Leave me alone!" he said to La Lupa. "For God's sake, leave me in peace! I've been face to face with death. Poor Maricchia is only driven wild. Now all the place knows about it. If I never see you again, it's better for you and for me."

And he would have liked to tear his eyes out so as not to see again those eyes of La Lupa, which, when they fixed themselves upon his, made him lose both body and soul. He didn't know what to do, to get free from the spell she put on him. He paid for Masses for the souls in Purgatory, and he went for help to the priest and to the Sergeant. At Easter he went to confession, and he publicly performed the penance of crawling on his belly and licking the stones of the sacred threshold before the church for a length of six feet.

After that, when La Lupa came back to tempt him: "Hark here!" he said. "Don't you come again into the stackyard; because if you keep on coming after me, as sure as God's above I'll kill you."

"Kill me, then," replied La Lupa. "It doesn't matter to me; I'm not going to live without thee."

He, when he perceived her in the distance, amid the fields of green young wheat, he left off hoeing the vines and went to take the ax from the elm tree. La Lupa saw him advancing toward her, pale and wild-eyed, with the ax glittering in the sun, but she did not hesitate in her step, nor lower her eyes, but kept on her way to meet him, with her hands full of red poppies, and consuming him with her black eyes.

"Ah! Curse your soul!" stammered Nanni.

Tomorrow and Tomorrow and So Forth

JOHN UPDIKE (1932-   )

WHIRLING, TALKING, 11D began to enter Room 109. From the quality of their excitement Mark Prosser guessed it would rain. He had been teaching high school for three years, yet his students still impressed him; they were such sensitive animals. They reacted so infallibly to merely barometric pressure.

In the doorway, Brute Young paused while little Barry Snyder giggled at his elbow. Barry's stagy laugh rose and fell, dipping down toward some vile secret that had to be tasted and retasted, then soaring artificially to proclaim that he, little Barry, shared such a secret with the school's fullback. Being Brute's stooge was precious to Barry. The fullback paid no attention to him; he twisted his neck to stare at something not yet coming through the door. He yielded heavily to the procession pressing him forward.

Right under Prosser's eyes, like a murder suddenly appearing in an annalistic frieze of kings and queens, someone stabbed a girl in the back with a pencil. She ignored the assault saucily. Another hand yanked out Geoffrey Langer's shirt-tail. Geoffrey, a bright student, was uncertain whether to laugh it off or defend himself with anger, and made a weak, half-turning gesture of compromise, wearing an expression of distant arrogance that Prosser instantly coördinated with feelings of fear he used to have. All along the line, in the glitter of key chains and the acute angles of turned-back shirt cuffs, an electricity was expressed which simple weather couldn't generate.

Mark wondered if today Gloria Angstrom wore that sweater, an ember-pink angora, with very brief sleeves. The virtual sleevelessness was the disturbing factor: the exposure of those two serene arms to the air, white as thighs against the delicate wool.

His guess was correct. A vivid pink patch flashed through the jiggle of arms and shoulders as the final knot of youngsters entered the room.

"Take your seats," Mr. Prosser said. "Come on. Let's go."

Most obeyed, but Peter Forrester, who had been at the center of the group around Gloria, still lingered in the doorway with her, finishing some story, apparently determined to make her laugh or gasp. When she did gasp, he tossed his head with satisfaction. His orange hair bobbed. Redheads are all alike, Mark thought, with their white eyelashes and pale puffy faces and thyroid eyes, their mouths always twisted with preposterous self-confidence. Bluffers, the whole bunch.

When Gloria, moving in a considered, stately way, had taken her seat, and Peter had swerved into his, Mr. Prosser said, "Peter Forrester."

"Yes?" Peter rose, scrabbling through his book for the right place.

"Kindly tell the class the exact meaning of the words 'Tomorrow, and tomorrow, and tomorrow/Creeps in this petty pace from day to day.'"

Peter glanced down at the high-school edition of *Macbeth* lying open on his desk. One of the duller girls tittered expectantly from the back of the room. Peter was popular with the girls; girls that age had minds like moths.

"Peter. With your book shut. We have all memorized this passage for today. Remember?" The girl in the back of the room squealed in delight. Gloria laid her own book face-open on her desk, where Peter could see it.

Peter shut his book with a bang and stared into Gloria's. "Why," he said at last, "I think it means pretty much what it says."

"Which is?"

"Why, that tomorrow is something we often think about. It creeps into our conversation all the time. We couldn't make any plans without thinking about tomorrow."

"I see. Then you would say that Macbeth is here referring to the, the date-book aspect of life?"

Geoffrey Langer laughed, no doubt to please Mr. Prosser. For a moment, he *was* pleased. Then he realized he had been playing for laughs at a student's expense.

His paraphrase had made Peter's reading of the lines seem more ridiculous than it was. He began to retract. "I admit—"

But Peter was going on; redheads never know when to quit. "Macbeth means that if we quit worrying about tomorrow, and just lived for today, we could appreciate all the wonderful things that are going on under our noses."

Mark considered this a moment before he spoke. He would not be sarcastic. "Uh, without denying that there is truth in what you say, Peter, do you think it likely that Macbeth, in his situation, would be expressing such"—he couldn't help himself—"such sunny sentiments?"

Geoffrey laughed again. Peter's neck reddened; he studied the floor. Gloria glared at Mr. Prosser, the anger in her face clearly meant for him to see.

Mark hurried to undo his mistake. "Don't misunderstand me, please," he told Peter. "I don't have all the answers myself. But it seems to me the whole speech, down to 'Signifying nothing,' is saying that life is—well, a *fraud*. Nothing wonderful about it."

"Did Shakespeare really think that?" Geoffrey Langer asked, a nervous quickness pitching his voice high.

Mark read into Geoffrey's question his own adolescent premonitions of the terrible truth. The attempt he must make was plain. He told Peter he could sit down and looked through the window toward the steadying sky. The clouds were gaining intensity. "There is," Mr. Prosser slowly began, "much darkness in Shakespeare's work, and no play is darker than 'Macbeth.' The atmosphere is poisonous, oppressive. One critic has said that in this play, humanity suffocates." This was too fancy.

"In the middle of his career, Shakespeare wrote plays about men like Hamlet and Othello and Macbeth—men who aren't allowed by their society, or bad luck, or some minor flaw in themselves, to become the great men they might have been. Even Shakespeare's comedies of this period deal with a world gone sour. It is as if he had seen through the bright, bold surface of his earlier comedies and histories and had looked upon something terrible. It frightened him, just as some day it may frighten some of you." In his determination to find the right words, he had been staring at Gloria, without meaning to. Embarrassed, she nodded, and, realizing what had happened, he smiled at her.

He tried to make his remarks gentler, even diffident. "But then I think Shakespeare sensed a redeeming truth. His last plays are serene and symbolical, as if he had pierced through the ugly facts and reached a realm where the facts are again beautiful. In this way, Shakespeare's total work is a more complete image of life than that of any other writer, except perhaps for Dante, an Italian poet who wrote several centuries earlier." He had been taken far from the Macbeth soliloquy. Other teachers had been happy to tell him how the kids made a game of getting him talking. He looked toward Geoffrey. The boy was doodling on his tablet, indifferent. Mr. Prosser concluded, "The last play Shakespeare wrote is an extraordinary poem called 'The Tempest.' Some of you may want to read it for your next book reports—the ones due May 10th. It's a short play."

The class had been taking a holiday. Barry Snyder was snicking BBs off the blackboard and glancing over at Brute Young to see if he noticed. "Once more, Barry," Mr. Prosser said, "and out you go." Barry blushed, and grinned to cover the blush, his eyeballs sliding toward Brute. The dull girl in the rear of the room was putting on lipstick. "Put that away, Alice," Mr. Prosser commanded. She giggled and obeyed. Sejak, the Polish boy who worked nights, was asleep at his desk, his cheek white with pressure against the varnished wood, his mouth sagging sidewise. Mr. Prosser had an impulse to let him sleep. But the impulse might not be true kindness, but just the self-congratulatory, kindly pose in which he sometimes discovered himself. Besides, one breach of discipline encouraged others. He strode down the aisle and shook Sejak awake. Then he turned his attention to the mumble growing at the front of the room.

Peter Forrester was whispering to Gloria, trying to make her laugh. The girl's face, though, was cool and solemn, as if a thought had been provoked in her head. Perhaps at least *she* had been listening to what Mr. Prosser had been saying. With a bracing sense of chivalrous intercession, Mark said, "Peter. I gather from this noise that you have something to add to your theories."

Peter responded courteously. "No, sir. I honestly don't understand the speech. Please, sir, what *does* it mean?"

This candid admission and odd request stunned the class. Every white, round face, eager, for once, to learn, turned toward Mark. He said, "I don't know. I was hoping *you* would tell *me*."

In college, when a professor made such a remark, it was with grand effect. The professor's humility, the necessity for creative interplay between teacher and student were dramatically impressed upon the group. But to 11D, ignorance in an instructor was as wrong as a hole in a roof. It was as if he had held forty strings pulling forty faces taut toward him and then had slashed the strings. Heads waggled, eyes dropped, voices buzzed. Some of the discipline problems, like Peter Forrester, smirked signals to one another.

"Quiet!" Mr. Prosser shouted. "All of you. Poetry isn't arithmetic. There's no single right answer. I don't want to force my own impression on you, even if I *have* had much more experience with literature." He made this last clause very loud and distinct, and some of the weaker students seemed reassured. "I know none of *you* want that," he told them.

Whether or not they believed him, they subsided, somewhat. Mark judged he could safely reassume his human-among-humans attitude again. He perched on the edge of the desk and leaned forward beseechingly. "Now, honestly. Don't any of you have some personal feeling about the lines that you would like to share with the class and me?"

One hand, with a flowered handkerchief balled in it, unsteadily rose. "Go ahead, Teresa," Mr. Prosser said encouragingly. She was a timid, clumsy girl whose mother was a Jehovah's Witness.

"It makes me think of cloud shadows," Teresa said.

Geoffrey Langer laughed. "Don't be rude, Geoff," Mr. Prosser said sideways, softly, before throwing his voice forward: "Thank you, Teresa. I think that's an interesting and valid impression. Cloud movement has something in it of the slow, monotonous rhythm one feels in the line 'Tomorrow, and tomorrow, and tomorrow.' It's a very gray line, isn't it, class?" No one agreed or disagreed.

Beyond the windows actual clouds were bunching rapidly, and erratic sections of sunlight slid around the room. Gloria's arm, crooked gracefully above her head, turned gold. "Gloria?" Mr. Prosser asked.

She looked up from something on her desk with a face of sullen radiance. "I think what Teresa said was very good," she said, glaring in the direction of Geoffrey Langer. Geoffrey chuckled defiantly. "And I have a question. What does 'petty pace' mean?"

"It means the trivial day-to-day sort of life that, say, a bookkeeper or a bank clerk leads. Or a schoolteacher," he added, smiling.

She did not smile back. Thought wrinkles irritated her perfect brow. "But Macbeth has been fighting wars, and killing kings, and being a king himself, and all," she pointed out.

"Yes, but it's just these acts Macbeth is condemning as 'nothing.' Can you see that?"

Gloria shook her head. "Another thing I worry about—isn't it silly for Macbeth to be talking to himself right in the middle of this war, with his wife just dead, and all?"

"I don't think so, Gloria. No matter how fast events happen, thought is faster."

His answer was weak; everyone knew it, even if Gloria hadn't mused, supposedly to herself, but in a voice the entire class could hear, "It seems so *stupid*."

Mark winced, pierced by the awful clarity with which his students saw him. Through their eyes, how queer he looked, with his long hands, and his horn-rimmed glasses, and his hair never slicked down, all wrapped up in "literature," where, when things get rough, the king mumbles a poem nobody understands. The delight Mr. Prosser took in such crazy junk made not only his good sense but his masculinity a matter of doubt. It was gentle of them not to laugh him out of the room. He looked down and rubbed his fingertips together, trying to erase the chalk dust. The class noise sifted into unnatural quiet. "It's getting late," he said finally. "Let's start the recitations of the memorized passage. Bernard Amilson, you begin."

Bernard had trouble enunciating, and his rendition began " 'T'mau 'n' t'mau 'n' t'mau.' " It was reassuring, the extent to which the class tried to repress its laughter. Mr. Prosser wrote "A" in his marking book opposite Bernard's name. He always gave Bernard A on recitations, despite the school nurse, who claimed there was nothing organically wrong with the boy's mouth.

It was the custom, cruel but traditional, to deliver recitations from the front of the room. Alice, when her turn came, was reduced to a helpless state by the first funny face Peter Forrester made at her. Mark let her hang up there a good minute while her face ripened to cherry redness, and at last forgave her. She may try it later. Many of the youngsters knew the passage gratifyingly well, though there was a tendency to leave out the line "To the last syllable of recorded time" and to turn "struts and frets" into "frets and struts" or simply "struts and struts." Even Sejak, who couldn't have looked at the passage before he came to class, got through it as far as "And then is heard no more."

Geoffrey Langer showed off, as he always did, by interrupting his own recitation with bright questions. " 'Tomorrow, and tomorrow, and tomorrow,' " he said, " 'creeps in'—shouldn't that be '*creep* in,' Mr. Prosser?"

"It is 'creep*s*.' The trio is in effect singular. Go on." Mr. Prosser was tired of coddling Langer. If you let them, these smart students will run away with the class. "Without the footnotes."

" 'Creep*sss* in this petty pace from day to day, to the last syllable of recorded time, and all our yesterdays have lighted fools the way to dusty death. Out, out—' "

"No, no!" Mr. Prosser jumped out of his chair. "This is poetry. Don't mushmouth it! Pause a little after "fools.'" Geoffrey looked genuinely startled this time, and Mark himself did not quite understand his annoyance and, mentally turning to see what was behind him, seemed to glimpse in the humid undergrowth the two stern eyes of the indignant look Gloria had thrown Geoffrey. He glimpsed himself in the absurd position of acting as Gloria's champion in her private war with this intelligent boy. He sighed apologetically. "Poetry is made up of lines," he began, turning to the class. Gloria was passing a note to Peter Forrester.

The rudeness of it! To pass notes during a scolding that she herself had caused! Mark caged in his hand the girl's frail wrist and ripped the note from her fingers. He read it to himself, letting the class see he was reading it, though he despised such methods of discipline. The note went:

> Pete— I think you're *wrong* about Mr. Prosser. I think he's wonderful and I get a lot out of his class. He's heavenly with poetry. I think I love him. I really do *love* him. So there.

Mr. Prosser folded the note once and slipped it into his side coat pocket. "See me after class, Gloria," he said. Then, to Geoffrey, "Let's try it again. Begin at the beginning."

While the boy was reciting the passage, the buzzer sounded the end of the period. It was the last class of the day. The room quickly emptied, except for Gloria. The noise of lockers slamming open and books being thrown against metal and shouts drifted in.

"Who has a car?"

"Lend me a cig, pig."

"We can't have practice in this slop."

Mark hadn't noticed exactly when the rain started, but it was coming down fast now. He moved around the room with the window pole, closing windows and pulling down shades. Spray bounced in on his hands. He began to talk to Gloria in a crisp voice that, like his device of shutting the windows, was intended to protect them both from embarrassment.

"About note passing." She sat motionless at her desk in the front of the room, her short, brushed-up hair like a cool torch. From the way she sat, her naked arms folded at her breasts and her shoulders hunched, he felt she was chilly. "It is not only rude to scribble when a teacher is talking, it is stupid to put one's words down on paper, where they look much more foolish than they might have sounded if spoken." He leaned the window pole in its corner and walked toward his desk.

"And about love. 'Love' is one of those words that illustrate what happens to an old, overworked language. These days, with movie stars and crooners and preachers and psychiatrists all pronouncing the word, it's come to mean nothing but a vague fondness for something. In this sense, I love the rain, this blackboard, these desks, you. It means nothing, you see, whereas once the word signified a quite explicit thing—a desire to share all you own and are with someone else. It is time we coined a new word to mean that, and when you think up the word *you* want to use, I suggest that you be economical with it. Treat it as something you can spend only once—if not for your own sake, for the good of the language." He walked over to his own desk and dropped two pencils on it, as if to say, "That's all."

"I'm sorry," Gloria said.

Rather surprised, Mr. Prosser said, "Don't be."

"But you don't understand."

"Of course I don't. I probably never did. At your age, I was like Geoffrey Langer."

"I bet you weren't." The girl was almost crying; he was sure of that.

"Come on, Gloria. Run along. Forget it." She slowly cradled her books between her bare arm and her sweater, and left the room with that melancholy shuffling teen-age gait, so that her body above her thighs seemed to float over the desks.

What was it, Mark asked himself, these kids were after? What did they want? Glide, he decided, the quality of glide. To slip along, always in rhythm, always cool, the little wheels humming under you, going nowhere special. If Heaven existed, that's the way it would be there. "He's heavenly with poetry." They loved the word. Heaven was in half their songs.

"Christ, he's humming." Strunk, the physical ed teacher, had come into the room without Mark's noticing. Gloria had left the door ajar.

"Ah," Mark said, "a fallen angel, full of grit."

"What the hell makes you so happy?"

"I'm not happy, I'm just serene. I don't know why you don't appreciate me."

"Say." Strunk came up an aisle with a disagreeably effeminate waddle, pregnant with gossip. "Did you hear about Murchison?"

"No." Mark mimicked Strunk's whisper.

"He got the pants kidded off him today."

"Oh dear."

Strunk started to laugh, as he always did before beginning a story. "You know what a goddam lady's man he thinks he is?"

"You bet," Mark said, although Strunk said that about every male member of the faculty.

"You have Gloria Angstrom, don't you?"

"You bet."

"Well, this morning Murky intercepts a note she was writing, and the note says what a damn neat guy she thinks Murchison is and how she *loves* him!" Strunk waited for Mark to say something, and then, when he didn't, continued, "You could see he was tickled pink. But—get this —it turns out at lunch that the same damn thing happened to Fryeburg in history yesterday!" Strunk laughed and cracked his knuckles viciously. "The girl's too dumb to have thought it up herself. We all think it was Peter Forrester's idea."

"Probably was," Mark agreed. Strunk followed him out to his locker, describing Murchison's expression when Fryeburg (in all innocence, mind you) told what had happened to him.

Mark turned the combination of his locker, 18–24–3. "Would you excuse me, Dave?" he said. "My wife's in town waiting."

Strunk was too thick to catch Mark's anger. "I got to get over to the gym. Can't take the little darlings outside in the rain; their mommies'll write notes to teacher." He clattered down the hall and wheeled at the far end, shouting, "Now don't tell You-know-who!"

Mr. Prosser took his coat from the locker and shrugged it on. He placed his hat upon his head. He fitted his rubbers over his shoes, pinching his fingers painfully, and lifted his umbrella off the hook. He thought of opening it right there in the vacant hall, as a kind of joke, and decided not to. The girl had been almost crying; he was sure of that.

The Apostate

GEORGE MILBURN (1906-   )

HARRY, YOU been jacking me up about how I been neglecting Rotary here lately, so I'm just going to break down and tell you something. Now I don't want you to take this personal, Harry, because it's not meant personal at all. No siree! Not *a*-tall! But, just between you and I, Harry, I'm not going to be coming out to Rotary lunches any more. I mean I'm quitting Rotary! . . .

Now whoa there! Whoa! Whoa just a minute and let me get in a word edgeways. Just let me finish my little say.

Don't you never take it into your head that I haven't been wrestling with this thing plenty. I mean I've argued it all out with myself. Now I'm going to tell you the whyfor and the whereof and the howcome about this, Harry, but kindly don't let what I say go no further. Please keep it strictly on the Q.T. Because I guess the rest of the boys would suspicion that I was turning highbrow on them. But you've always been a buddy to me, Harry, you mangy old son of a hoss thief, you, so what I'm telling you is the straight dope.

Harry, like you no doubt remember, up till a few months ago Rotary was about "the most fondest thing I is of," as the nigger says. There wasn't nothing that stood higher for me than Rotary.

Well, here, about a year ago last fall I took a trip down to the university to visit my son and go to a football game. You know Hubert Junior, my boy. Sure. Well, this is his second year down at the university. Yes sir, that boy is getting a college education. I mean, I'm all for youth having a college education.

Of course I think there is such a thing as too much education working a detriment. Take, for instance, some of these longhairs running around knocking the country right now. But what I mean is, a good, sound, substantial college education. I don't mean a string of letters a yard long for a man to write after his John Henry. I just mean that I want my boy to have his sheepskin, they call it, before he starts out in the world. Like the fellow says, I want him to get his A.B. degree, and then he can go out and get his J.O.B.

Now, Harry, I always felt like a father has got certain responsibilities to his son. That's just good Rotary. That's all that is. You know that that's just good Rotary yourself, Harry. Well, I always wanted Hubert to think about me just like I was a pal to him, or say an older brother, maybe. Hubert always knew that all he had to do was come to me, and I would act like a big buddy to him, irregardless.

Well, like I was telling you, Harry, I started Hubert in to the university two years ago, and after he had been there about two months, I thought I would run down and see how he was getting along and go to a football game. So I and Mrs. T. drove over one Friday. We didn't know the town very well, so we stopped at a filling station, and I give Hubert a ring, and he come right on down to where we was to show us the way. Just as soon as he come up, I could see right then that he had something on his mind bothering him.

He called me aside and took me into the filling-station rest-room, and says: "For the love of God, Dad, take that Rotary button out of your coat lapel," he says to me.

Harry, that come as a big surprise to me, and I don't mind telling you that it just about took the wind out of my sails. But I wasn't going to let on to him, so I rared back on my dignity, and says, "Why, what do you mean, take that Rotary button out of my lapel, young man?" I says to him.

"Dad," Hubert says to me, serious, "any frat house has always got a few cynics in it. If you was to wear that Rotary button in your lapel out to the frat house, just as soon as you got out of sight, some of those boys at the house would razz the life out of me," he says.

"Hubert," I says, "there's not a thing that this lapel badge represents that any decent, moral person could afford to make fun of. If that's the kind of Reds you got out at your fraternity, the kind that would razz a what you might call sacred thing—yes sir, a sacred thing—like Rotary, well I and your mamma can just go somewheres else and put up. I don't guess the hotels have quit running," I says to him.

By now I was on my high horse right, see?

"Now, Dad," Hubert says, "it's not that. I mean, person'ly I'm awful proud of you. It's just that I haven't been pledged to this fraternity long, see, and when some of those older members found out you was a Rotarian they would deal me a lot of misery, and I couldn't say nothing. Person'ly I think Rotary is all right," he says to me.

"Well, you better, son," I says, "or I'm going to begin to think that you're sick in the head."

The way he explained it, though, Harry, that made it a horse of a different tail, as the saying goes, so I give in and took off my Rotary button right there. Stuck it in my pocket, see? So we went on out and visited at Hubert's fraternity house, and do you know that those boys just got around there and treated we folks like we was princes of the blood. I ment you would of thought that I was an old ex-graduate of that university. And we saw the big pigskin tussle the next day, fourteen to aught, favor us, and we had such a scrumptious time all around I forgot all about what Hubert had said.

Ever'thing would of been all right, except for what happened later. I guess some of those older boys at the frat house begin using their form of psychology on Hubert. I mean they finely got his mind set against Rotary, because when he come home for the summer vacation that was about the size of things.

I mean all last summer, I thought Hubert never would let up. He just kept it up, making sarcastic remarks about Rotary, see? Even when we was on our vacation trip. You know we drove out to California and back last summer, Harry. Come back with the same air in the tires we started out with. Well, I thought it would be kind of nice to drop in and eat with the Hollywood Rotary—you know, just to be able to say I had. Well, do you know that that boy Hubert made so much fun of the idea I just had to give it up? That was the way it was the whole trip. He got his mother around on his side, too. Just to be frank with you, I never got so sick and tired of anything in all my born days.

Well, Harry, I had my dander up there for a while, and all the bickering in the world couldn't of shook me from my stand. But finely Hubert went back to college in September, and I thought I would have a little peace. Then I just got to thinking about it, and it all come over me. "Look here, Mister Man," I says to myself, "your faith and loyalty to Rotary may be a fine thing, and all that, but it's just costing you the fellowship of your own son." Now a man can't practice Rotary in the higher sense, and yet at the same time be letting his own son's fellowship get loose from him. So there it was. Blood's thicker than water, Harry. You'll have to admit that.

Right along in there, Harry, was the first time I begin to attending meetings irregular. I'll tell you—you might not think so—but it was a pretty tough struggle for me. I remember one Monday noon, Rotary-meeting day, I happened to walk past the Hotel Beckman just at lunchtime. The windows of the Venetian Room was open, and I could hear you boys singing a Rotary song. You know that one we sing set to the tune of "Last Night on the Back Porch." It goes:

> *I love the Lions in the morning,*
> *The Exchange Club at night,*
> *I love the Y's men in the evening,*
> *And Kiwanis are all right . . .*

Well, I couldn't carry a tune if I had it in a sack, but anyway that's the way it goes. So I just stopped in my tracks and stood there listening to that song coming out of the Hotel Beckman dining room. And when the boys come to the last verse,

> *I love the Optimists in the springtime,*
> *The Ad Club in the fall,*
> *But each day—and in every way—*
> *I love Rotary best of all. . . .*

I tell you, Harry, that just got me. I had a lump in my throat big enough to choke a cow. The tears begin coming up in my eyes, and it might sound ridiculous to hear me tell it now, but I could of broke down and bawled right there on the street. I got a grip on myself and walked on off, but right then I says to myself, "The hell with Hubert and his highbrow college-fraternity ideas; I'm going back to Rotary next week."

Well, I did go back the next week, and what happened decided me on taking the step I decided on. Here's what decided me. You know, I never got very well acquainted with Gay Harrison, the new secretary. I mean, of course, I know him all right, but he hasn't been in Rotary only but about a year. Well, on that particular day, I just happened to let my tongue slip and called him Mister Harrison, instead of by his nickname. Well, of course, the boys slapped a dollar fine on me right then and there. I haven't got no kick to make about that, but the point is, I had a letter from Hubert in my pocket right then, telling me that he had run short of money. So I just couldn't help but be struck by the idea "I wish I was giving Hubert this dollar." So that's what decided me on devoting my time and finances to another kind of fellowship, Harry.

I get down to the university to see Hubert more frequent now. I make it a point to. And the boys come to me, and I been helping them a little on their frat building fund. There's a fine spirit of fellowship in an organization like that. Some boys from the best families of the State are members, too. You might think from what I said that they'd be uppish, but they're not. No siree. Not a bit of it. I been down there enough for them to know me, now, and they all pound me on the back and call me H.T., just like I was one of them. And I do them, too. And I notice that when they sit down to a meal, they have some songs they sing just as lively and jolly as any we had at Rotary. Of course, like Hubert said, a few of them might have some wild-haired ideas about Rotary, but they're young yet. And as far as I can see there's not a knocker nor a sourbelly among them. Absolutely democratic.

It puts me in mind of a little incidence that happened last month when the frat threw a big Dad's Day banquet for us down there. All the fathers of the boys from all over the State was there. Well, to promote the spirit of fellowship between dad and son, the fraternity boys all agreed to call their dads by their first name, just treating the dads like big buddies. So at the table Hubert happened to forget for a minute, and says to me "Dad" something. Well sir, the president of the frat flashed right out, "All right, Hubie, we heard you call H.T. 'Dad.' So that'll just cost you a dollar for the ice-cream fund." Ever'body had a good laugh at Hubert getting caught like that, but do you know, that boy of mine just forked right over without making a kick. That shows the stuff, don't it, Harry? Nothing wrong with a boy like that.

And the whole bunch is like that, ever' one of them. I'll tell you, Harry, the boys at that frat of Hubert's are the builders in the coming generation. Any man of vision can see that.

Well, that's that. Now what was you going to say?

Daddy Wolf

JAMES PURDY (1923-   )

You AREN'T the first man to ask me what I am doing so long in the phone booth with the door to my flat open and all. Let me explain something, or if you want to use the phone, I'll step out for a minute, but I am trying to get Operator to re-connect me with a party she just cut me off from. If you're not in a big hurry would you let me just try to get my party again.

See I been home 2 days now just looking at them 2 or 3 holes in the linoleum in my flat, and those holes are so goddam big now—you can go in there and take a look—those holes are so goddam big that I bet my kid, if he was still here, could almost put his leg through the biggest one.

Maybe of course the rats don't use the linoleum holes as entrances or exits. They could come through the calcimine in the wall. But I kind of guess and I bet the super for once would back me up on this, the rats are using the linoleum holes. Otherwise what is the meaning of the little black specks in and near each hole in the linoleum. I don't see how you could ignore the black specks there. If they were using the wall holes you would expect black specks there, but I haven't found a single one.

The party I was just talking to on the phone when I got cut off was surprised when I told her how the other night after my wife and kid left me I came in to find myself staring right head-on at a fat, I guess a Mama rat, eating some of my uncooked cream of wheat. I was so took by surprise that I did not see which way she went out. She ran, is all I can say, the minute I come into the room.

I had no more snapped back from seeing the Mama rat when a teeny baby one run right between my legs and disappeared ditto.

I just stood looking at my uncooked cream of wheat knowing I would have to let it go to waste.

It was too late that evening to call the super or anybody and I know from a lot of sad experience how sympathetic he would be, for the rats, to quote him, is a *un-avoidable probability* for whatever party decides to rent one of these you-know-what linoleum apartments.

If you want something better than some old you-know-what linoleum-floor apartments, the super says, *you got the map of Newyorkcity to hunt with.*

Rats and linoleum go together, and when you bellyache about rats, remember you're living on linoleum.

I always have to go to the hall phone when I get in one of these states, but tonight instead of calling the super who has gone off by now anyhow to his night job (he holds down 2 jobs on account of, he says, the high cost of chicken and peas), I took the name of the first party my finger fell on in the telephone book.

This lady answered the wire.

I explained to her the state I was in, and that I was over in one of the linoleum apartments and my wife and kid left me.

She cleared her throat and so on.

Even for a veteran, I told her, this is rough.

She kind of nodded over the phone in her manner.

I could feel she was sort of half-friendly, and I told her how I had picked her name out from all the others in the telephone book.

It was rough enough, I explained to her, to be renting an apartment in the linoleum district and to not know nobody in Newyorkcity, and then only the other night after my wife and kid left me this Mama rat was in here eating my uncooked cream of wheat, and before I get over this, her offspring run right between my legs.

This lady on the wire seemed to say *I see* every so often but I couldn't be sure on account of I was talking so fast myself.

I would have called the super of the building, I explained to her, in an emergency like this, but he has 2 jobs, and as it is after midnight now he is on his night job. But it would be just as bad in the daytime as then usually he is out inspecting the other linoleum apartments or catching up on his beauty sleep and don't answer the door or phone.

When I first moved into this building, I told her, I had to pinch myself to be sure I was actually seeing it right. I seen all the dirt before I moved in, but once I was in, I really SEEN: all the traces of the ones who had been here before, people who had died or lost their jobs or found they was the wrong race or something and had had to vacate all of a sudden before they could clean the place up for the next tenant. A lot of them left in such a hurry they just give you a present of some of their belongings and under-

wear along with their dirt. But then after one party left in such a hurry, somebody else from somewhere moved in, found he could not make it in Newyorkcity, and lit out somewhere or maybe was taken to a hospital in a serious condition and never returned.

I moved in just like the others on the linoleum.

Wish you could have seen it then. Holes everywhere and that most jagged of the holes I can see clear over here from the phone booth is where the Mama rat come through, which seems now about 3,000 years ago to me.

I told the lady on the phone how polite she was to go on listening and I hoped I was not keeping her up beyond her bedtime or from having a nightcap before she did turn in.

I don't object to animals, see. If it had been a Mama bird, say, which had come out of the hole, I would have had a start, too, as a Mama bird seldom is about and around at that hour, not to mention it not nesting in a linoleum hole, but I think I feel the way I do just because you think of rats along with neglect and lonesomeness and not having nobody near or around you.

See my wife left me and took our kid with her. They could not take any more of Newyorkcity. My wife was very scared of disease, and she had heard the radio in a shoe-repair store telling that they were going to raise the V.D. rate, and she said to me just a few hours before she left, *I don't think I am going to stay on here, Benny, if they are going to have one of them health epidemics.* She didn't have a disease, but she felt she would if the city officials were bent on raising the V.D. rate. She said it would be her luck and she would be no exception to prove the rule. She packed and left with the kid.

Did I feel sunk with them gone, but Jesus it was all I could do to keep on here myself. A good number of times at night I did not share my cream of wheat with them. I told them to prepare what kind of food they had a yen for and let me eat my cream of wheat alone with a piece of warmed-over oleo and just a sprinkle of brown sugar on that.

My wife and kid would stand and watch me eat the cream of wheat, but they was entirely indifferent to food. I think it was partly due to the holes in the linoleum, and them knowing what was under the holes of course.

We have only the one chair in the flat, and so my kid never had any place to sit when I was to home.

I couldn't help telling this party on the phone then about my wife and DADDY WOLF.

I was the one who told my wife about DADDY WOLF and the TROUBLE PHONE in the first place, but at first she said she didn't want any old charity no matter if it was money or advice or just encouraging words.

Then when things got so rough, my wife did call DADDY WOLF. I think the number is CRack 8-7869 or something like that, and only ladies can call. You phone this number and say *Daddy Wolf, I am a lady in terrible trouble. I am in one of the linoleum apartments, and just don't feel I can go on another day. Mama rats are coming in and out of their holes with their babies, and all we have had to eat in a month is cream of wheat.*

DADDY WOLF would say he was listening and to go on, and then he would ask her if she was employed anywhere.

DADDY WOLF, *yes and no. I just do not seem to have the willpower to go out job-hunting any more or on these house-to-house canvassing jobs that I have been holding down lately, and if you could see this linoleum flat, I think you would agree,* DADDY WOLF, *that there is very little incentive for me and Benny.*

Then my wife would go on about how surprised we had both been, though she was the only one surprised, over the high rate of V.D. in Newyorkcity.

You see, DADDY WOLF, *I won't hold a thing back, I have been about with older men in order to tide my husband over this rough financial situation we're in. My husband works in the mitten factory, and he just is not making enough for the three of us to live on. He has to have his cream of wheat at night or he would not have the strength to go back to his day-shift, and our linoleum apartment costs 30 smackers a week.*

I leave the kid alone here and go out to try and find work, DADDY WOLF, *but I'm telling you, the only job I can find for a woman of my education and background is this house-to-house canvassing of Queen Bee royal jelly which makes* *older women look so much more appealing, but I hardly sell more than a single jar a day and am on my feet 12 hours at a stretch.*

The kid is glad when I go out to sell as he can have the chair to himself then. You see when I and his Daddy are home he either has to sit down on my lap, if I am sitting, or if his Daddy is sitting, just stand because I won't allow a little fellow like him to sit on that linoleum, it's not safe, and his Daddy will not let him sit on his lap because he is too dead-tired from the mitten factory.

That was the way she explained to DADDY WOLF on the TROUBLE PHONE, and that went on every night, night after night, until she left me.

DADDY WOLF always listened, I will give him credit for that. He advised Mabel too: *go to Sunday school and church and quit going up to strange men's hotel rooms. Devote yourself only to your husband's need, and you don't ever have to fear the rise in the V.D. rate.*

My wife, though, could just not take Newyorkcity. She was out selling that Queen Bee royal jelly every day, but when cold weather come she had only a thin coat and she went out less and less and that all added up to less cream of wheat for me in the evening.

It is funny thing about cream of wheat, you don't get tired of it. I think if I ate, say, hamburger and chop suey every night, I would get sick and tired of them. Not that I ever dine on them. But if I did, I would—get sick and tired, I mean. But there's something about cream of wheat, with just a daub of warm oleo on it, and a sprinkle of brown sugar that makes you feel you might be eatin' it for the first time.

My wife don't care for cream of wheat nearly so much as I do.

Our kid always ate with the old gentleman down the hall with the skullcap. He rung a bell when it was supper time, and the kid went down there and had his meal. Once in a while, he brought back something or other for us.

It's funny talking to you like this, Mister, and as I told this lady I am waiting to get reconnected with on the phone, if I didn't know any better I would think either one of you was DADDY WOLF on the TROUBLE PHONE.

Well, Mabel left me, then, and took the kid with her.

It was her silly fear of the V.D. rate that really made her light out. She could have stayed here indefinitely. She loved this here city at first. She was just crazy about Central Park.

Newyorkcity was just the place for me to find work in. I had a good job with the Singer sewing-machine people in one of their spare-parts rooms, then I got laid off and was without a thing for over 6 months and then was lucky to find this job at the mitten factory. I raise the lever that sews the inner lining to your mittens.

I don't think it is Mabel and the kid leaving me so much sometimes as it is the idea of that Mama rat coming through the holes in the linoleum that has got me so down-in-the-dumps today. I didn't even go to the mitten factory this A.M., and I have, like I say, got so down-in-the-dumps I almost felt like calling DADDY WOLF myself on the TROUBLE PHONE like she did all the time. But knowing he won't talk to nobody but ladies, as a kind of next-best-thing I put my finger down haphazard on top of this lady's name in the phone book, and I sure appreciated having that talk with her.

See DADDY WOLF would only talk with my wife for about one and a half minutes on account of other women were waiting to tell him their troubles. He would always say *Go back to your affiliation with the Sunday school and church of your choice, Mabel, and you'll find your burdens lighter in no time.*

DADDY said the same thing to her every night, but she never got tired hearing it, I guess.

DADDY WOLF told Mabel she didn't have to have any fear at all of the V.D. rate on account of she was a married woman and therefore did not have to go out for that relationship, but if she ever felt that DESIRE coming over her when her husband was gone, to just sit quiet and read an uplifting book.

Mabel has not had time, I don't think, to write me yet, taking care of the kid and all, and getting settled back home, and I have, well, been so goddam worried about everything. They are talking now about a shut-down at the mitten factory so that I hardly as a matter of fact have had time to think about my wife and kid, let alone miss them. There is, as a matter of fact, more cream of wheat now for supper, and I splurged today and bought a 5-pound box of that soft brown sugar that don't turn to lumps, which I wouldn't ever have done if they was still here.

The old gent down the hall with the skullcap misses my kid, as he almost entirely kept the boy in eats.

He never speaks to me in the hall, the old man. They said, I heard this somewhere, he don't have linoleum on his floor, but carpets, but I have not been invited in to see.

This building was condemned two years ago, but still isn't torn down, and the old man is leaving as soon as he can find the right neighborhood for his married daughter to visit him in.

Wait a minute. No, I thought I seen some action from under that one hole there in the linoleum.

Excuse me if I have kept you from using the phone with my talk but all I can say is you and this lady on the phone have been better for me tonight than DADDY WOLF on the TROUBLE PHONE ever was for my wife.

Up until now I have usually called the super when I was in one of these down-moods, but all he ever said was *Go back where you and Mabel got your own people and roots, Benny. You can't make it here in a linoleum apartment with your background and education.*

He has had his eyes opened—the super. He has admitted himself that he never thought Mabel and me could stick it out this long. (He don't know she is gone.)

But I won't give up. I WILL NOT give up. Mabel let a thing like the hike in the V.D. rates chase her out. I tried to show her that that was just statistics, but she always was superstitious as all get-out.

I judge when this scare I've had about the Mama rat dies down and I get some sleep and tomorrow if I go back to the mitten factory I will then really and truly begin to miss Mabel and the kid. The old man down the hall already misses the kid. That kid ate more in one meal with him than Mabel and me eat the whole week together. I don't begrudge it to him, though, because he was growing.

Well, Mister, if you don't want to use the phone after all, I think I will try to have

Operator re-connect me with that party I got disconnected from. I guess as this is the hour that Mabel always called DADDY WOLF I have just automatically caught her habit, and anyhow I sure felt in the need of a talk.

Do you hear that funny clicking sound? Here, I'll hold you the receiver so as you can hear it. Don't go away just yet: I think Operator is getting me that party again, so stick around awhile yet.

No, they cut us off again, hear? there is a bad connection or something.

Well, like I say, anyhow Mabel and the kid did get out of here, even if it was superstition. Christ, when I was a boy I had every one of those diseases and it never did me no hurt. I went right into the army with a clean bill of health, Korea, home again, and now Newyork-city.

You can't bullshit me with a lot of statistics.

Mabel, though, goddam it, I could knock the teeth down her throat, running out on me like this and taking the kid.

WHERE IS THAT GODDAM OPERATOR?

Hello. Look, Operator, what number was that I dialed and talked so long. Re-connect me please. That number I just got through talking with so long. I don't know the party's name or number. Just connect me back, will you please. This here is an emergency phone call, Operator.

The Lagoon

JOSEPH CONRAD (1857-1924)

THE WHITE man, leaning with both arms over the roof of the little house in the stern of the boat, said to the steersman:

"We will pass the night in Arsat's clearing. It is late."

The Malay only grunted, and went on looking fixedly at the river. The white man rested his chin on his crossed arms and gazed at the wake of the boat. At the end of the straight avenue of forests cut by the intense glitter of the river, the sun appeared unclouded and dazzling, poised low over the water that shone smoothly like a band of metal. The forests, somber and dull, stood motionless and silent on each side of the broad stream. At the foot of big, towering trees, trunkless nipa palms rose from the mud of the bank, in bunches of leaves enormous and heavy, that hung unstirring over the brown swirl of eddies. In the stillness of the air every tree, every leaf, every bough, every tendril of creeper and every petal of minute blossoms seemed to have been bewitched into an immobility perfect and final. Nothing moved on the river but the eight paddles that rose flashing regularly, dipped together with a single splash; while the steersman swept right and left with a periodic and sudden flourish of his blade describing a glinting semicircle above his head. The churned-up water frothed alongside with a confused murmur. And the white man's canoe, advancing upstream in the short-lived disturbance of its own making, seemed to enter the portals of a land from which the very memory of motion had forever departed.

The white man, turning his back upon the setting sun, looked along the empty and broad expanse of the sea-reach. For the last three miles of its course the wandering, hesitating river, as if enticed irresistibly by the freedom of an open horizon, flows straight into the sea, flows straight to the east—to the east that harbors both light and darkness. Astern of the boat the repeated call of some bird, a cry discordant and feeble, skipped along over the smooth water and lost itself, before it could reach the other shore, in the breathless silence of the world.

The steersman dug his paddle into the stream, and held hard with stiffened arms, his body thrown forward. The water gurgled aloud; and suddenly the long straight reach seemed to pivot on its center, the forests swung in a semicircle, and the slanting beams of sunset touched the broadside of the canoe with a fiery glow, throwing the slender and distorted shadows of its crew upon the streaked glitter of the river. The white man turned to look ahead. The course of the boat had been altered at right angles to the stream, and the carved dragon head of its prow was pointing now at a gap in the fringing bushes of the bank. It glided through, brushing the overhanging twigs, and disappeared from the river like some slim and amphibious creature leaving the water for its lair in the forests.

The narrow creek was like a ditch: tortuous, fabulously deep; filled with gloom under the thin strip of pure and shining blue of the heaven. Immense trees soared up, invisible behind the festooned draperies of creepers. Here and there, near the glistening blackness of the water, a twisted root of some tall tree showed amongst the tracery of small ferns, black and dull, writhing and motionless, like an arrested snake. The short words of the paddlers reverberated loudly between the thick and somber walls of vegetation. Darkness oozed out from between the trees, through the tangled maze of the creepers, from behind the great fantastic and unstirring leaves; the darkness, mysterious and invincible; the darkness scented and poisonous of impenetrable forests.

The men poled in the shoaling water. The creek broadened, opening out into a wide sweep of a stagnant lagoon. The forests receded from the marshy bank, leaving a level strip of bright green, reedy grass to frame the reflected blueness of the sky. A fleecy pink cloud drifted high above, trailing the delicate coloring of its image under the floating leaves and the silvery blossoms of the lotus. A little house, perched on high piles, appeared black in the distance. Near it, two tall nibong palms, that seemed to have come out of the forests in the background, leaned slightly over the ragged roof, with a suggestion of sad tenderness and care in the droop of their leafy and soaring heads.

The steersman, pointing with his paddle, said, "Arsat is there. I see his canoe fast between the piles."

The polers ran along the sides of the boat glancing over their shoulders at the end of the day's journey. They would have preferred to spend the night somewhere else than on this lagoon of weird aspect and ghostly reputation. Moreover, they disliked Arsat, first as a stranger, and also because he who repairs a ruined house, and dwells in it, proclaims that he is not afraid to live amongst the spirits that haunt the places abandoned by mankind. Such a man can disturb the course of fate by glances or words; while his familiar ghosts are not easy to propitiate by casual wayfarers upon whom they long to wreak the malice of their human master. White men care not for such things, being unbelievers and in league with the Father of Evil, who leads them unharmed through the invisible dangers of this world. To the warnings of the righteous they oppose an offensive pretense of disbelief. What is there to be done?

So they thought, throwing their weight on the end of their long poles. The big canoe glided on swiftly, noiselessly, and smoothly, towards Arsat's clearing, till, in a great rattling of poles thrown down, and the loud murmurs of "Allah be praised!" it came with a gentle knock against the crooked piles below the house.

The boatmen with uplifted faces shouted discordantly, "Arsat! O Arsat!" Nobody came. The white man began to climb the rude ladder giving access to the bamboo platform before the house. The juragan of the boat said sulkily, "We will cook in the sampan, and sleep on the water."

"Pass my blankets and the basket," said the white man, curtly.

He knelt on the edge of the platform to receive the bundle. Then the boat shoved off, and the white man, standing up, confronted Arsat, who had come out through the low door of his hut. He was a man young, powerful, with broad chest and muscular arms. He had nothing on but his sarong. His head was bare. His big, soft eyes stared eagerly at the white man, but his voice and demeanor were composed as he asked, without any words of greeting:

"Have you medicine, Tuan?"

"No," said the visitor in a startled tone. "No. Why? Is there sickness in the house?"

"Enter and see," replied Arsat, in the same calm manner, and turning short round, passed again through the small doorway. The white man, dropping his bundles, followed.

In the dim light of the dwelling he made out on a couch of bamboos a woman stretched on her back under a broad sheet of red cotton cloth. She lay still, as if dead; but her big eyes, wide open, glittered in the gloom, staring upwards at the slender rafters, motionless and unseeing. She was in a high fever, and evidently unconscious. Her cheeks were sunk slightly, her lips were partly open, and on the young face there was the ominous and fixed expression—the absorbed, contemplating expression of the unconscious who are going to die. The two men stood looking down at her in silence.

"Has she been long ill?" asked the traveler.

"I have not slept for five nights," answered the Malay, in a deliberate tone. "At first she heard voices calling her from the water and struggled against me who held her. But since the sun of today rose she hears nothing—she hears not me. She sees nothing. She sees not me—ME!"

He remained silent for a minute, then asked softly:

"Tuan, will she die?"

"I fear so," said the white man, sorrowfully. He had known Arsat years ago, in a far country in times of trouble and danger, when no friendship is to be despised. And since his Malay friend had come unexpectedly to dwell in the hut on the lagoon with a strange woman, he had slept many times there, in his journeys up and down the river. He liked the man who knew how to keep faith in council and how to fight without fear by the side of his white friend. He liked him—not so much perhaps as a man likes his favorite dog—but still he liked him well enough to help and ask no questions, to think sometimes vaguely and hazily in the midst of his own pursuits, about the lonely man and the long-haired woman with audacious face and triumphant eyes, who lived together hidden by the forests—alone and feared.

The white man came out of the hut in time to see the enormous conflagration of sunset put out by the swift and stealthy shadows that, rising like a black and impalpable vapor above the treetops, spread over the heaven, extinguishing the crimson glow of floating clouds and the red brilliance of departing daylight. In a few moments all the stars came out above the intense blackness of the earth and the great lagoon gleaming suddenly with reflected lights resembled an oval patch of night sky flung down into the hopeless and abysmal night of the wilderness. The white man had some supper out of the basket, then collecting a few sticks that lay about the platform, made up a small fire, not for warmth, but for the sake of the smoke, which would keep off the mosquitoes. He wrapped himself in the blankets and sat with his back against the reed wall of the house, smoking thoughtfully.

Arsat came through the doorway with noiseless steps and squatted down by the fire. The white man moved his outstretched legs a little.

"She breathes," said Arsat in a low voice, anticipating the expected question. "She breathes and burns as if with a great fire. She speaks not; she hears not—and burns!"

He paused for a moment, then asked in a quiet, incurious tone:

"Tuan . . . will she die?"

The white man moved his shoulders uneasily and muttered in a hesitating manner:

"If such is her fate."

"No, Tuan," said Arsat, calmly. "If such is my fate. I hear, I see, I wait. I remember. . . . Tuan, do you remember the old days? Do you remember my brother?"

"Yes," said the white man. The Malay rose suddenly and went in. The other, sitting still outside, could hear the voice in the hut. Arsat said: "Hear me! Speak!" His words were succeeded by a complete silence. "O Diamelen!" he cried, suddenly. After that cry there was a deep sigh. Arsat came out and sank down again in his old place.

They sat in silence before the fire. There was no sound within the house, there was no sound near them; but far away on the lagoon they could hear the voices of the boatmen ringing fitful and distinct on the calm water. The fire in the bows of the sampan shone faintly in the distance with a hazy red glow. Then it died out. The voices ceased. The land and the water slept invisible, unstirring and mute. It was as though there had been nothing left in the world but the glitter of stars streaming, ceaseless and vain, through the black stillness of the night.

The white man gazed straight before him into the darkness with wide-open eyes. The fear and fascination, the inspiration and the wonder of death—of death near, unavoidable, and unseen, soothed the unrest of his race and stirred the most indistinct, the most intimate of his thoughts. The ever-ready suspicion of evil, the gnawing suspicion that lurks in our hearts, flowed out into the stillness round him—into the stillness profound and dumb, and made it appear untrustworthy and infamous, like the placid and impenetrable mask of an unjustifiable violence. In that fleeting and powerful disturbance of his being the earth enfolded in the starlight peace became a shadowy country of inhuman strife, a battlefield of phantoms terrible and charming, august or ignoble, struggling ardently for the possession of our helpless hearts. An unquiet and mysterious country of inextinguishable desires and fears.

A plaintive murmur rose in the night; a murmur saddening and startling, as if the great solitudes of surrounding woods had tried to whisper into his ear the wisdom of their immense and lofty indifference. Sounds hesitating and vague floated in the air round him, shaped themselves slowly into words; and at last flowed on gently in a murmuring stream of soft and monotonous sentences. He stirred like a man waking up and changed his position slightly. Arsat, motionless and shadowy, sitting with bowed head under the stars, was speaking in a low and dreamy tone:

". . . for where can we lay down the heaviness of our trouble but in a friend's heart? A man must speak of war and of love. You, Tuan, know what war is, and you have seen me in time of danger seek death as other men seek life! A writing may be lost; a lie may be written; but what the eye has seen is truth and remains in the mind!"

"I remember," said the white man, quietly. Arsat went on with mournful composure:

"Therefore I shall speak to you of love. Speak in the night. Speak before both night and love are gone—and the eye of day looks upon my sorrow and my shame; upon my blackened face; upon my burnt-up heart."

A sigh, short and faint, marked an almost imperceptible pause, and then his words flowed on, without a stir, without a gesture.

"After the time of trouble and war was over and you went away from my country in the pursuit of your desires, which we, men of the islands, cannot understand, I and my brother became again, as we had been before, the sword bearers of the Ruler. You know we were men of family, belonging to a ruling race, and more fit than any to carry on our right shoulder the emblem of power. And in the time of prosperity Si Dendring showed us favor, as we, in time of sorrow, had showed to him the faithfulness of our courage. It was a time of peace. A time of deer hunts and cock fights; of idle talks and foolish squabbles between men whose bellies are full and weapons are rusty. But the sower watched the young rice shoots grow up without fear, and the traders came and went, departed lean and returned fat into the river of peace. They brought news, too. Brought lies and truth mixed together, so that no man knew when to rejoice and when to be sorry. We heard from them about you also. They had seen you here and had seen you there. And I was glad to hear, for I remembered the stirring times, and I always remembered you, Tuan, till the time came when my eyes could see nothing in the past, because they had looked upon the one who is dying there—in the house."

He stopped to exclaim in an intense whisper, "O Mara bahia! O Calamity!" then went on speaking a little louder:

"There's no worse enemy and no better friend than a brother, Tuan, for one brother knows another, and in perfect knowledge is strength for good or evil. I loved my brother. I went to him and told him that I could see nothing but one face, hear nothing but one voice. He told me: 'Open your heart so that she can see what is in it—and wait. Patience is wisdom. Inchi Midah may die or our Ruler may throw off his fear of a woman!' . . . I waited! . . . You remember the lady with the veiled face, Tuan, and the fear of our Ruler before her cunning and temper. And if she wanted her servant, what could I do? But I fed the hunger of my heart on short glances and stealthy words. I loitered on the path to the bathhouses in the daytime, and when the sun had fallen behind the forest I crept along the jasmine hedges of the women's courtyard. Unseeing, we spoke to one another through the scent of flowers, through the veil of leaves, through the blades of long grass that stood still before our lips; so great was our prudence, so faint was the murmur of our great longing. The time passed swiftly . . . and there were whispers amongst women—and our enemies watched—my brother was gloomy, and I began to think of killing and of a fierce death. . . . We are of a people who take what they want—like you whites. There is a time when a man should forget loyalty and respect. Might and authority are given to rulers, but to all men is given love and strength and courage. My brother said, 'You shall take her from their midst. We are two who are like one.' And I answered, 'Let it be soon, for I find no warmth in sunlight that does not shine upon her.' Our time came when the Ruler and all the great people went to the mouth of the river to fish by torchlight. There were hundreds of boats, and on the white sand, between the water and the forests, dwellings of leaves were built for the households of the Rajahs. The smoke of cooking fires was like a blue mist of the evening, and many voices rang in it joyfully. While they were making the boats ready to beat up the fish, my brother came to me and said, 'Tonight!' I looked to my weapons, and when the time came our canoe took its place in the circle of boats carrying the torches. The lights blazed on the water, but behind the boats there was darkness. When the shouting began and the excitement made them like mad we dropped out. The water swallowed our fire, and we floated back to the shore that was dark with only here and there the glimmer of embers. We could hear the talk of slave girls amongst the sheds. Then we found a place deserted and silent. We waited there. She came. She came running along the shore, rapid and leaving no trace, like a leaf driven by the wind into the sea. My brother said gloomily, 'Go and take her; carry her into our boat.' I lifted her in my arms. She panted. Her heart was beating against my breast. I said, 'I take you from those people. You came to the cry of my heart, but my arms take you into my boat against the will of the great!' 'It is right,' said my brother. 'We

are men who take what we want and can hold it against many. We should have taken her in daylight.' I said, 'Let us be off'; for since she was in my boat I began to think of our Ruler's many men. 'Yes. Let us be off,' said my brother. 'We are cast out and this boat is our country now—and the sea is our refuge.' He lingered with his foot on the shore, and I entreated him to hasten, for I remembered the strokes of her heart against my breast and thought that two men cannot withstand a hundred. We left, paddling downstream close to the bank; and as we passed by the creek where they were fishing, the great shouting had ceased, but the murmur of voices was loud like the humming of insects flying at noonday. The boats floated, clustered together, in the red light of torches, under a black roof of smoke; and men talked of their sport. Men that boasted, and praised, and jeered —men that would have been our friends in the morning, but on that night were already our enemies. We paddled swiftly past. We had no more friends in the country of our birth. She sat in the middle of the canoe with covered face; silent as she is now; unseeing as she is now—and I had no regret at what I was leaving because I could hear her breathing close to me —as I can hear her now."

He paused, listened with his ear turned to the doorway, then shook his head and went on:

"My brother wanted to shout the cry of challenge—one cry only—to let the people know we were freeborn robbers who trusted our arms and the great sea. And again I begged him in the name of our love to be silent. Could I not hear her breathing close to me? I knew the pursuit would come quick enough. My brother loved me. He dipped his paddle without a splash. He only said, 'There is half a man in you now—the other half is in that woman. I can wait. When you are a whole man again, you will come back with me here to shout defiance. We are sons of the same mother.' I made no answer. All my strength and all my spirit were in my hands that held the paddle—for I longed to be with her in a safe place beyond the reach of men's anger and of women's spite. My love was so great, that I thought it could guide me to a country where death was unknown, if I could only escape from Inchi

Midah's fury and from our Ruler's sword. We paddled with haste, breathing through our teeth. The blades bit deep into the smooth water. We passed out of the river; we flew in clear channels amongst the shallows. We skirted the black coast; we skirted the sand beaches where the sea speaks in whispers to the land; and the gleam of white sand flashed back past our boat, so swiftly she ran upon the water. We spoke not. Only once I said, 'Sleep, Diamelen, for soon you may want all your strength.' I heard the sweetness of her voice, but I never turned my head. The sun rose and still we went on. Water fell from my face like rain from a cloud. We flew in the light and heat. I never looked back, but I knew that my brother's eyes, behind me, were looking steadily ahead, for the boat went as straight as a bushman's dart, when it leaves the end of the sumpitan. There was no better paddler, no better steersman than my brother. Many times, together, we had won races in that canoe. But we never had put out our strength as we did then—then, when for the last time we paddled together! There was no braver or stronger man in our country than my brother. I could not spare the strength to turn my head and look at him, but every moment I heard the hiss of his breath getting louder behind me. Still he did not speak. The sun was high. The heat clung to my back like a flame of fire. My ribs were ready to burst, but I could no longer get enough air into my chest. And then I felt I must cry out with my last breath, 'Let us rest!' . . . 'Good!' he answered; and his voice was firm. He was strong. He was brave. He knew not fear and no fatigue . . . My brother!"

A murmur powerful and gentle, a murmur vast and faint; the murmur of trembling leaves, of stirring boughs, ran through the tangled depths of the forests, ran over the starry smoothness of the lagoon, and the water between the piles lapped the slimy timber once with a sudden splash. A breath of warm air touched the two men's faces and passed on with a mournful sound—a breath loud and short like an uneasy sigh of the dreaming earth.

Arsat went on in an even, low voice.

"We ran our canoe on the white beach of a little bay close to a long tongue of land that seemed to bar our road; a long wooded cape going far into the sea. My brother knew that place. Beyond the cape a river has its entrance, and through the jungle of that land there is a narrow path. We made a fire and cooked rice. Then we lay down to sleep on the soft sand in the shade of our canoe, while she watched. No sooner had I closed my eyes than I heard her cry of alarm. We leaped up. The sun was halfway down the sky already, and coming in sight in the opening of the bay we saw a prau manned by many paddlers. We knew it at once; it was one of our Rajah's praus. They were watching the shore, and saw us. They beat the gong, and turned the head of the prau into the bay. I felt my heart become weak within my breast. Diamelen sat on the sand and covered her face. There was no escape by sea. My brother laughed. He had the gun you had given him, Tuan, before you went away, but there was only a handful of powder. He spoke to me quickly: 'Run with her along the path. I shall keep them back, for they have no firearms, and landing in the face of a man with a gun is certain death for some. Run with her. On the other side of that wood there is a fisherman's house—and a canoe. When I have fired all the shots I will follow. I am a great runner, and before they can come up we shall be gone. I will hold out as long as I can, for she is but a woman—that can neither run nor fight, but she has your heart in her weak hands.' He dropped behind the canoe. The prau was coming. She and I ran, and as we rushed along the path I heard shots. My brother fired—once—twice—and the booming of the gong ceased. There was silence behind us. That neck of land is narrow. Before I heard my brother fire the third shot I saw the shelving shore, and I saw the water again; the mouth of a broad river. We crossed a grassy glade. We ran down to the water. I saw a low hut above the black mud, and a small canoe hauled up. I heard another shot behind me. I thought, 'That is his last charge.' We rushed down to the canoe; a man came running from the hut, but I leaped on him, and we rolled together in the mud. Then I got up, and he lay still at my feet. I don't know whether I had killed him or not. I and Diamelen pushed the canoe afloat. I heard yells behind me, and

I saw my brother run across the glade. Many men were bounding after him. I took her in my arms and threw her into the boat, then leaped in myself. When I looked back I saw that my brother had fallen. He fell and was up again, but the men were closing round him. He shouted, 'I am coming!' The men were close to him. I looked. Many men. Then I looked at her. Tuan, I pushed the canoe! I pushed it into deep water. She was kneeling forward looking at me, and I said, 'Take your paddle,' while I struck the water with mine. Tuan, I heard him cry. I heard him cry my name twice; and I heard voices shouting, 'Kill! Strike!' I never turned back. I heard him calling my name again with a great shriek, as when life is going out together with the voice—and I never turned my head. My own name! . . . My brother! Three times he called—but I was not afraid of life. Was she not there in that canoe? And could I not with her find a country where death is forgotten—where death is unknown!"

The white man sat up. Arsat rose and stood, an indistinct and silent figure above the dying embers of the fire. Over the lagoon a mist drifting and low had crept, erasing slowly the glittering images of the stars. And now a great expanse of white vapor covered the land: it flowed cold and gray in the darkness, eddied in noiseless whirls round the tree trunks and about the platform of the house, which seemed to float upon a restless and impalpable illusion of a sea. Only far away the tops of the trees stood outlined on the twinkle of heaven, like a somber and forbidding shore—a coast deceptive, pitiless and black.

Arsat's voice vibrated loudly in the profound peace.

"I had her there! I had her! To get her I would have faced all mankind. But I had her—and—"

His words went out ringing into the empty distances. He paused, and seemed to listen to them dying away very far—beyond help and beyond recall. Then he said quietly:

"Tuan, I loved my brother."

A breath of wind made him shiver. High above his head, high above the silent sea of mist the drooping leaves of the palms rattled together with a mournful and expiring sound.

The white man stretched his legs. His chin rested on his chest, and he murmured sadly without lifting his head:

"We all love our brothers."

Arsat burst out with an intense whispering violence:

"What did I care who died? I wanted peace in my own heart."

He seemed to hear a stir in the house—listened—then stepped in noiselessly. The white man stood up. A breeze was coming in fitful puffs. The stars shone paler as if they had retreated into the frozen depths of immense space. After a chill gust of wind there were a few seconds of perfect calm and absolute silence. Then from behind the black and wavy line of the forests a column of golden light shot up into the heavens and spread over the semicircle of the eastern horizon. The sun had risen. The mist lifted, broke into drifting patches, vanished into thin flying wreaths; and the unveiled lagoon lay, polished and black, in the heavy shadows at the foot of the wall of trees. A white eagle rose over it with a slanting and ponderous flight, reached the clear sunshine and appeared dazzlingly brilliant for a moment, then soaring higher, became a dark and motionless speck before it vanished into the blue as if it had left the earth forever. The white man, standing gazing upwards before the doorway, heard in the hut a confused and broken murmur of distracted words ending with a loud groan. Suddenly Arsat stumbled out with outstretched hands, shivered, and stood still for some time with fixed eyes. Then he said:

"She burns no more."

Before his face the sun showed its edge above the treetops rising steadily. The breeze freshened; a great brilliance burst upon the lagoon, sparkled on the rippling water. The forests came out of the clear shadows of the morning, became distinct, as if they had rushed nearer—to stop short in a great stir of leaves, of nodding boughs, of swaying branches. In the merciless sunshine the whisper of unconscious life grew louder, speaking in an incomprehensible voice round the dumb darkness of that human sorrow. Arsat's eyes wandered slowly, then stared at the rising sun.

"I can see nothing," he said half aloud to himself.

"There is nothing," said the white man, moving to the edge of the platform and waving his hand to his boat. A shout came faintly over the lagoon and the sampan began to glide towards the abode of the friend of ghosts.

"If you want to come with me, I will wait all the morning," said the white man, looking away upon the water.

"No, Tuan," said Arsat, softly. "I shall not eat or sleep in this house, but I must first see my road. Now I can see nothing—see nothing! There is no light and no peace in the world; but there is death—death for many. We are sons of the same mother—and I left him in the midst of enemies; but I am going back now."

He drew a long breath and went on in a dreamy tone:

"In a little while I shall see clear enough to strike—to strike. But she has died, and . . . now . . . darkness."

He flung his arms wide open, let them fall along his body, then stood still with unmoved face and stony eyes, staring at the sun. The white man got down into his canoe. The polers ran smartly along the sides of the boat, looking over their shoulders at the beginning of a weary journey. High in the stern, his head muffled up in white rags, the juragan sat moody, letting his paddle trail in the water. The white man, leaning with both arms over the grass roof of the little cabin, looked back at the shining ripple of the boat's wake. Before the sampan passed out of the lagoon into the creek he lifted his eyes. Arsat had not moved. He stood lonely in the searching sunshine; and he looked beyond the great light of a cloudless day into the darkness of a world of illusions.

Jerico, Jerico, Jerico

ANDREW NELSON LYTLE (1903-   )

SHE OPENED her eyes. She must have been asleep for hours or months. She could not reckon; she could only feel the steady silence of time. She had been Joshua and made it swing suspended in her room. Forever she had floated above the counterpane, between the tester and the counterpane she had floated until her hand, long and bony, its speckled-dried skin drawing away from the bulging blue veins, had reached and drawn her body under the covers. And now she was resting, clearheaded and quiet, her thoughts clicking like a new-greased mower. All creation could not make her lift her thumb or cross it over her finger. She looked at the bed, the bed her mother had died in, the bed her children had been born in, her marriage bed, the bed the General had drenched with his blood. Here it stood where it had stood for seventy years, square and firm on the floor, wide enough for three people to lie comfortable in, if they didn't sleep restless; but not wide enough for her nor long enough when her conscience scorched the cool wrinkles in the sheets. The two foot posts, octagonal-shaped and mounted by carved pieces that looked like absurd flowers, stood up to comfort her when the world began to crumble. Her eyes followed down the posts and along the basket-quilt. She had made it before her marriage to the General, only he wasn't a general then. He was a slight, tall young man with a rolling mustache and perfume in his hair. A many a time she had seen her young love's locks dripping with scented oil, down upon his collar . . . She had cut the squares for the baskets in January, and for stuffing had used the letters of old lovers, fragments of passion cut to warm her of a winter's night. The General would have his fun. *Miss Kate, I didn't sleep well last night. I heard Sam Buchanan make love to you out of that farthest basket. If I hear him again, I mean to toss this piece of quilt in the fire.* Then he would chuckle in his round, soft voice; reach under the covers and pull her over to his side of the bed. On a cold and frosting night he would sleep with his nose against her neck. His nose was so quick to turn cold, he said, and her neck was so warm. Sometimes her hair, the loose, unruly strands at the nape, would tickle his nostrils and he would wake up with a sneeze. This had been so long ago, and there had been so many years of trouble and worry. Her eyes, as apart from her as the mirror on the bureau, rested upon the half-tester, upon the enormous button that caught the rose-colored canopy and shot its folds out like the rays of the morning sun. She could not see but she could feel the heavy cluster of mahogany grapes that tumbled from the center of the head board—out of its vines curling down the sides it tumbled. How much longer would these never-picked grapes hang above her head? How much longer would she, rather, hang to the vine of this world, she who lay beneath as dry as any raisin. Then she remembered. She looked at the blinds. They were closed.

"You, Ants, where's my stick? I'm a great mind to break it over your trifling back."

"Awake? What a nice long nap you've had." said Doctor Ed.

"The boy? Where's my grandson? Has he come?"

"I'll say he's come. What do you mean taking to your bed like this? Do you realize, beautiful lady, that this is the first time I ever saw you in bed in my whole life? I believe you've taken to bed on purpose. I don't believe you want to see me."

"Go long, boy, with your foolishness."

That's all she could say, and she blushed as she said it—she blushing at the words of a snip of a boy, whom she had diapered a hundred times and had washed as he stood before the fire in the round tin tub, his little back swayed and his little belly sticking out in front, rosy from the scrubbing he had gotten. *Mammy, what for I've got a hole in my stummick; what for, Mammy?* Now he was sitting on the edge of the bed calling her beautiful lady, an old hag like her, beautiful lady. A good-looker the girls would call him, with his bold, careless face and his hands with their fine, long fingers. Soft, how soft they were, running over her rough,

skinny bones. He looked a little like his grandpa, but somehow there was something missing . . .

"Well, boy, it took you a time to come home to see me die."

"Nonsense. Cousin Edwin, I wouldn't wait on a woman who had so little faith in my healing powers."

"There an't nothing strange about dying. But I an't in such an all-fired hurry. I've got a heap to tell you about before I go."

The boy leaned over and touched her gently. "Not even death would dispute you here, on Long Gourd, Mammy."

He was trying to put her at her ease in his carefree way. It was so obvious a pretending, but she loved him for it. There was something nice in its awkwardness, the charm of the young's blundering and of their efforts to get along in the world. Their pretty arrogance, their patronizing airs, their colossal unknowing of what was to come. It was a quenching drink to a sin-thirsty old woman. Somehow his vitality had got crossed in her blood and made a dry heart leap, her blood that was almost water. Soon now she would be all water, water and dust, lying in the burying ground between the cedar—and fire. She could smell her soul burning and see it. What a fire it would make below, dripping with sin, like a rag soaked in kerosene. But she had known what she was doing. And here was Long Gourd, all its fields intact, ready to be handed on, in better shape than when she took it over. Yes, she had known what she was doing. How long, she wondered, would his spirit hold up under the trials of planting, of cultivating, and of the gathering time, year in and year out— how would he hold up before so many springs and so many autumns. The thought of him giving orders, riding over the place, or rocking on the piazza, and a great pain would pin her heart to her backbone. She had wanted him by her to train—there was so much for him to know: how the south field was cold and must be planted late, and where the orchards would best hold their fruit, and where the frosts crept soonest— that now could never be. She turned her head— who was that woman, that strange woman standing by the bed as if she owned it, as if . . .

"This is Eva, Mammy."

"Eva?"

"We are going to be married."

"I wanted to come and see—to meet Dick's grandmother . . ."

I wanted to come see her die. That's what she meant. Why didn't she finish and say it out. She had come to lick her chops and see what she would enjoy. That's what she had come for, the lying little slut. The richest acres in Long Gourd valley, so rich hit'd make yer feet greasy to walk over'm, Saul Oberly at the first tollgate had told the peddler once, and the peddler had told it to her, knowing it would please and make her trade. *Before you die.* Well, why didn't you finish it out? You might as well. You've given yourself away.

Her fierce thoughts dried up the water in her eyes, tired and resting far back in their sockets. They burned like a smothered fire stirred up by the wind as they traveled over the woman who would lie in her bed, eat with her silver, and caress her flesh and blood. The woman's body was soft enough to melt and pour about him. She could see that; and her firm, round breasts, too firm and round for any good to come from them. And her lips, full and red, her eyes bright and cunning. The heavy hair crawled about her head to tangle the poor, foolish boy in its ropes. She might have known he would do something foolish like this. He had a foolish mother. There warn't any way to avoid it. But look at her belly, small and no-count. There wasn't a muscle the size of a worm as she could see. And those hips—

And then she heard her voice: "What did you say her name was, son? Eva? Eva Callahan, I'm glad to meet you, Eva. Where'd your folks come from, Eva? I knew some Callahans who lived in the Goosepad settlement. They couldn't be any of your kin, could they?"

"Oh, no, indeed. My people . . ."

"Right clever people they were. And good farmers, too. Worked hard. Honest—that is, most of 'm. As honest as that run of people go. We always gave them a good name."

"My father and mother live in Birmingham. Have always lived there."

"Birmingham," she heard herself say with contempt. They could have lived there all their lives and still come from somewhere. I've got a mule older 'n Birmingham. "What's your pa's name?"

"Her father is Mister E. L. Callahan, Mammy."

"First name not Elijah by any chance? Lige they called him."

"No. Elmore, Mammy."

"Old Mason Callahan had a son they called Lige. Somebody told me he moved to Elyton. So you think you're going to live with the boy here."

"We're to be married . . . that is, if Eva doesn't change her mind."

And she saw his arm slip possessively about the woman's waist. "Well, take care of him, young woman, or I'll come back and han't you. I'll come back and claw your eyes out."

"I'll take very good care of him, Mrs. McCowan."

"I can see that." She could hear the threat in her voice, and Eva heard it.

"Young man," spoke up Doctor Edwin, "you should feel powerful set up, two such women pestering each other about you."

The boy kept an embarrassed silence.

"All of you get out now. I want to talk to him by himself. I've got a lot to say and precious little time to say it in. And he's mighty young and helpless and ignorant."

"Why, Mammy, you forget I'm a man now. Twenty-six. All teeth cut. Long trousers."

"It takes a heap more than pants to make a man. Throw open them blinds, Ants."

"Yes'm."

"You don't have to close the door so all-fired soft. Close it naturally. And you can tip about all you want to—later. I won't be hurried to the burying ground. And keep your head away from that door. What I've got to say to your new master is private."

"Listen at you, Mistiss."

"You listen to me. That's all. No, wait. I had something else on my mind—what is it? Yes. How many hens has Melissy set? You don't know? Find out. A few of the old hens ought to be setting. Tell her to be careful to turn the turkey eggs every day. No, you bring them and set them under my bed. I'll make sure. We got a mighty pore hatch last year. You may go now. I'm plumb worn out, boy, worn out thinking for these people. It's that that worries a body down. But you'll know all about it in good time. Stand out there and let me look at you good. You don't let me see enough of you, and I almost forget how you look. Not really, you understand. Just a little. It's your own fault. I've got so much to trouble me that you, when you're not here, naturally slip back in my mind. But that's all over now. You are here to stay, and I'm here to go. There will always be Long Gourd, and there must always be a McCowan on it. I had hoped to have you by me for several years, but you would have your fling in town. I thought it best to clear your blood of it, but as God is hard, I can't see what you find to do in town. And now you've gone and gotten you a woman. Well, they all have to do it. But do you reckon you've picked the right one—you must forgive the frankness of an old lady who can see the bottom of her grave—I had in mind one of the Carlisle girls. The Carlisle place lies so handy to Long Gourd and would give me a landing on the river. Have you seen Anna Belle since she's grown to be a woman? I'm told there's not a better housekeeper in the valley."

"I'm sure Anna Belle is a fine girl. But, Mammy, I love Eva."

"She'll wrinkle up on you, Son; and the only wrinkles land gets can be smoothed out by the harrow. And she looks sort of puny to me, Son. She's powerful small in the waist and walks about like she had worms."

Gee, Mammy, you're not jealous are you? That waist is in style."

"You want to look for the right kind of style in a woman. Old Mrs. Penter Matchem had two daughters with just such waists, but 'twarnt natural. She would tie their corset strings to the bed posts and whip'm out with a buggy whip. The poor girls never drew a hearty breath. Just to please that old woman's vanity. She got paid in kind. It did something to Eliza's bowels and she died before she was twenty. The other one never had any children. She used to whip'm out until they cried. I never liked that woman. She thought a whip could do anything."

"Well, anyway, Eva's small waist wasn't made by any corset strings. She doesn't wear any."

"How do you know, sir?"

"Well . . . I . . . What a question for a respectable woman to ask."

"I'm not a respectable woman. No woman can be respectable and run four thousand acres of land. Well, you'll have it your own way. I suppose the safest place for a man to take his folly is to bed."

"Mammy!"

"You must be lenient with your Cousin George. He wanders about night times talking about the War. I put him off in the west wing where he won't keep people awake, but sometimes he gets in the yard and gives orders to his troops. 'I will sweep that hill, General'—and many's the time he's done it when the battle was doubtful—'I'll sweep it with my iron brooms'; then he shouts out his orders, and pretty soon the dogs commence to barking. But he's been a heap of company for me. You must see that your wife humors him. It won't be for long. He's mighty feeble."

"Eva's not my wife yet, Mammy."

"You won't be free much longer—the way she looks at you, like a hungry hound."

"I was just wondering," he said hurriedly. "I hate to talk about anything like this . . ."

"Everybody has a time to die, and I'll have no maudlin nonsense about mine."

"I was wondering about Cousin George . . . if I could get somebody to keep him. You see, it will be difficult in the winters. Eva will want to spend the winters in town . . ."

He paused, startled, before the great bulk of his grandmother rising from her pillows, and in the silence that frightened the air, his unfinished words hung suspended about them.

After a moment he asked if he should call the doctor.

It was some time before she could find words to speak.

"Get out of the room."

"Forgive me, Mammy. You must be tired."

"I'll send for you," sounded the dead voice in the still room, "when I want to see you again. I'll send for you and—the woman."

She watched the door close quietly on his neat square back. Her head whirled and turned like a flying jennet. She lowered and steadied it on the pillows. Four thousand acres of the richest land in the valley he would sell and squander on that slut, and he didn't even know it and there was no way to warn him. This terrifying thought rushed through her mind, and she felt the bed shake with her pain, while before the footboard the spectre of an old sin rose up to mock her. How she had struggled to get this land and keep it together—through the War, the Reconstruction, and the pleasanter after days. For eighty-seven years she had suffered and slept and planned and rested and had pleasure in this valley, seventy of it, almost a turning century, on this place; and now that she must leave it . . .

The things she had done to keep it together. No. The one thing . . . from the dusty stacks the musty odor drifted through the room, met the tobacco smoke over the long table piled high with records, reports. Iva Louise stood at one end, her hat clinging perilously to the heavy auburn hair, the hard blue eyes and the voice:

"You promised Pa to look after me"—she had waited for the voice to break and scream—"and you have stolen my land!"

"Now, Miss Iva Louise," the lawyer dropped his empty eyes along the floor, "you don't mean . . ."

"Yes, I do mean it."

Her own voice had restored calm to the room: "I promised your pa his land would not be squandered."

"My husband won't squander my property. You just want it for yourself."

She cut through the scream with the sharp edge of her scorn: "What about that weakling's farm in Madison? Who pays the taxes now?"

The girl had no answer to that. Desperate, she faced the lawyer: "Is there no way, sir, I can get my land from the clutches of this unnatural woman?"

The man coughed; the red rim of his eyes watered with embarrassment: "I'm afraid," he cleared his throat, "you say you can't raise the money . . . I'm afraid—"

That trapped look as the girl turned away. It had come back to her, now trapped in her bed. As a swoon spreads, she felt the desperate terror of weakness, more desperate where there has been strength. Did the girl see right? Had she stolen the land because she wanted it?

Suddenly, like the popping of a thread in a loom, the struggles of the flesh stopped, and the years backed up and covered her thoughts like the spring freshet she had seen so many times creep over the dark soil. Not in order but, as if they were stragglers trying to catch up, the events of her life passed before her sight that had never been so clear. Sweeping over the mounds of her body rising beneath the quilts came the old familiar odors—the damp, strong, penetrating smell of a new-turned ground; the rank, clinging, resistless odor of green-picked feathers stuffed in a pillow by Guinea Nell, thirty-odd years ago; tobacco on the mantel, clean and sharp like smelling salts; her father's sweat, sweet like stale oil; the powerful ammonia of manure turned over in a stall; curing hay in the wind; the polecat's stink on the night air, almost pleasant, a sort of commingled scent of all the animals, man and beast; the dry smell of dust under a rug; the over-strong scent of too-sweet fruit trees blooming; the inhospitable wet ashes of a dead fire in a poor white's cabin; black Rebeccah in the kitchen; a wet hound steaming before a fire. There were other odors she could not identify, overwhelming her, making her weak, taking her body and drawing out of it a choking longing to hover over all that she must leave, the animals, the fences, the crops growing in the fields, the houses, the people in them . . .

It was early summer, and she was standing in the garden after dark—she had heard something after the small chickens. Mercy and Yellow Jane passed beyond the paling fence. Dark shadows—gay, full voices. *Where you gwine, gal? I dunno. Jest a-gwine. Where you? To the frolic, do I live. Well, stay off'n yoe back tonight.* Then out of the rich, gushing laughter: *All right, you stay off'n yourn. I done caught de stumbles.* More laughter.

The face of Uncle Ike, head man in slavery days, rose up. A tall Senegalese, he was standing in the crib of the barn unmoved before the bushwhackers. *Nigger, whar is that gold hid? You better tell us, nigger. Down in the well; in the far-place. By God, you black son of a bitch, we'll roast ye alive if you air too contrary to tell. Now, listen ole nigger, Miss McCowan ain't nothen to you no more. You been set free. We'll give ye some of it, a whole sack. Come on, now*—out of the dribbling, leering mouth—*whar air it?* Ike's tall form loomed towards the shadows. In the lamp flame his forehead shone like the point, the core of night. He stood there with no word for answer. As she saw the few white beads of sweat on his forehead, she spoke.

She heard her voice reach through the dark —*you turn that black man loose.* A pause and then—*I know your kind. In better days you'd slip around and set people's barns afire. You shirked the War to live off the old and weak. You don't spare me because I'm a woman. You'd shoot a woman quicker because she has the name of being frail. Well, I'm not frail, and my Navy Six ain't frail. Ike, take their guns.* Ike moved and one of them raised his pistol arm. He dropped it, and the acrid smoke stung her nostrils. *Now, Ike, get the rest of their weapons. Their knives, too. One of us might turn our backs.*

On top of the shot she heard the soft pat of her servants' feet. White eyeballs shining through the cracks in the barn. Then: *Caesar, Al, Zebedee, step in here and lend a hand to Ike.* By sun the people had gathered in the yard. Uneasy, silent, they watched her on the porch. She gave the word, and the whips cracked. The mules strained, trotted off, skittish and afraid, dragging the white naked bodies bouncing and cursing over the sod: *Turn us loose. We'll not bother ye no more, lady. You ain't no woman, you're a devil.* She turned and went into the house. It is strange how a woman gets hard when trouble comes a-gobbling after her people.

Worn from memory, she closed her eyes to stop the whirl, but closing her eyes did no good. She released the lids and did not resist. Brother Jack stood before her, handsome and shy, but ruined from his cradle by a cleft palate, until he came to live only in the fire of spirits. And she understood, so clear was life, down to the smallest things. She had often heard tell of this clarity that took a body whose time was spending on the earth. Poor Brother Jack, the gentlest of men, but because of his mark, made the butt and wit of the valley. She saw him leave for school, where he was sent to separate him from his drinking companions, to a church school where the boys buried their liquor in the

ground and sipped it up through straws. His letters: *Dear Ma, quit offering so much advice and send me more money. You send barely enough to keep me from stealing.* His buggy wheels scraping the gravel, driving up as the first roosters crowed. *Katharine, Malcolm, I thought you might want to have a little conversation.* Conversation two hours before sun! And down she would come and let him in, and the General would get up, stir up the fire, and they would sit down and smoke. Jack would drink and sing, *If the Little Brown Jug was mine, I'd be drunk all the time and I'd never be sob-er a-gin*—or, *Hog drovers, hog drovers, hog drovers we air, a-courting your darter so sweet and so fair.* They would sit and smoke and drink until she got up to ring the bell.

He stayed as long as the whiskey held out, growing more violent towards the end. She watered his bottles; begged whiskey to make camphor—*Gre't God, Sis Kate, do you sell camphor? I gave you a pint this morning.* Poor Brother Jack, killed in Breckinridge's charge at Murfreesboro, cut in two by a chain shot from an enemy gun. All night long she had sat up after the message came. His body scattered about a splintered black gum tree. She had seen that night, as if she had been on the field, the parties moving over the dark field hunting the wounded and dead. Clyde Bascom had fallen near Jack with a bad hurt. They were messmates. He had to tell somebody; and somehow she was the one he must talk to. The spectral lanterns, swinging towards the dirge of pain and the monotonous cries of *Water,* caught by the river dew on the before-morning air and held suspended over the field in its acrid quilt. There death dripped to mildew the noisy throats . . . and all the while relief parties, or maybe it was the burial parties, moving, blots of night, sullenly moving in the viscous blackness.

Her eyes widened, and she looked across the foot posts into the room. There was some mistake, some cruel blunder; for there now, tipping about the carpet, hunting in her wardrobe, under the bed, blowing down the fire to the ashes until they glowed in their dryness, stalked the burial parties. They stepped out of the ashes in twos and threes, hunting, hunting and shaking their heads. Whom were they searching for? Jack had long been buried. They moved more rapidly; looked angry. They crowded the room until she gasped for breath. One, gaunt and haggard, jumped on the foot of her bed; rose to the ceiling; gesticulated; argued in animated silence. He leaned forward; pressed his hand upon her leg. She tried to tell him to take it off. Cold and crushing heavy, it pressed her down to the bowels of the earth. Her lips trembled, but no sound came forth. Now the hand moved up to her stomach; and the haggard eyes looked gravely at her, alert, as if they were waiting for something. Her head turned giddy. She called to Dick, to Ants, to Doctor Ed; but the words struck her teeth and fell back in her throat. She concentrated on lifting the words, and the burial parties sadly shook their heads. Always the cries struck her teeth and fell back down. She strained to hear the silence they made. At last from a great distance she thought she heard . . . *too late* . . . *too late*. How exquisite the sound, like a bell swinging without ringing. Suddenly it came to her. She was dying.

How slyly death slipped up on a body, like sleep moving over the vague boundary. How many times she had lain awake to trick the unconscious there. At last she would know . . . But she wasn't ready. She must first do something about Long Gourd. That slut must not eat it up. She would give it to the hands first.

He must be brought to understand this. But the spectres shook their heads. Well let them shake. She'd be damned if she would go until she was ready to go. She'd be damned all right, and she smiled at the meaning the word took on now. She gathered together all the particles of her will; the spectres faded; and there about her were the anxious faces of kin and servants. Edwin had his hands under the cover feeling her legs. She made to raise her own hand to the boy. It did not go up. Her eyes wanted to roll upward and look behind her forehead, but she pinched them down and looked at her grandson.

"You want to say something, Mammy?"— she saw his lips move.

She had a plenty to say, but her tongue had somehow got glued to her lips. Truly it was now too late. Her will left her. Life withdrawing gathered like a frosty dew on her skin. The last breath blew gently past her nose. The dusty nostrils tingled. She felt a great sneeze coming. There was a roaring; the wind blew through her head once, and a great cotton field bent before it, growing and spreading, the bolls swelling as big as cotton sacks and bursting white as thunderheads. From a distance, out of the far end of the field, under a sky so blue that it was painful-bright, voices came singing, *Joshua fit the battle of Jerico, Jerico, Jerico— Joshua fit the battle of Jerico, and the walls come a-tumbling down.*

O Youth and Beauty!

JOHN CHEEVER (1912-   )

AT THE tag end of nearly every long, large Saturday-night party in the suburb of Shady Hill, when almost everybody who was going to play golf or tennis in the morning had gone home hours ago and the ten or twelve people remaining seemed powerless to bring the evening to an end although the gin and whiskey were running low, and here and there a woman who was sitting out her husband would have begun to

drink milk; when everybody had lost track of time, and the baby sitters who were waiting at home for these diehards would have long since stretched out on the sofa and fallen into a deep sleep, to dream about cooking-contest prizes, ocean voyages, and romance; when the bellicose drunk, the crapshooter, the pianist, and the woman faced with the expiration of her hopes had all expressed themselves; when every proposal—to go to the Farquarsons' for breakfast, to go swimming, to go and wake up the Townsends, to go here and go there—died as soon as it was made, then Trace Bearden would begin to chide Cash Bentley about his age and thinning hair. The chiding was preliminary to moving the living-room furniture. Trace and Cash moved the tables and the chairs, the sofas and the fire screen, the woodbox and the footstool; and when they had finished, you wouldn't know the place. Then if the host had a revolver, he would be asked to produce it. Cash would take off his shoes and assume a starting crouch behind a sofa. Trace would fire the weapon out of an open window, and if you were new to the community and had not understood what the preparations were about, you would then realize that you were watching a hurdle race. Over the sofa went Cash, over the tables, over the fire screen and the woodbox. It was not exactly a race, since Cash ran it alone, but it was extraordinary to see this man of forty surmount so many obstacles so gracefully. There was not a piece of furniture in Shady Hill that Cash could not take in his stride. The race ended with cheers, and presently the party would break up.

Cash was, of course, an old track star, but he was never aggressive or tiresome about his brilliant past. The college where he had spent his youth had offered him a paying job on the alumni council, but he had refused it, realizing that that part of his life was ended. Cash and his wife, Louise, had two children, and they lived in a medium-cost ranchhouse on Alewives Lane. They belonged to the country club, although they could not afford it, but in the case of the Bentleys nobody ever pointed this out, and Cash was one of the best-liked men in Shady Hill. He was still slender—he was careful about his weight —and he walked to the train in the morning with a light and vigorous step that marked him as an athlete. His hair was thin, and there were mornings when his eyes looked bloodshot, but this did not detract much from a charming quality of stubborn youthfulness.

In business Cash had suffered reverses and disappointments, and the Bentleys had many money worries. They were always late with their tax payments and their mortgage payments, and the drawer of the hall table was stuffed with un-paid bills; it was always touch and go with the Bentleys and the bank. Louise looked pretty enough on Saturday night, but her life was exacting and monotonous. In the pockets of her suits, coats, and dresses there were little wads and scraps of paper on which was written: "Oleomargarine, frozen spinach, Kleenex, dog biscuit, hamburger, pepper, lard . . ." When she was still half awake in the morning, she was putting on the water for coffee and diluting the frozen orange juice. Then she would be wanted by the children. She would crawl under the bureau on her hands and knees to find a sock for Toby. She would lie flat on her belly and wriggle under the bed (getting dust up her nose) to find a shoe for Rachel. Then there were the housework, the laundry, and the cooking, as well as the demands of the children. There always seemed to be shoes to put on and shoes to take off, snowsuits to be zipped and unzipped, bottoms to be wiped, tears to be dried, and when the sun went down (she saw it set from the kitchen window) there was the supper to be cooked, the baths, the bedtime story, and the Lord's Prayer. With the sonorous words of the Our Father in a darkened room the children's day was over, but the day was far from over for Louise Bentley. There were the darning, the mending, and some ironing to do, and after sixteen years of housework she did not seem able to escape her chores even while she slept. Snowsuits, shoes, baths, and groceries seemed to have permeated her subconscious. Now and then she would speak in her sleep—so loudly that she woke her husband. "I can't *afford* veal cutlets," she said one night. Then she sighed uneasily and was quiet again.

By the standards of Shady Hill, the Bentleys were a happily married couple, but they had their ups and downs. Cash could be very touchy at times. When he came home after a bad day at the office and found that Louise, for some good reason, had not started supper, he would be ugly. "Oh, for Christ sake!" he would say, and go into the kitchen and heat up some frozen food. He drank some whiskey to relax himself during this ordeal, but it never seemed to relax him, and he usually burned the bottom out of a pan, and when they sat down for supper the dining space would be full of smoke. It was only a question of time before they were plunged into a bitter quarrel. Louise would run upstairs, throw herself onto the bed, and sob. Cash would grab the whiskey bottle and dose himself. These rows, in spite of the vigor with which Cash and Louise entered into them, were the source of a great deal of pain for both of them. Cash would sleep downstairs on the sofa, but sleep never repaired the damage, once the trouble had begun, and if they met in the morning, they would be at one another's throats in a second. Then Cash would leave for the train, and, as soon as the children had been taken to nursery school, Louise would put on her coat and cross the grass to the Beardens' house. She would cry into a cup of warmed-up coffee and tell Lucy Bearden her troubles. What was the meaning of marriage? What was the meaning of love? Lucy always suggested that Louise get a job. It would give her emotional and financial independence, and that, Lucy said, was what she needed.

The next night, things would get worse. Cash would not come home for dinner at all, but would stumble in at about eleven, and the whole sordid wrangle would be repeated, with Louise going to bed in tears upstairs and Cash again stretching out on the living-room sofa. After a few days and nights of this, Louise would decide that she was at the end of her rope. She would decide to go and stay with her married sister in Mamaroneck. She usually chose a Saturday, when Cash would be at home, for her departure. She would pack a suitcase and get her War Bonds from the desk. Then she would take a bath and put on her best slip. Cash, passing the bedroom door, would see her. Her slip was transparent, and suddenly he was all repentance, tenderness, charm, wisdom, and love. "Oh, my darling!" he would groan, and when they went downstairs to get a bite to eat about an hour later, they would be sighing and making cow eyes at one another; they would be the happiest married couple in the whole Eastern United States. It was usually at about this time that Lucy Bearden turned up with the good news that she had found a job for Louise. Lucy would ring the doorbell, and Cash, wearing a bathrobe, would let her in. She would be brief with Cash, naturally, and hurry into the dining room to tell poor Louise the good news. "Well that's very nice of you to have

looked," Louise would say wanly, "but I don't think that I want a job any more. I don't think that Cash wants me to work, do you, sweetheart?" Then she would turn her big dark eyes on Cash, and you could practically smell smoke. Lucy would excuse herself hurriedly from this scene of depravity, but she never left with any hard feelings, because she had been married for nineteen years herself and she knew that every union has its ups and downs. She didn't seem to leave any wiser, either; the next time the Bentleys quarreled, she would be just as intent as ever on getting Louise a job. But these quarrels and reunions, like the hurdle race, didn't seem to lose their interest through repetition.

On a Saturday night in the spring, the Farquarsons gave the Bentleys an anniversary party. It was their seventeenth anniversary. Saturday afternoon, Louise Bentley put herself through preparations nearly as arduous as the Monday wash. She rested for an hour, by the clock, with her feet high in the air, her chin in a sling, and her eyes bathed in some astringent solution. The clay packs, the too tight girdle, and the plucking and curling and painting that went on were all aimed at rejuvenation. Feeling in the end that she had not been entirely successful, she tied a piece of veiling over her eyes—but she was a lovely woman, and all the cosmetics that she had struggled with seemed, like her veil, to be drawn transparently over a face where mature beauty and a capacity for wit and passion were undisguisable. The Farquarsons' party was nifty, and the Bentleys had a wonderful time. The only person who drank too much was Trace Bearden. Late in the party, he began to chide Cash about his thinning hair and Cash good-naturedly began to move the furniture around. Harry Farquarson had a pistol, and Trace went out onto the terrace to fire it up at the sky. Over the sofa went Cash, over the end table, over the arms of the wing chair and the fire screen. It was a piece of carving on a chest that brought him down, and down he came like a ton of bricks.

Louise screamed and ran to where he lay. He had cut a gash in his forehead, and someone made a bandage to stop the flow of blood. When he tried to get up, he stumbled and fell again, and his face turned a terrible green. Harry telephoned Dr. Parminter, Dr. Hopewell, Dr. Altman, and Dr. Barnstable, but it was two in the morning and none of them answered. Finally, a Dr. Yerkes—a total stranger—agreed to come. Yerkes was a young man—he did not seem old enough to be a doctor—and he looked around at the disordered room and the anxious company as if there was something weird about the scene. He got off on the wrong foot with Cash. "What seems to be the matter, old-timer?" he asked.

Cash's leg was broken. The doctor put a splint on it, and Harry and Trace carried the injured man out to the doctor's car. Louise followed them in her own car to the hospital, where Cash was bedded down in a ward. The doctor gave Cash a sedative, and Louise kissed him and drove home in the dawn.

Cash was in the hospital for two weeks, and when he came home he walked with a crutch and his broken leg was in a heavy cast. It was another ten days before he could limp to the morning train. "I won't be able to run the hurdle race any more, sweetheart," he told Louise sadly. She said that it didn't matter, but while it didn't matter to her, it seemed to matter to Cash. He had lost weight in the hospital. His spirits were low. He seemed discontented. He did not himself understand what had happened. He, or everything around him, seemed subtly to have changed for the worse. Even his senses seemed to conspire to damage the ingenuous world that he had enjoyed for so many years. He went into the kitchen late one night to make himself a sandwich, and when he opened the icebox door he noticed a rank smell. He dumped the spoiled meat into the garbage, but the smell clung to his nostrils. A few days later he was in the attic, looking for his old varsity sweater. There were no windows in the attic and his flashlight was dim. Kneeling on the floor to unlock a trunk, he broke a spider web with his lips. The frail web covered his mouth as if a hand had been put over it. He wiped it impatiently, but also with the feeling of having been gagged. A few nights later, he was walking down a New York side street in the rain and saw an old whore standing in a doorway. She was so sluttish and ugly that she looked like a cartoon of Death, but before he could appraise her—the instant his eyes took an impression of her crooked figure—his lips swelled, his breathing quickened, and he experienced all the other symptoms of erotic excitement. A few nights later, while he was reading *Time* in the living room, he noticed that the faded roses Louise had brought in from the garden smelled more of earth than of anything else. It was a putrid, compelling smell. He dropped the roses into a wastebasket, but not before they had reminded him of the spoiled meat, the whore, and the spider web.

He had started going to parties again, but without the hurdle race to run, the parties of his friends and neighbors seemed to him interminable and stale. He listened to their dirty jokes with an irritability that was hard for him to conceal. Even their countenances discouraged him, and, slumped in a chair, he would regard their skin and their teeth narrowly, as if he were himself a much younger man.

The brunt of his irritability fell on Louise, and it seemed to her that Cash, in losing the hurdle race, had lost the thing that had preserved his equilibrium. He was rude to his friends when they stopped in for a drink. He was rude and gloomy when he and Louise went out. When Louise asked him what was the matter, he only murmured, "Nothing, nothing, nothing," and poured himself some bourbon. May and June passed, and then the first part of July, without his showing any improvement.

Then it is a summer night, a wonderful summer night. The passengers on the eight-fifteen see Shady Hill—if they notice it at all—in a bath of placid golden light. The noise of the train is muffled in the heavy foliage, and the long car windows look like a string of lighted aquarium tanks before they flicker out of sight. Up on the hill, the ladies say to one another, "Smell the grass! Smell the trees!" The Farquarsons are giving another party, and Harry has hung a sign, WHISKEY GULCH, from the rose arbor, and is wearing a chef's white hat and an apron. His guests are still drinking, and the smoke from his meat fire rises, on this windless evening, straight up into the trees.

In the clubhouse on the hill, the first of the formal dances for the young people begins around nine. On Alewives Lane sprinklers continue to play after dark. You can smell the water. The air seems as fragrant as it is dark—it is a delicious element to walk through—and most of the windows on Alewives Lane are open to it. You can see Mr. and Mrs. Bearden, as you pass, looking at their television. Joe Lockwood, the young lawyer who lives on the corner, is practicing a speech to the jury before his wife. "I intend to show you," he says, "that a man of probity, a man whose reputation for honesty and reliability . . ." He waves his bare arms as he speaks. His wife goes on knitting. Mrs. Carver —Harry Farquarson's mother-in-law—glances up at the sky and asks, *"Where* did all the stars come from?" She is old and foolish, and yet she is right: Last night's stars seem to have drawn to themselves a new range of galaxies, and the night sky is not dark at all, except where there is a tear in the membrane of light. In the unsold house lots near the track a hermit thrush is singing.

The Bentleys are at home. Poor Cash has been so rude and gloomy that the Farquarsons have not asked him to their party. He sits on the sofa beside Louise, who is sewing elastic into the children's underpants. Through the open window he can hear the pleasant sounds of the summer night. There is another party, in the Rogerses' garden, behind the Bentleys'. The music from the dance drifts down the hill. The band is sketchy—saxophone, drums, and piano —and all the selections are twenty years old. The band plays "Valencia," and Cash looks tenderly toward Louise, but Louise, tonight, is a discouraging figure. The lamp picks out the gray in her hair. Her apron is stained. Her face seems colorless and drawn. Suddenly, Cash begins frenziedly to beat his feet in time to the music. He sings some gibberish—Jabajabajabajaba—to the distant saxophone. He sighs and goes into the kitchen.

Here a faint, stale smell of cooking clings to the dark. From the kitchen window Cash can see the lights and figures of the Rogerses' party. It is a young people's party. The Rogers girl has asked some friends in for dinner before the dance, and now they seem to be leaving. Cars are driving away. "I'm covered with grass stains," a girl says. "I hope the old man remembered to buy gasoline," a boy says, and a girl laughs. There is nothing on their minds but the passing summer night. Taxes and the elastic in underpants—all the unbeautiful facts of life that threaten to crush the breath out of Cash—have not touched a single figure in this garden. Then jealousy seizes him—such savage and bitter jealousy that he feels ill.

He does not understand what separates him from these children in the garden next door. He has been a young man. He has been a hero. He has been adored and happy and full of animal spirits, and now he stands in a dark kitchen, deprived of his athletic prowess, his impetuousness, his good looks—of everything that means anything to him. He feels as if the figures in the next yard are the specters from some party in that past where all his tastes and desires lie, and from which he has been cruelly removed. He feels like a ghost of the summer evening. He is sick with longing. Then he hears voices in the front of the house. Louise turns on the kitchen light. "Oh, here you are," she says. "The Beardens stopped in. I think they'd like a drink."

Cash went to the front of the house to greet the Beardens. They wanted to go up to the club, for one dance. They saw, at a glance, that Cash was at loose ends, and they urged the Bentleys to come. Louise got someone to stay with the children and then went upstairs to change.

When they got to the club, they found a few friends of their age hanging around the bar, but Cash did not stay in the bar. He seemed restless and perhaps drunk. He banged into a table on his way through the lounge to the ballroom. He cut in on a young girl. He seized her too vehemently and jigged her off in an ancient two-step. She signaled openly for help to a boy in the stag line, and Cash was cut out. He walked angrily off the dance floor onto the terrace. Some young couples there withdrew from one another's arms as he pushed open the screen door. He walked to the end of the terrace, where he hoped to be alone, but here he surprised another young couple, who got up from the lawn, where they seemed to have been lying, and walked off in the dark toward the pool.

Louise remained in the bar with the Beardens. "Poor Cash is tight," she said. And then, "He told me this afternoon that he was going to paint the storm windows," she said. "Well, he mixed the paint and washed the brushes and put on some old fatigues and went into the cellar. There was a telephone call for him at around five, and when I went down to tell him, do you know what he was doing? He was just sitting there in the dark with a cocktail shaker. He hadn't touched the storm windows. He was just sitting there in the dark, drinking Martinis."

"Poor Cash," Trace said.

"You ought to get a job," Lucy said. "That would give you emotional and financial independence." As she spoke, they all heard the noise of furniture being moved around in the lounge.

"Oh, my God!" Louise said. "He's going to run the race. Stop him, Trace, stop him! He'll hurt himself. He'll kill himself!"

They all went to the door of the lounge. Louise again asked Trace to interfere, but she could see by Cash's face that he was way beyond remonstrating with. A few couples left the dance floor and stood watching the preparations. Trace didn't try to stop Cash—he helped him. There was no pistol, so he slammed a couple of books together for the start.

Over the sofa went Cash, over the coffee table, the lamp table, the fire screen, and the hassock. All his grace and strength seemed to have returned to him. He cleared the big sofa at the end of the room and instead of stopping there, he turned and started back over the course. His face was strained. His mouth hung open. The tendons of his neck protruded hideously. He made the hassock, the fire screen, the lamp table, and the coffee table. People held their breath when he approached the final sofa, but he cleared it and landed on his feet. There was some applause. Then he groaned and fell. Louise ran to his side. His clothes were soaked with sweat and he gasped for breath. She knelt down beside him and took his head in her lap and stroked his thin hair.

Cash had a terrible hangover on Sunday, and Louise let him sleep until it was nearly time for church. The family went off to Christ Church together at eleven, as they always did. Cash sang, prayed, and got to his knees, but the most he ever felt in church was that he stood outside the realm of God's infinite mercy, and, to tell the truth, he no more believed in the Father, the Son, and the Holy Ghost than does my bull terrier. They returned home at one to eat the overcooked meat and stony potatoes that were their customary Sunday lunch. At around five, the Parminters called up and asked them over for a drink. Louise didn't want to go, so Cash went alone. (Oh, those suburban Sunday nights, those Sunday-night blues! Those departing weekend guests, those stale cocktails, those half-dead flowers, those trips to Harmon to catch the Century, those post-mortems and pickup suppers!) It was sultry and overcast. The dog days were beginning. He drank gin with the Parminters for an hour or two and then went over to the Townsends' for a drink. The Farquarsons called up the Townsends and asked them to come over and bring Cash with them, and at the Farquarsons' they had some more drinks and ate the leftover party food. The Farquarsons were glad to see that Cash seemed like himself again. It was half past ten or eleven when he got home. Louise was upstairs, cutting out of the current copy of *Life* those scenes of mayhem, disaster, and violent death that she felt might corrupt her children. She always did this. Cash came upstairs and spoke to her and then went down again. In a little while, she heard him moving the living-room furniture around. Then he called to her, and when she went down, he was standing at the foot of the stairs in his stocking feet, holding the pistol out to her. She had never fired it before, and the directions he gave her were not much help.

"Hurry up," he said. "I can't wait all night."

He had forgotten to tell her about the safety, and when she pulled the trigger nothing happened.

"It's that little lever," he said. "Press that little lever." Then, in his impatience, he hurdled the sofa anyhow.

The pistol went off and Louise got him in midair. She shot him dead.

In Dreams Begin Responsibilities

DELMORE SCHWARTZ (1913-   )

I

I THINK it is the year 1909. I feel as if I were in a moving-picture theater, the long arm of light crossing the darkness and spinning, my eyes fixed upon the screen. It is a silent picture, as if an old Biograph one, in which the actors are dressed in ridiculously old-fashioned clothes, and one flash succeeds another, with sudden jumps, and the actors, too, seem to jump about, walking too fast. The shots are full of rays and dots, as if it had been raining when the picture was photographed. The light is bad.

It is Sunday afternoon, June 12th, 1909, and my father is walking down the quiet streets of Brooklyn on his way to visit my mother. His clothes are newly pressed, and his tie is too tight in his high collar. He jingles the coins in his pocket, thinking of the witty things he will say. I feel as if I had by now relaxed entirely in the soft darkness of the theater; the organist peals out the obvious approximate emotions on which the audience rocks unknowingly. I am anonymous. I have forgotten myself: it is always so when one goes to a movie, it is, as they say, a drug.

My father walks from street to street of trees, lawns and houses, once in a while coming to an avenue on which a street-car skates and yaws, progressing slowly. The motorman, who has a handle-bar mustache, helps a young lady wearing a hat like a feathered bowl onto the car. He leisurely makes change and rings his bell as the passengers mount the car. It is obviously Sunday, for everyone is wearing Sunday clothes and the street-car's noises emphasize the quiet of the holiday (Brooklyn is said to be the city of churches). The shops are closed and their shades drawn but for an occasional stationery store or drugstore with great green balls in the window.

My father has chosen to take this long walk because he likes to walk and think. He thinks about himself in the future and so arrives at the place he is to visit in a mild state of exaltation. He pays no attention to the houses he is passing, in which the Sunday dinner is being eaten, nor to the many trees which line each street, now coming to their full green and the time when they will enclose the whole street in leafy shadow. An occasional carriage passes, the horses' hooves falling like stones in the quiet afternoon, and once in a while an automobile, looking like an enormous upholstered sofa, puffs and passes.

My father thinks of my mother, of how lady-like she is, and of the pride which will be his when he introduces her to his family. They are not yet engaged and he is not yet sure that he loves my mother, so that, once in a while, he becomes panicky about the bond already established. But then he reassures himself by thinking of the big men he admires who are married: William Randolph Hearst and William Howard Taft, who has just become the President of the United States.

My father arrives at my mother's house. He has come too early and so is suddenly embarrassed. My aunt, my mother's younger sister, answers the loud bell with her napkin in her hand, for the family is still at dinner. As my father enters, my grandfather rises from the table and shakes hands with him. My mother has run upstairs to tidy herself. My grandmother asks my father if he has had dinner and tells him that my mother will be down soon. My grandfather opens the conversation by remarking about the mild June weather. My father sits uncomfortably near the table, holding his hat in his hand. My grandmother tells my aunt to take my father's hat. My uncle, twelve years old, runs into the house, his hair tousled. He shouts a greeting to my father, who has often given him nickels, and then runs upstairs, as my grandmother shouts after him. It is evident that the respect in which my father is held in this house is tempered by a good deal of mirth. He is impressive, but also very awkward.

II

Finally my mother comes downstairs and my father, being at the moment engaged in conversation with my grandfather, is made uneasy by her entrance, for he does not know whether to greet my mother or to continue the conversation. He gets up from his chair clumsily and says "Hello" gruffly. My grandfather watches this, examining their congruence, such as it is, with a critical eye, and meanwhile rubbing his bearded cheek roughly, as he always does when he reasons. He is worried; he is afraid that my father will not make a good husband for his oldest daughter. At this point something happens to the film, just as my father says something funny to my mother: I am awakened to myself and my unhappiness just as my interest has become most intense. The audience begins to clap impatiently. Then the trouble is attended to, but the film has been returned to a portion just shown, and once more I see my grandfather rubbing his bearded cheek, pondering my father's character. It is difficult to get back into the picture once more and forget myself, but as my mother giggles at my father's words, the darkness drowns me.

My father and mother depart from the house, my father shaking hands with my grandfather once more, out of some unknown uneasiness. I stir uneasily also, slouched in the hard chair of the theater. Where is the older uncle, my mother's older brother? He is studying in his bedroom upstairs, studying for his final examinations at the College of the City of New York, having been dead of double pneumonia for the last twenty-one years. My mother and father walk down the same quiet streets once more. My mother is holding my father's arm and telling him of the novel she has been reading and my father utters judgments of the characters as the plot is made clear to him. This is a habit which he very much enjoys, for he feels the utmost superiority and confidence when he is approving or condemning the behavior of other people. At times he feels moved to utter a brief "Ugh," whenever the story becomes what

he would call sugary. This tribute is the assertion of his manliness. My mother feels satisfied by the interest she has awakened; and she is showing my father how intelligent she is and how interesting.

They reach the avenue, and the street-car leisurely arrives. They are going to Coney Island this afternoon, although my mother really considers such pleasures inferior. She has made up her mind to indulge only in a walk on the boardwalk and a pleasant dinner, avoiding the riotous amusements as being beneath the dignity of so dignified a couple.

My father tells my mother how much money he has made in the week just past, exaggerating an amount which need not have been exaggerated. But my father has always felt that actualities somehow fall short, no matter how fine they are. Suddenly I begin to weep. The determined old lady who sits next to me in the theater is annoyed and looks at me with an angry face, and being intimidated, I stop. I drag out my handkerchief and dry my face, licking the drop which has fallen near my lips. Meanwhile I have missed something, for here are my father and mother alighting from the street-car at the last stop, Coney Island.

III

They walk toward the boardwalk and my mother commands my father to inhale the pungent air from the sea. They both breathe in deeply, both of them laughing as they do so. They have in common a great interest in health, although my father is strong and husky, and my mother is frail. They are both full of theories about what is good to eat and not good to eat, and sometimes have heated discussions about it, the whole matter ending in my father's announcement, made with a scornful bluster, that you have to die sooner or later anyway. On the boardwalk's flagpole, the American flag is pulsing in an intermittent wind from the sea.

My father and mother go to the rail of the boardwalk and look down on the beach where a good many bathers are casually walking about. A few are in the surf. A peanut whistle pierces the air with its pleasant and active whine, and my father goes to buy peanuts. My mother remains at the rail and stares at the ocean. The ocean seems merry to her; it pointedly sparkles and again and again the pony waves are released. She notices the children digging in the wet sand, and the bathing costumes of the girls who are her own age. My father returns with the peanuts. Overhead the sun's lightning strikes and strikes, but neither of them are at all aware of it. The boardwalk is full of people dressed in their Sunday clothes and casually strolling. The tide does not reach as far as the boardwalk, and the strollers would feel no danger if it did. My father and mother lean on the rail of the boardwalk and absently stare at the ocean. The ocean is becoming rough; the waves come in slowly, tugging strength from far back. The moment before they somersault, the moment when they arch their backs so beautifully, showing white veins in the green and black, that moment is intolerable. They finally crack, dashing fiercely upon the sand, actually driving, full force downward, against it, bouncing upward and forward, and at last petering out into a small stream of bubbles which slides up the beach and then is recalled. The sun overhead does not disturb my father and my mother. They gaze idly at the ocean, scarcely interested in its harshness. But I stare at the terrible sun which breaks up sight, and the fatal merciless passionate ocean. I forget my parents. I stare fascinated, and finally, shocked by their indifference, I burst out weeping once more. The old lady next to me pats my shoulder and says: "There, there, young man, all of this is only a movie, only a movie," but I look up once more at the terrifying sun and the terrifying ocean, and being unable to control my tears I get up and go to the men's room, stumbling over the feet of the other people seated in my row.

IV

When I return, feeling as if I had just awakened in the morning sick for lack of sleep, several hours have apparently passed and my parents are riding on the merry-go-round. My father is on a black horse, my mother on a white one, and they seem to be making an eternal circuit for the single purpose of snatching the nickel rings which are attached to an arm of one of the posts. A hand organ is playing; it is inseparable from the ceaseless circling of the merry-go-round.

For a moment it seems that they will never get off the carousel, for it will never stop, and I feel as if I were looking down from the fiftieth story of a building. But at length they do get off; even the hand-organ has ceased for a moment. There is a sudden and sweet stillness, as if the achievement of so much motion. My mother has acquired only two rings, my father, however, ten of them, although it was my mother who really wanted them.

They walk on along the boardwalk as the afternoon descends by imperceptible degrees into the incredible violet of dusk. Everything fades into a relaxed glow, even the ceaseless murmuring from the beach. They look for a place to have dinner. My father suggests the best restaurant on the boardwalk and my mother demurs, according to her principles of economy and housewifeliness.

However they do go to the best place, asking for a table near the window so that they can look out upon the boardwalk and the mobile ocean. My father feels omnipotent as he places a quarter in the waiter's hand in asking for a table. The place is crowded and here too there is music, this time from a kind of string trio. My father orders with a fine confidence.

As their dinner goes on, my father tells of his plans for the future and my mother shows with expressive face how interested she is, and how impressed. My father becomes exultant, lifted up by the waltz that is being played and his own future begins to intoxicate him. My father tells my mother that he is going to expand his business, for there is a great deal of money to be made. He wants to settle down. After all, he is twenty-nine, he has lived by himself since his thirteenth year, he is making more and more money, and he is envious of his friends when he visits them in the security of their homes, surrounded, it seems, by the calm domestic pleasures, and by delightful children, and then as the waltz reaches the moment when the dancers all swing madly, then, then with awful daring, then he asks my mother to marry him, although awkwardly enough and puzzled as to how he had arrived at the question, and she, to make the whole business worse, begins to cry, and my father looks nervously about, not knowing at all what to do now, and my mother says:

"It's all I've wanted from the first moment I saw you," sobbing, and he finds all of this very difficult, scarcely to his taste, scarcely as he thought it would be, on his long walks over Brooklyn Bridge in the revery of a fine cigar, and it was then, at that point, that I stood up in the theater and shouted: "Don't do it! It's not too late to change your minds, both of you. Nothing good will come of it, only remorse, hatred, scandal, and two children whose characters are monstrous." The whole audience turned to look at me, annoyed, the usher came hurrying down the aisle flashing his searchlight, and the old lady next to me tugged me down into my seat, saying: "Be quiet. You'll be put out, and you paid thirty-five cents to come in." And so I shut my eyes because I could not bear to see what was happening. I sat there quietly.

V

But after a while I begin to take brief glimpses and at length I watch again with thirsty interest, like a child who tries to maintain his sulk when he is offered a bribe of candy. My parents are now having their picture taken in a photographer's booth along the boardwalk. The place is shadowed in the mauve light which is apparently necessary. The camera is set to the side on its tripod and looks like a Martian man. The photographer is instructing my parents in how to pose. My father has his arm over my mother's shoulder, and both of them smile emphatically. The photographer brings my mother a bouquet of flowers to hold in her hand, but she holds it at the wrong angle. Then the photographer covers himself with the black cloth which drapes the camera and all that one sees of him is one protruding arm and his hand with which he holds tightly to the rubber ball which he squeezes when the picture is taken. But he is not satisfied with their appearance. He feels that somehow there is something wrong in their pose. Again and again he comes out from his hiding place with new directions. Each suggestion merely makes matters worse. My father is becoming impatient. They try a seated pose. The photographer explains that he has his pride, he wants to make beautiful pictures, he is not merely interested in all of this for the money. My father says: "Hurry up, will you? We haven't got all

night." But the photographer only scurries about apologetically, issuing new directions. The photographer charms me, and I approve of him with all my heart, for I know exactly how he feels, and as he criticizes each revised pose according to some obscure idea of rightness, I become quite hopeful. But then my father says angrily: "Come on, you've had enough time, we're not going to wait any longer." And the photographer, sighing unhappily, goes back into the black covering, and holds out his hand, saying: "One, two, three, Now!" and the picture is taken, with my father's smile turned to a grimace and my mother's bright and false. It takes a few minutes for the picture to be developed and as my parents sit in the curious light they become depressed.

VI

They have passed a fortune-teller's booth and my mother wishes to go in, but my father does not. They begin to argue about it. My mother becomes stubborn, my father once more impatient. What my father would like to do now is walk off and leave my mother there, but he knows that that would never do. My mother refuses to budge. She is near tears, but she feels an uncontrollable desire to hear what the palm-reader will say. My father consents angrily and they both go into the booth which is, in a way, like the photographer's, since it is draped in black cloth and its light is colored and shadowed. The place is too warm, and my father keeps saying that this is all nonsense, pointing to the crystal ball on the table. The fortune-teller, a short, fat woman garbed in robes supposedly exotic, comes into the room and greets them, speaking with an accent, but suddenly my father feels that the whole thing is intolerable; he tugs at my mother's arm but my mother refuses to budge. And then, in terrible anger, my father lets go of my mother's arm and strides out, leaving my mother stunned. She makes a movement as if to go after him, but the fortune-teller holds her and begs her not to do so, and I in my seat in the darkness am shocked and horrified. I feel as if I were walking a tight-rope one hundred feet over a circus audience and suddenly the rope is showing signs of breaking, and I get up from my seat and begin to shout once more the first words I can think of to communicate my terrible fear, and once more the usher comes hurrying down the aisle flashing his searchlight, and the old lady pleads with me, and the shocked audience has turned to stare at me, and I keep shouting: "What are they doing? Don't they know what they are doing? Why doesn't my mother go after my father and beg him not to be angry? If she does not do that, what will she do? Doesn't my father know what he is doing?" But the usher has seized my arm, and is dragging me away, and as he does

so, he says: "What are *you* doing? Don't you know you can't do things like this, you can't do whatever you want to do, even if other people aren't about? You will be sorry if you do not do what you should do. You can't carry on like this, it is not right, you will find that out soon enough, everything you do matters too much," and as he said that, dragging me through the lobby of the theater, into the cold light, I woke up into the bleak winter morning of my twenty-first birthday, the window-sill shining with its lip of snow, and the morning already begun.

Disorder and Early Sorrow

THOMAS MANN (1875-1955)

THE PRINCIPAL dish at dinner had been croquettes made of turnip greens. So there follows a trifle, concocted out of one of those dessert powders we use nowadays, that taste like almond soap. Xaver, the youthful manservant, in his outgrown striped jacket, white woollen gloves, and yellow sandals, hands it round, and the "big folk" take this opportunity to remind their father, tactfully, that company is coming today.

The "big folk" are two, Ingrid and Bert. Ingrid is brown-eyed, eighteen, and perfectly delightful. She is on the eve of her exams, and will probably pass them, if only because she knows how to wind masters, and even headmasters, round her finger. She does not, however, mean to use her certificate once she gets it; having leanings towards the stage, on the ground of her ingratiating smile, her equally ingratiating voice, and a marked and irresistible talent for burlesque. Bert is blond and seventeen. He intends to get done with school somehow, anyhow, and fling himself into the arms of life. He will be a dancer, or a cabaret actor, possibly even a waiter—but not a waiter anywhere else save at the Cairo, the night-club, whither he has once already taken flight, at five in the morning, and been brought back crestfallen. Bert bears a strong resemblance to the youthful manservant Xaver Kleinsgutl, of about

the same age as himself; not because he looks common—in features he is strikingly like his father, Professor Cornelius—but by reason of an approximation of types, due in its turn to far-reaching compromises in matters of dress and bearing generally. Both lads wear their heavy hair very long on top, with a cursory parting in the middle, and give their heads the same characteristic toss to throw it off the forehead. When one of them leaves the house, by the garden gate, bareheaded in all weathers, in a blouse rakishly girt with a leather strap, and sheers off bent well over with his head on one side; or else mounts his push-bike—Xaver makes free with his employers', of both sexes, or even, in acutely irresponsible mood, with the Professor's own—Dr. Cornelius from his bedroom window cannot, for the life of him, tell whether he is looking at his son or his servant. Both, he thinks, look like young moujiks. And both are impassioned cigarette-smokers, though Bert has not the means to compete with Xaver, who smokes as many as thirty a day, of a brand named after a popular cinema star. The big folk call their father and mother the "old folk"—not behind their backs, but as a form of address and in all affection: "Hullo, old folks," they will say; though Cornelius is only forty-seven years old and his wife eight years younger. And the

Professor's parents, who lead in his household the humble and hesitant life of the really old, are on the big folks' lips the "ancients." As for the "little folk," Ellie and Snapper, who take their meals upstairs with blue-faced Ann—so-called because of her prevailing facial hue— Ellie and Snapper follow their mother's example and address their father by his first name, Abel. Unutterably comic it sounds, in its pert, confiding familiarity; particularly on the lips, in the sweet accents, of five-year-old Eleanor, who is the image of Frau Cornelius's baby pictures and whom the Professor loves above everything else in the world.

"Darling old thing," says Ingrid affably, laying her large but shapely hand on his, as he presides in proper middle-class style over the family table, with her on his left and the mother opposite: "Parent mine, may I ever so gently jog your memory, for you have probably forgotten: this is the afternoon we were to have our little jollification, our turkey-trot with eats to match. You haven't a thing to do but just bear up and not funk it; everything will be over by nine o'clock."

"Oh—ah!" says Cornelius, his face falling. "Good!" he goes on, and nods his head to show himself in harmony with the inevitable. "I only meant—is this really the day? Thursday, yes. How time flies! Well, what time are they coming?"

"Half past four they'll be dropping in, I should say," answers Ingrid, to whom her brother leaves the major rôle in all dealings with the father. Upstairs, while he is resting, he will hear scarcely anything, and from seven to eight he takes his walk. He can slip out by the terrace if he likes.

"Tut!" says Cornelius deprecatingly, as who should say: "You exaggerate." But Bert puts in: "It's the one evening in the week Wanja doesn't have to play. Any other night he'd have to leave by half past six, which would be painful for all concerned."

Wanja is Ivan Herzl, the celebrated young leading man at the Stadttheater. Bert and Ingrid are on intimate terms with him, they often visit him in his dressing-room and have tea. He is an artist of the modern school, who stands on the stage in strange and, to the Professor's mind, utterly affected dancing attitudes, and shrieks lamentably. To a professor of history, all highly repugnant; but Bert has entirely succumbed to Herzl's influence, blackens the lower rim of his eyelids—despite painful but fruitless scenes with the father—and with youthful carelessness of the ancestral anguish declares that not only will he take Herzl for his model if he becomes a dancer, but in case he turns out to be a waiter at the Cairo he means to walk precisely thus.

Cornelius slightly raises his brows and makes his son a little bow—indicative of the unassumingness and self-abnegation that befits his age. You could not call it a mocking bow or suggestive in any special sense. Bert may refer it to himself or equally to his so talented friend.

"Who else is coming?" next inquires the master of the house. They mention various people, names all more or less familiar, from the city, from the suburban colony, from Ingrid's school. They still have some telephoning to do, they say. They have to phone Max. This is Max Hergesell, an engineering student; Ingrid utters his name in the nasal drawl which according to her is the traditional intonation of all the Hergesells. She goes on to parody it in the most abandonedly funny and lifelike way, and the parents laugh until they nearly choke over the wretched trifle. For even in these times when something funny happens people have to laugh.

From time to time the telephone bell rings in the Professor's study, and the big folk run across, knowing it is their affair. Many people had to give up their telephones the last time the price rose, but so far the Corneliuses have been able to keep theirs, just as they have kept their villa, which was built before the war, by dint of the salary Cornelius draws as professor of history—a million marks, and more or less adequate to the chances and changes of post-war life. The house is comfortable, even elegant, though sadly in need of repairs that cannot be made for lack of materials, and at present disfigured by iron stoves with long pipes. Even so, it is still the proper setting of the upper middle class, though they themselves look odd enough in it, with their worn and turned clothing and altered way of life. The children, of course, know nothing else; to them it is normal and regular, they belong by birth to the "villa proletariat." The problem of clothing troubles them not at all. They and their like have evolved a costume to fit the time, by poverty out of taste for innovation: in summer it consists of scarcely more than a belted linen smock and sandals. The middle-class parents find things rather more difficult.

The big folk's table-napkins hang over their chair-backs, they talk with their friends over the telephone. These friends are the invited guests who have rung up to accept or decline or arrange; and the conversation is carried on in the jargon of the clan, full of slang and high spirits, of which the old folk understand hardly a word. These consult together meantime about the hospitality to be offered to the impending guests. The Professor displays a middle-class ambitiousness: he wants to serve a sweet—or something that looks like a sweet—after the Italian salad and brown-bread sandwiches. But Frau Cornelius says that would be going too far. The guests would not expect it, she is sure—and the big folk, returning once more to their trifle, agree with her.

The mother of the family is of the same general type as Ingrid, though not so tall. She is languid; the fantastic difficulties of the housekeeping have broken and worn her. She really ought to go and take a cure, but feels incapable; the floor is always swaying under her feet, and everything seems upside down. She speaks of what is uppermost in her mind: the eggs, they simply must be bought to-day. Six thousand marks apiece they are, and just so many are to be had on this one day of the week at one single shop fifteen minutes' journey away. Whatever else they do, the big folk must go and fetch them immediately after luncheon, with Danny, their neighbor's son, who will soon be calling for them; and Xaver Kleinsgutl will don civilian garb and attend his young master and mistress. For no single household is allowed more than five eggs a week; therefore the young people will enter the shop singly, one after another, under assumed names, and thus wring twenty eggs from the shopkeeper for the Cornelius family. This enterprise is the sporting event of the week for all participants, not excepting the

moujik Kleinsgutl, and most of all for Ingrid and Bert, who delight in misleading and mystifying their fellowmen and would revel in the performance even if it did not achieve one single egg. They adore impersonating fictitious characters; they love to sit in a bus and carry on long lifelike conversations in a dialect which they otherwise never speak, the most commonplace dialogue about politics and people and the price of food, while the whole bus listens open-mouthed to this incredibly ordinary prattle, though with a dark suspicion all the while that something is wrong somewhere. The conversation waxes ever more shameless, it enters into revolting detail about these people who do not exist. Ingrid can make her voice sound ever so common and twittering and shrill as she impersonates a shop-girl with an illegitimate child, said child being a son with sadistic tendencies, who lately out in the country treated a cow with such unnatural cruelty that no Christian could have borne to see it. Bert nearly explodes at her twittering, but restrains himself and displays a grisly sympathy; he and the unhappy shop-girl entering into a long, stupid, depraved, and shuddery conversation over the patricular morbid cruelty involved; until an old gentleman opposite, sitting with his ticket folded between his index finger and his seal ring, can bear it no more and makes public protest against the nature of the themes these young folk are discussing with such particularity. He uses the Greek plural: "themata." Whereat Ingrid pretends to be dissolving in tears, and Bert behaves as though his wrath against the old gentleman was with difficulty being held in check and would probably burst out before long. He clenches his fists, he gnashes his teeth, he shakes from head to foot; and the unhappy old gentleman, whose intentions had been of the best, hastily leaves the bus at the next stop.

Such are the diversions of the big folk. The telephone plays a prominent part in them: they ring up any and everybody—members of government, opera singers, dignitaries of the Church—in the character of shop assistants, or perhaps as Lord or Lady Doolittle. They are only with difficulty persuaded that they have the wrong number. Once they emptied their parents' card-tray and distributed its contents among the neighbors' letter-boxes, wantonly, yet not without impish sense of the fitness of things to make it highly upsetting. God only knowing why certain people should have called where they did.

Xaver comes to clear away, tossing the hair out of his eyes. Now that he has taken off his gloves you can see the yellow chain-ring on his left hand. And as the Professor finishes his watery eight-thousand-mark beer and lights a cigarette, the little folk can be heard scrambling down the stair, coming, by established custom, for their after-dinner call on Father and Mother. They storm the dining-room, after a struggle with the latch, clutched by both pairs of little hands at once; their clumsy small feet twinkle over the carpet, in red felt slippers with the socks falling down on them. With prattle and shoutings each makes for his own place: Snapper to Mother, to climb on her lap, boast of all he has eaten, and thump his fat little tum; Ellie to her Abel, so much hers because she is so very much his; because she consciously luxuriates in the deep tenderness—like all deep feeling, concealing a melancholy strain—with which he holds her small form embraced; in the love in his eyes as he kisses her little fairy hand or the sweet brow with its delicate tracery of tiny blue veins.

The little folk look like each other, with the strong undefined likeness of brother and sister. In clothing and hair-cut they are twins. Yet they are sharply distinguished after all, and quite on sex lines. It is a little Adam and a little Eve. Not only is Snapper the sturdier and more compact, he appears consciously to emphasize his four-year-old masculinity in speech, manner, and carriage, lifting his shoulders and letting the little arms hang down quite like a young American athlete, drawing down his mouth when he talks and seeking to give his voice a gruff and forthright ring. But all this masculinity is the result of effort rather than natively his. Born and brought up in these desolate, distracted times, he has been endowed by them with an unstable and hypersensitive nervous system and suffers greatly under life's disharmonies. He is prone to sudden anger and outbursts of bitter tears, stamping his feet at every trifle; for this reason he is his mother's special nursling and care. His round, round eyes are chestnut brown and already inclined to squint, so that he will need glasses in the near future. His little nose is long, the mouth small—the father's nose and mouth they are, more plainly than ever since the Professor shaved his pointed beard and goes smooth-faced. The pointed beard had become impossible—even professors must make some concession to the changing times.

But the little daughter sits on her father's knee, his Eleonorchen, his little Eve, so much more gracious a little being, so much sweeter-faced than her brother—and he holds his cigarette away from her while she fingers his glasses with her dainty wee hands. The lenses are divided for reading and distance, and each day they tease her curiosity afresh.

At bottom he suspects that his wife's partiality may have a firmer basis than his own: that Snapper's refractory masculinity perhaps is solider stuff than his own little girl's more explicit charm and grace. But the heart will not be commanded, that he knows; and once and for all his heart belongs to the little one, as it has since the day she came, since the first time he saw her. Almost always when he holds her in his arms he remembers that first time: remembers the sunny room in the Women's Hospital, where Ellie first saw the light, twelve years after Bert was born. He remembers how he drew near, the mother smiling the while, and cautiously put aside the canopy of the diminutive bed that stood beside the large one. There lay the little miracle among the pillows: so well formed, so encompassed, as it were, with the harmony of sweet proportions, with little hands that even then, though so much tinier, were beautiful as now; with wide-open eyes blue as the sky and brighter than the sunshine—and almost in that very second he felt himself captured and held fast. This was love at first sight, love everlasting: a feeling unknown, unhoped for, unexpected—insofar as it could be a matter of conscious awareness; it took entire possession of him, and he understood, with joyous amazement, that this was for life.

But he understood more. He knows, does Dr. Cornelius, that there is something not quite right about this feeling, so unaware, so un-dreamed of, so involuntary. He has a shrewd suspicion that it is not by accident it has so utterly mastered him and bound itself up with his existence; that he had—even subconsciously —been preparing for it, or, more precisely, been prepared for it. There is, in short, something in him which at a given moment was ready to issue in such a feeling; and this something, highly extraordinary to relate, is his essence and quality as a professor of history. Dr. Cornelius, however, does not actually say this, even to himself; he merely realizes it, at odd times, and smiles a private smile. He knows that history professors do not love history because it is something that comes to pass, but only be-cause it is something that *has* come to pass; that they hate a revolution like the present one be-cause they feel it is lawless, incoherent, irrelevant —in a word, unhistoric; that their hearts belong to the coherent, disciplined, historic past. For the temper of timelessness, the temper of eter-nity—thus the scholar communes with himself when he takes his walk by the river before sup-per—that temper broods over the past; and it is a temper much better suited to the nervous system of a history professor than are the ex-cesses of the present. The past is immortalized; that is to say, it is dead; and death is the root of all godliness and all abiding significance. Dr. Cornelius, walking alone in the dark, has a pro-found insight into this truth. It is this conserva-tive instinct of his, his sense of the eternal, that has found in his love for his little daughter a way to save itself from the wounding inflicted by the times. For father love, and a little child on its mother's breast—are not these timeless, and thus very, very holy and beautiful? Yet Cornelius, pondering there in the dark, descries something not perfectly right and good in his love. Theoretically, in the interests of science, he admits it to himself. There is something ul-terior about it, in the nature of it; that some-thing is hostility, hostility against the history of to-day, which is still in the making, and thus not history at all, in behalf of the genuine his-tory that has already happened—that is to say, death. Yes, passing strange though all this is, yet it is true; true in a sense, that is. His devo-tion to this priceless little morsel of life and new

growth has something to do with death, it clings to death as against life; and that is neither right nor beautiful—in a sense. Though only the most fanatical asceticism could be capable, on no other ground than such casual scientific perception, of tearing this purest and most precious of feelings out of his heart.

He holds his darling on his lap and her slim rosy legs hang down. He raises his brows as he talks to her, tenderly, with a half-teasing note of respect, and listens enchanted to her high, sweet little voice calling him Abel. He exchanges a look with the mother, who is caress-ing her Snapper and reading him a gentle lec-ture. He must be more reasonable, he must learn self-control; to-day again, under the mani-fold exasperations of life, he has given way to rage and behaved like a howling dervish. Cor-nelius casts a mistrustful glance at the big folk now and then, too; he thinks it not unlikely they are not unaware of those scientific preoccupa-tions of his evening walks. If such be the case they do not show it. They stand there leaning their arms on their chair-backs and with a benevolence not untinctured with irony look on at the parental happiness.

The children's frocks are of a heavy, brick-red stuff, embroidered in modern "arty" style. They once belonged to Ingrid and Bert and are precisely alike, save that little knickers come out beneath Snapper's smock. And both have their hair bobbed. Snapper's is a streaky blond, inclined to turn dark. It is bristly and sticky and looks for all the world like a droll, badly fitting wig. But Ellie's is chestnut brown, glossy and fine as silk, as pleasing as her whole little personality. It covers her ears—and these ears are not a pair, one of them being the right size, the other distinctly too large. Her father will some-times uncover this little abnormality and ex-claim over it as though he had never noticed it before, which both makes Ellie giggle and covers her with shame. Her eyes are now golden brown, set far apart and with sweet gleams in them— such a clear and lovely look! The brows above are blond; the nose still unformed, with thick nostrils and almost circular holes; the mouth large and expressive, with a beautifully arch-ing and mobile upper lip. When she laughs, dimples come in her cheeks and she shows her teeth like loosely strung pearls. So far she has lost but one tooth, which her father gently twisted out with his handkerchief after it had grown very wobbling. During this small operation she had paled and trembled very much. Her cheeks have the softness proper to her years, but they are not chubby; indeed, they are rather concave, due to her facial structure, with its somewhat prominent jaw. On one, close to the soft fall of her hair, is a downy freckle.

Ellie is not too well pleased with her looks —a sign that already she troubles about such things. Sadly she thinks it is best to admit it once for all, her face is "homely"; though the rest of her, "on the other hand," is not bad at all. She loves expressions like "on the other hand"; they sound choice and grown-up to her, and she likes to string them together, one after the other: "very likely," "probably," "after all." Snapper is self-critical too, though more in the moral sphere: he suffers from remorse for his attacks of rage and considers himself a tremendous sinner. He is quite certain that heaven is not for such as he; he is sure to go to "the bad place" when he dies, and no persuasions will convince him to the contrary—as that God sees the heart and gladly makes allowances. Obstinately he shakes his head, with the comic, crooked little peruke, and vows there is no place for him in heaven. When he has a cold he is immediately quite choked with mucus; rattles and rumbles from top to toe if you even look at him; his temperature flies up at once and he simply puffs. Nursy is pessimistic on the score of his constitution: such fat-blooded children as he might get a stroke any minute. Once she even thought she saw the moment at hand: Snapper had been in one of his berserker rages, and in the ensuing fit of penitence stood himself in the corner with his back to the room. Suddenly Nursy noticed that his face had gone all blue, far bluer, even, than her own. She raised the alarm, crying out that the child's all too rich blood had at length brought him to his final hour; and Snapper, to his vast astonishment, found himself, so far from being rebuked for evil-doing, encompassed in tenderness and anxiety—until it turned out that his color was not caused by

apoplexy but by the distempering on the nursery wall, which had come off on his tear-wet face.

Nursy had come downstairs too, and stands by the door, sleek-haired, owl-eyed, with her hands folded over her white apron, and a severely dignified manner born of her limited intelligence. She is very proud of the care and training she gives her nurslings and declares that they are "enveloping wonderfully." She has had seventeen suppurated teeth lately removed from her jaws and been measured for a set of symmetrical yellow ones in dark rubber gums; these now embellish her peasant face. She is obsessed with the strange conviction that these teeth of hers are the subject of general conversation, that, as it were, the sparrows on the housetops chatter of them. "Everybody knows I've had a false set put in," she will say; "there has been a great deal of foolish talk about them." She is much given to dark hints and veiled innuendo: speaks, for instance, of a certain Dr. Bleifuss, whom every child knows, and "there are even some in the house who pretend to be him." All one can do with talk like this is charitably to pass it over in silence. But she teaches the children nursery rhymes: gems like:

> Puff, puff, here comes the train!
> Puff, puff, toot, toot,
> Away it goes again.

Or that gastronomical jingle, so suited, in its sparseness, to the times, and yet seemingly with a blitheness of its own:

> Monday we begin the week,
> Tuesday there's a bone to pick.
> Wednesday we're half way through
> Thursday what a great do-do!
> Friday we eat what fish we're able,
> Saturday we dance round the table.
> Sunday brings us pork and greens—
> Here's a feast for kings and queens!

Also a certain four-line stanza with a romantic appeal, unutterable and unuttered:

> Open the gate, open the gate
> And let the carriage drive in.
> Who is it in the carriage sits?
> A lordly sir with golden hair.

Or, finally that ballad about golden-haired Marianne who sat on a, sat on a, sat on a stone, and combed out her, combed out her, combed out her hair; and about blood-thirsty Rudolph, who pulled out a, pulled out a, pulled out a knife—and his ensuing direful end. Ellie enunciates all these ballads charmingly, with her mobile little lips, and sings them in her sweet little voice—much better than Snapper. She does everything better than he does, and he pays her honest admiration and homage and obeys her in all things except when visited by one of his attacks. Sometimes she teaches him, instructs him upon the birds in the picture-book and tells him their proper names: "This is a chaffinch, Buddy, this is a bullfinch, this is a cowfinch." He has to repeat them after her. She gives him medical instruction too, teaches him the names of diseases, such as inflammation of the lungs, inflammation of the blood, inflammation of the air. If he does not pay attention and cannot say the words after her, she stands him in the corner. Once she even boxed his ears, but was so ashamed that she stood herself in the corner for a long time. Yes, they are fast friends, two souls with but a single thought, and have all their adventures in common. They come home from a walk and relate as with one voice that they have seen two moollies and a teenty-weenty baby calf. They are on familiar terms with the kitchen, which consists of Xaver and the ladies Hinterhofer, two sisters once of the lower middle class who, in these evil days, are reduced to living *"au pair"* as the phrase goes and officiating as cook and housemaid for their board and keep. The little ones have a feeling that Xaver and the Hinterhofers are on much the same footing with their father and mother as they are themselves. At least sometimes, when they have been scolded, they go downstairs and announce that the master and mistress are cross. But playing with the servants lacks charm compared with the joys of playing upstairs. The kitchen could never rise to the height of the games their father can invent. For instance, there is "four gentlemen taking a walk." When they play it Abel will crook his knees until he is the same height with themselves and go walking with them, hand in hand. They never get enough of this sport; they could walk round and round the dining-room a whole day on end, five gentlemen in all, counting the diminished Abel.

Then there is the thrilling cushion game. One of the children, usually Ellie, seats herself, unbeknownst to Abel, in his seat at table. Still as a mouse she awaits his coming. He draws near with his head in the air, descanting in loud, clear tones upon the surpassing comfort of his chair; and sits down on top of Ellie. "What's this, what's this?" says he. And bounces about, deaf to the smothered giggles exploding behind him. "Why have they put a cushion in my chair? And what a queer, hard, awkward-shaped cushion it is!" he goes on. "Frightfully uncomfortable to sit on!" And keeps pushing and bouncing about more and more on the astonishing cushion and clutching behind him into the rapturous giggling and squeaking, until at last he turns round, and the game ends with a magnificent climax of discovery and recognition. They might go through all this a hundred times without diminishing by an iota its power to thrill.

To-day is no time for such joys. The imminent festivity disturbs the atmosphere, and besides there is work to be done, and, above all, the eggs to be got. Ellie has just time to recite "Puff, puff," and Cornelius to discover that her ears are not mates, when they are interrupted by the arrival of Danny, come to fetch Bert and Ingrid. Xaver, meantime, has exchanged his striped livery for an ordinary coat, in which he looks rather rough-and-ready, though as brisk and attractive as ever. So then Nursy and the children ascend to the upper regions, the Professor withdraws to his study to read, as always after dinner, and his wife bends her energies upon the sandwiches and salad that must be prepared. And she has another errand as well. Before the young people arrive she has to take her shopping basket and dash into town on her bicycle, to turn into provisions a sum of money she has in hand, which she dares not keep lest it lose all value.

Cornelius reads, leaning back in his chair, with his cigar between his middle and index fingers. First he reads Macaulay on the origin of the English public debt at the end of the seventeenth century; then an article in a French periodical on the rapid increase in the Spanish debt towards the end of the sixteenth. Both these for his lecture on the morrow. He intends to compare the astonishing prosperity which accompanied the phenomenon in England with its fatal effects a hundred years earlier in Spain, and to analyze the ethical and psychological grounds of the difference in results. For that will give him a chance to refer back from the England of William III, which is the actual subject in hand, to the time of Philip II and the Counter-Reformation, which is his own special field. He has already written a valuable work on this period; it is much cited and got him his professorship. While his cigar burns down and gets strong, he excogitates a few pensive sentences in a key of gentle melancholy, to be delivered before his class next day: about the practically hopeless struggle carried on by the belated Philip against the whole trend of history: against the new, the kingdom-disrupting power of the Germanic ideal of freedom and individual liberty. And about the persistent, futile struggle of the aristocracy, condemned by God and rejected of man, against the forces of progress and change. He savors his sentences; keeps on polishing them while he puts back the books he has been using; then goes upstairs for the usual pause in his day's work, the hour with drawn blinds and closed eyes, which he so imperatively needs. But to-day, he recalls, he will rest under disturbed conditions, amid the bustle of preparations for the feast. He smiles to find his heart giving a mild flutter at the thought. Disjointed phrases on the theme of black-clad Philip and his times mingle with a confused consciousness that they will soon be dancing down below. For five minutes or so he falls asleep.

As he lies and rests he can hear the sound of the garden gate and the repeated ringing at the bell. Each time a little pang goes through him, of excitement and suspense, at the thought that the young people have begun to fill the floor below. And each time he smiles at himself again—though even his smile is slightly nervous, is tinged with the pleasurable anticipations people always feel before a party. At half past four—it is already dark—he gets up and washes at the wash-stand. The basin has been out of repair for two years. It is supposed to tip, but has broken away from its socket on one side

and cannot be mended because there is nobody to mend it; neither replaced because no shop can supply another. So it has to be hung up above the vent and emptied by lifting in both hands and pouring out the water. Cornelius shakes his head over this basin, as he does several times a day—whenever, in fact, he has occasion to use it. He finishes his toilet with care, standing under the ceiling light to polish his glasses till they shine. Then he goes downstairs.

On his way to the dining-room he hears the gramophone already going, and the sound of voices. He puts on a polite, society air; at his tongue's end is the phrase he means to utter: "Pray don't let me disturb you," as he passes directly into the dining-room for his tea. "Pray don't let me disturb you"—it seems to him precisely the *mot juste;* towards the guests cordial and considerate, for himself a very bulwark.

The lower floor is lighted up, all the bulbs in the chandelier are burning save one that has burned out. Cornelius pauses on a lower step and surveys the entrance hall. It looks pleasant and cosy in the bright light, with its copy of Marées over the brick chimney-piece, its wainscoted walls—wainscoted in soft wood—and red-carpeted floor, where the guests stand in groups, chatting, each with his tea-cup and slice of bread-and-butter spread with anchovy paste. There is a festal haze, faint scents of hair and clothing and human breath come to him across the room, it is all characteristic and familiar and highly evocative. The door into the dressing-room is open, guests are still arriving.

A large group of people is rather bewildering at first sight. The Professor takes in only the general scene. He does not see Ingrid, who is standing just at the foot of the steps, in a dark silk frock with a pleated collar falling softly over the shoulders, and bare arms. She smiles up at him, nodding and showing her lovely teeth.

"Rested?" she asks, for his private ear. With a quite unwarranted start he recognizes her, and she presents some of her friends.

"May I introduce Herr Zuber?" she says. "And this is Fräulein Plaichinger."

Herr Zuber is insignificant. But Fräulein Plaichinger is a perfect Germania, blond and voluptuous, arrayed in floating draperies. She has a snub nose, and answers the Professor's salutation in the high, shrill pipe so many stout women have.

"Delighted to meet you," he says. "How nice of you to come! A classmate of Ingrid's I suppose?"

And Herr Zuber is a golfing partner of Ingrid's. He is in business; he works in his uncle's brewery. Cornelius makes a few jokes about the thinness of the beer and professes to believe that Herr Zuber could easily do something about the quality if he would. "But pray don't let me disturb you," he goes on, and turns towards the dining-room.

"There comes Max," says Ingrid. "Max, you sweep, what do you mean by rolling up at this time of day?" For such is the way they talk to each other, offensively to an older ear; of social forms, of hospitable warmth, there is no faintest trace. They all call each other by their first names.

A young man comes up to them out of the dressing-room and makes his bow; he has an expanse of white shirt-front and a little black string tie. He is as pretty as a picture, dark, with rosy cheeks, clean-shaven of course, but with just a sketch of side-whisker. Not a ridiculous or flashy beauty, not like a gypsy fiddler, but just charming to look at, in a winning, well-bred way, with kind dark eyes. He even wears his dinner-jacket a little awkwardly.

"Please don't scold me, Cornelia," he says; "it's the idiotic lectures." And Ingrid presents him to her father as Herr Hergesell.

Well, and so this is Herr Hergesell. He knows his manners, does Herr Hergesell, and thanks the master of the house quite ingratiatingly for his invitation as they shake hands. "I certainly seem to have missed the bus," says he jocosely. "Of course I have lectures to-day up to four o'clock; I would have; and after that I had to go home to change." Then he talks about his pumps, with which he has just been struggling in the dressing-room.

"I brought them with me in a bag," he goes on. "Mustn't tramp all over the carpet in our brogues—it's not done. Well, I was ass enough not to fetch along a shoe-horn, and I find I simply can't get in! What a sell! They are the tightest I've ever had, the numbers don't tell

you a thing, and all the leather to-day is just cast iron. It's not leather at all. My poor finger" —he confidingly displays a reddened digit and once more characterizes the whole thing as a "sell," and a putrid sell into the bargain. He really does talk just as Ingrid said he did, with a peculiar nasal drawl, not affectedly in the least, but merely because that is the way of all the Hergesells.

Dr. Cornelius says it is very careless of them not to keep a shoe-horn in the cloak-room and displays proper sympathy with the mangled finger. "But now you *really* must not let me disturb you any longer," he goes on. "*Auf wiedersehen!*" And he crosses the hall into the dining-room.

There are guests there too, drinking tea; the family table is pulled out. But the Professor goes at once to his own little upholstered corner with the electric light bulb above it—the nook where he usually drinks his tea. His wife is sitting there talking with Bert and two other young men, one of them Herzl, whom Cornelius knows and greets; the other a typical "Wandervogel!" named Möller, a youth who obviously neither owns nor cares to own the correct evening dress of the middle classes (in fact, there is no such thing any more), nor to ape the manners of a gentleman (and, in fact, there is no such thing any more either). He has a wilderness of hair, horn spectacles, and a long neck, and wears golf stockings and a belted blouse. His regular occupation, the Professor learns, is banking, but he is by way of being an amateur folklorist and collects folk-songs from all localities and in all languages. He sings them, too, and at Ingrid's command has brought his guitar; it is hanging in the dressing-room in an oilcloth case. Herzl, the actor, is small and slight, but he has a strong growth of black beard, as you can tell by the thick coat of powder on his cheeks. His eyes are larger than life, with a deep and melancholy glow. He has put on rouge besides the powder— those dull carmine high-lights on the cheeks can be nothing but a cosmetic. "Queer," thinks the Professor. "You would think a man would be one thing or the other—not melancholic and use face paint at the same time. It's a psychological contradiction. How can a melancholy man rouge? But here we have a perfect illustration of the abnormality of the artist soul-form. It can make possible a contradiction like this—perhaps it even consists in the contradiction. All very interesting—and no reason whatever for not being polite to him. Politeness is a primitive convention—and legitimate. . . . Do take some lemon, Herr Hofschauspieler!"

Court actors and court theatres—there are no such things any more, really. But Herzl relishes the sound of the title, notwithstanding he is a revolutionary artist. This must be another contradiction inherent in his soul-form; so, at least, the Professor assumes, and he is probably right. The flattery he is guilty of is a sort of atonement for his previous hard thoughts about the rouge.

"Thank you so much—it's really too good of you, sir," says Herzl, quite embarrassed. He is so overcome that he almost stammers; only his perfect enunciation saves him. His whole bearing towards his hostess and the master of the house is exaggeratedly polite. It is almost as though he had a bad conscience in respect of his rouge; as though an inward compulsion had driven him to put it on, but now, seeing it through the Professor's eyes, he disapproves of it himself, and thinks, by an air of humility toward the whole of unrouged society, to mitigate its effect.

They drink their tea and chat: about Möller's folk-songs, about Basque folk-songs and Spanish folk-songs; from which they pass to the new production of *Don Carlos* at the Stadttheater, in which Herzl plays the title-rôle. He talks about his own rendering of the part and says he hopes his conception of the character has unity. They go on to criticize the rest of the cast, the setting, and the production as a whole; and Cornelius is struck, rather painfully, to find the conversation trending towards his own special province, back to Spain and the Counter-Reformation. He has done nothing at all to give it this turn, he is perfectly innocent, and hopes it does not look as though he had sought an occasion to play the professor. He wonders, and falls silent, feeling relieved when the little folk come up to the table. Ellie and Snapper have on their blue velvet Sunday frocks; they are permitted to partake in the festivities up to bedtime. They look

shy and large-eyed as they say how-do-you-do to the strangers and, under pressure, repeat their names and ages. Herr Möller does nothing but gaze at them solemnly, but Herzl is simply ravished. He rolls his eyes up to heaven and puts his hands over his mouth; he positively blesses them. It all, no doubt, comes from his heart, but he is so addicted to theatrical methods of making an impression and getting an effect that both words and behavior ring frightfully false. And even his enthusiasm for the little folk looks too much like part of his general craving to make up for the rouge on his cheeks.

The tea-table has meanwhile emptied of guests, and dancing is going on in the hall. The children run off, the Professor prepares to retire. "Go and enjoy yourselves," he says to Möller and Herzl, who have sprung from their chairs as he rises from his. They shake hands and he withdraws into his study, his peaceful kingdom, where he lets down the blinds, turns on the desk lamp, and sits down to work.

It is work which can be done, if necessary, under disturbed conditions: nothing but a few letters and a few notes. Of course, Cornelius's mind wanders. Vague impressions float through it: Herr Hergesell's refractory pumps, the high pipe in that plump body of the Plaichinger female. As he writes, or leans back in his chair and stares into space, his thoughts go back to Herr Möller's collection of Basque folk-songs, to Herzl's posings and humility, to "his" Carlos and the court of Philip II. There is something strange, he thinks, about conversations. They are so ductile, they will flow of their own accord in the direction of one's dominating interest. Often and often he has seen this happen. And while he is thinking, he is listening to the sounds next door—rather subdued, he finds them. He hears only voices, no sound of footsteps. The dancers do not glide or circle round the room; they merely walk about over the carpet, which does not hamper their movements in the least. Their way of holding each other is quite different and strange, and they move to the strains of the gramophone, to the weird music of the new world. He concentrates on the music and makes out that it is a jazz-band record, with various percussion instruments and the clack and clatter of castanets, which, however, are not even faintly suggestive of Spain, but merely jazz like the rest. No, not Spain. . . . His thoughts are back at the old round.

Half an hour goes by. It occurs to him it would be no more than friendly to go and contribute a box of cigarettes to the festivities next door. Too bad to ask the young people to smoke their own—though they have probably never thought of it. He goes into the empty dining-room and takes a box from his supply in the cupboard: not the best ones, nor yet the brand he himself prefers, but a certain long, thin kind he is not averse to getting rid of—after all, they are nothing but youngsters. He takes the box into the hall, holds it up with a smile, and deposits it on the mantel-shelf. After which he gives a look round and returns to his own room.

There comes a lull in dance and music. The guests stand about the room in groups or round the table at the window or are seated in a circle by the fireplace. Even the built-in stairs, with their worn velvet carpet, are crowded with young folk as in an amphitheatre: Max Herge-sell is there, leaning back with one elbow on the step above and gesticulating with his free hand as he talks to the shrill, voluptuous Plaichinger. The floor of the hall is nearly empty, save just in the centre: there, directly beneath the chandelier, the two little ones in their blue velvet frocks clutch each other in an awkward embrace and twirl silently round and round, oblivious of all else. Cornelius, as he passes, strokes their hair, with a friendly word; it does not distract them from their small solemn preoccupation. But at his own door he turns to glance round and sees young Hergesell push himself off the stair by his elbow—probably because he noticed the Professor. He comes down into the arena, takes Ellie out of her brother's arms, and dances with her himself. It looks very comic, without the music, and he crouches down just as Cornelius does when he goes walking with the four gentlemen, holding the fluttered Ellie as though she were grown up and taking little "shimmy-ing" steps. Everybody watches with huge enjoyment, the gramophone is put on again, dancing becomes general. The Professor stands and looks, with his hand on the door-knob. He nods and

laughs; when he finally shuts himself into his study the mechanical smile still lingers on his lips.

Again he turns over pages by his desk lamp, takes notes, attends to a few simple matters. After a while he notices that the guests have forsaken the entrance hall for his wife's drawing-room, into which there is a door from his own study as well. He hears their voices and the sounds of a guitar being tuned. Herr Möller, it seems, is to sing—and does so. He twangs the strings of his instrument and sings in a powerful bass a ballad in a strange tongue, possibly Swedish. The Professor does not succeed in identifying it, though he listens attentively to the end, after which there is great applause. The sound is deadened by the portière that hangs over the dividing door. The young bank-clerk begins another song. Cornelius goes softly in.

It is half-dark in the drawing-room; the only light is from the shaded standard lamp, beneath which Möller sits, on the divan, with his legs crossed, picking his strings. His audience is grouped easily about; as there are not enough seats, some stand, and more, among them many young ladies, are simply sitting on the floor with their hands clasped round their knees or even with their legs stretched out before them. Hergesell sits thus, in his dinner jacket, next the piano, with Fräulein Plaichinger beside him. Frau Cornelius is holding both children on her lap as she sits in her easy-chair opposite the singer. Snapper, the Bœotian, begins to talk loud and clear in the middle of the song and has to be intimidated with hushings and finger-shakings. Never, never would Ellie allow herself to be guilty of such conduct. She sits there daintily erect and still on her mother's knee. The Professor tries to catch her eye and exchange a private signal with his little girl; but she does not see him. Neither does she seem to be looking at the singer. Her gaze is directed lower down.

Möller sings the "joli tambour":

> "Sire, mon roi, donnez-moi votre fille—"

They are all enchanted. "How good!" Hergesell is heard to say, in the odd, nasally condescending Hergesell tone. The next one is a beggar ballad, to a tune composed by young Möller himself; it elicits a storm of applause:

Gypsy lassie a'goin' to the fair,
Huzza!
Gypsy laddie a-goin' to be there—
Huzza, diddlety umpty dido!

Laughter and high spirits, sheer reckless hilarity, reigns after this jovial ballad. "Frightfully good!" Hergesell comments again, as before. Follows another popular song, this time a Hungarian one; Möller sings it in his own outlandish tongue, and most effectively. The Professor applauds with ostentation. It warms his heart and does him good, this outcropping of artistic, historic, and cultural elements all amongst the shimmying. He goes up to young Möller and congratulates him, talks about the songs and their sources, and Möller promises to lend him a certain annotated book of folksongs. Cornelius is the more cordial because all the time, as fathers do, he has been comparing the parts and achievements of this young stranger with those of his own son, and being gnawed by envy and chagrin. This young Möller, he is thinking, is a capable bank-clerk (though about Möller's capacity he knows nothing whatever) and has this special gift besides, which must have taken talent and energy to cultivate. "And here is my poor Bert, who knows nothing and can do nothing and thinks of nothing except playing the clown, without even talent for that!" He tries to be just; he tells himself that, after all, Bert has innate refinement; that probably there is a good deal more to him than there is to the successful Möller; that perhaps he has even something of the poet in him, and his dancing and table-waiting are due to mere boyish folly and the distraught times. But paternal envy and pessimism win the upper hand; when Möller begins another song, Dr. Cornelius goes back to his room.

He works as before, with divided attention, at this and that, while it gets on for seven o'clock. Then he remembers a letter he may just as well write, a short letter and not very important, but letter-writing is wonderful for the way it takes up the time, and it is almost half past when he has finished. At half past eight the Italian salad will be served; so now is the prescribed moment for the Professor to go out into the wintry darkness to post his letters and take his daily quantum of fresh air and exercise. They are dancing again, and he will have to pass through the hall to get his hat and coat; but they are used to him now, he need not stop and beg them not to be disturbed. He lays away his papers, takes up the letters he has written, and goes out. But he sees his wife sitting near the door of his room and pauses a little by her easy-chair.

She is watching the dancing. Now and then the big folk or some of their guests stop to speak to her; the party is at its height, and there are more onlookers than these two: blue-faced Ann is standing at the bottom of the stairs, in all the dignity of her limitations. She is waiting for the children, who simply cannot get their fill of these unwonted festivities, and watching over Snapper, lest his all too rich blood be churned to the danger-point by too much twirling round. And not only the nursery but the kitchen takes an interest: Xaver and the two ladies Hinterhofer are standing by the pantry door looking on with relish. Fräulein Walburga, the elder of the two sunken sisters (the culinary section—she objects to being called a cook), is a whimsical, good-natured sort, brown-eyed, wearing glasses with thick circular lenses; the nose-piece is wound with a bit of rag to keep it from pressing on her nose. Fräulein Cecilia is younger, though not so precisely young either. Her bearing is as self-assertive as usual, this being her way of sustaining her dignity as a former member of the middle class. For Fräulein Cecilia feels acutely her descent into the ranks of domestic service. She positively declines to wear a cap or other badge of servitude, and her hardest trial is on the Wednesday evening when she has to serve the dinner while Xaver has his afternoon out. She hands the dishes with averted face and elevated nose—a fallen queen; and so distressing is it to behold her degradation that one evening when the little folk happened to be at table and saw her they both with one accord burst into tears. Such anguish is unknown to young Xaver. He enjoys serving and does it with an ease born of practice as well as talent, for he was once a "piccolo." But otherwise he is a thorough-paced good-for-nothing and windbag—with quite distinct traits of character of his own, as his long-suffering employers are always ready to concede, but perfectly impossible and a bag of wind for all that. One must just take him as he is, they think, and not expect figs from thistles. He is the child and product of the disrupted times, a perfect specimen of his generation, follower of the revolution, Bolshevist sympathizer. The Professor's name for him is the "minute-man," because he is always to be counted on in any sudden crisis, if only it address his sense of humour or love of novelty, and will display therein amazing readiness and resource. But he utterly lacks a sense of duty and can as little be trained to the performance of the daily round and common task as some kinds of dog can be taught to jump over a stick. It goes so plainly against the grain that criticism is disarmed. One becomes resigned. On grounds that appealed to him as unusual and amusing he would be ready to turn out of his bed at any hour of the night. But he simply cannot get up before eight in the morning, he cannot do it, he will not jump over the stick. Yet all day long the evidence of this free and untrammelled existence, the sound of his mouth-organ, his joyous whistle, or his raucous but expressive voice lifted in song, rises to the hearing of the world above-stairs; and the smoke of his cigarettes fills the pantry. While the Hinterhofer ladies work he stands and looks on. Of a morning while the Professor is breakfasting, he tears the leaf off the study calendar—but does not lift a finger to dust the room. Dr. Cornelius has often told him to leave the calendar alone, for he tends to tear off two leaves at a time and thus to add to the general confusion. But young Xaver appears to find joy in this activity, and will not be deprived of it.

Again, he is fond of children, a winning trait. He will throw himself into games with the little folk in the garden, make and mend their toys with great ingenuity, even read aloud from their books—and very droll it sounds in his thick-lipped pronunciation. With his whole soul he loves the cinema; after an evening spent there he inclines to melancholy and yearning and talking to himself. Vague hopes stir in him that some day he may make his fortune in that gay world and belong to it by rights—hopes based on his shock of hair and his physical agility and daring. He likes to climb the ash tree in the front garden, mounting branch by branch to the very top and frightening everybody to death who sees him. Once there he lights a cigarette and smokes it as he sways to and fro, keeping a look-out for a cinema director who might chance to come along and engage him.

If he changed his striped jacket for mufti, he might easily dance with the others and no one would notice the difference. For the big folk's friends are rather anomalous in their clothing: evening dress is worn by a few, but it is by no means the rule. There is quite a sprinkling of guests, both male and female, in the same general style as Möller the ballad-singer. The Professor is familiar with the circumstances of most of this young generation he is watching as he stands beside his wife's chair; he has heard them spoken of by name. They are students at the high school or at the School of Applied Art; they lead, at least the masculine portion, that precarious and scrambling existence which is purely the product of the time. There is a tall, pale, spindling youth, the son of a dentist, who lives by speculation. From all the Professor hears, he is a perfect Aladdin. He keeps a car, treats his friends to champagne suppers, and showers presents upon them on every occasion, costly little trifles in mother-of-pearl and gold. So to-day he has brought gifts to the young givers of the feast: for Bert a gold lead-pencil, and for Ingrid a pair of ear-rings of barbaric size, great gold circlets that fortunately do not have to go through the little ear-lobe, but are fastened over it by means of a clip. The big folk come laughing to their parents to display these trophies; and the parents shake their heads even while they admire—Aladdin bowing over and over from afar.

The young people appear to be absorbed in their dancing—if the performance they are carrying out with so much still concentration can be called dancing. They stride across the carpet, slowly, according to some unfathomable prescript, strangely embraced; in the newest attitude, tummy advanced and shoulders high, waggling the hips. They do not get tired, because nobody could. There is no such thing as heightened colour or heaving bosoms. Two girls may dance together or two young men—it is all the same. They move to the exotic strains of the gramophone, played with the loudest needles to procure the maximum of sound: shimmies, fox-trots, one-steps, double foxes, African shimmies, Java dances, and Creole polkas, the wild musky melodies follow one another, now furious, now languishing, a monotonous Negro programme in unfamiliar rhythm, to a clacking, clashing, and strumming orchestral accompaniment.

"What is that record?" Cornelius inquires of Ingrid, as she passes him by in the arms of the pale young speculator, with reference to the piece then playing, whose alternate languors and furies he finds comparatively pleasing and showing a certain resourcefulness in detail.

"*Prince of Pappenheim:* 'Console thee, dearest child,' " she answers, and smiles pleasantly back at him with her white teeth.

The cigarette smoke wreathes beneath the chandelier. The air is blue with a festal haze compact of sweet and thrilling ingredients that stir the blood with memories of green-sick pains and are particularly poignant to those whose youth—like the Professor's own—has been over-sensitive. . . . The little folk are still on the floor. They are allowed to stop up until eight, so great is their delight in the party. The guests have got used to their presence; in their own way, they have their place in the doings of the evening. They have separated, anyhow: Snapper revolves all alone in the middle of the carpet, in his little blue velvet smock, while Ellie is running after one of the dancing couples, trying to hold the man fast by his coat. It is Max Hergesell and Fräulein Plaichinger. They dance well, it is a pleasure to watch them. One has to admit that these mad modern dances, when the right people dance them, are not so bad after all—they have something quite taking. Young Hergesell is a capital leader, dances according to rule, yet with individuality. So it looks. With what aplomb can he walk backwards—when space permits! And he knows how to be graceful standing still in a crowd. And his partner supports him well, being unsuspectedly lithe and buoyant, as fat people

often are. They look at each other, they are talking, paying no heed to Ellie, though others are smiling to see the child's persistence. Dr. Cornelius tries to catch up his little sweetheart as she passes and draw her to him. But Ellie eludes him, almost peevishly; her dear Abel is nothing to her now. She braces her little arms against his chest and turns her face away with a persecuted look. Then escapes to follow her fancy once more.

The Professor feels an involuntary twinge. Uppermost in his heart is hatred for this party, with its power to intoxicate and estrange his darling child. His love for her—that not quite disinterested, not quite unexceptionable love of his—is easily wounded. He wears a mechanical smile, but his eyes have clouded, and he stares fixedly at a point in the carpet, between the dancers' feet.

"The children ought to go to bed," he tells his wife. But she pleads for another quarter of an hour; she has promised already, and they do love it so! He smiles again and shakes his head, stands so a moment and then goes across to the cloak-room, which is full of coats and hats and scarves and overshoes. He has trouble in rummaging out his own coat, and Max Hergesell comes out of the hall, wiping his brow.

"Going out, sir?" he asks, in Hergesellian accents, dutifully helping the older man on with his coat. "Silly business this, with my pumps," he says. "They pinch like hell. The brutes are simply too tight for me, quite apart from the bad leather. They press just here on the ball of my great toe"—he stands on one foot and holds the other in his hand—"it's simply unbearable. There's nothing for it but to take them off; my brogues will have to do the business. . . . Oh, let me help you, sir."

"Thanks," says Cornelius. "Don't trouble. Get rid of your own tormentors. . . . Oh, thanks very much!" For Hergesell has gone on one knee to snap the fasteners of his snowboots.

Once more the Professor expresses his gratitude; he is pleased and touched by so much sincere respect and youthful readiness to serve. "Go and enjoy yourself," he counsels. "Change your shoes and make up for what you have been suffering. Nobody can dance in shoes that pinch. Good-bye, I must be off to get a breath of fresh air."

"I'm going to dance with Ellie now," calls Hergesell after him. "She'll be a first-rate dancer when she grows up, and that I'll swear to."

"Think so?" Cornelius answers, already half out. "Well, you are a connoisseur, I'm sure. Don't get curvature of the spine with stooping."

He nods again and goes. "Fine lad," he thinks as he shuts the door. "Student of engineering. Knows what he's bound for, got a good clear head, and so well set up and pleasant too." And again paternal envy rises as he compares his poor Bert's status with this young man's, which he puts in the rosiest light that his son's may look the darker. Thus he sets out on his evening walk.

He goes up the avenue, crosses the bridge, and walks along the bank on the other side as far as the next bridge but one. The air is wet and cold, with a little snow now and then. He turns up his coat-collar and slips the crook of his cane over the arm behind his back. Now and then he ventilates his lungs with a long deep breath of the night air. As usual when he walks, his mind reverts to his professional preoccupations, he thinks about his lectures and the things he means to say to-morrow about Philip's struggle against the Germanic revolution, things steeped in melancholy and penetratingly just. Above all just, he thinks. For in one's dealings with the young it behoves one to display the scientific spirit, to exhibit the principles of enlightenment—not only for purposes of mental discipline, but on the human and individual side, in order not to wound them or indirectly offend their political sensibilities; particularly in these days, when there is so much tinder in the air, opinions are so frightfully split up and chaotic, and you may so easily incur attacks from one party or the other, or even give rise to scandal, by taking sides on a point of history. "And taking sides is unhistoric anyhow," so he muses. "Only justice, only impartiality is historic." And could not, properly considered, be otherwise. . . . For justice can have nothing of youthful fire and blithe, fresh, loyal conviction. It is by nature melancholy. And, being so, has secret affinity with the lost cause and the forlorn hope rather than with the fresh and blithe and loyal—perhaps this affinity is its very essence and without it it would not exist at all! . . . "And is there then no such thing as justice?" the Professor asks himself, and ponders the question so deeply that he absently posts his letters in the next box and turns round to go home. This thought of his is unsettling and disturbing to the scientific mind—but is it not after all itself scientific, psychological, conscientious, and therefore to be accepted without prejudice, no matter how upsetting? In the midst of which musings Dr. Cornelius finds himself back at his own door.

On the outer threshold stands Xaver, and seems to be looking for him.

"Herr Professor," says Xaver, tossing back his hair, "go upstairs to Ellie straight off. She's in a bad way."

"What's the matter?" asks Cornelius in alarm. "Is she ill?"

"No-o, not to say ill," answers Xaver. "She's just in a bad way and crying fit to bust her little heart. It's along o' that chap with the shirt-front that danced with her—Herr Hergesell. She couldn't be got to go upstairs peaceably, not at no price at all, and she's b'en crying bucketfuls."

"Nonsense," says the Professor, who has entered and is tossing off his things in the cloak-room. He says no more; opens the glass door and without a glance at the guests turns swiftly to the stairs. Takes them two at a time, crosses the upper hall and the small room leading into the nursery. Xaver follows at his heels, but stops at the nursery door.

A bright light still burns within, showing the gay frieze that runs all round the room, the large row of shelves heaped with a confusion of toys, the rocking-horse on his swaying platform, with red-varnished nostrils and raised hoofs. On the linoleum lie other toys—building blocks, railway trains, a little trumpet. The two white cribs stand not far apart, Ellie's in the window corner, Snapper's out in the room.

Snapper is asleep. He has said his prayers in loud, ringing tones, prompted by Nurse, and gone off at once into vehement, profound, and rosy slumber—from which a cannonball fired at close range could not rouse him. He lies with both fists flung back on the pillows on either side of the tousled head with its funny crooked little slumber-tossed wig.

A circle of females surrounds Ellie's bed: not only blue-faced Ann is there, but the Hinterhofer ladies too, talking to each other and to her. They make way as the Professor comes up and reveal the child sitting all pale among her pillows, sobbing and weeping more bitterly than he has ever seen her sob and weep in her life. Her lovely little hands lie on the coverlet in front of her, the nightgown with its narrow lace border has slipped down from her shoulder —such a thin, birdlike little shoulder—and the sweet head Cornelius loves so well, set on the neck like a flower on its stalk, her head is on one side, with the eyes rolled up to the corner between wall and ceiling above her head. For there she seems to envisage the anguish of her heart and even to nod to it—either on purpose or because her head wobbles as her body is shaken with the violence of her sobs. Her eyes rain down tears. The bow-shaped lips are parted, like a little *mater dolorosa's,* and from them issue long, low wails that in nothing resemble the unnecessary and exasperating shrieks of a naughty child, but rise from the deep extremity of her heart and wake in the Professor's own a sympathy that is well-nigh intolerable. He has never seen his darling so before. His feelings find immediate vent in an attack on the ladies Hinterhofer.

"What about the supper?" he asks sharply. "There must be a great deal to do. Is my wife being left to do it alone?"

For the acute sensibilities of the former middle class this is quite enough. The ladies withdraw in righteous indignation, and Xaver Kleingutl jeers at them as they pass out. Having been born to low life instead of achieving it, he never loses a chance to mock at their fallen state.

"Childie, childie," murmurs Cornelius, and sitting down by the crib enfolds the anguished Ellie in his arms. "What is the trouble with my darling?"

She bedews his face with her tears.

"Abel . . . Abel . . ." she stammers between sobs. "Why—isn't Max—my brother? Max ought to be—my brother!"

Alas, alas! What mischance is this? Is this

what the party has wrought, with its fatal atmosphere? Cornelius glances helplessly up at blue-faced Ann standing there in all the dignity of her limitations with her hands before her on her apron. She purses up her mouth and makes a long face. "It's pretty young," she says, "for the female instincts to be showing up."

"Hold your tongue," snaps Cornelius, in his agony. He has this much to be thankful for, that Ellie does not turn from him now; she does not push him away as she did downstairs, but clings to him in her need, while she reiterates her absurd, bewildered prayer that Max might be her brother, or with a fresh burst of desire demands to be taken downstairs so that he can dance with her again. But Max, of course, is dancing with Fräulein Plaichinger, that behemoth who is his rightful partner and has every claim upon him; whereas Ellie—never, thinks the Professor, his heart torn with the violence of his pity, never has she looked so tiny and birdlike as now, when she nestles to him shaken with sobs and all unaware of what is happening in her soul. No, she does not know. She does not comprehend that her suffering is on account of Fräulein Plaichinger, fat, overgrown, and utterly within her rights in dancing with Max Hergesell, whereas Ellie may only do it once, by way of a joke, although she is incomparably the more charming of the two. Yet it would be quite mad to reproach young Hergesell with the state of affairs or to make fantastic demands upon him. No, Ellie's suffering is without help or healing and must be covered up. Yet just as it is without understanding, so it is also without restraint—and that is what makes it so horribly painful. Xaver and blue-faced Ann do not feel this pain, it does not affect them—either because of native callousness or because they accept it as the way of nature. But the Professor's fatherly heart is quite torn by it, and by a distressful horror of this passion, so hopeless and so absurd.

Of no avail to hold forth to poor Ellie on the subject of the perfectly good little brother she already has. She only casts a distraught and scornful glance over at the other crib, where Snapper lies vehemently slumbering, and with fresh tears calls again for Max. Of no avail either the promise of a long, long walk to-morrow, all five gentlemen, round and round the dining-room table; or a dramatic description of the thrilling cushion games they will play. No, she will listen to none of all this, nor to lying down and going to sleep. She will not sleep, she will sit bolt upright and suffer. . . . But on a sudden they stop and listen, Abel and Ellie; listen to something miraculous that is coming to pass, that is approaching by strides, two strides, to the nursery door, that now over-whelmingly appears. . . .

It is Xaver's work, not a doubt of that. He has not remained by the door where he stood to gloat over the ejection of the Hinterhofers. No, he has bestirred himself, taken a notion; like-wise steps to carry it out. Downstairs he has gone, twitched Herr Hergesell's sleeve, and made a thick-lipped request. So here they both are. Xaver, having done his part, remains by the door; but Max Hergesell comes up to Ellie's crib; in his dinner-jacket, with his sketchy side-whisker and charming black eyes; obviously quite pleased with his rôle of swan knight and fairy prince, as one who should say: "See, here am I, now all losses are restored and sorrows end."

Cornelius is almost as much overcome as Ellie herself.

"Just look," he says feebly, "look who's here. This is uncommonly good of you, Herr Herge-sell."

"Not a bit of it," says Hergesell. "Why shouldn't I come to say good-night to my fair partner?"

And he approaches the bars of the crib, be-hind which Ellie sits struck mute. She smiles blissfully through her tears. A funny, high little note that is half a sigh of relief comes from her lips, then she looks dumbly up at her swan knight with her golden-brown eyes—tear-swollen though they are, so much more beautiful than the fat Plaichinger's. She does not put up her arms. Her joy, like her grief, is without under-standing; but she does not do that. The lovely little hands lie quiet on the coverlet, and Max Hergesell stands with his arms leaning over the rail as on a balcony.

"And now," he says smartly, "she need not 'sit the livelong night and weep upon her bed'!" He looks at the Professor to make sure he is

receiving due credit for the quotation. "Ha ha!" he laughs, "she's beginning young. 'Console thee, dearest child!' Never mind, you're all right! Just as you are you'll be wonderful! You've only got to grow up. . . . And you'll lie down and go to sleep like a good girl, now I've come to say good-night? And not cry any more, little Lorelei?"

Ellie looks up at him, transfigured. One birdlike shoulder is bare; the Professor draws the lace-trimmed nighty over it. There comes into his mind a sentimental story he once read about a dying child who longs to see a clown he had once, with unforgettable ecstasy, beheld in a circus. And they bring the clown to the bed-side marvellously arrayed, embroidered before and behind with silver butterflies; and the child dies happy. Max Hergesell is not embroidered, and Ellie, thank God, is not going to die, she has only "been in a bad way." But, after all, the effect is the same. Young Hergesell leans over the bars of the crib and rattles on, more for the father's ear than the child's, but Ellie does not know that—and the father's feelings towards him are a most singular mixture of thankful-ness, embarrassment, and hatred.

"Good night, little Lorelei," says Hergesell, and gives her his hand through the bars. Her pretty, soft, white little hand is swallowed up in the grasp of his big, strong, red one. "Sleep well," he says, "and sweet dreams! But don't dream about me—God forbid! Not at your age—ha ha!" And then the fairy clown's visit is at an end. Cornelius accompanies him to the door. "No, no, positively, no thanks called for, don't mention it," he large-heartedly protests; and Xaver goes downstairs with him, to help serve the Italian salad.

But Dr. Cornelius returns to Ellie, who is now lying down, with her cheek pressed into her flat little pillow.

"Well, wasn't that lovely?" he says as he smooths the covers. She nods, with one last little sob. For a quarter of an hour he sits beside her and watches while she falls asleep in her turn, beside the little brother who found the right way so much earlier than she. Her silky brown hair takes the enchanting fall it always does when she sleeps; deep, deep lie the lashes over the eyes that late so abundantly poured forth their sorrow; the angelic mouth with its bowed upper lip is peacefully relaxed and a little open. Only now and then comes a belated catch in her slow breathing.

And her small hands, like pink and white flowers, lie so quietly, one on the coverlet, the other on the pillow by her face—Dr. Cornelius, gazing, feels his heart melt with tenderness as with strong wine.

"How good," he thinks, "that she breathes in oblivion with every breath she draws! That in childhood each night is a deep, wide gulf between one day and the next. To-morrow, beyond all doubt, young Hergesell will be a pale shadow, powerless to darken her little heart. To-morrow, forgetful of all but present joy, she will walk with Abel and Snapper, all five gentlemen, round and round the table, will play the ever-thrilling cushion game."

Heaven be praised for that!

A Wife of Nashville

PETER TAYLOR (1917-   )

THE LOVELLS' old cook Sarah had quit to get married in the spring, and they didn't have anybody else for a long time—for several months, that is. It was during the depression, and when a servant quit, people in Nashville (and even people out at Thornton, where the Lovells came from) tried to see how long they could go before they got another. All through the summer, there would be knocks on the Lovells' front door or on the wooden porch floor, by the steps. And when one of the children or their mother went to the door, some Negro man or woman would be standing there, smiling and holding out a piece of paper. A recommendation it was supposed to be, but the illegible note scribbled with a blunt lead pencil was something no white person could have written if he had tried. If Helen Ruth, the children's mother, went to the door, she always talked awhile to whoever it was, but she hardly ever even looked at the note held out to her. She would give a piece of advice or say to meet her around at the back door for a handout. If one of the boys—there were three Lovell boys, and no girls—went to the door, he always brought the note in to Helen Ruth, unless John R., their father, was at home, sick with his back ailment. Helen Ruth would shake her head and say to tell whoever it was to go away, go away! "Tell him to go back home," she said once to the oldest boy, who was standing in the sun-parlor doorway with a smudged scrap of paper in his hand. "Tell him if he had any sense, he never would have left the country."

"He's probably not from the country, Mother."

"They're all from the country," Helen Ruth said. "When they knock on the porch floor like that, they're bound to be from the country, and they're better off at home, where somebody cares something about them. I don't care anything about them any more than you do."

But one morning Helen Ruth hired a cheerful-looking and rather plump, light-complexioned young Negress named Jess McGehee, who had come knocking on the front-porch floor just as the others had. Helen Ruth talked to her at the front door for a while; then she told her to come around to the kitchen, and they talked there for nearly an hour. Jess stayed to fix lunch and supper, and after she had been there a few days, the family didn't know how they had ever got along without her.

In fact, Jess got on so well with the Lovells that Helen Ruth even decided to let her come and live on the place, a privilege she had never before allowed a servant of hers. Together, she and Jess moved all of John R.'s junk—a grass duck-hunting outfit, two mounted stags' heads, an outboard motor, and so on—from the little room above the garage into the attic of the house. John R. lent Jess the money for the down payment on a "suit" of furniture, and

Jess moved in. "You would never know she was out there," Helen Ruth told her friends. "There is never any rumpus. And her room! It's as clean as yours or mine."

Jess worked for them for eight years. John R. got so one of his favorite remarks was "The honeymoon is over, but this is the real thing this time." Then he would go on about what he called Helen Ruth's "earlier affairs." The last one before Jess was Sarah, who quit to get married and go to Chicago at the age of sixty-eight. She was with them for six years and was famous for her pies and her banana dishes. Before Sarah, there was Carrie. Carrie had been with them when the two younger boys were born, and it was she who had once tried to persuade Helen Ruth not to go to the hospital but to let her act as midwife. She had quit them after five years, to become an undertaker. And before Carrie there was Jane Blakemore, the very first of them all, whom John R. and Helen Ruth had brought with them from Thornton to Nashville when they married. She lasted less than three years; she quit soon after John R., Jr., was born, because, she said, the baby made her nervous. "It's an honorable record," John R. would say. "Each of them was better than the one before, and each one stayed with us longer. It proves that experience is the best teacher."

Jess's eight years were the years when the boys were growing up; the boys were children when she came, and when she left them, the youngest, little Robbie, had learned to drive the car. In a sense, it was Jess who taught all three boys to drive. She didn't give them their first lessons, of course, because, like Helen Ruth, she had never sat at the wheel of an automobile in her life. She had not ridden in a car more than half a dozen times when she came to the Lovells, but just by chance, one day, she was in the car when John R. let John R., Jr., take the wheel. The car would jerk and lunge forward every time the boy shifted gears, and his father said, "Keep your mind on what you're doing."

"I am," John R., Jr., said, "but it just does that. What makes it do it?"

"Think!" John R. said. "Think! . . . *Think!*"

"*I am* thinking, but what makes it do it?"

Suddenly, Jess leaned forward from the back seat and said, "You letting the clutch out too fast, honey."

Both father and son were so surprised they could not help laughing. They laughed harder, of course, because what Jess said was true. And Jess laughed with them. When they had driven another block, they reached a boulevard stop, and in the process of putting on the brake John R., Jr., killed the engine and then flooded the motor. His father shouted, "Well, let it rest! We're just stuck here for about twenty minutes!"

Jess, who was seated with one arm around a big bag of groceries, began to laugh again. "Turn off the key," she said. "Press down on the starter a spell. Then torectly you turn on the key and she'll start."

John R. looked over his shoulder at her, not smiling but not frowning, either. Presently, he gave the order "Try it."

"Try what *Jess* said?" John R., Jr., asked.

"Try what Jess said."

The boy tried it, and in a moment he was racing the motor and grinning at his father. When they had got safely across the boulevard, John R. turned around to Jess again. He asked in a quiet, almost humble manner—the same manner he used when describing the pains in his back to Helen Ruth—where she had learned these things about an automobile. "Law," she said, "I learned them listening to my brother-in-law that drives a truck talk. I don't reckon I really know'm, but I can say them."

John R. was so impressed by the incident that he did not make it one of his stories. He told Helen Ruth about it, of course, and he mentioned it sometimes to his close friends when they were discussing "the good things" about Negroes. With his sons, he used it as an example of how much you can learn by listening to other people talk, and after that day he would permit John R., Jr., to go for drives in the car without him provided Jess went along in his place. Later on, when the other boys got old enough to drive, there were periods when he turned their instruction over to Jess. Helen Ruth even talked of learning to drive, herself, with the aid of Jess.

But it never came to more than talk with Helen Ruth, though John R. encouraged her, saying he thought driving was perhaps a serious strain on his back. She talked about it for several months, but in the end she said that the time had passed when she could learn new skills. When John R. tried to encourage her in the idea, she would sometimes look out one of the sun-parlor windows toward the street and think of how much she had once wanted to learn to drive. But that had been long ago, right after they were married, in the days when John R. had owned a little Ford coupé. John R. was on the road for the Standard Candy Company then, and during most of the week she was alone in their apartment at the old Vaux Hall. While he was away, John R. kept the coupé stored in a garage only two blocks east, on Broad Street; in those days travelling men still used the railroads, because Governor Peay hadn't yet paved Tennessee's highways. At that time, John R. had not believed in women's driving automobiles, and Helen Ruth had felt that he must be right about it; she had even made fun of women who went whizzing about town, blowing horns at every intersection. Yet in her heart she had longed to drive that coupé! Jane Blakemore was working for them then, and one day Jane had put Helen Ruth's longings into words. "Wouldn't it be dandy," she said, "if me and you clomb in that car one of these weekdays and toured out to Thornton to see all the folks—white and black?"

But without a moment's hesitation Helen Ruth gave the answer that she knew John R. would have given. "Now, *think* what you're saying, Jane!" she said. "Wouldn't we be a fool-looking pair pulling into the square at Thornton? *Think* about it. What if we should have a flat tire when we got out about as far as Nine Mile Hill? Who would change it? *You* certainly couldn't! Jane Blakemore, I don't think you use your head about anything!"

That was the way Helen Ruth had talked to Jane on more occasions than one. She was a plain-spoken woman, and she never spoke plainer to anyone than she did to Jane Blakemore during the days when they were shut up together in that apartment at the Vaux Hall.

Since Jane was from Thornton and knew how plain-spoken all Helen Ruth's family were, she paid little attention to the way Helen Ruth talked to her. She would smile, or else sneer, and go on with her work of cooking and cleaning. Sometimes she would rebel and speak just as plainly as Helen Ruth did. When Helen Ruth decided to introduce butter plates to their table, Jane said, "I ain't never heard tell of no butter dishes."

Helen Ruth raised her eyebrows. "That's because you are an ignoramus from Thornton, Tennessee," she said.

"I'm ignoramus enough to know ain't no need in nastying up all them dishes for me to wash."

Helen Ruth had, however, made Jane Blakemore learn to use butter plates and had made her keep the kitchen scrubbed and the other rooms of the apartment dusted and polished and in such perfect order that even John R. had noticed it when he came home on weekends. Sometimes he had said, "You drive yourself too hard, Helen Ruth."

Jess McGehee was as eager and quick to learn new things as Jane Blakemore had been unwilling and slow. She would even put finger bowls on the breakfast table when there was grapefruit. And how she did spoil the three boys about their food! There were mornings when she cooked eggs for each of them in a different way while John R. sat and shook his head in disgust at the way she pampered the boys. John R.'s "condition" in his back kept him at home a lot of the time during the eight years Jess was with them. He had long since left off travelling for the candy company; soon after the first baby came, he had opened an insurance agency of his own.

When Jane Blakemore left them and Helen Ruth hired Carrie (after fifteen or twenty interviews with other applicants), she had had to warn Carrie that John R.'s hours might be very irregular, because he was in business for himself and wasn't able merely to punch a time clock and quit when the day ended. "He's an onsurance man, ain't he?" Carrie had asked and had showed by the light in her eyes how favorably impressed she was. "I know about him," she had said. "He's the life-onsurance man, and that's the best kind to have."

At that moment, Helen Ruth thought perhaps she had made a mistake in Carrie. "I don't like my servant to discuss my husband's business," she said.

"No'm!" Carrie said with enthusiasm. "No, *Ma'am!*" Helen Ruth was satisfied, but often afterward she told herself that her first suspicion had been right. Carrie was nosy and prying and morbid—and she gossiped with other people's servants. Her curiosity and her gossiping were especially trying for Helen Ruth during her and John R.'s brief separation. They had actually separated for nearly two months right after Kenneth, the middle boy, was born. Helen Ruth had gone to her father's house at Thornton, taking the two babies and Carrie with her. The boys never knew about the trouble between their parents, of course, until Kenneth pried it out of his mother after they were all grown, and at the time people in Nashville and Thornton were not perfectly sure that it was a real separation. Helen Ruth tried to tell herself that perhaps Carrie didn't know it was a real separation. But she was never able to deny completely the significance of Carrie's behavior while they were at Thornton. Carrie's whole disposition had seemed to change the afternoon they left Nashville. Up till then, she had been a moody, shifty, rather loud-mouthed brown woman, full of darky compliments for white folks and of gratuitous promises of extra services she seldom rendered. But at Thornton she had put the old family servants to shame with her industriousness and her respectful, unassuming manner. "You don't find them like Carrie in Thornton any more," Helen Ruth's mother said. "The good ones all go to Nashville or Memphis." But Helen Ruth, sitting by an upstairs window one afternoon, saw her mother's cook and Carrie sauntering toward the back gate to meet a caller. She saw Carrie being introduced and then she recognized the caller as Jane Blakemore. Presently the cook returned to the kitchen and Helen Ruth saw Carrie and Jane enter the servants' house in the corner of the yard. During the hour that they visited there, Helen Ruth sat quietly by the window in the room

with her two babies. It seemed to her the most terrible hour of her separation from John R. When Carrie and Jane had reappeared on the stoop of the servants' house and Carrie was walking with Jane to the gate, there was no longer any doubt in Helen Ruth's mind but that she would return to her husband, and return without any complaints or stipulations. During that hour she had tried to imagine exactly what things the black Jane and the brown Carrie were talking about, or, rather, *how* and in what terms they were talking about the things they must be talking about. In her mind, she reviewed the sort of difficulties she had had with Jane and the sort she had with Carrie and tried to imagine what defense they would make for themselves—Jane for her laziness and contrariness, Carrie for her usual shiftiness and negligence. Would they blame her for these failings of theirs? Or would they blandly pass over their own failings and find fault with her for things that she was not even aware of, or that she could not help and could not begin to set right? Had she really misused these women, either the black one or the brown one? It seemed to her then that she had so little in life that she was entitled to the satisfaction of keeping an orderly house and to the luxury of efficient help. There was too much else she had not had—an "else" nameless to her, yet sorely missed—for her to be denied these small satisfactions. As she sat alone with her babies in the old nursery and thought of the two servants gossiping about her, she became an object of pity to herself. And presently John R., wherever he might be at that moment—in his office or at the club or, more likely, on a hunting or fishing trip somewhere—became an object of pity, too. And her two babies, one in his crib and the other playing on the carpet with a string of spools, were objects of pity. Even Carrie, standing alone by the gate after Jane had gone, seemed a lone and pitiful figure.

A few days later, Helen Ruth and Carrie and the two babies returned to Nashville.

In Nashville, Carrie was herself again; everything was done in her old slipshod fashion. Except during that interval at Thornton, Carrie was never known to perform any task to Helen Ruth's complete satisfaction. Hardly a meal came to the table without the soup or the dessert or some important sauce having been forgotten; almost every week something important was left out of the laundry; during a general cleaning the upper sashes of two or three windows were invariably left unwashed. Yet never in her entire five years did Carrie answer back or admit an unwillingness to do the most menial or the most nonessential piece of work. In fact, one of her most exasperating pronouncements was "You are exactly right," which was often followed by a lengthy description of how she would do the thing from then on, or an explanation of how it happened that she had forgotten to do it. Not only that, she would often undertake to explain to Helen Ruth Helen Ruth's reason for wanting it done. "You are exactly right, and I know how you mean. You want them drapes shut at night so it can seem like we're living in a house out in the Belle Meade instead of this here Vox Hall flat, and some fool might be able to look in from the yard."

"Never mind my reasons, Carrie," was Helen Ruth's usual answer. But her answers were not always so gentle—not when Carrie suggested that she have the second baby at home with Carrie acting as midwife, not when Carrie spoke to her about having the third baby circumcised. And the day that Helen Ruth began packing her things to go to Thornton, she was certain that Carrie would speak out of turn with some personal advice. That would have been more than she could bear, and she was prepared to dismiss Carrie from her service and make the trip alone. But neither then nor afterward did Carrie give any real evidence of understanding the reasons for the trip to Thornton.

In fact, it was not until long afterward, when Carrie had quit them to become an undertaker, that Helen Ruth felt that Carrie's gossip with other Nashville servants had, by accident, played a part in her separation from John R. She and John R. had talked of separation and a divorce more than once during the first two years they were married, in the era of Jane Blakemore. It was not that any quarrelling led to this talk but that each accused the other of being dissatisfied with their marriage. When

John R. came in from travelling, on a weekend or in the middle of the week—he was sometimes gone only two or three days at a time—he would find Helen Ruth sitting alone in the living room, without a book or even a deck of cards to amuse herself with, dressed perhaps in something new her mother had sent her, waiting for him. She would rise from her chair to greet him, and he would smile in frank admiration of the tall, graceful figure and of the countenance whose features seemed always composed, and softened by her hair, which was beginning to be gray even at the time of their marriage. But he had not come home many times before Helen Ruth was greeting him not with smiles but with tears. At first, he had been touched, but soon he began to complain that she was unhappy. He asked her why she did not see something of other people while he was away—the wives of his business and hunting friends, or some of the other Thornton girls who were married and living in Nashville. She replied that she did see them occasionally but that she was not the sort of woman who enjoyed having a lot of women friends. Besides, she was perfectly happy with her present life; it was only that she believed that he must be unhappy and that he no longer enjoyed her company. She understood that he had to be away most of the week, but even when he was in town, she saw very little of him. When he was not at his office, he was fishing out on Duck River or was off to a hunt up at Gallatin. And at night he either took her to parties with those hunting people, with whom she had nothing in common, or piled up on the bed after supper and slept. All of this indicated that he was not happy being married to her, she said, and so they talked a good deal about separating.

After the first baby came, there was no such talk for a long time—not until after the second baby. After the first baby came, Helen Ruth felt that their marriage must be made to last, regardless of her or John R.'s happiness. Besides, it was at that time that one of John R.'s hunting friends—a rich man named Rufus Brantley—had secured the insurance agency for him, and almost before John R. opened his office, he had sold policies to other hunting friends of his, among whom were the very richest men in Nashville. "Among the wealthiest in the whole South, for that matter," said John R. For a while, he was at home more than he had ever been before. But soon, when his business was established, he began to attend more and more meets and trials, all over Tennessee and Alabama and Kentucky. He even owned horses and dogs, which he kept at his friends' stables and kennels. And then his friends began to take him on trips to distant parts of the country. It seemed that when he was not deep-sea fishing in the Gulf, he was deerhunting in the State of Maine. Helen Ruth did sometimes go with him to the local horse shows, but one night, at the Spring Horse Show, she had told Mrs. Brantley that she had a new machine, and Mrs. Brantley had thought she meant an automobile, instead of a sewing machine. That, somehow, had been the last straw. She would never go out with "people like the Brantleys" after that. She was pregnant again before the first baby was a year old, and this soon became her excuse for going nowhere in the evening. The women she did visit with very occasionally in the daytime were those she had known as girls in Thornton, women whose husbands were bank tellers and office managers and were barely acquainted with John R. Lovell.

After the second baby came, Helen Ruth saw those women more frequently. She began to feel a restlessness that she could not explain in herself. There were days when she could not stay at home. With Carrie and the two babies, she would traipse about town, on foot or by streetcar, to points she had not visited since she was a little girl and was in Nashville with her parents to attend the State Fair or the Centennial. She went to the Capitol, to Centennial Park and the Parthenon, and even out to the Glendale Zoo. Once, with Nancy Lowder and Lucy Parkes, two of her old Thornton friends, she made an excursion to Cousin Mamie Lovell's farm, which was several miles beyond the town of Franklin. They went by the electric interurban to Franklin, and from there they took a taxi to the farm. Cousin Mamie's husband had been a second cousin of John R.'s father, and it was a connection the Thornton Lovells had once been very proud to claim. But for a generation this branch of the family had been in decline. Major Lovell had been a prominent lawyer in Franklin and had been in politics, but when he died, he left his family "almost penniless." His boys had not gone to college; since the farm was supposed to have been exhausted, they did not try to farm it but clerked in stores in Franklin. There was said to be a prosperous son-in-law in St. Louis, but the daughter was dead and Cousin Mamie was reported to have once called her son-in-law a parvenu to his face. Helen Ruth and her friends made the excursion because they wanted to see the house, which was one of the finest old houses in the county and full of antiques.

But Cousin Mamie didn't even let them inside the house. It was a hot summer day, and she had all the blinds closed and the whole L-shaped house shut up tight, so that it would be bearable at night. She received them on the long ell porch. Later, they moved their chairs out under a tree in the yard, where Cousin Mamie's cook brought them a pitcher of iced tea. While they were chatting under the tree that afternoon, they covered all the usual topics that are dealt with when talking to an old lady one doesn't know very well—the old times and the new times, mutual friends and family connections, country living and city living, and always, of course, the lot of woman as it relates to each topic.

"Where are you and John R. living?" Cousin Mamie asked Helen Ruth.

"We're still at the Vaux Hall, Cousin Mamie."

"I'd suppose the trains would be pretty bad for noise there, that close to the depot."

"They're pretty bad in the summer."

"I'd suppose you had a place out from town, seeing how often John R.'s name's in the paper as master of hounds here and horse judge there!"

"That's John R.'s life," Helen Ruth said, "not mine."

"He runs with a fine pack, I must say," said Cousin Mamie.

Nancy Lowder and Lucy Parkes nodded and smiled. Lucy said, "The swells of Nashville, Miss Mamie."

But Cousin Mamie said, "There was a day when they weren't the swells. Forty years ago, people like Major Lovell didn't know people like the Brantleys. I think the Brantleys quarried limestone, to begin with. I guess it don't matter, though, for when I was a girl in upper East Tennessee, people said the Lovells started as land speculators hereabouts and at Memphis. But I don't blame you for not wanting to fool with Brantleys, Helen Ruth."

"John R. and I each live our own life, Cousin Mamie."

"Helen Ruth is a woman with a mind of her own, Miss Mamie," Nancy Lowder said. "It's too bad more marriages can't be like theirs, each living their own life. Everyone admires it as a real achievement."

And Lucy Parkes said, "Because a woman's husband hunts is no reason for her to hunt, any more than because a man's wife sews is any reason for him to sew."

"Indeed not," Cousin Mamie said, actually paying little attention to what Lucy and Nancy were saying. Presently, she continued her own train of thought. "Names like Brantley and Partee and Havemeyer didn't mean a thing in this state even thirty years ago."

What Lucy and Nancy said about her marriage that day left Helen Ruth in a sort of daze and at the same time made her see her situation more clearly. She had never discussed her marriage with anybody, and hearing it described so matter-of-factly by these two women made her understand for the first time what a special sort of marriage it was and how unhappy she was in it. At the time, John R. was away on a fishing trip to Tellico Plains. She did not see him again before she took the babies and Carrie to Thornton. She sent a note to his office saying that she would return when he decided to devote his time to his wife and children instead of to his hounds and horses. While she was at Thornton, her letters from John R. made no mention of her note. He wrote about his business, about his hounds and horses, about the weather, and he always urged her to hurry home as soon as she had seen everybody and had a good visit. Meanwhile, he had a room at the Hermitage Club.

When Helen Ruth returned to Nashville,

their life went on as before. A year later, the third boy, Robbie, was born, and John R. bought a large bungalow on Sixteenth Avenue, not too far from the Tarbox School, where they planned to send the boys. Carrie was with them for three years after the separation, and though her work did not improve, Helen Ruth found herself making excuses for her. She began to attribute Carrie's garrulity to "a certain sort of bashfulness, or the Negro equivalent of bashfulness." And with the three small boys, and the yard to keep, too, there was so much more for Carrie to do than there had been before! Despite the excuses she made for her, Helen Ruth could see that Carrie was plainly getting worse about everything and that she now seemed to take pleasure in lying about the smallest, most unimportant things. But Helen Ruth found it harder and harder to confront Carrie with her lies or to reprimand her in any way.

During the last months before Carrie quit, she would talk sometimes about the nightwork she did for a Negro undertaker. To make Helen Ruth smile, she would report things she had heard about the mourners. Her job, Carrie always said, was to sweep the parlors after the funeral and to fold up the chairs. It was only when she finally gave notice to Helen Ruth that she told her what she professed was the truth. She explained that during all those months she had been learning to embalm. "Before you can get a certificate," she said, "you has to handle a bad accident, a sickness, a case of old age, a drowning, a burning, and a half-grown child or less. I been waiting on the child till last night, but now I'll be getting my certificate."

Helen Ruth would not even let Carrie go to the basement to get her hat and coat. "You send somebody for them," she said. "But *you*, you get off these premises, Carrie!" She was sincerely outraged by what Carrie had told her, and when she looked at Carrie's hands, she was filled with new horror. But something kept her from saying all the things that one normally said to a worthless, lying servant who had been guilty of one final outrage. "*Leave*, Carrie!" she said, consciously restraining herself. "*Leave* this place!" Carrie went out the kitchen door and down the driveway to the street, bareheaded, coatless, and wearing her kitchen slippers.

After Carrie, there was old Sarah, who stayed with them for six years and then quit them to get married and go to Chicago. Sarah was too old to do heavy work even when she first came, and before she had been there a week, John R. had been asked to help move the sideboard and to bring the ladder up from the basement. He said it seemed that every minute he was in the house, he was lifting or moving something that was too much for Sarah. Helen Ruth replied that perhaps she should hire a Negro man to help in the house and look after the yard. But John R. said no, he was only joking, he thought Sarah far and away the best cook they had ever had, and besides business conditions didn't look too good and it was no time to be taking on more help. But he would always add that he did not understand why Helen Ruth babied Sarah so. "From the first moment old Sarah set foot in this house, Helen Ruth has babied her," he would say to people in Helen Ruth's presence.

Sarah could neither read nor write. Even so, it took her only a short while to learn all Helen Ruth's special recipes and how to cook everything the way the Lovells liked it. For two weeks, Helen Ruth stayed in the kitchen with Sarah, reading to her from "How We Cook in Tennessee" and giving detailed instructions for every meal. It was during that time that her great sympathy for Sarah developed. Sarah was completely unashamed of her illiteracy, and it was this that first impressed Helen Ruth. She admired Sarah for having no false pride and for showing no resentment of her mistress's impatience. She observed Sarah's kindness with the children. And she learned from Sarah about Sarah's religious convictions and about her long, unhappy marriage to a Negro named Morse Wilkins, who had finally left her and gone up North.

While Sarah was working for them, John R. and Helen Ruth lived the life that Helen Ruth had heard her friends describe to John R.'s Cousin Mamie. It was not until after Sarah had come that Helen Ruth, recalling the afternoon at Cousin Mamie's, identified Lucy Parkes' words about a wife's sewing and a hus-

band's hunting as the very answer she had once given to some of Carrie's impertinent prying. That afternoon, the remark had certainly sounded familiar, but she had been too concerned with her own decision to leave her husband to concentrate upon anything so trivial. And after their reconciliation she tried not to dwell on the things that had led her to leave John R. Their reconciliation, whatever it meant to John R., meant to her the acceptance of certain mysteries—the mystery of his love of hunting, of his attraction to rich people, of his desire to maintain a family and home of which he saw so little, of his attachment to her, and of her own devotion to him. Her babies were now growing into little boys. She felt that there was much to be thankful for, not the least of which was a servant as fond of her and of her children as Sarah was. Sarah's affection for the three little boys often reminded Helen Ruth how lonely Sarah's life must be.

One day, when she had watched Sarah carefully wrapping up little Robbie in his winter play clothes before he went out to play in the snow, she said, "You love children so much, Sarah, didn't you ever have any of your own?"

Sarah, who was a yellow-skinned woman with face and arms covered with brown freckles, turned her gray eyes and fixed them solemnly on Helen Ruth. "Why, I had the cutest little baby you ever did see," she said, "and Morse went and killed it."

"Morse *killed* your baby?"

"He rolled over on it in his drunk sleep and smothered it in the bed."

After that, Helen Ruth would never even listen to Sarah when she talked about Morse, and she began to feel a hatred toward any and all of the men who came to take Sarah home at night. Generally, these men were the one subject Sarah did not discuss with Helen Ruth, and their presence in Sarah's life was the only serious complaint Helen Ruth made against her. They would come sometimes as early as four in the afternoon and wait on the back porch for Sarah to get through. She knew that Sarah was usually feeding one of them out of her kitchen, and she knew that Sarah was living with first one and then another of them, but when she told John R. she was going to put her foot down on it, he forbade her to do so. And so through nearly six years she tolerated this weakness of Sarah's. But one morning in the late spring Sarah told her that Morse Wilkins had returned from up North and that she had taken him back as her husband. Helen Ruth could not find anything to say for a moment, but after studying the large diamond on her engagement ring for a while she said, "My servant's private life is her own affair, but I give you warning now, Sarah, I want to see no more of your men friends—Morse or *any other*—on this place again."

From that time, she saw no more men on the place until Morse himself came, in a drunken rage, in the middle of a summer's day. Helen Ruth had been expecting something of the sort to happen. Sarah had been late to work several times during the preceding three weeks. She had come one morning with a dark bruise on her cheek and said she had fallen getting off the streetcar. Twice, Helen Ruth had found Sarah on her knees, praying, in the kitchen. The day Helen Ruth heard the racket at the back-porch door, she knew at once that it was Morse. She got up from her sewing machine and went directly to the kitchen. Sarah was on the back porch, and Morse was outside the screen door of the porch, which was hooked on the inside. He was a little old man, shrivelled up, bald-headed, not more than five feet tall, and of a complexion very much like Sarah's. Over his white shirt he wore a dark sleeveless sweater. "You come on home," he was saying as he shook the screen door.

Helen Ruth stepped to the kitchen door. "Is that her?" Morse asked Sarah, motioning his head toward Helen Ruth.

When Sarah turned her face around, her complexion seemed several shades lighter than Morse's. "I got to go," she said to Helen Ruth.

"No, Sarah, *he's* got to go. But *you* don't."

"He's gonna leave me again."

"That's the best thing that could happen to you, Sarah."

Sarah said nothing, and Morse began shaking the door again.

"Is he drunk, Sarah?" Helen Ruth asked.

"He's so drunk I don't know how he find his way here."

Helen Ruth went out onto the porch. "Now, you get off this place, and quick about it," she said to Morse.

He shook the screen door again. "You didn't make me come here, Mrs. Lovellel, and you can't make me leave, Mrs. Lovellel."

"*I* can't make you leave," Helen Ruth said at once, "but there's a bluecoat down on the corner who can."

Suddenly Sarah dropped to her knees and began praying. Her lips moved silently, and gradually she let her forehead come to rest on the top of the rickety vegetable bin. Morse looked at her through the screen, putting his face right against the wire. "Sarah," he said, "you come on home. You better come on now if you think I be there."

Sarah got up off her knees.

"I'm going to phone the police," Helen Ruth said, pretending to move toward the kitchen.

Morse left the door and staggered backward toward the driveway. "Come on, Sarah!" he shouted.

"I got to go," Sarah said.

"I won't let you go, Sarah!"

"She can't make you stay!" Morse shouted. "You better come on if you coming!"

"It will be the worst thing you ever did in your life, Sarah," said Helen Ruth. "And if you go with him, you can't ever come back here. He'll kill you someday, too—the way he did your baby."

Sarah was on her knees again, and Morse was out of sight but still shouting as he went down the driveway. Suddenly, Sarah was on her feet. She ran into the kitchen and on through the house to the front porch.

Helen Ruth followed, calling her back. She found Sarah on the front porch waving to Morse, who was halfway down the block, running in a zigzag down the middle of the street, still shouting at the top of his voice. Sarah cried out to him, "Morse! Morse!"

"Sarah!" Helen Ruth said.

"Morse!" Sarah cried again, and then she began mumbling words that Helen Ruth could not quite understand at the time. Afterward, going over it in her mind, Helen Ruth realized that what Sarah had been mumbling was "If I don't see you no more on this earth, Morse, I'll see you in Glory."

Sarah was with the Lovells for four more months, and then one night she called up on the telephone and asked John R., Jr., to tell his mother that she was going to get married to a man named Racecar and they were leaving for Chicago in the morning.

Jess McGehee came to them during the depression. Even before Sarah left the Lovells, John R. had had to give up all of his "activities" and devote his entire time to selling insurance. Rufus Brantley had shot himself through the head while cleaning a gun at his hunting lodge, and most of John R.'s other hunting friends were no longer rich men. The changes in their life had come so swiftly that Helen Ruth did not realize for a while what they meant in her relationship with John R. It seemed as though she woke up one day and discovered that she was not married to the same man. She found herself spending all her evenings playing Russian bank with a man who had no interest in anything but his home, his wife, and his three boys. Every night, he would give a brief summary of the things that had happened at his office or on his calls, and then he would ask her and the boys for an account of everything they had done that day. He took an interest in the house and the yard, and he and the boys made a lily pool in the back yard, and singlehanded he screened in the entire front porch. Sometimes he took the whole family to Thornton for a weekend, and he and Helen Ruth never missed the family reunions there in September.

In a sense, these were the happiest years of their married life. John R.'s business got worse and worse, of course, but since part of their savings were in the bank at Thornton that did not fail, they never had any serious money worries. Regardless of their savings, however, John R.'s loss of income and his having to give up his friends and his hunting wrought very real, if only temporary, changes in him. There were occasions when he would sit quietly and listen to his family's talk without correcting them or pointing out how foolish they were. He gave up saying "Think!" to the boys, and instead would say, "Now, let's see if we can't reason this thing out." He could never bring himself to ask for any sympathy from Helen Ruth for his various losses, but as it was during this time that he suffered so from the ailment in his back (he and Helen Ruth slept with boards under their mattress for ten years), the sympathy he got for his physical pain was more than sufficient. All in all, it was a happy period in their life, and in addition to their general family happiness they had Jess.

Jess not only cooked and cleaned, she planned the meals, did the marketing, and washed everything, from handkerchiefs and socks to heavy woollen blankets. When the boys began to go to dances, she even learned to launder their dress shirts. There was nothing she would not do for the boys or for John R. or for Helen Ruth. The way she idealized the family became the basis for most of the "Negro jokes" told by the Lovells during those years. In her room, she had a picture of the family, in a group beside the lily pool, taken with her own box Brownie; she had tacked it and also a picture of each of them on the wall above her washstand. In her scrapbook she had pasted every old snapshot and photograph that Helen Ruth would part with, as well as old newspaper pictures of John R. on horseback or with a record-breaking fish he had caught. She had even begged from Helen Ruth an extra copy of the newspaper notice of their wedding.

Jess talked to the family a good deal at mealtime, but only when they addressed her first and showed that they wanted her to talk. Her remarks were mostly about things that related to the Lovells. She told a sad story about a "very loving white couple" from Brownsville, her home town, who had been drowned in each other's arms when their car rolled off the end of a river ferry. The point of the story was that those two people were the same fine, loving sort of couple that John R. and Helen Ruth were. All three of the boys made good grades in school, and every month Jess would copy their grades in her scrapbook, which she periodically passed around for the family to appreciate. When Kenneth began to write stories and articles for his high-school paper, she would always borrow the paper overnight; soon it came out that she was copying everything he wrote onto the big yellow pages of her scrapbook.

After three or four years, John R. began to say that he thought Jess would be with them always and that they would see the day when the boys' children would call her "Mammy." Helen Ruth said that she would like to agree with him about that, but actually she worried, because Jess seemed to have no life of her own, which wasn't at all natural. John R. agreed that they should make her take a holiday now and then. Every summer, they would pack Jess off to Brownsville for a week's visit with her kinfolks, but she was always back in her room over the garage within two or three days; she said that her people fought and quarrelled so much that she didn't care for them. Outside her life with the Lovells, she had only one interest and only one friend. Her interest was the movies, and her friend was "the Mary who works for Mrs. Dunbar." Jess and Mary went to the movies together as often as three or four times a week, and on Sunday afternoons Mary came to see Jess or Jess went to see Mary, who lived over the Dunbars' garage. Jess always took along her scrapbook and her most recent movie magazines. She and Mary swapped movie magazines, and it was apparent from Jess's talk on Monday mornings that they also swapped eulogies of their white families.

Sometimes Helen Ruth would see Mrs. Dunbar downtown or at a P.T.A. meeting; they would discuss their cooks and smile over the reports that each had received of the other's family. "I understand that your boys are all growing into very handsome men," Mrs. Dunbar said once, and she told Helen Ruth that Jess was currently comparing one of the boys —Mrs. Dunbar didn't know which one—to Neil Hamilton, and that she was comparing Helen Ruth to Irene Rich, and John R. to Edmund Lowe. As the boys got older, they began to resent the amount of authority over them— though it was small—that Jess had been allowed by their parents and were embarrassed if anyone said Jess had taught them to drive the car. When John R., Jr., began at the University, he made his mother promise not to let Jess know what grades he received, and none of the boys would let Jess take snapshots of them any more. Their mother tried to comfort Jess by saying that the boys were only going through a phase and that it would pass in time. One day, she even said this in the presence of Robbie, who promptly reported it to the older boys, and it ended with John R., Jr.'s, complaining to his father that their mother ought not to make fun of them to Jess. His father laughed at him but later told Helen Ruth that he thought she was making a mistake.

She didn't make the same mistake again, but though Jess never gave any real sign of her feelings' being hurt, Helen Ruth was always conscious of how the boys were growing away from their good-natured servant. By the time Robbie was sixteen, they had long since ceased to have any personal conversation with Jess, and nothing would have induced Robbie to submit to taking drives with her but the knowledge that his father would not allow him to use the car on dates until he had had months of driving practice. Once, when Robbie and Jess returned from a drive, Jess reported, with a grin, that not a word had passed between them during the entire hour and a half. Helen Ruth only shook her head sadly. But the next day she bought Jess a new bedside radio.

The radio was the subject of much banter among the boys and their father. John R. said Helen Ruth had chosen the period of hard times and the depression to become more generous with her servant than she had ever been before in her life. They recalled other presents she had given Jess recently, and from that time on they teased her regularly about how she spoiled Jess. John R. said that if Jess had had his back trouble, Helen Ruth would have retired her at double pay and nursed her with twice the care that he received. The boys teased her by saying that at Christmas time she reversed the custom of shopping for the servant at the ten-cent stores and for the family at the department stores.

Yet as long as Jess was with them, they all agreed that she was the best help they had ever had. In fact, even afterward, during the war years, when John R.'s business prospered again and his back trouble left him entirely and the boys were lucky enough to be stationed near home and, later, continue their education at government expense, even then John R. and the boys would say that the years when Jess was with them were the happiest time of their life and that Jess was the best servant Helen Ruth had ever had. They said that, and then there would be a silence, during which they were probably thinking about the summer morning just before the war when Jess received a telephone call:

When the telephone rang that morning, Helen Ruth and John R. and the boys had just sat down to breakfast. As usual in the summertime, they were eating at the big drop-leaf table in the sun parlor. Jess had set the coffee urn by Helen Ruth's place and was starting from the room when the telephone rang. Helen Ruth, supposing the call was for a member of the family, and seeing that Jess lingered in the doorway, said for her to answer it there in the sun parlor instead of running to the telephone in the back hall.

Jess answered it, announcing whose residence it was in a voice so like Helen Ruth's that it made the boys grin. For a moment, everyone at the table kept silent. They waited for Jess's eyes to single out one of them. John R., Jr., and Kenneth even put down their grapefruit spoons. But the moment Jess picked up the instrument, she fixed her eyes on the potted fern on the window seat across the room. At once her nostrils began to twitch, her lower lip fell open, and it seemed only by an act of will that she was twice able to say "Yes, Ma'am," in answer to the small, metallic voice.

When she had replaced the telephone on its cradle, she turned quickly away and started into the dining room. But Helen Ruth stopped her. "Jess," she asked, her voice full of courtesy, "was the call for you?"

Jess stopped, and they all saw her hands go to her face. Without turning around, she leaned against the doorjamb and began sobbing aloud. Helen Ruth jumped up from the table, saying, "Jess, honey, what *is* the matter?" John R. and the boys stood up, too.

"It was a telegram for me—from Brownsville."

Helen Ruth took her in her arms. "Is someone dead?"

Between sobs, Jess answered, "My little brother—our baby brother—the only one of 'em I cared for." Then her sobs became more violent.

Helen Ruth motioned for John R. to move the morning paper from the big wicker chair, and she led Jess in that direction. But Jess would not sit down, and she could not be pulled away from Helen Ruth. She held fast to her, and Helen Ruth continued to pat her gently on the back and to try to console her with gentle words. Finally, she said, "Jess, you must go to Brownsville. Maybe there's been some mistake. Maybe he's not dead. But you must go, anyway."

Presently, Jess did sit in the chair, and dried her eyes on Helen Ruth's napkin. The boys shook their heads sympathetically and John R. said she certainly must go to Brownsville. She agreed, and said she believed there was a bus at ten that she would try to catch. Helen Ruth patted her hand, telling her to go along to her room when she felt like it, and said that *she* would finish getting breakfast.

"I want to go by to see Mary first," Jess said, "so I better make haste." She stood up, forcing a grateful smile. Then she burst into tears again and threw her arms about Helen Ruth, mumbling, "Oh, God! Oh, God!" The three boys and their father saw tears come into Helen Ruth's eyes, and through her tears Helen Ruth saw a change come over their faces. It was not exactly a change of expression. It couldn't be that, she felt, because it was exactly the same on each of the four faces. It hardly seemed possible that so similar a change could reflect four men's individual feelings. She concluded that her own emotion, and probably the actual tears in her eyes, had made her imagine the change, and when Jess now pulled away and hurried off to her room, Helen Ruth's tears had dried and she could see no evidence of the change she had imagined in her husband's and her sons' faces.

While Jess was in her room preparing to leave, they finished breakfast. Then Helen

Ruth began clearing the table, putting the dishes on the teacart. She had said little while they were eating, but in her mind she was all the while going over something that she knew she must tell her family. As she absent-mindedly stacked the dishes, her lips even moved silently over the simple words she would use in telling them. She knew that they were watching her, and when Robbie offered to take Jess to the bus station, she knew that the change she had seen in all their faces had been an expression of sympathy for *her* as well as of an eagerness to put this whole episode behind them. "I'll take Jess to her bus," he said.

But Helen Ruth answered, in the casual tone she had been preparing to use, that she thought it probably wouldn't be the thing to do.

"Why, what do you mean, Helen Ruth?" John R. asked her.

"It was very touching, Mother," Kenneth said in his new, manly voice, "the way she clung to you." He, too, wanted to express sympathy, but he also seemed to want to distract his mother from answering his father's question.

At that moment, Jess passed under the sun-parlor windows, walking down the drive-way, carrying two large suitcases. Helen Ruth watched her until she reached the sidewalk. Then, very quietly, she announced to her family that Jess had no baby brother and had never had one. "Jess and Mary are leaving for California. They think they're going to find themselves jobs out there."

"You knew that right along?" John R. asked.

"I knew it right along."

"Did she know you did, Helen Ruth?" he asked. His voice had in it the sternness he used when questioning the boys about something.

"No, John R., she did not. I didn't learn it from her."

"Well, I don't believe it's so," he said. "Why, I don't believe that for a minute. Her carrying-on was too real."

"They're going to California. They've already got their two tickets. Mrs. Dunbar got wind of it somehow, by accident, from Mrs. Lon Thompson's cook, and she called me on Monday. They've saved their money and they're going."

"And you let Jess get away with all that crying stuff just now?" John R. said.

Helen Ruth put her hands on the handle bar of the teacart. She pushed the cart a little way over the tile floor but stopped when he repeated his question. It wasn't to answer his question that she stopped, however. "Oh, my dears!" she said, addressing her whole family. Then it was a long time before she said anything more. John R. and the three boys remained seated at the table, and while Helen Ruth gazed past them and toward the front window of the sun parlor, they sat silent and still, as though they were in a picture. What could she say to them, she kept asking herself. And each time she asked the question, she received for answer some different memory of seemingly unrelated things out of the past twenty years of her life. These things presented themselves as answers to her question, and each of them seemed satisfactory to her. But how little sense it would make to her husband and her grown sons, she reflected, if she should suddenly begin telling them about the long hours she had spent waiting in that apartment at the Vaux Hall while John R. was on the road for the Standard Candy Company, and in the same breath should tell them about how plainly she used to talk to Jane Blakemore and how Jane pretended that the baby made her nervous and went back to Thornton. Or suppose she should abruptly remind John R. of how ill at ease the wives of his hunting friends used to make her feel and how she had later driven Sarah's worthless husband out of the yard, threatening to call a bluecoat. What if she should suddenly say that because a woman's husband hunts, there is no reason for *her* to hunt, any more than because a man's wife sews, there is reason for him to sew. She felt that she would be willing to say anything at all, no matter how cruel or absurd it was, if it would make them understand that everything that happened in life only reflected in some way the loneliness of people. She was ready to tell them about sitting in the old nursery at Thornton and waiting for Carrie and Jane Blakemore to come out of the cabin in the yard. If it would make them see what she had been so long in learning to see, she would even talk at last about the "so much else" that had been missing from her life and that she had not been able to name, and about the foolish mysteries she had so nobly accepted upon her reconciliation with John R. To her, these things were all one now; they were her loneliness, the loneliness from which everybody, knowingly or unknowingly, suffered. But she knew that her husband and her sons did not recognize her loneliness or Jess's or their own. She turned her eyes from the window to look at their faces around the table, and it was strange to see that they were still thinking in the most personal and particular terms of how they had been deceived by a servant, the ignorant granddaughter of an ignorant slave, a Negro woman from Brownsville who was crazy about the movies and who would soon be riding a bus, mile after mile, on her way to Hollywood, where she might find the friendly faces of the real Neil Hamilton and the real Irene Rich. It was with effort that Helen Ruth thought again of Jess's departure and the problem of offering an explanation to her family. At last, she said patiently, "My dears, don't you see how it was for Jess? How else can they tell us anything when there is such a gulf?" After a moment she said, "How can I make you understand this?"

Her husband and her three sons sat staring at her, their big hands, all so alike, resting on the breakfast table, their faces stamped with identical expressions, not of wonder but of incredulity. Helen Ruth was still holding firmly to the handle of the teacart. She pushed it slowly and carefully over the doorsill and into the dining room, dark and cool as an underground cavern, and spotlessly clean, the way Jess McGehee had left it.

POETRY

Introduction

There are so many misconceptions about poetry that any general statement on the subject, however short, must deal with them. First, then, what are some of the qualities which poetry does not have? It is not by nature soft or effeminate or remote from human experience. There is a great deal of bad poetry, of course, which exhibits these traits, just as there is a great deal of fiction and drama which exhibits them too; but such qualities are not typical of poetry any more than typical of fiction and drama. Moreover, poetry does not necessarily have to do with merely "poetic" subject matter, sheep grazing on a moonlit slope or the dawn just breaking over Mont Blanc or the first tremulous kiss of young love. Furthermore, poetry does not necessarily employ what are usually thought of as "poetic" words. Shakespeare, for instance, finds it necessary to use many words which many people would not regard as "nice," much less "poetic." The objection to the usual definition of poetry as "elevated thoughts expressed in beautiful language" is not only that it is too vague but also that it leads to this very misconception: *i.e.,* that poetry is limited to a special subject matter and a special vocabulary.

Our best approach to poetry is to regard it as we regard other forms of literature: that is, as the expression of a man's feelings and ideas about experience in such a form that his "vision" of the world is available to others, can be communicated to them. Some of the ways in which good poetry differs from bad poetry and bad literature in general have already been discussed in the "General Introduction." Good poetry, like all good literature, will attempt to avoid certain faults: sentimentality, the use of stock responses, worn-out comparisons, *clichés,* etc. But wherein does the good poem differ from, say, a good short story? This is the type of question which we must at least hold in mind here, even if we cannot finally answer it.

In the "General Introduction" we used Browning's poem, "Porphyria's Lover," in order to make the distinction in general terms between good literature and bad. We may use the same poem, however, to make the distinction which exists between poetry as a form of literature and the other forms. Suppose we compare this poem with other possible literary treatments of the same situation.

The first thing which one will notice in making such a comparison is that the poem is much *shorter* than any story or play based on the same situation could possibly be, and of course far shorter than any novel. We can make this perfectly plain if we reduce Browning's poem to a prose paraphrase:

I listened with breaking heart to the storm outside the cottage. As I listened, Porphyria glided into the room. She shut the door behind her, knelt by the grate and made up the fire. Then she took off her wet shawl and soiled gloves and her hat, and sat down beside me, calling my name, but I did not answer. She put her arm around my waist, and with her loosened yellow hair flowing about her, she pulled my cheek down against her bare shoulder, and told me how much she loved me. She was too weak to give up everything for me. I knew that. But tonight at the ball she had not been able to keep out of her mind the thought of me sitting here, pale and alone. And so she had come to me. I was happy and proud because I knew at last that Porphyria loved me, and I wondered what to do to keep her as she was at that moment. Therefore, I wound a cord of her yellow hair three times around her throat and strangled her. I am certain that she felt no pain, for, when I warily opened her eyes, their expression was quite normal. After my kisses brought the color back to her cheek, I propped her head on my shoulder. In this way we have both gained what we really wanted, and so we have sat here all night together without receiving any sign of God's displeasure.

In paraphrasing the poem, we have removed the verse and rhyme, and we have omitted the comparisons, but the paraphrase represents substantially all the detail represented in the poem, and in substantially the same order. The paraphrase obviously could not stand as a short story in its own right. The artist who wanted to turn it into a short story which would give an effect comparable to that given by the poem would have to alter it a great deal, and certainly one feels that he would have to *add things* here omitted—he would have to *expand* it, and give some of the detail of actuality which sometimes seems so irrelevant and, finally, so significant. As it stands, the paraphrase represents little more than an anecdote, not a story at all.

INTENSIFICATION AND CONCENTRATION

The first point that we notice then in our comparison is the relative concentration of the poem as compared with the story or play that might be based upon this situation. This is not to say, of course, that a poem is always shorter than a short story which deals with the same situation, or that on the other hand there may not be very fine long poems like Milton's *Paradise Lost,* for example. And it is not to say, of course, that the effect gained from the poem would ever be *exactly* the same as that gained from some other form. But a poem can give a *comparable* effect, that is, can provoke a significant emotional response in the reader, in much fewer words than can usually a story or play; and this fact points to a most important characteristic of the poetic method: it tends toward intensification and concentration.

If we compare the method of the poem with that of the story, we shall see that the poem tends to employ less detail than would the story; but, correspondingly, there is more emphasis on form or arrangement of the details in the poem. In other words, if the poet tends to use a smaller number of details, he must select them even more carefully, and must arrange them so as to get the maximum effect from them. The circumstance in the poem is relatively slight, therefore; the pattern of arrangement or the form, relatively complex.

The emphasis on figurative language in poetry may be interpreted as an aspect of the tendency toward concentration and intensification. That is, in poetry not only the denotations of words are important but the connotations as well. Consequently, since the poet is trying to

use all the qualities of his words, he often employs comparisons, for comparisons, as we shall see, allow us to depart further and further from the strict meaning of the word and at the same time concentrate and condense those additional meanings with the obvious ones. And this concentration and condensation gives that special flashing excitement of discovery which we think of as poetic.

We may set down then three items in our list of the special kinds of emphasis of the poetic method:

1. Selectivity
2. Form
3. Figurative language

Notice that in stating that poetry tends to stress these items we are not cutting off poetry from the other forms of literature by an impassable chasm. *Any* writer must select his detail—he cannot get down on paper all the possible infinite welter of detail, even if he wants to. *Any* writer imposes a form on his material—he cannot leave it in the meaningless disarrangement which it often seems to have in life. *Any* writer may make use of figurative language. But it is fair to say, as a preliminary and perhaps provisional statement, that the poetic method stresses these matters to a relatively higher degree than does any other method.

This emphasis on form, as we have seen, manifests itself in all aspects of poetry; but in one aspect, that of rhythm, it is so prominent that the student may have come to feel that this is the primary distinction of poetry. The use of measured rhythms or verse is, however, only one feature of poetry, and it may be wiser to postpone an examination of it, important as it is, for a few pages while we examine some other aspects of form.

If poetry represents a concentration and intensification of experience which depends upon an emphasis on the formal qualities of the poem, it is interesting to see how these formal qualities allow for condensation and how they aid in the business of intensification. In the paraphrase of "Porphyria's Lover" we carefully removed most of them, including the verse form, with the result that the paraphrase was robbed of nearly all force. How do some of these qualities of form function?

If, after reading Browning's poem, we compare our impressions of the room in the cottage with the actual details which have been given, we shall be surprised to see how few those details are. They have been carefully chosen to give an atmosphere. They *suggest* things in addition to themselves. For example, the storm outside which the poet intimates was possessed of a special quality of spite and vindictiveness, and the cold grate inside the cottage give an effect of a bleak and perhaps bare room—an effect which is vivid enough, but which is not based, we realize, on any detailed description of the room itself.

The descriptive details have also been chosen for their value in revealing to us the mood of the dominant character, and they thus help us to understand the motivation of the murder which he is to commit: In the "General Introduction" we pointed out the importance, in the poet's account of the murderer's motivation, of the murderer's emotional detachment from the normal world of right and wrong— and even from reality. We shall see that even the first details given in the poem prepare us for this feeling of isolation so that we, along with the lover himself, accept it. For example Porphyria's closing the door and shutting "the cold out and the storm" give the feeling of shutting out not only the cold but the whole normal world in which we live. The cottage becomes something isolated and apart from the real world of affairs—it becomes the small, private world of devotion which exists between the man and the woman. And Porphyria's act of stirring up the fire gives by a sort of comparison what spiritually she does for the man. The fire warms the room, and she warms her lover by her presence; and in warming him, in making him realize what happiness could be like, signs her own death warrant. If one objects that a person reading the poem could not possibly read all this into the lines in question, one must agree. But it is necessary to remember that such feelings given perhaps *unconsciously,* given only vaguely, are nevertheless a very powerful preparation for what follows, and that this unconscious preparation makes the latter part of the poem stir us with a much greater intensity than if the preparation were lacking. We must remember, in fact, as we analyze all sorts of poems that many of the most powerful means which the poet uses to influence us often accomplish their work without our being aware of them.

The form of poetry, then, is very closely knit, and in this poem details apparently so trivial as the description of the room are tied very tightly to the core of the poem.

In the "General Introduction" we have already pointed out how the arrangement of the details of the actual killing are calculated to imply the state of mind of the murderer: the methodical, calm, and apparently reasoned process of his mind. We noticed in the same place how important is the comparison which the poet uses here:

> As a shut bud that holds a bee,
> I warily oped her lids . . .

We pointed out the action referred to as that appropriate to the mischievous curiosity of a small boy—not that of a mature man; and that to intimate that the murderer could think of his murder in this way is to let us see, vividly and concretely, that his act as he committed it was not murder at all.

FIGURATIVE LANGUAGE

If one will reread the paraphrase of the poem from which this comparison was omitted, and then read the section in the poem in which it occurs, he will see how very important the comparison is. The case under discussion here is typical of poetry in general. Poets are continually using figures of speech, to make their most powerful and fundamental points. It is one of their most important devices for gaining intensity and concentration.

If this is true, we must perhaps revise some of our conceptions about the function of figurative language in poetry. At least we must make certain that we do not continue to entertain a widespread misconception of the use of figurative language which may prevent us from seeing the real service that figurative language renders. Figurative language is not used to give a pretty surface, though it may do so on occasion.

But even when it seems merely decorative, it often accomplishes something else more fundamental. Let us take, for example, a very famous and much admired passage from Shakespeare. It is a passage spoken by Macbeth upon hearing of the death of his wife:

> Tomorrow, and tomorrow, and tomorrow,
> Creeps in this petty pace from day to day,
> To the last syllable of recorded time;
> And all our yesterdays have lighted fools
> The way to dusty death. Out, out, brief candle;
> Life's but a walking shadow; a poor player,
> That struts and frets his hour upon the stage,
> And then is heard no more: it is a tale
> Told by an idiot, full of sound and fury,
> Signifying nothing.

Of the various things used in this passage for the purpose of comparison, only one, the candle, might be termed "pretty." And most of the other things, the idiot or the poor player, would be regarded as definitely ugly or unpleasant. The stories that idiots tell are not pretty, but this passage of poetry is universally recognized as one of the high points of Shakespeare's poetry. Therefore, if we can discover what general and fundamental function the figurative language serves in this case, we may arrive at a statement of the real purpose of figurative language in poetry.

All language is at basis figurative, of course; and we use all the time in our speech many terms which are clearly figurative in their origin. Thus we speak of the *eye* of a needle or the *mouth* of a river. We do not, of course, think of these objects as being eyes or mouths in any human sense as we use the terms today, but clearly the terms originated because the small hole in the needle was thought to be like a human eye and the entrance of a river like a human mouth.

In saying that all language is at basis figurative, we come very close to saying that at basis all language is *poetic*. It will be easy to show why. We have already said that poetry tends toward concentration and intensification. But so does figurative language, particularly when the images are not worn-out but fresh and new. Compare the two statements: "He is a distinctly unpleasant fellow," and "He is a swine." The latter is much sharper and more emphatic. It carries more force because it implies the figure of a hog with all the unpleasant attributes of a hog. But figures of speech, comparisons, are used of course sometimes, not because they carry a strong emotional coloring, but because they may be employed to make an idea clearer. For example, the author of a textbook in science may say that the human body is like a machine. He is interested in having the student see that the body derives energy from the food which it assimilates just as the machine derives energy from the fuel it burns. He uses the figure of the machine, therefore, as an *illustration*. Here, obviously, the author is not concerned with imparting an attitude, a feeling, at all. He is anxious merely to communicate an idea.

Now as we have seen, poetry, along with literature in general, differs from science in that it is interested, not in the communication of ideas merely, but of ideas *and* feelings about the ideas—or rather a fusion of the two in a heightened sense of meaningful life. The poet will be interested therefore in choosing comparisons which not only will state ideas but will carry feelings about the ideas. As a matter of fact, almost any comparison which we can think of does carry with it a feeling. Even the comparison of the body to a machine is not *mere* illustration of idea. It is colored by a certain kind of feeling. To compare the body to a tree rather than to a machine carries with it a certain change of feeling as well as of idea.

In addition to this function of *illustration*, critics sometimes speak of the function of *ornamentation*. For example, when the poet says

O my love is like a red, red rose

he attributes to his love the beauty and freshness of the flower. Poets often use comparisons thus to ennoble and dignify the things of which they speak. But they do not, as we have seen in the passage from *Macbeth*, always use comparisons to *ennoble* and *dignify*. This is only one aspect of the use of figurative language to influence our feelings about some object or idea. Indeed, the *general* function of the comparison of the girl to a rose is quite the same as that of the comparison of the man to a swine in such a statement of disgust as "He is a swine." The *general* function of both comparisons is to influence our feelings about, or attitude toward, the subjects under treatment, to heighten our awareness of the nature of the subject.

The passage quoted earlier from *Macbeth* will indicate how the poet uses a comparison to communicate not only idea but feeling, and feeling not restricted to the relatively narrow scope which it has in primarily decorative or ornamental comparisons. Macbeth says that life is a tale told by an idiot. Why? The idea of course is that life is meaningless. Macbeth feels, as his wife dies and all his plans begin to go to pieces, that life is meaningless. What else does the comparison tell us which the statement, "life is meaningless," would not?

In the first place, the picture of the idiot, raging and gibbering meaningless syllables, adds a horror and loathsomeness to the statement. It gives us something of the horror which Macbeth feels at his discovery that life has no meaning. But the figure also tells us more accurately than the mere abstract statement does just what kind of horror Macbeth feels. Though we do not expect a beast to utter intelligible speech, we do expect intelligible speech—a statement that has a meaning—from a human being. The incoherence of the idiot has a special horror, therefore, for the idiot is, after all, a human being. The idiot's babbling is felt, thus, as a hideous travesty on human nature. Macbeth feels, as do all human beings, that life *ought* to have a meaning. His horror at finding that his own life does not is therefore the sort of horror which one might feel at the babbling of an idiot.

It should be clear that the function of the comparison in the case just discussed is not merely that of making an idea clearer and simpler (the function of mere illustration); the poet is using his comparison in order to form and make expressible something which otherwise would not be available to the reader. This function of *intrinsic communication* (the communication of idea *plus* the attitude toward and feeling about the idea by means of embodiment in an image) is the great primary function of figurative language. It is perhaps because of this that we sometimes say that it is impossible to transpose what a good poet says into prose—that is, it is impossible to give the experience in any way other than by reading the poetry itself.

CLASSIFICATION OF FIGURATIVE LANGUAGE

Figurative language may be classified, for the sake of convenience in discussion, in a number of different ways. Two of the most common classifications are called the *simile* and the *metaphor*. A simile is a comparison announced by the use of *like* or *as*. For example:

> The Sea. . . .
> Lay like the folds of a bright girdle furl'd. . . .
>
> And we are here as on a darkling plain
> Swept with confused alarms of struggle and
>   flight. . . .
>   ("Dover Beach," ARNOLD)

A metaphor, however, is a comparison which is not announced, but appears in the form of an identification of one object with another. For example:

> Life's but a walking shadow
>   (*Macbeth,* SHAKESPEARE)

We have just said what comparisons in poetry (and in any other form of literature) accomplish for us. But on what grounds do we accept these comparisons? A comparison, we know, implies a similarity between the things compared. What is the nature of this similarity?

We know that a scientist, a botanist let us say, classifies the objects he deals with because of certain similarities. These similarities are not necessarily similarities of appearance, but depend on structure. For instance, the botanist classifies the grape or the tomato as a berry and the raspberry as an aggregate fruit. The botanist has discovered a system by which all plant life can be classified. But the writer has no such ready-made system for dealing with the similarities on which his comparisons are based. As we have already suggested, the use of figurative language in poetry is to convey feeling and attitude, but the scientist in making his system of similarities is absolutely unconcerned with this function; he is merely defining relationships of structure.

Since the poet, let us say, is not dealing with a fixed system, the similarities he embodies in his comparisons may be of many different kinds. For instance, in comparing his love to a red rose, Burns was dealing with the quality of freshness and fragility which was possessed by both the woman and the flower. He would never have maintained for a moment that they were alike in appearance. To take a more complicated case, notice the similarity found by Macbeth between life and the tale told by an idiot. In general, the poet is continually seizing upon some similarity of this sort and pointing it out to us, and the acceptability of the similarity in the final sense must be judged in the light of the poet's whole intention in the poem. A poet is not compelled to use similarities that strike us at first glance as clear and obvious, but he is compelled to prove to us that the similarity, in the sense in which he is using it, is a good one. Perhaps no one had ever thought of the similarity between life and the babblings of an idiot before Shakespeare wrote it down, but after we read the play and know how Macbeth's life had come to ruin, we know that the comparison is a good one. The great imaginative comparisons in poetry strike us with a sense of freshness—may even startle or shock us—and yet we feel, at the same time, that they ring true. To summarize all this, we may say that the pointing out of these similarities is one of the fundamental exercises of the imagination. The great poets are always pointing out connections and relationships in experience that other people never see—putting our experience into a pattern, into a form, so it comes to possess meaning.

Closely related to this imaginative use of figurative language, is the use of symbols. For if the metaphor is the identification of one thing with another, the symbol is the use of some concrete object which stands for something else, as the tiger in Blake's poem (p. 315) stands for the awesome and terrible energies of the universe. The artist seeks, or creates, symbols adequate to his vision of life. The principal characters in any really great story or novel or play, for example, always have a certain symbolic force. Poetry, then, with its insistence on metaphorical language and on symbolism is not an eccentric form of literature lying somewhere on the remote outskirts of fiction and drama, but is a form that lies very close to the heart of all literature—may even be said to be literature in a very pure and concentrated form.

The Basis of Verse in Human Experience

We have stated earlier in this introduction that regular rhythm is one aspect of the emphasis on form which we find in poetry. We have already seen how the poet binds together in closely knit patterns the various aspects of the words which he uses. It would be strange if we did not find him making use of the aspect of rhythm also, bringing it into the larger pattern of effects which is the poem. Some further comment on verse is necessary, however; for one reason, because there are so many confusions about the topic; for another, because verse, though it is only one element of poetry, is a very powerful one and its power calls for some sort of explanation.

All utterance has some sort of rhythm, of course. But in prose the rhythm is usually under relatively slight control of the author. He exerts some sort of control, of course, and some prose, much of that in the King James version of the Bible for instance, is very rhythmical indeed. But in poetry the rhythm is usually very carefully controlled. It is usually regularized; that is, it is strongly modified, or even controlled, by the regular pattern which we call *verse*. The poet, as we said, usually finds it an advantage to employ verse, and most poems are written in verse, but not all poetry. For example, examine the poem by William Carlos Williams on p. 303 in this collection. It is possible, then, to have a poem (that is, an experience thoroughly unified and intensified) which is not written in verse at all or which is written in what is called *free verse*, a relatively loose verse form. It is possible, on the other hand, to have verse which is not poetry at all. For example:

> Two and two equal four,
> Not any less nor any more.

The terms *verse* and *prose* are antithetical: something is written in verse or it is written in prose and it must be one thing or the other. But, as we have just seen, poetry is not identical with verse. The fact that something is not written in verse—the bit of doggerel just quoted above for example—does not insure our calling it poetry; but on the other hand, the absence of verse form ought not to prevent our applying the term poetry to passages which are otherwise entirely unified and present an experience with intensity and significance. Indeed, it is not always easy to decide whether to call a given passage poetry or simply exalted prose. For example consider the following sentences from the first chapter of the Book of Ecclesiastes.

What profit hath man of all his labor wherein he laboreth under the sun? One generation goeth, and another generation cometh; but the earth abideth forever. The sun also ariseth, and the sun goeth down, and hasteneth to its place where it ariseth. The wind goeth toward the south, and turneth about unto the north; it turneth about continually in its course, and the wind returneth again to its circuit. All the rivers run into the sea, yet the sea is not full; unto the place whither the rivers go, thither they go again.

Or to take another example, consider the last sentences of Melville's *Moby Dick:*

. . . and so the bird of heaven, with archangelic shrieks, and his imperial beak thrust upwards, and his captive form folded in the flag of Ahab, went down with his ship, which, like Satan, would not sink to hell till she had dragged a living part of heaven along with her, and helmeted herself with it.

Now small fowls flew screaming over the yet yawning gulf; a sullen white surf beat against its steep sides; then all collapsed, and the great shroud of the sea rolled on as it rolled five thousand years ago.

But the poet does usually employ verse. Why? One may be tempted to say that it is because of the connection of verse with emotional intensity. It is a fact that human beings do seem to fall naturally into a regular rhythm when speaking under great emotional stress. Here again it is not easy to give a good reason which will explain why this should be true. But it is a psychological fact which the student may check for himself. For example, if one has heard a woman speaking in deep grief, or a person speaking who is beside himself with rage, he will have noticed that the utterance begins to take on a regular rhythmical pattern: certain words tend to occur again and again with the same emphasis, and the whole speech tends to get a regular swing.

Now the poet does not employ a regular rhythmic pattern (that is, verse) because *he* is beside himself with emotion. As a matter of fact the situation is usually quite the contrary. But he often makes use of our association of high emotional intensity with a rhythmic pattern, using it to build up an emotional intensity in us.

One of the strange things about verse, however, is that, while we associate it with emotional intensity, it also has a marked hypnotic effect. The hypnotist uses rhythmic gesture and rhythmic utterance in order to induce a sort of trance in which the person hypnotized responds readily to the suggestions which the hypnotist wishes to implant. Realizing the connections which verse has with intense feeling and at the same time with hypnosis, we are better prepared to understand why it should be such a powerful tool in the poet's hand as he tries to make us share in an experience with himself, but also to see why it is a tool which must be used carefully and intelligently or else it will defeat the poet's own ends.

In the first place verse is simply one of several means which the poet has at his disposal. The sensitive and intelligent poet will not use verse at the expense of his other means for shaping and organizing and giving significance to the experience which is the poem. His handling of imagery, his choice of diction, his control of tone—all of these matters are important and the poet cannot neglect them simply because he is relying upon verse. Moreover, the intelligent poet will remember that overinsistence on the verse pattern may in fact produce an effect quite the opposite from that which he wants: verse stressed in this fashion will merely put people to sleep with its mechanical singsong. In general, if he uses a metrical pattern, he will use it, not rigidly and mechanically, but flexibly, relating it to the other formal arrangements which he employs, and always as a means to accomplishing the general intention of the poem—never as an end in itself. So also with rime, alliteration, and any other such devices which he may employ. Yeats's poem, "That the Night Come" (p. 318), will furnish a good example of the intelligent use of the verse in a poem, a use which makes it an organic element in the poem.

In Yeats's poem, the verse becomes an adjunct of meaning—one device among other devices for defining with precision the total meaning of the poem. The student in dealing with the specific poems in this book is urged to consider the aspect of verse in this light: that is, to consider how the verse works in that particular poem to point up and define the meaning of the poem. He must remember that, though verse can be considered as a device, it must be considered, too, as related to the natural pulse of our blood and of our emotional life. He ought to resist the temptation to treat the versification as an end in itself and the related temptation to conceive of the technicalities of meter as a formidable barrier to any intelligent appreciation of the poem. In the hope of mitigating these emphases, we have postponed any systematic discussion of meter to Section III. The technicalities of verse do come up for discussion in the poems of the first two sections.

SECTION I

All the poems in this first section tell (or imply) a story. Obviously they differ in many ways from a straight prose account of a story. Most prominent, of course, is the difference of metrical form. In the second place, there is a difference in the principle of organization: the treatment of the actual events in the poems is different from the treatment one would find in ordinary prose accounts. In approaching the poems in this section, the reader should constantly ask himself this question: "In what way might a prose account of the same event differ from the poem?" The reader may prepare a prose paraphrase of a given poem and then compare it with the poem itself. A good prose paraphrase will give a mastery of the facts of the case; but the poem is not attempting merely to give facts. What poetry does attempt is best appreciated by a good soaking in poem after poem—but a thoughtful soaking.

Sir Patrick Spens

ANONYMOUS

The king sits in Dumferling toune,
  Drinking the blude-reid wine:
"O whar will I get guid sailor,
  To sail this schip of mine."

Up and spake an eldern knicht,[1]   5
  Sat at the kings richt kne:
"Sir Patrick Spens is the best sailor,
  That sails upon the se."

The king has written a braid [2] letter,
  And signd it wi his hand,   10
And sent it to Sir Patrick Spens,
  Was walking on the sand.

The first line that Sir Patrick red,
  A loud lauch [3] lauchèd he;
The next line that Sir Patrick red,   15
  The teir blinded his ee.

"O wha [4] is this has don this deid,
  This ill deid don to me,
To send me out this time o' the yeir,
  To sail upon the se!   20

"Mak hast, mak hast, my mirry men all,
  Our guid ship sails the morne:"
"O say na sae,[5] my master deir,
  For I feir a deadlie storme."

"Late, late yestreen I saw the new moone,   25
  Wi the auld [6] moone in hir arme,
And I feir, I feir, my deir master,
  That we will cum to harme."

O our Scots nobles wer richt laith [7]
  To weet their cork-heild schoone;[8]   30

[1] knight [2] broad [3] laugh [4] who [5] so [6] old [7] loath [8] cork-heeled shoes

Bot lang owre a' [9] the play wer playd,
   Thair hats they swam aboone.[10]

O lang, lang may their ladies sit,
   Wi thair fans into their hand,
Or eir [11] they se Sir Patrick Spens   35
   Cum sailing to the land.

O lang, lang may the ladies stand,
   Wi thair gold kems [12] in their hair,
Waiting for thair ain [13] deir lords,
   For they'll se thame na mair.[14]   40

Haf owre, haf owre to Aberdour,[15]
   It's fiftie fadom deip,
And thair lies guid Sir Patrick Spens,
   Wi the Scots lords at his feit.

This is a *ballad;* that is, it is a poem which
tells a story. But it is important to notice *how*
it tells the story. In the first place, the poem
is not so much a detailed and ordered narrative as a *drama.* The poem is actually made up
of little dramatic scenes. The first of these scenes
portrays the king inquiring for the name of a
good sailor, learning of Sir Patrick, and writing
a letter to Sir Patrick, ordering him to undertake a voyage for him. There is no transition
from this to the second scene, which begins
abruptly with Sir Patrick pacing the seashore.
He receives the letter, and though he is shocked
at the folly of attempting a voyage at this time
of year, he passes on the order to his men. It is
only when we come to the eighth stanza that we
find the straight dramatic form abandoned in
favor of comment on the situation by the poet,
and even this comment is still close to drama.

The eighth stanza pictures—again without
any transition—the hats of the Scottish lords
floating on the sea. The ninth and tenth stanzas
picture the ladies in their fine houses waiting
for their lords to return to them. Not until
the last stanza does the poem state explicitly
that the ship was lost, and even here the poet
does not say "The ship foundered." Instead, he
paints a picture of the brave sailor lying on
the sea floor with the Scottish lords about him.

From this account one can see how much the
poem, simple though it may appear, differs from

flat prose statement. The prose statement would
probably go something like this: "The king,
deciding that a voyage had to be made, found
upon inquiry that Sir Patrick Spens was the
best sailor to be had, and ordered him to make
the voyage. Sir Patrick, though realizing that a
storm was brewing and that the trip was likely
to be disastrous, carried out the order. The ship
sank, and Sir Patrick went down with the crew
of noble passengers who had been entrusted to
his care."

Now, is the poem better than the prose
statement? We can draw up a sort of balance
sheet for the poem against our prose version. On
the debit side of the poem's account we must
first set down this: the prose statement seems,
at first glance, the clearer of the two. If one is in
a hurry to give the facts and if he merely wishes
to pass on the facts, he will naturally prefer to
use prose. But here we are not anxious to learn
these facts for their practical importance as one
needs to learn the price of eggs or the weather
forecast. And moreover, the tragedy as given in
the poem is clear enough—there is no great difficulty in finding out what really happened.

Now what is to be put to the credit side
of the account? What is gained by telling the
story in the form of the poem? In the first
place, everything is much more *vivid* in the poem.
By giving the story in little flashes or scenes,
we have a sharpness of detail—the sense of reality
—which would otherwise be missed. The prose
method is to make the flat statement that the king
was thoughtless and foolhardy, knowing nothing
of the sea, whereas Sir Patrick was an experienced
sailor. The method of the poem is, on the other
hand, to show the king actually in his characteristic surroundings. The poem shows him
sitting in his palace and drinking his wine at
his ease, in contrast to Sir Patrick walking on
the beach, within sight of his ship, then uttering a scornful laugh at the folly of the king's
orders.

In the same way, the ominous sense of disaster is given, and given vividly, by having the
sailor tell of the warning in the weather-signs.
The new moon with the old moon in her arms
is the folk way of describing what is sometimes
seen at the new moon: there is the thin cres-

9 all 10 above 11 ere 12 combs 13 own 14 more 15 Aberdeen

cent of the new moon with a thin ring of light outlining the rest of the circle of the moon. The picture is very effective here, for it is not only concrete; it has associations of mystery and foreboding. To analyze a little more closely, there is an ironical contrast embedded in the figure itself. The image of the new moon holding the old moon in her arms seems to be an image which suggests affectionate care; but to those who know the weather-signs, it means just the opposite—it means storms and disaster for those at sea.

Does the reader have to analyze consciously in such detail in order for the figure to be effective for him? No, much of the expressiveness of poetry depends upon effects made on the *unconscious* mind of the reader—effects which the reader cannot consciously analyze and explain and which are, therefore, accounted for under some such phrase as "the magic of poetry." And the reader loses a great deal that poetry has to give him if he is willing to accept only what he can immediately account for. Part of the difficulty in appreciating poetry is that the student is trained to read it only as he reads prose, looking only for the facts and not for what is implied.

The way in which the poem builds up to a climax at the end is a good example of this method of implication. There is a quality of suspense which the prose summary lacked. Not only does the poem avoid telling us what actually happened until we come to the last line; there is a connection of the tragic end with the forebodings of tragedy given in the earlier stanzas. For instance, after mentioning the consternation of the sailors, the poem brings us back to the Scottish lords for ironical comment. They didn't like to wet even the heels of their fine shoes, but before matters were over, their hats floated above them. Then the poem takes up their ladies, waiting for their husbands' return. They are pictured in their finery with their fans and their golden combs in their hands. But all their wealth could not bring their husbands back again. The irony built up here into a comment on the vanity of earthly power and riches is all the stronger for being merely hinted rather than stated in so many words in a moralizing fashion.

In the last stanza this rather generalized irony involving the lords and their ladies is brought to a sharp focus on Sir Patrick Spens himself. But with an important difference. The irony before the last stanza involves the ignorance of the lords and ladies; it is irony at their expense. The irony of the last stanza is not at the expense of Sir Patrick. He is a seasoned sailor. He knows the sea, and one feels that he knows life too. He knows that one can't beat the sea or nature or life. And he knows this because, unlike the fine lords, he has actually battled with life. In the end, of course, the disaster to the lords is his own disaster. As a loyal subject, he has to obey the king, even against his better knowledge. But he has his part in the general tragedy with a difference. At least he goes into it open-eyed. The tragic situation is the conflict between his loyalty and his knowledge.

On the basis of the last paragraphs, one may mention one more way in which the poem differs sharply from its prose paraphrase: the poem implies some kind of "meaning" in the experience and "feeling" about the experience. The paraphrase is interested in relating the facts. The poem is interested not merely in the facts, but in the way the author feels about the facts and the *meaning* of the facts.

Frankie and Johnny

ANONYMOUS

Frankie and Johnny were lovers, great God how
   they could love!
Swore to be true to each other, true as the stars
   up above.
He was her man, but he done her wrong.

Frankie she was his woman, everybody knows.
She spent her forty dollars for Johnny a suit of
   clothes.   5
He was her man, but he done her wrong.

Frankie and Johnny went walking, Johnny in
   his brand new suit.
"O good Lawd," said Frankie, "but don't my
   Johnny look cute?"
He was her man, but he done her wrong.

Frankie went down to the corner, just for a
bucket of beer.   10
Frankie said, "Mr. Bartender, has my loving
Johnny been here?
He is my man, he wouldn't do me wrong."

"I don't want to tell you no story, I don't want
to tell you no lie,
But your Johnny left here an hour ago with
that lousy Nellie Blye.
He is your man, but he's doing you wrong."   15

Frankie went back to the hotel, she didn't go
there for fun,
For under her red kimono she toted a forty-
four gun.
He was her man, but he done her wrong.

Frankie went down to the hotel and looked in
the window so high,
And there was her loving Johnny a-loving up
Nellie Blye.   20
He was her man, but he was doing her wrong.

Frankie threw back her kimono, took out that
old forty-four.
Root-a-toot-toot, three times she shot, right
through the hardwood door.
He was her man, but he was doing her wrong.

Johnny grabbed off his Stetson, crying, "O,
Frankie don't shoot!"   25
Frankie pulled that forty-four, went root-a-toot-
toot-toot-toot.
He was her man, but he done her wrong.

"Roll me over gently, roll me over slow,
Roll me on my right side, for my left side hurts
me so,
I was her man, but I done her wrong."   30

With the first shot Johnny staggered, with the
second shot he fell;
When the last bullet got him, there was a new
man's face in hell.
He was her man, but he done her wrong.

"O, bring out your rubber-tired hearses, bring
out your rubber-tired hacks;

Gonna take Johnny to the graveyard and ain't
gonna bring him back.   35
He was my man, but he done me wrong."

"O, put me in that dungeon, put me in that
cell,
Put me where the northeast wind blows from
the southeast corner of hell.
I shot my man, cause he done me wrong!"

This poem is a modern product of the same
impulse which produced "Sir Patrick Spens"
hundreds of years ago. People want more than
mere information; they want something that will
appeal to their emotions. "Frankie and Johnny,"
like "Sir Patrick Spens," grows out of a simple
and unsophisticated society, and in its make-up,
resembles closely the older ballad. "Frankie and
Johnny" raises at once for us, therefore, two important questions: (1) Can poetry grow out of
the present rather than merely the past? and (2)
can poetry deal with sordid materials; can it
use the subject matter of the backstreets of an
American city, material which we are inclined
to associate with tabloid headlines rather than
with poetry? Any reader can imagine how a
newspaper, whose function is to give the essential
facts, would treat such a story as the murder of
Johnny by his sweetheart. Since the answer to
such questions rests on what we think of the
poem, let us consider the poem first. In what
ways is it like "Sir Patrick Spens"?

In the first place, this poem, though not so
dramatic as the older poem, is told in terms
of little scenes. The links between the scenes
are left up to the reader's imagination, and
quite properly. The poem continually focuses
attention on the main problem. First there is
the statement of Frankie's love for Johnny; then
the scene of their walk together; the scene at
the saloon where Frankie learns that her lover
is unfaithful; then last, the scene in which she
kills him.

The scenes in themselves, moreover, are
vivid. Notice how concrete they are. A *hat* is
a "Stetson"; a *gun,* a "forty-four," etc. The
poem, crude as it may seem, shows a mastery of
this point: that if you give the reader a few
details sharply and vividly enough, his imagination will do the rest. The same holds true of the

understatement in the poem. We have the given understatement of Frankie's intention: "she didn't go there for fun." Or that about Johnny's burial: the hearse and hacks may take Johnny to the graveyard, but "they ain't gonna bring him back." Understatement, rather than exaggeration, puts the imagination to work, involves the reader in the process of the poem.

Moreover, the poem is not only real; it has a certain dignity. That is, it accepts the human values which the poem is based on. The poem is not interested in providing a great deal of dissecting of motives, nor is it interested in moralizing comment. The focus is kept where it should be here: on the core of the action itself but on the action as based on the observance of a strict code of honor. We don't ordinarily think of people of this sort as having such a code. The code of honor, however, is there; it is assumed throughout the poem; and it is the code which holds the poem together. It is right to kill the person who proves unfaithful. Johnny, himself, after he has been shot, admits it: "I was her man, but I done her wrong."

In this connection, notice how important the refrain is in binding the poem together, and the effect of the variations which occur in it: "He is my man, he wouldn't do me wrong," "He was your man, but he's doing you wrong," etc. The refrain affirms the idea from which the action springs.

The Star-Splitter

ROBERT FROST (1875-1963)

"You know Orion always comes up sideways.
Throwing a leg up over our fence of mountains,
And rising on his hands, he looks in on me
Busy outdoors by lantern-light with something
I should have done by daylight, and indeed,   5
After the ground is frozen, I should have done
Before it froze, and a gust flings a handful
Of waste leaves at my smoky lantern chimney
To make fun of my way of doing things,
Or else fun of Orion's having caught me.   10
Has a man, I should like to ask, no rights

These forces are obliged to pay respect to?"
So Brad McLaughlin mingled reckless talk
Of heavenly stars with hugger-mugger farming,
Till having failed at hugger-mugger farming,   15
He burned his house down for the fire insurance
And spent the proceeds on a telescope
To satisfy a life-long curiosity
About our place among the infinities.

"What do you want with one of those blame
    things?"   20
I asked him well beforehand. "Don't you get
one!"
"Don't call it blamed; there isn't anything
More blameless in the sense of being less
A weapon in our human fight," he said.
"I'll have one if I sell my farm to buy it."   25
There where he moved the rocks to plow the
    ground
And plowed between the rocks he couldn't
    move,
Few farms changed hands; so rather than spend
    years
Trying to sell his farm and then not selling,
He burned his house down for the fire
    insurance   30
And bought the telescope with what it came to.
He had been heard to say by several:
"The best thing that we're put here for's to see;
The strongest thing that's given us to see with's
A telescope. Someone in every town   35
Seems to me owes it to the town to keep one.
In Littleton it may as well be me."
After such loose talk it was no surprise
When he did what he did and burned his house
    down.

Mean laughter went about the town that
    day   40
To let him know we weren't the least imposed
    on,
And he could wait—we'd see to him to-morrow.
But the first thing next morning we reflected
If one by one we counted people out
For the least sin, it wouldn't take us long   45
To get so we had no one left to live with.
For to be social is to be forgiving.
Our thief, the one who does the stealing from
    us,

We don't cut off from coming to church supper
But what we miss we go to him and ask for.   50
He promptly gives it back, that is if still
Uneaten, unworn out, or undisposed of.
It wouldn't do to be too hard on Brad
About his telescope. Beyond the age
Of being given one's gift for Christmas,   55
He had to take the best way he knew how
To find himself in one. Well, all we said was
He took a strange thing to be roguish over.
Some sympathy was wasted on the house,
A good old-timer dating back along;   60
But a house isn't sentient; the house
Didn't feel anything. And if it did,
Why not regard it as a sacrifice,
And an old-fashioned sacrifice by fire?
Instead of a new-fashioned one at auction?   65

Out of a house and so out of a farm
At one stroke (of a match), Brad had to turn
To earn a living on the Concord railroad,
As under-ticket-agent at a station
Where his job, when he wasn't selling
    tickets,   70
Was setting out up track and down, not plants
As on a farm, but planets, evening stars
That varied in their hue from red to green.

He got a good glass for six hundred dollars.
His new job gave him leisure for star-gazing.   75
Often he bid me come and have a look
Up the brass barrel, velvet black inside,
At a star quaking in the other end.
I recollect a night of broken clouds
And underfoot snow melted down to ice,   80
And melting further in the wind to mud.
Bradford and I had out the telescope.
We spread our two legs as we spread its three,
Pointed our thoughts the way we pointed it,
And standing at our leisure till the day
    broke,   85
Said some of the best things we ever said.
That telescope was christened the Star-splitter,
Because it didn't do a thing but split
A star in two or three the way you split
A globule of quicksilver in your hand   90
With one stroke of your finger in the middle.
It's a star-splitter if there ever was one

And ought to do some good if splitting stars
'S a thing to be compared with splitting wood.

We've looked and looked, but after all where
    are we?   95
Do we know any better where we are,
And how it stands between the night to-night
And a man with a smoky lantern chimney?
How different from the way it ever stood?

    1. What kind of man is the narrator? How do
you know? What kind of man is Brad? How do you
know?
    2. Define as carefully as you can the narrator's at-
titude toward Brad. The community's. What attitude
is the reader invited to take?
    3. Is the narrator simply telling an amusing
story? Are there any glances at serious issues?
    4. Is Brad "justified" in taking the means he
does in order to get his telescope? In this connection, consider ll. 79-86 and ll. 93-99.
    5. How close does the language of the poem
seem to the kind of world that it describes?

Edward

ANONYMOUS

"Why dois your brand [1] sae [2] drap wi bluid,
             Edward, Edward?
"Why dois your brand sae drap wi bluid,
    And why sae sad gang [3] yee O?"
"O I hae killed my hauke [4] sae guid,   5
             Mither, mither,
O I hae killed my hauke sae guid,
    And I had nae mair bot hee O."

"Your haukis bluid was nevir sae reid,
             Edward, Edward,   10
Your haukis bluid was never sae reid,
    My deir son I tell thee O."
"O I hae killed my reid-roan steid, [5]
             Mither, mither,
O I hae killed my reid-roan steid,   15
    That erst was sae fair and frie O."
"Your steid was auld, [6] and ye hae gat mair, [7]
             Edward, Edward,

---

[1] sword   [2] so   [3] go   [4] hawk   [5] steed   [6] old   [7] more

Your steid was auld, and ye hae gat mair;
　　Sum other dule [8] ye drie O.”　　　　　20
“O I hae killed my fadir [9] deir,
　　　　　　　　Mither, mither,
O I hae killed my fadir deir,
　　Alas, and wae is mee O!”

“And whatten penance wul ye drie [10] for that, 25
　　　　　　　　Edward, Edward?
And whatten penance wul ye drie, for that?
　　My deir son, now tell me O.”
“Ile set my feit in yonder boat,
　　　　　　　　Mither, mither　　　30
Ile set my feit in yonder boat,
　　And Ile fare ovir the sea O.”

“And what wul ye doe wi your towirs and
　　your ha,[11]
　　　　　　　　Edward, Edward?
And what wul ye doe wi your towirs and your
　　ha,　　　　　　　　　　　　　　35
　　That were sae fair to see O?”
“Ile let thame stand tul they doun fa,
　　　　　　　　Mither, mither,
Ile let thame stand tul they doun fa,
　　For here nevir mair maun I bee O.”　　40

“And what wul ye leive to your bairns [12] and
　　your wife,
　　　　　　　　Edward, Edward?
And what wul ye leive to your bairns and your
　　wife,
　　Whan ye gang ovir the sea O?”
“The warldis [13] room, late them beg thrae
　　life,　　　　　　　　　　　　　45
　　　　　　　　Mither, mither,
The warldis room, late them beg thrae life,
　　For thame nevir mair wul I see O.”

“And what wul ye leive to your ain mither deir,
　　　　　　　　Edward, Edward?　50
And what wul ye leive to your ain mither deir?
　　My deir son, now tell me O.”
“The curse of hell frae me sall [14] ye beir,
　　　　　　　　Mither, mither,
The curse of hell frae me sall ye beir,　　55
　　Sic counseils ye gave to me O.”

[8] grief　[9] father　[10] undergo　[11] hall, manorhouse　[12] children　[13] world's　[14] shall

1

What is the story? Edward, the hero of the ballad, is a knight. His mother and father have presumably had a deadly quarrel. In any case we know of the desire of the mother to dispose of the father. The mother has gradually played on the son's feelings until he worked himself up to the point of killing the father. The mother has therefore accomplished her purpose without making herself actually guilty of murder. She discovers her son with a bloody sword in his hand; and in a mixture of curiosity, gratification, and horror, now that the deed is actually accomplished, she questions Edward on two points: why does the blade drip and why is he so sad? He at first says that he has killed his hawk. But she says the blood is too red (a reference to the first of her questions). Then he says that he has killed his steed. But she says in such a case he would not be sad because he has other and better ones (a reference to the second of her questions). Then, overcome with his growing remorse, he confesses to the crime. She then asks a question that seems to establish her detachment from the crime, but she does not express grief. What penance will *he* do? He answers that he will sail away, indicating a boat in harbor, and will become a wanderer. To the question about his estate he says that the tower and hall may fall into decay. And to that about his wife and children he says that they may beg through life. Then at the climax she asks him what he will leave to his own dear mother. He will leave her the curse of hell, he says, because she has been responsible for the crime.

2

But how do we know all this?

1. How do we know that Edward is a knight or nobleman? Because of the reference to his towers and hall.

2. How do we know of the relation of father and mother? The last line of the poem established the mother's desire to get rid of the father.

3. How do we know that Edward is suffering

remorse before he confesses? He refers to his "hawk so good," his only one, and to his "red-roan steed," that before was "fair and free"; but this regret for loss is really a statement of regret for the loss of the father, who may be taken to have been "so good" and "fair and free." There would have been no more reason for killing the father than for butchering the hawk or the horse which had served him well.

4. How do we know that the woman is a hard and calculating woman? Naturally, we know it from the accusation at the end. But there are three significant indications that do something to define her earlier in the poem and to give an effect of mounting suspense. First, when Edward says that he grieves over the horse, she says, "why, the horse was old," ignoring any sentiment a person might feel for a faithful animal. To her it is only a piece of property. Second, she asks, "what penance will *you* do?" She attempts by the way she frames the question to separate herself from all responsibility. The normal reaction would have been one of grief or at least momentary astonishment, but she is so cold and self-controlled that she first attempts to clear her own skirts. Third, when she addresses him in the last stanza she refers to herself as his "own mother dear," trying to ingratiate herself with him, when she is really his worst enemy and has ruined him.

3

How is the story handled?

The story of Edward is not given in the same way as the story of Sir Patrick Spens. In "Sir Patrick Spens" it is given in the normal chronological order: the action begins with the old knight's telling the king about Sir Patrick and ends with the picture of Sir Patrick on the sea floor. It has been pointed out in the discussion of "Sir Patrick Spens" that the story is not treated by a simple, unemphasized forward movement, as in ordinary narrative, but is presented by a series of scenes, glimpses of the key situations, significant flashes of action which fire the reader's imagination to fill in the continuity. The method is that of a little drama composed of several scenes. But "Edward" does not tell its story in chronological order; it has only one scene, a scene after the real action, and the content of that action has to be handled by implication. It is therefore more economical and unified.

"Sir Patrick Spens" is told from an omniscient point of view. The teller is not a person in any real sense, but he can see and describe a scene such as the sea floor, as no real person could ever do. But the story of "Edward" is not "told" at all. It is, rather, presented in direct form as a dialogue between the two principal persons of the story. It is therefore even more dramatic and objective than "Sir Patrick Spens," and makes even more exciting demands on the reader's imagination.

The action of "Sir Patrick Spens" is accounted for at the very first, when the king takes the advice of the old knight; and the conclusion is foreshadowed several times, once when Sir Patrick opens the letter and gives his sardonic laugh, and again when the new moon has the old moon in her arms. The method is exactly the opposite in "Edward." We know what has actually happened long before the end, but we do not know the reason, the motivation, until the very last line. There is a sense of foreboding and inevitability about "Sir Patrick Spens," and of surprise and shock about "Edward."

The psychological interest in "Edward" is more important than in "Sir Patrick Spens." Each question and answer in "Edward" brings out some new fact, not only of the story, but of the characters involved. In "Sir Patrick Spens" we learn at the very beginning all we ever know about the characters. This does not mean that "Edward" is necessarily superior to "Sir Patrick Spens"; it merely means that there is a different kind of effect.

In regard to the matter of the technique and structure of "Edward" one can observe that its stanza form is more complicated than that of "Sir Patrick Spens." It has, too, a very elaborate use of refrain and repetition. The very action of the ballad, as a matter of fact, is carried and emphasized by these two devices. The refrains of "Edward" and "mother" define the structure of each stanza, the question and answer arrangement. Further, the question and answer arrangement is well adapted to the building up of suspense, in regard to the nature of the crime, and to prepare for the surprise, in regard to the motivation of the crime, which comes at the end.

4

What is the meaning of the poem? We know the story, but what kind of effect does the story give? It gives an effect of tragic irony. A crime has been committed; and presumably the person most guilty, the mother, will suffer. But the son, whose moral nature is much superior to that of his mother but who has been influenced by her to commit the crime, must suffer too. Even the absolutely innocent persons, the wife and children, must suffer, for they will be abandoned to beg through life. The same question lies behind this story that lies behind the great tragedies: what is the nature of justice? But the ironical effect is not single, for it has certain cross references, as it were, within the situation. First, only when the father is dead does Edward realize the father's virtues and his own better nature that brings him to remorse and penance. Second, the mother, who should be the greatest guardian of the son, has ruined him. Third, the mother, who expected some profit or satisfaction from the crime, is left with only a curse from the son whom, in her way, she loves. Fourth, the wife and children, who are innocent, must suffer too. The irony of "Sir Patrick Spens" is more simple.

5

Let us ask one more question. With what feelings, what attitude, does Edward say of his wife and children that he leaves them the whole world's space in which they may beg through life?

Lord Randall

ANONYMOUS

"O where hae ye been, Lord Randall, my son?
O where hae ye been, my handsome young man?"
"I hae been to the wild wood; mother, make my bed soon,

1 would

For I'm weary wi hunting, and fain wald [1] lie down."
"Where gat ye your dinner, Lord Randall, my son?   5
Where gat ye your dinner, my handsome young man?"
"I dined wi my true-love; mother, make my bed soon,
For I'm weary wi hunting, and fain wald lie down."

"What gat ye to your dinner, Lord Randall, my son?
What gat ye to your dinner, my handsome young man?"   10
"I gat eels boiled in broo; mother, make my bed soon,
For I'm weary wi hunting, and fain wald lie down."

"What became of your bloodhounds, Lord Randall, my son?
What became of your bloodhounds, my handsome young man?"
"O they swelld and they died; mother, make my bed soon,   15
For I'm weary wi hunting, and fain wald lie down."

"O I fear ye are poisond, Lord Randall, my son!
O I fear ye are poisond, my handsome young man!"
"O yes! I am poisond; mother, make my bed soon,
For I'm sick at the heart, and I fain wald lie down."   20

Prepare a set of questions that you think might lead to a fuller understanding and appreciation of this poem. Compare your questions with those prepared by other students.

The Bonny Earl of Murray

ANONYMOUS

Ye Highlands, and ye Lawlands,
    Oh where have you been?

They have slain the Earl of Murray,
   And they layd him on the green.

"Now wae be to thee, Huntly!   5
   And wherefore did you sae?
I bade you bring him wi you,
   But forbade you him to slay."

He was a braw [1] gallant,
   And he rid at the ring;   10
And the bonny Earl of Murray,
   Oh he might have been a king!

He was a braw gallant,
   And he playd at the ba [2];
And the bonny Earl of Murray,   15
   Was the flower amang them a'.

He was a braw gallant,
   And he played at the glove;
And the bonny Earl of Murray,
   Oh he was the Queen's love!   20

Oh lang will his lady
   Look o'er the castle Down,
E'er she see the Earl of Murray
   Come sounding [3] thro the town.

This ballad is based upon an actual incident in Scottish history. But the ballad begins after the Earl has been killed, and limits itself to the speaker's (and others') reactions to the event.

1. Has the poem left too much to implication? Does it again force by this limitation? Upon what effect in the poem centered?

2. What sort of person was the dead man? How do the concrete details in the ballad serve to define his character?

3. Does the last stanza provide a fitting climax to the poem? If you think it does, why do you think so?

Danny Deever

RUDYARD KIPLING (1865-1936)

"What are the bugles blowin' for?" said Files-on-Parade.

"To turn you out, to turn you out," the Color-Sergeant said.
"What makes you look so white, so white?" said Files-on-Parade.
"I'm dreadin' what I've got to watch," the Color-Sergeant said.
   For they're hangin' Danny Deever, you can 'ear the Dead March play,   5
   The regiment's in 'ollow square—they're hangin' him today;
   They've taken of his buttons off an' cut his stripes away,
   An' they're hangin' Danny Deever in the mornin'.

"What makes the rear-rank breathe so 'ard?" said Files-on-Parade.
"It's bitter cold, it's bitter cold," the Color-Sergeant said.   10
"What makes that front-rank man fall down?" says Files-on-Parade.
"A touch of sun, a touch of sun," the Color-Sergeant said.
   They are hangin' Danny Deever, they are marchin' of 'im round.
   They 'ave 'alted Danny Deever by 'is coffin on the ground:
   And 'e'll swing in 'arf a minute for a sneakin' shootin' hound—   15
   O they're hangin' Danny Deever in the mornin'!

"'Is cot was right-'and cot to mine," said Files-on-Parade.
"'E's sleepin' out an' far tonight," the Color-Sergeant said.
"I've drunk 'is beer a score o' times," said Files-on-Parade.
"'E's drinkin' bitter beer alone," the Color-Sergeant said.   20
   They are hangin' Danny Deever, you must mark 'im to 'is place,
   For 'e shot a comrade sleepin'—you must look 'im in the face;
   Nine 'undred of 'is county an' the regiment's disgrace,
   While they're hangin' Danny Deever in the mornin'.

---

[1] brave   [2] ball   [3] riding

"What's that so black agin the sun?" said Files-
on-Parade.   25

"It's Danny fightin' 'ard for life," the Color-
Sergeant said.

"What's that that whimpers over'ead?" said
Files-on-Parade.

"It's Danny's soul that's passin' now," the Color-
Sergeant said.

  For they're done with Danny Deever, you
    can 'ear the quickstep play,
  The regiment's in column, an' they're
    marchin' us away;   30
  Ho! the young recruits are shakin', an'
    they'll want their beer today,
  After hangin' Danny Deever in the mornin'.

The two men who carry on the conversation in
this poem are noncommissioned officers in the British Army.

  1. What is the attitude of these two men toward
Danny Deever? What sort of person was Danny
Deever? How do you know? Is the poem primarily
concerned with the plight of Danny Deever as such,
or with the effect of the military execution upon the
typical soldier in the regiment?

  2. May the poem be said to set over against
each other the pathos of a weak and all-too-human
man and the grim and necessarily inhuman world of
military regulations? How is this contrast developed
in the detail of the poem? As one example we may
note that the poet never refers to the two cockney
soldiers by name but as the Color-Sergeant and as
Files-on-Parade. What are other examples?

  3. The regiment will, as a matter of fact, march
away from the execution at quick step. How is this
sense of a brisk movement away from the scene reflected in the last four lines? Does this sense of brisk
cheerfulness contradict the feeling built up in the
poem, or does it actually serve to enforce it?

My Last Duchess

Ferrara

ROBERT BROWNING
(1812-1889)

That's my last Duchess painted on the wall
Looking as if she were alive. I call
That piece a wonder, now: Frà Pandolf's hands
Worked busily a day, and there she stands.

Will't please you sit and look at her? I said   5
"Frà Pandolf" by design, for never read
Strangers like you that pictured countenance,
The depth and passion of its earnest glance,
But to myself they turned (since none puts by
The curtain I have drawn for you, but I)   10
And seemed as they would ask me, if they durst,
How such a glance came there; so, not the first
Are you to turn and ask thus. Sir, 'twas not
Her husband's presence only, called that spot
Of joy into the Duchess' cheek: perhaps   15
Frà Pandolf chanced to say, "Her mantle laps
Over my lady's wrist too much," or "Paint
Must never hope to reproduce the faint
Half-flush that dies along her throat." Such stuff
Was courtesy, she thought, and cause
  enough   20
For calling up that spot of joy. She had
A heart—how shall I say?—too soon made glad,
Too easily impressed; she liked whate'er
She looked on, and her looks went everywhere
Sir, 'twas all one! My favor at her breast,   25
The dropping of the daylight in the West,
The bough of cherries some officious fool
Broke in the orchard for her, the white mule
She rode with round the terrace—all and each
Would draw from her alike the approving
  speech,   30
Or blush, at least. She thanked men,—good!
  but thanked
Somehow—I know not how—as if she ranked
My gift of a nine-hundred-years-old name
With anybody's gift. Who'd stoop to blame
This sort of trifling? Even had you skill   35
In speech—(which I have not)—to make your
  will
Quite clear to such an one, and say, "Just this
Or that in you disgusts me; here you miss,
Or there exceed the mark"—and if she let
Herself be lessoned so, nor plainly set   40
Her wits to yours, forsooth, and made excuse,
—E'en then would be some stooping; and I
  choose
Never to stoop. Oh, sir, she smiled, no doubt,
Whene'er I passed her; but who passed without
Much the same smile? This grew; I gave com-
  mands;   45
Then all smiles stopped together. There she
  stands
As if alive. Will't please you rise? We'll meet

The company below then. I repeat,
The Count your master's known munificence
Is ample warrant that no just pretence   50
Of mine for dowry will be disallowed;
Though his fair daughter's self, as I avowed
At starting, is my object. Nay, we'll go
Together down, sir. Notice Neptune, though,
Taming a sea-horse, thought a rarity,   55
Which Claus of Innsbruck cast in bronze for
  me!

In this poem we have the Duke of Ferrara entertaining an emissary from an unnamed Count. The purpose of their business is to arrange a marriage between the Duke and the Count's daughter. The events actually begin with the Duke's pointing out a full-length portrait of his "last Duchess." He tells the story behind the painting: the artist portrayed a "certain look" in the Duchess' face. "The depth and passion of its earnest glance" displeased the Duke because he thought that that particular look should have been reserved for him alone. The Duchess, however, bestowed it upon any "officious fool" who happened to be courteous. The Duke "gave commands" (either to have the Duchess killed or sent to a convent) and "all smiles stopped."

The Duke's story is apparently ended. The two start to leave the room, and the Duke remarks on the dowry of the Count's daughter, protesting, however, that it is of minor importance. He insists that the emissary accompany rather than follow him; and he comments on another work of art, a bronze, "Neptune, taming a sea-horse, . . ."

The situation is dramatic. The emissary has come to arrange a marriage, although this point is not revealed until the last of the poem—a legitimate device for securing suspense. The success of the poem lies not so much in what is actually told by the poet as in the implications that the reader can draw from what is said.

We must realize that the poet faced at least two major difficulties: First, he was trying to reconstruct an incident, a crisis in the lives of several people, he himself not one of them, of another place and time. Second, the form chosen, the dramatic monologue, is not the simplest technical form. Only one person actually speaks in the poem, and he must not only bear his own side of the drama, but imply in his speech certain questions, gestures, and even attitudes of the person we infer to be present. The result is a compression that is difficult to obtain.

Suppose we examine the poem and see just how the Duke reveals his character. We know that he is proud; he refers continually to "my Duchess," "my favor at her breast," "my gift of a nine-hundred-years-old name." He is proud in another sense, proud of his possessions. His interest in the portrait is not that it is of his wife but that it is a masterpiece of Frà Pandolf's. He is proud in the same material way of a bronze by Claus of Innsbruck. And this pride, or vanity, lies behind the fate of the Duchess. Whether he had the Duchess killed or simply sent her away and let her die from humiliation and disgrace makes little difference. The smiles stopped, and he makes no apology or further explanation. He had not been able, in his cold egotism, to abide, much less appreciate, innocence. His jealousy was not caused by the loss of something but by his failure to possess completely every phase of his wife's life. As for his intelligence, we find him a shrewd, but superficial, person. He is interested in art, not for any relation that it might bear to his life, but as material possessions. He is desirous of a wife, not as a companion, but as a necessary ornament for his palace.

As for the Duchess, all we know of her is what we learn from the Duke. We would assume that any information from him would be derogatory, if only to justify himself. He, however, is not interested in justification but in revealing what he expects of a wife. She must have been of high rank, or the Duke would not have married her. She had a heart

    too soon made glad,
Too easily impressed; she liked what e'er
She looked on, and her looks went everywhere.

She was, then, a natural, innocent woman whom the Duke could not bend into the conventional form he thought his wife should have.

There are now two questions that arise: First, what was the impulse behind the writing of the poem, and second, why the indirection and compression rather than a straightforward presentation?

As for question one, the author had as his purpose the presentation of a scene of Renaissance Italy. He was not interested primarily in telling an incident, or he might have used another medium. He was not interested in presenting an accurate historical account and evaluating that period for us; therefore he even uses fictitious names. He is interested in presenting people to us at a crisis in their lives. He wishes to present a dramatic situation for its own sake and for the relation to experience it might promote. Notice that in the entire poem no direct judgments are passed on anyone or on the actions of anyone. The elements are arranged so that we make, as it were, the judgment.

As for question two, the monologue and indirection serve to compress the story, to create suspense, and to enrich the presentation. The poet cannot set the scene by means of elaborate description and exposition. He has to have the surface story and the real story behind it fused, moment by moment, in the Duke's words. For instance, the lines

> I said
> "Frà Pandolf" by design, for never read
> Strangers like you that pictured countenance—

tells us several things. First, we know that the emissary made some definite comment about the portrait or at least by some gesture revealed an interest greater than that usually expressed by guests. Second, we see the character of the Duke and his pride in presenting a masterpiece by a renowned artist. And we may justly see flattery and condescension in "never read strangers like you."

Notice the Duke's ironic disclaimer of any skill in speech:

> Even had you skill
> In speech (which I have not)—

It is true that he failed to make his will known to his first wife but that is only the surface of the matter. The real purpose of the entire story is to inform the emissary just what he expects of his wife. The Duke does not do his powers of speech justice. And the reader sees that he has considerable skill.

The success of this poem depends on this indirection and compression. In fact the interest in character, the conversational tone, the suspense and the clever phrasing of paradoxical statements make the poem successful.

1. What is the verse form?
2. Point out examples of irony and understatement. What is the effect of these instances?
3. What is revealed of the emissary's character?
4. Is there any evidence in the poem to suppose, as one critic has suggested, that the emissary and the Count's daughter were in love?
5. Why does the Duke tell the emissary this story?

Lucinda Matlock

EDGAR LEE MASTERS
(1869-1950)

I went to the dances at Chandlerville,
And played snap-out at Winchester.
One time we changed partners,
Driving home in the moonlight of middle June,
And then I found Davis. 5
We were married and lived together for seventy
  years,
Enjoying, working, raising the twelve children,
Eight of whom we lost
Ere I had reached the age of sixty.
I spun, I wove, I kept the house, I nursed the
  sick, 10
I made the garden, and for holiday
Rambled over the fields where sang the larks,
And by Spoon River gathering many a shell,
And many a flower and medicinal weed—
Shouting to the wooded hills, singing to the
  green valleys. 15
At ninety-six I had lived enough, that is all,
And passed to a sweet repose.
What is this I hear of sorrow and weariness,
Anger, discontent and drooping hopes?
Degenerate sons and daughters, 20
Life is too strong for you—
It takes life to love Life.

Spoon River Anthology, from which this poem is taken, purports to be a collection of epitaphs from the cemetery of a small Middle-Western town. The author imagines that in each such epitaph the character epitomizes his own life.

1. What is Lucinda Matlock's character? Are the

details given in the poem well chosen to present that character?

2. To whom does she address the last five lines? The sons and daughters are "degenerate" in what sense?

Bredon Hill

A. E. HOUSMAN (1859-1936)

In summertime on Bredon
  The bells they sound so clear;
Round both the shires they ring them
  In steeples far and near,
  A happy noise to hear.   5

Here of a Sunday morning
  My love and I would lie,
And see the colored counties,
  And hear the larks so high
  About us in the sky.   10

The bells would ring to call her
  In valleys miles away:
"Come all to church, good people;
  Good people, come and pray."
  But here my love would stay.   15

And I would turn and answer
  Among the springing thyme,
"Oh peal upon our wedding,
  And we will hear the chime,
  And come to church in time."   20

But when the snows at Christmas
  On Bredon top were strown,
My love rose up so early
  And stole out unbeknown
  And went to church alone.   25

They tolled the one bell only,
  Groom there was none to see,
The mourners followed after,
  And so to church went she,
  And would not wait for me.   30

The bells they sound on Bredon,
  And still the steeples hum.

"Come all to church, good people,—"
  Oh, noisy bells, be dumb;
  I hear you, I will come.   35

Prepare a set of questions for "Bredon Hill." Write an essay (500 words) based on your questions.

The True Lover

A. E. HOUSMAN (1859-1936)

The lad came to the door at night,
  When lovers crown their vows,
And whistled soft and out of sight
  In shadow of the boughs.

I shall not vex you with my face   5
  Henceforth, my love, for aye;
So take me in your arms a space
  Before the east is grey.

When I from hence away am past
  I shall not find a bride,   10
And you shall be the first and last
  I ever lay beside.

She heard and went and knew not why;
  Her heart to his she laid;
Light was the air beneath the sky   15
  But dark under the shade.

"Oh do you breathe, lad, that your breast
  Seems not to rise and fall,
And here upon my bosom prest
  There beats no heart at all?"   20

"Oh loud, my girl, it once would knock,
  You should have felt it then;
But since for you I stopped the clock
  It never goes again."

"Oh lad, what is it, lad, that drips   25
  Wet from your neck on mine?
What is it falling on my lips,
  My lad, that tastes of brine?"

"Oh like enough 'tis blood, my dear,
  For when the knife has slit   30

The throat across from ear to ear
'Twill bleed because of it."

Under the stars the air was light
  But dark below the boughs,
The still air of the speechless night,   35
  When lovers crown their vows.

This poem gives a single incident of a story,
the climax, and implies the rest of the story.
What is implied is, in summary, this much: a
lover who has been constantly rejected by his
sweetheart is prepared to go on a long journey.
When the poem begins, he has come to her
house at night and has whistled for her to come
out to tell him goodbye. He says:

> So take me in your arms a space
>   Before the east is grey.

To that point the story may be taken as a real
story which, like the preceding poems in this
section, might be understood as an actual incident. But in the third stanza the reader begins
to suspect that the journey the young man is to
take is not a real journey, for he says:

> When I from hence away am past
>   I shall not find a bride,
> And you shall be the first and last
>   I ever lay beside.

In other words, he asks his sweetheart to give
him her love so that his life may have some
meaning before he has to leave it.

But consider the speech of the girl in the
fifth stanza:

> Oh do you breathe, lad, that your breast
>   Seems not to rise and fall,

With that, and with the lad's answer, the reader
knows that the lover is already dead. The further question and answer merely make more
emphatic an ironic fact.

The story, then, is an impossible one, and
must not be understood as being realistic. To
take it as realistic would make it too disgusting
and horrible. It is a story invented by the poet
to present more dramatically the meaning of a
certain human relationship—the pathos and horror of realizing too late that one has rejected a
love that can never be recovered. One need not
even interpret the poem as meaning that the
"true lover" has actually committed suicide or
died. The love is merely lost beyond any recovery; and something within the lover has
died, never to be revived. The story of the poem
then stands for something beyond itself; the
story, then, stands as a concentrated representation of the feeling one might have about many
stories that were different in their circumstantial
incident and detail. It has a symbolic force.

How is the story told? The poem gives the
same impression as a ballad. It uses a very
simple stanza form, one that is common in the
folk ballads. Further, it uses devices of repetition (observe how the questions are built up)
and dialogue as do "Edward," and "Lord Randall." These devices have helped to concentrate
the presentation of the story so that it is unnecessary to tell it in full. The same kind of
ironic understatement appears in "The True
Lover" as in "Sir Patrick Spens." For instance,
the "true lover" says:

> But since for you I stopped the clock
>   It never goes again.

and:

> Oh like enough 'tis blood, my dear,
>   For when the knife has slit
> The throat across from ear to ear
>   'Twill bleed because of it.

This is the same effect one finds in "Sir
Patrick Spens" in the stanza:

> O our Scots nobles wer richt laith
>   To weet their cork-heild schoone;
> Bot lang owre a' the play wer playd,
>   Thair hats they swam aboone.

But there are certain obvious differences
from the folk ballads. The folk ballads usually
tell or imply a story that is to be taken as literal;
this ballad, however, gives a story of a symbolic
meaning. In the second place, the rhythm and
meter of "The True Lover" is more fluent and
musical than is common in the folk ballads.

The Farmer's Bride

CHARLOTTE MEW (1869-1928)

Three Summers since I chose a maid,
Too young maybe—but more's to do
At harvest-time than bide and woo.
    When us was wed she turned afraid
Of love and me and all things human;   5
Like the shut of a winter's day.
Her smile went out, and 'twasn't a woman—
    More like a little frightened fay.
        One night, in the Fall, she runned away.

"Out 'mong the sheep, her be," they said,   10
'Should properly have been abed;
But sure enough she wasn't there
Lying awake with her wide brown stare.
So over seven-acre field and up-along across the
        down
We chased her, flying like a hare   15
Before our lanterns. To Church-Town
    All in a shiver and a scare
We caught her, fetched her home at last
    And turned the key upon her, fast.

She does the work about the house   20
As well as most, but like a mouse:
    Happy enough to chat and play
    With birds and rabbits and such as they,
    So long as men-folk keep away.
"Not near, not near!" her eyes beseech   25
When one of us comes within reach.
    The women say that beasts in stall
    Look round like children at her call.
    I've hardly heard her speak at all.

Shy as a leveret, swift as he,   30
Straight and slight as a young larch tree,
Sweet as the first wild violets, she
To her wild self. But what to me?

The short days shorten and the oaks are brown,
    The blue smoke rises to the low gray sky, 35
One leaf in the still air falls slowly down,
    A magpie's spotted feathers lie
On the black earth spread white with rime,

The berries redden up to Christmas-time.
    What's Christmas-time without there be   40
Some other in the house than we!
She sleeps up in the attic there
Alone, poor maid. 'Tis but a stair
Betwixt us. Oh! my God! the down,
The soft young down of her, the brown,   45
The brown of her—her eyes, her hair, her
    hair . . .

    1. How does this poem suggest the pathos of the
situation of the girl?
    2. How does it suggest the pathos of the hus-
band's situation?
    3. Does the claim on our sympathy of one cancel
out the claim on our sympathy of the other?

Love on the Farm

D. H. LAWRENCE (1885-1930)

What large, dark hands are those at the window
Grasping in the golden light
Which weaves its way through the evening
        wind
    At my heart's delight?

Ah, only the leaves! But in the west   5
I see a redness suddenly come
Into the evening's anxious breast—
    'Tis the wound of love goes home!

The woodbine creeps abroad
Calling low to her lover: 10
    The sun-lit flirt who all the day
    Has poised above her lips in play
    And stolen kisses, shallow and gay
    Of pollen, now has gone away—
        She woos the moth with her sweet, low
            word;   15
And when above her his moth-wings hover
Then her bright breast she will uncover
And yield her honey-drop to her lover.
Into the yellow, evening glow
Saunters a man from the farm below;   20
Leans, and looks in at the low-built shed
Where the swallow has hung her marriage bed.
    The bird lies warm against the wall.

She glances quick her startled eyes
Towards him, then she turns away 25
Her small head, making warm display
Of red upon the throat. Her terrors sway
Her out of the nest's warm, busy ball,
Whose plaintive cry is heard as she flies
In one blue stoop from out the sties 30
Into the twilight's empty hall.
Oh, water-hen, beside the rushes,
Hide your quaintly scarlet blushes,
Still your quick tail, lie still as dead,
Till the distance folds over his ominous
  tread! 35

The rabbit presses back her ears,
Turns back her liquid, anguished eyes
And crouches low; then with wild spring
Spurts from the terror of his oncoming;
To be choked back, the wire ring 40
Her frantic effort throttling:
  Piteous brown ball of quivering fears!
Ah, soon in his large, hard hands she dies,
And swings all loose from the swing of his walk!
Yet calm and kindly are his eyes 45
And ready to open in brown surprise
Should I not answer to his talk
Or should he my tears surmise.

I hear his hand on the latch, and rise from my
  chair
Watching the door open; he flashes bare 50
His strong teeth in a smile, and flashes his eyes
In a smile like triumph upon me; then careless-
  wise
He flings the rabbit soft on the table board
And comes toward me: he! the uplifted sword

Of his hand against my bosom! and oh, the
  broad 55
Blade of his glance that asks me to applaud
His coming! With his hand he turns my face
  to him
And caresses me with his fingers that still smell
  grim
Of rabbit's fur! God, I am caught in a snare!
I know not what fine wire is round my
  throat; 60
I only know I let him finger there
My pulse of life, and let him nose like a stoat
Who sniffs with joy before he drinks the blood.
And down his mouth comes to my mouth! and
  down
His bright dark eyes come over me, like a
  hood 65
Upon my mind! his lips meet mine, and a flood
Of sweet fire sweeps across me, so I drown
Against him, die, and find death good.

In "The Farmer's Bride" it is the farmer who
speaks. In Lawrence's poem it is the farmer's wife
who speaks.

1. Compare and contrast the speaker in this poem
with the girl in "The Farmer's Bride." How are the
two women alike? How are they unlike? How do
their situations differ?

2. Notice how many of the items described in
ll. 1-44 have to do with love and fertility or with
death. Is it appropriate that for this observer the
objects of nature are seen in terms of love or of
death?

3. Why does the woman say "I am caught in a
snare"? Why does she compare her husband to a
stoat?

4. Are the last two lines of the poem a sudden
reversal of the woman's feelings or has her final
emotion actually been sufficiently prepared for?

SECTION II

The poems in this section do not tell the reader
a story, though some of them imply a situation
in which a story is potential. For instance, "The
Lotos Eaters," by Tennyson, is based on an incident out of the story of Ulysses' voyage home
after the Trojan War. But this poem is not concerned with the incident as such; it is, rather,
concerned with an attitude toward life. Such
poems as these appeal to some interest different
from that of situation or episode. Most of them
describe some natural object, or objects: an
eagle, a fly, a flock of wild swans, a tiger. But

there is always someone who is looking at the object, or objects. This observer may not be specified in the given poem (as in "The Eagle," by Tennyson); or he may be specified (as in "The Wild Swans at Coole," by Yeats). If he does appear, he may or may not be the poet himself (or the person that the poet, for the purpose of the poem, pretends to be at that moment). In "The Wild Swans at Coole," for instance, the observer is the poet himself, but in "The Lotos Eaters," the person involved is not the poet, but one of the wanderers. But in all cases the poet intends that the reader shall participate in the observation. In reading a poem one should always try to understand what kind of person the observer in the poem is, so that he himself may imaginatively enter this role.

The interest, however, that the observer and reader have in the object of the poem is not merely the interest one would have in looking at such an object in real life or in a photograph. The close observation of the poet may heighten the pleasure of the reader in recognition of the object. But even in poems in which there is no mention of an observer (that is, poems which are most objective), the reader, if he is at all sensitive, will find that the object, as the poet has presented it, awakens in him a certain feeling or mood.

What the poet expresses may be, as in the early poems in this section, a very vague and general feeling or mood. But the reader will observe that in this section the feeling becomes more and more closely defined and that the poems, more and more, tend to present an idea as well as a mood. That is, the objects the poet has chosen from nature tend to have more and more the force of a symbol. Sometimes the poet states definitely what he is symbolizing, or illustrating; but sometimes he merely gives clues so that the reader may discover the meaning for himself. This is the case with "The Wild Swans at Coole," by Yeats; for the poet, though he pretends to be merely telling about an encounter with the wild swans, is really telling a truth about his own life. And it is the case in "The Tiger," by Blake, in which one quickly discovers that the poet is not writing about an ordinary tiger, but about a beast that stands for something, for the power of evil in the world. One must remember that when a genuine poet gives description, that description inevitably comes with an expressive force: the image implies a feeling about life, and a feeling implies an idea.

The Eagle
ALFRED, LORD TENNYSON
(1809-1892)

He clasps the crag with crooked hands;
Close to the sun in lonely lands,
Ringed with the azure world, he stands.

The wrinkled sea beneath him crawls;
He watches from his mountain walls,   5
And like a thunderbolt he falls.

1.

This short poem comes about as close to the completely *objective* account of nature as a poem can. The poet is not using his description to illustrate a moral truth, or even a personal mood. He is giving a picture of an eagle, but we shall learn something about the aims and the method of poetry if we compare carefully this description with other possible descriptions. The definition in the dictionary reads as follows: "Any of various large diurnal birds of prey of the falcon family, noted for their strength, size, graceful figure, keenness of vision, and powers of flight. The typical eagles constitute a genus *Aquila* in which the legs are feathered to the toes." The scientist would be interested in giving such information as that in the last sentence. His account would have much to tell us about the eagle's diet, habitat, biological structure, etc. The poetic description is interested rather in such matters as the "graceful figure, keenness of vision, and powers of flight."

Notice in this poem that, although the poet emphasizes the elements given in the dictionary definition, he does so by presenting them vividly through concrete figures. As for the eagle's strength:

He clasps the crag with crooked hands.

The poet shows us the eagle actually exhibiting his strength, strength in this instance in repose but its latent powers suggested by its powerful talons, the crooked hands. As for the keenness of vision and powers of flight:

> Close to the sun in lonely lands.

One of the common folk-beliefs for a long time was that the eagle could look steadily at the sun. This is suggested by the phrase "close to the sun." But the loneliness and rugged power of the eagle are also suggested, "in lonely lands."

And in the next line the poet actually adopts the eagle's point of vantage. He does not describe the eagle as a man might look up at him, but describes the world as the eagle looks *down* on it.

> Ringed with the azure world, he stands.

When one is on a high place, the world seems to spread out in a ring around him, and in this case a distant ring; and "azure" indicates the bluish quality of far-off distances.

The next line continues from the eagle's vantage point—an eagle's-eye view:

> The wrinkled sea beneath him crawls.

Why *wrinkled?* Because seen from high above, the waves give the appearance of wrinkles, and as they move into shore, the sea seems to be a live thing with movement of its own.

The eagle's keenness of vision and terrible power are given an almost dramatic emphasis in the last two lines. The eagle is evidently watching for prey far below him, on the lower cliffs, or probably in the sea, and perceiving it, swoops toward it with the speed of lightning. And the swift and characteristic exit of the eagle from the poet's little picture of him affords the poet an appropriate ending for his poem.

But this is not the whole story. In interpreting, in trying to get the *meaning* of an experience, the poet, being a human being writing for human beings, is certain to interpret in human terms. The eagle, even in this objective poem, becomes something of a human being. He is, one might say, like a robber baron, exulting in his own liberty and fierceness and strength.

Unassailable in his own castle perched on the cliffs, he exacts toll at pleasure from the country below him. This is, as a matter of fact, what Tennyson does suggest to the reader. It is implied in the fact that he gives his eagle *hands* and in that he has him watch from his mountain *walls. Walls* is a human word. A wall is a fabric built by men. And so the phrase, "his mountain walls," implies a connection between the eagle and his human counterparts who owned rocky fastnesses which were indeed often as inaccessible as an eagle's aerie. Not least important is the word *his.* Animals do not properly own property. Tennyson's eagle owns his crag; and the bird becomes human enough for us, even in such a relatively objective poem, that we feel a sort of understanding of it, and therefore a sense of *meaning* to the whole. And in the poem one participates in the exhilaration of the eagle's distant view and the furious but controlled plunge downward. Observe how the poet has made the word *falls* the climactic (see Glossary) point of the poem, the word on which the whole effect of the poem is finally concentrated.

What are we to make of this poem? Are we to rest on the notion that this is merely some sort of poetic equating of eagles and robber barons? No, the poem is a celebration of power and grandeur, but a lonely power and an independent grandeur—a release of spirit into an ennobling moment.

2.

The instant we begin to analyze and interpret a poem, a certain question always comes to mind: how do we know that the poet "intended" this? We shall discuss this question more fully a little later (p. 303), but for the moment we may say that our concern is with the poem as it exists and not as it was "intended" to be. We put quotation marks around the word *intended* here to indicate that we must use it in a special sense. We can't use it about a poem in the way we use it about a house. An architect may draw the blueprint for a house and that blueprint represents his intention, his plan. Then the contractor goes and executes the plan. A man trained to read a blueprint can predict the house. That is not true of the "intention" of a poem—or, for that matter, of a novel or story or picture or piece of music. The artist, whatever kind he is, may have many ideas for his work, and many images in his head, and a kind of hunch about how he wants the finished work to feel. In his imagination he may—and to some degree must—project himself forward to the finished work. But the thing can't exist until it exists. That is, Tennyson could not "plan" the phrase "wrinkled sea." He may have an image in his mind of the sea as viewed from a great height, but that is not a "plan" or "intention" for the phrase. As soon as he has the phrase he does not have a plan, he has the thing itself. In poetry, the phrase, the rhythm, the associative relations of words are part of the meaning. Till we have them we do not have the full meaning.

This is not to say that a poet works only blindly and instinctively. It is simply to say that for the poet the composition of a poem may well be a process of exploration of his meaning, of creation of his meaning, and not the execution of a plan or intention. *Therefore, to put the matter somewhat paradoxically, we may say that, in the end, we go to the poem for the meaning of the poet and not to the poet for the meaning of the poem.* We must, of course, find out all we can about the poet and the world he lived in, what ideas and materials were available to him, what his experiences and concerns were. That information will undoubtedly help us in our reading of his poetry. But we can never take the poetry as a mere mechanical projection, the fulfilment of a plan, an intention, a blueprint.

Silver

WALTER DE LA MARE
(1873-   )

Slowly, silently, now the moon
Walks the night in her silver shoon;
This way, and that, she peers, and sees
Silver fruit upon silver trees;
One by one the casements catch   5
Her beams beneath the silvery thatch;
Couched in his kennel, like a log,
With paws of silver sleeps the dog;
From their shadowy cote the white breasts peep

Of doves in a silver-feathered sleep;   10
A harvest mouse goes scampering by,
With silver claws and a silver eye;
And moveless fish in the water gleam,
By silver reeds in a silver stream.

1. Is this poem merely objective description—a scene such as anyone could see upon a moonlit night—and presented without bias or interpretation?
2. Who is it that "sees" this world touched with silver? (See ll. 1-3)
3. Granted that the moon is a special observer—she herself *makes* the silver world that she *sees*—is it true that any observer colors the world that he sees in some degree by his very act of looking at it?

The Red Wheelbarrow
WILLIAM CARLOS WILLIAMS
(1883-1962)

so much depends
upon

a red wheel
barrow

glazed with rain   5
water

beside the white
chickens

Philip Wheelwright [1] makes the following comment upon this poem:

"A classical case (and apparently a classical failure) of the attempt to convey a simple experience through sheer simplicity of statement is to be found in Section xxi of William Carlos Williams' *Spring and All*. The eight short lines of the section, although they bear no distinguishing title, form an independent unit with no imagistic or thematic outside connections, and it may therefore be treated (as its author has, in fact, publicly spoken of it) as a single poem. The statement runs:

so much depends
upon

a red wheel
barrow

[1] Philip Wheelwright, *Metaphor and Reality* (Bloomington, Ind.: Indiana University Press, 1962), pp. 159-160.

glazed with rain
water

beside the white
chickens

That is all. To most readers it will be accepted as a pleasant pastiche [see Glossary], with no more than a fanciful justification for the opening words. To Dr. Williams, however, as he has repeatedly declared, the small remembered scene is of arresting and retaining importance. But quite obviously the personal associations and bubbles of memory that have stirred the poet's sensitive recollections are not shared by a reader whose only clues are to be found in the poem itself. The trouble is that in these lines the poet has tried to convey the simplicity of the remembered experience by a plain simplicity of utterance—by a simple simplicity, one might say, as opposed to a contextual [see Glossary] simplicity. The attempt was bound to fail. Simplicity, when it is fresh and not banal, can scarcely be conveyed to another mind, except in rare instances where, by happy accident, two diverse sensitivities happen to be attuned in just that respect."

1. Do you agree with Wheelwright?

2. Compare the Williams poem with "The Eagle" and with "Silver." Does "The Eagle" also represent an attempt to convey a simple experience through "plain simplicity of utterance"? If not, does "The Eagle" throw any light upon what Wheelwright means by "contextual simplicity"?

Inscription for a Fountain on a Heath

SAMUEL TAYLOR COLERIDGE
(1772-1834)

This Sycamore, oft musical with bees,—
Such tents the Patriarchs loved! O long
    unharmed
May all its agéd boughs o'er-canopy
The small round basin, which this jutting stone
Keeps pure from falling leaves! Long may the
    Spring,   5
Quietly as a sleeping infant's breath,
Send up cold waters to the traveller
With soft and even pulse! Nor ever cease
Yon tiny cone of sand its soundless dance,

Which at the bottom, like a Fairy's Page,   10
As merry and no taller, dances still,
Nor wrinkles the smooth surface of the Fount.
Here Twilight is and Coolness: here is moss,
A soft seat, and a deep and ample shade.
Thou may'st toil far and find no second tree.   15
Drink, Pilgrim, here; Here rest! and if thy heart
Be innocent, here too shalt thou refresh
Thy spirit, listening to some gentle sound,
Or passing gale or hum of murmuring bees!

1. Compare the kind of description used in this poem with that used in "The Red Wheelbarrow." Unlike Williams, Coleridge is not content to make a series of notations on the object. He interprets constantly, as in line 2. Does he, nevertheless, provide a vivid visualization of the scene he describes?

2. What is the "tiny cone of sand" in line 9? Is the comparison in lines 10 and 11 apt and effective?

3. What is the effect of the term "pilgrim" in line 16? Earlier in the poem Coleridge had been content with the term "traveler." Does the term "pilgrim" and the reference to a refreshment of the spirit serve to give the poem another dimension? Or does the poem become pretentious?

A Complaint

WILLIAM WORDSWORTH
(1770-1850)

There is a change—and I am poor;
Your love hath been, nor long ago,
A fountain at my fond heart's door,
Whose only business was to flow;
And flow it did; not taking heed   5
Of its own bounty, or my need.

What happy moments did I count!
Blest was I then all bliss above!
Now, for that consecrated fount
Of murmuring, sparkling, living love,   10
What have I? shall I dare to tell?
A comfortless and hidden well.

A well of love—it may be deep—
I trust it is,—and never dry:

What matter? if the waters sleep   15
In silence and obscurity.
—Such change, and at the very door
Of my fond heart, hath made me poor.

In his "Inscription for a Fountain" Coleridge is concerned to give us an account of the fountain for its own sake, even though he does hint that the fountain offers the wayfarer other refreshment than its cooling waters. Wordsworth, on the other hand, is primarily concerned to illustrate a human relationship. The poem has to do with the alteration in feelings between two friends—specifically between Wordsworth himself and Coleridge in 1806. A few years earlier the two men had shared an experience in which each stimulated the other intellectually and imaginatively, and in which each had the other's complete confidence. Now, as the poem tells us, there has been a change, a change which has left the speaker poor.

Wordsworth does not concern himself to tell us what has caused the change. The poem simply undertakes to describe it and to distinguish between the former and the present relation between the two men. But in doing so, the poet does not make use of any abstract (see Glossary) terms. He does not say that instead of the former warmth there is now coolness, or that affection has receded into respect. He has preferred to state the difference through an analogy—through the difference between a fountain and a well. The use of analogy can, however, be more effective than any set of abstract terms.

Most men would be happy in the possession of a well of love. The poet is evidently sincere in his belief that this well is very deep and in his confidence that it will never run dry. But a well does not make a spontaneous offering of itself. One must dip down into it to partake of its waters.

The contrast between fountain and well is apparently a simple one, but the poem itself is not really simple. It is interesting to see how delicately and yet richly the contrast may be used to point up the human relationship. In this connection it might be interesting for the student to put questions such as the following to himself.

1. Consider the adjectives in line 10. All of them refer to running waters. "Murmuring" and "sparkling" obviously do, but also "living": we speak, for example, of living waters, not only in the sense of fresh, unstagnant, pure because flowing from a source, but also in the sense of life-giving. May all three adjectives be applied to love, and if so, what do they imply?

2. Notice the adjectives in line 12. The well is comfortless and hidden, but is there a suggestion that it is comfortless *because* hidden? In the contrast between this well and the fountain just described, it would be presumably the waters themselves that were hidden, and yet the suggestion is that the well itself is hidden—as if the thirsty man not only had to seek the waters but was not even sure of the location of the well.

3. Notice that in stanza 3 the waters sleeping "in silence and obscurity" in both points contradict the characteristics of the fountain, whose waters are "murmuring" and "sparkling." How does the term "sleep" apply to water? Can it be properly applied at all? And even figuratively, is there anything wrong with waters sleeping? We might think of waters of a calm sea asleep beneath the moon, or a placid lake asleep under the sun. In this context, of course, where all the adjectives applying to the water also apply to love, sleep acquires a special sense of apathy and indifference.

4. Notice that the use of analogy allows Wordsworth to make the case against his friend without bitterness, as if he were merely describing a loss to himself with hurt and anguish, but with no sense of reproach. A well of deep affection is something so precious that it becomes a matter of regret only because once it was something more.

5. Though this poem is not primarily concerned with a description of a fountain for its own sake, not even to the extent to which Coleridge described his fountain for its own sake—the power of the poem depends upon the concrete detail which may suggest to our imaginations the sense of a fountain. How effectively has the poet done this?

Monody

HERMAN MELVILLE
(1819-1891)

To have known him, to have loved him
    After loneness long;
And then to be estranged in life,
    And neither in the wrong;

And now for death to set his seal—   5
    Ease me, a little ease, my song!

By wintry hills his hermit-mound
    The sheeted snow-drifts drape,
And houseless there the snow-bird flits
    Beneath the fir-trees' crape: 10
Glazed now with ice the cloistral vine
    That hid the shyest grape.

This poem refers to an estrangement between
Melville and Nathaniel Hawthorne, the author of
The Scarlet Letter and *The Marble Faun.* Now death
has made impossible a reconciliation of the two former friends.

    1. Compare this poem with "A Complaint."
    2. What function is served by the images in the
second stanza? In particular, what is the function
(and meaning) of "the shyest grape"?

Sonnet 18

WILLIAM SHAKESPEARE
(1564-1616)

Shall I compare thee to a summer's day?
Thou art more lovely and more temperate:
Rough winds do shake the darling buds of May,
And summer's lease hath all too short a date:
Sometime too hot the eye of heaven shines,   5
And often is his gold complexion dimmed;
And every fair from fair sometime declines,
By chance, or nature's changing course, un-
    trimmed;
But thy eternal summer shall not fade,
Nor lose possession of that fair thou owest;   10
Nor shall Death brag thou wander'st in his
    shade,
When in eternal lines to time thou growest:
    So long as men can breathe, or eyes can see,
    So long lives this, and this gives life to thee.

    1. The poem begins with a question: should he
use the summer's day comparison or not? What are
his arguments against it? To what does he finally
compare his friend?
    2. Are there other comparisons in this poem?
How are they related to the dominant comparison?
    3. Are the last lines of the poem boastful? If not,
why not?

Sonnet 73

WILLIAM SHAKESPEARE
(1564-1616)

That time of year thou mayst in me behold
When yellow leaves, or none, or few, do hang
Upon those boughs which shake against the
    cold,
Bare ruined choirs, where late the sweet birds
    sang.
In me thou seest the twilight of such day   5
As after sunset fadeth in the west;
Which by and by black night doth take away,
Death's second self, that seals up all in rest.
In me thou seest the glowing of such fire,
That on the ashes of his youth doth lie,   10
As the death-bed whereon it must expire,
Consum'd with that which it was nourished by.
    This thou perceiv'st, which makes thy love
    more strong,
    To love that well which thou must leave ere
    long.

    1. To what does the speaker compare himself?
Does he merely say I am like autumn, or does he develop the imagery of autumn?
    2. The speaker also compares himself to twilight
and to glowing coals. How are these comparisons
related to the comparison of himself to autumn?
What do the three comparisons have in common?
    3. What is the meaning of l. 12? How does the
meaning apply to the speaker?
    4. Relate the last two lines to the rest of the
poem. What is it that his friend "perceiv'st"?

Sonnet 97

WILLIAM SHAKESPEARE
(1564-1616)

How like a winter hath my absence been
From thee, the pleasure of the fleeting year!
What freezing have I felt, what dark days seen,
What old December's bareness everywhere!
And yet this time removed was summer's
    time;

The teeming autumn, big with rich increase,
Bearing the wanton burden of the prime,
Like widowed wombs after their lord's decease:
Yet this abundant issue seem'd to me
But hope of orphans, and unfathered fruit;   10
For summer and his pleasures wait on thee,
And, thou away, the very birds are mute;
   Or if they sing, 'tis with so dull a cheer,
   That leaves look pale, dreading the winter's
   near.

Develop a set of questions which would lead to an interpretation of this poem.

To Daffadills
ROBERT HERRICK (1591-1674)

Faire Daffadills, we weep to see
   You haste away so soone:
As yet the early-rising Sun
   Has not attain'd his Noone.
      Stay, stay,   5
     Until the hasting day
      Has run
     But to the Even-song;
And, having pray'd together, wee
     Will goe with you along.   10

We have short time to stay, as you,
   We have as short a Spring;
As quick a growth to meet Decay,
   As you, or any thing.
      We die,   15
     As your hours doe, and drie
      Away,
     Like to the Summers raine;
Or as the pearles of Mornings dew
     Ne'er to be found againe.   20

1. The speaker addresses the daffodils as if they were human beings. Does he justify this device in the analogies which he develops between the daffodils and men?
2. Note that "Even-song" technically means an evening church service and thus prepares for l. 9.
3. As the poem ends, is the emphasis upon the frailty of the flowers or of man?

Song
EDMUND WALLER (1606-1687)

Go, lovely Rose,
Tell her that wastes her time and me,
   That now she knows,
When I resemble her to thee,
How sweet and fair she seems to be.   5

Tell her that's young,
And shuns to have her graces spied,
   That hadst thou sprung
In deserts where no men abide,
Thou must have uncommended died.   10

Small is the worth
Of beauty from the light retired:
   Bid her come forth,
Suffer her self to be desired,
And not blush so to be admired.   15

Then die, that she
The common fate of all things rare
   May read in thee,
How small a part of time they share,
That are so wondrous sweet and faire.   20

Like the preceding poem, this one is addressed ostensibly to the flower, though the poet's real concern is with a human relation.

1. What does he gain by describing his sweetheart in terms of a rose?
2. Why is "wastes her time and me" (l. 2) superior to "wastes her time and mine"? What is the effect of "*Suffer* her self to be desired" (l. 14)?

The Bugle Song
ALFRED, LORD TENNYSON
(1809-1892)

The splendor falls on castle walls
   And snowy summits old in story;
The long light shakes across the lakes,
   And the wild cataract leaps in glory.

Blow, bugle, blow, set the wild echoes
    flying,   5
Blow, bugle; answer, echoes, dying, dying,
    dying.

O hark, O hear! how thin and clear,
    And thinner, clearer, farther going!
O sweet and far from cliff and scar
    The horns of Elfland faintly blowing!   10
Blow, let us hear the purple glens replying,
Blow, bugle; answer, echoes, dying, dying,
    dying.

O love, they die in yon rich sky,
    They faint on hill or field or river;
Our echoes roll from soul to soul,   15
    And grow forever and forever.
Blow, bugle, blow, set the wild echoes flying,
And answer, echoes, answer, dying, dying,
    dying.

The first two stanzas of this poem describe a bugle call at sunset. The poet who is apparently standing on some high place describes the country about him in the light of sunset, the castle in the distance, the waterfall, etc. Evidently, the country is mountainous, and not only are there the rich tones of the bugle, the hills throw back the echoes which gradually die away and which become at last so faint that one might imagine them as notes blown from the horns of the fairies. But an idea comes into the poet's mind as he listens to the dying echoes: these echoes of the bugle die away into nothingness, but the spiritual echoes which roll back and forth between him and his beloved do not decrease but actually increase as time goes on; that is, the poet seems to be saying, love does not become less with the years but grows greater.

It is easy to see why the poem has been very popular. The images are pretty and "poetical"; the rhythm (see Glossary) is emphatic; and there is a great deal of rhyme (see Glossary). The rich, even gaudy, description of the bugle call at sunset is made to serve true love. Beautiful as all this is, the poet seems to say, love is more beautiful, more enduring.

Suppose we read the poem carefully, however, and explore further the poet's experience. Does the idea in the last stanza grow out of what

has preceded it, or has it been added on as a sort of moralizing comment?

The first stanza contains some sharp and arresting phrases, for instance, "The long light shakes." "Long" suggests, vividly, the level beams of the setting sun, and "shakes" suggests a kind of dazzling quality, as if the light itself vibrated, shimmering over the water. But in addition to the visual element, the word "shakes" invokes the taut, vibrant quality of the bugle note. So sound and sight fuse and in that fusion excite our senses. Phrasings such as these more than make up for the rather vague and conventional (see Glossary) phrase "old in story" in line 2.

The second stanza, after the effective image of "cliff and scar," indulges a pleasant fancy: the sound of the bugle call, diminished by echo, causes the observer to imagine that he is hearing horns blown by the elves. But what about these "elves"? Isn't there something inevitably trivial and cute associated with them, to our modern mind at least, that debases the effect of the poem? And in any case, isn't the use of "Elfland" a kind of lazy shorthand for something the poet can achieve directly and powerfully in such phrases as "The long light shakes"?

Thus far, the poet has juxtaposed elements of sight and sound—the sunset gleam as reflected on far away castle walls and mountain summits, and the notes of the bugle as "reflected"—that is, echoed back—from these same distant points of the landscape. The experience is invested with a special kind of magical glamor—despite the reference to "Elfland." But the poet apparently felt that it was insufficient to let his poem stop with this kind of evocation and that he needed to bind the various descriptive elements together and to relate them to some assertion of obvious significance. He has attempted to bring this about in his last stanza. In judging his success in this matter, the student might put to himself the following questions.

1. Has the analogy—or contrast—between the echoes of the bugle and those which "roll from soul to soul" been adequately prepared for? Note that the romantic aura associated with the echoes of the bugle call comes from the fact that they are faint and are indeed "dying," but the lover surely would not admit that the spiritual "echoes" playing between him and his sweetheart will die away. It is possible that the poet wanted to make a point of the very difference

between the echoes, but in that case, has he made enough of the shock of contrast? Has he boldly dismissed the pretty magic of dying echoes in favor of the spiritual "echo"?

2. What is the sense of the word "grow" in line 16? Grow in intensity? In volume? Or grow in some way that would leave these echoes of the soul richer yet not deafening—magical yet ever and ever stronger?

3. How effectively does the poet use the refrain? It is an obvious means of tying the three stanzas together, but why does he want to have the "wild echoes" set flying in Stanza I? In Stanza II? And finally in Stanza III? Or is there any meaningful application in each case?

4. Granted that we are not to measure poetry by obviously logical standards, is not some kind of imaginative logic—some kind of coherence—called for in the poet's management of his images? If so, is there sufficient coherence of this kind manifested in "The Bugle Song"?

The Lotos Eaters

ALFRED, LORD TENNYSON
(1809-1892)

"Courage!" he said, and pointed toward the
     land,
"This mounting wave will roll us shoreward
     soon."
In the afternoon they came unto a land
In which it seemed always afternoon.
All round the coast the languid air did
     swoon,   5
Breathing like one that hath a weary dream.
Full-faced above the valley stood the moon;
And, like a downward smoke, the slender stream
     Along the cliff to fall and pause and fall
     did seem.

A land of streams! some, like a downward
     smoke,   10
Slow-drooping veils of thinnest lawn, did go;
And some through wavering lights and shadows
     broke,
Rolling a slumbrous sheet of foam below.
They saw the gleaming river seaward flow
From the inner land; far off, three mountain-
     tops,   15
Three silent pinnacles of aged snow,

Stood sunset-flushed; and, dewed with showery
     drops,
     Up-clomb the shadowy pine above the woven
     copse.

The charmed sunset lingered low adown
In the red West; through mountain clefts the
     dale   20
Was seen far inland, and the yellow down
Bordered with palm, and many a winding vale
And meadow, set with slender galingale;
A land where all things always seemed the
     same!
And round about the keel with faces pale,   25
Dark faces pale against that rosy flame,
     The mild-eyed melancholy Lotos-eaters came.

Branches they bore of that enchanted stem,
Laden with flower and fruit, whereof they gave
To each, but whoso did receive of them   30
And taste, to him the gushing of the wave
Far far away did seem to mourn and rave
On alien shores; and if his fellow spake,
His voice was thin, as voices from the grave;
And deep-asleep he seemed, yet all awake. 35
     And music in his ears his beating heart did
     make.

They sat them down upon the yellow sand,
Between the sun and moon upon the shore;
And sweet it was to dream of Fatherland,
Of child, and wife, and slave; but evermore 40
Most weary seemed the sea, weary the oar,
Weary the wandering fields of barren foam.
Then some one said, "We will return no more;"
And all at once they said, "Our island home
     Is far beyond the wave; we will no longer
     roam."   45

Tennyson here imagines a scene from one of the adventures of Odysseus (or Ulysses) in Homer's *Odyssey:* Ulysses is speaking as the poem opens. His mariners do make shore, and there find themselves in the land of the Lotos-eaters, a people who eat a fruit which begets a dreaming torpor.

1. How does the phrase "weary dream" (l. 6) set the tone for all the description that follows? Why is the description of the land as one "in which it seemed always afternoon" peculiarly appropriate?

2. How is the dreamlike quality of the landscape developed? The weary quality of the landscape?

3. Note the use of repetition in this poem, particularly of the word "weary" in the last stanza.

4. The sea in the first lines is associated with courageous effort. What has the sea become in the last stanza; see, for example, l. 42?

5. Compare the description in "The Lotos Eaters" with that in "The Bugle Song." Is it arguable that the descriptive detail in "The Lotos Eaters" is more significantly related to the meaning of the poem than in "The Bugle Song"? Note that in "The Lotos Eaters," as well as in "The Bugle Song," there is a reference to the effect of the light of sunset upon waterfalls and snow-clad summits. (See lines 10-17.) In "The Lotos Eaters" is the description of the "charmed sunset" merely decorative? Or is it rather directly related to the mood of the poem?

The Tree of Man

A. E. HOUSMAN (1859-1936)

On Wenlock Edge the wood's in trouble,
His forest fleece the Wrekin heaves;
The gale, it plies the saplings double,
And thick on Severn snow the leaves.

'Twould blow like this through holt and
   hanger   5
When Uricon the city stood:
'Tis the old wind in the old anger,
But then it threshed another wood.

Then, 'twas before my time, the Roman
At yonder heaving hill would stare: 10
The blood that warms an English yeoman,
The thoughts that hurt him, they were there.

There, like the wind through woods in riot,
Through him the gale of life blew high;
The tree of man was never quiet: 15
Then 'twas the Roman, now 'tis I.

The gale, it plies the saplings double,
It blows so hard, 'twill soon be gone;
Today the Roman and his trouble
Are ashes under Uricon.   20

Wenlock Edge and the Wrekin are hills in Shropshire.

The Severn is a river in the west of England.

1. This is a piece of description with an application of the scene to the poet's own life. In the description does the wind stand for anything else? What?

2. What does the wood stand for?

3. Compare and contrast this poem with "To Daffadills." With Sonnet 97. Is the use of imagery in this poem more subtle or less subtle than in the other two poems?

Nulla Fides

PATRICK CAREY (fl. 1651)

For God's sake mark that fly:
See what a poor, weak, little thing it is.
When thou has marked and scorned it, know
   that this,
This little, poor, weak fly
Has killed a pope; can make an emp'ror die.   5

Behold yon spark of fire;
How little hot! how near to nothing 'tis!
When thou hast done despising, know that this,
This contemned spark of fire,
Has burnt whole towns; can burn a world
   entire.   10

That crawling worm there see:
Ponder how ugly, filthy, vile it is.
When thou hast seen and loathed it, know that
   this,
This base worm thou dost see,
Has quite devoured thy parents; shall eat
   thee.   15

Honour, the world, and man,
What trifles are they; since most true it is
That this poor fly, this little spark, this
So much abhorred worm, can
Honour destroy; burn worlds; devour up
   man.   20

1. Is the description of the fly, the spark, and the worm sufficiently vivid? It could be argued that these objects are described in rather vague, general terms. If so, does this fact lessen the force of the poem? If not, why not?

2. Does the poem simply versify an obvious generalization? Is it therefore flat and trite?

3. What is the meaning of "For God's sake" (l. 1)? Is the phrase used merely to intensify the imperative? Or what is its function?

A Passer-By

ROBERT BRIDGES (1844-1930)

Whither, O splendid ship, thy white sails
    crowding,
    Leaning across the bosom of the urgent West,
That fearest nor sea rising, nor sky clouding,
    Whither away, fair rover, and what thy
    quest?
    Ah! soon, when Winter has all our vales
    opprest,   5
When skies are cold and misty, and hail is
    hurling,
    Wilt thou glide on the blue Pacific, or rest
In a summer haven asleep, thy white sails
    furling.

I there before thee, in the country that well
    thou knowest,
    Already arrived am inhaling the odorous
    air: 10
I watch thee enter unerringly where thou goest,
    And anchor queen of the strange shipping
    there,
    Thy sails for awnings spread, thy masts bare;
Nor is aught from the foaming reef to the snow-
    capped, grandest
    Peak, that is over the feathery palms more
    fair   15
Than thou, so upright, so stately, and still thou
    standest.

And yet, O splendid ship, unhailed and name-
    less,
    I know not if, aiming a fancy, I rightly divine
That thou hast a purpose joyful, a courage
    blameless,
    Thy port assured in a happier land than
    mine.   20
    But for all I have given thee, beauty enough
    is thine,
As thou, aslant with trim tackle, and shrouding,
    From the proud nostril curve of a prow's line

In the offing scatterest foam, thy white sails
    crowding.

Write an interpretive discussion of "A Passer-By." Try to base all your general notions on particulars in the poem.

The Wild Swans at Coole

WILLIAM BUTLER YEATS (1865-1939)

The trees are in their autumn beauty,
The woodland paths are dry;
Under the October twilight the water
Mirrors a still sky.
Upon the brimming water among the stones 5
Are nine and fifty swans.

The nineteenth autumn has come upon me
Since I first made my count.
I saw, before I had well finished,
All suddenly mount   10
And scatter wheeling in great broken rings
Upon their clamorous wings.

I have looked upon those brilliant creatures,
And now my heart is sore.
All's changed since I, hearing at twilight, 15
The first time on this shore,
The bell-beat of their wings above my head,
Trod with a lighter tread.

Unwearied still, lover by lover,
They paddle in the cold   20
Companionable streams, or climb the air.
Their hearts have not grown old;
Passion or conquest, wander where they will,
Attend upon them still.

But now they drift on the still water   25
Mysterious, beautiful.
Among what rushes will they build,
By what lake's edge or pool
Delight men's eyes, when I awake some day
To find they have flown away?   30

The poem begins as an apparently objective

and simple bit of description. One notices, however, the exactitude of it. It is autumn, at twilight. The paths through the woods are dry, and this suggests that the poet on a walk through the woods has just stepped out on the shore of the still pool, and has stood there long enough to count the swans. There are fifty-nine of them. It has been nineteen years since he counted them for the first time. At that time too it was the autumn of the year, and there was a particular incident connected with that first sight of the swans which may have impressed the whole scene on his memory and which may help account for his remembering it so exactly: the swans rose in flight on that occasion almost before he had finished counting them.

But the poet remembers other things connected with that first experience—how he responded to that first hearing of their wings with a resilience of step—of what he was then as compared to what he is now. And the swans, unchanged since that first meeting, become a sort of yard-stick against which the poet may measure the changes which have taken place in his own life.

The exactitude of description in the first stanzas—the poet's knowledge of the precise number of the swans, the reason for his having remembered them, etc.—has an importance therefore. These are particular swans; indeed, they are the poet's own swans because he has watched for them year after year. Because of this fact, there is no suggestion of affectation when the poet proceeds to contrast the immortality of the swans with his own mortality and change.

If the poet were to say "my heart is sore," prompted by some accidental or chance-met scene, we would be inclined to believe his grief was an easy or trivial one. The poet's restraint, or rather the effect of restraint which the poem gives us, is further reinforced by the poet's method of referring to his grief. He is content to describe the reasons for his soreness of heart and the quality of it by implied contrasts between himself and the swans. When he first saw the swans nineteen years before, he could identify himself to some extent with them. His step became lighter in exultation with them.

Now "All's changed," he tells us, and what has changed for him is suggested by what has remained unchanged with the swans: *they* are still unwearied; they are still lover beside lover; their hearts have not become old; they still find themselves at home in their world.

Notice how the poet has been able to suggest a great deal by his choice of words. Consider, for example, the phrase "companionable streams." *Companionable* suggests the qualities of security and comfort in a spacious, well-lighted room, with perhaps a great fire burning on the hearth. At first it may not seem appropriate to apply such a word to streams, especially since they have just been called "cold." And yet the adjective fits. The swans are at home in nature; they are not aliens in nature, but part of nature in a way in which the poet is not. The swans are not only at home in their world, they dominate it; "passion" and "conquest" wait upon them like servants wherever they choose to wander.

Indeed, the swans themselves are used as a symbol for the beautiful, mysterious, unwearied immortality of nature itself. The poem is an excellent example of the poet's making a bit of natural description carry emotional intensity by relating the description to his own feelings. But he does this by telling us about the swans and not about himself. He does not "pour out his heart" to us. We learn about his own loneliness in the world and his defeat by the implied contrast with the swans. This restraint of the poet gives an impression of intensity and manliness.

Hymn to Diana
BEN JONSON (1573-1637)

Queen and huntress, chaste and fair,
  Now the sun is laid to sleep,
Seated in thy silver chair,
    State in wonted manner keep:
      Hesperus entreats thy light,
      Goddess excellently bright.

Earth, let not thy envious shade
  Dare itself to interpose;

Cynthia's shining orb was made
  Heaven to clear when day did close:
    Bless us then with wishèd sight,
    Goddess excellently bright.

Lay thy bow of pearl apart,
  And thy crystal-shining quiver;
Give unto the flying hart
  Space to breathe, how short soever:
    Thou that mak'st a day of night—
    Goddess excellently bright.

Cynthia is one of the names for Diana, the moon goddess. She was a huntress and the goddess of chastity. Hesperus is the evening star.

1. The poem is addressed to Cynthia. In what ways does it resemble a prayer?
2. When Earth's "shade" interposes between the sun and moon, what occurs?
3. What qualities of a moonlit evening does the poem suggest? Though the poem does not undertake to describe such an evening, does it actually count as such a description? In what ways?

The Night-Piece to Julia
ROBERT HERRICK (1591-1674)

Her eyes the Glow-worm lend thee,
  The shooting Stars attend thee;
    And the Elves also,
    Whose little eyes glow,
Like the sparks of fire, befriend thee.   5

No Will-o'th'-Wisp mis-light thee;
  Nor Snake, or Slow-worm bite thee:
    But on, on thy way
    Not making a stay,
Since Ghost there's none to affright thee. 10

Let not the dark thee cumber;
  What though the Moon does slumber?
    The Stars of the night
    Will lend thee their light,
Like Tapers clear without number.   15

Then Julia let me woo thee,
  Thus, thus to come unto me:

    And when I shall meet
    Thy silvery feet,
My soul I'll pour into thee.   20

1. What is the effect of the poet's drawing all his descriptive detail from the imagery of night?
2. Why does he call the girl's feet "silvery"?
3. What is the effect upon the poem of the mention of the terrors of the night (the Will-o'-th'-Wisp, the Snake, the Slow-worm, etc.)? How seriously are we to take these terrors? Is the effect to make the poem less "flowery," more realistic? Or is it a blemish on the poem?
4. Can we more readily accept the "elves" of this poem than those of "The Bugle Song" (p. 307)?

The Mower
to the Glow-Worms
ANDREW MARVELL (1621-1678)

Ye living lamps, by whose dear light
The Nightingale does sit so late,
And studying all the Summer-night,
Her matchless Songs does meditate;

Ye Country Comets, that portend   5
No War, nor Princes funeral,
Shining unto no higher end
Than to presage the Grasses fall;

Ye Glow-worms, whose officious Flame
To wandering Mowers shows the way, 10
That in the Night have lost their aim,
And after foolish Fires do stray;

Your courteous Lights in vain you waste,
Since Juliana here is come,
For She my Mind hath so displaced 15
That I shall never find my home.

1. Compare and contrast the situation in this poem with that in "The Night-piece."
2. The speaker calls the glow-worms "living lamps"; but why does he call them "Country comets"? What is the force of "Country" here? (The appearance of comets was thought to presage the fall of kings and empires.)
3. "Officious" (l. 9) does not carry the modern

suggestion of "unwanted and distasteful service"; note that in l. 13, the glow-worms' lights are called "courteous." What are the "foolish Fires"? Is it implied that his love for Juliana (*cf.* l. 15) is a sort of Will-o'-th'-Wisp?

4. In this poem there is a good deal of description of the glow-worms, some of it playful, some of it charmingly fantastic. Is this description given primarily for its own sake? Why is it given? What concern does it serve?

God's Grandeur

GERARD MANLEY HOPKINS (1844-1889)

The world is charged with the grandeur of
  God.
  It will flame out, like shining from shook
    foil;
  It gathers to a greatness, like the ooze of oil
Crushed. Why do men then now not reck his
  rod?
Generations have trod, have trod, have trod;   5
  And all is seared with trade; bleared, smeared
    with toil;
  And wears man's smudge and shares man's
    smell: the soil
Is bare now, nor can foot feel, being shod.

And for all this, nature is never spent;
  There lives the dearest freshness deep down
    things;   10
And though the last lights off the black West
  went
  Oh, morning, at the brown brink eastward,
    springs—
Because the Holy Ghost over the bent
  World broods with warm breast and with ah!
    bright wings.

This poem begins with a general statement and it does not pretend to describe a particular scene. Yet many readers will feel that the poem is crammed with concrete particulars—details of description that are sharp and arresting.

1. Note that ll. 2 and 3 give two opposed ways in which the "grandeur" manifests itself. What do the images in these lines add to the statements?

2. What does the image of *treading* accomplish

in ll. 5-8? What has happened to the soil? To the foot that treads it?

3. "And for all this" (l. 9) means "And yet in spite of all this." What is the meaning of "spent" in l. 9? Why does the poet characterize the world as "bent" in l. 11?

4. Note that descriptions of various kinds of light ("flame," "shining," etc.) dominate the first lines of the poem. How is this description related to the last four lines of the poem? Is the dawn scene realized—made to come alive?

5. Read the poem aloud several times, trying to feel yourself into the rhythm and the verbal quality. Can you characterize the effect? Compare it to that of "Bugle Song" and that of "Night-Piece to Julia"?

The Lamb

WILLIAM BLAKE (1757-1827)

Little Lamb, who made thee?
  Dost thou know who made thee?
Gave thee life, and bid thee feed,
By the stream and o'er the mead;
Gave thee clothing of delight,   5
Softest clothing, woolly, bright;
Gave thee such a tender voice,
Making all the vales rejoice?
  Little Lamb, who made thee?
  Dost thou know who made thee?   10

  Little Lamb, I'll tell thee,
  Little Lamb, I'll tell thee:
He is callèd by thy name,
For he calls himself a Lamb.
He is meek, and he is mild;   15
He became a little child.
I a child, and thou a lamb,
We are callèd by his name.
  Little Lamb, God bless thee!
  Little Lamb, God bless thee!   20

This poem, from Blake's *Songs of Innocence*, is to be compared with "The Tiger," from his *Songs of Experience*.

1. Is this poem concerned primarily with a description of the lamb, or with a description of the mind of the child, who speaks the poem?

2. The child speaks to the lamb as if the lamb were a younger child. How does this dramatic device support the meaning of the poem? How are lamb

and child related to God (incarnate in Christ)? What facts does the child make the basis of the relationship? (For further questions, see those on "The Tiger.")

3. Can you see why the editors here preferred to place this poem *after* "God's Grandeur"?

The Tiger

WILLIAM BLAKE (1757-1827)

Tiger! Tiger! burning bright
In the forests of the night,
What immortal hand or eye
Could frame thy fearful symmetry?

In what distant deeps or skies   5
Burnt the fire of thine eyes?
On what wings dare he aspire?
What the hand dare seize the fire?

And what shoulder, and what art,
Could twist the sinews of thy heart?   10
And when thy heart began to beat,
What dread hand? and what dread feet?

What the hammer? what the chain?
In what furnace was thy brain?
What the anvil? what dread grasp   15
Dare its deadly terrors clasp?

When the stars threw down their spears,
And watered heaven with their tears,
Did he smile his work to see?
Did he who made the Lamb make thee?   20

Tiger! Tiger! burning bright
In the forests of the night,
What immortal hand or eye,
Dare frame thy fearful symmetry?

1. Like "The Lamb," this poem is concerned with the problem of authorship and creation. Lamb and Tiger represent, as it were, opposite poles of the creation. Do the two poems cancel each other out? Or do they illuminate each other? Do they complete each other?

2. Can you justify dramatically the unfinished sentences and the abrupt phrases of stanzas 3, 4 and 5? Who is speaking? Out of what emotional state is he speaking?

3. Are we made to "see" the tiger? Is this a realistic description? Are we made to sense the terrible power of the tiger? Is the tiger more than a literal animal? What does the tiger come to stand for?

4. What is this poem "about"? What is the "The Lamb-The Tiger" (considered as a double poem) about?

5. Compare this poem with "The Eagle," by Tennyson (p. 301).

Ode to the West Wind

PERCY BYSSHE SHELLEY (1792-1822)

I

O Wild West Wind, thou breath of Autumn's being
  Thou from whose unseen presence the leaves dead
Are driven like ghosts from an enchanter fleeing,

  Yellow, and black, and pale, and hectic red,
Pestilence-stricken multitudes! O thou   5
  Who chariotest to their dark wintry bed

The wingèd seeds, where they lie cold and low,
  Each like a corpse within its grave, until
Thine azure sister of the Spring shall blow

  Her clarion o'er the dreaming earth, and fill   10
(Driving sweet buds like flocks to feed in air)
  With living hues and odors plain and hill;

Wild Spirit, which art moving everywhere;
Destroyer and preserver; hear, O hear!

II

Thou on whose stream, 'mid the steep sky's commotion,   15
  Loose clouds like earth's decaying leaves are shed,
Shook from the tangled boughs of heaven and ocean.

  Angels of rain and lightning! there are spread
On the blue surface of thine airy surge,

Like the bright hair uplifted from the
   head   20

Of some fierce Maenad, even from the dim
   verge
Of the horizon to the zenith's height,
The locks of the approaching storm. Thou dirge

Of the dying year, to which this closing night
Will be the dome of a vast sepulchre,   25
   Vaulted with all thy congregated might

Of vapors, from whose solid atmosphere
Black rain, and fire, and hail, will burst: O
   hear!

III

Thou who didst waken from his summer
   dreams
   The blue Mediterranean, where he lay,   30
Lull'd by the coil of his crystalline streams,

   Beside a pumice isle in Baiae's bay,
And saw in sleep old palaces and towers
   Quivering within the wave's intenser day,

All overgrown with azure moss, and flowers   35
   So sweet, the sense faints picturing them!
   Thou
For whose path the Atlantic's level powers

   Cleave themselves into chasms, while far
   below
The sea-blooms and the oozy woods which wear
   The sapless foliage of the ocean, know   40

Thy voice, and suddenly grow gray with fear,
And tremble and despoil themselves: O hear!

IV

If I were a dead leaf thou mightest bear;
   If I were a swift cloud to fly with thee;

A wave to pant beneath thy power, and
   share   45

   The impulse of thy strength, only less free
Than thou, O uncontrollable! if even
   I were as in my boyhood, and could be
The comrade of thy wanderings over heaven,
   As then, when to outstrip thy skyey
   speed   50
Scarce seem'd a vision—I would ne'er have
   striven

   As thus with thee in prayer in my sore need.
O! lift me as a wave, a leaf, a cloud!
   I fall upon the thorns of life! I bleed!

A heavy weight of hours has chain'd and
   bow'd   55
One too like thee—tameless, and swift, and
   proud.

V

Make me thy lyre, even as the forest is:
   What if my leaves are falling like its own?
The tumult of thy mighty harmonies

   Will take from both a deep autumnal
   tone,   60
Sweet though in sadness. Be thou, Spirit fierce,
   My spirit! Be thou me, impetuous one!

Drive my dead thoughts over the universe,
   Like wither'd leaves, to quicken a new birth;
And, by the incantation of this verse,   65

   Scatter, as from an unextinguish'd hearth
Ashes and sparks, my words among mankind!
   Be through my lips to unawaken'd earth

The trumpet of a prophecy! O Wind,
If Winter comes, can Spring be far behind?   70

   Prepare a detailed set of questions that might
serve as a guide for an essay on this poem.

SECTION III

All poetry depends for an important part of its effect on the metrical[1] skill of the poet and on his skill in combining sound effects. The consideration of these matters is always necessary in studying any poetry, even though little has been said about these matters in our discussion of the poems in Sections I and II (See the closing paragraphs in the "Introduction to Poetry," p. 283.). Now that we are to consider metrics and sound effects, let us begin with a particular poem.

That the Night Come

WILLIAM BUTLER YEATS
(1865-1939)

She lived in storm and strife,
Her soul had such desire
For what proud death may bring
That it could not endure
The common good of life,   5
But lived as 'twere a king
That packed his marriage day
With banneret and pennon,
Trumpet and kettle drum,
And the outrageous cannon   10
To bundle time away
That the night come.

This poem is a character sketch. It portrays a woman of intense vitality, even a tragic vitality, which expressed itself in distracting but rather magnificent activity, as if life were merely an interlude to be passed over as quickly as possible before death, an event proud and terrible enough to match her own nature. The poem is really an expression of a paradox (see Glossary) of char-

acter. The fact of her excessive life and vitality is, in a way, but an expression of her hunger for death; and her hunger for death is but an expression of the intensity of her life. In cruder terms, people often comment upon this paradoxical situation. The most vital and energetic person is usually the one who indulges in dangerous sports and occupations and who flirts with death. Death and life define and fulfill each other.

In the first five lines of the poem the poet gives little more than a flat statement of the idea. But the poet not only wants to state the idea; he wants to make the reader grasp it in more concrete and dramatic terms. Therefore he shifts from a general statement to an incident, the incident of the nuptial celebration of a king, beginning with the sixth line.

The poet treats those two parts of his poem, short as it is, in different ways. This difference can be observed in (1) imagery, (2) rhythm.

In the first five lines, as has been pointed out, there is a general statement about the character. Here the images and figures used are not emphatic but are conventional. For instance, the phrase "storm and strife" is not original; it has been used for many years and has become really a *cliché* which has been absorbed into ordinary speech. The phrase "proud death" has not entered into general use as a figurative expression, but it has been used by poets and preachers for hundreds of years and is, also, a *cliché*. Usually, *clichés* impair the effect of a poem, but sometimes their use is justified. Here the very fact that they are conventional and somewhat flat or stale fits the easy, almost conversational, tone with which the poem begins. The same is true of "common good." The poet does not want to startle or surprise the reader. Instead, he wishes to start the poem with a subdued tone and then leap to a rapid climax. This contrast makes the final effect of surprise and splendor in the com-

[1] Technical terms such as this are defined in "The Mechanics of Verse" (pp. 319-25).

parison with the king's marriage day more emphatic.

In its meter and rhythm the poem has great variety for a piece so short. The prevailing metrical form of the poem is *iambic trimeter*. (The poem rhymes: a-b-c-b-a-c-d-e-f-e-d-f.) But the poem, as can be seen from the marking of accents below, is not perfectly regular:

1. She lived / in storm / and strife
2. Her soul / had such / desire
3. For what / proud death / may bring
4. That it / could not / endure
5. The com- / mon good / of life;
6. But lived / as 'twere / a king
7. That packed / his mar- / riage day
8. With ban- / neret / and pen- / non
9. Trumpet / and ket- / tle drum
10. And the / outra- / geous can- / non
11. To bun- / dle time / away
12. That / the night / come.

The normal line is composed of three iambic feet, that is, three divisions containing an unaccented and an accented syllable in that order. But the following lines have variations: 3, 8, 9, 10, 12. It will be observed that in the first section of the poem, that is, the first five lines, there is only one variation. That is the section which is somewhat flat and conventional and conversational in tone. The variations, most of which are highly expressive and do more than merely lend variety to the meter, are saved for the second section. In the first place, the most general effect of this is to make the second section more interesting metrically; it gives less effect of the cut-and-dried. In the second place, several of the variations are in themselves specially appropriate and expressive; that is, the

rhythm they establish bears a definite relation to the idea and feeling the poet wishes to convey. In line 9 the accent falls on the first syllable of *trumpet,* the first word in the line, which coming after the extra weak syllable at the end of the preceding line (*feminine ending*) gains an added emphasis. This effect is re-enforced by the tendency for the second syllable of *trumpet* to be drawn over to the next strong syllable, *ket-,* to make an anapaest and leave the syllable *trum-* isolated with a long drawn-out onomatopoeic emphasis. The reader who surrenders himself to the verse is forced by the metrical situation to pause and dwell upon the triumphant and exciting nature of the trumpet blast, now imaginatively fused with the special emphasis on the accented syllable. (Observe how the sound of that syllable is echoed again in *drum* at the end of the line, just as the first syllable of *kettle* echoes the last of *trumpet.*)

The forcing of the accent to *and* at the first of line 10 also has an expressive force. But first, it may be worth noting the process whereby the accent is forced on a conjunction, an unimportant word which normally would not be accented. If the syllable *out-* of *outrageous* carried a main metrical accent and were followed by a weak syllable, then the syllable *out-* would be the accented syllable of the first foot of the line, as in the following line:

And the out- / er bound / of space

But the main accent falls on the second syllable of *outrageous,* even if some of us may feel that here, in spite of the dictionary accentuation of the word, the first syllable *out-* carries some stress. In any case, a metrical accent tends to be forced back on *and.* This unusual situation has been prepared for by the similar pattern, more normally arrived at (the syllable *trum-* is always accented in *trumpet*), in the preceding line.

But what, then, is the effect of the accent on *and* in line 10? If a person in speaking is giving a list in the usual a, b, c, and d order and the items in the list are of equal importance, then the conjunction *and* is not emphasized. But assume a case where the first items in such a series or list are of equal importance; but the last item, the item introduced by *and,* is surprising and of far greater importance, so that it comes as an unexpected climax to the series. In such a case, in speaking, the *and,* which in the previous case was an unemphasized connective, receives an emphasis and is usually followed by a slight pause. For instance: At Mrs. Smith's house I saw John, Tom, Susie, *and—*Mary.

If one emphasizes the *and* in such a series, it implies that for some reason—let us say on account of a quarrel between the two—the appearance of Mary at the house of Mrs. Smith is a cause for astonishment. It forms a surprising climax to the series. The emphasis on *and* in the speaker's voice would cause the listeners to sit up and would create a momentary suspense, for it would be a signal for the climactic revelation. The *outrageous* cannon, the firing of salutes as it were, is the climax of the series in the poem, the banneret, pennon, trumpet, and kettle drum. The *cannon,* in addition to the emphasis it receives as the climax of the series, is supported by an adjective which calls special attention to it. The word *outrageous* works here in its ordinary sense of that which violates decorum or decency, but as applied to a cannon, which literally "rages out," the old metaphorical sense of the word is renewed, shockingly and thrillingly.

Let us turn to line 12. We expect the normal iambic line, but if we scan according to expectations, we get

/   /

That the night come.

The article *the* cannot accept an accent without making gibberish of the line. Furthermore, on the ground of sense *night* demands recognition —a demand supported by the fact that the meter of the poem is trimeter, and the third accent finds its natural place on *night.* We feel, too, the echo of the accented first syllable in lines 9 and 10. Therefore, the only reading for the line is:

/   /   /

That the night come.

But this line, we see, has other problems. It has only four instead of six syllables, the normal number of an iambic trimeter line. This means

that the accented syllables *night* and *come* are forced together instead of being separated normally by an unaccented syllable. This arrangement demands an unusually long pause between the two syllables, a pause that makes up for the missing unaccented syllable. The effect is one of weighty, deliberate, and inevitable conclusion —which is appropriate to the meaning of the line and the poem.

These examples may show how the metrical effects in a poem can emphasize the meaning. It cannot be said that the mere arrangement of sounds, which, in the abstract sense, the meter is, would give a specific meaning of its own. In these cases, however, it may be said that it bears an appropriate and emphasizing relation to the meaning; the rhythm works with the other elements of a good poem to give a single effect.

The Mechanics of Verse

METER

I. FOOT: The unit, or smallest, combination of accented and unaccented syllables occurring in verse. The regular recurrence of this syllable arrangement determines the rhythm of a verse line.

The kinds of feet are:

1. *Iamb:* One unaccented and one accented syllable.

    The following line is composed of iambic feet:

    ◡ / ◡ / ◡ / ◡ /

    She does / the work / about / the house

    1.   2.   3.   4.

2. *Anapest:* two unaccented and one accented syllable.

    This line is composed of anapestic feet:

    ◡ ◡ / ◡ ◡ / ◡ ◡ / ◡ ◡

    For I'm sick / at the heart / and I fain / would lie

    1.   2.   3.   4.

    /

    down

3. *Trochee:* one accented and one unaccented syllable.

    This line is composed of trochaic feet:

/ ⌣ / ⌣   / ⌣
Like a / rose em- / bowered
  1.   2.   3.

4. *Dactyl:* one accented and two unaccented
   syllables.
   This line is composed of dactylic feet:

/   ⌣⌣   /   ⌣⌣   /   ⌣⌣   / ⌣⌣
Where is my / lovely one / where is my / loveliest
   1.   2.   3.   4.

II. LINE: Meter marks off the prevailing rhythm
of a poem into *a verse* (a single line). It may
be said to define the *pattern of the line:* it gives
a principle of regularity and order. According
to their *metrical structure* (the number and
kinds of feet) lines may be defined as follows.
Number of feet: *monometer,* a line of one foot;
dimeter, a line of two feet; *trimeter,* a line of
three feet; *tetrameter,* a line of four feet; *pentameter,* a line of five feet; *hexameter,* a line of
six feet; *heptameter,* a line of seven feet; *oc-
tameter,* a line of eight feet.

A line is defined, therefore, as *iambic pentameter* (five iambic feet), *trochaic trimeter* (three
trochaic feet), *anapestic tetrameter* (four anapestic feet), etc. (See section under FOOT for examples.) Lines longer than five feet are extremely difficult to handle in verse. The important reason is that a line is really a unit of attention and must therefore be short enough for the
reader to grasp unconsciously the pattern, in itself, as a unit of composition. A seven-foot line
tends to break up into two units, one of four and
one of three feet.

III. VARIATION IN THE LINE: A line of verse
possesses a metrical order, but in any verse that
is even barely competent, it is not a mechanical
order. Variety arises from a number of causes.
The following are the most obvious:

1. *Substitution.* Sometimes a foot different from
that characteristic of the line may be *substituted.*
The following lines represent very common
varieties of metrical variation:

   1. With blackest moss the flower-pots
   2. Were thickly crusted, one and all;
   3. The rusted nails fell from the knots
   4. That held the pear to the gable-wall.

It is clear that the general metrical pattern

of the lines here is *iambic tetrameter.* But there
are two variations in lines 3 and 4. In line 3 there
are eight syllables, as in the preceding lines,
but the accents have a different arrangement:
the fifth syllable of the line, *fell,* is accented
although the fifth syllable of every other line is
unaccented. It is possible to argue that *fell
from* is a *trochaic* foot (/⌣), though some readers may argue that the word *from* really goes
with *the knots* to form an *anapestic foot* (⌣⌣/).

With the first interpretation the scansion of
the line would be:

⌣   /   ⌣   /   /   ⌣   ⌣   /
The rust- / ed nails / fell from / the knots

With the second interpretation the scansion
would be:

⌣   /   ⌣   /   /   ⌣   ⌣   /
The rust- / ed nails / fell / from the knots
                              ^

The caret (∧) marks an imperfect foot. (*Cf.*
l. 12 in "That the Night Come," p. 318.) But
note that under either interpretation, the accented syllables remain the same. Any system
of scansion is at some point arbitrary, and because it is arbitrary, it does not matter much
which we choose, provided that the chosen
interpretation does justice to the actual occurrence of stressed and unstressed syllables.

In line 4 of this passage there is another
kind of variation, for the line has nine syllables instead of the eight syllables common to the
other lines. Line 4 may be scanned as follows:

⌣   /   ⌣   /   ⌣   ⌣   /   ⌣   /
That held / the pear / to the ga- / ble wall

The third foot is an *anapestic* substitution
for the normal *iamb.*

2. *Rhetorical Variation.* It is clear that, even
in the case of a regular metrical line, the reader
does not put equal stress on all accented syllables. The actual meaning of the words prevents
any such mechanical reading. This creates another kind of movement in the line which does
not conform to the metrical pattern. For instance the following line is regular in meter:

The bird is on the wing the poet says

According to meter it might be graphed:

The bird is on the wing the poet says

But the two most emphatic words in the line according to the meaning are *bird* and *wing*, and the syllables *bird* and *wing* take the heaviest stresses in the line. The syllable *po-* is probably next in importance. *On,* though accented in the meter, is relatively unimportant, probably taking little more stress than the unaccented syllable *is*. The actual pattern of stresses in the line might be graphed in this way:

The bird is on the wing the poet says

Just as some accented syllables (accented, that is, by virtue of metrical position) actually do not receive much stress, so metrically unaccented syllables frequently, because of rhetorical considerations, actually receive a good deal of stress. Indeed, so important is this kind of variation that we shall make a special mark (″) to indicate these secondary accents. For example, in the passage quoted below, the normal foot (see p. 319) is *iambic;* but some of the secondary accents are almost as heavy as the heaviest accented syllables:

```
  ″    /        ″        /    ″  /    ᵕ    /
Few farms / changed hands; / so ra- / ther than /
  ″       /
spend years

/   ᵕ   ᵕ  /    ᵕ  /    ᵕ    /    ″  /
Trying / to sell / his farm / and then / not sel-
      ᵕ
ling

  ᵕ   /    ᵕ   /    ″   /    ᵕ   /
He  burned / his  house / down  for / the  fire /
  ᵕ  /   ᵕ
insur- ance
```

("The Star-Splitter," FROST)

There are a number of variations: the substituted *trochee* (*trying*) and the extra unaccented syllables (feminine endings) with which the second and third lines conclude. But the number of secondary accents and their disposition do as much as anything to give these lines

their characteristic rhythm. Indeed the use of the secondary accents is probably a more important form of rhetorical variation than is metrical substitution.

One further aspect of rhetorical variation remains to be treated. The pauses in verse tend to give it variety of movement. Every sentence in ordinary speech breaks up into word groups that constitute the units of the sentence (phrases and clauses) with pauses of different values between—with, or without, punctuation. The same is true of the sentence in verse. The pauses may or may not fit the verse pause, that is, the end of the line. If the sense pause falls at the end of the line, the unity of the metrical pattern of the line is strengthened. If the pause falls within a line, the metrical pattern tends to be broken. This is especially true if the pause falls *within a foot* and not at the end of a foot. Study the following examples. (The pauses are indicated by the mark / when light and // when heavy.)

1.   . . . . .thither he plies, /
2. Undaunted to meet there / whatever power
3. Or spirit / of the nethermost Abyss /
4. Might in that noise reside, // of whom to ask
5. Which way the nearest coast / of darkness lies
6. Bordering on light; // when straight behold the Throne
7. Of Chaos, / and his dark pavilion spread
8. Wide on the wasteful Deep; // with him enthroned
9. Sat sable-vested Night, / eldest of things, /
10. The consort of his reign; // and by them stood
11. Orcus and Ades, / and the dreaded name
12. Of Demogorgon; . . .

(*Paradise Lost,* Book II, MILTON)

Study, also, the variations in such blank verse poems as "The Star-Splitter" (p. 288) and "Inscription for a Fountain" (p. 304). There is no regular place where the pauses fall in the line, and the actual value of the pauses varies from instance to instance. When there is a definite pause at the end of a line it is called an *end-stopped line.* When there is no such pause it is called a *run-on line;* that is, when the sense-group spills over into the next line. This is also called *enjambement.* In the verses above most of the lines are run-on lines, the definite exceptions being lines 1 and 9, though the pause at the end of 3 is more marked than that at the end of any other of the remaining lines. Further, in the passage there are a great many heavy pauses within the lines. Consequently there is a kind of contest between the arrangement of the sense groups and the arrangement of the lines, which gives vitality and variety to the movement of the passage.

Such pauses as these in the passage above within the line are given the name *caesura*. Usually, the caesura falls toward the middle of the line, but there are exceptions here in lines 3 and 7.

More than one pause may occur in a line, although in such cases one pause is usually dominant. All pauses are not given in the name caesura.

3. *Length Variation*. It is obvious that some syllables require a longer *time* than others for pronunciation. In the following examples the difference in length is readily apparent even though the lines are all iambic pentameter: (Note: Example 4, however, is not precisely a regular line because of the light stress, if any, on the word *and*.)

(1) And wretches hang that jurymen may dine
    (*Rape of the Lock*, POPE)
(2) Thy hand, great Anarch, let the curtain fall,
(3) And universal dullness covers all. (*Dunciad*, POPE)
(4) Shield-breakings, and the clash of brands, the crash (*The Passing of Arthur*, TENNYSON)

Example 1 gives the impression of being very short; 4 of being very long; and 2 is longer than 3. Since the lines contain the same number of syllables and the same number of feet, the apparent differences in length derive from the nature of the syllables used, that is, from their differences in time value. These lines are extreme examples, with the effect of each line fairly consistent in itself, that is, tending to be all short or all long. But most lines of verse offer more fluctuation within themselves, a fluctuation of incidental variety often merely accidental, and more often unconscious.

ONOMATOPOEIA

Onomatopoeia is the imitation of sense by sound. The following words are onomatopoeic: *buzz, hiss, crackle, splash, bang, hum, whisper, rustle*. But the poet sometimes attempts to extend the effect of such imitation beyond a single word into a line or passage. One of the best known examples is from Tennyson:

The moan of doves in immemorial elms,
And murmuring of innumerable bees.
("Come Down O Maid," TENNYSON)

Here the poet is obviously trying to imitate, or at least suggest, in the actual sound of the word combination, the sounds he is describing. Or take another example, from Byron:

From peak to peak the rattling crags among
Leaps the live thunder.
(*Childe Harold*, BYRON)

In each of these examples the poet has based his effect on the use of two onomatopoeic words (*moan* and *murmuring* in the first, and *rattling* and *thunder* in the second) with the principle extended into words that, strictly speaking (for instance, *elms* or *leaps*), are not onomatopoeic. It might be said that a word like *leaps* is appropriate to the sense; that is, it is an *imitative* word, but such imitation is only of the vaguest and most general order. Sound combinations, such as "Leaps the live thunder," like metrical combinations, may in general be said to fit the sense only in the vaguest and most general way; they are appropriate to the *mood*, as we see after the mood has been defined by the meaning of the words. In themselves the sound or metrical combinations convey nothing specific. Of a line like the following, which is very fine, it would be difficult, for instance, to say that it *imitates* anything unless one is willing to go so far as to maintain that the word *white* or *gold* imitates the color in question:

Inexplicable splendour of Ionian white and gold
(*The Waste Land*, ELIOT)

Simply, the movement of the verse is vibrant and the sound combinations pleasing in themselves. It is well to talk about the *"union of sound and sense"* or the *"imitative quality of verse"* with the greatest caution and a clear notion of the limitations of such phrases in application to a specific instance in poetry. What does a passage of poetry from a foreign language convey if the words are not understood? In general, the movement of verse, rather than the imitative quality of words in themselves, is the more important factor. For instance, only in an extreme case like this:

> Death is here, death is there,
> Death is round us everywhere.

will it be obvious to everyone that the movement of the verse is clearly inappropriate to the sense.

RIME

Rime is a correspondence in sound between the last accented syllables of two or more words (blow-glow, address-repress). If the riming words end in one or more unaccented syllables, these also must correspond in sound (potato-Plato, pattering-scattering). Rime depends on sound, not on spelling, for instance, *buy—why, write—fight*. In all of the cases given, the introductory consonants are *different*, but the accented syllables and the vowels and succeeding consonants are identical in sound. Rimes are:

1. *Masculine* when the accented syllables that are rimed are the last syllables of the words in question: *address—repress*.
2. *Feminine* (or double) when the accented syllables that are rimed are followed by identical unaccented syllables: *lightly—brightly*.
3. *Triple* when the rimed accented syllables are each followed by two syllables that are identical: *tenderly—slenderly*. This type of rime is also called *feminine* because the words do not end with the syllable that takes the heavy accent.

Sometimes words that do not give perfect rime are used by poets. For instance, some words are spelled alike in the rime vowels and consonants, but are not pronounced alike: *stone—gone*. This may be called *eye rime* or *sight rime*. In other cases only the vowels are identical: *bone—dome*. (See ASSONANCE.) In other cases the necessary consonant arrangement is present, but the vowels differ: *study—lady*. This is variously called *half rime, slant rime, tangential rime,* or *suspended*

rime. When rimes occur within the line instead of at the ends of lines, the arrangement is called *internal rime:*

> So Lord Howard past *away* with five ships of war
>   that *day*

> The splendor *falls* on castle *walls*

The mere fact of rime in itself gives a kind of surprise and pleasure: but the poet uses it for definite effects. It serves a structural purpose in linking lines and building up stanzas by forming a pattern. When the reader grasps the pattern he anticipates the appearance of the rime. Thus, rime can become a principle of order in poetry. As the succession of consonant and vowel sounds in verse gives the *melody,* so the use of rime contributes to the *harmonic* effect.

There are other ways in which words may be linked and which may be discussed under the heading of rime: ALLITERATION, ASSONANCE, and CONSONANCE. ALLITERATION may be called initial rime, for the opening of the corresponding syllables is the same: *forest, farmer, furtive*. The use of alliteration links parts of a line together, or links one line to another. This is an example of the former use:

> *L*ie *l*ightless, all the sparkles *bl*eared and *bl*ack
>   and *bl*ind.

ASSONANCE may be called *interior rime,* for it means the identity of vowel sound in accented syllables without the identity of the following consonants. For instance, in the following line assonance appears:

> Upon the <u>lo</u>nely m<u>oa</u>ted grange.

Assonance is sometimes employed instead of ordinary rime at the end of lines, but usually it appears merely as a kind of internal linking and enrichment of sound effects within the line.

CONSONANCE differs from rime in that the consonants of the corresponding syllables are identical, though the vowels are different: *spilled—spelled; star—stir; gone—gun*. Consonance may be employed for the same general purpose as assonance.

STANZA

The stanza is a pattern of lines that usually, although not necessarily, is repeated in a poem as a unit of composition. The lines of a stanza may or may not rime. A stanza is described by the metrical pattern of lines and the *rime scheme,* if any. For example:

1. They sat them down upon the yellow sand, a.
2. Between the sun and moon upon the shore; b.
3. And sweet it was to dream of Fatherland, a.
4. Of child, and wife, and slave; but evermore b.
5. Most weary seemed the sea, weary the oar, b.
6. Weary the wandering fields of barren foam. c.
7. Then some one said, "We will return no more;" b.
8. And all at once they sang, "Our island home c.
9. Is far beyond the wave; we will no longer roam." c.

The normal foot in this stanza is *iambic,* though there are some *trochaic* substitutions, notably in lines 5 and 6, and several normally unaccented syllables carry rather heavy secondary accents. Lines 1-8 are *pentameter,* but line 9 is *hexameter* (the *iambic hexameter* is sometimes called an *alexandrine*). The rime scheme is a-b-a-b-b-c-b-c-c, the repetition of a letter indicating a rime. This stanza form (with eight iambic pentameter lines, plus an alexandrine, and rimed in the pattern just described) is called the *Spenserian stanza.*

The poet has the problem, after he adopts a stanza form for a poem, to thread his meaning, as it were, through it. Meaning groups (sentence, clause, or phrase) may or may not fall at corresponding points from stanza to stanza, and a sentence may run from one stanza into the next. That is, stanza, like the metrical scheme of a line, is a principle of order in a poem, but the movement of the verse within the stanza and the relation of meaning to the stanza afford perpetual variation.

Below are some of the more usual stanza forms:

I. Couplet: two paired lines riming or unriming. Whatever the length of the lines, the term applies. The lines do not have to be of the same length.

The *heroic couplet* is composed of two *iambic pentameter* lines riming:

See from the brake the whirring pheasant springs,
And mounts exultant on triumphant wings!
　　　　　　　　("Windsor Forest," Pope)

The *octosyllabic couplet (iambic tetrameter)* may be illustrated by the following lines:

Had we but world enough, and time,
This coyness, Lady, were no crime.
　　　　　　　("To His Coy Mistress," Marvell)

II. Quatrain: four lines rimed or unrimed and not necessarily of regular metrical length:

Oh loud, my girl, it once would knock,
　You should have felt it then;
But since for you I stopped the clock
　It never goes again.
　　　　　　　("The True Lover," Housman)

The first and third lines of this quatrain are *iambic tetrameter;* the second and fourth, *iambic trimeter.* The quatrain rimes a-b-a-b. The *ballad stanza* is of this type but calls for rimes only in the second and fourth lines, x-a-y-a. (See, for example, "Sir Patrick Spens, p. 284). The *heroic quatrain,* also very common, is *iambic pentameter* and rimes a-b-a-b-. (See "The Elegy in a Country Churchyard," p. 378.)

III. Three-Line Stanza.

1. *Triplet:* a stanza of three lines riming together; the length of the lines may vary (for one example, see "The Convergence of the Twain," p. 375).

2. *Terza rima:* stanzas of three lines linked together. The scheme is: a-b-a / b-c-b / c-d-c / d-e-d / etc.

The *terza rima* is not very common in English poetry; Shelley's "Ode to the West Wind," p. 315, the most famous English poem employing it, is in iambic pentameter, but the same rime scheme may be applied to lines of other length.

IV. Five- and Six-Line Stanzas: many five- and six-line combinations appear in English poetry (see "Bredon Hill," p. 297, "Song," p. 307, "The Bugle Song," p. 307), but most of these are not standardized and named.

V. The *Spenserian stanza* has been described above.

VI. SONNET: This is one of the most important forms in English. There are several types.

1. *Italian or legitimate:* this form consists of two parts, an *octet* or eight iambic pentameter lines riming a-b-b-a-a-b-b-a, and a *sestet* of six lines riming usually c-d-c-d-c-d. But in the *sestet* many other variations of riming may occur. The divisions of the sonnet are not purely artificial but correspond to the treatment of the thought involved. It may be said that the *octet* presents the *theme* of the sonnet, a question, a situation, a reflection, a problem, etc.; and that the *sestet* gives a resolution or conclusion, sometimes merely an acceptance without further protests of the situation defined in the *octet*. There may or may not be a definite break between the *octet* and *sestet;* when the break is not absolutely definite with a full pause, and when the thought spills over a little into the *sestet,* what is called *enjambement* occurs. (See, for example, "On the Late Massacre in Piedmont," p. 330.)

2. *Shakespearian or English:* this form is composed of three quatrains riming a-b-a-b-c-d-c-d-e-f-e-f-, and a couplet g-g. The lines are iambic pentameter. The turn in thought mentioned above does not occur in this form with the regularity which appears in the *legitimate* sonnet. But the couplet almost always offers a kind of conclusion or resolution of the theme developed in the three preceding quatrains. Sometimes, however, the conclusion or resolution may begin earlier in one of the quatrains; in such cases the psychological structure of the English sonnet approaches that of the legitimate.

VII. BLANK VERSE: *unrimed iambic pentameter.* Blank verse is a very flexible form, for it can be used for many different kinds of poetic effects (see, for example, "The Star-Splitter," p. 288, and "Macbeth Thinks of Murdering the King," p. 364). This flexibility made the form best adapted for plays, and so the Elizabethan drama is generally written in blank verse (see, for example, *Antony and Cleopatra,* p. 700).

Come Down, O Maid

ALFRED, LORD TENNYSON
(1809-1892)

Come down, O maid, from yonder mountain
    height:
What pleasure lives in height (the shepherd
    sang),
In height and cold, the splendor of the hills?
But cease to move so near the Heavens, and
    cease
To glide a sunbeam by the blasted Pine,   5
To sit a star upon the sparkling spire;
And come, for Love is of the valley, come,
For Love is of the valley, come thou down
And find him; by the happy threshold, he,
Or hand in hand with Plenty in the maize,   10
Or red with spirited purple of the vats,
Or foxlike in the vine; nor cares to walk
With Death and Morning on the silver horns,
Nor wilt thou snare him in the white ravine,
Nor find him dropt upon the firths of ice,   15
That huddling slant in furrow-cloven falls
To roll the torrent out of dusky doors:
But follow; let the torrent dance thee down
To find him in the valley; let the wild
Lean-headed Eagles yelp alone, and leave   20
The monstrous ledges there to slope, and spill
Their thousand wreaths of dangling water-
    smoke,
That like a broken purpose waste in air:
So waste not thou; but come; for all the vales
Await thee; azure pillars of the hearth   25
Arise to thee; the children call, and I
Thy shepherd pipe, and sweet is every sound,
Sweeter thy voice, but every sound is sweet;
Myriads of rivulets hurrying thro' the lawn,
The moan of doves in immemorial elms,   30
And murmuring of innumerable bees.

    1. For what purpose has the poet used the contrasting mountain-valley imagery? He has associated the mountain imagery with cold and lofty grandeur. With what has he associated the valley imagery? Is a death-life contrast implied? How?
    2. What is the function of the images of water? This imagery serves to bind the poem together, but

does it also serve to accentuate the system of contrasts?

3. The last lines of the poem have already been cited as an example of onomatopoeia (p. 322). Are there other examples in the poem of onomatopoeic effects?

4. How, specifically, is the handling of meter and of sound effects used to point up and support the development of the theme? (Deal with particular instances: pont out examples of assonance and consonance, of run-on lines, of metrical substitution, and rhetorical variation, etc.)

METRICAL EXERCISES

1. The first stanza of "Bredon Hill" (p. 297) may be scanned as follows:

˘ / ˘ / ˘ / ˘
In sum- / mertime / on Bre- / don

˘ / ˘ / " /
The bells / they sound / so clear;

" / ˘ / ˘ / ˘
Round both / the shires / they ring / them

˘ / ˘ / ˘ /
In stee- / ples far / and near,

˘ / ˘ / ˘ /
A hap- / py noise / to hear.

Note the secondary accents on *so* and *round*. Note also the manner of marking off feminine endings (ll. 1 and 3). Scan the next three stanzas, taking care to indicate substituted feet (if any) and secondary accents. Scan the last stanza. Do the secondary accents occurring in this stanza support the meaning?

2. Scan the first three stanzas of "The True Lover" (p. 297). In Exercise 1, the normal foot and the normal line length were determined for the student. In this exercise, the determination has to be made by the student. Read several lines aloud before trying to decide what is the normal foot. (Any one line may have irregularities. Read at least two stanzas before trying to decide what is the normal line pattern in each stanza.)

3. Scan the first two stanzas of "A Passer-By" (p. 311). Where do feminine endings occur? Are there any imperfect feet?

4. Scan the first two stanzas of "Danny Deever" (p. 293). What is the basic foot? Be careful to mark the substituted feet. Can you justify these substitutions in terms of the effect striven for by the poet?

5. Scan ll. 20-39 of "The Star-Splitter" (p. 288). What instances of rhetorical variation do you find in this passage?

6. Point out instances of rhetorical variation in the last 15 lines of "My Last Duchess" (p. 294). Why

has the poet chosen in this particular poem not to emphasize rime and not to stress any emphatic metrical pattern?

7. Discuss rhetorical variation and use of secondary accent in "The Wild Swans at Coole" (p. 311). Illustrate your discussion by a careful scanning of stanzas II and IV.

8. Does the author of "The Farmer's Bride" (p. 299) give an effect of actual conversation? In addition to her use of dialect words and colloquial phrases, what metrical devices support this effect? Note particularly rhetorical variation, secondary accents, and trochaic substitutions.

9. Do you find any instances of onomatopoeia in "The Lotos Eaters" (p. 309)? Do you find any instances of onomatopoeic effects? Discuss particularly stanza IV.

10. Is alliteration used in "Danny Deever" (p. 293) merely for decoration, or does it serve a more significant purpose in this poem? Contrast the movement of the first four lines of each stanza with the last four lines. How is the difference achieved metrically? For what purpose does the poet employ it?

11. Study the use of alliteration in "The Tree of Man" (p. 310). Is it used primarily as a device for emphasizing certain words? Is it used successfully?

12. Is the alliteration in "The Bugle Song" (p. 307) too emphatic? Why has the poet emphasized alliteration, feminine endings, and internal rimes? Do these devices as used here make for any particular effect?

13. Describe the stanza form used in "To Daffadills" (p. 307). Can you justify the poet's choice of this particular stanza pattern? What is the effect of the short lines following longer lines? Do we tend to read the shorter line more slowly or more rapidly?

14. What onomatopoeic effects are to be found in "Ode to the West Wind" (p. 315)? Describe the stanza form. Is the stanza form well chosen for this particular poem?

15. Point out among the poems read in Sections I and II four examples of the quatrain, an instance of Spenserian stanza, two examples of blank verse, an example of free verse, and an example of rimed couplet.

16. Describe the stanza form used in Waller's "Song" (p. 307). Is it well chosen for the effect given by the "Song"? Note particularly the metrical treatment of the short lines (the use of substituted feet and secondary accents).

17. Consider the last two lines of "Bredon Hill." Scan the lines carefully and indicate how the metrical situation supports, or fails to support, the concluding effect of the poem.

18. "The Tree of Man" (p. 310) and "The Mower to the Glow-Worm" (p. 313) employ the same basic stanza form and rime scheme. The two poems differ markedly in effect. How is this difference reflected in the metrical situation to be found in the two poems?

SECTION IV

We all know that the tone of voice in which a thing is said is important in defining what is said and may at times even reverse the literal meaning. The tone of a poem (that is, the speaker's attitude as reflected in the poem) is most important. In the poems that follow, the student ought to ask himself: what is the tone? How is it developed? Does it shift in the course of the poem? If tone seems an elusive term, he may transpose these questions to read: what is the speaker's attitude? How does his attitude color his statement? Does his attitude shift in the course of the poem?

Neutral Tones

THOMAS HARDY (1840-1928)

We stood by a pond that winter day,
And the sun was white, as though chidden of
    God,
And a few leaves lay on the starving sod;
  —They had fallen from an ash, and were
    gray.

Your eyes on me were as eyes that rove   5
Over tedious riddles solved years ago;
And some words played between us to and fro
  On which lost the more by our love.

The smile on your mouth was the deadest thing
Alive enough to have strength to die;   10
And a grin of bitterness swept thereby
  Like an ominous bird a-wing. . . .

Since then, keen lessons that love deceives,
And wrings with wrong, have shaped to me
Your face, and the God-curst sun, and a tree, 15
  And a pond edged with grayish leaves.

The situation in the poem is a simple one: a man recalls the occasion of a quarrel with his beloved, on a winter day, beside a pond where the gray leaves of an ash tree lay on the dead grass. This recollection is put in the form of a direct address, even though the woman, apparently, is absent and perhaps has been parted from him for many years; and this device of direct address gives a dramatic quality and force to a commonplace situation. But what really lifts the poem above the commonplace attempt to render the pathos of defeated love, and what defines the real theme of the poem, is the last stanza. The theme depends on the answer to this question implied in the last stanza: Why have the "keen lessons that love deceives" etc., always shaped for the speaker the face of the first beloved in that particular background . . . "the God-curst sun, and a tree, and a pond edged with grayish leaves"? The answer may run something like this: that early, and perhaps first, disappointment in love has become a symbol for all the later disappointments and frustrations of life; but it is more than that, being, as it were, in conjunction with the "God-curst" landscape also a symbol of all the curse of evil that hangs over man and nature—a curse which the speaker has, we sense, managed to endure with fortitude.

Therefore, this poem does in a very clear and apparently simple and direct way what all poetry tries to do: it takes a single incident, fact, or observation (the quarrel) and manages to link it with, or fuse it with, other things out of experience (the "starving sod," the dead leaves, the misty sun, etc.) to make a new kind of experience and perception of some kind of coordination or ordering of separate things. That is to say, the poet creates a symbolic experience, which means more than the mere experience of the incident originally chosen for the subject. It gives a meaning to the incident.

But there are other questions about this poem, or any other poem. For instance, what is the tone of the poem and, further, how does this tone relate to the meaning of the poem? The *tone* of a poem is really a metaphor based on the tone of a voice; and like the tone of voice, the tone of a poem modifies the literal statement by implying the speaker's attitude. Everybody knows that the same word spoken in different ways means different things. But a poet tries to convey the quality of tone across time and space to a reader who has never heard his voice. He conveys this in many ways, by his diction, by his rhythms and sentence structure, by the kind of similes and metaphors he uses, by the amount of direct speculation, moralizing, or philosophizing he puts into the poem, and by many other means. But take the first line of our present poem:

> We stood by a pond that winter day . . .

Then think what the difference in *tone* would be if the poet had said "pool" or "lake" instead of "pond." Yet a pond is after all a pool or a little lake. But *pond* is a more usual and homely word, a more realistic word, a less romantic word, a less "poetical" word. It implies a less formal tone, a less set and rhetorical tone, than would *lake* or *pool*.

Pond is a more usual word than *pool* and implies a more conversational tone in the poem. But observe the rhythms of the first stanza, and in fact, of the whole poem. The movement of the lines is more like that of ordinary conversation than of regular verse, such as we find in another poem by the same poet:

> I squared the broad foundations in
>   Of ashlared masonry;
> I moulded mullions thick and thin,
>   Hewed fillet and agee;
>   I circleted
>   Each sculptured head
> With nimb and canopy.

The rhythm of the first stanza of "Neutral Tones" continues the conversational tone and slows the movement as if the speaker were trying to recollect every detail of the scene by the pond. This is made very specific by the last line, "They had fallen from an ash and were gray," which is put on as though a kind of afterthought in the process of recollection. The sentence structure, too, is such that the loose groping movement of the mind trying to repicture a scene is perceived by the reader; for the whole sentence is not constructed with the proper subordination of detail to a main thought—the structure of a logical and planned-out sentence—but is constructed by the accumulation of detail, after a general statement, strung together by *and's* and then followed by a dash and an afterthought. The structure of the sentence by its very logical crudity implies that groping movement, the mind trying to recollect something that has already been mentioned. The tone here is conversational and meditative. The second and third stanzas give this effect less emphatically, but the last stanza makes it more emphatic even than the first. But here the effect is gained by a different kind of treatment. For instance, the line next to the last repeats the enumeration of details connected by *and's*, but in the last line:

> And a pond edged with grayish leaves

the difficulty of pronouncing these words at a normal speed again slows the line to a speed consonant with reflection.

But what is the poet's attitude underlying the situation? It might be summed up in the word *fatalism*. What will come, will come in spite of what a man can do. Love, like the ash tree or the seasons, grows and then dies. That is what the first stanza implies. The next two stanzas elaborate that idea with a different set of images: the beloved one like a riddle already solved and known too well to be interesting, the grin of bitterness so short-lived that it seemed like a bird of ill-omen flitting past. But the poet fuses all of this with the movement of nature in growth and death, the seasons, etc., and then with the evil in nature and in man's fate, things which must be accepted because man cannot change the course of events. Observe, further then, how the movement of the last stanza settles from a sharp movement of the two lines (which is made more emphatic by the alliteration) to the retarded movement, a movement appropriate to the fatalistic mood. It is by the tone, then, that we sense, as we have earlier suggested, the fortitude, the stoicism, with which the speaker looks back at the disappointments of life.

The Parting
MICHAEL DRAYTON
(1563-1631)

Since there's no help, come let us kiss and
    part—
Nay, I have done, you get no more of me;
And I am glad, yea, glad with all my heart,
That thus so cleanly I myself can free.
Shake hands for ever, cancel all our vows,   5
And when we meet at any time again,
Be it not seen in either of our brows
That we one jot of former love retain.
Now at the last gasp of Love's latest breath,
When, his pulse failing, Passion speechless
    lies,   10
When Faith is kneeling by his bed of death,
And Innocence is closing up his eyes,
    —Now if thou wouldst, when all have given
    him over,
    From death to life thou might'st him yet
    recover.

1. What is the attitude of the speaker toward his mistress?
2. Is the speaker really glad as he says he is in l. 3?
3. Do the last six lines contradict the first eight lines? Is the speaker aware of the contradiction? Does this partial contradiction make the speaker seem less serious or more serious in his comment on the situation?
4. Does the poem become sentimental? If not, why not?

Rose Aylmer
WALTER SAVAGE LANDOR
(1775-1864)

Ah, what avails the sceptred race!
    Ah, what the form divine!
What every virtue, every grace!
    Rose Aylmer, all were thine.

Rose Aylmer, whom these wakeful eyes   5
    May weep, but never see,
A night of memories and of sighs
    I consecrate to thee.

1. What is the dramatic situation implied by this poem? Would you judge that the speaker is a bereaved husband or a lover or that his relationship to Rose Aylmer was more distant?
2. Would the poem be more emphatic if the speaker promised to dedicate an *age* of memories and sighs to the beloved rather than "a night"? The speaker uses understatement here. Is that note of understatement corroborated elsewhere in the poem?
3. Describe the metrical situation in l. 7. *And* is ordinarily a lightly accented word. Is it proper that the meter should force a heavy accent here?

A Slumber Did My Spirit Seal
WILLIAM WORDSWORTH
(1770-1850)

A slumber did my spirit seal;
    I had no human fears—
She seemed a thing that could not feel
    The touch of earthly years.

No motion has she now, no force;   5
    She neither hears nor sees;
Rolled round in earth's diurnal course,
    With rocks, and stones, and trees.

1. This little poem deals with the shock felt by the lover at the sudden and unexpected loss of his beloved. How is the sense of shock conveyed? What is meant by "The touch of earthly years"?
2. The present motionless slumber of the girl has waked him out of the slumber that had possessed his spirit (l. 1). In what other ways does the poem point up this sense of reversal?
3. The inert body of the loved one now has no motion at all except as it partakes of the motion of the globe itself. How do the last two lines affect the tone of the poem? How would you describe the tone of the poem?

On the Late Massacre in Piedmont

JOHN MILTON (1608-1674)

Avenge, O Lord, thy slaughtered saints, whose
  bones
Lie scattered on the Alpine mountains cold;
Even them who kept thy truth so pure of old,
When all our fathers worshiped stocks and
  stones,
Forget not; in thy book record their groans   5
Who were thy sheep, and in their ancient fold
Slain by the bloody Piemontese, that rolled
Mother with infant down the rocks. Their
  moans
The vales redoubled to the hills, and they
To heaven. Their martyred blood and ashes
  sow   10
O'er all th' Italian fields, where still doth sway
The triple tyrant; that from these may grow
A hundredfold, who, having learnt thy way,
Early may fly the Babylonian woe.

    1. Is the tone of this sonnet that of a curse or of
a prayer?
    2. How does the poet's management of the metrical pattern of the sonnet support its tone? Be specific
in your answer.

The Day of Judgment

JONATHAN SWIFT (1667-1745)

With a whirl of thought oppressed,
I sunk from reverie to rest.
An horrid vision seized my head,
I saw the graves give up their dead!
Jove, armed with terrors, burst the skies,   5
And thunder roars, and lightning flies!
Amazed, confused, its fate unknown,
The world stands trembling at his throne!

While each pale sinner hung his head,
Jove, nodding, shook the heavens, and said: 10
"Offending race of humankind,
By nature, reason, learning, blind;
You who, through frailty, stepped aside;
And you who never fell, through pride;
You who in different sects were shamed,   15
And come to see each other damned
(So some folks told you, but they knew
No more of Jove's designs than you);
—The world's mad business now is o'er,
And I resent these pranks no more.   20
—I to such blockheads set my wit!
I damn such fools!—Go, go, you're bit."

    1. Jonathan Swift was himself a parson. Does this
poem suggest that he was too sceptical to be a good
parson? Or is this the kind of poem that a serious
man of God might on occasion feel the need to write?
    2. What is the effect on the tone of the poem of
the suggestion (in l. 14) that it was only pride which
prevented some of the souls from falling? And (l. 15)
that many of them are expectantly waiting to see the
others damned?
    3. The eighteenth-century expression "you're bit"
meant something like the present-day expression
"you've been had." Why is this last line of the poem
such an effective "punch line"? How would you define the tone of this poem?

To Ianthe

PERCY BYSSHE SHELLEY (1792-1822)

I love thee, Baby! for thine own sweet sake;
  Those azure eyes, that faintly dimpled cheek,
  Thy tender frame, so eloquently weak,
Love in the sternest heart of hate might wake;
But more when o'er thy fitfull slumber
    bending   5
  Thy mother folds thee to her wakeful heart,
  While love and pity, in her glances blending,
All that thy passive eyes can feel impart:
More, when some feeble lineaments of her,
  Who bore thy weight beneath her spotless
    bosom.   10
  As with deep love I read thy face, recur,—

More dear art thou, O fair and fragile blossom;
  Dearest when thy tender traits express
  The image of thy mother's loveliness.

The present poem has for its subject the love of a father for his child. The father says that he loves the child because the innocence and weakness of the child would provoke love in even the hardest heart; and that he loves it even more because its tender traits express something of the tenderness and appeal of the mother. That is what the poem says, and the feeling which is the subject of the poem must be a fairly usual one. But a poem is not good merely because it states a usual feeling, no matter how admirable that feeling may be. It must bring renewed strength to the subject, if the poem is to be better than a mere prose statement of the subject. As Wordsworth said, the poem must strip off "the veil of familiarity" from the subject. Shelley's poem presents no new body of perceptions and no enrichment of feeling for the subject. It stands in the same relation to a good poem on the subject as does a cheap picture of a mother and child on an advertising calendar to a good painting of the Madonna.

It fails, first, because the statement is flat, without any interest in developing or exploring the idea, and second, because there is no attempt to make the poem clear-cut and vivid to the reader. In almost every line the poet was content to take a second-hand and conventional way of expressing his idea. His phrases are *hackneyed* and are put in a hackneyed combination. Almost every line has one or more *clichés:* "sweet sake," "azure eyes," "dimpled cheek," "heart of hate," "fitfull slumber," "wakeful heart," "feeble lineaments," "spotless bosom," "deep love," "fair and fragile blossom." In each case the poet, apparently, took the first phrase that came to mind without any attempt to present to the reader an accurate and fresh perception; and only by accurate and fresh perceptions could he have made the reader feel the poem as a discovery. The poet simply assumed in a slovenly way that an adjective of a soft and agreeable nature would serve, and so the poem is burdened with them. There is no

variety. And to show how inaccurate and vague the use is one may rewrite the poem with all kinds of substitutions without impairing the effect.

I love thee, Baby! for thine own *dear* sake;
  Those *bluest* eyes, that *gently* dimpled cheek,
  Thy *budding* frame, so eloquently weak.
Love in the *cruelest* heart of hate might wake;
But more when o'er thy *troubled* slumber bending
  Thy mother folds thee to her *watchful* heart,
  While love and pity, in her glances blending,
All thy *receptive* eyes can feel impart:
More, when some *weakest* lineaments of her,
  Who bore thy weight beneath her *fairest* bosom,
  As with *great* love I read thy face, recur,—
More dear art thou, O *white* and *tender* blossom;
  Dearest when most thy *fragile* traits express
  The image of thy mother's loveliness.

Little or no harm has been done to the poem. A similar experiment with a good poem would immediately show the destructive effects of such transpositions and substitutions. The point is that Shelley was writing loosely and carelessly; consequently, he resorted to *clichés,* to the easy stereotypes of sentimentality. And this means that the tone is not his tone—and the poem, in the end, not his but an almost anonymous effusion.

Hymn of Apollo
PERCY BYSSHE SHELLEY
(1792-1822)

I

The sleepless Hours who watch me as I lie,
  Curtained with star-inwoven tapestries
From the broad moonlight of the sky,
  Fanning the busy dreams from my dim eyes,—
Waken me when their Mother, the gray Dawn, 5
Tells them that dreams and that the moon is
    gone.

II

Then I arise, and climbing Heaven's blue dome,
  I walk over the mountains and the waves,

Leaving my robe upon the ocean foam;
  My footsteps pave the clouds with fire; the
      caves   10
Are filled with my bright presence, and the air
Leaves the green Earth to my embraces bare.

III

The sunbeams are my shafts, with which I kill
  Deceit, that loves the night and fears the day;
All men who do or even imagine ill   15
  Fly me, and from the glory of my ray
Good minds and open actions take new might,
Until diminished by the reign of Night.

IV

I feed the clouds, the rainbows and the flowers
  With their aethereal colours; the moon's
      globe   20
And the pure stars in their eternal bowers
  Are cinctured with my power as with a robe;
Whatever lamps on Earth or Heaven may shine
Are portions of one power, which is mine.

V

I stand at noon upon the peak of Heaven,   25
  Then with unwilling steps I wander down
Into the clouds of the Atlantic even;
  For grief that I depart they weep and frown:
What look is more delightful than the smile
With which I soothe them from the western
     isle?   30

VI

I am the eye with which the Universe
  Beholds itself and knows itself divine;
All harmony of instrument or verse,
  All prophecy, all medicine is mine,
All light of art or nature;—to my song   35
Victory and praise in its own right belong.

Apollo, the Greek god of the sun, was also the god of medicine, music, and poetry. Notice that this is not a hymn sung to Apollo but a hymn sung by the sun god himself.

1. Compare this poem with Shelley's "To Ianthe." In this poem, can one make transpositions and substitutions without injury to the meaning and effectiveness of the poem?

2. Consider the statements made in Stanza IV. Are they literally true?

3. Notice the phrase in line 35: "All light of art or nature." Most of the poem has to do with the light of nature, the sunlight, through which directly or indirectly we have our visible world. What is the "light of art"?

4. What is the tone of this poem? Does the god Apollo seem to be boastful? If not, how has Shelley preserved the tone of calm, dignified, and exalted statement even though the sun god is here hymning his own glories? In this connection, look very carefully at Stanza VI.

Sonnet 87

WILLIAM SHAKESPEARE
(1564-1616)

Farewell! thou art too dear for my possessing,
And like enough thou know'st thy estimate:
The charter of thy worth gives thee releasing:
My bonds in thee are all determinate.
For how do I hold thee but by thy granting?   5
And for that riches where is my deserving?
The cause of this fair gift in me is wanting,
And so my patent back again is swerving.
Thyself thou gav'st, thy own worth then not
    knowing,
Or me, to whom thou gav'st it, else mis-
    taking;   10
So thy great gift, upon misprision growing,
Comes home again, on better judgment making.
  Thus have I had thee, as a dream doth flatter,
  In sleep a king, but waking, no such matter.

1. What is the speaker's attitude toward himself? Does he seem to grovel? Does he abandon his own proper self-esteem?

2. Is he helping his friend to rationalize the friend's abandonment of him, or is he rationalizing that abandonment to himself? What relation does the legal imagery (bonds, charter, patent, etc.) have to this question? In any case how seriously does he take his argument?

3. Is there any irony in this poem? Is there any bitterness? In what tone of voice ought the statement to be read?

4. Compare the tone of this sonnet with that of "The Parting."

Come Up from the Fields, Father

WALT WHITMAN (1819-1892)

Come up from the fields, father, here's a letter
from our Pete,
And come to the front door, mother, here's a
letter from thy dear son.

Lo, 'tis autumn,
Lo, where the trees, deeper green, yellower and
redder,
Cool and sweeten Ohio's villages with leaves
fluttering in the moderate wind,   5
Where apples ripe in the orchards hang and
grapes on the trellised vines,
(Smell you the smell of the grapes on the vines?
Smell you the buckwheat where the bees were
lately buzzing?)
Above all, lo, the sky so calm, so transparent
after the rain, and with wondrous clouds,
Below too, all calm, all vital and beautiful, and
the farm prospers well.   10

Down in the fields all prospers well,
But now from the fields come, father, come at
the daughter's call,
And come to the entry, mother, to the front
door come right away.

Fast as she can she hurries, something ominous,
her steps trembling,
She does not tarry to smooth her hair nor
adjust her cap.   15

Open the envelope quickly,
O this is not our son's writing, yet his name is
signed,
O a strange hand writes for our dear son, O
stricken mother's soul!
All swims before her eyes, flashes with black,
she catches the main words only,

Sentences broken, *gunshot wound in the breast,
cavalry skirmish, taken to hospital,*   20
At present low, but will soon be better.

Ah, now the single figure to me,
Amid all teeming and wealthy Ohio with all
its cities and farms,
Sickly white in the face and dull in the head,
very faint,
By the jamb of a door leans.   25

Grieve not so, dear mother (the just-grown
daughter speaks through her sobs,
The little sisters huddle around speechless and
dismayed),
*See, dearest mother, the letter says Pete will
soon be better.*

Alas, poor boy, he will never be better (nor
maybe needs to be better, that brave and
simple soul),
While they stand at home at the door he is
dead already,   30
The only son is dead.

But the mother needs to be better,
She with thin form presently drest in black,
By day her meals untouched, then at night fit-
fully sleeping, often waking,
In the midnight waking, weeping, longing with
one deep longing,   35

O that she might withdraw unnoticed, silent
from life escape and withdraw,
To follow, to seek, to be with her dear dead
son.

1. The incident described in this poem is typical
of the happenings of war, and the poet has actually
stressed its typicality. How has he then rendered it
concrete, vivid, and moving?
2. The poet puts himself into this poem as a
kind of commentator; that is, he does not simply present the whole incident objectively, nor does he simply let the characters speak for themselves. Even
when he seems, as in ll. 1 and 16, to be letting the
characters speak for themselves, we see that he is
really speaking for them, simply momentarily voic-
ing their thoughts. He knows more than they can
know; he goes on to predict and interpret. What is
his attitude as commentator? What tone does he
adopt?

3. What are the advantages of the poet's taking the role of a commentator brooding over the scene? What risks does he run by adopting this procedure? Does he, for example, risk sentimentalizing the incident? If not, how does he keep the tone firm and stable?

On an Invitation to the United States

THOMAS HARDY (1840-1928)

I

My ardors for emprize nigh lost
Since life has bared its bones to me,
I shrink to seek a modern coast
Whose riper times have yet to be;
Where the new regions claim them free   5
From that long drip of human tears
Which peoples old in tragedy
Have left upon the centuried years.

II

For, wonning in these ancient lands,
Enchased and lettered as a tomb,   10
And scored with prints of perished hands,
And chronicled with dates of doom,
Though my own Being bear no bloom
I trace the lives such scenes enshrine,
Give past exemplars present room,   15
And their experience count as mine.

His Books

ROBERT SOUTHEY (1774-1843)

My days among the Dead are past;
  Around me I behold,
Where'er these casual eyes are cast,
  The mighty minds of old:
My never-failing friends are they,   5
With whom I converse day by day.

With them I take delight in weal
  And seek relief in woe;
And while I understand and feel
  How much to them I owe,   10
My cheeks have often been bedewed
With tears of thoughtful gratitude.

My thoughts are with the Dead; with them
  I live in long-past years,
Their virtues love, their faults condemn,   15
  Partake their hopes and fears;
And from their lessons seek and find
Instruction with an humble mind.

My hopes are with the Dead; anon
  My place with them will be,   20
And I with them shall travel on
  Through all Futurity;
Yet leaving here a name, I trust,
That will not perish in the dust.

Here are two poems with much the same *themes* or basic *ideas*. Robert Southey and Thomas Hardy, both literary men and poets, are trying to express, in particular, their own relationships to the past, and in general, the relationship of the past to the present. They both say that they find the meaning of their own personal experience in the relationship of that experience to the lives that have gone before them.

This fact raises two questions of great importance in regard to the study of the real nature of a poem.

First, does this imply that the poems, as poems, *mean* the same thing?

Second, does this imply that they have, as poems, equal success? These two questions can only be answered at the end of the discussion of these two poems, and not at the beginning; but bear in mind that the answering of these two questions is the purpose of the present study. The study will have to take up several aspects of each poet's handling of the *theme:* (1) the situation, (2) attitude, (3) imagery and figures, (4) diction, (5) rhythm and meter.

1

Situation. The occasion of Hardy's poem is an invitation to the United States. The title tells us this much, and therefore provides a sort of framework of reference for the poem. That is, there is an incident behind the poem, the kernel of a little drama of which the poem is the expression. Hardy has had to make a decision to accept or reject his invitation; and decision is at the very core of dramatic interest. On the contrary, Southey's poem might have been written in his library at any time, for the only element of experience is the sight of his books, which, as he says, "Around me I behold." Nothing has happened in the library to make him *feel* the full force of the truth of what he is going to write. We do not get a notion that there is any choice to be made or any struggle in the poet's mind over anything. All of this means that Hardy's poem starts with a decided advantage: it is *dramatic* and *concrete,* while the other lacks *drama,* or *tension,* and is *abstract.*

(The situation or little drama a poet may use does not have to be drawn from his own experience; that is, it does not have to be autobiographical. There is no reason to suppose that it is better for a poem when it is drawn directly from experience. For the purpose in hand we do not need to know that Thomas Hardy ever did receive an invitation to the United States. As a matter of fact, some poets have written their worst poems about things that actually happened to them.)

The fact that Hardy's invitation is to the United States emphasizes the *dramatic* and *concrete* nature of his treatment of the *theme.* There is a contrast, not only in time between the past and the present, but in space between Europe and America. There is a contrast drawn between a civilization with a long past and a heavy burden of history, and a civilization with a short past and a light burden of history; between a civilization that is conservative and pessimistic, and one that is progressive and optimistic. This contrast reinforces the dramatic element. But there is still another contrast. The ordinary person, especially an American, may assume without much thought that a progressive and optimistic attitude is naturally more admirable and happy than a conservative and pessimistic one. Now, in this poem Hardy reverses the opinion and finds, not in being cut off from the past, but in being identified with

the pathos and tragedy of the continual struggle of mankind a nobility and a kind of satisfaction. He will not come to America—the Land of Promise. He has created in the poem a kind of *paradox.* The *tension* of the *paradox* adds to the *dramatic* quality.

All of these implications enrich Hardy's poem. Beside it Southey's poem appears very thin and poverty-stricken, for it says all it has to say about the situation at once and leaves nothing for the imagination of the reader to explore.

2

Attitude. In treating the *theme* Southey takes a much more limited attitude than does Hardy. The past he is talking about is merely the past seen through books. It is a *literary* past only. In the second place Southey gives some conventional and superficial moralizing. He takes the attitude of a teacher who will praise good behavior and correct bad:

> Their virtues love, their faults condemn.

Or he takes the attitude of a pupil and studies his lessons:

> And from their lessons seek and find
> Instruction with an humble mind.

On the other hand Hardy realizes that the true value of the past is to be gained through imaginative participation:

> I trace the lives such scenes enshrine.

To him the past means more than an excuse for passing a simple judgment or for learning simple moral lessons. He wants to reconstruct the past and feel himself into it in order to enrich his experience of the present:

> Though my own Being bear no bloom.

In the third place Southey is *sentimental,* because he professes a feeling toward the past which the poem does not communicate to the reader. The reader, therefore, feels that Southey is insincere. He says that he has often wept because he thought how much he owed to the past. The reader would be willing perhaps to believe him if he said some *one* particularly tragic or pathetic story had moved him so deeply; but nobody has ever wept over the past in *general.*

3

Imagery. Southey's poem is given as a straight statement in general, not specific, terms. Many good poems use a straight statement in general terms, in greater or less degree, but insofar as they are successful they find some way to attract the reader's attention and make him concentrate on the statement so that he will *feel* the weight and truth of it as if, for the moment, it were personal. The poet has to find some way to make the reader share the idea as an experience; that is, some way to establish a relation between the idea of the general statement and the reader's feelings. Perhaps the best and the most usual device the poet uses for this purpose is imagery. Notice how few pictures are presented in Southey's poem. The reader of a poem is like the man from Missouri: for him, seeing (or touching or hearing) is believing. Next, notice how few comparisons (figures of speech) there are in his poem. A comparison is one way of making the reader see, touch, or hear—and therefore believe in, or experience— the subject. For instance, in the last two lines of his poem Southey compares a name, or reputation, to a body decaying into the dust from which, as the Bible says, it came. But the figure of something decaying into dust is so worn out and has become so conventional that it is scarcely thought of as a comparison at all; it does not attract the interest of the reader and make him feel what the poet is trying to express. But contrast the treatment Southey makes of the dust figure with what another poet, James Shirley, makes:

> Only the actions of the just
> Smell sweet and blossom in their dust.

Here Shirley has taken as the basis for his figure the old one of "dust to dust," but has treated it with originality and has given it new meaning. The bodies of the just will decay into the nothingness of earth, but their actions are like flowers which, after a period when the seed is apparently lost or dead, will bloom again, nourished by the residue of decay. Further, the figure also carries as a kind of secondary meaning, the notion of the Christian resurrection. Shirley never uses the noun *flower,* but uses the verbs *smell* and *blossom.* This gives two advantages. First, it enables him to compress the meaning so that he does not have to explain by saying "like a flower." Second, by depending for his effect on *verbs* only he gets an active rather than a passive effect. These two things give the reader an impression of surprise or discovery and of vitality. The effect of Southey's last two lines is entirely general and passive:

> Yet leaving here a name, I trust,
> That will not perish in the dust.

Hardy's poem is very rich in imagery. Not only does he provide glimpses such as "bones," "drip of human tears," a highly ornamental medieval "tomb," etc., but he uses such things as a device for communicating his very meaning. For instance, he does not say, as a general statement, that a long life of observation and experience has taught him that man's lot is essentially tragic and painful and that the attitude that best equips man for facing his lot is a noble pessimism which makes him persist in the face of a recognized evil. But all of this, and more, is in the first stanza; and most of it is implied in the line: "Since Life has bared its bones to me." Or again, analyze the meaning of the line: "And scored with prints of perished hands." The very land is like something created, as it were, by the generations of the past. The fact that it bears their personal, though crude, marks gives it an added value; just as the geometrical imperfections of handmade pottery give an added value because they indicate the personal element in the creation in contrast with the impersonality of machine-made pottery. The "prints of perished hands" are at one level specific to the reader—farmhouses, old hedges, churches, tombs, stone walls, etc. At another level they are metaphorical—some object such as the piece of pottery with the fingerprint baked into the clay. Those prints, then, stand as a kind of symbol for the continuity of human experience and, further, as a symbol for human brotherhood.

Within the poem itself the images have a

continuity and interrelation. They are built up for a special effect. All of them for the first twelve lines build up the impression of a tragic destiny of fate which is finally summarized in the twelfth line by the phrase, "dates of doom." At that point exactly the opposite kind of image is introduced, the image of bloom and renewal of life, and the contrast is emphasized by the fact of the rhyme of *doom* with *bloom*. The contemplation of the tragic past gives the present a kind of spiritual renewal; that is the mysterious paradox on which the poem is built.

4

Diction. (You cannot separate the discussion of diction entirely from imagery, for if a reader dwells on the *connotations* (see Glossary) of one word as opposed to the *connotations* of a synonym a large part of the difference in the choice of diction will be found to be bound up with imagery.)

The diction of Southey's poem is, one might say, perfectly usual. *Anon, bedewed,* and *futurity* are the most unusual words in the poem. This is in itself nothing against the poem, and poems may be injured by the use of words too obscure or eccentric. But at least in Southey's case the reader feels a certain slovenliness in selection; there was no attempt to adapt vocabulary to idea; there was no attempt to create an interplay of connotation and suggestion. All of this means that the poem is flat in tone.

In Hardy's poem there is a definite attempt to work out some relation between idea and diction. The most emphatic case is the use of *wonning*. *Wonning* is an archaic word meaning *dwelling.* Hardy could have written the line this way:

For, dwelling in these ancient lands.

That would have expressed at the literal level exactly what he says in the line as it stands now; but the line would have lost a very rich part of its *connotative* meaning. The use of *wonning* connects by implication the poem to the Anglo-Saxon past of England; it gives an added meaning to *ancient* in the same line. (Hardy could use such a form with more natural-

ness than an American poet, for through the dialect of his native Wessex he had a more direct contact with the older language.) The use of *chronicled* carries another reinforcing implication. Try the meaning of the line revised:

And labeled with the dates of doom.

This is much inferior, for *labeled* has only one level of meaning for the poem. It says that the dates are attached to the lands, but that is all. *Chronicled* implies that the dates have been put down, not all at once, but in the long sequence of time as the events of "doom" occurred. Second, *chronicle* is the term used for the medieval attempts to write history; and so, something of the old manuscript is implied, with writing quaint and hard to decipher. But since the line follows on the comparison of the land to a tomb, the *chronicled* implies also the idea that the dates are engraved on stone or bronze. Therefore, *chronicled* is a very rich and appropriate word for the particular poem, which deals with the interpretation of the past. One might comment in the same way on *enshrine, centuried,* and *exemplars.*

5

Rhythm and meter. The movement of Southey's poem is very monotonous and mechanical. The regular movement of the meter is the prevailing movement of the poem, for there is no variety in meter itself, and little in (1) quantity or (2) rhetoric. In Hardy's poem there are metrical variations in lines 5, 8, 9, and 16. Further, Hardy's mixture of monosyllables and polysyllables, as opposed to the excess of monosyllables in Southey's poem, tends to give a variety of movement. But the greatest difference is in the verse-texture of the two pieces. The almost dead level of short vowel effects in Southey's poem gives a monotony and an impression of triviality. This analysis started with the question: Does the fact that "My Books" and "On an Invitation to the United States" have the same theme imply that they have the same meaning? The meaning of a poem depends to a large extent on the way the theme itself is realized. For instance, death as an idea and death as the sight of a corpse have two very different meanings. In the second case, the experience is much more vivid. Southey has not engaged the reader in an experience. He has simply stated an idea. Hardy has managed to get the idea involved with a complicated set of experiences (images, comparisons, rhythms, etc.) so that the idea can be felt.

This answers the second question with which this analysis started, the one concerning theme and success. A poem may be said to be successful when it accomplishes this fusion of idea and feeling; that is, when it makes the reader really *aware* of the idea.

On a Young Heir's Coming of Age

SAMUEL JOHNSON (1709-1784)

Long expected one-and-twenty,
  Ling'ring year, at length is flown;
Pride and pleasure, pomp and plenty,
  Great ———, are now your own.

Loosened from the minor's tether,   5
  Free to mortgage or to sell;
Wild as wind, and light as feather,
  Bid the sons of thrift farewell.

Call the Betseys, Kates, and Jennies,
  All the names that banish care;   10
Lavish of your grandsire's guineas,
  Show the spirit of an heir.

All that prey on vice or folly
  Joy to see their quarry fly:
There the gamester light and jolly,   15
  There the lender grave and sly.

Wealth, my lad, was made to wander,
  Let it wander as it will;
Call the jockey, call the pander,
  Bid them come, and take their fill.   20

When the bonny blade carouses,
  Pockets full and spirits high—
What are acres? what are houses?
  Only dirt, or wet or dry.

Should the guardian friend, or mother   25
  Tell the woes of wilful waste:
Scorn their counsel, scorn their pother,
  You can hang or drown at last.

1. This poem is ostensibly addressed to the young heir himself. The speaker pretends to urge the heir on to his dissipation of the estate. The poem is ironical then. But what is the quality of the irony? Bitter? Heavy-handed? Cynical?

2. Is there a shift in tone with ll. 15 and 16? Is the speaker here seeing the gamester and the lender as the heir sees them or as the speaker sees them or as they are in reality?

3. Does the tone break with the final stanza or is it sustained? How would you justify in terms of your answer the last two lines of the poem?

4. Is Dr. Johnson here pompous and oversolemn? If not, how has he kept the poem from becoming so? What does the metrical situation tell us on this score, if anything? Does the poet loathe the heir, or does he merely understand the heir? Is he wise in the ways of the world, or is he cynical?

Philomela

JOHN CROWE RANSOM (1888-   )

Procne, Philomela, and Itylus,
Your names are liquid, your improbable tale
Is recited in the classic numbers of the nightingale.
Ah, but our numbers are not felicitous,
It goes not liquidly for us.   5

Perched on a Roman ilex, and duly apostrophized,
The nightingale descanted unto Ovid;
She has even appeared to the Teutons, the swilled and gravid;
At Fontainebleau it may be the bird was gallicized;
Never was she baptized.   10

To England came Philomela with her pain,
Fleeing the hawk her husband; querulous ghost,
She wanders when he sits heavy on his roost,
Utters herself in the original again,
The untranslatable refrain.   15

Not to these shores she came! this other Thrace,
Environ barbarous to the royal Attic;
How could her delicate dirge run democratic,
Delivered in a cloudless boundless public place
To an inordinate race?   20

I pernoctated with the Oxford students once,
And in the quadrangles, in the cloisters, on the
    Cher,
Precociously knocked at antique doors ajar,
Fatuously touched the hems of the hierophants,
Sick of my dissonance.   25

I went out to Bagley Wood, I climbed the hill;
Even the moon had slanted off in a twinkling,
I heard the sepulchral owl and a few bells
    tinkling,
There was no more villainous day to unfulfil,
The diuturnity was still.   30

Up from the darkest wood where Philomela
    sat,
Her fairy numbers issued. What then ailed me?
My ears are called capacious but they failed me,
Her classics registered a little flat!
I rose, and venomously spat.   35

Philomela, Philomela, lover of song,
I am in despair if we may make us worthy,
A bantering breed sophistical and swarthy;
Unto more beautiful, persistently more young
Thy fabulous provinces belong.   40

The first line refers to the Greek myth about the
woman who was turned into a nightingale. Tereus
raped Philomela and then cut out her tongue and
cut off her hands to prevent her from communicating to her sister, Procne, Tereus's wife, what had happened to her. Philomela, however, was able to depict the scene in a tapestry, and showed it to Procne.
The sisters revenged themselves upon Tereus by killing his son, Itylus, and serving his flesh to Tereus
as food. Philomela was turned into a nightingale,
Procne into a swallow, and Tereus into the hawk
who pursues them.

1. What is the attitude of the speaker in the first
three stanzas? What is the effect of the witty expressions in such lines as 5 and 10? What is the effect of
the homely word "roost" in l. 13?

2. What is the poet's attitude toward his own
country? What is his attitude toward himself?

3. Is the poet mocking the pursuit of "culture"?
Is he debunking the Greek myth? Or is he after all
in some sense serious and quite in earnest?

4. Try to define the shifts of tone occurring at
l. 16, l. 21, and l. 36. On what note does the poem
end? Try to state the theme.

The Grasshopper

RICHARD LOVELACE
(1618-1658)

Oh thou that swing'st upon the waving ear
    Of some well-filled oaten beard,
Drunk ev'ry night with a delicious tear
    Dropped thee from Heav'n, where now th'art
    reared.

The joys of earth and air are thine entire,   5
    That with thy feet and wings dost hop and
    fly;
And when thy poppy works thou dost retire
    To thy carved acorn-bed to lie.

Up with the day, the sun thou welcom'st then,
    Sport'st in the guilt-plats of his beams,   10
And all these merry days mak'st merry men,
    Thy self, and melancholy streams.

But ah the sickle! Golden ears are cropped;
    Ceres and Bacchus bid goodnight;
Sharp frosty fingers all your flowers have
    topped,   15
    And what scythes spared, winds shave off
    quite.

Poor verdant fool! and now green ice! thy joys
    Large and as lasting as thy perch of grass,
Bid us lay in 'gainst winter rain, and poise
    Their floods, with an o'erflowing glasse.   20

Thou best of men and friends! we will create
    A genuine summer in each other's breast;

And spite of this cold time and frozen fate
  Thaw us a warm seat to our rest.

Our sacred hearths shall burn eternally   25
  As vestal flames; the North-wind, he
Shall strike his frost stretched wings, dissolve
    and fly
This Etna in epitome.

Dropping December shall come weeping in,
  Bewail th' usurping of his reign;   30
But when in showers of old Greek we begin,
  Shall cry, he hath his crown again!

Night as clear as Hesper shall our tapers whip
  From the light casements where we play,
And the dark Hag from her black mantle
    strip,   35
  And stick there everlasting day.

Thus richer than untempted kings are we,
  That asking nothing, nothing need:
Though lord of all what seas embrace, yet he
  That wants himself, is poor indeed.   40

1. What is the speaker's attitude toward the grasshopper? Note that it is *not* the attitude taken in the fable of the ant and the grasshopper. The poet is not blaming the grasshopper for being a wastrel and a happy-go-lucky time-killer.

2. What part does the imagery play in depicting the grasshopper's joys? How much of it has a human reference? The grasshopper is "drunk ev'ry night" (l. 3), has a "carved acorn-bed" (l. 8), etc.

3. What shift of tone occurs in l. 17? How does the phrase "green ice" epitomize the grasshopper's innocent gullibility? Does the image have a realistic basis? What are the associations of "green"? How are the associations of "green" played off against those of "golden"?

4. Is the poet arguing that the grasshopper enjoys only a spurious summer? That the only genuine summer is that which man can find within himself? Test this theory against ll. 21-40. In discussing the imagery, particularly that of the latter part of the poem, the student will probably require the following notes:

In classic mythology, Ceres was the goddess of grain; Bacchus, the god of wine. "Poise" (l. 19) means *to balance*. "Dropping" (l. 29) means dripping. The "old Greek" (l. 31) probably refers to Greek wine. The "crown" of December (l. 32) is apparently a reference to the Christmas festivities which in 1642 had been banned by the Puritan regime in England.

Fidele's Dirge

WILLIAM SHAKESPEARE
(1564-1616)

Fear no more the heat o' the sun,
  Nor the furious winter's rages;
Thou thy worldly task hast done,
  Home art gone, and ta'en thy wages;
Golden lads and girls all must,   5
As chimney-sweepers, come to dust.

Fear no more the frown o' the great,
  Thou art past the tyrant's stroke;
Care no more to clothe and eat;
  To thee the reed is as the oak;   10
The sceptre, learning, physic, must
All follow this, and come to dust.

Fear no more the lightning-flash,
  Nor the all-dreaded thunder-stone;
Fear not slander, censure rash;   15
  Thou hast finished joy and moan;
All lovers young, all lovers must
Consign to thee, and come to dust.

No exorciser harm thee!
Nor no witchcraft charm thee!   20
Ghost unlaid forbear thee!
Nothing ill come near thee!
Quiet consummation have;
And renownèd be thy grave!

1. What is the attitude toward death established in this poem?

2. What is the effect on the tone of the poem of the reiteration of the words "Fear no more"? On what basis has the poet selected the particular items which are no longer to be feared?

3. Does the poem succeed in making death seem a consolation and the grave a place of quiet and repose?

4. What is the effect of the emphasis upon the coming "to dust" of all things high and low, weak or powerful?

5. Can you account for the shift in style and tone in the last stanza? Is it meant to be a kind of charm against whatever might trouble the grave? Does it have the quality of a ritual? Does it make an effective ending for the dirge?

6. Scan Stanzas II and III. Can you justify the substitutions and variations of the metrical pattern?

in l. 4 gives the key to the poem? Why was it hard to believe that this child could die?

3. The poem makes use of irony and even of a kind of whimsy. Do these qualities cancel out any sense of tenderness? Or do they define and emphasize a special kind of tenderness?

4. Notice the rimes in this poem. Has the poet been careless, do you think, or are these slant and approximate rimes justified in what they contribute to the effect of the poem?

Bells for John Whiteside's Daughter

JOHN CROWE RANSOM
(1888-   )

There was such speed in her little body,
And such lightness in her footfall,
It is no wonder that her brown study
Astonishes us all.

Her wars were bruited in our high window.   5
We looked among orchard trees and beyond,
Where she took arms against her shadow,
Or harried unto the pond

The lazy geese, like a snow cloud
Dripping their snow on the green grass,   10
Tricking and stopping, sleepy and proud,
Who cried in goose, Alas,

For the tireless heart within the little
Lady with rod that made them rise
From their noon apple dreams, and scuttle   15
Goose-fashion under the skies!

But now go the bells, and we are ready;
In one house we are sternly stopped
To say we are vexed at her brown study,
Lying so primly propped.   20

1. Is this a poem of grief or not? If it is a poem of grief, why has the poet used phrases like "brown study" or such an expression as "Who cried in goose, Alas"? Why does the speaker say, not "We are saddened" or "We are hurt" but "We are vexed"? What is the speaker's attitude toward the death of the child?

2. Could it be argued that the word "astonishes"

At Her Window

FREDERICK LOCKER-
LAMPSON (1821-1895)

Beating Heart! we come again
    Where my Love reposes:
This is Mabel's window-pane;
    These are Mabel's roses.

Is she nested? Does she kneel   5
    In the twilight stilly,
Lily clad from throat to heel,
    She, my virgin Lily?

Soon the wan, the wistful stars,
    Fading, will forsake her;   10
Elves of light, on beamy bars,
    Whisper then, and wake her.

Let this friendly pebble plead
    At her flowery grating;
If she hear me will she heed?   15
    Mabel, I am waiting.

Mabel will be deck'd anon,
    Zoned in bride's apparel;
Happy zone! O hark to yon
    Passion-shaken carol!   20

Sing thy song, thou trancèd thrush,
    Pipe thy best, thy clearest;—
Hush, her lattice moves, O hush—
    Dearest Mabel!—dearest. . . .

What do you think of this poem?

Commemorative of a Naval Victory

HERMAN MELVILLE
(1819-1891)

Sailors there are of gentlest breed,
  Yet strong, like every goodly thing;
The discipline of arms refines,
  And the wave gives tempering.
  The damasked blade its beam can fling;   5
It lends the last grave grace:
The hawk, the hound, and sworded nobleman
  In Titian's picture for a king,
Are of hunter or warrior race.

In social halls a favored guest   10
  In years that follow victory won,
How sweet to feel your festal fame
  In woman's glance instinctive thrown:
  Repose is yours—your deed is known,
It musks the amber wine;   15
It lives, and sheds a light from storied days
  Rich as October sunsets brown,
Which make the barren place to shine.

But seldom the laurel wreath is seen
  Unmixed with pensive pansies dark;   20
There's a light and a shadow on every man
  Who at last attains his lifted mark—
  Nursing through night the ethereal spark.
Elate he never can be;
He feels that spirits which glad had hailed his
    worth,   25
  Sleep in oblivion.—The shark
Glides white through the phosphorous sea.

Each stanza of this poem represents a stage in the development of the theme. In the first stanza, against the background of an unspecified naval victory in the American Civil War, there is the comment on the gentleness mixed with strength in the "sailors." They are, the poet says, like a well-tempered steel blade that gives off a gleam and illuminates the place where it lies. In the last three lines of the stanza the description of the painting by Titian serves as another image for the sailor; the rich lordliness of the Renaissance figure is absorbed, as it were, into the modern hero. But we realize that the organization of this stanza is not very clear, the logical continuity is faulty. But do we make the leaps necessary to follow Melville despite his poor organization? Or can we say that the poor organization and loose syntax have a virtue of their own in this instance? In any case, we follow the drift of the stanza, and understand the kind of praise that Melville would give his sailors.

The second stanza is addressed, we learn, to the hero himself, the "you," who now, long after his great moment, still enjoys his "festal fame," the respect of men and the glances of women as a tribute to his now storied bravery that shines over his later life like rich October light. The hero deserves his fame. Melville is paying an honest compliment to the hero. There is no hint of irony, even if the hero seems to bask somewhat complacently in the old glory. His is an earned "repose."

But, as the last stanza puts it, the hero cannot enjoy his fame fully and easily. There is an irony after all. Even success has a shadow on it. The last three lines explain the nature of this shadow. Those who generously would best have appreciated his bravery are dead. Not only are they dead, but they died, we suddenly realize, in the naval battle for which the "you" now enjoys the fame. How do we know this? There is the image of the white shark that suddenly appears like a shocking vision across the scene of "festal fame," the savage creature drawn to the bleeding bodies of the wounded and dying in the sea, the image of evil.

There is one more step to take, one more question to ask. Does Melville mean the poem to apply merely to the naval hero? Or is he writing, finally, about all success, and the shadow over all success? Does he mean to imply that any successful man, if he is honest and has humanity, will understand that others as worthy as he have failed and sleep in oblivion? That, in a way, he lives off of their virtue and their generosity, for they would "glad" have "hailed his worth," and perhaps even by their death or failure have prepared the way for his success?

1. In each stanza of the poem we find an image of light. In the first, the finely tempered blade gives off a beam. In the second, the October light makes a barren landscape shine. In the third, there is light and shadow on every man, even in success. Interpret these three images as closely as possible. Is there any continuity of meaning among them? What do they imply about heroism and fame?

2. What is the meaning of the word *elate*? How does it apply here?

3. In the last two lines, we notice that "The shark" ends a line and is set off from the rest of the sentence to which it belongs and which composes the last line: "Glides white through the phosphorous sea." Is this arrangement effective?

The College Colonel

HERMAN MELVILLE
(1819-1891)

He rides at their head;
  A crutch by his saddle just slants in view,
One slung arm is in splints, you see,
  Yet he guides his strong steed—how coldly too.

He brings his regiment home—   5
  Not as they filed two years before,
But a remnant half-tattered, and battered, and worn,
Like castaway sailors, who—stunned
     By the surf's loud roar,
  Their mates dragged back and seen no more—   10
Again and again breast the surge,
  And at last crawl, spent, to shore.

A still rigidity and pale—
  An Indian aloofness lones his brow;
He has lived a thousand years   15
Compressed in battle's pains and prayers,
  Marches and watches slow.

There are welcoming shouts, and flags;
  Old men off hat to the Boy,
Wreaths from gay balconies fall at his feet,   20
But to *him*—there comes alloy.

It is not that a leg is lost,
  It is not that an arm is maimed,
It is not that the fever has racked—
  Self he has long disclaimed.   25

But all through the Seven Days' Fight,
  And deep in the Wilderness grim,
And in the field-hospital tent,
  And Petersburg crater, and dim
Lean brooding in Libby, there came—   30
  Ah Heaven!—what *truth* to him.

1. Compare the theme of this poem with that of "Commemorative of a Naval Victory."

2. What is the effect of the comparison that occupies stanza two? In what sense are the returning soldiers like cast-away sailors? Is the comparison overdone?

3. In the last stanza the poet names three famous battles that took place in Virginia during the Civil War and the Confederate prison at Richmond. What is gained by naming particularly the places?

4. What is the relation of the last line of the poem to the title of the poem?

The Need of Being Versed in Country Things

ROBERT FROST (1875-1963)

The house had gone to bring again
To the midnight sky a sunset glow.
Now the chimney was all of the house that stood,
Like a pistil after the petals go.

The barn opposed across the way,   5
That would have joined the house in flame
Had it been the will of the wind, was left
To bear forsaken the place's name.

No more it opened with all one end
For teams that came by the stony road   10
To drum on the floor with scurrying hoofs
And brush the mow with the summer load.

The birds that came to it through the air
At broken windows flew out and in,

Their murmur more like the sigh we sigh   15
From too much dwelling on what has been.

Yet for them the lilac renewed its leaf,
And the agèd elm, though touched with fire;
And the dry pump flung up an awkward arm;
And the fence post carried a strand of wire.   20

For them there was really nothing sad.
But though they rejoiced in the nest they kept,
One had to be versed in country things
Not to believe the phoebes wept.

This poem seems to confine itself largely to description: a rural scene in which the chimney of a burned farmhouse still stands, the barn, untouched by the fire, but with some of its windows broken, an old elm, one side of which had been scorched by the fire, a fence from which all but one strand of wire has fallen away, the now unused pump.

The details are well chosen, and their concrete vividness has been enforced by appropriate comparisons. The lone chimney, for example, stands like a pistil (the upright spike of certain flowers) after the cup-shaped part of the blossom has withered and fallen away. The arm of the pump has been left standing at an awkward angle—like a human arm thrown up in a clumsy gesture of protest and then arrested there.

The poem emphasizes the present scene, but there are several references to the past: there is a reference to the fire itself which caused a glow like that of sunset unseasonably at midnight; and there is a picture of the barn as it used to be when the hayloads were coming in at the end of summer. The sense of life and bustling, purposeful activity contrasts sharply with the present sense of deadness and desolation in the present scene. (The same contrast is unobtrusively implied in the fifth stanza: the pump is "dry"—the fence is in human practical terms now hardly a "fence" at all.)

The poem, we have remarked, seems to confine itself to description, and admirably detailed objective description; but the mention of the phoebes suggests an interpretation. For the scene is not completely desolate: the observer shares it with the birds, which have taken over the abandoned barn for their nesting place. The scene spells melancholy desolation, and the mournful cry of the birds seems to voice appropriately the quality of the scene.

Suppose that the poem ended with this fourth stanza. What sort of poem would it be? We should still have much of the descriptive detail (though we should sorely miss that of the fifth stanza); but the poem would seem a little predictable and trite in its interpretation of the scene, and might not entirely escape a certain hint of sentimentality.

But the poet does not stop with the fourth stanza. The speaker's realistic grasp on the situation is not relaxed; nor is his hold on the essential difference between man and nature. The phoebes are not weeping. Presumably, they are happy. And why should they not be? However desolate the setting in *human* terms, it is admirably accommodated to them. As a place to perch, *one* strand of wire is just as good as three or four. Nature, like the fire-damaged elm, has been only momentarily deflected by man's fortunes and misfortunes. Its flood of vitality perennially renews itself. What man abandons, nature casually repossesses.

Even the lines which may seem to tilt most dangerously over toward the sentimental effect (ll. 15-16) are seen actually to enforce this distinction between man and nature. If the "murmur" of the phoebes resembles a human sigh over the vanished past, it is like "the sigh *we* (i.e., human beings) sigh," and will seem so only to human beings.

The observer who speaks the poem is, then, tough-minded. He knows nature too well to attribute to it human concerns and human values. Nature does not weep over the abandoned home: it does not even know that the house is a house or that it has been abandoned. The—to human ears—mournful cry of the birds is only accidentally appropriate. But if the speaker is tough-minded and realistic, he is also sensitive; and he acknowledges the poignant sense of melancholy in the most powerful way possible: unless, he says, you really were "versed in country things," you would have been taken in—you might have believed that "the phoebes wept."

What is the advantage of having the scene reported through the lips of an observer who is, as this one is, evidently "versed in country things"? There is a great advantage. We properly discount the outburst of someone whose emotions are on hair-trigger—who responds easily and glibly to slight occasions—who has no sense of proportion. Conversely, we are impressed by the expression of emotion when it comes from a tough-grained sensibility, not prone to easy outburst.

In this poem, we may say that the poet succeeds in "having it both ways"—in doing justice to the hard realities of life and yet acknowledging the melancholy implicit in that life. But the use of the phrase "having it both ways" may smack of trickery, as if the poet were skilfully but coldly manipulating our feelings—palming off on us a trite and worn theme. Perhaps, then, we had better state in other terms what the poet accomplishes. The accomplishment may be put in this way: the poet has refused to make a vague and general appeal to our feelings by sketching in a conventionally melancholy scene in the hope that certain *clichés* of sentiment—the sadness of the past, of man's broken hopes, of simple rural life—will work. Instead he has defined for us in the poem quite precisely the quality and degree of melancholy which such a scene ought to elicit. In doing so, he has moreover refused to exploit this sentiment of regret as something to be dwelt upon for its own sake and in isolation from the hard facts of our world or from the hardest thinking that man can give to those facts. Last of all, he has merely implied his own attitude to the scene—not urging us to adopt it, but doing his reader the compliment of allowing him to apprehend it for himself.

1. Compare the theme of this poem with that of "The Woodpile" (p. 421). Are there any resemblances? How is the contrast between man and nature handled in the two poems?

2. Compare the theme of this poem with that of "The Wild Swans at Coole" (p. 311). Are there any resemblances? How does the tone of Yeats's poem differ from that of Frost's?

Sonnet 104

WILLIAM SHAKESPEARE
(1564-1616)

To me, fair friend, you never can be old;
For as you were when first your eye I eyed,
Such seems your beauty still. Three Winters cold
Have from the forests shook three Summers' pride;
Three beauteous Springs to yellow Autumn turned   5
In process of the seasons have I seen,
Three April perfumes in three hot Junes burned,
Since first I saw you fresh, which yet are green.
Ah! yet doth beauty, like a dial-hand,
Steal from his figure, and no pace perceived;   10
So your sweet hue, which methinks still doth stand,
Hath motion, and mine eye may be deceived:
  For fear of which, hear this, thou age unbred:
  Ere you were born was beauty's summer dead.

1. This poem, like Sonnets 18, 73, and 97 (see p. 306), makes elaborate use of the imagery of the seasons. How does it compare with those sonnets in tone? What relation does this imagery of the seasons have to the poet's attitude toward the fading of the friend's beauty?

2. The speaker begins by saying that his fair friend cannot age. The passage of three years has left him apparently unchanged. Yet the speaker faces the supposition that his friend has perhaps changed, though imperceptibly (see ll. 9-12). Do these lines contradict and weaken the emphatic statement with which the poem begins? Or do they really strengthen it?

3. What is the meaning of the last two lines? To whom or what are these lines addressed? How are they related to the statement made in the first eight lines and the reconsideration of that statement in the next four lines?

4. Some readers would characterize the tone of the poem as one of assurance and confidence. Do you agree? If it is confidence, confidence in what? That his friend cannot age? That his friend cannot be older to *him?* Or what?

In Memory of Major Robert Gregory

WILLIAM BUTLER YEATS
(1865-1939)

I

Now that we're almost settled in our house
I'll name the friends that cannot sup with us
Beside a fire of turf in th' ancient tower,
And having talked to some late hour
Climb up the narrow winding stair to bed: 5
Discoverers of forgotten truth
Or mere companions of my youth,
All, all are in my thoughts to-night being dead.

II

Always we'd have the new friend meet the old
And we are hurt if either friend seem cold,   10
And there is salt to lengthen out the smart
In the affections of our heart,
And quarrels are blown up upon that head;
But not a friend that I would bring
This night can set us quarrelling,   15
For all that come into my mind are dead.

III

Lionel Johnson comes first to mind,
That loved his learning better than mankind,
Though courteous to the worst; much falling he
Brooded upon sanctity   20
Till all his Greek and Latin learning seemed
A long blast upon the horn that brought
A little nearer to his thought
A measureless consummation that he dreamed.

IV

And that enquiring man John Synge comes next,
That dying chose the living world for text
And never could have rested in the tomb
But that, long travelling, he had come
Towards nightfall upon certain set apart
In a most desolate stony place,   30
Towards nightfall upon a race
Passionate and simple like his heart.

V

And then I think of old George Pollexfen,
In muscular youth well known to Mayo men
For horsemanship at meets or at race-
courses,   35
That could have shown how pure-bred horses
And solid men, for all their passion, live
But as the outrageous stars incline
By opposition, square and trine;
Having grown sluggish and contemplative.   40

VI

They were my close companions many a year,
A portion of my mind and life, as it were,
And now their breathless faces seem to look
Out of some old picture-book;
I am accustomed to their lack of breath,   45
But not that my dear friend's dear son,
Our Sidney and our perfect man,
Could share in that discourtesy of death.

VII

For all things the delighted eye now sees
Were loved by him; the old storm-broken
trees   50
That cast their shadows upon road and bridge;
The tower set on the stream's edge;
The ford where drinking cattle make a stir
Nightly, and startled by that sound
The water-hen must change her ground;   55
He might have been your heartiest welcomer

VIII

When with the Galway foxhounds he would
ride
From Castle Taylor to the Roxborough side
Or Esserkelly plain, few kept his pace;
At Mooneen he had leaped a place   60
So perilous that half the astonished meet
Had shut their eyes; and where was it
He rode a race without a bit?
And yet his mind outran the horses' feet.

IX

We dreamed that a great painter had been
born   65
To cold Clare rock and Galway rock and thorn,
To that stern colour and that delicate line
That are our secret discipline
Wherein the gazing heart doubles her might.

Soldier, scholar, horseman, he,   70
And yet he had the intensity
To have published all to be a world's delight.

X

What other could so well have counselled us
In all lovely intricacies of a house
As he that practised or that understood   75
All work in metal or in wood,
In moulded plaster or in carven stone?
Soldier, scholar, horseman, he,
And all he did done perfectly
As though he had but that one trade alone.   80

XI

Some burn damp faggots, others may consume
The entire combustible world in one small
    room
As though dried straw, and if we turn about
The bare chimney is gone black out
Because the work had finished in that flare. 85
Soldier, scholar, horseman, he,
As 'twere all life's epitome.
What made us dream that he could comb grey
    hair?

XII

I had thought, seeing how bitter is that wind
That shakes the shutter, to have brought to
    mind   90
All those that manhood tried, or childhood
    loved
Or boyish intellect approved,
With some appropriate commentary on each;
Until imagination brought
A fitter welcome; but a thought   95
Of that late death took all my heart for speech.

    The man commemorated was the son of
Yeats's close friend, Lady Augusta Gregory (1852-
1932), who joined Yeats in writing plays for the
Abbey Theatre, and at whose country place
Yeats frequently resided for long periods. Major
Gregory died in the first World War. Lionel
Johnson (1867-1902) was a minor poet of the
'nineties. John Synge (1871-1909) was the author
of *Riders to the Sea* and *The Playboy of the
Western World.* Yeats suggested to him that he
go to the Aran Islands off the western coast of
Ireland, and the Aran Islands furnish the locale
of Synge's best work. George Pollexfen, who
dabbled in astrology, was Yeats's maternal uncle.
Sir Philip Sidney (1554-1586), author of *Arcadia*
and *The Defence of Poesie,* was for the Elizabe-
thans a type of full-bodied manly excellence—
the perfect gentleman, courtier, and soldier.

    Yeats had refitted an ancient tower near
Lady Gregory's estate as a home. As the poem
opens, he and his wife have just moved in, and
he reflects upon the dead friends who cannot
come to welcome them to their new abode.

    1. How does the poet keep the imagery of the
house and the housewarming uppermost in our minds
throughout the poem?
    2. Is the poet cynical (see ll. 9-15)? Or cold to-
ward the dead friends? Does he emphasize their failures and limitations? What is the tone of his comments upon them?
    3. How does Major Gregory sum up the virtues
of Johnson, Synge, and Pollexfen? Are the comments
on these three really a preparation for the praise to
be accorded to Gregory? They have more or less
completely fulfilled themselves; Gregory's accomplishments are still merely potential. How does this fact
qualify the praise? Is the praise of Gregory fulsome
and excessive? If not, why not? Does part of the answer reside in the fact that the speaker has given
testimony (in his account of the other friends) to his
objectivity?
    4. What is the "discourtesy of death"? Can it
allude to the fact that the dead faces, though vividly
summoned up in memory, do not speak—give no
greeting—merely stare? Or to what? What is the
effect of this irony?
    5. Does the poem merely break off abruptly? Is
this an adequate ending? (The speaker says that he
had intended to summon up other friends.) Can you
defend the effectiveness of the ending?
    6. Scan Stanza XI. Do the substitutions and vari-
ations in this stanza serve to stress the key words?
Note, for example, the metrical situation in line 4.
    7. Locate examples of conversational tone in the
poem. Examples of realistic imagery. With what elements are these put in contrast? To what effect?

Lay Your Sleeping Head
W. H. AUDEN (1907-   )

Lay your sleeping head, my love,
Human on my faithless arm;
Time and fevers burn away

Individual beauty from
Thoughtful children, and the grave   5
Proves the child ephemeral:
But in my arms till break of day
Let the living creature lie,
Mortal, guilty but to me
The entirely beautiful.   10

Soul and body have no bounds:
To lovers as they lie upon
Her tolerant enchanted slope
In their ordinary swoon,
Grave the vision Venus sends   15
Of supernatural sympathy,
Universal love and hope;
While an abstract insight wakes
Among the glaciers and the rocks
The hermit's sensual ecstasy.   20

Certainty, fidelity
On the stroke of midnight pass
Like vibrations of a bell
And fashionable madmen raise
Their pedantic boring cry: 25
Every farthing of the cost,
All the dreaded cards foretell,
Shall be paid, but from this night
Not a whisper, not a thought,
Not a kiss nor look be lost.   30

Beauty, midnight, vision dies:
Let the winds of dawn that blow
Softly round your dreaming head
Such a day of sweetness show
Eye and knocking heart may bless,   35
Find the mortal world enough;
Noons of dryness see you fed
By the involuntary powers,
Nights of insult let you pass
Watched by every human love.   40

1. Is the speaker deliberately deceiving himself? For example, ll. 9-10 imply that the loved one is entirely beautiful perhaps only to himself. Line 31 acknowledges that "beauty, midnight, vision dies." Is the speaker saying in effect "I know that what I would like to believe is not true"? Or do these concessions actually strengthen his affirmation?

2. If the speaker acknowledges, as he does in l. 9, that the loved one is "mortal" and "guilty," is he likewise honest in the acknowledgment that he makes about himself? For example, in l. 2, he refers to his arm as "faithless." What then is his attitude toward himself and toward love?

3. Notice that the last stanza has almost the tone of a prayer. What does this final stanza contribute to the poem as a whole?

They Flee from Me

SIR THOMAS WYATT
(1503-1542)

They flee from me that sometime did me seek
    With naked foot, stalking in my chamber.
I have seen them gentle, tame, and meek,
    That now are wild, and do not remember
    That sometime they did put themselves in
      danger   5
To take bread at my hand; and now they range
Busily seeking with a continual change.

Thankèd be fortune, it hath been otherwise
    Twenty times better; but once in special,
In thin array, after a pleasant guise,   10
    When her loose gown from her shoulders
      did fall
    And she me caught in her arms long and
      small
Therewith all sweetly did me kiss
And softly said, 'Dear heart how like you this?'

It was no dream; I lay broad waking: 15
    But all is turned, through my gentleness,
Into a strange fashion of forsaking;
    And I have leave to go of her goodness,
    And she also to use newfangleness.
But since that I so kindly am served,   20
I would fain know what she hath deserved.

1. To what does the word "they" refer in l. 1? It would seem to refer to birds (or to any wild, shy, timorous creatures). But it seems also in view of stanza 2 to refer to women and to one woman in particular. How does the first stanza in its description of the actions of those that "flee from me" prepare for the specific reference to a woman in stanza 2?

2. What is the tone of the first two stanzas? It seems to be a relatively objective statement—not excited, not bitter, though the situation is evidently now, in the cold and altered present, so very different. What does l. 15 do for the tone? Is the speaker

saying in effect that "I have to pinch myself to believe that it was once otherwise, but I did not dream it. I was wide awake. I remember vividly that it actually happened"?

3. Try to characterize the tone of the last stanza. It evidently involves irony, but what kind of irony? Is it an irony primarily at the expense of the woman for whom love is merely a fashion—a mode of dress to be altered capriciously? Or does the irony also involve the speaker—as if he were intimating "how foolish of me to have expected anything else"? The word "kindly" in l. 20, in addition to its present

meaning, could mean in Wyatt's time "in accordance with nature," for the old original meaning of *kind* was "nature." One does not blame a bird for not coming up to the speaker's hand now that there is no bread to be offered. Is one to blame the woman for acting likewise in terms of her "nature"?

4. If this poem does involve a deeply sardonic account of inconstancy how has the poet kept it from seeming passionately bitter or glibly cynical? Does it become a more moving and powerful poem for having been kept free of a more superficial and obvious bitterness?

SECTION V

In the poems already studied attention has been called to the importance of the *imagery*. The poems in the present section do not differ in principle in their use of imagery from the preceding ones; for all poems, to a degree, use imagery, and it has been said that a poet thinks, to a large extent, by means of his images. Images, as has already been seen, are not merely pictures the poet describes; they are one of the most important instruments the poet can use for realizing the ideas and feelings which make up the poem. The poems in the present section, however, do give more complicated uses of imagery than appear in most of the previous poems.

Ode on Melancholy

JOHN KEATS (1795-1821)

No, no! go not to Lethe, neither twist
  Wolf's-bane, tight-rooted, for its poisonous wine;
Nor suffer thy pale forehead to be kist
  By nightshade, ruby grape of Proserpine;
Make not your rosary of yew-berries,   5
  Nor let the beetle, nor the death-moth be
    Your mournful Psyche, nor the downy owl
A partner in your sorrow's mysteries;
  For shade to shade will come too drowsily,
    And drown the wakeful anguish of the soul.   10

But when the melancholy fit shall fall
  Sudden from heaven like a weeping cloud,
That fosters the droop-headed flowers all,
  And hides the green hill in an April shroud:
Then glut thy sorrow on a morning rose,   15
  Or on the rainbow of a salt sand-wave,
    Or on the wealth of globèd peonies;
Or if thy mistress some rich anger shows,
  Imprison her soft hand, and let her rave,
    And feed deep, deep upon her peerless eyes.   20

She dwells with Beauty—Beauty that must die;
  And Joy, whose hand is ever at his lips
Bidding adieu; and aching Pleasure nigh,
  Turning to poison while the bee-mouth sips;
Ay, in the very temple of Delight   25
  Veiled Melancholy has her sovran shrine,
    Though seen of none save him whose strenuous tongue
Can burst Joy's grape against his palate fine;
  His soul shall taste the sadness of her might,
    And be among her cloudy trophies hung.   30

The poem begins with a rather simple statement: The intensity of sorrow is not to be found in the usual places in which one has been taught to expect it. On the contrary, melancholy haunts scenes of the greatest beauty; for beauty fades, it cannot endure.

The poet might have made his point more simply and directly, but he wants his reader to feel, as well as to understand, what he is saying, and one function of the imagery in this poem is to ensure the reader's experiencing the insight rather than merely noting it as an abstraction. In this poem Keats thinks *through* his images and expects us to do so.

The speaker is ordering someone *not* to do certain things. As the developing context makes clear, the person addressed wants to have the experience of melancholy, but the poet thinks that he is about to seek it in the wrong way. Thus the poem begins with a rather abrupt and dramatic dismissal of the conventional appurtenances of melancholy—death moths, the mournful owl, the berries of the yew, the tree so often seen in European graveyards, and so on. The poet's reason is this: a person who is really concerned with "sorrow's mysteries" will find that wolf's-bane and the grapes associated with Proserpine, the Greek death goddess, will simply dull his anguish rather than enable him to experience its intensity. The man who wants to savor the essence of melancholy is counselled to seek out the fresh but evanescent objects of beauty like the morning rose or the rainbow that hangs for a moment over the breaking wave.

The poet's advice is evidently addressed to someone who does not wish to *drown* his sorrow but rather wishes to explore it and come to understand what it means. This advice, it also becomes clear, is not given by a sentimentalist, nor is it advice suited to a sentimentalist, that is, to the kind of person who would like to enjoy a good cry—to indulge himself in a sweet sadness. For the man who speaks the advice in this poem, a love of melancholy is much more than a kind of self-indulgence. The procedure that he recommends is designed to relate the melancholy mood to some constant truths about human life, and it will turn the morbidly obsessive mood into insight and understanding.

In accomplishing this transformation, the poet (or the person through whom the poet speaks) depends heavily upon imagery. The first figure of the second stanza at once tends to mark off the melancholy mood from mere sentimentality, for the mood is identified with the inevitability of the processes of nature: not consciously sought, but allowed to come of itself. So the speaker describes the melancholy fit's falling "Sudden from heaven like a weeping cloud."

The fact that the cloud is a "weeping cloud" may seem to the reader to be the obvious point of the comparison, and it is this mournful note that seems to be carried forward in the figure of the shroud, two lines further on. But the shroud figure is much richer than a casual reader might think, and the poet is not content to depend merely upon its usual associations. Indeed the phrase "April shroud" is startling, for the word *April* brings in associations—the joyfulness and fruitfulness of spring—that seem to run counter to death and sorrow. The cloud is an emblem of mournfulness, but the poet is reminding the reader that it is also an emblem of fruitfulness, and the implication would seem to be that, like the cloud, melancholy has a fruitfulness of its own. Such a mood may help one see more clearly the meaning of life—to see the close connection of joy with sorrow, and to find in their contrast a kind of paradoxical unity. To sum up: the "weeping cloud" figure is not simple and "easy"; and in its own complication and richness it moves us away from the stock response and the sentimental effect.

With line 5 of Stanza II the speaker's positive recommendations begin. When the melancholy "fit shall fall," one ought to "glut" his "sorrow on a morning rose." Why *morning*? Because the rose at evening may not bear quite the exquisite bloom which it had at the beginning of the day. Or, he is to contemplate "the rainbow of a salt sand-wave." The rainbow made by the sunlight's falling on the spray of an ocean wave breaking on the sandy beach is another example of beauty perishing almost as quickly as seen.

The third instance, "the wealth of globèd peonies" does not stress the fleetingness of beauty, but perhaps the poet wants here a less striking—a more desultory—image before he reaches his climactic image, that of the woman in the fullness of her beauty, a woman agitated, filled with emotion, seen for a moment in all her pride of life.

The woman is treated like another object rather than like an equal human being. The imagined scene presents us with the rather Byronic young man, a connoisseur of beauty, treating the loved one as another and highest instance of his connoisseurship. When she shows some "rich anger" he is to seize her soft hand "and let her rave," paying no attention to what she says but looking deep into her matchless eyes.

The lady's anger is evidently not thought of here as a very serious matter but perhaps as a conscious pose which the lady knows will set off her beauty to better advantage. The connoisseur of melancholy, at any rate, is to savor her beauty as he would a particularly fine wine.

What is the poet's attitude here? Is it identical with that which he counsels his friend to adopt? Is he teasing the ladies here? Or is he teasing his friend? Or is he simply saying to the man who aspires to a knowledge of melancholy: the woman whom you adore, considered simply as a beautiful *object,* considered as a more precious morning rose, as a speaking flower, is a supreme instance of beauty that is fleeting and doomed to pass away?

Whatever we consider the tone of this second stanza to be, the tone of the third stanza modulates into the deepest kind of seriousness. The lady is the supreme instance of "Beauty that must die," beauty heightened by the very fact that it is not lasting. In Stanza III, Keats rather boldly associates the lady with personifications like Delight, Pleasure, Beauty, Joy, and Melancholy herself. How does he manage to do so and yet render the scene without a sense of artificiality or affectation? The answer may lie in the fact that the woman is considered to be a sort of priestess of Melancholy, though she resides in the "temple of Delight," where Joy and Pleasure abide, for in this temple "veiled Melancholy has her sovran shrine. . . ." The temple figure has been quietly prepared for in the first stanza. There the poet refers to one possessed by melancholy as a person indulging in a religious rite; he describes him as one seeking "a partner in your sorrow's mysteries." (*Mysteries* has among its meanings the rites of certain religions, specially secret and esoteric religions.) Indeed, in Stanza I, the whole assemblage of conventional objects associated with melancholy such as the "ruby grape of Proserine" and the "rosary of yew-berries" finds its proper counterpart and contrast in this last stanza. For the "poisonous wine" of the temple of Melancholy is something

so intensely pleasant that it makes the senses ache for it, but it turns "to poison while the bee-mouth sips" it. So with the other furnishings of the temple: there are no death-moths or downy owls but objects of joy and delight. The discerning person sees that melancholy is to be worshipped in no other temple than that of pleasure itself.

Throughout the poem, then, there is a thinking through images. We have yet to mention, however, the most forceful image of the poem. It occurs in the seventh and eighth lines of the last stanza: "Though seen of none save him whose strenuous tongue/Can burst Joy's grape against his palate fine." The image is not a sentimentally pretty one. The poet has not chosen the image for its superficial attractiveness, but because he needs the image for what he has to say. What does it say? It says that the requisites for feeling the full force of melancholy are sensitiveness on the part of the observer (the "palate fine") but also force and penetration of insight (the "strenuous tongue") which will allow the observer to taste the essence of joy, an act which will necessitate destroying it. The figure of the bursting of joy's grape is given dramatically: it is only the *strenuous* tongue that can burst that grape. The word *burst* gathers up into itself both elements of the comparison: a flood of rich sweetness tasted at the instant of bursting but also the necessity of bursting—the necessary destruction—of joy.

Even this account does not fully explain why the figure is so successful as it is. Though it has a dramatic element and comes with a hint of surprise, it has actually been prepared for very carefully from the earliest stanzas. One may go back and notice how many images of taste appear in the poem, images that prepare for this last great figure of tasting. Stanza I gives us two instances: the water of the river Lethe and the "poisonous wine." In Stanza II, the admonition to "glut" and to "feed" imply tasting. In the third stanza itself there is a tasting image in line 24. Pleasure turns to "poison while the bee-mouth sips." These and the great taste image of lines 27 and 28 are what supply the power for line 29: "His soul shall *taste* the sadness of her might" (italics ours). As a matter of fact, images of tasting and images of temple rites bind the poem together. The poem, very subtly, has been developed around these two basic images.

To Marguerite

MATTHEW ARNOLD
(1822-1888)

Yes: in the sea of life enisled,
  With echoing straits between us thrown.
Dotting the shoreless watery wild,
  We mortal millions live *alone*.
The islands feel the enclasping flow,   5
And then their endless bounds they know.

But when the moon their hollows lights,
  And they are swept by balms of spring,
And in their glens, on starry nights,
  The nightingales divinely sing;   10
And lovely notes, from shore to shore,
Across the sounds and channels pour;

O then a longing like despair
  Is to their farthest caverns sent!
For surely once, they feel we were   15
  Parts of a single continent.
Now round us spreads the watery plain—
O might our marges meet again!

Who order'd that their longing's fire
  Should be, as soon as kindled, cooled?   20
Who renders vain their deep desire?—
  A God, a God their severance ruled;
And bade betwixt their shores to be
The unplumb'd, salt, estranging sea.

    Write an interpretation of this poem, trying to indicate the relation of the imagery to the meaning.

Very Like a Whale

OGDEN NASH (1903-   )

One thing that literature would be greatly the better for
Would be a more restricted employment by authors of simile and metaphor.
Authors of all races, be they Greeks, Romans, Teutons or Celts,
Can't seem just to say that anything is the thing it is but have to go out of their way to say that it is like something else.
What does it mean when we are told   5
That the Assyrian came down like a wolf on the fold?
In the first place, George Gordon Byron had had enough experience
To know that it probably wasn't just one Assyrian, it was a lot of Assyrians.
However, as too many arguments are apt to induce apoplexy and thus hinder longevity,
We'll let it pass as one Assyrian for the sake of brevity.   10
Now then, this particular Assyrian, the one whose cohorts were gleaming in purple and gold,
Just what does the poet mean when he says he came down like a wolf on the fold?
In heaven and earth more than is dreamed of in our philosophy there are a great many things,
But I don't imagine that among them there is a wolf with purple and gold cohorts or purple and gold anythings.
No, no, Lord Byron, before I'll believe that this Assyrian was actually like a wolf I must have some kind of proof;   15
Did he run on all fours and did he have a hairy tail and a big red mouth and big white teeth and did he say Woof woof woof?
Frankly I think it very unlikely, and all you were entitled to say, at the very most,
Was that the Assyrian cohorts came down like a lot of Assyrian cohorts about to destroy the Hebrew host.
But that wasn't fancy enough for Lord Byron, oh dear me no, he had to invent a lot of figures of speech and then interpolate them,
With the result that whenever you mention Old Testament soldiers to people they say Oh yes, they're the ones that a lot of wolves dressed up in gold and purple ate them.   20
That's the kind of thing that's being done all the time by poets, from Homer to Tennyson;
They're always comparing ladies to lilies and veal to venison.
How about the man who wrote,

Her little feet stole in and out like mice beneath her petticoat?

Wouldn't anybody but a poet think twice 25
Before stating that his girl's feet were mice?

Then they always say things like that after a winter storm

The snow is a white blanket. Oh it is, is it, all right then, you sleep under a six-inch blanket of snow and I'll sleep under a half-inch blanket of unpoetical blanket material and we'll see which one keeps warm,

And after that maybe you'll begin to comprehend dimly

What I mean by too much metaphor and simile. 30

This poem is a humorous protest against the irresponsible use of simile and metaphor.

1. The first lines of Lord Byron's "Destruction of Sennacherib" are:

"The Assyrian came down like the wolf on the fold,
And his cohorts were gleaming in purple and gold. . . ."

What about Nash's literalistic and common-sense objections?

2. In l. 22 Nash says that poets are "always comparing ladies to lilies." One poem in this text, "At Her Window" (p. 341), makes use of this comparison. Is it well used in your opinion? Waller's "Song" (p. 307) compares a lady to a rose. Is this comparison well used in your opinion?

3. L. 24 refers to Sir John Suckling's "Ballad upon a Wedding": "Her feet beneath her petticoat like little mice stole in and out." Why did the poet make this comparison? Is it an apt comparison? What does it tell us about the poet's attitude?

4. What is the tone of Ogden Nash's poem? How is the tone indicated?

5. The title of the poem is taken from *Hamlet*, Act III, scene 2. What is the significance of the title?

You, Andrew Marvell

ARCHIBALD MacLEISH
(1892-   )

And here face down beneath the sun
And here upon earth's noonward height
To feel the always coming on
The always rising of the night

To feel creep up the curving East 5
The earthly chill of dusk and slow
Upon those under lands the vast
And ever climbing shadow grow

And strange at Ecbatan the trees
Take leaf by leaf the evening strange 10
The flooding dark about their knees
The mountains over Persia change

And now at Kermanshah the gate
Dark empty and the withered grass
And through the twilight now the late 15
Few travellers in the westward pass

And Baghdad darken and the bridge
Across the silent river gone
And through Arabia the edge
Of evening widen and steal on 20

And deepen on Palmyra's street
The wheel rut in the ruined stone
And Lebanon fade out and Crete
High through the clouds and overblown

And over Sicily the air 25
Still flashing with the landward gulls
And loom and slowly disappear
The sails above the shadowy hulls

And Spain go under and the shore
Of Africa the gilded sand 30
And evening vanish and no more
The low pale light across that land

Nor now the long light on the sea
And here face downward in the sun
To feel how swift how secretly 35
The shadow of the night comes on . . .

1. This poem traces the creeping shadow of night as the globe of the earth turns from west to east. Are the descriptive details well chosen? What do the details suggest?

2. The phrase "rising of the night" suggests the rising of flood waters. Is this hint developed as the poem goes on?

3. The poet uses the word *and* twenty-two times in this poem. Can you justify his insistence upon this word?

4. The rhythm changes in the last lines of the poem. Scan the last stanza. Try to define the nature of the change in rhythm. Is it justified?

5. Is the poet merely describing how the "shadow of the night comes on" or is he actually describing something else? What does the shadow of the night come to stand for?

Spring and Fall:

To a Young Child

GERARD MANLEY HOPKINS (1844-1889)

Márgarét, are you gríeving
Over Goldengrove unleaving?
Leáves, líke the things of man, you
With your fresh thoughts care for, can you?
Áh! ás the heart grows older   5
It will come to such sights colder
By and by, nor spare a sigh
Though worlds of wanwood leafmeal lie;
And yet you wíll weep and know why.
Now no matter, child, the name: 10
Sórrow's spríngs áre the same.
Nor mouth had, no nor mind, expressed
What heart heard of, ghost guessed:
It ís the blight man was born for,
It is Margaret you mourn for.   15

1. What is the situation implied by the poem? Who is speaking to Margaret? What is implied as to the character of the speaker?

2. The child is sorrowful at the falling of the leaves. But what do the leaves come to stand for that justifies the speaker's question? How can you say that you merely think you are weeping for the loss of the leaves, when actually you are mourning for yourself?

3. What is meant by "fresh" thoughts—particularly in this context? "Wanwood" suggests a leafless wood that is pale and gray. What else does it suggest? "Leafmeal" is a word made up presumably on the analogy of words like "piecemeal." What else does it imply? The word "ghost" in l. 13 is apparently used in the sense of spirit or soul. (Compare with the meaning as in "Holy Ghost," that is, "Holy Spirit.")

4. There are at least two interpretations for l. 9: either "Some day you will weep and know why you are weeping," or "You persist in weeping and in demanding an answer." Which is the more appropriate and significant interpretation?

Song

THOMAS CAREW (1595?-1639?)

Ask me no more where Jove bestows,
When June is past, the fading rose;
For in your beauty's orient deep
These flowers, as in their causes, sleep.

Ask me no more whither do stray   5
The golden atoms of the day;
For in pure love heaven did prepare
Those powders to enrich your hair.

Ask me no more whither doth haste
The nightingale when May is past;   10
For in your sweet dividing throat
She winters and keeps warm her note.

Ask me no more where those stars 'light
That downwards fall in dead of night;
For in your eyes they sit, and there   15
Fixèd become as in their sphere.

Ask me no more if east or west
The Phoenix builds her spicy nest;
For unto you at last she flies,
And in your fragrant bosom dies.   20

In this poem, the poet finds in his mistress the various beauties of nature. In her cheeks, he finds roses; in her hair, the golden light of day; in her voice, the music of the nightingale; in her eyes, the flash of stars. The poem is akin, as the reader will easily see, to many poems which undertake to praise a beautiful woman. One of the most interesting things about the poem, therefore, is the manner in which this poem is set off from other poems which intend to do the same sort of thing but which end in a mere series of *clichés*.

In the first place, the praise (like the praise of most love poems) is extravagant. And extravagant praise often sounds flat or glib. It gives one the impression of being glib if the reader feels that the poet is merely tossing off compliments. It gives the impression of being sentimental or flat if we feel that the poet, though perhaps sincere, is betrayed by his own enthusiasm so that he says things which, clear-eyed, he would not say; and which, we, unmoved by his personal enthusiasm, are ashamed for him to say.

The *tone* of the poem (which reflects the attitude of the poet towards his mistress and towards what he says about her) is, even in a relatively simple poem like this one, of great importance. What is that tone? And how does the poet establish it?

In attempting to determine this matter, an important point to notice is the complication which the poet introduces. By *complication* is meant the ways in which the poet adds to and develops the simple idea that his mistress is a compound of the most beautiful aspects of nature. Obviously, the particular twists, elaborations, etc., which the poet gives to the idea reveal much about his attitude.

One notices, in the first place, that there is considerable complication—more, indeed, than one hasty reading might indicate. The mistress is not merely a person possessing cheeks like roses and eyes like stars. She is a sort of repository or store-house where the aspects of nature which perish with the seasons or which die in a moment are kept safe. Notice that each element of natural beauty mentioned by the poet is one which is described in terms of its transience. The rose dies with summer, the golden light of day gives way to night, the nightingale is heard no more in the winter, the falling star shines for only a few seconds, the phoenix was remarkable in that when it was about to die, it burned itself in its nest, a new bird arising from the ashes; and here the phoenix is mentioned in the act of dying, building its "spicy nest." The mistress becomes, thus, a type of permanent beauty in a world of passing beauty. The poet, it is true, does not insist upon this interpretation, but he suggests it, and if we read the poem carefully, we feel the suggestion.

Notice too the complication involved in the individual comparisons. In the mistress's beauty the roses "as in their causes, sleep." A result may be said to sleep in its cause, for the cause contains the germ of the result which it operates to cause. The figure is rather daring; it

carries over to a philosophical idea. But notice the preceding line: "for in your beauty's orient deep." *Orient* comes from the Latin word meaning *rising,* and because the sun rises in the east, *orient* came to mean east, but the east primarily as we associate it with the dawn. The line refers to the girl's cheeks which are rosy like the dawn. But *orient* retains its meaning of *rising* and connects with the idea of the flowers sleeping in their causes. The images tie together very neatly, therefore. The poet is referring primarily to the dawn-like beauty of her cheeks, but the last line of the stanza develops a deeper meaning in addition to the surface meaning. Notice that the deeper meaning is *in addition to.* It does not contradict the surface meaning, but grows out of it. It is perhaps this sort of thing that critics have in mind when they speak of a poet's ability to carry a complex meaning in his poem without destroying the lyrical quality.

Notice too the third stanza. The nightingale with winter goes to a warmer place to wait until spring returns. The poet has the bird winter in her throat. She keeps her note warm there. And the adjective *warm* offers many suggestions. The music of the nightingale may be said to be warm; certainly the throat of the girl, it is suggested, is warm as may be the lively and tender speech that issues thence. And these suggestions of *warm* grow out of the poet's primary use of the term with regard to the nightingale's wintering.

Notice also the fourth stanza. In the old astronomy, the planets and the stars were thought to be fixed in transparent spheres which were concentric with the earth and which revolved around the earth. Each planet had a sphere to itself, and the "fixed stars," that is, heavenly bodies which did not appear to move with relation to other heavenly bodies as the planets did, occupied a special sphere of their own. The poet's mistress's eyes are spheres also. And the falling stars find there, the poet says, *their* sphere, becoming fixed stars. Many poets have said that a lady's eyes were like stars. The comparison has become a *cliché.* But Carew, by expanding it with new detail, makes it again fresh and real.

What does this neat, even ingenious, working out of the parallel between the beauties of nature and the poet's mistress tell us of the poet's attitude?

In the first place this complication removes any sense of glibness. The praise is measured, calculated, and fully realized by the poet. In the second place, ingenuity and sentimentality do not mix. Extravagant, the praise may be, but we have no sense of the poet's having been caught off guard—having been betrayed by his fervor.

Notice also that the recurring phrase, "ask me no more," which seems so simple, helps to define the poet's attitude too. The poet implies, as he opens each stanza, that he has arrived at a solution to a perplexing problem. There will be no need, he seems to say, to ask further what happens to beauty that dies. The phrase therefore implies the study of a problem, a calculated judgment, and a certain assurance as to the answer. And the implication of a problem thoroughly studied, carefully analyzed, and solved is corroborated by the elaboration of each point in the various stanzas. The poem does not give the sense, therefore, of a glib effusion.

One should also observe that the poem is a progression to a climax. It is not a haphazard bundle of compliments. The phoenix stanza gathers up the other compliments and caps the series with a final intensity. Heretofore, the poet has compared his mistress to various beauties of nature which perish. In this last stanza he uses the last and most extreme symbol of beauty which perishes only to renew itself in beauty. This image, like those before it, is related ingeniously to the living woman. Her "fragrant bosom" is like the phoenix's "spicy nest." Moreover, this comparison which makes her the source of beauty catches up and brings to an emphatic conclusion the hints of this given in earlier stanzas, "beauty's orient deep," and "as in their causes, sleep," and thus ties up the beginning of the poem with the end. In fact, to show how coherent the poem is, and how the last stanza refers to the first, one may consider the question: where did the phoenix die? It died (according to the legend) in the Orient, and therefore the death of the phoenix in the "fragrant bosom" of the mistress echoes the third line of the stanza, "For in your beauty's orient deep." The mistress, therefore, is not merely the repository of the fading beauties of nature; she is a source of beauty. And this twist of the thinking forms a contrast with what has gone before: the passive repository has become an active source.

Death the Leveler
JAMES SHIRLEY (1596-1666)

The glories of our blood and state
   Are shadows, not substantial things;
There is no armor against Fate;
   Death lays his icy hand on kings:
      Sceptre and Crown   5
      Must tumble down,
And in the dust be equal made
With the poor crooked scythe and spade.

Some men with swords may reap the field,
   And plant fresh laurels where they kill: 10
But their strong nerves at last must yield;
   They tame but one another still:
      Early or late
      They stoop to fate,
And must give up their murmuring breath   15
When they, pale captives, creep to death.

The garlands wither on your brow;
   Then boast no more your mighty deeds!
Upon Death's purple altar now
   See where the victor-victim bleeds.   20
      Your heads must come
      To the cold tomb:
Only the actions of the just
Smell sweet and blossom in their dust.

    Write an interpretation of "Death the Leveler."

Experience of the West
JOHN PEALE BISHOP
(1892-1944)

They followed the course of heaven, as before
Trojan in smoky armor westward fled
Disastrous walls and on his shoulders bore
A dotard recollection had made mad,

Depraved by years, Anchises: on the strong   5
Tall bronze upborne, small sack of impotence;
Yet still he wore that look of one who young
Had closed with Love in cloudy radiance.

So the discoverers when they wading came
From shallow ships and climbed the wooded
   shores;   10
They saw the west: a sky of falling flame
And by the streams savage ambassadors.

O happy, brave and vast adventure! Where
Each day the sun beat rivers of new gold;
The wild grape ripened; springs reflected
   fear;   15
The wild deer fled; the bright snake danger
   coiled.

They too, the stalwart conquerors of space,
Each on his shoulders wore a wise delirium
Of memory and age; ghostly embrace
Of fathers slanting toward a western tomb.   20

A hundred and a hundred years they stayed
Aloft, until they were as light as autumn
Shells of locusts. Where then were they laid?
And in what wilderness oblivion?

    According to Virgil's poem, the Trojan hero,
Aeneas, son of Anchises and Aphrodite, the Greek
goddess of love, escaped from Troy when it was captured by the Greeks and sailed westward to found
the new city of Rome. He carried his aged father on
his back through the burning city, though Anchises
was to die in Sicily before the new homeland was
reached.

    1. "They" in l. 1 refers to the American colo-
nists. Why does the poet compare them to Aeneas?
    2. Is there any contradiction to stanza 4: the ex-
ploration of America is called a "happy . . . adventure" yet it is said that "springs reflected fear" and
that the "bright snake danger coiled."
    3. The American colonists were again like
Aeneas, the poet says, in that each carried upon his
shoulders "a wise delirium/Of memory and age."
What is this Anchises that each bore upon his shoulders? What would a *wise* delirium be? The intimation is that this Anchises now no longer sits upon
the shoulders of the Americans. What is the poet
trying to say?
    4. Does the poem lean too hard upon this domi-
nant comparison of the American adventure to
Aeneas? Or is it through exploration of this comparison that we find what the poem is really about?

For Rhoda

DELMORE SCHWARTZ
(1913-   )

Calmly we walk through this April's day,
Metropolitan poetry here and there,
In the park sit pauper and rentier,
The screaming children, the motor car
Fugitive about us, running away,   5
Between the worker and the millionaire
Number provides all distances,
It is Nineteen Thirty-Seven now,
Many great dears are taken away,
What will become of you and me   10
(This is the school in which we learn . . .)
Besides the photo and the memory?
(. . . that time is the fire in which we burn.)

(This is the school in which we learn . . .)
What is the self amid this blaze?   15
What am I now that I was then
Which I shall suffer and act again,
The theodicy I wrote in my high school days
Restored all life from infancy,
The children shouting are bright as they
   run   20
(This is the school in which they learn . . .)
Ravished entirely in their passing play!
(. . . that time is the fire in which they burn.)

Avid its rush, that reeling blaze!
Where is my father and Eleanor?   25
Not where are they now, dead seven years,
But what they were then?
                No more? No more?
From Nineteen-Fourteen to the present day,
Bert Spira and Rhoda consume, consume
Not where they are now (where are they
   now?)   30
But what they were then, both beautiful;
Each minute bursts in the burning room,
The great globe reels in the solar fire,
Spinning the trivial and unique away.
(How all things flash! How all things
   flare!)   35
What am I now that I was then?

May memory restore again and again
The smallest color of the smallest day:
Time is the school in which we learn,
Time is the fire in which we burn.   40

    1. Several people are mentioned in this poem by name. Does it matter that we do not know who Eleanor is, or Bert Spira, or Rhoda? What is the advantage of using particular names even if the reader cannot be expected to know who the people are?
    2. The speaker of this poem is conscious of time. He looks back toward his childhood and forward to imagine what he and Rhoda and the others will some day become. It is easy to see why he regards time as a kind of school. How is time also a kind of fire? Look carefully at the fire imagery from line 24 to the end. What does the poet mean by "the burning room"? What does he mean when he exclaims "How all things flash!"? How can the great globe of earth be said to reel "in the solar fire"?
    3. Does the rest of the poem serve to indicate how we are to take the imagery of fire and burning? Or is the meaning of the poem as a whole heavily dependent upon this imagery of fire and burning?

Burning the Letters
RANDALL JARRELL (1914-   )

(The wife of a pilot killed in the Pacific is speaking several years after his death. She was once a Christian, a Protestant.)

Here in my head, the home that is left for you,
You have not changed; the flames rise from the
    sea
And the sea changes: the carrier, torn in two,
Sinks to its planes—the corpses of the carrier
Are strewn like ashes on the star-reflecting
    sea;   5
Are gathered, sewn with weights, are sunk.
The gatherers disperse.
                Here to my hands
From the sea's dark, incalculable calm,
The unchanging circle of the universe,   10
The letters float: the set yellowing face
Looks home to me, a child's at last,
From the cut-out paper; and the licked
Lips part in their last questioning smile.
The poor labored answers, still unanswer-
    ing;   15

The faded questions—questioning so much,
I thought then—questioning so little;
Grew younger, younger, as my eyes grew old,
As that dreamed-out and wept-for wife,
Your last unchanging country, changed   20
Out of your own rejecting life—a part
Of accusation and of loss, a child's eternally—
Into my troubled separate being.

A child has her own faith, a child's.
In its savage figures—worn down, now, to
    death—   25
Men's one life issues, neither out of earth
Nor from the sea, the last dissolving sea,
But out of death: by man came death
And his Life wells from death, the death of
    Man.
The hunting flesh, the broken blood   30
Glimmer within the tombs of earth, the food
Of the lives that burrow under the hunting
    wings
Of the light, of the darkness: dancing, dancing,
The flames grasp flesh with their last search-
    ing grace—
Grasp as the lives have grasped: the hunted   35
Pull down the hunter for his unused life
Parted into the blood, the dark, veined bread
Later than all law. The child shudders, aging:
The peering savior, stooping to her clutch,
His talons cramped with his own bartered
    flesh,   40
Pales, flickers, and flares out. In the darkness—
    darker
With the haunting after-images of light—
The dying God, the eaten Life
Are the nightmare I awaken from to night.

(The flames dance over life. The mourning
    slaves   45
In their dark secrecy, come burying
The slave bound in another's flesh, the slave
Freed once, forever, by another's flesh:
The Light flames, flushing the passive face
With its eternal life.)   50
                The lives are fed
Into the darkness of their victory;
The ships sink, forgotten; and the sea
Blazes to darkness: the unsearchable
Death of the lives lies dark upon the life   55

That, bought by death, the loved and tortured
    lives,
Stares westward, passive, to the blackening sea.
In the tables of the dead, in the unopened
    almanac,
The head, charred, featureless—the unknown
    mean—
Is thrust from the waters like a flame, is
    torn   60
From its last being with the bestial cry
Of its pure agony. O death of all my life
Because of you, because of you, I have not
    died,
By your death I have lived.
                    The sea is empty 65
As I am empty, stirring the charred and an-
    swered
Questions about your home, your wife, your cat
That stayed at home with me—that died at
    home
Gray with the years that gleam above you there
In the great green grave where you are
    young   70
And unaccepting still. Bound in your death,
I choose between myself and you, between your
    life
And my own life: it is finished.
                      Here in my head
There is room for your black body in its
    shroud   75
The dog-tags welded to your breastbone, and
    the flame
That winds above your death and my own life
And the world of my life. The letters and the
    face
That stir still, sometimes, with your fiery
    breath—
Take them, O grave! Great grave of all my
    years,   80
The unliving universe in which all life is lost,
Make yours the memory of that accepting
And accepted life whose fragments I cast here.

It is important in reading this poem to keep the dramatic situation in mind. The wife is burning the letters and throughout the poem there are references to the letters with their questions and answers, and to the flames leaping up as the letters burn. For example, see ll. 32-33, 45-50, or 78-79. But the flames have another reference, for they refer to the flaming aircraft carrier on which her husband has died. In the same way her vision of the sea in which he has been buried becomes the sea of death and oblivion to which she now finally consigns the young husband, still young and unchanged in her memory, though she feels that in the meantime she has grown old.

1. Why has the wife decided now to burn the letters? Note particularly ll. 63-64 and ll. 71-73.

2. What is the meaning of the first line—the statement that her head is the only "home that is left for you"? Note also that she calls herself in l. 20 "your last unchanging country." How can she say, as she does in ll. 9-11, that the letters float to her "from the sea's dark, incalculable calm"?

3. Section 3 of the poem deals with her childhood faith which she has (see the poet's note at the beginning of the poem) now lost. In that faith man lives, man's life issues from the death of man, from the Savior's death, "the eaten life" (l. 43). What light, if any, is thrown upon her decision to burn the letters by the statement which she makes in ll. 43-44?

4. What does she mean by saying that she is "bound in [his] death" (l. 71) and that she now chooses between his life and her own life? (Connect this passage with ll. 45-50.)

5. What is the meaning of ll. 74-75? Does it mean that she is now ready to accept him as dead—that she is ready to accept reality as she could not earlier accept it? In her head (see l. 1) he has heretofore had a country in which he has not changed. Now he still has a "home" there, but a burial place merely—not a place in which to live unchanged, but a place in which his dead body, his death now accepted, can rest. Does the last section of the poem mean that she has ceased to love him? Or does it mean something else?

A Prayer for My Daughter
WILLIAM BUTLER YEATS
(1865-1939)

Once more the storm is howling, and half hid
Under this cradle-hood and coverlid
My child sleeps on. There is no obstacle
But Gregory's wood and one bare hill
Whereby the haystack- and roof-leveling
    wind,   5
Bred on the Atlantic, can be stayed;
And for an hour I have walked and prayed
Because of the great gloom that is in my mind.

I have walked and prayed for this young child
    an hour

And heard the sea-wind scream upon the
    tower, 10
And under the arches of the bridge, and scream
In the elms above the flooded stream;
Imagining in excited reverie
That the future years had come,
Dancing to a frenzied drum, 15
Out of the murderous innocence of the sea.

May she be granted beauty, and yet not
Beauty to make a stranger's eye distraught,
Or hers before a looking-glass, for such,
Being made beautiful overmuch, 20
Consider beauty a sufficient end,
Lose natural kindness and maybe
The heart-revealing intimacy
That chooses right, and never find a friend.

Helen being chosen found life flat and dull 25
And later had much trouble from a fool,
While that great Queen, that rose out of the
    spray,
Being fatherless could have her way
Yet chose a bandy-legged smith for man.
It's certain that fine women eat 30
A crazy salad with their meat
Whereby the Horn of Plenty is undone.

In courtesy I'd have her chiefly learned;
Hearts are not had as a gift but hearts are
    earned
By those that are not entirely beautiful; 35
Yet many, that have played the fool
For beauty's very self, has charm made wise,
And many a poor man that has roved,
Loved and thought himself beloved,
From a glad kindness cannot take his eyes. 40

May she become a flourishing hidden tree
That all her thoughts may like the linnet be,
And have no business but dispensing round
Their magnanimities of sound,
Nor but in merriment begin a chase, 45
Nor but in merriment begin a quarrel.
Oh, may she live like some green laurel
Rooted in one dear perpetual place.

My mind, because the minds that I have loved,
The sort of beauty that I have approved, 50
Prosper but little, has dried up of late,

Yet knows that to be choked with hate
May well be of all evil chances chief.
If there's no hatred in a mind
Assault and battery of the wind 55
Can never tear the linnet from the leaf.

An intellectual hatred is the worst,
So let her think opinions are accursed.
Have I not seen the loveliest woman born
Out of the mouth of Plenty's horn, 60
Because of her opinionated mind
Barter that horn and every good
By quiet natures understood
For an old bellows full of angry wind?

Considering that, all hatred driven hence, 65
The soul recovers radical innocence
And learns at last that it is self-delighting,
Self-appeasing, self-affrighting,
And that its own sweet will is Heaven's will;
She can, though every face should scowl 70
And every windy quarter howl
Or every bellows burst, be happy still.

And may her bride-groom bring her to a house
Where all's accustomed, ceremonious;
For arrogance and hatred are the wares 75
Peddled in the thoroughfares.
How but in the custom and in ceremony
Are innocence and beauty born?
Ceremony's a name for the rich horn,
And custom for the spreading laurel tree. 80

In this poem a father prays for his infant daughter. The father's state of mind and the occasion which prompts his prayer are significant: they help us to understand the meaning of the prayer. The poet begins by presenting the circumstances vividly and dramatically.

It is night, and a storm is howling in from the Atlantic as the child sleeps. (Yeats actually lived at this time in an old tower near the west coast of Ireland (see p. 347), and details of the setting—"Gregory's wood" and the bridge which spanned the stream near which the tower stands—are mentioned in the description.) The child is safely asleep. Though the prayer is not for physical protection, the storm presumably does have something to do with the "great gloom" that fills the father's mind.

For him, the storm typifies the violence and uncertainty of the future—the violent and perhaps bloody future in which his daughter is to live.

The poem was written in 1919 and the years that have followed since then have indeed been confused and bloody years. One points this out, not to claim the gift of prophecy for the poet, but a realization of this fact may make it easier for present-day readers to feel that the insight that dictated the poem was no mere "excited reverie," in spite of the speaker's disclaimer, but rather a serious and realistic consideration of what sort of world probably lay before the child.

The phrase "murderous innocence of the sea" (l. 16) is sharp and arresting. Why has the poet used it? A natural force cannot literally be *murderous*. A lion, for instance, cannot commit murder, for it has no sense of right and wrong. And, by the same token, no natural force can be "innocent." And yet the phrase is justified, for it describes vividly a kind of aimless violence—not vindictive, not consciously evil, indeed without any purpose at all. Even a consciously malignant violence is somehow less ominous than this uncomprehending and unpitying force. We shall have to read further into the poem, however, before we see the full implications of the phrase.

After such an account of the father's sense of foreboding, the prayer itself (which begins with Stanza III) may seem rather anticlimactic. The father prays for rather simple and rather ordinary things. He prays that the girl may be granted beauty, though not great beauty; that she may be learned chiefly "in courtesy"; that she may "think opinions are accursed"; and that she may find a husband who will bring her into a house "where all's accustomed, ceremonious." But how can such gifts as these protect the girl in the kind of future that looms ahead of her?

The prayer may seem open to even more serious objections. Is the father simply asking that his daughter may find a sheltered and pleasant life, presumably by attracting a wealthy husband? Is he not praying that—the better to achieve this end—she may be "sweet" and pliant rather than thoughtful and forceful? The prayer, read in this fashion, may well seem shallow and cynical—even vulgarly snobbish.

To paraphrase the poem in this fashion is to distort it. For one thing, this paraphrase neglects entirely the images which run through the poem and which, as we shall see, are much more than bits of ornamentation. It is only through the dominant images that we may possess the poem and actually understand for what the father prays.

Why does the father hope that his child will not be granted "beauty to make a stranger's eye distraught" or to dazzle her own eyes? Because such beauty is a disruptive force. Helen of Troy (l. 25) brought on the Trojan War and the destruction of a great city because her beauty made distraught the eyes of Paris, the Trojan prince. The "great Queen" of l. 27 is Aphrodite, the Greek goddess of beauty, who, according to the myth, rose from the sea foam and was thus "fatherless." But she married the lame smith-god Hephaestus (Vulcan)—presumably because her beauty made her own eye distraught, so that, though free to choose, she could not choose well.

The "Horn of Plenty" (l. 32) is also from Greek legend: it is the cornucopia, the fabulous horn which poured out to the recipient anything for which he could ask. Those, however, who are granted all that they could want—perhaps just because they are sated with good things—seem to crave as a perverse relish "a crazy salad" which maddens them and cancels the gifts of abundance. The paradox of full abundance undoing the recipient is thus worked out primarily through this image of eating. But the sea image of the earlier stanzas is also echoed. Aphrodite rose out of the sea-foam, out of the sea, the character of which is a "murderous innocence."

Helen of Troy bears a special relation to Aphrodite. Helen was the prize that the goddess held out to Paris in order to persuade him to proclaim her most beautiful; but the prize was in a special way "murderously innocent." Through Helen, though she was innocent of any intent to destroy the Trojan State, Troy was destroyed, for the Greeks attacked Troy and finally burned it to avenge the honor of Helen's husband, the Greek prince Menelaus.

The Helen-Paris story is echoed in the fifth stanza: Helen, the poet says, "had much trouble from a fool," yet many that have "for beauty's very self," "played the fool" (l. 36) as Paris did, have recovered their senses and learned that there is something better than supernal beauty. Many a man whose eye has been made "distraught" (l. 18) as the eye of Paris was, "from a glad kindness cannot take his eyes" (l. 40).

Stanza VI introduces a new image, that of the "flourishing hidden tree," the "green laurel/Rooted in one dear perpetual place." This is the first positive image set over against the sea with its innocence and its murderous violence. The tree is rooted, unshifting, fixed, green with verdure, the pleasant home of the linnets. The figure receives a good deal of complication in the development which makes the linnet, sheltered by, and singing in, the tree, a type of the girl's thoughts. The thoughts-linnet comparison is an easy figure to sentimentalize, as if the poet were asking that the daughter might be merely charming and have ladylike "thoughts" which twitter like the linnets among the sheltering branches. And this misconception, if it occurs, may seem to be corroborated by the father's prayer in l. 58 that she may "think opinions are accursed."

But the poet has chosen his term carefully. Opinions are surmises, shifting, topical, usually tinctured with self-assertiveness (*cf.* "opinionated mind" in l. 61). They are associated with the screaming wind blowing off the restless, shifting sea and with anger and hate. The woman with her "opinionated mind" exchanges "every good" understood by "quiet natures" for "an old bellows full of angry wind." Hate is stultifying, and the worst kind of hate, the speaker observes, is an "intellectual hatred."

The "thoughts" that the father wishes his daughter to have make no strident screaming; they are like linnets' voices, "dispensing round/ Their magnanimities of sound." And the linnet comparison enforces the suggestion made in l. 40 of "glad kindness," a suggestion that is carried forward in ll. 45-46 with the reiteration of "merriment." Even her quarrels, he hopes, may begin "in merriment." But the difference between her mind and an "opinionated mind"

is not left to the contrast between the linnets' quiet voices and the screaming of the wind. For the laurel tree (in which the linnet lives) helps define that mind—not only in Stanzas VI and VII where the rooted tree is able to defy the "assault and battery of the wind," but also in Stanza IX in which the laurel tree image is still powerfully present.

The second line of the stanza (l. 66) contains the phrase "radical innocence." The word "radical" comes from the Latin *radix,* a root. A *radical* innocence is like the tree rooted, but of course it also is a *basic* and *fundamental* innocence, and the soul "recovers" it when it is purged of all hatred. The soul draws from its own resources the strength to withstand the howling wind.

Thus the images of the tree and wind suggest one of the basic themes of the poem: that the soul's reliance on its own integrity is the only protection against the blind and chaotic forces that are to dominate the future. In the recovery of "radical innocence," it "learns" that it makes its own joys, satisfactions, and fears (ll. 67-68). It learns that "its own sweet will is Heaven's will."

What keeps this last statement from being an expression of insufferable egotism and arrogance? Principally, the carefully developed contrast between arrogant self-assertion and a quiet dependence upon the resources of one's self. In the one case the self is imposed upon others; in the other, one finds joy in the depths of the self. But there are other elements that support the distinction. The phrase "its own sweet will," with its smack of the proverbial phrase for complete liberty of choice, suggests that the soul purged of hatred is perfectly free to choose, but "sweet will"—in the light of the preceding stanzas—must mean a will that is literally sweet—not arrogant or full of hate. If the soul's will is "sweet" it may be sure that "its own sweet will is Heaven's will." That last phrase itself is worth pondering. "Heaven's will" (with Heaven capitalized) means divine will—the will of Providence. But the phrase is also reminiscent of the figure used throughout the poem for blind destructive force—the sky's will, the wind that blows where it listeth and which may blow from any "quarter" of the heavens.

If the last comment seems to read too much into the phrase "Heaven's will," it need not be pressed. Suffice it to say that the contrast between angry self-assertion and joyful self-realization has been defined and developed through the imagery of the poem. But the imagery has done more: it has associated with these two views of self, contrasted views of innocence and of nature. The "murderous innocence" that is amoral is set over against a "radical innocence" out of which all that is good grows; nature as capricious and cruel, mere brute force, is set over against a nature which yields norms and archetypes of order, which indeed reflects the divine order.

The concluding stanza treats all these matters in their social aspect. Man lives in the society of his fellows. What, in terms of his life in human society, is the horn of plenty? What, the "spreading laurel tree"? Ceremony and custom, the poet boldly answers. The true dowering of gifts comes from ceremony—it is not a gift of nature; the true organic stability comes from custom, not from some inborn virtue.

The answer is a bold and somewhat surprising answer. We usually think of innocence and beauty as the gift of nature; and we oppose them to custom and ceremony, for we think of custom and ceremony as tending to sophisticate and perhaps corrupt the person who subjects himself to them. The last lines of the poem invert these relations; for they maintain that innocence and beauty are not the products of nature but of a disciplined life. They spring from order—they grow out of something—they are not the casual gifts of a blind and capricious force.

Does the poet make these assertions convincing? The student will have to decide for himself. But if they are rendered convincing, it is because "innocence" and "beauty" as used in this last stanza have been carefully defined. They have been defined in large part, however, through imagery—and so indeed it is with the whole argument of the poem: the poem is a "thinking out" in terms of images.

1. Are ll. 49-52 related to the tree imagery? How?
2. How, if at all, are the images of ll. 75-76 related to the field of imagery used earlier? Is the "old bellows" (l. 64) the sort of "ware" which a peddler would hawk through the streets? How are "thoroughfares" related to "One dear perpetual place" (l. 48)? What do the horn of plenty and the bellows have in common, if anything?
3. What is the tone of the first two stanzas? Of stanzas three through six? What shift in tone marks the beginning of the seventh stanza? What is the tone of the final stanza? How is the imagery used to modify and control the tone?
4. Notice how many expressions in the poem echo homely and colloquial phrases: "a crazy salad," "played the fool," "assault and battery," "own sweet will." Notice too that some of the images suggest the images that underlie modern slang expressions: *cf.* ll. 59-60 with "a nice dish" or "a peach," and *cf.* l. 64 with "an old windbag." Is this echoing of the colloquial and slangy a fault in this poem or a virtue? How does it affect the tone?

Hamlet Soliloquizes

(*Hamlet*, Act III, Scene I)
WILLIAM SHAKESPEARE
(1564-1616)

To be, or not to be: that is the question:
Whether 'tis nobler in the mind to suffer
The slings and arrows of outrageous fortune,
Or to take arms against a sea of troubles,
And by opposing end them? To die: to sleep;   5
No more; and by a sleep to say we end
The heart-ache and the thousand natural shocks
That flesh is heir to, 'tis a consummation
Devoutly to be wished. To die, to sleep;
To sleep: perchance to dream: ay, there's the rub;   10
For in that sleep of death what dreams may come
When we have shuffled off this mortal coil,
Must give us pause: there's the respect
That makes calamity of so long life;
For who would bear the whips and scorns of time,   15
The oppressor's wrong, the proud man's contumely,
The pangs of despised love, the law's delay,
The insolence of office, and the spurns

That patient merit of the unworthy takes,
When he himself might his quietus make 20
With a bare bodkin? who would fardels bear,
To grunt and sweat under a weary life,
But that the dread of something after death,
The undiscovered country from whose bourn
No traveler returns, puzzles the will, 25
And makes us rather bear those ills we have
Than fly to others that we know not of?
Thus conscience does make cowards of us all;
And thus the native hue of resolution
Is sicklied o'er with the pale cast of
    thought. 30

At this point in the play, Hamlet is debating suicide. But the debate that goes on in his mind is conducted, not through a series of statements, but through a series of metaphors.

1. Isolate and note down the separate metaphors that occur in this passage.

2. Are the metaphors consistent with each other? Are there any instances of mixed metaphor? Does the speaker's mind seem to leap from metaphor to metaphor, quite haphazardly? Or is there a discernible connected pattern of images?

3. One can conceive of troubles as missiles (slings and arrows); and the sea with its waves, rank on rank, pouring upon a beach may suggest an enormous army. But how can one take arms against a sea of troubles? Is the comparison absurd, or can you justify it in this context?

4. What image underlies l. 12? ("Rub" in l. 10 means "obstacle" or "hindrance.") What image underlies ll. 29-30?

Macbeth Thinks of Murdering the King

(*Macbeth*, Act I, Scene VII)

WILLIAM SHAKESPEARE (1564-1616)

If it were done when 'tis done, then 'twere
    well
It were done quickly: if the assassination
Could trammel up the consequence, and catch
With his surcease success; that but this blow
Might be the be-all and the end-all here, 5

But here, upon this bank and shoal of time,
We'd jump the life to come. But in these cases
We still have judgment here; that we but teach
Bloody instructions, which, being taught, return
To plague the inventor: this even-handed
    justice 10
Commends the ingredients of our poisoned
    chalice
To our own lips. He's here in double trust;
First, as I am his kinsman and his subject
Strong both against the deed; then, as his host,
Who should against his murderer shut the
    door, 15
Not bear the knife myself. Besides, this Duncan
Hath borne his faculties so meek, hath been
So clear in his great office that his virtues
Will plead like angels, trumpet-tongued, against
The deep damnation of his taking-off; 20
And pity, like a naked new-born babe,
Striding the blast, or heaven's cherubim, horsed
Upon the sightless couriers of the air,
Shall blow the horrid deed in every eye,
That tears shall drown the wind. I have no
    spur 25
To prick the sides of my intent, but only
Vaulting ambition, which o'erleaps itself
And falls on the other.

In this speech, Macbeth contemplates the murder of Duncan, the King, who is his kinsman, and who has just that day bestowed honors upon him. The King is spending the night in Macbeth's castle. There is opportunity; and Lady Macbeth has urged her husband to murder the King and seize the crown for himself.

1. Do ll. 1-4 convey the sense of excitement and conspiratorial whispering? How?

2. What is the meaning of ll. 2-7? What is the proviso that appeals to Macbeth—that would decide him if he could but be sure of it? ("Trammel" means to entangle as in a kind of net: *cf.* modern *trammel net.* "Jump" (l. 7) is interpreted by *A Shakespeare Glossary* to mean "risk," "hazard.") What image or images are to be found in these lines?

3. Pick out the various images that occur in the rest of the passage. How are the images related to each other? Do you find any mixed metaphors? Can you or can you not justify them?

4. Consider in particular the metaphors that occur in ll. 21-28. Babes, angels, horses, tears, and the wind occur in a remarkable mixture in these lines. What does the passage mean? How are the images interrelated? Is the poet confused? Or does the passage constitute great poetry?

The Leg in the Subway

OSCAR WILLIAMS (1900-   )

When I saw the woman's leg on the floor of the
    subway train,
Protrude beyond the panel (while her body
    overflowed my mind's eye),
When I saw the pink stocking, black shoe,
    curve bulging with warmth,
The delicate etching of the hair behind the
    flesh-colored gauze,
When I saw the ankle of Mrs. Nobody going
    nowhere for a nickel,   5
When I saw this foot motionless on the moving
    motionless floor,
My mind caught on a nail of a distant star, I
    was wrenched out
Of the reality of the subway ride, I hung in a
    socket of distance:
And this is what I saw:

The long tongue of the earth's speed was lick-
    ing the leg,   10
Upward and under and around went the long
    tongue of speed:
It was made of a flesh invisible, it dripped the
    saliva of miles:
It drank moment, lit shivers of insecurity in
    niches between bones:
It was full of eyes, it stopped licking to look
    at the passengers:
It was as alive as a worm, and busier than any-
    body in the train: 15

It spoke saying: To whom does this leg belong?
    Is it a bonus leg
For the rush hour? Is it a forgotten leg? Among
    the many
Myriads of legs did an extra leg fall in from
    the Out There?
O Woman, sliced off bodily by the line of the
    panel, shall I roll
Your leg into the abdominal nothing, among
    the digestive teeth?   20
Or shall I fit it in with the pillars that hold up
    the headlines?

But nobody spoke, though all the faces were
    talking silently,
As the train zoomed, a zipper closing up swiftly
    the seam of time.

Alas, said the long tongue of the speed of the
    earth quite faintly,
What is one to do with an incorrigible leg that
    will not melt—   25
But everybody stopped to listen to the train
    vomiting cauldrons
Of silence, while somebody's jolted-out after-
    thought trickled down
The blazing shirt-front solid with light bulbs,
    and just then
The planetary approach of the next station
    exploded atoms of light,
And when the train stopped, the leg had grown
    a surprising mate,   30
And the long tongue had slipped hurriedly
    out through the window:

I perceived through the hole left by the nail of
    the star in my mind
How civilization was as dark as a wood and di-
    mentional with things
And how birds dipped in chromium sang in
    the crevices of our deeds.

The sight of the leg, isolated and apparently detached from the body, stirs in the observer a kind
of nightmarish fantasy. The nightmare quality of
the experience accounts in part for the bizarre imagery; yet the nature of the imagery is not wholly explained in these terms. And if the reverie of the
observer makes—for all of its surrealistic quality—a
serious comment upon our civilization, there are further questions about the imagery to be explored.

1. Is the imagery wholly fantastic? Consider, for
example, l. 23.
2. Is the "reality of the subway ride" (l. 8) itself
so "unreal"—so much like a fantastic nightmare—that
it requires a violent and shocking imagery to present
it accurately?
3. What is the meaning of the puzzled comments
made by "the earth's speed" (ll. 16-21 and 24-25)?
Does speed try to reduce all things to a common
mass? Is speed baffled by the odd, the incommensurable, the persistently individual? Note that it regards
the leg as "incorrigible" (l. 25).
4. What does the observer mean by saying that
civilization is "as dark as a wood" (l. 33)? How does
his experience in the subway lead up to this statement?

The Good-Morrow

JOHN DONNE (1572-1631)

I wonder by my troth, what thou and I
Did, till we loved? Were we not weaned till
  then,
But sucked on country pleasures, childishly?
Or snorted we in the seven sleepers' den?
'Twas so; but this, all pleasures fancies be.   5
If ever any beauty I did see,
Which I desired, and got, 'twas but a dream
  of thee.

And now good morrow to our waking souls,
Which watch not one another out of fear;
For love all love of other sights controls,   10
And makes one little room, an everywhere.
Let sea-discoverers to new worlds have gone,
Let maps to other, worlds on worlds have
  shown;
Let us possess one world; each hath one, and
  is one.

My face in thine eye, thine in mine ap-
  pears,   15
And true plain hearts do in the faces rest;
Where can we find two better hemispheres
Without sharp north, without declining west?
Whatever dies was not mixed equally;
If our two loves be one, or thou and I   20
Love so alike that none do slacken, none can
  die.

The poem begins with an expression of
wonder. What, says the lover, to his loved one—
what could they have done—how did they spend
their time before this? In the light of this intensity, all previous experience pales into something drab and meaningless.

But the poet does not use a metaphor of
light (*intensity, pales, drab*) as we have done in
the preceding sentence. He has his own metaphor, and it is an important one for defining the
full and precise meaning of the poem. His metaphor involves a contrast between the life of an
infant (feeding and sleeping) and the full consciousness of adult life.

The lovers, until they found each other,
were "not weaned." They "sucked on" their
pleasures "childishly." They did not possess desirable things—they merely dreamed of them.
The dominant metaphor is, of course, complicated by other references. The pleasures on
which they sucked were "country" pleasures—the
sort that would appeal to naive rustics who do
not know the great world. Their sleeping reminds the speaker of the legend of the Seven
Sleepers of Ephesus, seven adults who drank enchanted wine and in their cave snored away for
centuries. The implication that the delights of
their earlier life were mere dreams receives special development and emphasis.

Except for this present delight into which
they have come, all pleasure is a mere figment
of the imagination. The lover appeals to his
own personal experience: whatever beauty heretofore attracted him was only a dream, a foreshadowing, of the loved one—not only all his
previous dreams of beauty, but even that beauty
which he came to possess turns out to be, in the
light of this experience, unsubstantial, shadowy,
and dreamlike.

Yet, in spite of the complications it receives,
the dominant figure is sustained; it is reaffirmed
in the first line of the second stanza. Their two
souls are waking up. Their long nonage—the
long sleep of their previous dreamlike experience—is over. They open their eyes and say
"good-morning" to each other.

The act of opening their eyes—implied in
the preceding line—is seized upon and emphasized in the lines that immediately follow. The
intensity of their gaze as they look at each other
is underscored in l. 9, by the mention of the
only other instance of the absolutely fixed intensity of watching—that of the person or animal
watching in wariness for the first hostile movement. The lovers' gaze embodies that riveted
attention—but it is directed not "out of fear,"
but out of loving wonder.

The intensity of the gaze is developed further in ll. 10-11: it is able to *see* in one little
place the whole world, making "one little room,
an everywhere." Let the explorers find the new
world of the Americas, and go on to explore

that new world. The lovers have found their new world in themselves. They have not only found it: they possess it, for each is such a world (in the eyes of the loved one) and possesses such a world (in the person of the other loved one).

The grammar of ll. 12-13 may be puzzling to the student. The sentences are not only highly condensed, but they embody a structure now archaic. Although we can still say: "Let discoverers *go* to new worlds," we should now have to say: "Grant that discoverers have gone to new worlds; well, let them," etc.

Stanza III carries forward the metaphor of the lovers as constituting a new world, discovered and possessed. But it also sustains the picture of the lovers watching each other with rapt attention (l. 9). For as the lovers look into each other's eyes, each sees his own face reflected in the other's eyes—two "hemispheres," two half globes, which contain himself. The poet has further enriched the metaphor with the statement that their hearts are reflected in their faces. In their eyes there is no dissimulation, but complete candor, complete disingenuousness, the heart reflected in the eyes. (*Cf.* the line that Milton was to write later in "Il Penseroso": "Thy rapt soul sitting in thine eyes.")

The technical word "hemispheres," with its special association with maps and globes, ties the image used here firmly to the earlier allusion to the "sea-discoverers" in l. 12. And the poet goes on to argue that the world which the lovers have discovered and possess is a better world than that which the voyagers have found. The lovers' world (which is themselves) has no north (with its implications of storm and cold) and no west (with its implications of sunset, evening, decline, and death).

Indeed, the last three lines of the poem go on to assert that the world discovered by the lovers carries the promise of immortality. The poet's argument rests upon the medieval belief that things which were completely one thing could not lose their perfection or that things "mixt equally," things possessing a perfect internal harmony, could not suffer change. If the love of each for the other has become merged in a love which is itself, one and undivided, or if their loves completely balance each other,

neither more nor less than the other, neither can die.

It is important to notice, however, that the speaker does not claim that their love will indeed last forever. The promise of immortality is conditioned by an *if*. The poet here does not prophesy. He is content to keep the whole poem focused upon the scene of waking, the fact of sudden initiation, the joyful but awed sense of discovery that the lover's experience in coming into possession of the new world which they did not know existed.

The images are abundant, and some of them may seem fantastic and bizarre. But it ought to be apparent that they are really tightly linked together. The "psychological line" through them is remarkably firm. The imagery is constantly shifted and extended, but the reader who grasps the dramatic situation will find that the shifts do not confuse.

One might make a further argument for the essential unity of the imagery. It could be claimed that all the images are simply variations on one dominant image, that implied in the title of the poem. For coming of age is itself a kind of waking up to the fullness of life, and Europe's discovery of the new world of the Americas can be regarded as a kind of coming of age, a kind of waking up to the fullness of the world. At least, one can argue that all three experiences have in common the sense of illumination and discovery, in the light of which the past experience becomes a sort of half-life —whether the life of dream or of childhood or (as Donne and other men of the Renaissance must have felt it) the more limited and confined life of the medieval world.

The last paragraph is not intended to imply that the poet consciously worked out variations and extensions of the metaphor of waking as a kind of preliminary blueprint for his poem, or that he was even conscious of all the interconnections among the images when he had completed the poem. The student is referred to the concluding paragraphs of our analysis of "The Eagle" (p. 301). Poets do not usually work by blueprint and formula. The process of writing a poem may be on the poet's part a work of exploration and discovery of "what he wants to say"—which he may come to know only *after* he has completed his poem. But the poet who possesses a disciplined sensibility may be able to accomplish quite intricate patternings of imagery "naturally" and without the self-consciousness which subsequent analysis of the imagery would imply.

Furthermore, we do not mean to imply that the relationship among the images that we have argued for is the only way of seeing them, *the* way in which they necessarily appear. But an examination of the imagery of this poem may suggest two things of some importance to the student: (1) that the imagery of a good poem may be studied with profit by the student, and that his further readings may result in his enriching his experience of the poem; and (2) that when the order of images seems somehow "right" in spite of apparently sharp and rapid shifts, the images may actually be aspects of a larger submerged image which gives a deeper coherence to the images than can be accounted for in examining merely their superficial relationships. And all this implies that the imagery of a poem may to a considerable extent be affecting us even before we have consciously explored it.

My Pictures Blacken

WALTER SAVAGE LANDOR
(1775-1864)

My pictures blacken in their frames
  As night comes on,
And youthful maids and wrinkled dames
  Are now all one.

Death of the day! a sterner Death   5
  Did worse before;
The fairest form, the sweetest breath,
  Away he bore.

1. The basic comparison in this little poem is obvious: death is a kind of night. How is the analogy "worked out"? The poem is simple. Is it also rich in its implications? What is the situation? What sort of man is the speaker? What is his attitude toward the loved one?

2. What advantages, if any, does the poet gain by relying upon one dominant controlling figure? What is the tone of the poem? How does the use of one dominant image affect the tone?

A Serenade at the Villa

ROBERT BROWNING
(1812-1889)

I

THAT was I, you heard last night,
  When there rose no moon at all,
Nor, to pierce the strained and tight
  Tent of heaven, a planet small:
Life was dead and so was light.   5

II

Not a twinkle from the fly,
  Not a glimmer from the worm;
When the crickets stopped their cry,
  When the owls forbore a term,
You heard music; that was I.   10

III

Earth turned in her sleep with pain,
  Sultrily suspired for proof:
In at heaven and out again,
  Lightning!—where it broke the roof,
Bloodlike, some few drops of rain.   15

IV

What they could my words expressed,
  O my love, my all, my one!
Singing helped the verses best,
  And when singing's best was done,
To my lute I left the rest.   20

V

So wore night; the East was gray,
  White the broad-faced hemlock-flowers:
There would be another day;
  Ere its first of heavy hours
Found me, I had passed away.   25

VI

What became of all the hopes,
  Words and song and lute as well?

Say, this struck you—"When life gropes
   "Feebly for the path where fell
"Light last on the evening slopes,   30

VII

"One friend in that path shall be,
   "To secure my step from wrong;
"One to count night day for me,
   "Patient through the watches long,
"Serving most with none to see."   35

VIII

Never say—as something bodes—
   "So, the worst has yet a worse!
"When life halts 'neath double loads,
   "Better the taskmaster's curse
"Than such music on the roads!   40

IX

"When no moon succeeds the sun,
   "Nor can pierce the midnight's tent
"Any star, the smallest one,
   "While some drops, where lightning rent,
"Show the final storm begun—   45

X

"When the fire-fly hides its spot,
   "When the garden-voices fail
"In the darkness thick and hot,—
   "Shall another voice avail,
"That shape be where these are not?   50

XI

"Has some plague a longer lease,
   "Proffering its help uncouth?
"Can't one even die in peace?
   "As one shuts one's eyes on youth,
"Is that face the last one sees?"   55

XII

Oh how dark your villa was,
   Windows fast and obdurate!
How the garden grudged me grass
   Where I stood—the iron gate
Ground its teeth to let me pass!   60

1. What is the story implied in this poem? Has the woman in the villa rejected the man who is singing to her? Is she to marry someone else? We are not told very much about the situation. Is it important, for the effect of the poem, that we should know no more than we do?

2. How does the poet make use of the fact that the night is dark and sultry and that the very earth seems to stir restlessly in its sleep? Notice that this description of the night dominates not only Stanzas I, II, and III, but is referred to in Stanzas IX and X.

3. The grammar in this poem is a little crabbed. Is the poet saying in Stanzas VI and VII: "I hope that my singing will mean, when you remember it in the future, such and such to you"? And in Stanzas VIII through IX, he is saying: "I hope that my remembered singing will *not* mean something very different to you—an annoyance, a troubling, a reminder of what you would really like to forget"?

4. What does the last stanza of the poem imply? Does the absolute lack of response suggest that maybe his more ominous feeling of what his song might have meant to her could be true? Notice how the house and the garden and the gate in this last stanza almost take on human personality—they are grudging, obdurate, resentful.

5. Compare with the imagery in this last stanza the images in Stanza V. What would be lost if the poet had written "So passed the night" rather than "So wore the night"? On what basis would you attempt to justify the violence of the imagery in the last stanza?

Kubla Khan:
Or A Vision in a Dream
SAMUEL TAYLOR COLERIDGE
(1772-1834)

In Xanadu did Kubla Khan
A stately pleasure-dome decree;
Where Alph, the sacred river, ran
Through caverns measureless to man
Down to a sunless sea.   5

So twice five miles of fertile ground
With walls and towers were girdled round:
And here were gardens bright with sinuous rills,
Where blossomed many an incense-bearing tree;
And here were forests ancient as the hills   10
Enfolding sunny spots of greenery.

But oh! that deep romantic chasm which slanted
Down the green hill athwart a cedarn cover!
A savage place! as holy and enchanted

As e'er beneath a waning moon was haunted   15
By woman wailing for her demon-lover!
And from this chasm, with ceaseless turmoil
    seething,
As if this earth in fast thick pants were
    breathing
A mighty fountain momently was forced:
Amid whose swift half-intermitted burst   20
Huge fragments vaulted like rebounding hail,
Or chaffy grain beneath the thresher's flail:
And 'mid these dancing rocks at once and ever
It flung up momently the sacred river.
Five miles meandering with a mazy motion   25
Through wood and dale the sacred river ran,
Then reached the caverns measureless to man,
And sank in tumult to a lifeless ocean:
And 'mid this tumult Kubla heard from far
Ancestral voices prophesying war!   30

    The shadow of the dome of pleasure
    Floated midway on the waves;
    Where was heard the mingled measure
    From the fountain and the caves.
It was a miracle of rare device,   35
A sunny pleasure-dome with caves of ice!

    A damsel with a dulcimer
    In a vision once I saw:
    It was an Abyssinian maid,
    And on her dulcimer she played,   40
    Singing of Mount Abora.
    Could I revive with me
    Her symphony and song,
    To such a deep delight 'twould win me,
That with music loud and long,   45
I would build that dome in air,
That sunny dome! those caves of ice!
And all who heard should see them there,—
And all should cry, Beware! Beware!—
His flashing eyes, his floating hair!   50
Weave a circle round him thrice,
And close your eyes with holy dread,
For he on honey-dew hath fed,
And drunk the milk of Paradise.

"Kubla Khan" raises in a most acute form the whole question of meaning in a poem and the poet's intention. We have already touched on this (p. 302), but now let us examine the matter a little more closely. We have Coleridge's account of how the poem was composed:

In the summer of the year 1797, the author, then in ill health, had retired to a lonely farmhouse between Porlock and Linton, on the Exmoor confines of Somerset and Devonshire. In consequence of a slight indisposition, an anodyne had been prescribed, from the effects of which he fell asleep in his chair at the moment that he was reading the following sentence, or words of the same substance, in *Purchas's Pilgrimage:* 'Here the Khan Kubla commanded a palace to be built, and a stately garden thereunto. And thus ten miles of fertile ground were inclosed within a wall.' The author continued for about three hours in a profound sleep, at least of the external senses, during which time he has the most vivid confidence, that he could not have composed less than from two to three hundrel lines; if that indeed can be called composition in which all the images rose up before him as *things,* with a parallel production of the correspondent expressions, without any sensation or consciousness of effort. On awaking he appeared to himself to have a distinct recollection of the whole, and taking his pen, ink, and paper, instantly and eagerly wrote down the lines that are here preserved. At this moment he was unfortunately called out by a person on business from Porlock, and detained by him above an hour, and on his return to his room, found, to his no small surprise and mortification, that though he still retained some vague and dim recollection of the general purport of the vision, yet, with the exception of some eight or ten scattered lines and images, all the rest has passed away like the images on the surface of a stream into which a stone has been cast, but, alas! without the after restoration of the latter.

Can a poem dreamed up in this fashion be said to have a meaning? Can it be the expression of some idea held by the poet? Suppose, however, that what was dreamed up was not a poem but a mathematical discovery or chemical formula. Would either of these have less validity because dreamed up? We should have to say, no, for the validity of the formula does not depend upon how it came to the scientist but upon its own nature. There are, in fact, many accounts of how important scientific discoveries did come in some flash of intuition or in dream. For instance, the great German chemist, Kekulé dreamed up two of his most important discoveries. But whether it is a poem or a chemical formula that is dreamed up, this important fact must be remembered: only poets dream up poems and only scientists dream up scientific discoveries. The dream, or the moment of inspiration, really sums up a long period of hard conscious work.

Wordsworth, in the Preface to the second edition of the *Lyrical Ballads,* has a very important remark on how meaning gets into poetry. Having just said that he hopes his poems to be distinguished by a "worthy purpose," he continues:

Not that I always began to write with a distinct purpose formally conceived: but habits of meditation have, I trust, so prompted and regulated my feelings, that my descriptions of such objects as strongly excite those feelings, will be found to carry along with them a *purpose.* If this opinion be erroneous, I can have little right to the name of a Poet. For all good poetry is the spontaneous overflow of powerful feelings: and though this be true, Poems to which any value can be attached were never produced on any variety of subjects but by a man who, being possessed of more than usual organic sensibility, had also thought long and deeply.

The important point is that Wordsworth takes a poem that happens to come in a flash as embodying the ideas carefully developed over a long period of time.

Sometimes, of course, a poet does start with a pretty clear notion of what he wants his poem to be and works systematically. Sometimes he starts with only the vaguest feeling and with no defined theme. Sometimes he may simply have a line or a phrase as a kind of germ. But no matter how he starts, he is working toward a conception of the poem that will hold all the parts in significant relation to each other. Therefore, as his general conception becomes clearer, he may find more and more need for going back and changing parts already composed. The process is a process of exploration and development. The poet is busy finding out his own full meanings, for the meanings themselves do not exist until they are composed. The poem isn't a way of saying something that could be said equally well another way. Its "saying" is the whole poem, the quality of the imagery, the feel of the rhythm, the dramatic force, the ideas, and the meaning does not exist until the words are all in their order.

It does not matter, then, whether the composition is slow and painful or easy and fast. We do not have two kinds of poetry, one spontaneous and one calculated. Without reference to the origin, we consider the quality of the poem, for the poem must deliver its own meaning. Some of those meanings may have entered in a flash, out of the poet's unconscious, but once they are absorbed into the poem they are part of the poem; they are ours and not the poet's.

To return to "Kubla Khan." It is possible that the poem was not dreamed up quite as literally as Coleridge said that it was. In 1934 there came to light another note by Coleridge telling how he wrote "Kubla Khan." The note reads as follows: "This fragment with a good deal more, not recoverable, composed in a sort of Reverie brought on by two grains of Opium, taken to check a dysentery, at a Farm House between Porlock & Linton, a quarter of a mile from Culbone Church, in the fall of the year, 1797." Miss Elizabeth Schneider believes that this is the earlier of the two accounts and probably the more accurate. In *Coleridge, Opium, and Kubla Khan* [1] she has argued quite persuasively against the idea that "Kubla Khan" was a "literal opium dream or any other extremely remarkable kind of automatic composition. . . ." But whether Miss Schneider is right or wrong on this point, "Kubla Khan" is the product of Coleridge's special experience and resembles his other poems. As a comparison with his "The Ancient Mariner" and his famous unfinished work "Christabel" will show, "Kubla Khan" is very similar to these poems in tone and method.

We know the origin of almost every image and of many phrases in "Kubla Khan," for John Livingston Lowes [2] has tracked them down in Coleridge's reading. The materials from Coleridge's reading do not give us the meaning of the poem any more than the fact of the composition under the influence of opium necessarily renders it meaningless. We have to look at the poem itself. The poem falls into two main sections. The first describes the dome of pleasure,

---

[1] Elizabeth Schneider, *Coleridge, Opium, and Kubla Khan* (Chicago, University of Chicago Press, 1953), p. 81.
[2] John L. Lowes, *The Road to Xanadu* (Boston, Houghton Mifflin Co., 1930), pp. 356-413.

the garden, the chasm, the great fountain and the ancestral voices prophesying war. The second, beginning with the line, "A damsel with a dulcimer," says that music might rebuild the world of Xanadu—or rather, that the special music of the Abyssinian maid might rebuild that world—and if the poet could recapture that music all who saw him would recognize his strange power as both beautiful and terrible. In other words, without treating the poem as an allegory and trying to make each detail equate with some notion, we can still take it to be a poem about creative imagination: "song," the imaginative power, the poetic power, could "build that dome in air" and recreate the enchanted and ominous world of Xanadu.

Does the fact that Coleridge called his poem a fragment argue against this interpretation? Probably not. Even though we can imagine that Coleridge might have planned to take the poem on through this or that line of development, we possess, nevertheless, a poem which is in itself coherent and which comes to a significant climax. Even though these fifty-four lines might have been envisaged as a section within a larger work the section can, in default of that larger work, stand alone.

How do we know that Coleridge "intended" the poem to mean what we have just suggested it means? Now we are back to our starting point. We do not know that he "intended" anything. He simply had a dream or perhaps it was a kind of waking reverie. But it is a product of the Coleridgean imagination. It embodies a meaningful structure. And for this meaning, the poem is its own best warrant.

1. This poem is celebrated for its suggestiveness —that is, its power to stimulate the imagination. Notice that a very large part of this power resides in the imagery. Examine the aura of association and suggestion that emanates from phrases such as "forests ancient as the hills," "deep romantic chasm," "holy and enchanted," "waning moon," etc.

2. Does the series of contrasts, stated or implied, help indicate what the poem is about: *i.e.*, "sunny" and "caves of ice," the tumultuous river and the "lifeless ocean," etc.?

3. The Khan seems to have chosen the site of his pleasure dome with great care. The spot exhibits a special kind of nature, rich, varied, and above all, numinous. May this poem be said to represent a kind

of union of art and nature? Or to hint that a special relation to nature must obtain if the artist, either as builder of pleasure dome or of poem, is to succeed?

A Valediction: Forbidding Mourning
JOHN DONNE (1573-1631)

As virtuous men pass mildly away,
   And whisper to their souls to go,
Whilst some of their sad friends do say,
   "The breath goes now," and some say, "No":

So let us melt, and make no noise,   5
   No tear-floods nor sigh-tempests move;
'Twere profanation of our joys
   To tell the laity our love.

Moving of the earth brings harms and fears;
   Men reckon what it did, and meant;   10
But trepidation of the spheres,
   Though greater far, is innocent.

Dull sublunary lovers' love
   —Whose soul is sense—cannot admit
Absence, because it doth remove   15
   Those things which elemented it.

But we by a love so far refined
   That ourselves know not what it is,
Inter-assurèd of the mind,
   Care less eyes, lips, and hands to miss.   20

Our two souls therefore, which are one,
   Though I must go, endure not yet
A breach, but an expansiön,
   Like gold to airy thinness beat.

If they be two, they are two so   25
   As stiff twin compasses are two;
Thy soul, the fixed foot, makes no show
   To move, but doth if the other do.

And though it in the center sit,
  Yet, when the other far doth roam,   30
It leans, and hearkens after it,
  And grows erect as that comes home.

Such wilt thou be to me, who must,
  Like the other foot, obliquely run;
Thy firmness makes my circle just,   35
  And makes me end where I begun.

    Draw up a set of questions that will have to do with the poet's choice and use of images in this poem and the way in which these images affect the tone of the poem. On the basis of these questions write an account of the poem.

The Abyss

THEODORE ROETHKE
(1908-1963)

I

Is the stair here?
Where's the stair?
"The stair's right there,
But it goes nowhere."

And the abyss? the abyss?   5
"The abyss you can't miss:
It's right where you are—
A step down the stair."

  Each time ever
  There always is   10
  Noon of failure,
  Part of a house.

  In the middle of,
  Around a cloud,
  On top a thistle   15
  The wind's slowing.

II

I have been spoken to variously
But heard little.
My inward witness is dismayed
By my unguarded mouth.   20
I have taken, too often, the dangerous path,

The vague, the arid,
Neither in nor out of this life.

  Among us, who is holy?
  What speech abides?   25
  I hear the noise of the wall.
  They have declared themselves,
  Those who despise the dove.

Be with me, Whitman, maker of catalogues:
For the world invades me again,   30
And once more the tongues begin babbling.
And the terrible hunger for objects quails me:
The sill trembles.
And there on the blind
A furred caterpillar crawls down a string.   35
My symbol!
For I have moved closer to death, lived with death;
Like a nurse he sat with me for weeks, a sly surly attendant,
Watching my hands, wary.
Who sent him away?   40
I'm no longer a bird dipping a beak into rippling water
But a mole winding through earth,
A night-fishing otter.

III

Too much reality can be a dazzle, a surfeit;
Too close immediacy an exhaustion: 45
As when the door swings open in a florist's storeroom—
The rush of smells strikes like a cold fire, the throat freezes,
And we turn back to the heat of August,
Chastened.

So the abyss—   50
The slippery cold heights,
After the blinding misery,
The climbing, the endless turning,
Strike like a fire,
A terrible violence of creation,   55
A flash into the burning heart of the abominable;
Yet if we wait, unafraid, beyond the fearful instant,
The burning lake turns into a forest pool,
The fire subsides into rings of water,
A sunlit silence.   60

IV

How can I dream except beyond this life?
Can I outleap the sea—
The edge of all the land, the final sea?
I envy the tendrils, their eyeless seeking,
The child's hand reaching into the coiled
    smilax,   65
And I obey the wind at my back
Bringing me home from the twilight fishing.

   In this, my half-rest,
   Knowing slows for a moment,
   And not-knowing enters, silent,   70
   Bearing being itself,
   And the fire dances
   To the stream's
   Flowing.

Do we move toward God, or merely another
    condition?   75
By the salt waves I hear a river's undersong,
In a place of mottled clouds, a thin mist morning
    and evening.
I rock between dark and dark,
My soul nearly my own,
My dead selves singing.   80
And I embrace this calm—
Such quiet under the small leaves!—
Near the stem, whiter at root,
A luminous stillness.

   The shade speaks slowly: 85
   'Adore and draw near.
   Who knows this—
   Knows all.'

V

I thirst by day. I watch by night.
I receive! I have been received!   90
I hear the flowers drinking in their light,
I have taken counsel of the crab and the sea-
    urchin,
I recall the falling of small waters,
The stream slipping beneath the mossy logs,
Winding down to the stretch of irregular
    sand,   95
The great logs piled like matchsticks.

I am most immoderately married:
The Lord God has taken my heaviness away;
I have merged, like the bird, with the bright air,
And my thought flies to the place by the
    bo-tree.   100

Being, not doing, is my first joy.

This poem obviously dramatizes a bout with madness. The speaker says that "Too much reality can be a dazzle, a surfeit." He observes that his "inward witness is dismayed/By [his] unguarded mouth." He cries out that "the world invades me again/And once more the tongues begin babbling."

   1. What is "the abyss"?
   2. Can you find any principle that seems to govern the poet's selection and deployment of the images in this poem?
   3. Does the last line of the poem signal a recovery from madness, or a relapse into madness, or what?

The Force that through the Green Fuse
DYLAN THOMAS (1914-1953)

The force that through the green fuse drives
    the flower
Drives my green age; that blasts the roots of trees
Is my destroyer.
And I am dumb to tell the crooked rose
My youth is bent by the same wintry fever.   5

The force that drives the water through the
    rocks
Drives my red blood; that dries the mouthing
    streams
Turns mine to wax.
And I am dumb to mouth unto my veins
How at the mountain spring the same mouth
    sucks.   10

The hand that whirls the water in the pool
Stirs the quicksand; that ropes the blowing
    wind
Hauls my shroud sail.
And I am dumb to tell the hanging man

How of my clay is made the hangman's lime.   15

The lips of time leech to the fountain head;
Love drips and gathers, but the fallen blood
Shall calm her sores.
And I am dumb to tell a weather's wind
How time has ticked a heaven round the
    stars.   20

And I am dumb to tell the lover's tomb
How at my sheet goes the same crooked worm.

   The imagery in this poem is bold and violent.
Frame a set of questions that will allow you to explore the poet's specific use of these images and
write, on the basis of these, an interpretation of this
poem.

SECTION VI

The poems in this section are closely related
to those in Section V. They may be studied,
however, with special reference to the poet's
treatment of an idea. Many of the poems which
we have already studied involve this same problem, but the poems of this section represent
special emphasis on the idea, and represent use
of relatively complex ideas. Obviously, the student should bring to bear in his study of these
poems all that has been said on the subjects of
imagery, verse, tone, etc., for, as we have seen
again and again, the poet attempts to convey
not an abstraction, but a concrete experience—
ideas and feelings about the ideas.

The Convergence
of the Twain

Lines on the Loss of the Titanic

THOMAS HARDY (1840-1928)

In a solitude of the sea
    Deep from human vanity,
And the Pride of Life that planned her, stilly
    couches she.

    Steel chambers, late the pyres
    Of her salamandrine fires,   5

Cold currents thrid, and turn to rhythmic tidal
    lyres.

    Over the mirrors meant
    To glass the opulent
The sea-worm crawls—grotesque, slimed, dumb,
    indifferent.

    Jewels in joy designed   10
    To ravish the sensuous mind
Lie lightless, all their sparkles bleared and black
    and blind.

    Dim moon-eyed fishes near
    Gaze at the gilded gear
And query: "What does this vaingloriousness
    down here?" . . .   15

    Well: while was fashioning
    This creature of cleaving wing,
The Immanent Will that stirs and urges every-
    thing

    Prepared a sinister mate
    For her—so gaily great—   20
A Shape of Ice, for the time far and dissociate.

    And as the smart ship grew
    In stature, grace, and hue,
In shadowy silent distance grew the Iceberg too.

    Alien they seemed to be: 25
    No mortal eye could see
The intimate welding of their later history,

    Or sign that they were bent
    By paths coincident
On being anon twin halves of one august
   event,   30

    Till the Spinner of the Years
    Said "Now!" And each one hears,
And consummation comes, and jars two hemispheres.

The subtitle of the poem tells us that it was
written upon the loss of the *Titanic,* which was
struck by an iceberg on her maiden voyage.
Many different kinds of poems might have been
written upon such a subject: this particular
poem, however, is not a narrative, nor is it an
objective description. It very frankly tries to
read a meaning or an interpretation into the
event. The meaning is, in part, the "vanity of
human wishes." The great ship, which represented the peak of man's ambition and attainment in his attempt to conquer nature, does not
conquer, but is conquered by, nature.

The poem begins, indeed, with the interpretation. The ship, planned by "the Pride of Life,"
finds its place of rest in the loneliness of the sea,
"Deep from human vanity." The reader expects
the more usual phrase, *"far* from human vanity."
But *deep* is correct. The ship is on the seafloor,
and the phrase is important for two considerations: it helps prevent the interpretation from
falling into a conventional moralization—the
poet twists the conventional phrase into a more
subtle and accurate one; and it directs our view
to the seafloor where the ship reposes.

The first two lines in each stanza (which are
short) give a sense of rapidity which contrasts
sharply with the slow and heavy march of the
long last line. Notice that Hardy, in the second
through the fifth stanzas, specifically associates
this rapidity with a sense of frail instability. He
uses the first two lines in each case to describe
some detail of the ship, and then the last line
for his ironical comment on that detail, thus
associating the long roll of the line with the sea
and with the dark irony of fate itself.

This is in general the plan of rhythmic effects in the poem: the contrast between the
rhythms supports the ironical contrasts in the
poem. But Hardy does not allow the rhythm to
become monotonous. For example, in the second
stanza there is a competition between *cold* and
current for the accent. To take another example,
in the third stanza it is impossible to read the
last line without giving a heavy and separate
emphasis to each of the adjectives: *grotesque,
slimed, dumb, indifferent.*

Not the least of the ironical effects which
Hardy employs in the earlier stanzas of the
poem is that of putting in the mouths of the
fishes, with a kind of grim comedy, a question
which in phrasing and rhythm might have come
out of Ecclesiastes: "What does this vaingloriousness down here?"

So much for the poet's comment on the
vanity of human wishes. Up to this point the
poem has occupied itself with the large, sardonic
handling of a conventional theme. But Hardy
does not risk tiring the reader. He has another
theme to state which is a matter for irony no
less than the theme just mentioned and which
forces the poem out of sardonic comment into
ironic interpretation—an interpretation not narrowed to one event but valid for the whole
wider implications of life.

The transition from the first section of the
poem to the second is afforded by the question
asked by the fishes. Hardy decides to answer
their question. The colloquial word *Well* is tremendously important. It is as if Hardy had said,
"I shall put a period to my sardonic play with
the idea. If you really want to know what happened, this is what happened." And the rhythm
supports this also. There is a heavy pause on the
word *Well,* and the pause effectively contrasts
with, and breaks the rhythm of, what has gone
before, and introduces the new section.

The reader should be warned here, that the
foregoing sentences do not mean that Hardy
has broken his poem in two. Far from it. The
irony built up in the preceding sections between
the vanity of man's frail works and the elemental strength of nature is employed in the
stanzas that follow. Fate, Hardy says, unknown
to man, had planned all along the meeting of
the iceberg and the *Titanic.* He proceeds then
to prove it, with irony again; this time, however, there is not only the ironical contrast be-

tween man's works and nature's, there is another contrast between the foreknowledge of man and that of fate. The eighth, ninth, and tenth stanzas develop the contrast between the iceberg and the ship, contrasting them in extremes, but each time, in the last lines, tying them together again. Our acceptance of the paradox is in large part the result of Hardy's figures in these stanzas. For example, "intimate welding": the figure is that of the most stable form of union possible, where one piece of metal becomes an integral part of another. And the further we explore the figure, the more appropriate it becomes. The ship and iceberg fuse into tragedy when they meet. The figure in the tenth stanza is drawn from mathematics, and gives to the meeting of the two objects the inevitability of mathematics. The paths which the two travel are in the purposes of fate, lines which are *coincident*. The phrase, "august event," in this stanza also deserves notice. *August* means imperial in splendor, impressive, commanding dignity. We are now far from the more conventional contrasts of the first part of the poem. The sinking of the great vessel is an *august* event, and Hardy having fully established the power and inevitability of fate, is prepared now to let man have his due to this extent at least.

The climax of the poem comes, of course, in the last stanza. Both man and nature are in the grip of a master power which uses the works of both indiscriminately. When fate, the Spinner of the Years, gives the command, they leap to their places. Here the rhythm of the lines rises to the situation. There is a pause after the heavy "Now" of command and the rest of the second line leaps forward with the first part of the last line to come to a momentary pause on *comes,* with another pause on *jars.* If one asks how the poet manages this, one can point out the effect of alliteration in the last line, and the fact that there can be only a partially heavy accent on the third syllable of *consummation. Comes* is the first word in the line which can be stressed heavily.

The whole poem is a splendid study in the variations of meter which a poet may use, as it is also a fine study in the effective use of contrasts of varying degree and of varying effect.

The ground plan of the poem is a system of contrasts and fusions of opposites—a ground plan used in many of the greatest poems. In the case of this poem, the welding of the ship and the iceberg into "one august event" is a sort of parable of the internal structure of the poem, so that the story of the poem itself reflects what the poet is doing beneath the surface.

Sonnet 55
WILLIAM SHAKESPEARE
(1564-1616)

Not marble, nor the gilded monuments
Of princes, shall outlive this powerful rhyme;
But you shall shine more bright in these contents
Than unswept stone besmeared with sluttish time.
When wasteful war shall statues overturn,   5
And broils root out the work of masonry,
Nor Mars his sword nor war's quick fire shall burn
The living record of your memory.
'Gainst death and all-oblivious enmity
Shall you pace forth; your praise shall still find room   10
Even in the eyes of all posterity
That wear this world out to the ending doom.
　So, till the judgment that yourself arise,
　You live in this, and dwell in lover's eyes.

1. The idea stated in this poem is a commonplace. Does the poet succeed in giving it dignity and seriousness?

2. Analyze the imagery used here in the light of this purpose. Note that the poet is asserting the endurance of his praise of the friend, that he has a vivid realization of the forces calculated to obliterate that praise.

3. Note that the "judgment" refers to judgment day when his friend will rise from the dead. How does the phrase "pace forth" give concreteness to the idea of his friend's living to posterity? How does it qualify "this powerful rhyme" (l. 2)? Does it focus attention upon the poet's prowess or on the friend's greatness?

Elegy

Written in a Country Churchyard

THOMAS GRAY (1716-1771)

The Curfew tolls the knell of parting day,
　The lowing herd wind slowly o'er the lea,
The plowman homeward plods his weary way,
　And leaves the world to darkness and to me.

Now fades the glimmering landscape on the
　　sight,　　　　　　　　　　　　　　　　5
And all the air a solemn stillness holds,
Save where the beetle wheels his droning flight,
　And drowsy tinklings lull the distant folds;

Save that from yonder ivy-mantled tower
　The moping owl does to the moon com-
　　plain　　　　　　　　　　　　　　　　10
Of such, as wandering near her secret bower,
　Molest her ancient solitary reign.

Beneath those rugged elms, that yew-tree's
　　shade,
　Where heaves the turf in many a mouldering
　　heap,
Each in his narrow cell for ever laid,　　15
　The rude forefathers of the hamlet sleep.

The breezy call of incense-breathing morn,
　The swallow twittering from the straw-built
　　shed,
The cock's shrill clarion, or the echoing horn,
　No more shall rouse them from their lowly
　　bed.　　　　　　　　　　　　　　　　20

For them no more the blazing hearth shall burn,
　Or busy housewife ply her evening care;
No children run to lisp their sire's return,
　Or climb his knees the envied kiss to share.

Oft did the harvest to their sickle yield,　25
　Their furrow oft the stubborn glebe has
　　broke;

How jocund did they drive their team afield!
　How bowed the woods beneath their sturdy
　　stroke!

Let not Ambition mock their useful toil,
　Their homely joys, and destiny obscure;　30
Nor Grandeur hear with a disdainful smile
　The short and simple annals of the poor.

The boast of heraldry, the pomp of power,
　And all that beauty, all that wealth o'er gave,
Awaits alike the inevitable hour.　　　35
　The paths of glory lead but to the grave.

Nor you, ye proud, impute to these the fault,
　If Memory o'er their tomb no trophies raise,
Where through the long-drawn aisle and fretted
　　vault
　The pealing anthem swells the note of
　　praise.　　　　　　　　　　　　　　40

Can storied urn or animated bust
　Back to its mansion call the fleeting breath?
Can Honor's voice provoke the silent dust,
　Or Flattery sooth the dull cold ear of Death?

Perhaps in this neglected spot is laid　45
　Some heart once pregnant with celestial fire;
Hands, that the rod of empire might have
　　swayed,
　Or waked to ecstasy the living lyre.

But Knowledge to their eyes her ample page
　Rich with the spoils of time did ne'er
　　unroll;　　　　　　　　　　　　　　50
Chill Penury repressed their noble rage,
　And froze the genial current of the soul.

Full many a gem of purest ray serene,
　The dark unfathomed caves of ocean bear:
Full many a flower is born to blush unseen,　55
　And waste its sweetness on the desert air.

Some village Hampden, that with dauntless
　　breast
　The little tyrant of his fields withstood;
Some mute inglorious Milton here may rest,
　Some Cromwell guiltless of his country's
　　blood.　　　　　　　　　　　　　　60

The applause of listening senates to command,
  The threats of pain and ruin to despise,
To scatter plenty o'er a smiling land,
  And read their history in a nation's eyes,

Their lot forbade: nor circumscribed alone   65
  Their growing virtues, but their crimes
    confin'd;
Forbade to wade through slaughter to a throne,
  And shut the gates of mercy on mankind,

The struggling pangs of conscious truth to hide,
  To quench the blushes of ingenuous
    shame,   70
Or heap the shrine of Luxury and Pride
  With incense kindled at the Muses's flame.

Far from the madding crowd's ignoble strife,
  Their sober wishes never learned to stray;
Along the cool sequestered vale of life   75
  They kept the noiseless tenor of their way.

Yet even these bones from insult to protect,
  Some frail memorial still erected nigh,
With uncouth rhymes and shapeless sculpture
    decked,
  Implores the passing tribute of a sigh.   80

Their names, their years, spelt by the unlettered
    muse,
  The place of fame and elegy supply:
And many a holy text around she strews,
  That teach the rustic moralist to die.

For who to dumb Forgetfulness a prey,   85
  This pleasing anxious being e'er resigned,
Left the warm precincts of the cheerful day,
  Nor cast one longing lingering look behind?

On some fond breast the parting soul relies,
  Some pious drops the closing eye re-
    quires;   90
Ev'n from the tomb the voice of Nature cries,
  Ev'n in our ashes live their wonted Fires.

For thee, who mindful of the unhonored dead
  Dost in these lines their artless tale relate,
If chance, by lonely contemplation led,   95
  Some kindred spirit shall inquire thy fate,

Haply some hoary-headed swain may say,
  "Oft have we seen him at the peep of dawn
Brushing with hasty steps the dews away
  To meet the sun upon the upland
    lawn.   100

"There at the foot of yonder nodding beech
  That wreathes its old fantastic roots so high,
His listless length at noontide would he stretch,
  And pore upon the brook that babbles by.

"Hard by yon wood, now smiling as in
    scorn,   105
  Muttering his wayward fancies he would
    rove,
Now drooping, woeful wan, like one forlorn,
  Or crazed with care, or crossed in hopeless
    love.

"One morn I missed him on the customed hill,
  Along the heath and near his favorite
    tree;   110
Another came; nor yet beside the rill,
  Nor up the lawn, nor at the wood was he;

"The next with dirges due in sad array
  Slow through the church-way path we saw
    him borne.
Approach and read (for thou can'st read) the
    lay,   115
  Graved on the stone beneath yon agèd
    thorn."

The Epitaph

Here rests his head upon the lap of earth
  A youth to fortune and to fame unknown.
Fair Science frowned not on his humble birth,
  And Melancholy marked him for her
    own.   120

Large was his bounty, and his soul sincere,
  Heav'n did a recompense as largely send:
He gave to Misery all he had, a tear,
  He gained from Heaven ('twas all he
    wished) a friend.

No farther seek his merits to disclose,   125
  Or draw his frailties from their dread abode,

(There they alike in trembling hope repose),
　The bosom of his Father and his God.

Prepare a set of questions calculated to further your understanding of this poem. Some of your questions will have to do, of course, with such matters as the development of the theme and the use of imagery, but you may need to ask also who such people as Hampton and Cromwell were. Look up these names in the library. You may also want to find in the library some account of the poet Gray and even of the "graveyard school" of English poets of the eighteenth century.

I Walked Out
to the Graveyard
to See the Dead

RICHARD EBERHART
(1904-　　)

I walked out to the graveyard to see the dead
The iron gates were locked, I couldn't get in,
A golden pheasant on the dark fir boughs
Looked with fearful method at the sunset,

Said I, Sir bird, wink no more at me　　　　5
I have had enough of my dark eye-smarting,
I cannot adore you, nor do I praise you,
But assign you to the rafters of Montaigne.

Who talks with the Absolute salutes a Shadow,
Who seeks himself shall lose himself;　　　10
And the golden pheasants are no help
And action must be learned from love of man.

Perhaps Montaigne (1533-1592) is referred to because of his association with speculations on man and nature carried out in a sceptical spirit. (His motto was *Que sais-je?*, "What do I know?")

1. Compare and contrast the mood of this poem with that of Gray's "Elegy."
2. Presumably the fact that the speaker encountered the pheasant was an accident, but the poet turns this fact to account in the poem. What does the bird symbolize?
3. Is this poem about the dead? Or about the way in which man is related to nature? Or what?

Dover Beach

MATTHEW ARNOLD
(1822-1888)

The sea is calm tonight,
The tide is full, the moon lies fair
Upon the straits;—on the French coast, the light
Gleams and is gone; the cliffs of England stand,
Glimmering and vast, out in the tranquil
　　bay.　　　　　　　　　　　　　　5
Come to the window, sweet is the night air!
Only, from the long line of spray
Where the sea meets the moon-blanch'd land,
Listen! you hear the grating roar
Of pebbles which the waves draw back, and
　　fling,　　　　　　　　　　　　　10
At their return, up the high strand,
Begin, and cease, and then again begin,
With tremulous cadence slow, and bring
The eternal note of sadness in.

Sophocles long ago　　　　　　　　15
Heard it on the Aegean, and it brought
Into his mind the turbid ebb and flow
Of human misery; we
Find also in the sound a thought,
Hearing it by this distant northern sea.　　20

The Sea of Faith
Was once, too, at the full, and round earth's
　　shore
Lay like the folds of a bright girdle furl'd.
But now I only hear
Its melancholy, long, withdrawing roar,　　25
Retreating, to the breath
Of the night-wind, down the vast edges drear
And naked shingles of the world.

Ah, love, let us be true
To one another! for the world, which
　　seems　　　　　　　　　　　　30
To lie before us like a land of dreams,
So various, so beautiful, so new,
Hath really neither joy, nor love, nor light,
Nor certitude, nor peace, nor help for pain;

And we are here as on a darkling plain   35
Swept with confused alarms of struggle and
  flight,
Where ignorant armies clash by night.

    1. What does the poet gain by using the symbol
of the ebb tide for the abstract statement, "decline
of faith"?
    2. Why does he wait until the second section of
the poem to declare his symbol?
    3. Does the poet use any onomatopoeic effects?
    4. What is the relation of the last section to the
rest of the poem? Why does the speaker take this
occasion in particular to say "let us be true/To one
another"?

The Secular Masque

JOHN DRYDEN (1631-1700)

JANUS: Chronos, Chronos, mend thy
            pace,
           An hundred times the rolling
            sun
           Around the radiant belt has run
           In his revolving race.
           Behold, behold, the goal in
            sight,   5
           Spread thy fans, and wing thy
            flight.

CHRONOS: Weary, weary of my weight,
           Let me, let me, drop my
            freight,
           And leave the world behind.
           I could not bear,   10
           Another year,
           The load of human-kind.

MOMUS: Ha! ha! ha! ha! ha! ha! well hast
           thou done
            To lay down thy pack,
            And lighten thy back,   15
           The world was a fool, e'er since
            it begun,
           And since neither Janus, nor
            Chronos, nor I,
           Can hinder the crimes,
           Or mend the bad times,

           'Tis better to laugh than to
            cry.   20

CHORUS OF
ALL THREE: 'Tis better to laugh than to cry.

JANUS: Since Momus comes to laugh
            below,
           Old Time, begin the show,
           That he may see, in every scene,
           What changes in this age have
            been.   25

CHRONOS: The goddess of the silver bow
           begin.

DIANA: With horns and with hounds, I
            waken the day:
           And hye to the woodland-
            walks away:
           I tuck up my robe, and am
            buskined soon,
           And tie to my forehead a
            wexing moon.   30
           I course the fleet stag, un-
            kennel the fox,
           And chase the wild goats o'er
            summits of rocks,
           With shouting and hooting
            we pierce through the sky,
           And Echo turns hunter, and
            doubles the cry.

CHORUS OF
ALL: With shouting and hooting we
           pierce through the sky,   35
           And Echo turns hunter, and
            doubles the cry.

JANUS: Then our age was in its prime:

CHRONOS: Free from rage:

DIANA: —And free from crime:

MOMUS: A very merry, dancing, drink-
           ing,
           Laughing, quaffing, and un-
            thinking time.   40

CHORUS OF
ALL: Then our age was in its prime,

Free from rage, and free from
    crime,
A very merry, dancing, drink-
    ing,
Laughing, quaffing, and un-
    thinking time.

MARS: Inspire the vocal brass, in-
                spire;   45
            The world is past its infant age:
                Arms and honor,
                Arms and honor,
            Set the martial mind on fire,
            And kindle manly rage;   50
            Mars has looked the sky to red;
            And Peace, the lazy good, is
                fled.
            Plenty, peace, and pleasure fly;
                The sprightly green,
            In woodland-walks, no more is
                seen;   55
            The sprightly green has drunk
                the
                Tyrian dye.

CHORUS OF
ALL: Plenty, peace, &c.

MARS: Sound the trumpet, beat the
                drum;
            Through all the world around,
            Sound   a   reveillé,   sound,
                sound,   60
            The warrior god is come.

CHORUS OF
ALL: Sound the trumpet, &c.

MOMUS: Thy sword within the scabbard
                keep,
                And let mankind agree;
            Better the world were fast
                asleep,   65
            Than kept awake by thee.
            The fools are only thinner,
                With all our cost and care;
            But neither side a winner,
                For   things   are   as   they
                    were.   70

CHORUS OF
ALL: The fools are only, &c.

VENUS: Calms appear, when storms are
                past;
            Love will have his hour at last:
            Nature is my kindly care;
            Mars   destroys,   and   I
                repair;   75
            Take me, take me, while you
                may,
            Venus comes not every day.

CHORUS OF
ALL: Take her, take her, &c.

CHRONOS: The world was then so light,
            I scarcely felt the weight;   80
            Joy ruled the day, and Love the
                night.
            But since the queen of pleasure
                left the ground,
                I faint, I lag,
                And feebly drag
            The pondrous orb around.   85

MOMUS: All, all of a piece throughout:
TO DIANA.   Thy chase had a beast in view.
TO MARS.   Thy wars brought nothing
                about;
TO VENUS.   Thy lovers were all untrue.

JANUS: 'Tis well an old age is out.   90

CHRONOS: And time to begin a new.

CHORUS OF
ALL: All, all of a piece throughout;
            Thy chase had a beast in view:
            Thy wars brought nothing
                about;
            Thy lovers were all untrue.   95
            'Tis well an old age is out,
            And time to begin a new.

In this poem, Dryden celebrates the turn of the
century. He employs allegorical figures (Janus, the
god of beginnings; Chronos, time; Momus, laughter,
etc.) to describe the passing seventeenth century and
his attitude toward it. He treats the century under
three main headings: the early century under James
I, the wars of Charles I, and the gay and licentious
courts of Charles II and James II.

1. What is the poet's attitude? Toward war? Toward love? Toward history?

2. Is the poet simply cynical? (See, for example,

"The fools are only thinner," l. 66.) Is he gloomy? Or gay? Does he regret the past? Or is he glad that it is past?

3. Is the poet's use of allegorical figures justified? Which figure comes closest to being a mouthpiece for the speaker himself?

4. How does the poet use rhythmical effects to express his attitude?

5. What "statement" about the dying century does the poet make? How are we to interpret the "statement"?

London

WILLIAM BLAKE (1757-1827)

I wander thro' each chartered street,
Near where the chartered Thames does flow
And mark in every face I meet
Marks of weakness, marks of woe.

In every cry of every man,   5
In every Infant's cry of fear,
In every voice; in every ban,
The mind-forged manacles I hear

How the Chimney-sweeper's cry
Every blackning Church appalls,   10
And the hapless Soldier's sigh
Runs in blood down Palace walls

But most thro' midnight streets I hear
How the youthful Harlot's curse
Blasts the new born Infant's tear   15
And blights with plagues the Marriage hearse

London, 1802

WILLIAM WORDSWORTH (1770-1850)

Milton! thou should'st be living at this hour:
England hath need of thee: she is a fen
Of stagnant waters: altar, sword, and pen,
Fireside, the heroic wealth of hall and bower,
Have forfeited their ancient English dower   5
Of inward happiness. We are selfish men:

Oh! raise us up, return to us again;
And give us manners, virtue, freedom, power.
Thy soul was like a Star, and dwelt apart:
Thou hadst a voice whose sound was like the
      sea: 10
Pure as the naked heavens, majestic, free,
So didst thou travel on life's common way,
In cheerful godliness; and yet thy heart
The lowliest duties on herself did lay.

Both poets are writing of the degradation which had befallen London near the turn of the eighteenth century. Both think of this degradation in spiritual terms: the fetters which London wears, according to Blake, are "mind-forged"; the happiness which Wordsworth wishes restored is an "inward happiness." And both poets think of the degradation as a loss of power: Blake says the city is "sold out" and that the inhabitants have been sold out; Wordsworth thinks of the city as a marsh full of stagnant waters. But in both cases energy, whether bound or reduced to torpor, is not able to exert itself. So far the poems run parallel, but in other respects they diverge widely, and a comparison of the two poets' intentions and accomplishments will indicate vividly the fact that poetry does not reside in a particular subject but in a treatment of the subject.

Blake's poem is essentially simpler than Wordsworth's. Blake organizes his poem on this scheme: what the poet sees, and more important, what he hears as he traverses London. Wordsworth makes his scheme of organization an appeal to Milton to return with his life-giving power to restore England to its spiritual health. Blake's method is not inherently superior to Wordsworth's, but in the case of these particular poems, Blake gives an effect of concentration and intensity which Wordsworth's poem lacks. In the next paragraphs we shall try to indicate why.

In the first place, notice the climactic order in Blake's poem. The first stanza is introductory as compared with the rest of the poem: that is, it gives the occasion for what is to follow. But though it is introductory, it does not postpone the poem; the poem begins with force. *Chartered* is used in two senses that mutually reinforce each other: first, in the sense of laid out and bound by a chart or plan; and second, in the sense of hired, or bought up. (It is possible to read even a third meaning into *chartered*: charters are documents which originally guarantee liberties to men, but which in the course of time become a means of enslavement.) The streets and the people whom the poet meets in them are not free, they are enslaved. The river itself down to which the streets lead is *chartered*, even though one thinks of a river as being a kind of symbol of natural and free movement. The three-fold repetition of *mark* in this first stanza suggests directness and simplicity:

> And mark in every face I meet
> Marks of weakness, marks of woe.

This is akin to the child's way of saying something: "I marked a mark," or "I bled blood." But the statement converts the elemental directness and simplicity of the child into a device of terrific emphasis, for the poet is dealing with a very complex and adult idea. (Observe also how the poet uses the repetitions of the word *cry* in the remainder of the poem.)

The climactic scale of the poem begins in the various cries which the poet hears, and the meaning of those cries. The second stanza states that in every cry that he hears, he hears the clanking of fetters. In the third and fourth stanzas he goes on to give concrete examples of particular cries and their particular meanings— all of them aspects of the great general meaning of self-enslavement.

The chimney-sweeper's cry appalls the church. Why? Because the child, enslaved in a deadening and disagreeable trade (the chimney-sweeps were often children at this time) shakes the church, the institution consecrated to fight against things so unchristian. Why *blackening church?* London churches are, as a matter of fact, blackened by soot, but the poet seizes upon this detail for a special reason: he suggests that they share in the degradation of the children whom they should protect—both are blackened by the soot. In the same way, the soldier's sigh runs like blood down the palace-walls. Sighs do not literally flow like blood, of course, but Blake is justified in saying so; for what he is really

saying is this: that soldiers mistreated by the state place a blood-guilt on the state, whether or not the blood is warm, red, and liquid.

Blake thus uses vivid, concrete images to make his indictment. He is daringly imaginative. How do the figures that Wordsworth uses compare with those that Blake uses? In exploring this matter the student might consider the following questions:

1. Milton's soul is said to be like a star and his voice like the sound of the sea. Milton was pure as the "naked heavens" as he traveled along life's "common way" in "cheerful godliness." What is the relation of these figures to that in which England is said to be a fen "of stagnant waters"?

2. Does Wordsworth through his images suggest how Milton is to be a cleansing or a restorative agent? Is there any principle which relates the images of the octave and the sestet of this sonnet?

3. What is Wordsworth attempting to do through his imagery? Is it more than loosely decorative? Vaguely ennobling?

Blake's indictment of London builds up to a terrific climax in the last stanza. Up to this, the fourth stanza, the poet has revealed an enslaved town, with the exploitation of both children and adults. In the last stanza he indicates that the very roots of life itself are poisoned. The fact that love is so misused that it can be bought and sold proclaims a curse on the child in the cradle and on love itself. The union of the sexes is the well-spring of life. To find poison there is the logical climax of the indictment. But Blake has pointed up the climax for us. "But most," he says, as this stanza begins. The phrase is not finished, and the fact that it is not and the resulting ambiguity are made use of by the poet. He may mean "But most frequent of all these cries," or "But most damning of all the cries of woe" or some other such phrase, and since he might mean any of them, and since he does not particularize any single one, the effect we receive is that of all of them combined. The ambiguity itself is *rich*. The phrase as it stands is ungrammatical, it is true, but it does not impress one as strained or affected—as a willful violation of grammar. Indeed, it gives the impression of a man speaking rapidly and forcefully, anxious to hurry on to something tremendously important, and so leaving unfinished an introductory phrase which will be supplied by the reader anyway. And this is just the effect appropriate to the force and power of the climax of the poem.

The student should compare the way in which Blake concludes his poem with the way in which Wordsworth concludes his.

1. Does "London, 1802" rise to a climax or does it trail off? Milton, though he is associated with the grand and elemental qualities of nature and had a soul that "dwelt apart," was willing to lay the "lowliest duties" upon his heart. Is this a startling contrast? What is its relation to the basic theme of the sonnet?

2. Is Wordsworth's poem simpler than Blake's or less simple? Which of the two poems is the more fully organized?

3. Compare the way in which the two poets have dramatized the degradation of London. Wordsworth says that "Altar, sword, and pen" have all alike "forfeited their ancient English dower." Blake uses utterances; he says that the cry of the infant and of the chimney sweep and the sigh of the soldier and the curse of the harlot—all of them testify to London's degradation. In which poem do we find the greater sense of concreteness?

We have commented upon the economy and organic quality of the structure of Blake's "London." Further instances might be given. "Midnight streets" applies literally. The poet is walking the streets at midnight, and it is then that he would be most likely to hear the harlot's curse; but "midnight" has an additional force. The streets of the damned city are midnight in the sense of dark—it is appropriate that the powers of evil should possess them. Again, "youthful" is an adjective which in English poetry is usually associated with joyfulness, freshness, springtime. Literally considered, the adjective does apply to *harlot,* but in applying it Blake is bringing these associations into contrast with the quite different associations which are usually related to *harlot.* The contrast has the effect of a bitter irony. Once more, the "harlot's curse" is apparently not directed by the harlot at love at all. It is merely an aspect of her degradation. But curses are supposed to blight. *Curse* is really being used in two senses, therefore. The curse refers primarily to the harlot's drunken profanity, but in another sense—and in a sense not intended by the harlot—it is a blighting and blasting anathema on all the institutions of love. The primary meanings in all three of these last examples fit the stanza literally; and yet in all three cases there are other meanings which supplement the indictment which Blake is making. We may say then that Blake is using the *denotations* of his words in straightforward enough fashion but that in addition these primary meanings draw along with them a whole train of *associations.* Blake's language is therefore very efficient. Blake extracts all the possible meaning from his words; Wordsworth makes only a superficial use of his. And this is probably the best explanation of two things: (1) why Blake's poem rings with such an intensity; and (2) why Blake's poem grows richer on further reading, whereas Wordsworth's grows dull.

In both of these poems the writer has expressed an indictment of the society in which he was living. The idea in each case may have been held with equal sincerity, and may have been equally justified by the different observations of the two poets. But in Blake's case the idea has been assimilated more fully and directly into the poem and comes to the reader in terms of the poet's observations. This means that the idea is no longer abstract and general, but has been expressed by the poet in concrete symbols; that is, the idea has been turned into poetry. Here one may generalize to this extent: an idea has no value for poetry until it can be made to appeal directly to the reader's feelings. The total effect of the poem must be directed toward this end.

Composed upon Westminster Bridge September 3, 1802
WILLIAM WORDSWORTH
(1770-1850)

Earth has not anything to show more fair:
Dull would he be of soul who could pass by

A sight so touching in its majesty:
This City now doth, like a garment, wear
The beauty of the morning; silent, bare,   5
Ships, towers, domes, theatres, and temples lie
Open unto the fields, and to the sky;
All bright and glittering in the smokeless air.
Never did sun more beautifully steep
In his first splendour, valley, rock, or hill;   10
Ne'er saw I, never felt, a calm so deep!
The river glideth at his own sweet will:
Dear God! the very houses seem asleep;
And all that mighty heart is lying still!

If there is, as we've already hinted, some question about the appropriateness of Wordsworth's images in his sonnet "London, 1802," there can be, in our opinion no question about the value and power of the imagery used in this poem, written also in 1802, and about London also.

1. If this poem shows a delighted surprise at the aspect that London presents in the morning light, what accounts for the surprise?

2. Could it be said that London has to become quiet almost as death, for the observer to notice that it is instinct with life?

3. How has the poet suggested that the city is not cut off from nature but is continuous with nature?

West London

MATTHEW ARNOLD
(1822-1888)

Crouched on the pavement close by Belgrave
     Square,
A tramp I saw, ill, moody, and tongue-tied;
A babe was in her arms, and at her side
A girl; their clothes were rags, their feet were
     bare.
Some labouring men, whose work lay somewhere
     there,   5
Passed opposite; she touched her girl, who hied
Across and begged, and came back satisfied.
The rich she had let pass with frozen stare.
Thought I: Above her state this spirit towers;

She will not ask of aliens, but of friends,   10
Of sharers in a common human fate.
She turns from that cold succor, which attends
The unknown little from the unknowing great,
And points us to a better time than ours.

1. This poem embodies a simple anecdote and the thought provoked by it. Is the theme stated too directly? Or is it given concreteness and the sense of reality by the descriptive detail and the drama of the anecdote?

2. How close is the theme of this poem to that of William Blake's "London"? Which poem is the more effective? Why?

An Elementary School Classroom in a Slum

STEPHEN SPENDER (1909-   )

Far far from gusty waves, these children's faces,
Like rootless weeds the torn hair round their
     paleness.
The tall girl with her weighed-down head. The
     paper-
seeming boy with rat's eyes. The stunted un-
     lucky heir
Of twisted bones, reciting a father's gnarled
     disease,   5
His lesson from his desk. At back of the dim
     class
One unnoted, mild and young: his eyes live in
     a dream
Of squirrels' game, in tree room, other than
     this.

On sour cream walls, donations. Shakespeare's
     head
Cloudless at dawn, civilized dome riding all
     cities.   10
Belled, flowery, Tyrolese valley. Open-handed
     map
Awarding the world its world. And yet, for
     these

For Mr. Taylor

page 386

doom.

Unless, governor, teacher, inspector, visitor,
This map becomes their window and these
 windows
That open on their lives like crouching tombs
Break, O break open, till they break the town
And show the children to the fields and all
 their world   30
Azure on their sands, to let their tongues
Run naked into books, the white and green
 leaves open
The history theirs whose language is the sun.

    1. Why does the poet say that "Surely Shake-
speare is wicked" (l. 17)? Is he saying that unless
some better life is offered to them, teaching these
children that there is a better life is worse than
meaningless?
    2. How effective is the imagery in this poem? In
what sense can the boy be said to be "reciting a
father's gnarled disease" (l. 5)? How are the windows
of the classroom related to the pictures and maps on
the classroom wall? Examine the imagery of the slag
heap in stanza 3.
    3. How is the last stanza related to the rest of
the poem? Is it a preachment, direct and explicit?
    4. Compare the theme of this poem with that
of "West London" and with that of Blake's "London." All three poems (not to mention Wordsworth's
"London, 1802") deal with one city, though in different ages, and involve the same or closely related
themes.

A Refusal to Mourn
the Death, by Fire,
of a Child in London
DYLAN THOMAS (1914-1953)

Never until the mankind making
Bird beast and flower
Fathering and all humbling darkness
Tells with silence the last light breaking
And the still hour   5
Is come of the sea tumbling in harness

And I must enter again the round
Zion of the water bead
And the synagogue of the ear of corn
Shall I let pray the shadow of a sound   10
Or sow my salt seed
In the least valley of sackcloth to mourn

The majesty and burning of the child's death.
I shall not murder
The mankind of her going with a grave truth   15
Nor blaspheme down the stations of the breath
With any further
Elegy of innocence and youth.

Deep with the first dead lies London's daughter,
Robed in the long friends,   20
The grains beyond age, the dark veins of her
 mother
Secret by the unmourning water
Of the riding Thames.
After the first death, there is no other.

    1. Why does the poet refuse to mourn the child's
death? Because the "majesty" of the child's death is
such that any attempt to celebrate it in words is a
sheer desecration? Because there is no death? Or does
the poet's refusal rest upon some other reason?
    2. The phrase "stations of the breath" is obvi-
ously modelled upon "stations of the cross." What
are some of the other religious terms that occur in
this poem? For what purpose does the poet use them?
    3. What is the tone of this poem?

The Lie

SIR WALTER RALEGH
(1552?-1618)

Go, Soul, the body's guest,
  Upon a thankless arrant: [1]
Fear not to touch the best;
  The truth shall be thy warrant:
Go, since I needs must die,   5
And give the world the lie.

Say to the court, it glows
  And shines like rotten wood;
Say to the church, it shows
  What's good, and doth no good: 10
If church and court reply,
Then give them both the lie.

Tell potentates, they live
  Acting by others' action;
Not loved unless they give,   15
  Not strong but by their faction:
If potentates reply,
Give potentates the lie.

Tell men of high condition,
  That manage the estate,   20
Their purpose is ambition,
  Their practice only hate:
And if they once reply,
Then give them all the lie.

Tell them that brave it most,   25
  They beg for more by spending,
Who, in their greatest cost,
  Seek nothing but commending:
And if they make reply,
Then give them all the lie.   30

Tell zeal it wants devotion;
  Tell love it is but lust;
Tell time it is but motion;
  Tell flesh it is but dust:

[1] errand

And wish them not reply,   35
For thou must give the lie.

Tell age it daily wasteth;
  Tell honor how it alters;
Tell beauty how she blasteth;
  Tell favor how it falters: 40
And as they shall reply,
Give every one the lie.

Tell wit how much it wrangles
  In tickle points of niceness;
Tell wisdom she entangles   45
  Herself in over-wiseness:
And when they do reply,
Straight give them both the lie.

Tell physic of her boldness;
  Tell skill it is pretension;   50
Tell charity of coldness;
  Tell law it is contention:
And as they do reply,
So give them still the lie.

Tell fortune of her blindness;   55
  Tell nature of decay;
Tell friendship of unkindness;
  Tell justice of delay;
And if they will reply,
Then give them all the lie.   60

Tell arts they have no soundness,
  But vary by esteeming;
Tell schools they want profoundness,
  And stand too much on seeming:
If arts and schools reply,   65
Give arts and schools the lie.

Tell faith it's fled the city;
  Tell how the country erreth;
Tell, manhood shakes off pity;
  Tell, virtue least preferreth: 70
And if they do reply,
Spare not to give the lie.

So when thou hast, as I
  Commanded thee, done blabbing,—

Although to give the lie   75
    Deserves no less than stabbing,—
Stab at thee he that will,
No stab the soul can kill.

1. What is the tone of this poem? Does the poet become hysterical in charging everything with rottenness?

2. Why does he use the word "blabbing" in the last stanza? Why not some more dignified word?

3. It is important to see to whom these directions about giving the lie are addressed. The soul is beyond human power to intimidate or to punish it. Moreover, it has nothing to gain by truckling for favor. Note how the first two lines in the last stanza make this point plain and thus emphasize the justification of this final truth telling.

4. Has the poet given variety to his indictment? What are some of the devices by which variety is gained? Does the poem fail in this matter and become monotonous?

5. Compare this poem with "The Secular Masque," which also has indictments to make of human society. Compare it with Blake's "London" which is quite as scathing in its picture of human society. "The Lie" will seem more direct and forthright in its use of statement than Blake's "London." Is it any more successful than Blake's poem? Any less successful? Is the difference in presentation justified—that is, is Ralegh's poem in its own way quite as dramatic as Blake's? For instance, can we characterize the speaker?

To His Coy Mistress
ANDREW MARVELL (1621-1678)

Had we but world enough, and time,
This coyness, Lady, were no crime.
We would sit down and think which way
To walk and pass our long love's day.
Thou by the Indian Ganges' side   5
Shouldst rubies find; I by the tide
Of Humber would complain. I would
Love you ten years before the Flood,
And you should, if you please, refuse
Till the conversion of the Jews.   10
My vegetable love would grow
Vaster than empires, and more slow;
An hundred years would go to praise

Thine eyes and on thy forehead gaze;
Two hundred to adore each breast,   15
But thirty thousand to the rest;
An age at least to every part,
And the last age should show your heart.
For, Lady, you deserve this state,
Nor would I love at lower rate.   20

But at my back I always hear
Time's winged chariot hurrying near;
And yonder all before us lie
Deserts of vast eternity.
Thy beauty shall no more be found,   25
Nor, in thy marble vault, shall sound
My echoing song; then worms shall try
That long preserved virginity,
And your quaint honor turn to dust,
And into ashes all my lust: 30
The grave's a fine and private place,
But none, I think, do there embrace.

Now therefore, while the youthful hue
Sits on thy skin like morning dew,[1]
And while thy willing soul transpires   35
At every pore with instant fires,
Now let us sport us while we may,
And now, like amorous birds of prey,
Rather at once our time devour
Than languish in his slow-chapped
    power.   40
Let us roll all our strength and all
Our sweetness up into one ball,
And tear our pleasures with rough strife
Through the iron gates of life:
Thus, though we cannot make our sun   45
Stand still, yet we will make him run.

The situation of the poem is this: a lover is trying to persuade his mistress to accept his suit. The three parts of the poem are really the three steps in his argument: (1) If life were not so short, the delays of your coyness would be appropriate, and I should be willing to gratify it by praising you for thousands of years before you eventually accepted my love. (2) But life is short, and in death both love and honor are meaningless. (3) Therefore, accept what pleasure there is in love while there is yet youth and

[1] "Dew" is a conjectural emendation. The *editio princeps* reads *glew*. H. M. Margoliouth suggests *lew* (a dialectal word meaning "warmth").

time. That is the bare outline of the argument, and is all of the poem that comes out in a direct and general statement.

The question is, what use does the poet make of such an outline of argument? In other words, how does the meaning of the poem differ, in the end, from the meaning of the argument?

It is a question that cannot be answered explicitly and at once. It can only be answered by investigating various aspects of the poem.

First, one may notice how the tone of the poem changes from section to section (see "Neutral Tones" and analysis). The poem starts with the tone of almost playful conversation, the tone of polite and not-too-serious verse, usually called *vers de société*. The poem introduces certain exaggerations so tremendous that they become a kind of playful and witty absurdity. While the lady picked up rubies by the Ganges in India, the lover, in England by the side of the Humber, would perform some of the polite preliminaries of his courtship by "complaining" on the subject of his love. All history, from before the Flood to the "conversion of the Jews," an event so remote as to be inconceivable, would be but the history of their courtship. But the phrase "vegetable love" introduces an exaggeration of another kind: why would such a kind of love be *vegetable*? The poet means *vegetable* in the sense of belonging to the vegetable kingdom, simply some great plant, like a sequoia, the life span of which would be greater than that of any other living thing. But vegetable growth is a kind of blind, aimless, and undirected growth, farther removed from the direction of the intelligence and will found in man than any form of animal life whatever. So the phrase serves as a kind of commentary, and a serious one, on the imagined courtship described. It implies the idea of an almost endless time, and as well the idea of the lack of intelligent direction in such a courtship. But on the surface, by the superficial absurdity of the phrase, the playful attitude is reënforced. The last two lines of the section give a kind of summarizing couplet which is a compliment to the lady.

But the poet has deliberately made the first section of the poem playful, conversational, and

absurd, not because he intended the poem to keep that level, but because he wanted the effect of sharp and dramatic contrast. Observe the sudden and shocking turn to the serious in the first couplet of the second section. The lover is haunted by the brevity of life. And observe the different kind of imagery used, imagery no longer absurd or playful but grand: "Time's wingèd chariot," "Deserts of vast eternity," and the stillness of the "marble vault" of the tomb. But then the poet again changes the tone, and the approach to his subject, by establishing another contrast. From the grand imagery of the marble vault, the chariot, and the desert, he turns to the worm, presenting, with a kind of suppressed sarcasm, the idea of the grave worm as a lover. The implied question to the lady is this: which lover does she prefer, the speaker or the worm—for the worm will later have the freedom of her body no matter how vigilantly she maintains her virtue in life? Then, as in the first section, the poet closes with a kind of summarizing couplet:

> The grave's a fine and private place,
> But none, I think, do there embrace.

The couplet is all the more effective because it says less than could be said. It is an understatement. The poet even pretends that he does not know, that he has only heard it reported, that there is no love in the grave. Furthermore, it is ironical, because the poet says that the grave has the very finest quality of a place for love, for it is "private." In the last six lines of the second section the poet repeats the playful and politely ironical manner of the first section, but now the subject matter, death and physical decay, is one of terrifying seriousness. But the poet refuses to surrender to that, and so treats it indirectly. The ironical overstatement, or exaggeration, of the first section is contrasted with the ironical understatement of the second section. The contrast gives an added point to each section after the reader is acquainted with the poem.

The third section, which gives the conclusion of the argument, also gives a resolution of the ironical contrasts built up in the preceding parts of the poem, just as a chord may resolve a musical composition. Observe the exciting quality of the imagery: "instant fires," "amorous birds of prey," "at once our time devour," "tear our pleasures," etc., the faster rhythm, etc. All of the imagery is directed, without irony or reservation on the part of the poet in the immediate statement, toward giving the effect of swiftness and exuberant vitality. But observe how the last couplet changes the effect from one of sheer exuberance and uncontrolled vitality by bringing the last section into a more complicated relation with the preceding sections. The last couplet is a kind of epigram, a paradox, a summary of the whole poem. It says: if we are not strong enough to conquer time and make ourselves immortal, we at least can be strong enough to make time pass faster. This connects the last section with the other two by emphasizing again the ideas of time and death. Furthermore, it makes the connection, by the very tone of the statement, for the couplet is again ironical and conversational, in contrast to the tone of the preceding ten lines; therefore, it echoes effects found earlier in the poem.

This discussion began with one question stated in two different ways. What use does the poet make of the outline of his argument? How does the meaning of the poem differ, in the end, from the meaning of the argument? It may now be easier to give some answer.

The poet merely uses the argument as a framework for the poem, for the situation of a lover speaking to his mistress is a fiction adopted by the poet to give a dramatic form to his theme. This theme may be stated in the form of a question: what should man's attitude be in the face of death and his ignorance of any life after death? He proposes this question, through the lips of the lover, to the mistress, and then gives the answer: man cannot master death, but he can attempt, by an exercise of his will, to master life by living as intensely as possible. But the poet wanted to indicate that his theme was important and his subject complicated and difficult. Therefore he used variations of tone, contrasted overstatement and understatement, and employed irony. He did not want the reader to feel that any one part of the poem was, as it were, ignorant of the rest of the poem. He did not want the poem to appear too glib and easy, for he believed that that would insult the underlying seriousness of his subject. He wanted the poem to appear controlled, and self-possessed; to give this effect he used overstatement only for the witty and playful part of the poem, and understatement for the most serious parts. He did not want to give an impression of simple pathos over the fact that beauty must fade and love must pass, etc. He wanted to give a more mature impression, one mixed with intelligence and will. After this examination, one may see that the prose paraphrase of the poem—the attempt to say the thing directly in so many words—will result in a forced and didactic effect. That is, the idea of the poem has to be communicated through the operation of many factors: tone, attitude, imagery, rhythm, etc. The paraphrase is not a true paraphrase, and can never be, because it must remain too simple; it omits most of the things that make the poem what it is—an experience in itself.

Other matters necessarily omitted in the foregoing account have to do with the relation of the poem to its historical and cultural background, the special literary conventions which it embodies, and certain traditional themes which it echoes. It might be interesting to point out briefly some of this conventional and traditional material which forms the special literary setting of this poem.

One might begin with the Petrarchan imagery. The term comes from the Italian poet Petrarch (1304-1374), whose sonnets to his mistress Laura greatly influenced Renaissance poetry, including the poetry of the English Renaissance. The typical Petrarchan mistress is beautiful and virtuous but cold-hearted and disdainful of love. Petrarchan imagery is usually extravagant: the mistress has teeth of pearl, lips of coral, hair of gold, cheeks in which roses bloom, but her breast is as cold and hard as marble. By Elizabethan times, the extravagance had gone so far and the images had become so trite, that a poet like Shakespeare sometimes mocked at the imagery. In Sonnet 130 he tells us that *his* mistress' eyes "are nothing like the sun" and that if hairs are wires, then black, not gold, wires grow upon his mistress' head.

During the latter part of the sixteenth and the first part of the seventeenth century the poetic lover sometimes tones down the extravagant imagery, sometimes makes fun of the very extravagance, and sometimes tries to give it freshness by giving it a new twist. Thomas Carew's song (p. 354) is a rather nice instance of the poet's success in paying high-flown compliments which yet seem fresh and charming. His mistress does not have gold wires upon her head but the golden atoms of day do find a lodging place in her hair. Her eyes are not merely like stars: they are the spheres in which the stars fallen from heaven find a welcome home.

Michael Drayton's sonnet "The Parting" (p. 329) shows another aspect of Petrarchan imagery, the use of the adventures of Cupid as a device for complimenting the lady. Though the little god of love is mortally sick and lies on his death bed, the poet's mistress is such that she could work the miracle of making him recover if she but would. Donne's "The Good Morrow" (p. 366) represents still another strategy for revivifying the Petrarchan mode. He uses its bloodless abstractions and trite absurdities as a foil for his own realism, cynicism, and gay wit. But in doing so he does not forego the ingenuity with which Petrarchan imagery was often so elaborately wrought.

Marvell's "To his Coy Mistress" exhibits a related method for turning to account the Petrarchan conventions of compliment. Notice, for example, the first twenty lines. The compliments to the lady are as extravagant as any Petrarchan sonneteer ever devised. But their very absurdity allows the poet to topple them over into an irony which perfectly fits his purpose.

We have already remarked that the lady of the Petrarchan convention, though beautiful and exciting ardent love, is herself cold and disdainful. Her diffidence calls to mind another convention, which was very popular in the poetry of the Renaissance. Many poems—though not necessarily worked out in Petrarchan imagery—plead with the mistress to put off coyness and accept love while the lovers are still young. Such poems are sometimes called *carpe diem* poems, for *carpe diem* means "seize the day." Robert

Herrick's little poem entitled "To the Virgins, to Make Much of Time" is a good instance. It begins "Gather ye Rose-buds while ye may, / Old Time is still a-flying: / And this same flower that smiles today, / Tomorrow will be dying." Waller's "Song" (p. 307) is another instance. So, in its own way, is "the True Lover" (p. 297), for in this poem the girl has not heeded her lover's plea. "To His Coy Mistress" obviously belongs to the *carpe diem* tradition, but it is a late and complicated instance, not a simple and joyous invitation to love. It is rich, massive, and almost "philosophical" in its power.

Sonnet 129

WILLIAM SHAKESPEARE
(1564-1616)

Th' expense of Spirit in a waste of shame
Is lust in action; and till action, lust
Is perjured, murderous, bloody, full of blame,
Savage, extreme, rude, cruel, not to trust;
Enjoyed no sooner but despisèd straight;   5
Past reason hunted; and, no sooner had,
Past reason hated, as a swallow'd bait
On purpose laid to make the taker mad:
Mad in pursuit, and in possession so;
Had, having, and in quest to have,
     extreme;   10
A bliss in proof, and proved, a very woe;
Before, a joy proposed; behind, a dream.
   All this the world well knows; yet none
      knows well
   To shun the heaven that leads men to this
      hell.

1. What is the theme of this sonnet? What does the imagery contribute to the theme?
2. Does the speaker make a series of "statements" about the nature of lust? Does he give a sense of dramatic force to his utterance? If so, how?
3. How complex is the idea expressed in this sonnet? Is the complexity justified?
4. What is the purpose of the frequent repetitions of particular words?
5. Compare this sonnet with "The World Is Too

Much With Us" with reference to: (a) the relation of image to statement, (b) the relation of image to image, and (c) the poet's success in giving a sense of dramatic utterance.

Sonnet 146

WILLIAM SHAKESPEARE
(1564-1616)

Poor soul, the center of my sinful earth,
Thrall to these rebel powers that thee array
Why dost thou pine within and suffer dearth,
Painting thy outward walls so costly gay?
Why so large cost, having so short a lease,   5
Dost thou upon thy fading mansion spend?
Shall worms, inheritors of this excess,
Eat up thy charge? is this thy bod's end?
Then, soul, live thou upon thy servant's loss,
And let that pine to aggravate thy store;   10
Buy terms divine in selling hours of dross;
Within be fed, without be rich no more:
   So shall thou feed on Death, that feeds on men,
   And Death once dead, there's no more dying then.

This sonnet is obviously based upon Christian theology. To say so is not, however, to imply that the sonnet is simply a bit of versified theology, that it does not have its own dramatic organization, or that it has nothing to say to people who are unable to accept its theology. As a work of art it has its own structure through which its meaning is presented. But it may be interesting—and useful—to see how this poem is related to the culture out of which it came, a culture which was shot through and through with theological concepts.

In the orthodox Christian conception, God created the world and what he created was good, including man's senses and his appetites. But though man was created good and sinless, he "fell," through pride, followed his own will rather than God's, and in so doing, cut himself off from the fountain of life. Hence the wages of sin was indeed death. (Milton was to put it thus in his *Paradise Lost:* Adam's sin of pride "Brought Death into the World, and all our woe.") In the Christian scheme, however, man is given a second chance when God, taking on human flesh in the person of Christ, becomes "the second Adam" and through his sacrificial death, promises to redeem man from the death which in his now corrupted nature he is doomed to suffer.

The notion that the flesh is in itself evil runs counter to the Hebraic-Christian conception of its originally divine origin; even so, the tendency to regard all matter as evil did appear early in the Christian era, and though vigorously condemned as heretical, is still to be met with. The reference to "my sinful earth" may suggest that Shakespeare's sonnet partakes of this heresy. But one must take into account the stress upon the "rebel powers" that hold the soul in thrall: in the general context, the rebellion is not merely against the soul but against God. Indeed, it can be argued that the emphasis here is not upon the essential wickedness of the flesh but upon the subversion that the rebel powers have effected, a subversion in which the master is being ruled by his own servant. In these terms the body can become a distraction and worse. At best, it is no permanent abiding place but "now to Death devote." Hence, the admonition given in this poem echoes St. Matthew 6:19-20: "Lay not up for yourselves treasures upon earth, where moth and rust doth corrupt, and where thieves break through and steal: but lay up for yourselves treasures in heaven, where neither moth nor rust doth corrupt, and where thieves do not break through nor steal."

So much for the general doctrinal basis. Consider how the poem manages to state and dramatize the theological position on which it rests.

1. Paraphrase the argument of the poem. What does even a careful paraphrase leave out?

2. The dominant metaphor is drawn from business life—investment in a house. Is this metaphor out of keeping with the solemnity of the theme? Or is it well chosen? How does it affect the tone of the poem?

3. How is the dominant metaphor related to the subsidiary imagery of the poem?

Sonnets at Christmas

1934

ALLEN TATE (1899-   )

I

This is the day His hour of life draws near,
Let me get ready from head to foot for it
Most handily with eyes to pick the year
For small feed to reward a feathered wit.
Some men would see it an epiphany   5
At ease, at food and drink, others at chase
Yet I, stung lassitude, with ecstasy
Unspent argue with the season's difficult case
So: Man, dull critter of enormous head,
What would he look at in the coiling sky?   10
But I must kneel again unto the Dead
While Christmas bells of paper white and red,
Figured with boys and girls spilt from a sled,
Ring out the silence I am nourished by.

II

Ah, Christ, I love you rings to the wild sky
And I must think a little of the past:
When I was ten I told a stinking lie
That got a black boy whipped; but now at last
The going years, caught in an accurate glow,   5
Reverse like balls englished upon green baize—
Let them return, let the round trumpets blow
The ancient crackle of the Christ's deep gaze.
Deafened and blind, with senses yet unfound,
Am I, untutored to the after-wit   10
Of knowledge, knowing a nightmare has no
   sound;
Therefore with idle hands and head I sit
In late December before the fire's daze
Punished by crimes of which I would be quit.

1. What is the situation portrayed in these sonnets? What sort of person is the speaker? If the Christmas season stirs him neither to simple holiday gaiety nor to fervent devotion, in what way does it affect him?

2. How has the poet used the circumstantial detail of the Christmas season? Consider, for example, this detail: Christmas bells have become holiday decoration of gaily colored paper; they "ring" out only silence, etc.

3. What is the season's "difficult case"? In what sense has the speaker argued it? Why is modern man said to be a creature of "enormous head"? Does the enormity of his head have anything to do with his plight? What light does the Christmas season shed upon his characteristic plight?

Christmas Eve Under Hooker's Statue

ROBERT LOWELL (1917-   )

Tonight in a blackout. Twenty years ago
I hung my stocking on the tree, and hell's
Serpent entwined the apple in the toe
To sting the child with knowledge. Hooker's
   heels
Kicking at nothing in the shifting snow,   5
A cannon and a cairn of cannon balls
Rusting before the blackened Statehouse, know
How the long horn of plenty broke like glass
In Hooker's gauntlets. Once I came from Mass;
Now storm-clouds shelter Christmas, once
   again   10
Mars meets his fruitless star with open arms,
His heavy sabre flashes with the rime,
The war-god's bronzed and empty forehead
   forms
Anonymous machinery from raw men;
The cannon on the Common cannot stun   15
The blundering butcher as he rides on Time—
The barrel clinks with holly. I am cold:
I ask for bread, my father gives me mould;

His stocking is full of stones. Santa in red
Is crowned with wizened berries. Man of
   war,   20
Where is the summer's garden? In its bed
The ancient speckled serpent will appear,
And black-eyed susan with her frizzled head.
When Chancellorsville mowed down the
   volunteer,
"All wars are boyish," Herman Melville
   said;   25

But we are old, our fields are running wild:
Till Christ again turn wanderer and child.

The scene is Boston ("the cannon on the Common"); the time 1944. Hooker, whose statue is alluded to, commanded the Army of the Potomac in its defeat at Chancellorsville.

1. Compare the situation presented here with that presented in the preceding sonnets by Tate. Compare and contrast the attitudes characterizing the speakers in these poems.
2. What comment does this poem make upon our civilization? How is this comment made? What part is played by the imagery and other devices of indirection? May it be said that in this poem references to childhood (the Christmas stocking, Santa Claus, etc.) are played off against images of brutality and war (Hooker's gauntlets, Mars, etc.)? To what effect?
3. The comparisons seem almost studiedly violent (*e.g.* "The barrel clinks with holly" l. 17). Is the violence justified?
4. What is the meaning of the last line of the poem? Does it summarize what the poem "says"? Does it depend for its precise meaning upon the rest of the poem?

A Psalm of Life

*What the Heart of the Young Man
Said to the Psalmist*

HENRY WADSWORTH
LONGFELLOW (1807-1882)

Tell me not in mournful numbers,
    Life is but an empty dream!—
For the soul is dead that slumbers,
    And things are not what they seem.

Life is real! Life is earnest!   5
    And the grave is not its goal;
Dust thou art, to dust returnest,
    Was not spoken of the soul.

Not enjoyment, and not sorrow,
    Is our destined end or way;   10
But to act, that each tomorrow
    Find us farther than today.

Art is long, and Time is fleeting,
    And our hearts, though stout and brave,
Still, like muffled drums, are beating   15
    Funeral marches to the grave.

In the world's broad field of battle,
    In the bivouac of Life,
Be not like dumb, driven cattle!
    Be a hero in the strife!   20

Trust no Future, howe'er pleasant!
    Let the dead Past bury its dead!
Act,—act in the living Present!
    Heart within, and God o'erhead!

Lives of great men all remind us   25
    We can make our lives sublime,
And, departing leave behind us
    Footprints on the sands of time;

Footprints, that perhaps another,
    Sailing o'er life's solemn main,   30
A forlorn and shipwrecked brother,
    Seeing, shall take heart again.

Let us, then, be up and doing,
    With a heart for any fate;
Still achieving, still pursuing,   35
    Learn to labor and to wait.

1. The morals proposed in this poem are excellent. Is the work, however, good poetry?
2. What is the relation of the figures used to the theme?
3. What is the tone?

The Funeral

JOHN DONNE (1573-1631)

Whoever comes to shroud me, do not harm
    Nor question much
That subtle wreath of hair about mine arm;
The mystery, the sign you must not touch,
    For 'tis my outward soul,   5
Viceroy to that which, unto heav'n being gone,
    Will leave this to control

And keep these limbs, her provinces, from dissolution.

For if the sinewy thread my brain lets fall
   Through every part   10
Can tie those parts, and make me one of all;
Those hairs, which upward grew, and strength
    and art
   Have from a better brain,
Can better do 't: except she meant that I
   By this should know my pain,   15
As prisoners then are manacled, when they're
   condemned to die.

Whate'er she meant by 't, bury it with me,
   For since I am
Love's martyr, it might breed idolatry
If into other hands these reliques came.   20
   As 'twas humility
T' afford to it all that a soul can do,
   So 'tis some bravery
That, since you would have none of me, I bury
   some of you.

The poet's mistress has given him a bracelet
woven out of her own hair. He wears it about his
arm, and asks that it be left upon his arm when his
body is buried. The motive for such an act is one
that most of us can take for granted: even in death
one wishes to cling to a precious memento of the
beloved. But it is precisely the motive (or the various motives) that the speaker here undertakes to
discuss.

1. The bracelet of hair is to be his "outward
soul" and is thus to serve to preserve his body. How
are the various analogies between nerves and hairs,
kings and viceroys, etc., worked out in ll. 1-14? What
is the tone of the passage? How does the elaborate
(and even fantastic) analogy qualify the tone?
2. What shift of tone occurs with "except she
meant" (l. 14)? Has it just occurred to him that she
may have given him the bracelet for purposes quite
different from those envisaged in ll. 1-14? What is
the speaker's attitude toward his mistress?
3. What is the tone of ll. 17ff.? How does his
new justification for burying the bracelet with him
grow out of the preceding lines? What is implied by
his calling himself "Love's martyr" (l. 19)?
4. Is his final gesture one of adoration or of
arrogance? What is the tone of ll. 21-24? Is he teasing his mistress? Persisting in his love for her in spite

of the fact that she will "have none of" him? Or
what?
5. What is the poet's final attitude toward his
mistress? What is the effect of the complex reasoning on the tone of the poem?

Eighth Air Force
RANDALL JARRELL (1914-   )

If, in an odd angle of the hutment,
A puppy laps the water from a can
Of flowers, and the drunk sergeant shaving
Whistles *O Paradiso!*—shall I say that man
Is not as men have said: a wolf to man?   5

The other murderers troop in yawning;
Three of them play Pitch, one sleeps, and one
Lies counting missions, lies there sweating
Till even his heart beats: One; One; One.
O murderers! . . . Still, this is how it's
   done: 10

This is war. . . . But since these play, before
   they die,
Like puppies with their puppy; since, a man,
I did as these have done, but did not die—
I will content the people as I can
And give up these to them: Behold the
   man!   15

I have suffered, in a dream, because of him,
Many things; for this last saviour, man,
I have lied as I lie now. But what is lying?
Men wash their hands, in blood, as best they
   can:
I find no fault in this just man.   20

This poem provides a very interesting example of how a poem makes its "statement" and
how the method of the presentation qualifies
and defines what is presented. This poem is,
we may say, "about" modern war. It is also
about the individual's sense of guilt and responsibility. It is also about the nature of Man
—especially as Man's nature is revealed by participation in modern war. But what does the

poem "say" about war, about guilt, about Man's essential nature?

To answer this question adequately, we shall have to examine, not only what is literally said by the speaker, but the implied character of the speaker, the circumstances under which he speaks, and the tone in which what he says is uttered. That is to say: we shall have to consider the speaker, not merely to be the mouth-piece of the poet—he may very well be that—but also as a dramatic character whose actions and utterances are rooted in a dramatic context. Let us consider this poem therefore as we would consider a play.

The scene is evidently an air base in England during World War II. The airmen in their hutment are casual enough and honest enough to be convincing. The raw building is domesticated: there are the flowers in water from which the mascot, a puppy, laps. There is the drunken sergeant, whistling an opera aria as he shaves. These "murderers," as the speaker is casually to call the airmen in the next stanza, display a touching regard for the human values. How, then, can one say that man is a wolf to man (cf. Benjamin Franklin's statement: "O that . . . men would cease to be as wolves to one another . . .") since these young soldiers "play before they die, like puppies with their puppy." But the casual presence of the puppy in the hutment allows us to take the stanza both ways, for the dog is a kind of tamed and domesticated wolf, and his presence may suggest that the hutment is a wolf den. After all, the timber wolf plays with its puppies.

The second stanza takes the theme to a perfectly explicit conclusion. If three of the men play pitch, and one is asleep, at least one man is awake and counts himself and his companions murderers. But his unvoiced cry "O murderers" is met, countered, and dismissed with the next two lines: ". . . Still this is how it is done: This is a war. . . ."

The note of casuistry and cynical apology prepares for a brilliant and rich resolving image, the image of Pontius Pilate, which is announced specifically in the third stanza:

I will content the people as I can
And give up these to them: Behold the man!

Yet if Pilate as he is first presented, is a jesting Pilate, who asks "What is truth?" it is a bitter and grieving Pilate who speaks the conclusion of the poem. It is the integrity of Man himself that is at stake. Is man a cruel animal, a wolf, or is he the last saviour, the Christ of our modern religion of humanity?

The Pontius Pilate metaphor, as the poet uses it, becomes a device for tremendous concentration. For the speaker (presumably the young airman who cried "O murderers") is himself the confessed murderer under judgment, and also the Pilate who judges, and he is, at least as a representative of man, the saviour whom the mob would condemn. He is even Pilate's better nature, his wife, for the lines "I have suffered, in a dream, because of him, Many things" is merely a rearrangement of Matthew 27:19, the speech of Pilate's wife to her husband. But this last item is more than a reminiscence of the scriptural scene. It reinforces the speaker's present dilemma. The modern has had high hopes for mankind: are the hopes merely a dream? Is man finally incorrigible, merely a cruel beast? The speaker's present torture springs from the hope and from his reluctance to dismiss it as an empty dream. This Pilate is even harder-pressed than was the Roman magistrate. For he must convince himself of this last saviour's innocence. But he has lied for him before. He will lie for him now.

Men wash their hands, in blood, as best they can:
I find no fault in this just man.

What is the meaning of "Men wash their hands, in blood, as best they can"? It can mean: since my own hands are bloody, I have no right to condemn the rest. It can mean: I know that man can love justice even though his hands are bloody, for there is blood on mine. It can mean: men are essentially decent; they try to keep their hands clean even if they have only blood in which to wash them. None of these meanings cancels out the others. All are relevant; and each meaning contributes to the total meaning of the poem.

Does the poem say that man is not a beast but essentially good? Yes, but the affirmation is qualified—qualified by the whole context of the situation—qualified by the fact that it is spoken by a Pilate who contents the people as he washes his own hands in blood. The sense of self-guilt, the yearning to believe in man's goodness, the knowledge of the difficulty in maintaining such a belief—all work to render accurately and sensitively the whole situation.

But the last paragraph may be misleading. To some students it may lead to a misapprehension of the function of irony; that is, the student may feel that the function of the irony in the poem is to pare the theme of man's goodness down to acceptable dimensions. We can accept it because the poet has indicated that he does not really believe in it himself. Such an account is, however, not what the editors intend to say.

A better way of stating the matter would be something like this: we do not ask the poet—in this or any other case—to bring his poem into line with our personal beliefs; still less ought we demand that he flatter our personal beliefs, whatever they may be. What we do ask is that the poet dramatize the situation so sensitively, so honestly, and with such fidelity to the total situation that it is no longer a question of our beliefs, but of our participation in the poetic experience. In "Eighth Air Force," the poet manages to bring us, by an act of imagination, to the most penetrating insight. Participating in that insight, we doubtless become better citizens. (One of the "uses" of poetry is to make us better citizens.) But poetry is not the eloquent rendition of the good citizen's creed. Poetry must carry us beyond the abstract creed into the very matrix out of which our creeds come and from which they are abstracted.

For the theme in a genuine poem does not confront us as abstraction—that is, as one man's generalization from the relevant particulars. Finding its proper symbol, defined and refined by the participating metaphors, the theme becomes a part of the reality in which we live—an insight, rooted in and growing out of concrete experience, many-sided, three-dimensional. Even the resistance to generalization has its part in this process—even the drag of the particulars away from the universal—even the tension of opposing themes—play their parts.

Hollywood

KARL SHAPIRO (1913-   )

Farthest from any war, unique in time
Like Athens or Baghdad, this city lies
Between dry purple mountains and the sea.
The air is clear and famous, every day
Bright as a postcard, bringing bungalows   5
   And sights. The broad nights advertise
For love and music and astronomy.

Heart of a continent, the hearts converge
On open boulevards where palms are nursed
With flare-pots like a grove, on villa roads   10
Where castles cultivated like a style
Breed fabulous metaphors in foreign stone,
   And on enormous movie lots
Where history repeats its vivid blunders.

Alice and Cinderella are most real.   15
Here may the tourist, quite sincere at last,
Rest from his dream of travels. All is new,
No ruins claim his awe, and permanence,
Despised like customs, fails at every turn.
   Here where the eccentric thrives,   20
Laughter and love are leading industries.

Luck is another. Here the body-guard,
The parasite, the scholar are well paid,
The quack erects his alabaster office,
The moron and the genius are enshrined,   25
And the mystic makes a fortune quietly;
   Here all superlatives come true
And beauty is marketed like a basic food.

O can we understand it? Is it ours,
A crude whim of a beginning people,   30
A private orgy in a secluded spot?
Or alien like the word *harem*, or true
Like hideous Pittsburgh or depraved Atlanta?
   Is adolescence just as vile
As this its architecture and its talk?   35

Or are they parvenus, like boys and girls?
Or ours and happy, cleverest of all?

Yes, Yes. Though glamorous to the ignorant
This is the simplest city, a new school.
What is more nearly ours? If soul can mean   40
  The civilization of the brain,
This is a soul, a possibly proud Florence.

    What do you make of this poem?

Colonel Shaw and the Massachusetts' 54th

"Relinquunt omnia servare rem publicam."

ROBERT LOWELL (1917-   )

The old South Boston Aquarium stands
in a Sahara of snow now. Its broken windows
  are boarded.
The bronze weathervane cod has lost half its
  scales.
The air tanks are dry.

Once my nose crawled like a snail on the
  glass;   5
my hand tingled
to burst the bubbles
drifting from the noses of the cowed, compliant
  fish.

My hand draws back. I often sigh still
for the dark downward and vegetating
  kingdom   10
of the fish and reptile. One morning last March,
I pressed against the new barbed and galvanized

fence on the Boston Common. Behind their cage,
yellow dinosaur steamshovels were grunting
as they cropped up tons of mush and grass   15
to gouge their underworld garage.

Parking-spaces luxuriate like civic
sandpiles in the heart of Boston.
A girdle of orange, Puritan-pumpkin colored
  girders
braces the tingling Statehouse,   20

shaking over the excavations, as it faces Colonel
  Shaw
and his bell-cheeked Negro infantry
on St. Gaudens' shaking Civil War relief,
propped by a plank splint against the garage's
  earthquake.

Two months after marching through Boston,   25
half the regiment was dead;
at the dedication,
William James could almost hear the bronze
  Negroes breathe.
Their monument sticks like a fishbone
in the City's throat.   30
Its Colonel is as lean
as a compass-needle.

He has an angry wrenlike vigilance,
a greyhound's gentle tautness;
he seems to wince at pleasure,   35
and suffocate for privacy.

He is out of bounds now. He rejoices in man's
  lovely,
peculiar power to choose life and die—
when he leads his black soldiers to death,
he cannot bend his back.   40

On a thousand small town New England greens,
the old white churches hold their air
of sparse, sincere rebellion; frayed flags
quilt the graveyards of the Grand Army of the
  Republic.

The stone statues of the abstract Union
  Soldier   45
grow slimmer and younger each year—
wasp-waisted, they doze over muskets
and muse through their sideburns . . .

Shaw's father wanted no monument
except the ditch,   50
where his son's body was thrown
and lost with his "niggers."

The ditch is nearer.
There are no statues for the last war here;
on Boyleston Street, a commercial
  photograph   55
shows Hiroshima boiling

over a Mosler Safe, the "Rock of Ages"
that survived the blast. Space is nearer.
When I crouch to my television set,
the drained faces of Negro children rise like
    balloons.   60

Colonel Shaw
is riding on his bubble,
he waits
for the blessed break.

The Aquarium is gone. Everywhere,   65
giant finned cars nose forward like fish;
a savage servility
slides by on grease.

Col. Robert Shaw left his friends and classmates
of the Harvard regiment to take command of a Negro
regiment and led it through heavy fighting during
the Civil War. He was killed in the War, and a
monument executed by St. Gaudens was erected to
his memory. William James, the celebrated psychologist and brother of the novelist, spoke at the dedication of the monument. But now, the modern poet
reflects, Colonel Shaw "is out of bounds." His monument faces a new world—of bulldozers, television
sets, atomic bombs, and fin-tailed automobiles.

1. In what senses is Shaw now "out of bounds"?
What does the poet mean? What does this poem
mean?

2. Why the contrast between the poet as boy
looking at the fish in the aquarium and the poet as
man watching the "dinosaur steamshovels"? Why the
contrast between the "cowed, compliant fish" and
the cars that "nose forward like fish"? What is the
principle that determines the choice of images in this
poem?

3. The Colonel is said to be like a wren and like
a greyhound. How does he—according to this poem
—define himself as a man and not a thing or an
animal?

4. What is the meaning of the last two lines of
the poem? How do these lines relate to the heroism
of Shaw and his men?

The Little Black Boy

WILLIAM BLAKE (1757-1827)

My mother bore me in the southern wild,
And I am black, but O! my soul is white;
White as an angel is the English child,
But I am black, as if bereav'd of light.

My mother taught me underneath a tree,   5
And sitting down before the heat of day,
She took me on her lap and kissed me,
And pointing to the east, began to say:

"Look on the rising sun: there God does live,
And gives his light, and gives his heat away;   10
And flowers and trees and beasts and men
    receive
Comfort in morning, joy in the noonday.

"And we are put on earth a little space,
That we may learn to bear the beams of love;
And these black bodies and this sunburnt
    face   15
Is but a cloud, and like a shady grove.

"For when our souls have learn'd the heat to
    bear,
The cloud will vanish; we shall hear his voice,
Saying: 'Come out from the grove, my love
    and care,
'And round my golden tent like lambs
    rejoice.' "   20

Thus did my mother say, and kissed me;
And thus I say to little English boy:
When I from black and he from white cloud
    free,
And round the tent of God like lambs we joy,

I'll shade him from the heat, till he can bear   25
To lean in joy upon our father's knee;
And then I'll stand and stroke his silver hair,
And be like him, and he will then love me.

1. This poem is ostensibly spoken by the "little
black boy." Does the poet attempt to suggest realistic speech? May it be said that the poem is spoken
not by an actual boy but by the spirit of the little
black boy? To whom is the poem addressed? To the
little English boy? Or to the speaker himself? Or to
whom?

2. Is the tone one of apology for his blackness?
Or defiant justification? Or quiet and confident explanation? Or what?

3. Note that though the blackness is described
as a cloud (to protect from the intensity of the sun),
the whiteness (of the little English boy) is described
as a cloud too. What is the cloud, whether black or
white? What is its relation to the sun?

4. What does the last stanza imply about the little English boy's attitude toward the little black boy?

Does the speaker take for granted that he is not now loved by the English boy? Does he speak wistfully? With degrading humility? Or in what tone of voice?

FROM

Song of Myself
WALT WHITMAN (1819-1892)

The wild gander leads his flock through the cool night,
Ya-honk he says, and sounds it down to me like an invitation,
The pert may suppose it meaningless, but I listening close,
Find its purpose and place up there toward the wintry sky.

The sharp-hoof'd moose of the north, the cat on the house-sill, the chickadee, the prairie-dog, 5
The litter of the grunting sow as they tug at her teats,
The brood of the turkey-hen and she with her half-spread wings,
I see in them and myself the same old law.

The press of my foot to the earth springs a hundred affections,
They scorn the best I can do to relate them.   10

I am enamour'd of growing out-doors,
Of men that live among cattle or taste of the ocean or woods,

Of the builders and steerers of ships and the wielders of axes and mauls, and the drivers of horses,
I can eat and sleep with them week in and week out.

What is commonest, cheapest, nearest, easiest, is Me,   15
Me going in for my chances, spending for vast returns,
Adorning myself to bestow myself on the first that will take me,
Not asking the sky to come down to my good will,
Scattering it freely forever.

The pure contralto sings in the organ loft,   20
The carpenter dresses his plank, the tongue of his foreplane whistles its wild ascending lisp,
The married and unmarried children ride home to their Thanksgiving dinner,
The pilot seizes the king-pin, he heaves down with a strong arm,
The mate stands braced in the whale-boat, lance and harpoon are ready,
The duck-shooter walks by silent and cautious stretches,   25
The deacons are ordain'd with cross'd hands at the altar,
The spinning-girl retreats and advances to the hum of the big wheel,
The farmer stops by the bars as he walks on a First-day loafe and looks at the oats and rye,
The lunatic is carried at last to the asylum a confirm'd case,
(He will never sleep any more as he did in the cot in his mother's bedroom;)   30
The jour printer with gray head and gaunt jaws works at his case,
He turns his quid of tobacco while his eyes blurr with the manuscript;
The malform'd limbs are tied to the surgeon's table,
What is removed drops horribly in a pail;
The quadroon girl is sold at the auction-stand, the drunkard nods by the bar-room stove,   35
The machinist rolls up his sleeves, the policeman travels his beat, the gate-keeper marks who pass,
The young fellow drives the express-wagon, (I love him, though I do not know him;)
The half-breed straps on his light boots to compete in the race,
The western turkey-shooting draws old and young, some lean on their rifles, some sit on logs,
Out from the crowd steps the marksman, takes his position, levels his piece;   40
The groups of newly-come immigrants cover the wharf or levee,
As the woolly-pates hoe in the sugar-field, the overseer views them from his saddle,
The bugle calls in the ball-room, the gentlemen run for their partners, the dancers bow to each other,

The youth lies awake in the cedar-roof'd garret
and harks to the musical rain,

The Wolverine sets traps on the creek that helps
fill the Huron,   45

The squaw wrapt in her yellow-hemm'd cloth
is offering moccasins and bead-bags for sale,

The connoisseur peers along the exhibition-
gallery with half-shut eyes bent sideways,

As the deck-hands make fast the steamboat the
plank is thrown for the shore-going passengers,

The young sister holds out the skein while the
elder sister winds it off in a ball, and stops now
and then for the knots,

The one-year wife is recovering and happy having a week ago borne her first child.   50

The clean-hair'd Yankee girl works with her
sewing-machine or in the factory or mill,

The paving-man leans on his two-handed ram-
mer, the reporter's lead flies swiftly over the
note-book, the sign-painter is lettering with
blue and gold,

The canal boy trots on the tow-path, the bookkeeper counts at his desk, the shoemaker waxes
his thread,

The conductor beats time for the band and all
the performers follow him,

The child is baptized, the convert is making his
first professions,   55

The regatta is spread on the bay, the race is
begun, (how the white sails sparkle!)

The drover watching his drove sings out to them
that would stray,

The pedler sweats with his pack on his back,
(the purchaser higgling about the odd cent;)

The bride unrumples her white dress, the
minute-hand of the clock moves slowly,

The opium-eater reclines with rigid head and
just-open'd lips,   60

The prostitute draggles her shawl, her bonnet
bobs on her tipsy and pimpled neck,

The crowd laugh at her blackguard oaths, the
men jeer and wink to each other,

(Miserable! I do not laugh at your oaths nor
jeer you;)

The President holding a cabinet council is surrounded by the great Secretaries,

On the piazza walk three matrons stately and
friendly with twined arms,   65

The crew of the fish-smack pack repeated layers
of halibut in the hold,

The Missourian crosses the plains toting his
wares and his cattle,

As the fare-collector goes through the train he
gives notice by the jingling of loose change,

The floor-men are laying the floor, the tinners
are tinning the roof, the masons are calling
for mortar,

In single file each shouldering his hod pass
onward the laborers;   70

Seasons pursuing each other the indescribable
crowd is gather'd, it is the fourth of Seventh-
month, (what salutes of cannon and small
arms!)

Seasons pursuing each other the plougher
ploughs, the mower mows, and the winter-
grain falls in the ground;

Off on the lakes the pike-fisher watches and waits
by the hole in the frozen surface,

The stumps stand thick round the clearing, the
squatter strikes deep with his axe,

Flatboatmen make fast towards dusk near the
cotton-wood or pecan-trees,   75

Coon-seekers go through the regions of the Red
River or through those drain'd by the Tennessee, or through those of the Arkansas,

Torches shine in the dark that hangs on the
Chattahooche or Altamahaw,

Patriarchs sit at supper with sons and grandsons
and great-grandsons around them,

In walls of adobie, in canvas tents, rest hunters
and trappers after their day's sport,

The city sleeps and the country sleeps,   80

The living sleep for their time, the dead sleep
for their time,

The old husband sleeps by his wife and the
young husband sleeps by his wife;

And these tend inward to me, and I tend outward to them,

And such as it is to be of these more or less I am,

And of these one and all I weave the song of
myself. . . .   85

I resist any thing better than my own
diversity,

Breathe the air but leave plenty after me,

And am not stuck up, and am in my place.

(The moth and the fish-eggs are in their place,

The bright suns I see and the dark suns I cannot
    see are in their place,   90

The palpable is in its place and the impalpable
    is in its place.)

These are really the thoughts of all men in all
    ages and lands, they are not original with me,

If they are not yours as much as mine they are
    nothing, or next to nothing,

If they are not the riddle and the untying of the
    riddle they are nothing,

If they are not just as close as they are distant
    they are nothing.   95

This is the grass that grows wherever the land
    is and the water is,

This is the common air that bathes the
    globe. . . .

Who goes there? hankering, gross, mystical,
    nude;

How is it I extract strength from the beef I
    eat?

What is a man anyhow? what am I? what are
    you?   100

All I mark as my own you shall offset it with
    your own,

Else it were time lost listening to me.

I do not snivel that snivel the world over,

That months are vacuums and the ground but
    wallow and filth.

Whimpering and truckling fold with powders
    for invalids, conformity goes to the fourth-
    remov'd,   105

I wear my hat as I please indoors or out.

Why should I pray? why should I venerate and
    be ceremonious?

Having pried through the strata, analyzed to a
    hair, counsel'd with doctors and calculated
    close,

I find no sweeter fat than sticks to my own
    bones.

In all people I see myself, none more and not
    one a barley-corn less,   110

And the good or bad I say of myself I say of
    them.

I know I am solid and sound,

To me the converging objects of the universe
    perpetually flow,

All are written to me, and I must get what the
    writing means.

I know I am deathless,   115

I know this orbit of mine cannot be swept by a
    carpenter's compass,

I know I shall not pass like a child's carlacue cut
    with a burnt stick at night.

I know I am august,

I do not trouble my spirit to vindicate itself or
    be understood,

I see that the elementary laws never apologize, 120

(I reckon I behave no prouder than the level
    I plant my house by, after all.)

I exist as I am, that is enough,

If no other in the world be aware I sit content,

And if each and all be aware I sit content.

One world is aware and by far the largest to me,
    and that is myself,   125

And whether I come to my own to-day or in
    ten thousand or ten million years,

I can cheerfully take it now, or with equal cheer-
    fulness I can wait.

My foothold is tenon'd and mortis'd in granite,

I laugh at what you call dissolution,

And I know the amplitude of time. . . .   130

Walt Whitman, a kosmos, of Manhattan the son,

Turbulent, fleshy, sensual, eating, drinking and
    breeding,

No sentimentalist, no stander above men and
    women or apart from them,

No more modest than immodest.

Unscrew the locks from the doors!   135

Unscrew the doors themselves from their jambs!

Whoever degrades another degrades me,

And whatever is done or said returns at last
    to me.

Through me the afflatus surging and surging,
    through me the current and index.

I speak the pass-word primeval, I give the sign
    of democracy,   140

By God! I will accept nothing which all cannot
    have their counterpart of on the same terms.

Through me many long dumb voices,
Voices of the interminable generations of pris-
 oners and slaves,
Voices of the diseas'd and despairing and of
 thieves and dwarfs,
Voices of cycles of preparation and accretion, 145
And of the threads that connects the stars, and
 of wombs and of the father-stuff,
And of the rights of them the others are down
 upon,
Of the deform'd, trivial, flat, foolish,
 despised,
Fog in the air, beetles rolling balls of dung.
To behold the day-break!   150
The little light fades the immense and diaph-
 anous shadows,
The air tastes good to my palate.

Hefts of the moving world at innocent gambols
 silently rising, freshly exuding,
Scooting obliquely high and low.

Something I cannot see puts upward libidinous
 prongs,   155
Seas of bright juice suffuse heaven.

The earth by the sky staid with, the daily close
 of their junction,
The heav'd challenge from the east that moment over my head,
The mocking taunt, See then whether you shall
 be master!

Dazzling and tremendous how quick the sun-
 rise would kill me,   160
If I could not now and always send sun-rise out
 of me.

We also ascend dazzling and tremendous as the
 sun,
We found our own O my soul in the calm and
 cool of the daybreak.

My voice goes after what my eyes cannot reach,
With the twirl of my tongue I encompass worlds
 and volumes of worlds.   165

Speech is the twin of my vision, it is unequal to
 measure itself,
It provokes me forever, it says sarcastically,
*Walt you contain enough, why don't you let it
 out then?*

Come now I will not be tantalized, you conceive
 too much of articulation,
Do you not know O speech how the buds be-
 neath you are folded?   170
Waiting in gloom, protected by frost,
The dirt receding before my prophetical screams,
I underlying causes to balance them at last,
My knowledge my live parts, it keeping tally
 with the meaning of all things,
Happiness, (which whoever hears me let him or
 her set out in search of this day.)   175

My final merit I refuse you, I refuse putting
 from me what I really am,
Encompass worlds, but never try to encompass
 me,
I crowd your sleekest and best by simply looking
 toward you.

Writing and talk do not prove me,
I carry the plenum of proof and every thing else
 in my face,   180
With the hush of my lips I wholly confound the
 skeptic. . . .

Space and Time! now I see it is true, what I
 guess'd at,
What I guess'd when I loaf'd on the grass,
What I guess'd while I lay alone in my bed,
And again as I walk'd the beach under the pal-
 ing stars of the morning.   185

My ties and ballasts leave me, my elbows rest
 in sea-gaps,
I skirt sierras, my palms cover continents,
I am afoot with my vision.

By the city's quadrangular houses—in log huts,
 camping with lunbermen,
Along the ruts of the turnpike, along the dry
 gulch and rivulet bed,   190
Weeding my onion-patch or hoeing rows of
 carrots and parsnips, crossing savannas, trailing in forests,
Prospecting, gold-digging, girdling the trees of a
 new purchase,
Scorch'd ankle-deep by the hot sand, hauling my
 boat down the shallow river,
Where the panther walks to and fro on a limb
 overhead, where the buck turns furiously at
 the hunter,

Where the rattlesnake suns his flabby length on a rock, where the otter is feeding on fish,   195
Where the alligator in his tough pimples sleeps by the bayou,
Where the black bear is searching for roots or honey, where the beaver pats the mud with his paddle-shaped tail;
Over the growing sugar, over the yellow-flower'd cotton plant, over the rice in its low moist field,
Over the sharp-peak'd farmhouse, with its scallop'd scum and slender shoots from the gutters,
Over the western persimmon, over the long-leav'd corn, over the delicate blue-flower flax,   200
Over the white and brown buckwheat, a hummer and buzzer there with the rest,
Over the dusky green of the rye as it ripples and shades in the breeze;

Scaling mountains, pulling myself cautiously up, holding on by low scragged limbs,
Walking the path worn in the grass and beat through the leaves of the brush,
Where the quail is whistling betwixt the woods and the wheat-lot,   205
Where the bat flies in the Seventh-month eve, where the great gold-bug drops through the dark,
Where the brook puts out of the roots of the old tree and flows to the meadow,
Where cattle stand and shake away flies with the tremulous shuddering of their hides,
Where the cheese-cloth hangs in the kitchen, where andirons straddle the hearth-slab, where cobwebs fall in festoons from the rafters;
Where trip-hammers crash, where the press is whirling its cylinders,   210
Where the human heart beats with terrible throes under its ribs,
Where the pear-shaped balloon is floating aloft, (floating in it myself and looking composedly down,)
Where the life-car is drawn on the slip-noose, where the heat hatches pale-green eggs in the dented sand,
Where the she-whale swims with her calf and never forsakes it,
Where the steam-ship trails hind-ways its long pennant of smoke,   215

Where the fin of the shark cuts like a black chip out of the water,
Where the half-burn'd brig is riding on unknown currents,
Where shells grow to her slimy deck, where the dead are corrupting below;
Where the dense-starr'd flag is borne at the head of the regiments,
Approaching Manhattan up by the long-stretching island,   220
Under Niagara, the cataract falling like a veil over my countenance,
Upon a door-step, upon the horse-block of hard wood outside,
Upon the race-course, or enjoying picnics or jigs or a good game of base-ball,
At he-festivals, with blackguard gibes, ironical license, bull-dances, drinking, laughter,
At the cider-mill tasting the sweets of the brown mash, sucking the juice through a straw,   225
At apple-peelings wanting kisses for all the red fruit I find,
At musters, beach-parties, friendly bees, huskings, house-raisings;
Where the mocking-bird sounds his delicious gurgles, cackles, screams, weeps,
Where the hay-rick stands in the barn-yard, where the dry-stalks are scatter'd, where the brood-cow waits in the hovel,
Where the bull advances to do his masculine work, where the stud to the mare, where the cock is treading the hen,   230
Where the heifers browse, where geese nip their food with short jerks,
Where sun-down shadows lengthen over the limitless and lonesome prairie,
Where herds of buffalo make a crawling spread of the square miles far and near,
Where the humming-bird shimmers, where the neck of the long-lived swan is curving and winding,
Where the laughing-gull scoots by the shore, where she laughs her near-human laugh,   235
Where bee-hives range on a gray bench in the garden half hid by the high weeds,
Where band-neck'd partridges roost in a ring on the ground with their heads out,
Where burial coaches enter the arch'd gates of a cemetery,

Where winter wolves bark amid wastes of snow
and icicled trees,

Where the yellow-crown'd heron comes to the
edge of the marsh at night and feeds upon
small crabs,   240

Where the splash of swimmers and divers cools
the warm noon,

Where the katy-did works her chromatic reed on
the walnut-tree over the well,

Through patches of citrons and cucumbers with
silver-wired leaves,

Through the salt-lick or orange glade, or under
conical firs,

Through the gymnasium, through the curtain'd
saloon, through the office or public hall;   245

Pleas'd with the native and pleas'd with the
foreign, pleas'd with the new and old,

Pleas'd with the homely woman as well as the
handsome,

Pleas'd with the quakeress as she puts off her
bonnet and talks melodiously,

Pleas'd with the tune of the choir of the white-
wash'd church,

Pleas'd with the earnest words of the sweating
Methodist preacher, impress'd seriously at the
camp-meeting;   250

Looking in at the shop-windows of Broadway the
whole forenoon, flatting the flesh of my nose
on the thick plate glass,

Wandering the same afternoon with my face
turn'd up to the clouds, or down a lane or
along the beach,

My right and left arms round the sides of two
friends, and I in the middle;

Coming home with the silent and dark-cheek'd
bush-boy, (behind me he rides at the drape of
the day,)

Far from the settlements studying the print of
animals' feet, or the moccasin print,   255

By the cot in the hospital reaching lemonade to
a feverish patient,

Nigh the coffin'd corpse when all is still, examining with a candle;

Voyaging to every port to dicker and adventure,

Hurrying with the modern crowd as eager and
fickle as any,

Hot toward one I hate, ready in my madness to
knife him,   260

Solitary at midnight in my back yard, my
thoughts gone from me a long while,

Walking the old hills of Judæa with the beautiful gentle God by my side,

Speeding through space, speeding through
heaven and the stars,

Speeding amid the seven satellites and the broad
ring, and the diameter of eighty thousand
miles,

Speeding with tail'd meteors, throwing fire-balls
like the rest,   265

Carrying the crescent child that carries its own
full mother in its belly,

Storming, enjoying, planning, loving, cautioning,

Backing and filling, appearing and disappearing,

I tread day and night such roads.

I visit the orchards of spheres and look at the
product,   270

And look at quintillions ripen'd and look at
quintillions green.

I fly those flights of a fluid and swallowing soul,

My course runs below the soundings of plummets.

I help myself to material and immaterial,

No guard can shut me off, no law prevent me.

I anchor my ship for a little while only,   275

My messengers continually cruise away or bring
their returns to me.

I go hunting polar furs and the seal, leaping
chasms with a pike-pointed staff, clinging to
topples of brittle and blue.

I ascend to the foretruck,

I take my place late at night in the crow's-nest,

We sail the arctic sea, it is plenty light
enough,   280

Through the clear atmosphere I stretch around
on the wonderful beauty,

The enormous masses of ice pass me and I pass
them, the scenery is plain in all directions,

The white-topt mountains show in the distance,
I fling out my fancies toward them,

We are approaching some great battle-field in
which we are soon to be engaged,   285

We pass the colossal outposts of the encamp-
ment, we pass with still feet and caution,

Or we are entering by the suburbs some vast
and ruin'd city,

The blocks and fallen architecture more than all
the living cities of the globe.

I am a free companion, I bivouac by invading
watchfires,
I turn the bridegroom out of bed and stay with
the bride myself,   290
I tighten her all night to my thighs and lips.

My voice is the wife's voice, the screech by the
rail of the stairs,
They fetch my man's body up dripping and
drown'd.

I understand the large hearts of heroes,
The courage of present times and all times,
How the skipper saw the crowded and rudderless wreck of the steamship, and Death chasing
it up and down the storm,   295
How he knuckled tight and gave not back an
inch, and was faithful of days and faithful of
nights,
And chalk'd in large letters on a board, *Be of
good cheer, we will not desert you;*
How he follow'd with them and tack'd with
them three days and would not give it up,
How he saved the drifting company at last,
How the lank loose-gown'd women look'd
when boated from the side of their pre-
pared graves,   300
How the silent old-faced infants and the lifted
sick, and the sharp-lipp'd unshaven men;
All this I swallow, it tastes good, I like it well,
it becomes mine,
I am the man, I suffer'd, I was there.

Read Randall Jarrell's "Some Lines From Whitman" (p. 538). What are Jarrell's main points? Do
you agree with them? Write a short essay (300 words)
on Jarrell's estimate of Whitman, taking your illustrations from this section of "Song of Myself."

The Idea of Order
at Key West
WALLACE STEVENS (1879-1955)

She sang beyond the genius of the sea.
The water never formed to mind or voice,
Like a body wholly body, fluttering

Its empty sleeves; and yet its mimic motion
Made constant cry, caused constantly a cry,   5
That was not ours although we understood,
Inhuman, of the veritable ocean.

The sea was not a mask. No more was she.
The song and water were not medleyed sound
Even if what she sang was what she heard,   10
Since what she sang was uttered word by word.
It may be that in all her phrases stirred
The grinding water and the gasping wind;
But it was she and not the sea we heard.

For she was the maker of the song she sang.   15
The ever-hooded, tragic-gestured sea
Was merely a place by which she walked to sing.
Whose spirit is this? we said, because we knew
It was the spirit that we sought and knew
That we should ask this often as she sang.   20

If it was only the dark voice of the sea
That rose, or even colored by many waves;
If it was only the outer voice of sky
And cloud, of the sunken coral water-walled,
However clear, it would have been deep air,   25
The heaving speech of air, a summer sound
Repeated in a summer without end
And sound alone. But it was more than that,
More even than her voice, and ours, among
The meaningless plungings of water and the
wind,   30
Theatrical distances, bronze shadows heaped
On high horizons, mountainous atmospheres
Of sky and sea.

It was her voice that made
The sky acutest at its vanishing.   35
She measured to the hour its solitude.
She was the single artificer of the world
In which she sang. And when she sang, the sea,
Whatever self it had, became the self
That was her song, for she was the maker. Then
we,   40
As we beheld her striding there alone,
Knew that there never was a world for her
Except the one she sang and, singing, made.

Ramon Fernandez, tell me, if you know,
Why, when the singing ended and we turned   45
Toward the town, tell why the glassy lights,

The lights in the fishing boats at anchor there,
As the night descended, tilting in the air,
Mastered the night and portioned out the sea,
Fixing emblazoned zones and fiery poles, 50
Arranging, deepening, enchanting night.

Oh! Blessed rage for order, pale Ramon,
The maker's rage to order words of the sea,
Words of the fragrant portals, dimly-starred,
And of ourselves and of our origins, 55
In ghostlier demarcations, keener sounds.

1. Notice that the poet very carefully specifies the relation of the singing girl to the sea by which she sings. He is not content to have it that she imitates the sea or expresses its spirit in her song, though he does not deny that she is perhaps inspired by the sea, and that something of the sea is in her song. Is he pedantic in insisting on his discriminations? What is the relation of the girl to the sea?

2. The older word for poet in English was *maker,* and so when the singing girl is called "the maker" we are being told that she is a type of the poet. Would you say that this poem is about, among things, the relation of the poet to nature?

3. Wallace Stevens has said that when he wrote "Ramon Fernandez," he was simply choosing a name, not referring to any particular person. (But it is a nice accident that there is a Ramon Fernandez who is an aesthetician and philosopher of art.) In any case, is not the question put to Fernandez a question that has to do with the function of art and the meaning of the imagination?

4. In what sense, if any, do lights seen at night —whether of a fishing boat or of something else— "arrange" and "deepen" night? Would their ability to do this be heightened in the mind of one who had been listening to the girl's song and reflecting upon the poet's "rage for order"?

Lines

Composed a Few Miles Above Tintern Abbey, on Revisiting the Banks of the Wye During a Tour, July 13, 1798

WILLIAM WORDSWORTH
(1770-1850)

Five years have past; five summers, with the length
Of five long winters! and again I hear

These waters, rolling from their mountain-springs
With a soft inland murmur.—Once again
Do I behold these steep and lofty cliffs, 5
That on a wild secluded impress
Thoughts of more deep seclusion; and connect
The landscape with the quiet of the sky.
The day is come when I again repose
Here, under this dark sycamore, and view 10
These plots of cottage-ground, these orchard-tufts,
Which at this season, with their unripe fruits,
Are clad in one green hue, and lose themselves
'Mid groves and copses. Once again I see
These hedge-rows, hardly hedge-rows, little lines 15
Of sportive wood run wild: these pastoral farms,
Green to the very door; and wreaths of smoke
Sent up, in silence from among the trees!
With some uncertain notice, as might seem
Of vagrant dwellers in the houseless woods, 20
Or of some Hermit's cave, where by his fire
The Hermit sits alone.

              These beauteous forms
Through a long absence, have not been to me
As is a landscape to a blind man's eye:
But oft, in lonely rooms, and 'mid the din 25
Of towns and cities, I have owed to them
In hours of weariness, sensations sweet,
Felt in the blood, and felt along the heart;
And passing even into my purer mind,
With tranquil restoration:—feeling too 30
Of unremembered pleasure: such, perhaps,
As have no slight or trivial influence
On that best portion of a good man's life.
His little, nameless, unremembered acts
Of kindness and of love. Nor less, I trust, 35
To them I may have owed another gift,
Of aspect more sublime; that blessed mood,
In which the burthen of the mystery,
In which the heavy and the weary weight
Of all this unintelligible world, 40
Is lightened:—that serene and blessed mood,
In which the affections gently lead us on,—
Until, the breath of this corporeal frame
And even the motion of our human blood
Almost suspended, we are laid asleep 45
In body, and become a living soul:
While with an eye made quiet by the power
Of harmony, and the deep power of joy,

We see into the life of things.
                                    If this
Be but a vain belief, yet, oh! how oft—   50
In darkness and amid the many shapes
Of joyless daylight; when the fretful stir
Unprofitable, and the fever of the world,
Have hung upon the beatings of my heart—
How oft, in spirit, have I turned to thee,   55
O sylvan Wye! thou wanderer thro' the woods,
How often has my spirit turned to thee!
      And now, with gleams of half-extinguished
         thought,
With many recognitions dim and faint,
And somewhat of a sad perplexity,   60
The picture of the mind revives again:
While here I stand, not only with the sense
Of present pleasure, but with pleasing thoughts
That in this moment there is life and food
For future years. And so I dare to hope,   65
Though changed, no doubt, from what I was
         when first
I came among these hills; when like a roe
I bounded o'er the mountains, by the sides
Of the deep rivers, and the lonely streams,
Wherever nature led: more like a man   70
Flying from something that he dreads, than one
Who sought the thing he loved. For nature then
(The coarser pleasures of my boyish days,
And their glad animal movements all gone by)
To me was all in all.—I cannot paint   75
What then I was. The sounding cataract
Haunted me like a passion: the tall rock,
The mountain, and the deep and gloomy wood,
Their colors and their forms, were then to me
An appetite; a feeling and a love,   80
That had no need of a remoter charm,
By thought supplied, nor any interest
Unborrowed from the eye.—That time is past,
And all its aching joys are now no more,
And all its dizzy raptures. Not for this   85
Faint I, nor mourn nor murmur; other gifts
Have followed; for such loss, I would believe,
Abundant recompense. For I have learned
To look on nature, not as in the hour
Of thoughtless youth; but hearing often-
         times   90
The still, sad music of humanity,
Nor harsh nor grating, though of ample power
To chasten and subdue. And I have felt
A presence that disturbs me with the joy

Of elevated thoughts; a sense sublime   95
Of something far more deeply interfused,
Whose dwelling is the light of setting suns,
And the round ocean and the living air,
And the blue sky, and in the mind of man;
A motion and a spirit, that impels   100
All thinking things, all objects of all thought,
And rolls through all things. Therefore am I
      still
A lover of the meadows and the woods,
And mountains; and of all that we behold
From this green earth; of all the mighty
      world   105
Of eye, and ear,—both what they half create,
And what perceive; well pleased to recognize
In nature and the language of the sense,
The anchor of my purest thoughts, the nurse,
The guide, the guardian of my heart, and
      soul   110
Of all my moral being.
                              Nor perchance,
If I were not thus taught, should I the more
Suffer my genial spirits to decay:
For thou art with me here upon the banks
Of this fair river; thou my dearest Friend,   115
My dear, dear Friend; and in thy voice I catch
The language of my former heart, and read
My former pleasures in the shooting lights
Of thy wild eyes. Oh! yet a little while
May I behold in thee what I was once,   120
My dear, dear Sister! and this prayer I make
Knowing that Nature never did betray
The heart that loved her; 'tis her privilege,
Through all the years of this our life, to lead
From joy to joy: for she can so inform   125
The mind that is within us, so impress
With quietness and beauty, and so feed
With lofty thoughts, that neither evil tongues,
Rash judgments, nor the sneers of selfish men,
Nor greetings where no kindness is, nor all   130
The dreary intercourse of daily life,
Shall e'er prevail against us, or disturb
Our cheerful faith, that all which we behold
Is full of blessings. Therefore let the moon
Shine on thee in thy solitary walk;   135
And let the misty mountain-winds be free
To blow against thee: and, in after years,
When these wild ecstasies shall be matured
Into a sober pleasure; when thy mind
Shall be a mansion for all lovely forms,   140

Thy memory be as a dwelling-place
For all sweet sounds and harmonies; oh! then,
If solitude, or fear, or pain, or grief,
Should be thy portion, with what healing
    thoughts
Of tender joy wilt thou remember me,   145
And these my exhortations! Nor, perchance—
If I should be where I no more can hear
Thy voice, nor catch from thy wild eyes these
    gleams
Of past existence—wilt thou then forget
That on the banks of this delightful stream   150
We stood together, and that I, so long
A worshipper of Nature, hither came
Unwearied in that service: rather say
With warmer love—oh! with far deeper zeal
Of holier love. Nor wilt thou then forget,   155
That after many wanderings, many years
Of absence, these steep woods and lofty cliffs,
And this green pastoral landscape, were to me
More dear, both for themselves and for thy sake!

This poem records an actual experience in the poet's life when he revisited the Wye valley in company with his sister Dorothy. Obviously the poem is an important document in the life of Wordsworth. Our immediate concern here, however, is with the poem as a poem. (That concern, it may be said, does not run counter to a concern with Wordsworth the man: a mastery of the poem as a work of art can contribute to any study of Wordsworth's spiritual development.)

1. What is the speaker trying to tell his companion about the meaning of nature to him? Has his attitude toward nature changed and developed during the course of his life? What are the various stages in that development?

2. Assuming that the student has worked out the "statement" of the poem in answering Question 1, how has the poet succeeded in dramatizing the statement? What, for example is the function of the scene which prompts the statement? Is the description of the valley simply decorative? Note the implied contrasts between "thought" and "joy." Cf. "joyless day-light," (l. 52), "aching joys" (l. 84), "thoughtless youth" (l. 90), "joy/ Of elevated thought" (l. 94), etc. Does the speaker honestly face the apparent antithesis between strong emotion and thought? Does he resolve the antithesis?

3. What has the memory of the "beauteous forms" of nature done for the speaker in the past? Have they been simply like a bouquet of cut flowers to brighten a dreary city room? Or does he make a more important claim for them? See, for example, l. 64; and relate your answer to "an eye made quiet by the power/Of harmony and the deep power of joy" (ll. 47-48).

4. What bearing, if any, on the answer to Question 3, has the following passage: "of all the mighty world/ Of eye, and ear,—both what they half create,/ And what perceive" (ll. 105-07). Does the passage argue that he is half "making up" the nature that means so much to him—that his vision of it is subjective? Or does it mean that "nature" is inside of him—part of his very makeup? Do our senses merely perceive and record an outside world that is already there? Or is there a creative element even in our sense apparatus?

5. At the very beginning of the poem, in ll. 7-8, the speaker says that once again, now that he has returned to this scene, he "connect[s] The landscape with the quiet of the sky." May the poem be regarded as a development of these lines? Do human beings ordinarily connect the landscape—the scenes in which they move on their various businesses—with the "quiet of the sky"? Does the poem dramatize for us the sense of such a connection?

6. Compare the attitude taken toward nature in this poem with the attitude toward nature expressed in "The Idea of Order at Key West." Wordsworth says that the eye and ear "half create" as well as "perceive" the mighty world that he loves. Stevens says of the singing girl that "the sea, / Whatever self it had, became the self / That was her song, for she was the maker." Compare the two poems on this point.

7. Wordsworth tells us that "with an eye made quiet" by the power of harmony and joy, we can see "into the life of things" and thus throw off the heavy burden of an otherwise "unintelligible world." Is this insight comparable to that exercised by Wallace Stevens' poet who has a "rage for order," a passion to confer meaning and order upon a world that lacks it?

SECTION VII

A Group of Poems by John Keats (1795-1821)

In Section V, we read and discussed Keats' "Ode on Melancholy" primarily as an example of the poet's handling of images (p. 349). We noticed how rich the imagery is, and how this richness gives the theme of the poem solidity and depth. But we also noticed how many of the images worked at several different levels, not only enriching the poem but tying the parts of it together. For example, when the melancholy fit was compared to a weeping cloud and the cloud itself to a kind of April shroud hiding the springtime hill, the metaphor associated the cloud not only with tears but with fruitfulness, implying that melancholy can feed the soul just as the rain can bring greenness to the springtime landscape. To mention another point: we noticed how the great figure having to do with the bursting of joy's grape gathered up in itself the allusions to tasting that occur throughout the poem.

Yet, as we have indicated earlier, the "Ode to Melancholy" has to be looked at in other ways than as an exercise in imagery. Indeed, the theme that dominates the "Ode to Melancholy" is one that runs through a great many poems by Keats. One way to study a poet is to see how his poems can help interpret each other and how the whole mass of poems sometimes has a unity of mood and even of technique, how, in fact, the body of a poet's work is a personal projection, an elaboration of some central and perhaps obsessive concern of the poet.

The theme of melancholy, though present in many of Keats' poems, is treated in different ways in such poems as the "Ode on a Grecian Urn," "Ode to Autumn," and "Ode to a Nightingale."

Ode to a Nightingale

I

My heart aches, and a drowsy numbness pains
   My sense, as though of hemlock I had drunk,
Or emptied some dull opiate to the drains
   One minute past, and Lethe-wards had sunk:
'Tis not through envy of thy happy lot,   5
   But being too happy in thine happiness,—
      That thou, light-winged Dryad of the trees,
        In some melodious plot
   Of beechen green, and shadows numberless,
      Singest of summer in full-throated ease.   10

II

O, for a draught of vintage! that hath been
   Cool'd a long age in the deep-delved earth,
Tasting of Flora and the country green,
   Dance, and Provencal song, and sunburnt
      mirth!
O for a beaker full of the warm South,   15
   Full of the true, the blushful Hippocrene,
      With beaded bubbles winking at the brim,
        And purple-stained mouth;
   That I might drink, and leave the world
      unseen,
      And with thee fade away into the forest
      dim: 20

III

Fade far away, dissolve, and quite forget
   What thou among the leaves hast never known,
The weariness, the fever, and the fret
   Here, where men sit and hear each other groan;

Where palsy shakes a few, sad, last gray hairs, 25
  Where youth grows pale, and spectre-thin,
    and dies;
    Where but to think is to be full of sorrow
    And leaden-eyed despairs,
  Where Beauty cannot keep her lustrous eyes,
    Or new Love pine at them beyond to-
      morrow.   30

IV

Away! away! for I will fly to thee,
  Not charioted by Bacchus and his pards,
But on the viewless wings of Poesy,
  Though the dull brain perplexes and retards:
Already with thee! tender is the night,   35
  And haply the Queen-Moon is on her throne,
    Cluster'd around by all her starry Fays;
      But here there is no light,
  Save what from heaven is with the breezes
    blown
    Through verdurous glooms and winding
      mossy ways.   40

V

I cannot see what flowers are at my feet,
  Nor what soft incense hangs upon the boughs,
But, in embalmed darkness, guess each sweet
  Wherewith the seasonable month endows
The grass, the thicket, and the fruit-tree wild; 45
  White hawthorn, and the pastoral eglantine;
    Fast fading violets cover'd up in leaves;
      And mid-May's eldest child,
  The coming musk-rose, full of dewy wine,
    The murmurous haunt of flies on summer
      eves.   50

VI

Darkling I listen; and, for many a time
  I have been half in love with easeful Death,
Call'd him soft names in many a mused rhyme,
  To take into the air my quiet breath;
Now more than ever seems it rich to die,   55
  To cease upon the midnight with no pain,
    While thou art pouring forth thy soul abroad
      In such an ecstacy!
  Still wouldst thou sing, and I have ears in
    vain—
    To thy high requiem become a sod.   60

VII

Thou wast not born for death, immortal Bird!
  No hungry generations tread thee down;
The voice I hear this passing night was heard
  In ancient days by emperor and clown:
Perhaps the self-same song that found a path 65
  Through the sad heart of Ruth, when, sick for
    home,
    She stood in tears amid the alien corn;
      The same that oft-times hath
  Charm'd magic casements, opening on the
    foam
    Of perilous seas, in faery lands forlorn. 70

VIII

Forlorn! the very word is like a bell
  To toll me back from thee to my sole self!
Adieu! the fancy cannot cheat so well
  As she is fam'd to do, deceiving elf.
Adieu! adieu! thy plaintive anthem fades   75
  Past the near meadows, over the still stream,
    Up the hill-side; and now 'tis buried deep
      In the next valley-glades:
  Was it a vision, or a waking dream?
    Fled is that music:—Do I wake or sleep? 80

The person who speaks this poem begins by saying that his heart aches, but the heartache in this instance is not simply a matter of sadness, and not so much a piercing ache as a sort of "drowsy numbness." It comes, the poet tells us, not from being sad but from being too happy—too happy in the bird's happiness as he hears it sing "of summer in full-throated ease." How a sense of pain which is also a sense of half-drugged torpor—a sense of forgetfulness and yet withal a sense of piercing joy in contemplating another creature's joy—how all of these are related (if indeed they are related) are matters that the student will have to determine after he has mastered the poem.

At this time it is enough to point out that the poet, charmed by the bird's song and delighting in the world of which it seems to speak, indulges in the fancy of flying away from the human world, with its disappointments, to the different world expressed through the bird's song. That world is so harmonious and so little haunted by anxiety that it might seem to be a world of pure imagination, though the speaker, under the influence of the nightingale's song, seems to identify it with the world of nature itself.

The means that the poet would use to reach the world of the nightingale are wine and the imagination. The first is contemplated and then rejected in favor of the second. The obstructing force that has to be overcome is not the poet's body but his brain. He writes (1. 34) that "the dull brain perplexes and retards." That the poet names the brain as the barrier to be overcome is significant: the wine would tend to release him from the inhibitions and discriminations made by the brain; the imagination would tend to transcend these discriminations.

The human world, the poem suggests, classified and categorized as it is by the analytic brain, is inimical to the rich, warm, undifferentiated world of nature. At this point the student may very well ask whether the poem really says anything like this, and his question will be well put, for the poem does not say this in so many words. But it can be argued that the poem does embody some such conception. Notice, for example, that the nightingale sings in darkness, that when the poet has imagined himself into the thicket in which the nightingale is singing, he cannot "see what flowers" are at his feet (1. 41), and that though the moon is shining and dominating the night, in the nightingale's thicket there is "no light, / Save what from heaven is by the breezes blown," and that the very heart of the nightingale's world is a place of "verdurous glooms" (1. 40) and of "embalmed darkness" (1. 43). Notice too that the poet, yearning to escape from the world of human anxiety and disappointment, wishes to "fade away" into this "forest dim" (1. 20)—into this place of "shadows numberless" (1. 9).

There is a pattern of related contrasts, the human being isolated and cut off from nature, in contrast to the nightingale, singing happily of nature; the world dominated by the dull brain—the analytic intellect—"where but to think is to be full of sorrow" (1. 27)—in contrast to the world of feeling and the imagination; the world of clear demarcations and sharp boundaries, in contrast to a world of rich warm darkness in which no boundaries exist. One must not, however, suppose that Keats, in his concern for a life of feelings and intense sensations, was celebrating mere brainlessness. By implication the poem, in repudiating a narrow notion of reason, affirms the deep unity of the human personality in which ideas and sensations flow together and the past, present, and future modify each other. The "Ode to a Nightingale" is, in fact, a thoughtful poem, for it concerns itself with the realms opened up to man by his consciousness and with the penalties imposed by consciousness.

At this point it might be interesting to consider another poem by Keats, a kind of blank-verse sonnet on knowledge and on what a bird's song may mean to a thoughtful man.

What the Thrush Said

O thou whose face hath felt the Winter's wind,
 Whose eye has seen the snow-clouds hung
  in mist,
 And the black elm tops 'mong the freezing
  stars,
 To thee the spring will be a harvest-time.
O thou whose only book has been the light   5
 Of supreme darkness, which thou feddest on
Night after night, when Phoebus was away!
 To thee the Spring shall be a triple morn.
O fret not after knowledge—I have none,
 And yet my song comes native with the
  warmth.   10
O fret not after knowledge—I have none,
 And yet the Evening listens. He who saddens
At thought of idleness cannot be idle,
And he's awake who thinks himself asleep.

This little poem was addressed to a friend of Keats' and forms part of a letter to him written on February 19, 1818. The bird is speaking to a young man who is wearied with the winter and longs for springtime. Since this young man is John Keats, we know that he too has been wearied with the waiting for his own talent as a poet to blossom and that he now hopes that his springtime as a writer will soon come. (The student might remember that Phoebus [1. 7] is not only the Greek god of the sun, for which the poet longs, but the god of poetry too.)

In Stanza 3 of "The Ode to a Nightingale," Keats describes the ills of life that he would happily forget: sickness, weariness, and age. These ills are all finally summed up in death. Yet one notes that the world out of which the nightingale sings is also touched by change and death. "The seasonable month" (1. 44), "Fast fading violets" (1. 47), "Mid-May's eldest child" (1. 48), and "The coming musk-rose" (1. 49) point to the passage of time. The nightingale's is not a world of ideal and unchanging forms, but a world of process; yet in the harmony of nature, death itself seems rid of its horror, and the poet, now listening to the voice of the nightingale, actually finds death attractive. He has, he tells us (1. 52), "been half in love with easeful Death, / Called him soft names in many a mused rhyme. . . ." The adjective "easeful" suggests why in the past death has seemed attractive: it offered a way out of the world of human fret and anxiety. But now death takes on a positive quality as if it were a sort of fulfillment. The poet says "Now more than ever seems it rich to die, . . . / While thou art pouring forth thy soul abroad / In such an ecstasy!" (ll. 55, 57-58).

Keats elsewhere expressed this notion of death as a fulfillment. In a sonnet, written in March, 1819, about two months before he wrote the "Ode to a Nightingale," he intimated that death, because it was more intense than any other human experience, was the most significant and even the most rewarding. Death, he wrote, "is Life's high meed," that is, high reward.

Why did I laugh to-night? No voice will tell:
   No God, no Demon of severe response,
Deigns to reply from heaven or from Hell.
   Then to my human heart I turn at once.
Heart! Thou and I are here sad and alone;   5
   Say, wherefore did I laugh? O mortal pain!
O Darkness! Darkness! ever must I moan,
   To question Heaven and Hell and Heart
      in vain.
Why did I laugh? I know this Being's lease,
   My fancy to its utmost blisses spreads;   10

Yet would I on this very midnight cease,
   And the world's gaudy ensigns see in shreds;
Verse, Fame, and Beauty are intense indeed,
   But Death intenser—Death is Life's high meed.

The meaning attached to death in this sonnet is not *necessarily*, of course, the same as that in the "Ode to a Nightingale," but a general parallelism is obvious and the student will do well to examine with some care the attitude toward death exhibited in the two poems.

   1. Does the poem suggest the quality of the poet's laugh? Merry? Thoughtless? Sardonic?
   2. What is the relation of the last four lines to the preceding ten?

The nightingale's song (see Stanza VI) renders even death attractive, but the listener, though tempted to "cease upon the midnight" to the bird's "high requiem," is fully aware of what death will mean to him: he will become oblivious to the requiem, being a mere senseless lump, "a sod." Though he yearns to attain the nightingale's world, he is inextricably linked to death as the nightingale is not. For the nightingale was "not born for death" and is an "immortal Bird."

What can be meant? Keats certainly knew that the small creature to whose song he listened had a shorter life span than his own, and yet he fancies the bird as having lived through the ages, having been heard, for example, by the Biblical character, Ruth, or by ladies in some fabled castle of the Middle Ages.

Why does the bird seem to be deathless? The answer lies in its harmonious rapport with nature. The human being's bitter conflict with time does not trouble the nightingale: "No hungry generations tread thee down" (1. 62). Earlier, the poet had expressed the desire to "forget / What thou among the leaves hast never known. . . ." What the bird has never known is the passage of time which leaves man, at the end, to shake "a few, sad, last gray hairs." The nightingale's immortality springs from the fact that it was "not born for death" (1. 61). Man, unfortunately, is born for death and speedily learns that fact. The shadow of death lies over all his activities, but the nightingale "among the leaves" truly has never known anything about death. He is so completely merged with nature that the life of nature seems to flow harmoniously through him and to find voice in his song.

We have seen in Stanza VI that the speaker makes a pointed contrast between the bird's continuing to sing and his own death-stopped ears, and at the beginning of Stanza VIII he sharpens the contrast between the bird and himself. "Forlorn," the last word in Stanza VII, conjures up the romantic world in which the nightingale sings, but the poet suddenly realizes that the word also applies to himself, for if *forlorn* means "romantically remote," it also literally means "lost, alienated," and describes his own dejected state—separated from nature and indeed born for death. With the clang of the word *forlorn,* the poet abandons the attempt to join the nightingale through an effort of the imagination. He realizes that he is irrevocably barred out of the world of the nightingale, and with this realization, what had been the nightingale's "high requiem" becomes a "plaintive anthem" (1. 75). Earlier, in response to the nightingale's song, the man had hoped to fade back into the world of nature; now (1. 75) it is the nightingale's song that *fades,* "Past the near meadows, over the still stream," and is finally "buried deep / In the next valley-glades. . . ." The song of the nightingale that the sad listener hoped might confer immortality upon him, now itself seems to sink into a grave. The listener is left questioning: "Was it a vision, or a waking dream? / Fled is that music:—Do I wake or sleep?"

What is the relevance of waking and sleeping to the meaning of this poem? Here, the student might profitably look back to "What the Thrush Said," with its last line: "And he's awake who thinks himself asleep." In both poems, Keats seems to be preoccupied with an experience which holds man in the trance-like state of dream and yet renders him peculiarly sensitive and receptive. (Cf. the account of the composition of "Kubla Khan," p. 370). Clearly, both poems turn upon the problem of consciousness and both celebrate a kind of knowledge which in its wholeness transcends the ordinary analytical procedures of the "dull brain." In the "Ode" of course, the insight into the nature of consciousness is more profound: the bird's harmony with nature and its happiness stem from the fact that it has practically no consciousness—very little memory of the past and almost no prevision of the future. Yet if self-consciousness is the source of man's anxiety and his disappointments, the world described in Stanza II—or in Stanza VII— is a world that is available only to man's consciousness. One might go further: the joy that the man takes in the nightingale's song is a joy peculiar to man and different from the thoughtless happiness of any natural creature.

1. What is the relation of the imagery in Stanza II to the theme of the poem as a whole? Are the associations that are summoned up by the idea of wine simply so much embroidery, charmingly rich, but presented for their own sake? Or are they also important for the theme of the poem? If so, how?

2. We have argued that in the "Ode to a Nightingale" the sense of sight is played down in favor of that of sound—that is, the song of the nightingale wells up out of a warm and engulfing darkness. In this connection, what about the sight imagery in Stanza III—"leaden-eyed despair" and beauty not able to keep her "lustrous eyes"? Do these visual references violate or substantiate the general pattern we have suggested?

3. In Stanza V, Keats uses the phrase "embalmed darkness." The adjective "embalmed" will, for many readers, suggest death. If so, is the notion necessarily inappropriate here? Do you think that Keats intended the association? Or if he did not, would he have been happy nevertheless if someone had later pointed it out to him?

4. In Stanza VII what is the force of the phrase "alien corn"? Why is this more moving, if it is so, than "alien sky" or "alien fields"?

The human situation in which joy is so intimately related to melancholy is also the theme of the "Ode on a Grecian Urn."

Ode on a Grecian Urn

I

Thou still unravish'd bride of quietness,
  Thou foster-child of silence and slow time,
Sylvan historian, who canst thus express
  A flowery tale more sweetly than our rhyme:
What leaf-fring'd legend haunts about thy
    shape   5

Of deities or mortals, or of both,
  In Tempe or the dales of Arcady?
What men or gods are these? What maidens
    loth?
What mad pursuit? What struggle to escape?
  What pipes and timbrels? What wild
    ecstasy?   10

II

Heard melodies are sweet, but those unheard
  Are sweeter; therefore, ye soft pipes, play on;
Not to the sensual ear, but, more endear'd,
  Pipe to the spirit ditties of no tone:
Fair youth, beneath the trees, thou canst not
    leave   15
  Thy song, nor ever can those trees be bare;
  Bold Lover, never, never canst thou kiss,
Though winning near the goal—yet, do not
    grieve;
  She cannot fade, though thou hast not thy
    bliss,
For ever wilt thou love, and she be fair!   20

III

Ah, happy, happy boughs! that cannot shed
  Your leaves, nor ever bid the Spring adieu;
And, happy melodist, unwearied,
  For ever piping songs for ever new;
More happy love! more happy, happy love!   25
  For ever warm and still to be enjoy'd,
  For ever panting, and for ever young;
All breathing human passion far above,
  That leaves a heart high-sorrowful and cloy'd,
  A burning forehead, and a parching
    tongue.   30

IV

Who are these coming to the sacrifice?
  To what green altar, O mysterious priest,
Lead'st thou that heifer lowing at the skies,
  And all her silken flanks with garlands drest?
What little town by river or sea shore,   35
  Or mountain-built with peaceful citadel,
    Is emptied of this folk, this pious morn?
And, little town, thy streets for evermore
  Will silent be; and not a soul to tell
    Why thou art desolate, can e'er return.   40

V

O Attic shape! Fair attitude! with brede
  Of marble men and maidens overwrought,

With forest branches and the trodden weed;
  Thou, silent form, dost tease us out of thought
As doth eternity: Cold Pastoral!   45
  When old age shall this generation waste,
  Thou shalt remain, in midst of other woe
Than ours, a friend to man, to whom thou
    say'st,
Beauty is truth, truth beauty,—that is all
    Ye know on earth, and all ye need to
    know.   50

In "Ode to a Nightingale," the speaker sought to achieve wholeness by merging himself into the rich, always changing, but ultimately unchanged world of natural process. In the "Ode on a Grecian Urn," Keats sets our human world, with its frustrations and disappointments, over against the world of art, which is immortal, not through unending process, but through stasis: a moment out of the flux of becoming has been frozen and perpetuated for our contemplation.

The "Ode" begins with an imaginative exploration of the world depicted upon the urn; but our human world lies in the background and remains a constant point of reference. Notice for example ll. 19-20 or ll. 26-30. The world of "breathing human passion" leaves the heart "high-sorrowful and cloyed," and it leaves too often a "burning forehead, and a parching tongue." In the actual human world within which we live, attainment of joy brings listlessness and satiety. Better the situation of the young lover figured on the urn who will never attain his love and therefore will never risk knowing the disappointment of a love that has lost its savor.

This general thesis dominates Stanzas II and III. The unattainable is better than the attained; the imagined melody is sweeter than that which actually strikes the eardrums. The implications of these stanzas are realistic and also pessimistic. (Line 30 comes close to being a description of a hangover on the morning after!) But the pessimistic note is not to the fore: the poet keeps our attention on the figures sculptured upon the urn. What we see there is recognizably human life, but life raised to an ideal plane, and, because it cannot change, not threatened by mortality. The scenes described in the first three stanzas are dynamic; there is "mad pursuit"; maidens "struggle to escape."

The dominant theme is that of romantic love—that of gods or men attempting to embrace the maidens or, as in the scene dwelt upon in Stanzas II and III that of the "fair youth, beneath the trees" who attempts to bestow a kiss.

Stanza IV presents another aspect of human activity. It is a religious rite. The population of some little Greek town has turned out to sacrifice to one of the gods. The urn does not, through some inscription or insignia, tell us the name of the town or to what god the altar is erected. In fact, the poet makes a point of this indefiniteness. The priest is a "mysterious" priest: that is, he could be a priest of Apollo or of Zeus or of some other god. The little town whose inhabitants we see in the procession might be "mountain-built" (1. 36) or else situated "by river or sea shore" (1. 35), and none of the figures that take part in the procession can move his marble lips to tell us the town's name.

The artist who sculptured the urn has captured for the imagination a vision of human life in some of its most significant and universal aspects, and the urn, which Keats calls a "sylvan historian" (1. 3), can silently relate a "flowery tale" more effectively, the poet modestly says, than his own rime can do. The urn presents human love and human worship, the individual assertion and the communal ceremony—and presents them with a fullness and vividness that stir our imagination.

By surviving the erosion of time, the urn has preserved the spirit of an older civilization. Two thousand and more years later, men can participate in the scenes depicted on it and feel the continuity of the human spirit. (It does not matter that we cannot locate on a map the town whose houses have been "emptied of this folk," or that we do not know whether the revellers in Stanza I are divine beings or mere mortals.) But time has been conquered only at a certain price: if the love celebrated in Stanza III, unlike mortal and human love, remains "forever warm and still to be enjoyed," it remains so only because it has been reduced to cold marble. This is the point that the poet is willing to recognize quite realistically in Stanza V, where he calls the urn a "Cold Pastoral." (A cold pastoral is something of a contradiction in terms, for "pastoral" suggests what is warm and simple—the elementary concerns of a pastoral society.)

Though it is a "silent form," the urn is capable of teasing "us out of thought." The phrase is rich and even ambiguous: it teases us, the poet says, "as doth eternity"—and the implication is that, through having conquered time, the urn partakes of the mystery of eternity. Perhaps the poet also implies that the urn provokes in us some deeper musing than is usually comprehended by the term "thought." Yet the urn, even if it "teases us," is regarded by the poet as friendly to man, to whom it has something comforting to say. What is the special revelation that the urn has to make? Something that has impressed some readers as a kind of high-flown nonsense: "Beauty is truth, truth beauty."

Much ink has been shed in the past over the meaning of this statement and some commentators have regarded this explicit statement as a blemish on the poem. Yet the thoughtful reader will perceive that the urn has been presented all along as a speaker. It was called a "historian" (1. 3), and its ability to express more sweetly than the poet can a flowery tale, is explicitly stated in ll. 4 and 5. Stanzas II, III, and IV are filled with the tales that the urn can tell, and the poet has indeed demonstrated how vividly and movingly the urn, for all its silence, can express them. There is really no break in the continuity of the poem in this last stanza when the speaker, stepping back, as it were, from the urn, and viewing it as an object ("O Attic shape") declares that it says, and will continue to say, something that man ought to hear.

In trying to determine the meaning of what the urn says, scholars have appealed to the letters of Keats—for example, to Keats' letter to his friend Bailey: "I am certain of nothing but the holiness of the Heart's affections and the truth of Imagination—what the imagination seizes as Beauty must be truth . . ."; or, to Keats' statement that he "never can feel certain of any truth but for a clear perception of its beauty." The truth with which Keats is concerned in these letters is obviously not scientific truth or historical truth, but the truth of man's nature and his relation to reality. Truth of that order might very well seem to a poet to possess the inevitability, harmony, and rightness of shape with which he associates beauty. But we do not need to go beyond the "Ode" itself in order to understand what Keats means in equating beauty with truth and truth with beauty. The visions of mankind as embodied in the sculptured form on the urn are beautiful in their harmony and clarity and ordered significance, but they are also "true." They do not give us "facts"—names, dates, and locations—but they do give us the essential dignity and pathos of man, the knowledge of himself that it suffices man to know.

The "Ode on a Grecian Urn" differs so much in emphasis and in tone from "Ode to a Nightingale" that the student may feel that the two poems have little in common. Yet a little reflection will indicate that in both poems the sadness and perplexity of human life is put in a special perspective. In the "Nightingale" it is contrasted with the fullness and harmony of nature as exhibited in a happy unconscious creature like the bird; in the "Urn," with the enduring but cold stasis of art. Both odes are also clearly related to the "Ode to Melancholy," for both imply that the man who is most aware of the threat of mortality and the frailty of beauty is the man who is most sensitive to the beauty of nature or of art. This is not to say that "Melancholy" or the "Urn" or the "Nightingale" is in the least sentimental; the poet does not whine or complain. He is very much aware of the intense beauty of both nature and art, but he is a realist too. Neither nature nor art is really a refuge for man. Neither will save man from old age, sickness, or sorrow, though they will give him something very precious. Moreover, man feels the power of nature and art as intensely as he does just because their immortality stands in contrast to his own mortality.

1. What is the appropriateness of "still unravish'd bride of quietness" as a description of the urn?

2. What has the poet gained by calling the urn the "foster-child of silence and slow time"?

3. What are some of the ways in which the poet has emphasized the advantages of the moment before enjoyment over the moment itself? Has the poet been fair in acknowledging the disadvantages? Give concrete instances here.

4. In Stanza IV, the poet suggests that the little town whose inhabitants have all gone forth to take part in the sacrificial rite will forever be silent and empty; that is, caught in their frozen stasis on the urn, they are always about to move forward and will never be able to go back into their town. Notice too that the poet has suggested that for this reason any person coming upon the silent little town will not be able to know why its inhabitants have left it. Is this last observation too fanciful? Too far-fetched? Someone carping at the poem would object that nobody will ever know that the little town is empty or indeed that it existed at all, except by inferring it from the urn. How would you reply to this objection?

5. In the preceding stanzas we have been close up to the scenes depicted on the urn, examining them and imaginatively participating in them. What is the stance of the observer in the last stanza? How is the change of stance marked?

6. Another question having to do with the last two lines of the poem has provoked a good deal of discussion. Does the urn speak all of the last two lines, or is only the statement "Beauty is truth, truth beauty" spoken by the urn, the rest spoken by the poet himself? Some commentators have argued that the poet, in the last line and a half, is telling the figures on the urn ("ye") that *they* know that beauty is truth and truth is beauty and that is all that *they* need to know, though living, breathing human beings need to know something besides this. (In our reading of the poem, we take the last two lines to be spoken by the urn.)

For a discussion of the reading and punctuation of the text as it survives in the manuscript copies, the student might look up Alvin Whitley's "The Message of the Grecian Urn," *Keats-Shelley Memorial Bulletin*, Vol. 5 (London, 1933), pp. 1-3. The student may well want to take into account the evidence of the manuscript copies as he tries to determine whether the last lines are divided between urn and poet, or are all spoken by the urn.

7. Mr. Whitley's essay has been reprinted in the volume entitled *Keats' Well-Read Urn*, edited by Harvey T. Lyon (New York, Holt, Rinehart and Winston, Inc., 1958). The student may want to consult this little book in order to see how many different interpretations of the "Ode on a Grecian Urn" have been proposed and try to decide for himself what an acceptable interpretation is.

Man's journey from childhood to maturity and then on to old age and death is part of the natural process. In spite of the pain with which the young poet contemplates old age and death, he has never blenched from the fact that they are inevitable and as we have seen, he accepts the fact in both the "Nightingale" and the "Urn." In another of his great odes, Keats treats the cycle of birth, growth and death with full acceptance.

To Autumn

I

Season of mists and mellow fruitfulness,
　Close bosom-friend of the maturing sun;
Conspiring with him how to load and bless
　With fruit the vines that round the thatch-eves
　　run;
To bend with apples the moss'd cottage-trees,　5
　And fill all fruit with ripeness to the core;
　　To swell the gourd, and plump the hazel
　　shells
With a sweet kernel; to set budding more,
And still more, later flowers for the bees,
Until they think warm days will never cease,　10
　　For Summer has o'er-brimm'd their clammy
　　cells.

II

Who hath not seen thee oft amid thy store?
　Sometimes whoever seeks abroad may find
Thee sitting careless on a granary floor,
　Thy hair soft-lifted by the winnowing wind;　15
Or on a half-reap'd furrow sound asleep,
　Drows'd with the fume of poppies, while thy
　　hook
　　Spares the next swath and all its twined
　　flowers:
And sometimes like a gleaner thou dost keep
　Steady thy laden head across a brook;　20
　Or by a cider-press, with patient look,
　　Thou watchest the last oozings hours by
　　hours.

III

Where are the songs of Spring? Ay, where are
　they?
　Think not of them, thou hast thy music too,—
While barréd clouds bloom the soft-dying day,　25
　And touch the stubble-plains with rosy hue;
Then in a wailful choir the small gnats mourn
　Among the river sallows, borne aloft
　　Or sinking as the light wind lives or dies;
And full-grown lambs loud bleat from hilly
　　bourn;　30

Hedge-crickets sing; and now with treble soft
The red-breast whistles from a garden-croft;
　And gathering swallows twitter in the skies.

In this poem, Keats' emphasis is not upon loss or decay but upon maturation and fulfillment. The mood is one of warmth and brightness: heavy with its fruitfulness, the season is suffused with drowsiness, but it is a drowsiness which is not so much dullness as the weight of plentitude.

Stanza II personifies autumn, turning her into a goddess. Rarely has a goddess ever been made to emerge from the landscape with more authority and authentic power. She is placid, sleepy, subdued by the very richness which she has produced and over which she reigns. She is even "careless" of the wealth which surrounds her simply because it is overpowering in its abundance. The whole tone is one of quiet fulfillment—there is nothing of nervous or anxious foreboding with reference to the cold winds and frost which are to descend upon the landscape. Time is made here to stand still, or to seem to stand still, because complete fulfillment makes one indifferent to time and what it can bring.

The last stanza does not, however, try to out-face approaching winter and death with a false optimism. The key of the stanza is definitely minor. It is evening now, and the stanza is full of hints—though they are no more than hints—of approaching death. The day in line 25 is seen as a *dying* day (even if it is "soft-dying"). And in line 27 the word *mourn* is used, though it is only the small gnats that mourn in their wailful choir. But there is clearly a touch of chill in the air, and the sense that something is over. The poet faces this fact, but he does so by finding the beauty and the charm that is in the season and exulting in it. He recognizes that the songs of spring are gone, but he exhorts autumn to disregard them, for "thou hast thy music too. . . ." The rest of the stanza evokes that music, and if the music is in part "wailful," it is nevertheless appropriate, has its own beauty, and is to be accepted on the assumption that all experience is good and that autumn too has in it something uniquely precious. None of this is said in so many words, nor need it be, but the relevance of the seasonal description to the human season will be perfectly plain to any sensitive reader.

1. Note that Stanzas I and II are filled with visual imagery but that auditory imagery dominates the last stanza. Is there any significance in this shift from sight to sound?

2. In Stanza I, autumn is associated with the sun —it is the "close bosom-friend" of the sun. How is the association actually reinforced by the imagery of Stanza I? Does the sun-association manage to give to autumn a special quality—linking it, not to the waning of the year, and rain, and cold winds, but to the ripe culmination of the year?

3. What is the force of words like "load," "bend," "swell," and "plump" in Stanza I?

4. In Stanza II, autumn is portrayed as a laborer in the harvest, on the granary floor: as a reaper with sickle, carrying a sheaf of grain, or watching the cider press. Does this labor seem to be one of weariness, languor, repletion, or what?

5. What is the mood of Stanza III? Is it implied that autumn needs consolation (see l. 24)? Is the character of the music to which the speaker alludes unhappy? Is it *all* mournful and minor in key?

6. What is the tone of "To Autumn"? Remember that tone, which has to do with the author's attitude toward his material and toward his reader, is different from mood, which has to do with the more general quality of feeling. To be specific: what is the poet's attitude toward the process of maturing? Toward the fulfillment of the period of growth and the onset of the period of decay? Does he dread it? Rejoice in it? Understand and accept it? Does he find—perhaps to his own surprise—a special beauty in it?

7. Are there any connections between this poem and Keats' "Ode on Melancholy"? How do the poems resemble each other? How do they differ?

In the discussion thus far we have been primarily concerned with linking one poem with another by way of comparison and contrast so that the student will have a better chance to see how the body of Keats' poetry forms a larger whole with its own unity and coherence. To this end, the student may want to explore further. He might look up, for example, Keats' sonnet "On the Grasshopper and the Cricket" as a slight but charming foreshadowing of one of the elements in "To Autumn." He might also enjoy

looking into Keats' letters for passages which throw light upon the poems and consulting other poems of Keats' to see their connection with the poems already examined. For example, remembering the first lines of the "Ode on Melancholy," he might find it interesting that Keats' sonnet "On Seeing the Elgin Marbles" uses the phrase "dizzy pain," or that line 275 of "The Eve of Saint Agnes" combines the idea of drowsing and aching: "For I shall drowse beside thee, so my soul does ache." With reference to the "Ode on a Grecian Urn," he might read Keats' "Sleep and Poetry."

The student might profitably go on to relate this group of poems, not only to the rest of Keats but to the other Romantic poets, such as Shelley, Byron, Wordsworth, and Coleridge. These poets shared a world view, characteristic attitudes toward nature, and, for all their differences, similar poetic methods. A recent and authoritative account of Romanticism sees it as constituting "a closely coherent body of thought and feeling," not only in England, but in Germany and France as well." [1] The fundamental characteristic is described as the endeavor "to overcome the split between subject and object, the self and the world, the conscious and the unconscious." In this connection, the student might recall what was said on pp. 412-13 above with regard to Keats' "Ode to a Nightingale," a poem in which the relation of the self and the world is of primary importance and which can be regarded as a dramatization of the whole problem of consciousness.

The literature dealing with Romanticism is immense. A handy guidebook is *The English Romantic Poets,* edited by T. M. Raysor (New York: Modern Language Association, 1956). During the last twenty-five years the Romantic poets have received renewed attention and their work has been reassessed. A sampling of recent discussion of these poets may be found in *English Romantic Poets,* edited by M. H. Abrams (New York: Oxford University Press, Inc., 1960).

---

[1] René Wellek, "Romanticism Re-examined," *Concepts of Criticism* (New Haven, Conn.: Yale University Press, 1963), p. 220.

A Group of Poems by Robert Frost (1874-1963)

On page 343 we discussed "The Need of Being Versed in Country Things" as an example of Frost's fine control of tone. But a discussion of tone always involves a consideration of the theme of a poem, and the theme of "The Need of Being Versed" turned out to be man's relation to nature. It is a theme frequently met with in Frost and occurs in poem after poem. Consider, for example, the following poem.

The Wood-Pile

Out walking in the frozen swamp one grey day,
I paused and said, 'I will turn back from here.
No, I will go on farther—and we shall see.'
The hard snow held me, save where now and then
One foot went through. The view was all in lines   5
Straight up and down of tall slim trees
Too much alike to mark or name a place by
So as to say for certain I was here
Or somewhere else: I was just far from home.   10
A small bird flew before me. He was careful
To put a tree between us when he lighted,
And say no word to tell me who he was
Who was so foolish as to think what *he* thought.
He thought that I was after him for a feather—   15
The white one in his tail; like one who takes
Everything said as personal to himself.
One flight out sideways would have undeceived him.
And then there was a pile of wood for which
I forgot him and let his little fear   20
Carry him off the way I might have gone,
Without so much as wishing him good-night.
He went behind it to make his last stand.
It was a cord of maple, cut and split
And piled—and measured, four by four by eight.   25
And not another like it could I see.
No runner tracks in this year's snow looped near it.
And it was older sure than this year's cutting,
Or even last year's or the year's before.
The wood was grey and the bark warping off it   30
And the pile somewhat sunken. Clematis
Had wound strings round and round it like a bundle.
What held it though on one side was a tree
Still growing, and on one a stake and prop,
These latter about to fall. I thought that only   35
Someone who lived in turning to fresh tasks
Could so forget his handiwork on which
He spent himself, the labour of his axe,
And leave it there far from a useful fireplace
To warm the frozen swamp as best it could   40
With the slow smokeless burning of decay.

This poem seems to describe a rather aimless walk. Nothing very much happens. The speaker tells how the frozen swamp looks on a gray winter day. He has no special place to go; he is simply taking a walk.

The bird that kept flitting in front of him and putting a tree between them is amusingly like certain human beings who, as the poet says, take "everything said as personal" to themselves. But the little incident is treated casually and is of no special importance. Finally the speaker comes upon the wood-pile, and here his walk terminates, or at least all that the poet has chosen to tell us about it.

What is the significance of the wood-pile? The cord is described with a countryman's eye: it is of maple wood; the wood is weathered gray, and the bark is warping off. The cord is held up, on one side by a growing tree and on the other by a stake and prop, though these last are about ready to fall.

What seems curious to the observer is that anyone would have taken the trouble to cut and split and pile a cord of wood and then abandon it, leaving it there in the swamp to rot away. The poem ends with this bit of speculation about the man who split and piled the wood: he must have been a man who kept irons in a good many fires—the sort of person who is always turning from one task to another. And with this observation the poem comes to an end. To some readers the poem will seem as aimless and inconsequential as the walk that ended with the discovery of the abandoned wood-pile.

Yet the reader may very well feel that the poem does have a point and that the pretense of a story, the account of the walk, and the description of the wood-pile all work together to maintain the interest of the reader as the poem goes along, but that none of them actually makes the point of the poem, a point which is given much less directly—almost glancingly—in the last three lines:

> . . . leave it there far from a useful fireplace
> To warm the frozen swamp as best it could
> With the slow smokeless burning of decay.

Having in mind what we learned about Frost's concern with nature in "The Need of Being Versed in Country Things," one might try to see what happens if we read these lines as a commentary on man's relation to nature. The abandoned wood-pile is presented with just a hint of pathos, the sort of pathos provoked by abandoned and forgotten objects which remain as evidence of the lives of nameless and unknown people. But we notice that the poet is not willing to leave the matter at that. The last two lines in particular take the concern one stage further. The wood-pile is, after all, on a fireplace, though it is not "a useful fireplace," and the wood is being burned, even though in the frozen swamp.

Thus the wood-pile, a common and homely object, is, for the purpose of this poem, something more than a wood-pile; it gains symbolic force and becomes a commentary, not only on the personality and temperament of the unknown man who set it up, but on the activities of all men. The implication is that if man

drops one activity in favor of another and forgets one accomplishment in his fever to get on with some other, nature, which never works in a hurry and never forgets anything, goes right on to take care of the tasks which man, in his forgetfulness, abandons.

This general point has already been hinted at earlier. The poet says of the wood-pile that

> . . . Clematis
> Had wound strings round and round it like a bundle.

The primary purpose of the comparison is to make us see the wood-pile more vividly and to emphasize the length of time that has elapsed since the cutting of the wood. But the comparison also suggests that nature is doing what the man has failed to do. Nature, in its own way, is man's collaborator and assistant. Nature seems to be tying the pile together and keeping it from falling. Or perhaps nature is claiming the wood-pile again for its own, taking possession of what man had tried to remove for his own purposes. Both of these meanings may seem to be involved in the comparison, and both meanings may be relevant. The implication that nature is both man's friend and man's enemy—and that it may finally be indifferent to him altogether—in the light of the whole poem, makes good sense.

Consider too the final comparison with which the poem closes. "The slow smokeless burning of decay" is actually an extremely accurate way of putting matters, for the decay of wood amounts to a slow oxidation. The difference between the wood's rotting in the swamp or burning on a useful fireplace is primarily a difference in the speed of the process. In fact, we have already suggested that the swamp is really a kind of fireplace and that nature will in its own way burn the wood that man forgot to burn.

If the point of the poem, then, has to do with man's relation to nature, it has been put subtly—so subtly that the attempt to phrase it briefly may appear to overstate it. Certainly we shall do well to go back and reread the poem carefully, letting the poem dramatize its point in its own way. But we must not make the mistake of thinking that the poem is without a point. Frost's method of approaching the true subject of "The Wood-Pile" is very cunning. This definition of the factual theme of the poem is delayed until the very end, with the result that the reader seems to stumble upon it unexpectedly just as the man discovered the wood-pile. Yet when the end of the poem is reached, one can see that the arrangement of materials in the poem, at first glance so casual, has actually been disposed to culminate in the final effect.

1. What is implied about the character of the man who takes this walk? How do you know that he is more than usually observant? How do you know that he has a sense of humor? *Philosophy* means literally "love of truth." What is the evidence that the observer in this poem is a "philosopher"?

2. Could one argue that the poem's trailing off into inconsequence at the end is only apparent—that is, that it is in reality a dramatic device to help make the essential point of the poem?

3. Can you see any relation in theme or attitude between this poem and "Ode to Autumn" by Keats?

The theme of man's relation to nature comes in for a characteristic statement in the following poem entitled:

A Leaf Treader

I have been treading on leaves all day until I
  am autumn-tired.
God knows all the color and form of leaves I have
  trodden on and mired.
Perhaps I have put forth too much strength and
  been too fierce from fear.
I have safely trodden underfoot the leaves of
  another year.

All summer long they were over head, more
  lifted up than I.   5
To come to their final place in earth they had
  to pass me by.
All summer long I thought I heard them
  threatening under their breath.
And when they came it seemed with a will to
  carry me with them to death.

They spoke to the fugitive in my heart as if it
  were leaf to leaf.
They tapped at my eyelids and touched my lips
  with an invitation to grief.   10

But it was no reason I had to go because they
  had to go.
Now up my knee to keep on top of another year
  of snow.

This poem begins almost as casually as "The Wood-Pile." It is an autumn day and the speaker, going about his chores on the farm, is conscious of having trodden leaves into the mud, golden, orange, crimson. Yet even as early as the second line of the poem, we get a hint that his experience had some deeper meaning for him. The hint is developed in ll. 3 and 4. Why does the speaker hazard the guess that perhaps he has put forth "too much strength"? And why does he remark that he has been "too fierce from fear"? Fear of what, if all he has done has been merely to tramp leaves down into the mud?

The adverb "safely" in l. 4 supplies the answer: to the casual glance, he was simply a man treading upon the autumn leaves, but to the man himself the action had a deeper meaning. He had just concluded a contest with nature as to whether he should be on top of the leaves at the end of this autumn or whether the leaves should be on top of him.

In the second stanza the summer leaves are made to take on an ominous quality. All summer long he thought he heard them threatening him "under their breath," and now as they fall past him on this autumn day, he imagines they wish to carry him with them to death. The threat in the seasonal change—the suggestion that man too is a leaf who has his season and finally must come to rest in the earth along with the other leaves—runs on into the third stanza, though there it takes on a rather different tone. In this stanza, the leaves do not so much threaten as cajole. A Freudian might find in this passage the death wish in man, but whether or not we use the term "death wish," most of us do feel, at some time or other, the attraction of subsiding into nature, of ceasing to strive against it.

The poet in this third stanza puts the point very well indeed. He says that the leaves spoke "to the fugitive in my heart as if it were leaf to leaf." The point is made graphically and concretely with the statement that the leaves "tapped at my eyelids and touched my lips with an invitation to grief." But one notices that even in this line the poet has not lost his hold on the concrete details of the situation. On a gusty autumn day some of the flying leaves would blow against one's eyelids or against one's lips.

The poem has moved a good long way from its rather casual opening. The term "autumn-tired" in the first line has been developed into a wistfulness attuned to the autumn, a season in which man is inclined to feel a kind of resignation knowing that he is doomed to pass from the scene even as the leaves do. But man, though a part of nature, is no mere leaf. The speaker asserts as much when suddenly (l. 11) there is a change of mood and a change of tone. He says "But it was no reason I had to go because they had to go." What is the tone? Well, it resembles as nearly as anything else the tone of one little boy taunting another little boy who had been called into the house by his mother: "It's no reason I've got to go in just because you've got to go in." But the student may prefer to supply his own, and perhaps better, analogy for the tone here. Perhaps the tone is not really taunting; but it is certainly colloquial, common-sensical, and sharp—sharp enough at least to break the somber mood into which the poem has gravitated.

The fact that the leaves have come to their dying time does not mean that the speaker has arrived at his. Yet if there is a slight note of cockiness here, the speaker is not carelessly over-confident. After all, he faces another season: soon the snowflakes will be flying and he will have to try to keep on top of them. As he says wryly in the last line, "Now up my knee to keep on top of another year of snow."

This little poem is a brilliant exercise in the use of imagery: the image of the falling leaves provides the speaker with all that he needs or wants to say. The poem is also a brilliant exercise in tone: if the tone were inept or oversimple, the poem would become something mawkishly sentimental or laboriously trivial. The manipulation of tone, and particularly the shift in tone in the last lines, keeps the poem nimble and graceful.

Does "A Leaf Treader" embody the same attitude toward nature and man's partial alienation from nature as that found in "The Need of Being Versed in Country Things"? Or in "The Wood-Pile"? The student ought to determine this for himself, but there can be no doubt that all three poems deal with the theme of man's relation to nature.

1. Is the man who recounts "A Leaf Treader" essentially the same man who took the walk in "The Wood-Pile"? If it is the same man, is his mood quite the same in the two poems? Look back at Housman's poem entitled "The Tree of Man" (p. 310) and compare the way in which the two poets have treated the analogy between man and leaf. How do the two poems differ in tone?

2. Compare "A Leaf Treader" with "Bells for John Whiteside's Daughter," by John Crowe Ransom (p. 341), on the basis of a fundamental attitude toward life.

The poem "To Earthward" looks at nature in a somewhat different way—though not in an entirely different way.

To Earthward

Love at the lips was touch
As sweet as I could bear;
And once that seemed too much;
I lived on air

That crossed me from sweet things,   5
The flow of—was it musk
From hidden grapevine springs
Down hill at dusk?

I had the swirl and ache
From sprays of honeysuckle   10
That when they're gathered shake
Dew on the knuckle.

I craved strong sweets, but those
Seemed strong when I was young;
The petal of the rose   15
It was that stung.

Now no joy but lacks salt
That is not dashed with pain
And weariness and fault;
I crave the stain   20

Of tears, the aftermark
Of almost too much love,
The sweet of bitter bark
And burning clove.

When stiff and sore and scarred   25
I take away my hand
From leaning on it hard
In grass and sand,

The hurt is not enough:
I long for weight and strength   30
To feel the earth as rough
To all my length.

The man who speaks records a change in his sensibility. Though even a delicate sweetness "seemed strong when I was young," he confesses that now he craves the "sweet of bitter bark." This comment on his change in tastes is made thoroughly believable. We are not dealing with any fussy aesthete. We are convinced because the poet has succeeded in making us participate imaginatively in the situation. The musk from the hidden grapevine reaching us, not from just anywhere or at just any time, but blown by the wind "down hill at dusk" is rendered poignant. The odor of honeysuckle is associated with a "swirl and ache" of the senses because the honeysuckle sprays are called up before our imaginations, wet with the dew which is shaken onto the knuckles of the hand that clasps them.

Presumably, the speaker is now no longer young, and pure sensual pleasure and mere sweetness are not enough. He needs a "salt" to bring out the flavor—"pain and weariness, and fault." The speaker tells us that he craves "the stain / Of tears, the aftermark / Of almost too much love. . . ."

Is the point that Frost is making here similar to that which Keats makes in his "Ode on Melancholy"? That is, is Frost like Keats suggesting that the only satisfying beauty is that which is connected with loss and suffering? In any case, Frost has his own characteristic way of making the point. He uses, in the last two stanzas, a homely but powerfully effective figure. Everybody knows how, lying on the grass, you prop yourself with your hand, not realizing how much weight it has to sustain until you find,

when you raise the hand, that grass stems or tiny pebbles have left their mark upon it, indenting the skin. Now the speaker craves to feel the earth as rough "to all my length."

Is he masochistic? Is he saying that now that his senses are dulled with age, he needs pain mixed with the sensation in order to feel with sufficient intensity? Or is he saying that he has learned to love the earth and reality as opposed to any mere dreams of it? That he wants reality, roughness and all, and that he finds that joy that is "not dashed with pain" now seems unreal?

The student may want to ponder these questions before arriving at his own conclusion. He may also want to read this poem in the light of the other Frost poems in this little group and see whether they can help him to make out what the poet is saying here. In any case, this much is plain: though Frost honestly faces the fact that man is alienated from nature, he loves nature, all of it, including its harshness and its ability to hurt. Indeed, these last may serve to guarantee his sense of real communion with it.

1. Notice how important in this poem are images of taste and smell—particularly of taste. Compare the use that Frost makes of taste imagery in this poem with that made by Keats in his "Ode to Melancholy."

2. How would you define the tone of this poem?

Come In

As I came to the edge of the woods,
Thrush music—hark!
Now if it was dusk outside,
Inside it was dark.

Too dark in the woods for a bird   5
By sleight of wing
To better its perch for the night,
Though it still could sing.

The last of the light of the sun
That had died in the west   10
Still lived for one song more
In a thrush's breast.

Far in the pillared dark
Thrush music went—
Almost like a call to come in   15
To the dark and lament.

But no, I was out for stars:
I would not come in.
I meant not even if asked,
And I hadn't been.   20

Out for a walk at evening, the speaker hears a thrush's music and thinks of the bird singing out of the now dark woods. With the fourth stanza he comes to a position very close to that reached in lines 9 and 10 of "A Leaf Treader." The thrush's music seems melancholy, the voice of nature itself, calling for man to join the lament rising out of the gathering darkness, the darkness that will eventually claim him and which, though frightening, exerts a positive attraction.

But the man out for the walk is one indeed versed in country things. He knows that the thrush is not really lamenting and phrases his comment very carefully. He says *Almost* like a call to come in / To the dark and lament." The last stanza—*cf.* "A Leaf Treader"—changes tone sharply and effectively. The speaker reminds himself that he did not come out for thrush music anyway, but to look at the stars. He refuses the invitation; he says "I would not come in." But then he remembers his manners, and with a further shift in tone, adds "I meant not even if asked, / And I hadn't been." He takes care not to presume upon an invitation that may not have been intended, for he knows that indeed no invitation has been given. Nature is supremely indifferent to man. Her thrush is not lamenting, and Nature does not care whether man himself laments or rejoices.

1. The description in this poem is not vague but quite detailed and exact. For example, notice such phrases as "By sleight of wing" (l. 6) or "To better its perch" (l. 7). Notice too that the observer is aware of the exact shades of light at this moment: "The last light of the sun," the dusk outside the wood, and the complete darkness within the wood. What is the effect on the poem of this sense of precise statement?

2. In line 15, what is the sense of "the pillared dark"?

3. How would you characterize the tone of this poem? What shifts of tone occur in the poem?

4. Do you gain any sense of the speaker's personality? How does it compare with that of the man who narrates "The Wood-Pile"? "The Star-Splitter"? Why is the speaker "out for stars"?

The Oven Bird

There is a singer everyone has heard,
Loud, a mid-summer and a mid-wood bird,
Who makes the solid tree trunks sound again.
He says that leaves are old and that for flowers
Mid-summer is to spring as one to ten.   5
He says the early petal-fall is past
When pear and cherry bloom went down in
   showers
On sunny days a moment overcast;
And comes that other fall we name the fall.
He says the highway dust is over all.   10
The bird would cease and be as other birds
But that he knows in singing not to sing.
The question that he frames in all but words
Is what to make of a diminished thing.

As this sonnet implies, the oven bird's song is not particularly musical, and since the oven bird really has very little to sing about, this fact is appropriate. His world is a world in which the spring flowers are gone, in which the leaves have lost their freshness, and "the highway dust is over all." What matters is that this bird manages to sing at all when the other birds, under such conditions, have given over. It may be amusing to compare Frost's account of the bird with that given in a technical bird guide. *A Guide to Birdsongs* by Aretas A. Saunders, (Garden City, N. Y.: Doubleday & Co., Inc., 1951) states that

"the Ovenbird is common in summer practically throughout the northeastern United States. . . . It sings from its arrival, the last of April, till the third week in July. . . . The common song of this bird is very distinctive and not easily mistaken for any other. It is a series of two-note phrases repeated to the end usually without variation in pitch or time, but increasing in loudness to the end of the song. The quality is not particularly musical, but the song is loud and one of the commonest sounds of the forest in early summer."

1. Frost's account is evidently accurate enough, even by technical standards. What does his poem give us that the prose exposition cannot give?

2. What does the poet mean in line 12 in saying that the oven bird "knows in singing not to sing"? What is the meaning of "singing" in this context?

3. What is the tone of this poem? What is the poet's attitude toward the bird? Amusement? Admiration? He apparently cannot give the oven bird high marks for singing. Does he award him an E for effort? Is it stupidity or intelligent taste that the bird displays in knowing "not to sing"?

4. Compare this poem to Keats' "Ode to Autumn." Is the season described by Keats a "diminished thing"? Or not? What is the relation of Keats' choir of "mournful gnats" and the no-song of the oven bird?

5. Is there any hint in this poem of Frost's attitude toward nature? Would you say that the human being in this instance feels perhaps a little closer to the oven bird than to some of the finer songsters? If you feel that this is hinted, why should he feel closer?

6. Read "Robert Frost," by W. H. Auden (p. 546). What connection do you see between these poems and Auden's ideas?

A Group of Poems by Emily Dickinson (1830-1886)

The eleven poems that follow are rather typical of the themes, methods, and metrical patterns used by this poet. A quality of sensibility—a special insight, a peculiar vision—is stamped upon nearly everything that Emily Dickinson ever wrote. Whether she is describing the weather, or a landscape, or the aspirations of human life and the disappointments to which it is subject, the poems bear her special signature. The student should examine them and try to see for himself how much unity this group of poems has.

If the student wishes, however, to go beyond a few very general observations, he will find it useful to frame some more particular questions and to re-examine the poem in the light of them. (The comments made and the questions put with reference to reading the Keats and the Frost poems earlier in this section will provide suggestions for the student.) For a start, here are two concrete observations, the first on the poet's themes, the other on her imagery. (1) Death informs a great deal of Emily Dickinson's poetry and lies at the background of many of her poems that ostensibly have nothing at all to do with it. (2) The concrete images for much of her poetry—even of that which deals with exalted and profound themes—is provided by the matter-of-fact of domestic life: household activities and the sights and smells of the yards and fields about the house. Test these comments against the poems themselves and see if you can frame others that will bring into focus the essential unity to be found in these poems.

Because Emily Dickinson's life and work were very intimately connected, it may be useful to gain some acquaintance with the poet's biography. The student may do well to examine such studies as George F. Whicher's *This Was a Poet* (New York: Charles Scribner's Sons, 1939); Richard Chase's *Emily Dickinson* (New York: William Morrow and Co., Inc., 1951); Thomas H. Johnson's *Emily Dickinson: An Interpretive Biography* (Cambridge, Mass: Harvard University Press, 1955); and Jay Leyda, *The Years and Hours of Emily Dickinson* (New Haven, Conn.: Yale University Press, 1960).

These are the days
when Birds come back

These are the days when Birds come back—
A very few—a Bird or two—
To take a backward look.

These are the days when skies resume
The old—old sophistries of June—   5
A blue and gold mistake.

Oh fraud that cannot cheat the Bee—
Almost thy plausibility
Induces my belief.

Till ranks of seeds their witness bear—   10
And softly thro' the altered air
Hurries a timid leaf.

Oh Sacrament of summer days,
Oh Last Communion in the Haze—
Permit a child to join.   15

Thy sacred emblems to partake—
Thy consecrated bread to take
And thine immortal wine!

The Sky is low—
the Clouds are mean

The Sky is low—the Clouds are mean.
A Travelling Flake of Snow
Across a Barn or through a Rut
Debates if it will go—

A Narrow Wind complains all Day   5
How some one treated him

Nature, like Us is sometimes caught
Without her Diadem.

The Mountains stood in Haze

The Mountains stood in Haze—
The Valleys stopped below
And went or waited as they liked
The River and the Sky.

At leisure was the Sun—   5
His interests of Fire
A little from remark withdrawn—
The Twilight spoke the Spire,

So soft upon the Scene
The Act of evening fell   10
We felt how neighborly a Thing
Was the Invisible.

I could not prove the Years
had feet

I could not prove the Years had feet—
Yet confident they run
Am I, from symptoms that are past
And Series that are done—

I find my feet have further Goals—   5
I smile upon the Aims
That felt so ample—Yesterday—
Today's—have vaster claims—

I do not doubt the self I was
Was competent to me—   10
But something awkward in the fit—
Proves that—outgrown—I see—

"Hope" is the thing with feathers

"Hope" is the thing with feathers—
That perches in the soul—
And sings the tune without the words—
And never stops—at all—

And sweetest—in the Gale—is heard—   5
And sore must be the storm—
That could abash the little Bird
That kept so many warm—

I've heard it in the chillest land—
And on the strangest Sea—   10
Yet, never, in Extremity,
It asked a crumb—of Me.

Success is counted sweetest

Success is counted sweetest
By those who ne'er succeed.
To comprehend a nectar
Requires sorest need.

Not one of all the purple Host   5
Who took the Flag today
Can tell the definition
So clear of Victory

As he defeated—dying—
On whose forbidden ear   10
The distant strains of triumph
Burst agonized and clear!

Our journey had advanced

Our journey had advanced—
Our feet were almost come

To that odd Fork in Being's Road—
Eternity—by Term—

Our pace took sudden awe—   5
Our feet—reluctant—led—
Before—were Cities—but Between—
The Forest of the Dead—

Retreat—was out of Hope—
Behind—a Sealed Route—   10
Eternity's White Flag—Before—
And God—at every Gate—

I Years had been from Home

I Years had been from Home
And now before the Door
I dared not enter, lest a Face
I never saw before

Stare stolid into mine   5
And ask my Business there—
"My Business but a Life I left
Was such remaining there?"

I leaned upon the Awe—
I lingered with Before—   10
The Second like an Ocean rolled
And broke against my ear—

I laughed a crumbling Laugh
That I could fear a Door
Who Consternation compassed   15
And never winced before.

I fitted to the Latch
My Hand, with trembling care
Lest back the awful Door should spring
And leave me in the Floor—   20

Then moved my Fingers off
As cautiously as Glass
And held my ears, and like a Thief
Fled gasping from the House—

Her final Summer was it

Her final Summer was it—
And yet We guessed it not—
If tenderer industriousness
Pervaded Her, We thought

A further force of life　　　　　　　5
Developed from within—
When Death lit all the shortness up
It made the hurry plain—

We wondered at our blindness
When nothing was to see　　　　　10
But Her Carrara Guide post—
At Our Stupidity—

When duller than our dullness
The Busy Darling lay—
So busy was she—finishing—　　　15
So Leisurely—were We—

Because I could not stop for Death

Because I could not stop for Death—
He kindly stopped for me—
The Carriage held but just Ourselves—
And Immortality.

We slowly drove—He knew no haste　　5
And I had put away
My labor and my leisure too,
For His Civility—

We passed the School, where Children strove
At Recess—in the Ring—　　　　　10
We passed the Fields of Gazing Grain—
We passed the Setting Sun—

Or rather—He passed Us—
The Dews drew quivering and chill—
For only Gossamer, my Gown—　　　15
My Tippet—only Tulle—

We paused before a House that seemed
A Swelling of the Ground—
The Roof was scarcely visible—
The Cornice—in the Ground—　　　20

Since then—'tis Centuries—and yet
Feels shorter than the Day
I first surmised the Horses' Heads
Were toward Eternity—

I heard a Fly buzz—when I died

I heard a Fly buzz—when I died—
The Stillness in the Room
Was like the Stillness in the Air—
Between the Heaves of Storm—

The Eyes around—had wrung them dry—　5
And Breaths were gathering firm
For that last Onset—when the King
Be witnessed—in the Room—

I willed my Keepsakes—Signed away
What portion of me be　　　　　　10
Assignable—and then it was
There interposed a Fly—

With Blue—uncertain stumbling Buzz—
Between the light—and me—
And then the Windows failed—and then　15
I could not see to see—

DISCURSIVE PROSE

Introduction

Our most common form of writing is what may be called discursive prose—the form of logical discourse. Inasmuch as our age prides itself on its recognition of the sanctity of "fact" and its respect for common sense, it is only to be expected that non-fictional prose should ordinarily be thought of as that form of writing that has to do with the presentation of facts and the handling of facts in relation to ideas. Typical examples would be a magazine article dealing with juvenile delinquency or with the prospects for a cure for cancer, an analysis of our foreign policy by a columnist or a political scientist, an argument for or against religion, or perhaps a psychological study of John Keats or of Adolf Hitler. Even when opinions or attitudes constitute the subject matter, we expect the logical marshalling of facts to be decisive. We claim that, as reasonable men, we will submit ourselves to the facts and to logical arguments based upon those facts. Clarity of presentation may thus plausibly seem to be the only virtue required for such writing, and writing that aims at a logical presentation of its material will often be thought of as worlds apart from "fine" literature—fancy things such as fiction and poetry.

Let us grant that clarity is the prime virtue of all writing. But, then, we must ask, in every instance, "What is it that is made clear?" and that is the rub. Does not a story or a poem have its own kind of clarity? Let us take, for example, Keats' "Ode on Melancholy." At a first reading it may seem very unclear to us—not at all as clear as the morning paper. Gradually, we may realize that the thing the poem aims to make "clear" is something very different from the facts the morning paper aims to make clear, and we may eventually realize that the way of the poem is the only way to make that particular subject clear. Criticism and discussion, the analysis of metrics or the study of psychology, the experience of day to day living plus a good thorough experience of literature in general—all of these may help pre-

pare us to read the poem. But these activities have not made the poem *clearer*; they "prepare" us to appreciate the "clarity" of the poem—that is, to appreciate the fullness and force with which the poem deals with its particular subject which is different from that of the morning paper.

To use a crude analogy, we may say that the process of preparation we are talking about here is rather like learning a foreign language. As we study the grammar of the language, listen to the spoken words, and twist our lips to make the unaccustomed sounds, we are changing ourselves, but we are not changing the nature of, say, the French language, we are not making it any "clearer." In fact, we may say that reading and studying a poem or story written in our own language is, fundamentally, a way of studying the nature of language itself, of coming to appreciate the expressive range and depth possible to words—of making ourselves ready to appreciate the "clarity" in a good literary work.

There are, of course, special languages—one here thinks of mathematics and science and some forms of logic—that dispense to a considerable degree, if not fully, with words: H_2O or $2 + 2 = 4$ will illustrate the non-verbal statements made in such special languages. There are, as we have already indicated in the General Introduction various other special languages with their own technical vocabularies and forms of statement. The inquest report on poor Porphyria, or the legal indictment of her lover (p. 2), is written in a special language and may seem to lie outside the bounds of literature. But wherever words, in the ordinary sense, enter, we have literary concerns—questions of form and style. And one may point out that even the most specialized technical languages are not completely divorced from these concerns: even mathematicians refer to the "elegance" of a demonstration, and lawyers to the "style" of a brief. The point is this: if technical language devised for precision in connection with some special subject carries with it the notions of form and style, then we shall misconceive form and style as they exist in ordinary discursive prose if we think of them as merely ornamental. Style may, to be sure, strike us as beautiful and please us aesthetically, but this does not mean that it is not fundamentally grounded in the writer's concern for precision and expressiveness, in his exploration and discrimination of meanings.

In fiction and poetry, of course, form and style have this same grounding. The difference between poetry, say, and discursive prose lies not in the difference between *belles lettres* and utilitarian writing but in the particular occasions which call them forth and which they serve. By "occasion" here, we mean that combination of the writer's various concerns—with the subject and his audience as well as with his more specific purposes and interests—that condition the piece of writing. For instance, we shall find among the essays in this general section, an eminent humorist, James Thurber, writing on French versions of the American Wild West stories; an eminent psychologist, B. F. Skinner, writing on the scientific control of human behavior; an eminent historian, Samuel Eliot Morison, writing on the youth of George Washington as a preparation for his greatness; and an eminent poet, T. S. Eliot, writing on literature in the modern world. Obviously, the problems of form and style—the problems of what constitutes the appropriate "clarity"—do not remain the same from one occasion to the next. Nor does the kind of preparation needed to appreciate that "clarity" remain the same from essay to essay.

In the essays to be studied we shall be concerned with differences in form and style, but we shall necessarily be concerned with them in relation to what writers are saying. What they are saying is important: many of these writers address themselves to the most crucial questions of our time. Indeed, many of the ideas discussed in the examples of discursive prose in our book underlie the literature of our time. We shall therefore try to see, for example, the relation between some of the essays to be studied here and some of the stories and poems that are printed earlier in this text.

SECTION I

The Personal Essay

In our general discussion we have just said that in our time we tend to think of non-fictional prose—let us say specifically the essay—as concerned with the presentation of facts and the handling of facts in relation to ideas. Let us, for example, return once more to the story of Porphyria and her lover which was treated in the "General Introduction." Suppose our writer, on the basis of this happening, decided to write not a poem or a story or a play, but an essay. What would be the nature of his essay? How would it differ from the other forms mentioned? It might, of course, treat any one of a number of aspects of the episode. It might turn out to be an essay on abnormal psychology, using the psychology of the murderer as an illustration. Or it might be an essay on marriage and marriage customs. Or it might be an essay on the attitudes which civilized people take towards such happenings as that involved in the story of Porphyria and her lover. Or it might be an essay on tragedy. But all the various possibilities which we have cited have one important thing in common: all tend to employ the facts of the original murder story as merely a starting point from which to go off into a discussion of a general idea, or to employ it as an illustration of a general idea. And this common trait separates the essay as a form of discursive prose rather sharply from fiction, drama, or poetry. In the story or the poem or the drama, the *particular* situation is the heart of the matter, the center of reference; in the essay the center of reference lies in some *general* idea or ideas, and any one of the possible treatments suggested above would conform to our ordinary notion of what an essay is.

The essay as a literary type is, however, much more various than our ordinary notion would indicate. As a matter of fact, when, at the end of the sixteenth century, the Frenchman Michel de Montaigne began writing what he called *essais*,[1] he was primarily concerned with expressing and revealing his own personality, and we can immediately see that this impulse is very close to that behind, say, lyric poetry and some fiction. Clearly, Montaigne's kind of essay established, as it were, one of the frontiers of the essay, for the essay occupies a broad sort of borderland which touches on one side the realm of "pure" literature (fiction, poetry, drama) and on the other the realm of practical and scientific writing (chemistry text books, medical prescriptions, cook books, etc.).

The kind of essay which Montaigne wrote established a type, a genre, called sometimes the *personal essay*, sometimes the *informal essay*, sometimes the *familiar essay*. It has existed for more than three hundred years, and some great names are associated with it—Addison, Steele, Lamb. It exists today, and has some brilliant practitioners, though the most popular form of it is now found in certain newspaper columnists —for instance, Art Buchwald, Harry Golden, and Robert Ruark. But in later years the personal essay has appeared less and less often. It may be said, by way of partial explanation, that the great masters of this form did their work before the development of the short story as we now know it. In the last two generations, the short story as developed by such writers as Anton Chekhov, Stephen Crane, Katherine Mansfield, Sherwood Anderson, James Joyce, Eudora Welty, Elizabeth Bowen, and Katherine Anne Porter has exploited psychological nuances, delicate shadings of personality and sensibility, and highly personal and sometimes poetic styles. Such writers have, in other words, appealed to the very tastes and interests which the writers of the personal essay once appealed to; and, with the freedom of fiction, they have been able to appeal to these tastes more concretely and variously. In making this observation we are not making an adverse criticism of such an essay as "Dream Children"—as if it were necessarily inferior to some of the later fiction which in some sense it foreshadows. What we are concerned to point out is the shadowiness of the line that separates Lamb's essay from such a story as "Araby."

Dream Children: A Reverie

CHARLES LAMB (1775-1834)

[1822]

CHILDREN LOVE to listen to stories about their elders, when *they* were children; to stretch their imagination to the conception of a traditionary great-uncle, or grandame, whom they never saw. It was in this spirit that my little ones crept about me the other evening to hear about their great-grandmother Field, who lived in a great house in Norfolk (a hundred times bigger than that in which they and papa lived) which had been the scene—so at least it was generally believed in that part of the country—of the tragic incidents which they had lately become familiar with from the ballad of the Children in the Wood. Certain it is that the whole story of the children and their cruel uncle was to be seen

[1] Our word *essay* comes from the word Montaigne used to describe what he was doing—making a trial, an attempt.

fairly carved out in wood upon the chimney-piece of the great-hall, the whole story down to the Robin Redbreasts; till a foolish rich person pulled it down to set up a marble one of modern invention in its stead, with no story upon it. Here Alice put out one of her dear mother's looks, too tender to be called upbraiding. Then I went on to say, how religious and how good their great-grandmother Field was, how beloved and respected by everybody, though she was not indeed the mistress of this great house, but had only the charge of it (and yet in some respects she might be said to be the mistress of it too) committed to her by the owner, who preferred living in a newer and more fashionable mansion which he had purchased somewhere in the adjoining county; but still she lived in it in a manner as if it had been her own, and kept up the dignity of the great house in a sort while she lived, which afterwards came to decay, and was nearly pulled down, and all its old ornaments stripped and carried away to the owner's other house, where they were set up, and looked as awkward as if some one were to carry away the old tombs they had seen lately at the Abbey, and stick them up in Lady C.'s tawdry gilt drawing-room. Here John smiled, as much as to say, "that would be foolish indeed." And then I told how, when she came to die, her funeral was attended by a concourse of all the poor, and some of the gentry, too, of the neighborhood, for many miles round, to show their respect for her memory, because she had been such a good and religious woman; so good indeed that she knew all the Psaltery by heart, aye, and a great part of the Testament besides. Here little Alice spread her hands. Then I told what a tall, upright, graceful person their great-grandmother Field once was; and how in her youth she was esteemed the best dancer—here Alice's little right foot played an involuntary movement, till, upon my looking grave, it desisted—the best dancer, I was saying, in the county, till a cruel disease, called a cancer, came, and bowed her down with pain; but it could never bend her good spirits, or make them stoop, but they were still upright, because she was so good and religious. Then I told how she was used to sleep by herself in a lone chamber of the great lone house; and how she believed that an apparition of two infants

was to be seen at midnight gliding up and down the great staircase near where she slept, but she said "those innocents would do her no harm"; and how frightened I used to be, though in those days I had my maid to sleep with me, because I was never half so good or religious as she—and yet I never saw the infants. Here John expanded all his eyebrows and tried to look courageous. Then I told how good she was to all her grandchildren, having us to the great house in the holidays, where I in particular used to spend many hours by myself, in gazing upon the old busts of the twelve Caesars, that had been Emperors of Rome, till the old marble heads would seem to live again, or I to be turned into marble with them; how I could never be tired with roaming about that huge mansion, with its vast empty rooms, with their worn-out hangings, fluttering tapestry, and carved oaken panels, with the gilding almost rubbed out—sometimes in the spacious old-fashioned gardens, which I had almost to myself, unless when now and then a solitary gardening man would cross me—and how the nectarines and peaches hung upon the walls, without my ever offering to pluck them, because they were forbidden fruit, unless now and then—and because I had more pleasure in strolling about among the old melancholy-looking yew-trees, or the firs, and picking up the red-berries, and the fir-apples, which were good for nothing but to look at—or in lying about upon the fresh grass with all the fine garden smells around me—or basking in the orangery, till I could almost fancy myself ripening too along with the oranges and the limes in that grateful warmth—or in watching the dace that darted to and fro in the fish pond, at the bottom of the garden, with here and there a great sulky pike hanging midway down the water in silent state, as if it mocked at their impertinent friskings; I had more pleasure in these busy-idle diversions than in all the sweet flavors of peaches, nectarines, oranges, and such-like common baits of children. Here John slily deposited back upon the plate a bunch of grapes, which, not unobserved by Alice, he had meditated dividing with her, and both seemed willing to relinquish them for the present as *irrelevant*. Then, in somewhat a more heightened tone, I told how, though their great-grandmother Field loved all her grand-children, yet in an especial manner she might be said to love their uncle John L——, because he was so handsome and spirited a youth, and a king to the rest of us; and, instead of moping about in solitary corners, like some of us, he would mount the most mettlesome horse he could get, when but an imp no bigger than themselves, and make it carry him half over the county in a morning, and join the hunters when there were any out; and yet he loved the old great house and gardens too, but had too much spirit to be always pent up within their boundaries—and how their uncle grew up to man's estate as brave as he was handsome, to the admiration of everybody, but of their great-grandmother Field most especially; and how he used to carry me upon his back when I was a lame-footed boy—for he was a good bit older than me—many a mile when I could not walk for pain; and how in after life he became lame-footed too, and I did not always (I fear) make allowances enough for him when he was impatient, and in pain, nor remember sufficiently how considerate he had been to me when I was lame-footed; and how when he died; though he had not been dead an hour, it seemed as if he had died a great while ago, such a distance there is betwixt life and death; and how I bore his death as I thought pretty well at first, but afterwards it haunted and haunted me; and though I did not cry or take it to heart as some do, and as I think he would have done if I had died, yet I missed him all day long, and knew not till then how much I had loved him. I missed his kindness, and I missed his crossness, and wished him to be alive again, to be quarrelling with him (for we quarrelled sometimes), rather than not have him again, and was as uneasy without him, as he their poor uncle must have been when the doctor took off his limb. Here the children fell a crying, and asked if their little mourning which they had on was not for uncle John, and they looked up, and prayed me not to go on about their uncle, but to tell them some stories about their pretty dead mother. Then I told how for seven long years, in hope sometimes, sometimes in despair, yet persisting ever, I courted the fair Alice W——n; and, as much as children could understand, I

explained to them what coyness, and difficulty, and denial, meant in maidens—when suddenly, turning to Alice, the soul of the first Alice looked out at her eyes with such a reality of re-presentment, that I became in doubt which of them stood there before me, or whose that bright hair was; and while I stood gazing, both the children gradually grew fainter to my view, receding, and still receding, till nothing at last but two mournful features were seen in the uttermost distance, which, without speech, strangely impressed upon me the effects of speech: "We are not of Alice, nor of thee, nor are we children at all. The children of Alice call Bartrum father. We are nothing, less than nothing, and dreams. We are only what might have been, and must wait upon the tedious shores of Lethe millions of ages before we have existence, and a name"—and immediately awakening, I found myself quietly seated in my bachelor armchair, where I had fallen asleep, with the faithful Bridget unchanged by my side; but John L. (or James Elia) was gone for ever.

EXERCISE

1. "Dream Children" lies at the very frontier that divides the essay from fiction. We have an immediate scene, the narrator talking to the children whom, as yet, we do not know to be dream children. The narrator's own character, and what we may take as the most significant facts of his life, gradually emerge for us. At the very end, however, there is a surprise, which gives an effect very much like that at the end of many stories. Furthermore, the whole essay is shot through with emotion, is governed by a dominant mood.

Taking all of these factors into account, what might be taken to distinguish "Dream Children" from a story? Compare it, for instance, with "An Episode of War," by Stephen Crane, "Araby," by James Joyce, "The Use of Force," by W. C. Williams, or "The Lottery Ticket," by Anton Chekhov. It is possible, of course, that, after all, you do feel that it is a short story, and that it is called an essay only because it was written before the rise of the story as we now understand it. If that is your view, defend it.

2. As we have said, "Dream Children" is shot through with emotion, and is governed by a dominant mood. How would you define this mood? How would you state the emotional relation of the tale the narrator tells the children, and the revelation about his own life at the end? Can you fix on any details along the way that might be considered emo-

tionally appropriate? For instance, the details of the narrator's life when, as a boy, he visited the estate presided over by his grandmother Field. What is the atmosphere of the garden of the estate? Locate details that support your generalization. In this connection, what relation do you see between the impression you get of the boy and that which you get of the narrator as a man?

3. Study the characteristic sentence structure. Read sections aloud and catch the natural rhythm of the prose. Do you see any relation between this style and the fact that most of what we have is a paraphrase of the tale to the children? Can you see any relation between the style, in this aspect, and the subject and mood? What is the prevailing tone of the whole? Are there any shifts of tone?

4. The dominant mood here, the pathos of the might-have-been, could readily lapse into sentimentality. Does Lamb, in your opinion, avoid this danger? Return to "The Fir Tree," by Hans Christian Andersen (p. 32). There we made some comment on the significance of the fact that the tale, presumably addressed to children, makes its impact on adult readers. Can you see any connection between that situation and the problem of avoiding sentimentality here? That is, in real life a certain tone acceptable in addressing children would be regarded as offensive or silly if used in addressing an adult.

5. Do you feel that the surprise ending is here justified? If so, has it been actually prepared for? How?

Farewell, My Lovely

LEE STROUT WHITE

(E. B. White and Richard Lee Strout)

[1936]

I SEE by the new Sears Roebuck catalogue that it is still possible to buy an axle for a 1909 Model T Ford, but I am not deceived. The great days have faded, the end is in sight. Only one page in the current catalogue is devoted to parts and accessories for the Model T; yet everyone remembers springtimes when the Ford gadget section was larger than men's clothing, almost as large as household furnishings. The last Model T was built in 1927, and the car is fading from what scholars call the American scene—which is an understatement, because to a few million people who grew up with it, the old Ford practically *was* the American scene.

It was the miracle God had wrought. And it was patently the sort of thing that could only happen once. Mechanically uncanny, it was like nothing that had ever come to the world before. Flourishing industries rose and fell with it. As a vehicle, it was hard-working, commonplace, heroic; and it often seemed to transmit those qualities to the persons who rode in it. My own generation identifies it with Youth,

with its gaudy irretrievable excitements; before it fades into the mist, I would like to pay it the tribute of the sigh that is not a sob, and set down random entries in a shape somewhat less cumbersome than a Sears Roebuck catalogue.

The Model T was distinguished from all other makes of cars by the fact that its transmission was of a type known as planetary—which was half metaphysics, half sheer friction. Engineers accepted the word "planetary" in its epicyclic sense, but I was always conscious that it also meant "wandering," "erratic." Because of the peculiar nature of this planetary element, there was always, in the Model T, a certain dull rapport between engine and wheels, and even when the car was in a state known as neutral, it trembled with a deep imperative and tended to inch forward. There was never a moment when the bands were not faintly egging the machine on. In this respect it was like a horse, rolling the bit on its tongue, and country people brought to it the same technique they used with draft animals.

Its most remarkable quality was its rate of

acceleration. In its palmy days the Model T could take off faster than anything on the road. The reason was simple. To get under way, you simply hooked the third finger of the right hand around a lever on the steering column, pulled down hard, and shoved your left foot forcibly against the low-speed pedal. These were simple, positive motions; the car responded by lunging forward with a roar. After a few seconds of this turmoil, you took your toe off the pedal, eased up a mite on the throttle, and the car, possessed of only two forward speeds, catapulted directly into high with a series of ugly jerks and was off on its glorious errand. The abruptness of this departure was never equalled in other cars of the period. The human leg was (and still is) incapable of letting in a clutch with anything like the forthright abandon that used to send Model T on its way. Letting in a clutch is a negative, hesitant motion, depending on delicate nervous control; pushing down the Ford pedal was a simple, country motion—an expansive act, which came as natural as kicking an old door to make it budge.

The driver of the old Model T was a man enthroned. The car, with top up, stood seven feet high. The driver sat on top of the gas tank, brooding it with his own body. When he wanted gasoline, he alighted, along with everything else in the front seat; the seat was pulled off, the metal cap unscrewed, and a wooden stick thrust down to sound the liquid in the well. There were always a couple of these sounding sticks kicking around in the ratty sub-cushion regions of a flivver. Refuelling was more of a social function then, because the driver had to unbend, whether he wanted to or not. Directly in front of the driver was the windshield—high, uncompromisingly erect. Nobody talked about air resistance, and the four cylinders pushed the car through the atmosphere with a simple disregard of physical law.

There was this about a Model T: the purchaser never regarded his purchase as a complete, finished product. When you bought a Ford, you figured you had a start—a vibrant, spirited framework to which could be screwed an almost limitless assortment of decorative and functional hardware. Driving away from the agency, hugging the new wheel between your knees, you were already full of creative worry. A Ford was born naked as a baby, and a flourishing industry grew up out of correcting its rare deficiencies and combating its fascinating diseases. Those were the great days of lily-painting. I have been looking at some old Sears Roebuck catalogues, and they bring everything back so clear.

First you bought a Ruby Safety Reflector for the rear, so that your posterior would glow in another car's brilliance. Then you invested thirty-nine cents in some radiator Moto Wings, a popular ornament which gave the Pegasus touch to the machine and did something godlike to the owner. For nine cents you bought a fan belt guide to keep the belt from slipping off the pulley.

You bought a radiator compound to stop leaks. This was as much a part of everybody's equipment as aspirin tablets are of a medicine cabinet. You bought special oil to prevent chattering, a clamp-on dash light, a patching outfit, a tool box which you bolted to the running board, a sun visor, a steering-column brace to keep the column rigid, and a set of emergency containers for gas, oil, and water—three thin, disc-like cans which reposed in a case on the running board during long, important journeys—red for gas, gray for water, green for oil. It was only a beginning. After the car was about a year old, steps were taken to check the alarming disintegration. (Model T was full of tumors, but they were benign.) A set of anti-rattlers (98¢) was a popular panacea. You hooked them on to the gas and spark rods, to the brake pull rod, and to the steering-rod connections. Hood silencers, of black rubber, were applied to the fluttering hood. Shock-absorbers and snubbers gave "complete relaxation." Some people bought rubber pedal pads, to fit over the standard metal pedals. (I didn't like these, I remember.) Persons of a suspicious or pugnacious turn of mind bought a rear-view mirror; but most Model T owners weren't worried by what was coming from behind because they would soon enough see it out in front. They rode in a state of cheerful catalepsy. Quite a large mutinous clique among Ford owners went over to a foot accelerator (you could buy one and screw it to the floor board), but there was a certain madness in these people, because the Model T, just as she stood, had a choice of three foot pedals to push, and there were plenty of moments when both feet were occupied in the routine performance of duty and when the only way to speed up the engine was with the hand throttle.

Gadget bred gadget. Owners not only bought ready-made gadgets, they invented gadgets to meet special needs. I myself drove my car directly from the agency to the blacksmith's, and had the smith affix two enormous iron brackets to the port running board to support an army trunk.

People who owned closed models builded along different lines; they bought ball grip handles for opening doors, window anti-rattlers, and deluxe flower vases of the cut-glass anti-splash type. People with delicate sensibilities garnished their car with a device called the Donna Lee Automobile Disseminator—a porous vase guaranteed, according to Sears, to fill the car with a "faint clean odor of lavender." The gap between open cars and closed cars was not as great then as it is now: for $11.95 Sears Roebuck converted your touring car into a sedan and you went forth renewed. One agreeable quality of the old Fords was that they had no bumpers, and their fenders softened and wilted with the years and permitted the driver to squeeze in and out of tight places.

Tires were 30 x 3½, cost about twelve dollars, and punctured readily. Everybody carried a Jiffy patching set, with a nutmeg grater to roughen the tube before the goo was spread on. Everybody was capable of putting on a patch, expected to have to, and did have to.

During my association with Model T's, self-starters were not a prevalent accessory. They were expensive and under suspicion. Your car came equipped with a serviceable crank, and the first thing you learned was how to Get Results. It was a special trick, and until you learned it (usually from another Ford owner, but sometimes by a period of appalling experimentation) you might as well have been winding up an awning. The trick was to leave the ignition switch off, proceed to the animal's head, pull the choke (which was a little wire protruding through the radiator), and give the crank

two or three nonchalant upward lifts. Then, whistling as though thinking about something else, you would saunter back to the driver's cabin, turn the ignition on, return to the crank, and this time, catching it on the down stroke, give it a quick spin with plenty of That. If this procedure was followed, the engine almost always responded—first with a few scattered explosions, then with a tumultuous gunfire, which you checked by racing around to the driver's seat and retarding the throttle. Often, if the emergency brake hadn't been pulled all the way back, the car advanced on you the instant the first explosions occurred and you would hold it back by leaning your weight against it. I can still feel my old Ford nuzzling me at the curb, as though looking for an apple in my pocket.

In zero weather, ordinary cranking became an impossibility, except for giants. The oil thickened, and it became necessary to jack up the rear wheels, which, for some planetary reason, eased the throw.

The lore and legend that governed the Ford were boundless. Owners had their own theories about everything; they discussed mutual problems in that wise, infinitely resourceful way old women discuss rheumatism. Exact knowledge was pretty scarce, and often proved less effective than superstition. Dropping a camphor ball into the gas tank was a popular expedient; it seemed to have a tonic effect on both man and machine. There wasn't much to base exact knowledge on. The Ford driver flew blind. He didn't know the temperature of his engine, the speed of his car, the amount of his fuel, or the pressure of his oil (the old Ford lubricated itself by what was amiably described as the "spash system"). A speedometer cost money and was an extra, like a windshield-wiper. The dashboard of the early models was bare save for an ignition key; later models, grown effete, boasted an ammeter which pulsated alarmingly with the throbbing of the car. Under the dash was a box of coils, with vibrators which you adjusted, or thought you adjusted. Whatever the driver learned of his motor, he learned not through instruments but through sudden developments. I remember that the timer was one of the vital organs about which there was ample doctrine. When everything else had been checked, you "had a look" at the timer. It was an extravagantly odd little device, simple in construction, mysterious in function. It contained a roller, held by a spring, and there were four contact points on the inside of the case against which, many people believed, the roller rolled. I have had a timer apart on a sick Ford many times, but I never really knew what I was up to—I was just showing off before God. There were almost as many schools of thought as there were timers. Some people, when things went wrong, just clenched their teeth and gave the timer a smart crack with a wrench. Other people opened it up and blew on it. There was a school that held that the timer needed large amounts of oil; they fixed it by frequent baptism. And there was a school that was positive it was meant to run dry as a bone; these people were continually taking it off and wiping it. I remember one spitting into a timer; not in anger, but in a spirit of research. You see, the Model T driver moved in the realm of metaphysics. He believed his car could be hexed.

One reason the Ford anatomy was never reduced to an exact science was that, having "fixed" it, the owner couldn't honestly claim that the treatment had brought about the cure. There were too many authenticated cases of Fords fixing themselves—restored naturally to health after a short rest. Farmers soon discovered this, and it fitted nicely with their draft-horse philosophy: "Let 'er cool off and she'll snap into it again."

A Ford owner had Number One Bearing constantly in mind. This bearing, being at the front end of the motor, was the one that always burned out, because the oil didn't reach it when the car was climbing hills. (That's what I was always told, anyway.) The oil used to recede and leave Number One dry as a clam flat; you had to watch that bearing like a hawk. It was like a weak heart—you could hear it start knocking, and that was when you stopped and let her cool off. Try as you would to keep the oil supply right, in the end Number One always went out. "Number One Bearing burned out on me and I had to have her replaced," you would say, wisely; and your companions always had a lot

to tell about how to protect and pamper Number One to keep her alive.

Sprinkled not too liberally among the millions of amateur witch doctors who drove Fords and applied their own abominable cures were the heaven-sent mechanics who could really make the car talk. These professionals turned up in undreamed-of spots. One time, on the banks of the Columbia River in Washington, I heard the rear end go out of my Model T when I was trying to whip it up a steep incline onto the deck of a ferry. Something snapped; the car slid backward into the mud. It seemed to me like the end of the trail. But the captain of the ferry, observing the withered remnant, spoke up.

"What's got her?" he asked.

"I guess it's the rear end," I replied, listlessly. The captain leaned over the rail and stared. Then I saw that there was a hunger in his eyes that set him off from other men.

"Tell you what," he said, carelessly, trying to cover up his eagerness, "let's pull the son of a bitch up onto the boat, and I'll help you fix her while we're going back and forth on the river."

We did just this. All that day I plied between the towns of Pasco and Kennewick, while the skipper (who had once worked in a Ford garage) directed the amazing work of resetting the bones of my car.

Springtime in the heyday of the Model T was a delirious season. Owning a car was still a major excitement, roads were still wonderful and bad. The Fords were obviously conceived in madness: any car which was capable of going from forward into reverse without any perceptible mechanical hiatus was bound to be a mighty challenging thing to the human imagination. Boys used to veer them off the highway into a level pasture and run wild with them, as though they were cutting up with a girl. Most everybody used the reverse pedal quite as much as the regular foot brake—it distributed the wear over the bands and wore them all down evenly. That was the big trick, to wear all the bands down evenly, so that the final chattering would be total and the whole unit scream for renewal.

The days were golden, the nights were dim and strange. I still recall with trembling those loud, nocturnal crises when you drew up to a signpost and raced the engine so the lights would be bright enough to read destinations by. I have never been really planetary since. I suppose it's time to say goodbye. Farewell, my lovely!

EXERCISE

1. With "Farewell, My Lovely," we have retreated from that frontier that separates fiction from the essay. Narrative is not the dominant mode here. Not a series of events but a series of aspects of a topic, the Model T Ford, provides the shape of the composition. Narrative does appear, but only in patchy or generalized form, and is used primarily for mood or for purposes of illustration. Do any elements that we ordinarily associate with fiction remain here? If so, what are they? It is clear why, on the basis of its loose, associative organization, if for nothing else, this might be called an informal essay, or a familiar essay; but why might we also call it a personal essay. Does one have to be interested in the Model T Ford to be interested in this essay?

2. What is the dominant mood of "Farewell, My Lovely"? How would you compare the mood here with that of "Dream Children"?

3. What is the effect of the literary allusions here? "What hath God wrought," was the first message sent over the telegraph wire, and the "tribute of a sigh" is from Gray's "Elegy in a Country Churchyard" (p. 378). What about the contrast between the solemnity in the allusions and their application to the Model T? In the application, there is, clearly, something of the burlesque, the mock-heroic. But if burlesque is not the whole effect, how do you account for the fact? What is the tone of the last paragraph? How would you relate this tone to the foregoing questions? Can you locate other allusions?

4. The Model T is compared to a horse. How dominant is this image in the essay? For what effect is it used? What does the comparison imply about the moment in the history of American civilization when the Model T appeared? What does it imply about the present?

5. What is the quality of humor in this essay? How does the comparison of the Model T to a horse relate to the humor? Go back to question 3 and consider it in relation to the quality of the humor here.

6. Consider the structure of the next to the last paragraph. By ordinary standards it is wandering and pointless. Do you find it effective here? If so, why?

Wild Bird Hickok and His Friends

JAMES THURBER (1894-1961)

IN ONE of the many interesting essays that make up his book called *Abinger Harvest*, Mr. E. M. Forster, discussing what he sees when he is reluctantly dragged to the movies in London, has set down a sentence that fascinates me. It is: "American women shoot the hippopotamus with eyebrows made of platinum." I have given that remarkable sentence a great deal of study, but I still do not know whether Mr. Forster means that American women have platinum eyebrows or that the hippopotamus has platinum eyebrows or that American women shoot platinum eyebrows into the hippopotamus. At any rate, it faintly stirred in my mind a dim train of elusive memories which were brightened up suddenly and brought into sharp focus for me when, one night, I went to see "The Plainsman," a hard-riding, fast-shooting movie dealing with warfare in the Far West back in the bloody seventies. I knew then what Mr. Forster's curious and tantalizing sentence reminded me of. It was nothing in the world so much as certain sentences which appeared in a group of French paperback dime (or, rather, twenty-five-centime) novels that I collected a dozen years ago in France. "The Plainsman" brought up these old pulp thrillers in all clarity for me because, like that movie, they dealt mainly with the stupendous activities of Buffalo Bill and Wild Bill Hickok; but in them were a unique fantasy, a special inventiveness, and an imaginative abandon beside which the movie treatment of the two heroes pales, as the saying goes, into nothing. In moving from one apartment to another some years ago, I somehow lost my priceless collection of *contes héroïques du*

Far-Ouest, but happily I find that a great many of the deathless adventures of the French Buffalo Bill and Wild Bill Hickok remain in my memory. I hope that I shall recall them, for anodyne, when with eyes too dim to read, I pluck finally at the counterpane.

In the first place, it should perhaps be said that in the eighteen-nineties the American dime-novel hero who appears to have been most popular with the French youth—and adult—given to such literature was Nick Carter. You will find somewhere in one of John L. Stoddard's published lectures—there used to be a set in almost every Ohio bookcase—an anecdote about how an American tourist, set upon by *apaches* in a dark *rue* in Paris in the nineties, caused them to scatter in terror merely by shouting, *"Je suis Nick Carter!"* But at the turn of the century, or shortly thereafter, Buffalo Bill became the favorite. Whether he still is or not, I don't know—perhaps Al Capone or John Dillinger has taken his place. Twelve years ago, however, he was going great guns—or perhaps I should say great dynamite, for one of the things I most clearly remember about the Buffalo Bill of the French authors was that he always carried with him sticks of dynamite which, when he was in a particularly tough spot—that is, surrounded by more than two thousand Indians—he hurled into their midst, destroying them by the hundred. Many of the most inspired paperbacks that I picked up in my quest were used ones I found in those little stalls along the Seine. It was there, for instance, that I came across one of my favorites, *Les Aventures du Wild Bill dans le Far-Ouest.*

Wild Bill Hickok was, in this wonderful and beautiful tale, an even more prodigious manipulator of the six-gun than he seems to have been in real life, which, as you must know, is saying a great deal. He frequently mowed down a hundred or two hundred Indians in a few minutes with his redoubtable pistol. The French author of this masterpiece for some mysterious but delightful reason referred to Hickok sometimes as Wild Bill and sometimes as Wild Bird. *"Bonjour, Wild Bill!"* his friend Buffalo Bill often said to him when they met, only to shout a moment later, *"Regardez, Wild Bird! Les Peaux-Rouges!"* The two heroes spent a great deal of their time, as in "The Plainsman," helping each other out of dreadful situations. Once, for example, while hunting Seminoles in Florida, Buffalo Bill fell into a tiger trap that had been set for him by the Indians—he stepped onto what turned out to be sticks covered with grass, and plunged to the bottom of a deep pit. At this point our author wrote, *" 'Mercy me!' s'écria Buffalo Bill."* The great scout was rescued, of course, by none other than Wild Bill, or Bird, who, emerging from the forest to see his old comrade in distress, could only exclaim *"My word!"*

It was, I believe, in another volume that one of the most interesting characters in all French fiction of the Far West appeared, a certain Major Preston, alias Preeton, alias Preslon (the paperbacks rarely spelled anyone's name twice in succession the same way). This hero, we were told when he was introduced, "had distinguished himself in the Civil War by capturing Pittsburgh," a feat which makes Lee's invasion of Pennsylvania seem mere child's play. Major Preeton (I always preferred that alias) had come out West to fight the Indians with cannon, since he believed it absurd that nobody had thought to blow them off the face of the earth with cannon before. How he made out with his artillery against the forest skulkers I have forgotten, but I have an indelible memory of a certain close escape that Buffalo Bill had in this same book. It seems that, through an oversight, he had set out on a scouting trip without his dynamite—he also carried, by the way, cheroots and a flashlight—and hence, when he stumbled upon a huge band of redskins, he had to ride as fast as he could for the nearest fort. He made it just in time. "Buffalo Bill," ran the story, "clattered across the drawbridge and into the fort just ahead of the Indians, who unable to stop in time, plunged into the moat and were drowned." It may have been in this same tale that Buffalo Bill was once so hard pressed that he had to send for Wild Bird to help him out. Usually, when one was in trouble, the other showed up by a kind of instinct, but this time Wild Bird was nowhere to be found. It was a long time, in fact, before his whereabouts were discovered. You will never guess where he was. He was "taking the baths at

Atlantic City under orders of his physician."
But he came riding across the country in one
day to Buffalo Bill's side, and all was well.
Major Preeton, it sticks in my mind, got bored
with the service in the Western hotels and went
"back to Philadelphia" (Philadelphia seems to
have been the capital city of the United States
at this time). The Indians in all these tales—
and this is probably what gave Major Preeton
his great idea—were seldom seen as individuals
or in pairs or small groups, but prowled about
in well-ordered columns of squads. I recall,
however, one drawing (the paperbacks were
copiously illustrated) which showed two *Peaux-
Rouges* leaping upon and capturing a scout who
had wandered too far from his drawbridge one
night. The picture represented one of the Indians as smilingly taunting his captive, and the
caption read, *"Vous vous promenez très tard ce
soir, mon vieux!"* This remained my favorite
line until I saw one night in Paris an old W. S.
Hart movie called "Le Roi du Far-Ouest," in
which Hart, insulted by a drunken ruffian,
turned upon him and said, in his grim, laconic
way, *"Et puis, après?"*

I first became interested in the French tales
of the Far West, when, one winter in Nice, a
French youngster of fifteen, who, it turned out,
devoted all his spending money to them, asked
me if I had ever seen a "wishtonwish." This
meant nothing to me, and I asked him where he
had heard about the wishtonwish. He showed
me a Far West paperback he was reading.
There was a passage in it which recounted an
adventure of Buffalo Bill and Wild Bill during
the course of which Buffalo Bill signalled to
Wild Bird "in the voice of the wishtonwish."
Said the author in a parenthesis which at that
time gave me as much trouble as Mr. Forster's

sentence about the platinum eyebrows does
now, "The wishtonwish was seldom heard west
of Philadelphia." It was some time—indeed, it
was not until I got back to America—that I
traced the wishtonwish to its lair, and in so
doing discovered the influence of James Feni-
more Cooper on all these French writers of Far
West tales. Cooper, in his novels, frequently
mentioned the wishtonwish, which was a Cad-
doan Indian name for the prairie dog. Cooper
erroneously applied it to the whippoorwill. An
animal called the "ouapiti" also figured occasionally in the French stories, and this turned
out to be the wapiti, or American elk, also mentioned in Cooper's tales. The French writer's
parenthetical note on the habitat of the wishtonwish only added to the delightful confusion and
inaccuracy which threaded these wondrous
stories.

There were, in my lost and lamented collection, a hundred other fine things, which I have
forgotten, but there is one that will forever
remain with me. It occurred in a book in which,
as I remember it, Billy the Kid, alias Billy the
Boy, was the central figure. At any rate, two
strangers had turned up in a small Western
town and their actions had aroused the suspicions of a group of respectable citizens, who
forthwith called on the sheriff to complain
about the newcomers. The sheriff listened
gravely for a while, got up and buckled on his
gun belt, and said, *"Alors, je vais demander ses
cartes d'identité!"* There are few things, in any
literature, that have ever given me a greater
thrill than coming across that line.

EXERCISE

Prepare a set of questions on "Wild Bird Hickok and
His Friends" that might serve as a guide to a discussion of the essay.

Let's See Who Salutes

ART BUCHWALD (1925-   )

HAVE YOU ever wondered what would have happened if the people who are in charge of television today were passing on the draft of the Declaration of Independence?

The scene is Philadelphia at WJULY TV. Several men are sitting around holding copies of the Declaration.

Thomas Jefferson comes in nervously.

"Tommy," says the producer, "it's just great. I would say it was a masterpiece."

"We love it, Tommy boy," the advertising agency man says. "It sings. Lots of drama, and it holds your interest. There are a few things that have to be changed, but otherwise it stays intact."

"What's wrong with it?" Mr. Jefferson asks.

There's a pause. Everyone looks at the man from the network.

"Well, frankly, Tommy, it smacks of being a little anti-British. I mean, we've got quite a few British listeners and something like this might bring in a lot of mail."

"Now don't get sore, Tommy boy," the agency man says. "You're the best declaration of independence writer in the business. That's why we hired you. But our sponsor the Boston Tea Company is interested in selling tea, not independence. Mr. Cornwallis, the sponsor's representative, is here, and I think he has a few thoughts on the matter. Go ahead, Corney. Let's hear what you think."

Mr. Cornwallis stands up. "Mr. Jefferson, all of us in this room want this to be a whale of a document. I think we'll agree on that."

Everyone in the room nods his head.

"At the same time we feel—I think I can speak for everybody—that we don't want to go over the heads of the mass of people who we hope will buy our product. You use words like despotism, annihilation, migration, and tenure. Those are all egghead words and don't mean a

damn thing to the public. Now I like your stuff about 'Life, Liberty, and the pursuit of Happiness.' They all tie in great with tea, particularly pursuit of happiness, but it's the feeling of all of us that you're really getting into controversial water when you start attacking the King of Britain."

Mr. Jefferson says, "But every word of it is true. I've got documentary proof."

"Let me take a crack at it, Corney," the agency man says. "Look, Tommy boy, it isn't a question of whether it's true or not. All of us here know what a louse George can be. But I don't think the people want to be reminded of it all the time. They have enough worries. They want escape. This thing has to be upbeat. If you remind people of all those taxes George has laid on us, they're not going to go out and buy tea. They're not going to go out and buy anything."

"Frankly," says the network man, "I have some strong objections on different grounds. I know you didn't mean it this way, but the script strikes me as pretty left-wing. I may have read the last paragraph wrong, but it seems to me that you're calling for the overthrow of the present government by force. The network could never allow anything like that."

"I'm sure Tommy didn't mean anything like that," the producer says. "Tommy's just a strong writer. Maybe he got a little carried away with himself. Suppose Tommy took out all references to the British and the King. Suppose we said in a special preamble this Declaration of Independence had nothing to do with persons living or dead, and the whole thing is fictitious. Wouldn't that solve it?"

Mr. Jefferson says, "Gentlemen, I was told to write a Declaration of Independence. I discussed it with many people before I did the actual writing. I've worked hard on this declaration—harder than I've worked on anything in my life. You either take it or leave it as it is."

"We're sorry you feel that way about it, Tommy," the agency man says. "We owe a responsibility to the country, but we owe a bigger responsibility to the sponsor. He's paying for it. We're not in the business of offending people, British people or any other kind of people. The truth is, the British are the biggest tea drinkers of anyone in the colonies. We're not going to antagonize them with a document like this. Isn't that so, Mr. Cornwallis?"

"Check—unless Mr. Jefferson changes it the way we want him to."

Mr. Jefferson grabs the Declaration and says, "Not for all the tea in China," and exits.

The producer shakes his head. "I don't know, fellows. Maybe we've made a mistake. We could at least have run it up a flagpole to see who saluted."

"As far as I'm concerned," Mr. Cornwallis said, "the subject is closed. Let's talk about an hour Western on the French and Indian War."

EXERCISE

1. How good a mimic is Buchwald? What are some of the various "languages" that he mimics here?

2. What is the tone of this short piece? Beneath the playfulness and the take-offs, is there any serious point?

3. In what sense is this a personal essay?

En Route to Chicago

JIM BROSNAN (1929-   )

MONDAY IS traditionally an off-day in Organized Baseball. It is a ballplayer's custom to go golfing, or swimming, or picnicking with the family on Mondays. Once in a while Monday is packing and traveling day, for managers tend to cut their rosters on Sunday night in the spring. They also like to announce trades then, too, so that on Monday the players can move to their new clubs. Ever since the Giants and Dodgers moved to California, however, Monday has lost some of its bright, cheery color on the ballplayer's calendar. Eight Mondays a season, we spend eight hours on an airplane. A hell of way to enjoy an off-day.

When airplanes were first discovered by baseball traveling secretaries—about five years ago—there was a minor revolt on some ball clubs. There will always be a number of people who think the best way to keep their feet on the ground is to stay out of airplanes. An extraordinary number—percentagewise—seemed to be making their living playing major league baseball. At first, these nonfliers were able to make their own way, from baseball town to town. But the shift to California forced them to revaluate their convictions. "If you want to play major league baseball now, you learn to fly. Think it over."

The soul-searching led one pitcher, Don Newcombe, to a psychiatrist, who apparently convinced Big Newk that flying was better than working for a living. Even Sal Maglie accepted his fate, although he frequently voiced objections to satisfy his conscience. "One close shave like this," said the Barber, "and I hang up my jock," as he exhibited clippings indicating that near-collisions between planes are a daily occurrence. Such morbid preoccupation with fatal accident statistics is food for idle gossip, and not worthy of a cool customer like Maglie. Moreover, trainers now carry tranquilizers to make plane-life bearable for the fly-shy.

You can sleep on the plane all day—it's easy to stay up the night before, on the Coast. Expensive, but pleasant. Or you can play cards. There's always a poker game in the back of the plane, and gin rummy is a popular, if monotonous way to pass the time. Occasionally, a bridge game is started, but that takes a lot of concentration, especially for a heavy head. United Airlines provides a rack full of popular magazines—*Mademoiselle, Harper's Bazaar, National Geographic,* etc., any one of which will put you to sleep in a hurry.

One consolation on the trip east is the thought that the plane flies faster coming back than going out. Because of the jet stream, or prevailing winds, or something. It proves, of course, that the wind can help as well as hinder the major league pitcher. On Sunday, in Frisco, the helpful aspect of the Seals Stadium wind was the topic of conversation in the Cardinal bullpen.

Howie Nunn was working on his knuckle ball, a pitch with erratic behavior in calm weather. When Nunn throws it into the wind, its fluttery movement is so unpredictable that it delights the pitcher as much as it confounds the catcher. Gene Green caught as many of Nunn's pitches on his knee as he did in his glove.

Most of the pitchers had already thrown, to loosen their arms, to work on control, or to practice a new pitch. It is customary during the middle innings of a ball game for the bullpen crew to talk shop about the pitching trade. "It never hurts to work on another pitch," say the veterans. And since many of the pitchers are in the bullpen because they weren't successful with the pitches they already were throwing, it becomes a brain-storming classroom. Bullpen sessions have produced some odd experiments.

"Where in hell did you come up with that pitch?" asks the manager the first time a new pitch fails. "Well, shove it under your hat, and forget about it." End of experiment.

I, personally, like to work on my spitball in the bullpen. The spitball is illegal, of course, although it's quite popular in the National League. (Also, the International, Texas, Pacific Coast, and most other leagues I've worked in.) It's not an easy pitch to control and requires constant practice. Most practitioners in the National, International, Texas, etc., leagues throw their spitballs most of the time they're pitching. Many of them are quite successful, and I've often wished that I could get away with spitballs, myself. However, there's a knack to it. I, personally, need a good stiff wind blowing straight out from the plate in order to get anything on the pitch.

As B. G. Smith was announced as a pinch-hitter for Larry Jackson, in the eighth, I felt greatly encouraged by the lump on Green's shin. My last spitter had just caromed off Gene's leg, as the bullpen bench laughed in appreciation. Pollet, who had feigned indifference to my illegal practicing, suddenly shocked me by saying, "You're in there, James. You ready?"

What ho! Jackson had pitched seven good innings, and we were behind by just two runs. Had I been promoted back to No. 1 relief once more? Four other guys had been shelled the night before, so it was really just my turn. I tried to forget my new, sensational spitter—it was no time to experiment on the mound during a game—and I pumped up a few fast balls as B. G. flied out to end the inning and force me into the game.

Ten minutes later, I had the bases loaded, with just one out and our bullpen was working seriously. In the Giant dugout, Rigney reached back into his memory, recalled one of my previous appearances in Seals Stadium, and sent Leon Wagner up to hit for Andy Rodgers. The crowd roared its approval as if they, too, had remembered.

In 1958 I started a game against the Giants and threw three home run pitches in four innings. One of the homers, hit by Wagner, had cleared the back wall of the right field bleachers, at the 425-foot mark, causing sportswriters to go dashing out of the press box with a tape measure. Leon hit the ball against the wind and into the trees . . . across the street. A goodly blast. I had reason to be proud of that one, if I viewed it in a purely objective manner. Which I try to do. Give the batter credit, I say. If he is better than you, make him a true giant among hitters.

Wagner is not, ordinarily, a good curve-ball hitter. The pitch he clobbered into the trees had had all the appearances of a pretty good curve. It was big, it broke down, and it was low and away. Perfect pitch, you say? I thought so when I let it go toward the plate. When Wagner golfed it out of sight I could only conclude that I really didn't have very good stuff that day. Fred Hutchinson, the manager, echoed my sentiments, exactly, and removed me for a relief pitcher.

So lightning doesn't strike twice, does it? I'd

been taught to believe it. "Wagner can't hit a good curve ball," Jackson had said in the pre-game meeting. Smitty signaled for a good curve, and I stepped back off the rubber to think. "Ten days ago I threw a similarly unlikely pitch and everyone in St. Louis encouraged me to regret it. What other choice do I have? He's a good fastball hitter. My slider is not working very well. These guys on the bases proved that. . . . When in doubt, curve him. . . . It's in the Book. Well, he sure can't hit the curve any further than the last time. Or, can he?"

I shrugged my doubts away and wound up, in one continuous motion. I threw the good curve

. . . same place . . . low and away. Did he hit it out again? He did not. He tapped it right back to me, like a good little boy, and we had a double play to retire the side. We still lost 3–1, but instead of being a bum, again . . .

"Nice going, Broz. That's the way to pitch."

Yes, sir, that's the way I did it last time. This game will drive you batty.

EXERCISE

"En Route to Chicago" is an entry in a diary which was published under the title *The Long Season*. Are the editors justified in putting it here among the personal essays? Explain your answer in detail.

The Stars

GEORGE SANTAYANA (1863-1952)

To MOST people, I fancy, the stars are beautiful; but if you ask why, they would be at a loss to reply, until they remembered what they had heard about astronomy, and the great size and distance and possible habitation of those orbs. The vague and illusive ideas thus aroused fall in so well with the dumb emotion we were already feeling, that we attribute this emotion to those ideas, and persuade ourselves that the power of the starry heavens lies in the suggestion of astronomical facts.

The idea of the insignificance of our earth and of the incomprehensible multiplicity of worlds is indeed immensely impressive; it may even be intensely disagreeable. There is something baffling about infinity; in its presence the sense of finite humility can never wholly banish the rebellious suspicion that we are being deluded. Our mathematical imagination is put on the rack by our attempted conception that has all the anguish of a nightmare and probably, could we but awake, all its laughable absurdity. But the obsession of this dream is an intellectual puzzle, not an æsthetic delight. Before the days of Kepler the heavens declared the glory of the Lord; and we needed no calculation of stellar distances, no fancies about a plurality of worlds,

no image of infinite spaces, to make the stars sublime.

Had we been taught to believe that the stars governed our fortunes, and were we reminded of fate whenever we looked at them, we should similarly tend to imagine that this belief was the source of their sublimity; and if the superstition were dispelled, we should think the interest gone from the apparition. But experience would soon undeceive us, and prove that the sensuous character of the object was sublime in itself. For that reason the parable of the natal stars governing our lives is such a natural one to express our subjection to circumstances, and can be transformed by the stupidity of disciples into a literal tenet. In the same way, the kinship of the emotion produced by the stars with the emotion proper to certain religious moments makes the stars seem a religious object. They become, like impressive music, a stimulus to worship. But fortunately there are experiences which remain untouched by theory, and which maintain the mutual intelligence of men through the estrangements wrought by intellectual and religious systems. When the superstructures crumble, the common foundation of human sentience and imagination is exposed beneath. Did not the infinite, by this initial assault upon our senses, awe us, and overwhelm us, as solemn music might, the idea of it would be abstract and mental like that of the infinitesimal, and nothing but an amusing curiosity. The knowledge that the universe is a multitude of minute spheres circling, like specks of dust, in a dark and boundless void, might leave us cold and indifferent, if not bored and depressed, were it not that we identify this hypothetical scheme with the visible splendor, the poignant intensity, and the baffling number of the stars. So far is the object from giving value to the impression, that it is here, as it must always ultimately be, the impression that gives value to the object. For all worth leads us back to actual feeling somewhere, or else evaporates into nothing—into a word and a superstition.

Now, the starry heavens are very happily designed to intensify the sensations on which their fascination must rest. The continuum of space is broken into points, numerous enough to give the utmost idea of multiplicity, and yet so distinct and vivid that it is impossible not to remain aware of their individuality. The sensuous contrast of the dark background—blacker the clearer the night and the more stars we can see—with the palpitating fire of the stars themselves, could not be exceeded by any possible device.

Fancy a map of the heavens and every star plotted upon it, even those invisible to the naked eye: why would this object, as full of scientific suggestions surely as the reality, leave us so comparatively cold? The sense of multiplicity is naturally in no way diminished by the representation; but the poignancy of the sensation, the life of the light, are gone; and with the dulled impression the keenness of the emotion disappears. Or imagine the stars, undiminished in number, without losing any of their astronomical significance and divine immutability, marshalled in geometrical patterns; say in a Latin cross, with the words *In hoc signo vinces* in a scroll around them. The beauty of the illumination would be perhaps increased, and its import, practical, religious, and cosmic, would surely be a little plainer; but where would be the sublimity of the spectacle? Irre-

trievably lost: and lost because the form of the object would no longer tantalize us with its sheer multiplicity, and with the consequent overpowering sense of suspense and awe. Accordingly things which have enough multiplicity, as the lights of a city seen across water, have an effect similar to that of the stars, if less intense; whereas a star, if alone, because the multiplicity is lacking, makes a wholly different impression. The single star is tender, beautiful, and mild; we can compare it to the humblest and sweetest of things:

> A violet by a mossy stone
> Half hidden from the eye,
> Fair as *a star when only one
> Is shining in the sky.*

It is, not only in fact but in nature, an attendant on the moon, associated with the moon, if we may be so prosaic here, not only by contiguity but also by similarity.

> Fairer than Phoebe's sapphire-regioned star
> Or vesper, amorous glow-worm of the sky.

The same poet can say elsewhere of a passionate lover:

> He arose
> Ethereal, flushed, and like a throbbing star,
> Amid the sapphire heaven's deep repose.

How opposite is all this from the cold glitter, the cruel and mysterious sublimity of the stars when they are many! With these we have no tender associations; they make us think rather of Kant who could hit on nothing else to compare with his categorical imperative, perhaps because he found in both the same baffling incomprehensibility and the same fierce actuality. Such ultimate feelings are sensations of physical tension.

EXERCISE

1. Here the central concern is, clearly, with the exposition of an idea. What is that idea? Outline the essay, paragraph by paragraph, indicating the stages by which the idea is presented. Identify Kepler and Kant, and determine the relevance of these references to the discussion. What is the significance of the last sentence in relation to the whole essay? Can it be said to summarize the essay?

2. With "The Stars" we are even farther from that frontier that separates fiction from the essay. Here, as we have already said, the central concern is

with the exposition of an idea—a concern which seems remote from that of the personal or familiar essay. How, then, can the editors justify putting "The Stars" among the personal essays? Do you think that a case might be made out for our having placed it here? If you do not, give your reasons. (Even if you do not regard "The Stars" as a personal essay, the fact that you and the editors disagree may serve to make a useful point: namely, that no hard-and-fast lines can be drawn among the various types of essays just as no hard-and-fast line can be drawn between fiction and the personal or familiar essay).

SECTION II

The Essay of Idea and Opinion

At the end of our Introduction to this general section of discursive prose, we said that questions of form and style can be properly considered only with reference to what we called the "occasion" of the particular piece of writing —the specific concerns of the writer as they are related to his subject and to the audience that he is addressing. So in our selection of these essays we have tried to exhibit not only a variety of method, but a number of distinguished writers and thinkers, treating subjects which are of fundamental importance to our time.

Nor is the order haphazard. We begin with an essay "Pulvis et Umbra," written (1888) at the time when the shock of modern scientific discovery, by throwing doubt upon the traditional religious interpretation of man's place in the universe, forced men to try to find in the natural world some basis for moral and other values. "Pulvis et Umbra" is followed by a pair of essays which really constitute the opposing sides of an argument on the function of science in controlling human behavior. These discussions of the general problem of modern man are followed by essays that examine the assumptions of democracy, the nature of culture in a democracy, and the role of literature in the modern world, and these essays are followed by discussion of still more specific problems that arise out of American society.

Pulvis et Umbra

ROBERT LOUIS STEVENSON (1850-1894)

WE LOOK for some reward for our endeavors and are disappointed; not success, not happiness, not even peace of conscience, crowns our ineffectual efforts to do well. Our frailties are invincible, our virtues barren; the battle goes sore against us to the going down of the sun. The canting moralist tells us of right and wrong; and we look abroad, even on the face of our small earth, and find them change with every climate, and no country where some action is not honored for a virtue and where it is not branded for a vice; and we look in our experience, and find no vital congruity in the wisest rules, but at the best a municipal fitness. It is not strange if we are tempted to despair of good. We ask too much. Our religions and moralities have been trimmed to flatter us, till they are all emasculate and sentimentalized, and only please and weaken. Truth is of a rougher strain. In the harsh face of life, faith can read a bracing gospel. The human race is a thing more ancient than the ten commandments; and the bones and revolutions of the Kosmos, in whose joints we are but moss and fungus, more ancient still.

I

Of the Kosmos in the last resort, science reports many doubtful things and all of them appalling. There seems no substance to this solid globe on which we stamp; nothing but symbols and ratios. Symbols and ratios carry us and bring us forth and beat us down; gravity that swings the incommensurable suns and worlds through space, is but a figment varying inversely as the squares of distances; and the suns and worlds themselves, imponderable figures of abstraction, NH_3 and H_2O. Consideration dares not dwell upon this view; that way madness lies; science carries us into zones of speculation, where there is no habitable city for the mind of man.

But take the Kosmos with a grosser faith, as our senses give it to us. We behold space sown with rotatory islands, suns and worlds and the shards and wrecks of systems: some, like the sun, still blazing; some rotting, like the earth; others, like the moon, stable in desolation. All of these we take to be made of something we call matter: a thing which no analysis can help us to conceive; to whose incredible properties no familiarity can reconcile our minds. This stuff, when not purified by the lustration of fire, rots uncleanly into something we call life; seized through all its atoms with a pediculous malady; swelling in tumors that become independent, sometimes even (by an abhorrent prodigy) locomotory; one splitting into millions, millions cohering into one, as the malady proceeds through varying stages. This vital putrescence of the dust, used as we are to it, yet strikes us with occasional disgust, and the profusion of worms in a piece of ancient turf, or the air of a marsh darkened with insects, will sometimes check our breathing so that we aspire for cleaner places. But none is clean: the moving sand is infected with lice; the pure spring, where it bursts out of the mountain, is a mere issue of worms; even in the hard rock the crystal is forming.

In two main shapes this eruption covers the countenance of the earth: the animal and the vegetable: one in some degree the inversion of the other: the second rooted to the spot; the first detached out of its natal mud, and scurrying abroad with the myriad feet of insects or towering into the heavens on the wings of birds: a thing so inconceivable that, if it be well considered, the heart stops. To what passes with the anchored vermin, we have little clue: doubtless they have their joys and sorrows, their delights and killing agonies: it appears not how. But of the locomotory, to which we ourselves belong, we can tell more. These share with us a thousand miracles: the miracles of sight, of hearing, of the projection of sound, things that bridge space; the miracles of memory and reason, by which the present is conceived, and when it is gone, its image kept living in the brains of man and brute; the miracle of reproduction, with its imperious desires and staggering consequences. And to put the last touch upon this mountain mass of the revolting and the inconceivable, all these prey upon each other, lives tearing other lives in pieces, cramming them inside themselves, and by that summary process, growing fat: the vegetarian, the whale, perhaps the tree, not less than the lion of the desert; for the vegetarian is only the eater of the dumb.

Meanwhile our rotatory island, loaded with predatory life, and more drenched with blood, both animal and vegetable, than ever mutinied ship, scuds through space with unimaginable speed, and turns alternate cheeks to the reverberation of a blazing world, ninety million miles away.

II

What a monstrous specter is this man, the disease of the agglutinated dust, lifting alternate feet or lying drugged with slumber; killing, feeding, growing, bringing forth small copies of himself; grown upon with hair like grass, fitted with eyes that move and glitter in his face; a thing to set children screaming;—and yet looked at nearlier, known as his fellows know him, how surprising are his attributes! Poor soul, here for so little, cast among so many hardships, filled with desires so incommensurate and so inconsistent, savagely surrounded, savagely descended, irremediably condemned to prey upon his fellow lives: who should have blamed him had he been of a piece with his destiny and a being merely barbarous? And we look and behold him instead filled with imperfect virtues: infinitely childish, often admirably valiant, often touchingly kind; sitting down, amidst his momentary life, to debate of right and wrong and the attributes of the deity; rising up to do battle for an egg or die for an idea; singling out his friends and his mate with cordial affection; bringing forth in pain, rearing with long-suffering solicitude, his young. To touch the heart of his mystery, we find in him one thought, strange to the point of lunacy: the thought of duty; the thought of something owing to himself, to his neighbor, to his God: an ideal of decency, to which he would rise if it were possible; a limit of shame, below which, if it be possible, he will not stoop. The design in most men is one of conformity; here and there, in picked natures, it transcends itself and soars on the other side, arming martyrs with independence; but in all, in their degrees, it is a bosom thought:—Not in man alone, for we trace it in dogs and cats whom we know fairly well, and doubtless some similar point of honor sways the elephant, the oyster, and the louse, of whom we know so little:—But in man, at least, it sways with so complete an empire that merely selfish things come second, even with the selfish: that appetites are starved, fears are conquered, pains supported; that almost the dullest shrinks from the reproof of a glance, although it were a child's; and all but the most cowardly stand amid the risks of war; and the more noble, having strongly conceived an act as due to their ideal, affront and embrace death. Strange enough if, with their singular origin and perverted practice, they think they are to be rewarded in some future life: stranger still, if they are persuaded of the contrary, and think this blow, which they solicit, will strike them senseless for eternity. I shall be reminded what a tragedy of misconception and misconduct man at large presents: of organized injustice, cowardly violence, and treacherous crime; and of the damning imperfections of the best. They cannot be too darkly drawn. Man is indeed marked for failure in his efforts to do right. But

where the best consistently miscarry, how tenfold more remarkable that all should continue to strive; and surely we should find it both touching and inspiriting, that in a field from which success is banished, our race should not cease to labor.

If the first view of this creature, stalking in his rotatory isle, be a thing to shake the courage of the stoutest, on this nearer sight he startles us with an admiring wonder. It matters not where we look, under what climate we observe him, in what stage of society, in what depth of ignorance, burthened with what erroneous morality; by camp-fires in Assiniboia, the snow powdering his shoulders, the wind plucking his blanket, as he sits, passing the ceremonial calumet and uttering his grave opinions like a Roman senator; in ships at sea, a man inured to hardship and vile pleasures, his brightest hope a fiddle in a tavern and a bedizened trull who sells herself to rob him, and he for all that simple, innocent, cheerful, kindly like a child, constant to toil, brave to drown, for others; in the slums of cities, moving among indifferent millions to mechanical employment, without hope of change in the future, with scarce a pleasure in the present, and yet true to his virtues, honest up to his lights, kind to his neighbors, tempted perhaps in vain by the bright gin-palace, perhaps long-suffering with the drunken wife that ruins him; in India (a woman this time) kneeling with broken cries and streaming tears as she drowns her child in the sacred river; in the brothel, the discard of society, living mainly on strong drink, fed with affronts, a fool, a thief, the comrade of thieves, and even here keeping the point of honor and the touch of pity, often repaying the world's scorn with service, often standing firm upon a scruple, and at a certain cost, rejecting riches: —everywhere some virtue cherished or affected, everywhere some decency of thought and carriage, everywhere the ensign of man's ineffectual goodness—ah! if I could show you this! if I could show you these men and women all the world over, in every stage of history, under every abuse of error, under every circumstance of failure, without hope, without health, without thanks, still obscurely fighting the lost fight of virtue, still clinging, in the brothel or on the scaffold, to some rag of honor, the poor jewel of their souls! They may seek to escape, and yet they cannot; it is not alone their privilege and glory, but their doom, they are condemned to some nobility all their lives long, the desire of good is at their heels, the implacable hunter.

Of all earth's meteors, here at least is the most strange and consoling; that this ennobled lemur, this hair-crowned bubble of the dust, this inheritor of a few years and sorrows, should yet deny himself his rare delights, and add to his frequent pains, and live for an ideal, however misconceived. Nor can we stop with man. A new doctrine, received with screams a little while ago by canting moralists, and still not properly worked into the body of our thoughts, lights us a step farther into the heart of this rough but noble universe. For nowadays the pride of man denies in vain his kinship with the original dust. He stands no longer like a thing apart. Close at his heels we see the dog, prince of another genus: and in him too, we see dumbly testified the same cultus of an unattainable ideal, the same constancy in failure. Does it stop with the dog? We look at our feet where the ground is blackened with the swarming ant; a creature so small, so far from us in the hierarchy of brutes, that we can scarce trace and scarce comprehend his doings; and here also, in his ordered polities and rigorous justice, we see confessed the law of duty and the fact of individual sin. Does it stop, then, with the ant? Rather this desire of well-doing and this doom of frailty run through all the grades of life: rather is this earth, from the frosty top of Everest to the next margin of the internal fire, one stage of ineffectual virtues and one temple of pious tears and perseverance. The whole creation groaneth and travaileth together. It is the common and godlike law of life. The browsers, the biters, the barkers, the hairy coats of field and forest, the squirrel in the oak, the thousand-footed creeper in the dust, as they share with us the gift of life, share with us the love of an ideal; strive like us—like us are tempted to grow weary of the struggle—to do well; like us receive at times unmerited refreshment, visitings of support, returns of courage; and are condemned like us to be crucified between that double law of the members and the will. Are they like us, I wonder, in the timid hope of some reward, some sugar with the drug? do they too stand aghast at unrewarded virtues, at the sufferings of those whom, in our partiality, we take to be just, and the prosperity of such as, in our blindness, we called wicked? It may be, and yet God knows what they should look for. Even while they look, even while they repent, the foot of man treads them by thousands in the dust, the yelping hounds burst upon their trail, the bullet speeds, the knives are heating in the den of the vivisectionist; or the dew falls, and the generation of a day is blotted out. For these are creatures, compared with whom our weakness is strength, our ignorance wisdom, our brief span eternity.

And as we dwell, we living things, in our isle of terror and under the imminent hand of death, God forbid it should be man the erected, the reasoner, the wise in his own eyes—God forbid it should be man that wearies in well-doing, that despairs of unrewarded effort, or utters the language of complaint. Let it be enough for faith, that the whole creation groans in mortal frailty, strives with unconquerable constancy: surely not all in vain.

DISCUSSION

In this essay Stevenson starts his discussion with a question: what is there in human life which reassures us when "we are tempted to despair of good"? The question is all the more difficult to answer when we realize that men cannot agree as to what goodness is; for standards vary from time to time, from place to place, from religion to religion, and from one set of social conventions to another set of social conventions.

Stevenson attempts to answer this question by looking at "the harsh face of life" itself. But this investigation leads to what is apparently a paradox: from one point of view life seems to be a merely casual and meaningless development in the solar system, a mere "fungus" or "putrescence" upon the "rotatory island," which is the earth; from another point of view life offers the spectacle of courage, sacrifice, and aspiration. The first view is based primarily on the picture of the cosmos which science gives, a description which is schematic, abstract, and mechanical, and which finds no place for courage, sacrifice, and aspiration, or, as Stevenson puts it, "affords no habitable city for the mind of man." For example, let us consider the definitions which various sciences might give of some person: chemistry would see that person as a chemical formula; biology would see the person in terms of anatomical structure and function; and so with the other sciences. But to one who loved or hated that person these descriptions would seem woefully inadequate; they would provide "no habitable city" for his mind. But the second view takes into account matters which elude, necessarily, the scientific formulation, matters which concern values and standards of conduct, honor, heroism, courage, pity, generosity, sympathy, etc. Man, even in the degraded conditions described in some of Stevenson's examples, retains some wish, however feeble, to "do good," some standard of conduct which he will not violate; and even the lower animals sometimes behave in ways which do not seem to be dictated by their mere appetites. In other words, all life seems to involve values beyond the merely materialistic interpretation. Stevenson's conclusion, therefore, does not imply a rejection of the first view (which within its own terms is perfectly sound), but it does involve a rejection of the idea that the first view exhausts the meaning of life.

We have just inspected the framework of ideas in this essay, but it will have occurred to the student that the essay enforces these points, not merely abstractly, but with a strong emotional coloring, a coloring which sets up attitudes toward the ideas, and which makes the effect of the essay go beyond the mere statement of ideas. How is this emotional coloring secured? Consider the section of the essay dealing with the "scientific" view of life. Stevenson, quite properly for his purposes, uses a very "unscientific" method of presenting the scientific view; that is, since he is anxious to appeal to our emotional attitudes, he is not content to offer an abstract description. Instead, notice how concrete is the description, and how much figurative language is used. Examine, for example, these comparisons: "This stuff . . . rots

uncleanly into something we call life . . . swelling in tumors that become independent, sometimes even . . . locomotory. . . ." These comparisons ("rots uncleanly," "tumors") are not used merely to help us understand more clearly the process by which life may have arisen on the earth; that is, they are not merely descriptive and neutral. Rather, they are used to imply an attitude toward life; their connotations suggest an unhealthy growth out of decay, the fouling of something clean, a disease; in other words, these comparisons imply a judgment, a judgment that life, if it does not transcend the purely materialistic level, is repulsive. But the comparisons and examples used in the second section of the essay, although they involve scenes of poverty, shame, and degradation, work in exactly the opposite direction: the savage passes his opinions "like a Roman senator." In general, it will be seen that the examples and the comparisons which Stevenson has used throughout the essay constantly suggest that the reader adopt certain attitudes toward the ideas which are being presented.

In the same way as Stevenson uses the comparisons and examples, Stevenson uses the rhythms of his sentences to suggest attitudes.

EXERCISE

1. Would Stevenson accept Hemingway's story, "The Killers," as an example of human value present in an unpromising context? Taking into account Bishop's "Homage to Hemingway" (and what you know of Hemingway's fiction), do you think that Hemingway would accept the vision of reality presented in "Pulvis et Umbra"? In what ways might Hemingway's vision of life differ?

2. Investigate the paradoxes involved in the following comparisons: "to some rag of honor, the poor jewel of their souls," "condemned to some nobility all their lives long," and "this hair-crowned bubble of the dust."

3. How would you describe the style of this essay? The first paragraph, for example, has a number of echoes from the King James version of the Bible. (Can you point them out?) In what other ways is the style "literary"? Compare and contrast it with the style of Hemingway, of Bishop, and of Lamb.

4. On the basis of this essay how would you describe the personality of Stevenson? Think of both content and style.

5. On what grounds would you compare and contrast this essay with "The Stars"?

Freedom and the Control of Men

B. F. SKINNER (1904-   )

I

THE SECOND half of the twentieth century may be remembered for its solution of a curious problem. Although Western democracy created the conditions responsible for the rise of modern science, it is now evident that it may never fully profit from that achievement. The so-called "democratic philosophy" of human behavior to which it also gave rise is increasingly in conflict with the application of the methods of science to human affairs. Unless this conflict is somehow resolved, the ultimate goals of democracy may be long deferred.

Just as biographers and critics look for external influences to account for the traits and achievements of the men they study, so science ultimately explains behavior in terms of "causes" or conditions which lie beyond the individual himself. As more and more causal relations are demonstrated, a practical corollary becomes difficult to resist: it should be possible to *produce* behavior according to plan simply by arranging the proper conditions. Now, among the specifications which might reasonably be submitted to a behavioral technology are these: Let men be happy, informed, skillful, well behaved, and productive.

This immediate practical implication of a science of behavior has a familiar ring, for it recalls the doctrine of human perfectibility of eighteenth- and nineteenth-century humanism. A science of man shares the optimism of that philosophy and supplies striking support for the working faith that men can build a better world and, through it, better men. The support comes just in time, for there has been little optimism of late among those who speak from the traditional point of view. Democracy has become "realistic," and it is only with some embarrassment that one admits today to perfectionistic or utopian thinking.

The earlier temper is worth considering, however. History records many foolish and unworkable schemes for human betterment, but almost all the great changes in our culture which we now regard as worthwhile can be traced to perfectionistic philosophies. Governmental, religious, educational, economic, and social reforms follow a common pattern. Someone believes that a change in a cultural practice—for example, in the rules of evidence in a court of law, in the characterization of man's relation to God, in the way children are taught to read and write, in permitted rates of interest, or in minimal housing standards—will improve the condition of men: by promoting justice, permitting men to seek salvation more effectively, increasing the literacy of a people, checking an inflationary trend, or improving public health and family relations, respectively. The underlying hypothesis is always the same: that a different physical or cultural environment will make a different and better man.

The scientific study of behavior not only justifies the general pattern of such proposals; it promises new and better hypotheses. The earliest cultural practices must have originated in sheer accidents. Those which strengthened the group survived with the group in a sort of natural selection. As soon as men began to propose and carry out changes in practice for the sake of possible consequences, the evolutionary process must have accelerated. The simple practice of making changes must have had survival value. A further acceleration is now to be expected. As laws of behavior are more precisely stated, the changes in the environment required to bring about a given effect may be more clearly specified. Conditions which have been neglected because their effects were slight or unlooked for may be shown to be relevant. New conditions may actually be created, as in the discovery and synthesis of drugs which affect behavior.

This is no time, then, to abandon notions of progress, improvement, or, indeed, human perfectibility. The simple fact is that man is able, and now as never before, to lift himself by his own bootstraps. In achieving control of the world of which he is a part, he may learn at last to control himself.

Timeworn objections to the planned improvement of cultural practices are already losing much of their force. Marcus Aurelius was probably right in advising his readers to be content with a haphazard amelioration of mankind. "Never hope to realize Plato's republic," he sighed, ". . . for who can change the opinions of men? And without a change of sentiments what can you make but reluctant slaves and hypocrites?" He was thinking, no doubt, of contemporary patterns of control based upon punishment or the threat of punishment which, as he correctly observed, breed only reluctant slaves of those who submit and hypocrites of those who discover modes of evasion. But we need not share his pessimism, for the opinions of men can be changed. The techniques of indoctrination which were being devised by the early Christian Church at the very time Marcus Aurelius was writing are relevant, as are some of the techniques of psychotherapy and of advertising and public relations. Other methods suggested by recent scientific analyses leave little doubt of the matter.

The study of human behavior also answers the cynical complaint that there is a plain "cussedness" in man which will always thwart efforts to improve him. We are often told that men do not want to be changed, even for the better. Try to help them, and they will outwit you and remain happily wretched. Dostoievsky claimed to see some plan in it. "Out of sheer ingratitude," he complained, or possibly boasted, "man will play you a dirty trick, just to prove that men are still men and not the keys of a piano. . . . And even if you could prove that a man is only a piano key, he would still do something out of sheer perversity—he would create destruction and chaos—just to gain his point. . . . And if all this could in turn be analyzed and prevented by predicting that it would occur, then man would deliberately go mad to prove his point." This is a conceivable neurotic reaction to inept control. A few men may have shown it, and many have enjoyed Dostoievsky's statement because they tend to show it. But that such perversity is a fundamental reaction of the human organism to controlling conditions is sheer nonsense.

So is the objection that we have no way of knowing what changes to make even though we have the necessary techniques. That is one of the great hoaxes of the century—a sort of booby trap left behind in the retreat before the advancing front of science. Scientists themselves have unsuspectingly agreed that there are two kinds of useful propositions about nature—facts and value judgments—and that science must confine itself to "what is," leaving "what ought to be" to others. But with what special sort of wisdom is the nonscientist endowed? Science is only effective knowing, no matter who engages in it. Verbal behavior proves upon analysis to be composed of many different types of utterances, from poetry and exhortation to logic and factual description, but these are not all equally useful in talking about cultural practices. We may classify useful propositions according to the degrees of confidence with which they may be asserted. Sentences about nature range from highly probable "facts" to sheer guesses. In general, future events are less likely to be correctly described than past. When a scientist talks about a projected experiment, for example, he must often resort to statements having only a moderate likelihood of being correct; he calls them hypotheses.

Designing a new cultural pattern is in many ways like designing an experiment. In drawing up a new constitution, outlining a new educational program, modifying a religious doctrine, or setting up a new fiscal policy, many statements must be quite tentative. We cannot be sure that the practices we specify will have the consequences we predict, or that the consequences will reward our efforts. This is in the nature of such proposals. They are not value judgments—they are guesses. To confuse and delay the improvement of cultural practices by quibbling about the word *improve* is itself not a useful practice. Let us agree, to start with, that health is better than illness, wisdom better than ignorance, love better than hate, and productive energy better than neurotic sloth.

Another familiar objection is the "political problem." Though we know what changes to make and how to make them, we still need to control certain relevant conditions, but these have long since fallen into the hands of selfish men who are not going to relinquish them for such purposes. Possibly we shall be permitted to develop areas which at the moment seem unimportant, but at the first signs of success the strong men will move in. This, it is said, has happened to Christianity, democracy, and communism. There will always be men who are fundamentally selfish and evil, and in the long run innocent goodness cannot have its way. The only evidence here is historical, and it may be misleading. Because of the way in which physical science developed, history could until very recently have "proved" that the unleashing of the energy of the atom was quite unlikely, if not impossible. Similarly, because of the order in which processes in human behavior have become available for purposes of control, history may seem to prove that power will probably be appropriated for selfish purposes. The first techniques to be discovered fell almost always to strong, selfish men. History led Lord Acton to believe that power corrupts, but he had probably never encountered absolute power, certainly not in all its forms, and had no way of predicting its effect.

An optimistic historian could defend a different conclusion. The principle that if there are not enough men of good will in the world the first step is to create more seems to be gaining recognition. The Marshall Plan (as originally conceived), Point Four, the offer of atomic materials to power-starved countries—these may or may not be wholly new in the history of international relations, but they suggest an increasing awareness of the power of governmental good will. They are proposals to make certain changes in the environments of men for the sake of consequences which should be rewarding for all concerned. They do not exemplify a disinterested generosity, but an interest which is the interest of everyone. We have not yet seen Plato's philosopher-king, and may not want to, but the gap between real and utopian government is closing.

But we are not yet in the clear, for a new and unexpected obstacle has arisen. With a world of their own making almost within reach, men of good will have been seized with distaste for their achievement. They have uneasily rejected opportunities to apply the techniques and findings of science in the service of men, and as the import of effective cultural design has come to be understood, many of them have voiced an outright refusal to have any part in it. Science has been challenged before when it has encroached upon institutions already engaged in the control of human behavior; but what are we to make of benevolent men, with no special interests of their own to defend, who nevertheless turn against the very means of reaching long-dreamed-of goals?

What is being rejected, of course, is the scientific conception of man and his place in nature. So long as the findings and methods of science are applied to human affairs only in a sort of remedial patchwork, we may continue to hold any view of human nature we like. But as the use of science increases, we are forced to accept the theoretical structure with which science represents its facts. The difficulty is that this structure is clearly at odds with the traditional democratic conception of man. Every discovery of an event which has a part in shaping a man's behavior seems to leave so much the less to be credited to the man himself; and as such explanations become more and more comprehensive, the contribution which may be claimed by the individual himself appears to approach zero. Man's vaunted creative powers, his original accomplishments in art, science, and morals, his capacity to choose and our right to hold him responsible for the consequences of his choice—none of these is conspicuous in this new self-portrait. Man, we once believed, was free to express himself in art, music, and literature, to inquire into nature, to seek salvation in his own way. He could initiate action and make spontaneous and capricious changes of course. Under the most extreme duress some sort of choice remained to him. He could resist any effort to control him, though it might cost him his life. But science insists that action is initiated by forces impinging upon the individual, and that caprice is only another name for behavior for which we have not yet found a cause.

In attempting to reconcile these views it is important to note that the traditional democratic conception was not designed as a description in the scientific sense but as a philosophy to be used in setting up and maintaining a governmental process. It arose under historical circumstances and served political purposes apart from which it cannot be properly understood. In rallying men against tyranny it was necessary that the individual be strengthened, that he be taught that he had rights and could govern himself. To give the common man a new conception of his worth, his dignity, and his power to save himself, both here and hereafter, was often the only resource of the revolutionist. When democratic principles were put into practice, the same doctrines were used as a working formula. This is exemplified by the notion of personal responsibility in Anglo-American law. All governments make certain forms of punishment contingent upon certain kinds of acts. In democratic countries these contingencies are expressed by the notion of responsible choice. But the notion may have no meaning under governmental practices formulated in other ways and would certainly have no place in systems which did not use punishment.

The democratic philosophy of human nature is determined by certain political exigencies and techniques, not by the goals of democracy. But exigencies and techniques change; and a conception which is not supported for its accuracy as a likeness—is not, indeed, rooted in fact at all—may be expected to change too. No matter how effective we judge current democratic practices to be, how highly we value them, or how long we expect them to survive, they are almost certainly not the *final* form of government. The philosophy of human nature which has been useful in implementing them is also almost certainly not the last word. The ultimate achievement of democracy may be long deferred unless we emphasize the real aims rather than the verbal devices of democratic thinking. A philosophy which has been appropriate to one set of political exigencies will defeat its purpose if, under other circumstances, it prevents us from applying to human affairs the science of man which probably nothing but democracy itself could have produced.

II

Perhaps the most crucial part of our democratic philosophy to be reconsidered is our attitude toward freedom—or its reciprocal, the control of human behavior. We do not oppose all forms of control because it is "human nature" to do so. The reaction is not characteristic of all men under all conditions of life. It is an attitude which has been carefully engineered, in large part by what we call the "literature" of democracy. With respect to some methods of control (for example, the threat of force), very little engineering is needed, for the techniques or their immediate consequences are objectionable. Society has suppressed these methods by branding them "wrong," "illegal," or "sinful." But to encourage these attitudes toward objectionable forms of control, it has been necessary to disguise the real nature of certain indispensable techniques, the commonest examples of which are education, moral discourse, and persuasion. The actual procedures appear harmless enough. They consist of supplying information, presenting opportunities for action, pointing out logical relationships, appealing to reason or "enlightened understanding," and so on. Through a masterful piece of misrepresentation, the illusion is fostered that these procedures do not involve the control of behavior; at most, they are simply ways of "getting someone to change his mind." But analysis not only reveals the presence of well-defined behavioral processes, it demonstrates a kind of control no less inexorable, though in some ways more acceptable, than the bully's threat of force.

Let us suppose that someone in whom we are interested is acting unwisely—he is careless in the way he deals with his friends, he drives too fast, or he holds his golf club the wrong way. We could probably help him by issuing a series of commands: don't nag, don't drive over sixty, don't hold your club that way. Much less objectionable would be "an appeal to reason." We could show him how people are affected by his treatment of them, how accident rates rise sharply at higher speeds, how a particular grip on the club alters the way the ball is struck and corrects a slice. In doing so we resort to verbal mediating devices which emphasize and support certain "contingencies of reinforcement"—that is, certain relations between behavior and its consequences—which strengthen the behavior we wish to set up. The same consequences would possibly set up the behavior without our help, and they eventually take control no matter which form of help we give. The appeal to reason has certain advantages over the authoritative command. A threat of punishment, no matter how subtle, generates emotional reactions and tendencies to escape or revolt. Perhaps the controllee merely "feels resentment" at being made to act in a given way, but even that is to be avoided. When we "appeal to reason," he "feels freer to do as he pleases." The fact is that we have exerted *less* control than in using a threat; since other conditions may contribute to the result, the effect may be delayed or, possibly in a given instance, lacking. But if we have worked a change in his behavior at all, it is because we have altered relevant environmental conditions, and the processes we have set in motion are just as real and just as inexorable, if not as comprehensive, as in the most authoritative coercion.

"Arranging an opportunity for action" is another example of disguised control. The power of the negative form has already been exposed in the analysis of censorship. Restriction of opportunity is recognized as far from harmless. As Ralph Barton Perry said in an article which appeared in the Spring, 1953, *Pacific Spectator,* "Whoever determines what alternatives shall be made known to man controls what that man shall choose *from.* He is deprived of freedom in proportion as he is denied access to *any* ideas, or is confined to any range of ideas short of the totality of relevant possibilities." But there is a positive side as well. When we present a relevant state of affairs, we increase the likelihood that a given form of behavior will be emitted. To the extent that the probability of action has changed, we have made a definite contribution. The teacher of history controls a student's behavior (or, if the reader prefers, "deprives him of freedom") just as much in *presenting* historical facts as in suppressing them.

Other conditions will no doubt affect the student, but the contribution made to his behavior by the presentation of material is fixed and, within its range, irresistible.

The methods of education, moral discourse, and persuasion are acceptable not because they recognize the freedom of the individual or his right to dissent, but because they make only *partial* contributions to the control of his behavior. The freedom they recognize is freedom from a more coercive form of control. The dissent which they tolerate is the possible effect of other determiners of action. Since these sanctioned methods are frequently ineffective, we have been able to convince ourselves that they do not represent control at all. When they show too much strength to permit disguise, we give them other names and suppress them as energetically as we suppress the use of force. Education grown too powerful is rejected as propaganda or "brain-washing," while really effective persuasion is decried as "undue influence," "demagoguery," "seduction," and so on.

If we are not to rely solely upon accident for the innovations which give rise to cultural evolution, we must accept the fact that some kind of control of human behavior is inevitable. We cannot use good sense in human affairs unless someone engages in the design and construction of environmental conditions which affect the behavior of men. Environmental changes have always been the condition for the improvement of cultural patterns, and we can hardly use the more effective methods of science without making changes on a grander scale. We are all controlled by the world in which we live, and part of that world has been and will be constructed by men. The question is this: Are we to be controlled by accident, by tyrants, or by ourselves in effective cultural design?

The danger of the misuse of power is possibly greater than ever. It is not allayed by disguising the facts. We cannot make wise decisions if we continue to pretend that human behavior is not controlled, or if we refuse to engage in control when valuable results might be forthcoming. Such measures weaken only ourselves, leaving the strength of science to others. The first step in a defense against tyranny is the fullest possible exposure of controlling techniques. A second step has already been taken successfully in restricting the use of physical force. Slowly, and as yet imperfectly, we have worked out an ethical and governmental design in which the strong man is not allowed to use the power deriving from his strength to control his fellow men. He is restrained by a superior force created for that purpose—the ethical pressure of the group, or more explicit religious and governmental measures. We tend to distrust superior forces, as we currently hesitate to relinquish sovereignty in order to set up an international police force. But it is only through such countercontrol that we have achieved what we call peace—a condition in which men are not permitted to control each other through force. In other words, control itself must be controlled.

Science has turned up dangerous processes and materials before. To use the facts and techniques of a science of man to the fullest extent without making some monstrous mistake will be difficult and obviously perilous. It is no time for self-deception, emotional indulgence, or the assumption of attitudes which are no longer useful. Man is facing a difficult test. He must keep his head now, or he must start again—a long way back.

III

Those who reject the scientific conception of man must, to be logical, oppose the methods of science as well. The position is often supported by predicting a series of dire consequences which are to follow if science is not checked. A recent book by Joseph Wood Krutch, *The Measure of Man,* is in this vein. Mr. Krutch sees in the growing science of man the threat of an unexampled tyranny over men's minds. If science is permitted to have its way, he insists, "we may never be able really to think again." A controlled culture will, for example, lack some virtue inherent in disorder. We have emerged from chaos through a series of happy accidents, but in an engineered culture it will be "impossible for the unplanned to erupt again." But there is no virtue in the accidental character of an accident, and the diversity which arises from disorder can not only be duplicated by design but vastly extended. The experimental method is superior to simple observation just because it

multiplies "accidents" in a systematic coverage of the possibilities. Technology offers many familiar examples. We no longer wait for immunity to disease to develop from a series of accidental exposures, nor do we wait for natural mutations in sheep and cotton to produce better fibers; but we continue to make use of such accidents when they occur, and we certainly do not prevent them. Many of the things we value have emerged from the clash of ignorant armies on darkling plains, but it is not therefore wise to encourage ignorance and darkness.

It is not always disorder itself which we are told we shall miss but certain admirable qualities in men which flourish only in the presence of disorder. A man rises above an unpropitious childhood to a position of eminence, and since we cannot give a plausible account of the action of so complex an environment, we attribute the achievement to some admirable faculty in the man himself. But such "faculties" are suspiciously like the explanatory fictions against which the history of science warns us. We admire Lincoln for rising above a deficient school system, but it was not necessarily something *in him* which permitted him to become an educated man in spite of it. His educational environment was certainly unplanned, but it could nevertheless have made a full contribution to his mature behavior. He was a rare man, but the circumstances of his childhood were rare too. We do not give Franklin Delano Roosevelt the same credit for becoming an educated man with the help of Groton and Harvard, although the same behavioral processes may have been involved. The founding of Groton and Harvard somewhat reduced the possibility that fortuitous combinations of circumstances would erupt to produce other Lincolns. Yet the founders can hardly be condemned for attacking an admirable human quality.

Another predicted consequence of a science of man is an excessive uniformity. We are told that effective control—whether governmental, religious, educational, economic, or social—will produce a race of men who differ from each other only through relatively refractory genetic differences. That would probably be bad design, but we must admit that we are not now pursuing another course from choice. In a modern school, for example, there is usually a syllabus which specifies what every student is to learn by the end of each year. This would be flagrant regimentation if anyone expected every student to comply. But some will be poor in particular subjects, others will not study, others will not remember what they have been taught, and diversity is assured. Suppose, however, that we someday possess such effective educational techniques that every student will in fact be put in possession of all the behavior specified in a syllabus. At the end of the year, all students will correctly answer all questions on the final examination and "must all have prizes." Should we reject such a system on the grounds that in making all students excellent it has made them all alike? Advocates of the theory of a special faculty might contend that an important advantage of the present system is that the good student learns *in spite of* a system which is so defective that it is currently producing bad students as well. But if really effective techniques are available, we cannot avoid the problem of design simply by preferring the status quo. At what point should education be deliberately inefficient?

Such predictions of the havoc to be wreaked by the application of science to human affairs are usually made with surprising confidence. They not only show a faith in the orderliness of human behavior; they presuppose an established body of knowledge with the help of which it can be positively asserted that the changes which scientists propose to make will have quite specific results—albeit not the results they foresee. But the predictions made by the critics of science must be held to be equally fallible and subject also to empirical test. We may be sure that many steps in the scientific design of cultural patterns will produce unforeseen consequences. But there is only one way to find out. And the test must be made, for if we cannot advance in the design of cultural patterns with absolute certainty, neither can we rest completely confident of the superiority of the status quo.

Apart from their possibly objectionable consequences, scientific methods seem to make no provision for certain admirable qualities and faculties which seem to have flourished in less explicitly planned cultures; hence they are called "degrading" or "lacking in dignity." (Mr. Krutch has called the author's *Walden Two* an "ignoble Utopia.") The conditioned reflex is the current whipping boy. Because conditioned reflexes may be demonstrated in animals, they are spoken of as though they were exclusively subhuman. It is implied, as we have seen, that no behavioral processes are involved in education and moral discourse or, at least, that the processes are exclusively human. But men do show conditioned reflexes (for example, when they are frightened by all instances of the control of human behavior because some instances engender fear), and animals do show processes similar to the human behavior involved in instruction and moral discourse. When Mr. Krutch asserts that " 'Conditioning' is achieved by methods which by-pass or, as it were, short-circuit those very reasoning faculties which education proposes to cultivate and exercise," he is making a technical statement which needs a definition of terms and a great deal of supporting evidence.

If such methods are called "ignoble" simply because they leave no room for certain admirable attributes, then perhaps the practice of admiration needs to be examined. We might say that the child whose education has been skillfully planned has been deprived of the right to intellectual heroism. Nothing has been left to be admired in the way he acquires an education. Similarly, we can conceive of moral training which is so adequate to the demands of the culture that men will be good practically automatically, but to that extent they will be deprived of the right to moral heroism, since we seldom admire automatic goodness. Yet if we consider the end of morals rather than certain virtuous means, is not "automatic goodness" a desirable state of affairs? Is it not, for example, the avowed goal of religious education? T. H. Huxley answered the question unambiguously: "If some great power would agree to make me always think what is true and do what is right, on condition of being a sort of clock and wound up every morning before I got out of bed, I should close instantly with the offer." Yet Mr. Krutch quotes this as the scarcely credible point of view of a "proto-modern" and seems himself to share T. S. Eliot's contempt for ". . . systems so perfect / That no one will need to be good."

"Having to be good" is an excellent example of an expendable honorific. It is inseparable from a particular form of ethical and moral control. We distinguish between the things we *have* to do to avoid punishment and those we *want* to do for rewarding consequences. In a culture which did not resort to punishment we should never "have" to do anything except with respect to the punishing contingencies which arise directly in the physical environment. And we are moving toward such a culture, because the neurotic, not to say psychotic, by-products of control through punishment have long since led compassionate men to seek alternative techniques. Recent research has explained some of the objectionable results of punishment and has revealed resources of at least equal power in "positive reinforcement." It is reasonable to look forward to a time when man will seldom "have" to do anything, although he may show interest, energy, imagination, and productivity far beyond the level seen under the present system (except for rare eruptions of the unplanned).

What we have to do we do with *effort*. We call it "work." There is no other way to distinguish between exhausting labor and the possibly equally energetic but rewarding activity of play. It is presumably good cultural design to replace the former with the latter. But an adjustment in attitudes is needed. We are much more practiced in admiring the heroic labor of a Hercules than the activity of one who works without having to. In a truly effective educational system the student might not "have to work" at all, but that possibility is likely to be received by the contemporary teacher with an emotion little short of rage.

We cannot reconcile traditional and scientific views by agreeing upon *what* is to be admired or condemned. The question is whether anything is to be so treated. Praise and blame are cultural practices which have been adjuncts of the prevailing system of control in Western democracy. All peoples do not engage in them for the same purposes or to the same extent, nor, of course, are the same behaviors always classified in the same way as subject to praise or blame. In admiring intellectual and moral heroism and unrewarding labor, and in rejecting a world in which these would be uncommon, we are simply demonstrating our own cultural conditioning. By promoting certain tendencies to admire and censure, the group of which we are a part has arranged for the social reinforcement and punishment needed to assure a high level of intellectual and moral industry. Under other and possibly better controlling systems, the behavior which we now admire would occur, but not under those conditions which make it admirable, and we should have no reason to admire it because the culture would have arranged for its maintenance in other ways.

To those who are stimulated by the glamorous heroism of the battlefield, a peaceful world may not be a better world. Others may reject a world without sorrow, longing, or a sense of guilt because the relevance of deeply moving works of art would be lost. To many who have devoted their lives to the struggle to be wise and good, a world without confusion and evil might be an empty thing. A nostalgic concern for the decline of moral heroism has been a dominating theme in the work of Aldous Huxley. In *Brave New World* he could see in the application of science to human affairs only a travesty on the notion of the Good (just as George Orwell, in *1984,* could foresee nothing but horror). In a recent issue of *Esquire,* Huxley has expressed the point this way: "We have had religious revolutions, we have had political, industrial, economic and nationalistic revolutions. All of them, as our descendants will discover, were but ripples in an ocean of conservatism—trivial by comparison with the psychological revolution toward which we are so rapidly moving. *That* will really be a revolution. When it is over, the human race will give no further trouble." (Footnote for the reader of the future: This was not meant as a happy ending. Up to 1956 men had been admired, if at all, either for causing trouble or alleviating it. Therefore—)

It will be a long time before the world can dispense with heroes and hence with the cultural practice of admiring heroism, but we move in that direction whenever we act to prevent war, famine, pestilence, and disaster. It will be a long time before man will never need to submit to punishing environments or engage in exhausting labor, but we move in that direction whenever we make food, shelter, clothing, and labor-saving devices more readily available. We may mourn the passing of heroes but not the conditions which make for heroism. We can spare the self-made saint or sage as we spare the laundress on the river's bank struggling against fearful odds to achieve cleanliness.

The two great dangers in modern democratic thinking are illustrated in a paper by former Secretary of State Dean Acheson. "For a long time now," writes Mr. Acheson, "we have gone along with some well-tested principles of conduct: That it was better to tell the truth than falsehoods; . . . that duties were older than and as fundamental as rights; that, as Justice Holmes put it, the mode by which the inevitable came to pass was effort; that to perpetrate a harm was wrong no matter how many joined in it . . . and so on . . . Our institutions are founded on the assumption that most people follow these principles most of the time because they want to, and the institutions work pretty well when this assumption is true. More recently, however, bright people have been fooling with the machinery in the human head and they have discovered quite a lot. . . . Hitler introduced new refinements [as the result of which] a whole people have been utterly confused and corrupted. Unhappily neither the possession of this knowledge nor the desire to use it was confined to Hitler. . . . Others dip from this same devil's cauldron."

The first dangerous notion in this passage is that most people follow democratic principles of conduct "because they want to." This does not account for democracy or any other form of government if we have not explained why people *want* to behave in given ways. Although it is tempting to assume that it is human nature to believe in democratic principles, we must not overlook the "cultural engineering" which produced and continues to maintain democratic practices. If we neglect the conditions which produce democratic *behavior,* it is useless to try to maintain a democratic *form* of government. And we cannot expect to export a democratic form of government successfully if we do not also provide for the cultural practices which will sustain it. Our forebears did not discover the essential nature of man; they evolved a pattern of behavior which worked remarkably well under the circumstances. The "set of principles" expressed in that pattern is not the only true set or necessarily the best. Mr. Acheson has presumably listed the most unassailable items; some of them are probably beyond question, but others—concerning duty and effort—may need to be revised as the world changes.

The second—and greater—threat to the democracy which Mr. Acheson is defending is his assumption that knowledge is necessarily on the side of evil. All the admirable things he mentions are attributed to the innate goodness of man, all the detestable to "fooling with the machinery in the human head." This is reminiscent of the position, taken by other institutions engaged in the control of men, that certain forms of knowledge are in themselves evil. But how out of place in a democratic philosophy! Have we come this far only to conclude that well-intentioned people cannot study the behavior of men without becoming tyrants or that informed men cannot show good will? Let us for once have strength and good will on the same side.

Far from being a threat to the tradition of Western democracy, the growth of a science of man is a consistent and probably inevitable part of it. In turning to the external conditions which shape and maintain the behavior of men, while questioning the reality of inner qualities and faculties to which human achievements were once attributed, we turn from the ill-defined and remote to the observable and manipulable. Though it is a painful step, it has far-reaching consequences, for it not only sets higher standards of human welfare but shows us how to meet them. A change in a theory of human nature cannot change the facts. The achievements of man in science, art, literature, music, and morals will survive any interpretation we place upon them. The uniqueness of the individual is unchallenged in the scientific view. Man, in short, will remain man. (There will be much to admire for those who are so inclined. Possibly the noblest achievement to which man can aspire, even according to present standards, is to accept himself for what he is, as that is revealed to him by the methods which he devised and tested on a part of the world in which he had only a small personal stake.)

If Western democracy does not lose sight of the aims of humanitarian action, it will welcome the almost fabulous support of its own science of man and will strengthen itself and play an important role in building a better world for everyone. But if it cannot put its "democratic philosophy" into proper historical perspective—if, under the control of attitudes and emotions which it generated for other purposes, it now rejects the help of science—then it must be prepared for defeat. For if we continue to insist that science has nothing to offer but a new and more horrible form of tyranny, we may produce just such a result by allowing the strength of science to fall into the hands of despots. And if, with luck, it were to fall instead to men of good will in other political communities, it would be perhaps a more ignominious defeat; for we should then, through a miscarriage of democratic principles, be forced to leave to others the next step in man's long struggle to control nature and himself.

EXERCISE

1. This essay is divided into three sections, each representing a main stage in the author's argument. Break down each of these stages into sub-stages, indicating the connection from each to the next. Having done this, write a brief statement of the intent of the argument.

2. "Freedom and Control of Men," like "Pulvis et Umbra," deals with the relation of science to human values and behavior. On what points are Stevenson and Skinner in agreement? On what in disagreement?

DISCUSSION

Skinner is presenting a case which he obviously intends to make convincing by closely reasoned argument rather than by the power of rhetoric. His sentences tend to be short and compactly organized, with little use of concessive clauses (such as "though one must admit that . . . ," "even if we recall that . . ." etc.) and constructions that would modify and qualify the line of argument (such as "but on the other hand . . . ," ". . . remembering that such distinctions are always necessary . . ." etc.). The drive is constantly forward, with the logical con-

nection between one sentence and the next almost always clearly marked. The rhythms are basically short, without a great range of variety, and are generally unassertive, but there is, by and large, a vibrance to the prose. Even the monotony of the movement in the first paragraph we feel to have some relation to the temper of the composition: this "dehumanized" rhythm puts, as it were, the basic issue at a cold distance, with mechanical precision. Then, in the next paragraph, as the mind begins to work over the issue, the vibration of thought enters the movement.

Let us, to prepare for our main point, set over against "Freedom and the Control of Men" a passage from a very undistinguished piece of expository prose. The author is discussing disarmament:

the second factor building up pressure for perseverance in the disarmament program springs from the response of people everywhere to the activities the program would generate. Probably this would manifest itself most plainly when the plan began to have a noticeable impact on the military, somewhere in the first stage. Three actions would signal it: cutbacks in calls for military service; reductions in military budgets; and the deposit for ultimate destruction in internationally supervised depots of military matériel in excess of the ceilings set. The third development would be the most dramatic; and doubtless each great power would strive to publicize its good faith in carrying out the plan by propaganda photographs of the vast parks of matériel it was building up. Yet more important, if less conspicuous, would be the concurrent measures reflecting the reduction in military budgets. These might take various forms, all welcome to the citizenry: investment in needed public works, educational and health programs, increases in the pay of government employees and teachers, and, in the United States at least, some reduction in taxes. As military cutbacks continued, sums released by these processes might begin to swell to tremendous dimensions. They would soon build up powerful vested interests for their continuation .

Here the lines of exposition are blurred. The tangle of modifying elements, with their loosely conceived syntax, makes us feel uncertain of what the writer is really driving at. The forward drive of reasoning—the unfolding shape of the argument—is lost. Read the passage aloud. The rhythm is sluggish and vague.

Let us come to our point. A good piece of prose discourse—exposition or argument—aims to state a problem, or to explain a situation, and then logically to move, stage by stage, to a solution, or resolution. This seems very remote from the excitement or delicate shading of emotion we may find in a good story or poem or play. A piece of prose discourse cannot, in fact, generate the emotional involvement characteristic of fiction, poetry, or drama: the human reaction to fate is not directly presented. But the movement of mind has its own dramatic structure, the curiosity of exposition, the involvement in analysis and the suspense as the subject gradually emerges into reasoned and manageable order, the crisis of solution and the sense of fulfilment and release.

This is not to say that all good discussion is fashioned alike, any more than all stories or poems are fashioned alike. It is to say, however, that the same principle underlies all good discursive prose. The good piece of prose will be an image of the mind at work on a certain kind of material. The difference from one good piece of prose to another will reflect the difference between the mind behind one and the mind be-hind the other, the difference between the demands of one subject and those of the other, the difference between one intended audience and the other. In other words, the piece of prose will reflect what we have called its particular occasion.

EXERCISE

1. Now, after this long preamble, try to distinguish the style of Skinner from that of Stevenson. Relate the style of each essay to what you take the author's attitude and personality to be. For instance, what turns of wit do you find in Skinner's essay? Do you find any in "Pulvis et Umbra"?

2. Compare Skinner's attitude with that in "The Gentleman from San Francisco," by Ivan Bunin (p. 143).

3. What, do you think, would Hemingway have made of Skinner's argument? What would Katherine Anne Porter make of it?

4. In the course of his essay Skinner refers to an attack made by the critic Joseph Wood Krutch on his book *Walden Two*, a book which had presented the same basic view as that we find in "Freedom and the Control of Men." Here is a section of Krutch's argument against the attitude of which Skinner is one of the most powerful proponents.

On Walden Two

JOSEPH WOOD KRUTCH (1893-   )

AMONG THEM [those who announce "our approaching scientific ability to control men's thoughts with precision" and are not appalled] may be included B. F. Skinner, Professor of Psychology at Harvard, one of the most able and esteemed leaders in his field, and author of a fantasy called *Walden Two* which describes the contented life led by the inmates of an institution—though Professor Skinner might dislike this designation—to which they have voluntarily committed themselves and where they are conditioned to like being conditioned. An analysis of Professor Skinner's thought will reveal very clearly in what direction some believe that the Science of Man is moving.

Walden Two is a utopian community created by an experimental psychologist named Frazier who has learned the techniques for controlling thought with precision and who has conditioned his subjects to be happy, obedient, and incapable of antisocial behavior. Universal benevolence and large tolerance of individual differences reign—not because it is assumed, as the founders of such utopias generally do assume, that they are natural to all innocent men uncorrupted by society—but because an experimental scientist, having at last mastered the "scientific ability to control men's thoughts with precision," has caused them to think benevolently and tolerantly.

An appeal to reason in contradistinction to passion, habit, or mere custom has been the usual basis of utopias from Plato to Sir Thomas More and even down to Samuel Butler. Mr. Skinner's is, on the other hand, distinctly modern in that it puts its faith in the conditioned reflex instead, and proposes to perfect mankind by making individual men incapable of anything except habit and prejudice. At Walden Two men behave in a fashion we are accustomed to call "reasonable," not because they reason, but because they do not; because "right responses" are automatic. At the very beginning of the story we are shown a flock of sheep confined to the area reserved for them by a single thread which long ago replaced the electric fence once employed to condition them not to wander. As predicted in official Communist theory, the State—represented here by electricity —has "withered away" and no actual restraint is necessary to control creatures in whom obedience has become automatic. Obviously the assumption is that what will work with sheep will work with men.

Now though men can reason, they are not exclusively reasoning creatures. None, therefore, of the classic utopias could be realized because each is based on the assumption that reason alone can be made to guide human behavior. Moreover—and what is perhaps more important —few people have ever seriously wished to be exclusively rational. The good life which most desire is a life warmed by passions and touched with that ceremonial grace which is impossible without some affectionate loyalty to traditional forms and ceremonies. Many have, nevertheless, been very willing to grant that a little more reason in the conduct of private and public affairs would not be amiss. That is why, as fantasies, the utopias of Plato and Sir Thomas More have seemed interesting, instructive, even inspiring. But who really wants, even in fancy, to be, as Walden Two would make him, more unthinking, more nearly automatic than he now is? Who, even in his imagination, would like to live in a community where, instead of thinking part of the time, one never found it possible to think at all?

Is it not more meaningful to say that whereas Plato's Republic and More's Utopia are noble absurdities, Walden Two is an ignoble one; that the first two ask men to be more than

human, while the second urges them to be less? When, in the present world, men behave well, that is no doubt sometimes because they are creatures of habit as well as, sometimes, because they are reasonable. But if one proposes to change Man as Professor Skinner and so many other cheerful mechanists propose, is it really so evident that he should be changed in the direction they advocate? Is he something which, in Nietzsche's phrase, "must be surpassed," or is he a creature to whom the best advice one can give is the advice to retreat—away from such reasoned behavior as he may be capable of and toward that automatism of which he is also capable?

Obviously Walden Two represents—glorified, perfected, and curiously modernized—that ideal of a "cloistered virtue" which European man has tended to find not only unsatisfactory as an ideal but almost meaningless in terms of his doubtless conflicting aspirations. Nevertheless it must be admitted that Thomas Henry Huxley, a proto-modern, once admitted in an often quoted passage that "if some great power would agree to make me always think what is true and do what is right, on condition of being turned into a sort of clock and wound up every morning before I got out of bed, I should instantly close with the offer." And what a Huxley would have agreed to, prospective candidates for admission into Walden Two might also find acceptable.

Frazier himself is compelled to make a significant confession: the motives which led him to undertake his successful experiment included a certain desire to exercise power over his fellows. That is not admirable in itself and is obviously not without its dangers. But he insists that the danger will disappear with him because those who succeed to his authority and inherit his techniques will have enjoyed, as he did not, the advantages of a scientific conditioning process and that therefore such potentially antisocial impulses as his will no longer exist. In other words, though the benevolent dictator is a rare phenomenon today, the happy chance which produced this one will not have to be relied on in the future. Walden Two will automatically produce the dictators necessary to carry it on.

Nevertheless and even if the skeptical reader will grant for the sake of argument that automatic virtue represents an ideal completely satisfactory, a multitude of other doubts and fears are likely to arise in his mind. He will remember of course that Brook Farm and the rest failed promptly and decisively. Perhaps he will remember also that Russian communism achieved at least some degree of permanence only by rejecting, more and more completely, everything which in any way parallels the mildness, the gentleness, and the avoidance of all direct restraints and pressures which is characteristic of Walden Two; that the makers of Soviet policy came to denounce and repress even that somewhat paradoxical enthusiasm for the culture of a different world which was as much encouraged in the earliest days of the experiment as it is at Walden Two.

Hence, if a Walden Two is possible it obviously has become so only because—and this is a point which presumably Mr. Skinner himself wishes to emphasize—it differs in several respects from all superficially similiar projects. Like the Russian experiment it assumes that, for all practical purposes, man is merely the product of society; but it also assumes a situation which did not exist when the Communist state was set up: namely one in which "the scientific ability to control men's thoughts with precision" has fully matured.

Thus if the man upon whom the experiment is performed is nothing but the limitlessly plastic product of external processes operating upon him and is, by definition, incapable of any significant autonomous activity, he is also, in this case, a creature who has fallen into the hands of an ideally competent dictator. His desires, tastes, convictions, and ideals are precisely what the experimenter wants to make them. He is the repository of no potentialities which can ever develop except as they are called forth by circumstances over which he has no control. Finally, of course, his happy condition is the result of the fortunate accident which determined that the "engineer" who created him and, indirectly, will create all of his progeny, was an experimenter whose own random conditioning happened to produce, not the monster who might just as likely have been the first to seize the power that science offered, but a genuinely benevolent dictator instead.

A propos this last premise it might, in passing, be remarked as a curious fact that though scientific method abhors the accidental, the uncontrollable, and the unpredicted; though Mr. Skinner's own ideal seems to be to remove forever any possible future intrusion of it into human affairs; yet the successful establishment of the first utopia depended ultimately on the decisive effect of just such an accident as will henceforth be impossible.

Critics of the assumption that technological advance is the true key to human progress have often urged that new powers are dangerous rather than beneficial unless the question of how they should be used is at least opened before the powers become available. With more than usual anxiety they might contemplate the situation in which we are now placed if it is true that only chance will answer the question by whom and in the interest of what "our approaching scientific ability to control men's thoughts with precision" is to be used. But this is only one of several desperate questions which the premises of *Walden Two* provoke. Most of them can also be related to points made by Mr. Skinner in less fanciful contexts and to one or two of them we may turn in connection with a more general consideration of problems raised if we are ready to assume that we actually do stand, at the threshold of a world in which men's thoughts will be controlled scientifically and as a matter of course.

To begin with, we must, of course, abandon the old platitude, "You can't change human nature," and accept its opposite, "You can change human nature as much and in whatever direction you wish"—because "human nature" does not exist in the sense which the phrase implies. Whatever desires, tastes, preferences, and tendencies have been so general and so persistent as to create the assumption that they are innate or "natural" must be, as a matter of fact, merely the most ancient and deeply graven of the conditionings to which the human animal has been subjected. As Pascal—an odd thinker to be invoked in defense of a mechanistic and completely relativistic ethic—once exclaimed in one of those terrifying speculations of which, no doubt, his own conditioning made him capable: "They say that habit is Second Nature; but perhaps Nature is only First Habit."

By eager reformers "You can't change human nature" has often been denounced as both a counsel of despair and a convenient excuse for lazy indifference in the face of the world's ills. Yet the fact or alleged fact which the phrase attempts to state has also its positive aspect. To say that human nature cannot be changed means that human nature is something in itself and there is at least the possibility that part of this something is valuable. If we say that it cannot be changed we are also saying that it cannot be completely corrupted; that it cannot be transformed into something which we would not recognize as human at all. This is what the eighteenth century allowed Pope to say for it, and as long as one holds the doctrine that the term Nature actually describes some enduring set of possibilities and values, then some limit is set, not only to human perfectibility, but also, and more encouragingly, to things which it can become or be made.

But once this view of "Nature" has been dismissed as an illusion and even what appear to be the most persistent of its traits are thought of as merely the result of conditioning, then there is no limit to the extent to which men may become different from what they now are. There is nothing against which it may be assumed that human nature will revolt. Only by a temporarily established convention is any kind of vice a "creature of so frightful mien." Anything can be made to seem "natural." Cruelty, treachery, slander, and deceit might come generally to seem not frightful but beautiful. And if it be said that the successful putting into practice of certain recent political philosophies supports the contention of determinists that man may, indeed, be taught to believe precisely this, it must be added that something more is also implied: namely that we must abandon—along with the conviction that human nature cannot be changed—all the hopes expressed in such phrases as "human nature will in the end revolt against" this or that.

Since no human nature capable of revolting against anything is now presumed to exist, then some other experimenter—conditioned perhaps as the son of the commandant of a Nazi labor camp—might decide to develop a race of men who found nothing more delightful than the infliction of suffering, and to establish for them a colony to be called Walden Three. By what standards could the dictator of Walden Two presume to judge that his utopia was any more desirable than its new rival? He could not appeal to God's revealed word; to the inner light of conscience; or to that eighteenth-century standby, the voice of Nature. He could say only that the accidents of his previous existence in a world where accident still played its part in determining how an individual should be conditioned had conditioned him to prefer what he would, in full realization of the unjustifiability of the metaphor, call "light rather than darkness." The life in Walden Two appears to him as "good" but the adjective would, of course, have no meaning in relation to anything outside himself.

In the light of such possibilities those who have not yet been molded by either Walden Two or Walden Three will tend to feel that before the "scientific ability to control men's thoughts with precision" has been fully utilized by whoever may seize the limitless power it will confer, we had better take a last look around—if not for that way of escape which may not exist, then at least in order to grasp certain implications and possible consequences as they appear to the minds of men who are still "free"—free at least in the limited sense that they are the product of conditions which were brought about, in part, through the presence of random factors destined to play a smaller and smaller part in determining human personality. That second generation of dictators to whom the dictator of Walden Two expects to pass on the control of affairs will be conditioners who have themselves been conditioned. The circle of cause and effect will have been closed and no man will ever again be anything which his predecessor has not consciously willed him to be.

According to the mechanist's own theories, everything which happened in the universe from its beginning down, at least until yesterday, was the result of chance. The chemical molecule didn't "want" or "plan" to grow more complex until it was a protein; the protein did not plan to become protoplasm; and the amoeba did not plan to become man. As a matter of fact, a theory very popular at the moment explains the fact that life seems to have arisen on our earth but once in all the billions of years of the planet's existence by saying that it could arise only as a result of a combination of circumstances so fantastically improbable that they have never occurred again. Yet though they owe to chance both their very existence and all progress from the protozoan to civilization, they are eager to take a step which would make it forever impossible for the unexpected and the unplanned to erupt again into the scheme which will pass completely under their own control.

No doubt many practical-minded people will object that such speculations as these are a waste of time. After all, they will say, even Walden Two does not exist except in fancy and no one has yet claimed that the "approaching scientific ability to control men's thoughts with precision" has already arrived. Logical dilemmas and metaphysical difficulties are cobwebs which will not entangle those who refuse to take seriously their gossamer threads. We have work to do and practical problems to solve.

But to all such it may be replied that practical problems and the metaphysical forms to which they may be reduced are not so unrelated as they may think, and that the logical extreme sometimes serves to make clear the real nature of a purely practical problem. It is true that no man has yet established a Walden Two or Walden Three, and that neither has any man yet controlled *with precision* men's thoughts. But it is also true that there has been a movement in a direction which suggests Walden Two as an ideal. Moreover, statesmen, educators and publicists have already achieved considerable success in their frankly admitted attempts to use the techniques already developed to control and condition large sections of the public and have increasingly declared their faith in the desirability and practicality of such methods in contradistinction to what used to be called education, on the one hand, and appeals to the enlightened understanding of the public, on the other. Already it has quite seriously and

without any conviction of cynicism been proposed that the advertisers' principle, "say a thing often enough and it will be believed," be utilized by those who have what they regard as "correct" or "healthy" or "socially useful" ideas to sell. Every time it is proposed that schools should develop certain attitudes in their pupils or that the government should undertake propaganda along a certain line, the question of the difficult distinction between education in some old-fashioned sense and "conditioning" definitely arises.

Moreover, it is because the techniques of the social scientist and the experimental psychologists do to some extent work that some attempt must be made to understand their implications. By their methods many men may be made to do and think many things. Already in the relatively simple case of education versus "useful conditioning," the difficult distinction ceases to be difficult once a border line has been definitely crossed. Writing to George Washington not long after our particular democracy had been founded, Thomas Jefferson remarked, "It is an axiom in my mind that our liberty can be safe but in the hands of the people themselves, and that, too, of the people with a certain degree of instruction." What would Jefferson have thought of the suggestion that "a certain degree of instruction" be interpreted to mean "a certain degree of conditioning"? Would he not have pointed out that the distinction between the two is clear and fundamental; that "conditioning" is achieved by methods which by-pass or, as it were, short-circuit those very reasoning faculties which education proposes to cultivate and exercise? And would he not have added that democracy can have no meaning or no function unless it is assumed that these faculties do lie within a realm of freedom where the sanctions of democracy arise?

Thus the whole future of mankind may well depend not only on the question whether man is entirely or only in part the product of conditionings, but also on the extent to which he is treated as though he were. Will we come ultimately to base what we call "education," in and out of schools, on the assumption that conditioning by propaganda as well as other methods is the most effective, even if it is not the only, method of influencing human beings?

To all such questions an answer in pragmatic terms has already been given at least positively enough to make it very pertinent to ask into whose hands the power already being exercised is to fall; to ask who is to decide in what direction the citizen is to be conditioned, and on what bases or what standards of value those decisions are to be made. That is simply the practical aspect of the theoretical question, "Who shall be master of Walden Two?"

In the totalitarian countries, where deterministic theories have been accepted in their most unqualified form and the techniques of control most systematically practiced, the question just posed has been answered in the simplest possible manner, and very much in the same way that it was answered at Walden Two. Power is exercised by those who seized it and, theoretically at least, this seizure was the last event which could "happen" because henceforward human destiny will be in the hands of those who are now in a position to control it. The question whether they ought to have done so and whether it is well for humanity that they did was either always meaningless or soon to become so since all the value judgments made in the future will be made by those who have been conditioned to approve what has happened to them.

EXERCISE

Summarize the argument of Krutch, stage by stage. To which position—that of Skinner or that of Krutch—do you incline? Why? Do you think that these two positions exhaust the possibilities? The collision between Skinner and Krutch points to one of the crucial problems of our time. Several of the essays to come touch on this problem, directly or indirectly. As you read, keep this issue in mind. If this problem is of special interest to you, you might look up and read *Brave New World,* by Aldous Huxley, or *1984,* by George Orwell.

Culture and Anarchy

SWEETNESS AND LIGHT

MATTHEW ARNOLD (1822-1888)

THE DISPARAGERS of culture make its motive curiosity; sometimes, indeed, they make its motive mere exclusiveness and vanity. The culture which is supposed to plume itself on a smattering of Greek and Latin is a culture which is begotten by nothing so intellectual as curiosity; it is valued either out of sheer vanity and ignorance or else as an engine of social and class distinction, separating its holder, like a badge or title, from other people who have not got it. No serious man would call this *culture,* or attach any value to it, as culture, at all. To find the real ground for the very different estimate which serious people will set upon culture, we must find some motive for culture in the terms of which may lie a real ambiguity; and such a motive the word *curiosity* gives us.

I have before now pointed out that we English do not, like the foreigners, use this word in a good sense as well as in a bad sense. With us the word is always used in a somewhat disapproving sense. A liberal and intelligent eagerness about the things of the mind may be meant by a foreigner when he speaks of curiosity, but with us the word always conveys a certain notion of frivolous and unedifying activity. In the *Quarterly Review,* some little time ago, was an estimate of the celebrated French critic, M. Sainte-Beuve, and a very inadequate estimate it in my judgment was. And its inadequacy consisted chiefly in this: that in our English way it left out of sight the double sense really involved in the word *curiosity,* thinking enough was said to stamp M. Sainte-Beuve with blame if it was said that he was impelled in his operations as a critic by curiosity, and omitting either to perceive that M. Sainte-Beuve himself, and many other people with him, would consider that this was praiseworthy and not blameworthy, or to point out why it ought really to be accounted worthy of blame and not of praise. For as there is a curiosity about intellectual matters which is futile, and merely a disease, so there is certainly a curiosity,—a desire after the things of the mind simply for their own sakes and for the pleasure of seeing them as they are,—which is, in an intelligent being, natural and laudable. Nay, and the very desire to see things as they are implies a balance and regulation of mind which is not often attained without fruitful effort, and which is the very opposite of the blind and diseased impulse of mind which is what we mean to blame when we blame curiosity. Montesquieu says: "The first motive which ought to impel us to study is the desire to augment the excellence of our nature, and to render an intelligent being yet more intelligent." This is the true ground to assign for the genuine scientific passion, however manifested, and for culture, viewed simply as a fruit of this passion; and it is a worthy ground, even though we let the term *curiosity* stand to describe it.

But there is of culture another view, in which not solely the scientific passion, the sheer desire to see things as they are, natural and proper in an intelligent being, appears as the ground of it. There is a view in which all the love of our neighbour, the impulses towards action, help, and beneficence, the desire for removing human error, clearing human confusion, and diminishing human misery, the noble aspiration to leave the world better and happier than we found it,—motives eminently such as are called social, come in as part of the grounds of culture, and the main and pre-eminent part. Culture is then properly described not as having its origin in curiosity, but as having its origin in the love of perfection; it is *a study of perfection*. It moves by the force, not merely or primarily of the scientific passion for pure knowledge, but also of the moral and social passion for doing good. As, in the first view of it, we took for its worthy motto Montesquieu's words: "To render an intelligent being yet more intelligent!" so, in the second view of it, there is no better motto which it can have than these words of Bishop Wilson: "To make reason and the will of God prevail!"

Only, whereas the passion for doing good is apt to be overhasty in determining what reason and the will of God say, because its turn is for acting rather than thinking and it wants to be beginning to act; and whereas it is apt to take its own conceptions, which proceed from its own state of development and share in all the imperfections and immaturities of this, for a basis of action; what distinguishes culture is, that it is possessed by the scientific passion as well as by the passion of doing good; that it demands worthy notions of reason and the will of God, and does not readily suffer its own crude conceptions to substitute themselves for them. And knowing that no action or institution can be salutary and stable which is not based on reason and the will of God, it is not so bent on acting and instituting, even with the great aim of diminishing human error and misery ever before its thoughts, but that it can remember that acting and instituting are of little use, unless we know how and what we ought to act and to institute.

This culture is more interesting and more far-reaching than that other, which is founded solely on the scientific passion for knowing. But it needs times of faith and ardour, times when the intellectual horizon is opening and widening all round us, to flourish in. And is not the close and bounded intellectual horizon within which we have long lived and moved now lifting up, and are not new lights finding free passage to shine in upon us? For a long time there was no passage for them to make their way in upon us, and then it was of no use to think of adapting the world's action to them. Where was the hope of making reason and the will of God prevail among people who had a routine which they had christened reason and the will of God, in which they were inextricably bound, and beyond which they had no power of looking? But now the iron force of adhesion to the old routine, —social, political, religious,—has wonderfully yielded; the iron force of exclusion of all which is new has wonderfully yielded. The danger now is, not that people should obstinately refuse to allow anything but their old routine to pass for reason and the will of God, but either that they should allow some novelty or other to pass for these too easily, or else that they should underrate the importance of them altogether, and think it enough to follow action for its own sake, without troubling themselves to make reason and the will of God prevail therein. Now, then, is the moment for culture to be of service, culture which believes in making reason and the will of God prevail, believes in perfection, is the study and pursuit of perfection, and is no longer debarred, by a rigid invincible exclusion of whatever is new, from getting acceptance for its ideas, simply because they are new.

The moment this view of culture is seized, the moment it is regarded not solely as the endeavor to see things as they are, to draw towards a knowledge of the universal order which seems to be intended and aimed at in the world, and which it is a man's happiness to go along with or his misery to go counter to,—to learn, in short, the will of God,—the moment, I say, culture is considered not merely as the endeavor to *see* and *learn* this, but as the endeavor, also, to make it *prevail,* the moral, social, and beneficent character of culture becomes manifest. The mere endeavor to see and learn the truth for our own personal satisfaction is indeed a commencement for making it prevail, a preparing the way for this, which always serves this, and is wrongly, therefore, stamped with blame absolutely in itself and not only in its caricature and degeneration. But perhaps it has got stamped with blame, and disparaged with the dubious title of curiosity, because in comparison with this wider endeavor of such great and plain utility it looks selfish, petty, and unprofitable.

And religion, the greatest and most important of the efforts by which the human race has manifested its impulse to perfect itself,—religion, that voice of the deepest human experience,—does not only enjoin and sanction the aim which is the great aim of culture, the aim of setting ourselves to ascertain what perfection is and to make it prevail; but also, in determining generally in what human perfection consists, religion comes to a conclusion identical with that which culture,—culture seeking the determination of this question through *all* the voices of human experience which have been heard upon it, of art, science, poetry, philosophy, history, as well as of religion, in order to give a greater fullness and certainty to its solution,—likewise reaches. Religion says: *The kingdom of God is within you;* and culture, in like manner, places human perfection in an *internal* condition, in the growth and predominance of our humanity proper, as distinguished from our animality. It places it in the ever-increasing efficacy and in the general harmonious expansion of those gifts of thought and feeling, which make the peculiar dignity, wealth, and happiness of human nature. As I have said on a former occasion: "It is in making endless additions to itself, in the endless expansion of its powers, in endless growth in wisdom and beauty, that the spirit of the human race finds its ideal. To reach this ideal, culture is an indispensable aid, and that is the true value of culture." Not a having and a resting, but a growing and a becoming, is the character of perfection as culture conceives it; and here, too, it coincides with religion.

And because men are all members of one great whole, and the sympathy which is in human nature will not allow one member to be indifferent to the rest or to have a perfect welfare independent of the rest, the expansion of our humanity, to suit the idea of perfection which culture forms, must be a *general* expansion. Perfection, as culture conceives it, is not possible while the individual remains isolated. The individual is required, under pain of being stunted and enfeebled in his own development if he disobeys, to carry others along with him in his march towards perfection, to be continually doing all he can to enlarge and increase the volume of the human stream sweeping thitherward. And here, once more, culture lays on us the same obligation as religion which says, as Bishop Wilson has admirably put it, that "to promote the kingdom of God is to increase and hasten one's own happiness."

But, finally, perfection,—as culture from a thorough disinterested study of human nature and human experience learns to conceive it,—

is a harmonious expansion of *all* the powers which make the beauty and worth of the human nature, and is not consistent with the over-development of any one power at the expense of the rest. Here culture goes beyond religion, as religion is generally conceived by us.

If culture, then, is a study of perfection, and of harmonious perfection, general perfection, and perfection which consists in becoming something rather than in having something, in an inward condition of the mind and spirit, not in an outward set of circumstances,—it is clear that culture, instead of being the frivolous and useless thing which Mr. Bright, and Mr. Frederic Harrison, and many other Liberals are apt to call it, has a very important function to fulfill for mankind. And this function is particularly important in our modern world, of which the whole civilization is, to a much greater degree than the civilization of Greece and Rome, mechanical and external, and tends constantly to become more so. But above all in our own country has culture a weighty part to perform, because here that mechanical character, which civilization tends to take everywhere, is shown in the most eminent degree. Indeed nearly all the characters of perfection, as culture teaches us to fix them, meet in this country with some powerful tendency which thwarts them and sets them at defiance.

The idea of perfection as an *inward* condition of the mind and spirit is at variance with the mechanical and material civilization in esteem with us, and nowhere, as I have said, so much in esteem as with us. The idea of perfection as a *general* expansion of the human family is at variance with our strong individualism, our hatred of all limits to the unrestrained swing of the individual's personality, our maxim of "every man for himself." Above all, the idea of perfection as a *harmonious* expansion of human nature is at variance with our want of flexibility, with our inaptitude for seeing more than one side of a thing, with our intense energetic absorption in the particular pursuit we happen to be following. So culture has a rough task to achieve in this country. Its preachers have, and are likely long to have, a hard time of it, and they will much oftener be regarded, for a great while to come, as elegant or spurious Jeremiahs than as friends and benefactors. That, however, will not prevent their doing in the end good service if they persevere. And, meanwhile, the mode of action they have to pursue, and the sort of habits they must fight against, ought to be made quite clear for every one to see, who may be willing to look at the matter attentively and dispassionately.

Faith in machinery is, I said, our besetting danger; often in machinery most absurdly disproportioned to the end which this machinery, if it is to do any good at all, is to serve; but always in machinery, as if it had a value in and for itself. What is freedom but machinery? what is population but machinery? what is coal but machinery? what are railroads but machinery? what is wealth but machinery? what are, even, religious organizations but machinery? Now almost every voice in England is accustomed to speak of these things as if they were precious ends in themselves, and therefore had some of the characters of perfection indisputably joined to them. I have before now noticed Mr. Roebuck's stock argument for proving the greatness and happiness of England as she is, and for quite stopping the mouths of all gainsayers. Mr. Roebuck is never weary of reiterating this argument of his, so I do not know why I should be weary of noticing it. "May not every man in England say what he likes?" —Mr. Roebuck perpetually asks; and that, he thinks, is quite sufficient, and when every man may say what he likes, our aspirations ought to be satisfied. But the aspirations of culture, which is the study of perfection, are not satisfied, unless what men say, when they may say what they like, is worth saying,—has good in it, and more good than bad. In the same way the *Times*, replying to some foreign strictures on the dress, looks and behavior of the English abroad, urges that the English ideal is that every one should be free to do and to look just as he likes. But culture indefatigably tries, not to make what each raw person may like the rule by which he fashions himself; but to draw ever nearer to a sense of what is indeed beautiful, graceful, and becoming, and to get the raw person to like that.

And in the same way with respect to rail-roads and coal. Every one must have observed the strange language current during the late discussions as to the possible failures of our supplies of coal. Our coal, thousands of people were saying, is the real basis of our national greatness; if our coal runs short, there is an end of the greatness of England. But what *is* greatness?—culture makes us ask. Greatness is a spiritual condition worthy to excite love, interest, and admiration. If England were swallowed up by the sea tomorrow, which of the two, a hundred years hence, would most excite the love, interest, and admiration of mankind,—would most, therefore, show the evidences of having possessed greatness,—the England of the last twenty years, or the England of Elizabeth, of a time of splendid spiritual effort, but when our coal, and our industrial operations depending on coal, were very little developed? Well, then, what an unsound habit of mind it must be which makes us talk of things like coal or iron as constituting the greatness of England, and how salutary a friend is culture, bent on seeing things as they are, and thus dissipating delusions of this kind and fixing standards of perfection that are real!

Wealth, again, that end to which our prodigious works for material advantage are directed, —the commonest of commonplaces tells us how men are always apt to regard wealth as a precious end in itself; and certainly they have never been so apt thus to regard it as they are in England at the present time. Never did people believe anything more firmly than nine Englishmen out of ten at the present day believe that our greatness and welfare are proved by our being so very rich. Now, the use of culture is that it helps us, by means of its spiritual standard of perfection, to regard wealth as but machinery, but really to perceive and feel that it is so. If it were not for this purging effect wrought upon our minds by culture, the whole world, the future as well as the present, would inevitably belong to the Philistines. The people who believe most that our greatness and welfare are proved by our being very rich, and who most give their lives and thoughts to becoming rich, are just the very people whom we call Philistines. Culture says: "Consider these people, then, their way of life, their habits, their manners, the very tones of their voice; look at them attentively; observe the literature they read, the things which give them pleasure, the words which come forth out of their mouths, the thoughts which make the furniture of their minds; would any amount of wealth be worth having with the condition that one was to become just like these people by having it?" And thus culture begets a dissatisfaction which is of the highest possible value in stemming the common tide of men's thoughts in a wealthy and industrial community, and which saves the future, as one may hope, from being vulgarized, even if it cannot save the present.

Population, again, and bodily health and vigour, are things which are nowhere treated in such an unintelligent, misleading, exaggerated way as in England. Both are really machinery; yet how many people all around us do we see rest in them and fail to look beyond them! Why, one has heard people, fresh from reading certain articles of the *Times* on the Registrar-General's returns of marriages and births in this country, who would talk of our large English families in quite a solemn strain, as if they had something in itself beautiful, elevating, and meritorious in them; as if the British Philistine would have only to present himself before the Great Judge with his twelve children, in order to be received among the sheep as a matter of right!

But bodily health and vigour, it may be said, are not to be classed with wealth and population as mere machinery; they have a more real and essential value. True; but only as they are more intimately connected with a perfect spiritual condition than wealth or population are. The moment we disjoin them from the idea of a perfect spiritual condition, and pursue them, as we do pursue them, for their own sake and as ends in themselves, our worship of them becomes as mere worship of machinery, as our worship of wealth or population, and as unintelligent and vulgarizing a worship as that is. Every one with anything like an adequate idea of human perfection has distinctly marked this subordination to higher and spiritual ends of the cultivation of bodily vigour and activity. "Bodily exercise profiteth little; but godliness is profitable unto all things," says the author of the Epistle to Timothy. And the utilitarian Franklin says just as explicitly: —"Eat and drink such an exact quantity as suits the constitution of thy body, *in reference to the services of the mind.*" But the point of view of culture, keeping the mark of human perfection simply and broadly in view, and not assigning to this perfection, as religion or utilitarianism assigns to it, a special and limited character, this point of view, I say, of culture is best given by these words of Epictetus:—"It is a sign of ἀφυΐα," says he,—that is, of a nature not finely tempered,—"to give yourselves up to things which relate to the body; to make, for instance, a great fuss about exercise, a great fuss about eating, a great fuss about drinking, a great fuss about walking, a great fuss about riding. All these things ought to be done merely by the way: the formation of the spirit and character must be our real concern." This is admirable; and, indeed, the Greek word εὐφυΐα, a finely tempered nature, gives exactly the notion of perfection as culture brings us to conceive it: a harmonious perfection, a perfection in which the characters of beauty and intelligence are both present, which unites "the two noblest of things,"—as Swift, who of one of the two, at any rate, had himself all too little, most happily calls them in his *Battle of the Books*,—"the two noblest of things, *sweetness and light.*" The εὐφυής is the man who tends towards sweetness and light; the ἀφυής, on the other hand, is our Philistine. The immense spiritual significance of the Greeks is due to their having been inspired with this central and happy idea of the essential character of human perfection; and Mr. Bright's misconception of culture, as a smattering of Greek and Latin, comes itself, after all, from this wonderful significance of the Greeks having affected the very machinery of our education, and is in itself a kind of homage to it.

In thus making sweetness and light to be characters of perfection, culture is of like spirit with poetry, follows one law with poetry. Far more than on our freedom, our population, and our industrialism, many amongst us rely upon our religious organizations to save us. I have called religion a yet more important manifestation of human nature than poetry, because it has worked on a broader scale for perfection, and with greater masses of men. But the idea of beauty and of a human nature perfect on all its sides, which is the dominant idea of poetry, is a true and invaluable idea, though it has not yet had the success that the idea of conquering the obvious faults of our animality, and of a human nature perfect on the moral side,— which is the dominant idea of religion,—has been enabled to have; and it is destined, adding to itself the religious idea of a devout energy, to transform and govern the other.

The best art and poetry of the Greeks, in which religion and poetry are one, in which the idea of beauty and of a human nature perfect on all sides adds to itself a religious and devout energy, and works in the strength of that, is on this account of such surpassing interest and instructiveness for us, though it was, —as, having regard to the human race in general, and, indeed, having regard to the Greeks themselves, we must own,—a premature attempt, an attempt which for success needed the moral and religious fiber in humanity to be more braced and developed than it had yet been. But Greece did not err in having the idea of beauty, harmony, and complete human perfection, so present and paramount; only, the moral fiber must be braced too. And we, because we have braced the moral fiber, are not on that account in the right way, if at the same time the idea of beauty, harmony, and complete human perfection, is wanting or misapprehended amongst us; and evidently it *is* wanting or misapprehended at present. And when we rely as we do on our religious organizations, which in themselves do not and cannot give us this idea, and think we have done enough if we make them spread and prevail, then, I say, we fall into our common fault of overvaluing machinery.

Nothing is more common than for people to confound the inward peace and satisfaction which follows the subduing of the obvious faults of our animality with what I may call absolute inward peace and satisfaction,—the peace and satisfaction which are reached as we draw near to complete spiritual perfection, and not merely to moral perfection, or rather to relative moral perfection. No people in the world have done more and struggled more to attain this relative moral perfection than our English race has. For no people in the world has the command to *resist the devil, to overcome the wicked one,* in the nearest and most obvious sense of those words, had such a pressing force and reality. And we have had our reward, not only in the great worldly prosperity which our obedience to this command has brought us, but also, and far more, in great inward peace and satisfaction. But to me few things are more pathetic than to see people, on the strength of the inward peace and satisfaction which their rudimentary efforts towards perfection have brought them, employ, concerning their incomplete perfection and the religious organizations within which they have found it, language which properly applies only to complete perfection, and is a far-off echo of the human soul's prophecy of it. Religion itself, I need hardly say, supplies them in abundance with this grand language. And very freely do they use it; yet it is really the severest possible criticism of such an incomplete perfection as alone we have yet reached through our religious organizations.

The impulse of the English race towards moral development and self-conquest has nowhere so powerfully manifested itself as in Puritanism. Nowhere has Puritanism found so adequate an expression as in the religious organization of the Independents. The modern Independents have a newspaper, the *Nonconformist,* written with great sincerity and ability. The motto, the standard, the profession of faith which this organ of theirs carries aloft, is: "The Dissidence of Dissent and the Protestantism of the Protestant religion." There is sweetness and light, and an ideal of complete harmonious human perfection! One need not go to culture and poetry to find language to judge it. Religion, with its instinct for perfection, supplies language to judge it, language, too, which is in our mouths every day. "Finally, be of one mind, united in feeling," says St. Peter. There is an ideal which judges that Puritan ideal: "The Dissidence of Dissent and the Protestantism of the Protestant religion!"

And religious organizations like this are what people believe in, rest in, would give their lives for! Such, I say, is the wonderful virtue of even the beginnings of perfection, of having conquered even the plain faults of our animality, that the religious organization which has helped us to do it can seem to us something precious, salutary, and to be propagated, even when it wears such a brand of imperfection on its forehead as this. And men have got such a habit of giving to the language of religion a special application, of making it a mere jargon, that for the condemnation which religion itself passes on the shortcomings of their religious organizations they have no ear; they are sure to cheat themselves and to explain this condemnation away. They can only be reached by the criticism which culture, like poetry, speaking a language not to be sophisticated, and resolutely testing these organizations by the idea of a human perfection complete on all sides, applies to them.

But men of culture and poetry, it will be said, are again and again failing, and failing conspicuously, in the necessary first stage to a harmonious perfection, in the subduing of the great obvious faults of our animality, which it is the glory of these religious organizations to have helped us to subdue. True, they do often so fail. They have often been without the virtues as well as the faults of the Puritan; it has been one of their dangers that they so felt the Puritan's faults that they too much neglected the practice of his virtues. I will not, however, exculpate them at the Puritan's expense. They have often failed in morality, and morality is indispensable. And they have been punished for their failure, as the Puritan has been rewarded for his performance. They have been punished wherein they erred; but their ideal of beauty, of sweetness and light, and a human nature complete on all its sides, remains the true ideal of perfection still; just as the Puritan's ideal of perfection remains narrow and inadequate, although for what he did well he has been richly rewarded. Notwithstanding the mighty results of the Pilgrim Fathers' voyage, they and their standard of perfection are rightly judged when we figure to ourselves Shakspeare or Virgil,—souls in whom sweetness and light, and all that in human nature is most humane, were eminent,—accompanying them on their voyage, and think what intolerable company Shakspeare and Virgil would have found them! In the same way let us judge the religious organizations which we see all around us. Do not let us deny the good and the happiness which they have accomplished; but do not let us fail to see clearly that their idea of human perfection is narrow and inadequate, and that the Dissidence of Dissent and the Protestantism of the Protestant religion will never bring humanity to its true goal. As I said with regard to wealth: Let us look at the life of those who live in and for it,—so I say with regard to the religious organizations. Look at the life imaged in such a newspaper as the *Nonconformist,*—a life of jealousy of the Establishment, disputes, tea-meeting, openings of chapels, sermons; and then think of it as an ideal of a human life completing itself on all sides, and aspiring with all its organ after sweetness, light, and perfection!

Another newspaper, representing, like the *Nonconformist,* one of the religious organizations of this country, was a short time ago giving an account of the crowd at Epsom on the Derby day, and of all the vice and hideousness which was to be seen in that crowd; and then the writer turned suddenly round upon Professor Huxley, and asked him how he proposed to cure all this vice and hideousness without religion. I confess I felt disposed to ask the asker this question: and how do you propose to cure it with such a religion as yours? How is the ideal of a life so unlovely, so unattractive, so incomplete, so narrow, so far removed from a true and satisfying ideal of human perfection, as is the life of your religious organization as you yourself reflect it, to conquer and transform all this vice and hideousness? Indeed, the strongest plea for the study of perfection as pursued by culture, the clearest proof of the actual inadequacy of the idea of perfection held by the religious organizations,—expressing, as I have said, the most widespread effort which the human race has yet made after perfection, —is to be found in the state of our life and society with these in possession of it, and having been in possession of it I know not how

many hundred years. We are all of us included in some religious organization or other; we all call ourselves, in the sublime and aspiring language of religion which I have before noticed, *children of God.* Children of God;— it is an immense pretension!—and how are we to justify it? By the works which we do, and the words which we speak. And the work which we collective children of God do, our grand center of life, our *city* which we have builded for us to dwell in, is London! London, with its unutterable external hideousness, and with its internal canker of *publicè egestas, privatim opulentia,*—to use the words which Sallust puts into Cato's mouth about Rome,—unequalled in the world! The word, again, which we children of God speak, the voice which most hits our collective thought, the newspaper with the largest circulation in England, nay, with the largest circulation in the whole world, is the *Daily Telegraph!* I say that when our religious organizations,—which I admit to express the most considerable effort after perfection that our race has yet made,—land us in no better result than this, it is high time to examine carefully their idea of perfection, to see whether it does not leave out of account sides and forces of human nature which we might turn to great use; whether it would not be more operative if it were more complete. And I say that the English reliance on our religious organizations and on their ideas of human perfection just as they stand, is like our reliance on freedom, on muscular Christianity, on population, on coal, on wealth,—mere belief in machinery, and unfruitful; and that it is wholesomely counter-acted by culture, bent on seeing things as they are, and on drawing the human race onwards to a more complete, a harmonious perfection.

Culture, however, shows its singleminded love of perfection, its desire simply to make reason and the will of God prevail, its freedom from fanaticism, by its attitude towards all this machinery, even while it insists that it *is* machinery. Fanatics, seeing the mischief men do themselves by their blind belief in some machinery or other,—whether it is wealth and industrialism, or whether it is the cultivation of bodily strength and activity, or whether it is a political organization,—or whether it is a religious organization,—oppose with might and main the tendency to this or that political and religious organization, or to games and athletic exercises, or to wealth and industrialism, and try violently to stop it. But the flexibility which sweetness and light give, and which is one of the rewards of culture pursued in good faith, enables a man to see that a tendency may be necessary, and even, as a preparation for something in the future, salutary, and yet that the generations or individuals who obey this tendency are sacrificed to it, that they fall short of the hope of perfection by following it; and that its mischiefs are to be criticized, lest it should take too firm a hold and last after it has served its purpose.

Mr. Gladstone well pointed out, in a speech at Paris,—and others have pointed out the same thing,—how necessary is the present great movement towards wealth and industrialism, in order to lay broad foundations of material well-being for the society of the future. The worst of these justifications is, that they are generally addressed to the very people engaged, body and soul, in the movement in question; at all events, that they are always seized with the greatest avidity by these people, and taken by them as quite justifying their life; and that thus they tend to harden them in their sins. Now, culture admits the necessity of the movement towards fortune-making and exaggerated industrialism, readily allows that the future may derive benefit from it; but insists, at the same time, that the passing generations of industrialists,—forming, for the most part, the stout main body of Philistinism,—are sacrificed to it. In the same way, the result of all the games and sports which occupy the passing generation of boys and young men may be the establishment of a better and sounder physical type for the future to work with. Culture does not set itself against the games and sports; it congratulates the future, and hopes it will make a good use of its improved physical basis; but it points out that our passing generation of boys and young men is, meantime, sacrificed. Puritanism was perhaps necessary to develop the moral fiber of the English race, Nonconformity to break the yoke of ecclesiastical domination

over men's minds and to prepare the way for freedom of thought in the distant future; still, culture points out that the harmonious perfection of generations of Puritans and Nonconformists has been, in consequence, sacrificed. Freedom of speech may be necessary for the society of the future, but the young lions of the *Daily Telegraph* in the meanwhile are sacrificed. A voice for every man in his country's government may be necessary for the society of the future, but meanwhile Mr. Beales and Mr. Bradlaugh are sacrificed.

Oxford, the Oxford of the past, has many faults; and she has heavily paid for them in defeat, in isolation, in want of hold upon the modern world. Yet we in Oxford, brought up amidst the beauty and sweetness of that beautiful place, have not failed to seize one truth,— the truth that beauty and sweetness are essential characters of a complete human perfection. When I insist on this, I am all in the faith and tradition of Oxford. I say boldly that this our sentiment for beauty and sweetness, our sentiment against hideousness and rawness, has been at the bottom of our attachment to so many beaten causes, of our opposition to so many triumphant movements. And the sentiment is true, and has never been wholly defeated, and has shown its power even in its defeat. We have not won our political battles, we have not carried our main points, we have not stopped our adversaries' advance, we have not marched victoriously with the modern world; but we have told silently upon the mind of the country, we have prepared currents of feeling which sap our adversaries' position when it seems gained, we have kept up our own communications with the future. Look at the course of the great movement which shook Oxford to its center some thirty years ago! It was directed, as any one who reads Dr. Newman's *Apology* may see, against what in one word may be called "Liberalism." Liberalism prevailed; it was the appointed force to do the work of the hour; it was necessary, it was inevitable that it should prevail. The Oxford movement was broken, it failed; our wrecks are scattered on every shore:—

Quæ regio in terris nostri non plena laboris?

But what was it, this liberalism, as Dr. Newman saw it, and as it really broke the Oxford movement? It was the great middle-class liberalism, which had for the cardinal points of its belief the Reform Bill of 1832, and local self-government, in politics; in the social sphere, free-trade, unrestricted competition, and the making of large industrial fortunes; in the religious sphere, the Dissidence of Dissent and the Protestantism of the Protestant religion. I do not say that other and more intelligent forces than this were not opposed to the Oxford movement: but this was the force which really beat it; this was the force which Dr. Newman felt himself fighting with; this was the force which till only the other day seemed to be the paramount force in this country, and to be in possession of the future; this was the force whose achievements fill Mr. Lowe with such inexpressible admiration, and whose rule he was so horror-struck to see threatened. And where is this great force of Philistinism now? It is thrust into the second rank, it is become a power of yesterday, it has lost the future. A new power has suddenly appeared, a power which it is impossible yet to judge fully, but which is certainly a wholly different force from middle-class liberalism; different in its cardinal points of belief, different in its tendencies in every sphere. It loves and admires neither the legislation of middle-class Parliaments, nor the local self-government of middle-class vestries, nor the unrestricted competition of middle-class industrialists, nor the dissidence of middle-class Dissent and the Protestantism of middle-class Protestant religion. I am not now praising this new force, or saying that its own ideals are better; all I say is, that they are wholly different. And who will estimate how much the currents of feeling created by Dr. Newman's movement, the keen desire for beauty and sweetness which it nourished, the deep aversion it manifested to the hardness and vulgarity of middle-class liberalism, the strong light it turned on the hideous and grotesque illusions of middle-class Protestantism,—who will estimate how much all these contributed to swell the tide of secret dissatisfaction which has mined the ground under self-confident liberalism of the last thirty years, and has prepared the way for its sudden collapse and supersession? It is in this manner that the sentiment of Oxford for beauty and sweetness conquers, and in this manner long may it continue to conquer! . . .

The pursuit of perfection, then, is the pursuit of sweetness and light. He who works for sweetness and light, works to make reason and the will of God prevail. He who works for machinery, he who works for hatred, works only for confusion. Culture looks beyond machinery, culture hates hatred; culture has one great passion, the passion for sweetness and light. It has one even yet greater!—the passion for making them *prevail*. It is not satisfied till we *all* come to a perfect man; it knows that the sweetness and light of the few must be imperfect until the raw and unkindled masses of humanity are touched with sweetness and light. If I have not shrunk from saying that we must work for sweetness and light, so neither have I shrunk from saying that we must have a broad basis, must have sweetness and light for as many as possible. Again and again I have insisted how those are the happy moments of humanity, how those are the marking epochs of a people's life, how those are the flowering times for literature and art and all the creative power of genius, when there is a *national* glow of life and thought, when the whole of society is in the fullest measure permeated by thought, sensible to beauty, intelligent and alive. Only it must be *real* thought and *real* beauty; *real* sweetness and *real* light. Plenty of people will try to give the masses, as they call them, an intellectual food prepared and adapted in the way they think proper for the actual condition of the masses. The ordinary popular literature is an example of this way of working on the masses. Plenty of people will try to indoctrinate the masses with the set of ideas and judgments constituting the creed of their own profession or party. Our religious and political organizations give an example of this way of working on the masses. I condemn neither way; but culture works differently. It does not try to teach down to the level of inferior classes; it does not try to win them for this or that sect of its own, with ready-made judgments and watchwords. It seeks to do away with classes; to make the best that has been thought and known in the world current everywhere; to make all men live in an atmosphere of sweetness and light, where they may use ideas, as it uses them itself, freely,— nourished, and not bound by them.

This is the *social idea;* and the men of culture are the true apostles of equality. The great men of culture are those who have had a passion for diffusing, for making prevail, for carrying from one end of society to the other, the best knowledge, the best ideas of their time; who have labored to divest knowledge of all that was harsh, uncouth, difficult, abstract, professional, exclusive; to humanize it, to make it efficient outside the clique of the cultivated and learned, yet still remaining the *best* knowledge and thought of the time, and a true source, therefore, of sweetness and light. Such a man was Abelard in the Middle Ages, in spite of all his imperfections; and thence the boundless emotion and enthusiasm which Abelard excited. Such were Lessing and Herder in Germany, at the end of the last century; and their services to Germany were in this way inestimably precious. Generations will pass, and literary monuments will accumulate, and works far more perfect than the works of Lessing and Herder will be produced in Germany; and yet the names of these two men will fill a German with a reverence and enthusiasm such as the names of the most gifted masters will hardly awaken. And why? Because they *humanized* knowledge; because they broadened the basis of life and intelligence; because they worked powerfully to diffuse sweetness and light, to make reason and the will of God prevail. With Saint Augustine they said: "Let us not leave thee alone to make in the secret of thy knowledge, as thou didst before the creation of the firmament, the division of light from darkness; let the children of thy spirit, placed in their firmament, make their light shine upon the earth, make the division of night and day, and announce the revolution of the times; for the old order is passed, and the new arises; the night is spent, the day is come forth; and thou shalt crown the year with thy blessing, when thou shalt send forth laborers into thy harvest sown by other hands than theirs; when thou shalt send forth new laborers to new seed-times, whereof the harvest shall be not yet."

DISCUSSION

This essay, though written a century ago, remains of fundamental importance in dealing with problems of modern society. For one thing, Arnold attempts definitions of certain key words. Notice the number of things, such as "culture," "religion," and "poetry," which Arnold undertakes to define. But Arnold attempts to give more than a set of definitions, though one must understand the definitions before one can understand Arnold's basic view. That basic view may be summarized as follows: the "good life" cannot be led merely by emphasizing one aspect of the human personality; rather, it must depend upon a harmonious development of all the individual's powers. It is easy to see the reasonableness of this view in its application to certain concrete examples which Arnold cites. For instance, Arnold says of machinery: "Faith in machinery is . . . our besetting danger; often in machinery most absurdly disproportioned to the end which this machinery, if it is to do any good at all, is to serve." In other words, mechanical ability may be set to the task of perfecting an iron lung or a bomb; the mechanical ability in itself does not determine which is to be created or for what purpose either is to be used. Something beyond mechanical ability must decide which ends are valuable. In the same way, mere wealth cannot insure the attainment of the good life; that, for either an individual or a nation, must depend upon how the wealth is used.

But Arnold not only applies his view to such things as wealth and machinery, but to such an activity as theoretical science itself. Science increases our knowledge of the world about us and gives us means to manipulate that world, but it cannot, as science, assign objectives for that manipulation.

Arnold goes on to apply this view to codes of conduct, and even to religion. Religion, particularly a puritanical religion, because it emphasizes a moral code, tends to develop certain aspects of the human personality to the exclusion of others. People who are merely moral "confound the inward peace and satisfaction which follows the subduing of the obvious faults of our animality with what I may call absolute inward peace and satisfaction—the peace and satisfaction which are reached as we draw near to complete spiritual perfection. . . . " This complete spiritual perfection would involve, not only moral virtue, but also the development of a sense of beauty, the power of reason, etc. In other words, morality is not an end in itself, but a means toward an end.

Up to this point the emphasis has been on the development of the individual. But Arnold says that the bearers of the idea of culture are the true apostles of equality. And: "The great men of culture are those who have had a passion for diffusing, for making prevail, for carrying from one end of society to the other, the best knowledge, the best ideas of their time. . . ."

Arnold's concern with definitions has already been mentioned. Looking back upon the essay, we can see the reason for this, for the very essence of Arnold's culture is that it does not consist in the application of any ready-made, abstract formula or code. Rather, it is a sense of taste and judgment operating in the light of certain principles, but making each application individual and concrete. Any mere code might be defined briefly and clearly.

EXERCISE

1. The essay has been analyzed in order to examine certain central points. It may be interesting to reread the essay with a special view to Arnold's method of presentation and argument. What has he gained by the special ordering of his ideas? What important ideas have been omitted in the "Discussion"?

2. Notice the numerous illustrations in the essay. Do these become irrelevant digressions?

3. Notice the metaphors and similes which Arnold uses. How do these contribute to the persuasiveness of the essay?

4. Consider, for example, the difference in style between the concluding paragraphs of the essay and, say, the section on Puritanism and the Non-conformists. What accounts for this difference?

5. Arnold attacks what he calls our "faith in machinery." Compare his position on this point with the position which Skinner takes with regard to the function of science in a civilization and with that presumably held by Boorstin (p. 484).

6. Compare Arnold's basic attitude with that of Stevenson.

7. Attempt to state in your own terms what Arnold means by "humanized knowledge." Has he given the phrase a definite content, or does it remain merely a pleasantly emotional epithet?

8. What does Arnold mean by non-conformity? Compare his notion with that of T. S. Eliot.

9. Arnold writes: "The danger now is, not that people should obstinately refuse to allow anything but their old routine to pass for reason and the will of God, but . . . that they should allow some novelty or other to pass for these too easily," etc. (p. 470). Do you think this true today?

Literature and the Modern World

T. S. ELIOT (1888-   )

PEOPLE MAY be conscious of their age without knowing very much about it. I believe that most of us are influenced, more than we realize, by a kind of deterministic conception of history. That may be all right for the Marxian, who has a reasoned theory about it; but it has no advantage as an unconscious assumption. The assumption of the inevitability of progress has, we all know, been discarded in its nineteenth-century form: it is the butt of popular philosophers like Dean Inge. But actually, what we have discarded is a particular variety of the theory of progress: that which is associated with Darwin, Tennyson, free-trade, and the industrial development of the latter part of the last century: in short, with Liberalism. Our beliefs have been shaken in detail: for instance, no one now is convinced of the automatic beneficence of scientific invention. Invention may be applied to destructive, rather than to creative activity; and it throws people out of work and it stimulates production while it diminishes consumption: these are commonplaces. Nevertheless, we retain the essential of the doctrine of progress: we have no faith in the present.

In popularizing the belief in the future in a crude form we have, I think, a good deal for which to thank Mr. H. G. Wells. His superficial philosophy has had an extensive influence. Whatever Mr. Wells may explicitly disclaim, I think that the effect of his writing has been something like this: to propagate a belief that the value of the present resides in its service to the future, and nowhere else. Morality consists in working to forward the happiness of future generations, "happiness" of a not remarkably spiritualized kind. We are to find our happiness in scientific work which will benefit future humanity, and for the rest get anything out of life that we can. I do not want to let my words be twisted to suggest that we should take no concern with the lives of future generations. It is very much our business. What I object to is the complete dislocation of values. It is important not only that we should try to want the right things for the future. It is important also that we should have just as much respect for ourselves; and remember that we, as human beings, are individually just as valuable as the men of the future. Mr. Wells seems to propagate a strange false humility of evolutionism: as the higher apes are to us, he says in effect, so are we to the men of the future; and as we regard our animal ancestors, whether apes, lemurs, or opossums, so will they of the future regard us. This is, of course, the quite natural corollary of a naïf faith in perpetual evolution, combined with a denial of any sharp dividing line between the human and the animal: that is, a denial of the human soul.

Now, one effect of this is to justify a contempt for humanity as we find it today, and the admission of any means, at whatever cost to human dignity, which will bring about the kind of future which Mr. Wells contemplates with such rapture. I confess that I cannot see why we should take such pains to produce a race of men, millennia hence, who will only look down upon *us* as apes, lemurs, or opossums. It seems a thankless labor. We must affirm that there is no more value in the future than there is in the present. That is to say, we must affirm the eternal against the transient; the eternal which has been realized in the past, can be realized in the present; and it is our business to try to bring about a future in which the obstacles to this realization will be less, for the mass of humanity, than they are today. And these obstacles are not all of a material kind; they are in ourselves too. Our attitude may seem less ambitious than that of Mr. Wells; but it is more definite. It is simply that of the humble parent who wants his child to have a better chance in life than he had, and to lead a better life than he has led.

I said at the beginning that this modern eschatology begins in optimism and easily ends in despair. But I do not draw the moral of the proprietor whose granary was full. We are obviously at the end of an age, oppressed by the sense of corruption and decay, and fearful of the kinds of change which may come, since some change must. And since our minds must needs be filled with thought about the future, thought affecting our own action tomorrow perhaps, and our consciences disturbed by what we find about us and within us, it is all the more important to keep our heads, our sense of values; all the more important that we should hold fast to the things which were, and are, and shall be, world without end.

My immediate occupation, however, is with the effect upon modern literature of this dislocation of values and this moral subservience of the present to the future. As a kind of consultant, as well as a potential impresario, I have to see a good deal of what is being written, in some forms, by those much younger than myself. In the better writers there is strongly developed a kind of social conscience, a notion that literature ought to be useful to society. In the inferior writers this conscience may, of course, take the form merely of a determination not to miss the boat; but I confidently assure you of the existence of a fair proportion of sincerity. Now this devotion to society may involve precisely the same dislocation of values as the devotion to the future; and I propose to try to come to a conclusion about the proper relation of the poet today to himself and to society. The preoccupation of which I speak is inevitable, it is right; but how is it to be adjusted to the permanent values which literature is supposed to realize?

Here we get to the point. Should a literary artist have this acute sense of a social duty obliging him to convey a message; and if so, when is the "message" beneficial and when detrimental to the "art"?

I believe that the man of letters at the present day ought to have this sense. But the great danger for the artist is always that of conscientiously trying to feel what he does not feel. I will venture the following formulation: What is desirable is a harmony between the individual and sub-individual passions of the artist, and the social ideas and feelings which he wishes to propagate. In this harmony, he neither exploits the conscious doctrine as a vehicle for his personality, nor cramps or distorts his personality to adapt it to a social doctrine. This requires some little amplification.

A man is both an individual and a member. Instead of "individual" I shall use the word "person." His *personality* is unique and not to be violated; but he is equally created to be a *member* of society. When society is conceived as merely a sum of individuals, you get the chaos of liberal democracy. When the person is wholly subordinated to society, you get the dehumanization of fascism or communism. The extremes, however, may meet. For what liberal democracy really recognizes is a sum, not of persons, but of individuals: that is to say, not the variety and uniqueness of persons, but the purely material individuation of the old-fashioned or Democritean atom. And this is a disrespect to the person. For the person is no longer a person if wholly isolated from the community; and the community is no longer a community if it does not consist of persons. A man is not himself unless he is a member; and he cannot be a member unless he is also something alone. Man's membership and his solitude must be taken together. There are moments, perhaps not known to everyone, when a man may be nearly crushed by the terrible awareness of his isolation from every other human being; and I pity him if he finds himself only alone with himself and his meanness and futility, alone without God. It is after these moments, alone *with* God and aware of our worthiness, but for Grace, of nothing but damnation, that we turn with most thankfulness and appreciation to the awareness of our *membership:* for we appreciate and are thankful for nothing fully until we see where it begins and where it ends. All that I have been saying is recognized by the Church, and the balance is maintained only by the Church: it is not recognized, but is made manifest by, the endless seesaw of political tendency between anarchy and tyranny: a seesaw which, in the secular world, I believe has no end.

Now all this may sound perfectly irrelevant to my subject; but it is not so. This same balance ought to exist, on its plane, in the activity of the artist. For the artist cannot devote himself truly to any cause unless by that devotion he is also most truly being, and becoming, himself. The artist may, as Remy de Gourmont profoundly says, "in writing himself, write his age"; but I think that we should add that he may sometimes in writing his age, write himself: which will come to the same thing. But it is from himself that he must start. It is sometimes helpful to put things in an extreme, and therefore dangerous way. So I may say that in one aspect the true artist may be said to be simply *exploiting* the things he believes in for the purpose of making art:—only if he does this *consciously* is he a false artist.

Whereas a man like D. H. Lawrence is in danger of manipulating his philosophy to fit his private needs and to justify his private weaknesses, the adherent of an objective creed is in danger of denying, or distorting himself to fit his beliefs; and the opposite insincerity becomes possible. This is equally a danger for the Christian and for the communist, and especially at those moments when personal inspiration fails. How far can one go in identifying a creed with oneself, or oneself with a creed? The development of the person may be twisted, or the purity of the creed may be polluted. I believe, naturally, that the Christian, if he understands his Christianity, has safeguards which the mere social revolutionist cannot have: safeguards of the personal emotion. For instance: social enthusiasm alone, however intense, does not seem to have the substance needed to make poetry. What is the difference between Dante's denunciation of the vices of his time, and Shelley's denunciation of kings, tyrants, and priests? Shelley's excitement is in his head, and therefore emits rather shrill and inapplicable head noises; whereas Dante's is involved with all his own sufferings—definite grievances and definite humiliations at the hands of particular people, of all of which he is conscious: self-interested grudges and deprivations, earthly if you like, but primarily *real,* and that is the first thing. Only the greatest, the Hebrew Prophets, seem to be utterly caught up and possessed by God as mouthpieces; in ordinary human poets the human personal loss, the private grievance and bitterness and loneliness, must be present. Even when the poet is aware of nothing, interested in nothing, beyond his personal feelings, these may have, by their intensity, a representative value, so that we envisage him, like Villon, not as wrapped up in his private griefs, but reliving them, holding nothing back, in a passionate cry to God—and there is, in the end, no one else to cry to. But in the greatest poets these private passions are completed in a passionate belief in objective moral values, in a striving towards justice and the life of the spirit among men.

Now the tendency of secular revolution today seems to me to be to diminish the value of the person. Of what importance, we may say currently, is all this expression of personal feeling and private suffering, in a world of so much general injustice and oppression? and this is the secular point of view: of what importance one man, when the life of society is at stake! We are back with the modern eschatology of which Mr. Wells is the popular preacher. The present order is damned, let us snatch what satisfaction we can, say some; and, the present order is damned, let us sacrifice—not our pleasure, but our *selves*—to the future, say others; and one may perhaps maintain both conclusions at once. And behind is the master idea which has been working unobtrusively throughout our time, an idea which in the forms of heresy has always been waiting for us: the idea of the *"group consciousness"*—modest, and scientific and certain it sounds under that name.

In a recent article called "The Real Issue," which I have read with interest and approval, Mr. Christopher Dawson makes some pertinent remarks about the position of the individual in the classless society:

. . . the orthodox Communist will deny that this total subordination and sacrifice of humanity to the State machine is of the essence of Communism, for did not Marx and Lenin expressly teach that the dictatorship of the proletariat is only a temporary phase, and that the State itself will eventually wither away and give place to a classless and Stateless society? But how will this end be attained? Only when the individual is so completely socialized that he will instinctively devote all his energies to working for society and will be unable to conceive of any other end than that of the economic organism of which he forms part. In such an order there will be no need for a State any more than it is necessary for ants or bees to have a State. But is it a human order, and is it possible for humanity to rise or sink to such a level?

I do not, any more than Mr. Dawson, think such a consummation likely; but if I did not think it possible I should not take the trouble of attacking the idea of it. It would be brought about, not by the diabolic cleverness of scheming philosophers and politicians, but by the natural aversion of human beings to the responsibility and strain of being *human*. For we must remember that it *is* a great strain for the erect animal to persist in being erect, a physical and still more a moral strain. With or without mechanical aids of movement and noise, most people spend a good deal of their time avoiding the human responsibility; and we only remain human because of the continual vicarious sacrifice of a few dedicated lives. And the "group consciousness," the heresy bred within the antithetical heresy of liberalism, has a great seductive charm; for it helps to release us from the burden of responsibility. It would more likely, I think, be a reversion to a lower kind of consciousness, than an ascent to a higher one; it is largely, in fact, to the speculations, which profess to be based on the study of primitive races, of such writers as Durkheim and Levy-Bruhl, that we owe the conceptions. That such a state of humanity would be unfavorable to poetry follows from what I have said earlier. That is not perhaps of the utmost importance in itself; there are matters more important than the perpetual produtcion of new poetry, though we must remember that a people which ceases to create the new will also lose the power to appreciate the *old*. What is important is that the creation of poetry depends upon the maintenance of the person, of the person in relation to other individuals, to God, and to society.

There is much, however, in the aspirations of poetry today with which I am in full sympathy. When we compare the state of poetry now with that of forty years ago, towards the end of the last century, I think we may see, without drawing any comparison between the merits of individual poets (and even if that comparison were to result to our disadvantage), that the social earnestness and dissatisfaction which have been lately expressing themselves have been all to the good; and poetry has taken on a new seriousness and a new social importance. It is perhaps not insignificant that the one great poet we have who belongs to both periods, Mr. William Butler Yeats, has been writing his finest poetry within recent years. With all we owe him, I find it difficult to regard Mr. Yeats as anything but a *contemporary;* and if anyone said that of me, when I arrive at his present age, I should consider it the highest of compliments. What I think we have missed, and have been struggling for, is the recognition of poetry as something other than exquisite pleasure for a small number of people who have the taste for it—as something having a function of social value. The poet must assume his rôle of moralist, and thus manifest his relation to society.

I think however that the passion for social righteousness will prove in the end not enough in itself. The danger of what I have called the modern eschatology, the danger of neglecting the permanent for the transitory, the personal for the social, is one to which the poet is exposed in common with everyone else: but he has a peculiar responsibility not to be deluded. Yet I would ask you to have some sympathy with his difficulties. An age of change, and a period of incessant apprehension of war, do not form a favorable environment. There is a temp-tation to welcome change for its own sake, to sink our minds in some desperate philosophy of *action;* and several such philosophies are being urged upon us. Contempt for the past, and even ignorance of it, is on the increase, and many are ready for the unlimited experiment. We cannot effect intelligent change, unless we hold fast to the permanent essentials; and a clear understanding of what we should hold fast to, and what abandon, should make us all the better prepared to carry out the changes that are needed. Thus we can look back upon the past without regret, and to the future without fear.

EXERCISE

1. Eliot writes: "We are obviously at the end of an age, oppressed by the sense of corruption and decay. . . ." (p. 480). Compare with Bishop's ". . . the disintegration of the social fabric . . . became apparent to almost anyone" (p. 527). What common assumptions, if any, are shared by this essay and Bishop's "Homage to Hemingway"? And which are shared by Stevenson?

2. How does Eliot connect the deterministic conception of history with belief in progress? With Liberalism?

3. How does Eliot's conception of the political process differ from that of Skinner?

4. What similarities in ideas do you find between Arnold and Eliot? What differences? How do they feel about the social usefulness of literature? How do you feel about it?

5. Ought "literature . . . to be useful to society"? What are the dangers in trying to make literature carry a "message"? Or is a "message" unavoidable? Focus your discussion on the meaning to be given the word *message*.

6. How much of Eliot's criticism of H. G. Wells, in your opinion, would apply to Skinner?

7. Is Eliot, in asking us not to have a contempt for the past, counseling us to neglect the future? Compare his attitude toward the past with that of Arnold and of Skinner.

8. How does Eliot's conception of a "person" differ from that of Skinner? From that of Hemingway? From that of Krutch?

From Hero to Celebrity

DANIEL J. BOORSTIN (1914-   )

OUR AGE has produced a new kind of eminence. This is as characteristic of our culture and our century as was the divinity of Greek gods in the sixth century B.C. or the chivalry of knights and courtly lovers in the middle ages. It has not yet driven heroism, sainthood, or martyrdom completely out of our consciousness. But with every decade it overshadows them more. All older forms of greatness now survive only in the shadow of this new form. This new kind of eminence is "celebrity."

The word "celebrity" (from the Latin *celebritas* for "multitude" or "fame" and *celeber* meaning "frequented," "populous," or "famous") originally meant not a person but a condition— as the Oxford English Dictionary says, "the condition of being much talked about; famousness, notoriety." In this sense its use dates from at least the early seventeenth century. Even then it had a weaker meaning than "fame" or "renown." Matthew Arnold, for example, remarked in the nineteenth century that while the philosopher Spinoza's followers had "celebrity," Spinoza himself had "fame."

For us, however, "celebrity" means primarily a person—"a person of celebrity." This usage of the word significantly dates from the early years of the Graphic Revolution, the first example being about 1850. Emerson spoke of "the celebrities of wealth and fashion" (1848). Now American dictionaries define a celebrity as "a famous or well-publicized person."

The celebrity in the distinctive modern sense could not have existed in any earlier age, or in America before the Graphic Revolution. *The celebrity is a person who is known for his well-knownness.*

His qualities—or rather his lack of qualities —illustrate our peculiar problems. He is neither good nor bad, great nor petty. He is the human pseudo-event. He has been fabricated on purpose to satisfy our exaggerated expectations of human greatness. He is morally neutral. The product of no conspiracy, of no group promoting vice or emptiness, he is made by honest, industrious men of high professional ethics doing their job, "informing" and educating us. He is made by all of us who willingly read about him, who like to see him on television, who buy recordings of his voice, and talk about him to our friends. His relation to morality and even to reality is highly ambiguous. He is like the woman *in* an Elinor Glyn novel who describes another by saying, "She is like a figure in an Elinor Glyn novel."

The massive *Celebrity Register* (1959), compiled by Earl Blackwell and Cleveland Amory, now gives us a well-documented definition of the word, illustrated by over 2,200 biographies. "We think we have a better yardstick than the *Social Register,* or *Who's Who,* or any such book," they explain. "Our point is that it is impossible to be accurate in listing a man's social standing—even if anyone cared; and it's impossible to list accurately the success or value of men; but you *can* judge a man as a celebrity —all you have to do is weigh his press clippings." The *Celebrity Register's* alphabetical order shows Mortimer Adler followed by Polly Adler, the Dalai Lama listed beside TV comedienne Dagmar, Dwight Eisenhower preceding Anita Ekberg, ex-President Herbert Hoover following ex-torch singer Libby Holman, Pope John XXIII coming after Mr. John the hat designer, and Bertrand Russell followed by Jane Russell. They are all celebrities. The well-knownness which they have in common overshadows everything else.

The advertising world has proved the market appeal of celebrities. In trade jargon celebrities are "big names." Endorsement advertising not only uses celebrities; it helps make them. Anything that makes a well-known name still better known automatically raises its status as a celebrity. The old practice, well established before the nineteenth century, of declaring the prestige of a product by the phrase "By Appointment to His Majesty" was, of course, a kind of use of the testimonial endorsement. But the King was in fact a great person, one of illustrious lineage and with impressive actual and symbolic powers. The King was not a venal endorser, and he was likely to use only superior products. He was not a mere celebrity. For the test of celebrity is nothing more than well-knownness.

Studies of biographies in popular magazines suggest that editors, and supposedly also readers, of such magazines not long ago shifted their attention away from the old-fashioned hero. From the person known for some serious achievement, they have turned their biographical interests to the new-fashioned celebrity. Of the subjects of biographical articles appearing in the *Saturday Evening Post* and the now-defunct *Collier's* in five sample years between 1901 and 1914, 74 per cent came from politics, business, and the professions. But after about 1922 well over half of them came from the world of entertainment. Even among the entertainers an ever decreasing proportion has come from the serious arts—literature, fine arts, music, dance, and theater. An ever increasing proportion (in recent years nearly all) comes from the fields of light entertainment, sports, and the night club circuit. In the earlier period, say before World War I, the larger group included figures like the President of the United States, a Senator, a State Governor, the Secretary of the Treasury, the banker J. P. Morgan, the railroad magnate James J. Hill, a pioneer in aviation, the inventor of the torpedo, a Negro educator, an immigrant scientist, an opera singer, a famous poet, and a popular fiction writer. By the 1940's the larger group included figures like the boxer Jack Johnson, Clark Gable, Bobby Jones, the movie actresses Brenda Joyce and Brenda Marshall, William Powell, the woman matador Conchita Cintron, the night club entertainer Adelaide Moffett, and the gorilla Toto. Some analysts say the shift is primarily the sign of a new focus of popular attention away from production and toward consumption. But this is oversubtle.

A simpler explanation is that the machinery of information has brought into being a new substitute for the hero, who is the celebrity, and whose main characteristic is his well-knownness. In the democracy of pseudo-events, anyone can become a celebrity, if only he can get into the news and stay there. Figures from the world of entertainment and sports are most apt to be well known. If they are successful enough, they actually overshadow the real figures they portray. George Arliss overshadowed Disraeli, Vivian Leigh overshadowed Scarlett O'Hara, Fess Parker overshadowed Davy Crockett. Since their stock in trade is their well-knownness, they are most apt to have energetic press agents keeping them in the public eye.

It is hardly surprising then that magazine and newspaper readers no longer find the lives of their heroes instructive. Popular biographies can offer very little in the way of solid information. For the subjects are themselves mere figments of the media. If their lives are empty of drama or achievement, it is only as we might have expected, for they are not known for drama or achievement. They are celebrities. Their chief claim to fame is their fame itself. They are notorious for their notoriety. If this is puzzling or fantastic, if it is mere tautology, it is no more puzzling or fantastic or tautologous than much of the rest of our experience. Our experience tends more and more to become tautology—needless repetition of the same in different words and images. Perhaps what ails us is not so much a vice as a "nothingness." The vacuum of our experience is actually made emptier by our anxious straining with mechanical devices to fill it artificially. What is remarkable is not only that we manage to fill experience with so much emptiness, but that we manage to give the emptiness such appealing variety.

We can hear ourselves straining. "He's the greatest!" Our descriptions of celebrities overflow with superlatives. In popular magazine biographies we learn that a Dr. Brinkley is the "best-advertised doctor in the United States"; an actor is the "luckiest man in the movies today"; a Ringling is "not only the greatest, but the first real showman in the Ringling family"; a general is "one of the best mathematicians this side of Einstein"; a columnist has "one of the strangest of courtships"; a statesman has "the world's most exciting job"; a sportsman is "the loudest and by all odds the most abusive"; a newsman is "one of the most consistently resentful men in the country"; a certain ex-King's mistress is "one of the unhappiest women that ever lived." But, despite the "supercolossal" on the label, the contents are very ordinary. The lives of celebrities which we like to read, as Leo Lowenthal remarks, are a mere catalogue of "hardships" and "breaks." These men and women are "the proved specimens of the average."

No longer external sources which fill us with purpose, these new-model "heroes" are receptacles into which we pour our own purposelessness. They are nothing but ourselves seen in a magnifying mirror. Therefore the lives of entertainer-celebrities cannot extend our horizon. Celebrities populate our horizon with men and women we already know. Or, as an advertisement for the *Celebrity Register* cogently puts it, celebrities are "the 'names' who, once made by news, now make news by themselves." Celebrity is made by simple familiarity, induced and re-enforced by public means. The celebrity therefore is the perfect embodiment of tautology: the most familiar is the most familiar.

II

The hero was distinguished by his achievement; the celebrity by his image or trademark. The hero created himself; the celebrity is created by the media. The hero was a big man; the celebrity is a big name.

Formerly, a public man needed a *private* secretary for a barrier between himself and the public. Nowadays he has a *press* secretary, to keep him properly in the public eye. Before the Graphic Revolution (and still in countries which have not undergone that revolution) it was a mark of solid distinction in a man or a family to keep out of the news. A lady of aristocratic pretensions was supposed to get her name in the papers only three times: when she was born, when she married, and when she died. Now the families who are Society are by definition those always appearing in the papers. The man of truly heroic stature was once supposed to be marked by scorn for publicity. He quietly relied on the power of his character or his achievement.

In the South, where the media developed more slowly than elsewhere in the country, where cities appeared later, and where life was dominated by rural ways, the celebrity grew more slowly. The old-fashioned hero was romanticized. In this as in many other ways, the Confederate General Robert E. Lee was one of the last surviving American models of the older type. Among his many admirable qualities, Southern compatriots admired none more than his retirement from public view. He had the reputation for never having given a newspaper interview. He steadfastly refused to write his memoirs. "I should be trading on the blood of my men," he said. General George C. Marshall (1880-1959) is a more recent and more anachronistic example. He, too, shunned publicity and refused to write his memoirs, even while other generals were serializing theirs in the newspapers. But by his time, few people any longer considered this reticence a virtue. His old-fashioned unwillingness to enter the publicity arena finally left him a victim of the slanders of Senator Joseph McCarthy and others.

The hero was born of time: his gestation required at least a generation. As the saying went, he had "stood the test of time." A maker of tradition, he was himself made by tradition. He grew over the generations as people found new virtues in him and attributed to him new exploits. Receding into the misty past he became more, and not less, heroic. It was not necessary that his face or figure have a sharp, well-delineated outline, nor that his life be footnoted. Of course there could not have been any photographs of him, and often there was not even a likeness. Men of the last century were more heroic than those of today; men of antiquity were still more heroic; and those of prehistory became demigods. The hero was always somehow ranked among the ancients.

The celebrity, on the contrary, is always a contemporary. The hero is made by folklore, sacred texts, and history books, but the celebrity is the creature of gossip, of public opinion, of magazines, newspapers, and the ephemeral images of movie and television screen. The passage of time, which creates and establishes the hero, destroys the celebrity. One is made, the other unmade, by repetition. The celebrity is born in the daily papers and never loses the mark of his fleeting origin.

The very agency which first makes the celebrity in the long run inevitably destroys him. He will be destroyed, as he was made, by publicity. The newspapers make him, and they unmake him—not by murder but by suffocation or starvation. No one is more forgotten than the last generation's celebrity. This fact explains the newspaper feature "Whatever Became Of . . . ?" which amuses us by accounts of the present obscurity of former celebrities. One can always get a laugh by referring knowingly to the once-household names which have lost their celebrity in the last few decades: Mae Bush, William S. Hart, Clara Bow. A woman reveals her age by the celebrities she knows.

There is not even any tragedy in the celebrity's fall, for he is a man returned to his proper anonymous station. The tragic hero, in Aristotle's familiar definition, was a man fallen from great estate, a great man with a tragic flaw. He had somehow become the victim of his own greatness. Yesterday's celebrity, however, is a commonplace man who has been fitted back into his proper commonplaceness not by any fault of his own, but by time itself.

The dead hero becomes immortal. He becomes more vital with the passage of time. The celebrity even in his lifetime becomes passé: he passes out of the picture. The white glare of publicity, which first gave him his specious brilliance, soon melts him away. This was so even when the only vehicles of publicity were the magazine and the newspaper. Still more now with our vivid round-the-clock media, with radio and television. Now when it is possible, by bringing their voices and images daily into our living rooms, to make celebrities more quickly than ever before, they die more quickly than ever. This has been widely recognized by entertainment celebrities and politicians. President Franklin Delano Roosevelt was careful to space out his fireside chats so the citizenry would not tire of him. Some comedians (for example, Jackie Gleason in the mid-1950's) have found that when they have weekly programs they reap quick and remunerative notoriety, but that they soon wear out their images. To extend their celebrity-lives, they offer their images more sparingly—once a month or once every two months instead of once a week.

There is a subtler difference between the personality of the hero and that of the celebrity. The figures in each of the two classes become assimilated to one another, but in two rather different ways. Heroes standing for greatness in the traditional mold tend to become colorless and cliché. The greatest heroes have the least distinctiveness of face or figure. We may show our reverence for them, as we do for God, by giving them beards. Yet we find it hard to imagine that Moses or Jesus could have had other special facial characteristics. The hero while being thus idealized and generalized loses his individuality. The fact that George Washington is not a vivid personality actually helps him serve as the heroic Father of Our Country. Perhaps Emerson meant just this when he said that finally every great hero becomes a great bore. To be a great hero is actually to become lifeless; to become a face on a coin or a postage stamp. It is to become a Gilbert Stuart's Washington. Contemporaries, however, and the celebrities made of them, suffer from idiosyncrasy. They are too vivid, too individual to be polished into a symmetrical Greek statue. The Graphic Revolution, with its klieg lights on face and figure, makes the images of different men more distinctive. This itself disqualifies them from becoming heroes or demigods.

While heroes are assimilated to one another by the great simple virtues of their character, celebrities are diffentiated mainly by trivia of personality. To be known for your personality actually proves you a celebrity. Thus a synonym for "a celebrity" is "a personality." Entertainers, then, are best qualified to become celebrities because they are skilled in the marginal differentiation of their personalities. They succeed by skillfully distinguishing themselves from others essentially like them. They do this by minutiae of grimace, gesture, language, and voice. We identify Jimmy ("Schnozzola") Durante by his nose, Bob Hope by his fixed smile, Jack Benny by his stinginess, Jack Paar by his rudeness, Jackie Gleason by his waddle, Imogene Coca by her bangs.

With the mushroom-fertility of all pseudo-events, celebrities tend to breed more celebrities.

They help make and celebrate and publicize one another. Being known primarily for their well-knownness, celebrities intensify their celebrity images simply by becoming widely known for relations among themselves. By a kind of symbiosis, celebrities live off one another. One becomes better known by being the habitual butt of another's jokes, by being another's paramour or ex-wife, by being the subject of another's gossip, or even by being ignored by another celebrity. Elizabeth Taylor's celebrity appeal has consisted less perhaps in her own talents as an actress than in her connections with other celebrities—Nick Hilton, Mike Todd, and Eddie Fisher. Arthur Miller, the playwright, became a "real" celebrity by his marriage to Marilyn Monroe. When we talk or read or write about celebrities, our emphasis on their marital relations and sexual habits, on their tastes in smoking, drinking, dress, sports cars, and interior decoration is our desperate effort to distinguish among the indistinguishable. How can those commonplace people like us (who, by the grace of the media, happened to become celebrities) be made to seem more interesting or bolder than we are?

III

As other pseudo-events in our day tend to overshadow spontaneous events, so celebrities (who are human pseudo-events) tend to overshadow heroes. They are more up-to-date, more nationally advertised, and more apt to have press agents. And there are far more of them. Celebrities die quickly but they are still more quickly replaced. Every year we experience a larger number than the year before.

Just as real events tend to be cast in the mold of pseudo-events, so in our society heroes survive by acquiring the qualities of celebrities. The best-publicized seems the most authentic experience. If someone does a heroic deed in our time, all the machinery of public information—press, pulpit, radio, and television—soon transform him into a celebrity. If they cannot succeed in this, the would-be hero disappears from public view.

A dramatic, a tragic, example is the career of Charles A. Lindbergh. He performed single-handed one of the heroic deeds of this century.

His deed was heroic in the best epic mold. But he became degraded into a celebrity. He then ceased to symbolize the virtues to which his heroic deed gave him a proper claim. He became filled with emptiness; then he disappeared from view. How did this happen?

On May 21, 1927, Charles A. Lindbergh made the first nonstop solo flight from Roosevelt Field, New York, to Le Bourget Air Field, Paris, in a monoplane, "The Spirit of St. Louis." This was plainly a heroic deed in the classic sense; it was a deed of valor—alone against the elements. In a dreary, unheroic decade Lindbergh's flight was a lightning flash of individual courage. Except for the fact of his flight, Lindbergh was a commonplace person. Twenty-five years old at the time, he had been born in Detroit and raised in Minnesota. He was not a great inventor or a leader of men. He was not extraordinarily intelligent, eloquent, or ingenious. Like many another young man in those years, he had a fanatical love of flying. The air was his element. There he showed superlative skill and extraordinary courage—even to foolhardiness.

He was an authentic hero. Yet this was not enough. Or perhaps it was too much. For he was destined to be made into a mere celebrity; and he was to be the American celebrity par excellence. His rise and fall as a hero, his tribulations, his transformation, and his rise and decline as a celebrity are beautifully told in Kenneth S. Davis' biography.

Lindbergh himself had not failed to predict that his exploit would put him in the news. Before leaving New York he had sold to *The New York Times* the exclusive story of his flight. A supposedly naive and diffident boy, on his arrival in Paris he was confronted by a crowd of newspaper reporters at a press conference in Ambassador Myron T. Herrick's residence. But he would not give out any statement until he had clearance from the *Times* representative. He had actually subscribed to a newspaper clipping service, the clippings to be sent to his mother, who was then teaching school in Minnesota. With uncanny foresight, however, he had limited his subscriptions to clippings to the value of $50. (This did not prevent the company, doubtless seeking publicity as well as money, from suing him for not paying them for clippings beyond the specified amount.) Otherwise he might have had to spend the rest of his life earning the money to pay for clippings about himself.

Lindbergh's newspaper success was unprecedented. The morning after his flight *The New York Times,* a model of journalistic sobriety, gave him the whole of its first five pages, except for a few ads on page five. Other papers gave as much or more. Radio commentators talked of him by the hour. But there was not much hard news available. The flight was a relatively simple operation, lasting only thirty-three and a half hours. Lindbergh had told reporters in Paris just about all there was to tell. During his twenty-five years he had led a relatively uneventful life. He had few quirks of face, of figure, or of personality; little was known about his character. Some young women called him "tall and handsome," but his physical averageness was striking. He was the boy next door. To tell about this young man on the day after his flight, the nation's newspapers used 25,000 tons of newsprint more than usual. In many places sales were two to five times normal, and might have been higher if the presses could have turned out more papers.

When Lindbergh returned to New York on June 13, 1927, *The New York Times* gave its first sixteen pages the next morning almost exclusively to news about him. At the testimonial dinner in Lindbergh's honor at the Hotel Commodore (reputed to be the largest for an individual "in modern history") Charles Evans Hughes, former Secretary of State, and about to become Chief Justice of the United States, delivered an extravagant eulogy. With unwitting precision he characterized the American hero-turned-celebrity: "We measure heroes as we do ships, by their displacement. Colonel Lindbergh has displaced everything."

Lindbergh was by now the biggest human pseudo-event of modern times. His achievement, actually because it had been accomplished so neatly and with such spectacular simplicity, offered little spontaneous news. The biggest news about Lindbergh was that he was such big news. Pseudo-events multiplied in more than the usual geometric progression, for Lindbergh's well-knownness was so sudden and so overwhelming. It was easy to make stories about

what a big celebrity he was; how this youth, unknown a few days before, was now a household word; how he was received by Presidents and Kings and Bishops. There was little else one could say about him. Lindbergh's singularly impressive heroic deed was soon far overshadowed by his even more impressive publicity. If well-knownness made a celebrity, here was the greatest. Of course it was remarkable to fly the ocean by oneself, but far more remarkable thus to dominate the news. His stature as hero was nothing compared with his stature as celebrity. All the more because it had happened, literally, overnight.

A large proportion of the news soon consisted of stories of how Lindbergh reacted to the "news" and to the publicity about himself. People focused their admiration on how admirably Lindbergh responded to publicity, how gracefully he accepted his role of celebrity. "Quickie" biographies appeared. These were little more than digests of newspaper accounts of the publicity jags during Lindbergh's ceremonial visits to the capitals of Europe and the United States. This was the celebrity after-life of the heroic Lindbergh. This was the tautology of celebrity.

During the next few years Lindbergh stayed in the public eye and remained a celebrity primarily because of two events. One was his marriage on May 27, 1929, to the cultivated and pretty Anne Morrow, daughter of Dwight Morrow, a Morgan partner, then Ambassador to Mexico. Now it was "The Lone Eagle and His Mate." As a newlywed he was more than ever atractive raw material for news. The maudlin pseudo-events of romance were added to all the rest. His newsworthiness was revived. There was no escape. Undaunted newsmen, thwarted in efforts to secure interviews and lacking solid facts, now made columns of copy from Lindbergh's efforts to keep out of the news! Some newspapermen, lacking other material for speculation, cynically suggested that Lindbergh's attempts to dodge reporters were motivated by a devious plan to increase his news-interest. When Lindbergh said he would co-operate with sober, respectable papers, but not with others, those left out pyramided his rebuffs into more news than his own statements would have made.

The second event which kept Lindbergh alive as a celebrity was the kidnaping of his infant son. This occurred at his new country house at Hopewell, New Jersey, on the night of March 1, 1932. For almost five years "Lindbergh" had been an empty receptacle into which news makers had poured their concoctions—saccharine, maudlin, legendary, slanderous, adulatory, or only fantastic. Now, when all other news-making possibilities seemed exhausted, his family was physically consumed. There was a good story in it. Here was "blood sacrifice," as Kenneth S. Davis calls it, to the gods of publicity. Since the case was never fully solved, despite the execution of the supposed kidnaper, no one can know whether the child would have been returned unharmed if the press and the public had behaved differently. But the press (with the collaboration of the bungling police) who had unwittingly destroyed real clues, then garnered and publicized innumerable false clues, and did nothing solid to help. They exploited Lindbergh's personal catastrophe with more than their usual energy.

In its way the kidnaping of Lindbergh's son was as spectacular as Lindbergh's transatlantic flight. In neither case was there much hard news, but this did not prevent the filling of newspaper columns. City editors now gave orders for no space limit on the kidnaping story. "I can't think of any story that would compare with it," observed the general news manager of the United Press, "unless America should enter a war." Hearst's INS photo service assigned its whole staff. They chartered two ambulances which, with sirens screaming, shuttled between Hopewell and New York City carrying photographic equipment out to the Lindbergh estate, and on the way back to the city served as mobile darkrooms in which pictures were developed and printed for delivery on arrival. For on-the-spot reporting at Hopewell, INS had an additional five men with three automobiles. United Press had six men and three cars; the Associated Press had four men, two women, and four cars. By midnight of March 1 the New York *Daily News* had nine reporters at Hopewell, and three more arrived the next day; the New York *American* had a dozen (including William Randolph Hearst, Jr., the paper's president); the New York

Herald Tribune, four; the New York *World-Telegram, The New York Times,* and the Philadelphia *Ledger,* each about ten. This was only a beginning.

The next day the press agreed to Lindbergh's request to stay off the Hopewell grounds in order to encourage the kidnaper to return the child. The torrent of news did stop. Within twenty-four hours INS sent over its wires 50,000 words (enough to fill a small volume) about the crime, 30,000 words the following day, and for some time thereafter 10,000 or more words a day. The Associated Press and United Press served their subscribers just as well. Many papers gave the story the whole of the front page, plus inside carry-overs, for a full week. There were virtually no new facts available. Still the news poured forth—pseudo-events by the score—clues, rumors, local color features, and what the trade calls "think" pieces.

Soon there was almost nothing more to be done journalistically with the crime itself. There was little more to be reported, invented, or conjectured. Interest then focused on a number of sub-dramas created largely by newsmen themselves. These were stories about how the original event was being reported, about the mix-up among the different police that had entered the case, and about who would or should be Lindbergh's spokesman to the press world and his go-between with the kidnaper. Much news interest still centered on what a big story all the news added up to, and on how Mr. and Mrs. Lindbergh reacted to the publicity.

At this point the prohibition era crime celebrities came into the picture. "Salvy" Spitale and Irving Bitz, New York speakeasy owners, briefly held the spotlight. They had been suggested by Morris Rosner, who, because he had underworld connections, soon became a kind of personal secretary to the Lindberghs. Spitale and Bitz earned headlines for their effort to make contact with the kidnapers, then suspected to be either the notorious Purple Gang of Detroit or Al Capone's mob in Chicago. The two go-betweens became big names, until Spitale bowed out, appropriately enough, at a press conference. There he explained: "If it was someone I knew, I'll be God-damned if I wouldn't name him. I been in touch all around, and I come to the conclusion that this one was pulled by an independent." Al Capone himself, more a celebrity than ever, since he was about to begin a Federal prison term for income-tax evasion, increased his own newsworthiness by trying to lend a hand. In an interview with the "serious" columnist Arthur Brisbane of the Hearst papers, Capone offered $10,000 for information leading to the recovery of the child unharmed and to the capture of the kidnapers. It was even hinted that to free Capone might help recover the child.

The case itself produced a spate of new celebrities, whose significance no one quite understood but whose newsworthiness itself made them important. These included Colonel H. Norman Schwarzkopf, commander of the New Jersey State Police; Harry Wolf, Chief of Police in Hopewell; Betty Gow, the baby's nurse; Colonel Breckenridge, Lindbergh's personal counsel; Dr. J. F. ("Jafsie") Condon, a retired Bronx schoolteacher who was a volunteer go-between (he offered to add to the ransom money his own $1,000 life savings "so a loving mother may again have her child and Colonel Lindbergh may know that the American people are grateful for the honor bestowed on them by his pluck and daring"); John Hughes Curtis, a half-demented Norfolk, Virginia, boatbuilder, who pretended to reach the kidnapers; Gaston B. Means (author of *The Strange Death of President Harding*), later convicted of swindling Mrs. Evalyn Walsh McLean out of $104,000 by posing as a negotiator with the kidnapers; Violet Sharpe, a waitress in the Morrow home, who married the Morrow butler and who had had a date with a young man not her husband on the night of the kidnaping (she committed suicide on threat of being questioned by the police); and countless others.

Only a few years later the spotlight was turned off Lindbergh as suddenly as it had been turned on him. *The New York Times Index*—a thick volume published yearly which lists all references to a given subject in the pages of the newspaper during the previous twelve months—records this fact with statistical precision. Each volume of the index for the years 1927 to 1940 contains several columns of fine print merely itemizing the different news stories which referred to Lindbergh. The 1941 volume shows

over three columns of such listings. Then suddenly the news stream dries up, first to a mere trickle, then to nothing at all. The total listings for all seventeen years from 1942 through 1958 amount to less than two columns—only about half that found in the single year 1941. In 1951 and 1958 there was not even a single mention of Lindbergh. In 1957 when the movie *The Spirit of St. Louis,* starring James Stewart, was released, it did poorly at the box office. A poll of the preview audiences showed that few viewers under forty years of age knew about Lindbergh.

A *New Yorker* cartoon gave the gist of the matter. A father and his young son are leaving a movie house where they have just seen *The Spirit of St. Louis.* "If everyone thought what he did was so marvelous," the boy asks his father, "how come he never got famous?"

The hero thus died a celebrity's sudden death. In his fourteen years he had already long outlasted the celebrity's usual life span. An incidental explanation of this quick demise of Charles A. Lindbergh was his response to the pressure to be "all-around." Democratic faith was not satisfied that its hero be only a dauntless flier. He had to become a scientist, an outspoken citizen, and a leader of men. His celebrity status unfortunately had persuaded him to become a public spokesman. When Lindbergh gave in to these temptations, he offended. But his offenses (unlike those, for example, of Al Capone and his henchmen, who used to be applauded when they took their seats in a ball park) were not in themselves dramatic or newsworthy enough to create a new notoriety. His pronouncements were dull, petulant, and vicious. He acquired a reputation as a pro-Nazi and a crude racist; he accepted a decoration from Hitler. Very soon the celebrity was being uncelebrated. The "Lindbergh Beacon" atop a Chicago skyscraper was renamed the "Palmolive Beacon," and high in the Colorado Rockies "Lindbergh Peak" was rechristened the noncommittal, "Lone Eagle Peak."

EXERCISE

Frame a set of questions on "From Hero to Celebrity," that would serve as a guide to a critical discussion of both content and method. Be sure to make, when possible, comparisons with content or method of other essays in this section.

The Meaning of Treason

REBECCA WEST (1892-   )
(CICILY ISABEL FAIRFIELD)

[1947]

FROM TIME to time during my career as a journalist I have reported notable law cases, and I know that it is not only morbidity which makes the public enjoy following the trial of a serious crime. It is very difficult for those who study life to find a story that comes to its end under their eyes. When we select an individual whose course we want to trace, it is as likely as not that he covers his tracks with secrecy, or moves to a field outside our view, or delays his end until we ourselves have ended. That is why classical history is a valuable study; we can see the whole story, the beginning, the middle, and the end of Greece and Rome, Egypt, and Persia. That is why the lives of great men in the past teach us more than knowledge of great men in the present; we know their remoter consequences. The dock brings a like illumination.

Here an individual story comes to its end in a collision with the community. Every case has its unique intellectual and spiritual significance. The appearance of the accused person, the changes in his face and voice, his agreement with society as disclosed by the witnesses who approve of him, his conflict with society as disclosed by the witnesses who disapprove of him, his relation to the crime of which he is truly or falsely accused, always reveal a special case. But the crime which he committed, if he was justly accused, or the other crime which was committed by the representatives of society if he was falsely accused, has always the same cause; refusal to respect the individuality of another or others. A world in which each man respected the soul of all other men, no matter how little they seemed to merit respect, would be crimeless.

There is an obvious political implication to be drawn from this. The authoritarian state is *ipso facto* criminal. When I covered the trial of William Joyce ("Lord Haw-Haw") for the *New Yorker* I saw a man in the dock who was doubly criminal. He had committed crimes against the law out of his desire to substitute a criminal state for a state which, if not completely innocent, aimed at the innocence of freedom. It was obviously doubtful if he would ever have been guilty of any offense had he not been tainted by this political guilt. But when his actual offense against the law was examined it was seen that he had acted in a manner which had long been extolled by many who were in theory pure of that guilt and firmly opposed to the authoritarian state.

Almost all contemporary left-wing writers of this generation and the last attacked the idea of nationalism. It was true that many of these attacks were made under the delusion that the words nationalism and imperialism mean the same thing, whereas nationalism—which means simply a special devotion of a people to its own material and spiritual achievements—implies no desire for the annexation of other territories and enslavement of other peoples. But a great many of these attacks were made under no such apprehension. It was genuinely felt that it was pure superstition which required a man to feel any warmer emotion about his own land, race, and people than about any other. Why then should any man feel a lump in his throat when he saw his flag or the statue at the harbor gate of his native land, or feel that in a dispute between his people and another he must obey the will of his kin and not aid their enemy?

I watched the trial of William Joyce, and of all traitors who were charged in courts which I could conveniently attend. They had all cleared their throats of that lump, they had all made that transit of frontiers recommended by the nationalists; and this had landed them in the service of the persecutors of reason, the fanatical believers in frontiers as the demarcation lines between the saved and the damned. But as their lives were unfolded it appeared that none of them had cast off their nationalist prejudice because of their strength, but had been divested of it by maladjusted ambition, by madness, by cowardice, by weakness. It seemed as if contemporary rationalists had been wrong, and I remembered that the trouble about man is twofold. He cannot learn truths which are too complicated; he forgets truths which are too simple. After I had seen twenty traitors tried it seemed to me that the reason why they were in the dock, why intellectuals preach against nationalism, is that we have forgotten certain simple truths.

We have forgotten that we live outward from the center of a circle and that what is nearest to the center is most real to us. If a man cut his hand, it hurts him more than if he cut some other man's hand; therefore he is more careful to guard his own. Even if he spend his whole life in teaching himself that we are all of one body, and that therefore his neighbor's pain is his also, he will still suffer more when his own hand is hurt, for the message then runs straight from his palm and fingers to his brain, traveling at a speed faster than light or sound, which bear the news of others' accidents. Throughout his life it remains true that what is nearest to his body is of greatest interest to his mind. When a baby is given food and held warmly by a certain woman, he grows up to feel a closer concern for her than for other women of her generation, and at her death will feel greatly disturbed. Should he be institution-bred and have no woman as his particular slave and tyrant, grievance will sour him till his last day.

If in his maturity he should live with a woman for any considerable period of time, he and she are apt, unless they are overtaken by certain obviously disagreeable circumstances, to behave as though there were a complete community of interest between them. There must have been some instinctive liking between them or they would never have been drawn together

in the first place; they became involved in each other's prosperity; experience has taught each how the other will behave in most eventualities. Therefore they do better by one another than strangers would. Should he have children by this or any other woman, they will have great power over him, while other children will have little or none. He will know so much more about them. The veiled moment of their conception is his secret, and resemblances to him, to a familiar woman, or to his kin enable him to trace their inner lives, disguised though they be first by their inarticulateness and then by their articulateness. He can read his own nature by their light, and will have a sense of fusion between himself and those who are so inextricably tangled with that self.

If that man live in a house during the days of his childhood, he will know it better than any house he lives in later, though it shelter him forty years longer; and though the staircase wind as deviously as any in the world he will find his way down it in the darkness as surely as if it were straight. All his life long, when he hears talk of woods, he shall see beechwoods, if he come from a Buckinghamshire village, and a castle to him shall stand on Castle Rock, if Edinburgh was his home, and in the one case he shall know Southern English country folk, and in the other Lowland Scottish townsfolk, better than any other Britons. Born and bred in England, he will find it easier to understand the English than the rest of men, not for any mystical reason, but because their language is his, because he is fully acquainted with their customs, and because he is the product of their common history. So also each continent enjoys a vague unity of self-comprehension, and is divided from the others by a sharp disunity; and even those who profess the closest familiarity with the next world speak with more robust certainty of this world and seem not to want to leave it.

This is not to say that a man loves what is nearest to him. He may hate his parents, his wife, and his children. Millions have done so. On the tables of the Law it was written "Honor thy father and thy mother, as the Lord God hath commanded thee; that thy days may be prolonged, and that it may go well with thee in the land which the Lord thy God giveth thee," and it is advice of almost gross practicality aimed at preventing the faithful from abandoning themselves to their natural impulses and wasting all their force on family rows. St. Paul, that great artist who perpetually betrayed his art because he was also a great man of action, and constantly abandoned the search for truth to seek instead a myth to inspire vigorous action, tried to gild bondage of man to the familiar. "Who that loveth his wife loveth himself. For no man ever yet hated his own flesh, but nourished it and cherisheth it, even as the Lord of the Church." But countless men have hated their own flesh. Everywhere and at all times men have carried such hatred to the point of slaying it, and still more have persecuted it by abstinence and mortification and debauchery. It has a value to them far above their loathing or their liking. It is their own flesh and they can have no direct experience of any other. Not with all the gold in the world or by incessant prayer can we obtain another instrument-case, packed with these our only instruments, the five senses, by which alone we can irradiate the universe that is a black void around us, and build a small platform in that darkness. A wife is someone who has stood on that irradiated platform long enough to be fully examined and to add the testimony of her own sense as to the nature of that encircling mystery. She may be loved or hated, or loved and hated, and serve in that research.

A child knows that what is near is easier for him to handle than what is far. All men took it for granted till recent times, when it was challenged, together with some other traditional assumptions, not because they had proved unsound, but because a number of urbanized populations from which the intellectual classes were largely drawn had lost their sense of spiritual as well as material process. They had lost their sense of material process owing to the development of the machine; goods which had formerly been produced by simple and comprehensible processes, often carried on where they could be witnessed by the consumer, were now produced by elaborate processes, not to be grasped by people without mechanical train-

ing, and carried on in the privacy of the large factories.

The reason for their ignorance of spiritual process was the urban lack of the long memory and the omniscient gossip enjoyed by the village. The townsman is surrounded by people whose circumstances he does not know and whose heredities are the secrets of other districts; and he is apt to take their dissimulating faces and their clothed bodies as the sum of them. People began to think of each other in a new way; as simple with a simplicity in fact unknown in organic life. They ignored the metabolism of human nature, by which experiences are absorbed into the mind and magically converted into personality, which rejects much of the material life brings to it and handles the rest to serve the interests of love or hate, good or evil, life or death, according to an inhabiting daemon, whose reasons are never given. Man conceived himself as living reasonably under the instruction of the five senses, which tell him to seek pleasure and avoid pain.

The first effect of this rational conception of life was cheerful vulgarity; and there are worse things than that. Man might well have felt this view of his destiny as a relief after the Christian philosophy, which abased his origin to criminality, and started him so low only to elevate him to the height, most disagreeable to most people, of company with godhead, after dragging him through all sorts of unpalatable experiences, including participation in a violent and apparently unnecessary death. Insofar as a man adopted the new and rationalist philosophy he could be compared to an actor who, after spending a lifetime playing Hamlet and Othello and King Lear, retires to keep a country pub. All was thenceforward to go at a peaceable jog-trot. Children were to grow up straight striplings of light, undeformed by repression, unscarred by conflicts, because their parents would hand them over in their earliest years to the care of pedagogic experts. Divorce was not to be reckoned as a disgrace nor as a tragedy nor even as a failure, but as a pleasurable extension of experience, like travel. Furthermore—and this was considered as the sanest adjustment of all—the ardors of patriotism were to be abandoned, and replaced by a cool resolution to place one's country on a level with all others in one's affections, and to hand it over without concern to the dominion of any other power which could offer it greater material benefits. It was not out of cynicism that the benefits demanded were material: it was believed that the material automatically produced the intellectual and the spiritual. These reasonable steps having been taken, there was to follow harmony. The only peril was that it might become too sweet.

But the five senses had evidently not been rightly understood. Such children as were surrendered by their parents to expert treatment, complained against that surrender as if it had been any other kind of abandonment. They quarreled with the pedagogues as much as they would have quarreled with their parents; but, the bond of the flesh being absent, there was something sapless in their quarrels, and there was less energy engendered. Sexual life was not noticeably smoother than it had been. The epic love of marriage and the lyric love-song of the encounter both lost much by the pretense that they were the same. Nor, as patriotism was discredited, did peace come nearer. Indeed, the certainty of war now arched over the earth like a second sky, inimical to the first. If harmony had been our peril, we were preserved from it, both within and without. For it was plain that, as Christian philosophy had so harshly averred, the world was a stage on which an extraordinary drama, not yet fully comprehended by the intellect, was being performed; and its action was now an agony. But, owing to the adoption of rationalist philosophy, some of the actors filling the most important parts were now incapable of speaking their lines. It appeared that *Hamlet* and *Othello* and *King Lear* would be no longer cathartic tragedies but repellent and distressing farces if the leading characters had, in the climactic scenes, been overtaken by the delusion that they had retired and were keeping country pubs.

So the evil moment came and was clear: not surpassed in evil since the days of the barbarian invasions. The devil of nationalism had been driven out of man, but he had not become the headquarters of the dove. Instead there had entered into him the seven devils of internationalism, and he was torn by their frenzies. Then

what is against all devils came to his aid. The achievement (which, as yet, is unfinished, since peace does not reign) was accomplished by a continuance of the drama in spite of the difficulties created by the rationalist philosophy. Since the actors cast to play the leading parts would not speak, the action was carried on by the peoples, who used to walk to and fro at the back of the scene, softly laughing or softly weeping, or simply quietly being. Now these people streamed across the continents, inscribing their beliefs on the surface of the earth by the course of their flights, and on the sites of their martyrdoms. They defeated fascism by not being fascist. They showed the contrast between fascism and nonfascism so clearly that the world, wishing to live, defended their side because it could be seen that they were the representatives of life. As they exorcised the devils from the body of Europe they seemed to affirm certain values. It was perhaps true that the origin of man was in criminality, for once a community refused to make the effort of seeking the company of godhead it certainly became criminal. It was perhaps true that hedonism is an impotent gospel, for now it could be seen that pleasure means nothing to many men. As fast as those who ran to save their lives ran those who ran to slay them, even if their pursuit, pressed too hard, might change them into fugitives, whose own lives were in danger. Now the scorned bonds of the flesh asserted their validity. It was the final and unbearable misery of these flights that husbands were separated from their wives, and parents lost sight of their children. The men who performed the cruelest surgery on these families, who threw the husband and wife into the gas chamber while the children traveled by train to an unknown destination, had themselves been brought up to condemn their own ties of blood. The anguish of the divided was obviously holy. The contentment of those who felt no reluctance to divide was plainly damned.

In this day of exposition those who made the other sacrifice of the near for the far, and preferred other countries to their own, proved also to be unholy. The relationship between a man and a fatherland is always disturbed by conflict, if either man or fatherland is highly developed. A man's demands for liberty must at some point challenge the limitations the state imposes on the individual for the sake of the mass. If he is to carry on the national tradition he must wrestle with those who, speaking in its name, desire to crystallize it at the point reached by the previous generation. In any case national life itself must frequently exasperate him, because it is the medium in which he is expressing himself, and every craftsman or artist is repelled by the resistance of his medium to his will. All men should have a drop or two of treason in their veins, if the nations are not to go soft like so many sleepy bears.

Yet to be a traitor is most miserable. All the men I saw in the prisoner's dock were sad as they stood their trials, not only because they were going to be punished. They would have been sad even if they had never been brought to justice. They had forsaken the familiar medium; they had trusted themselves to the mercies of those who had no reason to care for them; knowing their custodians' indifference they had lived for long in fear; and they were aware that they had thrown away their claim on those who might naturally have felt affection for them. Strangers, as King Solomon put it, were filled with their wealth, and their labors were in the house of a stranger, and they mourned at the last when their flesh and body were consumed. As a divorce sharply recalls what a happy marriage should be, so the treachery of these men recalled what a nation should be; a shelter where all talents are generously recognized, all forgivable oddities forgiven, all viciousness quietly frustrated, and those who lack talent honored for equivalent contributions of graciousness. Each of these men was as dependent on the good opinion of others as one is oneself; they needed a nation which was also a hearth, and their capacity for suffering made it tragic that they had gone out from their own hearth to suffer among strangers, because the intellectual leaders of their time had professed a philosophy which was scarcely more than a lapse of memory, and had forgotten, that a hearth gives out warmth.

EXERCISE

1. Like the essays by Bishop, Skinner, and Eliot, this essay deals quite specifically with the values and ideas of our time—with the dominant state of mind of the educated man of the last generation. Do you feel that Rebecca West would be most sympathetic with the ideas expressed in Bishop's essay, in Skinner's, or in Eliot's?

2. To whom is this essay addressed? The author writes "We have forgotten, etc." Who is we? What is the tone of the essay?

3. What is it that "contemporary rationalists" have forgotten? Is Miss West an "irrationalist"? Is she attacking rationality and glorifying the emotions, blind instincts, and habits? Or does she ask us to choose between reason and emotion?

4. Is Miss West a sentimentalist? Note that she writes: "This is not to say that a man loves what is nearest to him. He may hate his parents, his wife. . . ." What is her point?

5. Discuss the style of this essay, noting particularly the means by which the author establishes a particular tone.

The Death-In-Life of Benjamin Reid

WILLIAM STYRON (1925-   )

THE CONNECTICUT STATE PRISON at Wethersfield is a huge, gloomy Victorian structure whose very appearance seems calculated to implant in the mind of the onlooker the idea of justice in its most retributive sense. It is one of the oldest prisons in America. Uncompromisingly sober, the penitentiary suggests not only that crime does not pay but that whosoever is a wrongdoer is quite conceivably beyond redemption. On Death Row, the condemned cells were built for an epoch when, after a man was told he must die, the supreme penalty was administered far more swiftly than in these present days of interminable legal postponements. Each cell still measures only seven by seven feet, implying momentary residence. A strong electric light shines in the face of the condemned all day and all night. The condemned are not allowed to communicate with one another and until recently, unlike their fellow convicts in the prison at large, were denied even the solace of an earphone radio. To live on Death Row at Wethersfield is in effect to dwell in solitary confinement until the day of one's execution. As I write these words (mid-October, 1961), the state of Connecticut is preparing to kill a twenty-four year old felon named Benjamin Reid. Reid is no Caryl Chessman; as a matter of fact, he is sub-literate, and possesses an intelligence which, if not so low as to be called defective, can only be described as marginal. The condemned at Wethersfield are allowed to read and to write letters, but it is doubtful that Ben Reid has availed himself much of these privileges; and this is a circumstance which must have made his confinement all the more forsaken, because Reid has lived in the presence of the electric chair for four years and three months.

On a bitterly cold night in Hartford in January of 1957, Ben Reid, who was nineteen at the time, waylaid a middle-aged woman in a parking lot and beat her to death with a hammer. His avowed and premeditated motive was profit (the woman was a friend of his mother's, and had been known to carry large sums of money with her), but this aspect of his crime he so ruinously botched that he got nothing. Over two thousand dollars were discovered on the woman's frozen body, which Reid in his final panic had jammed into a car. It would appear that Reid scarcely bothered to conceal his tracks, fleeing to the house of a relative in New Haven where he was found in short order by the police. He seemed rather relieved to be caught. He made several confessions and, in the summer of that same year, was brought to trial by jury in the Superior Court at Hartford. The trial was a fairly brief one, as murder trials go. On June 27, 1957, Reid was sentenced to die by electrocution. He was taken to Wethersfield (a suburb of Hartford and, except for the eyesore of its prison and several small factories, a lovely elm-lined New England town) and there in a cell seven feet by seven feet, brightly illuminated night and day, he has been for over four years, awaiting what must be, for him, the ever-present but always undiscoverable moment of his death.

There is of course no such thing as absolute justice, but even advocates of capital punishment will grant that, when a human's life is at stake, there should be the closest approximation of absolute justice the law can attain. In terms of absolute justice, to make evident the reasonableness of Ben Reid's execution for murder it would have to be proved that his crime was morally more reprehensible than a similar crime, for which some other murderer received a lesser sentence. There have been, and still are, murderers whose crimes repel us by their violence and brutality quite as strongly as does Ben Reid's. Some of these criminals have been put to death as creatures past salvation; more frequently sparing their lives, the State has sentenced them to serve a life term, with the possibility of parole, or a number of years, and by this relative leniency has granted, at least theoretically, the rather more lucid assumption that some men's crimes are not so depraved as to place them forever beyond redemption. But the logic of this random choice is as fearful as it is mysterious. The wickedness, the inherent immorality, of any crime is a quality which it is beyond the power of any of us to weigh or measure. Ben Reid's crime, however, has been weighed, and Reid himself has been found completely and irrevocably wanting. Neither absolute justice nor any kind of justice, so far as the eye can see, has been served. It might be interesting to learn something about this young man, and perhaps discover why the State has judged him irredeemable, past hope of recovery.

Warden Lewis E. Lawes of Sing Sing, an expert foe of the death penalty, once said that in order to be executed in America a person had to be three things: poor, a man, and black. He was speaking of the North as well as the South. He was also admittedly generalizing, if not being somewhat facetious, for a great many white men and a few women of both races have, of course, been executed and, on exquisitely rare occasions, the State has taken the life of a criminal of wealth. But the implication of his remark, it is safe to say, is borne out by the statistics—North and South—and Ben Reid fills the bill: he is a poor black man. To read of his background and career is to read not only of poverty and neglect and a mire of futile, petty crime and despair, but, in the end, of a kind of wretched archetype: the Totally Damned American. If one wished to make a composite portrait of the representative criminal upon whom the State enacts its legal vengeance, one's result would be a man who looked very much like Ben Reid. Like his victim, who was also a Negro, he was born in a dilapidated slum area on the north side of Hartford. When he was two his father died, leaving his mother virtually destitute and with several children to support besides Ben. These years toward the end of the Depression were bleak enough for a large number of Americans; for people in the situation of Ben Reid and his family the times were catastrophic, and left ineradicable scars. When Reid was almost eight his mother got into a shooting scrape and was grievously wounded; she was left crippled for life and partially paralyzed. At this point Reid was forced to enter the Hartford County Home, and there he remained for eight years. He was not alone among his family to become a ward of the People; during the time he was at the county home his twin brother was committed to the state hospital for the insane at Norwich, while an older sister, adjudged to be mentally deficient, was sent to the Mansfield State Training School. Most children are released from the county home at the age of fifteen, but since no one wanted Reid he received the dispensation granted, in special cases, to the totally unwanted, and was privileged to stay an extra year. One pauses to speculate, hesitates, goes on, feeling presumptuous (there is no other word) as one tries to imagine Ben Reid's thoughts during this weary, bedraggled era. He was never too bright, so probably—unlike other adolescents somewhat more richly endowed in mind as well as circumstance—he entertained no Deep Thoughts about life at all. To Reid, coming out of oblivion into this existence which, so far as one can tell, had seemed to guarantee the unfulfillment and frustration of every ordinary childish yearning, life must have begun to appear simply and demonstrably lacking in significance. Lack-

ing in significance, it must necessarily have lacked any values whatever, and it is not at all surprising that Reid, soon after he was sent away from the county home, began feloniously and empty-headedly to trifle with those values in life which society so highly regards.

When the county home finally discharged him, the nation was experiencing a time of prosperity such as no country has ever seen, but very little of this abundance rubbed off on Ben Reid. For a year or so he was shunted from one foster home to another; he went hungry again from time to time, and there were occasions when he was reduced to foraging from garbage cans on the back streets of Hartford. It was during this period that Reid had his first brush with the law, in an involvement which has come to seem numbingly typical of his age and background: he was caught acting as a runner for a narcotics peddler, and for his offense was placed on probation. A few months later he tried to rob a store, hopelessly bungled the endeavor, and was sentenced to serve a term in the state reformatory at Cheshire. It is apparent that he was in no way reformed. However, it may be said that, after his release from the reformatory, an episode occurred in Reid's life which tends in some small way to alleviate the harshness and ugliness of his career until then. He met a girl. She was a few years older than he, but they began seeing each other and, presumably fell in love, and they were married in 1956. It might have been an answer to Reid's trouble, but it wasn't. He was unable to get a job. Not long after their marriage, Ben began to brood about money and commenced hitting the wine bottle. His wife apparently did her best to straighten him out, but these efforts led to nothing. She was pregnant, and had just left him, when Reid, thinking about money, went out into the snow that night and committed the crime for which he was now scheduled to die.

Often, it seems, what appears to be justice is merely a shadow-image of justice, determined by queer circumstances which can only be discerned in retrospect. This sinister element in the law might alone be enough to cast final doubts upon the infliction of the death penalty; for only under conditions of absolute justice— a kind of aseptic legal vacuum completely invulnerable to fleeting social panic, hysteria, shifts in the public temper—could we presume to condemn a man utterly, and absolute justice nowhere exists. It of course cannot strictly be proven, but it seems at least probable that had Ben Reid not come to trial at the particular time he did, he would not have been condemned to die. The reason for this conjecture is the existence in Hartford at that same time of two particularly vicious criminals: a huge, lantern-jawed ex-con and ex-resident of Death Row named Joseph ("The Chin") Taborsky, and his moronic accomplice, Arthur Culombe. Taborsky, who was a psychopath of fearfully sadistic dimensions, and Culombe, a kind of torpid, blinky-eyed caricature of the dim-witted henchman, had finally been apprehended after a series of holdup-murders which had terrorized central Connecticut and, quite literally, sent many of the people of Hartford in off the streets. A notable feature of their *modus operandi* was to make their victims kneel down at their feet before shooting them. Taborsky and Culombe had been dubbed by the newspapers, with scant originality though in luminous headlines, "The Mad Dog Killers," and when they came to be tried there can be no doubt that the public, which attended the trial in droves, was in something less than a mood of composure. Ben Reid was tried at the same time and in the same building. His mother, crippled and woefully concerned, was the only spectator on the first day of the trial, when the jurors were sworn in, and except for Reid's wife and one or two interested onlookers, remained the only spectator until the trial's end. The People's interest was in the Mad Dogs, not in Ben Reid. There seems little doubt that the Taborsky-Culombe affair next door, with its public hubbub and its reverberant atmosphere of mass outrage, did nothing to help Ben Reid's case, and in fact subtly contaminated his own courtroom with the odor of vengeance.

The trial, as I have said, lasted only a few days. Reid's defense was almost nonexistent; he had, after all, killed someone with what in the legal sense is surely malice and premeditation. His defense counsel (since Reid had no money, this job fell to the Public Defender) made strenuous efforts in his client's behalf, outlining his squalid background and the nature of his up-

bringing. But the jury (Respectability in its pure, concentrated essence, disarmingly mild-eyed and benign, like a Norman Rockwell tableau: five Christian housewives and among the rest, as might be anticipated in Hartford, a clutch of insurance adjusters) was not terribly moved. Testifying in his own behalf, Reid seemed confused. Once when asked why, after his first blow, he continued to strike the woman, he replied that she had seemed to be suffering so that he wanted to put her out of her pain. Now, asked the same question by the prosecutor, he could only mumble hopelessly: "I don't know. I started to shake. I lost control of myself. I didn't want her to die." In his final summation, the prosecuting attorney expressed a few personal regrets, but went on to add that we must not be swayed by the fact of a person's sordid environment; after all, some of our most valued citizens have struggled up to eminence from the lower depths, fighting their way to fame and fortune, ladies and gentlemen, while people like this criminal sitting here, etc. It had the echo of a thousand courtrooms: Look at Al Jolson and Eddie Cantor. Look at Joe Louis! It was the old American death-cry, and there is no reply to it, save the negative one, to be spoken in a whisper, that when life is an issue we have no God-given right to measure the gallant strength of a few men against the imponderable weakness of a foundling like Ben Reid. The jury was asked if it would like to retire and deliberate right away, or if it would like to have lunch first. It replied that it would like to have lunch. After it fed itself it retired and came back with the verdict in a little over an hour. As happens with rather enigmatic frequency in capital trials, the judge flubbed the reading of the death sentence. In setting the date of the execution, he said "the year 1958," instead of "the year 1957," and the entire pronouncement, for the record, had to be read over again. Up until this time, Reid had showed very little emotion during the trial, except for the moment when the prosecutor began to describe his crime in its bloody detail, at which point, in a gesture which can only be described as childlike, he furiously clapped his hands over his ears. Now perhaps he felt that the judge was damning him twice. At any rate, he broke down and wept.

One curious fact which tends to underline the basic senselessness of capital punishment is the way in which we are regularly brought into touch with an evil apart from the nagging, chronic, yet somehow endurable distress which the death penalty itself causes us: this is the almost unendurable incongruity it manifests in its choice of victims. If in Caryl Chessman, for instance, we were confronted with a plucky, dogged, intelligent man (so intelligent in fact, as to have blurred in the minds of many people the nature of his morality, which was that of a cynical, self-justifying hoodlum; he verged as close to the embodiment of the perfect son of a bitch as the mind can conceive) who possessed the right at least to the possibility of redemption, in Ben Reid we are faced with a man so egregiously lacking in gifts, so totally desolate in circumstance, in quality of mind and spirit, that though he bears an almost antipodean relationship to Chessman as a man, we find ourselves questioning by this very contradistinction his implacable abandonment by society. Of course, the facts of heredity and environment cannot be allowed completely to eliminate responsibility and guilt. Reid's crime was an appalling one—one of such blind ruthlessness that it should have been apparent at the outset that he must be removed from the community until that time when it might reasonably be made certain that he could take his place again among his fellow men. Failing this approximate certainty, it would have to be made sure that he was incarcerated for good. But here we are not speaking of correction. We are not even speaking of that reasonable punishment which might carry with it vitalizing connotations of remorse and contrition. We are speaking of total abandonment. Perhaps not so wise but no less unfortunate than Chessman, Reid too had been judged beyond salvation. It is this abrupt, irrevocable banishment, this pre-emption by the state of the single final judgment which is in the providence of God alone—and the subtle but disastrous effect this act has upon the whole philosophy of crime and punishment—that wrecks the possibility of any lasting, noble concept of justice, and causes the issue of the death penalty to become, not peripheral, but central to an understanding of a moral direction in our time.

Against an awesome contemporary backdrop of domestic trouble and crisis, and the lingering image of concentration camps, and the threat of mass annihilation, the case of Ben Reid might seem an event of such small moment that there is hardly any wonder that it has commanded no one's attention. It is a case little enough known in Hartford, much less in the state of Connecticut or the broad, busy world. If it is true that crime in general, save in its most garish, tabloid aspects, fails to gain our serious regard, it may also be said that the question of capital punishment commands even less interest on the part of thinking people, especially in America. It becomes one of those lofty moral issues relegated to high school debates. To most thinking people, crime is something we read about at breakfast. The infliction of the death penalty, even further removed from our purview, is a ceremony which takes place in the dead of night, enacted, like some unnameable perversion, in shame and secrecy, and reported the next morning, on a back page, with self-conscious and embarrassed brevity. Our feelings are usually mixed; conditioned by two decades of James Cagney movies, and the memory of the jaunty wisecrack when the warden comes and the last mile commences, few of us can escape a shiver of horrid fascination which the account of a man's judicial execution affords us. But the truth is that few of us, at the same time, are left without a sense of queasiness and discomfort, and indeed there are some—not simply the quixotic or the "bleeding hearts," as Mr. J. Edgar Hoover describes those who abhor the death penalty—who are rendered quite inescapably bereft. "For certain men, more numerous than is supposed," wrote Albert Camus, "knowing what the death penalty really is and being unable to prevent its application is physically insupportable. In their own way, they suffer this penalty, too, and without any justification. If at least we lighten the weight of the hideous images that burden these men, society will lose nothing by our actions." This is not alone an interior, personal viewpoint which would subvert a general evil in the name of delicate feelings; Camus' other arguments against capital punishment are too fierce and telling for that. The fact remains that all of us, to some degree, are spiritually and physically diminished by the doctrine of legal vengeance, even though it manifests itself as nothing more than a chronic, insidious infection beneath the public skin. We need only the occurrence of a sudden Chessman, flaunting his anguish like a maddened carbuncle, to make evident the ultimate concern we have with our own debilitating and corrupting sickness. That we do not discuss this problem until a Chessman appears is only an indication of one of our most ruinous human failings—our inability to think about any great issue except in the light of the unique, the glamorous, the celebrity. Chessman was indisputably unique as a criminal and as one condemned; it is not to demean that uniqueness to declare that we shall never resolve the issue of the capital punishment until we ponder it in terms, not alone of Chessman, but of Ben Reid.

It has been argued that opponents of capital punishment are swayed by emotion, that they are sentimental. To the degree that sentimentality may be considered a state of mind relying more upon emotion than reason, it would seem plain that it was the defenders of the death penalty who are the sentimentalists. If for example, it could be proved that capital punishment was an effective deterrent to crime, even the most emotionally vulnerable, diehard humanitarian would be forced to capitulate in favor of it. But, unable to fend off the statistical proof that it is no deterrent at all, proponents of capital punishment find themselves backed into a corner, espousing emotional, last-ditch arguments. In the present instance, its lack of deterrent effect may be shown in the fact that it did not deter Ben Reid. Even more strikingly it is true in the case of the terrible Taborsky, finally executed, who had barely escaped electrocution for murder once (he was released from Death Row on a judicial error and freed from prison), whereupon he committed the series of brutal slayings I have mentioned. If it is evident that Taborsky should never have been released into society, it seems almost as clear that he is a case in point of that theory, proposed by a number of serious observers, that the death

penalty in significant and not-too-rare instances actually exerts a fatal lure, impelling certain unbalanced people to crimes which ordinarily they would not commit. (In a recent English case, one Frederick Cross of Stockport, near Manchester, said in testimony: "When I saw the man in his car I got the idea that if I was to kill him I would be hanged . . . I don't wish to be defended at all. I killed him so that I would be hanged." The victim was a complete stranger. Cross achieved his desire: he was hanged.) Finally, in order to make reasonable the argument that capital punishment is a deterrent, why is it that the public is not incessantly exposed to its horrible finality, forced to witness the barbarous rite itself, and thereby made to reflect on the gruesome fate awaiting malefactors? But it remains a secret, shameful ceremony and, except for the most celebrated cases, it is even indifferently reported in the press. Until by legislative mandate all executions are carried on the television networks of the states involved (they could be sponsored by the gas and electric companies), in a dramatic fashion which will enable the entire population—men, women and all children over the age of five—to watch the final agonies of those condemned, even the suggestion that we inflict the death penalty to deter people from crime is a farcical one.

Shorn of all rational, practical arguments, those who favor the death penalty must confront those who would eliminate it upon the solitary grounds of vengeance, and it is here upon these grounds, and these grounds alone, that the issue will have to be resolved. There is no doubt that the urge for revenge is a strong human emotion. But whether this is an emotion to be encouraged by the State is a different matter. As for Ben Reid, how much actual vengeance society still harbors toward him can only be a matter of conjecture. It would be a disgrace to all of us to say that it could be much. Having dwelt in his seven by seven cell on Death Row, as I have said, for over four years, he would seem to have endured such a torture of bewilderment, anxiety and terror as to make the question of vengeance academic. Since that day in June, 1957, when he entered his cell on Death Row, there have been numberless writs, reprieves, reversals, stays of execution, all carried out in that admirable spirit of Fair Play which marks American justice but which, like a pseudo-smile masking implacable fury, must seem to a condemned man pitiless and sadistic beyond any death sentence. A year-and-a-half ago, indeed, it appeared that Ben Reid would have his opportunity for redemption; the judge of the U. S. District Court vacated his conviction on the grounds that his trial had been "fundamentally unfair," because the police had exacted his confessions without informing him of his rights to counsel or, for that matter, of any of his rights. At this point, Reid's attorney told him the good news: it looked as if he were going to live. This past September, however, the U. S. Circuit Court of Appeals in New York took a different view: since counsel had not brought up the point of illegal confessions at the trial, Ben had in effect "waived his rights." Thus the lower court was overruled—not without, however, a vigorous dissenting opinion by one of the justices, Judge Charles E. Clark, one time dean of the Yale Law School, who said that the view that Reid waived his rights "borders on the fantastic in any human or practical or, indeed, legal sense." Reid has just recently been granted a reprieve, until April 30, 1962, in order that his case may be argued before the U. S. Supreme Court. Especially in the light of Judge Clark's angry dissent, it seems likely that Reid's case will at least be accepted for review. Whether by these nine old metaphysicians, as Mencken called them, the legal point will be resolved in Reid's favor remains, as usual, a mystery. In any event, for Reid it has been a splendid ordeal. His present lawyer (who incidentally is also a Negro) has protested to the State, asking his removal from the tiny cell. After four years there, he contends, Ben's mind has badly deteriorated. Nowhere else on earth is a man dragged by such demoralizing extremes to the very edge of the abyss.

"The little man, despite the pratings of Democracy," Judge Curtis Bok has written of the death penalty, "is still the scapegoat." And he added this observation: "Someday we will look back upon our criminal and penal processes with the same horrified wonder as we now look back upon the Spanish Inquisition." Should the U.S. Supreme Court turn down his appeal, I am told that there is an outside chance, at least, that Ben Reid—due to those considerations of environment and mentality which his lawyer initially argued for in vain—may have his sentence commuted by the State Board of Pardons. This is highly unlikely: the Board of Pardons has never commuted a death sentence of a man convicted under the same Connecticut law. But there is a chance. If this comes to pass and Reid is allowed to live, he will gain, aside from the fragments of his life, an ironic kind of victory: nothing could demonstrate more cruelly the travesty of justice which is capital punishment than this shabby and belated mercy, predicated upon the identical arguments which were advanced in his favor in a court of law nearly five years before. On the other hand, should the fact if not the spirit of justice be served, and Ben Reid goes to the electric chair one night this spring, it may be said that the soul which is taken will have been already so diminished by our own inhumanity that what shall be lost is hardly a soul at all, and that the death penalty, having divested a man not alone of his life but of that dignity with which even the humblest of men must be allowed to face death itself, has achieved its ultimate corruption. *Or when saw we Thee sick, or in prison, and came unto Thee?* It is perhaps a late date in history to summon up the gospel in behalf of a derelict Negro boy; having abandoned him, it does not become a Christian society to waste a shred of its jealously guarded piety upon him whom it has cast out into darkness. Only the condemned can truly know the heaviness of guilt; it settles upon their spirits like the weight of all the universe, and the quality of their bereavement is solitary and unique among humankind. To attempt to sooth this bereavement through Christian homilies would seem to be, like that final promenade with the chaplain whispering from Holy Writ, an act of outrageous hypocrisy. Yet somehow, try as we might to evade the verdict, we find ourselves being measured: *Inasmuch as ye have done it unto one of the least of these My brethren, ye have done it unto Me.* Until, searching our hearts, we can reconcile these words with the murder we inflict, in the name of justice, upon Ben Reid, and his fellows likewise outcast and

condemned, we stand ourselves utterly condemned.

EXERCISE

The publication of this essay had the practical effect
of setting into motion a chain of events that saved
the life of Ben Reid. His death sentence was changed
to imprisonment with the possibility of parole. List
the arguments that presumably led to this. How effective do you think such arguments presented abstractly—that is, without the particular history of Ben
Reid—would have been?

In Favor of Capital Punishment

JACQUES BARZUN (1902-   )

A PASSING remark of mine in the *Mid-Century*
magazine has brought me a number of letters
and a sheaf of pamphlets against capital punishment. The letters, sad and reproachful, offer me
the choice of pleading ignorance or being proved
insensitive. I am asked whether I know that there
exists a worldwide movement for the abolition of
capital punishment which has everywhere enlisted able men of every profession, including the
law. I am told that the death penalty is not only
inhuman but also unscientific, for rapists and
murderers are really sick people who should be
cured, not killed. I am invited to use my imagination and acknowledge the unbearable horror of
every form of execution.

I am indeed aware that the movement for
abolition is widespread and articulate, especially
in England. It is headed there by my old friend
and publisher, Mr. Victor Gollancz, and it numbers such well-known writers as Arthur Koestler,
C. H. Rolph, James Avery Joyce and Sir John
Barry. Abroad as at home the profession of
psychiatry tends to support the cure principle,
and many liberal newspapers, such as the *Observer*, are committed to abolition. In the United
States there are at least twenty-five state leagues
working to the same end, plus a national league
and several church councils, notably the Quaker
and the Episcopal.

The assemblage of so much talent and enlightened goodwill behind a single proposal must
give pause to anyone who supports the other side,
and in the attempt to make clear my views,
which are now close to unpopular, I start out
by granting that my conclusion is arguable; that

is, I am still open to conviction, *provided* some
fallacies and frivolities in the abolitionist argument are first disposed of and the difficulties not
ignored but overcome. I should be glad to see
this happen, not only because there is pleasure
in the spectacle of an airtight case, but also because I am not more sanguinary than my neighbor and I should welcome the discovery of safeguards—for society *and* the criminal—other than
killing. But I say it again, these safeguards must
really meet, not evade or postpone, the difficulties
I am about to describe. Let me add before I begin
that I shall probably not answer any more letters
on this arousing subject. If this printed exposition does not do justice to my cause, it is not
likely that I can do better in the hurry of private
correspondence.

I readily concede at the outset that present
ways of dealing out capital punishment are as
revolting as Mr. Koestler says in his harrowing
volume, *Hanged by the Neck*. Like many of our
prisons, our modes of execution should change.
But this objection to barbarity does not mean
that capital punishment—or rather, judicial
homicide—should not go on. The illicit jump we
find here, on the threshold of the inquiry, is
characteristic of the abolitionist and must be
disallowed at every point. Let us bear in mind
the possibility of devising a painless, sudden and
dignified death, and see whether its administration is justifiable.

The four main arguments advanced against
the death penalty are: *1.* punishment for crime
is a primitive idea rooted in revenge; *2.* capital

punishment does not deter; *3*. judicial error being possible, taking life is an appalling risk; *4*. a civilized state, to deserve its name, must uphold, not violate, the sanctity of human life.

I entirely agree with the first pair of propositions, which is why, a moment ago, I replaced the term capital punishment with "judicial homicide." The uncontrollable brute whom I want put out of the way is not to be punished for his misdeeds, nor used as an example or a warning; he is to be killed for the protection of others, like the wolf that escaped not long ago in a Connecticut suburb. No anger, vindictiveness or moral conceit need preside over the removal of such dangers. But a man's inability to control his violent impulses or to imagine the fatal consequences of his acts should be a presumptive reason for his elimination from society. This generality covers drunken driving and teenage racing on public highways, as well as incurable obsessive violence; it might be extended (as I shall suggest later) to other acts that destroy, precisely, the moral basis of civilization.

But why kill? I am ready to believe the statistics tending to show that the prospect of his own death does not stop the murderer. For one thing he is often a blind egotist, who cannot conceive the possibility of his own death. For another, detection would have to be infallible to deter the more imaginative who, although afraid, think they can escape discovery. Lastly, as Shaw long ago pointed out, hanging the wrong man will deter as effectively as hanging the right one. So, once again, why kill? If I agree that moral progress means an increasing respect for human life, how can I oppose abolition?

I do so because on this subject of human life, which is to me the heart of the controversy, I find the abolitionist inconsistent, narrow or blind. The propaganda for abolition speaks in hushed tones of the sanctity of human life, as if the mere statement of it as an absolute should silence all opponents who have any moral sense. But most of the abolitionists belong to nations that spend half their annual income on weapons of war and that honor research to perfect means of killing. These good people vote without a qualm for the political parties that quite sensibly arm their country to the teeth. The West today does not seem to be the time or place to invoke the absolute sanctity of human life. As for the clergymen in the movement, we may be sure from the experience of two previous world wars that they will bless our arms and pray for victory when called upon, the sixth commandment notwithstanding.

"Oh, but we mean the sanctity of life *within* the nation!" Very well: is the movement then campaigning also against the principle of self-defense? Absolute sanctity means letting the cutthroat have his sweet will of you, even if you have a poker handy to bash him with, for you might kill. And again, do we hear any protest against the police firing at criminals on the street—mere bank robbers usually—and doing this, often enough, with an excited marksmanship that misses the artist and hits the bystander? The absolute sanctity of human life is, for the abolitionist, a slogan rather than a considered proposition.

Yet it deserves examination, for upon our acceptance or rejection of it depend such other highly civilized possibilities as euthanasia and seemly suicide. The inquiring mind also wants to know, why the sanctity of *human* life alone? My tastes do not run to household pets, but I find something less than admirable in the uses to which we put animals—in zoos, laboratories and space machines—without the excuse of the ancient law, "Eat or be eaten."

It should moreover be borne in mind that this argument about sanctity applies—or would apply—to about ten persons a year in Great Britain and to between fifty and seventy-five in the United States. These are the average numbers of those executed in recent years. The count by itself should not, of course, affect our judgment of the principle: one life spared or forfeited is as important, morally, as a hundred thousand. But it should inspire a comparative judgment: there are hundreds and indeed thousands whom, in our concern with the horrors of execution, we forget: on the one hand, the victims of violence; on the other, the prisoners in our jails.

The victims are easy to forget. Social science tends steadily to mark a preference for the troubled, the abnormal, the problem case. Whether it is poverty, mental disorder, delinquency or crime, the "patient material" monopolizes the interest of increasing groups of people among the most generous and learned. Psychiatry and moral liberalism go together; the application of law as we have known it is thus coming to be regarded as an historic prelude to social work, which may replace it entirely. Modern literature makes the most of this same outlook, caring only for the disturbed spirit, scorning as bourgeois those who pay their way and do *not* stab their friends. All the while the determinism of natural science reinforces the assumption that society causes its own evils. A French jurist, for example, says that in order to understand crime we must first brush aside all ideas of Responsibility. He means the criminal's and takes for granted that of society. The murderer kills because reared in a broken home or, conversely, because at an early age he witnessed his parents making love. Out of such cases, which make pathetic reading in the literature of modern criminology, is born the abolitionist's state of mind: we dare not kill those we are beginning to understand so well.

If, moreover, we turn to the accounts of the crimes committed by these unfortunates, who are the victims? Only dull ordinary people going about their business. We are sorry, of course, but they do not interest science on its march. Balancing, for example, the sixty to seventy criminals executed annually in the United States, there were the seventy to eighty housewives whom George Cvek robbed, raped and usually killed during the months of a career devoted to proving his virility. "It is too bad." Cvek alone seems instructive, even though one of the law officers who helped track him down quietly remarks: "As to the extent that his villainies disturbed family relationships, or how many women are still haunted by the specter of an experience they have never disclosed to another living soul, these questions can only lend themselves to sterile conjecture."

The remote results are beyond our ken, but it is not idle to speculate about those whose death by violence fills the daily two inches at the back of respectable newspapers—the old man sunning himself on a park bench and beaten to death by four hoodlums, the small children abused and strangled, the middle-aged ladies on a hike assaulted and killed, the family terrorized by a released or escaped lunatic, the half-dozen working people massacred by the sudden maniac, the boatload of persons dispatched by the skipper, the mindless assaults upon schoolteachers and shopkeepers by the increasing horde of dedicated killers in our great cities. Where does the sanctity of life begin?

It is all very well to say that many of these killers are themselves "children," that is, minors. Doubtless a nine-year-old mind is housed in that 150 pounds of unguided muscle. Grant, for argument's sake, that the misdeed is "the fault of society," trot out the broken home and the slum environment. The question then is, What shall we do, not in the Utopian city of tomorrow, but here and now? The "scientific" means of cure are more than uncertain. The apparatus of detention only increases the killer's antisocial animus. Reformatories and mental hospitals are full and have an understandable bias toward discharging their inmates. Some of these are indeed "cured"—so long as they stay under a rule. The stress of the social free-for-all throws them back on their violent modes of self-expression. At that point I agree that society has failed—twice: it has twice failed the victims, whatever may be its guilt toward the killer.

As in all great questions, the moralist must choose, and choosing has a price. I happen to think that if a person of adult body has not been endowed with adequate controls against irrationally taking the life of another, that person must be judicially, painlessly, regretfully killed before that mindless body's horrible automation repeats.

I say "irrationally" taking life, because it is often possible to feel great sympathy with a murderer. Certain *crimes passionnels* can be forgiven without being condoned. Blackmailers invite direct retribution. Long provocation can be an excuse, as in that engaging case of some years ago, in which a respectable carpenter of seventy found he could no longer stand the incessant nagging of his wife. While she excoriated him from her throne in the kitchen—a daily exercise for fifty years—the husband went to his bench and came back with a hammer in each hand to settle the score. The testimony to his character, coupled with the sincerity implied by the two hammers, was enough to have him sent into quiet and brief seclusion.

But what are we to say of the type of motive disclosed in a journal published by the inmates of one of our Federal penitentiaries? The author is a bank robber who confesses that money is not his object:

My mania for power, socially, sexually, and otherwise can feel no degree of satisfaction until I feel sure I have struck the ultimate of submission and terror in the minds and bodies of my victims. . . . It's very difficult to explain all the queer fascinating sensations pounding and surging through me while I'm holding a gun on a victim, watching his body tremble and sweat. . . . This is the moment when all the rationalized hypocrisies of civilization are suddenly swept away and two men stand there facing each other morally and ethically naked, and right and wrong are the absolute commands of the man behind the gun.

This confused echo of modern literature and modern science defines the choice before us. Anything deserving the name of cure for such a man presupposes not only a laborious individual psychoanalysis, with the means to conduct and to sustain it, socially and economically, but also a re-education of the mind, so as to throw into correct perspective the garbled ideas of Freud and Nietzsche, Gide and Dostoevski, which this power-seeker and his fellows have derived from the culture and temper of our times. Ideas are tenacious and give continuity to emotion. Failing a second birth of heart and mind, we must ask: How soon will this sufferer sacrifice a bank clerk in the interests of making civilization less hypocritical? And we must certainly question the wisdom of affording him more than one chance. The abolitionists' advocacy of an unconditional "let live" is in truth part of the same cultural tendency that animates the killer. The Western peoples' revulsion from power in domestic and foreign policy has made of the state a sort of counterpart of the bank robber: both having power and neither knowing how to use it. Both waste lives because hypnotized by irrelevant ideas and crippled by contradictory emotions. If psychiatry were sure of its ground in diagnosing the individual case, a philosopher might consider whether such dangerous obsessions should not be guarded against by judicial homicide *before* the shooting starts.

I raise the question not indeed to recommend the prophylactic execution of potential murderers, but to introduce the last two perplexities that the abolitionists dwarf or obscure by their concentration on changing an isolated penalty. One of these is the scale by which to judge the offenses society wants to repress. I can for example imagine a truly democratic state in which it would be deemed a form of treason punishable by death to create a disturbance in any court or deliberative assembly. The aim would be to recognize the sanctity of orderly discourse in arriving at justice, assessing criticism and defining policy. Under such a law, a natural selection would operate to remove permanently from the scene persons who, let us say, neglect argument in favor of banging on the desk with their shoe. Similarly, a bullying minority in a diet, parliament or skupshtina would be prosecuted for treason to the most sacred institutions when fists or flying inkwells replace rhetoric. That the mere suggestion of such a law sounds ludicrous shows how remote we are from civilized institutions, and hence how gradual should be our departure from the severity of judicial homicide.

I say gradual and I do not mean standing still. For there is one form of barbarity in our law that I want to see mitigated before any other. I mean imprisonment. The enemies of capital punishment—and liberals generally—seem to be satisfied with any legal outcome so long as they themselves avoid the vicarious guilt of shedding blood. They speak of the sanctity of life, but have no concern with its quality. They give no impression of ever having read what it is certain they have read, from Wilde's *De Profundis* to the latest account of prison life by a convicted homosexual. Despite the infamy of concentration camps, despite Mr. Charles Burney's remarkable work, *Solitary Confinement,* despite riots in prisons, despite the round of escape, recapture and return in chains, the abolitionists' imagination tells them nothing about the reality of being caged. They read without a qualm, indeed they read with rejoicing, the hideous irony of "Killer Gets Life"; they sigh with relief instead of horror. They do not see and suffer the cell, the drill, the clothes, the stench, the food; they do not feel the sexual racking of young and old bodies, the hateful promiscuity, the insane monotony, the mass degradation, the impotent hatred. They do not remember from Silvio Pellico that only a strong political faith, with a hope of final victory, can steel a man to endure long detention. They forget that Joan of Arc, when offered "life," preferred burning at the stake. Quite of another mind, the abolitionists point with pride to the "model prisoners" that murderers often turn out to be. As if a model prisoner were not, first, a contradiction in terms, and second, an exemplar of what a free society should not want.

I said a moment ago that the happy advocates of the life sentence appear not to have understood what we know they have read. No more do they appear to read what they themselves write. In the preface to his useful volume of cases, *Hanged in Error,* Mr. Leslie Hale, M.P., refers to the tardy recognition of a minor miscarriage of justice—one year in jail: "The prisoner emerged to find that his wife had died and that his children and his aged parents had been removed to the workhouse. By the time a small payment had been assessed as 'compensation' the victim was incurably insane." So far we are as indignant with the law as Mr. Hale. But what comes next? He cites the famous Evans case, in which it is very probable that the wrong man was hanged, and he exclaims: "While such mistakes are possible, should society impose an irrevocable sentence?" Does Mr. Hale really ask us to believe that the sentence passed on the first man, whose wife died and who went insane, was in any sense *revocable?* Would not any man rather be Evans dead than that other wretch "emerging" with his small compensation and his reasons for living gone?

Nothing is revocable here below, imprisonment least of all. The agony of a trial itself is punishment, and acquittal wipes out nothing. Read the heart-rending diary of William Wallace, accused quite implausibly of having murdered his wife and "saved" by the Court of Criminal Appeals—but saved for what? Brutish ostracism by everyone and a few years of solitary despair. The cases of Adolf Beck, of Oscar Slater, of the unhappy Brooklyn bank teller who vaguely resembled a forger and spent eight years in Sing Sing only to "emerge" a broken, friendless, useless, "compensated" man—all these, if the dignity of the individual has any meaning, had better have been dead before the prison door ever opened for them. This is what counsel always says to the jury in the course of a murder trial and counsel is right: far better hang this man than "give him life." For my part, I would choose death without hesitation. If that option is abolished, a demand will one day be heard to claim it as a privilege in the name of human dignity. I shall believe in the abolitionist's present views only after he has emerged from twelve months in a convict cell.

The detached observer may want to interrupt here and say that the argument has now passed from reasoning to emotional preference. Whereas the objector to capital punishment *feels* that death is the greatest of evils, I *feel* that imprisonment is worse than death. A moment's thought will show that feeling is the appropriate arbiter. All reasoning about what is right, civilized and moral rests upon sentiment, like mathematics. Only, in trying to persuade others, it is important to single out the fundamental feeling, the prime intuition, and from it to reason justly. In my view, to profess respect for human life and be willing to see it spent in a penitentiary is to entertain liberal feelings frivolously. To oppose the death penalty because, unlike a prison term, it is irrevocable is to argue fallaciously.

In the propaganda for abolishing the death sentence the recital of numerous miscarriages of justice commits the same error and implies the same callousness: what is at fault in our present system is not the sentence but the fallible procedure. Capital cases being one in a thousand or more, who can be cheerful at the thought of all the "revocable" errors? What the miscarriages point to is the need for reforming the jury system, the rules of evidence, the customs of prosecution, the machinery of appeal. The failure to see that this is the great task reflects the sentimentality I spoke of earlier, that which responds chiefly to the excitement of the unusual. A writer on Death and the Supreme Court is at pains to point out that when that tribunal reviews a capital case, the judges are particularly anxious and careful. What a left-handed compliment to the highest judicial conscience of the country! Fortunately, some of the champions of the misjudged see the issue more clearly. Many of those who are thought wrongly convicted now languish in jail because the jury was uncertain or because a doubting governor commuted the death sentence. Thus Dr. Samuel H. Sheppard, Jr., convicted of his wife's murder in the second degree is serving a sentence that is supposed to run for the term of his natural life. The story of his numerous trials, as told by Mr. Paul Holmes, suggests that police incompetence, newspaper demagogy, public envy of affluence and the mischances of legal procedure fashioned the result. But Dr. Sheppard's vindicator is under no illusion as to the conditions that this "lucky" evader of the electric chair will face if he is granted parole after ten years: "It will carry with it no right to resume his life as a physician. His privilege to practice medicine was blotted out with his conviction. He must all his life bear the stigma of a parolee, subject to unceremonious return to confinement for life for the slightest misstep. More than this, he must live out his life as a convicted murderer."

What does the moral conscience of today think it is doing? If such a man is a dangerous repeater of violent acts, what right has the state to let him loose after ten years? What is, in fact, the meaning of a "life sentence" that peters out long before life? Paroling looks suspiciously like an expression of social remorse for the pain of incarceration, coupled with a wish to avoid "unfavorable publicity" by freeing a suspect. The man is let out when the fuss has died down; which would mean that he was not under lock and key for our protection at all. He *was* being punished, just a little—for so prison seems in the abolitionist's distorted view, and in the jury's and the prosecutor's, whose "second-degree" murder suggests killing someone "just a little." *

If, on the other hand, execution and life imprisonment are judged too severe and the accused is expected to be harmless hereafter—punishment being ruled out as illiberal—what has society gained by wrecking his life and damaging that of his family?

What we accept, and what the abolitionist will clamp upon us all the more firmly if he succeeds, is an incoherence which is not remedied by the belief that second-degree murder merits a kind of second-degree death; that a doubt as to the identity of a killer is resolved by commuting real death into intolerable life; and that our ignorance whether a maniac will strike again can be hedged against by measuring "good behavior" within the gates and then releasing the subject upon the public in the true spirit of experimentation.

These are some of the thoughts I find I cannot escape when I read and reflect upon this grave subject. If, as I think, they are relevant to any discussion of change and reform, resting as they do on the direct and concrete perception of what happens, then the simple meliorists who expect to breathe a purer air by abolishing the death penalty are deceiving themselves and us. The issue is for the public to judge; but I for one shall not sleep easier for knowing that in England and America and the West generally a hundred more human beings are kept alive in degrading conditions to face a hopeless future; while others—possibly less conscious, certainly less controlled—benefit from a premature freedom dangerous alike to themselves and society. In short, I derive no comfort from the illusion that in giving up one manifest protection of the law-abiding, we who might well be in any of these three roles—victim, prisoner, licensed killer—have struck a blow for the sanctity of human life.

EXERCISE

1. This essay and "The Death-In-Life of Benjamin Reid" may be taken as constituting the two sides of a debate. You have already made an outline of the arguments presented by Styron. Now make an outline of those presented by Barzun. Indicate each point of Barzun that may be taken as responsive to one by Styron. Can you suggest any point which has been omitted by either side?

2. How would you assess the two lines of argument?

3. Undoubtedly some readers would say that Styron introduces much material that is emotionally

---

* The British Homicide Act of 1957, Section 2, implies the same reasoning in its definition of "diminished responsibility" for certain forms of mental abnormality. The whole question of irrationality and crime is in utter confusion, on both sides of the Atlantic.

disturbing but is not logically relevant. (For instance, the treatment of a man in the death cell; we can conceive of his being treated differently, more humanely.) Do you find any elements in Barzun's essay that might, conceivably, be said to distract from the logical line?

4. Compare the two essays on the grounds of style and tone.

Artists in Uniform

MARY MC CARTHY (1912-   )

The Colonel went out sailing,
He spoke with Turk and Jew . . .

"POUR IT on Colonel," cried the young man in the Dacron suit excitedly, making his first sortie into the club-car conversation. His face was white as Roquefort and of a glistening, cheese-like texture; he had a shock of tow-colored hair, badly cut and greasy, and a snub nose with large gray pores. Under his darting eyes were two black craters. He appeared to be under some intense nervous strain and had sat the night before in the club car drinking bourbon with beer chasers and leafing through magazines which he frowningly tossed aside, like cards into a discard heap. This morning he had come in late, with a hangdog, hangover look, and had been sitting tensely forward on a settee, smoking cigarettes and following the conversation with little twitches of the nose and quivers of the body, as a dog follows a human conversation, veering its mistrustful eyeballs from one speaker to another and raising its head eagerly at its master's voice. The colonel's voice, rich and light and plausible, had in fact abruptly risen and swollen, as he pronounced his last sentence. "I can tell you one thing," he had said harshly. "They weren't named Ryan or Murphy!"

A sort of sigh, as of consummation, ran through the club car. "Pour it on, Colonel, give it to them, Colonel, that's right, Colonel," urged the young man in a transport of admiration. The colonel fingered his collar and modestly smiled. He was a thin, hawklike, black-haired handsome man with a bright blue bloodshot eye and a well-pressed, well-tailored uniform that did not show the effects of the heat—the train, west-bound for St. Louis, was passing through Indiana, and, as usual in a heat wave, the air-conditioning had not met the test. He wore the Air Force insignia, and there was something in his light-boned, spruce figure and keen, knifelike profile that suggested a classic image of the aviator, ready to cut, piercing, into space. In base fact, however, the colonel was in procurement, as we heard him tell the mining engineer who had just bought him a drink. From several silken hints that parachuted into the talk, it was patent to us that the colonel was a man who knew how to enjoy this earth and its pleasures: he led, he gave us to think, a bachelor's life of abstemious dissipation and well-rounded sensuality. He had accepted the engineer's drink with a mere nod of the glass in acknowledgment, like a genial Mars quaffing a libation; there was clearly no prospect of his buying a second in return, not if the train were to travel from here to the Mojave Desert. In the same way, an understanding had arisen that I, the only woman in the club car, had become the colonel's perquisite; it was taken for granted, without an invitation's being issued, that I was to lunch with him in St. Louis, where we each had a wait between trains—my plans for seeing the city in a taxicab were dished.

From the beginning, as we eyed each other over my volume of Dickens ("*The Christmas Carol?*" suggested the colonel, opening relations), I had guessed that the colonel was of Irish stock, and this, I felt, gave me an advantage, for he did not suspect the same of me; strangely so, for I am supposed to have the map of Ireland written on my features. In fact, he had just wagered, with a jaunty, sidelong grin at the mining engineer, that my people "came from Boston from way

back," and that I—narrowed glance, running, like
steel measuring-tape, up and down my form—
was a professional sculptress. I might have
laughed this off, as a crudely bad guess like his
Christmas Carol, if I had not seen the engineer
nodding gravely, like an idol, and the peculiar
young man bobbing his head up and down in
mute applause and agreement. I was wearing a
bright apple-green raw silk blouse and a dark-
green rather full raw silk skirt, plus a pair of
pink glass earrings; my hair was done up in a
bun. It came to me, for the first time, with a sort
of dawning horror, that I had begun, in the
course of years, without ever guessing it, to look
irrevocably Bohemian. Refracted from the three
men's eyes was a strange vision of myself as an
artist, through and through, stained with my occupation like the dyer's hand. All I lacked, apparently, was a pair of sandals. My sick heart
sank to my Ferragamo shoes; I had always particularly preened myself on being an artist in
disguise. And it was not only a question of personal vanity—it seemed to me that the writer or
intellectual had a certain missionary usefulness
in just such accidental gatherings as this, if he
spoke not as an intellectual but as a normal
member of the public. Now, thanks to the
colonel, I slowly became aware that my contributions to the club-car conversation were being
watched and assessed as coming from *a certain
quarter.* My costume, it seemed, carefully assembled as it had been at an expensive shop, was
to these observers simply a uniform that blazoned
a caste and allegiance just as plainly as the
colonel's khaki and eagles. *"Gardez,"* I said to
myself. But, as the conversation grew tenser and
I endeavored to keep cool, I began to writhe
within myself, and every time I looked down,
my contrasting greens seemed to be growing
more and more lurid and taking on an almost
menacing light, like leaves just before a storm
that lift their bright undersides as the air becomes darker. We had been speaking, of course,
of Russia, and I had mentioned a study that had
been made at Harvard of political attitudes
among Iron Curtain refugees. Suddenly, the
colonel had smiled. "They're pretty Red at
Harvard, I'm given to understand," he observed
in a comfortable tone, while the young man
twitched and quivered urgently. The eyes of all

the men settled on me and waited. I flushed as I
saw myself reflected. The woodland greens of my
dress were turning to their complementary red,
like a color-experiment in psychology or a traffic
light changing. Down at the other end of the
club car, a man looked up from his paper. I
pulled myself together. "Set your mind at rest,
Colonel," I remarked dryly. "I know Harvard
very well and they're conservative to the point
of dullness. The only thing crimson is the football team." This disparagement had its effect.
"So . . . ?" queried the colonel. "I thought there
was some professor. . . ." I shook my head.
"Absolutely not. There used to be a few fellow-
travelers, but they're very quiet these days, when
they haven't absolutely recanted. The general
atmosphere is more anti-Communist than the
Vatican." The colonel and the mining engineer
exchanged a thoughtful stare and seemed to agree
that the Delphic oracle that had just pronounced
knew whereof it spoke. "Glad to hear it," said
the colonel. The engineer frowned and shook his
fat wattles; he was a stately, gray-haired, plump
man with small hands and feet and the pampered,
finical tidiness of a small-town widow. "There's
so much hearsay these days," he exclaimed
vexedly. "You don't know *what* to believe."

I reopened my book with an air of having
closed the subject and read a paragraph three
times over. I exulted to think that I had made a
modest contribution to sanity in our times, and
I imagined my words pyramiding like a chain
letter—the colonel telling a fellow-officer on the
veranda of a club in Texas, the engineer halting
a works-superintendent in a Colorado mine shaft:
"I met a woman on the train who claims . . .
Yes, absolutely. . . ." Of course, I did not know
Harvard as thoroughly as I pretended, but I
forgave myself by thinking it was the convention
of such club-car symposia in our positivistic
country to speak from the horse's mouth.

Meanwhile, across the aisle, the engineer and
the colonel continued their talk in slightly lowered voices. From time to time, the colonel's
polished index-fingernail scratched his burnished
black head and his knowing blue eye forayed occasionally toward me. I saw that still I was a
doubtful quantity to them, a movement in the
bushes, a noise, a flicker, that was figuring in

their crenelated thought as "she." The subject of Reds in our colleges had not, alas, been finished; they were speaking now of another university and a woman faculty-member who had been issuing Communist statements. This story somehow, I thought angrily, had managed to appear in the newspapers without my knowledge, while these men were conversant with it; I recognized a big chink in the armor of my authority. Looking up from my book, I began to question them sharply, as though they were reporting some unheard-of natural phenomenon. "When?" I demanded. "Where did you see it? What was her name?" This request for the professor's name was a head-long attempt on my part to buttress my position, the implication being that the identities of all university professors were known to me and that if I were but given the name I could promptly clarify the matter. To admit that there was a single Communist in our academic system whose activities were hidden from me imperiled, I instinctively felt, all the small good I had done here. Moreover, in the back of my mind, I had a supreme confidence that these men were wrong: the story, I supposed, was some tattered piece of misinformation they had picked up from a gossip column. Pride, as usual, preceded my fall. To the colonel, the demand for the name was not specific but generic: what *kind* of name was the question he presumed me to be asking. "Oh," he said slowly with a luxurious yawn, "Finkelstein or Fishbein or Feinstein." He lolled back in his seat with a side glance at the engineer, who deeply nodded. There was a voluptuary pause, as the implication sank in. I bit my lip, regarding this as a mere diversionary tactic. "Please!" I said impatiently. "Can't you remember exactly?" The colonel shook his head and then his spare cheekbones suddenly reddened and he looked directly at me. "I can tell you one thing," he exclaimed irefully. "They weren't named Ryan or Murphy."

The colonel went no further; it was quite unnecessary. In an instant, the young man was at his side, yapping excitedly and actually picking at the military sleeve. The poor thing was transformed, like some creature in a fairy tale whom a magic word releases from silence. "That's right, Colonel," he happily repeated. "I know them. *I* was at Harvard in the business school,

studying accountancy. I left. I couldn't take it." He threw a poisonous glance at me, and the colonel, who had been regarding him somewhat doubtfully, now put on an alert expression and inclined an ear for his confidences. The man at the other end of the car folded his newspaper solemnly and took a seat by the young man's side. "They're all Reds, Colonel," said the young man. "They teach it in the classroom. I came back here to Missouri. It made me sick to listen to the stuff they handed out. If you didn't hand it back, they flunked you. Don't let anybody tell you different." "You are wrong," I said coldly and closed my book and rose. The young man was still talking eagerly, and the three men were leaning forward to catch his every gasping word, like three astute detectives over a dying informer, when I reached the door and cast a last look over my shoulder at them. For an instant, the colonel's eye met mine and I felt his scrutiny processing my green back as I tugged open the door and met a blast of hot air, blowing my full skirt wide. Behind me, in my fancy, I saw four sets of shrugging brows.

In my own car, I sat down, opposite two fat nuns, and tried to assemble my thoughts. I ought to have spoken, I felt, and yet what could I have said? It occurred to me that the four men had perhaps not realized why I had left the club car with such abruptness: was it possible that they thought I was a Communist, who feared to be unmasked? I spurned this possibility, and yet it made me uneasy. For some reason, it troubled my *amour-propre* to think of my anti-Communist self living on, so to speak, green in their collective memory as a Communist or fellow-traveler. In fact, though I did not give a fig for the men, I hated the idea, while a few years ago I should have counted it a great joke. This, it seemed to me, was a measure of the change in the social climate. I had always scoffed at the notion of liberals "living in fear" of political dema-goguery in America, but now I had to admit that if I was not fearful, I was at least un-comfortable in the supposition that anybody, any-body whatever, could think of me, precious me, as a Communist. A remoter possibility was, of course, that back there my departure was being ascribed to Jewishness, and this too annoyed me.

I am in fact a quarter Jewish, and though I did not "hate" the idea of being taken for a Jew, I did not precisely like it, particularly under these circumstances. I wished it to be clear that I had left the club car for intellectual and principled reasons; I wanted those men to know that it was not I, but my principles, that had been offended. To let them conjecture that I had left because I was Jewish would imply that only a Jew could be affronted by an anti-Semitic outburst; a terrible idea. Aside from anything else, it voided the whole concept of transcendence, which was very close to my heart, the concept that man is more than his circumstances, more even than himself.

However you looked at the episode, I said to myself nervously, I had not acquitted myself well. I ought to have done or said something concrete and unmistakable. From this, I slid glassily to the thought that those men ought to be punished, the colonel, in particular, who occupied a responsible position. In a minute, I was framing a businesslike letter to the Chief of Staff, deploring the colonel's conduct as unbecoming to an officer and identifying him by rank and post, since unfortunately I did not know his name. Earlier in the conversation, he had passed some comments on "Harry" that bordered positively on treason, I said to myself triumphantly. A vivid image of the proceedings against him presented itself to my imagination: the long military tribunal with a row of stern soldierly faces glaring down at the colonel. I myself occupied only an inconspicuous corner of this tableau, for, to tell the truth, I did not relish the role of the witness. Perhaps it would be wiser to let the matter drop . . . ? We were nearing St. Louis now; the colonel had come back into my car, and the young accountant had followed him, still talking feverishly. I pretended not to see them and turned to the two nuns, as if for sanctuary from this world and its hatred and revenges. Out of the corner of my eye, I watched the colonel, who now looked wry and restless; he shrank against the window as the young man made a place for himself amid the colonel's smart luggage and continued to express his views in a pale breathless voice. I smiled to think that the colonel was paying the piper. For the colonel, anti-Semitism was simply an aspect of urbanity,

like a knowledge of hotels or women. This frantic psychopath of an accountant was serving him as a nemesis, just as the German people had been served by their psychopath, Hitler. Colonel, I adjured him, you have chosen, between him and me; measure the depth of your error and make the best of it! No intervention on my part was now necessary; justice had been meted out. Nevertheless, my heart was still throbbing violently, as if I were on the verge of some dangerous action. What was I to do, I kept asking myself, as I chatted with the nuns, if the colonel were to hold me to that lunch? And I slowly and apprehensively revolved this question, just as though it were a matter of the most serious import. It seemed to me that if I did not lunch with him—and I had no intention of doing so—I had the dreadful obligation of telling him why.

He was waiting for me as I descended the car steps. "Aren't you coming to lunch with me?" he called out and moved up to take my elbow. I began to tremble with audacity. "No," I said firmly, picking up my suitcase and draping an olive-green linen duster over my arm. "I can't lunch with you." He quirked a wiry black eyebrow. "Why not?" he said. "I understood it was all arranged." He reached for my suitcase. "No," I said, holding on to the suitcase. "I can't." I took a deep breath. "I have to tell you. I think you should be *ashamed* of yourself, Colonel, for what you said in the club car." The colonel stared: I mechanically waved for a redcap, who took my bag and coat and went off. The colonel and I stood facing each other on the emptying platform. "What do you mean?" he inquired in a low, almost clandestine tone. "Those anti-Semitic remarks," I muttered, resolutely. "You ought to be *ashamed*." The colonel gave a quick, relieved laugh. "Oh, come now," he protested. "I'm sorry," I said. "I can't have lunch with anybody who feels that way about the Jews." The colonel put down his attaché case and scratched the back of his lean neck. "Oh, come now," he repeated, with a look of amusement. "You're not Jewish, are you?" "No," I said quickly. "Well, then . . ." said the colonel, spreading his hands in a gesture of bafflement. I saw that he was truly surprised and slightly hurt by my criticism, and this made me feel wretchedly embarrassed and even apologetic, on my side, as though I had called attention to some physical defect in him, of which he himself was unconscious. "But I might have been," I stammered. "You had no way of knowing. You oughtn't to talk like that." I recognized, too late, that I was strangely reducing the whole matter to a question of etiquette: "Don't start anti-Semitic talk before making sure there are no Jews present." "Oh, hell," said the colonel, easily. "I can tell a Jew." "No, you can't," I retorted, thinking of my Jewish grandmother, for by Nazi criteria I was Jewish. "Of course I can," he insisted. "So can you." We had begun to walk down the platform side by side, disputing with a restrained passion that isolated us like a pair of lovers. All at once, the colonel halted, as though struck with a thought. "What *are* you, anyway?" he said meditatively, regarding my dark hair, green blouse, and pink earrings. Inside myself, I began to laugh. "Oh," I said gaily, playing out the trump I had been saving. "I'm Irish, like you, Colonel." "How did you know?" he said amazedly. I laughed aloud. "I can tell an Irishman," I taunted. The colonel frowned. "What's your family name?" he said brusquely. "McCarthy." He lifted an eyebrow, in defeat, and then quickly took note of my wedding ring. "That your maiden name?" I nodded. Under this peremptory questioning, I had the peculiar sensation that I get when I am lying; I began to feel that "McCarthy" was a nom de plume, a coinage of my artistic personality. But the colonel appeared to be satisfied. "Hell," he said, "come on to lunch, then. With a fine name like that, you and I should be friends." I still shook my head, though by this time we were pacing outside the station restaurant; my baggage had been checked in a locker; sweat was running down my face and I felt exhausted and hungry. I knew that I was weakening and I wanted only an excuse to yield and go inside with him. The colonel seemed to sense this. "Hell," he conceded. "You've got me wrong. I've nothing against the Jews. Back there in the club car, I was just stating a simple fact: you won't find an Irishman sounding off for the Commies. You can't deny that, can you?"

His voice rose persuasively; he took my arm. In the heat, I wilted and we went into the air-conditioned cocktail lounge. The colonel ordered two old-fashioneds. The room was dark as a cave and produced, in the midst of the hot midday, a hallucinated feeling, as though time had ceased, with the weather, and we were in eternity together. As the colonel prepared to relax, I made a tremendous effort to guide the conversation along rational, purposive lines; my only justification for being here would be to convert the colonel. "There *have* been Irishmen associated with the Communist party." I said suddenly, when the drinks came. "I can think of two." "Oh, hell," said the colonel, "every race and nation has its traitors. What I mean is, you won't find them in numbers. You've got to admit the Communists in this country are ninety per cent Jewish." "But the Jews in this country aren't ninety per cent Communist," I retorted.

As he stirred his drink, restively, I began to try to show him the reasons why the Communist movement in America had attracted such a large number, relatively, of Jews: how the Communists had been anti-Nazi when nobody else seemed to care what happened to the Jews in Germany; how the Communists still capitalized on a Jewish fear of fascism; how many Jews had become, after Buchenwald, traumatized by this fear. . . .

But the colonel was scarcely listening. An impatient frown rested on his jaunty features. "I don't get it," he said slowly. "Why should you be for them, with a name like yours?" "I'm *not* for the Communists," I cried. "I'm just trying to explain to you—" "For the Jews," the colonel interrupted, irritable now himself. "I've heard of such people but I never met one before." "I'm not 'for' them," I protested. "You don't understand. I'm not for *any* race or nation. I'm against those who are against them." This word, *them*, with a sort of slurring circle drawn round it, was beginning to sound ugly to me. Automatically, in arguing with him, I seemed to have slipped into the colonel's style of thought. It occurred to me that defense of the Jews could be a subtle and safe form of anti-Semitism, an exercise of patronage: as a rational Gentile, one could feel superior both to the Jews and the anti-Semites. There could be no doubt that the Jewish question evoked a curious stealthy lust or concupiscence. I could feel it now vibrating between us over the dark table. If I had been a good person, I should unquestionably have got up and left.

"I don't get it," repeated the colonel. "How were you brought up? Were your people this way too?" It was manifest that an odd reversal had taken place; each of us regarded the other as "abnormal" and was attempting to understand the etiology of a disease. "Many of my people think just as you do," I said, smiling coldly. "It seems to be a sickness to which the Irish are prone. Perhaps it's due to the potato diet," I said sweetly, having divined that the colonel came from a social stratum somewhat lower than my own.

But the colonel's hide was tough. "You've got me wrong," he reiterated, with an almost plaintive laugh. "I don't dislike the Jews. I've got a lot of Jewish friends. Among themselves, they think just as I do, mark my words. I tell you what it is," he added ruminatively, with a thoughtful prod of his muddler, "I draw a distinction between a kike and a Jew." I groaned. "Colonel, I've never heard an anti-Semite who didn't draw that distinction. You know what Otto Kahn said? 'A kike is a Jewish gentleman who has just left the room.'" The colonel did not laugh. "I don't hold it against some of them," he persisted, in a tone of pensive justice. "It's not their fault if they were born that way. That's what I tell them, and they respect me for my honesty. I've had a lot of discussions; in procurement, you have to do business with them, and the Jews are the first to admit that you'll find more chiselers among their race than among the rest of mankind." "It's not a race," I interjected wearily, but the colonel pressed on. "If I deal with a Jewish manufacturer, I can't bank on his word. I've seen it again and again, every damned time. When I deal with a Gentile, I can trust him to make delivery as promised. That's the difference between the two races. They're just a different breed. They don't have standards of honesty, even among each other." I sighed, feeling unequal to arguing the colonel's personal experience.

"Look," I said, "you may be dealing with an industry where the Jewish manufacturers are the most recent comers and feel they have to cut corners to compete with the established firms. I've heard that said about Jewish cattle-dealers, who are supposed to be extra sharp. But what I think, really, is that you notice it when a Jewish firm fails to meet an agreement and don't notice it when it's a Yankee." "Hah," said the colonel. "They'll tell you what I'm telling you themselves, if you get to know them and go into their homes. You won't believe it, but some of my best friends are Jews," he said, simply and thoughtfully, with an air of originality. "They may be *your* best friends, Colonel," I retorted, "but you are not theirs. I defy you to tell me that you talk to them as you're talking now." "Sure," said the Colonel, easily. "More or less." "They must be very queer Jews you know." I observed tartly, and I began to wonder whether there indeed existed a peculiar class of Jews whose function in life was to be "friends" with such people as the colonel. It was difficult to think that all the anti-Semites who made the colonel's assertion were the victims of a cruel self-deception.

A dispirited silence followed. I was not one of those liberals who believed that the Jews, alone among peoples, possessed no characteristics whatever of a distinguishing nature—this would mean they had no history and no culture, a charge which should be leveled against them only by an anti-Semite. Certainly, types of Jews could be noted and patterns of Jewish thought and feeling: Jewish humor, Jewish rationality, and so on, not that every Jew reflected every attribute of Jewish life or history. But somehow, with the colonel, I dared not concede that there was such a thing as a Jew: I saw the sad meaning of the assertion that a Jew was a person whom other people thought was Jewish.

Hopeless, however, to convey this to the colonel. The desolate truth was that the colonel was extremely stupid, and it came to me, as we sat there, glumly ordering lunch, that for extremely stupid people anti-Semitism was a form of intellectuality, the sole form of intellectuality of which they were capable. It represented, in a rudimentary way, the ability to make categories, to generalize. Hence a thing I had noted before but never understood: the fact that anti-Semitic statements were generally delivered in an atmosphere of profundity. Furrowed brows attended these speculative distinctions between a kike and a Jew, these little empirical laws that you can't know one without knowing them all. To arrive, indeed, at the idea of a Jew was, for these grouping minds, an exercise in Platonic thought, a discovery of essence, and to be able to add the great corollary, "Some of my best friends are Jews," was to find the philosopher's cleft between essence and existence. From this, it would seem, followed the querulous obstinacy with which the anti-Semite clung to his concept; to be deprived of this intellectual tool by missionaries of tolerance would be, for persons like the colonel, the equivalent of Western man's losing the syllogism: a lapse into animal darkness. In the club car, we had just witnessed an example: the colonel with his anti-Semitic observation had come to the mute young man like the paraclete, bearing the gift of tongues.

Here in the bar, it grew plainer and plainer that the colonel did not regard himself as an anti-Semite but merely as a heavy thinker. The idea that I considered him anti-Semitic sincerely outraged his feelings. "Prejudice" was the last trait he could have imputed to himself. He looked on me, almost respectfully, as a "Jew-lover," a kind of being he had heard of but never actually encountered, like a centaur or a Siamese twin, and the interest of relating this prodigy to the natural state of mankind overrode any personal distaste. There I sat, the exception which was "proving" or testing the rule, and he kept pressing me for details of my history that might explain my deviation in terms of the norm. On my side, of course, I had become fiercely resolved that he would learn nothing from me that would make it possible for him to dismiss my anti-anti-Semitism as the product of special circumstances: I was stubbornly sitting on the fact of my Jewish grandmother like a hen on a golden egg. I was bent on making *him* see himself as a monster, a deviation, a heretic from Church and State. Unfortunately, the colonel, owing perhaps to his military training, had not the glimmering of an idea of what democracy meant; to him, it was simply a slogan that was sometimes useful in war. The notion of an ordained inequality was to him "scientific."

"Honestly," he was saying in lowered tones, as our drinks were taken away and the waitress set down my sandwich and his corned-beef hash,

"don't you, brought up the way you were, feel about them the way I do? Just between ourselves, isn't there a sort of inborn feeling of horror that the very word, Jew, suggests?" I shook my head, roundly. The idea of an *innate* anti-Semitism was in keeping with the rest of the colonel's thought, yet it shocked me more than anything he had yet said. "No," I sharply replied. "It doesn't evoke any feeling one way or the other." "Honest Injun?" said the colonel. "Think back; when you were a kid, didn't the word, Jew, make you feel sick?" There was a dreadful sincerity about this that made me answer in an almost kindly tone. "No, truthfully, I assure you. When we were children, we learned to call the old-clothes man a sheeny, but that was just a dirty word to us, like 'Hun' that we used to call after workmen we thought were Germans."

"I don't get it," pondered the colonel, eating a pickle. "There must be something wrong with you. Everybody is born with that feeling. It's natural; it's part of nature." "On the contrary," I said. "It's something very unnatural that you must have been taught as a child." "It's not something you're *taught*," he protested. "You must have been," I said. "You simply don't remember it. In any case, you're a man now; you must rid yourself of that feeling. It's psychopathic, like that horrible young man on the train." "You thought he was crazy?" mused the colonel, in an idle, dreamy tone. I shrugged my shoulders. "Of course. Think of his color. He was probably just out of a mental institution. People don't get that tattletale gray except in prison or mental hospitals." The colonel suddenly grinned. "You might be right," he said. "He was quite a case." He chuckled.

I leaned forward. "You know, Colonel," I said quickly, "anti-Semitism is contrary to the Church's teaching. God will make you do penance for hating the Jews. Ask your priest; he'll tell you I'm right. You'll have a long spell in Purgatory, if you don't rid yourself of this sin. It's a deliberate violation of Christ's commandment, 'Love thy neighbor.' The Church holds that the Jews have a sacred place in God's design. Mary was a Jew and Christ was a Jew. The Jews are under God's special protection. The Church teaches that the millennium can't come until the conversion of the Jews; therefore, the

Jews must be preserved that the Divine Will may be accomplished. Woe to them that harm them, for they controvert God's Will!" In the course of speaking, I had swept myself away with the solemnity of the doctrine. The Great Reconciliation between God and His chosen people, as envisioned by the Evangelist, had for me at that moment a piercing, majestic beauty, like some awesome Tintoretto. I saw a noble spectacle of blue sky, thronged with gray clouds, and a vast white desert, across which God and Israel advanced to meet each other, while below in hell the demons of disunion shrieked and gnashed their teeth.

"Hell," said the colonel, jovially, "I don't believe in all that. I lost my faith when I was a kid. I saw that all this God stuff was a lot of bushwa." I gazed at him in stupefaction. His confidence had completely returned. The blue eyes glittered debonairly, the eagles glittered; the narrow polished head cocked and listened to itself like a trilling bird. I was up against an airman with a bird's-eye view, a man who believed in nothing but the law of kind: the epitome of godless materialism. "You still don't hold with that bunk?" the colonel inquired in an undertone, with an expression of stealthy curiosity. "No," I confessed, sad to admit to a meeting of minds. "You know what got me?" exclaimed the colonel. "That birth-control stuff. Didn't it kill you?" I made a neutral sound. "I was beginning to play around," said the colonel, with a significant beam of the eye, "and I just couldn't take that guff. When I saw through the birth-control talk, I saw through the whole thing. They claimed it was against nature, but I claim, if that's so, an operation's against nature. I told my old man that when he was having his kidney stones out. You ought to have heard him yell!" A rich, reminiscent satisfaction dwelt in the colonel's face.

This period of his life, in which he had thrown off the claims of the spiritual and adopted a practical approach, was evidently one of those "turning points" to which a man looks back with pride. He lingered over the story of his break with church and parents with a curious sort of heat, as though the flames of old sexual conquests stirred within his body at the memory of those old quarrels. The looks he rested on me, as a sharer of that experience, grew more and more lickerish and assaying. "What got *you* down?" he finally inquired, settling back in his chair and pushing his coffee cup aside. "Oh," I said wearily, "it's a long story. You can read it when it's published." "You're an author?" cried the colonel, who was really very slow-witted. I nodded, and the colonel regarded me afresh. "What do you write? Love stories?" He gave a half-wink. "No," I said. "Various things. Articles. Books. Highbrowish stories." A suspicion darkened in the colonel's sharp face. "That McCarthy," he said. "Is that your pen name?" "Yes," I said, "but it's my real name too. It's the name I write under *and* my maiden name." The colonel digested this thought. "Oh," he concluded.

A new idea seemed to visit him. Quite cruelly, I watched it take possession. He was thinking of the power of the press and the indiscretions of other military figures, who had been rewarded with demotion. The consciousness of the uniform he wore appeared to seep uneasily into his body. He straightened his shoulders and called thoughtfully for the check. We paid in silence, the colonel making no effort to forestall my dive into my pocketbook. I should not have let him pay in any case, but it startled me that he did not try to do so, if only for reasons of vanity. The whole business of paying, apparently, was painful to him; I watched his facial muscles contract as he pocketed the change and slipped two dimes for the waitress onto the table, not daring quite to hide them under the coffee cup —he had short-changed me on the bill and the tip, and we both knew it. We walked out into the steaming station and I took my baggage out of the checking locker. The colonel carried my suitcase and we strolled along without speaking. Again, I felt horribly embarrassed for him. He was meditative, and I supposed that he too was mortified by his meanness about the tip.

"Don't get me wrong," he said suddenly, setting the suitcase down and turning squarely to face me, as though he had taken a big decision. "I may have said a few things back there about the Jews getting what they deserved in Germany." I looked at him in surprise; actually, he had not said that to me. Perhaps he had let it drop in the club car after I had left. "But that doesn't mean I approve of Hitler." "I should hope not," I said. "What I mean is," said the colonel, "that they probably gave the Germans a lot of provocation, but that doesn't excuse what Hitler did." "No," I said, somewhat ironically, but the colonel was unaware of anything satiric in the air. His face was grave and determined; he was sorting out his philosophy for the record. "I mean, I don't approve of his methods," he finally stated. "No," I agreed. "You mean, you don't approve of the gas chamber." The colonel shook his head very severely. "Absolutely not! That was terrible." He shuddered and drew out a handkerchief and slowly wiped his brow. "For God's sake," he said, "don't get me wrong. I think they're human beings." "Yes," I assented, and we walked along to my track. The colonel's spirits lifted, as though, having stated his credo, he had both got himself in line with public policy and achieved an autonomous thought. "I mean," he resumed, "you may not care for them, but that's not the same as killing them, in cold blood, like that." "No, Colonel," I said.

He swung my bag onto the car's platform and I climbed up behind it. He stood below, smiling, with upturned face. "I'll look for your article," he cried, as the train whistle blew. I nodded, and the colonel waved, and I could not stop myself from waving back at him and even giving him the corner of a smile. After all, I said to myself, looking down at him, the colonel was "a human being." There followed one of those inane intervals in which one prays for the train to leave. We both glanced at our watches. "See you some time," he called. "What's your married name?" "Broadwater," I called back. The whistle blew again. "Brodwater?" shouted the colonel, with a dazed look of unbelief and growing enlightenment; he was not the first person to hear it as a Jewish name, on the model of Goldwater. "B-r-o-a-d," I began, automatically, but then I stopped. I disdained to spell it out for him; the victory was his. "One of the chosen, eh?" his brief grimace seemed to commiserate. For the last time, and in the final fullness of understanding, the hawk eye patrolled the green dress, the duster, and the earrings; the narrow flue of his nostril contracted as he curtly turned away. The train commenced to move.

EXERCISE

1. Since we have here an event which is treated very much in the spirit of fiction—with all the concreteness and dramatic detail—and since the account is, presumably, autobiographical, with the author giving, step by step, her own responses to the course of the episode, do you think that the editors are justified in putting "Artists in Uniform" here and not among the personal essays?

2. How does the author intend for us to interpret the last paragraph? In what way may it be taken as summing up the essay?

3. What role does the young man in the Dacron suit have in the episode? As a character and personality? With reference to ideas?

4. Indicate certain bits of description, turns of phrase, or bits of dialogue that seem particularly effective.

5. What character does the author give herself?

The Deliverance of Dunkirk

WINSTON CHURCHILL (1874-   )

May 26 to June 4, 1940

THERE WAS a short service of intercession and prayer in Westminster Abbey on May 26. The English are loth to expose their feelings, but in my stall in the choir I could feel the pent-up, passionate emotion, and also the fear of the congregation, not of death or wounds or material loss, but of the defeat and the final ruin of Britain.

It was Tuesday, May 28, and I did not attend the House until that day week. There was no advantage to be gained by a further statement in the interval, nor did Members express a wish for one. But everyone realised that the fate of our Army and perhaps much else might be decided by then. "The House," I said, "should prepare itself for hard and heavy tidings. I have only to add that nothing which may happen in this battle can in any way relieve us of our duty to defend the world cause to which we have vowed ourselves; nor should it destroy our confidence in our power to make our way, as on former occasions in our history, through disaster and through grief to the ultimate defeat of our enemies." I had not seen many of my colleagues outside the War Cabinet, except individually, since the formation of the Government, and I thought it right to have a meeting in my room at the House of Commons of all Ministers of Cabinet rank other than the War Cabinet Members. We were perhaps twenty-five round the table. I described the course of events, and I showed them plainly where we were, and all that was in the balance. Then I said quite casually, and not treating it as a point of special significance: "Of course, whatever happens at Dunkirk, we shall fight on."

There occurred a demonstration which, considering the character of the gathering—twenty-five experienced politicians and Parliament men, who represented all the different points of view, whether right or wrong, before the war—surprised me. Quite a number seemed to jump up from the table and come running to my chair, shouting and patting me on the back. There is no doubt that had I at this juncture faltered at all in the leading of the nation, I should have been hurled out of office. I was sure that every Minister was ready to be killed quite soon, and have all his family and possessions destroyed rather than give in. In this they represented the House of Commons and almost all the people. It fell to me in these coming days to express their sentiments on suitable occasions. This I was able to do, because they were mine also. There was a white glow, overpowering, sublime, which ran through our island from end to end.

Accurate and excellent accounts have been written of the evacuation of the British and French armies from Dunkirk. Ever since the 20th the gathering of shipping and small craft had been proceeding under the control of Admiral Ramsay, who commanded at Dover. On the evening of the 26th (6.57 P.M.) an Admiralty signal put "Operation Dynamo" into play, and the first troops were brought home that night. After the loss of Boulogne and Calais only the remains of the port of Dunkirk and the open beaches next to the Belgian frontier were in our hands. At this time it was thought that the most we could rescue was about 45,000 men in two days. Early the next morning, May 27, emergency measures were taken to find additional small craft "for a special requirement." This was no less than the full evacuation of the British Expeditionary Force. It was plain that large numbers of such craft would be required for work on the beaches, in addition to bigger ships which could load in Dunkirk Harbour. On the suggestion of Mr. H. C. Riggs, of the Ministry of Shipping, the various boatyards, from Teddington to Brightlingsea, were searched by Admiralty officers, and yielded upwards of forty serviceable motor-boats or launches, which were assembled at Sheerness on the following day. At the same time lifeboats from liners in the London docks, tugs from the Thames, yachts, fishing-craft, lighters, barges, and pleasure-boats—anything that could be of use along the beaches—were called into service. By the night of the 27th a great tide of small vessels began to flow towards the sea, first to our Channel ports, and thence to the beaches of Dunkirk and the beloved Army.

Once the need for secrecy was relaxed, the Admiralty did not hesitate to give full rein to the spontaneous movement which swept the seafaring population of our south and southeastern shores. Everyone who had a boat of any kind, steam or sail, put out for Dunkirk, and the preparations, fortunately begun a week earlier, were now aided by the brilliant improvisation of volunteers on an amazing scale. The numbers arriving on the 29th were small, but they were the forerunners of nearly four hundred small craft which from the 31st were destined to play a vital part by ferrying from the beaches to the off-lying ships almost a hundred thousand men. In these days I missed the head of my Admiralty map room, Captain Pim, and one or two other familiar faces. They had got hold of a Dutch *schuit* which in four days brought off eight hundred soldiers. Altogether there came to the rescue of the Army under the ceaseless air bombardment of the enemy about 860 vessels, of which nearly seven hundred were British and the rest Allied.

Here is the official list in which ships not engaged in embarking troops are omitted:

BRITISH SHIPS

	Total Engaged	Sunk	Damaged
A.A. cruiser	1	–	1
Destroyers	39	6	19
Sloops, corvettes and gunboats	5	1	1
Minesweepers	36	5	7
Trawlers and drifters	77	17	6
Special service vessels	3	1	–
Armed boarding vessels	3	1	1
Motor torpedo boats and Motor anti-submarine boats	4	–	–
Ex-Dutch schuits (naval crews)	40	4 }	(Not
Yachts (naval crews)	26	3 }	recorded)
Personnel ships	45	8	8
Hospital carriers	8	1	5
Naval motor-boats	12	6	
Tugs	22	3 }	(Not
Other small craft *	372	170 }	recorded)
Total	693	226	

ALLIED SHIPS

Warships (all types)	49	8 }	(Not
Other ships and craft	119	9 }	recorded)
Total	168	17	
Grand Total	861	243	

* Omitting ships' lifeboats and some other privately owned small craft of which no record is available.

Meanwhile ashore around Dunkirk the occupation of the perimeter was effected with precision. The troops arrived out of chaos and were formed in order along the defences, which even in two days had grown. Those men who were in best shape turned about to form the line. Divisions like the 2d and 5th, which had suffered most, were held in reserve on the beaches and were then embarked early. In the first instance there were to be three corps on the front, but by the 29th we shortened it so that two sufficed. The enemy had closely followed the withdrawal, and hard fighting was incessant, especially on the flanks near Nieuport and Bergeus. As the evacuation went on, the steady decrease in the number of troops, both British and French, was accompanied by a corresponding contraction of the defence. On the beaches among the sand dunes, for three, four, or five days scores of thousands of men dwelt under unrelenting air attack. Hitler's belief that the German Air Force would render escape impossible, and that therefore he should keep his armoured formations for the final stroke of the campaign, was a mistaken but not unreasonable view.

Three factors falsified his expectations. First, the incessant air-bombing of the masses of troops along the seashore did them very little harm. The bombs plunged into the soft sand which muffled their explosions. In the early stages, after a crashing air raid, the troops were astonished to find that hardly anybody had been killed or wounded. Everywhere there had been explosions, but scarcely anyone was the worse. A rocky shore would have produced far more deadly results. Presently the soldiers regarded the air attacks with contempt. They crouched in the sand dunes with composure and growing hope. Before them lay the grey but not unfriendly sea. Beyond, the rescuing ships and—Home.

The second factor which Hitler had not foreseen was the slaughter of his airmen. British and German air quality was put directly to the test. By intense effort Fighter Command maintained successive patrols over the scene, and fought the enemy at long odds. Hour after hour they bit into the German fighter and bomber squadrons, taking a heavy toll, scattering them and driving them away. Day after day this went on, till the glorious victory of the Royal Air Force was gained. Wherever German aircraft were encountered, sometimes in forties and fifties, they were instantly attacked, often by single squadrons or less, and shot down in scores, which presently added up into hundreds. The whole Metropolitan Air Force, our last sacred reserve, was used. Sometimes the fighter pilots made four sorties a day. A clear result was obtained. The superior enemy were beaten or killed, and for all their bravery mastered, or even cowed. This was a decisive clash. Unhappily, the troops on the beaches saw very little of this epic conflict in the air, often miles away or above the clouds. They knew nothing of the loss inflicted on the enemy. All they felt was the bombs scourging the beaches, cast by the foes who had got through, but did not perhaps return. There was even a bitter anger in the Army against the Air Force, and some of the troops landing at Dover or at Thames ports in their ignorance insulted men in Air Force uniform. They should have clasped their hands; but how could they know? In Parliament I took pains to spread the truth.

But all the aid of the sand and all the prowess in the air would have been vain without the sea. The instructions given ten or twelve days before had under the pressure and emotion of events borne amazing fruit. Perfect discipline prevailed ashore and afloat. The sea was calm. To and fro between the shore and the ships plied the little boats, gathering the men from the beaches as they waded out or picking them from the water, with total indifference to the air bombardment, which often claimed its victims. Their numbers alone defied air attack. The Mosquito Armada as a whole was unsinkable. In the midst of our defeat glory came to the island people, united and unconquerable; and the tale of the Dunkirk beaches will shine in whatever records are preserved of our affairs.

Notwithstanding the valiant work of the small craft, it must not be forgotten that the heaviest burden fell on the ships plying from Dunkirk Harbour where two-thirds of the men were embarked. The destroyers played the predominant part as the casualty lists on page 519 show. Nor must the great part played by the personnel ships with their mercantile crews be overlooked.

The progress of the evacuation was watched with anxious eyes and growing hope. On the evening of the 27th, Lord Gort's position appeared critical to the Naval authorities, and Captain Tennant, R.N., from the Admiralty, who had assumed the duties of Senior Naval Officer at Dunkirk, signalled for all available craft to be sent to the beaches immediately, as "evacuation tomorrow night is problematical." The picture presented was grim, even desperate. Extreme efforts were made to meet the call, and a cruiser, eight destroyers and twenty-six other vessels were sent. The 28th was a day of tension, which gradually eased as the position on land was stabilised with the powerful help of the Royal Air Force. The naval plans were carried through despite severe losses on the 29th, when three destroyers and twenty-one other vessels were sunk and many others damaged.

There was never any question of our leaving the French behind. Here was my order before any request or complaint from the French was received:

Prime Minister to Secretary of State for War,
29.V.40

C.I.G.S. and GENERAL ISMAY.
  (Original to C.I.G.S.)

It is essential that the French should share in such evacuations from Dunkirk as may be possible. Nor must they be dependent only upon their own shipping resources. Arrangements must be concerted at once with the French Missions in this country, or, if necessary, with the French Government, so that no reproaches, or as few as possible, may arise. It might perhaps be well if we evacuated the two French divisions from Dunkirk, and replaced them pro tem. with our own troops, thus simplifying the command. But let me have the best proposals possible, and advise me whether there is any action I should take.

Prime Minister to GENERAL SPEARS (Paris).
29.V.40.

Following for Reynaud for communication to Weygand and Georges:

We have evacuated nearly 50,000 from Dunkirk and beaches, and hope another 30,000 tonight. Front may be beaten in at any time, or piers, beaches, and shipping rendered unusable by air attack, and also by artillery fire from the southwest. No one can tell how long present good flow will last, or how much we can save for future. We wish French troops to share in evacuation to fullest possible extent, and Admiralty have been instructed to aid French Marine as required. We do not know how many will be forced to capitulate, but we must share this loss together as best we can, and, above all, bear it without reproaches arising from inevitable confusion, stresses, and strains.

As soon as we have reorganised our evacuated troops, and prepared forces necessary to safeguard our life against threatened and perhaps imminent invasion, we shall build up a new B.E.F. from St. Nazaire. I am bringing Regulars from India and Palestine; Australians and Canadians are arriving soon. At present we are removing equipment south of Amiens, beyond what is needed for five divisions. But this is only to get into order and meet impending shock, and we shall shortly send you a new scheme for reinforcement of our troops in France. I send this in all comradeship. Do not hesitate to speak frankly to me.

On the 30th I held a meeting of the three Service Ministers and the Chiefs of Staff in the Admiralty War Room. We considered the events of the day on the Belgian coast. The total number of troops brought off had risen to 120,000, including only 6000 French; 850 vessels of all kinds were at work. A message from Admiral Wake Walker at Dunkirk said that, in spite of intense bombardment and air attack, 4000 men had been embarked in the previous hour. He also thought that Dunkirk itself would probably be untenable by the next day. I emphasized the urgent need of getting off more French troops. To fail to do so might do irreparable harm to the relations between ourselves and our ally. I also said that when the British strength was reduced to that of a corps we ought to tell Lord Gort to embark and return to England, leaving a corps commander in charge. The British Army would have to stick it out as long as possible so that the evacuation of the French could continue.

Knowing well the character of Lord Gort, I wrote out in my own hand the following order to him, which was sent officially by the War Office at 2 P.M. on the 30th:

Continue to defend the present perimeter to the utmost in order to cover maximum evacuation now proceeding well. Report every three hours through La Panne. If we can still communicate we shall send you an order to return to England with such officers as you may choose at the moment when we deem your command so reduced that it can be handed over to a corps commander. You should now nominate this commander. If communications are broken, you are to hand over and return as specified when your effective fighting force does not exceed the equivalent of three divisions. This is in accordance with correct military procedure, and no personal discretion is left you in the matter. On political grounds it would be a needless triumph to the enemy to capture you when only a small force remained under your orders. The corps commander chosen by you should be ordered to carry on the defence in conjunction with the French and evacuation whether from Dunkirk or the beaches, but when in his judgment no further organised evacuation is possible and no further proportionate damage can be inflicted on the enemy, he is authorised in consultation with the senior French commander to capitulate formally to avoid useless slaughter.

It is possible that this last message influenced other great events and the fortunes of another valiant commander. When I was at the White House at the end of December, 1941, I learned from the President and Mr. Stimson of the approaching fate of General MacArthur at the American garrison at Corregidor. I thought it right to show them the way in which we had dealt with the position of a Commander-in-Chief whose force was reduced to a small fraction of his original command. The President and Mr. Stimson both read the telegram with profound attention, and I was struck by the impression it seemed to make upon them. A little later in the day Mr. Stimson came back and asked for a copy of it, which I immediately gave him. It may be (for I do not know) that this influenced them in the right decision which they took in ordering General MacArthur to hand over his command to one of his subordinate generals, and thus saved for all his future glorious services the great Commander who would otherwise have perished or passed the war as a Japanese captive. I should live to think this was true.

On the 30th members of Lord Gort's staff in conference with Admiral Ramsay at Dover informed him that daylight on June 1 was the latest time up to which the eastern perimeter might be expected to hold. Evacuation was therefore pressed on with the utmost urgency to ensure, so far as possible, that a British rearguard of no more than about four thousand men would then remain ashore. Later it was found that this number would be insufficient to defend the final covering positions, and it was decided to hold the British sector until midnight June 1/2, evacuation proceeding meanwhile on the basis of full equality between French and British forces.

Such was the situation when on the evening of May 31 Lord Gort in accordance with his orders handed over his command to Major-General Alexander and returned to England.

To avoid misunderstandings by keeping personal contact it was necessary for me to fly to Paris on May 31 for a meeting of the Supreme War Council. With me in the plane came Mr. Attlee and Generals Dill and Ismay. I also took

General Spears, who had flown over on the 30th with the latest news from Paris. This brilliant officer and Member of Parliament was a friend of mine from the First Great War. Liaison officer between the left of the French and the right of the British Armies, he had taken me round the Vimy Ridge in 1916, and had made me friends with General Fayolle, who commanded the Thirty-Third French Corps. Speaking French with a perfect accent and bearing five wound stripes on his sleeve, he was a personality at this moment fitted to our anxious relations. When Frenchmen and Englishmen are in trouble together and arguments break out, the Frenchman is often voluble and vehement, and the Englishman unresponsive or even rude. But Spears could say things to the high French personnel with an ease and force which I have never seen equalled.

This time we did not go to the Quai d'Orsay, but to M. Reynaud's room at the War Office in the Rue Saint-Dominique. Attlee and I found Reynaud and Marshal Pétain opposite to us as the only French Ministers. This was the first appearance of Pétain, now Vice-President of the Council, at any of our meetings. He wore plain clothes. Our Ambassador, Dill, Ismay, and Spears were with us, and Weygand and Darlan, Captain de Margerie, head of Reynaud's private office, and a M. Baudouin of the Secretariat represented the French.

The first question was the position in Norway. I said that the British Government was of the considered opinion that the Narvik area should be evacuated at once. Our troops there, the destroyers involved, and a hundred anti-aircraft guns were badly wanted elsewhere. We therefore proposed an evacuation beginning on June 2. The British Navy would transport and repatriate the French forces, the King of Norway and any Norwegian troops who wished to come. Reynaud said that the French Government agreed with this policy. The destroyers would be urgently required in the Mediterranean in the event of war with Italy. The sixteen thousand men would be very valuable on the line of the Aisne and the Somme. This matter was therefore settled.

I then turned to Dunkirk. The French seemed to have no more idea of what was hap-pening to the northern armies than we had about the main French front. When I told them that 165,000 men, of whom 15,000 were French, had been taken off, they were astonished. They naturally drew attention to the marked British preponderance. I explained that this was due largely to the fact that there had been many British administrative units in the back area who had been able to embark before fighting troops could be spared from the front. Moreover, the French up to the present had had no orders to evacuate. One of the chief reasons why I had come to Paris was to make sure that the same orders were given to the French troops as to the British. The three British divisions now holding the centre would cover the evacuation of all the Allied forces. That, and the sea-transport, would be the British contribution to offset the heavy Allied losses which now must be faced. His Majesty's Government had felt it necessary in the dire circumstances to order Lord Gort to take off fighting men and leave the wounded behind. If present hopes were confirmed, 200,000 able-bodied troops might be got away. This would be almost a miracle. Four days ago I would not have wagered on more than 50,000 as a maximum. I dwelt upon our terrible losses in equipment. Reynaud paid a handsome tribute to the work of the British Navy and Air Force, for which I thanked him. We then spoke at some length upon what could be done to rebuild the British forces in France.

Meanwhile, Admiral Darlan had drafted a telegram to Admiral Abrial at Dunkirk:

(1) A bridgehead shall be held round Dunkirk with the divisions under your command and those under British command.

(2) As soon as you are convinced that no troops outside the bridgehead can make their way to the points of embarkation, the troops holding the bridgehead shall withdraw and embark, the British forces embarking first.

I intervened at once to say that the British would not embark first, but that the evacuation should proceed on equal terms between the British and the French—"Bras-dessus, bras-dessous." The British would form the rear guard. This was agreed.

The conversation next turned to Italy. I expressed the British view that if Italy came in we should strike at her at once in the most effective manner. Many Italians were opposed to war, and all should be made to realise its severity. I proposed that we should strike by air-bombing at the northwestern industrial triangle enclosed by the three cities of Milan, Turin, and Genoa. Reynaud agreed that the Allies must strike at once; and Admiral Darlan said he had a plan ready for the naval and aerial bombardment of Italy's oil supplies, largely stored along the coast between the frontier and Naples. The necessary technical discussions were arranged.

I then mentioned my desire that more Ministers of the Administration I had just formed should become acquainted with their French opposite numbers as soon as possible. For instance, I should like Mr. Bevin, the Minister of Labour and trade-union leader, to visit Paris. Mr. Bevin was showing great energy, and under his leadership the British working class was now giving up holidays and privileges to a far greater extent than in the last war. Reynaud cordially assented.

After some talk about Tangier and the importance of keeping Spain out of the war, I spoke on the general outlook. I said:

The Allies must maintain an unflinching front against all their enemies. . . . The United States had been roused by recent events, and even if they did not enter the war, would soon be prepared to give us more powerful aid. An invasion of England, if it took place, would have a still more profound effect on the United States. England did not fear invasion, and would resist it most fiercely in every village and hamlet. It was only after her essential need of troops had been met that the balance of her armed forces could be put at the disposal of her French ally. . . . I was absolutely convinced we had only to carry on the fight to conquer. Even if one of us should be struck down, the other must not abandon the struggle. The British Government were prepared to wage war from the New World, if through some disaster England herself were laid waste. If Germany defeated either ally or both, she would give no mercy; we should be reduced to the status of vassals and slaves forever. It would be better far that the civilisation of Western Europe with all its achievements should come to a tragic but splendid end than that the two great democracies should linger on, stripped of all that made life worth living.

Mr. Attlee then said that he entirely agreed with my view.

The British people now realise the danger with which they are faced, and know that in the event of a German victory everything they have built up will be destroyed. The Germans kill not only men, but ideas. Our people are resolved as never before in their history.

Reynaud thanked us for what we had said. He was sure that the morale of the German people was not up to the level of the momentary triumph of their army. If France could hold the Somme with the help of Britain and if American industry came in to make good the disparity in arms, then we could be sure of victory. He was most grateful, he said, for my renewed assurance that if one country went under the other would not abandon the struggle.

The formal meeting then ended.

After we rose from the table, some of the principals talked together in the bay window in a somewhat different atmosphere. Chief among these was Marshal Pétain. Spears was with me helping me out with my French and speaking himself. The young Frenchman, Captain de Margerie, had already spoken about fighting it out in Africa. But Marshal Pétain's attitude, detached and sombre, gave me the feeling that he would face a separate peace. The influence of his personality, his reputation, his serene acceptance of the march of adverse events, apart from any words he used, was almost overpowering to those under his spell. One of the Frenchmen, I cannot remember who, said in their polished way that a continuance of military reverses might in certain eventualities enforce a modification of foreign policy upon France. Here Spears rose to the occasion and addressing himself particularly to Marshal Pétain said in perfect French: "I suppose you understand, M. le Maréchal, that that would mean blockade?" Someone else said: "That would perhaps be inevitable." But then Spears to Pétain's face: "That would not only mean blockade but bombardment of all French ports in German hands." I was glad to have this said. I sang my usual song: we would fight on whatever happened or whoever fell out.

Again we had a night of petty raids, and in the morning I departed. Here was the information that awaited me on my return:

Prime Minister to GENERAL WEYGAND.   1.VI.40

Crisis in evacuation now reached. Five Fighter Squadrons, acting almost continuously, is the most we can do, but six ships, several filled with troops, sunk by bombing this morning. Artillery fire menacing only practicable channel. Enemy closing in on reduced bridgehead. By trying to hold on till tomorrow we may lose all. By going tonight much may certainly be saved, though much will be lost. Nothing like numbers of effective French troops you mention believed in bridgehead now, and we doubt whether such large numbers remain in area. Situation cannot be fully judged by Admiral Abrial in the fortress, nor by you, nor by us here. We have therefore ordered General Alexander, commanding British sector of bridgehead, to judge, in consultation with Admiral Abrial, whether to try to stay over tomorrow or not. Trust you will agree.

May 31 and June 1 saw the climax though not the end at Dunkirk. On these two days over 132,000 men were safely landed in England, nearly one-third of them having been brought from the beaches in small craft under fierce air attack and shell fire. On June 1 from early dawn onward the enemy bombers made their greatest efforts, often timed when our own fighters had withdrawn to refuel. These attacks took heavy toll of the crowded shipping, which suffered almost as much as in all the previous week. On this single day our losses by air attack, by mines, E-boats, or other misadventure were thirty-one ships sunk and eleven damaged.

The final phase was carried through with much skill and precision. For the first time it became possible to plan ahead instead of being forced to rely on hourly improvisations. At dawn on June 2, about four thousand British with seven anti-aircraft guns and twelve anti-tank guns remained with the considerable French forces holding the contracting perimeter of Dunkirk. Evacuation was now possible only in darkness, and Admiral Ramsay determined to make a massed descent on the harbour that night with all his available resources. Besides tugs and small craft, forty-four ships were sent that evening from England, including eleven destroyers and fourteen mine-sweepers. Forty French and Belgian vessels also participated. Before midnight the British rearguard was embarked.

This was not, however, the end of the Dunkirk story. We had been prepared to carry considerably greater numbers of French that night than had offered themselves. The result was that when our ships, many of them still empty, had to withdraw at dawn, thirty thousand French troops, many still in contact with the enemy, remained ashore. One more effort had

BRITISH AND ALLIED TROOPS LANDED IN ENGLAND †

Date	From the Beaches	From Dunkirk Harbour	Total	Accumulated Total
May 27	Nil	7,669	7,669	7,669
28	5,930	11,874	17,804	25,473
29	13,752	33,558	47,310	72,783
30	29,512	24,311	53,823	126,606
31	22,942	45,072	68,014	194,620
June 1	17,348	47,081	64,429	259,049
2	6,695	19,561	26,256	285,305
3	1,870	24,876	26,746	312,051
4	622	25,553	26,175	338,226
Grand Total	98,780	239,446	338,226	

† These figures are taken from a final analysis of the Admiralty records. The War Office figure for the total number of men landed in England is 336,427.

to be made. Despite the exhaustion of ships' companies after so many days without rest or respite, the call was answered. On June 4, 26,175 Frenchmen were landed in England, over 21,000 of them in British ships.

Finally, at 2.23 P.M. that day the Admiralty in agreement with the French announced that "Operation Dynamo" was now completed. Unfortunately several thousands remained who had gallantly protected the evacuation of their comrades.

Parliament assembled on June 4, and it was my duty to lay the story fully before them both in public and later in secret session. The narrative requires only a few extracts from my speech, which is extant. It was imperative to explain not only to our own people but to the world that our resolve to fight on was based on serious grounds, and was no mere despairing effort. It was also right to lay bare my own reasons for confidence.

We must be very careful not to assign this deliverance the attributes of a victory. Wars are not won by evacuations. But there was a victory inside this deliverance, which should be noted. It was gained by the Air Force. Many of our soldiers coming back have not seen the Air Force at work; they saw only the bombers which escaped its protective attack. They underrate its achievements. I have heard much talk of this; that is why I go out of my way to say this. I will tell you about it.

This was a great trial of strength between the British and German Air Forces. Can you conceive a greater objective for the Germans in the air than to make evacuation from these beaches impossible, and to sink all these ships which were displayed, almost to the extent of thousands? Could there have been an objective of greater military importance and significance for the whole purpose of the war than this? They tried hard, and they were beaten back; they were frustrated in their task. We got the Army away; and they have paid fourfold for any losses which they have inflicted . . . All of our types and all our pilots have been vindicated as superior to what they have at present to face.

When we consider how much greater would be our advantage in defending the air above this island against an overseas attack, I must say that I find in these facts a sure basis upon which practical and reassuring thoughts may rest. I will pay my tribute to these young airmen. The great French Army was very largely, for the time being, cast back and disturbed by the on-rush of a few thousands of armoured vehicles. May it not also be that the cause of civilisation itself will be defended by the skill and devotion of a few thousand airmen?

We are told that Herr Hitler has a plan for invading the British Isles. This has often been thought of before. When Napoleon lay at Boulogne for a year with his flat-bottomed boats and his Grand Army, he was told by someone, "There are bitter weeds in England." There are certainly a great many more of them since the British Expeditionary Force returned.

The whole question of Home Defence against invasion is, of course, powerfully affected by the fact that we have for the time being in this island incomparably stronger military forces than we have ever had at any moment in this war or the last. But this will not continue. We shall not be content with a defensive war. We have our duty to our Ally. We have to reconstitute and build up the British Expeditionary Force once again, under its gallant Commander-in-Chief, Lord Gort. All this is in train; but in the interval we must put our defences in this island into such a high state of organisation that the fewest possible numbers will be required to give effective security and that the largest possible potential of offensive effort may be realised. On this we are now engaged.

I ended in a passage which was to prove, as will be seen, a timely and important factor in United States decisions.

Even though large tracts of Europe and many old and famous States have fallen or may fall into the grip of the Gestapo and all the odious apparatus of Nazi rule, we shall not flag or fail. We shall go on to the end, we shall fight in France, we shall fight in the seas and oceans, we shall fight with growing confidence and growing strength in the air, we shall defend our island, whatever the cost may be, we shall fight on the beaches, we shall fight on the landing-grounds, we shall fight in the fields and in the streets, we shall fight in the hills; we shall never surrender, and even if, which I do not for a moment believe, this island or a large part of it were subjugated and starving, then our Empire beyond the seas, armed and guarded by the British Fleet, would carry on the struggle, until, in God's good time, the New World, with all its power and might, steps forth to the rescue and the liberation of the Old.

EXERCISE

1. Rebecca West writes (p. 495): "So the evil moment came and was clear: not surpassed in evil since the days of the barbarian invasions." "The Deliverance of Dunkirk" is a chapter from Churchill's history of the "evil" time of which Miss West speaks. Is Churchill's account addressed to precisely the same audience as "The Meaning of Treason"? What is the difference in tone of the two essays?

2. How much of the explicit matter of Rebecca West's essay is implied and presented dramatically in "The Deliverance of Dunkirk"?

3. As a historian, Churchill is necessarily interested in giving facts—precise dates, places, even tables of statistics. Does he manage to make his facts "come alive"? Does he succeed in presenting the dramatic excitement as felt by himself and the British people? If so, how has he done this? Consider carefully the diction, the comparisons, and the rhythms of the relevant passages.

4. Is there any difference in style between Churchill writing as historian and Churchill speaking as orator? In this connection, consider very carefully the style of the last paragraph of "The Deliverance of Dunkirk."

SECTION III

The Critical Essay

The critical essay, and that minor variant of it, the book review, is really a special type of the essay of ideas and opinion. For the critical essay is nothing but ideas and opinions about some particular literary work (or group of works), some particular writer or group of writers, or some literary question.

Criticism is a vague and inclusive term, and a critical essay may involve many different, though often related, kinds of intentions. It may explain, or analyze, or compare, or interpret, or advertise, or give impressions about, or make paraphrases of, or evaluate. It may do other things, too, for criticism is nothing more than a more or less systematic statement of the critic's reactions, intellectual and otherwise, to the subject before him. It may, in fact, become so personal that its only interest may be in the critic himself and not in the thing criticized. The intention of criticism may vary, in fact, from moment to moment in the same essay.

As we find a variety of intentions in criticism, so we find a variety of styles and methods. For here, as always, the relation between the occasion and the form is of crucial importance.

Homage to Hemingway

JOHN PEALE BISHOP (1892-1944)

I

ERNEST HEMINGWAY had the chance to become the spokesman of the war generation, or, more particularly, he came to be regarded as the spokesman of that generation by those who had not, in their own persons, known the experience of war. The phrase which he had culled from one of his many conversations with Gertrude Stein and printed opposite the title page of *The Sun Also Rises*—"You are all a lost generation"—was destined to *faire fortune*. And to this he appended another quotation from the aged and charming cynic of Ecclesiastes, which not only pointed the title of his book, but linked its own disillusionment with another so old and remote in time as to seem a permanent proclamation of the vanity of things.

His own generation admired him, but could also appraise how special his experience had been. It was a still younger generation, those who were schoolboys at the time of the War, who were infatuated with him. Hemingway not only supplied them with the adventures they had missed; he offered them an attitude with which to meet the disorders of the postwar decade. It was they who accepted the Hemingway legend and by their acceptance gave it a reality it had not had.

It is as one who dictated the emotions to contemporary youth that Hemingway has been compared to Lord Byron. The comparison is in many ways an apt one. The years of Byron's fame were not unlike the decade after the last war. The hopes raised by the French Revolution had then been frustrated and all possibilities of action were being rapidly destroyed by those in power. In the 1920's, the disintegration of the social fabric which began before the War became apparent to almost anyone. Here and there were new faces in politics, but Hemingway, who had worked on a Midwestern paper in his youth, gone abroad shortly after the War as a correspondent to a Canadian newspaper, come into contact with the literary diplomats at the Quai d'Orsay, followed the French troops of M. Poincaré into the Ruhr, known Mussolini when he too was a journalist, seen war and government from both sides in the Turkish-Greek conflict, was not likely to rate the new gangsters above the old gangs. It should have been obvious to a disinterested observer in 1922 that there was no longer much prospect of immediate revolution in the countries of Europe. It was in 1922 that Hemingway seriously began his career as a writer.

He was to become, like Byron, a legend while he was still in his twenties. But when I first met him in the summer of 1922 there could be no possibility of a legend. I had just come abroad and, calling on Ezra Pound, had asked him about American writers of talent then in Paris. Pound's answer was a taxi, which carried us with decrepit rapidity across the Left Bank, through the steep streets rising toward Mont Saint-Geneviève, and brought us to the Rue du Cardinal Lemoine. There we climbed four flights of stairs to find Ernest Hemingway. He had then published nothing except his newspaper work, none of which I had ever seen; so that my impressions could be only personal. From that time until 1930 I saw Hemingway fairly constantly. Since then he has retired to Florida, and I have seen him but once. Any later impressions I have are gathered entirely from his books. I say this to make clear what I shall have to say about the legendary figure.

The legend is, in some ways, astounding. Nothing is more natural than that the imaginative man should at times envy the active one. Stendhal would have liked to be a handsome lieutenant of hussars. But the born writer is, by his very imagination, cut off from the satisfactions of the man of action; he can emulate him only by a process of deliberate stultification.

Hemingway, as he then appeared to me, had many of the faults of the artist, some, such as vanity, to an exaggerated degree. But these are faults which from long custom I easily tolerate. And in his case they were compensated for by extraordinary literary virtues. He was instinctively intelligent, disinterested and not given to talking nonsense. Toward his craft, he was humble, and had, moreover, the most complete literary integrity it has ever been my lot to encounter. I say the most complete, for while I have known others who were not to be corrupted, none of them was presented with the opportunities for corruption that assailed Hemingway. His was that innate and genial honesty which is the very chastity of talent; he knew that to be preserved it must constantly be protected. He could not be bought. I happened to be with him on the day he turned down an offer from one of Mr. Hearst's editors, which, had he accepted it, would have supported him handsomely for years. He was at the time living back of the Montparnasse cemetery, over the studio of a friend, in a room small and bare except for a bed and table, and buying his midday meal for five sous from street vendors of fried potatoes.

The relation of a living writer to his legend may become curiously complicated. If we take the account that Mr. Peter Quennell has recently given us in *Byron: The Years of Fame,* it would seem that superficially the poet had at twenty-two only a very slight resemblance to the picture which the public presently began to compose of him. On the contrary, he seemed to his friends a personable, gay young man, an excellent drinking companion; there was, of course, the limp; and he had, as they may not have known, the consciousness of a bad heredity. *Childe Harold* was made of emotions only latent in Byron. It was a corollary of his fame that the poet should be identified with Childe Harold in the minds of his admirers. But it was not long before in his own imagination he became Childe Harold. And presently Lord Byron is committing incest with his sister. His conscience required that he complete the fiction by a private action. Byron's public stood as panders beside Augusta's bed.

In attempting to say what has happened to

Hemingway, I might suggest that, for one thing, he has become the legendary Hemingway. He appears to have turned into a composite of all those photographs he has been sending out for years: sunburned from snows, on skis; in fishing get-up, burned dark from the hot Caribbean; the handsome, stalwart hunter crouched smiling over the carcass of some dead beast. Such a man could not have written Hemingway's early books; he might have written most of *Green Hills of Africa*. He is proud to have killed the great kudu. It is hard not to wonder whether he has not, hunting, brought down an even greater victim.

Byron's legend is sinister and romantic, Hemingway's manly and low-brow. One thing is certain. This last book is hard-boiled. If that word is to mean anything, it must mean indifference to suffering and, since we are what we are, can signify a callousness to others' pain. When I say that the young Hemingway was among the tenderest of mortals, I do not speak out of private knowledge, but from the evidence of his writings. He could be, as any artist must in this world, if he is to get his work done, ruthless. He wrote courageously, but out of pity; having been hurt, and badly hurt, he could understand the pain of others. His heart was worn, as was the fashion of the times, up his sleeve and not on it. It was always there and his best tricks were won with it. Now, according to the little preface to *Green Hills of Africa,* he seems to think that, having discarded that half-concealed card, he plays more honestly. He does not. For with the heart the innate honesty of the artist is gone. And he loses the game.

II

The problem of style is always a primary one, for to each generation it is presented anew. It is desirable, certainly, that literature reflect the common speech; it is even more necessary that it set forth a changed sensibility, since that is the only living change from one generation to another. But to an American who, like Hemingway, was learning the craft of prose in the years that followed the War, that problem was present in a somewhat special way. He must achieve a style that could record an American experience, and neither falsify the world without nor betray the world within.

How difficult that might be, he could see from his immediate predecessors; they had not much else to teach. On the one side there was Mr. Hergesheimer, whose style falsified every fact he touched. On the other was Mr. Dreiser, a worthy, lumbering workman who could deliver the facts of American existence, all of them, without selection, as a drayman might deliver trunks. Where, then, to start? To anyone who felt there was an American tradition to be carried on, there was but one writer who was on the right track: Sherwood Anderson. When he was in his stride, there was no doubt about it, he was good. The trouble with Anderson was there was never any telling just how long he could keep up his pace. He had a bad way of stumbling. And when he stumbled he fell flat.

So did Mark Twain, who loomed out of the American past. All authentic American writing, Hemingway has said, stems from one book: *Huckleberry Finn.* How much was he prepared to learn from it may be ascertained by comparing the progress of the boy's raft down the Mississippi with the journey of Jake and his friend from France to Spain in *The Sun Also Rises.* Mark Twain is the one literary ancestor whom Hemingway has openly acknowledged; but what neither he nor Sherwood Anderson, who was Hemingway's first master, could supply was a training in discipline.

It was here that chance served. But it was a chance from which Hemingway carefully profited. There was one school which for discipline surpassed all others: that of Flaubert. It still had many living proponents, but none more passionate than Ezra Pound. In Paris, Hemingway submitted much of his apprentice work in fiction to Pound. It came back to him blue-penciled, most of the adjectives gone. The comments were unsparing. Writing for a newspaper was not at all the same as writing for a poet.

Pound was not the young American's only critical instructor. If Hemingway went often to 70 bis, Rue Nôtre Dame des Champs, he was presently to be found also at 12, Rue de Fleurus. There he submitted his writings to the formidable scrutiny of Gertrude Stein. It was of this period that Hemingway said to me later: "Ezra was right half the time, and when he was wrong, he was so wrong you were never in doubt about it. Gertrude was always right."

Miss Stein, for all her long residence abroad, was American. As she sat in one of the low chairs in the pavilion of the Rue de Fleurus, she was as unmistakably American as Mark Hanna; the walls were covered with Picassos; but with her closely clipped masculine head and old-fashioned dress, she might have been an adornment to the McKinley era. And if the problem was to combine Mark Twain and Gustave Flaubert—to convert a common American speech to the uses of the French tradition—it could hardly be doubted that Miss Stein had done it. She had taken up, in her *Three Lives,* where Flaubert left off. In *Un Coeur Simple,* he had presented the world through the eyes of a servant girl; but the words through which her vision is conveyed are not her own, but Flaubert's. Miss Stein had rendered her servant girls in an idiom which, if not exactly theirs, is supposed to be appropriate to their mentality. It is, so to speak, a transcript of dumb emotions. Having made it, Miss Stein discovered that she had arrived at a curious formalization of the common speech, which, she presently decided, might be put to other uses than the one for which it was originally intended.

If Gertrude Stein is always interesting in what she sets out to do, the result, once her writing is done, is all too often unsurpassed for boredom. She has told us in her *Autobiography of Alice B. Toklas* that she is a genius. We would have preferred that the statement had been made by someone else, but it happens to be true. Miss Stein has a mature intelligence; her genius, unfortunately, has not yet arrived at the age of three years. Ernest Hemingway, at the time he came under her influence, was a young man of twenty-four. But he was all of that. Miss Stein had developed a literary medium; but she had no material, at least none that was available to that strangely infantile genius of hers. She had at last realized that proud jest of Villiers de l'Isle-Adam; she had had, quite literally, to let her servants live for her. The relation between a writer and his material is much more mysterious than most critics

would like to admit. Miss Stein had led, in Paris and elsewhere, what anyone would call an interesting life. She could never write of it until, leaving the genial baby behind, she assumed the proportions of Miss Alice B. Toklas, her companion, and began writing as an intelligent being of her own years.

Hemingway had an abundance of material. There was a boyhood in the Midwest, with summers in the forests of Michigan, where he had come in contact with the earliest American way of life. There were the love affairs of a young man. There was not one war, but two. He had known in his own person an experience for which Gertrude Stein had vainly sought a substitute in words.

What she taught Hemingway must be in part left to conjecture. Like Pound, she undoubtedly did much for him simply by telling him what he must not do, for a young writer perhaps the most valuable aid he can receive. More positively, it was from her prose he learned to employ the repetitions of American speech without monotony. (I say this quite aware that Miss Stein's repetitions are monotonous in the extreme.) She also taught him how to adapt its sentence structure, inciting in him a desire to do what Hemingway calls "loosening up the language." She did not teach him dialogue. The Hemingway dialogue is pure invention. He does not talk like his characters and neither does Miss Stein. And it was not until they had read Hemingway's books that the two ladies of the Rue de Fleurus acquired those dramatic tricks of speech.

They are brilliant. But they have deafened Hemingway to the way people talk. In *The Sun Also Rises,* each of the characters has his own particular speech, but by the time we reach *Death in the Afternoon* and the extraordinary conversations with the Old Lady, there is no longer even the illusion that there is more than one way of talking. It is a formula, in that book employed with great dexterity and no small power; but it is dramatic only in words; in terms of character it is not dramatic at all.

There is no space here to appraise Hemingway's style with accuracy. It is enough to say that, as no one before him had done, he made Midwestern speech into a prose, living and alert, capable of saying at all times exactly what he wanted it to say. It is no longer the lean unlovely thing it was. Just as Eliot, in such a poem as "Sweeney Among the Nightingales," had shown how by controlling the sound apart from the sense the most prosaic statements could be turned to poetry, Hemingway made this American speech into prose by endowing it with a beauty of accurate motion. It is changed, as a gawky boy may change in a few years to an accomplished athlete; its identity is not destroyed. And here I am reminded of a remark of Hemingway's that it was Napoleon who taught Stendhal how to write. It may be that more than one of the best qualities of this prose were acquired from a careful watching of Spanish bullfighters.

III

> We were in the garden at Mons. Young Buckley came in with his patrol from across the river. The first German I saw climbed up over the garden wall. We waited until he got one leg over and then potted him. He had so much equipment on and looked awfully surprised and fell down in the garden. Then three more came over further down the wall. We shot them. They all came just like that.

It is easy to see how a story like this could convey the impression that Hemingway is indifferent alike to cruelty and suffering. And yet this tale is a precise record of emotion. What we have here is not callousness, but the Flaubertian discipline carried to a point Flaubert never knew—just as in the late war military control was brought to such perfection that dumb cowed civilians in uniform, who cared nothing for fighting and little for the issues of battle, could be held to positions that the professional soldiers of the nineteenth century would have abandoned without the slightest shame. Flaubert describing an incident, despite his pretending to be aloof, or even absent throughout, is continually intent on keeping his emotions implicit within the scene. The reader is never left in the slightest doubt as to what he is supposed to feel from the fiction. But in this account of the Germans coming over the wall and being shot, one by one, all emotion is kept out, unless it is the completely inadequate surprise of the victims. The men who kill feel nothing. And yet what Hemingway was doing in the summer of 1922, lying on a bed in a room where the old Verlaine had once had lodging, was first remembering that he had been moved, and then trying to find out what had happened to cause the emotion. It is the bare happening that is set down, and only the happening that must arouse in the reader whatever emotion he is capable of according to his nature: pity, horror, disgust.

But this was a point beyond which Hemingway himself could not go. And in the stories that follow the first little volume, published in Paris and called *In Our Time*, he is almost always present in one guise or another. That is not to say, as might be assumed, that these stories are necessarily autobiographical. Wounded in the War, Hemingway was a very apprehensive young man. Indeed, his imagination could hardly be said to exist apart from his apprehension. I should not call this fear. And yet he could hardly hear of something untoward happening to another that he did not instantly, and without thought, attach this event to himself, or to the woman he loved. The narration is still remarkably pure. But there is always someone subject to the action.

For this is another distinction. In Flaubert, people are always planning things that somehow fail to come off—love affairs, assignations, revolutions, schemes for universal knowledge. But in Hemingway, men and women do not plan; it is to them that things happen. In the telling phrase of Wyndham Lewis, the "I" in Hemingway's stories is "the man that things are done to." Flaubert already represents a deterioration of the romantic will, in which both Stendhal and Byron, with the prodigious example of Napoleon before them, could not but believe. Waterloo might come, but before the last battle there was still time for a vast, however destructive, accomplishment of the will. Flaubert had before him Louis Philippe, whose green umbrella and thrifty bourgeois mind would not save him from flight; Louis Napoleon, whose plans were always going astray. But even Sedan was a better end than Woodrow Wilson had, with his paralytic chair and his closed room on a side street in Washington. And in Hemingway, the will is lost to action.

There are actions, no lack of them but, as when the American lieutenant shoots the sergeant in *A Farewell to Arms,* they have only the significance of chance. Their violence does not make up for their futility. They may be, as this casual murder is, shocking; they are not incredible; but they are quite without meaning. There is no destiny but death.

It is because they have no will and not because they are without intelligence that the men and women in Hemingway are devoid of spiritual being. Their world is one in time with the War and the following confusion, and is a world without traditional values. That loss has been consciously set down.

IV

It is the privilege of literature to propose its own formal solutions for problems which in life have none. In many of the early stories of Hemingway the dramatic choice is between death and a primitive sense of male honor. The nineteen-year-old Italian orderly in "A Simple Enquiry" is given to choose between acceding to his major's corrupt desires and being sent back to his platoon. Dishonor provides no escape, for in "The Killers" the old heavyweight prizefighter who has taken that course must at last lie in his room, trying to find the courage to go out and take what is coming to him from the two men who are also waiting in tight black overcoats, wearing gloves that leave no fingerprints. One can make a good end, or a bad end, and there are many deaths besides the final one. In "Hills Like White Elephants," love is dead no matter what the lovers decide. "I don't feel any way," the girl says. "I just know things." And what she knows is her own predicament.

The Spaniards stand apart, and particularly the bullfighters, not so much because they risk their lives in a spectacular way, with beauty and skill and discipline, but because as members of a race still largely, though unconsciously, savage, they retain the tragic sense of life. In *The Sun Also Rises,* the young Romero, courteous, courageous, born knowing all the things that the others—wise-cracking Americans, upper-class British or intellectual Jews—will never learn, is a concentration of contrast. And yet the character in that novel who most nearly represents the author is aware, as soon as he has crossed the border back into France, that it is here that he belongs, in the contemporary world. He is comfortable only where all things have a value that can be expressed and paid for in paper money.

The best one can do is to desert the scene, as every man and woman must do sooner or later, to make, while the light is still in the eyes, a separate peace. And is this not just what Hemingway has done? Is there a further point to which he can retire than Key West? There he is still in political America, but on its uttermost island, no longer attached to his native continent.

His vision of life is one of perpetual annihilation. Since the will can do nothing against circumstance, choice is precluded; those things are good which the senses report good; and beyond their brief record there is only the remorseless devaluation of nature, which, like the vast blue flowing of the Gulf Stream beyond Havana, bears away of our great hopes, emotions and ambitions only a few and soon disintegrating trifles. Eternity—horribly to paraphrase Blake—is in love with the garbage of time.

What is there left? Of all man's activities, the work of art lasts longest. And in this morality there is little to be discerned beyond the discipline of the craft. This is what the French call the sense of the *métier* and their conduct in peace and war has shown that it may be a powerful impulse to the right action; if I am not mistaken, it is the main prop of French society. In "The Undefeated," the old bullfighter, corrupt though he is with age, makes a good and courageous end, and yet it is not so much courage that carries him as a proud professional skill. It is this discipline, which Flaubert acquired from the traditions of his people and which Pound transmitted to the young Hemingway, that now, as he approaches forty, alone sustains him. He has mastered his *métier* as has no American among his contemporaries. That is his pride and his distinction.

EXERCISE

This account of Hemingway is best studied in relation to the subsequent essay on Hemingway by Dwight Macdonald. Bishop's estimate was written at the very center of Hemingway's creative career (1936), Macdonald's shortly after his suicide in 1961, and comparison of the two essays highlights certain features of the career. But for the moment we shall confine ourselves to an inspection of Bishop's essay.

1. Test this account of Hemingway's work against the Hemingway stories that you have read. How just is the account? If you think it is just, can you supply further illustrations from "The Killers" and "In Another Country"?

2. In this essay, Bishop undertakes to deal with Hemingway's development as a writer and with the background of mood and ideas out of which Hemingway's stories grow. With how much of it can you agree? Bishop writes (p. 527). "In the 1920's, the dis-

integration of the social fabric which began before the War became apparent to everyone." This is clearly Bishop's own view. On p. 531 he writes: "His vision of life is one of perpetual annihilation." This view is attributed to Hemingway, and not put down as necessarily a view that the author shares. Has Bishop fairly and convincingly depicted the intellectual situation of the 'twenties and Hemingway's own special modifications of that complex of ideas?

3. What devices has Bishop used as a means of organizing his account of Hemingway? Discuss his use of analogy (Byron is compared to Hemingway), personal anecdote, historical allusion, metaphor (the Gulf Stream comparison on p. 531), etc. How do you relate the element of personal recollection to the more strictly critical part of the essay?

Ernest Hemingway

DWIGHT MACDONALD (1906-   )

HE WAS a big man with a bushy beard and everybody knew him. The tourists knew him and the bar-tenders knew him and the critics knew him too. He enjoyed being recognised by the tourists and he liked the bar-tenders but he never liked the critics very much. He thought they had his number. Some of them did. The hell with them. He smiled a lot and it should have been a good smile, he was so big and bearded and famous, but it was not a good smile. It was a smile that was uneasy around the edges as if he was not sure he deserved to be quite as famous as he was famous.

He liked being a celebrity and he liked celeb-

rities. At first it was Sherwood Anderson and Ezra Pound and Gertrude Stein. He was an athletic young man from Oak Park, Illinois, who wanted to write and he made friends with them. He was always good at making friends with celebrities. They taught him about style. Especially Gertrude Stein. The short words, the declarative sentences, the repetition, the beautiful absence of subordinate clauses. He always worked close to the bull in his writing. In more senses than one, señor. It was a kind of inspired baby-talk when he was going good.* When he was not going good, it was just baby-talk.† Or so the critics said and the hell with

---

* "And what if she should die? She won't die. People don't die in childbirth nowadays. That was what all husbands thought. Yes, but what if she should die? She won't die. She's just having a bad time. The initial labour is usually protracted. She's only having a bad time. Afterwards we'd say what a bad time, and Catherine would say it wasn't really so bad. But what if she should die? She can't die. Yes, but what if she should die? She can't, I tell you. Don't be a fool. It's just a bad time. It's just nature giving her hell. It's only the first labor, which is almost always protracted. Yes, but what if she should die? She can't die. Why should she die? What reason is there for her to die? . . . But what if she should die? She won't. She's all right. But what if she should die? She can't die. But what if she should die? Hey, what about that? What if she should die?" *A Farewell to Arms* (pp. 245-6, Penguin ed.).

† I remember waking in the morning. Catherine was asleep and the sun was coming in through the window. The rain had stopped and I stepped out of bed and across the floor to the window. . . .

"How are you, darling?" she said. "Isn't it a lovely day?"

"How do you feel?"

"I feel very well. We had a lovely night."

"Do you want breakfast?"

She wanted breakfast. So did I and we had it in bed, the November sunlight coming in through the window, and the breakfast tray across my lap.

"Don't you want the paper? You always wanted the paper in the hospital."

"No," I said. "I don't want the paper now." *A Farewell to Arms* (p. 193).

them. Most of the tricks were good tricks and they worked fine for a while especially in the short stories. Ernest was fast and stylish in the hundred-yard dash but he didn't have the wind for the long stuff. Later on the tricks did not look so good. They were the same tricks but they were not fresh any more and nothing is worse than a trick that has gone stale. He knew this but he couldn't invent any new tricks. It was a great pity and one of the many things in life that you can't do anything about. Maybe that was why his smile was not a good smile.

After 1930, he just didn't have it any more. His legs began to go and his syntax became boring and the critics began to ask why he didn't put in a few subordinate clauses just to make it look good. But the bar-tenders still liked him and the tourists liked him too. He got more and more famous and the big picture magazines photographed him shooting a lion and catching a tuna and interviewing a Spanish Republican militiaman and fraternising with bullfighters and helping liberate Paris and always smiling bushily and his stuff got worse and worse. Mr. Hemingway the writer was running out of gas but no one noticed it because Mr. Hemingway the celebrity was such good copy. It was all very American and in 1954 they gave him the Nobel Prize and it wasn't just American any more. The judges were impressed by "the style-forming mastery of the art of modern narration" he had shown in *The Old Man and the Sea,* which he had published in *Life* two years earlier. *Life* is the very biggest of the big picture magazines and *Life* is exactly where *The Old Man and the Sea* belonged. Literary prize judges are not always clever. This is something you know and if you don't know it you should know it. They gave him the prize and he went to Stockholm and the King of Sweden put the medal around his neck and they shook hands. Mr. Hemingway meet Mr. Bernadotte.

After 1930 his friends were not named Anderson or Pound or Stein. They are named Charles Ritz and Toots Shor and Leonard Lyons and Ava Gardner and Marlene Dietrich and Gary Cooper. He almost had a fight with Max Eastman because he thought Max Eastman had questioned his virility and he almost fought a duel with someone he thought might have in-

sulted the honor of Ava Gardner but he didn't have the fight and he decided that Ava Gardner's honor had not been insulted after all. It is often difficult to tell about honor. It is something you feel in your *cojones.* Or somewhere. He liked Marlene Dietrich very much. They had good times together. He called her "The Kraut" and she called him "Papa." His wife called him "Papa" too. Many other people called him "Papa." He liked being called "Papa."

He wrote a novel called *Across the River and Into the Trees.* It was not a good novel. It was a bad novel. It was so bad that all the critics were against it. Even the ones who had liked everything else. The trouble with critics is that you can't depend on them in a tight place and this was a very tight place indeed. They scare easy because their brains are where their *cojones* should be and because they have no loyalty and because they have never stopped a charging lion with a Mannlicher double-action .34 or done any of the other important things. The hell with them. Jack Dempsey thought *Across the River* was OK. So did Joe Di Maggio. The Kraut thought it was terrific. So did Toots Shor. But it was not OK and he knew it and there was absolutely nothing he could do about it.

He was a big man and he was famous and he drank a great deal now and wrote very little. He lived in Havana and often went game fishing and *Life* photographed him doing it. Sometimes he went to Spain for the bullfights and he made friends with the famous bullfighters and wrote it up in three instalments for *Life.* He had good times with his friends and his admirers and his wife and the tourists and the bar-tenders and everybody talked and drank and laughed and was gay but it all went away when he was alone. It was bad when he was alone. Nothing helped then. He knew he had been very good once, he knew he had been as good as they come at the special kind of thing he was good at, and he knew he had not been good for a long time. He talked to interviewers: "I trained hard and I beat Mr. De Maupassant. I've fought two draws with Mr. Stendhal, but nobody is going to get me in any ring with Mr. Tolstoy unless I'm crazy or keep getting better." But he knew he was getting worse, and not better. He was a writer and his writing had gone soft a long time ago and he knew this no matter what the Nobel Prize judges and the editors of *Life* told him and he was a writer and nothing else interested him much. He took shock treatments for depression at the Mayo Clinic. He went twice and he stayed there a long time but they didn't work. He was overweight and his blood pressure was high and his doctor made him cut down on the eating and drinking. Last spring his friend Gary Cooper died. He took it hard. The position is outflanked the lion can't be stopped the sword won't go into the bull's neck the great fish is breaking the line and it is the fifteenth round and the champion looks bad.

Now it is that morning in the house in Ketchum, Idaho. He takes his favourite gun down from the rack. It is a 12-gauge double-barrelled shotgun and the stock is inlaid with silver. It is a very beautiful gun. He puts the end of the gun-barrel into his mouth and he pulls both triggers. There is nothing much left above the chin.

That week his great shaggy head looks down from the covers of the picture magazines on the news-stands and the graduate students smile thinly as they realise that a definitive study of the complete *œuvre* of Ernest Hemingway is now possible.

II

A professor of English in North Carolina State College recently called Hemingway "essentially a philosophical writer." This seems to me a foolish statement even for a professor of literature. It is true that Hemingway originated a romantic attitude which was as seductive to a whole generation, and as widely imitated, as Byron's had been. (It is still attractive: Norman Mailer, for instance, is a belated Hemingway type, though his prose style is different.) But Hemingway was no more a philosopher than Byron was; in fact, he was considerably less of one. A feeling that loyalty and bravery are the cardinal virtues and that physical action is the basis of the good life—even when reinforced with the kind of nihilism most of us get over by the age of twenty—these don't add up to a philoso-phy. There is little evidence of thought in Hemingway's writing and much evidence of the reverse—the kind of indulgence in emotion and prejudice which the Nazis used to call "blood-thinking." For all the sureness of his instinct as a writer, he strikes one as not particularly intelligent. Byron wrote *Manfred* but he also wrote *Don Juan* and the letters and journals; underneath the romantic pose there was a tough, vigorous, and sceptical mind, a throwback to the 18th century and the Age of Reason. There were two Byrons but there was (alas) only one Hemingway. He was hopelessly sincere. His life, his writing, his public personality and his private thoughts were all of a piece. Unlike Byron, he believed his own propaganda. I hate to think what his letters and journals must be like. I suspect he kept no journals, since to do so implies reflection and self-awareness; also that one has a private life as apart from one's professional and public existence; I don't think Hemingway did—indeed I think it was this lack of private interests which caused him to kill himself when his professional career had lost its meaning.

We know what his conversation was like, in his later years at least, from Lillian Ross's minute account of two days spent with Hemingway and his entourage (*The New Yorker*, May, 13th, 1950). The article presents a Hemingway who sounds as fatuous and self-consciously he-man as his general in *Across the River*. At least that is how it sounds to me. But Miss Ross has a different ear. She insists, and I believe her, that (a) she simply reported what Hemingway said and did, and (b) that she liked and respected him (and what he said and did). She also states that she showed advance proofs to Hemingway and that he made no objections to the article and in fact was pleased with it. One can only admire his objectivity and good nature. But perhaps his reaction was a little *too* objective. Perhaps it shows an alienation from himself that is neurotic—one should feel a certain amount of prejudice in favour of one's self, after all. Or perhaps, worse, it means that Hemingway by then had accepted the public personality that had been built up for him by the press—a well-trained lion, he jumped through all the hoops—and even gloried in the grotesque (but virile) philistine Miss Ross had innocently depicted. This latter possibility is suggested by a letter from Hemingway which Miss Ross quoted in *The New Republic* of August 7th last when she protested against Irving Howe's assumption that she had been out to "smear" Hemingway in her *New Yorker* piece. "The hell with them," Hemingway wrote her after the piece had been published, apropos of people who had found it "devastating" (as I must confess I still do). "Think one of the 'devastating' things was that I drink a little in it and that makes them think I am a rummy. But of course if they (the devastate people) drank what we drink in that piece they would die or something. Then (I should not say it) there is a lot of jealousy around and because I have fun a lot of the time and am not really spooky and so far always get up when they count over me some people are jealous. They can't understand you being a serious writer and not solemn." This seems to me, taken in conjunction with Miss Ross's reportage, to indicate the opposite to what the writer intended to indicate.

III

Hemingway's importance, I think, is almost entirely as a stylistic innovator. I have just re-read *A Farewell to Arms* and *Men Without Women* and what strikes me most is their extreme mannerism. I don't know which is the more surprising, after twenty years, the virtuosity of the style or its lack of emotional resonance to-day. Consider the opening paragraphs of *In Another Country:*

In the fall the war was always there, but we did not go to it any more. It was cold in the fall in Milan and the dark came very early. Then the electric lights came on, and it was pleasant along the streets looking in the windows. There was much game hanging outside the shops, and the snow powdered in the fur of the foxes and the wind blew their tails. The deer hung stiff and heavy and empty, and small birds blew in the wind and the wind turned their feathers. It was a cold fall and the wind came down from the mountains.

We were all at the hospital every afternoon, and there were different ways of walking across the town through the dusk to the hospital. Two of the ways were alongside canals, but they were long. Always, though you crossed a bridge across a canal to enter the hospital. There was a choice of three bridges. On

one of them a woman sold roasted chestnuts. It was warm, standing in front of the charcoal fire, and the chestnuts were warm afterwards in your pocket. The hospital was very old and very beautiful, and you entered through a gate on the other side. There were usually funerals starting from the courtyard. Beyond the old hospital were the new brick pavilions, and there we met every afternoon and were all very polite and interested in what was the matter, and sat in the machines that were to make so much difference.

This is a most peculiar way to begin a story. Nothing "happens" until the last sentence of the second paragraph. Up to then everything is simply atmosphere but not atmosphere as it was generally known before Hemingway, except for the wonderful two sentences about the game hanging outside the shops. It is an original mixture of the abstract and the concrete, as in the first sentence, and the effect is to describe not a particular state of mind but rather a particular way of looking at experience, one which makes as sharp a break with previous literary methods as Jackson Pollock made with previous ways of painting. The primitive syntax is the equivalent of Pollock's "drip and dribble" technique and, like it, is a declaration of war against the genteel and academic style. There is also a parallel with the architecture of Mies Van Der Rohe, whose "Less is more" applies to Hemingway's style, which gets its effect from what it leaves out. (Maybe this is the characteristic 20th-century manner in the arts: I'm told that in the music of Webern and the jazz of Thelonius Monk one should listen not to the notes but to the silences between them.) Because Van Der Rohe's buildings are simple in form and without ornamentation many people think they are functional, but in fact they are as aggressively unfunctional as the wildest baroque. The same goes for Hemingway's style which is direct and simple on the surface but is actually as complexly manneristic as the later James.

"Refinements in the use of subordinate clauses are a mark of maturity in style," writes Albert C. Baugh in *A History of the English Language*. "As the loose association of clauses (parataxis) gives way to more precise indications of logical relationship and subordination (hypotaxis), there is need for a greater variety of words effecting the union." Hemingway was a most paratactical writer. Not because he was primitive but because he was stylistically sophisticated to the point of decadence. Supremely uninterested in "precise indications of logical relationship," he needed very few words; his vocabulary must be one of the smallest in literary history.

I can see why, in the 'twenties, the two paragraphs quoted above were fresh and exciting, but in 1961 they seem as academically mannered as *Euphues* or *Marius the Epicurean*. This is, of course, partly because Hemingway's stylistic discoveries have become part of our natural way of writing, so that they are at once too familiar to cause any excitement and at the same time, in the extreme form in which Hemingway used them, they now sound merely affected. This kind of writing is lost unless it can create a mood in the reader, since it deliberately gives up all the resources of logic and reason. But I was, in 1961, conscious of the tricks—and impatient with them. *Why* must we be told about the two ways of walking to the hospital and the three bridges and the chestnut seller? The aim is probably to create tension by lingering over the prosaic—writers of detective stories, a highly artificial literary form, have learned much from Hemingway—just as the purpose of stating that it is warm in front of a fire and that newly roasted chestnuts feel warm in one's pocket is to suggest the coldness of Milan that fall. But these effects didn't "carry" with me, I just felt impatient.

IV

A Farewell to Arms is generally considered Hemingway's best novel. It has aged and shrivelled from what I remembered. I found myself skipping yards and yards of this sort of thing:

> "We could walk or take a tram," Catherine said. "One will be along," I said. "They go by here." "Here comes one," she said.
> The driver stopped his horse and lowered the metal sign on his meter. The top of the carriage was up and there were drops of water on the driver's coat. His varnished hat was shining in the wet. We sat back in the seat and the top of the carriage made it dark.
> (Half a page omitted)
> At the hotel I asked Catherine to wait in the carriage while I went in and spoke to the manager. There were plenty of rooms. Then I went out to the carriage, paid the driver, and Catherine and I walked in together. The small boy in buttons carried the package. The manager bowed us towards the elevator. There was much red plush and brass. The manager went up in the elevator with us.

There is a great deal of paying cab drivers and finding it dark at night inside a closed carriage.

I found both the military part and the love-story tedious except at moments of ordeal or catastrophe. The wounding of the narrator, Lieutenant Henry, and his escape after Caporetto are exciting, and the chapters on the retreat from Caporetto are as good as I remembered, especially the four pages about the shooting of the officers by the battle police. As long as the lieutenant and Catherine Baker are making love and having "a good time" together, one is bored and sceptical. To my surprise, I found that Catherine was like the heroines of *For Whom the Bell Tolls* and *Across the River and Into the Trees,* not a person but an adolescent day-dream—utterly beautiful and utterly submissive and utterly in love with the dreamer: "You see I'm happy, darling, and we have a lovely time. . . . You are happy, aren't you? Is there anything I do you don't like? Can I do anything to please you? Would you like me to take down my hair? Do you want to play?" "Yes and come to bed." "All right. I'll go and see the patients first." The conversation of these lovers is even more protracted and boring than that of real lovers. (It is curious how verbose Hemingway's laconic style can become.) But at the end when Catherine dies in childbed, the feeling comes right and one is moved—just as the preceding ordeal of the escape to Switzerland by rowing all night is well done. This deathbed scene is one of the few successful ones in literary history; it is the stylistic antithesis to Dickens' Death of Little Nell (of which Oscar Wilde remarked, "One must have a heart of stone to read it without laughing").

The fact is Hemingway is a short-story writer and not a novelist. He has little understanding of the subject-matter of the novel: character, social setting, politics, money matters, human relations, all the prose of life. Only the climactic moments interest him, and of those only ordeal, suffering, and death. (Except for a lyrical feeling about hunting and fishing.) In a novel he gets lost, wandering around aimlessly in a circle as lost people are said to do, and the alive parts are really short stories, such as the lynching of the fascists and the blowing up of the bridge in *For Whom the Bell Tolls.* In the short story he knows just where he is going and his style, which becomes tedious in a novel, achieves the intensity appropriate to the shorter form. The difference may be seen in comparing the dialogue in *A Farewell to Arms* with that in the little short story, "Hills Like White Elephants." The former is often aimlessly repetitious because the writer sees nowhere to go (except at peak moments of crisis) but the latter is directed with superb craftsmanship to the single bitter point the story makes. Every line of this apparently random conversation between a man and a girl waiting at a Spanish railway station—she is going to Madrid for an abortion he wants but she doesn't—develops the theme and when towards the end she asks, "Would you do something for me now?" and he replies, "I'd do anything for you," and she says "Would you please please please please please please please stop talking?"—then one feels that tightening of the scalp that tells one an artist has made his point.

V

"Hemingway's tragedy as an artist," Cyril Connolly writes in *Enemies of Promise,* "is that he has not had the versatility to run away fast enough from his imitators. . . . A Picasso would have done something different; Hemingway could only indulge in invective against his critics—and do it again." The list of Hemingwayesque writers includes James M. Cain, Erskine Caldwell, John O'Hara, and a whole school of detective fiction headed by Dashiel Hammett and Raymond Chandler. It also includes Hemingway. Connolly wrote before Hemingway had begun to parody himself in *The Old Man and the Sea*—which is simply his early short story, "The Undefeated," perhaps the best thing he ever did, re-told in terms of fishing instead of bullfighting and transposed from a spare, austere style into a slack, fake-

biblical style which retains the mannerisms and omits the virtues—and above all in *Across the River and Into the Trees,* an unconscious self-parody of almost unbelievable fatuity. The peculiar difficulty American creative writers have in maturing has often been commented on. Emotionally, Hemingway was adolescent all his life; intellectually, he was a Philistine on principle. His one great talent was æsthetic—a feeling for style, in his writing and in his life, that was remarkably sure. But the limits of æstheticism unsupported by thought or feeling are severe. Hemingway made one big, original stylistic discovery—or rather he worked it out most consciously with the aid of Gertrude Stein—but when he had gotten everything there was to be gotten out of it (and a bit more) he was unable, as Connolly notes, to invent anything else. He was trapped in his style as a miner might be trapped underground; the oxygen is slowly used up without any new air coming in.

Hemingway's opposites are Stendhal and Tolstoy—interesting he should feel especially awed by them—who had no style at all, no effects. Stendhal wrote the way a police sergeant would write if police sergeants had imagination—a dry, matter-of-fact style. Tolstoy's writing is clear and colourless, interposing no barrier between the reader and the narrative, the kind of direct prose, businesslike and yet Olympian, that one imagines the Recording Angel uses for entries in *his* police blotter. There is no need for change or innovation with such styles, but the more striking and original a style is, obviously the greater such necessity. Protean innovators like Joyce and Picasso invent, exploit, and abandon dozens of styles; Hemingway had only one; it was not enough. But he did write some beautiful short stories while it was working. Perhaps they are enough.

EXERCISE

1. Macdonald says, in Section 3, that Hemingway's importance is almost entirely that of a stylistic innovator. With that opinion in mind, let us turn to Section 1. The content here is, in brief, an account of Hemingway's inner failure as an artist as his importance as a celebrity increased, a failure which, Macdonald implies, has a moral basis and which ends with the suicide. Here is a sad and desperate human story. What effect does Macdonald expect from presenting this desperate story in a parody of Heming-

way's own style? What implied criticism is there, for instance, of the style itself—the thing on which Macdonald says that Hemingway's importance rests? In other words, is Macdonald saying that Hemingway's style would have been adequate for the rendering of his own deeper experience? Do you think Macdonald would have made his points more effectively by general statements?

2. How would you relate implications of this first section to Bishop's comparison of Hemingway and Byron? How would you relate it to Boorstin's essay "From Hero to Celebrity"? (p. 484). What other material in Macdonald's essay could be drawn into relation to Boorstin's essay?

3. In Section I, Macdonald gives two long quotations from Hemingway. One he considers "inspired baby-talk," the other "just baby-talk." Can you see why he approves of one and not of the other? Though this question is unanswerable, in any deep sense, unless you have read *A Farewell to Arms,* try to make a provisional answer.

4. On what points do Bishop and Macdonald agree? From Macdonald's estimate, written after Hemingway's death, how prophetic of the second half of the career do you think Bishop's essay to be? Both Bishop and Macdonald discuss at some length the question of Hemingway's style. Which critic seems to feel more clearly that style is rooted in the period and the general occasion of an author's work? Or is there no difference here between the view of Bishop and that of Macdonald—merely a difference in the way the notion of style is applied to a particular case?

5. There are a good many examples of wit in the essay by Macdonald. Locate them. How do they relate to the tone of the essay? What do you take Macdonald's basic feeling toward Hemingway to be? Does it differ from Bishop's?

6. Merely on the basis of these two essays, how would you describe Bishop's personality? Macdonald's?

Some Lines from Whitman

RANDALL JARRELL (1914-   )

WHITMAN, DICKINSON, and Melville seem to me the best poets of the nineteenth century here in America. Melville's poetry has been grotesquely underestimated, but of course it is only in the last four or five years that it has been much read; in the long run, in spite of the awkwardness and amateurishness of so much of it, it will surely be thought well of. (In the short run it will probably be thought entirely too well of. Melville is a great poet only in the prose of *Moby Dick*.) Dickinson's poetry has been thoroughly read, and well though undifferentiatingly loved—after a few decades or centuries almost everybody will be able to see through Dickinson to her poems. But something odd has happened to the living changing part of Whitman's reputation: nowadays it is people who are not particularly interested in poetry, people who say that they read a poem for what it says, not for how it says it, who admire Whitman most. Whitman is often written about, either approvingly or disapprovingly, as if he were the Thomas Wolfe of nineteenth-century democracy, the hero of a de Mille movie about Walt Whitman. (People even talk about a war in which Walt Whitman and Henry James chose up sides, to begin with, and in which you and I will go on fighting till the day we die.) All this sort of thing, and all the bad poetry that there of course is in Whitman—for any poet has written enough bad poetry to scare away anybody—has helped to scare away from Whitman most "serious readers of modern poetry." They do not talk of his poems, as a rule, with any real liking of knowledge. Serious readers, people who are ashamed of not knowing all of Hopkins by heart, are not at all ashamed to say, "I don't really know Whitman very well." This may harm Whitman in your eyes, they know, but that is a chance that poets have to take. Yet "their" Hopkins, that good critic and great poet, wrote about Whitman, after seeing five or six of his poems in a newspaper review: "I may as well say what I should not otherwise have said, that I always knew in my heart Walt Whitman's mind to be more like my own than any other man's living. As he is a very great scoundrel this is not a very pleasant confession." And Henry James, the leader of "their" side in that awful imaginary war of which I spoke, once read Whitman to Edith Wharton (much as Mozart used to imitate, on the piano, the organ) with such power and solemnity that both sat shaken and silent; it was after this reading that James expressed his regret at Whitman's "too extensive acquaintance with the foreign languages." Almost all the most "original and advanced" poets and critics and readers of the last part of the nineteenth century thought Whitman as original and advanced as themselves, in manner as well as in matter. Can Whitman really be a sort of Thomas Wolfe or Carl Sandburg or Robinson Jeffers or Henry Miller—or a sort of Balzac of poetry, whose every part is crude but whose whole is somehow good? He is not, nor could he be; a poem, like Pope's spider, "lives along the line," and all the dead lines in the world will not make one live poem. As Blake says, "all sublimity is founded on minute discrimination," and it is in these "minute particulars" of Blake's that any poem has its primary existence.

To show Whitman for what he is one does not need to praise or explain or argue, one needs simply to quote. He himself said, "I and mine do not convince by arguments, similes, rhymes,/ We convince by our presence." Even a few of his phrases are enough to show us that Whitman was no sweeping rhetorician, but a poet of the greatest and oddest delicacy and originality and sensitivity, so far as words are concerned. This is, after all, the poet who said, "Blind loving wrestling touch, sheath'd hooded sharptooth'd touch"; who said, "Smartly attired, countenance smiling, form upright, death under the breast-bones, hell under the skull-bones"; who said, "Agonies are one of my changes of garments"; who saw grass as the "flag of my disposition," saw "the sharp-peak'd farmhouse, with its scallop'd scum and slender shoots from the gutters," heard a plane's "wild ascending lisp," and saw and heard how at the amputation "what is removed drops horribly in a pail." This is the poet for whom the sea was "howler and scooper of storms," reaching out to us with "crooked inviting fingers"; who went "leaping chasms with a pike-pointed staff, clinging to topples of

brittle and blue"; who, a runaway slave, saw how "my gore dribs, thinn'd with the ooze of my skin"; who went "lithographing Kronos . . . buying drafts of Osiris"; who stared out at the "little plentiful mannikins skipping around in collars and tail'd coats,/I am aware who they are, (they are positively not worms or fleas)." For he is, at his best, beautifully witty: he says gravely, "I find I incorporate gneiss, coals, longthreaded moss, fruits, grain, esculent roots,/And am stucco'd with quadrupeds and birds all over"; and of these quadrupeds and birds "not one is respectable or unhappy over the whole earth." He calls advice: "Unscrew the locks from the doors! Unscrew the doors from their jambs!" He publishes the results of research: "Having pried through the strata, analyz'd to a hair, counsel'd with doctors and calculated close,/I find no sweeter fat than sticks to my own bones." Everybody remembers how he told the Muse to "cross out please those immensely overpaid accounts,/ That matter of Troy and Achilles' wrath, and Aeneas', Odysseus' wanderings," but his account of the arrival of the "illustrious emigré" here in the New World is even better: "Bluff'd not a bit by drainpipe, gasometer, artificial fertilizers,/Smiling and pleas'd with palpable intent to stay,/She's here, install'd amid the kitchenware." Or he sees, like another Breughel, "the mechanic's wife with the babe at her nipple interceding for every person born,/Three scythes at harvest whizzing in a row from three lusty angels with shirts bagg'd out at their waists,/ The snag-toothed hostler with red hair redeeming sins past and to come"—the passage has enough wit not only (in Johnson's phrase) to keep it sweet, but enough to make it believable. He says:

I project my hat, sit shame-faced, and beg.
Enough! Enough! Enough!
Somehow I have been stunn'd. Stand back!
Give me a little time beyond my cuff'd head, slumbers,
                                    dreams, gaping,
I discover myself on the verge of a usual mistake.

There is in such changes of tone as these the essence of wit. And Whitman is even more farfetched than he is witty; he can say about Doubters, in the most improbable and explosive of juxtapositions: "I know every one of you, I know the sea of torment, doubt, despair and unbelief./How the flukes splash! How they contort rapid as lightning, with splashes and spouts of blood!" Who else would have said about God: "As the hugging and loving bed-fellow sleeps at my side through the night, and withdraws at the break of day with stealthy tread,/ Leaving me baskets cover'd with white towels, swelling the house with their plenty"?—the Psalmist himself, his cup running over, would have looked at Whitman with dazzled eyes. (Whitman was persuaded by friends to hide the fact that it was God he was talking about.) He says, "Flaunt of the sunshine I need not your bask—lie over!" This unusual employment of verbs is usual enough in participle-loving Whitman, who also asks you to "look in my face while I snuff the sidle of evening," or tells you, "I effuse my flesh in eddies, and drift it in lacy jags." Here are some typical beginnings of poems: "City of orgies, walks, and joys. . . . Not heaving from my ribb'd breast only. . . . O take my hand Walt Whitman! Such gliding wonders! Such sights and sounds! Such join'd unended links. . . ." He says to the objects of the world, "You have waited, you always wait, you dumb, beautiful ministers"; sees "the sun and stars that float in the open air,/The apple-shaped earth"; says, "O suns— O grass of graves— O perpetual transfers and promotions,/If you do not say anything how can I say anything?" Not many poets have written better, in queerer and more convincing and more individual language, about the world's *gliding wonders:* the phrase seems particularly right for Whitman. He speaks of those "circling rivers the breath," of the "savage old mother incessantly crying,/To the boy's soul's questions sullenly timing, some drown'd secret hissing"—ends a poem, once, "We have voided all but freedom and our own joy." How can one quote enough? If the reader thinks that all this is like Thomas Wolfe he *is* Thomas Wolfe; nothing else could explain it. Poetry like this is as far as possible from the work of any ordinary rhetorician, whose phrases cascade over us like suds of the oldest and most-advertised detergent.

The interesting thing about Whitman's worst language (for, just as few poets have ever written better, few poets have ever written worse) is how unusually absurd, how really ingeniously bad, such language is. I will quote none of the most famous examples; but even a line like O *culpable! I acknowledge. I exposé!* is not anything that you and I could do—only a man with the most extraordinary feel for language, or none whatsoever, could have cooked up Whitman's worst messes. For instance: what other man in all the history of this planet would have said, "I am a habitan of Vienna"? (One has an immediate vision of him as a sort of French-Canadian halfbreed to whom the Viennese are offering, with trepidation, through the bars of a zoological garden, little mounds of whipped cream.) And *enclaircise*—why, it's as bad as *explicate!* We are right to resent his having made up his own horrors, instead of sticking to the ones that we ourselves employ. But when Whitman says, "I dote on myself, there is that lot of me and all so luscious," we should realize that we are not the only ones who are amused. And the queerly bad and the merely queer and the queerly good will often change into one another without warning: "Hefts of the moving world, at innocent gambols silently rising, freshly exuding,/Scooting obliquely high and low"—not good, but *queer!*—suddenly becomes, "Something I cannot see puts up libidinous prongs,/Seas of bright juice suffuse heaven," and it is sunrise.

But it is not in individual lines and phrases, but in passages of some length, that Whitman is at his best. In the following quotation Whitman has something difficult to express, something that there are many formulas, all bad, for expressing; he expresses it with complete success, in language of the most dazzling originality:

The orchestra whirls me wider than Uranus flies,
It wrenches such ardors from me I did not know I
    possess'd them,
It sails me, I dab with bare feet, they are lick'd by
    the indolent waves,
I am cut by bitter and angry hail, I lose my breath,
Steep'd amid honey'd morphine, my windpipe throt-
    tled in fakes of death,
At length let up again to feel the puzzle of puzzles,
And that we call Being.

One hardly knows what to point at—everything works. But *wrenches* and *did not know I possess'd them;* the incredible *it sails me, I dab with bare feet; lick'd by the indolent; steep'd amid honey'd morphine; my windpipe throttled in fakes of death*—no wonder Crane admired Whitman! This originality, as absolute in its way as that of Berlioz' orchestration, is often at Whitman's command:

I am a dance—play up there! the fit is whirling me
  fast!
I am the ever-laughing—it is new moon and twilight,
I see the hiding of douceurs, I see nimble ghosts
  whichever way I look,
Cache and cache again deep in the ground and sea,
  and where it is neither ground nor sea.
Well do they do their jobs those journeymen divine,
Only from me can they hide nothing, and would not
  if they could,
I reckon I am their boss and they make me a pet
  besides,
And surround me and lead me and run ahead when
  I walk,
To lift their sunning covers to signify me with
  stretch'd arms, and resume the way;
Onward we move, a gay gang of blackguards! with
  mirth-shouting music and wild-flapping pennants
  of joy!

If you did not believe Hopkins' remark about Whitman, that *gay gang of blackguards* ought to shake you. Whitman shares Hopkins' passion for "dappled" effects, but he slides in and out of them with ambiguous swiftness. And he has at his command a language of the calmest and most prosaic reality, one that seems to do no more than present:

The little one sleeps in its cradle.
I lift the gauze and look a long time, and silently
  brush away flies with my hand.

The youngster and the red-faced girl turn aside up
  the bushy hill,
I peeringly view them from the top.

The suicide sprawls on the bloody floor of the bedroom.
I witness the corpse with its dabbled hair, I note
  where the pistol has fallen.

It is like magic: that is, something has been done to us without our knowing how it was done; but if we look at the lines again we see the *gauze, silently, youngster, red-faced, bushy, peeringly, dabbled*—not that this is all we see. "Present! present!" said James; these are presented, put down side by side to form a little "view of life," from the cradle to the last bloody floor of the

bedroom. Very often the things presented form nothing but a list:

The pure contralto sings in the organ loft,
The carpenter dresses his plank, the tongue of his
  foreplane whistles its wild ascending lisp,
The married and unmarried children ride home to
  their Thanksgiving dinner,
The pilot seizes the king-pin, he heaves down with
  a strong arm,
The mate stands braced in the whale-boat, lance
  and harpoon are ready,
The duck-shooter walks by silent and cautious
  stretches,
The deacons are ordained with cross'd hands at the
  altar,
The spinning-girl retreats and advances to the hum
  of the big wheel,
The farmer stops by the bars as he walks on a First-
  day loafe and looks at the oats and rye.
The lunatic is carried at last to the asylum a con-
  firm'd case,
(He will never sleep any more as he did in the cot
  in his mother's bed-room;)
The jour printer with gray head and gaunt jaws
  works at his case,
He turns his quid of tobacco while his eyes blur with
  the manuscript,
The malform'd limbs are tied to the surgeon's table,
What is removed drops horribly in a pail. . . .

It is only a list—but what a list! And how delicately, in what different ways—likeness and opposition and continuation and climax and anticlimax—the transitions are managed, whenever Whitman wants to manage them. Notice them in the next quotation, another "mere list":

The bride unrumples her white dress, the minute-
  hand of the clock moves slowly,
The opium-eater reclines with rigid head and just-
  open'd lips,
The prostitute draggles her shawl, her bonnet bobs
  on her tipsy and pimpled neck. . . .

The first line is joined to the third by *unrumples* and *draggles, white dress* and *shawl*; the second to the third by *rigid head, bobs, tipsy, neck*; the first to the second by *slowly, just-open'd,* and the slowing-down of time in both states. And occasionally one of these lists is metamorphosed into something we have no name for; the man who would call the next quotation a mere list—anybody will feel this—would boil his babies up for soap:

Ever the hard unsunk ground,
Ever the eaters and drinkers, ever the upward and
    downward sun,
Ever myself and my neighbors, refreshing, wicked,
    real,
Ever the old inexplicable query, ever that thorned
    thumb, that breath of itches and thirsts,
Ever the vexer's hoot! hoot! till we find where the
    sly one hides and bring him forth,
Ever the sobbing liquid of life,
Ever the bandage under the chin, ever the trestles
    of death.

Sometimes Whitman will take what would generally be considered an unpromising subject (in this case, a woman peeping at men bathing naked) and treat it with such tenderness and subtlety and understanding that we are ashamed of ourselves for having thought it unpromising, and murmur that Chekhov himself couldn't have treated it better:

Twenty-eight young men bathe by the shore,
Twenty-eight young men and all so friendly,
Twenty-eight years of womanly life and all so lone-
    some.

She owns the fine house by the rise of the bank,
She hides handsome and richly drest aft the blinds of
    the window.

Which of the young men does she like the best?
Ah the homeliest of them is beautiful to her.

Where are you off to, lady? for I see you,
You splash in the water there, yet stay stock still in
    your room.

Dancing and laughing along the beach came the
    twenty-ninth bather,
The rest did not see her, but she saw them and loved
    them.

The beards of the young men glistened with wet, it
    ran from their long hair,
Little streams pass'd all over their bodies.

An unseen hand also pass'd over their bodies,
It descended tremblingly from their temples and ribs.

The young men float on their backs, their white bel-
    lies bulge to the sun, they do not ask who seizes
    fast to them,
They do not know who puffs and declines with
    pendant and bending arch,
They do not know whom they souse with spray.

And in the same poem (that "Song of My-

self" in which one finds half his best work) the writer can say of a sea-fight:

Stretched and still lies the midnight,
Two great hulls motionless on the breast of the
    darkness,
Our vessel riddled and slowly sinking, preparations
    to pass to the one we have conquer'd,
The captain on the quarter-deck coldly giving his
    orders through a countenance white as a sheet,
Near by the corpse of the child that serv'd in the
    cabin,
The dead face of an old salt with long white hair and
    carefully curl'd whiskers,
The flames spite of all that can be done flickering
    aloft and below,
The husky voices of the two or three officers yet fit
    for duty,
Formless stacks of bodies and bodies by themselves,
    dabs of flesh upon the masts and spars,
Cut of cordage, dangle of rigging, slight shock of the
    soothe of waves,
Black and impassive guns, litter of powder-parcels,
    strong scent,
A few large stars overhead, silent and mournful
    shining,
Delicate snuffs of sea-breeze, smells of sedgy grass
    and fields by the shore, death-messages given in
    charge to survivors,
The hiss of the surgeon's knife, the gnawing teeth
    of his saw,
Wheeze, cluck, swash of falling blood, short wild
    scream, and long, dull, tapering groan,
These so, these irretrievable.

There are faults in this passage, and they *do not matter:* the serious truth, the complete realization of these last lines make us remember that few poets have shown more of the tears of things, and the joy of things, and of the reality beneath either tears or joy. Even Whitman's most general or political statements often are good: everybody knows his "When liberty goes out of a place it is not the first to go, nor the second or third to go,/It waits for all the rest to go, it is the last"; these sentences about the United States just before the Civil War may be less familiar:

Are those really Congressmen? are those the great
    Judges? is that the President?
Then I will sleep awhile yet, for I see that these
    States sleep, for reasons;
(With gathering murk, with muttering thunder and
    lambent shoots we all duly awake,
South, North, East, West, inland and seaboard,
    we will surely awake.)

How well, with what firmness and dignity and command, Whitman does such passages! And Whitman's doubts that he has done them or anything else well—ah, there is nothing he does better:

The best I had done seemed to me blank and sus-
picious,
My great thoughts as I supposed them, were they not
in reality meagre?
I am he who knew what it was to be evil,
I too knitted the old knot of contrariety . . .
Saw many I loved in the street or ferry-boat or pub-
lic assembly, yet never told them a word,
Lived the same life with the rest, the same old laugh-
ing, gnawing, sleeping,
Played the part that still looks back on the actor
and actress,
The same old role, the role that is what we make
it . . .

Whitman says once that the "look of the bay mare shames silliness out of me." This is true—sometimes it is true; but more often the silliness and affectation and cant and exaggeration are there shamelessly, the Old Adam that was in Whitman from the beginning and the awful new one that he created to keep it company. But as he says, "I know perfectly well my own egotism,/Know my omnivorous lines and must not write any less." He says over and over that there are in him good and bad, wise and foolish, anything at all and its antonym, and he is telling the truth; there is in him almost everything in the world, so that one responds to him, willingly or unwillingly, almost as one does to the world, that world which makes the hairs of one's flesh stand up, which seems both evil beyond any rejection and wonderful beyond any acceptance. We cannot help seeing that there is something absurd about any judgment we make of its whole—for there is no "point of view" at which we can stand to make the judgment, and the moral categories that mean most to us seem no more to apply to its whole than our spatial or temporal or causal categories seem to apply to its beginning or its end. (But we need no arguments to make our judgments seem absurd—we feel their absurdity without argument.) In some like sense Whitman is a world, a waste with, here and there, systems blazing at random out of the darkness. Only an innocent and rigidly methodical mind will reject it for this disorganization, particularly since there are in it, here and there, little systems as beautifully and astonishingly organized as the rings and satellites of Saturn:

I understand the large hearts of heroes,
The courage of present times and all times,
How the skipper saw the crowded and rudderless
wreck of the steam-ship, and Death chasing it up
and down the storm,
How he knuckled tight and gave not back an inch,
and was faithful of days and faithful of nights,
And chalked in large letters on a board, Be of good
cheer, we will not desert you;
How he follow'd with them and tack'd with them
three days and would not give it up,
How he saved the drifting company at last,
How the lank loose-gown'd women looked when
boated from the side of their prepared graves,
How the silent old-faced infants and the lifted sick,
and the sharp-lipp'd unshaved men;
All this I swallow, it tastes good, I like it well, it be-
comes mine,
I am the man, I suffered, I was there.

In the last lines of this quotation Whitman has reached—as great writers always reach—a point at which criticism seems not only unnecessary but absurd: these lines are so good that even admiration feels like insolence, and one is ashamed of anything that one can find to say about them. How anyone can dismiss or accept patronizingly the man who wrote them, I do not understand.

The enormous and apparent advantage of form, of omission and selection, of the highest degree of organization, are accompanied by important disadvantages—and there are far greater works than *Leaves of Grass* to make us realize this. But if we compare Whitman with that very beautiful poet Alfred Tennyson, the most skillful of all Whitman's contemporaries, we are at once aware of how limiting Tennyson's forms have been, of how much Tennyson has had to leave out, even in those discursive poems where he is trying to put everything in. Whitman's poems *represent* his world and himself much more satisfactorily than Tennyson's do his. In the past a few poets have both formed and represented, each in the highest degree; but in modern times what controlling, organizing, selecting poet has created a world with as much in it as Whitman's, a world that so plainly *is* the world? Of all modern poets he has, quantitatively speaking, "the most comprehensive soul"—and, qualitatively, a most comprehensive and comprehending one, with charities and concessions and qualifications that are rare in any time.

"Do I contradict myself? Very well then I contradict myself," wrote Whitman, as everybody remembers, and this is not naïve, or something he got from Emerson, or a complacent pose. When you organize one of the contradictory elements out of your work of art, you are getting rid not just of it, but of the contradiction of which it was a part; and it is the contradictions in works of art which make them able to represent to us—as logical and methodical generalizations cannot—our world and our selves, which are also full of contradictions. In Whitman we do not get the controlled, compressed, seemingly concordant contradictions of the great lyric poets, of a poem like, say, Hardy's "During Wind and Rain"; Whitman's contradictions are sometimes announced openly, but are more often scattered at random throughout the poems. For instance: Whitman specializes in ways of saying that there is in some sense (a very Hegelian one, generally) no evil—he says a hundred times that evil is not Real; but he also specializes in making lists of the evil of the world, lists of an unarguable reality. After his minister has recounted "the rounded catalogue divine complete," Whitman comes home and puts down what has been left out: "the countless (nineteen-twentieths) low and evil, crude and savage . . . the barren soil, the evil men, the slag and hideous rot." He ends another such catalogue with the plain unexcusing "All these—all meanness and agony without end I sitting look out upon,/See, hear, and am silent." Whitman offered himself to everybody, and said brilliantly and at length what a good thing he was offering:

Sure as the most certain sure, plumb in the uprights,
  well entretied, braced in the beams,
Stout as a horse, affectionate, haughty, electrical,
I and this mystery here we stand.

Just for oddness, characteristicalness, differentness, what more could you ask in a letter of recommendation? (Whitman sounds as if he were recommending a house—haunted, but what foundations!) But after a few pages he is oddly different:

Apart from the pulling and hauling stands what I am,
Stands amused, complacent, compassionating, idle,
  unitary,
Looks down, is erect, or bends an arm on an impalpable certain rest
Looking with side curved head curious what will
  come next,
Both in and out of the game and watching and wondering at it.

Tamburlaine is already beginning to sound like Hamlet: the employer feels uneasily, *Why, I might as well hire myself* . . . And, a few pages later, Whitman puts down in ordinary-sized type, in the middle of the page, this warning to any *new person drawn toward me:*

Do you think I am trusty and faithful?
Do you see no further than this façade, this smooth
  and tolerant manner of me?
Do you suppose yourself advancing on real ground
  toward a real heroic man?
Have you no thought O dreamer that it may be all
  maya, illusion?

Having wonderful dreams, telling wonderful lies, was a temptation Whitman could never resist; but telling the truth was a temptation he could never resist, either. When you buy him you know what you are buying. And only an innocent and solemn and systematic mind will condemn him for his contradictions: Whitman's catalogues of evils represent realities, and his denials of their reality represent other realities, of feeling and intuition and desire. If he is faithless to logic, to Reality As It Is—whatever that is—he is faithful to the feel of things, to reality as it seems; this is all that a poet has to be faithful to, and philosophers even have been known to leave logic and Reality for it.

Whitman is more co-ordinate and parallel than anybody, is *the* poet of parallel present participles, of twenty verbs joined by a single subject: all this helps to give his work its feeling of raw hypnotic reality, of being that world which also streams over us joined only by *ands,* until we supply the subordinating conjunctions; and since as children we see the *ands* and not the *becauses,* this method helps to give Whitman some of the freshness of childhood. How inexhaustibly *interesting* the world is in Whitman! Arnold all his life kept wishing that we could see the world "with a plainness as near, as flashing" as that with which Moses and Rebekah and the Argonauts saw it. He asked with elegiac nostalgia, "Who can see the green earth any more/As she was by the sources of Time?"—and all the time there was somebody alive who saw it so, as plain and near and flashing, and with a kind of calm, pastoral, biblical dignity and elegance as well, sometimes. The *thereness* and *suchness* of the world are incarnate in Whitman as they are in few other writers.

They might have put on his tombstone WALT WHITMAN: HE HAD HIS NERVE. He is the rashest, the most inexplicable and unlikely—the most impossible, one wants to say—of poets. He somehow *is* in a class by himself, so that one compares him with other poets about as readily as one compares *Alice* with other books. (Even his free verse has a completely different effect from anybody else's.) Who would think of comparing him with Tennyson or Browning or Arnold or Baudelaire?—it is Homer, or the sagas, or something far away and long ago, that comes to one's mind only to be dismissed; for sometimes Whitman *is* epic, just as *Moby Dick* is, and it surprises us to be able to use truthfully this word that we have misused so many times. Whitman *is* grand, and elevated, and comprehensive, and real with an astonishing reality, and many other things—the critic points at his qualities in despair and wonder, all method failing, and simply calls them by their names. And the range of these qualities is the most extraordinary thing of all. We can surely say about him, "He was a man, take him for all in all. I shall not look upon his like again"—and wish that people had seen this and not tried to be his like: one Whitman is miracle enough, and when he comes again it will be the end of the world.

I have said so little about Whitman's faults because they are so plain: baby critics who have barely learned to complain of the lack of ambiguity in *Peter Rabbit* can tell you all that is wrong with *Leaves of Grass*. But a good many of my readers must have felt that it is ridiculous to write an essay about the obvious fact that Whitman is a great poet. It is ridiculous— just as, in 1851, it would have been ridiculous for anyone to write an essay about the obvious fact that Pope was no "classic of our prose" but a great poet. Critics have to spend half their

time reiterating whatever ridiculously obvious things their age or the critics of their age have found it necessary to forget: they say despairingly, at parties, that Wordsworth is a great poet, and *won't* bore you, and tell Mr. Leavis that Milton is a great poet whose deposition *hasn't* been accomplished with astonishing ease by a few words from Eliot and Pound . . . There is something essentially ridiculous about critics, anyway: what is good is good without our saying so, and beneath all our majesty we know this.

Let me finish by mentioning another quality of Whitman's—a quality, delightful to me, that I have said nothing of. If some day a tourist notices, among the ruins of New York City, a copy of *Leaves of Grass*, and stops and picks it up and reads some lines in it, she will be able to say to herself: "How very American! If he and his country had not existed, it would have been impossible to imagine them."

EXERCISE

1. Compare the method of this essay with that of Macdonald's. To approach the matter in another way, which of the two, Jarrell or Macdonald, places more confidence in the critic's analyses and in his judgment?

2. What different kinds of style does Whitman, according to this critic, employ? What examples of critical analysis do you find Jarrell using in distinguishing these styles?

3. Macdonald attacks Hemingway's style because it is lacking in precisely articulated logical relationships—because it is "paratactical." Yet Whitman's style is "paratactical," too, and Jarrell, without using the technical term, praises him for this. What are we to make of this? Or can we make anything of it unless we go behind the mere syntax of the work and relate the work, to its general basis on feeling and ideas? How would you undertake to defend Whitman on this count? How does Jarrell defend him?

4. You have read some of Jarrell's own poetry. On the basis of that do you find it natural that he should admire Whitman?

5. Jarrell, as a critic, is well known for his wit. What instances do you find in this essay? For what purpose is it used? At whose expense? How does this differ from Macdonald's practice?

6. At the end of the essay Jarrell says: "There is something essentially ridiculous about critics, anyway." What does he mean? Having decided what he means, what do you think of what he means?

Robert Frost

W. H. AUDEN (1907-   )

> *But Islands of the Blessed, bless you son,*
> *I never came upon a blessed one.*

IF ASKED who said *Beauty is Truth, Truth Beauty!*, a great many readers would answer "Keats." But Keats said nothing of the sort. It is what he said the Grecian Urn said, his description and criticism of a certain kind of work of art, the kind from which the evils and problems of this life, the "heart high sorrowful and cloyed," are deliberately excluded. The Urn, for example, depicts, among other beautiful sights, the citadel of a hill town; it does not depict warfare, the evil which makes the citadel necessary.

Art arises out of our desire for both beauty and truth and our knowledge that they are not identical. One might say that every poem shows some sign of a rivalry between Ariel and Prospero; in every good poem their relation is more or less happy, but it is never without its tensions. The Grecian Urn states Ariel's position; Prospero's has been equally succinctly stated by Dr. Johnson: *The only end of writing is to enable the readers better to enjoy life or better to endure it.*

We want a poem to be beautiful, that is to say, a verbal earthly paradise, a timeless world of pure play, which gives us delight precisely because of its contrast to our historical existence with all its insoluble problems and inescapable suffering; at the same time we want a poem to be true, that is to say, to provide us with some kind of revelation about our life which will show us what life is really like and free us from self-enchantment and deception, and a poet cannot bring us any truth without introducing into his poetry the problematic, the painful, the disorderly, the ugly. Though every poem involves *some* degree of collaboration between Ariel and Prospero, the role of each varies in importance from one poem to another: it is usually possible to say of a poem and, sometimes, of the whole output of a poet, that it is Ariel-dominated or Prospero-dominated.

> Hot sun, cool fire, tempered with sweet air,
> Black shade, fair nurse, shadow my white hair:
> Shine, sun; burn, fire; breathe, air, and ease me;
> Black shade, fair nurse, shroud me and please me:
> Shadow, my sweet nurse, keep me from burning,
> Make not my glad cause, cause for mourning,
> > Let not my beauty's fire
> > Inflame unstaid desire,
> > Nor pierce any bright eye
> > That wandereth lightly.
> > > (GEORGE PEELE, "Bathsabe's Song.")

> The road at the top of the rise
> Seems to come to an end
> And take off into the skies.
> So at a distant bend
>
> It seems to go into a wood,
> The place of standing still
> As long as the trees have stood.
> But say what Fancy will,
>
> The mineral drops that explode
> To drive my ton of car
> Are limited to the road.
> They deal with the near and far,
>
> And have almost nothing to do
> With the absolute flight and rest
> The universal blue
> And local green suggest.
> > (ROBERT FROST,
> > > "The Middleness of the Road.")

Both poems are written in the first person singular, but the Peele-Bathsabe *I* is very different from the Frost *I*. The first seems anonymous, hardly more than a grammatical form; one cannot imagine meeting Bathsabe at a dinner party. The second *I* names a historical individual in a specific situation—he is driving an automobile in a certain kind of landscape.

Take away what Bathsabe says and she

vanishes, for what she says does not seem to be a response to any situation or event. If one asks what her song is about, one cannot give a specific answer, only a vague one:—a beautiful young girl, any beautiful girl, on any sunny morning, half-awake and half-asleep, is reflecting on her beauty with a mixture of self-admiration and pleasing fear, pleasing because she is unaware of any real danger; a girl who was really afraid of a Peeping Tom would sing very differently. If one tries to explain why one likes the song, or any poem of this kind, one finds oneself talking about language, the handling of the rhythm, the pattern of vowels and consonants, the placing of caesuras, epanorthosis, etc.

Frost's poem, on the other hand, is clearly a response to an experience which preceded any words and without which the poem could not have come into being, for the purpose of the poem is to define that experience and draw wisdom from it. Though the beautiful verbal element is not absent—it is a poem, not a passage of informative prose—this is subordinate in importance to the truth of what it says.

If someone suddenly asks me to give him an example of good poetry, it is probably a poem of the Peele sort which will immediately come to my mind: but if I am in a state of emotional excitement, be it joy or grief, and try to think of a poem which is relevant and illuminating to my condition, it is a poem of the Frost sort which I shall be most likely to recall.

Ariel, as Shakespeare has told us, has no passions. That is his glory and his limitation. The earthly paradise is a beautiful place but nothing of serious importance can occur in it.

An anthology selected by Ariel, including only poems like the *Eclogues* of Vergil, *Las Soledades* of Góngora and poets like Campion, Herrick, Mallarmé, would, in the long run, repel us by its narrowness and monotony of feeling: for Ariel's other name is Narcissus.

It can happen that a poem which, when written, was Prospero-dominated, becomes an Ariel poem for later generations. The nursery rhyme *I will sing you One O* may very well originally have been a mnemonic rhyme for teaching sacred lore of the highest importance. The sign that, for us, it has become an Ariel poem is that we have no curiosity about the

various persons it refers to: it is as anthropologists not as readers of poetry that we ask who the lily-white boys really were. On the other hand, anything we can learn about the persons whom Dante introduces into *The Divine Comedy*, contributes to our appreciation of his poem.

It is also possible for a poet himself to be mistaken as to the kind of poem he is writing. For example, at first reading, *Lycidas* seems to be by Prospero, for it purports to deal with the most serious matters possible—death, grief, sin, resurrection. But I believe this to be an illusion. On closer inspection, it seems to me that only the robes are Prospero's and that Ariel has dressed up in them for fun, so that it is as irrelevant to ask, "Who is the Pilot of the Galilean Lake?" as it is to ask, "Who is the Pobble who has no toes?" and He who walks the waves is merely an Arcadian shepherd whose name happens to be Christ. If *Lycidas* is read in this way, as if it were a poem by Edward Lear, then it seems to me one of the most beautiful poems in the English language: if, however, it is read as the Prospero poem it apparently claims to be, then it must be condemned, as Dr. Johnson condemned it, for being unfeeling and frivolous, since one expects wisdom and revelation and it provides neither.

The Ariel-dominated poet has one great advantage; he can only fail in one way—his poem may be trivial. The worst one can say of one of his poems is that it needn't have been written. But the Prospero-dominated poet can fail in a number of different ways. Of all English poets, Wordsworth is perhaps the one with the least element of Ariel that is compatible with being a poet at all, and so provides the best examples of what happens when Prospero tries to write entirely by himself.

The Bird and Cage they both were his:
'Twas my Son's bird: and neat and trim
He kept it; many voyages
This singing bird has gone with him:
When last he sailed he left the bird behind;
As it might be, perhaps from bodings in his mind.

Reading such a passage, one exclaims, "The man can't write," which is something that can never be said about Ariel; when Ariel can't write, he doesn't. But Prospero is capable of graver errors than just being ridiculous; since he is trying to say something which is true, if he fails, the result can be worse than trivial. It can be false, compelling the reader to say, not "This poem need not have been written," but "This poem should not have been written."

Both in theory and practice Frost is a Prospero-dominated poet. In the preface to his *Collected Poems,* he writes:

The sound is the gold in the ore. Then we will have the sound out alone and dispense with the inessential. We do till we make the discovery that the object in writing poetry is to make all poems sound as different as possible from each other, and the resources for that of vowels, consonants, punctuation, syntax, words, sentences, meter are not enough. We need the help of context—meaning—subject matter. . . . And we are back in poetry as merely one more art of having something to say, sound or unsound. Probably better if sound, because deeper and from wider experience. [A poem] begins in delight and ends in wisdom . . . a clarification of life—not necessarily a great clarification such as sects and cults are founded on, but in a momentary stay against confusion.

His poetic style is what I think Professor C. S. Lewis would call Good Drab. The music is always that of the speaking voice, quiet and sensible, and I cannot think of any other modern poet, except Cavafy, who uses language more simply. He rarely employs metaphors, and there is not a word, not a historical or literary reference in the whole of his work which would be strange to an unbookish boy of fifteen. Yet he manages to make this simple kind of speech express a wide variety of emotion and experience.

> Be that as may be, she was in their song.
> Moreover her voice upon their voices crossed
> Had now persisted in the woods so long
> That probably it would never be lost.
> Never again would bird's song be the same.
> And to do that to birds was why she came.
>
> .   .   .   .   .
>
> I hope if he is where he sees me now
> He's so far off he can't see what I've come to.
> You *can* come down from everything to nothing.
> All is, if I'd a-known when I was young
> And full of it, that this would be the end,
> It doesn't seem as if I'd had the courage
> To make so free and kick up in folk's faces.
> I might have, but it doesn't seem as if.

The emotions in the first passage are tender, happy, and its reflections of a kind which could

only be made by an educated man. The emotions in the second are violent and tragic, and the speaker a woman with no schooling. Yet the diction in both is equally simple. There are a few words the man uses which the woman would not use herself, but none she could not understand; her syntax is a little cruder than his, but only a little. Yet their two voices sound as distinct as they sound authentic.

Frost's poetic speech is the speech of a mature mind, fully awake and in control of itself; it is not the speech of dream or of uncontrollable passion. Except in reported speech, interjections, imperatives and rhetorical interrogatives are rare. This does not mean, of course, that his poems are lacking in feeling; again and again, one is aware of strong, even violent, emotion behind what is actually said, but the saying is reticent, the poetry has, as it were, an auditory chastity. It would be impossible for Frost, even if he wished, to produce an unabashed roar of despair, as Shakespeare's tragic heroes so often can, but the man who wrote the following lines has certainly been acquainted with despair.

> I have stood still and stopped the sound of feet
> When far away an interrupted cry
> Came over houses from another street,
> But not to call me back or say good-bye.
> And further still at an unearthly height
> One luminary clock against the sky
> Proclaimed the time was neither wrong nor right.
> I have been one acquainted with the night.

Every style has its limitations. It would be as impossible to write "Ebauche d'un Serpent" in the style of Frost as it would be to write "The Death of the Hired Man" in the style of Valéry. A style, like Frost's which approximates to ordinary speech is necessarily contemporary, the style of a man living in the first half of the twentieth century; it is not well suited, therefore, to subjects from the distant past, in which the difference between then and today is significant, or to mythical subjects which are timeless.

Neither Frost's version of the Job story in *A Masque of Reason* nor his version of the Jonah story in *A Masque of Mercy* seems to me quite to come off; both are a little self-consciously in modern dress.

Nor is such a style well-suited to official

public occasions when a poet must speak about and on behalf of the *Civitas Terrenae*. Frost's tone of voice, even in his dramatic pieces, is that of a man talking to himself, thinking aloud and hardly aware of an audience. This manner is, of course, like all manners, calculated, and more sophisticated than most. The calculation is sound when the poems are concerned with personal emotions, but when the subject is one of public affairs or ideas of general interest, it may be a miscalculation. "Build Soil, a Political Pastoral" which Frost composed for the National Party Convention at Columbia University in 1932, was much criticized at the time by the Liberal-Left for being reactionary. Reading it today, one wonders what all their fuss was about, but the fireside-chat I'm-a-plain-fellow manner is still irritating. One finds oneself wishing that Columbia had invited Yeats instead; he might have said the most outrageous things, but he would have put on a good act, and that is what we want from a poet when he speaks to us of what concerns us, not as private persons but as citizens. Perhaps Frost himself felt uneasy, for the last two lines of the poem, and the best, run thus:

> We're too unseparate. And going home
> From company means coming to our senses.

Any poetry which aims at being a clarification of life must be concerned with two questions about which all men, whether they read poetry or not, seek clarification.

1) *Who am I?* What is the difference between man and all other creatures? What relations are possible between them? What is man's status in the universe? What are the conditions of his existence which he must accept as his fate which no wishing can alter?

2) *Whom ought I to become?* What are the characteristics of the hero, the authentic man whom everybody should admire and try to become? Vice versa, what are the characteristics of the churl, the unauthentic man whom everybody should try to avoid becoming?

We all seek answers to these questions which shall be universally valid under all circumstances, but the experiences to which we put them are always local both in time and place. What any poet has to say about man's status in nature, for example, depends in part upon the landscape and climate he happens to live in and in part upon the reactions to it of his personal temperament. A poet brought up in the tropics cannot have the same vision as a poet brought up in Hertfordshire and, if they inhabit the same landscape, the chirpy social endomorph will give a different picture of it from that of the melancholic withdrawn ectomorph.

The nature in Frost's poetry is the nature of New England. New England is made of granite, is mountainous, densely wooded, and its soil is poor. It has a long severe winter, a summer that is milder and more pleasant than in most parts of the States, a short and sudden Spring, a slow and theatrically beautiful fall. Since it adjoins the eastern seaboard, it was one of the first areas to be settled but, as soon as the more fertile lands to the West were opened up, it began to lose population. Tourists and city dwellers who can afford a summer home may arrive for the summer, but much land which was once cultivated has gone back to the wild.

One of Frost's favorite images is the image of the abandoned house. In Britain or Europe, a ruin recalls either historical change, political acts like war or enclosure, or, in the case of abandoned mine buildings, a successful past which came to an end, not because nature was too strong, but because she had been robbed of everything she possessed. A ruin in Europe, therefore, tends to arouse reflections about human injustice and greed and the nemesis that overtakes human pride. But in Frost's poetry, a ruin is an image of human heroism, of a defense in the narrow pass against hopeless odds.

> I came an errand one cloud-blowing morning
> To a slab-built, black-paper-covered house
> Of one room and one window and one door,
> The only dwelling in a waste cut over
> A hundred square miles round it in the mountains:
> And that not dwelt in now by men or women.
> (It never had been dwelt in, though, by women.)
>
> .   .   .   .   .
>
> Here further up the mountain slope
> Than there was ever any hope,
> My father built, enclosed a spring,
> Strung chains of wall round everything,

Subdued the growth of earth to grass,
And brought our various lives to pass.
A dozen girls and boys we were.
The mountain seemed to like the stir
And made of us a little while—
With always something in her smile.
To-day she wouldn't know our name.
(No girl's of course has stayed the same.)
The mountain pushed us off her knees.
And now her lap is full of trees.

Thumbing through Frost's *Collected Poems,* I find twenty-one in which the season is winter as compared with five in which it is spring, and in two of these there is still snow on the ground; I find twenty-seven in which the time is night and seventeen in which the weather is stormy.

The commonest human situation in his poetry is of one man, or a man and wife, alone in a small isolated house in a snowbound forest after dark.

Where I could think of no thoroughfare,
Away on the mountain up far too high,
A blinding headlight shifted glare
And began to bounce down a granite stair
Like a star fresh-fallen out of the sky,
And I away in my opposite wood
Am touched by that unintimate light
And made feel less alone than I rightly should,
For traveler there could do me no good
Were I in trouble with night tonight.

     .   .   .   .   .

We looked and looked, but after all where are we?
Do we know any better where we are,
And how it stands between the night tonight
And a man with a smokey lantern chimney,
How different from the way it ever stood?

In "Two Look at Two," nature, as represented by a buck stag and a doe, responds in sympathy to man, as represented by a boy and girl, but the point of the poem is that this sympathetic response is a miraculous exception. The normal response is that described in "The Most of It."

Some morning from the boulder-broken beach
He would cry out on life that what it wants
Is not its own love back in copy speech,
But counter-love, original response.
And nothing ever came of what he cried
Unless it was the embodiment that crashed
In the cliff's talus on the other side,
And then in the far distant water splashed,
But after a time allowed for it to swim,
Instead of proving human when it neared
And some one else additional to him,
As a great buck it powerfully appeared . . .

Nature, however, is not to Frost, as she was to Melville, malignant.

It must be a little more in favor of man,
Say a fraction of one per cent at least,
Or our number living wouldn't be steadily more.

She is, rather, the Dura Virum Nutrix who, by her apparent indifference and hostility, even, calls forth all man's powers and courage and makes a real man of him.

Courage is not to be confused with romantic daring. It includes caution and cunning,

All we who prefer to live
Have a little whistle we give,
And flash at the least alarm
We dive down under the farm

and even financial prudence,

Better to do down dignified
With boughten friendship at your side
Then none at all. Provide, provide!

There have been European poets who have come to similar conclusions about the isolation of the human condition, and nature's indifference to human values, but, compared with an American, they are at a disadvantage in expressing them. Living as they do in a well, even overpopulated, countryside where, thanks to centuries of cultivation, Mother Earth has acquired human features, they are forced to make abstract philosophical statements or use uncommon atypical images, so that what they say seems to be imposed upon them by theory and temperament rather than by facts. An American poet like Frost, on the other hand, can appeal to facts for which any theory must account and which any temperament must admit.

The Frostian man is isolated not only in space but also in time. In Frost's poems the nostalgic note is seldom, if ever, struck. When he writes a poem about childhood like "Wild Grapes," childhood is not seen as a magical Eden which will all too soon, alas, be lost, but as a school in which the first lessons of adult life are learned. The setting of one of his best long poems, "The Generations of Man," is the ancestral home of the Stark family in the town of Bow, New Hampshire. Bow is a rock-strewn township where farming has fallen off and sproutlands flourish since the axe has gone. The Stark family mansion is by now reduced to an old cellar-hole at the side of a by-road. The occasion described in the poem is a gathering together from all over of the Stark descendants, an advertising stunt thought up by the governor of the state. The characters are a boy Stark and a girl Stark, distant cousins, who meet at the cellar-hole and are immediately attracted to each other. Their conversation turns, naturally, to their common ancestors, but, in fact, they know nothing about them. The boy starts inventing stories and doing imaginary imitations of their voices as a way of courtship, making their ancestors hint at marriage and suggest building a new summer home on the site of the old house. The real past, that is to say, is unknown and unreal to them; its role in the poem is to provide a lucky chance for the living to meet.

Like Gray, Frost has written a poem on a deserted graveyard. Gray is concerned with the possible lives of the unknown dead; the past is more imaginatively exciting to him than the present. But Frost does not try to remember anything; what moves him is that death, which is always a present terror, is no longer present here, having moved on like a pioneer.

> It would be easy to be clever
> And tell the stones; men hate to die
> And have stopped dying now for ever.
> I think they would believe the lie.

What he finds valuable in man's temporal existence is the ever-recurrent opportunity of the present moment to make a discovery or a new start.

> One of the lies would make it out that nothing
> Ever presents itself before us twice.
> Where would we be at last if that were so?
> Our very life depends on everything's
> Recurring till we answer from within.
> The thousandth time may prove the charm.

Frost has written a number of pastoral eclogues and, no doubt, has taken a sophisticated pleasure in using what is, by tradition, the most aristocratic and idyllic of all literary forms to depict democratic realities. If the landscape of New England is unarcadian, so is its social life; the leisured class with nothing to do but cultivate its sensibility which the European pastoral presupposes, is simply not there. Of course, as in all societies, social distinctions exist. In New Eng-

land, Protestants of Anglo-Scotch stock consider themselves a cut above Roman Catholics and those of a Latin race, and the most respectable Protestant denominations are the Congregationalists and the Unitarians. Thus, in "The Ax-Helve," the Yankee farmer is aware of his social condescension in entering the house of his French-Canadian neighbor, Baptiste.

> I shouldn't mind his being overjoyed
> (If overjoyed he was) at having got me
> Where I must judge if what he knew about an ax
> That not everybody else knew was to count
> For nothing in the measure of a neighbor.
> Hard if, though cast away for life with Yankees,
> A Frenchman couldn't get his human rating!

And in "Snow," Mrs. Cole passes judgment upon the Evangelical preacher, Meserve.

> I detest the thought of him
> With his ten children under ten years old.
> I hate his wretched little Racker Sect,
> All's ever I heard of it, which isn't much.

Yet in both poems the neighbor triumphs over the snob. The Yankee acknowledges Baptiste's superior skill, and the Coles stay up all night in concern until they hear that Meserve has reached home safely through the storm.

In the Frost pastoral, the place of the traditional worldly-wise, world-weary courtier is taken by the literary city dweller, often a college student who has taken a job for the summer on a farm; the rustics he encounters are neither comic bumpkins nor noble savages.

In "A Hundred Collars," a refined shy college professor meets in a small town hotel bedroom a fat whisky-drinking vulgarian who canvasses the farms around on behalf of a local newspaper. If, in the end, the reader's sympathies go to the vulgarian, the vulgarian is not made aesthetically appealing nor the professor unpleasant. The professor means well—he is a democrat, if not at heart, in principle—but he is the victim of a way of life which has narrowed his human sympathies and interests. The vulgarian is redeemed by his uninhibited friendliness which is perfectly genuine, not a professional salesman's manner. Though vulgar, he is not a go-getter.

> 'One would suppose they might not be as glad
> to see you as you are to see them.'
>   'Oh,

Because I want their dollar? I don't want
Anything they've got. I never dun.
I'm there, and they can pay me if they like.
I go nowhere on purpose: I happen by.'

In "The Code," a town-bred farmer unwittingly offends one of his hired hands.

'What is there wrong?'
        'Something you just now said.'
'What did I say?'
        'About our taking pains.'
'To cock the hay—because it's going to
        shower?
I said that more than half an hour ago.
I said it to myself as much as you.'
'You didn't know. But James is one big fool.
He thought you meant to find fault with his
        work,
That's what the average farmer would have
        meant.' . . .
'He's a fool if that's the way he takes me.'
'Don't let it bother you. You've found out
        something.
The hand that knows his business won't be
        told
To do work better or faster—those two
        things. . . .'

The ignorance of the town-bred farmer is made use of, not to blame him, but to praise the quality which, after courage, Frost ranks as the highest of the virtues, the self-respect which comes from taking a pride in something. It may be a pride in one's own skill, the pride of the axe-maker Baptiste, the pride of the Hired Man who dies from a broken heart since old age has taken from him the one accomplishment, building a load of hay, which had hitherto prevented him from feeling utterly worthless, or it may be a pride which, from a worldly point of view, is a folly, the pride of the man who has failed as a farmer, burned his house down for the insurance money, bought a telescope with the proceeds and taken a lowly job as a ticket agent on the railroad. The telescope is not a good one, the man is poor, but he is proud of his telescope and happy.

Every poet is at once a representative of his culture and its critic. Frost has never written satires, but it is not hard to guess what, as an American, he approves and disapproves of in his own countrymen. The average American is a stoic and, contrary to what others are apt to conclude from his free-and-easy friendly manner, reticent, far more reticent than the average Englishman about showing his feelings. He believes in independence because he has to; life is too mobile and circumstances change too fast for him to be supported by any fixed frame of family or social relations. In a crisis he will help his neighbor, whoever he may be, but he will regard someone who is always coming for help as a bad neighbor, and he disapproves of all self-pity and nostalgic regret. All these qualities find their expression in Frost's poetry, but there are other American characteristics which are not to be found there, the absence of which implies disapproval; the belief, for instance, that it should be possible, once the right gimmick has been found, to build the New Jerusalem on earth in half an hour. One might describe Frost as a Tory, provided that one remembers that all American political parties are Whigs.

Hardy, Yeats and Frost have all written epitaphs for themselves.

Hardy
I never cared for life, life cared for me.
And hence I owe it some fidelity. . . .

Yeats
Cast a cold eye
On life and death.
Horseman, pass by.

Frost
I would have written of me on my stone
I had a lover's quarrel with the world.

Of the three, Frost, surely, comes off best. Hardy seems to be stating the Pessimist's Case rather than his real feelings. I never cared . . . *Never?* Now, Mr. Hardy, really! Yeats' horseman is a stage prop; the passer-by is much more likely to be a motorist. But Frost convinces me that he is telling neither more nor less than the truth about himself. And, when it comes to wisdom, is not having a lover's quarrel with life more worthy of Prospero than not caring or looking coldly?

EXERCISE

Compose a set of questions on this essay, touching on its line of thought, comparing it in method and intention with other essays you have here read, and using what you know about Frost's work from other sources.

Why Do We Read Fiction?

ROBERT PENN WARREN (1905-   )

WHY DO we read fiction? The answer is simple. We read it because we like it. And we like it because fiction, as an image of life, stimulates and gratifies our interest in life. But whatever interests may be appealed to by fiction, the special and immediate interest that takes us to fiction is always our interest in a story.

A story is not merely an image of life, but of life in motion—specifically, the presentation of individual characters moving through their particular experiences to some end that we may accept as meaningful. And the experience that is characteristically presented in a story is that of facing a problem, a conflict. To put it bluntly: No conflict, no story.

It is no wonder that conflict should be at the center of fiction, for conflict is at the center of life. But why should we, who have the constant and often painful experience of conflict in life and who yearn for inner peace and harmonious relation with the outer world, turn to fiction, which is the image of conflict? The fact is that our attitude toward conflict is ambivalent. If we do find a totally satisfactory adjustment in life, we tend to sink into the drowse of the accustomed. Only when our surroundings—or we ourselves—become problematic again do we wake up and feel that surge of energy which is life. And life more abundantly lived is what we seek.

So we, at the same time that we yearn for peace, yearn for the problematic. The adventurer, the sportsman, the gambler, the child playing hide-and-seek, the teen-age boys choosing up sides for a game of sandlot baseball, the old grad cheering in the stadium—we all, in fact, seek out or create problematic situations of greater or lesser intensity. Such situations give us a sense of heightened energy, of life. And fiction, too, gives us that heightened awareness of life, with all the fresh, uninhibited opportunity to vent the rich emotional charge—tears, laughter, tenderness, sympathy, hate, love, and irony—that is stored up in us and short-circuited in the drowse of the accustomed. Furthermore, this heightened awareness can be more fully relished now, because what in actuality would be the threat of the problematic is here tamed to mere imagination, and because some kind of resolution of the problem is, owing to the very nature of fiction, promised.

The story promises us a resolution, and we wait in suspense to learn how things will come out. We are in suspense, not only about what will happen, but even more about what the event will mean. We are in suspense about the story in fiction because we are in suspense about another story far closer and more important to us —the story of our own life as we live it. We do not know how that story of our own life is going to come out. We do not know what it will mean. So, in that deepest suspense of life, which will be shadowed in the suspense we feel about the story in fiction, we turn to fiction for some slight hint about the story in the life we live. The relation of our life to the fictional life is what, in a fundamental sense, takes us to fiction.

Even when we read, as we say, to "escape," we seek to escape not from life but to life, to a life more satisfying than our own drab version. Fiction gives us an image of life—sometimes of a life we actually have and like to dwell on, but often and poignantly of one we have had but do not have now, or one we have never had and can never have. The ardent fisherman, when his rheumatism keeps him housebound, reads stories from *Field and Stream*. The baseball fan reads *You Know Me, Al,* by Ring Lardner. The little co-ed, worrying about her snub nose and her low mark in Sociology 2, dreams of being a debutante out of F. Scott Fitzgerald; and the thin-chested freshman, still troubled by acne, dreams of being a granite-jawed Neanderthal out of Mickey Spillane. When the Parthians in 53 B.C. beat Crassus, they found in the baggage of Roman officers some very juicy items called *Milesian Tales,* by a certain Aristides of Miletus; and I have a friend who in A.D. 1944, supplemented his income as a GI by reading aloud *Forever Amber,* by a certain Kathleen Winsor, to buddies who found that the struggle over three-syllable words somewhat impaired their dedication to that improbable daydream.

And that is what, for all of us, fiction, in one sense, is—a daydream. It is, in other words, an imaginative enactment. In it we find, in imagination, not only the pleasure of recognizing the world we know and of reliving our past, but also the pleasure of entering worlds we do not know and of experimenting with experiences which we deeply crave but which the limitations of life, the fear of consequences, or the severity of our principles forbid to us. Fiction can give us this pleasure without any painful consequences, for there is no price tag on the magic world of imaginative enactment. But fiction does not give us only what we want; more importantly, it may give us things we hadn't even known we wanted.

In this sense then, fiction painlessly makes up for the defects of reality. Long ago Francis Bacon said that poetry—which, in his meaning, would include our fiction—is "agreeable to the spirit of man" because it affords "a greater grandeur of things, a more perfect order, and a more beautiful variety" than can "anywhere be found in nature. . . ." More recently we find Freud putting it that the "meagre satisfactions" that man "can extract from reality leave him starving," and John Dewey saying that art "was born of need, lack, deprivation, incompleteness." But philosophers aside, we all know entirely too well how much we resemble poor Walter Mitty.

If fiction is—as it clearly is for some readers —merely a fantasy to redeem the liabilities of our private fate, it is flight from reality and therefore the enemy of growth, of the life process. But is it necessarily this? Let us look at the matter in another way.

The daydream which is fiction differs from the ordinary daydream in being publicly available. This fact leads to consequences. In the private daydream you remain yourself—though nobler, stronger, more fortunate, more beautiful than in life. But when the little freshman settles cozily with his thriller by Mickey Spillane, he finds that the granite-jawed hero is not named Slim Willett, after all—as poor Slim, with his thin chest, longs for it to be. And Slim's college instructor, settling down to *For Whom the Bell Tolls,* finds sadly that this other college instructor who is the hero of the famous tale of sleeping bags, bridge demolition, tragic love and lonely valor, is named Robert Jordan.

In other words, to enter into that publicly available daydream which fiction is, you have to accept the fact that the name of the hero will never be your own; you will have to surrender something of your own identity to him, have to let it be absorbed in him. But since that kind of daydream is not exquisitely custom-cut to the exact measure of your secret longings, the identification can never be complete. In fact, only a very naïve reader tries to make it thrillingly complete. The more sophisticated reader plays a deep double game with himself; one part of him is identified with a character—or with several in turn—while another part holds aloof to respond, interpret and judge. How often have we heard some sentimental old lady say of a book: "I just loved the heroine—I mean I just went through everything with her and I knew exactly how she felt. Then when she died I just cried." The sweet old lady, even if she isn't very sophisticated, is instinctively playing the double game too: She identifies herself with the heroine, but she survives the heroine's death to shed the delicious tears. So even the old lady knows how to make the most of what we shall call her role-taking. She knows that doubleness, in the very act of identification, is of the essence of role-taking: There is the taker of the role and there is the role taken. And fiction is, in imaginative enactment, a role-taking.

For some people—those who fancy themselves hardheaded and realistic—the business of role-taking is as reprehensible as indulgence in a daydream. But in trying to understand our appetite for fiction, we can see that the process of role-taking not only stems from but also affirms the life process. It is an essential part of growth.

Role-taking is, for instance, at the very center of children's play. This is the beginning of the child's long process of adaptation to others, for only by feeling himself into another person's skin can the child predict behavior; and the stakes in the game are high, for only thus does he learn whether to expect the kiss or the cuff. In this process of role-taking we find, too, the roots of many of the massive intellectual structures we later rear—most obviously psychology and ethics, for it is only by role-taking that the child comes to know, to know "inwardly" in the only way that finally counts, that other people really exist and are, in fact, persons with needs, hopes, fears and even rights. So the role-taking of fiction, at the same time that it gratifies our deep need to extend and enrich our own experience, continues this long discipline in human sympathy. And this discipline in sympathy, through the imaginative enactment of role-taking, gratifies another need deep in us: our yearning to enter and feel at ease in the human community.

Play when we are children, and fiction when we are grown up, lead us, through role-taking, to an awareness of others. But all along the way role-taking leads us, by the same token, to an awareness of ourselves; it leads us, in fact, to the creation of the self. For the individual is not born with a self. He is born as a mysterious bundle of possibilities which, bit by bit, in a long process of trial and error, he sorts out until he gets some sort of unifying self, the ring-master self, the official self.

The official self emerges, but the soul, as Plato long ago put it, remains full of "ten thousand opposites occurring at the same time," and modern psychology has said nothing to contradict him. All our submerged selves, the old desires and possibilities, are lurking deep in us, sleepless and eager to have another go. There is knife-fighting in the inner dark. The fact that most of the time we are not aware of trouble does not mean that trouble is any the less present and significant; and fiction, most often in subtly disguised forms, liberatingly reenacts for us such inner conflict. We feel the pleasure of liberation even when we cannot specify the source of the pleasure.

Fiction brings up from their dark oubliettes our shadowy, deprived selves and gives them an airing in, as it were, the prison yard. They get a chance to participate, each according to his nature, in the life which fiction presents. When in Thackeray's *Vanity Fair* the girl Becky Sharp, leaving school for good, tosses her copy of Doctor Johnson's *Dictionary* out of the carriage, something in our own heart leaps gaily up, just as something rejoices at her later sexual and pecuniary adventures in Victorian society, and suffers, against all our sense of moral justice, when she comes a cropper. When Holden Caulfield, of Salinger's *Catcher in the Rye,* undertakes his gallant and absurd little crusade against the "phony" in our world, our own nigh-doused idealism flares up again, for the moment without embarrassment. When in Faulkner's *Light in August* Percy Grimm pulls the trigger of the black, blunt-nosed automatic and puts that tight, pretty little pattern of slugs in the top of the overturned table behind which Joe Christmas cowers, our trigger finger tenses, even while, at the same time, with a strange joy of release and justice satisfied, we feel those same slugs in our heart. When we read Dostoevski's *Crime and Punishment,* something in our nature participates in the bloody deed, and later, something else in us experiences, with the murderer Raskolnikov, the bliss of repentance and reconciliation.

For among our deprived selves we must confront the redeemed as well as the damned, the saintly as well as the wicked; and strangely enough, either confrontation may be both humbling and strengthening. In having some awareness of the complexity of self we are better-prepared to deal with that self. As a matter of fact, our entering into the fictional process helps to redefine this dominant self—even, as it were, to recreate, on a sounder basis—sounder because better understood—that dominant self, the official "I." As Henri Bergson says, fiction "brings us back into our own presence"—the presence in which we must make our final terms with life and death.

The knowledge in such confrontations does not come to us with intellectual labels. We don't say, "Gosh, I've got 15 percent of sadism in me" —or 13 percent of unsuspected human charity. No, the knowledge comes as enactment; and as imaginative enactment, to use our old phrase, it comes as knowledge. It comes, rather, as a heightened sense of being, as the conflict in the story evokes the conflict in ourselves, evokes it with some hopeful sense of meaningful resolution, and with, therefore, an exhilarating sense of freedom.

Part of this sense of freedom derives, to repeat ourselves, from the mere fact that in imagination we are getting off scot-free with something which we, or society, would never permit in real life; from the fact that our paradoxical relation to experience presented in fiction—our involvement and noninvolvement at the same time—gives a glorious feeling of mastery over the game of life. But there is something more important that contributes to this sense of freedom, the expansion and release that knowledge always brings; and in fiction we are permitted to know in the deepest way, by imaginative participation, things we would otherwise never know—including ourselves. We are free from the Garden curse: We may eat of the Tree of Knowledge, and no angel with flaming sword will appear.

But in the process of imaginative enactment we have, in another way, that sense of freedom that comes from knowledge. The image that fiction presents is purged of the distractions, confusions and accidents of ordinary life. We can now gaze at the inner logic of things—of a personality, of the consequences of an act or a thought, of a social or historical situation, of a lived life. One of our deepest cravings is to find logic in experience, but in real life how little of our experience comes to us in such a manageable form!

We have all observed how a person who has had a profound shock needs to tell the story of the event over and over again, every detail. By telling it he objectifies it, disentangling himself, as it were, from the more intolerable effects. This objectifying depends, partly at least, on the fact that the telling is a way of groping for the logic of the event, an attempt to make the experience intellectually manageable.

If a child—or a man—who is in a state of blind outrage at his fate can come to understand that the fate which had seemed random and gratuitous is really the result of his own previous behavior or is part of the general pattern of life, his emotional response is modified by that intellectual comprehension. What is intellectually manageable is, then, more likely to be emotionally manageable.

This fiction is a "telling" in which we as readers participate and is, therefore, an image of the process by which experience is made manageable. In this process experience is foreshortened, is taken out of the ruck of time, is put into an ideal time where we can scrutinize it, is given an interpretation. In other words, fiction shows, as we have said, a logical structure which implies a meaning. By showing a logical structure, it relieves us, for the moment at least, of what we sometimes feel as the greatest and most mysterious threat of life—the threat of the imminent but "unknowable," of the urgent but "unsayable." Insofar as a piece of fiction is original and not merely a conventional repetition of the known and predictable, it is a movement through the "unknowable" toward the "knowable"—the imaginatively knowable. It says the "unsayable."

This leads us, as a sort of aside, to the notion that fiction sometimes seems to be, for the individual or for society, prophetic. Now looking back we can clearly see how Melville, Dostoevski, James, Proust, Conrad and Kafka tried to deal with some of the tensions and problems which have become characteristic of our time. In this sense they foretold our world—and even more importantly, forefelt it. They even forefelt us.

Or let us remember that F. Scott Fitzgerald and Hemingway did not merely report a period, they predicted it in that they sensed a new mode of behavior and feeling. Fiction, by seizing on certain elements in its time and imaginatively pursuing them with the unswerving logic of projected enactment, may prophesy the next age. We know this from looking back on fiction of the past. More urgently we turn to fiction of our own time to help us envisage the time to come and our relation to it.

But let us turn to more specific instances of that inner logic which fiction may reveal. In *An American Tragedy* Dreiser shows us in what subtle and pitiful ways the materialism of America and the worship of what William James called the "bitch-goddess Success" can corrupt an ordinary young man and bring him to the death cell. In *Madame Bovary* Flaubert shows us the logic by which Emma's yearning for color and meaning in life leads to the moment when she gulps the poison. In both novels we sense this logic most deeply because we, as we have seen, are involved, are accomplices. We, too, worship the bitch-goddess—as did Dreiser. We, too, have yearnings like Emma's, and we remember that Flaubert said that he himself was Emma Bovary.

We see the logic of the enacted process, and we also see the logic of the end. Not only do we have now, as readers, the freedom that leads to a knowledge of the springs of action; we have also the more difficult freedom that permits us to contemplate the consequences of action and the judgment that may be passed on it. For judgment, even punishment, is the end of the logic we perceive. In our own personal lives, as we well know from our endless secret monologues of extenuation and alibi, we long to escape from judgment; but here, where the price tag is only that of imaginative involvement, we can accept judgment. We are reconciled to the terrible necessity of judgment—upon our surrogate self in the story, our whipping boy and scapegoat. We find a moral freedom in this fact that we recognize a principle of justice, with also perhaps some gratification of the paradoxical desire to suffer.

It may be objected here that we speak as though all stories were stories of crime and punishment. No, but all stories, from the gayest farce to the grimmest tragedy, are stories of action and consequence—which amounts to the same thing. All stories, as we have said, are based on conflict; and the resolution of the fictional conflict is, in its implications, a judgment too, a judgment of values. In the end some shift of values has taken place. Some new awareness has dawned, some new possibility of attitude has been envisaged.

Not that the new value is necessarily "new" in a literal sense. The point, to come back to an old point, is that the reader has, by imaginative enactment, lived through the process by which the values become valuable. What might have been merely an abstraction has become vital, has been lived, and is, therefore, "new"—new because newly experienced. We can now rest in the value as experienced; we are reconciled in it, and that is what counts.

It is what counts, for in the successful piece of fiction, a comic novel by Peter de Vries or a gut-tearing work like Tolstoy's *War and Peace,* we feel, in the end, some sense of reconciliation with the world and with ourselves. And this process of moving through conflict to reconciliation is an echo of our own life process. The life process, as we know it from babyhood on, from our early relations with our parents on to our adult relation with the world, is a long process of conflict and reconciliation. This process of enriching and deepening experience is a pattern of oscillation—a pattern resembling that of the lovers' quarrel: When lovers quarrel, each asserts his special ego against that of the beloved and then in the moment of making up finds more keenly than before the joy of losing the self in the love of another. So in fiction we enter imaginatively a situation of difficulty and estrangement—a problematic situation that, as we said earlier, sharpens our awareness of life—and move through it to a reconciliation which seems fresh and sweet.

Reconciliation—that is what we all, in some depth of being, want. All religion, all philosophy, all psychiatry, all ethics involve this human fact. And so does fiction. If fiction begins in daydream, if it springs from the cramp of the world, if it relieves us from the burden of being ourselves, it ends, if it is good fiction and we are good readers, by returning us to the world and to ourselves. It reconciles us with reality.

Let us pause to take stock. Thus far what we have said sounds as though fiction were a combination of opium addiction, religious conversion without tears, a home course in philosophy and the poor man's psychoanalysis. But it is not; it is fiction.

It is only itself, and that *itself* is not, in the

end, a mere substitute for anything else. It is an art—an image of experience formed in accordance with its own laws of imaginative enactment, laws which, as we have seen, conform to our deep needs. It is an "illusion of life" projected through language, and the language is that of some individual man projecting his own feeling of life.

The story, in the fictional sense, is not something that exists of and by itself, out in the world like a stone or a tree. The materials of stories—certain events or characters, for example—may exist out in the world, but they are not fictionally meaningful to us until a human mind has shaped them. We are, in other words, like the princess in one of Hans Christian Andersen's tales; she refuses her suitor when she discovers that the bird with a ravishing song which he has offered as a token of love is only a real bird after all. We, like the princess, want an artificial bird—an artificial bird with a real song. So we go to fiction because it is a *created* thing.

Because it is created by a man, it draws us, as human beings, by its human significance. To begin with, it is an utterance, in words. No words, no story. This seems a fact so obvious, and so trivial, as not to be worth the saying, but it is of fundamental importance in the appeal fiction has for us. We are creatures of words, and if we did not have words we would have no inner life. Only because we have words can we envisage and think about experience. We find our human nature through words. So in one sense we may say that insofar as the language of the story enters into the expressive whole of the story we find the deep satisfaction, conscious or unconscious, of a fulfillment of our very nature.

As an example of the relation of words, of style, to the expressive whole which is fiction, let us take Hemingway. We readily see how the stripped, laconic, monosyllabic style relates to the tight-lipped, stoical ethic, the cult of self-discipline, the physicality and the anti-intellectualism and the other such elements that enter into his characteristic view of the world. Imagine Henry James writing Hemingway's story *The Killers*. The complicated sentence structure of James, the deliberate and subtle rhythms of James, the careful parentheses—all these things express the delicate intellectual, social and aesthetic discriminations with which James concerned himself. But what in the Lord's name would they have to do with the shocking blankness of the moment when the gangsters enter the lunchroom, in their tight-buttoned identical blue overcoats, with gloves on their hands so as to leave no fingerprints when they kill the Swede?

The style of a writer represents his stance toward experience, toward the subject of his story; and it is also the very flesh of our experience of the story, for it is the flesh of our experience as we read. Only through his use of words does the story come to us. And with language, so with the other aspects of a work of fiction. Everything there—the proportioning of plot, the relations among the characters, the logic of motivation, the speed or retardation of the movement—is formed by a human mind into what it is, into what, if the fiction is successful, is an expressive whole, a speaking pattern, a form. And in recognizing and participating in this form, we find a gratification, though often an unconscious one, as fundamental as any we have mentioned.

We get a hint of the fundamental nature of this gratification in the fact that among primitive peoples decorative patterns are developed long before the first attempts to portray the objects of nature, even those things on which the life of the tribe depended. The pattern images a rhythm of life and intensifies the tribesman's sense of life.

Or we find a similar piece of evidence in psychological studies made of the response of children to comic books. "It is not the details of development," the researchers tell us, "but rather the general aura which the child finds fascinating." What the child wants is the formula of the accelerating buildup of tension followed by the glorious release when the righteous Superman appears just in the nick of time. What the child wants, then, is a certain "shape" of experience. Is his want, at base, different from our own?

At base, no. But if the child is satisfied by a nearly abstract pattern for the feelings of tension and release, we demand much more. We, too, in the build and shape of experience, catch the echo of the basic rhythm of our life. But we know that the world is infinitely more complicated than the child thinks. We, unlike the child, must scrutinize the details of development, the contents of life and of fiction. So the shaping of experience to satisfy us must add to the simplicity that satisfies the child something of the variety, roughness, difficulty, subtlety and delight which belongs to the actual business of life and our response to it. We want the factual richness of life absorbed into the pattern so that content and form are indistinguishable in one expressive flowering in the process that John Dewey says takes "life and experience in all its uncertainties, mystery, doubt and half-knowledge and turns that experience upon itself to deepen and intensify its own qualities." Only then will it satisfy our deepest need—the need of feeling our life to be, in itself, significant.

EXERCISE

1. This essay, unlike those earlier in this section, is not concerned with a particular writer. It undertakes to answer a question of general theoretical interest. Break the essay into its main parts, and summarize the argument under each part.

2. In what form here does the distinction appear that Auden treats under the figures of Ariel and Prospero? Would the two essays seem to take the same view of the distinction?

3. How does Jarrell's notion of whom the writer writes for relate to this essay?

4. What connection do you see between the last two paragraphs of this essay and the last line of "The Stars," by Santayana? (p. 446)

5. What ideas that appear in the General Introduction (p. 1) do you find here in other forms?

6. In what sense can it be said that all stories are "dream children"?

SECTION IV

Biography

History is one of the most extensive, important, and fascinating branches of literature. But there are kinds and kinds of history, and they lie at different distances from that frontier which, as with the essay, can be taken to separate history from "pure literature." An economic history of the United States will certainly lie far from the frontier, no matter with what clarity and cogency it is written. A history of the American Revolution will, almost certainly, lie much closer. For one thing, it will more immediately concern itself with the world of hopes, fears, ideals, illusions, vices, prejudices, and prides, in which human conduct is germinated. It will be specifically a human story in which the whole man plays a part—not a story in which only the "economic man" is protagonist. And this human story is bound to be shot through with matters of feeling and matters of value judgments. For another thing, this kind of material in which the historian of the Revolution must be inter-

ested naturally invites—though the invitation is all too rarely accepted—a fuller and deeper use of language than one is apt to find in the economic history.

If some kinds of history, such as our history of the Revolution, lie close to the frontier of pure literature, then that sub-species of history which we call biography can, in general, be taken to lie closer still. Like history it aims to depict and interpret a place and a time, and to unveil the springs and meaning of human actions. But it goes beyond ordinary history in that, with its concentration upon an individual, it tends to give a more complete and coherent picture of character in action, and invites, with reference to the character presented, an imaginative involvement that makes for dramatic tension. The story tends to be, in the emotional sense, rounder, the problems of human values more fully explored. As for biography as an art, much that we have said of fiction, and some things that we have said of poetry, apply here with equal force. Like fiction, biography is concerned with the pattern of action woven by a human character. Like fiction and poetry, it is concerned with creating a compelling verbal picture, an imaginative event.

The main difference between biography and fiction is obvious. The writer of fiction is not wedded to fact in the sense in which the biographer is. He may use an actual happening to give him the suggestion for a story, but he need not abide by the detail of the happening. This liberty, obviously, the biographer does not possess. He must abide by the ascertainable facts. They are the facts, and they limit his treatment. To illustrate, Shakespeare read the story of Macbeth in Holinshed's *Chronicles,* a history book. It happened that in the same book Shakespeare read a very vivid account of a murder committed in Macbeth's time. Shakespeare, seeing that the murder furnished fine material for his purpose, in the play makes Macbeth commit the murder, and thus violates history.

Now as a dramatist Shakespeare is quite justified in doing this. He is writing a play, not a biography; and consequently his incidental violation of historical fact makes no difference. But if Shakespeare were undertaking to give us biography, he could not have Macbeth commit a murder of which he was innocent.

This limitation which is imposed on every biographer—and we may add, on every historian—may seem to make the writing of biography a cut-and-dried affair, the assemblage of known facts in a chronological order. Certainly the business of ascertaining the facts is a most important matter. Much of the work of the biographer consists in this most important "spade work" of unearthing and collecting the facts. But after the facts have been assembled and classified, the business of interpretation remains; and we have already seen in the "Introduction to Fiction" and the "Introduction to Poetry" that interpretation brings us into the realm of literary values.

To use an example already employed in the "Introduction to Fiction": one catches a glimpse from a train window of a man standing under a streetlamp at night striking a woman who is standing beside him. This fragment of action in itself, it was pointed out, is meaningless. The literary man might find in it, however, we said, the germ of a story, and in turning it into fiction (that is, a unified and meaningful action) might give us an imaginative account of what happened, relating it to earlier events, making us see the motivation behind the action.

Now the biographer, when he is presented with a set of facts, has something of the same problem. He must put the facts with which he deals into some sort of pattern so that they may have a meaning. How does his task differ from that of the writer of fiction? We noticed and stated in the "Introduction to Fiction" that the bit of action seen under the streetlamp might be interpreted in dozens of ways—might become in the hands of twenty different writers, twenty different stories. But the biographer is anxious to get the one story, the historically true story. He is not at liberty to alter the facts; he must if possible discover many more facts. He must find out the previous history of the man and woman. He must take into account all sorts of information which may throw light on their feelings toward each other, their temperaments, their attitudes, etc. Having collected all the items of relevant information which he can, he still is faced with the problem of interpretation; and here his task, though it must be executed within different limits, is essentially the same kind of task as that imposed upon the writer of fiction.

Obviously the scene which we have been using for illustration will hardly call for the services of the biographer. But we can illustrate the general problem from an actual instance in biography. The biographer writing the life of Stonewall Jackson is faced with such a problem, for example, when he must explain why Jackson at the Seven Days' Battle delayed to attack at the time that Lee ordered him to. Obviously, he will try to find a clear reason or reasons in the records which have been preserved; he will try to find out all he can about the condition of Jackson's army, the conditions of roads, the state of the maps which Jackson possessed, the vagueness or precision of the orders. Furthermore, he will try to find out to the best of his ability the state of Jackson himself at the time: his physical condition (fatigue, possible illness, etc.) and his mental condition. But more than this, he will take into account Jackson's record as a soldier before this battle and his subsequent record, his attitude toward Lee, his attitude toward the general strategy of the battle, etc. With these last items, however, he will have come down to dealing with the problem of Jackson himself. What sort of man was he? What is the dominant motivation of his actions? Can this particular matter, his failure to advance as ordered, be fitted into some sort of logic? It may be, as in this case, that the facts do not dictate positively a particular explanation of his conduct and that he will have to attempt to reconstruct imaginatively what probably went on in Jackson's mind. (If he has to do this, he will as a good historian, caution his reader that his explanation is of this sort.) But his general task, whether or not in an extreme case such as this, will call always for a use of his imagination as he attempts to order his facts into a pattern—as he tries to make them fit into a logic growing out of the character of the man whose life he is attempting to reconstruct. He must of course always test his conception of the character by the facts; but his picture of the man is arrived at, nonetheless, by an act of the imagination.

In fiction, the writer may select and arrange his material as an expression of the theme which he cares to state. He may, of course, choose—or in the course of composition discover and embody—whatever theme he will. The biographer is, of course, far more limited. He begins, not with a theme which he has adopted, but with the circumstantial material. His task is to find what the theme—the "meaning" of the life—is. But even with the limitation just stated, there remain a number of possible arrangements of his material from which the biographer may choose. His choice will depend primarily on his interest in his subject. For example, he may be interested in his subject's life itself, or he may be interested in it as representative of some larger process; he may wish to give us a careful statement of the

influences which combined to form the character whom he is studying, or he may wish to glide over his subject's development very rapidly in order to focus attention on some period of his mature life. He may wish to use the life of his subject as a way of affirming some body of moral, or other, convictions. He may be drawn to his subject by some peculiar personal affinity. And in any case, the biographer is not exploring only the theme of the subject's life: he is, inevitably, exploring his own feelings and values. So biography, in that sense also, lies close to the boundary of fiction and poetry.

To end this discussion, let us ask, and try to answer, a question. If biography lies so close to the realm of "pure literature"—if, in fact, narrative must bulk so large in it—why do we place it here under the heading of "discursive prose"? Our answer here is by way of reference to the basic intention of biography. That basic aim is to arrive at a "truth" by way of reasoning from the available facts of the case. The decisive element here is not the mere use of facts. As we have said before, fiction or poetry may use—and in fact, in one sense, must use—facts, some facts. But in biography the use of facts is, to begin with, "factual." However numerous and well validated are the facts in a piece of fiction, we are concerned, in the end, with the imaginative coherence. In this imaginative coherence, the fact enters at the same level as a piece of invention: probability is the test here for acceptance. By probability we mean the affirmative answer to this question: is the item consistent with (1) what we know of the external world (say the problem of human desires and motivations) and with (2) the logic and pattern of the particular work in which it appears?

To state the matter succinctly, we may say that in fiction the facts are to be tested by the imagination, in biography the imagination is to be tested by the facts. No, we should say that the imagination is to be tested by the reasoning from the facts. And that is the discursive process.

Lady Olga

JOSEPH MITCHELL (1908-   )

JANE BARNELL occasionally considers herself an outcast and feels that there is something vaguely shameful about the way she makes a living. When she is in this mood, she takes no pride in the fact that she has had a longer career as a sideshow performer than any other American woman and wishes she had never left the drudgery of her grandmother's cotton farm in North Carolina. Miss Barnell is a bearded lady. Her thick, curly beard measures thirteen and a half inches, which is the longest it has ever been. When she was young and more entranced by life under canvas, she wore it differently every year; in those days there was a variety of styles in beards—she remembers the Icicle, the Indian Fighter, the Whisk Broom, and the Billy Goat—and at the beginning of a season she would ask the circus barber to trim hers in the style most popular at the moment. Since it became gray, she has worn it in the untrimmed, House of David fashion.

The business of exhibiting her beard has taken her into every state in the Union. In fact, she has undoubtedly travelled as widely in the United States as any other person, but she has always been too bored to take much notice of her surroundings and probably would not do well with a grammar-school geography quiz. "I been all over everywhere, up, down, and sideways," she says. "I've hit thousands of towns, but I don't remember much about any of them. Half the time I didn't even know what state I was in. Didn't know or care." Miss Barnell is sixty-nine years old and was first put on exhibition shortly after her fourth birthday; she claims she has been bearded since infancy. As Princess Olga, Madame Olga, or Lady Olga, she has worked in the sideshows of at least twenty-five circuses and carnivals for wages ranging between twenty and a hundred dollars a week. She has forgotten the names of some of these outfits; one circus she remembers only as "that ten-car mess on the West Coast where I and my third husband had to knock the sideshow manager on the noggin with a tent stake to get my pay." She started out with a tramp circus, or "mud show," whose rickety, louse-infested wagons were pulled by oxen, and worked her way up to Ringling Brothers and Barnum & Bailey.

She spent six years in the Ringling circus. She was with it last in 1938, when its season was cut short by a strike in Scranton, an occurrence which made her hysterical. Ringling's sideshow, the Congress of Strange People, is as highly esteemed by freaks as the Palace used to be by vaudeville actors, but she would not sign a contract for the 1939 season. It pained her to make this decision; for six consecutive seasons she had occupied the same berth in Old Ninety-six, the Ringling sleeping car for sideshow people, and had grown attached to it. "Once I heard about a man in the penitentiary who broke down and cried when he finished his term and had to leave his cell for the last time," she says. "It had got to be a home to him. That's how I felt about my berth." She turned down the 1939 contract because she had become obsessed with a notion that out on the road she would somehow be forced to join the circus union. Unions frighten her. Although she has never voted, she is a violently opinionated Republican. Also, she is a veteran reader of Hearst newspapers and believes everything she reads in them. She thinks the average union organizer carries a gun and will shoot to kill. When she sees pickets, she immediately crosses to the other side of the street. "Just as sure as I go back to Ringling's, that union will get me," she told a circus official who tried for hours to reason with her, and added, "To tell you the truth, I think that old union is a corporation, like everything else these days." She also has a fear of corporations; to her, they are as sinister as unions. Since she left, Ringling's has been without a bearded lady. Fred Smythe, manager of the Congress, offers her a contract every spring, but she always tells him that she will never again work for the Big Show. This never surprises Smythe. "Short of blasting," he says, "there's no way of getting a fool notion out of the head of a freak. I'd sure like to get her back. She's the only real, old-fashioned bearded lady left in the country. Most bearded ladies are men. Even when they're women, they look like men. Lady Olga is a woman, and she looks like a woman." Smythe says that bearded ladies are not particularly sensational but they are traditional in sideshows, like clowns in the circus itself. "People don't laugh at clowns any more but they want to see them around," he says. "Likewise, if there isn't a bearded lady in a sideshow, people feel there's something lacking."

Miss Barnell has not been on the road since leaving the Big Show but has stuck pretty close to New York City, which, as much as any other place, she considers home. In the winter she works intermittently in the basement sideshow of Hubert's Museum on West Forty-second Street. She has shown her beard in practically every dime museum in the country and likes Hubert's best of all; she has come to look upon it as her winter headquarters. Professor Le Roy Heckler, who operates the Flea Circus concession in Hubert's, is an old friend of hers. They once lived in the same farming community in Mecklenburg County, North Carolina, and she worked in circuses long ago with his father, the late Professor William Heckler, who was a sideshow strong man before he developed a method of educating fleas and established the family business. She has great respect for Le Roy; she calls him "the young Professor" and says she has known him since he was "diaper size." In the summer she divides her time between Hubert's and Professor Sam Wagner's World Circus Side Show, also a dime museum, in Coney Island. She likes Coney because she feels that salt air is good for her asthma; also, she has a high regard for the buttered roasting-ear corn that is sold in stands down there.

On the dime museum circuit she does not work steadily; she works two or three weeks in a row and then lays off for a week. "I don't want to go nuts," she says. In museums, her hours are from 11 A.M. to 11 P.M. There is an average of two shows an hour and during a show she is on the platform from five to ten minutes. Between appearances, she is free. At Hubert's she kills most of this time dozing in a rocking chair in her dressing room. Sometimes she visits with other performers, usually with Albert-Alberta, the half-man-half-woman. Twice a week she goes into Professor Heckler's booth and watches him feed his fleas. This spectacle always amazes her, although she has seen it scores of times. The Professor rolls up one sleeve, picks the fleas out of their mother-of-pearl boxes with tweezers, and drops them, one by one, on a forearm, where they browse for fifteen minutes. While the fleas are feeding, the Professor reads a newspaper and she smokes a cigarette. They seldom say anything to each other. Taciturn herself, Miss Barnell does not care for talkative people. At least once an afternoon she wraps a scarf around her beard and goes out for coffee or a mug of root beer. She usually goes to the lunchroom in the American Bus Depot, a few doors west of Hubert's. She finds the atmosphere of a bus terminal soothing to her nerves. When showing in Coney Island, she takes brisk turns on the boardwalk between appearances.

In the past, while filling engagements in or around the city, Miss Barnell always lived in small Broadway hotels. A year or so ago she gave up hotel life. One Saturday night, after working late in Hubert's, she walked into a hotel off Times Square in which she had been living since the Ringling strike and a drunk in the lobby saw her and said, "By God, it's the bearded lady!" He followed her to the elevator, shouting, "Beaver! Beaver!" Next day she moved out and took a furnished apartment in a theatrical rooming house on Eighth Avenue, not far from the Garden. The house was recommended by a colleague, a man who eats electric-light bulbs. Among the other tenants are a magician, an old burlesque comedian, a tattooed woman, and a retired circus cook. Surrounded by such people, she feels at ease; when she meets them on the stairs they simply take her for granted and do not look startled. "If an old baboon was to walk down the hall tooting on a cornet, nobody in my house would give him a second look," she says.

Miss Barnell would like to spend the rest of her life in the city, but she knows that sooner or later she will become a stale attraction in the dime museums and will have to run an "At Liberty" notice in *Billboard* and get a job with a circus or carnival again. She wants to put this off as long as possible because she has grown to like apartment life; it has given her a chance, she says, really to get acquainted with Thomas O'Boyle, her fourth husband, and with Edelweiss, her cat. O'Boyle is a veteran Joey, or clown, but recently he has been employed as a talker—the sideshow term for barker—on the box at the gate at Hubert's. He is nineteen years younger than Miss Barnell and, unlike her, is enthralled by sideshow life. He wears dark-blue shirts, lemon-yellow neckties, and Broadway suits. He believes Miss Barnell is one of the great women of all time and treats her accordingly. When she comes into a room he leaps to his feet, and when she takes out a cigarette he hurriedly strikes a match for her. They were married after working together during the season of 1931 in the Johnny J. Jones Exposition, a carnival. Both are short-wave-radio fans, and O'Boyle says that this mutual interest is what brought them together. "Since our marriage, I and Mr. O'Boyle have travelled with the same outfits," Miss Barnell said recently, "but I never felt like I really knew him until we settled in an apartment. In a sleeping car you just don't feel married. To get to know a husband, you have to cook and wash for him." Next to O'Boyle, Edelweiss is her chief concern. Edelweiss is a sullen, over-fed, snow-white Persian, for which she paid twenty-five dollars when it was a kitten and which now weighs sixteen pounds. She has nicknamed it Edie, and when she speaks to it she uses baby talk. She owns a comfortable old canvas chair—it came out of a circus dressing tent—and she likes to loll in this chair, hold the cat in her lap, and sing to it. Interminably, one after the other, she sings "Eadie Was a Lady" and "Root, Hog, or Die," an old circus

song. Cats and dogs are not permitted in the sleeping cars of most circuses, so when she is on the road she usually has to board Edie in a pet store. "Sometimes out in the sticks," she says, "I get so lonesome for Edie I feel like I just can't bear it." She thinks Hubert's is much nicer than other museums because the manager there understands how she feels about the cat and lets her bring it with her to work. While she is on the platform, Edie stands beside her, purring. After cats, Miss Barnell likes horses best. She is one of those women who cannot pass a horse standing at a curb without trying to stroke its head; she keeps a handful of wrapped cube sugar in her bag for horses. Once a month, no matter how lean the season, she sends a contribution to the A.S.P.C.A. "To an animal, if you're bearded, it don't make no difference," she says.

Miss Barnell has not only a beard but side whiskers and a droopy mustache. In a white, loose-fitting house dress, she looks like an Old Testament prophet. Her appearance is more worldly when she dresses for a party; on such occasions she uses lipstick and rouge. Monty Woolley saw her once when she was dressed for the evening and said she looked like Elsa Maxwell in a property beard. Someone repeated Woolley's remark to her and she snorted with indignation. "Mr. Woolley must not have good eyesight," she said. She is not as plump as Miss Maxwell. She is five feet five and weighs a hundred and eighty-three pounds. She does not look her age; she has few wrinkles and she walks with a firm step. Her face is round and gloomy. Her bobbed gray hair is brushed pompadour style, and on the platform she wears a Spanish comb and two side combs. Once a year she gets a permanent wave. Before going on the street, she always covers her face with a veil and wraps a Paisley scarf around her neck, hiding her beard. To keep it curly, she sleeps with her beard in a pigtail plait; on days off she does not unplait it. She wears a thick gold wedding ring. Her voice is low and feminine.

Years of listening to barkers has had an effect on her speech; she makes long words longer. To her, a monstrosity is a "monsterosity." She uses some circus slang. The men who haunt the pinball machines on the first floor of Hubert's and never spend a dime to visit the sideshow in the basement are "lot lice" to her; in circuses, this term is applied to townspeople who do not buy tickets but stand around the lot, gaping at everything and getting in the way. She uses the word "old" to express contempt. She once said, "If that old Mayor they have here can't think up anything better than that old sales tax, he ought to lay down and quit." She consistently says "taken" for "took." This is a sample of her conversation: "When I was a young'un I taken the name Princess Olga. After I first got married I changed to Madame, but when every confounded swami-woman and mitt-reader in the nation taken to calling herself Madame So-and-So, I decided Lady was more ree-fined." She has a dim but unmistakable Southern accent, and many of her habits of speech are North Carolinian. She heavily accents the first syllable in words like "hotel" and "police." She uses "one" as a contraction for "one or the other." She says, "I'm going to the movie pitchers this afternoon, or down to Coney Island, one." When she gets ready to do her kitchen shopping, she doesn't say, "I'm going up the street"; she says, "I'm going up street," or, "I'm going down street." Another heritage from her years in rural North Carolina is a liking for snuff. She and O'Boyle own an automobile, and occasionally they get it out of storage and take a long trip. While riding along with the windows lowered, they both dip snuff. "Out in the country, snuff is better than cigarettes," she says. "Of course, I'd never think of using it indoors." She smokes a pack and a half of cigarettes a day. The use of tobacco is her only bad habit. As a rule, sideshow performers are fond of the bottle, but she is a teetotaler and a believer in prohibition.

On a sideshow platform or stage, Miss Barnell is rather austere. To discourage people from getting familiar, she never smiles. She dresses conservatively, usually wearing a plain black evening gown. "I like nice clothes, but there's no use wasting money," she says. "People don't notice anything but my old beard." She despises pity and avoids looking into the eyes of the people in her audiences; like most freaks, she has cultivated a blank, unseeing stare. When

people look as if they feel sorry for her, especially women, it makes her want to throw something. She does not sell photographs of herself and does not welcome questions from spectators. She will answer specific questions about her beard as graciously as possible, but when someone becomes inquisitive about her private life—"You ever been married?" is the most frequent query—she gives the questioner an icy look or says quietly, "None of your business." Audiences seem to think that this is admirable. Now and then, after she has told off a persistent or insulting questioner, people will applaud. Miss Barnell's temper has been a blessing; it has kept her from succumbing to utter apathy, which is the occupational disease of freaks. "I don't take no back talk from nobody," she says. She guards her dignity jealously. Once she slapped an apology out of a carnival owner who had suggested that she dye her beard so he could bill her as "Olga, the Lady Bluebeard." Wisecracking professors, or talkers, annoy her; she prefers to be introduced by one who is deadly serious and able to use long medical words. Except for midgets, the majority of freaks in American sideshows are natives, but talkers hate to admit this. Consequently, at one time or another, Miss Barnell has been introduced as having been born in Budapest, Paris, Moscow, Shanghai, and Potsdam. In one carnival she was "the daughter of a Hungarian general," and in another "the half sister of a French duke." She does not have a high opinion of foreigners and is sorely vexed by such introductions. She was grateful to the late Clyde Ingalls, who was once married to Lillian Leitzel and preceded Smythe as manager of Ringling's Congress, because he never seemed to resent the fact that she was born in North Carolina. Ingalls would bow to her, turn to the audience, click his heels, and say, "It gives me the greatest pleasure at this time to introduce a little woman who comes to us from an aristocratic plantation in the Old South and who is recognized by our finest doctors, physicians, and medical men as the foremost unquestioned, and authentic fee-male bearded lady in medical history. Ladies and gentlemen, Lay-dee Oolgah!"

Among freaks it is axiomatic that Coney

Island audiences are the most inhuman, but Miss Barnell has found that a Surf Avenue dime museum on a Saturday night is peaceful compared with a moving-picture studio at any time. She talks bitterly about her experiences in Hollywood, where she has been used in a number of horror and circus pictures. Her most important rôle was in "Freaks," a Metro-Goldwyn-Mayer study of sideshow life filmed in 1932. It was probably the most frightening picture ever made. In it, among other things, a beautiful trapeze girl of a European circus permits a dwarf to fall in love with her in order to obtain some money he has inherited. At their wedding feast, with a fantastic group of sideshow people around the table, she gets drunk and lets slip the fact that she despises the dwarf. A few nights later, during a terrible storm when the troupe is on the road, the freaks climb into her private wagon and mutilate her, turning *her* into a freak. Miss Barnell thinks this picture was an insult to all freaks everywhere and is sorry she acted in it. When it was finished, she swore she would never again work in Hollywood.

Her self-esteem suffers least of all when she is working in circuses, where sideshow class distinctions are rigidly observed. She herself divides freaks into three classes: born freaks are the aristocrats of the sideshow world. She, of course, is a member of this class. So are Siamese twins, pinheads, fat girls, dwarfs, midgets, giants, living skeletons, and men with skulls on which rocks can be broken. Made freaks include tattooed people, sword-swallowers, snake charmers, and glass-eaters. Normal people who obtain sideshow engagements because of past glory or notoriety are two-timers to her. Examples are reformed criminals, old movie stars, and retired athletes like Jack Johnson, the old pug, and Grover Cleveland Alexander, the old ballplayer, both of whom starred for a while on the dime museum circuit. Because Johnson wears a beret and because she has heard that he sips beer through a straw, she particularly dislikes him. "To the general public, old Jack Johnson may be a freak," she says, "but to a freak, he ain't a freak." Paradoxically, she bears no animosity toward fake bearded ladies. They amuse her. She was greatly amused when Frances Murphy, the Gorilla Lady in the "Strange As It Seems" sideshow at the New York World's Fair in 1940, got into an altercation with a truck-driver and was exposed as a male. "If any man is fool enough to be a bearded lady," she says, "it's all right with me."

Some of Miss Barnell's genuine but less gifted colleagues are inclined to think that she is haughty, but she feels that a woman with a beard more than a foot long has a right to be haughty. She undoubtedly does have the most flamboyant female beard in American sideshow history. The beard of Joséphine Boisdechêne, a native of Switzerland and one of P. T. Barnum's most lucrative freaks, was only eight inches long, and she had no mustache. She did, however, have a bearded son—Albert, billed as "Esau, the Hairy Boy" who helped make up for this shortcoming. Grace Gilbert, who came from Kalkaska, Michigan, and spent most of her professional life in Barnum & Bailey's Circus had a lush beard, but it was only six inches long. Miss Gilbert used peroxide and was billed as "Princess Gracie, the Girl with the Golden Whiskers." Records of non-professional female beards are scarce. Margaret of Parma, Regent of the Netherlands from 1559 to 1567, had a "coarse, bushy beard." She was proud of it, believing it gave her a regal appearance, and she required court physicians to mix tonics for it. Charles XII of Sweden had a bearded female grenadier in his army, a reputedly beautiful amazon, who was captured by the Russians in the battle of Poltava in 1709 and subsequently taken to St. Petersburg and presented to the Czar at whose court she was popular for several years. There was a Spanish nun called St. Paula the Bearded, who grew a miraculous beard, according to sacred history. She was being pursued one night by a man with evil intent when hair suddenly sprouted from her chin. She turned and confronted the man and he fled. No reliable statistics on the length of these beards have come down to us.

Most freaks are miserable in the company of non-freaks, but unless she is sunk in one of the morose spells she suffers from occasionally, Miss Barnell welcomes the opportunity to go out among ordinary people. One morning in the winter of 1940 Cole Porter went to her dressing room at Hubert's and asked her to go with him to a cocktail party Monty Woolley was giving at the Ritz-Carlton. Porter told her that Woolley was a student of beards, that he was known as The Beard by his friends, and that he had always wanted to meet a bearded lady. "I'll have to ask my old man," Miss Barnell said. O'Boyle told her to go ahead and enjoy herself. Porter offered to pay for the time she would lose at the museum. "Well, I tell you," she said, "I and you and Mr. Woolley are all in show business, and if this party is for members of the profession, I won't charge a cent." Porter said non-professionals would be present, so she set a fee of eight dollars. Late that afternoon he picked her up at her house. She had changed into a rhinestone-spangled gown. In the Ritz-Carlton elevator she took off the scarf she was wearing around her beard, astonishing the other passengers. There were more than a hundred stage and society people at the party, and Porter introduced her to most of them. Woolley, who got quite interested in her, asked her to have a drink. She hesitated and then accepted a glass of sherry, remarking that it was her first drink in nine years. "I like to see people enjoying theirselves," she said after finishing the sherry. "There's too confounded much misery in this world." She was at the party an hour and a half and said she wished she could stay longer but she had to go home and cook a duck dinner for her husband. Next day, at Hubert's, she told a colleague she had never had a nicer time. "Some of the better class of the Four Hundred were there," she said, "and when I was introduced around I recognized their names. I guess I was a curiosity to them. Some of them sure were a curiosity to me. I been around peculiar people most of my life, but I never saw no women like them before." She was able to recognize the names of the society people because she is a devoted reader of the Cholly Knickerbocker column in the *Journal & American*. She is, in fact, a student of society scandals. "The Four Hundred sure is one cutting-up set of people," she says.

Several endocrinologists have tried vainly to argue Miss Barnell into letting them examine her. She is afraid of physicians. When sick, she depends on patent medicines. "When they get their hands on a monsterosity the medical profession don't know when to stop," she says. "There's nobody so indecent and snoopy as an old doctor." Her hirsuteness is undoubtedly the result of distorted glandular activity. The abnormal functioning of one of the endocrine, or ductless, glands is most often responsible for excessive facial hair in females. Hypertrichosis and hirsutism are the medical terms for the condition. Miss Barnell once read a book called "The Human Body" and is familiar with the glandular explanation, but does not take much stock in it. She says that her parentage was Jewish, Irish, and American Indian, and she believes vaguely that this mixture of bloods is in some way to blame, although she had three beardless sisters.

Miss Barnell has to be persuaded to talk about her early life. "What's the use?" she tells people. "You won't believe me." She says that her father, George Barnell, an itinerant buggy- and wagon-maker, was a Russian Jew who had Anglicized his name. Around 1868, while wandering through the South, he visited a settlement of Catawba Indians on the Catawba River in York County, South Carolina, and fell in love with and was married to a girl who had a Catawba mother and an Irish father. They settled in Wilmington, the principal port of North Carolina, where Barnell established himself in the business of repairing drays on the docks. Miss Barnell was their second child; she was born in 1871 and named Jane, after her Indian grandmother. At birth her chin and cheeks were covered with down. Before she was two years old she had a beard. Her father was kind to her, but her mother, who was superstitious, believed she was bewitched and took her to a succession of Negro granny-women and conjure doctors. Around her fourth birthday, her father inherited some money from a relative and went up to Baltimore to see about starting a business there. While he was away a dismal little six-wagon circus came to Wilmington. It was called the Great Orient Family Circus and Menagerie, and was operated by a family of small, dark foreigners; Miss Barnell calls them "the Mohammedans." The family was composed of a mother, who was a snake charmer; two daughters, who danced; and three sons, who were jugglers and fire-walkers. The wagons were pulled by oxen, and the show stock consisted of three old lions, a few sluggish snakes, some monkeys, a cage of parrots, an educated goat, and a dancing bear. There were many tramp circuses of this type in the country at that time. On the last day of the Great Orient's stay, Mrs. Barnell sold or gave Jane to the Mohammedan mother. "I never been able to find out if Mamma got any money for me or just gave me away to get rid of me," Miss Barnell says bitterly. "She hated me, I know that. Daddy told me years later that he gave her a good beating when he got home from Baltimore and found out what had happened. He had been in Baltimore two months, and by the time he got home I and the Mohammedans were long gone. He and the sheriff of New Hanover County searched all over the better part of three states for us, but they didn't find hide or hair."

She does not remember much about her life with the Great Orient. "My entire childhood was a bad dream," she says. The Mohammedans exhibited her in a small tent separate from the circus, and people had to pay extra to see her. On the road she slept with the Mohammedan mother in the same wagon in which the snakes were kept. Her pallet on the floor was filthy. She was homesick and cried a lot. The Mohammedans were not intentionally cruel to her. "They did the best they could, I guess," she says. "They were half starved themselves. I didn't understand their talk and their rations made me sick. They put curry in everything. After a while the old Mohammedan mother taken to feeding me on eggs and fruits." The circus wandered through the South for some months, eventually reaching a big city, which she thinks was New Orleans. There the Mohammedans sold their stock and wagons to another small circus and got passage on a boat to Europe, taking her along. In Europe, they joined a German circus. In Berlin, in the summer 1876, after Jane had been exhibited by the German circus for four or five months, she got sick. She thinks she had typhoid fever. She was placed in a charity hospital. "I was nothing but skin and bones," she says. "The day they put me in the hospital was the last I ever saw of the Mohammedans. They thought I was due to die." She does not remember how long she was in the hospital. After she recovered she was transferred to an institution which she thinks was an orphanage. One morning her father appeared and took her away. "I disremember how Daddy located me," she says, "but I think he said the old Mohammedan mother went to the chief of police in Berlin and told who I was. I guess he somehow got in touch with the chief of police in Wilmington. That must have been the way it happened."

Barnell brought Jane back to North Carolina but did not take her home; she did not want to see her mother. Instead, he put her in the care of her Indian grandmother, who, with other Catawbas, had moved up from the settlement in South Carolina to a farming community in Mecklenburg County, near Charlotte. Jane worked on her grandmother's farm, chopping cotton, milking cows, and tending pigs. She never went to school but was taught to read and write by a Presbyterian woman who did missionary work among the Catawbas. Jane remembers stories this woman told her about Florence Nightingale; they made her long to become a nurse. In her teens she taught herself to shave with an old razor that had belonged to her grandfather. When she was around seventeen she went to Wilmington to visit her father, and a doctor he knew got her a place as a student nurse in the old City Hospital. She worked in the hospital for perhaps a year, and she still thinks of this as the happiest period of her life. Eventually, however, something unpleasant happened which caused her to leave; what it was, she will not tell. "I just figured I could never have a normal life," she says, "so I went back to Grandma's and settled down to be a farm hand the rest of my days." Three or four years later she became acquainted with the senior Professor Heckler, who owned a farm near her grandmother's; he worked in circuses in the summer and lived on the farm in the winter. Heckler convinced her she would be happier in a sideshow than on a farm and helped her get a job with the John Robinson Circus. As well as she can remember, she got this job in the spring of 1892, when she was twenty-one. "Since that time," she says, "my beard has been my meal ticket." Until the death of her grandmother, around 1899, Miss Barnell went back to North Carolina every winter. She had three sisters and two brothers in Wilmington, and she visited them occasionally. "They all thought I was a disgrace and seeing them never gave me much enjoyment," she says. "Every family of a freak I ever heard of was the same. I've known families that lived off a freak's earnings but wouldn't be seen with him. My parents passed on long ago, and I reckon my brothers and sisters are all dead by now. I haven't seen any of them for twenty-two years. I had one sister I liked. I used to send her a present every Christmas, and sometimes she'd drop me a card. She was a nurse. She went to China twenty-some-odd years ago to work in a hospital for blind Chinese children, and that's the last I ever heard of her. I guess she's dead."

Miss Barnell was with the Robinson Circus for fourteen years. While with it, she was married to a German musician in the circus band. By him she had two children, both of whom died in infancy. Soon after the death of her second child, her husband died. "After that," she says, "I never got any more pleasure out of circus life. I had to make a living, so I kept on. It's been root, hog, or die. When I got sick of one outfit, I moved on to another. Circuses are all the same—dull as ditch water." She left Robinson's to go with the Forepaugh-Sells Brothers' Circus and Menagerie, leaving it to marry a balloon ascensionist. He was killed about a year after they were married; how, she will not say. "He was just killed," she says, shrugging her shoulders. Her third marriage also ended unhappily. "That one treated me shamefully," she says. "If he was in a bottle, I wouldn't pull out the stopper to give him air. I taken out a divorce from him the year before I and Mr. O'Boyle got married."

Miss Barnell is disposed to blame circuses for much of the unhappiness in her life. Consequently she does not share her present husband's enthusiasm for them. O'Boyle was an orphan who ran away to work with a circus, and has never become disenchanted. Every

week he reads *Billboard* from cover to cover, and he keeps a great stack of back copies of the magazine in their apartment; she rarely reads it. Like most old circus men, he is garrulous about the past. He often tries to get his wife to talk about her circus experiences, but she gives him little satisfaction. O'Boyle is proud of her career. Once he begged her to give him a list of the circuses and carnivals she has worked for; he wanted to send the list to the letters-to-the-editor department of *Billboard*. She mentioned Ringling, Barnum & Bailey, Forepaugh-Sells, Hagenbeck-Wallace, the World of Mirth Carnival, the Royal American Shows, the Rubin & Cherry Exposition, and the Beckmann & Gerety Shows, and then yawned and said, "Mr. O'Boyle, please go turn on the radio." He has never been able to get the full list.

In the last year or so Miss Barnell has become a passionate housekeeper and begrudges every moment spent away from her apartment. About once a week she rearranges the furniture in her two small rooms. On a window sill she keeps two geranium plants in little red pots. On sunny afternoons during her days off she places a pillow on the sill, rests her elbows on it, and stares for hours into Eighth Avenue. People who see her in the window undoubtedly think she is a gray-bearded old man. She spends a lot of time in the kitchen, trying out recipes clipped from newspapers. O'Boyle has gained eleven pounds since they moved into the apartment. Before starting work in the kitchen, she turns on four electric fans in various corners of the apartment and opens all the windows; she does not trust gas and believes that stirring up the air is good for her asthma. While the fans are on, she keeps Edie, the cat, who is susceptible to colds, shut up in a closet. She has developed a phobia about New York City tap water; she is sure there is a strange, lethal acid in it, and boils drinking water for fifteen minutes. She even boils the water in which she gives Edie a bath. In her opinion, the consumption of unboiled water is responsible for most of the sickness in the city. On her bureau she keeps two radios, one of them a short-wave set. On her days off she turns on the short-wave radio right after she gets up and leaves it on until she goes to bed. While in the kitchen, she listens to police calls. The whirring of the fans and the clamor of the radio do not bother her in the least. The walls are thin, however, and once the burlesque comedian who lives in the next apartment rapped on the door and said, "Pardon me, Madam, but it sounds like you're murdering a mule in there, or bringing in an oil well."

Miss Barnell's attitude toward her work is by no means consistent. In an expansive mood, she will brag that she has the longest female beard in history and will give the impression that she feels superior to less spectacular women. Every so often, however, hurt by a snicker or a brutal remark made by someone in an audience, she undergoes a period of depression which may last a few hours or a week. "When I get the blues, I feel like an outcast from society," she once said. "I used to think when I got old my feelings wouldn't get hurt, but I was wrong. I got a tougher hide than I once had, but it ain't tough enough." On the road she has to keep on working, no matter how miserable she gets, but in a museum she simply knocks off and goes home. Until she feels better, she does not go out of her apartment, but passes the time listening to the police calls, playing with Edie, reading the *Journal & American,* and studying an old International Correspondence Schools course in stenography which she bought in a secondhand-bookstore in Chicago years ago. Practicing shorthand takes her mind off herself. She is aware that such a thing is impossible, but she daydreams about becoming a stenographer the way some women daydream about Hollywood. She says that long ago she learned there is no place in the world outside of a sideshow for a bearded lady. When she was younger she often thought of joining the Catholic Church and going into a nunnery; she had heard of sideshow women who became nuns, although she had never actually known one. A lack of religious conviction deterred her. Religion has been of little solace to her. "I used to belong to the Presbyterians, but I never did feel at home in church," she says. "Everybody eyed me, including the preacher. I rather get my sermons over the radio."

Most of Miss Barnell's colleagues are touchy about the word "freak," preferring to be called artistes or performers. Years ago, because of this, Ringling had to change the name of its sideshow from the Congress of Freaks to the Congress of Strange People. Miss Barnell would like to be considered hardboiled and claims she does not care what she is called. "No matter how nice a name was put on me," she says, "I would still have a beard." Also, she has a certain professional pride. Sometimes, sitting around with other performers in a dressing room, she will say, with a slight air of defiance, that a freak is just as good as any actor, from the Barrymores on down. "If the truth was known, we're all freaks together," she says.

EXERCISE

This is quite literally a biography. "Lady Olga" existed at the time Joseph Mitchell wrote this essay, and may still exist, and he undertook to give the facts of her strange life. Since she was a private person, of no historical importance, what led him to write her story? That basic question underlies the following questions.

1. Note the first sentence of "Lady Olga." Does it set the tone for what follows? Does it establish the theme? Does this account have a theme?

2. The author does not follow a strictly chronological scheme. For example, we are not told about Lady Olga's babyhood and childhood until we are over halfway through the account of her life. Can you justify this and other departures from chronology?

3. What is the author's attitude toward the bearded lady? Does he pity her? Admire her? Make fun of her? Is his attitude more complex than any of these?

4. What is the quality of the humor? Part of the humorous effect comes from the perspective with which pride, self-esteem, etc., are viewed from the odd and bizarre world which Lady Olga inhabits. Is all the laughter at the expense of Lady Olga and her sideshow companions?

5. Is Lady Olga's life pathetic? Tragic? Comic? Or what? Does the author suggest an answer to this question? Or is he completely noncommittal and "objective"? Justify in the light of your answer to this question, the author's method of presentation. Compare "Lady Olga" to "Clay," by James Joyce (p. 60). To "Keela," by Eudora Welty (p. 109).

6. Might this essay be placed among the personal essays? Perhaps it should be placed there. Why?

The Young Man Washington

SAMUEL ELIOT MORISON (1887-   )

WASHINGTON IS the last person you would ever suspect of having been a young man, with all the bright hopes and black despairs to which youth is subject. In American folklore he is known only as a child or a general or an old, old man: priggish hero of the cherry-tree episode, commander-in-chief, or the Father of his Country, writing a farewell address. By some freak of fate, Stuart's Athenæum portrait of an ideal and imposing, but solemn and weary, Washington at the age of sixty-four has become the most popular. It has been placed in every school in the country; so we may expect that new generations of American school children will be brought up with the idea that Washington was a solemn old bore. If only Charles Willson Peale's portrait of him as a handsome and gallant young soldier could have been used instead! His older biographers, too, have conspired to create the legend; and the recent efforts to "popularize" Washington have taken the unfortunate line of trying to make him out something that he was not: a churchman, politician, engineer, businessman, or realtor. These attempts to degrade a hero to a go-getter, an aristocrat to a vulgarian, remind one of the epitaph that Aristotle wished to have carved on the tomb of Plato: *Hic jacet homo, quem non licet, non decet, impiis vel ignorantibus laudare* (Here lies a man whom it is neither permissible nor proper for the irreverent or the ignorant to *praise*).

Perhaps it is not the fault of the painters and biographers that we think of Washington as an old man, but because his outstanding qualities—wisdom, poise, and serenity—are not those commonly associated with youth. He seemed to have absorbed, wrote Emerson, "all the serenity of America, and left none for his restless, rickety, hysterical countrymen." The Comte de Chastellux, one of the French officers in the war, said that Washington's most char-

acteristic feature was balance: "the perfect harmony existing between the physical and moral attributes of which he is made up." Yet Gilbert Stuart, after painting his first portrait of Washington, said that "all his features were indicative of the most ungovernable passions, and had he been born in the forests, it was his opinion that he would have been the fiercest man among the savage tribes." Both men were right. Washington's qualities were so balanced that his talents, which were great but nothing extraordinary, were more effective in the long run than those of greater generals like Napoleon, or of bolder and more original statesmen like Hamilton and Jefferson. Yet as a young man Washington was impatient and passionate, eager for glory in war, wealth in land, and success in love. Even in maturity his fierce temper would sometimes get the better of him. At his headquarters in the Craigie House, Cambridge, he once became so exasperated at the squabbling of drunken soldiers in the front yard that, forgetting the dignity of a general, he rushed forth and laid out a few of the brawlers with his own fists; and then, much relieved, returned to his office. Under great provocation he would break out with a torrent of Olympian oaths that terrified the younger men on his staff. Tobias Lear, the smooth young Harvard graduate who became Washington's private secretary, admitted that the most dreadful experience in his life was hearing the General swear!

It was only through the severest self-discipline that Washington attained his characteristic poise and serenity. Discipline is not a popular word nowadays, for we associate it with schoolmasters, drill sergeants, and dictators; and it was certainly not discipline of that sort that made the passionate young Washington into an effective man. His discipline came in a very small part from parents, masters, or superiors; and in no respect from institutions. It came from environment, from a philosophy of life that he imbibed at an impressionable age; but most of all from his own will. He apprehended the great truth that man can only be free through mastery of himself. Instead of allowing his passions to spend themselves, he restrained them. Instead of indulging himself in a life of pleasure—for which he had ample means at the age of twenty—he placed duty first. In fact he followed exactly that course of conduct which, according to the second-hand popularizers of Freud, makes a person "thwarted," "inhibited," and "repressed." Yet Washington became a liberated, successful, and serene man. The process can hardly fail to interest young men who are struggling with the same difficulties as Washington—although, I am bound to say, under more difficult circumstances.

Whence came this impulse to self-discipline? We can find nothing to account for it in the little we know of Washington's heredity. His family was gentle, but undistinguished. George knew little of his forebears and cared less, although he used the family coat of arms. Lawrence Washington, sometime Fellow of Brasenose College, Oxford, was ejected from his living by the Roundheads as a "malignant Royalist." His son John came to Virginia by way of Barbados as mate of a tobacco ship, and settled there. As an Indian fighter, John Washington was so undisciplined as to embarrass the Governor of Virginia almost as much as did the Indians. His son, Lawrence, father of Augustine and grandfather of George, earned a competence in the merchant marine and settled down to planting. Love of the land was a trait which all Washingtons had in common: they might seek wealth at sea or glory in war, but happiness they found only in the work and sport that came from owning and cultivating land.

Usually the Washingtons married their social betters, but the second marriage of George's father, Augustine, was an exception. Mary Ball, the mother of Washington, has been the object of much sentimental writing; but the cold record of her own and her sons' letters shows her to have been grasping, querulous, and vulgar. She was a selfish and exacting mother, whom most of her children avoided as early as they could; to whom they did their duty, but rendered little love. It was this sainted mother of Washington who opposed almost everything that he did for the public good, who wished his sense of duty to end with his duty to her, who pestered him in his campaigns by complaining letters, and who at a dark moment of the Revolutionary War increased his anxieties by strident complaints of neglect and starvation. Yet for one thing Americans may well be grateful to Mary Ball: her selfishness lost George an opportunity to become midshipman in the Royal Navy, a school whence few Americans emerged other than as loyal subjects of the King.

There is only one other subject connected with Washington upon which there has been more false sentiment, misrepresentation, and mendacity than on that of his mother, and that is his religion. Washington's religion was that of an eighteenth-century gentleman. Baptized in the Church of England, he attended service occasionally as a young man, and more regularly in middle age, as one of the duties of his station. He believed in God: the eighteenth-century Supreme Being, a Divine Philosopher who ruled all things for the best. He was certain of a Providence in the affairs of men. By the same token, he was completely tolerant of other people's beliefs, more so than the American democracy of today; for in a letter to the Swedenborgian church of Baltimore he wrote: "In this enlightened age and in the land of equal liberty it is our boast that a man's religious tenets will not forfeit the protection of the law, nor deprive him of the right of attaining and holding the highest offices that are known in the United States." But Washington never became an active member of any church. Even after his marriage to a devout churchwoman, and when as President of the United States the eyes of all men were upon him, he never joined Martha in the beautiful and comforting sacrament of the body and blood of Christ. Considering the pressure always placed on a man to conform by a religious wife, this abstention from Holy Communion is very significant. Christianity had little or no part in that discipline which made Washington more humble and gentle than any of the great captains, less proud and ambitious than most of the statesmen who have proclaimed themselves disciples of the

Nazarene. His inspiration, as we shall see, came from an entirely different source.

Washington gained little discipline from book learning; but like all Virginian gentlemen of the day he led an active outdoor life, which gave him a magnificent physique. When fully grown he stood a little over six feet, and weighed between 175 and 200 pounds. Broad-shouldered and straight-backed, he carried his head erect and his chin up, and showed a good leg on horse-back. There is no reason to doubt the tradition of his prowess at running, leaping, wrestling, and horsemanship. The handling of horses, in which Washington was skilled at an early age, is one of the finest means of discipline that a youngster can have: for he who cannot control himself can never handle a spirited horse; and for the same reason fox hunting, which was Washington's favorite sport, is the making—or the breaking— of a courageous and considerate gentleman. His amazing physical vitality is proved by an in-cident of his reconnaissance to the Ohio. At the close of December, 1753, he and the scout Christopher Gist attempted to cross the river just above the site of Pittsburgh, on a raft of their own making. The river was full of floating ice, and George, while trying to shove the raft away from an ice floe with his setting-pole, fell overboard, but managed to climb aboard again. They were forced to land on an island and spend the night there without fire or dry clothing. Gist, the professional woodsman, who had not been in the water, froze all his fingers and some of his toes; but Washington suffered no ill effects from the exposure. For that, his healthy Virginia boyhood may be thanked.

His formal education was scanty. The colonial colleges provided a classical discipline more severe and selective than that of their suc-cessors, but George had none of these "ad-vantages." There were no means to prepare him for William and Mary, the college of the Virginia gentry; his father died when he was eleven years old, and as a younger son in a land-poor family, his only schoolmasters were chosen haphazardly. Endowed with the blood and the instincts of a gentleman, he was not given a gentleman's educa-tion, as he became painfully aware when at adolescence he went to live with his half brother at Mount Vernon.

In modern phrase, George was "parked" on the estate which would one day be his. Evidently there had been some sort of family consultation about what to do with him; and Lawrence good-naturedly offered to take his young brother in hand, if only to get him away from the termagant mother. Lawrence Washington, Augustine's favorite son and fondest hope, had been sent to England for his schooling, had served under Admiral Vernon in the war with Spain, and had inherited the bulk of his father's property, to the exclusion of George and the four younger brothers and sisters. The proximity of Mount Vernon to the vast estates of the Fairfax family in the Northern Neck of Virginia gave Lawrence his opportunity. He married a Fairfax, and was admitted to the gay, charmed circle of the First Families of Virginia. He was already a well-established gentleman of thirty when the hob-bledehoy half brother came to stay.

George was then a tall, gangling lad of six-teen years, with enormous hands and feet that were continually getting in his way. Young girls giggled when he entered a room, and burst out laughing at his awkward attempts to court them. He was conscious that he did not "belong," and made every effort to improve his manners. About three years before, a schoolmaster had made him copy out one hundred and ten Rules of Civility from a famous handbook by one Hawkins—a popular guide to good manners already a cen-tury and a half old; and George was probably glad to have this manuscript manual of social etiquette ready to consult. One of the most touching and human pictures of Washington is that of the overgrown schoolboy solemnly conn-ing old Hawkins' warnings against scratching oneself at table, picking one's teeth with a fork, or cracking fleas in company, lest he commit serious breaks in the houses of the great.

These problems of social behavior no doubt occupied much space in Washington's adolescent thoughts. But he was also preparing to be a man of action. At school he had cared only for mathe-matics. He procured more books, progressed further than his schoolmaster could take him, and so qualified to be surveyor to Lord Fairfax. This great gentleman and landowner required an immense amount of surveying in the Shen-andoah Valley, and found it difficult to obtain men with enough mathematics to qualify as surveyors, or sufficient sobriety to run a line straight and see a job through. So George at sixteen earned as Lord Fairfax's surveyor the high salary of a doubloon (about $7.50) a day, most of which he saved up and invested in land. For he had early decided that in the fresh lands of the Virginia Valley and the West lay the road to position, competence, and happiness. His personality as well as his excellent surveying earned him the friendship of the Fairfaxes, liberal and intelligent gentlemen; and this, as we shall see, was of first importance in Washington's moral and intellectual development.

That friendship, not the doubloon a day, was the first and most fortunate gain from this surveying job; the second was the contact which it gave young Washington with frontiersmen, with Indians, and with that great teacher of self-reliance, the wilderness. He had the advantage of a discipline that few of us can obtain today. We are born in crowded cities, and attend crowded schools and colleges; we take our pleasure along crowded highways and in crowded places of amusement; we are tempted to assert ourselves by voice rather than deed, to advertise, to watch the clock, escape responsibility, and leave decisions to others. But a hungry woodsman could not afford to lose patience with a deer he was trying to shoot, or with a trout he was trying to catch; and it did not help him much to bawl out an Indian. If you cannot discipline yourself to quiet and caution in the wilderness, you won't get far; and if you make the wrong decision in woods infested with savages, you will probably have no opportunity to make another. What our New England forebears learned from the sea, Washington learned from the wilderness.

His life from sixteen to twenty was not all spent on forest trails. This was the golden age of the Old Dominion, the fifteen years from 1740 to the French and Indian War. The old roughness and crudeness were passing away. Peace reigned over the land, high prices ruled for tobacco, immigrants were pouring into the back country; the traditional Virginia of Thackeray and Vachel Lindsay—"Land of the gauntlet and the glove"—came into being. Living in Virginia at that time was like riding on the sparkling crest of a great wave just before it breaks and spreads into dull, shallow pools. At Mount Vernon, on the verge of the wilderness, one felt the zest of sharp contrasts, and one received the discipline that comes from life. On the one side were mansion houses where young Washington could learn manners and philosophy from gentlefolk. He took part in all the sports and pastimes of his social equals: dancing and card playing and flirting with the girls. When visiting a town like Williamsburg he never missed a show; and later as President he was a patron of the new American drama. He loved shooting, fox hunting, horse racing, and all the gentlemen's field sports of the day; he bet small sums at cards, and larger sums on the ponies, and was a good loser. He liked to make an impression by fine new clothes, and by riding unruly steeds when girls were looking on; for though ungainly afoot, he was a graceful figure on horseback. He belonged to clubs of men who dined at taverns and drank like gentlemen; that is to say, they drank as much wine as they could hold without getting drunk. Tobacco, curiously enough, made George's head swim; but he learned to smoke the peace pipe with Indians when necessary without disgracing himself.

On the other side of Mount Vernon were log cabins, and all the crude elements of American life: Scots-Irish, Pennsylvania German pioneers, and other poor whites who as insubordinate soldiers would prove the severest test of Washington's indefatigable patience. The incidents of roughing it, such as the "one threadbear blanket with double its weight of vermin, such as lice, fleas, etc." which he records in the journal of his first surveying trip, were not very pleasant, but he took it all with good humor and good sportsmanship. A little town called Alexandria sprang up about a tobacco warehouse and wharf, and young Washington made the first survey of it. There was a Masonic Lodge at Fredericksburg, and George, always a good "joiner," became brother to all the rising journalists and lawyers of the northern colonies. The deep Potomac flowed past Mount Vernon, bearing ships of heavy burthen to the Chesapeake and overseas; you sent your orders to England every year with your tobacco, and ships returned with the latest modes and manners, books and gazettes, and letters full of coffee-house gossip. London did not seem very far away, and young George confessed in a letter that he hoped to visit that "gay Matrapolis" before long.

It was probably just as well that he did not visit London, for he had the best and purest English tradition in Virginia. When Washington was in his later teens, just when a youth is fumbling for a philosophy of life, he came into intimate contact with several members of the Fairfax family. They were of that eighteenth-century Whig gentry who conformed outwardly to Christianity, but derived their real inspiration from Marcus Aurelius, Plutarch, and the Stoic philosophers. Thomas, sixth Lord Fairfax, was a nobleman devoted to "Revolution Principles"—the Glorious Revolution of 1688, in which his father had taken an active part. Of the same line was that General Lord Fairfax, commander-in-chief of the New Model Army, who of all great soldiers in English history most resembles Washington. The ideal of this family was a noble simplicity of living, and a calm acceptance of life: duty to the Commonwealth, generosity to fellow men, unfaltering courage, and enduring virtue; in a word, the Stoic philosophy, which overlaps Christian ethics more than any other discipline of the ancients. A Stoic never evaded life: he faced it. A Stoic never avoided responsibility: he accepted it. A Stoic not only believed in liberty: he practiced it.

It is not necessary to suppose that young Washington read much Stoic philosophy, for he was no great reader at any time; but he must have absorbed it from constant social intercourse with the Fairfaxes of Belvoir, neighbors whom he saw constantly. At Belvoir lived George William Fairfax, eight years Washington's senior, and his companion in surveying expeditions. Anne, the widow of Lawrence Washington, was Fairfax's sister, and Sally, the lady with whom George Washington was so happy (and so miserable) as to fall in love, was his wife. Books were there, if he wanted them. North's Plutarch was in every gentleman's library, and it was Plutarch who wrote the popular life of Cato, Washington's favorite character in history—not crabbed Cato the Censor, but Cato of pent-up Utica. At the age of seventeen, Washington himself owned an outline, in English, of the principal Dialogues of Seneca the younger, "sharpest of all the Stoics." The mere chapter headings are the moral axioms that Washington followed through life:

"An Honest Man can never be outdone in Courtesy"
"A Good man can never be Miserable, nor a Wicked man Happy"
"A Sensual Life is a Miserable Life"
"Hope and Fear are the Bane of Human Life"
"The Contempt of Death makes all the Miseries of Life Easy to us"

And of the many passages that young Washington evidently took to heart, one may select this:

No man is born wise: but Wisdom and Virtue require a Tutor; though we can easily learn to be Vicious without a Master. It is Philosophy that gives us a Veneration for God; a Charity for our Neighbor; that teaches us our Duty to Heaven, and Exhorts us to an Agreement one with another. It unmasks things that are terrible to us, asswages our Lusts, refutes our Errors, restrains our Luxury, Reproves our avarice, and works strangely on tender Natures.

Washington read Addison's tragedy *Cato* in company with his beloved; and if they did not act it together in private theatricals, George expressed the wish that they might. At Valley Forge, when the morale of the army needed a stimulus, Washington caused *Cato* to be performed and attended the performance. It was his favorite play, written, as Pope's prologue says,

To make mankind in conscious virtue bold,
Live o'er each scene, and be what they behold.

Portius, Cato's son, whose "steddy temper"

Can look on guilt, rebellion, fraud, and Cæsar
In the calm lights of mild Philosophy

declares (I, ii, 40-5):

I'll animate the soldiers' drooping courage
With love of freedom, and contempt of Life:
I'll thunder in their ears their country's cause
And try to rouse up all that's Roman in 'em.
'Tis not in Mortals to Command Success
But we'll do more, Sempronius, we'll Deserve it.

These last two lines sound the note that runs through all Washington's correspondence in the dark hours of the Revolutionary struggle; and these same lines are almost the only literary quotations found in the vast body of Washington's writings. Many years after, when per-plexed and wearied by the political squabbles of his Presidency and longing to retire to Mount Vernon, Washington quoted the last lines of Cato's advice to Portius (IV, iv, 146-54):

Let me advise thee to retreat betimes
To thy paternal seat, the Sabine field,
Where the great Censor toil'd with his own hands,
And all our frugal Ancestors were blest
In humble virtues, and a rural life.
There lived retired, pray for the peace of Rome:
Content thy self to be obscurely good.
When vice prevails, and impious men bear sway,
The post of honour is a private station.

From his camp with General Forbes's army in the wilderness, Washington wrote to Sally Fairfax, September 25, 1758: "I should think our time more agreeably spent, believe me, in playing a part in Cato with the Company you mention, and myself doubly happy in being the Juba to such a Marcia as you must take." Marcia was the worthy daughter of Cato, and Juba her lover, the young Numidian prince to whom Syphax says:

You have not read mankind, your youth admires
The throws and swellings of a Roman soul,
Cato's bold flights, th' extravagance of Virtue.

And Juba had earlier said, (I, iv, 49-58):

Turn up thy eyes to Cato!
There may'st thou see to what a godlike height
The Roman virtues lift up mortal man.
While good, and just, and anxious for his friends,
He's still severely bent against himself;
Renouncing sleep, and rest, and food, and ease,
He strives with thirst and hunger, toil and heat;
And when his fortune sets before him all
The pomps and pleasures that his soul can wish,
His rigid virtue will accept of none.

So, here we have a young man of innate noble qualities, seeking a philosophy of life, thrown in contact during his most impressionable years with a great gentleman whom he admired, a young gentleman who was his best friend, and a young lady whom he loved, all three steeped in the Stoical tradition. What would you ex-pect? Can it be a mere coincidence that this characterization of the Emperor Antoninus Pius by his adopted son Marcus Aurelius, the Im-perial Stoic, so perfectly fits the character of Washington?

Take heed lest thou become a Cæsar indeed; lest the purple stain thy soul. For such things have been. Then keep thyself simple, good, pure, and serious; a friend to justice and the fear of God; kindly, affec-tionate, and strong to do the right. Reverence Heaven and succour man. Life is short; and earthly exist-ence yields but one harvest, holiness of character and altruism of action. Be in everything a true disciple of Antoninus. Emulate his constancy in all rational activity, his unvarying equability, his purity, his cheerfulness of countenance, his sweetness, his con-tempt for notoriety, and his eagerness to come at the root of the matter.

Remember how he would never dismiss any sub-ject until he had gained a clear insight into it and grasped it thoroughly; how he bore with the injus-tice of his detractors and never retorted in kind; how he did nothing in haste, turned a deaf ear to the professional tale-bearers, and showed himself an acute judge of characters and actions, devoid of all re-proachfulness, timidity, suspiciousness, and sophistry; how easily he was satisfied—for instance, with lodg-ing, bed, clothing, food, and servants—how fond of work and how patient; capable, thanks to his frugal diet, of remaining at his post from morning till night, having apparently subjected even the operations of nature to his will; firm and constant in friendship, tolerant of the most outspoken criticism of his opin-ions, delighted if any one could make a better sug-gestion than himself, and, finally, deeply religious without any trace of superstition.

When Washington was twenty years old, his brother Lawrence died. George, next heir by their father's will, stepped into his place as proprietor of Mount Vernon. At this stage of his life, George did not greatly enjoy the exact-ing task of running a great plantation; he thirsted for glory in war. But he soon began to enlarge and improve his holdings, and in the end came to love the land as nothing else. Late in life, when the First Citizen of the World, he wrote: "How much more delightful is the task of making improvements on the earth than all the vain-glory which can be acquired from ravaging it by the most uninterrupted career of conquests." And again: "To see plants rise from the earth and flourish by the superior skill and bounty of the laborer fills a contemplative mind with ideas which are more easy to be conceived than expressed." That was the way with all Washington's ideas: they were more easily con-ceived and executed than expressed on paper. Ideas did not interest him, nor was he interested in himself. Hence the disappointing matter-of-fact objectiveness of his letters and diaries.

Nevertheless, it is clear from Washington's diaries that farming was a great factor in his discipline. For the lot of a Virginia planter was not as romance has colored it. Slaves had to be driven, or they ate out your substance; overseers had to be watched, or they slacked and stole; accounts had to be balanced, or you became poorer every year. There were droughts, and insect pests, and strange maladies among the cattle. Washington's life at Mount Vernon was one of constant experiment, unremitting labor, unwearying patience. It was a continual war against human error, insect enemies, and tradition. He might provide improved flails and a clean threshing floor in his new barn; when his back was turned the overseer would have the wheat out in the yard, to be trod into the muck by the cattle. His books prove that he was an eager and bold experimenter in that "new husbandry" of which Coke of Norfolk was the great exponent. There were slave blacksmiths, carpenters, and bricklayers; a cider press and a still-house, where excellent corn and rye whisky were made, and sold in barrels made by the slaves from plantation oak. Herring and shad fisheries in the Potomac provided food for the slaves; a gristmill turned Washington's improved strain of wheat into flour, which was taken to market in his own schooner, which he could handle like any down-East skipper. Indeed, it is in his husbandry that we can earliest discern those qualities that made Washington the first soldier and statesman of America. As landed proprietor no less than as commander-in-chief he showed executive ability, the power of planning for a distant end, and a capacity for taking infinite pains. Neither drought nor defeat could turn him from a course that he discerned to be proper and right; but in farming as in war he learned from failure, and grew in stature from loss and adversity.

Not long after inheriting Mount Vernon, Washington had an opportunity to test what his brother had taught him of military tactics and the practice of arms. Drilling and tactics, like surveying, were a projection of Washington's mathematical mind; like every born strategist he could see moving troops in his mind's eye, march and deploy them and calculate the time to a minute. He devoured accounts of Frederick's campaigns, and doubtless dreamt of directing a great battle on a grassy plain, a terrain he was destined never to fight on in this shaggy country. As one of the first landowners in the county, at twenty he was commissioned major of militia. He then asked for and obtained the post of adjutant of militia for the county. The settlement of his brother's affairs brought him into contact with Governor Dinwiddie, a shrewd Scot who knew a dependable young man when he saw one; and from this came his first great opportunity.

At twenty-one he was sent on a highly confidential and difficult thousand-mile reconnaissance through the back country from western Virginia to the Ohio, and almost to the shores of Lake Erie. This young man just past his majority showed a caution in wilderness work, a diplomatic skill in dealing with Indians, and a courteous firmness in dealing with French commanders that would have done credit to a man twice his age. But on his next mission, one notes with a feeling of relief, youthful impetuosity prevailed. Unmindful that one must always let the enemy make the first aggression, our young lieutenant colonel fired the shot that began the Seven Years' War.

A phrase of the young soldier's blithe letter to his younger brother: "I heard the bullets whistle, and believe me, there is something charming in the sound," got into the papers, and gave sophisticated London a good laugh. Even King George II heard it and remarked: "He would not say so, if he had been used to hear many!" That time would come soon enough. Washington's shot in the silent wilderness brought the French and Indians buzzing about his ears. He retired to Fort Necessity, which he had caused to be built in a large meadow, hoping to tempt the enemy to a pitched battle. But the enemy was very inconsiderate. He swarmed about the fort in such numbers that Washington was lucky to be allowed to capitulate and go home; for this was one of those wars that was not yet a war; it was not declared till two years after the fighting began. The enemy was so superior in numbers that nobody blamed Washington; and when General Braddock arrived with an army of regulars, he invited the young frontier leader to accompany his expedition into the wilderness.

There is no need for me to repeat the tale of Braddock's defeat, except to say that the general's stupidity and the colonel's part in saving what could be saved have both been exaggerated. Parkman wrote in his classic *Montcalm and Wolfe:* "Braddock has been charged with marching blindly into an ambuscade; but it was not so. There was no ambuscade; and had there been one, he would have found it." That is the truth of the matter; and whilst Washington's behavior was creditable in every respect, he did not save Braddock's army; the French and Indians were simply too busy despoiling the dead and wounded to pursue.

Shortly after Washington reached Alexandria, the annual electoral campaign began for members of the Virginia Assembly. In a political dispute the colonel said something insulting to a quick-tempered little fellow named Payne, who promptly knocked him down with a hickory stick. Soldiers rushed up to avenge Washington, who recovered just in time to tell them he was not hurt, and could take care of himself, thank you! The next day he wrote to Payne requesting an interview at a tavern. The little man arrived, expecting a demand for an apology, or a challenge. Instead, Washington apologized for the insult which had provoked the blow, hoped that Payne was satisfied, and offered his hand. Some of Washington's biographers cannot imagine or understand such conduct. One of them brackets this episode with the cherry-tree yarn as "stories so silly and so foolishly impossible that they do not deserve an instant's consideration." Another explains Washington's conduct as a result of his defeat at Fort Necessity: "Washington was crushed into such meekness at this time that . . . instead of retaliating or challenging the fellow to a duel, he apologized." But the incident, which has been well substantiated, occurred after Braddock's defeat, not Washington's; and it was due to Stoical magnanimity, not Christian meekness. "It is the Part of a Great Mind to despise Injuries," says Seneca the younger, in the L'Estrange translation that Washington owned. The Payne affair was merely an early instance of what Washington was doing all his life: admitting he was wrong when he was convinced he was in the wrong, and doing the handsome thing in a gentlemanly manner. A man who took that attitude became impregnable to attack by politicians or anyone else. For a young man of twenty-three to take it meant that he had firm hold of a great philosophy.

During the next two years Washington had charge of the frontier defenses of Virginia, and a chain of thirty garrisoned stockades which followed the Shenandoah Valley and its outer bulwarks from Winchester to the North Carolina line. In the execution of this command he showed a prodigious physical activity, often riding thirty miles a day for several days over wilderness trails. His letters show a youthful touchiness about rank and recognition; he sorely tried the patience of Governor Dinwiddie, who, to Washington's evident surprise, accepted a proffered resignation; but he was soon reappointed and took a leading part in General Forbes's expedition against Fort Duquesne. It was merely to settle a question of precedence that Washington undertook a long journey to interview Governor Shirley, the commander-in-chief, at Boston. Two aides, and two servants clad in new London liveries of the Washington colors and mounted on horses with the Washington arms embroidered on their housings, accompanied their colonel; for George had a young man's natural desire to make an impressive appearance. He stopped with great folk at Philadelphia and New York and gave generous tips to their servants. At New London the exhausted horses had to be left behind, and the colonel and suite proceeded by sea to Boston, where George ordered a new hat and uniform, a mass of silver lace, and two pair of gloves. But Washington never made the mistake of wearing splendid clothes on the wrong occasion. In the French and Indian War he wore a plain, neutral-colored uniform instead of royal scarlet, and dressed his soldiers as frontiersmen, in buckskin and moccasins, so that they carried no superfluous weight and offered no mark to the Indians.

As a young officer he often became impatient with the frontier folk—their shortsighted selfishness in refusing to unite under his command, their lack of discipline and liability to panic, and the American militiaman's propensity to offer unwanted advice and sulk if it were not taken.

But he found something to like in them as he did in all men, and learned to work with and through them. Militia deserted Washington as they deserted other officers, despite the flogging of sundry and the hanging of a few to encourage the rest. Here is plenty of material for a disparaging biographer to describe Washington as a military martinet who had not even the merit of a notable victory; and some of the "debunkers," who have never known what it is to command troops, have said just that. A sufficient reply to them, as well as striking proof of the amazing confidence, even veneration, which Washington inspired at an early age, is the "Humble Address" of the twenty-seven officers of his regiment, beseeching him to withdraw his resignation:

SIR,

We your most obedient and affectionate Officers, beg leave to express our great Concern, at the disagreeable News we have received of your Determination to resign the Command of that Corps, in which we have under you long served. . . .

In our earliest Infancy you took us under your Tuition, train'd us up in the Practice of that Discipline, which alone can constitute good Troops, from the punctual Observance of which you never suffer'd the least Deviation.

Your steady adherence to impartial Justice, your quick Discernment and invariable Regard to Merit . . . first heighten'd our natural Emulation, and our Desire to excel. . . .

Judge then, how sensibly we must be Affected with the loss of such an excellent Commander, such a sincere Friend, and so affable a Companion. . . .

It gives us an additional Sorrow, when we reflect, to find, our unhappy Country will receive a loss, no less irreparable, than ourselves. Where will it meet a Man so experienc'd in military Affairs? One so renown'd for Patriotism, Courage and Conduct? Who has so great knowledge of the Enemy we have to deal with? Who so well acquainted with their Situation and Strength? Who so much respected by the Soldiery? Who in short so able to support the military Character of Virginia? . . .

We with the greatest Deference, presume to entreat you to suspend those Thoughts [of resigning] for another Year. . . . In you we place the most implicit Confidence. Your Presence only will cause a steady Firmness and Vigor to actuate in every Breast, despising the greatest Dangers, and thinking light of Toils and Hardships, while lead on by the Man we know and Love. . . .

Fully persuaded of this, we beg Leave to assure you, that as you have hitherto been the actuating Soul of the whole Corps, we shall at all times pay the most invariable Regard to your Will and Pleasure, and will always be happy to demonstrate by our Actions, with how much Respect and Esteem we are,
Sir,

Fort Loudoun   Your most affectionate
Decr 31st 1758   and most obedient humble Servants
[Followed by twenty-seven signatures]

There stands the young man Washington, reflected in the hearts of his fellows. As one reads this youthfully sincere composition of the officers' mess at Fort Loudoun, one imagines it addressed to a grizzled veteran of many wars, a white-whiskered colonel of fifty. Colonel Washington was just twenty-six.

A farewell to arms Washington was determined it must be. Fort Duquesne was won, and his presence at the front was no longer needed. Virginia, the colony which had received the first shock of the war, could justly count on British regulars and the northern colonies to carry it to a glorious conclusion on the Plains of Abraham.

In four years Washington had learned much from war. He found it necessary to discipline himself before he could handle men. He had learned that the interminable boredom of drill, arguing about supplies, and begging for transportation was ill rewarded by the music of whistling bullets; that war was simply hard, beastly work. The sufferings of the border people, the bloody shambles on the Monongahela, the frozen evidence of torture on the road to Fort Duquesne, cured his youthful appetite for glory, completely. When Washington again drew his sword, in 1775, it was with great reluctance, and only because he believed, like Cato (II, v, 85):

> The hand of fate is over us, and Heaven
> Exacts severity from all our thoughts.
> It is not now a time to talk of aught
> But chains, or conquest; liberty, or death.

From one woman he learned perhaps as much as from war. Sally Cary, his fair tutor in Stoicism and the love of this youth, was eighteen and married to his friend and neighbor George William Fairfax, when at sixteen he first met her. Beautiful, intelligent, and of gentle birth, Mrs. Fairfax took a more than sisterly interest in the callow young surveyor; and as near neighbors they saw much of each other. Cryptic jottings in his diary for 1748 show that he was already far gone in love. His pathetic letter to her from Fort Cumberland in 1755, begging for a reply to "make me happier than the day is long," strikes a human note in the midst of his businesslike military correspondence. No letters from her to him have been preserved, but from the tone of his replies I gather that Sally was somewhat more of a tease than befitted Cato's daughter. Whatever her sentiments may have been toward him, Washington's letters leave no doubt that he was passionately in love with her; yet gentlemanly standards were then such that while her husband lived she could never be his wife, much less his mistress. What anguish he must have suffered, any young man can imagine. It was a situation that schooled the young soldier-lover in manners, moderation, and restraint—a test case of his Stoical philosophy. His solution was notable for its common sense: when on a hurried visit to Williamsburg in the spring of 1758, to procure clothes for his ragged soldiers, he met, wooed, and won a housewifely little widow of twenty-seven named Martha Custis. She wanted a manager for her property and a stepfather for her children; he needed a housekeeper for Mount Vernon. It was a *mariage de convenance* that developed into a marriage of affection. But Martha well knew that she was not George's first or greatest love, nor he hers.

Thirty years later, when Mrs. Fairfax was a poor and childless widow in London, crushing the memories of a Virginia springtime in her heart, there came a letter from Washington. The First Citizen of the World writes that the crowded events of the more than a quarter-century since they parted have not "been able to eradicate from my mind the recollection of those happy moments, the happiest in my life, which I have enjoyed in your company." Martha Washington enclosed a letter under the same cover, in order to show that she, too, understood.

Let us neither distort nor exaggerate this relation, the most beautiful thing in Washington's life. Washington saw no visions of Sally Fairfax in the battle smoke. He did not regard himself as her knightly champion, or any such romantic nonsense; Walter Scott had not yet revived the age of chivalry. Women occupied a small part in Washington's thoughts, as in those of most men of action. No more than Cato did he indulge in worry or bitter thoughts about his ill fortune in love. Suppose, however, Washington had turned out a failure or shown some fault of character at a critical moment, instead of superbly meeting every test. Every yapping biographer of the last decade would have blamed the three members of this blameless triangle. Since he turned out otherwise, we can hardly fail to credit both women with an important share in the formation of Washington's character. And who will deny that Washington attained his nearly perfect balance and serenity, not through self-indulgence but through restraint?

Plutarch wrote of Cato: "He had not taken to public life, like some others, casually or automatically or for the sake of fame or personal advantage. He chose it because it was the function proper to a good man." That was why Washington allowed himself to be elected in 1758 to the Virginia Assembly, an office proper to a gentleman of his station. He had no gift for speaking or for wirepulling; he showed no talent or desire for political leadership. But he learned at first hand the strange behavior of *Homo sapiens* in legislative assemblies. Everyone marvels at the long-suffering patience shown by Washington in his dealings with Congress during the war; few remember that he had been for many years a burgess of Virginia, and for several months a member of the very Congress to which he was responsible.

So at twenty-seven George Washington was not only a veteran colonel who had won the confidence and affection of his men, but a member of the Virginia Assembly, a great landowner, and a husband. His youth was over, and he had the means for a life of ease and competence; but the high example of antique virtue would not let him ignore another call to duty. When it came, his unruly nature had been disciplined by the land and the wilderness, by philosophy and a noble woman, and by his own indomitable will, to become a fit instrument for a great cause. There were other colonial soldiers in 1775 who from better opportunity had gained more glory in the last war than he; but there was none who inspired so much confidence as this silent, capable man of forty-three. So that when the political need of the moment required a Virginian, there was no question but that Colonel Washington should be commander-in-chief.

If he had failed, historians would have blamed the Continental Congress for a political appointment of a provincial colonel with an indifferent war record. If he had failed, the American Revolution would have been something worse than futile—a Rebellion of '98 that would have soured the American character, made us another Ireland, with a long and distressful struggle for freedom ahead. If, like so many leaders of revolutions, he had merely achieved a personal triumph, or inoculated his country with ambition for glory, the world would have suffered from his success. His country could and almost did fail Washington; but Washington could not fail his country, or disappoint the expectations of his kind. A simple gentleman of Virginia with no extraordinary talents had so disciplined himself that he could lead an insubordinate and divided people into ordered liberty and enduring union.

EXERCISE

In "Lady Olga," Mitchell gives us a portrait of a woman of no importance. Here Morison describes the youth of the most famous American. A certain tone, a certain feeling, dominates "Lady Olga." There is pathos in her story; yet admiration is evoked. We can, presumably, see what attracted the attention of the author. The historical importance of Washington might very well attract Morison to this subject: whatever Washington was would, naturally, prove of some interest. But what is the special attraction that draws Morison? What, shall we ask, is the theme, the idea, of the essay, the values of which Washington is, finally, but an embodiment? Show how the structure of the essay relates to this idea.

The Life of Samuel Johnson

(Selection)

JAMES BOSWELL (1740-1795)

THIS IS to me a memorable year; for in it I had the happiness to obtain the acquaintance of that extraordinary man whose memoirs I am now writing; an acquaintance which I shall ever esteem as one of the most fortunate circumstances in my life. Though then but two-and-twenty, I had for several years read his work with delight and instruction, and had the highest reverence for their author, which had grown up in my fancy into a kind of mysterious veneration, by figuring to myself a state of solemn elevated abstraction, in which I supposed him to live in the immense metropolis of London. Mr. Gentleman, a native of Ireland, who passed some years in Scotland as a player, and as an instructor in the English language, a man whose talents and worth were depressed by misfortunes, had given me a representation of the figure and manner of DICTIONARY JOHNSON! as he was then generally called, and during my first visit to London, which was for three months in 1760, Mr. Derrick the poet, who was Gentleman's friend and countryman, flattered me with hopes that he would introduce me to Johnson, an honor of which I was very ambitious. But he never found an opportunity; which made me doubt that he had promised to do what was not in his power; till Johnson some years afterwards told me, "Derrick, Sir, might very well have introduced you. I had a kindness for Derrick, and am sorry he is dead."

In the summer of 1761 Mr. Thomas Sheridan was at Edinburgh, and delivered lectures upon the English Language and Public Speaking to large and respectable audiences. I was often in his company, and heard him frequently expatiate upon Johnson's extraordinary knowledge, talents, and virtues, repeat his pointed sayings, describe his particularities, and boast of his being his guest sometimes till two or three in the morning. At his house I hoped to have many opportunities of seeing the sage, as Mr. Sheridan obligingly assured me I should not be disappointed.

When I returned to London in the end of

1762, to my surprise and regret I found an irreconcileable difference had taken place between Johnson and Sheridan. A pension of two hundred pounds a year had been given to Sheridan. Johnson, who as has been already mentioned, thought slightingly of Sheridan's art, upon hearing that he was also pensioned, exclaimed, "What! have they given *him* a pension? Then it is time for me to give up mine." Whether this proceeded from a momentary indignation, as if it were an affront to his exalted merit that a player should be rewarded in the same manner with him, or was the sudden effect of a fit of peevishness, it was unluckily said, and, indeed, cannot be justified. Mr. Sheridan's pension was granted to him not as a player, but as a sufferer in the cause of government, when he was manager of the Theatre Royal in Ireland, when parties ran high in 1753. And it must also be allowed that he was a man of literature, and had considerably improved the arts of reading and speaking with distinctness and propriety.

Besides, Johnson should have recollected that Mr. Sheridan taught pronunciation to Mr. Alexander Wedderburne, whose sister was married to Sir Harry Erskine, an intimate friend of Lord Bute, who was the favorite of the King; and surely the most outrageous Whig will not maintain, that, whatever ought to be the principle in the disposal of *offices,* a *pension* ought never to be granted from any bias of court connection. Mr. Macklin, indeed, shared with Mr. Sheridan the honor of instructing Mr. Wedderburne; and though it was too late in life for a Caledonian to acquire the genuine English cadence, yet so successful were Mr. Wedderburne's instructors, and his own unabating endeavors, that he got rid of the coarse part of his Scotch accent, retaining only as much of the "native woodnote wild," as to mark his country; which, if any Scotchman should effect to forget, I should heartily despise him. Notwithstanding the difficulties which are to be encountered by those who had not had the advantage of an English education, he by degrees formed a mode of speaking to which Englishmen do not deny the praise of elegance. Hence his distinguished oratory, which he exerted in his own country as an advocate in the Court of Session, and a ruling elder of the *Kirk,* has had its fame and ample reward, in much higher sphere. When I look back on this noble person at Edinburgh, in situations so unworthy of his brilliant powers, and behold LORD LOUGHBOROUGH at London, the change seems almost like one of the metamorphoses in *Ovid;* and as his two preceptors, by refining his utterance, gave currency to his talents, we may say in the words of that poet, *"Nam vos mutastis."*

I have dwelt the longer upon this remarkable instance of successful parts and assiduity; because it affords animating encouragement to other gentlemen of North-Britain to try their fortunes in the southern part of the Island, where they may hope to gratify their utmost ambition; and now that we are one people by the Union, it would surely be illiberal to maintain, that they have not an equal title with the natives of any other part of his Majesty's dominions.

Johnson complained that a man who disliked him repeated his sarcasm to Mr. Sheridan, without telling him what followed, which was, that after a pause he added, "However, I am glad that Mr. Sheridan has a pension, for he is a very good man." Sheridan could never forgive this hasty contemptuous expression. It rankled in his mind; and though I informed him of all that Johnson said, and that he would be very glad to meet him amicably, he positively declined repeated offers which I made, and once went off abruptly from a house where he and I were engaged to dine, because he was told that Dr. Johnson was to be there. I have no sympathetic feeling with such persevering resentment. It is painful when there is a breach between those who had lived together socially and cordially; and I wonder that there is not, in all such cases, a mutual wish that it should be healed. I could perceive that Mr. Sheridan was by no means satisfied with Johnson's acknowledging him to be a good man. That could not soothe his injured vanity. I could not but smile, at the same time that I was offended, to observe Sheridan in *The Life of Swift,* which he afterwards published, attempting, in the writhings of resentment, to depreciate Johnson, by characterizing him as "A writer of gigantic fame in these days of little men"; that very Johnson whom he once so highly admired and venerated.

This rupture with Sheridan deprived Johnson of one of his most agreeable resources for amusement in his lonely evenings; for Sheridan's well-informed, animated, and bustling mind never suffered conversation to stagnate; and Mrs. Sheridan was a most agreeable companion to an intellectual man. She was sensible, ingenious, unassuming, yet communicative. I recollect, with satisfaction, many pleasing hours which I passed with her under the hospitable roof of her husband, who was to me a very kind friend. Her novel, entitled *Memoirs of Miss Sydney Biddulph,* contains an excellent moral while it inculcates a future state of retribution; and what it teaches is impressed upon the mind by a series of as deep distress as can effect humanity, in the amiable and pious heroine who goes to her grave unrelieved, but resigned, and full of hope of "heaven's mercy." Johnson paid her this high compliment upon it: "I know not, Madam, that you have a right, upon moral principles, to make your readers suffer so much."

Mr. Thomas Davies the actor, who then kept a bookseller's shop in Russel-street, Covent-garden, told me that Johnson was very much his friend, and came frequently to his house, where he more than once invited me to meet him; but by some unlucky accident or other he was prevented from coming to us.

Mr. Thomas Davies was a man of good understanding and talents, with the advantage of a liberal education. Though somewhat pompous, he was an entertaining companion; and his literary performances have no inconsiderable share of merit. He was a friendly and very hospitable man. Both he and his wife, (who has been celebrated for her beauty,) though upon the stage for many years, maintained an uniform decency of character; and Johnson esteemed them, and lived in as easy an intimacy with them, as with any family which he used to visit. Mr. Davies recollected several of Johnson's remarkable sayings, and was one of the best of the many imitators of his voice and manner, while relating them. He increased my impatience more and more to see the extraordinary man whose works I highly valued, and

whose conversation was reported to be so peculiarly excellent.

At last, on Monday the 16th of May, when I was sitting in Mr. Davies's back-parlor, after having drunk tea with him and Mrs. Davies, Johnson unexpectedly came into the shop; and Mr. Davies having perceived him through the glass-door in the room in which we were sitting, advancing towards us,—he announced his aweful approach to me, somewhat in the manner of an actor in the part of Horatio, when he addresses Hamlet on the appearance of his father's ghost, "Look, my Lord, it comes." I found that I had a very perfect idea of Johnson's figure, from the portrait of him painted by Sir Joshua Reynolds soon after he had published his *Dictionary,* in the attitude of sitting in his easy chair in deep meditation, which Sir Joshua very kindly presented to me, and from which an engraving has been made for this work. Mr. Davies mentioned my name, and respectfully introduced me to him. I was much agitated; and recollecting his prejudice against the Scotch, of which I had heard much, I said to Davies, "Don't tell where I come from."—"From Scotland," cried Davies roguishly. "Mr. Johnson, (said I) I do indeed come from Scotland, but I cannot help it." I am willing to flatter myself that I meant this as light pleasantry to soothe and conciliate him, and not as an humiliating abasement at the expense of my country. But however that might be, this speech was somewhat unlucky; for with that quickness of wit for which he was so remarkable, he seized the expression "come from Scotland," which I used in the sense of being of that country; and, as if I had said that I had come away from it, or left it, retorted, "That, Sir, I find, is what a very great many of your countrymen cannot help." This stroke stunned me a good deal; and when we had sat down, I felt myself not a little embarrassed, and apprehensive of what might come next. He then addressed himself to Davies: "What do you think of Garrick? He has refused me an order for the play for Miss Williams, because he knows the house will be full, and that an order would be worth three shillings." Eager to take any opening to get into conversation with him, I ventured to say, "O, Sir, I cannot think Mr. Garrick would grudge such a trifle to you." "Sir, (said he, with a stern look,) I have known David Garrick longer than you have done: and I know no right you have to talk to me on the subject." Perhaps I deserved this check; for it was rather presumptuous in me, an entire stranger, to express any doubt of the justice of his animadversion upon his old acquaintance and pupil. I now felt myself much mortified, and began to think that the hope which I had long indulged of obtaining his acquaintance was blasted. And, in truth, had not my ardor been uncommonly strong, and my resolution uncommonly persevering, so rough a reception might have deterred me for ever from making any further attempts. . . .

A few days afterwards I called on Davies, and asked him if he thought I might take the liberty of waiting on Mr. Johnson at his Chambers in the Temple. He said I certainly might, and that Mr. Johnson would take it as a compliment. So upon Tuesday the 24th of May, after having been enlivened by the witty sallies of Messieurs Thornton, Wilkes, Churchill and Lloyd, with whom I had passed the morning, I boldly repaired to Johnson. His Chambers were on the first floor of No. 1, Inner-Temple-lane, and I entered them with an impression given me by the Reverend Dr. Blair, of Edinburgh, who had been introduced to him not long before, and described his having "found the Giant in his den," an expression, which, when I came to be pretty well acquainted with Johnson, I repeated to him, and he was diverted at this picturesque account of himself. Dr. Blair had been presented to him by Dr. James Fordyce. At this time the controversy concerning the pieces published by Mr. James Macpherson, as translations of *Ossian*, was at its height. Johnson had all along denied their authenticity; and, what was still more provoking to their admirers, maintained that they had no merit. The subject having been introduced by Dr. Fordyce, Dr. Blair, relying on the internal evidence of their antiquity, asked Dr. Johnson whether he thought any man of a modern age could have written such poems? Johnson replied, "Yes, Sir, many men, many women, and many children." Johnson, at this time, did not know that Dr. Blair had just published a *Dissertation*, not only defending their authenticity,

but seriously ranking them with the poems of *Homer and Virgil;* and when he was afterwards informed of this circumstance, he expressed some displeasure at Dr. Fordyce's having suggested the topic, and said, "I am not sorry that they got thus much for their pains. Sir, it was like leading one to talk of a book when the author is concealed behind the door."

He received me very courteously; but, it must be confessed, that his apartment, and furniture, and morning dress, were sufficiently uncouth. His brown suit of clothes looked very rusty; he had on a little old shrivelled unpowdered wig, which was too small for his head; his shirt-neck and knees of his breeches were loose; his black worsted stockings ill drawn up; and he had a pair of unbuckled shoes by way of slippers. But all these slovenly particularities were forgotten the moment that he began to talk. Some gentlemen, whom I do not recollect, were sitting with him; and when they went away, I also rose; but he said to me, "Nay, don't go." "Sir, (said I,) I am afraid that I intrude upon you. It is benevolent to allow me to sit and hear you." He seemed pleased with this compliment, which I sincerely paid him, and answered, "Sir, I am obliged to any man who visits me." I have preserved the following short minute of what passed this day:—

"Madness frequently discovers itself merely by unnecessary deviation from the usual modes of the world. My poor friend Smart showed the disturbance of his mind, by falling upon his knees, and saying his prayers in the street, or in any other unusual place. Now although, rationally speaking, it is greater madness not to pray at all, than to pray as Smart did, I am afraid there are so many who do not pray, that their understanding is not called in question."

Concerning this unfortunate poet, Christopher Smart, who was confined in a mad-house, he had, at another time, the following conversation with Dr. Burney:—BURNEY. "How does poor Smart do, Sir; is he likely to recover?" JOHNSON. "It seems as if his mind had ceased to struggle with the disease; for he grows fat upon it." BURNEY. "Perhaps, Sir; he has partly as much exercise as he used to have, for he digs in the garden. Indeed, before his confinement, he used for exercise to walk to the ale-house;

but he was *carried* back again. I did not think he ought to be shut up. His infirmities were not noxious to society. He insisted on people praying with him; and I'd as lief pray with Kit Smart as any one else. Another charge was, that he did not love clean linen; and I have no passion for it."—Johnson continued. "Mankind have a great aversion to intellectual labor; but even supposing knowledge to be easily attainable, more people would be content to be ignorant than would take even a little trouble to acquire it."

"The morality of an action depends on the motive from which we act. If I fling half a crown to a beggar with intention to break his head, and he picks it up and buys victuals with it, the physical effect is good; but, with respect to me, the action is very wrong. So, religious exercises, if not performed with an intention to please GOD, avail us nothing. As our Savior says of those who perform them from other motives, 'Verily they have their reward.'

"The Christian religion has very strong evidences. It, indeed, appears in some degree strange to reason; but in History we have undoubted facts, against which, reasoning *a priori*, we have more arguments than we have for them; but then, testimony has great weight, and casts the balance. I would recommend to every man whose faith is yet unsettled, Grotius,—Dr. Pearson,—and Dr. Clarke."

Talking of Garrick, he said, "He is the first man in the world for sprightly conversation."

When I rose a second time he again pressed me to stay, which I did.

He told me, that he generally went abroad at four in the afternoon, and seldom came home till two in the morning. I took the liberty to ask if he did not think it wrong to live thus, and not make more use of his great talents. He owned it was a bad habit. On reviewing, at the distance of many years, my journal of this period, I wonder how, at my first visit, I ventured to talk to him so freely, and that he bore it with so much indulgence.

Before we parted, he was so good as to promise to favor me with his company one evening at my lodgings; and, as I took my leave, shook me cordially by the hand. It is almost needless to add, that I felt no little elation at having now so happily established an acquaintance of which I had been so long ambitious.

My readers will, I trust, excuse me for being thus minutely circumstantial, when it is considered that the acquaintance of Dr. Johnson was to me a most valuable acquisition, and laid the foundation of whatever instruction and entertainment they may receive from my collections concerning the great subject of the work which they are now perusing.

I did not visit him again till Monday, June 13, at which time I recollect no part of his conversation, except that when I told him I had been to see Johnson ride upon three horses, he said, "Such a man, Sir, should be encouraged; for his performances show the extent of the human powers in one instance, and thus tend to raise our opinion of the faculties of man. He shows what may be attained by persevering application; so that every man may hope, that by giving as much application, although perhaps he may never ride three horses at a time, or dance upon a wire, yet he may be equally expert in whatever profession he has chosen to pursue."

He again shook me by the hand at parting, and asked me why I did not come oftener to him. Trusting that I was now in his good graces, I answered, that he had not given me much encouragement, and reminded him of the check I had received from him at our first interview. "Poh, poh! (said he, with a complacent smile,) never mind these things. Come to me as often as you can. I shall be glad to see you."

I had learnt that his place of frequent resort was the Mitre tavern in Fleet-street, where he loved to sit up late, and I begged I might be allowed to pass an evening with him there soon, which he promised I should. A few days afterwards I met him near Temple-bar, about one o'clock in the morning, and asked if he would then go to the Mitre. "Sir, (said he,) it is too late; they won't let us in. But I'll go with you another night with all my heart."

A revolution of some importance in my plan of life had just taken place; for instead of procuring a commission in the foot-guards, which was my own inclination, I had, in compliance with my father's wishes, agreed to study the law; and was soon to set out for Utrecht, to hear the lectures of an excellent Civilian in that University, and then to proceed on my travels. Though very desirous of obtaining Dr. Johnson's advice and instructions on the mode of pursuing my studies, I was at this time so occupied, shall I call it? or so dissipated, by the amusements of London, that our next meeting was not till Saturday, June 25, when happening to dine at Clifton's eating-house, in Butcher-row, I was surprised to perceive Johnson come in and take his seat at another table. The mode of dining, or rather being fed, at such houses in London, is well known to many to be particularly unsocial, as there is no Ordinary, or united company, but each person has his own mess, and is under no obligation to hold any intercourse with any one. A liberal and full-minded man, however, who loves to talk, will break through this churlish and unsocial restraint. Johnson and an Irish gentleman got into a dispute concerning the cause of some part of mankind being black. "Why, Sir, (said Johnson,) it has been accounted for in three ways: either by supposing that they are the posterity of Ham, who was cursed; or that GOD at first created two kinds of men, one black and another white; or that by the heat of the sun the skin is scorched, and so acquires a sooty hue. This matter has been much canvassed among naturalists, but has never been brought to any certain issue." What the Irishman said is totally obliterated from my mind; but I remember that he became very warm and intemperate in his expressions; upon which Johnson rose, and quietly walked away. When he had retired, his antagonist took his revenge, as he thought, by saying, "He has a most ungainly figure, and an affectation of pomposity, unworthy of a man of genius."

Johnson had not observed that I was in the room. I followed him, however, and he agreed to meet me in the evening at the Mitre. I called on him, and we went thither at nine. We had a good supper, and port wine, of which he then sometimes drank a bottle. The orthodox high-church sound of the MITRE,—the figure and manner of the celebrated SAMUEL JOHNSON,—the extraordinary power and precision of his conversation, and the pride arising from finding myself admitted as his companion, pro-

duced a variety of sensations, and a pleasing elevation of mind beyond what I had ever before experienced. . . .

Finding him in a placid humor, and wishing to avail myself of the opportunity which I fortunately had of consulting a sage, to hear whose wisdom, I conceived in the ardor of youthful imagination, that men filled with a noble enthusiasm for intellectual improvement would gladly have resorted from distant lands;—I opened my mind to him ingenuously, and gave him a little sketch of my life, to which he was pleased to listen with great attention.

I acknowledged, that though educated very strictly in the principles of religion, I had for some time been misled into a certain degree of infidelity; but that I was come now to a better way of thinking, and was fully satisfied of the truth of the Christian revelation, though I was not clear as to every point considered to be orthodox. Being at all times a curious examiner of the human mind, and pleased with an undisguised display of what had passed in it, he called to me with warmth, "Give me your hand; I have taken a liking to you." He then began to descant upon the force of testimony, and the little we could know of final causes; so that the objections of, why was it so? or why was it not so? ought not to disturb us: adding, that he himself had at one period been guilty of a temporary neglect of religion, but that it was not the result of argument, but mere absence of thought.

After having given credit to reports of his bigotry, I was agreeably surprized when he expressed the following very liberal sentiment, which has the additional value of obviating an objection to our holy religion, founded upon the discordant tenets of Christians themselves: "For my part, Sir, I think all Christians, whether Papists or Protestants, agree in the essential articles, and that their differences are trivial, and rather political than religious."

We talked of belief in ghosts. He said, "Sir, I make a distinction between what a man may experience by the mere strength of his imagination, and what imagination cannot possibly produce. Thus, suppose I should think that I saw a form, and heard a voice cry 'Johnson, you are a very wicked fellow, and unless you repent you will certainly be punished'; my own unworthiness is so deeply impressed upon my mind, that I might *imagine* I thus saw and heard, and therefore I should not believe that an external communication had been made to me. But if a form should appear, and a voice should tell me that a particular man had died at a particular place, and a particular hour, a fact which I had no apprehension of, nor any means of knowing, and this fact, with all its circumstances, should afterwards be unquestionably proved, I should, in that case, be persuaded that I had supernatural intelligence imparted to me."

Here it is proper, once for all, to give a true and fair statement of Johnson's way of thinking upon the question, whether departed spirits are ever permitted to appear in this world, or in any way to operate upon human life. He has been ignorantly misrepresented as weakly credulous upon that subject; and, therefore, though I feel an inclination to disdain and treat with silent contempt so foolish a notion concerning my illustrious friend, yet as I find it has gained ground, it is necessary to refute it. The real fact then is, that Johnson had a very philosophical mind, and such a rational respect for testimony, as to make him submit his understanding to what was authentically proved, though he could not comprehend why it was so. Being thus disposed, he was willing to inquire into the truth of any relation of supernatural agency, a general belief of which has prevailed in all nations and ages. But so far was he from being the dupe of implicit faith, that he examined the matter with a jealous attention, and no man was more ready to refute its falsehood when he had discovered it. Churchill, in his poem entitled *The Ghost,* availed himself of the absurd credulity imputed to Johnson, and drew a caricature of him under the name of "POMPOSO," representing him as one of the believers of the story of a Ghost in Cock-lane, which, in the year 1762, had gained very general credit in London. Many of my readers, I am convinced, are to this hour under an impression that Johnson was thus foolishly deceived. It will therefore surprise them a good deal when they are informed upon undoubted authority, that Johnson was one of those by whom the imposture was detected. The story had become so popular, that he thought it should be investigated; and in this research he was assisted by the Reverend Dr. Douglas, now Bishop of Salisbury, the great detector of impostures; who informs me, that after the gentlemen who went and examined into the evidence were satisfied of its falsity, Johnson wrote in their presence an account of it, which was published in the Newspapers and *Gentleman's Magazine,* and undeceived the world. . . .

As Dr. Oliver Goldsmith will frequently appear in this narrative, I shall endeavor to make my readers in some degree acquainted with his singular character. He was a native of Ireland, and a contemporary with Mr. Burke at Trinity College, Dublin, but did not then give much promise of future celebrity. He, however, observed to Mr. Malone, that "though he made no great figure in mathematics, which was a study in much repute there, he could turn an Ode of Horace into English better than any of them." He afterwards studied physic at Edinburgh, and upon the Continent; and I have been informed, was enabled to pursue his travels on foot, partly by demanding at Universities to enter the lists as a disputant, by which, according to the custom of many of them, he was entitled to the premium of a crown, when luckily for him his challenge was not accepted; so that, as I once observed to Dr. Johnson, he *disputed* his passage through Europe. He then came to England, and was employed successively in the capacities of an usher to an academy, a corrector of the press, a reviewer, and a writer for a news-paper. He had sagacity enough to cultivate assiduously the acquaintance of Johnson, and his faculties were gradually enlarged by the contemplation of such a model. To me and many others it appeared that he studiously copied the manner of Johnson, though, indeed, upon a smaller scale.

At this time I think he had published nothing with his name, though it was pretty generally known that *one Dr. Goldsmith* was the author of *An Enquiry into the present State of polite Learning in Europe,* and of *The Citizen of the World,* a series of letters supposed to be written from London by a Chinese. No man had the art of displaying with more advantage as a writer, whatever literary acquisitions he made. *"Nihil quod tetigit non ornavit."* His mind resembled a fertile, but thin soil. There was a quick, but not a strong vegetation, of whatever chanced to be thrown upon it. No deep root could be struck. The oak of the forest did not grow there; but the elegant shrubbery and the fragrant parterre appeared in gay succession. It has been generally circulated and believed that he was a mere fool in conversation; but, in truth, this has been greatly exaggerated. He had, no doubt, a more than common share of that hurry of ideas which we often find in his countrymen, and which sometimes produces a laughable confusion in expressing them. He was very much what the French call *un étourdi,* and from vanity and an eager desire of being conspicuous wherever he was, he frequently talked carelessly without knowledge of the subject, or even without thought. His person was short, his countenance coarse and vulgar, his deportment that of a scholar awkwardly affecting the easy gentleman. Those who were in any way distinguished, excited envy in him to so ridiculous an excess, that the instances of it are hardly credible. When accompanying two beautiful young ladies with their mother on a tour in France, he was seriously angry that more attention was paid to them than to him; and once at the exhibition of the *Fantoccini* in London, when those who sat next him observed with what dexterity a puppet was made to toss a pike, he could not bear that it should have such praise, and exclaimed with some warmth, "Pshaw! I can do it better myself."

He, I am afraid, had no settled system of any sort, so that his conduct must not be strictly scrutinized; but his affections were social and generous, and when he had money he gave it away very liberally. His desire of imaginary consequence predominated over his attention to truth. When he began to rise into notice, he said he had a brother who was Dean of Durham, a fiction so easily detected, that it is wonderful how he should have been so inconsiderate as to hazard it. He boasted to me at this time of the power of his pen in commanding money, which I believe was true in a certain degree, though in the instance he gave he was by no means correct. He told me that he had

sold a novel for four hundred pounds. This was his *Vicar of Wakefield.* But Johnson informed me, that he had made the bargain for Goldsmith, and the price was sixty pounds. "And, Sir, (said he,) a sufficient price too, when it was sold; for then the fame of Goldsmith had not been elevated, as it afterwards was, by his *Traveller;* but the bookseller had such faint hopes of profit by his bargain, that he kept the manuscript by him a long time, and did not publish it till after *The Traveller* had appeared. Then, to be sure, it was accidentally worth more money."

Mrs. Piozzi and Sir John Hawkins have strangely misstated the history of Goldsmith's situation and Johnson's friendly interference, when this novel was sold. I shall give it authentically from Johnson's own exact narration:— "I received one morning a message from poor Goldsmith that he was in great distress, and as it was not in his power to come to me, begging that I would come to him as soon as possible. I sent him a guinea, and promised to come to him directly. I accordingly went as soon as I was drest, and found that his landlady had arrested him for his rent, at which he was in a violent passion. I perceived that he had already changed my guinea, and had got a bottle of Madeira and a glass before him. I put the cork into the bottle, desired he would be calm, and began to talk to him of the means by which he might be extricated. He then told me that he had a novel ready for the press, which he produced to me. I looked into it, and saw its merit; told the landlady I should soon return, and having gone to a bookseller, sold it for sixty pounds. I brought Goldsmith the money, and he discharged his rent, not without rating his landlady in a high tone for having used him so ill."

My next meeting with Johnson was on Friday the 1st of July, when he and I and Dr. Goldsmith supped together at the Mitre. I was before this time pretty well acquainted with Goldsmith, who was one of the brightest ornaments of the Johnsonian school. Goldsmith's respectful attachment to Johnson was then at its height; for his own literary reputation had not yet distinguished him so much as to excite a vain desire of competition with his great Master. He had increased my admiration of the goodness of Johnson's heart, by incidental remarks in the course of conversation, such as, when I mentioned Mr. Levet, whom he entertained under his roof, "He is poor and honest, which is recommendation enough to Johnson"; and when I wondered that he was very kind to a man of whom I had heard a very bad character, "He is now become miserable, and that insures the protection of Johnson."

Goldsmith attempted this evening to maintain, I suppose from an affectation of paradox, "that knowledge was not desirable on its own account, for it often was a source of unhappiness." JOHNSON. "Why, Sir, that knowledge may in some cases produce unhappiness, I allow. But, upon the whole, knowledge, *per se,* is certainly an object which every man would wish to attain, although perhaps, he may not take the trouble necessary for attaining it. . . ."

I had as my guests this evening at the Mitre tavern, Dr. Johnson, Dr. Goldsmith, Mr. Thomas Davies, Mr. Eccles, an Irish gentleman, for whose agreeable company I was obliged to Mr. Davies, and the Reverend Mr. John Ogilvie, who was desirous of being in company with my illustrious friend, while I, in my turn, was proud to have the honor of showing one of my countrymen upon what easy terms Johnson permitted me to live with him.

Goldsmith, as usual, endeavored, with too much eagerness, to *shine,* and disputed very warmly with Johnson against the well-known maxim of the British constitution, "the King can do no wrong"; affirming, that "what was morally false could not be politically true; and as the King might, in the exercise of regal power, command and cause the doing of what was wrong, it certainly might be said, in sense and in reason, that he could do wrong." JOHNSON. "Sir, you are to consider, that in our constitution, according to its true principles, the King is the head; he is supreme; he is above every thing, and there is no power by which he can be tried. Therefore, it is, Sir, that we hold the King can do no wrong; that whatever may happen to be wrong in government may not be above our reach, by being ascribed to Majesty. Redress is always to be had against oppression, by punishing the immediate agents. The King, though he should command, cannot

force a Judge to condemn a man unjustly; therefore it is the Judge whom we prosecute and punish. Political institutions are formed upon the consideration of what will most frequently tend to the good of the whole, although now and then exceptions may occur. Thus it is better in general that a nation should have a supreme legislative power, although it may at times be abused. And then, Sir, there is this consideration, that *if the abuse be enormous, Nature will rise up, and claiming her original rights, overturn a corrupt political system.*" I mark this animated sentence with peculiar pleasure, as a noble instance of that truly dignified spirit of freedom which ever glowed in his heart, though he was charged with slavish tenets by superficial observers; because he was at all times indignant against that false patriotism, that pretended love of freedom, that unruly restlessness, which is inconsistent with the stable authority of any good government. . . .

Mr. Ogilvie was unlucky enough to choose for the topic of his conversation the praises of his native country. He began with saying, that there was very rich land round Edinburgh. Goldsmith, who had studied physic there, contradicted this, very untruly, with a sneering laugh. Disconcerted a little by this, Mr. Ogilvie then took new ground, where, I suppose, he thought himself perfectly safe; for he observed, that Scotland had a great many noble wild prospects. JOHNSON. "I believe, Sir, you have a great many. Norway, too, has noble wild prospects; and Lapland is remarkable for prodigious noble wild prospects. But, Sir, let me tell you, the noblest prospect which a Scotchman ever sees, is the high road that leads him to England!" This unexpected and pointed sally produced a roar of applause. After all, however, those who admire the rude grandeur of Nature, cannot deny it to Caledonia.

On Saturday, July 9, I found Johnson surrounded with a numerous levee, but have not preserved any part of his conversation. On the 14th we had another evening by ourselves at the Mitre. It happening to be a very rainy night, I made some commonplace observations on the relaxation of nerves and depression of spirits which such weather occasioned; adding, however, that it was good for the vegetable creation. Johnson, who, as we have already seen, denied that the temperature of the air had any influence on the human frame, answered, with a smile of ridicule, "Why yes, Sir, it is good for vegetables, and for the animals who eat those vegetables, and for the animals who eat those animals." This observation of his aptly enough introduced a good supper; and I soon forgot in Johnson's company, the influence of a moist atmosphere.

Feeling myself now quite at ease as his companion, though I had all possible reverence for him, I expressed a regret that I could not be so easy with my father, though he was not much older than Johnson, and certainly, however respectable, had not more learning and greater abilities to depress me. I asked him the reason of this. JOHNSON. "Why, Sir, I am a man of the world. I live in the world, and I take, in some degree, the color of the world as it moves along. Your father is a Judge in a remote part of the island, and all his notions are taken from the old world. Besides, Sir, there must always be a struggle between a father and son, while one aims at power and the other at independence." I said, I was afraid my father would force me to be a lawyer. JOHNSON. "Sir, you need not be afraid of his forcing you to be a laborious practicing lawyer; that is not in his power. For as the proverb says, 'One man may lead a horse to the water, but twenty cannot make him drink.' He may be displeased that you are not what he wishes you to be; but that displeasure will not go far. If he insists only on your having as much law as is necessary for a man of property, and then endeavors to get you into Parliament, he is quite in the right."

He enlarged very convincingly upon the excellence of rhyme over blank verse in English poetry. I mentioned to him that Dr. Adam Smith, in his lectures upon composition, when I studied under him at the College of Glasgow, had maintained the same opinion strenuously, and I repeated some of his arguments. JOHNSON. "Sir, I was once in company with Smith, and we did not take to each other; but had I known that he loved rhyme as much as you tell me he does, I should have HUGGED him."

Talking of those who denied the truth of Christianity, he said, "It is always easy to be on the negative side. If a man were now to deny that there is salt upon the table, you could not reduce him to an absurdity. Come, let us try this a little further. I deny that Canada is taken, and I can support my denial by pretty good arguments. The French are a much more numerous people than we; and it is not likely that they would allow us to take it. 'But the ministry have assured us, in all the formality of *The Gazette,* that it is taken.'—Very true. But the ministry have put us to an enormous expense by the war in America, and it is their interest to persuade us that we have got something for our money.—'But the fact is confirmed by thousands of men who were at the taking of it.'—Ay, but these men have still more interest in deceiving us. They don't want that you should think the French have beat them, but that they have beat the French. Now suppose you should go over and find that it is really taken, that would only satisfy yourself; for when you come home we will not believe you. We will say, you have been bribed.—Yet, Sir, notwithstanding all these plausible objections, we have no doubt that Canada is really ours. Such is the weight of common testimony. How much stronger are the evidences of the Christian religion!"

"Idleness is a disease which must be combated; but I would not advise a rigid adherence to a particular plan of study. I myself have never persisted in any plan for two days together. A man ought to read just as inclination leads him; for what he reads as a task will do him little good. A young man should read five hours in a day, and so may acquire a great deal of knowledge."

To a man of vigorous intellect and arduous curiosity like his own, reading without a regular plan may be beneficial; though even such a man must submit to it, if he would attain a full understanding of any of the sciences.

To such a degree of unrestrained frankness had he now accustomed me, that in the course of this evening I talked of the numerous reflections which had been thrown out against him on account of his having accepted a pension from his present Majesty. "Why, Sir, (said he, with a hearty laugh,) it is a mighty foolish noise that they make. I have accepted of a pension as a reward which has been thought due to my literary merit; and now that I have this pension, I am the same man in every respect that I have ever been; I retain the same principles. It is true, that I cannot now curse (smiling) the House of Hanover; nor would it be decent for me to drink King James's health in the wine that King George gives me money to pay for. But, Sir, I think that the pleasure of cursing the House of Hanover, and drinking King James's health, are amply over-balanced by three hundred pounds a year."

There was here, most certainly, an affectation of more Jacobitism than he really had; and indeed an intention of admitting, for the moment, in a much greater extent than it really existed, the charge of disaffection imputed to him by the world, merely for the purpose of showing how dexterously he could repel an attack, even though he were placed in the most disadvantageous position; for I have heard him declare, that if holding up his right hand would have secured victory at Culloden to Prince Charles's army, he was not sure he would have held it up; so little confidence had he in the right claimed by the house of Stuart, and so fearful was he of the consequences of another revolution on the throne of Great-Britain; and Mr. Topham Beauclerk assured me, he had heard him say this before he had his pension. At another time he said to Mr. Langton, "Nothing has ever offered, that has made it worth my while to consider the question fully." He, however, also said to the same gentleman, talking of King James the Second, "It was become impossible for him to reign any longer in this country." He no doubt had an early attachment to the House of Stuart; but his zeal had cooled as his reason strengthened. Indeed I heard him once say, that "after the death of a violent Whig, with whom he used to contend with great eagerness, he felt his Toryism much abated." I suppose he meant Walmsley.

Yet there is no doubt that at earlier periods he was wont often to exercise both his pleasantry and ingenuity in talking Jacobitism. My much respected friend, Dr. Douglas, now Bishop of Salisbury, has favored me with the following admirable instance from his Lordship's own recollection. One day when dining at old Mr. Langton's where Miss Roberts, his niece, was one of the company, Johnson, with his usual complacent attention to the fair sex, took her by the hand and said, "My dear, I hope you are a Jacobite." Old Mr. Langton, who, though a high and steady Tory, was attached to the present Royal Family, seemed offended, and asked Johnson, with great warmth, what he could mean by putting such a question to his niece? "Why, Sir, (said Johnson) I meant no offence to your niece, I meant her a great compliment. A Jacobite, Sir, believes in the divine right of the Kings. He that believes in the divine right of Kings believes in a Divinity. A Jacobite believes in the divine right of Bishops. He that believes in the divine right of Bishops believes in the divine authority of the Christian religion. Therefore, Sir, a Jacobite is neither an Atheist nor a Deist. That cannot be said of a Whig; for *Whiggism is a negation of all principle*."

He advised me, when abroad, to be as much as I could with the Professors in the Universities, and with the Clergy; for from their conversation I might expect the best accounts of every thing in whatever country I should be, with the additional advantage of keeping my learning alive.

It will be observed, that when giving me advice as to my travels, Dr. Johnson did not dwell upon cities, and palaces, and pictures, and shows, and Arcadian scenes. He was of Lord Essex's opinion, who advises his kinsman Roger Earl of Rutland, "rather to go an hundred miles to speak with one wise man, than five miles to see a fair town."

I described to him an impudent fellow from Scotland, who affected to be a savage, and railed at all established systems. JOHNSON. "There is nothing surprising in this, Sir. He wants to make himself conspicuous. He would tumble in a hogstye, as long as you looked at him and called to him to come out. But let him alone, never mind him, and he'll soon give it over."

I added, that the same person maintained that there was no distinction between virtue and vice. JOHNSON. "Why, Sir, if the fellow does not think as he speaks, he is lying; and I see not what honor he can propose to himself from having the character of a liar. But if he does really think that there is no distinction between virtue and vice, why, Sir, when he leaves our houses let us count our spoons. . . ."

Mr. Levet this day showed me Dr. Johnson's library, which was contained in two garrets over his Chambers, where Lintot, son of the celebrated bookseller of that name, had formerly his warehouse. I found a number of good books, but very dusty and in great confusion. The floor was strewed with manuscript leaves, in Johnson's own handwriting, which I beheld with a degree of veneration, supposing they perhaps might contain portions of *The Rambler* or of *Rasselas.* I observed an apparatus for chemical experiments, of which Johnson was all his life very fond. The place seemed to be very favorable for retirement and meditation. Johnson told me, that he went up thither without mentioning it to his servant, when he wanted to study, secure from interruption; for he would not allow his servant to say he was not at home when he really was. "A servant's strict regard for truth, (said he) must be weakened by such a practice. A philosopher may know that it is merely a form of denial; but few servants are such nice distinguishers. If I accustom a servant to tell a lie for me, have I not reason to apprehend that he will tell many lies for *himself.*"

I am, however, satisfied that every servant, of any degree of intelligence, understands saying his master is not at home, not at all as the affirmation of a fact, but as customary words, intimating that his master wishes not to be seen; so that there can be no bad effect from it.

Mr. Temple, now vicar of St. Gluvias, Cornwall, who had been my intimate friend for many years, had at this time Chambers in Farrar's-buildings, at the bottom of Inner Temple-lane, which he kindly lent me upon my quitting my lodgings, he being to return to Trinity Hall, Cambridge. I found them particularly convenient for me, as they were so near Dr. Johnson's.

On Wednesday, July 20, Dr. Johnson, Dr. Dempster, and my uncle Dr. Boswell, who happened to be now in London, supped with me at these Chambers. JOHNSON. "Pity is not natural to man. Children are always cruel. Savages are always cruel. Pity is acquired and improved by the cultivation of reason. We may have un-easy sensations from seeing a creature in distress, without pity; for we have not pity unless we wish to relieve them. When I am on my way to dine with a friend, and finding it late, have bid the coachman make haste, if I happen to attend when he whips his horses, I may feel unpleasantly that the animals are put to pain, but I do not wish him to desist. No, Sir, I wish him to drive on. . . ."

Next morning I found him alone, and have preserved the following fragments of his conversation. Of a gentleman who was mentioned, he said, "I have not met with any man for a long time who has given me such general displeasure. He is totally unfixed in his principles, and wants to puzzle other people." I said his principles had been poisoned by a noted infidel writer, but that he was, nevertheless, a benevolent good man. JOHNSON. "We can have no dependence upon that instinctive, that constitutional goodness which is not founded upon principle. I grant you that such a man may be a very amiable member of society. I can conceive him placed in such a situation that he is not much tempted to deviate from what is right; and as every man prefers virtue, when there is not some strong incitement to transgress its precepts, I can conceive him doing nothing wrong. But if such a man stood in need of money, I should not like to trust him; and I should certainly not trust him with young ladies, for *there* there is always temptation. Hume, and other sceptical innovators, are vain men, and will gratify themselves at any expense. Truth will not afford sufficient food to their vanity; so they have betaken themselves to error. Truth, Sir, is a cow which will yield such people no more milk, and so they are gone to milk the bull. If I could have allowed myself to gratify my vanity at the expense of truth, what fame might I have acquired. Every thing which Hume has advanced against Christianity had passed through my mind long before he wrote. Always remember this, that after a system is well settled upon positive evidence, a few partial objections ought not to shake it. The human mind is so limited, that it cannot take in all the parts of a subject, so that there may be objections raised against any thing. There are objections against a *plenum,* and objections against a *vacuum;* yet one of them must certainly be true."

I mentioned Hume's argument against the belief of miracles, that it is more probable that the witnesses to the truth of them are mistaken, or speak falsely, than that the miracles should be true. JOHNSON. "Why, Sir, the great difficulty of proving miracles should make us very cautious in believing them. But let us consider, although God has made Nature to operate by certain fixed laws, yet it is not unreasonable to think that he may suspend those laws, in order to establish a system highly advantageous to mankind. Now the Christian religion is a most beneficial system, as it gives us light and certainty where we were before in darkness and doubt. The miracles which prove it are attested by men who had no interest in deceiving us; but who, on the contrary, were told that they should suffer persecution, and did actually lay down their lives in confirmation of the truth of the facts which they asserted. Indeed, for some centuries the heathens did not pretend to deny the miracles; but said they were performed by the aid of evil spirits. This is a circumstance of great weight. Then, Sir, when we take the proofs derived from prophecies which have been so exactly fulfilled, we have most satisfactory evidence. Supposing a miracle possible, as to which, in my opinion, there can be no doubt, we have as strong evidence for the miracles in support of Christianity, as the nature of the thing admits."

At night Mr. Johnson and I supped in a private room at the Turk's Head coffee-house, in the Strand. "I encourage this house, (said he;) for the mistress of it is a good civil woman, and has not much business."

"Sir, I love the acquaintance of young people; because in the first place, I don't like to think myself growing old. In the next place, young acquaintances must last longer, if they do last; and then, Sir, young men have more virtue than old men; they have more generous sentiments in every respect. I love the young dogs of this age: they have more wit and humor and knowledge of life than we had; but then the dogs are not so good scholars. Sir, in my early years I read very hard. It is a sad reflection, but a true one, that I knew almost as much at eighteen

as I do now. My judgment, to be sure, was not so good; but I had all the facts. I remember very well, when I was at Oxford, an old gentleman said to me, 'Young man, ply your book diligently now, and acquire a stock of knowledge; for when years come upon you, you will find that poring upon books will be but an irksome task.' "

This account of his reading, given by himself in plain words, sufficiently confirms what I have already advanced upon the disputed questions as to his application. It reconciles any seeming inconsistency in his way of talking upon it at different times; and shows that idleness and reading hard were with him relative terms, the import of which, as used by him, must be gathered from a comparison with what scholars of different degrees of ardor and assiduity have been known to do. And let it be remembered, that he was now talking spontaneously, and expressing his genuine sentiments; whereas at other times he might be induced from his spirit of contradiction, or more properly from his love of argumentative contest, to speak lightly of his own application to study. It is pleasing to consider that the old gentleman's gloomy prophecy as to the irksomeness of books to men of an advanced age, which is too often fulfilled, was so far from being verified in Johnson, that his ardor for literature never failed, and his last writing had more ease and vivacity than any of his earlier productions.

He mentioned to me now, for the first time, that he had been distrest by melancholy, and for that reason had been obliged to fly from study and meditation, to the dissipating variety of life. Against melancholy he recommended constant occupation of mind, a great deal of exercise, moderation in eating and drinking, and especially to shun drinking at night. He said melancholy people were apt to fly to intemperance for relief, but that it sunk them much deeper in misery. He observed, that laboring men who work hard, and live sparingly, are seldom or never troubled with low spirits.

He again insisted on the duty of maintaining subordination of rank. "Sir, I would no more deprive a nobleman of his respect, than of his money. I consider myself as acting a part in the great system of society, and I do to others as I would have them to do to me. I would behave to a nobleman as I should expect he would behave to me, were I a nobleman and he Sam. Johnson. Sir, there is one Mrs. Macaulay in this town, a great republican. One day when I was at her house, I put on a very grave countenance, and said to her, 'Madam, I am now become a convert to your way of thinking. I am convinced that all mankind are upon an equal footing; and to give you an unquestionable proof, Madam, that I am in earnest, here is a very sensible, civil well-behaved fellow citizen, your footman; I desire that he may be allowed to sit down and dine with us.' I thus, Sir, showed her the absurdity of the levelling doctrine. She has never liked me since. Sir, your levellers wish to level *down* as far as themselves; but they cannot bear levelling *up* to themselves. They would all have some people under them; why not then have some people above them?" I mentioned a certain author who disgusted me by his forwardness, and by showing no deference to noblemen into whose company he was admitted. JOHNSON. "Suppose a shoemaker should claim an equality with him, as he does with a Lord; how he would stare. 'Why, Sir, do you stare? (says the shoemaker,) I do great service to society. 'Tis true I am paid for doing it; but so are you, Sir: and I am sorry to say it, paid better than I am, for doing something not so necessary. For mankind could do better without your books, than without my shoes.' Thus, Sir, there would be a perpetual struggle for precedence, were there no fixed invariable rules for the distinction of rank, which creates no jealousy, as it is allowed to be accidental. . . ."

We concluded the day at the Turk's Head coffeehouse very socially. He was pleased to listen to a particular account which I gave him of my family, and of its hereditary estate, as to the extent and population of which he asked questions, and made calculations; recommending, at the same time, a liberal kindness to the tenantry, as people over whom the proprietor was placed by Providence. He took delight in hearing my description of the romantic seat of my ancestors. "I must be there, Sir, (said he) and we will live in the old castle; and if there is not a room in it remaining, we will build

one." I was highly flattered, but could scarcely indulge a hope that Auchinleck would indeed be honored by his presence, and celebrated by a description, as it afterwards was, in his *Journey to the Western Islands.*

After we had again talked of my setting out for Holland, he said, "I must see thee out of England; I will accompany you to Harwich." I could not find words to express what I felt upon this unexpected and very great mark of his affectionate regard.

Next day, Sunday, July 31, I told him I had been that morning at a meeting of the people called Quakers, where I had heard a woman preach. JOHNSON. "Sire, a woman's preaching is like a dog's walking on his hinder legs. It is not done well; but you are surprized to find it done at all."

On Tuesday, August 2 (the day of my departure from London having been fixed for the 5th,) Dr. Johnson did me the honour to pass a part of the morning with me at my Chambers. He said, that "he always felt an inclination to do nothing." I observed, that it was strange to think that the most indolent man in Britain had written the most laborious work, *The English Dictionary.*

I mentioned an imprudent publication, by a certain friend of his, at an early period of life, and asked him if he thought it would hurt him. JOHNSON. "No, Sir; not much. It may, perhaps, be mentioned at an election."

I had now made good my title to be a privileged man, and was carried by him in the evening to drink tea with Miss Williams, whom, though under the misfortune of having lost her sight, I found to be agreeable in conversation; for she had a variety of literature, and expressed herself well; but her peculiar value was the intimacy in which she had long lived with Johnson, by which she was well acquainted with his habits, and knew how to lead him on to talk.

After tea he carried me to what he called his walk, which was a long narrow paved court in the neighbourhood, overshadowed by some trees. There we sauntered a considerable time; and I complained to him that my love of London and of his company was such, that I shrunk almost from the thought of going away, even to travel, which is generally so much desired by young men. He roused me by manly and spirited conversation. He advised me, when settled in any place abroad, to study with an eagerness after knowledge, and to apply to Greek an hour every day; and when I was moving about, to read diligently the great book of mankind.

DISCUSSION

Boswell was conscious of the fact that his method of treating the life of Samuel Johnson was rather unusual, and in the opening pages of the life he undertakes to give a statement of his method and a justification of it. The following paragraphs will indicate the principles on which he worked:

"Instead of melting down my materials into one mass, and constantly speaking in my own person, by which I might have appeared to have more merit in the execution of the work, I have resolved to adopt and enlarge upon the excellent plan of Mr. Mason, in his Memoirs of Gray. Wherever narrative is necessary to explain, connect, and supply, I furnish it to the best of my abilities; but in the chronological series of Johnson's life, which I trace as distinctly as I can, year by year, I produce, wherever it is in my power, his own minutes, letters or conversation, being convinced that this mode is more lively, and will make my readers better acquainted with him, than even most of those were who actually knew him, but could know him only partially; whereas there is here an accumulation of intelligence from various points, by which his character is more fully understood and illustrated.

"Indeed I cannot conceive a more perfect mode of writing any man's life, than not only relating all the most important events of it in their order, but interweaving what he privately wrote, and said, and thought; by which mankind are enabled as it were to see him live, and to 'live o'er each scene' with him, as he actually advanced through the several stages of his life. Had his other friends been as diligent and ardent as I was, he might have been almost entirely preserved. As it is, I will venture to say that he will be seen in his work more completely than any man who has ever yet lived.

"And he will be seen as he really was; for I profess to write, not his panegyric, which must be all praise, but his Life; which, great and good as he was, must not be supposed to be entirely perfect. To be as he was, is indeed subject of panegyric enough to any man in this state of being; but in every picture there should be shade as well as light, and when I delineate him without reserve, I do what he himself recommended, both by his precept and his example. . . .

"If authority be required, let us appeal to Plutarch, the prince of ancient biographers. . . . 'Nor is it always in the most distinguished achievements that men's virtues or vices may be best discerned; but very often an action of small note, a short saying, or a jest, shall distinguish a person's real character more than the greatest sieges, or the most important battles.'

"To this may be added the sentiments of the very man whose life I am about to exhibit.

" 'The business of the biographer is often to pass slightly over those performances and incidents which produce vulgar greatness, to lead the thoughts into domestick privacies, and display the minute details of daily life, where exterior appendages are cast aside, and men excel each other only by prudence and by virtue. . . .'

"I am fully aware of the objections which may be made to the minuteness on some occasions of my detail of Johnson's conversation, and how happily it is adapted for the petty exercise of ridicule, by men of superficial understanding and ludicrous fancy; but I remain firm and confident in my opinion, that minute particulars are frequently characteristic, and always amusing, when they relate to a distinguished man. I am therefore exceedingly unwilling that any thing, however slight, which my illustrious friend thought it worth his while to express, with any degree of point, should perish."

It will be seen that a life written on this plan will not have the logical structure of, say, the account of Washington's early life by Morison. Any fact about Johnson, or any remark by Johnson, no matter how trivial it might seem, would, according to this principle of biographical writing, be incorporated in the work. For this reason, the method as applied to many figures of history and literature, and as applied by many writers, might result in works, not only dull, but relatively formless, with the interpretation of idea completely confused by incident and conversation in no way relevant to it. Boswell, in fact, was scarcely concerned with the interpretation of his subject. It is true that Boswell makes comments and judgments upon Johnson, but he is primarily concerned with recording Johnson and not with defining the central idea of his life, or of assessing the civilization which would produce such a man, or of determining his effect upon history. This can be readily seen if one contrasts the work of Boswell with that of Strachey.

Moreover, in discussing Boswell's method, one must realize, as Boswell himself did, that he was peculiarly fortunate in his subject. For instance, one can see how difficult it would be to apply the method to the biography of a man of action, like Napoleon, or a statesman, like Woodrow Wilson, the interest in whom would be more objective. But the method is appropriate to the life of a man like Johnson, whose greatness, to a considerable extent, lay in his personality.

Boswell, furthermore, makes a virtue out of the apparent necessities of his method. For example, since Boswell does not pretend to be shaping the book in any particular order or according to any particular idea, we are not disappointed at the lack of these things, and the impression of Johnson's day-to-day life is actually heightened by the casualness and veracity of the treatment. To take another example, Boswell finds it impossible to keep himself out of the account, but by putting himself into it so frankly and objectively, on the same level, as it were, as any other character, he avoids any impression that he is coloring the total effect.

EXERCISE

1. In the selections given above how does Boswell present Johnson's brusqueness? His essential kindliness? His humor?

2. What would you judge to be Johnson's real attitude toward the Scottish people?

3. How do some of the anecdotes given in these selections indicate Johnson's basic common sense?

4. Compare Boswell's method of presenting individual scenes with that of Morison or Mitchell. Which method is nearer to that of fiction?

5. Boswell kept a journal or diary for a good part of his life. That covering his first stay in London was published in 1950 as *Boswell's London Journal, 1762-1763,* edited by Frederick A. Pottle. The student may find it interesting to compare with the corresponding sections in the *Life of Johnson,* the Journal entries for 24 May and for 31st July through 3rd of August. The comparison will suggest the principles upon which Boswell made his selection of materials to go into the *Life.* Note not only what Boswell chose to transfer to the *Life* but what he chose to omit.

The Life of Marcus Antonius

(Selections)

PLUTARCH (FIRST CENTURY, A.D.)

Translated by SIR THOMAS NORTH (c. 1535-c. 1601)

ANTONIUS BEING thus inclined, the last and extremest mischief of all other (to wit, the love of Cleopatra) lighted on him, who did waken and stir up many vices yet hidden in him, and were never seen to any: and, if any spark of goodness or hope of rising were left him, Cleopatra quenched it straight, and made it worse than before. The manner how he fell in love with her was this. Antonius, going to make war with the Parthians, sent to command Cleopatra to appear personally before him when he came into Cilicia, to answer unto such accusations as were laid against her, being this: that she had aided Cassius and Brutus in their war against him. The messenger sent unto Cleopatra to make this summons unto her was called Dellius: who when he had thoroughly considered her beauty, the excellent grace and sweetness of her tongue, he nothing mistrusted that Antonius would do any hurt to so noble a lady, but rather assured himself that within few days she should be in favor with him. Thereupon he did her great honor, and persuaded her to come into Cilicia as honorably furnished as she could possible, and bade her not to be afraid at all of Antonius, for he was a more courteous lord than any that she had ever seen. Cleopatra, on the other side, believing Dellius' words, and guessing by the former access and credit she had with Julius Caesar and Cneius Pompey (the son of Pompey the Great) only for her beauty, she began to have good hope that she might more easily win Antonius. For Caesar and Pompey knew her when she was but a young thing, and knew not then what the world meant: but now she went to Antonius at the age when a woman's beauty is at the prime, and she also of best judgment. So she furnished herself with a world of gifts, store of gold and silver, and of riches and other sumptuous ornaments, as is credible enough she might bring from so great a house, and from so wealthy and rich a realm as Egypt was. But yet she carried nothing with her wherein she trusted more than in herself, and in the charms and enchantment of her passing beauty and grace. Therefore when she was sent unto by divers letters, both from Antonius himself, and also from his friends, she made so light of it and mocked Antonius so much, that she disdained to set forward otherwise, but to take her barge in the river of Cydnus, the poop whereof was of gold, the sails of purple, and the oars of silver, which kept stroke in rowing after the sound of the music of flutes, howboys, citherns, viols, and such other instruments as they played upon in the barge. And now for the person of herself: she was laid under a pavilion of cloth of gold of tissue, apparelled and attired like the goddess Venus commonly drawn in picture: and hard by her, on either hand of her, pretty fair boys apparelled as painters do set forth god Cupid, with little fans in their hands, with the which they fanned wind upon her. Her ladies and gentlewomen also, the fairest of them were apparelled like the nymphs Nereids (which are the mermaids of the waters) and like the Graces, some steering the helm, others tending the tackle and ropes of the barge, out of the which there came a wonderful passing sweet savor of perfumes, that perfumed the wharf's side, pestered with innumerable multitudes of people. Some of them followed the barge all alongst the river-side: others also ran out of the city to see her coming in. So that in the end there ran such multitudes of people one after another to see her, that Antonius was left post alone in the market-place in his imperial seat to give audience: and there went a rumor in the people's mouths, that the goddess Venus was come to play with the god Bacchus, for the general good of all Asia. When Cleopatra landed, Antonius sent to invite her to supper to him. But she sent him word again, he should do better rather to come and sup with her. Antonius therefore, to show himself courteous unto her at her arrival, was contented to obey her, and went to supper to her: where he found such passing sumptuous fare, that no tongue can express it. But, amongst all other things, he most wondered at the infinite number of lights and torches hanged on the top of the house, giving light in every place, so artificially set and ordered by devices, some round, some square, that it was the rarest thing to behold that eye could discern, or that ever books could mention. The next night, Antonius feasting her contended to pass her in magnificence and fineness: but she overcame him in both. So that he himself began to scorn the gross service of his house, in respect of Cleopatra's sumptuousness and fineness. And, when Cleopatra found Antonius' jests and slents to be but gross and soldierlike in plain manner, she gave it him finely, and without fear taunted him throughly. Now her beauty (as it is reported) was not so passing, as unmatchable of other women, nor yet such as upon present view did enamor men with her: but so sweet was her company and conversation, that a man could not possibly but be taken. And, besides her beauty, the good grace she had to talk and discourse, her courteous nature that tempered her words and deeds, was a spur that pricked to the quick. Furthermore, besides all these, her voice and words were marvellous pleasant: for her tongue was an instrument of music to divers sports and pastimes, the which she easily turned to any language that pleased her. She spake unto few barbarous people by interpreter, but made them answer herself, or at the least the most part of them: as the Ethiopians, the Arabians, the Troglodytes, the Hebrews, the Syrians, the Medes, and the Parthians, and to many others also, whose languages she had learned. Whereas divers of her progenitors, the kings of Egypt, could scarce learn the Egyptian tongue only, and many of them forgot to speak the Macedonian. Now Antonius was so ravished with the love of Cleopatra, that though his wife Fulvia had great wars, and much ado with Caesar for his affairs, and that the army of the Parthians (the which the king's lieutenants had given to the only leading of Labienus) was now assembled in Mesopotamia ready to invade Syria: yet, as though all this had nothing touched him, he yielded himself to go with Cleopatra into Alexandria, where he spent and lost in childish sports (as a man might say) and idle pastimes the most precious thing a man can spend, as Antiphon saith: and that is, time.

But now again to Cleopatra. Plato writeth that there are four kinds of flattery, but Cleopatra divided it into many kinds. For she, were it in sport or in matters of earnest, still devised sundry new delights to have Antonius at commandment, never leaving him night nor day, nor once letting him go out of her sight. For she would play at dice with him, drink with him, and hunt commonly with him, and also be with him when he went to any exercise or activity of body. And sometime also, when he would go up and down the city disguised like a slave in the night, and would peer into poor men's windows and their shops, and scold and brawl with them within the house: Cleopatra would be also in a chamber-maid's array, and amble up and down the streets with him, so that oftentimes Antonius bare away both mocks and blows. Now, though most men misliked this manner, yet the Alexandrians were commonly glad of this jollity, and liked it well,

saying very gallantly and wisely, that Antonius showed them a comical face, to wit, a merry countenance: and the Romans a tragical face, to say, a grim look. But to reckon up all the foolish sports they made, revelling in this sort, it were too fond a part of me, and therefore I will only tell you one among the rest. On a time he went to angle for fish, and when he could take none he was as angry as could be, because Cleopatra stood by. Wherefore he secretly commanded the fishermen, that when he cast in his line they should straight dive under the water, and put a fish on his hook which they had taken before: and so snatched up his angling rod, and brought up fish twice or thrice. Cleopatra found it straight, yet she seemed not to see it, but wondered at his excellent fishing: but, when she was alone by herself among her own people, she told them how it was, and bade them the next morning to be on the water to see the fishing. A number of people came to the haven, and got into the fisher-boats to see this fishing. Antonius then threw in his line, and Cleopatra straight commanded one of her men to dive under water before Antonius' men, and to put some old salt-fish upon his bait, like unto those that are brought out of the country of Pont. When he had hung the fish on his hook, Antonius, thinking he had taken a fish indeed, snatched up his line presently. Then they all fell a-laughing. Cleopatra laughing also, said unto him: "Leave us (my Lord) Egyptians (which dwell in the country of Pharus and Canopus) your angling rod: this is not thy profession: thou must hunt after conquering of realms and countries." Now Antonius delighting in these fond and childish pastimes, very ill news were brought him from two places. The first from Rome, that his brother Lucius and Fulvia his wife fell out first between themselves, and afterwards fell to open war with Caesar, and had brought all to nought, that they were both driven to fly out of Italy. The second news, as bad as the first: that Labienus conquered all Asia with the army of the Parthians, from the river of Euphrates, and from Syria, unto the countries of Lydia and Ionia. Then began Antonius with much ado a little to rouse himself, as if he had been wakened out of a deep sleep, and, as a man may say, coming out of a great drunkenness. So first of all he bent himself against the Parthians, and went as far as the country of Phoenicia: but there he received lamentable letters from his wife Fulvia. Whereupon he straight returned towards Italy with two hundred sail: and, as he went, took up his friends by the way that fled out of Italy to come to him. By them he was informed, that his wife Fulvia was the only cause of this war: who, being of a peevish, crooked, and troublesome nature, had purposely raised this uproar in Italy, in hope thereby to withdraw him from Cleopatra. But by good fortune his wife Fulvia, going to meet with Antonius, sickened by the way, and died in the city of Sicyon: and therefore Octavius Caesar and he were the easilier made friends together. For when Antonius landed in Italy, and that men saw Caesar asked nothing of him, and that Antonius on the other side laid all the fault and burden on his wife Fulvia: the friends of both parties would not suffer them to unrip any old matters, and to prove or defend who had the wrong or right, and who was the first procurer of this war, fearing to make matters worse between them: but they made them friends together, and divided the empire of Rome between them, making the sea Ionium the bounds of their division. For they gave all the provinces eastward unto Antonius: and the countries westward, unto Caesar: and left Africk unto Lepidus: and made a law, that they three one after another should make their friends Consuls, when they would not be themselves. This seemed to be a sound counsel, but yet it was to be confirmed with a straiter bond, which fortune offered thus. There was Octavia the eldest sister of Caesar, not by one mother, for she came of Ancharia, and Caesar himself afterwards of Attia. It is reported that he dearly loved his sister Octavia, for indeed she was a noble lady, and left the widow of her first husband Caius Marcellus, who died not long before: and it seemed also that Antonius had been widower ever since the death of his wife Fulvia. For he denied not that he kept Cleopatra, but so did he not confess that he had her as his wife: and so with reason he did defend the love he bare unto this Egyptian Cleopatra. Thereupon

every man did set forward this marriage, hoping thereby that this lady Octavia, having an excellent grace, wisdom, and honesty joined unto so rare a beauty, that when she were with Antonius (he loving her as so worthy a lady deserveth) she should be a good mean to keep good love and amity betwixt her brother and him.

Sextus Pompeius at that time kept in Sicily, and so made many an inroad into Italy with a great number of pinnaces and other pirates' ships, of the which were captains two notable pirates, Menas and Menecrates, who so scoured all the sea thereabouts, that none durst peep out with a sail. Furthermore, Sextus Pompeius had dealt very friendly with Antonius, for he had courteously received his mother, when she fled out of Italy with Fulvia: and therefore they thought good to make peace with him. So they met all three together by the mount of Misenum, upon a hill that runneth far into the sea: Pompey having his ships riding hard by at anker, and Antonius and Caesar their armies upon the shore side, directly over against him. Now, after they had agreed that Sextus Pompeius should have Sicily and Sardinia, with this condition, that he should rid the sea of all thieves and pirates, and make it safe for passengers, and withal that he should send a certain of wheat to Rome: one of them did feast another, and drew cuts who should begin. It was Pompeius' chance to invite them first. Whereupon Antonius asked him: "And where shall we sup?" "There," said Pompey, and showed him his admiral galley which had six banks of oars: "That" (said he) "is my father's house they have left me." He spake it to taunt Antonius, because he had his father's house, that was Pompey the Great. So he cast ankers enow into the sea to make his galley fast, and then built a bridge of wood to convey them to his galley from the head of Mount Misenum: and there he welcomed them, and made them great cheer. Now in the midst of the feast, when they fell to be merry with Antonius' love unto Cleopatra, Menas the Pirate came to Pompey, and, whispering in his ear, said unto him: "Shall I cut the cables of the ankers, and make thee lord not only of Sicily and Sardinia, but of the whole empire of Rome besides?" Pompey, having paused awhile upon it, at length answered him: "Thou shouldest have done it, and never have told it me, but now we must content us with that we have. As for myself, I was never taught to break my faith, nor to be counted a traitor." The other two also did likewise feast him in their camp, and then he returned into Sicily. Antonius, after this agreement made, sent Ventidius before into Asia to stay the Parthians, and to keep them they should come no further: and he himself in the meantime, to gratify Caesar, was contented to be chosen Julius Caesar's priest and sacrificer, and so they jointly together dispatched all great matters concerning the state of the empire. But in all other manner of sports and exercises, wherein they passed the time away the one with the other, Antonius was ever inferior unto Caesar, and always lost, which grieved him much. With Antonius there was a soothsayer or astronomer of Egypt, that could cast a figure, and judge of men's nativities, to tell them what should happen to them. He, either to please Cleopatra, or else for that he found it so by his art, told Antonius plainly, that his fortune (which of itself was excellent good, and very great) was altogether blemished and obscured by Caesar's fortune: and therefore he counselled him utterly to leave his company, and to get him as far from him as he could. "For thy demon," said he, (that is to say, the good angel and spirit that keepeth thee) "is afraid of his: and, being courageous and high when he is alone, becometh fearful and timorous when he cometh near unto the other." Howsoever it was, the events ensuing proved the Egyptian's words true. For it is said that as often as they two drew cuts for pastime, who should have anything, or whether they played at dice, Antonius alway lost. Oftentimes, when they were disposed to see cockfight, or quails that were taught to fight one with another, Caesar's cocks or quails did ever overcome. The which spited Antonius in his mind, although he made no outward show of it: and therefore he believed the Egyptian the better. In fine, he recommended the affairs of his house unto Caesar, and went out of Italy with Octavia his wife, whom he carried into Greece, after he had had a daughter by her.

Then began this pestilent plague and mischief of Cleopatra's love (which had slept a long time, and seemed to have been utterly forgotten, and that Antonius had given place to better counsel) again to kindle, and to be in force, so soon as Antonius came near unto Syria. And in the end, the horse of the mind, as Plato termeth it, that is so hard of rein, (I mean the unreined lust of concupiscence), did put out of Antonius' head all honest and commendable thoughts: for he sent Fonteius Capito to bring Cleopatra into Syria. Unto whom, to welcome her, he gave no trifling things: but unto that she had already he added the provinces of Phoenicia, those of the nethermost Syria, the Isle of Cyprus, and a great part of Cilicia, and that country of Jewry where the true balm is, and that part of Arabia where the Nabataeans do dwell, which stretcheth out towards the ocean. These great gifts much misliked the Romans. But now, though Antonius did easily give away great seigniories, realms, and mighty nations unto some private men, and that also he took from other kings their lawful realms, (as from Antigonus king of the Jews, whom he openly beheaded, where never king before had suffered like death), yet all this did not so much offend the Romans, as the unmeasurable honors which he did unto Cleopatra. But yet he did much more aggravate their malice and ill-will towards him, because that, Cleopatra having brought him two twins, a son and a daughter, he named his son Alexander, and his daughter Cleopatra, and gave them to their surnames, the Sun to the one, and the Moon to the other.

Cleopatra knowing that Octavia would have Antonius from her, and fearing also that if with her virtue and honest behavior (besides the great power of her brother Caesar) she did add thereunto her modest kind love to please her husband, that she would then be too strong for her, and in the end win him away: she subtilly seemed to languish for the love of Antonius, pining her body for lack of meat. Furthermore, she every way so framed her countenance that, when Antonius came to see her, she cast her eyes upon him like a woman ravished for joy. Straight again, when he went from her, she fell a-weeping and blubbering, looked ruefully of the matter, and still found the means that Antonius should oftentimes find her weeping: and then, when he came suddenly upon her, she made as though she dried her eyes, and turned her face away, as if she were unwilling that he should see her weep. All these tricks she used, Antonius being in readiness to go into Syria to speak with the king of Medes. Then the flatterers that furthered Cleopatra's mind blamed Antonius, and told him that he was a hard-natured man, and that he had small love in him, that would see a poor lady in such torment for his sake, whose life depended only upon him alone. For Octavia, said they, that was married unto him as it were of necessity, because her brother Caesar's affairs so required it, hath the honor to be called Antonius' lawful spouse and wife: and Cleopatra, being born a queen of so many thousands of men, is only named Antonius' leman, and yet that she disdained not so to be called, if it might please him she might enjoy his company and live with him, but, if he once leave her, that then it is unpossible she should live. To be short, by these their flatteries and enticements they so wrought Antonius' effeminate mind that, fearing lest she would make herself away, he returned again unto Alexandria, and referred the king of Medes to the next year following, although he received news that the Parthians at that time were at civil wars among themselves. This notwithstanding, he went afterwards and made peace with him. For he married his daughter, which was very young, unto one of the sons that Cleopatra had by him: and then returned, being fully bent to make war with Caesar. When Octavia was returned to Rome from Athens, Caesar commanded her to go out of Antonius' house, and to dwell by herself, because he had abused her. Octavia answered him again, that she would not forsake her husband's house, and that if he had no other occasion to make war with him she prayed him then to take no thought for her: for, said she, it were too shameful a thing that two so famous captains should bring in civil wars among the Romans, the one for the love of a woman, and the other for the jealousy betwixt one another. Now, as she spake the word, so did she also perform the deed. For she kept still in Antonius' house, as if he had been there, and very honestly and honorably kept his children, not those only she had by him, but the other which her husband had by Fulvia. Furthermore, when Antonius sent any of his men to Rome to sue for any office in the commonwealth, she received him very courteously, and so used herself unto her brother that she obtained the thing she requested. Howbeit thereby, thinking no hurt, she did Antonius great hurt. For her honest love and regard to her husband made every man hate him, when they saw he did so unkindly use so noble a lady: but yet the greatest cause of their malice unto him was for the division of lands he made amongst his children in the city of Alexandria.

Then he went unto the city of Athens, and there gave himself again to see plays and pastimes, and to keep the theatres. Cleopatra, on the other side, being jealous of the honors which Octavia had received in this city, where indeed she was marvellously honored and beloved of the Athenians: to win the people's good-will also at Athens, she gave them great gifts: and they likewise gave her many great honors, and appointed certain ambassadors to carry the decree to her house, among the which Antonius was one, who as a citizen of Athens reported the matter unto her, and made an oration in the behalf of the city. Afterwards he sent to Rome to put his wife Octavia out of his house, who (as it is reported) went out of his house with all Antonius' children, saving the eldest of them he had by Fulvia, who was with his father, bewailing and lamenting her cursed hap that had brought her to this, that she was accounted one of the chiefest causes of this civil war. The Romans did pity her, but much more Antonius, and those specially that had seen Cleopatra, who neither excelled Octavia in beauty, nor yet in young years. Octavius Caesar understanding the sudden and wonderful great preparation of Antonius, he was not a little astonied at it (fearing he should be driven to fight that summer), because he wanted many things, and the great and grievous exactions of money did sorely oppress the people. For all manner of men else were driven to pay the fourth part of their goods and revenue: but the libertines, (to wit, those whose fathers or other predecessors had sometime been bondmen), they were sessed to pay the eighth part of all their goods at one payment. Hereupon there rose a wonderful exclamation and great uproar all Italy over: so that, among the greatest faults that ever Antonius committed, they blamed him most for that he delayed to give Caesar battle. For he gave Caesar leisure to make his preparations, and also to appease the complaints of the people.

Now after that Caesar had made sufficient preparation, he proclaimed open war against Cleopatra, and made the people to abolish the power and empire of Antonius, because he had before given it up unto a woman. And Caesar said furthermore, that Antonius was not master of himself, but that Cleopatra had brought him beside himself by her charms and amorous poisons, and that they that should make war with them should be Mardian the Eunuch, Pothinus, and Iras, a woman of Cleopatra's bed-chamber, that frizzled her hair and dressed her head, and Charmion, the which were those that ruled all the affairs of Antonius' empire. Before this war, as it is reported, many signs and wonders fell out. First of all, the city of Pisaurum, which was made a colony to Rome and replenished with people by Antonius, standing upon the shore side of the sea Adriatic, was by a terrible earthquake sunk into the ground. One of the images of stone which was set up in the honor of Antonius, in the city of Alba, did sweat many days together: and, though some wiped it away, yet it left not sweating still. In the city of Patras, whilst Antonius was there, the temple of Hercules was burnt with lightning. And at the city of Athens also, in a place where the war of the giants against the gods is set out in imagery, the statue of Bacchus with a terrible wind was thrown down in the theatre. It was said that Antonius came of the race of Hercules, as you have heard before, and in the manner of his life he followed Bacchus: and therefore he was called the new Bacchus. Furthermore, the same blustering storm of wind overthrew the great monstrous images at Athens, that were made in the honor of Eumenes and Attalus, the which men had names and entitled the Antonians, and yet they did hurt none of the other images which were many besides. The admiral galley of Cleopatra was called Antoniad, in the which there chanced a marvellous ill sign. Swallows had bred under the poop of her ship, and there came others after them that drave away the first, and plucked down their nests. Now, when all things were ready, and that they drew near to fight, it was found that Antonius had no less than five hundred good ships of war, among which there were many galleys that had eight and ten banks of oars, the which were sumptuously furnished, not so meet for fight as for triumph, a hundred thousand footmen, and twelve thousand horsemen, and had with him to aid him these kings and subjects following: Bocchus king of Libya, Tarcondemus king of high Cilicia, Archelaus king of Cappadocia, Philadephus king of Paphlagonia, Mithridates king of Commagena, and Adallas king of Thrace. All which were there every man in person. The residue that were absent sent their armies, as Polemon king of Pont, Malchus king of Arabia, Herodes king of Jewry: and, furthermore, Amyntas king of Lycaonia and of the Galatians: and, besides all these, he had all the aid the king of Medes sent unto him. Now for Caesar, he had two hundred and fifty ships of war, fourscore thousand footmen, and well near as many horsemen as his enemy Antonius. Antonius for his part had all under his dominion from Armenia and the river of Euphrates unto the sea Ionium and Illyricum. Octavius Caesar had also for his part all that which was in our hemisphere, or half-part of the world, from Illyria unto the ocean sea upon the west: then all from the ocean unto Mare Siculum: and from Africk all that which is against Italy, as Gaul and Spain. Furthermore, all from the province of Cyrene to Ethiopia was subject unto Antonius. Now Antonius was made so subject to a woman's will, that, though he was a great deal the stronger by land, yet for Cleopatra's sake he would needs have this battle tried by sea:

though he saw before his eyes, that, for lack of watermen, his captains did press by force all sorts of men out of Greece that they could take up in the field, as travellers, muleteers, reapers, harvest men, and young boys, and yet could they not sufficiently furnish his galleys: so that the most part of them were empty, and could scant row, because they lacked watermen enow. But on the contrary side Caesar's ships were not built for pomp, high and great, only for a sight and bravery: but they were light of yarage, armed and furnished with watermen as many as they needed, and had them all in readiness in the havens of Tarentum and Brundusium. So Octavius Caesar sent unto Antonius, to will him to delay no more time, but to come on with his army into Italy: and that for his own part he would give him safe harbor, to land without any trouble, and that he would withdraw his army from the sea as far as one horse could run, until he had put his army ashore, and had lodged his men. Antonius on the other side bravely sent him word again, and challenged the combat of him man to man, though he were the elder: and that, if he refused him so, he would then fight a battle with him in the fields of Pharsalia, as Julius Caesar and Pompey had done before. Now, whilst Antonius rode at anker, lying idly in harbor at the head of Actium, in the place where the city of Nicopolis standeth at this present, Caesar had quickly passed the sea Ionium, and taken a place called Toryne, before Antonius understood that he had taken ship. Then began his men to be afraid, because his army by land was left behind. But Cleopatra making light of it, "And what danger, I pray you," said she, "if Caesar keep at Toryne?" The next morning by break of day, his enemies coming with full force of oars in battle against him, Antonius was afraid that if they came to join they would take and carry away his ships, that had no men of war in them. So he armed all his watermen, and set them in order of battle upon the fore-castle of their ships, and then lift up all his ranks of oars towards the element, as well on the one side as on the other, with the proes against the enemies, at the entry and mouth of the gulf which beginneth at the point of Actium, and so kept

them in order of battle, as if they had been armed and furnished with watermen and soldiers. Thus Octavius Caesar, being finely deceived by this stratagem, retired presently, and therewithal Antonius very wisely and suddenly did cut him off from fresh water. For, understanding that the places where Octavius Caesar landed had very little store of water, and yet very bad: he shut them in with strong ditches and trenches he cast, to keep them from sallying out at their pleasure, and so to go seek water farther off. Furthermore, he dealt very friendly and courteously with Domitius, and against Cleopatra's mind. For, he being sick of an ague when he went and took a little boat to go unto Caesar's camp, Antonius was very sorry for it, but yet he sent after him all his carriage, train, and men: and the same Domitius, as though he gave him to understand that he repented his open treason, he died immediately after. There were certain kings also that forsook him, and turned on Caesar's side: as Amyntas and Deiotarus. Furthermore his fleet and navy that was unfortunate in all things, and unready for service, compelled him to change his mind, and to hazard battle by land. And Canidius also, who had charge of his army by land, when time came to follow Antonius' determination, he turned him clean contrary, and counselled him to send Cleopatra back again, and himself to retire into Macedon, to fight there on the mainland. And furthermore told him, that Dicomes king of the Getae promised him to aid him with a great power: and that it should be no shame nor dishonor to him to let Caesar have the sea, (because himself and his men both had been well practised and exercised in battles by sea, in the war of Sicily against Sextus Pompeius), but rather that he should do against all reason, he having so great skill and experience of battles by land as he had, if he should not employ the force and valiantness of so many lusty armed footmen as he had ready, but would weaken his army by dividing them into ships. But now, notwithstanding all these good persuasions, Cleopatra forced him to put all to the hazard of battle by sea: considering with herself how she might fly and provide for her safety, not to help him to win the victory, but to fly more easily after the battle lost. Betwixt Antonius' camp and his fleet of ships there was a great high point of firm land that ran a good way into the sea, the which Antonius used often for a walk without mistrust of fear or danger. One of Caesar's men perceived it, and told his master that he would laugh if they could take up Antonius in the midst of his walk. Thereupon Caesar sent some of his men to lie in ambush for him, and they missed not much of taking of him: for they took him that came before him, because they discovered too soon, and so Antonius scaped very hardly. So, when Antonius had determined to fight by sea, he set all the other ships on fire but threescore ships of Egypt, and reserved only but the best and greatest galleys, from three banks unto ten banks of oars. Into them he put two-and-twenty thousand fighting men, with two thousand darters and slingers. Now, as he was setting his men in order of battle, there was a captain, and a valiant man, that had served Antonius in many battles and conflicts, and had all his body hacked and cut: who, as Antonius passed by him, cried out unto him and said: "O noble emperor, how cometh it to pass that you trust to these vile brittle ships? What, do you mistrust these wounds of mine and this sword? Let the Egyptians and Phoenicians fight by sea, and set us on the mainland, where we used to conquer, or to be slain on our feet." Antonius passed by him and said never a word, but only beckoned to him with his hand and head, as though he willed him to be of good courage, although indeed he had no great courage himself. For, when the masters of the galleys and pilots would have let their sails alone, he made them clap them on, saying to color the matter withal, that not one of his enemies should scape. All that day and the three days following, the sea rose so high and was so boisterous, that the battle was put off. The fifth day the storm ceased and the sea calmed again, and then they rowed with force of oars in battle one against the other, Antonius leading the right wing with Publicola, and Caelius the left, and Marcus Octavius and Marcus Justeius the midst. Octavius Caesar, on the other side, had placed Agrippa in the left wing of his army, and had kept the right wing for himself. For the armies by land, Canidius was general of Antonius' side, and Taurus of Caesar's side: who kept their men in battle ray the one before the other, upon the seaside, without stirring one against the other.

About noon there rose a little gale of wind from the sea, and then Antonius' men waxing angry with tarrying so long, and trusting to the greatness and height of their ships, as if they had been invincible, they began to march forward with their left wing. Caesar seeing that was a glad man, and began a little to give back from the right wing, to allure them to come farther out of the strait and gulf, to the end that he might with his light ships well manned with watermen turn and environ the galleys of the enemies, the which were heavy of yarage, both for their bigness as also for lack of watermen to row them. When the skirmish began, and that they came to join, there was no great hurt at the first meeting, neither did the ships vehemently hit one against the other, as they do commonly in fight by sea. For, on the one side, Antonius' ships for their heaviness could not have the strength and swiftness to make their blows of any force: and Caesar's ships, on the other side, took great heed not to rush and shock with the forecastles of Antonius' ships, whose proes were armed with great brazen spurs. Furthermore they durst not flank them, because their points were easily broken, which way so ever they came to set upon his ships, that were made of great main square pieces of timber, bound together with great iron pins: so that the battle was much like to a battle by land, or, to speak more properly, to the assault of a city. For there were always three or four of Caesar's ships about one of Antonius' ships, and the soldiers fought with their pikes, halberds, and darts, and threw pots and darts with fire. Antonius' ships on the other side bestowed among them, with their cross-bows and engines of battery, great store of shot from their high towers of wood that were upon their ships.

Howbeit the battle was yet of even hand, and the victory doubtful, being indifferent to both: when suddenly they saw the threescore ships of Cleopatra busy about their yard-masts, and hoisting sail to fly. So they fled through the midst of them that were in fight, for they had been placed behind the great ships, and did marvellously disorder the other ships. For the enemies themselves wondered much to see them said in that sort with full sail towards Peloponnesus. There Antonius showed plainly, that he had not only lost the courage and heart of an emperor, but also of a valiant man, and that he was not his own man, (proving that true which an old man spake in mirth, that the soul of a lover lived in another body, and not in his own): he was so carried away with the vain love of this woman, as if he had been glued unto her, and that she could not have removed without moving of him also. For, when he saw Cleopatra's ship under sail, he forgot, forsook, and betrayed them that fought for him, and embarked upon a galley with five banks of oars, to follow her that was already begun to overthrow him, and would in the end be his utter destruction. When she knew his galley afar off, she lift up a sign in the poop of her ship, and so Antonius coming to it was plucked up where Cleopatra was: howbeit he saw her not at his first coming, nor she him, but went and sat down alone in the prow of his ship, and said never a word, clapping his head between both his hands. In the meantime came certain light brigantines of Caesar's that followed him hard.

Antonius sent unto Canidius to return with his army into Asia by Macedon. Now, for himself, he determined to cross over into Africk, and took one of her carects or hulks loaden with gold and silver and other rich carriage, and gave it unto his friends: commanding them to depart, and to seek to save themselves. They answered him weeping, that they would neither do it, not yet forsake him. Then Antonius very courteously and lovingly did comfort them, and prayed them to depart: and wrote unto Theophilus governor of Corinth, that he would see them safe, and help to hide them in some secret place, until they had made their way and peace with Caesar. This Theophilus was the father of Hipparchus, who was had in great estimation about Antonius. He was the first of all his enfranchised bondmen that revolted from him and yielded unto Caesar, and afterwards went and dwelt at Corinth. And thus it stood with Antonius. Now, for his army by sea, that fought before the head or foreland of Actium, they held out a long time, and nothing troubled them more than a great boisterous wind that rose full in the prows of their ships, and yet with much ado his navy was at length overthrown, five hours within night. There were not slain above five thousand men: but yet there were three hundred ships taken, as Octavius Caesar writeth himself in his commentaries. Many plainly saw Antonius fly, and yet could very hardly believe it, that he, that had nineteen legions whole by land and twelve thousand horsemen upon the seaside, would so have forsaken them, and have fled so cowardly: as if he had not oftentimes proved both the one and the other fortune, and that he had not been throughly acquainted with the diverse changes and fortunes of battles. And yet his soldiers still wished for him, and ever hoped that he would come by some means or other unto them. Furthermore they showed themselves so valiant and faithful unto him, that after they certainly knew he was fled they kept themselves whole together seven days. In the end Canidius, Antonius' lieutenant, flying by night, and forsaking his camp, when they saw themselves thus destitute of their heads and leaders, they yielded themselves unto the stronger.

Antonius being arrived in Libya, he sent Cleopatra before into Egypt from the city of Paraetonium: and he himself remained very solitary, having only two of his friends with him, with whom he wandered up and down, both of them orators, the one Aristocrates a Grecian, and the other Lucilius a Roman: of whom we have written in another place, that, at the battle where Brutus was overthrown by the city of Philippi, he came and willingly put himself into the hands of those that followed Brutus, saying that it was he: because Brutus in the meantime might have liberty to save himself. And, afterwards, because Antonius saved his life, he still remained with him: and was very faithful and friendly unto him till his death. But when Antonius heard that he whom he had trusted with the government of Libya, and unto whom he had given the charge of his army there, had yielded unto Caesar: he was so mad withal, that he would have slain himself for anger, had not his friends about him withstood him, and kept him from it. So he went unto Alexandria, and there found Cleopatra about a wonderful enterprise, and of great attempt. Betwixt the Red Sea and the sea between the lands that point upon the coast of Egypt there is a little piece of land, that divideth both the seas and separateth Africk from Asia: the which strait is so narrow at the end where the two seas are narrowest, that it is not above three hundred furlongs over. Cleopatra went about to lift her ships out of the one sea, and to hale them over the strait into the other sea: that, when her ships were come into the Gulf of Arabia, she might then carry all her gold and silver away, and so with a great company of men go and dwell in some place about the ocean sea far from the sea Mediterranean, to scape the danger and bondage of this war. But now, because the Arabians dwelling about the city of Petra did burn the first ships that were brought to land, and that Antonius thought that his army by land, which he left at Actium, was yet whole: she left off her enterprise, and determined to keep all the ports and passages of her realm. Antonius, he forsook the city and company of his friends, and built him a house in the sea, by the Isle of Pharos, upon certain forced amounts which he caused to be cast into the sea, and dwelt there, as a man that banished himself from all men's company: saying that he would lead Timon's life, because he had the like wrong offered him, that was before offered unto Timon: and that for the unthankfulness of those he had done good unto, and whom he took to be his friends, he was angry with all men, and would trust no man.

Canidius himself came to bring him news, that he had lost all his army by land at Actium: on the other side he was advertised also, that Herodes king of Jewry, who had also certain legions and bands with him, was revolted unto Caesar, and all the other kings in like manner: so that, saving those that were about him, he had none left him. All this notwithstanding did nothing trouble him, and it seemed that he

was contented to forgo all his hope, and so to be rid of all his care and troubles. Thereupon he left his solitary house he had built by the sea which he called Timoneon, and Cleopatra received him into her royal palace. He was no sooner come thither, but he straight set all the city on rioting and banqueting again, and himself to liberality and gifts. He caused the son of Julius Caesar and Cleopatra to be enrolled (according to the manner of the Romans) amongst the number of young men: and gave Antyllus, his eldest son he had by Fulvia, the man's gown, the which was a plain gown without guard or embroidery of purple. For these things there was kept great feasting, banqueting, and dancing in Alexandria many days together.

Cleopatra in the meantime was very careful in gathering all sorts of poisons together, to destroy men. Now, to make proof of those poisons which made men die with least pain, she tried it upon condemned men in prison. For, when she saw the poisons that were sudden and vehement, and brought speedy death with grievous torments, and, in contrary manner, that such as were more mild and gentle had not that quick speed and force to make one die suddenly, she afterwards went about to prove the stinging of snakes and adders, and made some to be applied unto men in her sight, some in one sort and some in another. So, when she had daily made divers and sundry proofs, she found none of them all she had proved so fit as the biting of an aspic, the which causeth only a heaviness of the head, without swooning or complaining, and bringeth a great desire also to sleep, with a little sweat in the face, and so by little and little taketh away the senses and vital powers, no living creature perceiving that the patients feel any pain. For they are so sorry when anybody awaketh them, and taketh them up, as those that being taken out of a sound sleep are very heavy and desirous to sleep. This notwithstanding, they sent ambassadors unto Octavius Caesar in Asia, Cleopatra requesting the realm of Egypt for their children, and Antonius praying that he might be suffered to live at Athens like a private man, if Caesar would not let him remain in

Egypt. And, because they had no other men of estimation about them, for that some were fled, and, those that remained, they did not greatly trust them: they were enforced to send Euphronius the schoolmaster of their children.

Caesar would not grant unto Antonius' requests: but, for Cleopatra, he made her answer, that he would deny her nothing reasonable, so that she would either put Antonius to death, or drive him out of her country. Therewithal he sent Thyreus one of his men unto her, a very wise and discreet man, who, bringing letters of credit from a young lord unto a noble lady, and that besides greatly liked her beauty, might easily by his eloquence have persuaded her. He was longer in talk with her than any man else was, and the queen herself also did him great honor: insomuch as he made Antonius jealous of him. Whereupon Antonius caused him to be taken and well-favoredly whipped, and so sent him unto Caesar: and bade him tell him that he made him angry with him, because he showed himself proud and disdainful towards him, and now specially when he was easy to be angered, by reason of his present misery. "To be short, if this mislike thee," said he, "thou hast Hipparchus one of my enfranchised bondmen with thee: hang him if thou wilt, or whip him at thy pleasure that we may cry quittance." From thenceforth Cleopatra, to clear herself of the suspicion he had of her, she made more of him than ever she did. For first of all, where she did solemnize the day of her birth very meanly and sparingly, fit for her present misfortune, she now in contrary manner did keep it with such solemnity, that she exceeded all measure of sumptuousness and magnificence: so that the guests that were bidden to the feasts, and came poor, went away rich. Now, things passing thus, Agrippa by divers letters sent one after another unto Caesar prayed him to return to Rome, because the affairs there did of necessity require his person and presence. Thereupon he did defer the war till the next year following: but, when winter was done, he returned again through Syria by the coast of Africk, to make wars against Antonius, and his other captains. When the city of Pelusium was taken, there ran a rumor in the city, that Seleucus, by Cleopatra's consent, had surrendered the same. But, to clear herself that she did not, Cleopatra brought Seleucus' wife and children unto Antonius, to be revenged of them at his pleasure. Furthermore, Cleopatra had long before made many sumptuous tombs and monuments, as well for excellency of workmanship as for height and greatness of building, joining hard to the temple of Isis. Thither she caused to be brought all the treasure and precious things she had of the ancient kings her predecessors: as gold, silver, emeralds, pearls, ebony, ivory, and cinnamon, and besides all that, a marvellous number of torches, faggots, and flax. So Octavius Caesar being afraid to lose such a treasure and mass of riches, and that this woman for spite would set it afire, and burn it every whit: he always sent some one or other unto her from him, to put her in good comfort, whilst he in the meantime drew near the city with his army. So Caesar came, and pitched his camp hard by the city, in the place where they run and manage their horses. Antonius made a sally upon him, and fought very valiantly, so that he drave Caesar's horsemen back, fighting with his men even into their camp. Then he came again to the palace, greatly boasting of this victory, and sweetly kissed Cleopatra, armed as he was when he came from the fight, recommending one of his men of arms unto her, that had valiantly fought in this skirmish. Cleopatra to reward his manliness gave him an armor and head-piece of clean gold: howbeit the man at arms, when he had received this rich gift, stale away by night, and went to Caesar. Antonius sent again to challenge Caesar to fight with him hand to hand. Caesar answered him, that he had many other ways to die than so. Then Antonius, seeing there was no way more honorable for him to die than fighting valiantly, he determined to set up his rest, both by sea and land. So, being at supper (as it is reported), he commanded his officers and household servants that waited on him at his board, that they should fill his cups full, and make as much of him as they could: "For," said he, "you know not whether you shall do so much for me to-morrow or not, or whether you shall serve another master: and it may be you shall see me no more, but a dead body." This notwithstanding, perceiving that his friends and men fell a-weeping to hear him say so: to salve that he had spoken, he added this more unto it, that he would not lead them to battle, where he thought not rather safely to return with victory, than valiantly to die with honor. Furthermore, the self same night within little of midnight, when all the city was quiet, full of fear and sorrow, thinking what would be the issue and end of this war: it is said that suddenly they heard a marvellous sweet harmony of sundry sorts of instruments of music, with the cry of a multitude of people, as they had been dancing, and had sung as they use in Bacchus' feasts, with movings and turnings after the manner of the Satyrs: and it seemed that this dance went through the city unto the gate that opened to the enemies, and that all the troop that made this noise they heard went out of the city at that gate. Now, such as in reason sought the depth of the interpretation of this wonder, thought that it was the god unto whom Antonius bare singular devotion to counterfeit and resemble him, that did forsake them. The next morning by break of day, he went to set those few footmen he had in order upon the hills adjoining unto the city: and there he stood to behold his galleys which departed from the haven, and rowed against the galleys of his enemies, and so stood still, looking what exploit his soldiers in them would do. But, when by force of rowing they were come near unto them, they first saluted Caesar's men, and then Caesar's men resaluted them also, and of two armies made but one, and then did all together row toward the city. When Antonius saw that his men did forsake him, and yielded unto Caesar, and that his footmen were broken and overthrown: he then fled into the city, crying out that Cleopatra had betrayed him unto them, with whom he had made war for her sake. Then she, being afraid of his fury, fled into the tomb which she caused to be made, and there locked the doors unto her, and shut all the springs of the locks with great bolts, and in the meantime sent unto Antonius to tell him that she was dead. Antonius, believing it, said unto himself: "What dost thou look for further, Antonius, sith spiteful fortune hath taken from thee the only joy thou hadst, for whom thou yet reservedst thy life?" When he had said these words, he went into a chamber and unarmed himself, and being naked said thus: "O Cleopatra, it grieveth me not that I have lost thy company, for I will not be long from thee: but I am sorry that, having been so great a captain and emperor, I am indeed condemned to be judged of less courage and noble mind than a woman." Now he had a man of his called Eros, whom he loved and trusted much, and whom he had long before caused to swear unto him, that he should kill him when he did command him: and then he willed him to keep his promise. His man drawing his sword lift it up as though he had meant to have stricken his master: but turning his head at one side he thrust his sword into himself, and fell down dead at his master's foot. Then said Antonius, "O noble Eros, I thank thee for this, and it is valiantly done of thee, to show me what I should do to myself, which thou couldst not do for me." Therewithal he took his sword, and thrust it into his belly, and so fell down upon a little bed. The wound he had killed him not presently, for the blood stinted a little when he was laid: and, when he came somewhat to himself again, he prayed them that were about him to dispatch him. But they all fled out of the chamber, and left him crying out and tormenting himself: until at last there came a secretary unto him called Diomedes, who was commanded to bring him into the tomb or monument where Cleopatra was. When he heard that she was alive, he very earnestly prayed his men to carry his body thither, and so he was carried in his men's arms into the entry of the monument. Notwithstanding, Cleopatra would not open the gates, but came to the high windows, and cast out certain chains and ropes, in the which Antonius was trussed: and Cleopatra her own self, with two women only, which she had suffered to come with her into these monuments, triced Antonius up. They that were present to behold it said they never saw so pitiful a sight. For they plucked up poor Antonius all bloody as he was, and drawing on with pangs of death, who holding up his hands to Cleopatra raised up himself as well as he could. It was a hard thing for these women to do, to lift him up: but Cleopatra stooping down with her head, putting to all her strength to her uttermost power, did lift him up with much ado, and never let go her hold, with the help of the women beneath that bade her be of good courage, and were as sorry to see her labor so, as she herself. So when she had gotten him in after that sort, and laid him on a bed, she rent her garments upon him, clapping her breast, and scratching her face and stomach. Then she dried up his blood that had berayed his face, and called him her lord, her husband, and emperor, forgetting her own misery and calamity, for the pity and compassion she took of him. Antonius made her cease her lamenting, and called for wine, either because he was athirst, or else for that he thought thereby to hasten his death. When he had drunk, he earnestly prayed her, and persuaded her, that she would seek to save her life, if she could possible, without reproach and dishonor: and that chiefly she should trust Proculeius above any man else about Caesar. And, as for himself, that she should not lament nor sorrow for the miserable change of his fortune at the end of his days: but rather that she should think him the more fortunate for the former triumphs and honors he had received, considering that while he lived he was the noblest and greatest prince of the world, and that now he was overcome not cowardly, but valiantly, a Roman by another Roman. As Antonius gave the last gasp, Proculeius came that was sent from Caesar. For, after Antonius had thrust his sword in himself, as they carried him into the tombs and monuments of Cleopatra, one of his guard called Dercetaeus took his sword with the which he had striken himself, and hid it: then he secretly stale away, and brought Octavius Caesar the first news of his death, and showed him his sword that was bloodied. Caesar hearing these news straight withdrew himself into a secret place of his tent, and there burst out with tears, lamenting his hard and miserable fortune that had been his friend and brother-in-law, his equal in the empire, and companion with him in sundry great exploits and battles. Then he called for all his friends, and showed them the letters Antonius had written to him, and his

answers also sent him again, during their quarrel and strife: and how fiercely and proudly the other answered him, to all just and reasonable matters he wrote unto him. After this, he sent Proculeius, and commanded him to do what he could possible to get Cleopatra alive, fearing lest otherwise all the treasure would be lost: and furthermore, he thought that if he could take Cleopatra, and bring her alive to Rome, she would marvellously beautify and set out his triumph. But Cleopatra would never put herself into Proculeius' hands, although they spake together. For Proculeius came to the gates that were very thick and strong, and surely barred, but yet there were some cranews through the which her voice might be heard, and so they without understood, that Cleopatra demanded the kingdom of Egypt for her sons: and that Proculeius answered her, that she should be of good cheer, and not be afraid to refer all unto Caesar. After he had viewed the place very well, he came and reported her answer unto Caesar. Who immediately sent Gallus to speak once again with her, and bade him purposely hold her with talk, whilst Proculeius did set up a ladder against that high window by the which Antonius was triced up, and came down into the monument with two of his men, hard by the gate where Cleopatra stood to hear what Gallus said unto her. One of her women which was shut in her monuments with her saw Proculeius by chance as he came down, and shrieked out. "O poor Cleopatra, thou art taken." Then, when she saw Proculeius behind her as she came from the gate, she thought to have stabbed herself in with a short dagger she wore of purpose by her side. But Proculeius came suddenly upon her, and taking her by both the hands said unto her: "Cleopatra, first thou shalt do thyself great wrong, and secondly unto Caesar, to deprive him of the occasion and opportunity openly to show his bounty and mercy, and to give his enemies cause to accuse the most courteous and noble prince that ever was, and to appeach him, as though he were a cruel and merciless man that were not to be trusted." So even as he spake the word he took her dagger from her, and shook her clothes for fear of any poison hidden about her. Afterwards Caesar sent one of his enfranchised men called Epaphroditus, whom he straightly charged to look well unto her, and to beware in any case that she made not herself away: and, for the rest, to use her with all the courtesy possible.

Many princes, great kings, and captains did crave Antonius' body of Octavius Caesar, to give him honorable burial: but Caesar would never take it from Cleopatra, who did sumptuously and royally bury him with her own hands, whom Caesar suffered to take as much as she would to bestow upon his funerals. Now was she altogether overcome with sorrow and passion of mind, for she had knocked her breast so pitifully, that she had martyred it, and in divers places had raised ulcers and inflammations, so that she fell into a fever withal: whereof she was very glad, hoping thereby to have good color to abstain from meat, and that so she might have died easily without any trouble. She had a physician called Olympus, whom she made privy of her intent, to the end he should help her to rid her out of her life: as Olympus writeth himself, who wrote a book of all these things. But Caesar mistrusted the matter, by many conjectures he had, and therefore did put her in fear, and threatened her to put her children to shameful death. With these threats Cleopatra for fear yielded straight, as she would have yielded unto strokes, and afterwards suffered herself to be cured and dieted as they listed. Shortly after, Caesar came himself in person to see her, and to comfort her. Cleopatra being laid upon a little low bed in poor state, when she saw Caesar come into her chamber, she suddenly rose up, naked in her smock, and fell down at his feet marvellously disfigured: both for that she had plucked her hair from her head, as also for that she had martyred all her face with her nails, and besides, her voice was small and trembling, her eyes sunk into her head with continual blubbering, and moreover they might see the most part of her stomach torn in sunder. To be short, her body was not much better than her mind: yet her good grace and comelines and the force of her beauty was not altogether defaced. But, notwithstanding this ugly and pitiful state of hers, yet she showed herself within by her outward looks and countenance. When Caesar had made her lie down again, and sat by her bedside, Cleopatra began to clear and excuse herself for that she had done, laying all to the fear she had of Antonius: Caesar, in contrary manner, reproved her in every point. Then she suddenly altered her speech, and prayed him to pardon her, as though she were afraid to die, and desirous to live. At length, she gave him a brief and memorial of all the ready money and treasure she had. But by chance there stood Seleucus by, one of her treasurers, who, to seem a good servant, came straight to Caesar to disprove Cleopatra, that she had not set in all, but kept many things back of purpose. Cleopatra was in such a rage with him, that she flew upon him, and took him by the hair of the head, and boxed him well-favoredly. Caesar fell a-laughing, and parted the fray. "Alas," said she, "O Caesar, is not this a great shame and reproach, that thou having vouchsafed to take the pains to come unto me, and hast done me this honor, poor wretch and caitiff creature brought into this pitiful and miserable state, and that mine own servants should come now to accuse me: though it may be I have reserved some jewels and trifles meet for women, but not for me (poor soul) to set out myself withal, but meaning to give some pretty presents and gifts unto Octavia and Livia, that, they making means and intercession for me to thee, thou mightest yet extend thy favor and mercy upon me?" Caesar was glad to hear her say so, persuading himself thereby that she had yet a desire to save her life. So he made her answer, that he did not only give her that to dispose of at her pleasure which she had kept back, but further promised to use her more honorably and bountifully than she would think for: and so he took his leave of her, supposing he had deceived her, but indeed he was deceived himself. There was a young gentleman Cornelius Dolabella, that was one of Caesar's very great familiars, and besides did bear no evil will unto Cleopatra. He sent her word secretly as she had requested him, that Caesar determined to take his journey through Syria, and that within three days he would send her away before with her children. When this was told Cleopatra, she requested Caesar that it would please him to suffer her to offer the last oblations of the dead unto the soul of Antonius. This being granted her, she was carried to the place where his tomb was, and there falling down on her knees, embracing the tomb with her women, the tears running down her cheeks, she began to speak in this sort: "O my dear Lord Antonius, not long sithence I buried thee here, being a freewoman: and now I offer unto thee the funeral sprinklings and oblations, being a captive and prisoner, and yet I am forbidden and kept from tearing and murthering this captive body of mine with blows, which they carefully guard and keep, only to triumph of thee: look therefore henceforth for no other honors, offerings, nor sacrifices from me, for these are the last which Cleopatra can give thee, sith now they carry her away. Whilst we lived together, nothing could sever our companies: but now at our death I fear me they will make us change our countries. For as thou being a Roman has been buried in Egypt, even so wretched creature I, an Egyptian, shall be buried in Italy, which shall be all the good that I have received by thy country. If therefore the gods where thou art now have any power and authority, sith our gods here have forsaken us, suffer no thy true friend and lover to be carried away alive, that in me they triumph of thee: but receive me with thee, and let me be buried in one self tomb with thee. For though my griefs and miseries be infinite, yet none hath grieved me more, now that I could less bear withal, than this small time which I have been driven to live alone without thee." Then, having ended these doleful plaints, and crowned the tomb with garlands and sundry nosegays, and marvellous lovingly embraced the same, she commanded they should prepare her bath, and when she had bathed and washed herself she fell to her meat, and was sumptuously served. Now whilst she was at dinner there came a countryman, and brought her a basket. The soldiers that warded at the gates asked him straight what he had in his basket. He opened the basket, and took out the leaves that covered the figs, and showed them that they were figs he brought. They all of them marvelled to see so goodly figs. The countryman laughed to hear them, and bade

them take some if they would. They believed he told them truly, and so bade him carry them in. After Cleopatra had dined, she sent a certain table written and sealed unto Caesar, and commanded them all to go out of the tombs where she was, but the two women: then she shut the doors to her. Caesar, when he received this table, and began to read her lamentation and petition, requesting him that he would let her be buried with Antonius, found straight what she meant, and thought to have gone thither himself: howbeit he sent one before in all haste that might be, to see what it was. Her death was very sudden. For those whom Caesar sent unto her ran thither in all haste possible, and found the soldiers standing at the gate, mistrusting nothing, nor understanding of her death. But when they had opened the doors they found Cleopatra stark dead, laid upon a bed of gold, attired and arrayed in her royal robes, and one of her two women, which was called Iras, dead at her feet: and her other woman called Charmion half-dead, and trembling, trimming the diadem which Cleopatra ware upon her head. One of the soldiers, seeing her, angrily said unto her: "Is that well done, Charmion?" "Very well," said she again, "and meet for a princess descended from the race of so many noble kings." She said no more, but fell dead hard by the bed. Some report that this aspic was brought unto her in the basket with figs, and that she had commanded them to hide it under the figleaves, that, when she should think to take out the figs, the aspic should bite her before she should see her: howbeit that, when she would have taken away the leaves for the figs, she perceived it, and said, "Art thou here then?" And so, her arm being naked, she put it to the aspic to be bitten. Others say again, she kept it in a box, and that she did prick and thrust it with a spindle of gold, so that the aspic, being angered withal, leapt out with great fury, and bit her in the arm. Howbeit few can tell the troth. For they report also, that she had hidden poison in a hollow razor which she carried in the hair of her head: and yet was there no mark seen of her body, or any sign discerned that she was poisoned, neither also did they find this serpent in her tomb. But it was reported only, that there were seen certain fresh steps or tracks where it had gone, on the tomb side toward the sea, and specially by the door side. Some say also, that they found two little pretty bitings in her arm, scant to be discerned: the which it seemeth Caesar himself gave credit unto, because in his triumph he carried Cleopatra's image, with an aspic biting of her arm. And thus goeth the report of her death. Now Caesar, though he was marvellous sorry for the death of Cleopatra, yet he wondered at her noble mind and courage, and therefore commanded she should be nobly buried, and laid by Antonius: and willed also that her two women should have honorable burial. Cleopatra died being eight-and-thirty years old, after she had reigned two-and-twenty years, and governed above fourteen of them with Antonius. And for Antonius, some say that he lived three-and-fifty years: and others say, six-and-fifty.

EXERCISE

1. Antony's life is closely bound up with great events in the history of the Roman Empire. How much interest does Plutarch show here in the course of the Roman Empire? What is his focus of interest? Locate certain events that illustrate this focus of interest with special force.

2. What is Plutarch's attitude toward Antony? Does he pity him? Does he attempt to condone his actions? Does he make Antony a hero?

3. Cleopatra turned the whole course of Antony's career. Does Plutarch make us feel Cleopatra's fascination sufficiently to account for her influence on Antony?

4. Shakespeare used North's translation of Plutarch's Antony in writing his play, *Antony and Cleopatra*. Some of Plutarch's description, Shakespeare altered hardly more than by putting it into blank verse. Do you consider Plutarch's description as good as Shakespeare apparently did?

5. Look up something about Plutarch. How do his origins, moment in history and philosophy, condition his biographical interests?

~DRAMA~

Introduction

The dramatic method of presenting an experience is to let the characters speak for themselves and perform their actions before our eyes. A drama is, then, a dialogue spoken by the characters, with directions from the author telling what the characters do and perhaps how they speak their lines, and with directions (usually fairly brief) describing the background against which they perform their action.

Dramas are written to be performed, of course, and it may be argued that the appreciation of a play gained from reading it is not quite the same thing as that gained from seeing it on the stage. This is true. But the actors who through their performance help the dramatist to interpret his action for us had to shape their interpretation of the play from their reading of it. Good direction and excellent acting can indeed make the play richer and more meaningful for us. But if we have imagination, the lack of proper stage sets and the gestures and voices of the actors should not be a crippling handicap.

The dramatic mode, since it is merely one of the several modes possible to the writer, has certain strong points and certain limitations; that is, through drama the writer can present certain things more vividly and intensely than through other literary forms, but on the other hand, drama has certain limitations within which a skillful writer will develop his action. The great problem of the artist, of course, remains the same in drama as in poetry and fiction, the problem of creating for the reader an experience with intensity and meaning. The dramatic method of organizing his material is properly only one of a number of means to this end.

Some of the general problems which the dramatist shares with writers in other literary forms have been discussed in the Introduction to Fiction. The student might do well at this point to go back to that introduction and recall what was said under such topics as conflict, action and plot, point of view, exposition, and so on. The dramatist shares with the writer of fiction the problem, to begin with a very general one, of building up characters in whom we can believe, and relating them to each other and to the story so that we can feel that their conduct is properly motivated and reveals its own logic. Common to both drama and fiction is the problem of choosing a beginning point, and the problem of exposition—the problem of telling the audience who the characters are and what the original situation is. There is the problem of movement, that of deciding how the various stages of the action are to be presented to the reader, and the problem of complicating the action. Above all, there is the general problem of making the play express the theme which the author wishes to present to his audience.

Some of these problems which allow a number of choices to the writer of fiction admit of only one type of solution in drama. For example, the point of view for the dramatist is always the same—the objective view. Narration cannot be used as a basic method; we must see the events before our eyes, by and large, and, by and large, infer their meaning. Furthermore, for the dramatist, certain problems rather easily solved in fiction present additional complications. Perhaps, however, our best method for setting forth briefly the differences which separate drama from the novel or short story is to see how the situation in "Porphyria's Lover" would be handled by the dramatist.

Suppose the writer mentioned in the "General Introduction" decided to turn this situation into a play rather than into a story or poem. How, in general, would he go about it?

PORPHYRIA'S LOVER

Dramatis Personæ

PORPHYRIA

HER LOVER

Time: The late nineteenth century. Night.

Place: The interior of a small English cottage. There is a small table to the left, covered with books and papers. On it a small lamp burns, throwing a dull glow over the room. Two plain straight-backed chairs are placed against the wall. To the right there is a small fireplace in which a few coals smoulder. The windows back stage are streaked with rain. Before the fireplace there is a large chair in which a young man sits. He is plainly dressed. His eyes are closed, and he appears either to be asleep or in a coma of inattention. There is a soft knock at the door to the left. The man does not stir. The knock is repeated, and the door opens to admit Porphyria. She is a pretty girl, dressed for a party. Over her dress is thrown a shawl which is wet with the rain. She closes the door softly, and walks toward the man.

PORPHYRIA. John? (*He looks up at her silently, but does not rise*) Oh, darling, I'm so sorry. (*She throws off her shawl and pulls off her gloves*) You look so sad, and (*shivering*) you must be cold! (*She hurries over to the fireplace, and begins to build up the fire. The man remains silent while she tends the fire.*) Now. This will be better. You mustn't take it in this way. You make me feel guilty—guiltier than I already feel.

JOHN (*bitterly*). Can you feel guilty, Porphyria?

So much for the setting of the play. The dramatist must now by conversation between Porphyria and her lover reveal to us the background of the situation, the characters of the two people involved, their emotional states at the time that this action takes place, and most of all the motivation which makes the killing of the girl possible and even inevitable. The core of the dramatist's problem lies here. He must make the lover's action credible so that when he strangles Porphyria, we shall accept the act as flowing from what has already occurred. The problem is not an easy one to solve, and our dramatist might well feel that it is impossible to make the death of the girl credible to us merely on the basis of conversation which takes place between the lovers on this last evening. In that case, the dramatist might want to develop their characters further by lengthening the play and introducing an earlier scene or scenes so that

his auditors might know more about the lovers before they come to the fatal night, and the dramatist might also want to complicate the action further—that is, introduce other characters and other events leading up to the murder, so that this final act, the climax of the situation, will be made real and acceptable to us.

But even from so slight a sketch of the possible play that might be written on this subject it will be possible to illustrate some of the special features of the dramatic form.

Suppose we list first some of the limitations of the form.

1. *Description.* The author who depends a great deal upon descriptive writing for securing his effects will probably choose some other form, though some writers, like Eugene O'Neill, for example, describe the setting in much more detail than is usual with playwrights. But although we may often read the stage directions with enjoyment, they are essentially *stage directions*—directions as to how the performers are to arrange the stage, or, if we are merely reading the play, hints to us of the setting—something, after all, outside the play proper.

2. *Comment.* The dramatist in writing a play gives up the right to comment on the characters and events. The interpretation otherwise given by such comment must be *implied* by the speeches of the various characters or by their actions. The dramatist gives up his identity, as it were, and speaks only in the person of his characters. But the dramatist's inability to comment on the action directly is far from a crippling handicap, as we have seen in the "Introduction to Fiction." Ernest Hemingway, for example, in his short story, "The Killers," forbears to comment on the action as author and merely implies his comment by the action which he objectively reveals. This lack of direct comment eliminates certain types of material from dramatic treatment. But this means not that drama is an inferior form to fiction, but only that it is a more specialized form.

3. *Direct penetration into the characters' minds.* Perhaps most important of all, the dramatist gives up his right to tell us directly what his characters are thinking or feeling. He limits himself to one means of revelation: the knowledge of their thoughts and feelings

which we can draw from what they say and do. There are exceptions, of course: one character may confide in another character what he thinks and feels. And there is the soliloquy in which the character speaks aloud to himself, exposing thus directly to the audience his thoughts. But the confession and the soliloquy are the exception, not the rule. The essence of the dramatic method is to reveal to the audience the feelings of the character not explicitly but by implication—through his conversation with the other characters and through his behavior.

If the dramatist must limit himself rather severely by his methods, what are the corresponding compensations? Where does he really come into his own? What is the characteristic virtue of his method? To answer this, one must define the essential nature of drama. It may be put simply. The basis of drama is conflict. Earlier we remarked in the Introduction to Fiction (p. 9): "No conflict, no story." But if fiction requires conflict, in drama the requirement is paramount. The most obvious feature of a good drama is the clash of wills as the various characters come into conflict with each other's purposes and desires. *Melodrama* (which corresponds in drama to the crude action story in fiction) will clearly illustrate the point: the wicked villain attempts to win the beautiful heroine, and the handsome hero struggles in the face of tremendous odds to circumvent him, succeeding only in the nick of time. In tragedy, though problems of character and of human fate are explored, the struggle may be as violent as that of melodrama. Modes other than melodrama and tragedy may involve less violent conflict, but the dramatic effect—even in light comedy—derives, ultimately, from conflict.

This quality of tension and conflict is to be found to some degree in all forms of literature. Hence it is that one finds critics speaking of a "dramatic situation" or a "dramatic story" or even a "dramatic lyric." But obviously the dramatic form allows the author to display most directly and forcibly such a struggle, for he can represent it, not as one might meditate about it long after, but with all the immediacy, intensity, and vividness of the present. He can make the conflict develop and come to its climax, literally before our eyes. Obviously, one can put the most undramatic tale into the *form* of a play; but this is very different from using the dramatic form as the appropriate vehicle for dramatic material. And if we realize that struggle and conflict lie at the basis of drama, we shall better realize why the great tragedies deal so often with violence and why the great comedies move with such swiftness.

The two great classifications of drama are *tragedy* and *comedy*. These are, of course, not the only possible classifications; nor, on the other hand, do we often find either in an absolutely pure state. They are often mixed; plays partake of both elements. But the comic and the tragic do represent two extremes of drama, and it is important to define them and to say something about their relationship to each other. It is all the more important to define them because the terms are used to apply not only to drama but to other forms of literature. We speak of a "comic story," for example, or of a "tragic ballad."

Tragedy and comedy, though at so many points antithetical, may involve actions which are fundamentally very much alike. Indeed, the same general circumstance may be interpreted as comedy or as tragedy. A commonplace example will illustrate. Suppose someone slips on a banana peeling and falls into a puddle of mud. We laugh. We laugh all the more if the person who slips into the puddle is dressed in evening clothes. The situation is incongruous. Men dressed in evening clothes have nothing in common with mud puddles. If the person who slipped into the puddle wears patched overalls, the matter is not nearly so funny, perhaps because not nearly so incongruous.

But more than incongruity is involved in our reaction. Our sympathy or lack of sympathy for the person and the seriousness of the consequences which his fall entails have a great deal to do with our reaction. The student might contemplate such variations as these. The person who slips is a feeble old man; or the person who slips, though not feeble but hearty and cocky, suffers a serious injury; or the person who slips is a little girl on crutches.

There are also the instances in which we have conflicting and even alternating attitudes. The person who slips is a good friend of ours. He is wearing a fresh linen suit. We laugh when we see the surprise and chagrin on his face, but we happen to know that his errand is really an important one, and we are genuinely sorry for him. We tell him so, and hurry to render help, but as we observe him gazing woefully on his muddy suit, his plight becomes very funny again and once more we laugh until a realization that he has been put to real trouble silences our laughter once more.

If this particular example of an incongruous situation seems too farfetched to provide a useful illustration of the differences between tragedy and comedy, suppose we apply the same principles to a real play.

Othello, Shakespeare's story of how a fine man is so moved to jealousy by a scoundrel as to kill his wife whom he dearly loves, is surely an example of tragedy. The incongruity is shocking in the extreme. Here is a great and finely endowed man who seems to deserve well of life come to a sorry and miserable end. How would we go about changing the play into a comedy?

Let us consider our two principles. First, we make our audience less sympathetic with Othello. He is somewhat pompous and a braggart after all. He does not really love his wife with a fine and sincere love. Second, we make the consequences of his fall less serious. He does not kill his wife. He is simply badly enough fooled to have his ego thoroughly deflated. But the essential situation we need not change. We need to change only our treatment of it in order to have a comedy. And as a matter of fact the jealous husband who is duped by his enemy is one of the stock themes of comedy.

So much for the kinship of tragedy and comedy. They both spring from some fundamental incongruity—some shocking discrepancy between what we think should be and what has actually come to pass. And they become tragic or comic in proportion as we sympathize with the protagonist (the dominant character) or fail to sympathize—in proportion as the consequences are serious or trivial. It is not, then, the bare situation which makes a play tragic or comic—*it is largely the interpretation and treatment of the situation by the dramatist himself.*

If the examples given make this point, they have served their purpose. One feature which the examples lack, however, is this: they do not take into account the fact that in drama the characters are not static but dynamic; they are not merely acted on or have things happen to them, they act. As we have already said, the essence of drama is a struggle, a conflict.

It is especially necessary to make this point in order to see the very important distinction which exists between *tragedy* and *pathos.* It is a distinction which the critics who handle these terms do not make often enough, and yet it is a distinction vital to the whole conception of tragedy. The difference between the pathetic and the tragic may be stated briefly as follows: in the pathetic there is no emphasis on struggle. The protagonist suffers almost passively or struggles so ineffectually that the reader's attitude is one of pity. In the tragic action there is a definite emphasis on the struggle. The protagonist fights back and fights so effectively that at times the issue of the conflict seems in doubt. He may win, we feel, after all. True tragedy can never be, therefore, merely a matter of pity. The death of a child, for instance, may be pathetic; it cannot be tragic.

From this general principle a number of conclusions may be drawn.

1. The character must not be spineless. Weaknesses he may have, as all human beings do have. But he must be able to put up a fight and a good one.

2. The protagonist must not be sent up against overpowering odds. We must feel that he has a chance to win. For this reason, the struggle of a man against a disease, or a machine, or a completely overpowering environment is hardly tragic. The tragic character is not a worm ground under the heel of fate. He is a man, and a modern critic, Bonamy Dobrée, defines tragedy as the trial of a man's individual strength.

3. The fate of the protagonist must flow from his character. One must not feel that it is merely the result of accident. The dramatist may make use of accident, but as we have pointed out in the "Introduction to Fiction," even then he must still provide us with a "logic" of character. In Shakespeare's tragedies we often speak of the "tragic fault," the one grave defect

of character which is responsible for the protagonist's ruin. Whether or not we call it the "tragic fault," the dramatist, no less than the writer of fiction, must relate the characters of his drama to the events which take place in the drama. To sum up, the tragic character is in some deep sense responsible for his own fate. For example, he cannot be merely a sick man. He cannot be an insane man. We must be able to recognize, in his plight, the problem of moral awareness.

4. The dramatist cannot afford to rest in mere character analysis. Tragedy often involves a great deal of psychological study, but it is always more than mere psychological analysis. For example, in the *Emperor Jones,* by Eugene O'Neill, the dramatist offers us a very interesting psychological case study of the disintegration of a man under certain powerful influences. The psychology involved is sound enough and the process of disintegration has its own interest. But we never imaginatively identify ourselves with the basic character. There is an air of clinical detachment. We stand aside, as it were, and consequently, the *Emperor Jones* is hardly a tragedy for us.

This identification of ourselves with the tragic protagonist so that he stands for universal human traits—stands indeed for us—brings us back to one of the primary differences between the tragic attitude and the comic—namely, our sympathy for the hero. If in tragedy we stand side by side with the protagonist, even with a protagonist like Macbeth, in comedy we stand in our sympathies with society itself, the laws or customs which the primary figure in the comedy is breaking. And this fact explains why many of the critics who have written on comedy in the past have described the function of comedy as that of a social corrective. In comedy we make vivid and dramatic the breaking of the laws of society, but we stand by the laws, by the average good sense of mankind, and we laugh at the individual who breaks them—laugh at his clumsiness, or his egotism, or his ridiculous vanity. In tragedy, when the protagonist violates the principles on which human society is based, we find our interests sharply divided, for we realize the necessity of the principles but sympathize with the protagonist. In tragedy,

then, the defeat of the protagonist produces tragic irony; in comedy, the defeat of the protagonist provokes us to satiric mirth.

To set off tragedy and comedy in such neat antithetical fashion is of course to oversimplify matters. Thornton Wilder's *The Skin of Our Teeth,* for example, does not fit readily and obviously into the general pattern we have suggested. Again, as we shall see a little later in this section, Bernard Shaw's *Saint Joan* does not neatly fit into this pattern. The generalizations about tragedy and comedy that we have made above and which we have, for purposes of clarity, stated in rather extreme terms, are true of only the extreme cases, and, of course, many actual cases lie somewhere between the extremes. Shakespeare's Falstaff, for example, is a figure so human and in his way so magnificent, and we sympathize with him so much, that our laughter in his case is anything but satiric. Moreover, much of the time the satire is double-edged. We laugh not merely at Falstaff as he breaks the conventions of society; we often laugh with him at the conventions of society. Furthermore, we are moved to a feeling of pathos at his fall—so close he stands to the great figures of tragedy.

But what has been said is sufficiently true to indicate that in comedy, a vivid sense of the laws, the conventions, the rules of conduct in a society, is present. It is no accident therefore that the most brilliant comedy has usually come out of an urbane, sophisticated society like that of the Restoration Period in England. Nor is it an accident, remembering what we have said about the relative lack of sympathy with the protagonist in comedy, that comedy is usually thought of as a more intellectual, less emotional mode than is tragedy. In the main this is true, subject always of course to the reservations which any student of literature must be prepared to make: the constant realization that definitions and schemes of literary modes are only *tools* to help the reader in exploring literature and are not exact blueprints of literature itself. And we must remember that tragedy and comedy are ways of looking at life—ways of interpreting it.

There are special terms used in dealing with drama which need mention, or if they have already been mentioned, further comment. Perhaps the best way to define them is to relate them to one of the plays included in this text, *Hedda Gabler*. As a matter of fact many of the terms used in discussing drama, such as *exposition, motivation, movement*, etc., are used with reference to fiction as well as drama and have already been discussed in the "Introduction to Fiction." Their special application to drama is usually apparent at once on a consideration of the obvious differences which separate the dramatic form from that of fiction. For example, as has already been indicated in the "Introduction to Fiction," *movement* in drama is limited by the nature of drama production to one type. The dramatist must present his material in *scenes*. He cannot give us a continuous narrative; he can only give us certain selected sections of it. Obviously, he must choose rather carefully how many scenes he will use, and what materials he will give us in these scenes. (Most plays are divided into acts as well as scenes. For the distinction between an act and a scene, see the Glossary.)

The function of the first scene or scenes in a play is obviously that of *exposition*. We must be introduced to the characters and the general problem with which the play deals. From the nature of drama, exposition must be a relatively integral part of the plot, for the exposition must be communicated to the audience by the action and conversation of the characters. In the case of *Hedda Gabler,* it is necessary for the audience to have the following information before the play can go forward. We must know: that Hedda has been married for a few months to the pedantic scholar, Tesman; that they have returned to make their home in Christiania; that Tesman is in some need of money in order to support his bride in the style in which she prefers to live; that Tesman hopes to win a university appointment; that Eilert Lövborg, a brilliant young scholar who has been in love with Hedda and who has thrown himself away, has been helped by Mrs. Elvsted, another former acquaintance of Hedda's, to get a grip on himself and to write a brilliant book; that Eilert Lövborg has just come to town. Most of all, we must know something about Hedda's pride and independence and of her dissatis-

faction at the prospect of a dull, middle-class life.

How does Ibsen present this information to us? We have just said that the dramatist must weave his exposition into the plot. Ibsen has the information come out in the conversation between the various people who come to the Tesmans' house the morning after their arrival in town. In the talk between such *minor characters* as the old servant, Berta, and Tesman's aunt, as well as that between these characters and Tesman and Hedda herself, we learn much about the situation between Hedda and her husband. Mrs. Elvsted's call on this same morning may be thought to smack a little of coincidence. But the dramatist must bring her in in order to tell us about Lövborg, and he has provided her with a motive for making her call just at this time. Lövborg is going to attempt to establish himself as a scholar again, and she has come to ask Tesman's help.

The arrival of Judge Brack, a friend of the family who might be expected to call on the couple soon after their arrival, gives Ibsen an opportunity to bring out the final piece of information necessary to link tightly together the Lövborg-Elvsted and the Tesman-Hedda groups. It seems there is going to be some difficulty about Tesman's appointment after all. There is to be a competition for the post, and Lövborg, with his brilliant new book, will be Tesman's rival.

With this last piece of information, the characters are defined in relation to each other, the situation is set, and the play is ready to go forward.

Obviously, this is only one of a number of possible ways in which the exposition in drama may be set forth; but the present case will illustrate aspects of dramatic exposition which are general: the relative compression of the material and the closeness with which it is related to the plot. Suspense begins, then, with this news that there is to be a competition for the university appointment, that is, with the first *complication*. This first complication is speedily *resolved,* resolved in part at least, in the second act when it is learned that Tesman's appointment will not be interfered with by Lövborg's competition; but in the meantime a number of other complications have taken place, some of which are not resolved until the very end of the play.

The emphasis in this play is on the character of Hedda—not on some general social problem which the situation outlined in the play illustrates. We generally reserve the term *problem play* for plays of the latter type; but this use of the term should not blind us to the fact that in one sense, of course, almost every serious play, including *Hedda Gabler,* is a "problem play." For, since drama is based primarily on conflict, the protagonist is always faced with a problem. But if the dramatist does choose to emphasize a general idea rather than the particular situation, he should, of course, take care that he does not turn his play into mere propaganda. For in drama, as in all literature, the author attempts to give his theme a concrete statement rather than merely an abstract one.

We have emphasized the fact that the special virtue of the dramatic method is that it allows the author to throw conflict into very sharp focus, and have commented on some of the ways in which this fact influences the various aspects of drama. One further general influence should be mentioned. The emphasis on conflict in drama tends to force the dramatist to bring us on the scene when the problem is well advanced and near its culmination in *direct* conflict. Since he is interested in the actual conflict, he tends to open his play just early enough before the actual clash to allow time for the exposition of the characters, the primary situation of the characters, and the nature of the problem. This tendency toward compression may account for much of the discussion of the *unities of time and place* which is to be met with frequently in criticism of drama. Problems *are* settled and decisions *are* made in a particular place and at a particular time, and if we take up the action near enough to its climax, the action of the play will *tend* to occur in a particular place and within a short time. This much truth resides, then, in the doctrine of the unities, and only this much. There is obviously nothing sacrosanct about observing the unity of place or of time as such.

To state that dramatic plots tend toward a high degree of unity and compression is not to say, however, that there are not many exceptions. Furthermore, it is not to say that there may be no development of character in drama, or that a dramatist, like Shakespeare for example, may not often give us glimpses of characters over a period of months and even years. Moreover, whereas dramatic plots do tend to be relatively tightly unified, the plots of some plays are very complex, sometimes having in addition to the main plot a *subplot,* a secondary plot which is linked to the main action. But the tendency of drama is toward compression, and even Shakespeare's plays which seem to violate this tendency most give an effect of far greater compression than a narrative treatment of the same actions would give. *Hedda Gabler,* then, which represents a rather highly unified and relatively simple plot, is typical of the dramatic method of organization in that it represents this tendency toward compression.

Hedda Gabler

HENRIK IBSEN (1828-1906)

Characters

GEORGE TESMAN.

HEDDA TESMAN, *his wife.*

MISS JULIANA TESMAN, *his aunt.*

MRS. ELVSTED.

JUDGE BRACK.

EILERT LÖVBORG.

BERTA, *servant at the Tesmans'.*

The scene of the action is Tesman's villa, in the west end of Christiania.

Act I

SCENE: *A spacious, handsome, and taste-fully furnished drawing-room, decorated in dark colors. In the back, a wide doorway with curtains drawn back, leading into a smaller room decorated in the same style as the drawing-room. In the right-hand wall of the front room, a folding door leading out to the hall. In the opposite wall, on the left, a glass door, also with curtains drawn back. Through the panes can be seen part of a veranda outside, and trees covered with autumn foliage. An oval table, with a cover on it, and surrounded by chairs, stands well forward. In front, by the wall on the right, a wide stove of dark porcelain, a high-backed arm-chair, a cushioned foot-rest, and two foot-stools. A settee, with a small round table in front of it, fills the upper right-hand corner. In front, on the left, a little way from the wall, a sofa. Farther back than the glass door, a piano. On either side of the doorway at the back a whatnot with terra-cotta and majolica ornaments.—Against the back wall of the inner room a sofa, with a table, and one or two chairs. Over the sofa hangs the portrait of a handsome elderly man in a general's uniform. Over the table a hanging lamp, with an opal glass shade.—A number of bouquets are arranged about the drawing-room, in vases and glasses. Others lie upon the tables. The floors in both rooms are covered with thick carpets.—Morning light. The sun shines in through the glass door.*

(MISS JULIANA TESMAN, *with her bonnet on and carrying a parasol, comes in from the hall, followed by* BERTA, *who carries a bouquet wrapped in paper.* MISS TESMAN *is a comely and pleasant-looking lady of about sixty-five. She is nicely but simply dressed in a gray walk-ing-costume.* BERTA *is a middle-aged woman of plain and rather countrified appearance.*)

MISS TESMAN (*stops close to the door, listens, and says softly*). Upon my word, I don't believe they are stirring yet!

BERTA (*also softly*). I told you so, Miss. Remember how late the steamboat got in last night. And then, when they got home!—good Lord, what a lot the young mistress had to unpack before she could get to bed.

MISS TESMAN. Well, well—let them have their sleep out. But let us see that they get a good breath of the fresh morning air when they do appear. (*She goes to the glass door and throws it open*)

BERTA (*beside the table, at a loss what to do with the bouquet in her hand*). I declare there isn't a bit of room left. I think I'll put it down here, Miss. (*She places it on the piano*)

MISS TESMAN. So you've got a new mistress now, my dear Berta. Heaven knows it was a wrench to me to part with you.

BERTA (*on the point of weeping*). And do you think it wasn't hard for me too, Miss? After all the blessed years I've been with you and Miss Rina.

MISS TESMAN. We must make the best of it, Berta. There was nothing else to be done. George can't do without you, you see—he absolutely can't. He has had you to look after him ever since he was a little boy.

BERTA. Ah, but, Miss Julia, I can't help thinking of Miss Rina lying helpless at home there, poor thing. And with only that new girl, too! She'll never learn to take proper care of an invalid.

MISS TESMAN. Oh, I shall manage to train her. And of course, you know, I shall take most of it upon myself. You needn't be uneasy about my poor sister, my dear Berta.

BERTA. Well, but there's another thing, Miss. I'm so mortally afraid I shan't be able to suit the young mistress.

MISS TESMAN. Oh, well—just at first there may be one or two things——

BERTA. Most like she'll be terrible grand in her ways.

MISS TESMAN. Well, you can't wonder at that —General Gabler's daughter! Think of the sort of life she was accustomed to in her father's time. Don't you remember how we used to see her riding down the road along with the General? In that long black habit—and with feathers in her hat?

BERTA. Yes, indeed—I remember well enough—! But good Lord, I should never have dreamt in those days that she and Master George would make a match of it.

MISS TESMAN. Nor I.—But, by-the-bye, Berta —while I think of it: in future you mustn't say Master George. You must say Dr. Tesman.

BERTA. Yes, the young mistress spoke of that too—last night—the moment they set foot in the house. Is it true, then, Miss?

MISS TESMAN. Yes, indeed it is. Only think, Berta—some foreign university has made him a doctor—while he has been abroad, you understand. I hadn't heard a word about it, until he told me himself upon the pier.

BERTA. Well, well, he's clever enough for anything, he is. But I didn't think he'd have gone in for doctoring people too.

MISS TESMAN. No, no, it's not that sort of doctor he is. (*Nods significantly*) But let me tell you, we may have to call him something still grander before long.

BERTA. You don't say so! What can that be, Miss?

MISS TESMAN (*smiling*). H'm—wouldn't you like to know! (*With emotion*) Ah, dear, dear— if my poor brother could only look up from his grave now, and see what his little boy has grown into! (*Looks around*) But bless me, Berta —why have you done this? Taken the chintz covers off all the furniture?

BERTA. The mistress told me to. She can't abide covers on the chairs, she says.

MISS TESMAN. Are they going to make this their everyday sitting-room then?

BERTA. Yes, that's what I understood—from the mistress. Master George—the doctor—he said nothing.

(GEORGE TESMAN *comes from the right into the inner room, humming to himself, and carrying an unstrapped empty portmanteau. He is a middle-sized, young-looking man of thirty-three, rather stout, with a round, open, cheerful face, fair hair and beard. He wears spectacles, and is somewhat carelessly dressed in comfortable indoor clothes.*)

MISS TESMAN. Good morning, good morning, George.

TESMAN (*in the doorway between the rooms*). Aunt Julia! Dear Aunt Julia! (*Goes up to her and shakes hands warmly*) Come all this way— so early! Eh?

MISS TESMAN. Why of course I had to come and see how you were getting on.

TESMAN. In spite of your having had no proper night's rest?

MISS TESMAN. Oh, that makes no difference to me.

TESMAN. Well, I suppose you got home all right from the pier? Eh?

MISS TESMAN. Yes, quite safely, thank goodness. Judge Brack was good enough to see me right to my door.

TESMAN. We were so sorry we couldn't give

you a seat in the carriage. But you saw what a pile of boxes Hedda had to bring with her.

MISS TESMAN. Yes, she had certainly plenty of boxes.

BERTA (*to* TESMAN). Shall I go in and see if there's anything I can do for the mistress?

TESMAN. No, thank you, Berta—you needn't. She said she would ring if she wanted anything.

BERTA (*going towards the right*). Very well.

TESMAN. But look here—take this portmanteau with you.

BERTA (*taking it*). I'll put it in the attic.

(*She goes out by the hall door*)

TESMAN. Fancy, Aunty—I had the whole of that portmanteau chock full of copies of documents. You wouldn't believe how much I have picked up from all the archives I have been examining—curious old details that no one has had any idea of——

MISS TESMAN. Yes, you don't seem to have wasted your time on your wedding trip, George.

TESMAN. No, that I haven't. But do take off your bonnet, Aunty. Look here! Let me untie the strings—eh?

MISS TESMAN (*while he does so*). Well, well —this is just as if you were still at home with us.

TESMAN (*with the bonnet in his hand, looks at it from all sides*). Why, what a gorgeous bonnet you've been investing in!

MISS TESMAN. I bought it on Hedda's account.

TESMAN. On Hedda's account? Eh?

MISS TESMAN. Yes, so that Hedda needn't be ashamed of me if we happened to go out together.

TESMAN (*patting her cheek*). You always think of everything, Aunt Julia (*Lays the bonnet on a chair beside the table*) And now, look here—suppose we sit comfortably on the sofa and have a little chat, till Hedda comes.

(*They seat themselves. She places her parasol in the corner of the sofa*)

MISS TESMAN (*takes both his hands and looks at him*). What a delight it is to have you again, as large as life, before my very eyes, George! My George—my poor brother's own boy!

TESMAN. And it's a delight for me, too, to see you again, Aunt Julia! You, who have been father and mother in one to me.

MISS TESMAN. Oh, yes, I know you will al-

ways keep a place in your heart for your old aunts.

TESMAN. And what about Aunt Rina? No improvement—eh?

MISS TESMAN. Oh, no—we can scarcely look for any improvement in her case, poor thing. There she lies, helpless, as she has lain for all these years. But heaven grant I may not lose her yet awhile! For if I did, I don't know what I should make of my life, George—especially now that I haven't you to look after any more.

TESMAN (*patting her back*). There, there, there——!

MISS TESMAN (*suddenly changing her tone*). And to think that here you a married man, George!—And that you should be the one to carry off Hedda Gabler—the beautiful Hedda Gabler! Only think of it—she, that was so beset with admirers!

TESMAN (*hums a little and smiles complacently*). Yes, I fancy I have several good friends about town who would like to stand in my shoes—eh?

MISS TESMAN. And then this fine long wedding-tour you have had! More than five—nearly six months——

TESMAN. Well, for me it has been a sort of tour of research as well. I have had to do so much grubbing among old records—and to read no end of books too, Auntie.

MISS TESMAN. Oh, yes, I suppose so. (*More confidentially, and lowering her voice a little*) But listen now, George—have you nothing—nothing special to tell me?

TESMAN. As to our journey?

MISS TESMAN. Yes.

TESMAN. No, I don't know of anything except what I have told you in my letters. I had a doctor's degree conferred on me—but that I told you yesterday.

MISS TESMAN. Yes, yes, you did. But what I mean is—haven't you any—any—expectations——?

TESMAN. Expectations?

MISS TESMAN. Why, you know, George—I'm your old auntie!

TESMAN. Why, of course I have expectations.

MISS TESMAN. Ah!

TESMAN. I have every expectation of being a professor one of these days.

MISS TESMAN. Oh, yes, a professor——

TESMAN. Indeed, I may say I am certain of it. But my dear Auntie—you know all about that already!

MISS TESMAN (*laughing to herself*). Yes, of course I do. You are quite right there. (*Changing the subject*) But we were talking about your journey. It must have cost a great deal of money, George?

TESMAN. Well, you see—my handsome traveling-scholarship went a good way.

MISS TESMAN. But I can't understand how you can have made it go far enough for two.

TESMAN. No, that's not so easy to understand —eh?

MISS TESMAN. And especially traveling with a lady—they tell me that makes it ever so much more expensive.

TESMAN. Yes, of course—it makes it a little more expensive. But Hedda had to have this trip, Auntie! She really had to. Nothing else would have done.

MISS TESMAN. No, no, I suppose not. A wedding-tour seems to be quite indispensable nowadays.—But tell me now—have you gone thoroughly over the house yet?

TESMAN. Yes, you may be sure I have. I have been afoot ever since daylight.

MISS TESMAN. And what do you think of it all?

TESMAN. I'm delighted! Quite delighted! Only I can't think what we are to do with the two empty rooms between this inner parlor and Hedda's bedroom.

MISS TESMAN (*laughing*). Oh, my dear George, I dare say you may find some use for them—in the course of time.

TESMAN. Why of course you are quite right, Aunt Julia! You mean as my library increases— eh?

MISS TESMAN. Yes, quite so, my dear boy. It was your library I was thinking of.

TESMAN. I am specially pleased on Hedda's account. Often and often, before we were engaged, she said that she would never care to live anywhere but in Secretary Falk's villa.

MISS TESMAN. Yes, it was lucky that this very house should come into the market, just after you had started.

TESMAN. Yes, Aunt Julia, the luck was on our side, wasn't it—eh?

MISS TESMAN. But the expense, my dear George! You will find it very expensive, all this.

TESMAN (*looks at her, a little cast down*). Yes, I suppose I shall, Aunt!

MISS TESMAN. Oh, frightfully!

TESMAN. How much do you think? In round numbers?—Eh?

MISS TESMAN. Oh, I can't even guess until all the accounts come in.

TESMAN. Well, fortunately, Judge Brack has secured the most favorable terms for me,—so he said in a letter to Hedda.

MISS TESMAN. Yes, don't be uneasy, my dear boy.—Besides, I have given security for the furniture and all the carpets.

TESMAN. Security? You? My dear Aunt Julia —what sort of security could you give?

MISS TESMAN. I have given a mortgage on our annuity.

TESMAN (*jumps up*). What! On your—and Aunt Rina's annuity!

MISS TESMAN. Yes, I knew of no other plan, you see.

TESMAN (*placing himself before her*). Have you gone out of your senses, Auntie! Your annuity—it's all that you and Aunt Rina have to live upon.

MISS TESMAN. Well, well, don't get so excited about it. It's only a matter of form you know—Judge Brack assured me of that. It was he that was kind enough to arrange the whole affair for me. A mere matter of form, he said.

TESMAN. Yes, that may be all very well. But nevertheless——

MISS TESMAN. You will have your own salary to depend upon now. And, good heavens, even if we did have to pay up a little——! To eke things out a bit at the start——! Why, it would be nothing but a pleasure to us.

TESMAN. Oh, Auntie—will you never be tired of making sacrifices for me!

MISS TESMAN (*rises and lays her hands on his shoulders*). Have I had any other happiness in this world except to smooth your way for you, my dear boy? You, who have had neither father nor mother to depend on. And now we have reached the goal, George! Things have looked black enough for us, sometimes; but, thank heaven, now you have nothing to fear.

TESMAN. Yes, it is really marvelous how everything has turned out for the best.

MISS TESMAN. And the people who opposed you—who wanted to bar the way for you—now you have them at your feet. They have fallen, George. Your most dangerous rival—his fall was the worst.—And now he has to lie on the bed he has made for himself—poor misguided creature.

TESMAN. Have you heard anything of Eilert? Since I went away, I mean.

MISS TESMAN. Only that he is said to have published a new book.

TESMAN. What! Eilert Lövborg! Recently—eh?

MISS TESMAN. Yes, so they say. Heaven knows whether it can be worth anything! Ah, when your new book appears—that will be another story, George! What is it to be about?

TESMAN. It will deal with the domestic industries of Brabant during the Middle Ages.

MISS TESMAN. Fancy—to be able to write on such a subject as that!

TESMAN. However, it may be some time before the book is ready. I have all these collection to arrange first, you see.

MISS TESMAN. Yes, collecting and arranging —no one can beat you at that. There you are my poor brother's own son.

TESMAN. I am looking forward eagerly to setting to work at it; especially now that I have my own delightful home to work in.

MISS TESMAN. And, most of all, now that you have got the wife of your heart, my dear George.

TESMAN (embracing her). Oh, yes, yes, Aunt Julia. Hedda—she is the best part of all! (Looks toward the doorway) I believe I hear her coming —eh?

(HEDDA enters from the left through the inner room. She is a woman of nine-and-twenty. Her face and figure show refinement and distinction. Her complexion is pale and opaque. Her steel-gray eyes express a cold, unruffled repose. Her hair is of an agreeable medium brown, but not particularly abundant. She is dressed in a tasteful, somewhat loose-fitting morning-gown.)

MISS TESMAN (going to meet HEDDA). Good morning, my dear Hedda! Good morning, and a hearty welcome.

HEDDA (holds out her hand). Good morning, dear Miss Tesman! So early a call! That is kind of you.

MISS TESMAN (with some embarrassment). Well—has the bride slept well in her new home?

HEDDA. Oh yes, thanks. Passably.

TESMAN (laughing). Passably! Come, that's good, Hedda! You were sleeping like a stone when I got up.

HEDDA. Fortunately. Of course one has always to accustom one's self to new surroundings, Miss Tesman—little by little. (Looking towards the left) Oh—there the servant has gone and opened the veranda door, and let in a whole flood of sunshine.

MISS TESMAN (going towards the door). Well, then, we will shut it.

HEDDA. No, no, not that! Tesman, please draw the curtains. That will give a softer light.

TESMAN (at the door). All right—all right. There now, Hedda, now you have both shade and fresh air.

HEDDA. Yes, fresh air we certainly must have, with all these stacks of flowers—— But—won't you sit down, Miss Tesman?

MISS TESMAN. No, thank you. Now that I have seen that everything is all right here—thank heaven!—I must be getting home again. My sister is lying longing for me, poor thing.

TESMAN. Give her my very best love, Auntie; and say I shall look in and see her later in the day.

MISS TESMAN. Yes, yes, I'll be sure to tell her. But by-the-bye, George—(feeling in her dress pocket)—I have almost forgotten—I have something for you here.

TESMAN. What is it, Auntie? Eh?

MISS TESMAN (produces a flat parcel wrapped in newspaper and hands it to him). Look here, my dear boy.

TESMAN (opening the parcel). Well, I declare! —Have you really saved them for me, Aunt Julia! Hedda! Isn't this touching—eh?

HEDDA (beside the whatnot on the right). Well, what is it?

TESMAN. My old morning-shoes! My slippers.

HEDDA. Indeed. I remember you often spoke of them while we were abroad.

TESMAN. Yes, I missed them terribly. (Goes up to her) Now you shall see them, Hedda!

HEDDA (going towards the stove). Thanks, I

really don't care about it.

TESMAN (*following her*). Only think—ill as she was, Aunt Rina embroidered these for me. Oh you can't think how many associations cling to them.

HEDDA (*at the table*). Scarcely for me.

MISS TESMAN. Of course not for Hedda, George.

TESMAN. Well, but now that she belongs to the family; I thought——

HEDDA (*interrupting*). We shall never get on with this servant, Tesman.

MISS TESMAN. Not get on with Berta?

TESMAN. Why, dear, what puts that in your head? Eh?

HEDDA (*pointing*). Look there! She has left her old bonnet lying about on a chair.

TESMAN (*in consternation, drops the slippers on the floor*). Why, Hedda——

HEDDA. Just fancy, if any one should come in and see it!

TESMAN. But Hedda—that's Aunt Julia's bonnet.

HEDDA. Is it!

MISS TESMAN (*taking up the bonnet*). Yes, indeed it's mine. And, what's more, it's not old, Madame Hedda.

HEDDA. I really did not look closely at it, Miss Tesman.

MISS TESMAN (*trying on the bonnet*). Let me tell you it's the first time I have worn it—the very first time.

TESMAN. And a very nice bonnet it is too— quite a beauty!

MISS TESMAN. Oh, it's no such great things, George. (*Looks around her*) My parasol——? Ah, here. (*Takes it*) For this is mine too— (*mutters*) —not Berta's.

TESMAN. A new bonnet and a new parasol! Only think, Hedda!

HEDDA. Very handsome indeed.

TESMAN. Yes, isn't it? But Aunty, take a good look at Hedda before you go! See how handsome she is!

MISS TESMAN. Oh, my dear boy, there's nothing new in that. Hedda was always lovely. (*She nods and goes towards the right*)

TESMAN (*following*). Yes, but have you noticed what splendid condition she is in? How she has filled out on the journey?

HEDDA (*crossing the room*). Oh, do be quiet——!

MISS TESMAN (*who has stopped and turned*). Filled out?

TESMAN. Of course you don't notice it so much now that she has that dress on. But I, who can see——

HEDDA (*at the glass door, impatiently*). Oh, you can't see anything.

TESMAN. It must be the mountain air in the Tyrol——

HEDDA (*curtly, interrupting*). I am exactly as I was when I started.

TESMAN. So you insist; but I'm quite certain you are not. Don't you agree with me, Aunty?

MISS TESMAN (*who has been gazing at her with folded hands*). Hedda is lovely—lovely— lovely. (*Goes up to her, takes her head between both hands, draws it downwards, and kisses her hair*) God bless and preserve Hedda Tesman —for George's sake.

HEDDA (*gently freeing herself*). Oh—! Let me go.

MISS TESMAN (*in quiet emotion*). I shall not let a day pass without coming to see you.

TESMAN. No you won't, will you, Auntie? Eh?

MISS TESMAN. Good-bye—good-bye!

(*She goes out by the hall door. TESMAN accompanies her. The door remains half open. TESMAN can be heard repeating his message to Aunt Rina and his thanks for the slippers.*

In the meantime, HEDDA walks about the room raising her arms and clenching her hands as if in desperation. Then she flings back the curtains from the glass door, and stands there looking out.

Presently TESMAN returns and closes the door behind him.)

TESMAN (*picks up the slippers from the floor*). What are you looking at, Hedda?

HEDDA (*once more calm and mistress of herself*). I am only looking at the leaves. They are so yellow—so withered.

TESMAN (*wraps up the slippers and lays them on the table*). Well you see, we are well into September now.

HEDDA (*again restless*). Yes, to think of it!— Already in—in September.

TESMAN. Don't you think Aunt Julia's manner was strange, dear? Almost solemn? Can you imagine what was the matter with her? Eh?

HEDDA. I scarcely know her, you see. Is she often like that?

TESMAN. No, not as she was today.

HEDDA (*leaving the glass door*). Do you think she was annoyed about the bonnet?

TESMAN. Oh, scarcely at all. Perhaps a little, just at the moment——

HEDDA. But what an idea, to pitch her bonnet about in the drawing-room! No one does that sort of thing.

TESMAN. Well you may be sure Aunt Julia won't do it again.

HEDDA. In any case, I shall manage to make my peace with her.

TESMAN. Yes, my dear, good Hedda, if you only would.

HEDDA. When you call this afternoon, you might invite her to spend the evening here.

TESMAN. Yes, that I will. And there's one thing more you can do that would delight her heart.

HEDDA. What is it?

TESMAN. If you could only prevail on yourself to say *du*[1] to her. For my sake, Hedda? Eh?

HEDDA. No, no, Tesman—you really mustn't ask that of me. I have told you so already. I shall try to call her "Aunt"; and you must be satisfied with that.

TESMAN. Well, well. Only I think now that you belong to the family, you——

HEDDA. H'm—I can't in the least see why——

(*She goes up towards the middle doorway*)

TESMAN (*after a pause*). Is there anything the matter with you, Hedda? Eh?

HEDDA. I'm only looking at my old piano. It doesn't go at all well with all the other things.

TESMAN. The first time I draw my salary, we'll see about exchanging it.

HEDDA. No, no—no exchanging. I don't want to part with it. Suppose we put it there in the inner room, and then get another here in its place. When it's convenient, I mean.

TESMAN (*a little taken aback*). Yes—of course we could do that.

HEDDA (*takes up the bouquet from the piano*). These flowers were not here last night when we arrived.

TESMAN. Aunt Julia must have brought them for you.

HEDDA (*examining the bouquet*). A visiting-card. (*Takes it out and reads*) "Shall return later in the day." Can you guess whose card it is?

TESMAN. No. Whose? Eh?

HEDDA. The name is "Mrs. Elvsted."

TESMAN. Is it really? Sheriff Elvsted's wife? Miss Rysing that was.

HEDDA. Exactly. The girl with the irritating hair, that she was always showing off. An old flame of yours, I've been told.

TESMAN (*laughing*). Oh, that didn't last long; and it was before I knew you, Hedda. But fancy her being in town!

HEDDA. It's odd that she should call upon us. I have scarcely seen her since we left school.

TESMAN. I haven't seen her either for—heaven knows how long. I wonder how she can endure to live in such an out-of-the-way hole—eh?

HEDDA (*after a moment's thought says suddenly*). Tell me, Tesman—isn't it somewhere near there that he—that—Eilert Lövborg is living?

TESMAN. Yes, he is somewhere in that part of the country.

(BERTA *enters by the hall door*)

BERTA. That lady, ma'am, that brought some flowers a little while ago, is here again. (*Pointing*) The flowers you have in your hand, ma'am.

HEDDA. Ah, is she? Well, please show her in.

(BERTA *opens the door for* MRS. ELVSTED, *and goes out herself.—*MRS. ELVSTED *is a woman of fragile figure, with pretty, soft features. Her eyes are light blue, large, round, and somewhat prominent, with a startled, inquiring expression. Her hair is remarkably light, almost flaxen, and unusually abundant and wavy. She is a couple of years younger than* HEDDA. *She wears a dark visiting dress, tasteful, but not quite in the latest fashion.*)

HEDDA (*receives her warmly*). How do you do, my dear Mrs. Elvsted? It's delightful to see you again.

MRS. ELVSTED (*nervously, struggling for self-control*). Yes, it's a very long time since we met.

---

[1] *Du* = thou; Tesman means, "If you could persuade yourself to *tutoyer* her."

Tesman (*gives her his hand*). And we too—eh?

Hedda. Thanks for your lovely flowers——

Mrs. Elvsted. Oh, not at all—— I would have come straight here yesterday afternoon; but I heard that you were away——

Tesman. Have you just come to town? Eh?

Mrs. Elvsted. I arrived yesterday, about midday. Oh, I was quite in despair when I heard that you were not at home.

Hedda. In despair! How so?

Tesman. Why, my dear Mrs. Rysing—I mean Mrs. Elvsted——

Hedda. I hope that you are not in any trouble?

Mrs. Elvsted. Yes, I am. And I don't know another living creature here that I can turn to.

Hedda (*laying the bouquet on the table*). Come—let us sit here on the sofa——

Mrs. Elvsted. Oh, I am too restless to sit down.

Hedda. Oh no, you're not. Come here. (*She draws* Mrs. Elvsted *down upon the sofa and sits at her side*)

Tesman. Well? What is it, Mrs. Elvsted?

Hedda. Has anything particular happened to you at home?

Mrs. Elvsted. Yes—and no. Oh—I am so anxious you should not misunderstand me——

Hedda. Then your best plan is to tell us the whole story, Mrs. Elvsted.

Tesman. I suppose that's what you have come for—eh?

Mrs. Elvsted. Yes, yes—of course it is. Well then, I must tell you—if you don't already know —that Eilert Lövborg is in town, too.

Hedda. Lövborg——!

Tesman. What! Has Eilert Lövborg come back? Fancy that, Hedda!

Hedda. Well, well—I hear it.

Mrs. Elvsted. He has been here a week already. Just fancy—a whole week! In this terrible town, alone! With so many temptations on all sides.

Hedda. But my dear Mrs. Elvsted—how does he concern you so much?

Mrs. Elvsted (*looks at her with a startled air, and says rapidly*). He was the children's tutor.

Hedda. Your children's?

Mrs. Elvsted. My husband's. I have none.

Hedda. Your step-children's, then?

Mrs. Elvsted. Yes.

Tesman (*somewhat hesitatingly*). Then was he—I don't know how to express it—was he— regular enough in his habits to be fit for the post? Eh?

Mrs. Elvsted. For the last two years his conduct has been irreproachable.

Tesman. Has it indeed? Fancy that, Hedda!

Hedda. I hear it.

Mrs. Elvsted. Perfectly irreproachable. I assure you! In every respect. But all the same— now that I know he is here—in this great town —and with a large sum of money in his hands— I can't help being in mortal fear for him.

Tesman. Why did he not remain where he was? With you and your husband? Eh?

Mrs. Elvsted. After his book was published he was too restless and unsettled to remain with us.

Tesman. Yes, by-the-bye, Aunt Julia told me he had published a new book.

Mrs. Elvsted. Yes, a big book, dealing with the march of civilization—in broad outline, as it were. It came out about a fortnight ago. And since it has sold so well, and been so much read —and made such a sensation——

Tesman. Has it indeed? It must be something he has had lying by since his better days.

Mrs. Elvsted. Long ago, you mean?

Tesman. Yes.

Mrs. Elvsted. No, he has written it all since he has been with us—within the last year.

Tesman. Isn't that good news, Hedda? Think of that.

Mrs. Elvsted. Ah, yes, if only it would last!

Hedda. Have you seen him here in town?

Mrs. Elvsted. No, not yet. I have had the greatest difficulty in finding out his address. But this morning I discovered it at last.

Hedda (*looks searchingly at her*). Do you know, it seems to me a little odd of your husband—h'm——

Mrs. Elvsted (*starting nervously*). Of my husband. What?

Hedda. That he should send you to town on such an errand—that he does not come himself and look after his friend.

Mrs. Elvsted. Oh no, no—my husband has no time. And besides, I—I had some shopping to do.

Hedda (*with a slight smile*). Ah, that is a different matter.

MRS. ELVSTED (*rising quickly and uneasily*). And now I beg and implore you, Mr. Tesman—receive Eilert Lövborg kindly if he comes to you! And that he is sure to do. You see you were such great friends in the old days. And then you are interested in the same studies—the same branch of science—so far as I can understand.

TESMAN. We used to be, at any rate.

MRS. ELVSTED. That is why I beg so earnestly that you—you too—will keep a sharp eye upon him. Oh, you will promise me that, Mr. Tesman—won't you?

TESMAN. With the greatest of pleasure, Mrs. Rysing——

HEDDA. Elvsted.

TESMAN. I assure you I shall do all I possibly can for Eilert. You may rely upon me.

MRS. ELVSTED. Oh, how very, very kind of you! (*Presses his hands*) Thanks, thanks, thanks! (*Frightened*) You see, my husband is very fond of him!

HEDDA (*rising*). You ought to write to him, Tesman. Perhaps he may not care to come to you of his own accord.

TESMAN. Well, perhaps it would be the right thing to do, Hedda? Eh?

HEDDA. And the sooner the better. Why not at once?

MRS. ELVSTED (*imploringly*). Oh, if you only would!

TESMAN. I'll write this moment. Have you his address, Mrs.—Mrs. Elvsted?

MRS. ELVSTED. Yes. (*Takes a slip of paper from her pocket, and hands it to him*) Here it is.

TESMAN. Good, good. Then I'll go in—— (*Looks about him*) By-the-bye,—my slippers? Oh, here. (*Takes the packet, and is about to go*)

HEDDA. Be sure you write him a cordial, friendly letter. And a good long one too.

TESMAN. Yes, I will.

MRS. ELVSTED. But please, please don't say a word to show that I have suggested it.

TESMAN. No, how could you think I would? Eh?

(*He goes out to the right, through the inner room*)

HEDDA (*goes up to* MRS. ELVSTED, *smiles, and says in a low voice*). There. We have killed two birds with one stone.

MRS. ELVSTED. What do you mean?

HEDDA. Could you not see that I wanted him to go?

MRS. ELVSTED. Yes, to write the letter——

HEDDA. And that I might speak to you alone.

MRS. ELVSTED (*confused*). About the same thing?

HEDDA. Precisely.

MRS. ELVSTED (*apprehensively*). But there is nothing more, Mrs. Tesman! Absolutely nothing!

HEDDA. Oh, yes, but there is. There is a great deal more—I can see that. Sit here—and we'll have a cozy, confidential chat. (*She forces* MRS. ELVSTED *to sit in the easy-chair beside the stove, and seats herself on one of the footstools*)

MRS. ELVSTED (*anxiously, looking at her watch*). But, my dear Mrs. Tesman—I was really on the point of going.

HEDDA. Oh, you can't be in such a hurry.—Well? Now tell me something about your life at home.

MRS. ELVSTED. Oh, that is just what I care least to speak about.

HEDDA. But to me, dear——? Why, weren't we schoolfellows?

MRS. ELVSTED. Yes, but you were in the class above me. Oh, how dreadfully afraid of you I was then!

HEDDA. Afraid of me?

MRS. ELVSTED. *Yes,* dreadfully. For when we met on the stairs you used always to pull my hair.

HEDDA. Did I, really?

MRS. ELVSTED. Yes, and once you said you would burn it off my head.

HEDDA. Oh, that was all nonsense, of course.

MRS. ELVSTED. Yes, but I was so silly in those days.—And since then, too—we have drifted so far—far apart from each other. Our circles have been so entirely different.

HEDDA. Well then, we must try to drift together again. Now listen! At school we said *du* to each other; and we called each other by our Christian names——

MRS. ELVSTED. No, I am sure you must be mistaken.

HEDDA. No, not at all! I can remember quite distinctly. So now we are going to renew our old friendship. (*Draws the footstool closer to* MRS. ELVSTED) There now! (*Kisses her cheek*)

You must say *du* to me and call me Hedda.

MRS. ELVSTED (*presses and pats her hands*). Oh, how good and kind you are! I am not used to such kindness.

HEDDA. There, there, there! And I shall say *du* to you, as in the old days, and call you my dear Thora.

MRS. ELVSTED. My name is Thea.

HEDDA. Why, of course! I meant Thea. (*Looks at her compassionately*) So you are not accustomed to goodness and kindness, Thea? Not in your own home?

MRS. ELVSTED. Oh, if I only had a home! But I haven't any; I have never had a home.

HEDDA (*looks at her for a moment*). I almost suspected as much.

MRS. ELVSTED (*gazing helplessly before her*). Yes—yes—yes.

HEDDA. I don't quite remember—was it not as housekeeper that you first went to Mr. Elvsted's?

MRS. ELVSTED. I really went as governess. But his wife—his late wife—was an invalid,—and rarely left her room. So I had to look after the housekeeping as well.

HEDDA. And then—at last—you became mistress of the house.

MRS. ELVSTED (*sadly*). Yes, I did.

HEDDA. Let me see—about how long ago was that?

MRS. ELVSTED. My marriage?

HEDDA. Yes.

MRS. ELVSTED. Five years ago.

HEDDA. To be sure; it must be that.

MRS. ELVSTED. Oh, those five years——! Or at all events the last two or three of them! Oh, if you [2] could only imagine——

HEDDA (*giving her a little slap on the hand*). De? Fie, Thea!

MRS. ELVSTED. Yes, yes, I will try—— Well if—you could only imagine and understand——

HEDDA (*lightly*). Eilert Lövborg has been in your neighborhood about three years, hasn't he?

MRS. ELVSTED (*looks at her doubtfully*). Eilert Lövborg? Yes—he has.

HEDDA. Had you known him before, in town here?

MRS. ELVSTED. Scarcely at all. I mean—I knew him by name of course.

HEDDA. But you saw a good deal of him in the country?

MRS. ELVSTED. Yes, he came to us every day. You see, he gave the children lessons; for in the long run I couldn't manage it all myself.

HEDDA. No, that's clear.—And your husband——? I suppose he is often away from home?

MRS. ELVSTED. Yes. Being sheriff, you know, he has to travel about a good deal in his district.

HEDDA (*leaning against the arm of the chair*). Thea—my poor, sweet Thea— now you must tell me everything—exactly as it stands.

MRS. ELVSTED. Well, then, you must question me.

HEDDA. What sort of a man is your husband, Thea? I mean—you know—in everyday life. Is he kind to you?

MRS. ELVSTED (*evasively*). I am sure he means well in everything.

HEDDA. I should think he must be altogether too old for you. There is at least twenty years' difference between you, is there not?

MRS. ELVSTED (*irritably*). Yes, that is true, too. Everything about him is repellent to me! We have not a thought in common. We have no single point of sympathy—he and I.

HEDDA. But is he not fond of you all the same? In his own way?

MRS. ELVSTED. Oh, I really don't know. I think he regards me simply as a useful property. And then it doesn't cost much to keep me. I am not expensive.

HEDDA. That is stupid of you.

MRS. ELVSTED (*shakes her head*). It cannot be otherwise—not with him. I don't think he really cares for any one but himself—and perhaps a little for the children.

HEDDA. And for Eilert Lövborg, Thea.

MRS. ELVSTED (*looking at her*). For Eilert Lövborg? What puts that into your head?

HEDDA. Well, my dear—I should say, when he sends you after him all the way to town—— (*Smiling almost imperceptibly*) And besides, you said so yourself, to Tesman.

MRS. ELVSTED (*with a little nervous twitch*). Did I? Yes, I suppose I did. (*Vehemently, but not loudly*) No—I may just as well make a clean breast of it at once! For it must all come

---

[2] Mrs. Elvsted here uses the formal pronoun *De,* whereupon Hedda rebukes her. In her next speech Mrs. Elvsted says *du.*

out in any case.

HEDDA. Why, my dear Thea——?

MRS. ELVSTED. Well, to make a long story short: My husband did not know that I was coming.

HEDDA. What! Your husband didn't know it!

MRS. ELVSTED. No, of course not. For that matter, he was away from home himself—he was traveling. Oh, I could bear it no longer, Hedda! I couldn't indeed—so utterly alone as I should have been in future.

HEDDA. Well? And then?

MRS. ELVSTED. So I put together some of my things—what I needed most—as quietly as possible. And then I left the house.

HEDDA. Without a word?

MRS. ELVSTED. Yes—and took the train straight to town.

HEDDA. Why, my dear, good Thea—to think of you daring to do it!

MRS. ELVSTED (rises and moves about the room). What else could I possibly do?

HEDDA. But what do you think your husband will say when you go home again?

MRS. ELVSTED (at the table, looks at her). Back to him?

HEDDA. Of course.

MRS. ELVSTED. I shall never go back to him again.

HEDDA (rising and going towards her). Then you have left your home—for good and all?

MRS. ELVSTED. Yes. There was nothing else to be done.

HEDDA. But then—to take flight so openly.

MRS. ELVSTED. Oh, it's impossible to keep things of that sort secret.

HEDDA. But what do you think people will say of you, Thea?

MRS. ELVSTED. They may say what they like for aught I care. (Seats herself wearily and sadly on the sofa) I have done nothing but what I had to do.

HEDDA (after a short silence). And what are your plans now? What do you think of doing?

MRS. ELVSTED. I don't know yet. I only know this, that I must live here, where Eilert Lövborg is—if I am to live at all.

HEDDA (takes a chair from the table, seats herself beside her, and strokes her hands). My dear Thea—how did this—this friendship—be-

tween you and Eilert Lövborg come about?

MRS. ELVSTED. Oh, it grew up gradually. I gained a sort of influence over him.

HEDDA. Indeed?

MRS. ELVSTED. He gave up his old habits. Not because I asked him to, for I never dared do that. But of course he saw how repulsive they were to me; and so he dropped them.

HEDDA (concealing an involuntary smile of scorn). Then you have reclaimed him—as the saying goes—my little Thea.

MRS. ELVSTED. So he says himself, at any rate. And he, on his side, has made a real human being of me—taught me to think, and to understand so many things.

HEDDA. Did he give you lessons too, then?

MRS. ELVSTED. No, not exactly lessons. But he talked to me—talked about such an infinity of things. And then came the lovely, happy time when I began to share in his work—when he allowed me to help him!

HEDDA. Oh, he did, did he?

MRS. ELVSTED. Yes! He never wrote anything without my assistance.

HEDDA. You were two good comrades, in fact?

MRS. ELVSTED (eagerly). Comrades! Yes, fancy, Hedda—that is the very word he used!—Oh, I ought to feel perfectly happy; and yet I cannot; for I don't know how long it will last.

HEDDA. Are you no surer of him than that?

MRS. ELVSTED (gloomily). A woman's shadow stands between Eilert Lövborg and me.

HEDDA (looks at her anxiously). Who can that be?

MRS. ELVSTED. I don't know. Some one he knew in his—in his past. Some one he has never been able wholly to forget.

HEDDA. What has he told you—about this?

MRS. ELVSTED. He has only once—quite vaguely—alluded to it.

HEDDA. Well! And what did he say?

MRS. ELVSTED. He said that when they parted, she threatened to shoot him with a pistol.

HEDDA (with cold composure). Oh, nonsense! No one does that sort of thing here.

MRS. ELVSTED. No. And that is why I think it must have been that red-haired singing woman whom he once——

HEDDA. Yes, very likely.

MRS. ELVSTED. For I remember they used to

say of her that she carried loaded firearms.

HEDDA. Oh—then of course it must have been she.

MRS. ELVSTED (*wringing her hands*). And now just fancy, Hedda—I hear that this singing-woman—that she is in town again! Oh, I don't know what to do——

HEDDA (*glancing towards the inner room*). Hush! Here comes Tesman. (*Rises and whispers*) Thea—all this must remain between you and me.

MRS. ELVSTED (*springing up*). Oh, yes, yes! for heaven's sake——!

(GEORGE TESMAN, *with a letter in his hand, comes from the right through the inner room.*)

TESMAN. There now—the epistle is finished.

HEDDA. That's right. And now Mrs. Elvsted is just going. Wait a moment—I'll go with you to the garden gate.

TESMAN. Do you think Berta could post the letter, Hedda dear?

HEDDA (*takes it*). I will tell her to.

(BERTA *enters from the hall*)

BERTA. Judge Brack wishes to know if Mrs. Tesman will receive him.

HEDDA. Yes, ask Judge Brack to come in. And look here—put this letter in the post.

(BERTA *taking the letter. Yes, ma'am. She opens the door for* JUDGE BRACK *and goes out herself.* BRACK *is a man of forty-five; thick-set, but well-built and elastic in his movements. His face is roundish with an aristocratic profile. His hair is short, still almost black, and carefully dressed. His eyes are lively and sparkling. His eyebrows thick. His moustaches are also thick, with short-cut ends. He wears a well-cut walking-suit, a little too youthful for his age. He uses an eye-glass, which he now and then lets drop.*)

JUDGE BRACK (*with his hat in his hand, bowing*). May one venture to call so early in the day?

HEDDA. Of course one may.

TESMAN (*presses his hand*). You are welcome at any time. (*Introducing him*) Judge Brack—Miss Rysing——

HEDDA. Oh——!

BRACK (*bowing*). Ah—delighted——

HEDDA (*looks at him and laughs*). It's nice to have a look at you by daylight, Judge!

BRACK. Do you find me—altered?

HEDDA. A little younger, I think.

BRACK. Thank you so much.

TESMAN. But what do you think of Hedda—eh? Doesn't she look flourishing? She has actually——

HEDDA. Oh, do leave me alone. You haven't thanked Judge Brack for all the trouble he has taken——

BRACK. Oh, nonsense—it was a pleasure to me——

HEDDA. Yes, you are a friend indeed. But here stands Thea all impatience to be off—so *au revoir* Judge. I shall be back again presently.

(*Mutual salutations.* MRS. ELVSTED *and* HEDDA *go out by the hall door*)

BRACK. Well,—is your wife tolerably satisfied——

TESMAN. Yes, we can't thank you sufficiently. Of course she talks a little re-arrangement here and there; and one or two things are still wanting. We shall have to buy some additional trifles.

BRACK. Indeed!

TESMAN. But we won't trouble you about these things. Hedda says she herself will look after what is wanting.——Shan't we sit down? Eh?

BRACK. Thanks, for a moment. (*Seats himself beside the table*) There is something I wanted to speak to you about, my dear Tesman.

TESMAN. Indeed? Ah, I understand! (*Seating himself*) I suppose it's the serious part of the frolic that is coming now. Eh?

BRACK. Oh, the money question is not so very pressing; though, for that matter, I wish we had gone a little more economically to work.

TESMAN. But that would never have done, you know! Think of Hedda, my dear fellow! You, who know her so well——. I couldn't possibly ask her to put up with a shabby style of living!

BRACK. No, no—that is just the difficulty.

TESMAN. And then—fortunately—it can't be long before I receive my appointment.

BRACK. Well, you see—such things are often apt to hang fire for a time.

TESMAN. Have you heard anything definite? Eh?

BRACK. Nothing exactly definite—— (*Interrupting himself*) But, by-the-bye—I have one piece of news for you.

TESMAN. Well?

BRACK. Your old friend, Eilert Lövborg, has returned to town.

TESMAN. I know that already.

BRACK. Indeed! How did you learn it?

TESMAN. From that lady who went out with Hedda.

BRACK. Really? What was her name? I didn't quite catch it.

TESMAN. Mrs. Elvsted.

BRACK. Aha—Sheriff Elvsted's wife? Of course —he has been living up in their regions.

TESMAN. And fancy—I'm delighted to hear that he is quite a reformed character!

BRACK. So they say.

TESMAN. And then he has published a new book—eh?

BRACK. Yes, indeed he has.

TESMAN. And I hear it has made some sensation!

BRACK. Quite an unusual sensation.

TESMAN. Fancy—isn't that good news! A man of such extraordinary talents—— I felt so grieved to think that he had gone irretrievably to ruin.

BRACK. That was what everybody thought.

TESMAN. But I cannot imagine what he will take to now! How in the world will he be able to make his living? Eh?

(*During the last words,* HEDDA *has entered by the hall door*)

HEDDA (*to* BRACK, *laughing with a touch of scorn*). Tesman is forever worrying about how people are to make their living.

TESMAN. Well, you see, dear—we were talking about poor Eilert Lövborg.

HEDDA (*glancing at him rapidly*). Oh, indeed? (*Seats herself in the arm-chair beside the stove and asks indifferently*) What is the matter with him?

TESMAN. Well—no doubt he has run through all his property long ago; and he can scarcely write a new book every year—eh? So I really can't see what is to become of him.

BRACK. Perhaps I can give you some information on that point.

TESMAN. Indeed!

BRACK. You must remember that his relations have a good deal of influence.

TESMAN. Oh, his relations, unfortunately, have entirely washed their hands of him.

BRACK. At one time they called him the hope of the family.

TESMAN. At one time, yes! But he has put an end to all that.

HEDDA. Who knows? (*With a slight smile*) I hear they have reclaimed him up at Sheriff Elvsted's——

BRACK. And then this book that he has published——

TESMAN. Well, well, I hope to goodness they may find something for him to do. I have just written to him. I asked him to come and see us this evening, Hedda dear.

BRACK. But, my dear fellow, you are booked for my bachelors' party this evening. You promised on the pier last night.

HEDDA. Had you forgotten, Tesman?

TESMAN. Yes, I had utterly forgotten.

BRACK. But it doesn't matter, for you may be sure he won't come.

TESMAN. What makes you think that? Eh?

BRACK (*with a little hesitation, rising and resting his hands on the back of his chair*). My dear Tesman—and you too, Mrs. Tesman—I think I ought not to keep you in the dark about something that—that——

TESMAN. That concerns Eilert——?

BRACK. Both you and him.

TESMAN. Well, my dear Judge, out with it.

BRACK. You must be prepared to find your appointment deferred longer than you desired or expected.

TESMAN (*jumping up uneasily*). Is there some hitch about it? Eh?

BRACK. The nomination may perhaps be made conditional on the result of a competition——

TESMAN. Competition! Think of that, Hedda!

HEDDA (*leans farther back in the chair*). Aha —aha!

TESMAN. But who can my competitor be? Surely not——?

BRACK. Yes, precisely—Eilert Lövborg.

TESMAN (*clasping his hands*). No, no—it's quite inconceivable! Quite impossible! Eh?

BRACK. H'm—that is what it may come to, all the same.

TESMAN. Well but, Judge Brack—it would show the most incredible lack of consideration for me. (*Gesticulates with his arms*) For—just think—I'm a married man. We have been married on the strength of these prospects, Hedda and I; and run deep into debt; and borrowed money from Aunt Julia too. Good heavens, they had as good as promised me the appointment. Eh?

BRACK. Well, well, well—no doubt you will get it in the end; only after a contest.

HEDDA (*immovable in her arm-chair*). Fancy, Tesman, there will be a sort of sporting interest in that.

TESMAN. Why, my dearest Hedda, how can you be so indifferent about it.

HEDDA (*as before*). I am not at all indifferent. I am most eager to see who wins.

BRACK. In any case, Mrs. Tesman, it is best that you should know how matters stand. I mean—before you set about the little purchases I hear you are threatening.

HEDDA. This can make no difference.

BRACK. Indeed! Then I have no more to say. Good-bye! (*To* TESMAN) I shall look in on my way back from my afternoon walk, and take you home with me.

TESMAN. Oh, yes, yes—your news has quite upset me.

HEDDA (*reclining, holds out her hand*). Good-bye, Judge; and be sure you call in the afternoon.

BRACK. Many thanks. Good-bye, good-bye!

TESMAN (*accompanying him to the door*). Good-bye, my dear Judge! You must really excuse me—— (JUDGE BRACK *goes out by the hall door*)

TESMAN (*crosses the room*). Oh, Hedda—one should never rush into adventures. Eh?

HEDDA (*looks at him, smiling*). Do you do that?

TESMAN. Yes, dear—there is no denying—it was adventurous to go and marry and set up house upon mere expectations.

HEDDA. Perhaps you are right there.

TESMAN. Well—at all events, we have our delightful home, Hedda! Fancy, the home we both dreamed of—the home we were in love with, I may almost say. Eh?

HEDDA (*rising slowly and wearily*). It was part of our compact that we were to go into society—to keep open house.

TESMAN. Yes, if you only knew how I had been looking forward to it! Fancy—to see you as hostess—in a select circle? Eh? Well, well, well—for the present we shall have to get on without society, Hedda—only to invite Aunt Julia now and then.—Oh, I intended you to lead such an utterly different life, dear——!

HEDDA. Of course I cannot have my man in livery just yet.

TESMAN. Oh no, unfortunately. It would be out of the question for us to keep a footman, you know.

HEDDA. And the saddle-horse I was to have had——

TESMAN (*aghast*). The saddle-horse!

HEDDA. ——I suppose I must not think of that now.

TESMAN. Good heavens, no!—that's as clear as daylight.

HEDDA (*goes up the room*). Well, I shall have one thing at least to kill time with in the meanwhile.

TESMAN (*beaming*). Oh, thank heaven for that! What is it, Hedda? Eh?

HEDDA (*in the middle doorway, looks at him with covert scorn*). My pistols, George.

TESMAN (*in alarm*). Your pistols!

HEDDA (*with cold eyes*). General Gabler's pistols. (*She goes out through the inner room, to the left*)

TESMAN (*rushes up to the middle doorway and calls after her*). No, for heaven's sake, Hedda darling—don't touch those dangerous things! For my sake, Hedda! Eh?

Act II

SCENE: *The room at the* TESMANS' *as in the first act, except that the piano has been removed, and an elegant little writing-table with bookshelves put in its place. A smaller table stands near the sofa at the left. Most of the bouquets have been taken away.* MRS. ELVSTED'S *bouquet is upon the large table in front.—It is afternoon.*

(Hedda, *dressed to receive callers, is alone in the room. She stands by the open glass door, loading a revolver. The fellow to it lies in an open pistol-case on the writing-table.*)

Hedda (*looks down the garden, and calls*). So you are here again, Judge!

Brack (*is heard calling from a distance*). As you see, Mrs. Tesman!

Hedda (*raises the pistol and points*). Now I'll shoot you, Judge Brack!

Brack (*calling unseen*). No, no, no! Don't stand aiming at me!

Hedda. This is what comes of sneaking in by the back way.[1] (*She fires*)

Brack (*nearer*). Are you out of your senses——!

Hedda. Dear me—did I happen to hit you?

Brack (*still outside*). I wish you would let these pranks alone!

Hedda. Come in then, Judge.

(Judge Brack, *dressed as though for a men's party, enters by the glass door. He carries a light overcoat over his arm.*)

Brack. What the deuce—haven't you tired of that sport, yet? What are you shooting at?

Hedda. Oh, I am only firing in the air.

Brack (*gently takes the pistol out of her hand*). Allow me, madam! (*Looks at it*) Ah—I know this pistol well! (*Looks around*) Where is the case? Ah, here it is. (*Lays the pistol in it, and shuts it*) Now we won't play at that game any more today.

Hedda. Then what in heaven's name would you have me do with myself?

Brack. Have you had no visitors?

Hedda (*closing the glass door*). Not one. I suppose all our set are still out of town.

Brack. And is Tesman not at home either?

Hedda (*at the writing-table, putting the pistol-case in a drawer which she shuts*). No. He rushed off to his aunt's directly after lunch; he didn't expect you so early.

Brack. H'm—how stupid of me not to have thought of that!

Hedda (*turning her head to look at him*). Why stupid?

Brack. Because if I had thought of it I should have come a little—earlier.

Hedda (*crossing the room*). Then you would have found no one to receive you; for I have been in my room changing my dress ever since lunch.

Brack. And is there no sort of little chink that we could hold a parley through?

Hedda. You have forgotten to arrange one.

Brack. That was another piece of stupidity.

Hedda. Well, we must just settle down here —and wait. Tesman is not likely to be back for some time yet.

Brack. Never mind; I shall not be impatient.

(Hedda *seats herself in the corner of the sofa.* Brack *lays his overcoat over the back of the nearest chair, and sits down, but keeps his hat in his hand. A short silence. They look at each other.*)

Hedda. Well?

Brack (*in the same tone*). Well?

Hedda. I spoke first.

Brack (*bending a little forward*). Come, let us have a cozy little chat, Mrs. Hedda.

Hedda (*leaning further back in the sofa*). Does it not seem like a whole eternity since our last talk? Of course I don't count those few words yesterday evening and this morning.

Brack. You mean since our last confidential talk? Our last tête-à-tête?

Hedda. Well, yes—since you put it so.

Brack. Not a day has passed but I have wished that you were home again.

Hedda. And I have done nothing but wish the same thing.

Brack. You? Really, Mrs. Hedda? And I thought you had been enjoying your tour so much!

Hedda. Oh, yes, you may be sure of that!

Brack. But Tesman's letters spoke of nothing but happiness.

Hedda. Oh, Tesman! You see, he thinks nothing so delightful as grubbing in libraries and making copies of old parchments, or whatever you call them.

Brack (*with a spice of malice*). Well, that is his vocation in life—or part of it at any rate.

Hedda. Yes, of course; and no doubt when it's your vocation—— But I! Oh, my dear Mr. Brack, how mortally bored I have been.

Brack (*sympathetically*). Do you really say

[1] Bagueje means both "back ways" and "underhand courses."

so? In downright earnest?

HEDDA. Yes, you can surely understand it——! To go for six whole months without meeting a soul that knew anything of our circle, or could talk about the things we are interested in.

BRACK. Yes, yes—I too should feel that a deprivation.

HEDDA. And then, what I found most intolerable of all——

BRACK. Well?

HEDDA. ——was being everlastingly in the company of—one and the same person——

BRACK (with a nod of assent). Morning, noon, and night, yes—at all possible times and seasons.

HEDDA. I said "everlastingly."

BRACK. Just so. But I should have thought, with our excellent Tesman, one could——

HEDDA. Tesman is—a specialist, my dear Judge.

BRACK. Undeniably.

HEDDA. And specialists are not at all amusing to travel with. Not in the long run at any rate.

BRACK. Not even—the specialist one happens to love?

HEDDA. Faugh—don't use that sickening word!

BRACK (taken aback). What do you say, Mrs. Hedda?

HEDDA (half laughing, half irritated). You should just try it! To hear of nothing but the history of civilization, morning, noon, and night——

BRACK. Everlastingly.

HEDDA. Yes, yes, yes! And then all this about the domestic industry of the Middle Ages——! That's the most disgusting part of it!

BRACK (looks searchingly at her). But tell me —in that case, how am I to understand your——? H'm——

HEDDA. My accepting George Tesman, you mean?

BRACK. Well, let us put it so.

HEDDA. Good heavens, do you see anything so wonderful in that?

BRACK. Yes and no—Mrs. Hedda.

HEDDA. I had positively danced myself tired, my dear Judge. My day was done—— (With a slight shudder) Oh no—I won't say that; nor think it either!

BRACK. You have assuredly no reason to.

HEDDA. Oh, reasons—— (Watching him closely)

And George Tesman—after all, you must admit that he is correctness itself.

BRACK. His correctness and respectability are beyond all question.

HEDDA. And I don't see anything absolutely ridiculous about him.—Do you?

BRACK. Ridiculous? N—no—I shouldn't exactly say so——

HEDDA. Well—and his powers of research, at all events, are untiring.—I see no reason why he should not one day come to the front, after all.

BRACK (looks at her hesitatingly). I thought that you, like every one else, expected him to attain the highest distinction.

HEDDA (with an expression of fatigue). Yes, so I did.—And then, since he was bent, at all hazards, on being allowed to provide for me—I really don't know why I should not have accepted his offer?

BRACK. No—if you look at it in that light——

HEDDA. It was more than my other adorers were prepared to do for me, my dear Judge.

BRACK (laughing). Well, I can't answer for all the rest; but as for myself, you know quite well that I have always entertained a—a certain respect for the marriage tie—for marriage as an institution, Mrs. Hedda.

HEDDA (jestingly). Oh, I assure you I have never cherished any hopes with respect to you.

BRACK. All I require is a pleasant and intimate interior, where I can make myself useful in every way, and am free to come and go as—as a trusted friend——

HEDDA. Of the master of the house, do you mean?

BRACK (bowing). Frankly—of the mistress first of all; but of course of the master, too, in the second place. Such a triangular friendship—if I may call it so—is really a great convenience for all parties, let me tell you.

HEDDA. Yes, I have many a time longed for some one to make a third on our travels. Oh— those railway-carriage tête-à-têtes——!

BRACK. Fortunately your wedding journey is over now.

HEDDA (shaking her head). Not by a long— long way. I have only arrived at a station on the line.

BRACK. Well, then the passengers jump out and move about a little, Mrs. Hedda.

HEDDA. I never jump out.

BRACK. Really?

HEDDA. No—because there is always some one standing by to——

BRACK (*laughing*). To look at your ankles, do you mean?

HEDDA. Precisely.

BRACK. Well but, dear me——

HEDDA (*with a gesture of repulsion*). I won't have it. I would rather keep my seat where I happen to be—and continue the tête-à-tête.

BRACK. But suppose a third person were to jump in and join the couple.

HEDDA. Ah—that is quite another matter!

BRACK. A trusted, sympathetic friend——

HEDDA. ——with a fund of conversation on all sorts of lively topics——

BRACK. ——and not the least bit of a specialist!

HEDDA (*with an audible sigh*). Yes, that would be a relief indeed.

BRACK (*hears the front door open, and glances in that direction*). The triangle is completed.

HEDDA (*half aloud*). And on goes the train.

(GEORGE TESMAN, *in a gray walking-suit, with a soft felt hat, enters from the hall. He has a number of unbound books under his arm and in his pockets.*)

TESMAN (*goes up to the table beside the corner settee*). Ouf—what a load for a warm day —all these books. (*Lays them on the table*) I'm positively perspiring, Hedda. Hallo—are you there already, my dear Judge? Eh? Berta didn't tell me.

BRACK (*rising*). I came in through the garden.

HEDDA. What books have you got there?

TESMAN (*stands looking them through*). Some new books on my special subjects—quite indispensable to me.

HEDDA. Your special subjects?

BRACK. Yes, books on his special subjects, Mrs. Tesman. (BRACK *and* HEDDA *exchange a confidential smile*)

HEDDA. Do you need still more books on your special subjects?

TESMAN. Yes, my dear Hedda, one can never have too many of them. Of course one must keep up with all that is written and published.

HEDDA. Yes, I suppose one must.

TESMAN (*searching among his books*). And look here—I have got hold of Eilert Lövborg's new book too. (*Offering it to her*) Perhaps you would like to glance through it, Hedda? Eh?

HEDDA. No, thank you. Or rather—afterwards perhaps.

TESMAN. I looked into it a little on the way home.

BRACK. Well, what do you think of it—as a specialist?

TESMAN. I think it shows quite remarkable soundness of judgment. He never wrote like that before. (*Putting the books together*) Now I shall take all these into my study. I'm longing to cut the leaves——! And then I must change my clothes. (*To* BRACK) I suppose we needn't start just yet? Eh?

BRACK. Oh, dear no—there is not the slightest hurry.

TESMAN. Well then, I will take my time. (*Is going with his books, but stops in the doorway and turns*) By-the-bye, Hedda—Aunt Julia is not coming this evening.

HEDDA. Not coming? Is it that affair of the bonnet that keeps her away?

TESMAN. Oh, not at all. How could you think such a thing of Aunt Julia? Just fancy——! The fact is, Aunt Rina is very ill.

HEDDA. She always is.

TESMAN. Yes, but today she is much worse than usual, poor dear.

HEDDA. Oh, then it's only natural that her sister should remain with her. I must bear my disappointment.

TESMAN. And you can't imagine, dear, how delighted Aunt Julia seemed to be—because you had come home looking so flourishing!

HEDDA (*half aloud, rising*). Oh, those everlasting aunts!

TESMAN. What?

HEDDA (*going to the glass door*). Nothing.

TESMAN. Oh, all right. (*He goes through the inner room, out to the right*)

BRACK. What bonnet were you talking about?

HEDDA. Oh, it was a little episode with Miss Tesman this morning. She had laid down her bonnet on the chair there—(*Looks at him and smiles*)—and I pretended to think it was the servant's.

BRACK (*shaking his head*). Now my dear Mrs. Hedda, how could you do such a thing? To that excellent old lady, too!

HEDDA (*nervously crossing the room*). Well, you see—these impulses come over me all of a sudden; and I cannot resist them. (*Throws herself down in the easy-chair by the stove*) Oh, I don't know how to explain it.

BRACK (*behind the easy-chair*). You are not really happy—that is at the bottom of it.

HEDDA (*looking straight before her*). I know of no reason why I should be—happy. Perhaps you can give me one?

BRACK. Well—amongst other things, because you have got exactly the home you had set your heart on.

HEDDA (*looks up at him and laughs*). Do you too believe in that legend?

BRACK. Is there nothing in it, then?

HEDDA. Oh, yes, there is something in it.

BRACK. Well?

HEDDA. There is this in it, that I made use of Tesman to see me home from evening parties last summer——

BRACK. I, unfortunately, had to go quite a different way.

HEDDA. That's true. I know you were going a different way last summer.

BRACK (*laughing*). Oh fie, Mrs. Hedda! Well, then—you and Tesman——?

HEDDA. Well, we happened to pass here one evening; Tesman, poor fellow, was writhing in the agony of having to find conversation; so I took pity on the learned man——

BRACK (*smiles doubtfully*). You took pity? H'm——

HEDDA. Yes, I really did. And so—to help him out of his torment—I happened to say, in pure thoughtlessness, that I should like to live in this villa.

BRACK. No more than that?

HEDDA. Not that evening.

BRACK. But afterwards?

HEDDA. Yes, my thoughtlessness had consequences, my dear Judge.

BRACK. Unfortunately that too often happens, Mrs. Hedda.

HEDDA. Thanks! So you see it was this enthusiasm for Secretary Falk's villa that first constituted a bond of sympathy between George Tesman and me. From that came our engagement and our marriage, and our wedding journey, and all the rest of it. Well, well, my dear Judge—as you make your bed so you must lie, I could almost say.

BRACK. This is exquisite! And you really cared not a rap about it all the time.

HEDDA. No, heaven knows I didn't.

BRACK. But now? Now that we have made it so homelike for you?

HEDDA. Ugh—the rooms all seem to smell of lavender and dried love-leaves.—But perhaps it's Aunt Julia that has brought that scent with her.

BRACK (*laughingly*). No, I think it must be a legacy from the late Mrs. Secretary Falk.

HEDDA. Yes, there is an odor of mortality about it. It reminds me of a bouquet—the day after the ball. (*Clasps her hands behind her head, leans back in her chair and looks at him*) Oh, my dear Judge—you cannot imagine how horribly I shall bore myself here.

BRACK. Why should not you, too, find some sort of vocation in life, Mrs. Hedda?

HEDDA. A vocation—that should attract me?

BRACK. If possible, of course.

HEDDA. Heaven knows what sort of a vocation that could be. I often wonder whether—— (*Breaking off*) But that would never do either.

BRACK. Who can tell? Let me hear what it is.

HEDDA. Whether I might not get Tesman to go into politics, I mean.

BRACK (*laughing*). Tesman? No, really now, political life is not the thing for him—not at all in his line.

HEDDA. No, I daresay not.—But if I could get him into it all the same?

BRACK. Why—what satisfaction could you find in that? If he is not fitted for that sort of thing, why should you want to drive him into it?

HEDDA. Because I am bored, I tell you! (*After a pause*) So you think it quite out of the question that Tesman should ever get into the ministry?

BRACK. H'm—you see, my dear Mrs. Hedda—to get into the ministry, he would have to be a tolerably rich man.

HEDDA (*rising impatiently*). Yes, there we have it! It is this genteel poverty I have managed to drop into——! (*Crosses the room*) That is what makes life so pitiable! So utterly ludicrous!—For that's what it is.

BRACK. Now *I* should say the fault lay elsewhere.

HEDDA. Where, then?

BRACK. You have never gone through any really stimulating experience.

HEDDA. Anything serious, you mean?

BRACK. Yes, you may call it so. But now you may perhaps have one in store.

HEDDA (*tossing her head*). Oh, you're thinking of the annoyances about this wretched professorship! But that must be Tesman's own affair. I assure you I shall not waste a thought upon it.

BRACK. No, no, I daresay not. But suppose now that what people call—in elegant language—a solemn responsibility were to come upon you? (*Smiling*) A new responsibility, Mrs. Hedda?

HEDDA (*angrily*). Be quiet! Nothing of that sort will ever happen!

BRACK (*warily*). We will speak of this again a year hence—at the very outside.

HEDDA (*curtly*). I have no turn for anything of the sort, Judge Brack. No responsibilities for me!

BRACK. Are you so unlike the generality of women as to have no turn for duties which——?

HEDDA (*beside the glass door*). Oh, be quiet, I tell you!—I often think there is only one thing in the world I have any turn for.

BRACK (*drawing near to her*). And what is that, if I may ask?

HEDDA (*stands looking out*). Boring myself to death. Now you know it. (*Turns, looks towards the inner room, and laughs*) Yes, as I thought! Here comes the Professor.

BRACK (*softly, in a tone of warning*). Come, come, come, Mrs. Hedda!

(GEORGE TESMAN, *dressed for the party, with his gloves and hat in his hand, enters from the right through the inner room*)

TESMAN. Hedda, has no message come from Eilert Lövborg? Eh?

HEDDA. No.

TESMAN. Then you'll see he'll be here presently.

BRACK. Do you really think he will come?

TESMAN. Yes, I am almost sure of it. For what you were telling us this morning must have been a mere floating rumor.

BRACK. You think so?

TESMAN. At any rate, Aunt Julia said she did not believe for a moment that he would ever stand in my way again. Fancy that!

BRACK. Well then, that's all right.

TESMAN (*placing his hat and gloves on a chair on the right*). Yes, but you must really let me wait for him as long as possible.

BRACK. We have plenty of time yet. None of my guests will arrive before seven or half-past.

TESMAN. Then meanwhile we can keep Hedda company, and see what happens. Eh?

HEDDA (*placing* BRACK's *hat and overcoat upon the corner settee*). And at the worst Mr. Lövborg can remain here with me.

BRACK (*offering to take his things*). Oh, allow me, Mrs. Tesman!—What do you mean by "At the worst"?

HEDDA. If he won't go with you and Tesman.

TESMAN (*looks dubiously at her*). But, Hedda dear—do you think it would quite do for him to remain with you? Eh? Remember, Aunt Julia can't come.

HEDDA. No, but Mrs. Elvsted is coming. We three can have a cup of tea together.

TESMAN. Oh, yes, that will be all right.

BRACK (*smiling*). And that would perhaps be the safest plan for him.

HEDDA. Why so?

BRACK. Well, you know, Mrs. Tesman, how you used to gird at my little bachelor parties. You declared they were adapted only for men of the strictest principles.

HEDDA. But no doubt Mr. Lövborg's principles are strict enough now. A converted sinner—— (BERTA *appears at the hall door*)

BERTA. There's a gentleman asking if you are at home, ma'am——

HEDDA. Well, show him in.

TESMAN (*softly*). I'm sure it is he! Fancy that!

(EILERT LÖVBORG *enters from the hall. He is slim and lean; of the same age as* TESMAN, *but looks older and somewhat worn-out. His hair and beard are of a blackish brown, his face long and pale, but with patches of color on the cheekbones. He is dressed in a well-cut black visiting suit, quite new. He has dark gloves and a silk hat. He stops near the door, and makes a rapid bow, seeming somewhat embarrassed.*)

TESMAN (*goes up to him and shakes him warmly by the hand*). Well, my dear Eilert—so at last we meet again!

EILERT LÖVBORG (*speaks in a subdued voice*). Thanks for your letter, Tesman. (*Approaching* HEDDA) Will you too shake hands with me, Mrs. Tesman?

HEDDA (*taking his hand*). I am glad to see you, Mr. Lövborg. (*With a motion of her hand*) I don't know whether you two gentlemen——?

LÖVBORG (*bowing slightly*). Judge Brack, I think.

BRACK (*doing likewise*). Oh, yes,—in the old days——

TESMAN (*to* LÖVBORG, *with his hands on his shoulders*). And now you must make yourself entirely at home, Eilert! Mustn't he, Hedda?—For I hear you are going to settle in town again? Eh?

LÖVBORG. Yes, I am.

TESMAN. Quite right, quite right. Let me tell you, I have got hold of your new book; but I haven't had time to read it yet.

LÖVBORG. You may spare yourself the trouble.

TESMAN. Why so?

LÖVBORG. Because there is very little in it.

TESMAN. Just fancy—how can you say so?

BRACK. But it has been much praised, I hear.

LÖVBORG. That was what I wanted; so I put nothing into the book but what everyone would agree with.

BRACK. Very wise of you.

TESMAN. Well but, my dear Eilert——!

LÖVBORG. For now I mean to win myself a position again—to make a fresh start.

TESMAN (*a little embarrassed*). Ah, that is what you wish to do? Eh?

LÖVBORG (*smiling, lays down his hat, and draws a packet, wrapped in paper, from his coat pocket*). But when this one appears, George Tesman, you will have to read it. For this is the real book—the book I have put my true self into.

TESMAN. Indeed? And what is it?

LÖVBORG. It is the continuation.

TESMAN. The continuation? Of what?

LÖVBORG. Of the book.

TESMAN. Of the new book?

LÖVBORG. Of course.

TESMAN. Why, my dear Eilert—does it not come down to our own days?

LÖVBORG. Yes, it does; and this one deals with the future.

TESMAN. With the future! But, good heavens, we know nothing of the future!

LÖVBORG. No; but there is a thing or two to be said about it all the same. (*Opens the packet*) Look here——

TESMAN. Why, that's not your handwriting.

LÖVBORG. I dictated it. (*Turning over the pages*) It falls into two sections. The first deals with the civilizing forces of the future. And here is the second— (*running through the pages towards the end*)—forecasting the probable line of development.

TESMAN. How odd now! I should never have thought of writing anything of that sort.

HEDDA (*at the glass door, drumming on the pane*). H'm—I daresay not.

LÖVBORG (*replacing the manuscript in its paper and laying the packet on the table*). I brought it, thinking I might read you a little of it this evening.

TESMAN. That was very good of you, Eilert. But this evening——? (*Looking at* BRACK) I don't quite see how we can manage it——

LÖVBORG. Well then, some other time. There is no hurry.

BRACK. I must tell you, Mr. Lövborg—there is a little gathering at my house this evening—mainly in honor of Tesman, you know——

LÖVBORG (*looking for his hat*). Oh—then I won't detain you——

BRACK. No, but listen—will you not do me the favor of joining us?

LÖVBORG (*curtly and decidedly*). No, I can't—thank you very much.

BRACK. Oh, nonsense—do! We shall be quite a select little circle. And I assure you we shall have a "lively time" as Mrs. Hed—as Mrs. Tesman says.

LÖVBORG. I have no doubt of it. But nevertheless——

BRACK. And then you might bring your manuscript with you, and read it to Tesman at my house. I could give you a room to yourselves.

TESMAN. Yes, think of that, Eilert,—why shouldn't you? Eh?

HEDDA (*interposing*). But, Tesman, if Mr. Lövborg would really rather not! I am sure Mr. Lövborg is much more inclined to remain here and have supper with me.

LÖVBORG (*looking at her*). With you, Mrs.

Tesman?

HEDDA. And with Mrs. Elvsted.

LÖVBORG. Ah—— (*Lightly*) I saw her for a moment this morning.

HEDDA. Did you? Well, she is coming this evening. So you see you are almost bound to remain, Mr. Lövborg, or she will have no one to see her home.

LÖVBORG. That's true. Many thanks, Mrs. Tesman—in that case I will remain.

HEDDA. Then I have one or two orders to give the servant——

(*She goes to the hall door and rings. BERTA enters. HEDDA talks to her in a whisper, and points towards the inner room. BERTA nods and goes out again.*)

TESMAN (*at the same time, to LÖVBORG*). Tell me, Eilert—is it this new subject—the future—that you are going to lecture about?

LÖVBORG. Yes.

TESMAN. They told me at the bookseller's, that you are going to deliver a course of lectures this autumn.

LÖVBORG. That is my intention. I hope you won't take it ill, Tesman.

TESMAN. Oh no, not in the least! But——?

LÖVBORG. I can quite understand that it must be disagreeable to you.

TESMAN (*cast down*). Oh, I can't expect you, out of consideration for me, to——

LÖVBORG. But I shall wait till you have received your appointment.

TESMAN. Will you wait? Yes, but—yes, but—are you not going to compete with me? Eh?

LÖVBORG. No; it is only the moral victory I care for.

TESMAN. Why, bless me—then Aunt Julia was right after all! Oh yes—I knew it! Hedda! Just fancy—Eilert Lövborg is not going to stand in our way!

HEDDA (*curtly*). Our way? Pray leave me out of the question.

(*She goes up towards the inner room, where BERTA is placing a tray with decanters and glasses on the table. HEDDA nods approval, and comes forward again. BERTA goes out.*)

TESMAN (*at the same time*). And you, Judge Brack—what do you say to this? Eh?

BRACK. Well, I say that a moral victory—h'm

—may be all very fine——

TESMAN. Yes, certainly. But all the same——

HEDDA (*looking at TESMAN with a cold smile*). You stand there looking as if you were thunderstruck——

TESMAN. Yes—so I am—I almost think——

BRACK. Don't you see, Mrs. Tesman, a thunderstorm has just passed over?

HEDDA (*pointing towards the inner room*) Will you not take a glass of cold punch, gentlemen?

BRACK (*looking at his watch*). A stirrup-cup? Yes, it wouldn't come amiss.

TESMAN. A capital idea, Hedda! Just the thing! Now that the weight has been taken off my mind——

HEDDA. Will you not join them, Mr. Lövborg?

LÖVBORG (*with a gesture of refusal*). No, thank you. Nothing for me.

BRACK. Why, bless me—cold punch is surely not poison.

LÖVBORG. Perhaps not for everyone.

HEDDA. I will keep Mr. Lövborg company in the meantime.

TESMAN. Yes, yes, Hedda dear, do.

(*He and BRACK go into the inner room, seat themselves, drink punch, smoke cigarettes, and carry on a lively conversation during what follows. EILERT LÖVBORG remains beside the stove. HEDDA goes to the writing-table.*)

HEDDA (*raising her voice a little*). Do you care to look at some photographs, Mr. Lövborg? You know Tesman and I made a tour in the Tyrol on our way home?

(*She takes up an album, and places it on the table beside the sofa, in the farther corner of which she seats herself. EILERT LÖVBORG approaches, stops, and looks at her. Then he takes a chair and seats himself at her left, with his back towards the inner room.*)

HEDDA (*opening the album*). Do you see this range of mountains, Mr. Lövborg? It's the Ortler group. Tesman has written the name underneath. Here it is: "The Ortler group near Meran."

LÖVBORG (*who has never taken his eyes off her, says softly and slowly*). Hedda—Gabler!

HEDDA (*glancing hastily at him*). Ah, hush!

LÖVBORG (*repeats softly*). Hedda Gabler!

HEDDA (*looking at the album*). That was my name in the old days—when we two knew each other.

LÖVBORG. And I must teach myself never to say Hedda Gabler again—never, as long as I live.

HEDDA (*still turning over the pages*). Yes, you must. And I think you ought to practice in time. The sooner the better, I should say.

LÖVBORG (*in a tone of indignation*). Hedda Gabler married? And married to—George Tesman!

HEDDA. Yes—so the world goes.

LÖVBORG. Oh, Hedda, Hedda—how could you [2] throw yourself away!

HEDDA (*looks sharply at him*). What? I can't allow this!

LÖVBORG. What do you mean? (TESMAN *comes into the room and goes toward the sofa*)

HEDDA (*hears him coming and says in an indifferent tone*). And this is a view from the Val d'Ampezzo, Mr. Lövborg. Just look at these peaks! (*Looks affectionately up at* TESMAN) What's the name of these curious peaks, dear?

TESMAN. Let me see? Oh, those are the Dolomites.

HEDDA. Yes, that's it!—Those are the Dolomites, Mr. Lövborg.

TESMAN. Hedda dear,—I only wanted to ask whether I shouldn't bring you a little punch after all? For yourself at any rate—eh?

HEDDA. Yes, do, please; and perhaps a few biscuits.

TESMAN. No cigarettes?

HEDDA. No.

TESMAN. Very well.

(*He goes into the inner room and out to the right.* BRACK *sits in the inner room, and keeps an eye from time to time on* HEDDA *and* LÖVBORG.)

LÖVBORG (*softly, as before*). Answer me, Hedda—how could you go and do this?

HEDDA (*apparently absorbed in the album*). If you continue to say *du* to me I won't talk to you.

LÖVBORG. May I not say *du* when we are alone?

HEDDA. No. You may think it; but you mustn't say it.

LÖVBORG. Ah, I understand. It is an offense against George Tesman, whom you [3]—love.

HEDDA (*glances at him and smiles*). Love? What an idea!

LÖVBORG. You don't love him then!

HEDDA. But I won't hear of any sort of unfaithfulness! Remember that.

LÖVBORG. Hedda—answer me one thing——

HEDDA. Hush!

(TESMAN *enters with a small tray from the inner room*)

TESMAN. Here you are! Isn't this tempting? (*He puts the tray on the table*)

HEDDA. Why do you bring it yourself?

TESMAN (*filling the glasses*). Because I think it's such fun to wait upon you, Hedda.

HEDDA. But you have poured out two glasses. Mr. Lövborg said he wouldn't have any——

TESMAN. No, but Mrs. Elvsted will soon be here, won't she?

HEDDA. Yes, by-the-bye—Mrs. Elvsted——

TESMAN. Had you forgotten her? Eh?

HEDDA. We were so absorbed in these photographs. (*Shows him a picture*) Do you remember this little village?

TESMAN. Oh, it's that one just below the Brenner Pass. It was there we passed the night——

HEDDA. ——and met that lively party of tourists.

TESMAN. Yes, that was the place. Fancy—if we could only have had you with us, Eilert! Eh? (*He returns to the inner room and sits beside* BRACK)

LÖVBORG. Answer me this one thing, Hedda——

HEDDA. Well?

LÖVBORG. Was there no love in your friendship for me either? Not a spark—not a tinge of love in it?

HEDDA. I wonder if there was? To me it seems as though we were two good comrades—two thoroughly intimate friends. (*Smilingly*) You especially were frankness itself.

---

2 He uses the familiar *du*.

3 From this point onward Lövborg uses the formal *De*.

LÖVBORG. It was you that made me so.

HEDDA. As I look back upon it all, I think there was really something beautiful, something fascinating—something daring—in—in that secret intimacy—that comradeship which no living creature so much as dreamed of.

LÖVBORG. Yes, yes, Hedda! Was there not? —When I used to come to your father's in the afternoon—and the General sat over at the window reading his papers—with his back towards us——

HEDDA. And we two on the corner sofa——

LÖVBORG. Always with the same illustrated paper before us——

HEDDA. For want of an album, yes.

LÖVBORG. Yes, Hedda, and when I made my confessions to you—told you about myself, things that at that time no one else knew! There I would sit and tell you of my escapades —my days and nights of devilment. Oh, Hedda —what was the power in you that forced me to confess these things?

HEDDA. Do you think it was any power in me?

LÖVBORG. How else can I explain it? And all those—those roundabout questions you used to put to me——

HEDDA. Which you understood so particularly well——

LÖVBORG. How could you sit and question me like that? Question me quite frankly——

HEDDA. In roundabout terms, please observe.

LÖVBORG. Yes, but frankly nevertheless. Cross-question me about—all that sort of thing?

HEDDA. And how could you answer, Mr. Lövborg?

LÖVBORG. Yes, that is just what I can't understand—in looking back upon it. But tell me now, Hedda—was there not love at the bottom of our friendship? On your side, did you not feel as though you might purge my stains away if I made you my confessor? Was it not so?

HEDDA. No, not quite.

LÖVBORG. What was your motive, then?

HEDDA. Do you think it quite incomprehensible that a young girl—when it can be done —without any one knowing——

LÖVBORG. Well?

HEDDA. ——should be glad to have a peep,

now and then, into a world which——

LÖVBORG. Which——?

HEDDA. ——which she is forbidden to know anything about?

LÖVBORG. So that was it?

HEDDA. Partly. Partly—I almost think.

LÖVBORG. Comradeship in the thirst for life. But why should not that, at any rate, have continued?

HEDDA. The fault was yours.

LÖVBORG. It was you that broke with me.

HEDDA. Yes, when our friendship threatened to develop into something more serious. Shame upon you, Eilert Lövborg! How could you think of wronging your—your frank comrade?

LÖVBORG (clenching his hands). Oh, why did you not carry out your threat? Why did you not shoot me down?

HEDDA. Because I have such a dread of scandal.

LÖVBORG. Yes, Hedda, you are a coward at heart.

HEDDA. A terrible coward. (Changing her tone) But it was a lucky thing for you. And now you have found ample consolation at the Elvsteds'.

LÖVBORG. I know what Thea has confided to you.

HEDDA. And perhaps you have confided to her something about us?

LÖVBORG. Not a word. She is too stupid to understand anything of that sort.

HEDDA. Stupid?

LÖVBORG. She is stupid about matters of that sort.

HEDDA. And I am cowardly. (Bends over towards him, without looking him in the face, and says more softly) But now I will confide something to you.

LÖVBORG (eagerly). Well?

HEDDA. The fact that I dared not shoot you down——

LÖVBORG. Yes!

HEDDA. ——that was not my most arrant cowardice—that evening.

LÖVBORG (looks at her a moment, understands, and whispers passionately). Oh, Hedda! Hedda Gabler! Now I begin to see a hidden reason beneath our comradeship! You[4] and

4 In this speech he once more says du. Hedda addresses him throughout as De.

I——! After all, then, it was your craving for life——

HEDDA (*softly, with a sharp glance*). Take care! Believe nothing of the sort!

(*Twilight has begun to fall. The hall door is opened from without by* BERTA.)

HEDDA (*closes the album with a bang and calls smilingly*). Ah, at last! My darling Thea, —come along!

(MRS. ELVSTED *enters from the hall. She is in evening dress. The door is closed behind her.*)

HEDDA (*on the sofa, stretches out her arms towards her*). My sweet Thea—you can't think how I have been longing for you!

(MRS. ELVSTED, *in passing, exchanges slight salutations with the gentlemen in the inner room, then goes up to the table and gives* HEDDA *her hands.* EILERT LÖVBORG *has risen. He and* MRS. ELVSTED *greet each other with a silent nod.*)

MRS. ELVSTED. Ought I to go in and talk to your husband for a moment?

HEDDA. Oh, not at all. Leave those two alone. They will soon be going.

MRS. ELVSTED. Are they going out?

HEDDA. Yes, to a supper-party.

MRS. ELVSTED (*quickly, to* LÖVBORG). Not you?

LÖVBORG. No.

HEDDA. Mr. Lövborg remains with us.

MRS. ELVSTED (*takes a chair and is about to seat herself at his side*). Oh, how nice it is here!

HEDDA. No, thank you, my little Thea! Not there! You'll be good enough to come over here to me. I will sit between you.

MRS. ELVSTED. Yes, just as you please.

(*She goes around the table and seats herself on the sofa on* HEDDA's *right.* LÖVBORG *reseats himself on his chair.*)

LÖVBORG (*after a short pause, to* HEDDA). Is not she lovely to look at?

HEDDA (*lightly stroking her hair*). Only to look at?

LÖVBORG. Yes. For we two—she and I—we are two real comrades. We have absolute faith in each other; so we can sit and talk with perfect frankness——

HEDDA. Not roundabout, Mr. Lövborg?

LÖVBORG. Well——

MRS. ELVSTED (*softly clinging close to* HEDDA). Oh, how happy I am, Hedda; for, only think, he says I have inspired him too.

HEDDA (*looks at her with a smile*). Ah! Does he say that, dear?

LÖVBORG. And then she is so brave, Mrs. Tesman!

MRS. ELVSTED. Good heavens—am I brave?

LÖVBORG. Exceedingly—where your comrade is concerned.

HEDDA. Ah, yes—courage! If one only had that!

LÖVBORG. What then? What do you mean?

HEDDA. Then life would perhaps be livable, after all. (*With a sudden change of tone*) But now, my dearest Thea, you really must have a glass of cold punch.

MRS. ELVSTED. No, thanks—I never take anything of that kind.

HEDDA. Well then, you, Mr. Lövborg.

LÖVBORG. Nor I, thank you.

MRS. ELVSTED. No, he doesn't either.

HEDDA (*looks fixedly at him*). But if I say you shall?

LÖVBORG. It would be no use.

HEDDA (*laughing.*) Then I, poor creature, have no sort of power over you?

LÖVBORG. Not in that respect.

HEDDA. But seriously, I think you ought to —for your own sake.

MRS. ELVSTED. Why, Hedda——!

LÖVBORG. How so?

HEDDA. Or rather on account of other people.

LÖVBORG. Indeed?

HEDDA. Otherwise people might be apt to suspect that—in your heart of hearts—you did not feel quite secure—quite confident of yourself.

MRS. ELVSTED (*softly*). Oh please, Hedda——

LÖVBORG. People may suspect what they like —for the present.

MRS. ELVSTED (*joyfully*). Yes, let them!

HEDDA. I saw it plainly in Judge Brack's face a moment ago.

LÖVBORG. What did you see?

HEDDA. His contemptuous smile, when you dared not go with them into the inner room.

LÖVBORG. Dared not? Of course I preferred to stop here and talk to you.

MRS. ELVSTED. What could be more natural,

Hedda?

HEDDA. But the Judge could not guess that. And I saw, too, the way he smiled and glanced at Tesman when you dared not accept his invitation to this wretched little supper-party of his.

LÖVBORG. Dared not! Do you say I dared not?

HEDDA. *I* don't say so. But that was how Judge Brack understood it.

LÖVBORG. Well, let him.

HEDDA. Then you are not going with them?

LÖVBORG. I will stay here with you and Thea.

MRS ELVSTED. Yes, Hedda—how can you doubt that?

HEDDA (*smiles and nods approvingly to* LÖVBORG). Firm as a rock! Faithful to your principles, now and forever! Ah, that is how a man should be! (*Turns to* MRS. ELVSTED *and caresses her*) Well now, what did I tell you, when you came to us this morning in such a state of distraction——

LÖVBORG (*surprised*). Distraction!

MRS. ELVSTED (*terrified*). Hedda—oh Hedda——!

HEDDA. You can see for yourself; you haven't the slightest reason to be in such mortal terror —— (*Interrupting herself*) There! Now we can all three enjoy ourselves!

LÖVBORG (*who has given a start*). Ah—what is all this, Mrs. Tesman?

MRS. ELVSTED. Oh my God, Hedda! What are you saying? What are you doing?

HEDDA. Don't get excited! That horrid Judge Brack is sitting watching you.

LÖVBORG. So she was in mortal terror! On my account!

MRS. ELVSTED (*softly and piteously*). Oh, Hedda—now you have ruined everything!

LÖVBORG (*looks fixedly at her for a moment. His face is distorted.*). So that was my comrade's frank confidence in me?

MRS. ELVSTED (*imploringly*). Oh, my dearest friend—only let me tell you——

LÖVBORG (*takes one of the glasses of punch, raises it to his lips, and says in a low, husky voice*). Your health, Thea!

(*He empties the glass, puts it down, and takes the second*)

MRS. ELVSTED (*softly*). Oh, Hedda, Hedda—how could you do this?

HEDDA. *I* do it? *I?* Are you crazy?

LÖVBORG. Here's to your health too, Mrs. Tesman. Thanks for the truth. Hurrah for the truth!

(*He empties the glass and is about to refill it*)

HEDDA (*lays her hand on his arm*). Come, come—no more for the present. Remember you are going out to supper.

MRS. ELVSTED. No, no, no!

HEDDA. Hush! They are sitting watching you.

LÖVBORG (*putting down the glass*). Now, Thea—tell me the truth——

MRS. ELVSTED. Yes.

LÖVBORG. Did your husband know that you had come after me?

MRS. ELVSTED (*wringing her hands*). Oh, Hedda—do you hear what he is asking?

LÖVBORG. Was it arranged between you and him that you were to come to town and look after me? Perhaps it was the Sheriff himself that urged you to come? Aha, my dear—no doubt he wanted my help in his office! Or was it at the card-table that he missed me?

MRS. ELVSTED (*softly, in agony*). Oh, Lövborg, Lövborg——!

LÖVBORG (*seizes a glass and is on the point of filling it*). Here's a glass for the old Sheriff too!

HEDDA (*preventing him*). No more just now. Remember you have to read your manuscript to Tesman.

LÖVBORG (*calmly, putting down the glass*). It was stupid of me—all this, Thea—to take it in this way, I mean. Don't be angry with me, my dear, dear comrade. You shall see—both you and the others—that if I was fallen once—now I have risen again! Thanks to you, Thea.

MRS. ELVSTED (*radiant with joy*). Oh, heaven be praised——!

(BRACK *has in the meantime looked at his watch. He and* TESMAN *rise and come into the drawing-room.*)

BRACK (*takes his hat and overcoat*). Well, Mrs. Tesman, our time has come.

HEDDA. I suppose it has.

LÖVBORG (*rising*). Mine too, Judge Brack.

MRS. ELVSTED (*softly and imploringly*). Oh, Lövborg, don't do it!

HEDDA (*pinching her arm*). They can hear you!

MRS. ELVSTED (*with a suppressed shriek*). Ow!

LÖVBORG (*to* BRACK). You were good enough to invite me.

BRACK. Well, are you coming after all?

LÖVBORG. Yes, many thanks.

BRACK. I'm delighted——

LÖVBORG (*to* TESMAN, *putting the parcel of MS. in his pocket*). I should like to show you one or two things before I send it to the printers.

TESMAN. Fancy—that will be delightful. But, Hedda dear, how is Mrs. Elvsted to get home? Eh?

HEDDA. Oh, that can be managed somehow.

LÖVBORG (*looking towards the ladies*). Mrs. Elvsted? Of course, I'll come again and fetch her. (*Approaching*) At ten or thereabouts, Mrs. Tesman? Will that do?

HEDDA. Certainly. That will do capitally.

TESMAN. Well, then, that's all right. But you must not expect me so early, Hedda.

HEDDA. Oh, you may stop as long—as long as ever you please.

MRS. ELVSTED (*trying to conceal her anxiety*). Well then, Mr. Lövborg—I shall remain here until you come.

LÖVBORG (*with his hat in his hand*). Pray do, Mrs. Elvsted.

BRACK. And now off goes the excursion train, gentlemen! I hope we shall have a lively time, as a certain fair lady puts it.

HEDDA. Ah, if only the fair lady could be present unseen——!

BRACK. Why unseen?

HEDDA. In order to hear a little of your liveliness at first hand, Judge Brack.

BRACK (*laughingly*). I should not advise the fair lady to try it.

TESMAN (*also laughing*). Come, you're a nice one Hedda! Fancy that!

BRACK. Well, good-bye, good-bye, ladies.

LÖVBORG (*bowing*). About ten o'clock, then.

(BRACK, LÖVBORG, *and* TESMAN *go out by the hall door. At the same time* BERTA *enters from the inner room with a lighted lamp, which she places on the dining-room table; she goes out by the way she came.*)

MRS. ELVSTED (*who has risen and is wandering restlessly about the room*). Hedda—Hedda—what will come of all this?

HEDDA. At ten o'clock—he will be here. I can see him already—with vine-leaves in his hair—flushed and fearless——

MRS. ELVSTED. Oh, I hope he may.

HEDDA. And then, you see—then he will have regained control over himself. Then he will be a free man for all his days.

MRS. ELVSTED. Oh God!—if he would only come as you see him now!

HEDDA. He will come as I see him—so, and not otherwise! (*Rises and approaches* THEA) You may doubt him as long as you please; I believe in him. And now we will try——

MRS ELVSTED. You have some hidden motive in this, Hedda!

HEDDA. Yes, I have. I want for once in my life to have power to mold a human destiny.

MRS. ELVSTED. Have you not the power?

HEDDA. I have not—and have never had it.

MRS. ELVSTED. Not your husband's?

HEDDA. Do you think that is worth the trouble? Oh, if you could only understand how poor I am. And fate has made you so rich! (*Clasps her passionately in her arms*) I think I must burn your hair off, after all.

MRS. ELVSTED. Let me go! Let me go! I am afraid of you, Hedda!

BERTA (*in the middle doorway*). Tea is laid in the dining room, ma'am.

HEDDA. Very well. We are coming.

MRS. ELVSTED. No, no, no! I would rather go home alone! At once!

HEDDA. Nonsense? First you shall have a cup of tea, you little stupid. And then—at ten o'clock—Eilert Lövborg will be here—with vine-leaves in his hair.

(*She drags* MRS. ELVSTED *almost by force towards the middle doorway.*)

Act III

SCENE: The room at the TESMANS'. *The curtains are drawn over the middle doorway, and also over the glass door. The lamp, half turned down, and with a shade over it, is burning on the table. In the stove, the door of which stands open, there has been a fire, which is now nearly burnt out.*

(MRS. ELVSTED, *wrapped in a large shawl, and with her feet upon a foot-rest, sits close to the stove, sunk back in the arm-chair.* HEDDA, *fully dressed, lies sleeping upon the sofa, with a sofa-blanket over her.*)

MRS. ELVSTED (*after a pause, suddenly sits up in her chair, and listens eagerly. Then she sinks back again wearily, moaning to herself.*). Not yet!—Oh God—oh God—not yet!

(BERTA *slips in by the hall door. She has a letter in her hand.*)

MRS. ELVSTED (*turns and whispers eagerly*). Well—has anyone come?

BERTA (*softly*). Yes, a girl has brought this letter.

MRS. ELVSTED (*quickly, holding out her hand*). A letter! Give it to me!

BERTA. No, it's for Dr. Tesman, ma'am.

MRS. ELVSTED. Oh, indeed.

BERTA. It was Miss Tesman's servant that brought it. I'll lay it here on the table.

MRS. ELVSTED. Yes, do.

BERTA (*laying down the letter*). I think I had better put out the lamp. It's smoking.

MRS. ELVSTED. Yes, put it out. It must soon be daylight now.

BERTA (*putting out the lamp*). It is daylight already, ma'am.

MRS. ELVSTED. Yes, broad day! And no one come back yet——!

BERTA. Lord bless you, ma'am! I guessed how it would be.

MRS. ELVSTED. You guessed?

BERTA. Yes, when I saw that a certain person had come back to town—and that he went off with them. For we've heard enough about that gentleman before now.

MRS. ELVSTED. Don't speak so loud. You will waken Mrs. Tesman.

BERTA (*looks towards the sofa and sighs*). No, no—let her sleep, poor thing, Shan't I put some wood on the fire?

MRS. ELVSTED. Thanks, not for me.

BERTA. Oh, very well. (*She goes softly out by the hall door*)

HEDDA (*is awakened by the shutting of the door, and looks up*). What's that——?

MRS. ELVSTED. It was only the servant——

HEDDA (*looking about her*). Oh, we're here——! Yes now I remember. (*Sits erect upon the sofa, stretches herself, and rubs her eyes*) What o'clock is it, Thea?

MRS. ELVSTED (*looks at her watch*). It's past seven.

HEDDA. When did Tesman come home?

MRS. ELVSTED. He has not come.

HEDDA. Not come home yet?

MRS. ELVSTED (*rising*). No one has come.

HEDDA. Think of our watching and waiting here till four in the morning——

MRS. ELVSTED (*wringing her hands*). And how I watched and waited for him!

HEDDA (*yawns, and says with her hand before her mouth*). Well, well—we might have spared ourselves the trouble.

MRS. ELVSTED. Did you get a little sleep?

HEDDA. Oh yes; I believe I have slept pretty well. Have you not?

MRS. ELVSTED. Not for a moment. I couldn't, Hedda!—not to save my life.

HEDDA (*rises and goes towards her*). There, there, there! There's nothing to be so alarmed about. I understand quite well what has happened.

MRS. ELVSTED. Well, what do you think? Won't you tell me?

HEDDA. Why, of course it has been a very late affair at Judge Brack's——

MRS. ELVSTED. Yes, yes, that is clear enough. But all the same——

HEDDA. And then, you see, Tesman hasn't cared to come home and ring us up in the middle of the night. (*Laughing*) Perhaps he wasn't inclined to show himself either—immediately after a jollification.

MRS. ELVSTED. But in that case—where can he have gone?

HEDDA. Of course he has gone to his aunts' and slept there. They have his old room ready for him.

MRS. ELVSTED. No, he can't be with them; for a letter has just come for him from Miss Tesman. There it lies.

HEDDA. Indeed? (*Looks at the address*) Why yes, it's addressed in Aunt Julia's own hand. Well then, he has remained at Judge Brack's. And as for Eilert Lövborg—he is sitting, with vine-leaves in his hair, reading his manuscript.

MRS. ELVSTED. Oh Hedda, you are just saying things you don't believe a bit.

HEDDA. You really are a little blockhead, Thea.

MRS. ELVSTED. Oh yes, I suppose I am.

HEDDA. And how mortally tired you look.

MRS. ELVSTED. Yes, I am mortally tired.

HEDDA. Well then, you must do as I tell you. You must go into my room and lie down for a little while.

MRS. ELVSTED. Oh no, no—I shouldn't be able to sleep.

HEDDA. I am sure you would.

MRS. ELVSTED. Well, but your husband is certain to come soon now; and then I want to know at once——

HEDDA. I shall take care to let you know when he comes.

MRS. ELVSTED. Do you promise me, Hedda?

HEDDA. Yes, rely upon me. Just you go in and have a sleep in the meantime.

MRS. ELVSTED. Thanks; then I'll try to. (*She goes off through the inner room*)

(HEDDA *goes up to the glass door and draws back the curtains. The broad daylight streams into the room. Then she takes a little hand-glass from the writing-table, looks at herself in it, and arranges her hair. Next she goes to the hall door and presses the bell-button.*

BERTA *presently appears at the hall door.*)

BERTA. Did you want anything, ma'am?

HEDDA. Yes; you must put some more wood in the stove. I am shivering.

BERTA. Bless me—I'll make up the fire at once. (*She rakes the embers together and lays a piece of wood upon them; then stops and listens*) That was a ring at the front door, ma'am.

HEDDA. Then go to the door. I will look after the fire.

BERTA. It'll soon burn up. (*She goes out by the hall door*)

(HEDDA *kneels on the foot-rest and lays some more pieces of wood in the stove. After a short pause, GEORGE TESMAN enters from the hall. He looks tired and rather serious. He steals on tiptoe towards the middle doorway and is about to slip through the curtains.*)

HEDDA (*at the stove, without looking up*). Good morning.

TESMAN (*turns*). Hedda! (*Approaching her*) Good heavens—are you up so early? Eh?

HEDDA. Yes, I am up very early this morning.

TESMAN. And I never doubted you were still sound asleep! Fancy that, Hedda!

HEDDA. Don't speak so loud. Mrs. Elvsted is resting in my room.

TESMAN. Has Mrs. Elvsted been here all night?

HEDDA. Yes, since no one came to fetch her.

TESMAN. Ah, to be sure.

HEDDA (*closes the door of the stove and rises*). Well, did you enjoy yourself at Judge Brack's?

TESMAN. Have you been anxious about me? Eh?

HEDDA. No, I should never think of being anxious. But I asked if you had enjoyed yourself.

TESMAN. Oh yes,—for once in a way. Especially the beginning of the evening; for then Eilert read me part of his book. We arrived more than an hour too early—fancy that! And Brack had all sorts of arrangements to make— so Eilert read to me.

HEDDA (*seating herself by the table on the right*). Well? Tell me, then——

TESMAN (*sitting on a footstool near the stove*). Oh Hedda, you can't conceive what a book that is going to be! I believe it is one of the most remarkable things that have ever been written. Fancy that!

HEDDA. Yes, yes; I don't care about that——

TESMAN. I must make a confession to you, Hedda. When he had finished reading—a horrid feeling came over me.

HEDDA. A horrid feeling?

TESMAN. I felt jealous of Eilert for having had it in him to write such a book. Only think,

Hedda!

HEDDA. Yes, yes, I am thinking!

TESMAN. And then how pitiful to think that he—with all his gifts—should be irreclaimable after all.

HEDDA. I suppose you mean that he has more courage than the rest?

TESMAN. No, not at all—I mean that he is incapable of taking his pleasures in moderation.

HEDDA. And what came of it all—in the end?

TESMAN. Well, to tell the truth, I think it might best be described as an orgy, Hedda.

HEDDA. Had he vine-leaves in his hair?

TESMAN. Vine-leaves? No, I saw nothing of the sort. But he made a long, rambling speech in honor of the woman who had inspired him in his work—that was the phrase he used.

HEDDA. Did he name her?

TESMAN. No, he didn't; but I can't help thinking he meant Mrs. Elvsted. You may be sure he did.

HEDDA. Well—where did you part from him?

TESMAN. On the way to town. We broke up —the last of us at any rate—all together; and Brack came with us to get a breath of fresh air. And then, you see, we agreed to take Eilert home; for he had had far more than was good for him.

HEDDA. I daresay.

TESMAN. But now comes the strange part of it, Hedda; or, I should rather say, the melancholy part of it. I declare I am almost ashamed —on Eilert's account—to tell you——

HEDDA. Oh, go on——

TESMAN. Well, as we were getting near town, you see, I happened to drop a little behind the others. Only for a minute or two—fancy that!

HEDDA. Yes, yes, yes, but——?

TESMAN. And then, as I hurried after them —what do you think I found by the wayside? Eh?

HEDDA. Oh, how should I know!

TESMAN. You mustn't speak of it to a soul, Hedda! Do you hear! Promise me, for Eilert's sake. (*Draws a parcel, wrapped in paper, from his coat pocket*) Fancy, dear—I found this.

HEDDA. Is not that the parcel he had with him yesterday?

TESMAN. Yes, it is the whole of his precious, irreplaceable manuscript! And he had gone and lost it, and knew nothing about it. Only fancy, Hedda! So deplorably——

HEDDA. But why did you not give him back the parcel at once?

TESMAN. I didn't dare to—in the state he was then in——

HEDDA. Did you not tell any of the others that you had found it?

TESMAN. Oh, far from it. You can surely understand that, for Eilert's sake, I wouldn't do that.

HEDDA. So no one knows that Eilert Lövborg's manuscript is in your possession?

TESMAN. No. And no one must know it.

HEDDA. Then what did you say to him afterwards?

TESMAN. I didn't talk to him again at all; for when we got in among the streets, he and two or three of the others gave us the slip and disappeared. Fancy that!

HEDDA. Indeed! They must have taken him home then.

TESMAN. Yes, so it would appear. And Brack, too, left us.

HEDDA. And what have you been doing with yourself since?

TESMAN. Well, I and some of the others went home with one of the party, a jolly fellow, and took our morning coffee with him; or perhaps I should rather call it our night coffee—eh? But now, when I have rested a little, and given Eilert, poor fellow, time to have his sleep out, I must take this back to him.

HEDDA (*holds out her hand for the packet*). No—don't give it to him! Not in such a hurry, I mean. Let me read it first.

TESMAN. No, my dearest Hedda, I mustn't, I really mustn't.

HEDDA. You must not?

TESMAN. No—for you can imagine what a state of despair he will be in when he awakens and misses the manuscript. He has no copy of it, you know! He told me so.

HEDDA (*looking searchingly at him*). Can such a thing not be reproduced? Written over again?

TESMAN. No, I don't think that would be possible. For the inspiration, you see——

HEDDA. Yes, yes—I suppose it depends on that. (*Lightly*) But, by-the-bye—here is a letter for you.

TESMAN. Fancy——!

HEDDA (*handing it to him*). It came early this morning.

TESMAN. It's from Aunt Julia! What can it be? (*He lays the packet on the other footstool, opens the letter, runs his eye through it, and jumps up*) Oh, Hedda—she says that poor Aunt Rina is dying!

HEDDA. Well, we were prepared for that.

TESMAN. And that if I want to see her again, I must make haste. I'll run in to them at once.

HEDDA (*suppressing a smile*). Will you run?

TESMAN. Oh, dearest Hedda—if you could only make up your mind to come with me! Just think!

HEDDA (*rises and says wearily, repelling the idea*). No, no, don't ask me. I will not look upon sickness and death. I loathe all sorts of ugliness.

TESMAN. Well, well, then——! (*Bustling around*) My hat—My overcoat——? Oh, in the hall—I do hope I mayn't come too late, Hedda! Eh?

HEDDA. Oh, if you run——

BERTA. Judge Brack is at the door, and wishes to know if he may come in.

TESMAN. At this time! No, I can't possibly see him.

HEDDA. But I can. (*To* BERTA) Ask Judge Brack to come in. (BERTA *goes out*)

HEDDA (*quickly whispering*). The parcel, Tesman! (*She snatches it up from the stool*)

TESMAN. Yes, give it to me!

HEDDA. No, no, I will keep it till you come back.

(*She goes to the writing-table and places it in the bookcase.* TESMAN *stands in a flurry of haste, and cannot get his gloves on.*

JUDGE BRACK *enters from the hall.*)

HEDDA (*nodding to him*). You are an early bird, I must say.

BRACK. Yes, don't you think so? (*To* TESMAN) Are you on the move, too?

TESMAN. Yes, I must rush off to my aunts'. Fancy—the invalid one is lying at death's door, poor creature.

BRACK. Dear me, is she indeed? Then on no account let me detain you. At such a critical moment——

TESMAN. Yes, I must really rush—Good-bye! Good-bye! (*He hastens out by the hall door*)

HEDDA (*approaching*). You seem to have made a particularly lively night of it at your rooms, Judge Brack.

BRACK. I assure you I have not had my clothes off, Mrs. Hedda.

HEDDA. Not you, either?

BRACK. No, as you may see. But what has Tesman been telling you of the night's adventures?

HEDDA. Oh, some tiresome story. Only that they went and had coffee somewhere or other.

BRACK. I have heard about that coffee-party already. Eilert Lövborg was not with them, I fancy?

HEDDA. No, they had taken him home before that.

BRACK. Tesman, too?

HEDDA. No, but some of the others, he said.

BRACK (*smiling*). George Tesman is really an ingenuous creature, Mrs. Hedda.

HEDDA. Yes, heaven knows he is. Then is there something behind all this?

BRACK. Yes, perhaps there may be.

HEDDA. Well then, sit down, my dear Judge, and tell your story in comfort.

(*She seats herself to the left of the table.* BRACK *sits near her, at the long side of the table.*)

HEDDA. Now then?

BRACK. I had special reasons for keeping track of my guests—or rather of some of my guests—last night.

HEDDA. Of Eilert Lövborg among the rest, perhaps?

BRACK. Frankly, yes.

HEDDA. Now you make me really curious——

BRACK. Do you know where he and one or two of the others finished the night, Mrs. Hedda?

HEDDA. If it is not quite unmentionable, tell me.

BRACK. Oh no, it's not at all unmentionable. Well, they put in an appearance at a particularly animated soirée.

HEDDA. Of the lively kind?

BRACK. Of the very liveliest——

HEDDA. Tell me more of this, Judge Brack——

BRACK. Lövborg, as well as the others, had

been invited in advance. I knew all about it. But he had declined the invitation; for now, as you know, he has become a new man.

HEDDA. Up at the Elvsteds', yes. But he went after all, then?

BRACK. Well, you see, Mrs. Hedda—unhappily the spirit moved him at my rooms last evening——

HEDDA. Yes, I hear he found inspiration.

BRACK. Pretty violent inspiration. Well, I fancy that altered his purpose; for we men folk are unfortunately not always so firm in our principles as we ought to be.

HEDDA. Oh, I am sure you are an exception, Judge Brack. But as to Lövborg——?

BRACK. To make a long story short—he landed at last in Mademoiselle Diana's rooms.

HEDDA. Mademoiselle Diana's?

BRACK. It was Mademoiselle Diana that 'was giving the soirée, to a select circle of her admirers and her lady friends.

HEDDA. Is she a red-haired woman?

BRACK. Precisely.

HEDDA. A sort of a—singer?

BRACK. Oh yes—in her leisure moments. And moreover a mighty huntress—of men—Mrs. Hedda. You have no doubt heard of her. Eilert Lövborg was one of her most enthusiastic protectors—in the days of his glory.

HEDDA. And how did all this end?

BRACK. Far from amicably, it appears. After a most tender meeting, they seem to have come to blows——

HEDDA. Lövborg and she?

BRACK. Yes. He accused her or her friends of having robbed him. He declared that his pocket-book had disappeared—and other things as well. In short, he seems to have made a furious disturbance.

HEDDA. And what came of it all?

BRACK. It came to a general scrimmage, in which the ladies as well as the gentlemen took part. Fortunately the police at last appeared on the scene.

HEDDA. The police too?

BRACK. Yes. I fancy it will prove a costly frolic for Eilert Lövborg, crazy being that he is.

HEDDA. How so?

BRACK. He seems to have made a violent resistance—to have hit one of the constables on the head and torn the coat off his back. So they had to march him off to the police station with the rest.

HEDDA. How have you learnt all this?

BRACK. From the police themselves.

HEDDA (gazing straight before her). So that is what happened. Then he had no vine-leaves in his hair.

BRACK. Vine-leaves, Mrs. Hedda?

HEDDA (changing her tone). But tell me now, Judge—what is your real reason for tracking out Eilert Lövborg's movements so carefully?

BRACK. In the first place, it could not be entirely indifferent to me if it should appear in the police-court that he came straight from my house.

HEDDA. Will the matter come into court, then?

BRACK. Of course. However, I should scarcely have troubled so much about that. But I thought that, as a friend of the family, it was my duty to supply you and Tesman with a full account of his nocturnal exploits.

HEDDA. Why so, Judge Brack?

BRACK. Why, because I have a shrewd suspicion that he intends to use you as a sort of blind.

HEDDA. Oh, how can you think such a thing!

BRACK. Good heavens, Mrs. Hedda—we have eyes in our head. Mark my words! This Mrs. Elvsted will be in no hurry to leave town again.

HEDDA. Well, even if there should be anything between them, I suppose there are plenty of other places where they could meet.

BRACK. Not a single home. Henceforth, as before, every respectable house will be closed against Eilert Lövborg.

HEDDA. And so ought mine to be, you mean?

BRACK. Yes. I confess it would be more than painful to me if this personage were to be made free of your house. How superfluous, how intrusive, he would be, if he were to force his way into——

HEDDA. ——into the triangle?

BRACK. Precisely. It would simply mean that I should find myself homeless.

HEDDA (looks at him with a smile). So you want to be the one cock in the basket—that is your aim.

BRACK (nods slowly and lowers his voice). Yes, that is my aim. And for that I will fight—with every weapon I can command.

HEDDA (her smile vanishing). I see you are a dangerous person—when it comes to the point.

BRACK. Do you thing so?

HEDDA. I am beginning to think so. And I am exceedingly glad to think—that you have no sort of hold over me.

BRACK (laughing equivocally). Well, well, Mrs. Hedda—perhaps you are right there. If I had, who knows what I might be capable of?

HEDDA. Come, come now, Judge Brack. That sound almost like a threat.

BRACK (rising). Oh, not at all! The triangle, you know, ought, if possible, to be spontaneously constructed.

HEDDA. There I agree with you.

BRACK. Well, now I have said all I had to say; and I had better be getting back to town. Goodbye, Mrs. Hedda. (He goes towards the glass door)

HEDDA (rising). Are you going through the garden?

BRACK. Yes, it's a short cut for me.

HEDDA. And then it is the back way, too.

BRACK. Quite so. I have no objection to back ways. They may be piquant enough at times.

HEDDA. When there is ball practice going on, you mean?

BRACK (in the doorway, laughing to her). Oh, people don't shoot their tame poultry, I fancy.

HEDDA (also laughing). Oh no, when there is only one cock in the basket——

(They exchange laughing nods of farewell. He goes. She closes the door behind him. HEDDA, who has become quite serious, stands for a moment looking out. Presently she goes and peeps through the curtain over the middle doorway. Then she goes to the writing-table, takes Löv-BORG's packet out of the bookcase, and is on the point of looking through its contents. BERTA is heard speaking loudly in the hall. HEDDA turns and listens. Then she hastily locks up the packet in the drawer, and lays the key on the inkstand.

EILERT LÖVBORG, with his great coat on

and his hat in his hand, tears open the hall door. He looks somewhat confused and irritated.)

LÖVBORG (looking towards the hall). And I tell you I must and will come in! There!

(He closes the door, turns and sees HEDDA, at once regains his self-control, and bows)

HEDDA (at the writing table). Well, Mr. Löv-borg, this is rather a late hour to call for Thea.

LÖVBORG. You mean rather an early hour to call on you. Pray pardon me.

HEDDA. How do you know that she is still here?

LÖVBORG. They told me at her lodgings that she had been out all night.

HEDDA (going to the oval table). Did you notice anything about the people of the house when they said that?

LÖVBORG (looks inquiringly at her). Notice anything about them?

HEDDA. I mean, did they seem to think it odd?

LÖVBORG (suddenly understanding). Oh yes, of course! I am dragging her down with me! However, I didn't notice anything.—I suppose Tesman is not up yet?

HEDDA. No—I think not——

LÖVBORG. When did he come home?

HEDDA. Very late.

LÖVBORG. Did he tell you anything?

HEDDA. Yes, I gathered that you had had an exceedingly jolly evening at Judge Brack's.

LÖVBORG. Nothing more?

HEDDA. I don't think so. However, I was so dreadfully sleepy——

(MRS. ELVSTED enters through the curtains of the middle doorway)

MRS. ELVSTED (going towards him). Ah, Löv-borg! At last——!

LÖVBORG. Yes, at last. And too late!

MRS. ELVSTED (looks anxiously at him). What is too late?

LÖVBORG. Everything is too late now. It is all over with me.

MRS. ELVSTED. Oh no, no—don't say that.

LÖVBORG. You will say the same when you hear——

MRS. ELVSTED. I won't hear anything!

HEDDA. Perhaps you would prefer to talk to her alone! If so, I will leave you.

LÖVBORG. No, stay—you too. I beg you to stay.

MRS. ELVSTED. Yes, but I won't hear anything, I tell you.

LÖVBORG. It is not last night's adventures that I want to talk about.

MRS. ELVSTED. What is it then——?

LÖVBORG. I want to say that now our ways must part.

MRS. ELVSTED. Part!

HEDDA (*involuntarily*). I knew it!

LÖVBORG. You can be of no more service to me, Thea.

MRS. ELVSTED. How can you stand there and say that! No more service to you! Am I not to help you now, as before? Are we not to go on working together?

LÖVBORG. Henceforward I shall do no work.

MRS. ELVSTED (*despairingly*). Then what am I to do with my life?

LÖVBORG. You must try to live your life as if you had never known me.

MRS. ELVSTED. But you know I cannot do that!

LÖVBORG. Try if you cannot, Thea. You must go home again——

MRS. ELVSTED (*in vehement protest*). Never in this world! Where you are, there will I be also! I will not let myself be driven away like this! I will remain here! I will be with you when the book appears.

HEDDA (*half aloud, in suspense*). Ah yes—the book!

LÖVBORG (*looks at her*). My book and Thea's; for that is what it is.

MRS. ELVSTED. Yes, I feel that it is. And that is why I have a right to be with you when it appears! I will see with my own eyes how respect and honor pour in upon you afresh. And the happiness—the happiness—oh, I must share it with you!

LÖVBORG. Thea—our book will never appear.

HEDDA. Ah!

MRS. ELVSTED. Never appear!

LÖVBORG. Can never appear.

MRS. ELVSTED (*in agonized foreboding*). Lövborg—what have you done with the manuscript?

HEDDA (*looks anxiously at him*). Yes, the manuscript——?

MRS. ELVSTED. Where is it?

LÖVBORG. Oh Thea—don't ask me about it!

MRS. ELVSTED. Yes, yes, I will know. I demand to be told at once.

LÖVBORG. The manuscript— Well then—I have torn the manuscript into a thousand pieces.

MRS. ELVSTED (*shrieks*). Oh no, no——!

HEDDA (*involuntarily*). But that's not——

LÖVBORG (*looks at her*). Not true, you think?

HEDDA (*collecting herself*). Oh well, of course —since you say so. But it sounded so improbable——

LÖVBORG. It is true, all the same.

MRS. ELVSTED (*wringing her hands*). Oh God —oh God, Hedda—torn his own work to pieces!

LÖVBORG. I have torn my own life to pieces. So why should I not tear my life-work too——?

MRS. ELVSTED. And you did this last night?

LÖVBORG. Yes, I tell you! Tore it into a thousand pieces and scattered them on the fiord— far out. There there is cool sea-water at any rate —let them drift upon it—drift with the current and the wind. And then presently they will sink —deeper and deeper—as I shall, Thea.

MRS. ELVSTED. Do you know, Lövborg, that what you have done with the book—I shall think of it to my dying day as though you had killed a little child.

LÖVBORG. Yes, you are right. It is a sort of child-murder.

MRS. ELVSTED. How could you, then——! Did not the child belong to me too?

HEDDA (*almost inaudibly*). Ah, the child——

MRS. ELVSTED (*breathing heavily*). It is all over then. Well, well, now I will go, Hedda.

HEDDA. But you are not going away from town?

MRS. ELVSTED. Oh, I don't know what I shall do. I see nothing but darkness before me. (*She goes out by the hall door*)

HEDDA (*stands waiting for a moment*). So you are not going to see her home, Mr. Lövborg?

LÖVBORG. I? Through the streets? Would you have people see her walking with me?

HEDDA. Of course I don't know what else may have happened last night. But is it so utterly irretrievable?

LÖVBORG. It will not end with last night—I know that perfectly well. And the thing is that now I have no taste for that sort of life either. I won't begin it anew. She has broken my courage and my power of braving life out.

HEDDA (*looking straight before her*). So that

pretty little fool has had her fingers in a man's destiny. (*Looks at him*) But all the same, how could you treat her so heartlessly?

LÖVBORG. Oh, don't say that it was heartless!

HEDDA. To go and destroy what has filled her whole soul for months and years! You do not call that heartless!

LÖVBORG. To you I can tell the truth, Hedda.

HEDDA. The truth?

LÖVBORG. First promise me—give me your word—that what I now confide to you Thea shall never know.

HEDDA. I give you my word.

LÖVBORG. Good. Then let me tell you that what I said just now was untrue.

HEDDA. About the manuscript?

LÖVBORG. Yes. I have not torn it to pieces—nor thrown it into the fiord.

HEDDA. No, n— But—where is it then?

LÖVBORG. I have destroyed it none the less—utterly destroyed it, Hedda!

HEDDA. I don't understand.

LÖVBORG. Thea said that what I had done seemed to her like a child-murder.

HEDDA. Yes, so she said.

LÖVBORG. But to kill his child—that is not the worst thing a father can do to it.

HEDDA. Not the worst?

LÖVBORG. No. I wanted to spare Thea from hearing the worst.

HEDDA. Then what is the worst?

LÖVBORG. Suppose now, Hedda, that a man—in the small hours of the morning—came home to his child's mother after a night of riot and debauchery, and said: "Listen—I have been here and there—in this place and in that. And I have taken our child with me—to this place and to that. And I have lost the child—utterly lost it. The devil knows into what hands it may have fallen—who may have had their clutches on it."

HEDDA. Well—but when all is said and done, you know—that was only a book——

LÖVBORG. Thea's pure soul was in that book.

HEDDA. Yes, so I understand.

LÖVBORG. And you can understand, too, that for her and me together no future is possible.

HEDDA. What path do you mean to take then?

LÖVBORG. None. I will only try to make an end of it all—the sooner the better.

HEDDA (*a step nearer to him*). Eilert Lövborg—listen to me. Will you not try to—to do it beautifully?

LÖVBORG. Beautifully? (*Smiling*) With vine-leaves in my hair, as you used to dream in the old days——?

HEDDA. No, no. I have lost my faith in the vine-leaves. But beautifully, nevertheless! For once in a way!—Good-bye! You must go now—and do not come here any more.

LÖVBORG. Good-bye, Mrs. Tesman. And give George Tesman my love. (*He is on the point of going*)

HEDDA. No, wait! I must give you a memento to take with you.

(*She goes to the writing-table and opens the drawer and the pistol-case; then returns to* LÖVBORG *with one of the pistols*)

LÖVBORG (*looks at her*). This? Is this the memento?

HEDDA (*nodding slowly*). Do you recognize it? It was aimed at you once.

LÖVBORG. You should have used it then.

HEDDA. Take it—and do you use it now.

LÖVBORG (*puts the pistol in his breast pocket*). Thanks!

HEDDA. And beautifully, Eilert Lövborg. Promise me that!

LÖVBORG. Good-bye, Hedda Gabler. (*He goes out by the hall door*)

(HEDDA *listens for a moment at the door. Then she goes up to the writing-table, takes out the packet of manuscript, peeps under the cover, draws a few of the sheets half out, and looks at them. Next she goes over and seats herself in the armchair beside the stove, with the packet in her lap. Presently she opens the stove door, and then the packet.*)

HEDDA (*throws one of the quires into the fire and whispers to herself*). Now I am burning your child, Thea!—Burning it, curly-locks! (*Throwing one or two more quires into the stove*) Your child and Eilert Lövborg's. (*Throws the rest in*) I am burning—I am burning your child.

Act IV

SCENE: The same rooms at the TESMANS'. *It is evening. The drawing-room is in darkness. The back room is lighted by the hanging lamp over the table. The curtains over the glass door are drawn close.*

(HEDDA, *dressed in black, walks to and fro in the dark room. Then she goes into the back room and disappears for a moment to the left. She is heard to strike a few chords on the piano. Presently she comes in sight again, and returns to the drawing-room.*

BERTA *enters from the right, through the inner room, with a lighted lamp, which she places on the table in front of the corner settee in the drawing-room. Her eyes are red with weeping, and she has black ribbons in her cap. She goes quietly and circumspectly out to the right.*

HEDDA *goes up to the glass door, lifts the curtain a little aside, and looks out into the darkness.*

Shortly afterwards, MISS TESMAN, *in mourning, with a bonnet and veil on, comes in from the hall.* HEDDA *goes towards her and holds out her hand.*)

MISS TESMAN. Yes, Hedda, here I am, in mourning and forlorn; for now my poor sister has at last found peace.

HEDDA. I have heard the news already, as you see. Tesman sent me a card.

MISS TESMAN. Yes, he promised me he would. But nevertheless I thought that to Hedda—here in the house of life—I ought myself to bring the tidings of death.

HEDDA. That was very kind of you.

MISS TESMAN. Ah, Rina ought not to have left us just now. This is not the time for Hedda's house to be a house of mourning.

HEDDA (*changing the subject*). She died quite peacefully, did she not, Miss Tesman?

MISS TESMAN. Oh, her end was so calm, so beautiful. And then she had the unspeakable happiness of seeing George once more—and bidding him good-bye.—Has he come home yet?

HEDDA. No. He wrote that he might be detained. But won't you sit down?

MISS TESMAN. No thank you, my dear, dear Hedda. I should like to, but I have so much to do. I must prepare my dear one for her rest as well as I can. She shall go to her grave looking her best.

HEDDA. Can I not help you in any way?

MISS TESMAN. Oh, you must not think of it! Hedda Tesman must have no hand in such mournful work. Nor let her thoughts dwell on it either—not at this time.

HEDDA. One is not always mistress of one's thoughts——

MISS TESMAN (*continuing*). Ah yes, it is the way of the world. At home we shall be sewing a shroud; and here there will soon be sewing too, I suppose—but of another sort, thank God!

(GEORGE TESMAN *enters by the hall door*)

HEDDA. Ah, you have come at last!

TESMAN. You here, Aunt Julia? With Hedda? Fancy that!

MISS TESMAN. I was just going, my dear boy. Well, have you done all you promised?

TESMAN. No; I'm really afraid I have forgotten half of it. I must come to you again tomorrow. Today my brain is all in a whirl. I can't keep my thoughts together.

MISS TESMAN. Why, my dear George, you mustn't take it in this way.

TESMAN. Mustn't——? How do you mean?

MISS TESMAN. Even in your sorrow you must rejoice, as I do—rejoice that she is at rest.

TESMAN. Oh yes, yes—you are thinking of Aunt Rina.

HEDDA. You will feel lonely now, Miss Tesman.

MISS TESMAN. Just at first, yes. But that will not last very long, I hope. I daresay I shall soon find an occupant for poor Rina's little room.

TESMAN. Indeed? Who do you think will take it? Eh?

MISS TESMAN. Oh, there's always some poor invalid or other in want of nursing, unfortunately.

HEDDA. Would you really take such a burden upon you again?

MISS TESMAN. A burden! Heaven forgive you, child—it has been no burden to me.

HEDDA. But suppose you had a total stranger on your hands——

MISS TESMAN. Oh, one soon makes friends with sick folk; and it's such an absolute necessity for me to have some one to live for. Well, heaven be praised, there may soon be something in this house, too, to keep an old aunt busy.

HEDDA. Oh, don't trouble about anything here.

TESMAN. Yes, just fancy what a nice time we three might have together, if——?

HEDDA. If——?

TESMAN (*uneasily*). Oh, nothing. It will all come right. Let us hope so—eh?

MISS TESMAN. Well, well, I daresay you two want to talk to each other. (*Smiling*) And perhaps Hedda may have something to tell you too, George. Good-bye! I must go home to Rina. (*Turning at the door*) How strange it is to think that now Rina is with me and with my poor brother as well!

TESMAN. Yes, fancy that, Aunt Julia! Eh?

(MISS TESMAN *goes out by the hall door*)

HEDDA (*follows* TESMAN *coldly and searchingly with her eyes*). I almost believe your Aunt Rina's death affects you more than it does your Aunt Julia.

TESMAN. Oh, it's not that alone. It's Eilert I am so terribly uneasy about.

HEDDA (*quickly*). Is there anything new about him?

TESMAN. I looked in at his rooms this afternoon, intending to tell him the manuscript was in safe keeping.

HEDDA. Well, did you not find him?

TESMAN. No. He wasn't at home. But afterwards I met Mrs. Elvsted, and she told me that he had been here early this morning.

HEDDA. Yes, directly after you had gone.

TESMAN. And he said that he had torn his manuscript to pieces—eh?

HEDDA. Yes, so he declared.

TESMAN. Why, good heavens, he must have been completely out of his mind! And I suppose you thought it best not to give it back to him, Hedda?

HEDDA. No, he did not get it.

TESMAN. But of course you told him that we had it?

HEDDA. No. (*Quickly*) Did you tell Mrs. Elvsted?

TESMAN. No; I thought I had better not. But you ought to have told him. Fancy, if, in

desperation, he should go and do himself some injury! Let me have the manuscript, Hedda! I will take it to him at once. Where is it?

HEDDA (*cold and immovable, leaning on the armchair*). I have not got it.

TESMAN. Have not got it? What in the world do you mean?

HEDDA. I have burnt it—every line of it.

TESMAN (*with a violent movement of terror*). Burnt! Burnt Eilert's manuscript!

HEDDA. Don't scream so. The servant might hear you.

TESMAN. Burnt! Why, good God——! No, no, no! It's impossible!

HEDDA. It is so, nevertheless.

TESMAN. Do you know what you have done, Hedda? It's unlawful appropriation of lost property. Fancy that! Just ask Judge Brack, and he'll tell you what it is.

HEDDA. I advise you not to speak of it—either to Judge Brack, or to any one else.

TESMAN. But how could you do anything so unheard-of? What put it into your head? What possessed you? Answer me that—eh?

HEDDA (*suppressing an almost imperceptible smile*). I did it for your sake, George.

TESMAN. For my sake!

HEDDA. This morning, when you told me about what he had read to you——

TESMAN. Yes, yes—what then?

HEDDA. You acknowledged that you envied him his work.

TESMAN. Oh, of course I didn't mean that literally.

HEDDA. No matter—I could not bear the idea that any one should throw you into the shade.

TESMAN (*in an outburst of mingled doubt and joy*). Hedda! Oh, is this true? But—but— I never knew you to show your love like that before. Fancy that!

HEDDA. Well, I may as well tell you that— just at this time—— (*Impatiently, breaking off*) No, no; you can ask Aunt Julia. She will tell you, fast enough.

TESMAN. Oh, I almost think I understand you, Hedda! (*Clasps his hands together*) Great heavens! do you really mean it! Eh?

HEDDA. Don't shout so. The servant might hear.

TESMAN (*laughing in irrepressible glee*). The

servant! Why, how absurd you are, Hedda. It's only my old Berta! Why, I'll tell Berta myself.

HEDDA (*clenching her hands together in desperation*). Oh, it is killing me,—it is killing me, all this!

TESMAN. What is, Hedda? Eh?

HEDDA (*coldly, controlling herself*). All this—absurdity—George.

TESMAN. Absurdity! Do you see anything absurd in my being overjoyed at the news! But after all perhaps I had better not say anything to Berta.

HEDDA. Oh—why not that too?

TESMAN. No, no, not yet! But I must certainly tell Aunt Julia. And then that you have begun to call me George too! Fancy that! Oh, Aunt Julia will be so happy—so happy.

HEDDA. When she hears that I have burnt Eilert Lövborg's manuscript—for your sake?

TESMAN. No, by-the-bye—that affair of the manuscript—of course nobody must know about that. But that you love me so much, Hedda—Aunt Julia must really share my joy in that! I wonder, now, whether this sort of thing is usual in young wives? Eh?

HEDDA. I think you had better ask Aunt Julia that question too.

TESMAN. I will indeed, some time or other. (*Looks uneasy and downcast again*) And yet the manuscript—the manuscript! Good God! it is terrible to think what will become of poor Eilert now.

(MRS. ELVSTED, *dressed as in the first act, with hat and cloak, enters by the hall door*)

MRS. ELVSTED (*greets them hurriedly, and says in evident agitation*). Oh, dear Hedda, forgive my coming again.

HEDDA. What is the matter with you, Thea?

TESMAN. Something about Eilert Lövborg again—eh?

MRS. ELVSTED. Yes! I am dreadfully afraid some misfortune has happened to him.

HEDDA (*seizes her arm*). Ah,—do you think so?

TESMAN. Why, good Lord—what makes you think that, Mrs. Elvsted?

MRS. ELVSTED. I heard them talking of him at my boarding-house—just as I came in. Oh, the most incredible rumors are afloat about him to-day.

TESMAN. Yes, fancy, so I heard too! And I can bear witness that he went straight home to bed last night. Fancy that!

HEDDA. Well, what did they say at the boarding-house?

MRS. ELVSTED. Oh, I couldn't make out anything clearly. Either they knew nothing definite, or else—— They stopped talking when they saw me; and I did not dare to ask.

TESMAN (*moving about uneasily*). We must hope—we must hope that you misunderstood them, Mrs. Elvsted.

MRS. ELVSTED. No, no; I am sure it was of him they were talking. And I heard something about the hospital or——

TESMAN. The hospital?

HEDDA. No—surely that cannot be!

MRS. ELVSTED. Oh, I was in such mortal terror! I went to his lodgings and asked for him there.

HEDDA. You could make up your mind to that, Thea!

MRS. ELVSTED. What else could I do? I really could bear the suspense no longer.

TESMAN. But you didn't find him either—eh?

MRS. ELVSTED. No. And the people knew nothing about him. He hadn't been home since yesterday afternoon, they said.

TESMAN. Yesterday! Fancy, how could they say that?

MRS. ELVSTED. Oh, I am sure something terrible must have happened to him.

TESMAN. Hedda dear—how would it be if I were to go and make inquiries——?

HEDDA. No, no—don't you mix yourself up in this affair.

(JUDGE BRACK, *with his hat in his hand, enters by the hall door, which* BERTA *opens, and closes behind him. He looks grave and bows in silence.*)

TESMAN. Oh, is that you, my dear Judge? Eh?

BRACK. Yes. It was imperative I should see you this evening.

TESMAN. I can see you have heard the news about Aunt Rina.

BRACK. Yes, that among other things.

TESMAN. Isn't it sad—eh?

BRACK. Well, my dear Tesman, that depends on how you look at it.

TESMAN (*looks doubtfully at him*). Has anything else happened?

BRACK. Yes.

HEDDA (*in suspense*). Anything sad, Judge Brack?

BRACK. That, too, depends on how you look at it, Mrs. Tesman.

MRS. ELVSTED (*unable to restrain her anxiety*). Oh! it is something about Eilert Lövborg!

BRACK (*with a glance at her*). What makes you thing that, Madam? Perhaps you have already heard something——?

MRS. ELVSTED (*in confusion*). No, nothing at all, but——

TESMAN. Oh, for heaven's sake, tell us!

BRACK (*shrugging his shoulders*). Well, I regret to say Eilert Lövborg has been taken to the hospital. He is lying at the point of death.

MRS. ELVSTED (*shrieks*). Oh God! Oh God——

TESMAN. To the hospital! And at the point of death.

HEDDA (*involuntarily*). So soon then——

MRS. ELVSTED (*wailing*). And we parted in anger, Hedda!

HEDDA (*whispers*). Thea—Thea—be careful!

MRS. ELVSTED (*not heeding her*). I must go to him! I must see him alive!

BRACK. It is useless, Madam. No one will be admitted.

MRS. ELVSTED. Oh, at least tell me what has happened to him? What is it?

TESMAN. You don't mean to say that he has himself—— Eh?

HEDDA. Yes, I am sure he has.

TESMAN. Hedda, how can you——?

BRACK (*keeping his eyes fixed upon her*). Unfortunately you have guessed quite correctly, Mrs. Tesman.

MRS. ELVSTED. Oh, how horrible!

TESMAN. Himself, then! Fancy that!

HEDDA. Shot himself!

BRACK. Rightly guessed again, Mrs. Tesman.

MRS. ELVSTED (*with an effort at self-control*). When did it happen, Mr. Brack?

BRACK. This afternoon—between three and four.

TESMAN. But, good Lord, where did he do it? Eh?

BRACK (*with some hesitation*). Where? Well —I suppose at his lodgings.

MRS. ELVSTED. No, that cannot be; for I was there between six and seven.

BRACK. Well, then, somewhere else. I don't know exactly. I only know that he was found——. He had shot himself—in the breast.

MRS. ELVSTED. Oh, how terrible! That he should die like that!

HEDDA (*to* BRACK). Was it in the breast?

BRACK. Yes—as I told you.

HEDDA. Not in the temple?

BRACK. In the breast, Mrs. Tesman.

HEDDA. Well, well—the breast is a good place, too.

BRACK. How do you mean, Mrs. Tesman?

HEDDA (*evasively*). Oh, nothing—nothing.

TESMAN. And the wound is dangerous, you say—eh?

BRACK. Absolutely mortal. The end has probably come by this time.

MRS. ELVSTED. Yes, yes, I feel it. The end! The end! Oh, Hedda——!

TESMAN. But tell me, how have you learnt all this?

BRACK (*curtly*). Through one of the police. A man I had some business with.

HEDDA (*in a clear voice*). At last a deed worth doing!

TESMAN (*terrified*). Good heavens, Hedda; what are you saying?

HEDDA. I say there is beauty in this.

BRACK. H'm, Mrs. Tesman——

TESMAN. Beauty! Fancy that!

MRS. ELVSTED. Oh, Hedda, how can you talk of beauty in such an act!

HEDDA. Eilert Lövborg has himself made up his account with life. He has had the courage to do—the one right thing.

MRS. ELVSTED. No, you must never think that was how it happened! It must have been in delirium that he did it.

TESMAN. In despair!

HEDDA. That he did not. I am certain of that.

MRS. ELVSTED. Yes, yes! In delirium! Just as when he tore up our manuscript.

BRACK (*starting*). The manuscript? Has he torn that up?

MRS. ELVSTED. Yes, last night.

TESMAN (*whispers softly*). Oh, Hedda, we shall never get over this.

BRACK. H'm, very extraordinary.

TESMAN (*moving about the room*). To think

of Eilert going out of the world in this way! And not leaving behind him the book that would have immortalized his name——

MRS. ELVSTED. Oh, if only it could be put together again!

TESMAN. Yes, if it only could! I don't know what I would not give——

MRS. ELVSTED. Perhaps it can, Mr. Tesman.

TESMAN. What do you mean?

MRS. ELVSTED (searches in the pocket of her dress). Look here. I have kept all the loose notes he used to dictate from.

HEDDA (a step forward). Ah——!

TESMAN. You have kept them, Mrs. Elvsted! Eh?

MRS. ELVSTED. Yes, I have them here. I put them in my pocket when I left home. Here they still are——

TESMAN. Oh, do let me see them!

MRS. ELVSTED (hands him a bundle of papers). But they are in such disorder—all mixed up.

TESMAN. Fancy, if we could make something out of them, after all! Perhaps if we two put our heads together——

MRS. ELVSTED. Oh, yes, at least let us try——

TESMAN. We will manage it! We must! I will dedicate my life to this task.

HEDDA. You, George! Your life?

TESMAN. Yes, or rather all the time I can spare. My own collections must wait in the meantime. Hedda—you understand, eh? I owe this to Eilert's memory.

HEDDA. Perhaps.

TESMAN. And so, my dear Mrs. Elvsted, we will give our whole minds to it. There is no use in brooding over what can't be undone—eh? We must try to control our grief as much as possible, and——

MRS. ELVSTED. Yes, yes, Mr. Tesman, I will do the best I can.

TESMAN. Well then, come here. I can't rest until we have looked through the notes. Where shall we sit? Here? No, in there, in the back room. Excuse me, my dear Judge. Come with me, Mrs. Elvsted.

MRS. ELVSTED. Oh, if only it were possible!

(TESMAN and MRS. ELVSTED go into the back room. She takes off her hat and cloak. They both sit at the table under the hanging lamp, and are soon deep in an eager examination of the papers. HEDDA crosses to the stove and sits in the armchair. Presently BRACK goes up to her.)

HEDDA (in a low voice). Oh, what a sense of freedom it gives one, this act of Eilert Lövborg's.

BRACK. Freedom, Mrs. Hedda? Well, of course, it is a release for him——

HEDDA. I mean for me. It gives me a sense of freedom to know that a deed of deliberate courage is still possible in this world,—a deed of spontaneous beauty.

BRACK (smiling). H'm—my dear Mrs. Hedda——

HEDDA. Oh, I know what you are going to say. For you are a kind of a specialist too, like—you know!

BRACK (looking hard at her). Eilert Lövborg was more to you than perhaps you are willing to admit to yourself. Am I wrong?

HEDDA. I don't answer such questions. I only know Eilert Lövborg has had the courage to live his life after his own fashion. And then—the last great act, with its beauty! Ah! that he should have the will and the strength to turn away from the banquet of life—so early.

BRACK. I am sorry, Mrs. Hedda,—but I fear I must dispel an amiable illusion.

HEDDA. Illusion.

BRACK. Which could not have lasted long in any case.

HEDDA. What do you mean?

BRACK. Eilert Lövborg did not shoot himself voluntarily.

HEDDA. Not voluntarily?

BRACK. No. The thing did not happen exactly as I told it.

HEDDA (in suspense). Have you concealed something? What is it?

BRACK. For poor Mrs. Elvsted's sake I idealized the facts a little.

HEDDA. What are the facts?

BRACK. First, that he is already dead.

HEDDA. At the hospital?

BRACK. Yes—without regaining consciousness.

HEDDA. What more have you concealed?

BRACK. This—the event did not happen at his lodgings.

HEDDA. Oh, that can make no difference.

BRACK. Perhaps it may. For I must tell you— Eilert Lövborg was found shot in—in Mademoiselle Diana's boudoir.

HEDDA (*makes a motion as if to rise, but sinks back again*). That is impossible, Judge Brack! He cannot have been there again today.

BRACK. He was there this afternoon. He went there, he said, to demand the return of something which they had taken from him. Talked wildly about a lost child——

HEDDA. Ah—so that was why——

BRACK. I thought probably he meant his manuscript; but now I hear he destroyed that himself. So I suppose it must have been his pocketbook.

HEDDA. Yes, no doubt. And there—there he was found?

BRACK. Yes, there. With a pistol in his breast-pocket, discharged. The ball had lodged in a vital part.

HEDDA. In the breast—yes.

BRACK. No—in the bowels.

HEDDA (*looks up at him with an expression of loathing*). That too! Oh, what curse is it that makes everything I touch turn ludicrous and mean?

BRACK. There is one point more, Mrs. Hedda —another disagreeable feature in the affair.

HEDDA. And what is that?

BRACK. The pistol he carried——

HEDDA (*breathless*). Well? What of it?

BRACK. He must have stolen it.

HEDDA (*leaps up*). Stolen it! That is not true! He did not steal it!

BRACK. No other explanation is possible. He must have stolen it—— Hush!

(TESMAN *and* MRS. ELVSTED *have risen from the table in the back room, and come into the drawing room*)

TESMAN (*with the papers in both his hands*). Hedda dear, it is almost impossible to see under that lamp. Think of that!

HEDDA. Yes, I am thinking.

TESMAN. Would you mind our sitting at your writing-table—eh?

HEDDA. If you like. (*Quickly*) No, wait! Let me clear it first!

TESMAN. Oh, you needn't trouble, Hedda. There is plenty of room.

HEDDA. No, no; let me clear it, I say! I will take these things in and put them on the piano. There!

(*She has drawn out an object, covered with sheet music, from under the bookcase, places several other pieces of music upon it, and carries the whole into the inner room, to the left.* TESMAN *lays the scraps of paper on the writing-table, and moves the lamp there from the corner table.* HEDDA *returns.*)

HEDDA (*behind* MRS. ELVSTED'S *chair, gently ruffling her hair*). Well, my sweet Thea,—how goes it with Eilert Lövborg's monument?

MRS. ELVSTED (*looks dispiritedly up at her*). Oh, it will be terribly hard to put in order.

TESMAN. We must manage it. I am determined. And arranging other people's papers is just the work for me.

(HEDDA *goes over to the stove, and seats herself on one of the foot-stools.* BRACK *stands over her, leaning on the armchair.*)

HEDDA (*whispers*). What did you say about the pistol?

BRACK (*softly*). That he must have stolen it.

HEDDA. Why stolen it?

BRACK. Because every other explanation ought to be impossible, Mrs. Hedda.

HEDDA. Indeed?

BRACK (*glances at her*). Of course Eilert Lövborg was here this morning. Was he not?

HEDDA. Yes.

BRACK. Were you alone with him?

HEDDA. Part of the time.

BRACK. Did you not leave the room whilst he was here?

HEDDA. No.

BRACK. Try to recollect. Were you not out of the room a moment?

HEDDA. Yes, perhaps just a moment—out in the hall.

BRACK. And where was your pistol-case during that time?

HEDDA. I had it locked up in——

BRACK. Well, Mrs. Hedda?

HEDDA. The case stood there on the writing-table.

BRACK. Have you looked since, to see whether both the pistols are there?

HEDDA. No.

BRACK. Well, you need not. I saw the pistol found in Lövborg's pocket, and I knew it at once as the one I had seen yesterday—and before, too.

HEDDA. Have you it with you?

BRACK. No; the police have it.

HEDDA. What will the police do with it?

BRACK. Search till they find the owner.

HEDDA. Do you think they will succeed?

BRACK (*bends over her and whispers*). No, Hedda Gabler—not so long as I say nothing.

HEDDA (*looks frightened at him*). And if you do not say nothing,—what then?

BRACK (*shrugs his shoulders*). There is always the possibility that the pistol was stolen.

HEDDA (*firmly*). Death rather than that.

BRACK (*smiling*). People say such things—but they don't do them.

HEDDA (*without replying*). And supposing the pistol was stolen, and the owner is discovered? What then?

BRACK. Well, Hedda—then comes the scandal.

HEDDA. The scandal!

BRACK. Yes, the scandal—of which you are mortally afraid. You will, of course, be brought before the court—both you and Mademoiselle Diana. She will have to explain how the thing happened—whether it was an accidental shot or murder. Did the pistol go off as he was trying to take it out of his pocket, to threaten her with? Or did she tear the pistol out of his hand, shoot him, and push it back into his pocket? That would be quite like her; for she is an able-bodied young person, this same Mademoiselle Diana.

HEDDA. But *I* have nothing to do with all this repulsive business.

BRACK. No. But you will have to answer the question: Why did you give Eilert Lövborg the pistol? And what conclusions will people draw from the fact that you did give it to him?

HEDDA (*lets her head sink*). That is true. I did not think of that.

BRACK. Well, fortunately, there is no danger, so long as I say nothing.

HEDDA (*looks up at him*). So I am in your power, Judge Brack. You have me at your beck and call, from this time forward.

BRACK (*whispers softly*). Dearest Hedda—believe me—I shall not abuse my advantage.

HEDDA. I am in your power none the less. Subject to your will and your demands. A slave, a slave then! (*Rises impetuously*) No, I cannot endure the thought of that! Never!

BRACK (*looks half-mockingly at her*). People generally get used to the inevitable.

HEDDA (*returns his look*). Yes, perhaps. (*She crosses to the writing-table. Suppressing an involuntary smile, she imitates* TESMAN's *intonations.*) Well? Are you getting on, George? Eh?

TESMAN. Heaven knows, dear. In any case it will be the work of months.

HEDDA (*as before*). Fancy that! (*Passes her hands softly through* MRS. ELVSTED's *hair*) Doesn't it seem strange to you, Thea? Here are you sitting with Tesman—just as you used to sit with Eilert Lövborg?

MRS. ELVSTED. Ah, if I could only inspire your husband in the same way.

HEDDA. Oh, that will come too—in time.

TESMAN. Yes, do you know, Hedda—I really think I begin to feel something of the sort. But won't you go and sit with Brack again?

HEDDA. Is there nothing I can do to help you two?

TESMAN. No, nothing in the world. (*Turning his head*) I trust to you to keep Hedda company, my dear Brack.

BRACK (*with a glance at* HEDDA). With the very greatest of pleasure.

HEDDA. Thanks. But I am tired this evening. I will go in and lie down a little on the sofa.

TESMAN. Yes, do dear—eh?

(HEDDA *goes into the back room and draws the curtains. A short pause. Suddenly she is heard playing a wild dance on the piano.*)

MRS. ELVSTED (*starts from her chair*). Oh—what is that?

TESMAN (*runs to the doorway*). Why, my dearest Hedda—don't play dance music tonight! Just think of Aunt Rina! And of Eilert too!

HEDDA (*puts her head out between the curtains*). And of Aunt Julia. And of all the rest of them.—After this, I will be quiet. (*Closes the curtains again*)

TESMAN (*at the writing-table*). It's not good for her to see us at this distressing work. I'll tell you what, Mrs. Elvsted,—you shall take the empty room at Aunt Julia's, and then I will come over in the evenings, and we can sit and work there—eh?

HEDDA (*in the inner room*). I hear what you are saying, Tesman. But how am *I* to get through the evenings out here?

TESMAN (*turning over the papers*). Oh, I daresay Judge Brack will be so kind as to look in now and then, even though I am out.

BRACK (*in the armchair, calls out gaily*). Every blessed evening, with all the pleasure in life, Mrs. Tesman! We shall get on capitally together, we two!

HEDDA (*speaking loud and clear*). Yes, don't you flatter yourself we will, Judge Brack? Now that you are the one cock in the basket——

(*A shot is heard within. TESMAN, MRS. ELVSTED, and BRACK leap to their feet.*)

TESMAN. Oh, now she is playing with those pistols again.

(*He throws back the curtains and runs in, followed by MRS. ELVSTED. HEDDA lies stretched on the sofa, lifeless. Confusion and cries. BERTA enters in alarm from the right.*)

TESMAN (*shrieks to BRACK*). Shot herself! Shot herself in the temple! Fancy that!

BRACK (*half-fainting in the armchair*). Good God!—people don't do such things.

DISCUSSION

In the Introduction to Drama we have already discussed this play at some length. Our discussion there was primarily devoted to the method of dramatic organization and compression, though we did give some attention to the motivation of the characters. It remains now to speak further of the characters in their relations to each other and about the meaning of the play.

We may begin by considering Hedda herself. She is the main character and a consideration of what Ibsen would have us make of her may lead us to what he would have us make of the play. We already know about her pride and independence and her dissatisfaction with the dull life that seems to be closing around her. We can have some sympathy with her dissatisfaction. Tesman is an amiable dullard, an academic grubber without ideas, a cautious careerist. His attachment to Hedda seems to be primarily—or at least in part—vanity in her aristocratic background as a kind of mark of his own success: he would like to see her, his wife, the center of a "select" little circle. Ibsen has been careful to give us the full value of Tesman's conventionality of mind, his fussy "Eh's," his constantly reiterated fatuous bafflement in his "Fancy that now," his triviality of feeling. His knitted morning shoes, which he had so much missed all during the long honeymoon trip, sum up, at the very beginning of the play, the husband of Hedda. We shall come back to Tesman, but for the moment we are concerned with the general picture of the husband and the kind of life he will probably make for Hedda.

Hedda rebels at the thought of life with Tesman, and we can scarcely blame her. But on second thought we realize, remembering her talk with Judge Brack, that the situation is one of her own creating. She had danced herself tired, as she tells Judge Brack, had become bored with life, had found no man to excite her, and in full awareness of Tesman's qualities had married him, just because he wanted, as she puts it, to provide for her. Thus cynically and somewhat desperately she has made her bargain. But she does not keep it. She lacks sportsmanship and honor, the very virtues which we would assume to be the virtues of her aristocratic heritage.

Not that she is overtly unfaithful to Tesman. She is far too afraid of social pressures for that. For one thing, it is not virtue but conventionality of mind that makes her a faithful wife. In a sense she is just as conventional in mind and as trivial in feeling as her husband. We see, for example, how astonished and even envious she is that Thea, seemingly a much more timid creature than she, has been willing to make a bold decision and follow Lövborg. We know from Hedda's early relations with Lövborg that she had been drawn to him, partly at least, by her curiosity about his dissipations, a kind of dishonest curiosity, for she had wanted vicarious satisfactions from his wild life without the risks. And we know that when Judge Brack, in the end, intrudes himself as her prospective lover, he does so by a blackmail based on her fear of the conventions. He is clever enough to sense this fear in her character, and to guess that if anything would make her take the risk of an illicit affair with him it would be, ironically enough, the threat of scandal.

Yet Hedda, with all this timorousness and conventionality of mind, longs for some moment of noble and fulfilling freedom. She has thought of Lövborg as a person who, by his very dissipations, his willingness to throw away respectability and his career, might achieve freedom: the free pagan with vine leaves in his hair. But for Hedda, freedom means destruction, for she has found no positive value of any kind in life. She cannot conceive of Lövborg's redemption and his fulfillment through his work as an achievement of freedom. So she drives Lövborg to his ruin and to death to gratify her desire for freedom, to make him affirm by his death that at least a kind of freedom is possible.

But we may notice here that her attitude toward Lövborg's suicide as she drives him toward it is very much like her earlier attitude toward his dissipations: she would get a vicarious satisfaction out of his experience at no risk to herself. This vicarious satisfaction, however, fails her too. Instead of dying with a noble gesture, the pistol ball through his head or heart, Lövborg falls with a wound in the bowels, and not even with the dignity of suicide. The noble gesture that Hedda had planned—at somebody else's expense, of course—has, as she puts it, turned, "ludicrous and mean." Her faith in the possibility of significance in life is destroyed. We must emphasize the phrase "her faith," for we are not to equate her view with the dramatist's view. Her faith comes to nothing. Even her own suicide, though the ball is in her head, is scarcely a free act: she is driven to it by desperation, by the closing in of the world on her. Her faith comes to nothing, because her whole approach to the question of freedom and significance had been negative, merely destructive.

Thinking along this line, we can turn back to earlier elements in the play. For one thing, Ibsen's first presentation of Hedda describes her hair as "not particularly abundant." This at first may strike us as a peculiarly irrelevant detail, but its apparent irrelevance may point to a deeper relevance. Then we find Thea, who is played off as the opposite (the ordinary word is *foil*) of Hedda, given hair that is "unusually abundant and wavy." Later on we learn how back in school, Hedda had tortured the little Thea by pulling her hair, as though driven by an unconscious envy, and how she had threatened to burn it off her head. In Act II, in the episode with Hedda, Thea, and Lövborg, Hedda strokes Thea's hair (as she will do at the very end of the play as she goes into the next room to her own death). At the end of Act II, when Hedda has won the victory over Thea and sent Lövborg off to the party at Judge Brack's establishment, we find the following passage:

MRS. ELVSTED. You have some hidden motive in this, Hedda!
HEDDA. Yes, I have. I want for once in my life to have power to mold a human destiny.
MRS. ELVSTED. Have you not the power?
HEDDA. I have not—and have never had it.
MRS. ELVSTED. Not your husband's?
HEDDA. Do you think that is worth the trouble? Oh, if you could only understand how poor I am. And fate has made you so rich! (*Clasps her passionately in her arms*) I think I must burn your hair off, after all.

Here Hedda, in her first moment of triumph over Thea, cries out in envy of Thea, whom fate has made "rich." But rich in what sense? At first thought, it may seem that Hedda is saying that she herself is poor because she has only George Tesman while Thea has Lövborg. But at this moment Hedda has control of Lövborg, and if she were courageous enough, as courageous as Thea, might have him as a lover. But it is not merely the possession of Lövborg that is in question. It is the particular kind of relation to Lövborg. Hedda's relation is sterile, destructive. Thea's has been fruitful, creative. In this connection we remember that the book on which Thea had worked with Lövborg is called their "child," and that much is made of the fact. At the very end of Act III, when Hedda seems to have scored her greatest triumph, she has sent Lövborg out to shoot himself "beautifully," when he is, as it seems now, completely hers and Thea is vanquished, Hedda burns the manuscript:

HEDDA. Now I am burning your child, Thea!—Burning it, curly-locks! (*Throwing one or two more quires into the stove*) Your child and Eilert Lövborg's. (*Throws the rest in*) I am burning—I am burning your child.

The last mark of Hedda's moment of triumph is to destroy the "child," the sign of Thea's creative relation with Lövborg. But we see that here, too, Hedda comes back to the subject of Thea's hair, and we see how closely it is associated with the subject of Thea's creativity. So the hair has been used as a symbol for creativity, for fertility, the mark of the power that Thea has and Hedda lacks. Ibsen, of course, did not "make up" this symbol: woman's hair has, for thousands of years, had this symbolic significance, the mark of the fully and fruitfully feminine.

To return to Hedda, we may recall that in her first private conversation with Judge Brack, in Act II, she says that she does not want children: "no responsibilities for me!" Yet we are given to understand that she is pregnant, as she implies to her husband significantly in the same breath as she tells him that she has destroyed the manuscript, the "child" of Thea and Lövborg. So with this idea, another motive enters into Hedda's suicide. After she has found that Lövborg's beautiful gesture is nothing but a ludicrous and mean accident, she can find no significance in life. Her own unwanted burden of creativity is something she cannot bear, and in one sense her suicide is a flight from it.

We have said that Hedda, in her first appearance in the play, is described as having hair "not particularly abundant." She lacks, as it were, something of the specially feminine quality, and in the end, as we have seen, she refuses her natural feminine role as mother. Now, in a symbolic sense, we can bring General Gabler's pistols into the play. They are several things at once in their overtones of meaning. For one thing, they are reminders of Hedda's aristocratic background, a mark of her pride. For another, they imply the dangerous, destructive quality inherent in her. But for a third thing, the pistols carry some symbolic implication of masculinity. And in this connection we can see that three times in the play the pistols are used to indicate a relation between Hedda and a man. Tesman is afraid of them. Hedda fires at Judge Brack to make him jump, to scare him. She had once threatened Lövborg with a pistol, at the time when he was trying to pass from the role of comrade to that of lover. So all of this

implies that because of some unnatural masculine quality, some defect in femininity, in creativity, Hedda has rejected love. And if we take this line of reasoning, her suicide is also a rejection of Judge Brack. It is a declaration of her independence, a refusal to accept the role of the "molded" instead of the "molder," a desperate gesture to affirm significance—but all this does not prevent the act from being a last and characteristic rejection of love. It does not matter that Judge Brack's love is of a rather debasing and tawdry order; it is still a kind of love, and Hedda rejects it.

Over against Hedda, we have, as we have said, little Thea as a kind of foil. There are various conflicts in the play (between Judge Brack and Hedda, between Tesman and Hedda, between Lövborg and Tesman), but the main conflict is between Hedda and Thea for the possession of Lövborg. What is Thea like? We have already learned that she is "curly-locks," and in the first presentation of her we find the adjectives *fragile, pretty,* and *soft,* adjectives carrying implications of the feminine. With these qualities, with her feminine devotion, she has, to a degree, regenerated and gained possession of Lövborg. At least she has possession of him until he comes again into Hedda's orbit, where Hedda can play upon the old attraction between them and can challenge his manhood by taunting him about his cowardice in not going to the party and in being, in a way, under the thumb of Thea. But, as Lövborg says to Hedda, Thea is "stupid" about certain things, about the hidden significance, for instance, of the relation that had existed between Hedda and Lövborg and about the streak of desperation in Lövborg's character and his wild appetite for experience. She does not fully understand Lövborg, and therefore fails to regenerate or possess him fully.

Thea seems to be the very image of feminine devotion and self-abnegation, but is she quite that simple? Let us remember her own situation, an unloved wife, childless, on a lonely country estate. Lövborg brings to her the single possibility of fulfilment. It is not merely selfless devotion to him that spurs her to her act of courage; it is also her only chance for life. She says to Hedda: "I only know this, that I must live here, where Eilert Lövborg is—if I am to live at all." Then we must ask ourselves if Thea's desertion of Lövborg when he tells her that he has destroyed the manuscript is a mark of self-less love and devotion. Instead of taking his act as an indication of his desperate condition and realizing that now is his moment of greatest need for her, she says: "Do you know, Lövborg, that what you have done with the book—I shall think of it to my dying day as though you had killed a little child." And then, after his reply, she says: "How could you, then——! Did not the child belong to me too?" With that she leaves him. Here we have an element of resentment. However well justified it may be, it is resentment still, and in a sense outraged egotism. And this brings us to another thought: Thea is not really interested in ideas and books, and the work done with Lövborg is a kind of substitute for the real children of which she has been deprived.

We recall how when Thea parts from Lövborg she says: "I see nothing but darkness before me." She goes out, we assume at that moment, to her own tragedy. But later when she returns to the Tesman house and learns of Lövborg's death and hears Tesman say that Lövborg has gone without leaving the book to immortalize his name, she produces the notes and she and Tesman fall to work to reconstruct Lövborg's book. Both do this in memory of Lövborg. Tesman has his bad conscience about the destruction of the manuscript which, in a way, he had been party to. But also he is fulfilling his natural function: ". . . arranging other people's papers is just the work for me," he says happily. So with Thea, the work is done in memory of Lövborg, but we know that as soon as Hedda and Lövborg are well cold underground, the common work of Thea and Tesman will lead to a match. How do we know this? Hedda implies as much as she goes out of the room to her death, but the little tableau of the two with their heads together under the lamp speaks louder than words. Thea will get her home and family, after all, and Lövborg's book about the future will have done it for her. Tesman will suit her perfectly. She will never know what Hedda had known with such desperate clarity, that Tesman is a fatuous dull-ard. Tesman will serve her purpose, and that

is all, in the end, that she will ask. Poor Lövborg, whom she had not understood, will be forgotten.

Is this a way of saying that Thea's virtues are not real virtues? No, her virtues remain virtues. She had been devoted to Lövborg; she had performed acts of great courage for him. But this is a way of saying that people are complicated, and that we do not have with Thea merely the "good" Thea over against the "bad" Hedda. Thea, in her own fashion, had used Lövborg.

This brings us to another, and more general, consideration. How are the characters to be "grouped" in the play? What kind of pattern do they make in relation to the central idea of the play? We can say, from one standpoint, that Hedda is the central character, and that we are to see other characters in relation to her. She is a study in a certain kind of neurotic frustration, a certain kind of destructiveness masquerading under a romantic idealism, under her passion for the noble and beautiful gesture. The pattern of characters may be taken in terms of the effect of her destructiveness upon each. But is the play to be taken, then, just as a case history, a clinical report cleverly dramatized?

The play is more than that. For one thing, Hedda's story is a comment on our human capacity for self-deception and destructiveness. It makes a judgment, implicitly of course, on conduct and values. But we can go beyond that. If we take Lövborg as the central figure, we arrive at a broader conception of the meaning of the play. Lövborg is the creative force, the creative personality, in the world of the play. This world is so bound by convention, so barren of ideas, and so lacking in courage, that a man like Lövborg is out of place. In a blind rebellion —and in his own weakness, we may add—he throws away his talents, the force that would shape the "future." But everybody around him, aware of barrenness and lack of creativity, preys on Lövborg in one way or another. Hedda, in the old days, had sought experience vicariously through him, and finally drives him to his death to affirm her dream of the noble gesture. Thea had used him to fill up her childless life, had made his book her "child." Tesman, with Lövborg's death, gets his own proper occupation, "arranging other people's papers," mechanical scholarship devoid of ideas. In this perspective the play becomes a comment on the frustration of creativity of various kinds in the modern world. Lövborg's work will survive, the vision of the future, but it will survive, ironically enough, through Tesman and Thea, two decent, dull people who do not really grasp the meaning of the work they are reconstructing from Lövborg's notes.

Now we may turn to a more general question: is *Hedda Gabler* a tragedy? Certainly, it is a serious play, and it is a play involving violence and death. But seriousness of meaning and violence of action are not enough to constitute what we ordinarily think of as tragedy. To take things at the simplest level, we expect to give the tragic character some sympathy or admiration. It is easy to see why we sympathize with a tragic character like Romeo in Shakespeare's play. He is an attractive personality. It is only a little less easy to see why we admire him. He is willing to take great risks, to pay the highest price, for what he values most, the love of Juliet. There is some largeness in his character. It is more difficult to see how we sympathize with a tragic character like Richard III of Shakespeare's play by that name, when Richard is bloodthirsty, and ambitious, and cunning. But in his play he is set in a world largely populated by vicious, confused, or self-deceiving weaklings, and he at least has the strength of mind and honesty to see his own position quite clearly and not to flinch or apologize to himself or for himself. So he draws, against our will and our ultimate moral judgment, our sympathy and admiration.

But how does Ibsen first present Hedda? It is in the performance of a mean-spirited act. First, she complains about the scent of the flowers, the very flowers that are there as a tribute to her. Second, and quite deliberately as we later learn, she hurts old Aunt Juliana's feelings about her new bonnet. Ibsen poisons us against Hedda from the very start. It will be difficult to see any largeness of mind or spirit after this. All Hedda's talk about nobility and beauty comes to us against this recollection. And when she complains that all she touches turns "mean and ludicrous," we already know why: the meanness of spirit is in her.

The only character here who might serve as the central figure of a tragedy is Lövborg himself. He has some largeness, and we can sympathize with him. But the step to his ruin is a step forced on him by Hedda, and forced on him by her playing on a weak and mean streak in his character. He is, we are tempted to say, too much the victim to be a tragic hero. But when he discovers the loss of his manuscript the lie he tells Thea has something of the tragic quality—even if it is. a lie. In the end, however, he dies with the pistol ball in his bowels, not in his head or heart, and he dies by accident in a sordid house. It is as though Ibsen were saying: "This is the only kind of end possible in this kind of world." The play, then, instead of being a tragedy, is a kind of parody, an intended parody, of tragedy, a kind of antitragedy, a way of indicating that the tragic scale is not possible in a world that has forfeited, or lost, its sense of mission, its creativity.

EXERCISE

1. Aunt Juliana is a good woman, we grant that. But can you discover anything in her make-up to lead you to sympathize with Hedda's distaste for her? Can it be said that she has more than a trace of George Tesman's fatuousness? What is her attitude toward Lövborg? Does this make us modify our notion of her goodness?

2. Very early in the first act Tesman says to his aunt: "We were so sorry we couldn't give you a seat in the carriage. But you saw what a pile of boxes Hedda had to bring with her." What is the purpose of this bit in the play?

3. After Juliana goes, in Act I, Hedda looks out at the yellowing leaves and comments on them. What is the meaning of this?

4. In the first act, before Hedda appears, Tesman and his aunt have discussed Lövborg. But later, with no prompting from anyone, Hedda mentions him. The reference to the home of the Elvsteds suggests him to her. She says: "Tell me, Tesman—isn't it somewhere near there that he—that—Eilert Lövborg is living?" What is the significance of the fact that she says "he" before she mentions Lövborg's name, or before it has been mentioned in her presence? What lies behind her unprovoked question?

5. What is the significance of the fact that everyone who comes to the Tesman house the first morning must mention Lövborg?

6. What are we to make of the fact that Hedda, when she hears that there may be a competition for the post that Tesman seeks, says, "Fancy, Tesman, there will be a sort of sporting interest in that"?

7. Define the dramatic intention of the last few speeches in Act I.

8. Interpret the fact that Lövborg has put into his current book about the present nothing but "what everyone would agree with," and into the book about the future has put his "true self."

9. In Act II, when Hedda is showing Lövborg the photographs taken during the honeymoon trip, she looks up once at Tesman "affectionately." How does Ibsen mean this stage direction to be understood? If this is only simulated affection, why does Hedda simulate it at this particular moment?

10. More than one impulse is involved in Lövborg's taking his glass of punch in Act II. What are these several impulses?

11. The end of Act II is a triumphant statement by Hedda; she sees Lövborg returning with "vine-leaves in his hair." What is the tone of the opening of Act III? What is the value of this shift of tone?

12. What is Tesman's attitude toward Lövborg's new book, the book still in manuscript? When he tells Hedda, in Act III, that he has picked up the manuscript and intends to take it back to Lövborg, is he entirely sincere in the statement of intention? Or does he really hope, in some obscure and unadmitted way, that Hedda will prevent him? Hedda tempts him in this scene. Compare the scene with the scene in Shakespeare's *Macbeth* when Lady Macbeth tempts her husband to kill Duncan (Act I, Scene vii).

13. In Act III, about two thirds of the way into the act, Hedda and Judge Brack have had a quiet conversation about their relationship. Just after Brack has left, Lövborg suddenly bursts into the room. What dramatic contrasts are involved here?

14. When Tesman, in Act IV, asks for Lövborg's manuscript from Hedda and she tells him that she has burnt it, he cries out, "Burnt! Burnt Eilert's manu-

script!" The stage direction indicates that this is accompanied by a "violent movement of terror." Of what is Tesman terrified? A little later Tesman says to Hedda: "Do you know what you have done, Hedda? It's unlawful appropriation of lost property." Is "unlawful appropriation of lost property" an accurate description of the content of Hedda's act in destroying the manuscript? If it is not, why does Ibsen put this in the mouth of Tesman? What does it tell us about Tesman? What does it imply about the nature and depth of his shock when he discovers the manuscript to be destroyed? On the same point, what does his sudden joy tell us when he thinks that Hedda has done the deed for love of him? How fundamental had been his moral distress? Later, when Tesman finds that Thea has the notes of Lövborg's book he undertakes to reconstruct the work, and says: "I owe this to Eilert's memory." Why does he "owe" something to Lövborg's memory? Are his motives mixed in undertaking this project?

15. At the very end of the play we see Thea and Tesman together with the notes, hear Tesman suggesting that he and Thea work at Aunt Juliana's house, and see Judge Brack's confidence that he at last has the upper hand with Hedda. Does all this suggest a kind of new sympathy and justification for Hedda?

16. When the death shot is heard, Tesman says: "Oh, now she is playing with those pistols again." What ironical elements are involved in the word *playing?*

17. What ironical elements are involved in Judge Brack's final words: "Good God!—people don't do such things"?

18. If you have read Gustave Flaubert's novel *Madame Bovary,* how would you compare Emma Bovary and Hedda Gabler?

Oedipus Rex

SOPHOCLES

An English Version by Dudley Fitts and Robert Fitzgerald

Characters

OEDIPUS
A PRIEST
CREON
TEIRESIAS
IOCASTE

MESSENGER
SHEPHERD OF LAIOS
SECOND MESSENGER
CHORUS OF THEBAN ELDERS

SCENE: Before the palace of Oedipus, King of Thebes. A central door and two lateral doors open onto a platform which runs the length of the façade. On the platform, right and left, are altars; and three steps lead down into the "orchestra," or chorus-ground. At the beginning of the action these steps are crowded by suppliants who have brought branches and chaplets of olive leaves and who lie in various attitudes of despair. OEDIPUS *enters.*

Prologue

OEDIPUS.

My children, generations of the living
In the line of Kadmos, nursed at his ancient
  hearth:
Why have you strewn yourselves before these
  altars
In supplication, with your boughs and garlands?
The breath of incense rises from the city
With a sound of prayer and lamentation.
                              Children,
I would not have you speak through messengers,
And therefore I have come myself to hear you—
I, Oedipus, who bear the famous name.
                              (*To a* PRIEST)
You, there, since you are eldest in the company,
Speak for them all, tell me what preys upon you,
Whether you come in dread, or crave some
  blessing:

Tell me, and never doubt that I will help you
In every way I can; I should be heartless
Were I not moved to find you suppliant here.

PRIEST.

Great Oedipus, O powerful King of Thebes!
You see how all the ages of our people
Cling to your altar steps: here are boys
Who can barely stand alone, and here are priests
By weight of age, as I am a priest of God,
And young men chosen from those yet
  unmarried;
As for the others, all that multitude,
They wait with olive chaplets in the squares,
At the two shrines of Pallas, and where Apollo
Speaks in the glowing embers.
                              Your own eyes
Must tell you: Thebes is tossed on a murdering
  sea
And can not lift her head from the death surge.
A rust consumes the buds and fruits of the earth;
The herds are sick; children die unborn,
And labor is vain. The god of plague and pyre
Raids like detestable lightning through the city,
And all the house of Kadmos is laid waste,
All emptied, and all darkened: Death alone
Battens upon the misery of Thebes.

You are not one of the immortal gods, we know;
Yet we have come to you to make our prayer
As to the man surest in mortal ways
And wisest in the ways of God. You saved us

From the Sphinx, that flinty singer, and the
tribute
We paid to her so long; yet you were never
Better informed than we, nor could we teach
you:
It was some god breathed in you to set us free.

Therefore, O mighty King, we turn to you:
Find us our safety, find us a remedy,
Whether by counsel of the gods or men.
A king of wisdom tested in the past
Can act in a time of troubles, and act well.
Noblest of men, restore
Life to your city! Think how all men call you
Liberator for your triumph long ago;
Ah, when your years of kingship are remembered,
Let them not say *We rose, but later fell*—
Keep the State from going down in the storm!
Once, years ago, with happy augury,
You brought us fortune; be the same again!
No man questions your power to rule the land:
But rule over men, not over a dead city!
Ships are only hulls, citadels are nothing,
When no life moves in the empty passageways.

OEDIPUS.

Poor children! You may be sure I know
All that you longed for in your coming here.
I know that you are deathly sick; and yet,
Sick as you are, not one is as sick as I.
Each of you suffers in himself alone
His anguish, not another's; but my spirit
Groans for the city, for myself, for you.

I was not sleeping, you are not waking me.
No, I have been in tears for a long while
And in my restless thought walked many ways.
In all my search, I found one helpful course,
And that I have taken: I have sent Creon,
Son of Menoikeus, brother of the Queen,
To Delphi, Apollo's place of revelation,
To learn there, if he can,
What act or pledge of mine may save the city.
I have counted the days, and now, this very day,
I am troubled, for he has overstayed his time.
What is he doing? He has been gone too long.
Yet whenever he comes back, I should do ill
To scant whatever duty God reveals.

PRIEST.

It is a timely promise. At this instant

They tell me Creon is here.

OEDIPUS.

O Lord Apollo!
May his news be fair as his face is radiant!

PRIEST.

It could not be otherwise: he is crowned with
bay,
The chaplet is thick with berries.

OEDIPUS.

We shall soon know;
He is near enough to hear us now.
(*Enter* CREON)
O Prince:
Brother: son of Menoikeus:
What answer do you bring us from the god?

CREON.

A strong one. I can tell you, great afflictions
Will turn out well, if they are taken well.

OEDIPUS.

What was the oracle? These vague words
Leave me still hanging between hope and fear.

CREON.

Is it your pleasure to hear me with all these
Gathered around us? I am prepared to speak,
But should we not go in?

OEDIPUS.

Let them all hear it.
It is for them I suffer, more than for myself.

CREON.

Then I will tell you what I heard at Delphi.

In plain words
The god commands us to expel from the land of
Thebes
An old defilement we are sheltering.
It is a deathly thing, beyond cure;
We must not let it feed upon us longer.

OEDIPUS.

What defilement? How shall we rid ourselves of
it?

CREON.

By exile or death, blood for blood. It was

Murder that brought the plague-wind on the city.

OEDIPUS.

Murder of whom? Surely the god has named him?

CREON.

My lord: long ago Laïos was our king,
Before you came to govern us.

OEDIPUS.

I know;
I learned of him from others; I never saw him.

CREON.

He was murdered; and Apollo commands us now
To take revenge upon whoever killed him.

OEDIPUS.

Upon whom? Where are they? Where shall we
find a clue
To solve that crime, after so many years?

CREON.

Here in this land, he said.
If we make enquiry,
We may touch things that otherwise escape us.

OEDIPUS.

Tell me: Was Laïos murdered in his house,
Or in the fields, or in some foreign country?

CREON.

He said he planned to make a pilgrimage.
He did not come home again.

OEDIPUS.

And was there no one,
No witness, no companion, to tell what
happened?

CREON.

They were all killed but one, and he got away
So frightened that he could remember one thing
only.

OEDIPUS.

What was that one thing? One may be the key
To everything, if we resolve to use it.

CREON.

He said that a band of highwaymen attacked
them,
Outnumbered them, and overwhelmed the King.

OEDIPUS.

Strange, that a highwayman should be so
daring—
Unless some faction here bribed him to do it.

CREON.

We thought of that. But after Laïos' death
New troubles arose and we had no avenger.

OEDIPUS.

What troubles could prevent your hunting down
the killers?

CREON.

The riddling Sphinx's song
Made us deaf to all mysteries but her own.

OEDIPUS.

Then once more I must bring what is dark to
light.
It is most fitting that Apollo shows,
As you do, this compunction for the dead.
You shall see how I stand by you, as I should,
To avenge the city and the city's god,
And not as though it were for some distant
friend,
But for my own sake, to be rid of evil.
Whoever killed King Laïos might—who knows?—
Decide at any moment to kill me as well.
By avenging the murdered king I protect myself.

Come, then, my children: leave the altar steps,
Lift up your olive boughs!
One of you go
And summon the people of Kadmos to gather
here.
I will do all that I can; you may tell them that.
(*Exit a* PAGE)
So, with the help of God,
We shall be saved—or else indeed we are lost.

PRIEST.

Let us rise, children. It was for this we came,
And now the King has promised it himself.
Phoibos has sent us an oracle; may he descend
Himself to save us and drive out the plague.

(*Exeunt* OEDIPUS *and* CREON *into the palace
by the central door. The* PRIEST *and the*
SUPPLIANTS *disperse R and L. After a
short pause the* CHORUS *enters the orchestra.*)

Párodos

CHORUS.

(STROPHE 1)

What is God singing in his profound
Delphi of gold and shadow?
What oracle for Thebes, the sunwhipped city?

Fear unjoints me, the roots of my heart tremble.

Now I remember, O Healer, your power, and
　wonder:
Will you send doom like a sudden cloud, or
　weave it
Like nightfall of the past?

Speak, speak to us, issue of holy sound:
Dearest to our expectancy: be tender!

(ANTISTROPHE 1)

Let me pray to Athenê, the immortal daughter
　of Zeus,
And to Artemis her sister
Who keeps her famous throne in the market
　ring,
And to Apollo, bowman at the far butts of
　heaven—

O gods, descend! Like three streams leap against
The fires of our grief, the fires of darkness;
Be swift to bring us rest!

As in the old time from the brilliant house
Of air you stepped to save us, come again!

Now our afflictions have no end,　　(STROPHE 2)
Now all our stricken host lies down
And no man fights off death with his mind;

The noble plowland bears no grain,
And groaning mothers can not bear—

See, how our lives like birds take wing,
Like sparks that fly when a fire soars,
To the shore of the god of evening.

(ANTISTROPHE 2)

The plague burns on, it is pitiless,
Though pallid children laden with death
Lie unwept in the stony ways,

And old gray women by every path
Flock to the strand about the altars

There to strike their breasts and cry
Worship of Phoibos in wailing prayers:
Be kind, God's golden child!

(STROPHE 3)

There are no swords in this attack by fire,
No shields, but we are ringed with cries.

Send the besieger plunging from our homes
Into the vast sea-room of the Atlantic
Or into the waves that foam eastward of Thrace—

For the day ravages what the night spares—

Destroy our enemy, lord of the thunder!
Let him be riven by lightning from heaven!

(ANTISTROPHE 3)

Phoibos Apollo, stretch the sun's bowstring,
That golden cord, until it sing for us,
Flashing arrows in heaven!

　　　　　　　　Artemis, Huntress,
Race with flaring lights upon our mountains!

O scarlet god, O golden-banded brow,
O Theban Bacchos in a storm of Maenads,
　　　　　　(*Enter* OEDIPUS, *C.*)
Whirl upon Death, that all the Undying hate!
Come with blinding torches, come in joy!

Scene I

OEDIPUS.

Is this your prayer? It may be answered. Come,
Listen to me, act as the crisis demands,
And you shall have relief from all these evils.

Until now I was a stranger to this tale,
As I had been a stranger to the crime.
Could I track down the murderer without a clue?
But now, friends,
As one who became a citizen after the murder,
I make this proclamation to all Thebans:

If any man knows by whose hand Laïos, son of
　Labdakos,

Met his death, I direct that man to tell me
  everything,
No matter what he fears for having so long
  withheld it.
Let it stand as promised that no further trouble
Will come to him, but he may leave the land in
  safety.

Moreover: If anyone knows the murderer to be
  foreign,
Let him not keep silent: he shall have his reward
  from me.
However, if he does conceal it; if any man
Fearing for his friend or for himself disobeys this
  edict,
Hear what I propose to do:

I solemnly forbid the people of this country,
Where power and throne are mine, ever to
  receive that man
Or speak to him, no matter who he is, or let him
Join in sacrifice, lustration, or in prayer.
I decree that he be driven from every house,
Being, as he is, corruption itself to us: the
  Delphic
Voice of Zeus has pronounced this revelation.
Thus I associate myself with the oracle
And take the side of the murdered king.

As for the criminal, I pray to God—
Whether it be a lurking thief, or one of a
  number—
I pray that that man's life be consumed in evil
  and wretchedness.
And as for me, this curse applies no less
If it should turn out that the culprit is my guest
  here,
Sharing my hearth.
                    You have heard the penalty.

I lay it on you now to attend to this
For my sake, for Apollo's, for the sick
Sterile city that heaven has abandoned.
Suppose the oracle had given you no command:
Should this defilement go uncleansed for ever?
You should have found the murderer: your king,
A noble king, had been destroyed!
                    Now I,
Having the power that he held before me,
Having his bed, begetting children there

Upon his wife, as he would have, had he lived—
Their son would have been my children's
  brother,
If Laïos had had luck in fatherhood!
(But surely ill luck rushed upon his reign)—
I say I take the son's part, just as though
I were his son, to press the fight for him
And see it won! I'll find the hand that brought
Death to Labdakos' and Polydoros' child,
Heir of Kadmos' and Agenor's line.
And as for those who fail me,
May the gods deny them the fruit of the earth,
Fruit of the womb, and may they rot utterly!
Let them be wretched as we are wretched, and
  worse!

For you, for loyal Thebans, and for all
Who find my actions right, I pray the favor
Of justice, and of all the immortal gods.

  CHORAGOS.

Since I am under oath, my lord, I swear
I did not do the murder, I can not name
The murderer. Might not the oracle
That has ordained the search tell where to find
  him?

  OEDIPUS.

An honest question. But no man in the world
Can make the gods do more than the gods will.

  CHORAGOS.

There is one last expedient—

  OEDIPUS.

                    Tell me what it is.
Though it seem slight, you must not hold it back.

  CHORAGOS.

A lord clairvoyant to the lord Apollo,
As we all know, is the skilled Teiresias.
One might learn much about this from him,
  Oedipus.

  OEDIPUS.

I am not wasting time:
Creon spoke of this, and I have sent for him—
Twice, in fact; it is strange that he is not here.

  CHORAGOS.

The other matter—that old report—seems useless.

OEDIPUS.

Tell me. I am interested in all reports.

CHORAGOS.

The King was said to have been killed by
highwaymen.

OEDIPUS.

I know. But we have no witnesses to that.

CHORAGOS.

If the killer can feel a particle of dread,
Your curse will bring him out of hiding!

OEDIPUS.

                         No.

The man who dared that act will fear no curse.
(Enter the blind seer TEIRESIAS, *led by a*
PAGE)

CHORAGOS.

But there is one man who may detect the
criminal.
This is Teiresias, this is the holy prophet
In whom, alone of all men, truth was born.

OEDIPUS.

Teiresias: seer: student of mysteries,
Of all that's taught and all that no man tells,
Secrets of Heaven and secrets of the earth:
Blind though you are, you know the city lies
Sick with plague; and from this plague, my lord,
We find that you alone can guard or save us.

Possibly you did not hear the messengers?
Apollo, when we sent to him,
Sent us back word that this great pestilence
Would lift, but only if we established clearly
The identity of those who murdered Laïos.
They must be killed or exiled.
                        Can you use
Birdflight or any art of divination
To purify yourself, and Thebes, and me
From this contagion? We are in your hands.
There is no fairer duty
Then that of helping others in distress.

TEIRESIAS.

How dreadful knowledge of the truth can be
When there's no help in truth! I knew this well,
But made myself forget. I should not have come.

OEDIPUS.

What is troubling you? Why are your eyes so
cold?

TEIRESIAS.

Let me go home. Bear your own fate, and I'll
Bear mine. It is better so: trust what I say.

OEDIPUS.

What you say is ungracious and unhelpful
To your native country. Do not refuse to speak.

TEIRESIAS.

When it comes to speech, your own is neither
temperate
Nor opportune. I wish to be more prudent.

OEDIPUS.

In God's name, we all beg you—

TEIRESIAS.

                       You are all ignorant.
No; I will never tell you what I know.
Now it is my misery; then, it would be yours.

OEDIPUS.

What! You do know something, and will not
tell us?
You would betray us all and wreck the State?

TEIRESIAS.

I do not intend to torture myself, or you.
Why persist in asking? You will not persuade me.

OEDIPUS.

What a wicked old man you are! You'd try a
stone's
Patience! Out with it! Have you no feeling at all?

TEIRESIAS.

You call me unfeeling. If you could only see
The nature of your own feelings . . .

OEDIPUS.

                           Why,
Who would not feel as I do? Who could endure
Your arrogance toward the city?

TEIRESIAS.

                    What does it matter!
Whether I speak or not, it is bound to come.

OEDIPUS.

Then, if "it" is bound to come, you are bound to
tell me.

TEIRESIAS.

No, I will not go on. Rage as you please.

OEDIPUS.

Rage? Why not!
        And I'll tell you what I think:
You planned it, you had it done, you all but
Killed him with your own hands: if you had eyes,
I'd say the crime was yours, and yours alone.

TEIRESIAS.

So? I charge you, then,
Abide by the proclamation you have made:
From this day forth
Never speak again to these men or to me;
You yourself are the pollution of this country.

OEDIPUS.

You dare say that! Can you possibly think you
  have
Some way of going free, after such insolence?

TEIRESIAS.

I have gone free. It is the truth sustains me.

OEDIPUS.

Who taught you shamelessness? It was not your
  craft.

TEIRESIAS.

You did. You made me speak. I did not want to.

OEDIPUS.

Speak what? Let me hear it again more clearly.

TEIRESIAS.

Was it not clear before? Are you tempting me?

OEDIPUS.

I did not understand it. Say it again.

TEIRESIAS.

I say that you are the murderer whom you seek.

OEDIPUS.

Now twice you have spat out infamy. You'll pay
  for it!

TEIRESIAS.

Would you care for more? Do you wish to be
really angry?

OEDIPUS.

Say what you will. Whatever you say is worthless.

TEIRESIAS.

I say you live in hideous shame with those
Most dear to you. You can not see the evil.

OEDIPUS.

It seems you can go on mouthing like this for
ever.

TEIRESIAS.

I can, if there is power in truth.

OEDIPUS.

                There is:
But not for you, not for you,
You sightless, witless, senseless, mad old man!

TEIRESIAS.

You are the madman. There is no one here
Who will not curse you soon, as you curse me.

OEDIPUS.

You child of endless night! You can not hurt me
Or any other man who sees the sun.

TEIRESIAS.

True: it is not from me your fate will come.
That lies within Apollo's competence,
As it is his concern.

OEDIPUS.

        Tell me:
Are you speaking for Creon, or for yourself?

TEIRESIAS.

Creon is no threat. You weave your own doom.

OEDIPUS.

Wealth, power, craft of statesmanship!
Kingly position, everywhere admired!
What savage envy is stored up against these,
If Creon, whom I trusted, Creon my friend,
For this great office which the city once
Put in my hands unsought—if for this power
Creon desires in secret to destroy me!

He has bought this decrepit fortune-teller, this
Collector of dirty pennies, this prophet fraud—
Why, he is no more clairvoyant than I am!
                Tell us:

Has your mystic mummery ever approached the
    truth?
When that hellcat the Sphinx was performing
    here,
What help were you to these people?
Her magic was not for the first man who came
    along:
It demanded a real exorcist. Your birds—
What good were they? or the gods, for the matter
    of that?
But I came by,
Oedipus, the simple man, who knows nothing—
I thought it out for myself, no birds helped me!
And this is the man you think you can destroy,
That you may be close to Creon when he's king!
Well, you and your friend Creon, it seems to me,
Will suffer most. If you were not an old man,
You would have paid already for your plot.

CHORAGOS.

We can not see that his words or yours
Have been spoken except in anger, Oedipus,
And of anger we have no need. How can God's
    will
Be accomplished best? That is what most con-
    cerns us.

TEIRESIAS.

You are a king. But where argument's concerned
I am your man, as much a king as you.
I am not your servant, but Apollo's.
I have no need of Creon to speak for me.

Listen to me. You mock my blindness, do you?
But I say that you, with both your eyes, are blind:
You can not see the wretchedness of your life,
Nor in whose house you live, no, nor with whom.
Who are your father and mother? Can you tell
    me?
You do not even know the blind wrongs
That you have done them, on earth and in the
    world below.
But the double lash of your parents' curse will
    whip you
Out of this land some day, with only night
Upon your precious eyes.
Your cries then—where will they not be heard?
What fastness of Kithairon will not echo them?
And that bridal-descant of yours—you'll know it
    then,

The song they sang when you came here to
    Thebes
And found your misguided berthing.
All this, and more, that you can not guess at
    now,
Will bring you to yourself among your children.

Be angry, then. Curse Creon. Curse my words.
I tell you, no man that walks upon the earth
Shall be rooted out more horribly than you.

OEDIPUS.

Am I to bear this from him?—Damnation
Take you! Out of this place! Out of my sight!

TEIRESIAS.

I would not have come at all if you had not
asked me.

OEDIPUS.

Could I have told that you'd talk nonsense, that
You'd come here to make a fool of yourself, and
of me?

TEIRESIAS.

A fool? Your parents thought me sane enough.

OEDIPUS.

My parents again!—Wait: who were my parents?

TEIRESIAS.

This day will give you a father, and break your
heart.

OEDIPUS.

Your infantile riddles! Your damned
abracadabra!

TEIRESIAS.

You were a great man once at solving riddles.

OEDIPUS.

Mock me with that if you like; you will find it
true.

TEIRESIAS.

It was true enough. It brought about your ruin.

OEDIPUS.

But if it saved this town?

TEIRESIAS.

(*To the* PAGE)
Boy, give me your hand.

OEDIPUS.

Yes, boy; lead him away.

          —While you are here
We can do nothing. Go; leave us in peace.

TEIRESIAS.

I will go when I have said what I have to say.
How can you hurt me? And I tell you again:
The man you have been looking for all this time,
The damned man, the murderer of Laïos,
That man is in Thebes. To your mind he is
    foreign-born,
But it will soon be shown that he is a Theban,
A revelation that will fail to please.

                     A blind man,
Who has his eyes now; a penniless man, who is
    rich now;
And he will go tapping the strange earth with
    his staff
To the children with whom he lives now he
    will be
Brother and father—the very same; to her
Who bore him, son and husband—the very same
Who came to his father's bed, wet with his
    father's blood.

Enough. Go think that over.
If later you find error in what I have said,
You may say that I have no skill in prophecy.

    (*Exit* TEIRESIAS, *led by his* PAGE. OEDIPUS
      goes into the palace)

Ode I

CHORUS.

The Delphic stone of prophecies   (STROPHE 1)
Remembers ancient regicide
And a still bloody hand.
That killer's hour of flight has come.
He must be stronger than riderless
Coursers of untiring wind,
For the son of Zeus armed with his father's
    thunder
Leaps in lightning after him;
And the Furies follow him, the sad Furies.

Holy Parnassos' peak of snow   (ANTISTROPHE 1)
Flashes and blinds that secret man,
That all shall hunt him down:
Though he may roam the forest shade
Like a bull gone wild from pasture
To rage through glooms of stone.
Doom comes down on him; flight will not avail
    him;
For the world's heart calls him desolate,
And the immortal Furies follow, for ever follow.

But now a wilder thing is heard   (STROPHE 2)
From the old man skilled at hearing Fate in the
    wing-beat of a bird.
Bewildered as a blown bird, my soul hovers and
    can not find
Foothold in this debate, or any reason or rest of
    mind.
But no man ever brought—none can bring
Proof of strife between Thebes' royal house,
Labdakos' line, and the son of Polybos;
And never until now has any man brought word
Of Laïos' dark death staining Oedipus the King.

Divine Zeus and Apollo hold   (ANTISTROPHE 2)
Perfect intelligence alone of all tales ever told;
And well though this diviner works, he works in
    his own night;
No man can judge that rough unknown or trust
    in second sight,
For wisdom changes hands among the wise.
Shall I believe my great lord criminal
At a raging word that a blind old man let fall?
I saw him, when the carrion woman faced him
    of old,
Prove his heroic mind! These evil words are lies.

Scene II

CREON.

Men of Thebes:
I am told that heavy accusations
Have been brought against me by King Oedipus.

I am not the kind of man to bear this tamely.

If in these present difficulties
He holds me accountable for any harm to him
Through anything I have said or done—why,
    then,
I do not value life in this dishonor.

It is not as though this rumor touched upon
Some private indiscretion. The matter is grave.

The fact is that I am being called disloyal
To the State, to my fellow citizens, to my friends.

CHORAGOS.

He may have spoken in anger, not from his mind.

CREON.

But did you not hear him say I was the one
Who seduced the old prophet into lying?

CHORAGOS.

The thing was said; I do not know how seriously.

CREON.

But you were watching him! Were his eyes
    steady?
Did he look like a man in his right mind?

CHORAGOS.

                                    I do not know.
I can not judge the behavior of great men.
But here is the King himself.

                                    (*Enter* OEDIPUS)

OEDIPUS.

                        So you dared come back.
Why? How brazen of you to come to my house,
You murderer!

                        Do you think I do not know
That you plotted to kill me, plotted to steal my
    throne?
Tell me, in God's name: am I coward, a fool,
That you should dream you could accomplish
    this?
A fool who could not see your slippery game?
A coward, not to fight back when I saw it?
You are the fool, Creon, are you not? hoping
Without support or friends to get a throne?
Thrones may be won or bought: you could do
    neither.

CREON.

Now listen to me. You have talked; let me talk,
    too.
You can not judge unless you know the facts.

OEDIPUS.

You speak well: there is one fact; but I find it
    hard
To learn from the deadliest enemy I have.

CREON.

That above all I must dispute with you.

OEDIPUS.

That above all I will not hear you deny.

CREON.

If you think there is anything good in being
    stubborn
Against all reason, then I say you are wrong.

OEDIPUS.

If you think a man can sin against his own kind
And not be punished for it, I say you are mad.

CREON.

I agree. But tell me: what have I done to you?

OEDIPUS.

You advised me to send for that wizard, did you
    not?

CREON.

I did. I should do it again.

OEDIPUS.

                            Very well. Now tell me:
How long has it been since Laïos—

CREON.

                            What of Laïos?

OEDIPUS.

Since he vanished in that onset by the road?

CREON.

It was long ago, a long time.

OEDIPUS.

                            And this prophet,
Was he practicing here then?

CREON.

                        He was; and with honor, as now.

OEDIPUS.

Did he speak of me at that time?

CREON.

                                    He never did;
At least, not when I was present.

OEDIPUS.

                                But . . . the enquiry?
I suppose you held one?

CREON.

                        We did, but we learned nothing.

OEDIPUS.

Why did the prophet not speak against me then?

CREON.

I do not know; and I am the kind of man
Who holds his tongue when he has no facts to
go on.

OEDIPUS.

There's one fact that you know, and you could
tell it.

CREON.

What fact is that? If I know it, you shall have it.

OEDIPUS.

If he were not involved with you, he could not
say
That it was I who murdered Laïos.

CREON.

If he says that, you are the one that knows it!—
But now it is my turn to question you.

OEDIPUS.

Put your questions. I am no murderer.

CREON.

First, then: You married my sister?

OEDIPUS.

                              I married your sister.

CREON.

And you rule the kingdom equally with her?

OEDIPUS.

Everything that she wants she has from me.

CREON.

And I am the third, equal to both of you?

OEDIPUS.

That is why I call you a bad friend.

CREON.

No. Reason it out, as I have done.
Think of this first: Would any sane man prefer
Power, with all a king's anxieties,
To that same power and the grace of sleep?
Certainly not I.
I have never longed for the king's power—only
his rights.
Would any wise man differ from me in this?

As matters stand, I have my way in everything
With your consent, and no responsibilities.
If I were king, I should be a slave to policy.

How could I desire a scepter more
Than what is now mine—untroubled influence?
No, I have not gone mad; I need no honors,
Except those with the perquisites I have now.
I am welcome everywhere; every man salutes me,
And those who want your favor seek my ear,
Since I know how to manage what they ask.
Should I exchange this ease for that anxiety?
Besides, no sober mind is treasonable.
I hate anarchy
And never would deal with any man who likes it.

Test what I have said. Go to the priestess
At Delphi, ask if I quoted her correctly.
And as for this other thing: if I am found
Guilty of treason with Teiresias,
Then sentence me to death! You have my word
It is a sentence I should cast my vote for—
But not without evidence!
                              You do wrong
When you take good men for bad, bad men for
good.
A true friend thrown aside—why, life itself
Is not more precious!
                              In time you will know this well:
For time, and time alone, will show the just man,
Though scoundrels are discovered in a day.

CHORAGOS.

This is well said, and a prudent man would
ponder it.
Judgments too quickly formed are dangerous.

OEDIPUS.

But is he not quick in his duplicity?
And shall I not be quick to parry him?
Would you have me stand still, hold my peace,
and let
This man win everything, through my inaction?

CREON.

And you want—what is it, then? To banish me?

OEDIPUS.

No, not exile. It is your death I want,
So that all the world may see what treason means.

CREON.

You will persist, then? You will not believe me?

OEDIPUS.

How can I believe you?

CREON.

Then you are a fool.

OEDIPUS.

To save myself?

CREON.

In justice, think of me.

OEDIPUS.

You are evil incarnate.

CREON.

But suppose that you are wrong?

OEDIPUS.

Still I must rule.

CREON.

But not if you rule badly.

OEDIPUS.

O city, city!

CREON.

It is my city, too!

CHORAGOS.

Now, my lords, be still. I see the Queen,
Iocastê, coming from her palace chambers;
And it is time she came, for the sake of you both.
This dreadful quarrel can be resolved through
  her.

(*Enter* IOCASTE)

IOCASTE.

Poor foolish men, what wicked din is this?
With Thebes sick to death, is it not shameful
That you should rake some private quarrel up?

(*To* OEDIPUS)

Come into the house.

—And you, Creon, go now:
Let us have no more of this tumult over nothing.

CREON.

Nothing? No, sister: what your husband plans
  for me

Is one of two great evils: exile or death.

OEDIPUS.

He is right.
          Why, woman I have caught him squarely
Plotting against my life.

CREON.

No! Let me die
Accurst if ever I have wished you harm!

IOCASTE.

Ah, believe it, Oedipus!
In the name of the gods, respect this oath of his
For my sake, for the sake of these people here!

CHORAGOS.   (STROPHE 1)

Open your mind to her, my lord. Be ruled by
  her, I beg you!

OEDIPUS.

What would you have me do?

CHORAGOS.

Respect Creon's word. He has never spoken like
  a fool,
And now he has sworn an oath.

OEDIPUS.

You know what you ask?

CHORAGOS.

I do.

OEDIPUS.

Speak on, then.

CHORAGOS.

A friend so sworn should not be baited so,
In blind malice, and without final proof.

OEDIPUS.

You are aware, I hope, that what you say
Means death for me, or exile at the least.

CHORAGOS.   (STROPHE 2)

No, I swear by Helios, first in Heaven!
    May I die friendless and accurst,
The worst of deaths, if ever I meant that!
    It is the withering fields
      That hurt my sick heart:
    Must we bear all these ills,
      And now your bad blood as well?

OEDIPUS.

Then let him go. And let me die, if I must,
Or be driven by him in shame from the land of
  Thebes.
It is your unhappiness, and not his talk,
That touches me.
                As for him—
Wherever he goes, hatred will follow him.

CREON.

Ugly in yielding, as you were ugly in rage!
Natures like yours chiefly torment themselves.

OEDIPUS.

Can you not go? Can you not leave me?

CREON.

                                I can.
You do not know me; but the city knows me,
And in its eyes I am just, if not in yours.
                        (*Exit* CREON)

CHORAGOS.   (ANTISTROPHE 1)

Lady Iocastê, did you not ask the King to go to
  his chambers?

IOCASTE.

First tell me what has happened.

CHORAGOS.

There was suspicion without evidence; yet it
  rankled
As even false charges will.

IOCASTE.

                    On both sides?

CHORAGOS.

                            On both.

IOCASTE.

                    But what was said?

CHORAGOS.

Oh let it rest, let it be done with!
Have we not suffered enough?

OEDIPUS.

You see to what your decency has brought you:
You have made difficulties where my heart saw
  none.

CHORAGOS.   (ANTISTROPHE 2)

Oedipus, it is not once only I have told you—

You must know I should count myself unwise
To the point of madness, should I now forsake
        you—
    You, under whose hand,
      In the storm of another time,
    Our dear land sailed out free.
      But now stand fast at the helm!

IOCASTE.

In God's name, Oedipus, inform your wife as
  well:
Why are you so set in this hard anger?

OEDIPUS.

I will tell you, for none of these men deserves
My confidence as you do. It is Creon's work,
His treachery, his plotting against me.

IOCASTE.

Go on, if you can make this clear to me.

OEDIPUS.

He charges me with the murder of Laïos.

IOCASTE.

Has he some knowledge? Or does he speak from
  hearsay?

OEDIPUS.

He would not commit himself to such a charge,
But he has brought in that damnable soothsayer
To tell his story.

IOCASTE.

                Set your mind at rest.
If it is a question of soothsayers, I tell you
That you will find no man whose craft gives
  knowledge
Of the unknowable.

                    Here is my proof:

An oracle was reported to Laïos once
(I will not say from Phoibos himself, but from
His appointed ministers, at any rate)
That his doom would be death at the hands of
  his own son—
His son, born of his flesh and of mine!

Now, you remember the story: Laïos was killed
By marauding strangers where three highways
  meet;

But his child had not been three days in this
  world
Before the King had pierced the baby's ankles
And left him to die on a lonely mountainside.

Thus, Apollo never caused that child
To kill his father, and it was not Laïos' fate
To die at the hands of his son, as he had feared.
This is what prophets and prophecies are worth!
Have no dread of them.
                              It is God himself
Who can show us what he wills, in his own way.

OEDIPUS.

How strange a shadowy memory crossed my
  mind,
Just now while you were speaking; it chilled my
  heart.

IOCASTE.

What do you mean? What memory do you speak
of?

OEDIPUS.

If I understand you, Laïos was killed
At a place where three roads meet.

IOCASTE.

                              So it was said;
We have no later story.

OEDIPUS.

                    Where did it happen?

IOCASTE.

Phokis, it is called: at a place where the Theban
  Way
Divides into the roads toward Delphi and Daulia.

OEDIPUS.

When?

IOCASTE.

      We had the news not long before you came
And proved the right to your succession here.

OEDIPUS.

Ah, what net has God been weaving for me?

IOCASTE.

Oedipus! Why does this trouble you?

OEDIPUS.

                        Do not ask me yet.

First, tell me how Laïos looked, and tell me
How old he was.

IOCASTE.

              He was tall, his hair just touched
With white; his form was not unlike your own.

OEDIPUS.

I think that I myself may be accurst
By my own ignorant edict.

IOCASTE.

                        You speak strangely.
It makes me tremble to look at you, my King.

OEDIPUS.

I am not sure that the blind man can not see.
But I should know better if you were to tell me—

IOCASTE.

Anything—though I dread to hear you ask it.

OEDIPUS.

Was the King lightly escorted, or did he ride
With a large company, as a ruler should?

IOCASTE.

There were five men with him in all: one was a
  herald,
And a single chariot, which he was driving.

OEDIPUS.

Alas, that makes it plain enough!
                              But who—
Who told you how it happened?

IOCASTE.

                        A household servant,
The only one to escape.

OEDIPUS.

                    And is he still
A servant of ours?

IOCASTE.

                No; for when he came back at last
And found you enthroned in the place of the
  dead king,
He came to me, touched my hand with his, and
  begged
That I would send him away to the frontier
  district
Where only the shepherds go—

As far away from the city as I could send him.
I granted his prayer; for although the man was
    a slave,
He had earned more than this favor at my hands.

OEDIPUS.

Can he be called back quickly?

IOCASTE.

Easily.

But why?

OEDIPUS.

I have taken too much upon myself
Without enquiry; therefore I wish to consult
    him.

IOCASTE.

Then he shall come.
                But am I not one also
To whom you might confide these fears of yours?

OEDIPUS.

That is your right; it will not be denied you,
Now least of all; for I have reached a pitch
Of wild foreboding. Is there anyone
To whom I should sooner speak?

Polybos of Corinth is my father.
My mother is a Dorian: Meropê.
I grew up chief among the men of Corinth
Until a strange thing happened—
Not worth my passion, it may be, but strange.

At a feast, a drunken man maundering in his
    cups
Cries out that I am not my father's son!

I contained myself that night, though I felt anger
And a sinking heart. The next day I visited
My father and mother, and questioned them.
    They stormed,
Calling it all the slanderous rant of a fool;
And this relieved me. Yet the suspicion
Remained always aching in my mind;
I knew there was talk; I could not rest;
And finally, saying nothing to my parents,
I went to the shrine at Delphi.
The god dismissed my question without reply;
He spoke of other things.
                Some were clear,

Full of wretchedness, dreadful, unbearable:
As, that I should lie with my own mother, breed
Children from whom all men would turn their
    eyes;
And that I should be my father's murderer.

I heard all this, and fled. And from that day
Corinth to me was only in the stars
Descending in that quarter of the sky,
As I wandered farther and farther on my way
To a land where I should never see the evil
Sung by the oracle. And I came to this country
Where, so you say, King Laïos was killed.

I will tell you all that happened there, my lady.

There were three highways
Coming together at a place I passed;
And there a herald came towards me, and a
    chariot
Drawn by horses, with a man such as you
    describe
Seated in it. The groom leading the horses
Forced me off the road at his lord's command;
But as this charioteer lurched over towards me
I struck him in my rage. The old man saw me
And brought his double goad down upon my
    head
As I came abreast.
                He was paid back, and more!
Swinging my club in this right hand I knocked
    him
Out of his car, and he rolled on the ground.
                I killed him.

I killed them all.
Now if that stranger and Laïos were—kin,
Where is a man more miserable than I?
More hated by the gods? Citizen and alien alike
Must never shelter me or speak to me—
I must be shunned by all.
                And I myself
Pronounced this malediction upon myself!

Think of it: I have touched you with these
    hands,
These hands that killed your husband. What
    defilement!

Am I all evil, then? It must be so,

Since I must flee from Thebes, yet never again
See my own countrymen, my own country,
For fear of joining my mother in marriage
And killing Polybos, my father.

                            Ah,
If I was created so, born to this fate,
Who could deny the savagery of God?

O holy majesty of heavenly powers!
May I never see that day! Never!
Rather let me vanish from the race of men
Than know the abomination destined me!

    CHORAGOS.

We too, my lord, have felt dismay at this.
But there is hope: you have yet to hear the
   shepherd.

    OEDIPUS.

Indeed, I fear no other hope is left me.

    IOCASTE.

What do you hope from him when he comes?

    OEDIPUS.

                       This much:
If his account of the murder tallies with yours,
Then I am cleared.

    IOCASTE.

              What was it that I said
Of such importance?

    OEDIPUS.

             Why, "marauders," you said,
Killed the King, according to this man's story.
If he maintains that still, if there were several,
Clearly the guilt is not mine: I was alone.
But if he says one man, singlehanded, did it,
Then the evidence all points to me.

    IOCASTE.

You may be sure that he said there were several;
And can he call back that story now? He cán not.
The whole city heard it as plainly as I.
But suppose he alters some detail of it:
He can not ever show that Laïos' death
Fulfilled the oracle: for Apollo said
My child was doomed to kill him; and my child—
Poor baby!—it was my child that died first.

No. From now on, where oracles are concerned,

I would not waste a second thought on any.

    OEDIPUS.

You may be right.

                  But come: let someone go
For the shepherd at once. This matter must be
   settled.

    IOCASTE.

I will send for him.
I would not wish to cross you in anything,
And surely not in this.—Let us go in.

                (Exeunt into the palace)

Ode II

    CHORUS.   (STROPHE 1)

Let me be reverent in the ways of right,
Lowly the paths I journey on;
Let all my words and actions keep
The laws of the pure universe
From highest Heaven handed down.
For Heaven is their bright nurse,
Those generations of the realms of light;
Ah, never of mortal kind were they begot,
Nor are they slaves of memory, lost in sleep:
Their Father is greater than Time, and ages not.

The tyrant is a child of Pride   (ANTISTROPHE 1)
Who drinks from his great sickening cup
Recklessness and vanity,
Until from his high crest headlong
He plummets to the dust of hope.
That strong man is not strong.
But let no fair ambition be denied;
May God protect the wrestler for the State
In government, in comely policy,
Who will fear God, and on His ordinance wait.

                    (STROPHE 2)
Haughtiness and the high hand of disdain
Tempt and outrage God's holy law;
And any mortal who dares hold
No immortal Power in awe
Will be caught up in a net of pain:
The price for which his levity is sold.
Let each man take due earnings, then,
And keep his hands from holy things,
And from blasphemy stand apart—
Else the crackling blast of heaven

Blows on his head, and on his desperate heart;
Though fools will honor impious men,
In their cities no tragic poet sings.

(ANTISTROPHE 2)

Shall we lose faith in Delphi's obscurities,
We who have heard the world's core
Discredited, and the sacred wood
Of Zeus at Elis praised no more?
The deeds and the strange prophecies
Must make a pattern yet to be understood.
Zeus, if indeed you are lord of all,
Throned in light over night and day,
Mirror this in your endless mind:
Our masters call the oracle
Words on the wind, and the Delphic vision
  blind!
Their hearts no longer know Apollo,
And reverence for the gods has died away.

Scene III

(Enter IOCASTE)

IOCASTE.

Prince of Thebes, it has occurred to me
To visit the altars of the gods, bearing
These branches as a suppliant, and this incense.
Our King is not himself: his noble soul
Is overwrought with fantasies of dread,
Else he would consider
The new prophecies in the light of the old.
He will listen to any voice that speaks disaster,
And my advice goes for nothing.
                 (She approaches the altar, R.)
                 To you, then, Apollo,
Lycean lord, since you are nearest, I turn in
  prayer.
Receive these offerings, and grant us deliverance
From defilement. Our hearts are heavy with fear
When we see our leader distracted, as helpless
  sailors
Are terrified by the confusion of their helmsman.
                 (Enter MESSENGER)

MESSENGER.

Friends, no doubt you can direct me:
Where shall I find the house of Oedipus,
Or, better still, where is the King himself?

CHORAGOS.

It is this very place, stranger; he is inside.
This is his wife and mother of his children.

MESSENGER.

I wish her happiness in a happy house,
Blest in all the fulfillment of her marriage.

IOCASTE.

I wish as much for you: your courtesy
Deserves a like good fortune. But now, tell me:
Why have you come? What have you to say to us?

MESSENGER.

Good news, my lady, for your house and your
  husband.

IOCASTE.

What news? Who sent you here?

MESSENGER.

                 I am from Corinth.
The news I bring ought to mean joy for you,
Though it may be you will find some grief in it.

IOCASTE.

What is it? How can it touch us in both ways?

MESSENGER.

The word is that the people of the Isthmus
Intend to call Oedipus to be their king.

IOCASTE.

But old King Polybos—is he not reigning still?

MESSENGER.

No. Death holds him in his sepulchre.

IOCASTE.

What are you saying? Polybos is dead?

MESSENGER.

If I am not telling the truth, may I die myself.

IOCASTE.   *(To a* MAIDSERVANT)

Go in, go quickly; tell this to your master.

O riddlers of God's will, where are you now!
This was the man whom Oedipus, long ago,
Feared so, fled so, in dread of destroying him—
But it was another fate by which he died.
                 (Enter OEDIPUS, *C.)*

OEDIPUS.

Dearest Iocastê, why have you sent for me?

IOCASTE.

Listen to what this man says, and then tell me
What has become of the solemn prophecies.

OEDIPUS.

Who is this man? What is his news for me?

IOCASTE.

He has come from Corinth to announce your
father's death!

OEDIPUS.

Is it true, stranger? Tell me in your own words.

MESSENGER.

I can not say it more clearly: the King is dead.

OEDIPUS.

Was it by treason? Or by an attack of illness?

MESSENGER.

A little thing brings old men to their rest.

OEDIPUS.

It was sickness, then?

MESSENGER.

                              Yes, and his many years.

OEDIPUS.

Ah!
Why should a man respect the Pythian hearth, or
Give heed to the birds that jangle above his
     head?
They prophesied that I should kill Polybos,
Kill my own father; but he is dead and buried,
And I am here—I never touched him, never,
Unless he died of grief for my departure,
And thus, in a sense, through me. No. Polybos
Has packed the oracles off with him
     underground.
They are empty words.

IOCASTE.

                              Had I not told you so?

OEDIPUS.

You had; it was my faint heart that betrayed me.

IOCASTE.

From now on never think of those things again.

OEDIPUS.

And yet—must I not fear my mother's bed?

IOCASTE.

Why should anyone in this world be afraid,
Since Fate rules us and nothing can be foreseen?
A man should live only for the present day.

Have no more fear of sleeping with your mother:
How many men, in dreams, have lain with their
     mothers!
No reasonable man is troubled by such things.

OEDIPUS.

That is true; only—
If only my mother were not still alive!
But she is alive. I can not help my dread.

IOCASTE.

Yet this news of your father's death is wonderful.

OEDIPUS.

Wonderful. But I fear the living woman.

MESSENGER.

Tell me, who is this woman that you fear?

OEDIPUS.

It is Meropê, man; the wife of King Polybos.

MESSENGER.

Meropê? Why should you be afraid of her?

OEDIPUS.

An oracle of the gods, a dreadful saying.

MESSENGER.

Can you tell me about it or are you sworn to
silence?

OEDIPUS.

I can tell you, and I will.
Apollo said through his prophet that I was the
     man
Who should marry his own mother, shed his
     father's blood
With his own hands. And so, for all these years
I have kept clear of Corinth, and no harm has
     come—
Though it would have been sweet to see my
     parents again.

MESSENGER.

And is this the fear that drove you out of Corinth?

OEDIPUS.

Would you have me kill my father?

MESSENGER.

As for that You must be reassured by the news I gave you.

OEDIPUS.

If you could reassure me, I would reward you.

MESSENGER.

I had that in mind, I will confess: I thought I could count on you when you returned to Corinth.

OEDIPUS.

No: I will never go near my parents again.

MESSENGER.

Ah, son, you still do not know what you are doing—

OEDIPUS.

What do you mean? In the name of God tell me!

MESSENGER.

—If these are your reason for not going home.

OEDIPUS.

I tell you, I fear the oracle may come true.

MESSENGER.

And guilt may come upon you through your parents?

OEDIPUS.

That is the dread that is always in my heart.

MESSENGER.

Can you not see that all your fears are groundless?

OEDIPUS.

How can you say that? They are my parents, surely?

MESSENGER.

Polybos was not your father.

OEDIPUS.

Not my father?

MESSENGER.

No more your father than the man speaking to you.

OEDIPUS.

But you are nothing to me!

MESSENGER.

Neither was he.

OEDIPUS.

Then why did he call me son?

MESSENGER.

I will tell you: Long ago he had you from my hands, as a gift.

OEDIPUS.

Then how could he love me so, if I was not his?

MESSENGER.

He had no children, and his heart turned to you.

OEDIPUS.

What of you? Did you buy me? Did you find me by chance?

MESSENGER.

I came upon you in the crooked pass of Kithairon.

OEDIPUS.

And what were you doing there?

MESSENGER.

Tending my flocks.

OEDIPUS.

A wandering shepherd?

MESSENGER.

But your savior, son, that day.

OEDIPUS.

From what did you save me?

MESSENGER.

Your ankles should tell you that.

OEDIPUS.

Ah, stranger, why do you speak of that childhood pain?

MESSENGER.

I cut the bonds that tied your ankles together.

OEDIPUS.

I have had the mark as long as I can remember.

MESSENGER.

That was why you were given the name you bear.

OEDIPUS.

God! Was it my father or my mother who did it?
Tell me!

MESSENGER.

  I do not know. The man who gave you to me
Can tell you better than I.

OEDIPUS.

It was not you that found me, but another?

MESSENGER.

It was another shepherd gave you to me.

OEDIPUS.

Who was he? Can you tell me who he was?

MESSENGER.

I think he was said to be one of Laïos' people.

OEDIPUS.

You mean the Laïos who was king here years ago?

MESSENGER.

Yes; King Laïos; and the man was one of his
herdsmen.

OEDIPUS.

Is he still alive? Can I see him?

MESSENGER.

              These men here
Know best about such things.

OEDIPUS.

             Does anyone here
Know this shepherd that he is talking about?
Have you seen him in the fields, or in the town?
If you have, tell me. It is time things were made
plain.

CHORAGOS.

I think the man he means is that same shepherd
You have already asked to see. Iocastê perhaps
Could tell you something.

OEDIPUS.

            Do you know anything
About him, Lady? Is he the man we have
summoned?
Is that the man this shepherd means?

IOCASTE.

            Why think of him?
Forget this herdsman. Forget it all.
This talk is a waste of time.

OEDIPUS.

            How can you say that,
When the clues to my true birth are in my hands?

IOCASTE.

For God's love, let us have no more questioning!
Is your life nothing to you?
My own is pain enough for me to bear.

OEDIPUS.

You need not worry. Suppose my mother a slave,
And born of slaves: no baseness can touch you.

IOCASTE.

Listen to me, I beg you: do not do this thing!

OEDIPUS.

I will not listen; the truth must be made known.

IOCASTE.

Everything that I say is for you own good!

OEDIPUS.

            My own good
Snaps my patience, then; I want none of it.

IOCASTE.

You are fatally wrong! May you never learn who
you are!

OEDIPUS.

Go, one of you, and bring the shepherd here.
Let us leave this woman to brag of her royal
name.

IOCASTE.

Ah, miserable!
That is the only word I have for you now.
That is the only word I can ever have.

            (*Exit into the palace*)

CHORAGOS.

Why has she left us, Oedipus? Why has she gone

In such a passion of sorrow? I fear this silence:
Something dreadful may come of it.

OEDIPUS.

Let it come!
However base my birth, I must know about it.
The Queen, like a woman, is perhaps ashamed
To think of my low origin. But I
Am a child of Luck; I can not be dishonored.
Luck is my mother; the passing months, my
    brothers,
Have seen me rich and poor.

If this is so,
How could I wish that I were someone else?
How could I not be glad to know my birth?

Ode III

CHORUS.

If ever the coming time were known   (STROPHE)
To my heart's pondering,
Kithairon, now by Heaven I see the torches
At the festival of the next full moon,
And see the dance, and hear the choir sing
A grace to your gentle shade:
Mountain where Oedipus was found,
O mountain guard of a noble race!
May the god who heals us lend his aid,
And let that glory come to pass
For our king's cradling-ground.

(ANTISTROPHE)
Of the nymphs that flower beyond the years,
Who bore you, royal child,
To Pan of the hills or the timberline Apollo,
Cold in delight where the upland clears,
Or Hermês for whom Kyllenê's heights are
    piled?
Or flushed as evening cloud,
Great Dionysos, roamer of mountains,
He—was it he who found you there,
And caught you up in his own proud
Arms from the sweet god-ravisher
Who laughed by the Muses' fountains?

Scene IV

OEDIPUS.
Sirs: though I do not know the man,
I think I see him coming, this shepherd we want:
He is old, like our friend here, and the men

Bringing him seem to be servants of my house.
But you can tell, if you have ever seen him.
(*Enter* SHEPHERD *escorted by Servants*)

CHORAGOS.
I know him, he was Laïos' man. You can trust
him.

OEDIPUS.
Tell me first, you from Corinth: is this the
shepherd
We were discussing?

MESSENGER.

This is the very man.

OEDIPUS.   (*To* SHEPHERD)
Come here. No, look at me. You must answer
Everything I ask.—You belonged to Laïos?

SHEPHERD.
Yes: born his slave, brought up in his house.

OEDIPUS.
Tell me: what kind of work did you do for him?

SHEPHERD.
I was a shepherd of his, most of my life.

OEDIPUS.
Where mainly did you go for pasturage?

SHEPHERD.
Sometimes Kithairon, sometimes the hills near-by.

OEDIPUS.
Do you remember ever seeing this man out
there?

SHEPHERD.
What would he be doing there? This man?

OEDIPUS.
This man standing here. Have you ever seen him
before?

SHEPHERD.
No. At least, not to my recollection.

MESSENGER.
And that is not strange, my lord. But I'll refresh
His memory: he must remember when we two
Spent three whole seasons together, March to
    September,
On Kithairon or thereabouts. He had two flocks;

I had one. Each autumn I'd drive mine home
And he would go back with his to Laïos'
    sheepfold.—
Is this not true, just as I have described it?

SHEPHERD.

True, yes; but it was all so long ago.

MESSENGER.

Well, then: do you remember, back in those days,
That you gave me a baby boy to bring up as my
    own?

SHEPHERD.

What if I did? What are you trying to say?

MESSENGER.

King Oedipus was once that little child.

SHEPHERD.

Damn you, hold your tongue!

OEDIPUS.

                              No more of that!
It is your tongue needs watching, not this man's.

SHEPHERD.

My King, my Master, what is it I have done
    wrong?

OEDIPUS.

You have not answered his question about the
    boy.

SHEPHERD.

He does not know . . . He is only making
    trouble . . .

OEDIPUS.

Come, speak plainly, or it will go hard with you.

SHEPHERD.

In God's name, do not torture an old man!

OEDIPUS.

Come here, one of you; bind his arms behind
    him.

SHEPHERD.

Unhappy king! What more do you wish to learn?

OEDIPUS.

Did you give this man the child he speaks of?

SHEPHERD.

                                        I did.
And I would to God I had died that very day.

OEDIPUS.

You will die now unless you speak the truth.

SHEPHERD.

Yet if I speak the truth, I am worse than dead.

OEDIPUS.

Very well; since you insist upon delaying—

SHEPHERD.

No! I have told you already that I gave him the
    boy.

OEDIPUS.

Where did you get him? From your house? From
    somewhere else?

SHEPHERD.

Not from mine, no. A man gave him to me.

OEDIPUS.

Is that man here? Do you know whose slave he
    was?

SHEPHERD.

For God's love, my King, do not ask me any
    more!

OEDIPUS.

You are a dead man if I have to ask you again.

SHEPHERD.

Then . . . Then the child was from the palace of
    Laïos.

OEDIPUS.

A slave child? or a child of his own line?

SHEPHERD.

Ah, I am on the brink of dreadful speech!

OEDIPUS.

And I of dreadful hearing. Yet I must hear.

SHEPHERD.

If you must be told, then . . .
                        They said it was Laïos' child;
But it is your wife who can tell you about that.

OEDIPUS.

My wife!—Did she give it to you?

SHEPHERD.

My lord, she did.

OEDIPUS.

Do you know why?

SHEPHERD.

I was told to get rid of it.

OEDIPUS.

An unspeakable mother!

SHEPHERD.

There had been prophecies . . .

OEDIPUS.

Tell me.

SHEPHERD.

It was said that the boy would kill his own
father.

OEDIPUS.

Then why did you give him over to this old
man?

SHEPHERD.

I pitied the baby, my King,
And I thought that this man would take him far
away
To his own country.
He saved him—but for what a fate!
For if you are what this man says you are,
No man living is more wretched than Oedipus.

OEDIPUS.

Ah God!
It was true!
All the prophecies!
—Now,
O Light, may I look on you for the last time!
I, Oedipus,
Oedipus, damned in his birth, in his marriage
damned,
Damned in the blood he shed with his own hand!

(*He rushes into the palace*)

Ode IV

CHORUS.

Alas for the seed of men. (STROPHE 1)

What measure shall I give these generations
That breathe on the void and are void
And exist and do not exist?

Who bears more weight of joy
Than mass of sunlight shifting in images,
Or who shall make his thought stay on
That down time drifts away?

Your splendor is all fallen.

O naked brow of wrath and tears,
O change of Oedipus!
I who saw your days call no man blest—
Your great days like ghósts góne.

That mind was a strong bow. (ANTISTROPHE 1)

Deep, how deep you drew it then, hard archer,
At a dim fearful range,
And brought dear glory down!

You overcame the stranger—
The virgin with her hooking lion claws—
And though death sang, stood like a tower
To make pale Thebes take heart.

Fortress against our sorrow!

True king, giver of laws,
Majestic Oedipus!
No prince in Thebes had ever such renown,
No prince won such grace of power.

And now of all men ever known (STROPHE 2)
Most pitiful is this man's story:
His fortunes are most changed, his state
Fallen to a low slave's
Ground under bitter fate.

O Oedipus, most royal one!
The great door that expelled you to the light
Gave at night—ah, gave night to your glory:
As to the father, to the fathering son.

All understood too late.

How could that queen whom Laïos won,
The garden that he harrowed at his height,
Be silent when that act was done?

(ANTISTROPHE 2)

But all eyes fail before time's eye,
All actions come to justice there.
Though never willed, though far down the deep
    past,
Your bed, your dread sirings,
Are brought to book at last.

Child by Laïos doomed to die,
Then doomed to lose that fortunate little death,
Would God you never took breath in this air
That with my wailing lips I take to cry:

For I weep the world's outcast.

I was blind, and now I can tell why:
Asleep, for you had given ease of breath
To Thebes, while the false years went by.

Éxodos

(*Enter, from the palace,* SECOND MESSENGER)

SECOND MESSENGER.

Elders of Thebes, most honored in this land,
What horrors are yours to see and hear, what
    weight
Of sorrow to be endured, if, true to your birth,
You venerate the line of Labdakos!
I think neither Istros nor Phasis, those great
    rivers,
Could purify this place of the corruption
It shelters now, or soon must bring to light—
Evil not done unconsciously, but willed.

The greatest griefs are those we cause ourselves.

CHORAGOS.

Surely, friend, we have grief enough already;
What new sorrow do you mean?

SECOND MESSENGER.

                    The Queen is dead.

CHORAGOS.

Iocastê? Dead? But at whose hand?

SECOND MESSENGER.

                    Her own.
The full horror of what happened you can not
    know,

For you did not see it; but I, who did, will tell
    you
As clearly as I can how she met her death.

When she had left us,
In passionate silence, passing through the court,
She ran to her apartment in the house,
Her hair clutched by the fingers of both hands.
She closed the doors behind her; then, by that bed
Where long ago the fatal son was conceived—
That son who should bring about his father's
    death—
We heard her call upon Laïos, dead so many
    years,
And heard her wail for the double fruit of her
    marriage,
A husband by her husband, children by her child.

Exactly how she died I do not know:
For Oedipus burst in moaning and would not
    let us
Keep vigil to the end: it was by him
As he stormed about the room that our eyes
    were caught.
From one to another of us he went, begging a
    sword,
Cursing the wife who was not his wife, the
    mother
Whose womb had carried his own children and
    himself.
I do not know: it was none of us aided him,
But surely one of the gods was in control!
For with a dreadful cry
He hurled his weight, as though wrenched out
    of himself,
At the twin doors: the bolts gave, and he rushed
    in.
And there we saw her hanging, her body swaying
From the cruel cord she had noosed about her
    neck.
A great sob broke from him, heartbreaking to
    hear,
As he loosed the rope and lowered her to the
    ground.

I would blot out from my mind what happened
    next!
For the King ripped from her gown the golden
    brooches

That were her ornament, and raised them, and
  plunged them down
Straight into his own eyeballs, crying, "No more,
No more shall you look on the misery about me,
The horrors of my own doing! Too long you
  have known
The faces of those whom I should never have
  seen,
Too long been blind to those for whom I was
  searching!
From this hour, go in darkness!" And as he spoke,
He struck at his eyes—not once, but many times;
And the blood spattered his beard,
Bursting from his ruined sockets like red hail.

So from the unhappiness of two this evil has
  sprung,
A curse on the man and woman alike. The old
Happiness of the house of Labdakos
Was happiness enough: where is it today?
It is all wailing and ruin, disgrace, death—all
The misery of mankind that has a name—
And it is wholly and for ever theirs.

CHORAGOS.
Is he in agony still? Is there no rest for him?

SECOND MESSENGER.
He is calling for someone to lead him to the gates
So that all the children of Kadmos may look
  upon
His father's murderer, his mother's—no,
I can not say it!
          And then he will leave Thebes,
Self-exiled, in order that the curse
Which he himself pronounced may depart from
  the house.
He is weak, and there is none to lead him,
So terrible is his suffering.
              But you will see:
Look, the doors are opening; in a moment
You will see a thing that would crush a heart of
  stone.
          (The central door is opened; OEDIPUS,
          blinded, is led in)

CHORAGOS.
Dreadful indeed for men to see.
Never have my own eyes
Looked on a sight so full of fear.

Oedipus!
What madness came upon you, what daemon
Leaped on your life with heavier
Punishment than a mortal man can bear?
No: I can not even
Look at you, poor ruined one.
And I would speak, question, ponder,
If I were able. No.
You make me shudder.

OEDIPUS.
God.   God.
Is there a sorrow greater?
Where shall I find harbor in this world?
My voice is hurled far on a dark wind.
What has God done to me?

CHORAGOS.
Too terrible to think of, or to see.

OEDIPUS.
O cloud of night,   (STROPHE 1)
Never to be turned away: night coming on,
I can not tell how: night like a shroud!

My fair winds brought me here.
                          O God. Again
The pain of the spikes where I had sight,
The flooding pain
Of memory, never to be gouged out.

CHORAGOS.
This is not strange.
You suffer it all twice over, remorse in pain,
Pain in remorse.

OEDIPUS.
Ah dear friend   (ANTISTROPHE 1)
Are you faithful even yet, you alone?
Are you still standing near me, will you stay
  here,
Patient, to care for the blind?
                          The blind man!
Yet even blind I know who it is attends me,
By the voice's tone—
Though my new darkness hide the comforter.

CHORAGOS.
Oh fearful act!
What god was it drove you to rake black
Night across your eyes?

OEDIPUS.

Apollo. Apollo. Dear   (STROPHE 2)
Children, the god was Apollo.
He brought my sick, sick fate upon me.
But the blinding hand was my own!
How could I bear to see
When all my sight was horror everywhere?

CHORAGOS.

Everywhere; that is true.

OEDIPUS.

And now what is left?
Images? Love? A greeting even,
Sweet to the senses? Is there anything?
Ah, no, friends: lead me away.
Lead me away from Thebes.
                        Lead the great wreck
And hell of Oedipus, whom the gods hate.

CHORAGOS.

Your fate is clear, you are not blind to that.
Would God you had never found it out!

OEDIPUS.   (ANTISTROPHE 2)

Death take the man who unbound
My feet on that hillside
And delivered me from death to life! What life?
If only I had died,
This weight of monstrous doom
Could not have dragged me and my darlings
    down.

CHORAGOS.

I would have wished the same.

OEDIPUS.

Oh never to have come here
With my father's blood upon me! Never
To have been the man they call his mother's
    husband!
Oh accurst! Oh child of evil,
To have entered that wretched bed—
                        the selfsame one!
More primal than sin itself, this fell to me.

CHORAGOS.

I do not know how I can answer you.
You were better dead than alive and blind.

OEDIPUS.

Do not counsel me any more. This punishment

That I have laid upon myself is just.
If I had eyes,
I do not know how I could bear the sight
Of my father, when I came to the house of
    Death,
Or my mother: for I have sinned against them
    both
So vilely that I could not make my peace
By strangling my own life.
                    Or do you think my children,
Born as they were born, would be sweet to my
    eyes?
Ah never, never! Nor this town with its high
    walls,
Nor the holy images of the gods.
                                For I,
Thrice miserable!—Oedipus, noblest of all the
    line
Of Kadmos, have condemned myself to enjoy
These things no more, by my own malediction
Expelling that man whom the gods declared
To be a defilement in the house of Laïos.
After exposing the rankness of my own guilt,
How could I look men frankly in the eyes?
No, I swear it,
If I could have stifled my hearing at its source,
I would have done it and made all this body
A tight cell of misery, blank to light and sound:
So I should have been safe in a dark agony
Beyond all recollection.
                        Ah Kithairon!
Why did you shelter me? When I was cast upon
    you,
Why did I not die? Then I should never
Have shown the world my execrable birth.

Ah Polybos! Corinth, city that I believed
The ancient seat of my ancestors: how fair
I seemed, your child! And all the while this evil
Was cancerous within me!
                        For I am sick
In my daily life, sick in my origin.

O three roads, dark ravine, woodland and way
Where three roads met: you, drinking my father's
    blood,
My own blood, spilled by my own hand: can you
    remember
The unspeakable things I did there, and the
    things

I went on from there to do?

                O marriage, marriage!

The act that engendered me, and again the act

Performed by the son in the same bed—

                      Ah, the net

Of incest, mingling fathers, brothers, sons,

With brides, wives, mothers: the last evil

That can be known by men: no tongue can say

How evil!

          No. For the love of God, conceal me

Somewhere far from Thebes; or kill me; or hurl
  me

Into the sea, away from men's eyes for ever.

Come, lead me. You need not fear to touch me.

Of all men, I alone can bear this guilt.

                   (*Enter* CREON)

CHORAGOS.

We are not the ones to decide; but Creon here

May fitly judge of what you ask. He only

Is left to protect the city in your place.

OEDIPUS.

Alas, how can I speak to him? What right have I

To beg his courtesy whom I have deeply
  wronged?

CREON.

I have not come to mock you, Oedipus,

Or to reproach you, either.

                (*To* ATTENDANTS)

          —You, standing there:

If you have lost all respect for man's dignity,

At least respect the flame of Lord Helios:

Do not allow this pollution to show itself

Openly here, an affront to the earth

And Heaven's rain and the light of day. No, take
  him

Into the house as quickly as you can.

For it is proper

That only the close kindred see his grief.

OEDIPUS.

I pray you in God's name, since your courtesy

Ignores my dark expectation, visiting

With mercy this man of all men most execrable:

Give me what I ask—for your good, not for mine.

CREON.

And what is it that you would have me do?

OEDIPUS.

Drive me out of this country as quickly as may be

To a place where no human voice can ever greet
  me.

CREON.

I should have done that before now—only,

God's will had not been wholly revealed to me.

OEDIPUS.

But his command is plain: the parricide

Must be destroyed. I am that evil man.

CREON.

That is the sense of it, yes; but as things are,

We had best discover clearly what is to be done.

OEDIPUS.

You would learn more about a man like me?

CREON.

You are ready now to listen to the god.

OEDIPUS.

I will listen. But it is to you

That I must turn for help. I beg you, hear me.

The woman in there—

Give her whatever funeral you think proper:

She is your sister.

          —But let me go, Creon!

Let me purge my father's Thebes of the pollution

Of my living here, and go out to the wild hills,

To Kithairon, that has won such fame with me,

The tomb my mother and father appointed for
  me,

And let me die there, as they willed I should.

And yet I know

Death will not ever come to me through sickness

Or in any natural way: I have been preserved

For some unthinkable fate. But let that be.

As for my sons, you need not care for them.

They are men, they will find some way to live.

But my poor daughters, who have shared my
  table,

Who never before have been parted from their
  father—

Take care of them, Creon; do this for me.

And will you let me touch them with my hands

A last time, and let us weep together?

Be kind, my lord,
Great prince, be kind!
     Could I but touch them,
They would be mine again, as when I had my
 eyes.
    (*Enter* ANTIGONE *and* ISMENE, *attended*)
Ah, God!
Is it my dearest children I hear weeping?
Has Creon pitied me and sent my daughters?

CREON.

Yes, Oedipus: I knew that they were dear to you
In the old days, and know you must love them
 still.

OEDIPUS.

May God bless you for this—and be a friendlier
Guardian to you than he has been to me!

Children, where are you?
Come quickly to my hands: they are your
 brother's—
Hands that have brought your father's once clear
 eyes
To this way of seeing—
     Ah dearest ones,
I had neither sight nor knowledge then, your
 father
By the woman who was the source of his own
 life!
And I weep for you—having no strength to see
 you—,
I weep for you when I think of the bitterness
That men will visit upon you all your lives.
What homes, what festivals can you attend
Without being forced to depart again in tears?
And when you come to marriageable age,
Where is the man, my daughters, who would dare
Risk the bane that lies on all my children?
Is there any evil wanting? Your father killed
His father; sowed the womb of her who bore
 him;
Engendered you at the fount of his own
 existence!
That is what they will say of you.

      Then, whom
Can you ever marry? There are no bridegrooms
 for you,
And your lives must wither away in sterile
 dreaming.

O Creon, son of Menoikeus!
You are the only father my daughters have,
Since we, their parents, are both of us gone for
 ever.
They are your own blood: you will not let them
Fall into beggary and loneliness;
You will keep them from the miseries that are
 mine!
Take pity on them; see, they are only children,
Friendless except for you. Promise me this,
Great Prince, and give me your hand in token
 of it.

    (CREON *clasps his right hand*)

Children:
I could say much, if you could understand me,
But as it is, I have only this prayer for you:
Live where you can, be as happy as you can—
Happier, please God, than God has made your
 father!

CREON.

Enough. You have wept enough. Now go within.

OEDIPUS.

I must; but it is hard.

CREON.

      Time eases all things.

OEDIPUS.

But you must promise—

CREON.

      Say what you desire.

OEDIPUS.

Send me from Thebes!

CREON.

      God grant that I may!

OEDIPUS.

But since God hates me . . .

CREON.

     No, he will grant your wish.

OEDIPUS.

You promise?

CREON.

    I can not speak beyond my knowledge.

OEDIPUS.

Then lead me in.

CREON.

Come now, and leave your children.

OEDIPUS.

No! Do not take them from me!

CREON.

Think no longer
That you are in command here, but rather think
How, when you were, you served your own
    destruction.

> (*Exeunt into the house all but the* CHORUS;
> *the* CHORAGOS *chants directly to the audi-*
> *ence*)

CHORAGOS.

Men of Thebes: look upon Oedipus.

This is the king who solved the famous riddle
And towered up, most powerful of men.
No mortal eyes but looked on him with envy,
Yet in the end ruin swept over him.

Let every man in mankind's frailty
Consider his last day; and let none
Presume on his good fortune until he find
Life, at his death, a memory without pain.

DISCUSSION

The *Oedipus the King* of Sophocles was
produced at Athens between 430 and 411 B.C.
This play has for long been regarded as one of
the great masterpieces of Greek tragedy, and
Aristotle, in his *Poetics,* seems to have regarded
it as a sort of touchstone for tragedy. Through
the centuries *Oedipus the King* has drawn special
praise for the brilliance of its plotting.

In the Introduction to Drama (p. 619) we
made the point that if the dramatist begins his
play at a point not far removed from the climax
of the action—near the finish line of the race, as
it were—the total action need not involve any
long span of time. This play begins at a point
quite close to the revelation that will bring
down Oedipus from his proud position as ruler
of his city to the plight of a miserable, blinded
man, begging to be exiled.

Yet there are problems and difficulties in
beginning a play so close to its climactic point—
for example, the difficulty of providing adequate
exposition and complication. The disaster that
befalls Oedipus has its beginnings in events that
go far back in time, to a period before his very
birth. Since all of this material must be marshalled and deployed in what had to be a relatively short play, the problem of plotting becomes most important. The student, at this point,
might well go back and reread what was said in
the Introduction to Fiction about *suspense*
(p. 10) and about the relation of *plot* to *action*
(p. 12).

Sophocles, it is true, had some special advantages in the matter of plotting. Like most
Greek tragedies, *Oedipus the King* was founded
on an ancient Greek myth, and the Athenian
audience could be counted on to be thoroughly
familiar with it. Even so, one notices that
Sophocles has taken care to weave every bit of
information relevant to the plot into the fabric
of the play.

The real advantage of writing for an audience that knew the story of Oedipus comes out in
a rather different way. From the beginning, the
audience knows what will be the outcome of
Oedipus's attempt to discover the murderer of
Laios. The situation is one, therefore, which
legitimately allows for all sorts of ironies, and
especially for what has come to be called "Soph-
oclean irony," where a speech that has one import for the character in the play carries a very
different meaning to the ears of the audience.
When Oedipus curses the murderer of Laios,
whoever that murderer may be, the audience is
aware that he is cursing himself. Or when Jocasta,
trying to describe Laios, her former husband, to
Oedipus, tells him that Laios was tall, his hair
just touched with white, and that his form "was
not unlike your own," the audience knows exactly why the two men resembled each other.

Yet granted a brilliant compression of the
plot of the play, and granted the stunning effect
of some of the ironic reversals, what did this play
have to say to a Greek audience of the fifth century B.C.? And what does it have to say to us?

As for the meaning that the play had for the
Greeks: we must remember that the Greek gods
do not correspond to our modern notion of
divinity. They are immanent rather than tran-

scendent, and they are closer to impersonal forces than to beings like the God of Abraham or the Christian God. H. B. F. Kitto, in his *Sophocles: Dramatist and Philosopher* (Oxford University Press, 1958) points out that the Greek gods, "the *theoi* individually or collectively, were never intended as a pattern of what *ought* to be; they are a statement of what *is*. . . . [Greek tragedy] is continually saying: '*These* are the permanent conditions of human life; these are the gods.' "

It behooves the modern reader, therefore, to be cautious in reading into this play his own ideas and valuations, for if he does so, he may very well misconstrue the meaning. Is the modern reader, then, barred out from the play? Is the play so tightly tied to the value assumptions of the civilization out of which it comes that it has little to say to us in the twentieth century? The modern reader, for instance, does not believe in oracles; yet in this play Sophocles—so it has been argued—is pounding home to his Athenian audience the necessity for such belief. Sophocles may in fact have believed in oracles; many intelligent Greeks did, though others did not. But the modern reader certainly does not.

An even greater obstacle for the modern reader may be the nature of the justice or injustice meted out to Oedipus. The modern reader may feel that Oedipus is punished quite savagely and beyond any crime that can be conceivably attributed to him. How are we to relate the ironic fall of Oedipus to the general human situation or see it as having meaning and relevance for our own time?

Here again Professor Kitto is helpful: the matter of importance, as he makes plain, is not the detail of Greek religion or the special nature of the warning sign—whether dreams, oracles, or portents—but the kind of universe that the poetry reveals, and it is a universe which has some relevance to twentieth-century man. It is a universe ordered by law and the man who breaks its laws, though in ignorance, will suffer the consequences. When Oedipus, by killing his father and marrying his mother, offends against the *theoi* who guard the purity of the race, he incurs the penalty even though his offense is unwitting. To use Kitto's words: "If, in all innocence, a man eats potassium cyanide, thinking that it is

sugar, his innocence and ignorance will not save him." Seen in such terms as these, the fall of Oedipus does have meaning for a man of the twentieth century, perhaps a most significant meaning for twentieth-century man, who lives under the threat of world disaster and may very well be vaporized through a wrong triggering of the machinery which he is just learning to manipulate to his potential benefit, but also at great potential peril to himself and his fellows.

One way to view the play, then, is as a commentary on knowledge—on man's splendid aspiration to knowledge, his inability ever to achieve full knowledge, and the perils of all partial knowledge. The prophecies of the Delphic oracle concerning Laios and Jocasta and Oedipus present themselves as full knowledge, knowledge as of the gods who know all things and cannot be mistaken. The oracles do not compel the people concerned to act in a particular way: they simply foretell what the people concerned are in fact going to do. Naturally, Laios and Jocasta and Oedipus try to avoid what is foretold of them, but their knowledge, because human, is necessarily imperfect and partial. Ironically, their very attempts to avoid the prophecies result in fulfilling them. If the consequences are terrible, and go beyond our notion of just deserts, the basic pattern nevertheless is grounded in human experience. As we know, human beings, in their very anxiety to avoid certain happenings, sometimes bring them about.

Though the parents of Oedipus were cruel in their attempt to avoid the prophecy, they were not cruel enough: they did not ensure the death of their baby son by having him killed before their eyes. In his attempt to avoid the prophecy, Oedipus too acted drastically and perhaps cruelly, for he deserted home and parents. But his action was not sufficiently drastic either. A more careful and prudent man would have tried to avoid killing any man and marrying any woman. Yet even if the human characters had taken every precaution, the dread oracles might have fulfilled themselves, nevertheless. Who knows?

It was not Oedipus's fault that he was the child of Laios and Jocasta, or that his parents sent him out to die, or that he was adopted by foster parents who did not tell him the secret of his birth. Oedipus is blameworthy only in his pride and in his confidence that he does know who he is and that with his human knowledge he can outwit the prophecies and manipulate the future. The tragic flaw of the Greek protagonist is overweening pride, or, to give it its Greek name, *hybris*. The man guilty of *hybris* forgets his humanity and thinks of himself as a man of unlimited—that is, godlike—powers. If we regard *Oedipus the King* as a commentary on knowledge, Oedipus's presumption is in thinking that his own knowledge is as full and deep as that of the gods.

There are reasons—and they are perfectly natural human reasons—for Oedipus's taking pride in his powers. By solving the riddle of the Sphinx, the answer to which no one else had been able to discover, he had saved the city of Thebes. Now the people of Thebes are appealing to their ruler to save them once more. As Oedipus speedily learns, the salvation of Thebes will turn again on the solution of an intellectual problem: the plague can be ended only by discovering the murderer of Laios. This is a problem after Oedipus's own heart. His past success gives him confidence, but more than that, Oedipus is a man who honestly values the truth. His faults and his virtues are all of a piece: he craves knowledge, and later in the play will prove that he is willing to suffer in order to gain it.

Another reason for Oedipus's pride in his own abilities lies in the way in which he had attained kingly power. The play should actually not be called *Oedipus the King,* but ought to be given its proper Greek title, *Oedipus Tyrannos,* for the word *tyrannos* had a special significance for the Athenians. The *tyrannos* was the man who held power not because he had inherited it but because he had won it through sheer ability and skill. Ignorant that he possesses princely blood, or that he has any claim to the throne of Thebes, Oedipus thinks of himself as indeed the self-made man.

Because he is a *tyrannos,* Oedipus tends to suspect that other people might like to seize power too, and speedily becomes suspicious of Creon, his brother-in-law. His conduct may be in part accounted for by his impetuousness and his hot temper, traits that revealed themselves long before this, when he killed the man and his servants at the crossroads. But now his tempera-mental edginess is heightened by his being aware that his position as ruler is not secured by claims of blood and "legitimacy."

It is important, however, to make a distinction here. Oedipus does not come to grief because he has a high temper—though a more prudent and less touchy man might have handled the encounter with Laios somewhat differently. Nor does he come to grief because he is suspicious of Creon. When the play opens, Oedipus, as the audience knows (though as he himself cannot know), is already guilty of parricide and incest. But these unwitting crimes simply point up the *hybris* that is not responsible for these crimes but that, in view of them, is seen as indeed presumptuous. Even the shrewdest human being, using that shrewdness for the best of motives, cannot know the consequences of all of his acts, and, what may be even more disastrous, cannot fully know himself.

There is something pathetic in watching this great towering figure, so confident in his own good intentions and in his own abilities, reassuring his people by telling them that he is going to find out who the murderer of Laios is, and woe be to that person when he finds him; or pronouncing a curse upon the murderer who has brought the taint upon the city, and, in his ignorance, cursing himself. Though the spectacle is pitiable, it also has an aspect of heroism, particularly when Oedipus refuses to give up the search even when it has begun to take a darker and more personal direction, and attention has shifted to the problem of finding out who he himself is and where he came from. But the spectacle is also terrifying inasmuch as we can see in the action of Oedipus something of our own limitations and blindness, for we too, though we do not really know ourselves, are constantly forced to try to settle the affairs of ourselves and others.

Aristotle in his *Poetics* said that tragedy excited pity and terror, and whatever he meant by these terms (and whether or not he would apply them in just this fashion to Oedipus) he clearly regarded the case of Oedipus as providing "the spectacle of a virtuous man brought from prosperity to adversity," and not at all as the spectacle of "a bad man" suffering misfortune, or of the downfall of an "utter villain." As Aristotle put it, the proper tragic hero is "a man who is not eminently good and just, yet whose misfortune is brought about not by vice or depravity, but by some error or frailty. . . ."

Kitto, in summing up on this play, remarks that "the gods can see the whole pattern of this Universe; Man cannot. . . . We should (therefore) remember how blind we are, avoiding *hybris,* arrogance, cocksureness." But Kitto, of course, does not mean to imply that the play is a moral tract presenting this "message" to its Athenian audience and to ourselves. The meaning of the play is much more massive than this, and not only more massive but richer and more complicated in the ramifications of its meanings. It does not preach a moral but rather dramatizes a very important aspect of man's fate: man finds himself in a universe that imposes terrible penalties upon those who break its laws though these are laws that no human being can fully understand.

EXERCISE

1. Notice that rather early in the play Teiresias, though he would avoid saying anything if he could, tells Oedipus the truth about himself. Is this an inartistic, because too early, divulging of the mystery? If not, why not? Why does Oedipus not believe the truth here told to him?

2. Three people try very hard during the course of the play to persuade Oedipus to desist from his inquiry. The first is Teiresias, the second is Jocasta. Who is the third?

3. Observe that not once but twice people trying to reassure Oedipus actually involve him in greater doubts. Jocasta (p. 679), in her anxiety to assuage Oedipus's fears about soothsayers, tells him that a prophecy concerning the death of her first husband failed to come true, but some of the details of this pronouncement of the oracle disturb Oedipus greatly —not at the thought that Laios is his father, but that it might have been he who killed Jocasta's first husband. What is the second instance of an attempt to reassure Oedipus that actually disturbs him the more? These reversals of expectation (Aristotle's term is *peripeteia*) have what effect upon the general theme of the play? What is their function in terms of the plot?

4. A modern commentator writes that Oedipus has some warrant for being suspicious of Creon, since Oedipus has felt "from the beginning that the death of Laios is attributable to treachery and bribery at work within the state—and in his mind lies also the thought that he himself may be the victim of a similar plot. These are the natural suspicions of any tyran-

nos. . . ." Does this comment help to account for the promptness with which Oedipus expects the worst of Creon?

5. Is not Oedipus's act of blinding himself symbolically appropriate? Remember that the oracles have been pronounced by Apollo the god of light.

6. Note how many of the speeches in this play have to do with the matter of seeing and of blindness. For example, Oedipus says to Creon: "Then once more I must bring what is dark to light" (p. 669). Teiresias says to Oedipus: "You mock my blindness, do you? / I say that you, with both your eyes, are blind: / You cannot see the wretchedness of your life. . . ." (p. 674). Oedipus says to Jocasta: "I am not sure that the blind man [that is, Teiresias] cannot see" (p. 680), and this is the first hint on Oedipus's part that the man with good eyes may not be able to discern what the man without eyes can discern. The chorus sing: "But all eyes fail before time's eye" (p. 690). Notice particularly the comments on blindness and seeing in the last scene of the play.

7. Early in the play (p. 671), someone suggests that the oracle that "ordained the search" for the murderer of Laios might be appealed to to tell where the murderer now is. Oedipus replies that this solution is too easy, for "No man in the world / Can make the gods do more than the gods will." Yet Oedipus's whole adult life has been based upon the supposition that a mortal man can evade what the gods have foretold will happen. Notice how this double attitude toward the knowledge of the gods runs through the play, so that we have at one point the attempt to prove an oracle false, then reliance upon an oracle, then confidence that oracles do not tell truth, and finally the awesome knowledge that they do. Trace the pattern of attitudes toward oracular pronouncements and give special attention to the statements of the chorus (pp. 682-83) and to the speeches of Jocasta and Oedipus (pp. 681-82).

8. One of the more interesting ironies in the play is that which contrasts the role of king (that is, the man who inherits rule) and *tyrannos* (the man who wins it by his own achievements). More than once Oedipus boasts of the fact that he is a self-made man who has won the rulership of Thebes through his own accomplishment. Yet Oedipus is to find that he is indeed the true king of Thebes, the child of Laios and Jocasta. What is the bearing, if there is any, of this ironic reversal upon the conduct of Oedipus? Upon the theme of the tragedy? In pondering your answer, take into account Scene III of the play in which Oedipus mistakes the reason for Jocasta's dread of any revelation about his ancestry.

9. The horrible truth about Oedipus dawns on Jocasta before it becomes clear to Oedipus. When she first becomes sure that Oedipus is her son, can it be said that from this point onward she tries with—ironically—something of a mother's concern to save her child?

10. Consider carefully the Second Messenger's speech on p. 690. What do you make of Oedipus's attitude toward Jocasta? Why does he beg for a sword? What is his attitude toward his children?

11. Oedipus wishes to leave Thebes. What motives does he give for wanting to go? Are these his only motives?

12. Creon says to Oedipus: "You are ready now to listen to the god" (p. 693), and Oedipus replies that he is ready. What is the bearing of this exchange upon Oedipus's attitude toward the gods? Upon his attitude toward his new-found knowledge? Upon the theme of the play? Note that Creon, though he would like to grant Oedipus's wish, and hopes that he will be able to do so, refuses to grant it until he has consulted the oracle once more.

13. Would you say from a review of this play that Sophocles is an "anti-intellectual"? Would he discourage the active pursuit of the truth that Oedipus exemplifies? Or would the implied attitude toward man's pursuit of knowledge be better put in other terms? Is it implied, for example, that though truth is precious, it cannot always be won simply by confident seeking? That truth is more mysterious and intractable than we are wont to think? That the hardest truth to come by is the truth about ourselves?

The following are some recent publications on Greek tragedy and the work of Sophocles: S. M. Adams, *Sophocles the Playwright* (Toronto, 1957); H. D. F. Kitto, *Greek Tragedy* (New York: Anchor Books, 1954); C. H. Whitman, *Sophocles: A Study of Heroic Humanism* (Cambridge, Mass., 1951); and Bernard M. W. Knox, *Oedipus at Thebes* (New Haven, 1957). The latter work in particular will be interesting to the student who would like to see how the very diction and imagery of the Greek play are used to develop the many ironies that attach to the search for truth that Oedipus so heroically makes. (Some of this material is included in Knox's "Sophocles' Oedipus," one of the essays in *Tragic Themes in Western Literature,* ed. Cleanth Brooks (Yale University Press, 1955).

Antony and Cleopatra

WILLIAM SHAKESPEARE (1564-1616)

Characters

MARK ANTONY,	} triumvirs	MENAS,	} friends to
OCTAVIUS CAESAR,		MENECRATES,	Pompey
M. AEMILIUS LEPIDUS,		VARRIUS,	
SEXTUS POMPEIUS.		TAURUS, *Lieutenant-General to Caesar*	
DOMITIUS ENOBARBUS,		CANIDIUS, *Lieutenant-General to Antony*	
VENTIDIUS,		SILIUS, *an Officer under Ventidius*	
EROS,	*friends to Antony*	EUPHRONIUS, *Ambassador from Antony to Caesar*	
SCARUS,		ALEXAS,	
DERCETAS,		MARDIAN,	} attendants on Cleopatra
DEMETRIUS,		SELEUCUS,	
PHILO,		DIOMEDES,	
MECAENAS,		*A Soothsayer*	
AGRIPPA,		A Clown	
DOLABELLA,	*friends to Caesar*	CLEOPATRA, *Queen of Egypt*	
PROCULEIUS,		OCTAVIA, *sister to Caesar, and wife to Antony*	
THYREUS,		CHARMIAN,	} attendants on Cleopatra
GALLUS,		IRAS,	

Officers, Soldiers, Messengers, and other Attendants

SCENE: In several parts of the Roman Empire.

Act I

SCENE I. *Alexandria. A room in* CLEOPATRA'S *palace.*

(*Enter* DEMETRIUS *and* PHILO)

PHILO. Nay, but this dotage of our general's
O'erflows the measure; those his goodly eyes,
That o'er the files and musters of the war
Have glowed like plated [1] Mars, now bend, now turn
The office and devotion of their view   5
Upon a tawny front; his captain's heart,
Which in the scuffles of great fights hath burst
The buckles on his breast, reneges all temper.[2]
And is become the bellows and the fan
To cool a gypsy's lust.

(*Flourish. Enter* ANTONY *and* CLEOPATRA,
with their trains; eunuchs fanning her.)
                              Look! where they come.   10
Take but good note, and you shall see in him
The triple pillar of the world transformed
Into a strumpet's fool; behold and see.
    CLEOPATRA. If it be love indeed, tell me how
        much.
    ANTONY. There's beggary in the love that can
        be reckoned.   15
    CLEOPATRA. I'll set a bourn [3] how far to be
        beloved.
    ANTONY. Then must thou needs find out new
        heaven, new earth.

---

1 armored   2 renounces all self-restraint   3 boundary

(*Enter an* ATTENDANT)

ATTENDANT. News, my good lord, from Rome.

ANTONY. Grates me; the sum.

CLEOPATRA. Nay, hear them, Antony.
Fulvia perchance is angry; or, who knows   20
If the scarce-bearded Caesar have not sent
His powerful mandate to you, "Do this, or this;
Take in that kingdom, and enfranchise that;
Perform't, or else we damn thee."

ANTONY.   How, my love!

CLEOPATRA. Perchance! nay, and most like;   25
You must not stay here longer; your dismission
Is come from Caesar; therefore hear it, Antony.
Where's Fulvia's process? [4] Caesar's I would say?
   both?
Call in the messengers. As I am Egypt's queen,
Thou blushest, Antony, and that blood of
   thine,   30
Is Caesar's homager; else so thy cheek pays
   shame
When shrill-tongued Fulvia scolds. The messen-
   gers!

ANTONY. Let Rome in Tiber melt, and the
   wide arch
Of the ranged empire fall! Here is my space.
Kingdoms are clay; our dungy earth alike   35
Feeds beast as man; the nobleness of life
Is to do thus; when such a mutual pair
   (*Embracing*)
And such a twain can do 't, in which I bind,
On pain of punishment, the world to weet [5]
We stand up peerless.

CLEOPATRA.   Excellent falsehood!   40
Why did he marry Fulvia and not love her?
I'll seem the fool I am not; Antony
Will be himself.

ANTONY.   But stirred by Cleopatra.
Now, for the love of Love and her soft hours,
Let's not confound the time with conference
   harsh: 45
There's not a minute of our lives should stretch
Without some pleasure now. What sport tonight?

CLEOPATRA. Hear the ambassadors.

ANTONY.   Fie, wrangling queen!
Whom every thing becomes, to chide, to laugh,
To weep; whose every passion fully strives   50
To make itself, in thee, fair and admired.
No messenger, but thine; and all alone,

Tonight we'll wander through the streets and
   note
The qualities of people. Come, my queen;
Last night you did desire it: speak not to us.   55
   (*Exeunt* ANTONY *and* CLEOPATRA,
                           with their train)

DEMETRIUS. Is Caesar with Antonius prized
   so slight?

PHILO. Sir, sometimes, when he is not Antony,
He comes too short of that great property
Which still should go with Antony.

DEMETRIUS.   I am full sorry
That he approves [6] the common liar, who   60
Thus speaks of him at Rome; but I will hope
Of better deeds tomorrow. Rest you happy!
   (*Exeunt*)

SCENE II. *The same. Another room.*

   (*Enter* CHARMIAN, IRAS, ALEXAS,
                  and a SOOTHSAYER)

CHARMIAN. Lord Alexas, sweet Alexas, most
any thing Alexas, almost most absolute Alexas,
where's the soothsayer that you praised so to
the queen? O! that I knew this husband, which,
you say, must charge his horns with garlands!   5

ALEXAS. Soothsayer!

SOOTHSAYER. Your will?

CHARMIAN. Is this the man? Is't you, sir, that
know things?

SOOTHSAYER. In nature's infinite book of secrecy
A little I can read.

ALEXAS.   Show him your hand.   10
   (*Enter* ENOBARBUS)

ENOBARBUS. Bring in the banquet quickly;
   wine enough
Cleopatra's health to drink.

CHARMIAN. Good sir, give me good fortune.

SOOTHSAYER. I make not, but foresee.

CHARMIAN. Pray then, foresee me one.   15

SOOTHSAYER. You shall be yet far fairer than
you are.

CHARMIAN. He means in flesh.

IRAS. No, you shall paint when you are old.

CHARMIAN. Wrinkles forbid!

ALEXAS. Vex not his prescience; be attentive.

CHARMIAN. Hush!   21

---

4 command   5 know   6 justifies

SOOTHSAYER. You shall be more beloving than
beloved.

CHARMIAN. I had rather heat my liver with
drinking.

ALEXAS. Nay, hear him.   24

CHARMIAN. Good now, some excellent fortune! Let me be married to three kings in a
forenoon, and widow them all; let me have a
child at fifty, to whom Herod of Jewry may do
homage; find me to marry me with Octavius
Caesar, and companion me with my mistress.

SOOTHSAYER. You shall outlive the lady whom
you serve.   31

CHARMIAN. O excellent! I love long life better
than figs.

SOOTHSAYER. You have seen and proved a
    fairer former fortune
Than that which is to approach.   34

CHARMIAN. Then, belike, my children shall
have no names; prithee, how many boys and
wenches must I have?

SOOTHSAYER. If every of your wishes had a
    womb,
And fertile every wish, a million.

CHARMIAN. Out, fool! I forgive thee for a
witch.   40

ALEXAS. You think none but your sheets are
privy to your wishes.

CHARMIAN. Nay, come, tell Iras hers.

ALEXAS. We'll know all our fortunes.

ENOBARBUS. Mine, and most of our fortunes,
tonight, shall be,—drunk to bed.   46

IRAS. There's a palm presages chastity, if
nothing else.

CHARMIAN. E'en as the overflowing Nilus
presageth famine.   50

IRAS. Go, you wild bedfellow, you cannot
soothsay.

CHARMIAN. Nay, if an oily palm be not a fruitful prognostication, I cannot scratch mine ear.
Prithee, tell her but a worky-day [1] fortune.   55

SOOTHSAYER. Your fortunes are alike.

IRAS. But how? but how? give me particulars.

SOOTHSAYER. I have said.

IRAS. Am I not an inch of fortune better than
she?   60

CHARMIAN. Well, if you were but an inch of
fortune better than I, where would you choose
it?

[1] every-day, ordinary

IRAS. Not in my husband's nose.

CHARMIAN. Our worser thoughts Heavens
mend! Alexas,—come, his fortune, his fortune. O!
let him marry a woman that cannot go, sweet
Isis, I beseech thee; and let her die too, and
give him a worse; and let worse follow worse,
till the worst of all follow him laughing to his
grave, fiftyfold a cuckold! Good Isis, hear me
this prayer, though thou deny me a matter of
more weight; good Isis, I beseech thee!   73

IRAS. Amen. Dear goddess, hear that prayer
of the people! for, as it is a heart-breaking to
see a handsome man loose-wived, so it is a deadly
sorrow to behold a foul knave uncuckolded:
therefore, dear Isis, keep decorum, and fortune
him accordingly!

CHARMIAN. Amen.   80

ALEXAS. Lo, now! if it lay in their hands to
make me a cuckold, they would make themselves whores, but they'd do't.

            (*Enter* CLEOPATRA)

ENOBARBUS. Hush! here comes Antony.

CHARMIAN.   Not he; the queen.

CLEOPATRA. Saw you my lord?   86

ENOBARBUS. No, lady.

CLEOPATRA. Was he not here?

CHARMIAN. No, madam.

CLEOPATRA. He was disposed to mirth; but
    on the sudden   90
A Roman thought hath struck him. Enobarbus!

ENOBARBUS. Madam!

CLEOPATRA. Seek him, and bring him hither.
    Where's Alexas?

ALEXAS. Here, at your service. My lord   95
    approaches.

        (*Enter* ANTONY, *with a* MESSENGER
                and ATTENDANTS)

CLEOPATRA. We will not look upon him; go
    with us.

        (*Exeunt* CLEOPATRA, ENOBARBUS, ALEXAS,
            IRAS, CHARMIAN, SOOTHSAYER, *and*
                            ATTENDANTS)

MESSENGER. Fulvia thy wife first came into
    the field.

ANTONY. Against my brother Lucius?

MESSENGER. Ay:
But soon that war had end, and the time's
    state   101
Made friends of them, jointing their force

'gainst Caesar,
Whose better issue [2] in the war, from Italy
Upon the first encounter drave them.

ANTONY. Well, what worst? 105

MESSENGER. The nature of bad news infects the teller.

ANTONY. When it concerns the fool, or coward. On;
Things that are past are done with me. 'Tis thus:
Who tells me true, though in his tale lay death,
I hear him as [3] he flattered.

MESSENGER. Labienus— 111
This is stiff news—hath, with his Parthian force
Extended Asia; from Euphrates
His conquering banner shook from Syria
To Lydia and to Ionia: whilst— 115

ANTONY. Antony, thou wouldst say,—

MESSENGER. O! my lord.

ANTONY. Speak to me home, mince not the general tongue;
Name Cleopatra as she is called in Rome;
Rail thou in Fulvia's phrase; and taunt my faults 120
With such full licence as both truth and malice
Have power to utter. O! then we bring forth weeds
When our quick minds lie still; and our ills told us
Is as our earing.[4] Fare thee well awhile. 124

MESSENGER. At your noble pleasure. (Exit)

ANTONY. From Sicyon, ho, the news! Speak there!

FIRST ATTENDANT. The man from Sicyon, is there such an one?

SECOND ATTENDANT. He stays upon your will.

ANTONY. Let him appear.
These strong Egyptian fetters I must break, 130
Or lose myself in dotage.

(Enter another MESSENGER)
What are you?

SECOND MESSENGER. Fulvia thy wife is dead.

ANTONY. Where died she?

SECOND MESSENGER. In Sicyon: 135
Her length of sickness, with what else more serious
Importeth thee to know, this bears.
(Giving a letter)

ANTONY. Forbear me.

2 fortune 3 as though 4 plowing

(Exit SECOND MESSENGER)
There's a great spirit gone! Thus did I desire it:
What our contempts do often hurl from us 140
We wish it ours again; the present pleasure,
By revolution lowering, does become
The opposite of itself: she's good, being gone;
The hand could pluck her back that shoved her on.
I must from this enchanting queen break off; 145
Ten thousand harms, more than the ills I know,
My idleness doth hatch. How now! Enobarbus!

(Re-enter ENOBARBUS)

ENOBARBUS. What's your pleasure, sir?

ANTONY. I must with haste from hence. 149

ENOBARBUS. Why, then, we kill all our women. We see how mortal an unkindness is to them; if they suffer our departure, death's the word.

ANTONY. I must be gone.

ENOBARBUS. Under a compelling occasion let women die; it were pity to cast them away for nothing; though between them and a great cause they should be esteemed nothing. Cleopatra, catching but the least noise of this, dies instantly; I have seen her die twenty times upon far poorer moment. I do think there is mettle in death which commits some loving act upon her, she hath such a celerity in dying. 163

ANTONY. She is cunning past man's thought.

ENOBARBUS. Alack! sir, no; her passions are made of nothing but the finest part of pure love. We cannot call her winds and waters sighs and tears; they are greater storms and tempests than almanacs can report: this cannot be cunning in her; if it be, she makes a shower of rain as well as Jove. 171

ANTONY. Would I had never seen her!

ENOBARBUS. Oh, sir! you had then left unseen a wonderful piece of work which not to have been blessed withal would have discredited your travel. 176

ANTONY. Fulvia is dead.

ENOBARBUS. Sir?

ANTONY. Fulvia is dead.

ENOBARBUS. Fulvia! 180

ANTONY. Dead.

ENOBARBUS. Why, sir, give the gods a thankful sacrifice. When it pleaseth their deities to take the wife of a man from him, it shows to man the tailors of the earth; comforting therein, that when old robes are worn out, there are members to make new. If there were no more women but Fulvia, then had you indeed a cut, and the case to be lamented: this grief is crowned with consolation; your old smock brings forth a new petticoat; and indeed the tears live in an onion that should water this sorrow.   193

ANTONY. The business she hath broachèd [5] in the state
Cannot endure my absence.

ENOBARBUS. And the business you have broached here cannot be without you; especially that of Cleopatra's, which wholly depends on your abode.   199

ANTONY. No more light answers. Let our officers
Have notice what we purpose. I shall break
The cause of our expedience [6] to the queen,
And get her leave to part. For not alone
The death of Fulvia, with more urgent touches,
Do strongly speak to us, but the letters too   206
Of many our contriving friends in Rome
Petition us at home. Sextus Pompeius
Hath given the dare to Caesar, and commands
The empire of the sea; our slippery people—
Whose love is never linked to the deserver
Till his deserts are past—begin to throw
Pompey the Great and all his dignities
Upon his son; who, high in name and power,
Higher than both in blood and life, stands up
For the main soldier, whose quality, going on,
The sides o' the world may danger. Much is breeding,
Which, like the courser's hair,[7] hath yet but life,
And not a serpent's poison. Say, our pleasure,
To such whose place is under us, requires   220
Our quick remove from hence.

ENOBARBUS. I shall do it.   (*Exeunt*)

SCENE III. *The same. Another room.*

(*Enter* CLEOPATRA, CHARMIAN, IRAS, *and* ALEXAS)

CLEOPATRA. Where is he?
CHARMIAN.   I did not see him since.

CLEOPATRA. See where he is, who's with him, what he does;
I did not send you: if you find him sad,
Say I am dancing; if in mirth, report
That I am sudden sick: quick, and return.   5
                    (*Exit* ALEXAS)
CHARMIAN. Madam, methinks, if you did love him dearly,
You do not hold the method to enforce
The like from him.
CLEOPATRA.   What should I do I do not?
CHARMIAN. In each thing give him way, cross him in nothing.
CLEOPATRA. Thou teachest like a fool; the way to lose him.   10
CHARMIAN. Tempt him not so too far; I wish, forbear:
In time we hate that which we often fear.
But here comes Antony.
                (*Enter* ANTONY)
CLEOPATRA.   I am sick and sullen.
ANTONY. I am sorry to give breathing to my purpose,—
CLEOPATRA. Help me away, dear Charmian, I shall fall: 15
It cannot be thus long, the sides of nature
Will not sustain it.
ANTONY.   Now, my dearest queen,—
CLEOPATRA. Pray you, stand further from me.
ANTONY.   What's the matter?
CLEOPATRA. I know, by that same eye, there's some good news.
What says the married woman? You may go: 20
Would she had never given you leave to come!
Let her not say 'tis I that keep you here;
I have no power upon you; hers you are.
ANTONY. The gods best know,—
CLEOPATRA.   O! never was there queen
So mightily betrayed; yet at the first   25
I saw the treasons planted.
ANTONY.   Cleopatra,—
CLEOPATRA. Why should I think you can be mine and true,
Though you in swearing shake the thronèd gods,
Who have been false to Fulvia? Riotous madness,   29
To be entangled with those mouth-made vows,

---

[5] begun   [6] enterprise
[7] horse's hair, with a reference to the old superstition that a horse hair dropped into a pond turned into a serpent

Which break themselves in swearing!

ANTONY.   Most sweet queen,—

CLEOPATRA. Nay, pray you, seek no colour
    for your going,

But bid farewell, and go: when you sued stay-
    ing [1]

Then was the time for words; no going then:

Eternity was in our lips and eyes,   35

Bliss in our brows bent; none our parts so poor

But was a race of heaven; they are so still,

Or thou, the greatest soldier of the world,

Art turned the greatest liar.

ANTONY.   How now, lady!

CLEOPATRA. I would I had thy inches; thou
    shouldst know   40

There were a heart in Egypt.

ANTONY.   Hear me, queen:

The strong necessity of time commands

Our services awhile, but my full heart

Remains in use with you. Our Italy

Shines o'er with civil swords; Sextus Pompeius

Makes his approaches to the port of Rome;   46

Equality of two domestic powers

Breeds scrupulous faction. The hated, grown to
    strength,

Are newly grown to love; the condemned
    Pompey,

Rich in his father's honour, creeps apace   50

Into the hearts of such as have not thrived

Upon the present state, whose numbers
    threaten;

And quietness, grown sick of rest, would purge [2]

By any desperate change. My more particular,

And that which most with you should safe [3] my
    going,   55

Is Fulvia's death.

CLEOPATRA. Though age from folly could not
    give me freedom,

It does from childishness: can Fulvia die?

ANTONY. She's dead, my queen:

Look here, and at thy sovereign leisure read   60

The garboils [4] she awaked; at the last, best,

See when and where she died.

CLEOPATRA.   O most false love!

Where be the sacred vials thou shouldst fill

With sorrowful water? Now I see, I see,

In Fulvia's death, how mine received shall be.

ANTONY. Quarrel no more, but be prepared
    to know   66

The purposes I bear, which are or cease

As you shall give the advice. By the fire

That quickens Nilus' slime, I go from hence

Thy soldier, servant, making peace or war   70

As thou affect'st.[5]

CLEOPATRA.   Cut my lace, Charmian, come;

But let it be: I am quickly ill, and well;

So Antony loves.

ANTONY.   My precious queen, forbear,

And give true evidence to his love which stands

An honourable trial.

CLEOPATRA.   So Fulvia told me.   75

I prithee, turn aside and weep for her;

Then bid adieu to me, and say the tears

Belong to Egypt: good now, play one scene

Of excellent dissembling, and let it look

Like perfect honour.

ANTONY.   You'll heat my blood; no more.

CLEOPATRA. You can do better yet, but this
    is meetly.   81

ANTONY. Now, by my sword,—

CLEOPATRA.   And target. Still he mends;

But this is not the best. Look, prithee, Char-
    mian,

How this Herculean Roman does become

The carriage of his chafe.   85

ANTONY. I'll leave you, lady.

CLEOPATRA.   Courteous lord, one word.

Sir, you and I must part, but that's not it:

Sir, you and I have loved, but there's not it;

That you know well: something it is I
    would,—

O! my oblivion is a very Antony,   90

And I am all forgotten.

ANTONY.   But that your royalty

Holds idleness your subject, I should take you

For idleness itself.

CLEOPATRA.   'Tis sweating labour

To bear such idleness so near the heart

As Cleopatra this. But, sir, forgive me;   95

Since my becomings [6] kill me when they do not

Eye [7] well to you: your honour calls you hence;

Therefore be deaf to my unpitied folly,

And all the gods go with you! Upon your sword

Sit laurel victory! and smooth success   100

Be strewed before your feet!

ANTONY.   Let us go. Come;

Our separation so abides and flies,

That thou, residing here, go'st yet with me,

---

[1] begged to stay [2] restore itself to healthy activity [3] make safe [4] commotions [5] art inclined [6] graces [7] appear

And I, hence fleeting, here remain with thee.
Away!　　　　　　　　　　(*Exeunt*)　105

SCENE IV: *Rome. A room in Caesar's house.*

(*Enter* OCTAVIUS CAESAR, LEPIDUS,
and ATTENDANTS)

CAESAR. You may see, Lepidus, and hence-
　　forth know,
It is not Caesar's natural vice to hate
Our great competitor. From Alexandria
This is the news: he fishes, drinks, and wastes
The lamps of night in revel; is not more man-
　　like　　　　　　　　　　　　　　5
Than Cleopatra, nor the queen of Ptolemy
More womanly than he; hardly gave audience,
　　or
Vouchsafed to think he had partners: you shall
　　find there
A man who is the abstract of all faults
That all men follow.

LEPIDUS.　　　　　　I must not think there are
Evils enow to darken all his goodness;　11
His faults in him seem as the spots of heaven,
More fiery by night's blackness; hereditary
Rather than purchased; what he cannot change
Than what he chooses.　　　　　　15

　　CAESAR. You are too indulgent. Let us grant
　　it is not
Amiss to tumble on the bed of Ptolemy,
To give a kingdom for a mirth, to sit
And keep the turn of tippling with a slave,
To reel the streets at noon, and stand the buffet
With knaves that smell of sweat; say this be-
　　comes him,—　　　　　　　　　21
As his composure [1] must be rare indeed
Whom these things cannot blemish,—yet must
　　Antony
No way excuse his foils, when we do bear
So great weight in his lightness. If he filled　25
His vacancy with his voluptuousness,
Full surfeits and the dryness of his bones
Call on him for 't; but to confound such time
That drums him from his sport, and speaks as
　　loud
As his own state and ours, 'tis to be chid　30
As we rate [2] boys, who, being mature in knowl-
　　edge,
Pawn their experience to their present pleasure,

And so rebel to judgment.

(*Enter a* MESSENGER)

LEPIDUS.　　　　　　　Here's more news.
MESSENGER. Thy biddings have been done,
　　and every hour,
Most noble Caesar, shalt thou have report　35
How 'tis abroad. Pompey is strong at sea,
And it appears he is beloved of those
That only have feared Caesar; to the ports
The discontents repair, and men's reports
Give him much wronged.

CAESAR.　　　　I should have known no less.　40
It hath been taught us from the primal state,
That he which is was wished until he were;
And the ebbed man, ne'er loved till ne'er worth
　　love,
Comes deared [3] by being lacked. This common
　　body,
Like to a vagabond flag upon the stream,　45
Goes to and back, lackeying the varying tide,
To rot itself with motion.

MESSENGER.　　　　Caesar, I bring thee word,
Menecrates and Menas, famous pirates,
Make the sea serve them, which they ear and
　　wound
With keels of every kind: many hot inroads
They make in Italy; the borders maritime　51
Lack blood to think on 't, and flush [4] youth
　　revolt;
No vessel can peep forth, but 'tis as soon
Taken as seen; for Pompey's name strikes more
Than could his war resisted.

CAESAR.　　　　　　　Antony,　55
Leave thy lascivious wassails. When thou once
Wast beaten from Modena, where thou slew'st
Hirtius and Pansa, consuls, at thy heel
Did famine follow, whom thou fought'st
　　against,
Though daintily brought up, with patience
　　more　　　　　　　　　　　　60
Than savages could suffer; thou didst drink
The stale of horses and the gilded puddle
Which beasts would cough at; thy palate then
　　did deign
The roughest berry on the rudest hedge;
Yea, like the stag, when snow the pasture
　　sheets,　　　　　　　　　　　65
The barks of trees thou browsed'st; on the Alps
It is reported thou didst eat strange flesh,

[1] disposition　[2] berate, scold　[3] becomes endeared, valued　[4] lusty　[5] did not become shrunken

Which some did die to look on; and all this—
It wounds thy honour that I speak it now—
Was borne so like a soldier, that thy cheek   70
So much as lanked [5] not.

LEPIDUS.   'Tis pity of him.

CAESAR. Let his shames quickly
Drive him to Rome. 'Tis time we twain
Did show ourselves i' the field; and to that end
Assemble we immediate council; Pompey   75
Thrives in our idleness.

LEPIDUS.   Tomorrow, Caesar,
I shall be furnished to inform you rightly
Both what by sea and land I can be able
To front this present time.

CAESAR.   Till which encounter,
It is my business too. Farewell.   80

LEPIDUS. Farewell, my lord. What you shall
      know meantime
Of stirs abroad, I shall beseech you, sir,
To let me be partaker.

CAESAR.   Doubt not, sir;
I knew it for my bond.   (Exeunt)

SCENE V. Alexandria. A room in the palace.

(Enter CLEOPATRA, CHARMIAN, IRAS
      and MARDIAN)

CLEOPATRA. Charmian!

CHARMIAN. Madam!

CLEOPATRA. Ha, ha!
Give me to drink mandragora.[1]

CHARMIAN.   Why, madam?

CLEOPATRA. That I might sleep out this great
      gap of time   5
My Antony is away.

CHARMIAN.   You think of him too much.

CLEOPATRA. O! 'tis treason.

CHARMIAN.   Madam, I trust, not so.

CLEOPATRA. Thou, eunuch Mardian!

MARDIAN. What's your highness' pleasure?

CLEOPATRA. Not now to hear thee sing; I
      take no pleasure
In aught a eunuch has. 'Tis well for thee,   10
That, being unseminared,[2] thy freer thoughts
May not fly forth of Egypt. Hast thou affections?

MARDIAN. Yes, gracious madam.

CLEOPATRA. Indeed!

MARDIAN. Not in deed, madam: for I can do
      nothing   15

But what indeed is honest to be done;
Yet have I fierce affections, and think
What Venus did with Mars.

CLEOPATRA. O Charmian!
Where think'st thou he is now? Stands he, or
      sits he?
Or does he walk? or is he on his horse?   20
O happy horse, to bear the weight of Antony!
Do bravely, horse, for wot'st [3] thou whom thou
      mov'st?
The demi-Atlas of this earth, the arm
And burgonet of men. He's speaking now,
Or murmuring 'Where's my serpent of old
      Nile?'   25
For so he calls me. Now I feed myself
With most delicious poison. Think on me,
That am with Phoebus' amorous pinches black,
And wrinkled deep in time? Broad-fronted
      Caesar,   29
When thou wast here above the ground I was
A morsel for a monarch, and great Pompey
Would stand and make his eyes grow in my
      brow;
There would he anchor his aspect [4] and die
With looking on his life.

      (Enter ALEXAS)

ALEXAS.   Sovereign of Egypt, hail!

CLEOPATRA. How much unlike art thou Mark
      Antony!   35
Yet, coming from him, that great medicine hath
With his tinct gilded thee.
How goes it with my brave Mark Antony?

ALEXAS. Last thing he did, dear queen,
He kissed, the last of many doubled kisses,   40
This orient pearl. His speech sticks in my heart.

CLEOPATRA. Mine ear must pluck it thence.

ALEXAS.   "Good friend," quoth he,
"Say, the firm Roman to great Egypt sends
This treasure of an oyster; at whose foot,
To mend the petty present, I will piece   45
Her opulent throne with kingdoms; all the east,
Say thou, shall call her mistress." So he nodded,
And soberly did mount an arm-gaunt [5] steed,
Who neighed so high that what I would have
      spoke
Was beastly dumbed by him.

CLEOPATRA.   What! was he sad or merry?

ALEXAS. Like to the time o' the year between
      the extremes   51

1 a narcotic   2 destitute of seed   3 knowest   4 gaze   5 lean from bearing arms (?)

Of hot and cold; he was nor sad nor merry.

CLEOPATRA. O well-divided disposition! Note him,

Note him, good Charmian, 'tis the man; but note him:

He was not sad, for he would shine on those   55

That make their looks by his; he was not merry,

Which seemed to tell them his remembrance lay

In Egypt with his joy; but between both:

O heavenly mingle! Be'st thou sad or merry.

The violence of either thee becomes,   60

So does it no man else. Mett'st thou my posts?

ALEXAS. Ay, madam, twenty several messengers.

Why do you send so thick?

CLEOPATRA.   Who's born that day

When I forget to send to Antony,   64

Shall die a beggar. Ink and paper, Charmian.

Welcome, my good Alexas. Did I, Charmian,

Ever love Caesar so?

CHARMIAN.   O! that brave Caesar.

CLEOPATRA. Be choked with such another emphasis!

Say the brave Antony.

CHARMIAN.   The valiant Caesar!

CLEOPATRA. By Isis, I will give thee bloody teeth,   70

If thou with Caesar paragon [6] again

My man of men.

CHARMIAN. By your most gracious pardon,

I sing but after you.

CLEOPATRA.   My salad days,

When I was green in judgment, cold in blood,

To say as I said then! But come, away;   75

Get me ink and paper:

He shall have every day a several greeting,

Or I'll unpeople Egypt.   (*Exeunt*)

Act II

SCENE I. *Messina. A room in* POMPEY's *house.*

(*Enter* POMPEY, MENECRATES, *and* MENAS)

POMPEY. If the great gods be just, they shall assist

The deeds of justest men.

MENECRATES.   Know, worthy Pompey,

That what they do delay, they not deny.

POMPEY. Whiles we are suitors to their throne, decays

The thing we sue for.

MENECRATES.   We, ignorant of ourselves,

Beg often our own harms, which the wise powers   6

Deny us for our good; so find we profit

By losing of our prayers.

POMPEY.   I shall do well:

The people love me, and the sea is mine;

My powers are crescent,[1] and my auguring hope

Says it will come to the full. Mark Antony   11

In Egypt sits at dinner, and will make

No wars without doors; Caesar gets money where

He loses hearts; Lepidus flatters both,

Of both is flattered; but he neither loves,   15

Nor either cares for him.

MENECRATES.   Caesar and Lepidus

Are in the field; a mighty strength they carry.

POMPEY. Where have you this? 'tis false.

MENECRATES. From Silvius, sir.

POMPEY. He dreams; I know they are in Rome together,

Looking for Antony. But all the charms of love,

Salt [2] Cleopatra, soften thy wanèd [3] lip!   21

Let witchcraft join with beauty, lust with both!

Tie up the libertine in a field of feasts,

Keep his brain fuming; Epicurean cooks

Sharpen with cloyless sauce his appetite,   25

That sleep and feeding may prorogue his honour

Even till a Lethe'd dulness!

(*Enter* VARRIUS)

                    How now, Varrius!

VARRIUS. This is most certain that I shall deliver:

Mark Antony is every hour in Rome

Expected; since he went from Egypt 'tis   30

A space for further travel.

POMPEY.   I could have given less matter

A better ear. Menas, I did not think

This amorous surfeiter would have donned his helm

For such a petty war; his soldiership

Is twice the other twain. But let us rear   35

The higher our opinion,[4] that our stirring

---

[6] compare   [1] in the ascendant   [2] lecherous   [3] withered   [4] self-confidence

Can from the lap of Egypt's widow pluck
The ne'er-lust-wearied Antony.

MENECRATES.   I cannot hope
Caesar and Antony shall well greet together;
His wife that's dead did trespasses to Caesar,   40
His brother warred upon him, although I think
Not moved by Antony.

POMPEY.   I know not, Menas,
How lesser enmities may give way to greater.
Were 't not that we stand up against them all
'Twere pregnant they should square between
    themselves,   45
For they have entertained cause enough
To draw their swords; but how the fear of us
May cement their divisions and bind up
The petty difference, we yet not know.
Be it as our gods have 't! It only stands   50
Our lives upon, to use our strongest hands.
Come, Menas.   (*Exeunt*)

SCENE II. *Rome. A room in* LEPIDUS' *house.*

(*Enter* ENOBARBUS *and* LEPIDUS)

LEPIDUS. Good Enorbarbus, 'tis a worthy deed,
And shall become you well, to entreat your
    captain
To soft and gentle speech.

ENOBARBUS.   I shall entreat him
To answer like himself: if Caesar move him,
Let Antony look over Caesar's head,   5
And speak as loud as Mars. By Jupiter,
Were I the wearer of Antonius' beard,
I would not shave 't to-day.

LEPIDUS.   'Tis not a time
For private stomaching.[1]

ENOBARBUS.   Every time
Serves for the matter that is then born in 't.

LEPIDUS. But small to greater matters must
    give way.   11

ENOBARBUS. Not if the small come first.

LEPIDUS.   Your speech is passion;
But, pray you, stir no embers up. Here comes
The noble Antony.

(*Enter* ANTONY *and* VENTIDIUS)

ENOBARBUS.   And yonder, Caesar.

(*Enter* CAESAR, MECAENAS, *and* AGRIPPA)

ANTONY. If we compose [2] well here, to
    Parthia: 15
Hark ye, Ventidius.

CAESAR.   I do not know,
Mecaenas; ask Agrippa.

LEPIDUS.   Noble friends,
That which combined us was most great, and
    let not
A leaner action rend us. What's amiss,
May it be gently heard; when we debate   20
Our trivial difference loud, we do commit
Murder in healing wounds; then, noble
    partners,—
The rather, for I earnestly beseech,—
Touch you the sourest points with sweetest
    terms,
Nor curstness [3] grow to the matter.

ANTONY.   'Tis spoken well.
Were we before our armies, and to fight,   26
I should do thus. (ANTONY *embraces* CAESAR)

CAESAR. Welcome to Rome.

ANTONY.   Thank you.

CAESAR.   Sit.

ANTONY.   Sit, sir.

CAESAR.   Nay, then.

ANTONY. I learn, you take things ill which
    are not so,
Or being, concern you not.

CAESAR.   I must be laughed at
If, or for nothing or a little, I   31
Should say myself offended, and with you
Chiefly i' the world; more laughed at that I
    should
Once name you derogately, when to sound your
    name
It not concerned me.

ANTONY.   My being in Egypt, Caesar,
What was 't to you?   36

CAESAR. No more than my residing here at
    Rome
Might be to you in Egypt; yet, if you there
Did practice on my state,[4] your being in Egypt
Might be my question.

ANTONY.   How intend [5] you, practiced?

CAESAR. You may be pleased to catch at mine
    intent   41
By what did here befall me. Your wife and
    brother
Made wars upon me, and their contestation
Was theme for you, you were the word of war.

ANTONY. You do mistake your business; my
    brother never   45

---

[1] resenting   [2] agree   [3] bad humor   [4] plot against my government   [5] mean   [6] disposition

Did urge me in his act: I did inquire it;
And have my learning from some true reports,
That drew their swords with you. Did he not
    rather
Discredit my authority with yours,   49
And make the wars alike against my stomach,[6]
Having alike your cause? Of this my letters
Before did satisfy you. If you'll patch a quarrel,
As matter whole you have not to make it with,
It must not be with this.

CAESAR.   You praise yourself
By laying defects of judgment to me, but   55
You patched up your excuses.

ANTONY.   Not so, not so;
I know you could not lack, I am certain on 't,
Very necessity of this thought, that I,
Your partner in the cause 'gainst which he
    fought,   59
Could not with graceful eyes attend those wars
Which fronted mine own peace. As for my wife,
I would you had her spirit in such another:
The third o' the world is yours, which with a
    snaffle
You may pace easy, but not such a wife.

ENOBARBUS. Would we had all such wives, that
the men might go to wars with the women!   66

ANTONY. So much uncurbable, her garboils,
    Caesar,
Made out of her impatience,—which not wanted
Shrewdness of policy too,—I grieving grant
Did you too much disquiet; for that you must
But say I could not help it.

CAESAR.   I wrote to you   71
When rioting in Alexandria; you
Did pocket up my letters, and with taunts
Did gibe my missive [7] out of audience.

ANTONY.   Sir,
He fell upon me, ere admitted: then   75
Three kings I had newly feasted, and did want
Of what I was i' the morning; but next day
I told him of myself, which was as much
As to have asked him pardon. Let this fellow
Be nothing of our strife; if we contend,   80
Out of our question wipe him.

CAESAR.   You have broken
The article of your oath, which you shall never
Have tongue to charge me with.

LEPIDUS.   Soft, Caesar!

ANTONY.   No,
Lepidus, let him speak:
The honour's sacred which he talks on now,   85
Supposing that I lacked it. But on, Caesar;
The article of my oath.

CAESAR. To lend me arms and aid when I re-
    quired them,
The which you both denied.

ANTONY.   Neglected, rather;
And then, when poisoned hours had bound me
    up   90
From mine own knowledge. As nearly as I may,
I'll play the penitent to you; but mine honesty
Shall not make poor my greatness, nor my
    power
Work without it. Truth is, that Fulvia,
To have me out of Egypt, made wars here;   95
For which myself, the ignorant motive, do
So far ask pardon as befits mine honour
To stoop in such a case.

LEPIDUS.   'Tis noble spoken.

MECAENUS. If it might please you, to enforce
    no further
The griefs between ye: to forget them quite
Were to remember that the present need   101
Speaks to atone [8] you.

LEPIDUS.   Worthily spoken, Mecaenas.

ENOBARBUS. Or, if you borrow one another's
love for the instant, you may, when you hear
no more words of Pompey, return it again: you
shall have time to wrangle in when you have
nothing else to do.   107

ANTONY. Thou art a soldier only; speak no
    more.

ENOBARBUS. That truth should be silent I had
    almost forgot.

ANTONY. You wrong this presence; therefore
    speak no more.

ENOBARBUS. Go to, then; your considerate
    stone.

CAESAR. I do not much dislike the matter, but
The manner of his speech; for it cannot be
We shall remain in friendship, our conditions [9]
So differing in their acts. Yet, if I knew   116
What hoop should hold us stanch,[10] from edge
    to edge
O' the world I would pursue it.

AGRIPPA.   Give me leave, Caesar.

CAESAR. Speak, Agrippa.

AGRIPPA. Thou hast a sister by the mother's

---

[7] messenger   [8] reconcile   [9] characters   [10] firm

side,   120
Admired Octavia; great Mark Antony
Is now a widower.

    CAESAR.   Say not so, Agrippa:
If Cleopatra heard you, your reproof
Were well deserved of rashness.

    ANTONY. I am not married, Caesar; let me hear
        Agrippa further speak.   126

    AGRIPPA. To hold you in perpetual amity,
To make you brothers, and to knit your hearts
With an unslipping knot, take Antony
Octavia to his wife; whose beauty claims   130
No worse a husband than the best of men,
Whose virtue and whose general graces speak
That which none else can utter. By this mar-
    riage,
All little jealousies which now seem great,
And all great fears which now import[11] their
    dangers,   135
Would then be nothing; truths would be but
    tales
Where now half tales be truths; her love to both
Would each to other and all loves to both
Draw after her. Pardon what I have spoke,
For 'tis a studied, not a present thought,   140
By duty ruminated.

    ANTONY.   Will Caesar speak?

    CAESAR. Not till he hears how Antony is
    touched
With what is spoke already.

    ANTONY.   What power is in Agrippa,
If I would say, "Agrippa, be it so,"
To make this good?

    CAESAR.   The power of Caesar, and
His power unto Octavia.

    ANTONY.   May I never   146
To this good purpose, that so fairly shows,
Dream of impediment! Let me have thy hand;
Further this act of grace, and from this hour
The heart of brothers govern in our loves
And sway our great designs!

    CAESAR.   There is my hand. 151
A sister I bequeath you, whom no brother
Did ever love so dearly; let her live
To join our kingdoms and our hearts, and never
Fly off our loves again!

    LEPIDUS.   Happily, amen!   155

    ANTONY. I did not think to draw my sword
    'gainst Pompey,

For he hath laid strange courtesies and great
Of late upon me; I must thank him only,
Lest my remembrance suffer ill report;
At heel of that, defy him.

    LEPIDUS.   Time calls upon 's:
Of us must Pompey presently be sought,   161
Or else he seeks out us.

    ANTONY.   Where lies he?

    CAESAR. About the Mount Misenum.

    ANTONY.   What's his strength
By land?

    CAESAR. Great and increasing; but by sea   165
He is an absolute master.

    ANTONY.   So is the fame.[12]
Would we had spoke[13] together! Haste we for
    it;
Yet, ere we put ourselves in arms, dispatch we
The business we have talked of.

    CAESAR.   With most gladness;
And do invite you to my sister's view,   170
Whither straight I'll lead you.

    ANTONY.   Let us, Lepidus,
Not lack your company.

    LEPIDUS.   Noble Antony,
Not sickness should detain me.

        (*Flourish. Exeunt* CAESAR, ANTONY,
                   and LEPIDUS.)

    MECAENAS. Welcome from Egypt, sir.

    ENOBARBUS. Half the heart of Caesar, worthy
Mecaenas!   175
My honourable friend, Agrippa!

    AGRIPPA. Good Enobarbus!

    MECAENAS. We have cause to be glad that
matters are so well digested. You stayed well
by 't in Egypt.   180

    ENOBARBUS. Ay, sir; we did sleep day out of
countenance, and made the night light with
drinking.

    MECAENAS. Eight wild boars roasted whole at
a breakfast, and but twelve persons there; is
this true?   185

    ENOBARBUS. This was but as a fly by an eagle;
we had much more monstrous matter of feast,
which worthily deserved noting.

    MECAENAS. She's a most triumphant lady, if
report be square to her.   190

    ENOBARBUS. When she first met Mark Antony
she pursed[14] up his heart, upon the river of
Cydnus.

---

11 bring with them 12 report 13 fought 14 pocketed

AGRIPPA. There she appeared indeed, or my reporter devised well for her.

ENOBARBUS. I will tell you.   195
The barge she sat in, like a burnished throne,
Burned on the water; the poop was beaten gold,
Purple the sails, and so perfumed, that
The winds were love-sick with them, the oars
      were silver,
Which to the tune of flutes kept stroke, and
      made   200
The water which they beat to follow faster,
As amorous of their strokes. For her own person,
It beggared all description; she did lie
In her pavilion,—cloth-of-gold of tissue,—
O'er-picturing that Venus where we see   205
The fancy outwork nature; on each side her
Stood pretty-dimpled boys, like smiling Cupids,
With divers-coloured fans, whose wind did seem
To glow the delicate cheeks which they did
      cool,   209
And what they undid did.

AGRIPPA.   O! rare for Antony.

ENOBARBUS. Her gentlewomen, like the Ne-
      reides,
So many mermaids, tended her i' the eyes,
And made their bends adornings; at the helm
A seeming mermaid steers; the silken tackle
Swell with the touches of those flower-soft
      hands,   215
That yarely [15] frame the office. From the barge
A strange invisible perfume hits the sense
Of the adjacent wharfs. The city cast
Her people out upon her, and Antony,   219
Enthroned i' the market-place, did sit alone,
Whistling to the air; which, but for vacancy,
Had gone to gaze on Cleopatra too
And made a gap in nature.

AGRIPPA.   Rare Egyptian!

ENOBARBUS. Upon her landing, Antony sent to
      her,
Invited her to supper; she replied   225
It should be better he became her guest,
Which she entreated. Our courteous Antony,
Whom ne'er the word of "No" woman heard
      speak,
Being barbered ten times o'er, goes to the feast,

AGRIPPA.   Royal wench!
And, for his ordinary [16] pays his heart   230
For what his eyes eat only.

She made great Caesar lay his sword to bed.
He ploughed her, and she cropped.

ENOBARBUS. I saw her once
Hop forty paces through the public street;
And having lost her breath, she spoke, and
      panted   235
That [17] she did make defect perfection,
And, breathless, power breathe forth.

MECAENAS. Now Antony must leave her ut-
      terly.

ENOBARBUS. Never; he will not:
Age cannot wither her, nor custom stale   240
Her infinite variety; other women cloy
The appetites they feed, but she makes hungry
Where most she satisfies; for vilest things
Become themselves [18] in her, that the holy
      priests
Bless her when she is riggish.[19]   245

MECAENAS. If beauty, wisdom, modesty, can
      settle
The heart of Antony, Octavia is
A blessed lottery to him.

AGRIPPA.   Let us go.
Good Enobarbus, make yourself my guest
Whilst you abide here.

ENOBARBUS.   Humbly, sir, I thank you. 250
                                          (Exeunt)

SCENE III. The same. A room in CAESAR'S
                  house.

(Enter CAESAR, ANTONY, OCTAVIA
            between them; ATTENDANTS)

ANTONY. The world and my great office will
      sometimes.
Divide me from your bosom.

OCTAVIA.   All which time
Before the gods my knee shall bow my prayers
To them for you.

ANTONY.   Good night, sir, My Octavia,
Read not my blemishes in the world's report;   5
I have not kept my square,[1] but that to come
Shall all be done by the rule. Good night, dear
      lady.

OCTAVIA. Good night, sir.

CAESAR. Good night; (Exeunt CAESAR and OC-
                                          TAVIA)

            (Enter SOOTHSAYER)

ANTONY. Now, sirrah; you do wish yourself
      in Egypt?   10

---

[15] nimbly   [16] dinner   [17] so that   [18] are becoming, delightful   [19] wanton

SOOTHSAYER. Would I had never come from
    thence, nor you
Thither!
    ANTONY. If you can, your reason?
    SOOTHSAYER.   I see it in
My motion,[2] have it not in my tongue: but yet
Hie you to Egypt again.
    ANTONY.   Say to me,   15
Whose fortunes shall rise higher, Caesar's or
    mine?
    SOOTHSAYER. Caesar's.
Therefore, O Antony! stay not by his side;
Thy demon—that's thy spirit which keeps thee,
    —is
Noble, courageous, high, unmatchable,   20
Where Caesar's is not; but near him thy angel
Becomes a fear, as being o'erpowered; therefore
Make space enough between you.
    ANTONY.   Speak this no more.
    SOOTHSAYER. To none but thee; no more but
    when to thee.
If thou dost play with him at any game   25
Thou art sure to lose, and, of that natural luck,
He beats thee 'gainst the odds; thy lustre thick-
    ens [3]
When he shines by. I say again, thy spirit
Is all afraid to govern thee near him,
But he away, 'tis noble.
    ANTONY.   Get thee gone: 30
Say to Ventidius I would speak with him.
                      (*Exit* SOOTHSAYER)
He shall to Parthia. Be it art or hap [4]
He hath spoken true; the very dice obey him.
And in our sports my better cunning faints
Under his chance; if we draw lots he speeds,[5]
His cocks do win the battle still of mine   36
When it is all to nought, and his quails [6] ever
Beat mine, inhooped, at odds. I will to Egypt;
And though I make this marriage for my peace,
I' the east my pleasure lies.
               (*Enter* VENTIDIUS)
               O! come, Ventidius, 40
You must to Parthia; your commission's ready;
Follow me, and receive 't.   (*Exeunt*)

SCENE IV. *The same. A street.*

(*Enter* LEPIDUS, MECAENAS, *and* AGRIPPA)

LEPIDUS. Trouble yourselves no further; pray
you hasten
Your generals after.
    AGRIPPA.   Sir, Mark Antony
Will e'en but kiss Octavia, and we'll follow.
    LEPIDUS. Till I shall see you in your soldier's
    dress,
Which will become you both, farewell.
    MECAENAS.   We shall, 6
As I conceive the journey, be at the Mount
Before you, Lepidus.
    LEPIDUS.   Your way is shorter;
My purposes do draw me much about:
You'll win two days upon me.

MECAENAS. ⎫
               ⎬ Sir, good success!
AGRIPPA. ⎭

    LEPIDUS. Farewell.   (*Exeunt*) 10

SCENE V. *Alexandria. A Room in the Palace.*

(*Enter* CLEOPATRA, CHARIMAN, IRAS,
    ALEXAS, *and* ATTENDANT)
CLEOPATRA. Give me some music; music,
moody food
Of us that trade in love.
    ATTENDANT.   The music, ho!
              (*Enter* MARDIAN)
CLEOPATRA. Let it alone; let's to billiards:
    come, Charmian.
    CHARMIAN. My arm is sore; best play with
    Mardian.
    CLEOPATRA. As well a woman with a eunuch
    played   5
As with a woman. Come, you'll play with me,
    sir?
    MARDIAN. As well as I can, madam.
    CLEOPATRA. And when good will is showed,
    though 't come too short,
The actor may plead pardon. I'll none now.
Give me mine angle; we'll to the river; there—
My music playing far off—I will betray   11
Tawny-finned fishes; my bended hook shall
    pierce
Their slimy jaws; and, as I draw them up,
I'll think them every one an Antony,
And say, "Ah, ha!" you're caught.
    CHARMIAN.   'Twas merry when
You wagered on your angling; when your diver
Did hang a salt-fish on his hook, which he   17

---

[1] due proportion in conduct [2] intuitively [3] dims [4] chance [5] wins [6] pitted against each other in a hoop or ring

With fervency drew up.

CLEOPATRA.　　　　　　That time—O times!—
I laughed him out of patience; and that night
I laughed him into patience: and next morn,　20
Ere the ninth hour, I drunk him to his bed;
Then put my tires [1] and mantles on him whilst
I wore his sword Philippan.[2]
　　　　　　(*Enter a* MESSENGER)
　　　　　　　　　　O! from Italy;
Ram thou thy fruitful tidings in mine ears,
That long time have been barren.

MESSENGER.　　　　　　Madam, madam—

CLEOPATRA. Antony's dead! if you say so, vil-
　lain,　26
Thou kill'st thy mistress; but well and free,
If thou so yield him, there is gold, and here
My bluest veins to kiss; a hand that kings
Have lipped, and trembled kissing.　30

MESSENGER. First, madam, he is well.

CLEOPATRA.　　　　　Why, there's more gold.
But, sirrah, mark, we use
To say the dead are well: bring it to that,
The gold I give thee will I melt, and pour
Down thy ill-uttering throat.　35

MESSENGER. Good madam, hear me.

CLEOPATRA.　　　　　Well, go to, I will;
But there's no goodness in thy face; if Antony
Be free and healthful, so tart a favour [3]
To trumpet such good tidings! if not well,
Thou shouldst come like a Fury crowned with
　snakes,　40
Not like a formal man.[4]

MESSENGER.　　　Will 't please you hear me?

CLEOPATRA. I have a mind to strike thee ere
　thou speak'st:
Yet, if thou say Antony lives, is well,
Or friends with Caesar, or not captive to him,
I'll set thee in a shower of gold, and hail　45
Rich pearls upon thee.

MESSENGER.　　　Madam, he's well.

CLEOPATRA.　　　　　　Well said.

MESSENGER. And friends with Caesar.

CLEOPATRA.　　　　Thou'rt an honest man.

MESSENGER. Caesar and he are greater friends
　than ever.

CLEOPATRA. Make thee a fortune from me.

MESSENGER.　　　　But yet, madam,—

CLEOPATRA. I do not like "but yet," it does

allay　　　　　　　　　　　　　　51
The good precedence; [5] fie upon "but yet!"
"But yet" is as a gaoler to bring forth
Some monstrous malefactor. Prithee, friend,
Pour out the pack of matter to mine ear,
The good and bad together. He's friends with
　Caesar;　55
In state of health, thou sayst; and thou sayst,
　free.

MESSENGER. Free, madam! no; I made no such
　report:
He's bound unto Octavia.

CLEOPATRA.　　　　　For what good turn?

MESSENGER. For the best turn i' the bed.

CLEOPATRA. I am pale, Charmian.

MESSENGER. Madam, he's married to Octavia.

CLEOPATRA. The most infectious pestilence
　upon thee!　61
　　(*Strikes him down*)

MESSENGER. Good madam, patience.

CLEOPATRA.　　　　What say you? Hence,
　　(*Strikes him again*)
Horrible villain! or I'll spurn thine eyes
Like balls before me; I'll unhair thy head:
　　(*She hales him up and down*)
Thou shalt be whipped with wire, and stewed
　in brine,　65
Smarting in lingering pickle.

MESSENGER.　　　　Gracious madam,
I, that do bring the news made not the match.

CLEOPATRA. Say 'tis not so, a province I will
　give thee,
And make thy fortunes proud; the blow thou
　hadst　69
Shall make thy peace for moving me to rage,
And I will boot [6] thee with what gift beside
Thy modesty can beg.

MESSENGER.　　　He's married, madam.

CLEOPATRA. Rogue! thou hast lived too long.
　　(*Draws a knife*)

MESSENGER.　　　　Nay, then I'll run.
What mean you, madam? I have made no fault.
　　　　　　　　　　　　　　　(*Exit*)

CHARMIAN. Good madam, keep yourself with-
　in yourself;　75
The man is innocent.

CLEOPATRA. Some innocents 'scape not the
　thunder-bolt.

---

[1] head-dresses　[2] the sword Antony had wielded at his victory at Philippi
[3] sour an aspect　[4] man in form　[5] thing said before　[6] enrich in addition

Melt Egypt into Nile! and kindly creatures
Turn all to serpents! Call the slave again: 79
Though I am mad, I will not bite him. Call.
  CHARMIAN. He is afeared to come.
  CLEOPATRA.   I will not hurt him.
                        (*Exit* CHARMIAN)
These hands do lack nobility, that they strike
A meaner than myself; since I myself
Have given myself the cause.
      (*Re-enter* CHARMIAN, *and* MESSENGER)
                     Come hither, sir.
Though it be honest, it is never good   85
To bring bad news; give to a gracious message
A host of tongues, but let ill tidings tell
Themselves when they be felt.
  MESSENGER.   I have my duty.
  CLEOPATRA. Is he married?
I cannot hate thee worser than I do   90
If thou again say "Yes."
  MESSENGER.   He's married, madam.
  CLEOPATRA. The gods confound thee! dost
    thou hold there still?
  MESSENGER. Should I lie, madam?
  CLEOPATRA.   O! I would thou didst,
So [7] half my Egypt were submerged and made
A cistern for scaled snakes. Go, get thee hence;
Hadst thou Narcissus in thy face, to me   96
Thou wouldst appear most ugly. He is married?
  MESSENGER. I crave your highness' pardon.
  CLEOPATRA.   He is married?
  MESSENGER. Take no offence that I would not
    offend you;
To punish me for what you make me do   100
Seems much unequal; he's married to Octavia.
  CLEOPATRA. O! that his fault should make a
    knave of thee,
That art not what thou 'rt sure of. Get thee
    hence;
The merchandise which thou hast brought from
    Rome
Are all too dear for me; lie they upon thy
    hand   105
And be undone by 'em!   (*Exit* MESSENGER)
  CHARMIAN.   Good your highness, patience.
  CLEOPATRA. In praising Antony I have dis-
    praised Caesar.
  CHARMIAN. Many times, madam.
  CLEOPATRA.   I am paid for 't now.
Lead me from hence;   109

[7] even though   [8] disposition

I faint. O Iras! Charmian! 'Tis no matter.
Go to the fellow, good Alexas; bid him
Report the feature of Octavia, her years,
Her inclination,[8] let him not leave out
The colour of her hair: bring me word quickly.
                      (*Exit* ALEXAS)
Let him for ever go:—let him not—Charmian!—
Though he be painted one way like a Gorgon,
The other way's a Mars. (*To* MARDIAN) Bid
    you Alexas   117
Bring me word how tall she is. Pity me, Char-
    mian,
But do not speak to me. Lead me to my cham-
    ber.   (*Exeunt*)

SCENE VI. *Near Misenum.*

    (*Flourish. Enter* POMPEY *and* MENAS, *at
    one side, with drum and trumpet; at
    the other,* CAESAR, ANTONY, LEPIDUS,
    ENOBARBUS, MECAENAS, *with* Soldiers
    marching.*)
  POMPEY. Your hostages I have, so have you
    mine;
And we shall talk before we fight.
  CAESAR.   Most meet
That first we come to words, and therefore have
    we
Our written purposes before us sent;
Which if thou hast considered, let us know   5
If 'twill tie up thy discontented sword,
And carry back to Sicily much tall youth
That else must perish here.
  POMPEY.   To you all three,
The senators alone of this great world,
Chief factors [1] for the gods, I do not know   10
Wherefore my father should revengers want,
Having a son and friends; since Julius Caesar,
Who at Philippi the good Brutus ghosted,
There saw you labouring for him. What was 't
That moved pale Cassius to conspire? and what 15
Made the all-honoured, honest Roman, Brutus,
With the armed rest, courtiers of beauteous free-
    dom,
To drench the Capitol, but that they would
Have one man but a man? And that is it   19
Hath made me rig my navy, at whose burden
The angered ocean foams, with which I meant
To scourge the ingratitude that despiteful Rome

Cast on my noble father.

CAESAR.   Take your time.

ANTONY. Thou canst not fear [2] us, Pompey,
   with thy sails;

We'll speak with thee at sea: at land, thou
   know'st   25

How much we do o'er-count [3] thee.

POMPEY.   At land, indeed,

Thou dost o'er-count me of my father's house;

But, since the cuckoo builds not for himself,

Remain in't as thou mayst.

LEPIDUS.   Be pleased to tell us—

For this is from the present—how you take   30

The offers we have sent you.

CAESAR.   There's the point.

ANTONY. Which do not be entreated to, but
   weigh

What it is worth embraced.

CAESAR.   And what may follow,

To try a larger fortune.

POMPEY.   You have made me offer

Of Sicily, Sardinia; and I must   35

Rid all the sea of pirates; then, to send

Measures of wheat to Rome; this 'greed upon,

To part with unhacked edges, and bear back

Our targets undinted.

CAESAR. ⎤
ANTONY. ⎬ That's our offer.
LEPIDUS. ⎦

POMPEY.   Know, then,

I came before you here a man prepared   41

To take this offer; but Mark Antony

Put me to some impatience. Though I lose

The praise of it by telling, you must know,

When Caesar and your brother were at blows, 45

Your mother came to Sicily and did find

Her welcome friendly.

ANTONY.   I have heard it, Pompey;

And am well studied for a liberal thanks

Which I do owe you.

POMPEY.   Let me have your hand:

I did not think, sir, to have met you here.   50

ANTONY. The beds i' the east are soft; and
   thanks to you,

That called me timelier than my purpose hither,

For I have gained by 't.

CAESAR.   Since I saw you last,

There is a change upon you.

POMPEY.   Well, I know not

What counts [4] harsh Fortune casts upon my
   face,   55

But in my bosom shall she never come

To make my heart her vassal.

LEPIDUS.   Well met here.

POMPEY. I hope so, Lepidus. Thus we are
   agreed.

I crave our composition may be written

And sealed between us.

CAESAR.   That's the next to do.

POMPEY. We'll feast each other ere we part;
   and let's   61

Draw lots who shall begin.

ANTONY.   That will I, Pompey.

POMPEY. No, Antony, take the lot:

But, first or last, your fine Egyptian cookery

Shall have the fame. I have heard that Julius
   Caesar   65

Grew fat with feasting there.

ANTONY.   You have heard much.

POMPEY. I have fair meanings, sir.

ANTONY.   And fair words to them.

POMPEY. Then, so much have I heard;

And I have heard Apollodorus carried—

ENOBARBUS. No more of that: he did so.

POMPEY.   What, I pray you?

ENOBARBUS. A certain queen to Caesar in a
   mattress.   71

POMPEY. I know thee now; how far'st thou,
   soldier?

ENOBARBUS.   Well;

And well am like to do; for I perceive

Four feasts are toward.

POMPEY.   Let me shake thy hand;

I never hated thee. I have seen thee fight,   76

When I have envied thy behaviour.

ENOBARBUS.   Sir,

I never loved you much, but I ha' praised ye

When you have well deserved ten times as
   much

As I have said you did.

POMPEY.   Enjoy thy plainness, 80

It nothing ill becomes thee.

Aboard my galley I invite you all:

Will you lead, lords?

CAESAR. ⎤
ANTONY. ⎬ Show us the way, sir.
LEPIDUS. ⎦

POMPEY.   Come.

1 agents   2 frighten   3 over-reach   4 reckonings

(*Exeunt all except* MENAS *and* ENOBARBUS)

MENAS. Thy father, Pompey, would ne'er have made this treaty. You and I have known, sir. 86

ENOBARBUS. At sea, I think.

MENAS. We have, sir.

ENOBARBUS. You have done well by water.

MENAS. And you by land. 90

ENOBARBUS. I will praise any man that will praise me: though it cannot be denied what I have done by land.

MENAS. Nor what I have done by water. 94

ENOBARBUS. Yes, something you can deny for your own safety; you have been a great thief by sea.

MENAS. And you by land.

ENOBARBUS. There I deny my land service. But give me your hand, Menas; if our eyes had authority,[5] here they might take two thieves kissing. 101

MENAS. All men's faces are true, whatsoe'er their hands are.

ENOBARBUS. But there is never a fair woman has a true face. 105

MENAS. No slander; they steal hearts.

ENOBARBUS. We came hither to fight with you.

MENAS. For my part, I am sorry it is turned to a drinking. Pompey doth this day laugh away his fortune. 110

ENOBARBUS. If he do, sure, he cannot weep it back again.

MENAS. You have said, sir. We looked not for Mark Antony here: pray you, is he married to Cleopatra? 115

ENOBARBUS. Caesar's sister is called Octavia.

MENAS. True, sir; she was the wife of Caius Marcellus.

ENOBARBUS. But she is now the wife of Marcus Antonius.

MENAS. Pray ye, sir? 120

ENOBARBUS. 'Tis true.

MENAS. Then is Caesar and he for ever knit together.

ENOBARBUS. If I were bound to divine of this unity, I would not prophesy so. 125

MENAS. I think the policy of that purpose made more in the marriage than the love of the parties.

ENOBARBUS. I think so too; but you shall find

[5] legal power to arrest [6] quiet behavior [7] opportunity

the band that seems to tie their friendship together will be the very strangler of their amity. Octavia is of a holy, cold, and still conversation.[6] 131

MENAS. Who would not have his wife so?

ENOBARBUS. Not he that himself is not so; which is Mark Antony. He will to his Egyptian dish again; then, shall the sighs of Octavia blow the fire up in Caesar, and, as I said before, that which is the strength of their amity shall prove the immediate author of their variance. Antony will use his affection where it is; he married but his occasion[7] here. 140

MENAS. And thus it may be. Come, sir, will you aboard? I have a health for you.

ENOBARBUS. I shall take it, sir: we have used our throats in Egypt.

MENAS. Come; let's away. (*Exeunt*) 145

SCENE VII. *On board* POMPEY's *Galley off Misenum.*

(*Music. Enter two or three* SERVANTS, *with a banquet.*)

FIRST SERVANT. Here they'll be, man. Some o' their plants are ill-rooted already; the least wind i' the world will blow them down.

SECOND SERVANT. Lepidus is high-coloured.

FIRST SERVANT. They have made him drink alms-drink.[1] 6

SECOND SERVANT. As they pinch[2] one another by the disposition, he cries out, "No more;" reconciles them to his entreaty, and himself to the drink.

FIRST SERVANT. But it raises the greater war between him and his discretion. 11

SECOND SERVANT. Why, this it is to have a name in great men's fellowship; I had as lief have a reed that will do me no service as a partisan I could not heave.[3] 15

FIRST SERVANT. To be called into a huge sphere, and not to be seen to move in 't, are the holes where eyes should be, which pitifully disaster[4] the cheeks.

(*A sennet sounded. Enter* CAESAR, ANTONY, LEPIDUS, POMPEY, AGRIPPA, MECAENAS, ENOBARBUS, MENAS, *with other* Captains.)

ANTONY. Thus do they, sir. They take the flow o' the Nile 20

By certain scales i' the pyramid; they know
By the height, the lowness, or the mean, if
   dearth
or foison [5] follow. The higher Nilus swells
The more it promises; as it ebbs, the seedsman
Upon the slime and ooze scatters his grain,   25
And shortly comes to harvest.

   LEPIDUS. You've strange serpents there.

   ANTONY. Ay, Lepidus.

   LEPIDUS. Your serpent of Egypt is bred now
of your mud by the operation of your sun; so
is your crocodile.   31

   ANTONY. They are so.

   POMPEY. Sit,—and some wine! A health to
Lepidus!

   LEPIDUS. I am not so well as I should be, but
I'll ne'er out.   36

   ENOBARBUS. Not till you have slept; I fear me
you'll be in till then.

   LEPIDUS. Nay, certainly, I have heard the
Ptolemies' pyramises are very goodly things;
without contradiction, I have heard that.   41

   MENAS. Pompey, a word.

   POMPEY. Say in mine ear; what is 't?

   MENAS. Forsake thy seat, I do beseech thee,
   captain,
And hear me speak a word.

   POMPEY.   Forbear me till anon.
This wine for Lepidus!   45

   LEPIDUS. What manner o' thing is your crocodile?

   ANTONY. It is shaped, sir, like itself, and it is
as broad as it hath breadth; it is just so high as
it is, and moves with it own organs; it lives by
that which nourisheth it; and the elements once
out of it, it transmigrates.   51

   LEPIDUS. What colour is it of?

   ANTONY. Of it own colour too.

   LEPIDUS. 'Tis a strange serpent.

   ANTONY. 'Tis so; and the tears of it are wet.

   CAESAR. Will this description satisfy him?   56

   ANTONY. With the health that Pompey gives
him, else he is a very epicure.

   POMPEY. Go hang, sir, hang! Tell me of that?
   away!
Do as I bid you. Where's this cup I called for?

   MENAS. If for the sake of merit thou wilt hear
   me,   61
Rise from thy stool.

   POMPEY. I think thou 'rt mad. The matter?
   (Walks aside)

   MENAS. I have ever held my cap off to thy
   fortunes.

   POMPEY. Thou hast served me with much
   faith. What's else to say?
Be jolly, lords.

   ANTONY. These quick-sands, Lepidus,   65
Keep off them, for you sink.

   MENAS. Wilt thou be lord of all the world?

   POMPEY.   What sayst thou?

   MENAS. Wilt thou be lord of the whole
world? That's twice.

   POMPEY. How should that be?

   MENAS.   But entertain it,
And though thou think me poor, I am the man
Will give thee all the world.   71

   POMPEY.   Hast thou drunk well?

   MENAS. No, Pompey, I have kept me from
   the cup.
Thou art, if thou dar'st be, the earthly Jove:
Whate'er the ocean pales,[6] or sky inclips,[7]
Is thine, if thou wilt ha't.

   POMPEY.   Show me which way.

   MENAS. These three world-sharers, these com-
   petitors,   76
Are in thy vessel: let me cut the cable;
And, when we are put off, fall to their throats:
All there is thine.

   POMPEY. Ah! this thou shouldst have done,
And not have spoke on't. In me 'tis villany;
In thee't had been good service. Thou must
   know   81
'Tis not my profit that does lead mine honour;
Mine honour, it. Repent that e'er thy tongue
Hath so betrayed thine act; being done un-
   known,   84
I should have found it afterwards well done,
But must condemn it now. Desist, and drink.

   MENAS (aside). For this,
I'll never follow thy palled fortunes more.
Who seeks, and will not take when once 'tis
   offered,
Shall never find it more.

   POMPEY.   This health to Lepidus!

   ANTONY. Bear him ashore. I'll pledge it for
   him, Pompey.   91

   ENOBARBUS. Here's to thee, Menas!

   MENAS.   Enobarbus, welcome!

---

[1] leavings   [2] irritate   [3] weapon I could not lift   [4] ruin   [5] scarcity or abundance   [6] encloses   [7] embraces

POMPEY. Fill till the cup be hid.

ENOBARBUS. There's a strong fellow, Menas.
(*Pointing to the* Attendant *who carries off*
LEPIDUS)   95

MENAS. Why?

ENOBARBUS. A'[8] bears the third part of the
world, man; see'st not?

MENAS. The third part then is drunk; would
it were all,
That it might go on wheels!

ENOBARBUS. Drink thou; increase the reels.

MENAS. Come.   101

POMPEY. This is not yet an Alexandrian feast.

ANTONY. It ripens towards it. Strike the vessels, ho!
Here is to Caesar!

CAESAR.   I could well forbear 't.
It's monstrous labour, when I wash my brain,
And it grows fouler.

ANTONY.   Be a child o' the time.

CAESAR. Possess it, I'll make answer;   107
But I had rather fast from all four days
Than drink so much in one.

ENOBARBUS (*to* ANTONY). Ha! my brave
emperor;   110
Shall we dance now the Egyptian Bacchanals,
And celebrate our drink?

POMPEY.   Let's ha't, good soldier.

ANTONY. Come, let's all take hands,
Till that the conquering wine hath steeped our
sense
In soft and delicate Lethe.

ENOBARBUS.   All take hands.   ·115
Make battery to our ears with the loud music;
The while I'll place you: then the boy shall
sing,
The holding[9] every man shall bear as loud
As his strong sides can volley.
(*Music plays.* ENOBARBUS *places them hand
in hand.*)

SONG.

Come, thou monarch of the vine,
Plumpy Bacchus, with pink eyne![10]   120
In thy fats[11] our cares be drowned,
With thy grapes our hairs be crowned:
    Cup us, till the world go round,
    Cup us, till the world go round!   125

CAESAR. What would you more? Pompey,
good night. Good brother,
Let me request you off; our graver business
Frowns at this levity. Gentle lords, let's part;
You see we have burnt our cheeks; strong
Enobarb
Is weaker than the wine, and mine own tongue
Splits what it speaks; the wild disguise hath
almost   131
Anticked[12] us all. What needs more words?
Good night.
Good Antony, your hand.

POMPEY.   I'll try you on the shore.

ANTONY. And shall, sir. Give's your hand.

POMPEY.   O, Antony!
You have my father's house,—But, what? we are
friends.   135
Come down into the boat.

ENOBARBUS.   Take heed you fall not.
(*Exeunt* POMPEY, CAESAR, ANTONY,
and Attendants)
Menas, I'll not on shore.

MENAS.   No, to my cabin.
These drums! these trumpets, flutes! what!
Let Neptune hear we bid a loud farewell
To these great fellows: sound and be hanged!
sound out!   140
(*A flourish of trumpets with drums*)

ENOBARBUS. Hoo! says a'. There's my cap.

MENAS. Hoo! noble captain! come. (*Exeunt*)

Act III

SCENE I. *A plain in Syria.*

(*Enter* VENTIDIUS, *in triumph, with* SILIUS
and other Romans, Officers, *and* Soldiers;
the dead body of PACORUS *borne before
him*)

VENTIDIUS. Now, darting Parthia, art thou
struck; and now
Pleased fortune does of Marcus Crassus' death
Make me revenger. Bear the king's son's body
Before our army. Thy Pacorus, Orodes,
Pays this for Marcus Crassus.

8 he   9 chorus   10 half-shut eyes   11 vats   12 made us all like buffoons

SILIUS.   Noble Ventidius,
Whilst yet with Parthian blood thy sword is
    warm,   6
The fugitive Parthians follow; spur through
    Media,
Mesopotamia, and the shelters whither
The routed fly; so thy grand captain Antony
Shall set thee on triumphant chariots and   10
Put garlands on thy head.
    VENTIDIUS.   O Silius, Silius!
I have done enough; a lower place, note well,
May make too great an act; for learn this, Silius,
Better to leave undone than by our deed
Acquire too high a fame when him we serve's
    away.   15
Caesar and Antony have ever won
More in their officer than person; Sossius,
One of my place in Syria, his lieutenant,
For quick accumulation of renown,
Which he achieved by the minute,[1] lost his
    favour.   20
Who does i' the wars more than his captain can
Becomes his captain's captain; and ambition,
The solider's virtue, rather makes choice of loss
Than gain which darkens him.
I could do more to do Antonius good,   25
But 'twould offend him; and in his offence
Should my performance perish.
    SILIUS.   Thou hast, Ventidius, that
Without the which a soldier, and his sword,
Grants scarce distinction. Thou wilt write to
    Antony?
    VENTIDIUS. I'll humbly signify what in his
    name,   30
That magical word of war, we have effected;
How, with his banners and his well-paid ranks,
The ne'er-yet-beaten horse of Parthia
We have jaded [2] out o' the field.
    SILIUS.   Where is he now?
    VENTIDIUS. He purposeth to Athens; whither,
    with what haste   35
The weight we must convey with's will permit,
We shall appear before him. On, there; pass
    along.   (*Exeunt*)

SCENE II. *Rome. A room in* CAESAR's *house.*

(*Enter* AGRIPPA *and* ENOBARBUS, *meeting*)
AGRIPPA. What! are the brothers parted?

ENOBARBUS. They have dispatched with Pom-
    pey; he is gone;
The other three are sealing.[1] Octavia weeps
To part from Rome; Caesar is sad; and Lepidus,
Since Pompey's feast, as Menas says, is troubled
With the green sickness.   5
    AGRIPPA.   'Tis a noble Lepidus.
ENOBARBUS. A very fine one. O! how he loves
    Caesar.
AGRIPPA. Nay, but how dearly he adores
    Mark Antony!
ENOBARBUS. Caesar? Why, he's the Jupiter
    of men.
AGRIPPA. What's Antony? The god of Jupiter.
ENOBARBUS. Spake you of Caesar? How! the
    nonpareil!   11
AGRIPPA. O, Antony! O thou Arabian bird!
ENOBARBUS. Would you praise Caesar, say,
"Caesar," go no further.
AGRIPPA. Indeed, he plied them both with
excellent praises.
ENOBARBUS. But he loves Caesar best; yet he
    loves Antony.   15
Hoo! hearts, tongues, figures, scribes, bards
    poets, cannot
Think, speak, cast,[2] write, sing, number; hoo!
His love to Antony. But as for Caesar,
Kneel down, kneel down, and wonder.
    AGRIPPA.   Both he loves.
ENOBARBUS.   They are his shards, and he
    their beetle. (*Trumpets within*) So;   20
This is to horse. Adieu, noble Agrippa.
    AGRIPPA. Good fortune, worthy soldier, and
    farewell.

        (*Enter* CAESAR, ANTONY, LEPIDUS,
                and OCTAVIA)
    ANTONY. No further, sir.
    CAESAR. You take from me a great part of
    myself;
Use me well in 't. Sister, prove such a wife   25
As my thoughts make thee, and as my furthest
    band
Shall pass on thy approof. Most noble Antony,
Let not the piece of virtue, which is set
Betwixt us as the cement of our love
To keep it builded, be the ram to batter   30
The fortress of it; for better might we
Have loved without this mean, if on both parts
This be not cherished.

---

[1] every moment   [2] driven exhausted   [1] setting seals to an argument   [2] calculate   [3] particular

ANTONY.   Make me not offended
In your distrust.
   CAESAR.   I have said.
   ANTONY.   You shall not find,
Though you be therein curious,[3] the least cause
For what you seem to fear. So, the gods keep
   you,   36
And make the hearts of Romans serve your
   ends!
We will here part.
   CAESAR. Farewell, my dearest sister, fare thee
   well:
The elements be kind to thee, and make   40
Thy spirits all of comfort! fare thee well.
   OCTAVIA. My noble brother!
   ANTONY. The April's in her eyes; it is love's
   spring,
And these the showers to bring it on. Be cheer-
   ful.
   OCTAVIA. Sir, look well to my husband's
   house; and—
   CAESAR.   What,   45
Octavia.
   OCTAVIA. I'll tell you in your ear.
   ANTONY. Her tongue will not obey her heart,
   nor can
Her heart inform her tongue; the swan's down-
   feather,
That stands upon the swell at full of tide,
And neither way inclines.   49
   ENOBARBUS (aside to AGRIPPA). Will Caesar
   weep?
   AGRIPPA.   He has a cloud in 's face.
   ENOBARBUS. He were the worse for that were
   he a horse;
So is he, being a man.
   AGRIPPA.   Why, Enobarbus,
When Antony found Julius Caesar dead
He cried almost to roaring; and he wept   55
When at Philippi he found Brutus slain.
   ENOBARBUS. That year, indeed, he was trou-
   bled with a rheum,[4]
What willingly he did confound [5] he wailed,
Believ't, till I wept too.
   CAESAR.   No, sweet Octavia,
You shall hear from me still; the time shall not 60
Out-go my thinking on you.
   ANTONY.   Come, sir, come;
I'll wrestle with you in my strength of love:

4 cold   5 ruin

Look, here I have you; thus I let you go,
And give you to the gods.
   CAESAR.   Adieu; be happy!
   LEPIDUS. Let all the number of the stars give
   light   65
To thy fair way!
   CAESAR.   Farewell, farewell! (Kisses OC-
TAVIA)
   ANTONY.   Farewell!
                    (Trumpets sound. Exeunt.)

SCENE III. Alexandria. A room in the palace.

            (Enter CLEOPATRA, CHARMIAN, IRAS,
                      and ALEXAS)
   CLEOPATRA. Where is the fellow?
   ALEXAS.   Half afeared to come.
   CLEOPATRA. Go to, go to.
                    (Enter a MESSENGER)
                         Come hither, sir.
   ALEXAS.   Good majesty,
Herod of Jewry dare not look upon you
But when you are well pleased.
   CLEOPATRA.   That Herod's head
I'll have; but how, when Antony is gone   5
Through whom I might command it? Come
   thou near.
   MESSENGER. Most gracious majesty!
   CLEOPATRA.   Didst thou behold
Octavia?
   MESSENGER. Ay, dread queen.
   CLEOPATRA.   Where?   10
   MESSENGER.   Madam, in Rome;
I looked her in the face, and saw her led
Between her brother and Mark Antony.
   CLEOPATRA. Is she as tall as me?
   MESSENGER.   She is not, madam.
   CLEOPATRA. Didst hear her speak? is she
   shrill-tongued, or low?   15
   MESSENGER. Madam, I heard her speak; she
   is low-voiced.
   CLEOPATRA. That's not so good. He cannot
   like her long.
   CHARMIAN. Like her! O Isis! 'tis impossible.
   CLEOPATRA. I think so, Charmian: dull of
   tongue, and dwarfish!
What majesty is in her gait? Remember,   20
If e'er thou look'dst on majesty.

MESSENGER.   She creeps;
Her motion and her station [1] are as one;
She shows a body rather than a life,
A statue than a breather.

     CLEOPATRA.   Is this certain?   24

     MESSENGER. Or I have no observance.

     CHARMIAN.   Three in Egypt
Cannot make better note.

     CLEOPATRA.   He's very knowing,
I do perceive 't. There's nothing in her yet.
The fellow has good judgment.

     CHARMIAN.   Excellent.

     CLEOPATRA. Guess at her years, I prithee.

     MESSENGER.   Madam,
She was a widow,—

     CLEOPATRA.   Widow! Charmian, hark.

     MESSENGER. And I do think she's thirty.   31

     CLEOPATRA. Bear'st thou her face in mind? is
     't long or round?

     MESSENGER. Round even to faultiness.

     CLEOPATRA. For the most part, too, they are
     foolish that are so.
Her hair, what colour?   35

     MESSENGER. Brown, madam; and her fore-
     head
As low as she would wish it.

     CLEOPATRA.   There's gold for thee:
Thou must not take my former sharpness ill.
I will employ thee back again; I find thee
Most fit for business. Go, make thee ready;   40
Our letters are prepared.   (*Exit* MESSENGER)

     CHARMIAN.   A proper man.

     CLEOPATRA. Indeed, he is so; I repent me
     much
That so I harried him. Why, methinks, by him,
This creature's no such thing.

     CHARMIAN.   Nothing, madam.

     CLEOPATRA. The man hath seen some
     majesty, and should know.   45

     CHARMIAN. Hath he seen majesty? Isis else
     defend,
And serving you so long!

     CLEOPATRA. I have one thing more to ask him
     yet, good Charmian:
But 'tis no matter; thou shalt bring him to me
Where I will write. All may be well enough.   50

     CHARMIAN. I warrant you, madam.

                             (*Exeunt*)

SCENE IV. *Athens. A room in* ANTONY's *house.*

(*Enter* ANTONY *and* OCTAVIA)

     ANTONY. Nay, nay, Octavia, not only that,
That were excusable, that, and thousands more
Of semblable import,[1] but he hath waged
New wars 'gainst Pompey; made his will, and
     read it
To public ear: 5
Spoke scantly of me; when perforce he could
     not
But pay me terms of honour, cold and sickly
He vented them; most narrow measure lent me; [2]
When the best hint was given him, he not
     took 't,
Or did it from his teeth.[3]

     OCTAVIA.   O my good lord!   10
Believe not all; or, if you must believe,
Stomach [4] not all. A more unhappy lady,
If this division chance, ne'er stood between,
Praying for both parts:
The good gods will mock me presently,   15
When I shall pray, "O! bless my lord and hus-
     band;"
Undo that prayer, by crying out as loud,
"O! bless my brother!" Husband win, win
     brother,
Prays, and destroys the prayer; no midway
'Twixt these extremes at all.

     ANTONY.   Gentle Octavia,
Let your best love draw to that point which
     seeks   21
Best to preserve it. If I lose mine honour
I lose myself; better I were not yours
Than yours so branchless. But, as you requested.
Yourself shall go between 's; the mean time,
     lady,   25
I'll raise the preparation of a war
Shall stain your brother; make your soonest
     haste,
So your desires are yours.

     OCTAVIA.   Thanks to my lord.
The Jove of power make me most weak, most
     weak,
Your reconciler! Wars 'twixt you twain would
     be   30
As if the world should cleave, and that slain
     men

---

[1] manner of standing   [1] like meaning   [2] gave as little credit as possible to me   [3] grudgingly   [4] resent

Should solder up the rift.

ANTONY. When it appears to you where this begins,
Turn your displeasure that way; for our faults
Can never be so equal that your love   35
Can equally move with them. Provide [5] your going;
Choose your own company, and command what cost
Your heart has mind to.   (*Exeunt*)

SCENE V. *The same. Another room.*

(*Enter* ENOBARBUS *and* EROS, *meeting*)
ENOBARBUS. How now, friend Eros!
EROS. There's strange news come, sir.
ENOBARBUS. What, man?
EROS. Caesar and Lepidus have made wars upon Pompey.   5
ENOBARBUS. This is old; what is the success? [1]
EROS. Caesar, having made use of him in the wars 'gainst Pompey, presently denied him rivality, [2] would not let him partake in the glory of the action; and not resting here, accuses him of letters he had formerly wrote to Pompey; upon his own appeal, seizes him: so the poor third is up, till death enlarge his confine.
ENOBARBUS. Then, world, thou hast a pair of chaps, [3] no more;   14
And throw between them all the food thou hast,
They'll grind the one the other. Where's Antony?
EROS. He's walking in the garden—thus: and spurns
The rush that lies before him; cries, "Fool, Lepidus!"
And threats the throat of that his officer
That murdered Pompey.
ENOBARBUS.   Our great navy's rigged.
EROS. For Italy and Caesar. More, Domitius;
My lord desires you presently: [4] my news   22
I might have told hereafter.
ENOBARBUS.   'Twill be naught;
But let it be. Bring me to Antony.
EROS. Come, sir.   (*Exeunt*)   25

SCENE VI. *Rome. A room in* CAESAR'S *house.*

(*Enter* CAESAR, AGRIPPA, *and* MECAENAS)

CAESAR. Contemning Rome, he has done all this and more
In Alexandria; here's the manner of 't;
I' the market-place, on a tribunal [1] silvered,
Cleopatra and himself in chairs of gold
Were publicly enthroned; at the feet sat   5
Caesarion, whom they call my father's son,
And all the unlawful issue that their lust
Since then hath made between them. Unto her
He gave the 'stablishment [2] of Egypt; made her
Of Lower Syria, Cyprus, Lydia,   10
Absolute queen.
MECAENAS.   This in the public eye?
CAESAR. I' the common show-place, where they exercise.
His sons he there proclaimed the kings of kings;
Great Media, Parthia, and Armenia
He gave to Alexander; to Ptolemy he assigned
Syria, Cilicia, and Phoenicia. She   16
In the habiliments of the goddess Isis
That day appeared; and oft before gave audience,
As 'tis reported, so.
MECAENAS.   Let Rome be thus
Informed.
AGRIPPA. Who, queasy [3] with his insolence   20
Already, will their good thoughts call from him.
CAESAR. The people know it; and have now received.
His accusations.
AGRIPPA.   Whom does he accuse?
CAESAR. Caesar; and that, having in Sicily
Sextus Pompeius spoiled, we had not rated [4] him   25
His part o' the isle; then does he say, he lent me
Some shipping unrestored; lastly, he frets
That Lepidus of the triumvirate
Should be deposed; and, being, that we detain
All his revenue.
AGRIPPA.   Sir, this should be answered.   30
CAESAR. 'Tis done already, and the messenger gone.
I have told him, Lepidus was grown too cruel;
That he his high authority abused,
And did deserve his change: for what I have conquered,
I grant him part; but then, in his Armenia,   35
And other of his conquered kingdoms, I

---

[5] make provision for   [1] outcome   [2] partnership   [3] jaws   [4] at once   [1] dais   [2] settled possession of
[3] nauseated   [4] allotted   [5] anticipated   [6] display

Demand the like.

MECAENAS.   He'll never yield to that.

CAESAR. Nor must not then be yielded to in
this.

(*Enter* OCTAVIA, *with her train*)

OCTAVIA. Hail, Caesar, and my lord! hail,
most dear Caesar!

CAESAR. That ever I should call thee cast-
away!   40

OCTAVIA. You have not called me so, nor
have you cause.

CAESAR. Why have you stol'n upon us thus?
You come not

Like Caesar's sister; the wife of Antony
Should have an army for an usher, and
The neighs of horse to tell of her approach   45
Long ere she did appear; the trees by the way
Should have borne men; and expectation
      fainted,
Longing for what it had not; nay, the dust
Should have ascended to the roof of heaven,
Raised by your populous troops. But you are
      come   50
A market-maid to Rome, and have prevented [5]
The ostentation [6] of our love, which, left un-
      shown,
Is often left unloved: we should have met you
By sea and land, supplying every stage
With an augmented greeting.

OCTAVIA.   Good my lord,   55
To come thus was I not constrained, but did it
On my free-will. My lord, Mark Antony,
Hearing that you prepared for war, acquainted
My grieved ear withal; whereon, I begged
His pardon for return.

CAESAR.   Which soon he granted,
Being an obstruct 'tween his lust and him.   61

OCTAVIA. Do not say so, my lord.

CAESAR.   I have eyes upon him,
And his affairs come to me on the wind.
Where is he now?

OCTAVIA.   My lord, in Athens.

CAESAR. No, my most wronged sister; Cleo-
patra   65
Hath nodded him to her. He hath given his
      empire
Up to a whore; who now are levying
The kings o' the earth for war. He hath as-
      sembled

Bocchus, the King of Libya; Archelaus,
Of Cappadocia; Philadelphos, King   70
Of Paphlagonia; the Thracian king, Adallas;
King Malchus of Arabia; King of Pont;
Herod of Jewry; Mithridates, King
Of Comagene; Polemon and Amyntas,
The Kings of Mede and Lycaonia,   75
With a more larger list of sceptres.

OCTAVIA.   Ay me, most wretched,
That have my heart parted betwixt two friends
That do afflict each other!

CAESAR.   Welcome hither:
Your letters did withhold our breaking forth,
Till we perceived both how you were wrong
      led   80
And we in negligent danger. Cheer your heart;
Be you not troubled with the time, which drives
O'er your content these strong necessities,
But let determined things to destiny
Hold unbewailed their way. Welcome to Rome;
Nothing more dear to me. You are abused   86
Beyond the mark of thought, and the high gods,
To do you justice, make them ministers
Of us and those that love you. Best of comfort,
And ever welcome to us.

AGRIPPA.   Welcome, lady.   90

MECAENAS. Welcome, dear madam.
Each heart in Rome does love and pity you;
Only the adulterous Antony, most large [7]
In his abominations, turns you off,
And gives his potent regiment to a trull,[8]   95
That noises it against us.

OCTAVIA.   Is it so, sir?

CAESAR. Most certain. Sister, welcome; pray
you,
Be ever known to patience; my dearest sister!

(*Exeunt*)

SCENE VII. ANTONY's *camp, near to the promontory of Actium.*

(*Enter* CLEOPATRA *and* ENOBARBUS)

CLEOPATRA. I will be even with thee, doubt
it not.

ENOBARBUS. But why, why, why?

CLEOPATRA. Thou hast forspoke [1] my being
in these wars,
And sayst it is not fit.

ENOBARBUS.   Well, is it, is it?

───────────

[7] gross   [8] powerful rule of a wanton   [1] spoken against   [2] proclaimed   [3] military command

CLEOPATRA. If not denounced [2] against us,
why should not we   5
Be there in person?

ENOBARBUS (aside). Well, I could reply.
If we should serve with horse and mares to-
gether
The horse were merely lost; the mares would
bear
A soldier and his horse.

CLEOPATRA. What is 't you say?

ENOBARBUS. Your presence needs must puzzle
Antony;   10
Take from his heart, take from his brain, from
's time,
What should not then be spared. He is already
Traduced for levity, and 'tis said in Rome
That Photinus a eunuch and your maids
Manage this war.   15

CLEOPATRA.   Sink Rome, and their tongues
rot
That speak against us! A charge [3] we bear i' the
war,
And, as the president of my kingdom, will
Appear there for a man. Speak not against it;
I will not stay behind.

ENOBARBUS.   Nay, I have done.
Here comes the emperor.   20

(Enter ANTONY and CANIDIUS)

ANTONY.   Is it not strange, Canidius,
That from Tarentum and Brundusium
He could so quickly cut the Ionian sea,
And take in Toryne? You have heard on 't,
sweet?

CLEOPATRA. Celerity is never more admired
Than by the negligent.

ANTONY.   A good rebuke,   26
Which might have well becomed the best of
men,
To taunt at slackness. Canidius, we
Will fight with him by sea.

CLEOPATRA.   By sea! What else?

CANIDIUS. Why will my lord do so?

ANTONY.   For that he dares us to 't.   30

ENOBARBUS. So hath my lord dared him to
single fight.

CANIDIUS. Ay, and to wage his battle at
Pharsalia,
Where Caesar fought with Pompey; but these
offers,

Which serve not for his vantage, he shakes off;
And so should you.

ENOBARBUS.   Your ships are not well
manned;   35
Your mariners are muleters, reapers, people
Ingrossed by swift impress,[4] in Caesar's fleet
Are those that often have 'gainst Pompey
fought:
Their ships are yare,[5] yours, heavy. No disgrace
Shall fall [6] you for refusing him at sea,   40
Being prepared for land.

ANTONY.   By sea, by sea.

ENOBARBUS. Most worthy sir, you therein
throw away
The absolute soldiership you have by land;
Distract your army, which doth most consist
Of war-marked footmen; leave unexecuted   45
Your own renowned knowledge; quite forego
The way which promises assurance; and
Give up yourself merely to chance and hazard
From firm security.

ANTONY.   I'll fight at sea.

CLEOPATRA. I have sixty sails, Caesar none
better.   50

ANTONY. Our overplus of shipping will we
burn;
And with the rest, full-manned, from the head
of Actium
Beat the approaching Caesar. But if we fail,
We then can do 't at land.

(Enter a MESSENGER)
                    Thy business?

MESSENGER. The news is true, my lord; he is
descried;   55
Caesar has taken Toryne.

ANTONY. Can he be there in person? 'tis im-
possible;
Strange that his power should be. Canidius,
Our nineteen legions thou shalt hold by land,
And our twelve thousand horse. We'll to our
ship: 60
Away, my Thetis!

(Enter a SOLDIER)
                    How now, worthy soldier!

SOLDIER. O noble emperor! do not fight by
sea;
Trust not to rotten planks: do you misdoubt
This sword and these my wounds? Let the
Egyptians

4 collected by sudden conscription   5 easily handled   6 befall

And the Phoenicians go a-ducking; we   65
Have used to conquer, standing on the earth,
And fighting foot to foot.

ANTONY.   Well, well: away!
                    (*Exeunt* ANTONY, CLEOPATRA,
                            and ENOBARBUS)
    SOLDIER. By Hercules, I think I am i' the
    right.
    CANIDIUS. Soldier, thou art; but his whole
    action grows
Not in the power on 't: so our leader's led,   70
And we are women's men.
    SOLDIER.   You keep by land
The legions and the horse whole, do you not?
    CANIDIUS. Marcus Octavius, Marcus Justeius,
Publicola, and Caelius, are for sea;
But we keep whole by land. This speed of
    Caesar's   75
Carries beyond belief.
    SOLDIER.   While he was yet in Rome
His power went out in such distractions [7] as
Beguiled all spies.
    CANIDIUS.   Who's his lieutenant, hear you?
    SOLDIER. They say, one Taurus.
    CANIDIUS.   Well I know the man.
                    (*Enter a* MESSENGER)
    MESSENGER. The emperor calls Canidius.   80
    CANIDIUS. With news the time's with labour,
    and throes forth
Each minute some.   (*Exeunt*)

SCENE VIII. *A plain near Actium.*

(*Enter* CAESAR, TAURUS, Officers, *and others*)
    CAESAR. Taurus!
    TAURUS. My lord?
    CAESAR. Strike not by land; keep whole:
    provoke not battle,
Till we have done at sea. Do not exceed
The prescript of this scroll: our fortune lies   5
Upon this jump.[1]   (*Exeunt*)
            (*Enter* ANTONY *and* ENOBARBUS)
    ANTONY. Set we our squadrons on yond side
    o' the hill,
In eye of Caesar's battle; from which place
We may the number of the ships behold,
And so proceed accordingly.   (*Exeunt*)   10
    (*Enter* CANIDIUS, *marching with his land
    army one way over the stage; and* TAURUS,

the lieutenant of CAESAR, *the other way.
After their going in is heard the noise of a
sea-fight.*)
    (*Alarum. Re-enter* ENOBARBUS.)
    ENOBARBUS. Naught, naught, all naught! I
    can behold no longer.
The Antoniad, the Egyptian admiral,[2]
With all their sixty, fly, and turn the rudder;
To see 't mine eyes are blasted.
                    (*Enter* SCARUS)
    SCARUS.   Gods and goddesses,
All the whole synod of them!
    ENOBARBUS.   What's thy passion?
    SCARUS. The greater cantle [3] of the world is
    lost   16
With very ignorance; we have kissed away
Kingdoms and provinces.
    ENOBARBUS.   How appears the fight?
    SCARUS. On our side like the tokened pesti-
    lence,[4]
Where death is sure. Yon ribaudred [5] nag of
    Egypt,   20
Whom leprosy o'ertake! i' the midst o' the fight,
When vantage like a pair of twins appeared,
Both as the same, or rather ours the elder,
The breese [6] upon her, like a cow in June,
Hoists sails and flies.
    ENOBARBUS.   That I beheld: 25
Mine eyes did sicken at the sight, and could not
Endure a further view.
    SCARUS.   She once being loofed,[7]
The noble ruin of her magic, Antony,
Claps on his sea-wing, and like a doting mal-
    lard,
Leaving the fight in height, flies after her.   30
I never saw an action of such shame;
Experience, manhood, honour, ne'er before
Did violate so itself.
    ENOBARBUS.   Alack, alack!
                    (*Enter* CANIDIUS)
    CANIDIUS. Our fortune on the sea is out of
    breath,
And sinks most lamentably. Had our general   35
Been what he knew himself, it had gone well:
O! he has given example for our flight
Most grossly by his own.
    ENOBARBUS.   Ay, are you thereabouts?
Why, then, good night, indeed.
    CANIDIUS. Towards Peloponnesus are they

---

[7] detachments [1] hazard [2] flagship [3] portion [4] the plague [5] lewd [6] goadfly [7] luffed

fled. 40

SCARUS. 'Tis easy to 't; and there I will attend
What further comes.

CANIDIUS.   To Caesar will I render
My legions and my horse; six kings already
Show me the way of yielding.

ENOBARBUS.   I'll yet follow
The wounded chance of Antony, though my
reason 45
Sits in the wind against me.   (*Exeunt*)

SCENE IX. *Alexandria. A room in the palace.*

(*Enter* ANTONY *and* ATTENDANTS)

ANTONY. Hark! the land bids me tread no
more upon 't;
It is ashamed to bear me. Friends, come hither:
I am so lated [1] in the world that I
Have lost my way for ever. I have a ship
Laden with gold; take that, divide it; fly, 5
And make your peace with Caesar.

ATTENDANTS.   Fly! not we.

ANTONY. I have fled myself, and have in-
structed cowards
To run and show their shoulders. Friends, be
gone;
I have myself resolved upon a course
Which has no need of you; be gone: 10
My treasure's in the harbour, take it. O!
I followed that I blush to look upon:
My very hairs do mutiny, for the white
Reprove the brown for rashness, and they them
For fear and doting. Friends, be gone; you
shall 15
Have letters from me to some friends that will
Sweep your way for you. Pray you, look not sad,
Nor make replies of loathness; take the hint
Which my despair proclaims; let that be left
Which leaves itself; to the sea-side straight-
way; 20
I will possess you of that ship and treasure.
Leave me, I pray, a little; pray you now:
Nay, do so; for, indeed, I have lost command,
Therefore I pray you. I'll see you by and by.
     (*Sits down*)
     (*Enter* EROS *following* CLEOPATRA, *led by*
     CHARMIAN *and* IRAS)

EROS. Nay, gentle madam, to him, comfort
him. 25

IRAS. Do, most dear queen.

CHARMIAN. Do! Why, what else?

CLEOPATRA. Let me sit down. O Juno!

ANTONY. No, no, no, no, no.

EROS. See you here, sir? 30

ANTONY. O fie, fie, fie!

CHARMIAN. Madam!

IRAS. Madam; O good empress!

EROS. Sir, sir!

ANTONY. Yes, my lord, yes. He, at Philippi
kept 35
His sword e'en like a dancer, while I struck
The lean and wrinkled Cassius; and 'twas I
That the mad Brutus ended: he alone
Dealt on lieutenantry,[2] and no practice had
In the brave squares of war: yet now—No
matter. 40

CLEOPATRA. Ah! stand by.

EROS. The queen, my lord, the queen.

IRAS. Go to him, madam, speak to him;
He is unqualited [3] with very shame.

CLEOPATRA. Well then, sustain me: O! 45

EROS. Most noble sir, arise; the queen approaches:
Her head's declined, and death will seize her,
but
Your comfort makes the rescue.

ANTONY. I have offended reputation,
A most unnoble swerving.

EROS.   Sir, the queen. 50

ANTONY. O! whither hast thou led me, Egypt?
See,
How I convey my shame out of thine eyes
By looking back what I have left behind
'Stroyed in dishonour.

CLEOPATRA.   O my lord, my lord!
Forgive my fearful sails: I little thought 55
You would have followed.

ANTONY.   Egypt, thou knew'st too well
My heart was to thy rudder tied by the strings,
And thou shouldst tow me after; o'er my spirit
Thy full supremacy thou knew'st, and that
Thy beck might from the bidding of the gods 60
Command me.

CLEOPATRA. O! my pardon.

ANTONY.   Now I must
To the young man send humble treaties, dodge
And palter [4] in the shifts of lowness, who
With half the bulk o' the world played as I

[1] belated [2] acted by proxy [3] divested of his character [4] use tricks [5] is worth

pleased,   64
Making and marring fortunes. You did know
How much you were my conqueror, and that
My sword, made weak by my affection, would
Obey it on all cause.

CLEOPATRA.   Pardon, pardon!

ANTONY. Fall not a tear, I say; one of them
    rates [5]
All that is won and lost. Give me a kiss;   70
Even this repays me. We sent our schoolmaster;
Is he come back? Love, I am full of lead.
Some wine, within there, and our viands! For-
    tune knows,
We scorn her most when most she offers blows.

                                    (*Exeunt*)

SCENE X. *Egypt.* CAESAR'S *camp.*

(*Enter* CAESAR, DOLABELLA, THYREUS,
                and others)

CAESAR. Let him appear that's come from
    Antony.
Know you him?

DOLABELLA. Caesar, 'tis his schoolmaster:
An argument that he is plucked, when hither
He sends so poor a pinion of his wing,
Which had superfluous kings for messengers   5
Not many moons gone by.

                (*Enter* EUPHRONIUS)

CAESAR.   Approach, and speak.

EUPHRONIUS. Such as I am, I come from
    Antony:
I was of late as petty to his ends
As is the morn-dew on the myrtle-leaf
To his grand sea.

CAESAR.   Be 't so. Declare thine office.   10

EUPHRONIUS. Lord of his fortunes he salutes
    thee, and
Requires to live in Egypt; which not granted,
He lessens his requests, and to thee sues
To let him breathe between the heavens and
    earth,
A private man in Athens; this for him.   15
Next, Cleopatra does confess thy greatness,
Submits her to thy might, and of thee craves
The circle [1] of the Ptolemies for her heirs,
Now hazarded to thy grace.

CAESAR.   For Antony,

I have no ears to his request. The queen   20
Of audience nor desire shall fail, so she
From Egypt drive her all-disgracèd friend,
Or take his life there; this if she perform,
She shall not sue unheard. So to them both.

EUPHRONIUS. Fortune pursue thee!

CAESAR.   Bring him through the bands.

                        (*Exit* EUPHRONIUS)

(*To* THYREUS) To try thy eloquence, now
    'tis time; dispatch.   26
From Antony win Cleopatra; promise,
And in our name, what she requires; add more,
From thine invention, offers. Women are not
In their best fortunes strong, but want will per-
    jure   30
The ne'er-touched vestal. Try thy cunning,
    Thyreus;
Make thine own edict for thy pains, which we
Will answer as a law.

THYREUS.   Caesar, I go.

CAESAR. Observe how Antony becomes his
    flaw,[2]   34
And what thou think'st his very action speaks
In every power that moves.

THYREUS.   Caesar, I shall.

                                    (*Exeunt*)

SCENE XI. *Alexandria. A room in the palace.*

(*Enter* CLEOPATRA, ENOBARBUS,
            CHARMIAN, *and* IRAS)

CLEOPTRA. What shall we do, Enobarbus?

ENOBARBUS.   Think, and die.

CLEOPATRA. Is Antony or we, in fault for
    this?

ENOBARBUS. Antony only, that would make
    his will
Lord of his reason. What though you fled
From that great face of war, whose several
    ranges   5
Frighted each other, why should he follow?
The itch of his affection should not then
Have nicked [3] his captainship; at such a point,
When half to half the world opposed, he being
The mered question.[4] 'Twas a shame no less   10
Than was his loss, to course [5] your flying flags,
And leave his navy gazing.

---

1 crown   2 crock, ruin   3 cut off   4 the matter to which the dispute is limited   5 chase   6 advantages   7 weakened
8 deprive of dignity   9 part

CLEOPATRA. Prithee, peace.
(*Enter* ANTONY, *with* EUPHRONIUS)
ANTONY. Is that his answer?
EUPHRONIUS. Ay, my lord.
ANTONY. The queen shall then have courtesy,
so she 15
Will yield us up?
EUPHRONIUS. He says so.
ANTONY. Let her know 't.
To the boy Caesar send this grizzled head,
And he will fill thy wishes to the brim
With principalities.
CLEOPATRA. That head, my lord?
ANTONY. To him again. Tell him he wears
the rose 20
Of youth upon him, from which the world
should note
Something particular; his coin, ships, legions,
May be a coward's, whose ministers would
prevail
Under the service of a child as soon
As i' the command of Caesar: I dare him there-
fore 25
To lay his gay comparisons 6 apart,
And answer me declined,7 sword against sword,
Ourselves alone. I'll write it: follow me.
(*Exeunt* ANTONY *and* EUPHRONIUS)
ENOBARBUS (*aside*). Yes, like enough, high-
battled Caesar will
Unstate 8 his happiness, and be staged to the
show 30
Against a sworder! I see men's judgments are
A parcel 9 of their fortunes, and things outward
Do draw the inward quality after them,
To suffer all alike. That he should dream,
Knowing all measures, the full Caesar will 35
Answer his emptiness! Caesar, thou hast sub-
dued
His judgment too.
(*Enter an* ATTENDANT)
ATTENDANT. A messenger from Caesar.
CLEOPATRA. What! no more ceremony? See!
my women;
Against the blown rose may they stop their
nose,
That kneeled unto the buds. Admit him, sir.
(*Exit* ATTENDANT)
ENOBARBUS (*aside*). Mine honesty and I
begin to square. 41

The loyalty well held to fools does make
Our faith mere folly; yet he that can endure
To follow with allegiance a fall'n lord,
Does conquer him that did his master conquer,
And earns a place i' the story. 46
(*Enter* THYREUS)
CLEOPATRA. Caesar's will?
THYREUS. Hear it apart.
CLEOPATRA. None but friends; say boldly.
THYREUS. So, haply,10 are they friends to
Antony.
ENOBARBUS. He needs as many, sir, as Caesar
has,
Or needs not us. If Caesar please, our master 50
Will leap to be his friend; for us, you know
Whose he is we are, and that is Caesar's.
THYREUS. So.
Thus then, thou most renowned: Caesar en-
treats,
Not to consider in what case thou stand'st,
Further than he is Caesar.
CLEOPATRA. Go on; right royal.
THYREUS. He knows that you embrace not
Antony 56
As you did love, but as you feared him.
CLEOPATRA. O!
THYREUS. The scars upon your honour there-
fore he
Does pity, as constrained blemishes,
Not as deserved.
CLEOPATRA. He is a god and knows 60
What is most right. Mine honour was not
yielded,
But conquered merely.
ENOBARBUS (*aside*). To be sure of that,
I will ask Antony. Sir, sir, thou'rt so leaky,
That we must leave thee to thy sinking, for
Thy dearest quit thee. (*Exit*)
THYREUS. Shall I say to Caesar 65
What you require of him? for he partly begs
To be desired to give. It much would please
him,
That of his fortunes you should make a staff
To lean upon; but it would warm his spirits
To hear from me you had left Antony, 70
And put yourself under his shroud,11
The universal landlord.
CLEOPATRA. What's your name?
THYREUS. My name is Thyreus.

10 perhaps 11 cloak, protection 12 by proxy 13 scramble

CLEOPATRA.   Most kind messenger,
Say to great Caesar this: in deputation [12]
I kiss his conqu'ring hand; tell him, I am
    prompt   75
To lay my crown at 's feet, and there to kneel;
Tell him, from his all-obeying breath I hear
The doom of Egypt.
    THYREUS.   'Tis your noblest course.
Wisdom and fortune combating together,
If that the former dare but what it can,   80
No chance may shake it. Give me grace to lay
My duty on your hand.
    CLEOPATRA.   Your Caesar's father oft,
When he hath mused of taking kingdoms in,
Bestowed his lips on that unworthy place,
As it rained kisses.   84
    (*Re-enter* ANTONY *and* ENOBARBUS)
    ANTONY.   Favours, by Jove that thunders!
What art thou, fellow?
    THYREUS.   One that but performs
The bidding of the fullest man, and worthiest
To have command obeyed.
    ENOBARBUS (*aside*). You will be whipped.
    ANTONY. Approach there! Ah, you kite! Now,
    gods and devils!
Authority melts from me: of late, when I cried
    "Ho!"   90
Like boys unto a muss,[13] kings would start
    forth,
And cry, "Your will?" Have you no ears? I am
Antony yet.
    (*Enter* ATTENDANTS)
        Take hence this Jack and whip him.
    ENOBARBUS (*aside*). 'Tis better playing with
    a lion's whelp
Than with an old one dying.
    ANTONY.   Moon and stars!
Whip him. Were 't twenty of the greatest trib-
    utaries   96
That do acknowledge Caesar, should I find
    them
So saucy with the hand of—she here, what's
    her name,
Since she was Cleopatra? Whip him, fellows,
Till, like a boy, you see him cringe his face   100
And whine aloud for mercy; take him hence.
    THYREUS. Mark Antony,—
    ANTONY.   Tug him away; being whipped,
Bring him again; this Jack of Caesar's shall

Bear us an errand to him.
    (*Exeunt* ATTENDANTS *with* THYREUS)
You were half blasted ere I knew you: ha!   105
Have I my pillow left unpressed in Rome,
Forborne the getting of a lawful race,
And by a gem of women, to be abused
By one that looks on feeders?
    CLEOPATRA.   Good my lord,—
    ANTONY. You have been a boggler ever: 110
But when we in our viciousness grow hard,—
O misery on 't!—the wise gods seel our eyes;
In our own filth drop our clear judgments; make
    us
Adore our errors; laugh at 's while we strut
To our confusion.
    CLEOPATRA.   O! is 't come to this?   115
    ANTONY. I found you as a morsel, cold upon
Dead Caesar's trencher; nay, you were a frag-
    ment
Of Cneius Pompey's; besides what hotter hours,
Unregistered in vulgar fame, you have
Luxuriously picked out; for, I am sure,   120
Though you can guess what temperance should
    be,
You know not what it is.
    CLEOPATRA.   Wherefore is this?
    ANTONY. To let a fellow that will take re-
    wards
And say "God quit [14] you!" be familiar with
My playfellow, your hand; this kingly seal   125
And plighter of high hearts. O! that I were
Upon the hill of Basan,[15] to outroar
The hornèd [16] herd; for I have savage cause;
And to proclaim it civilly were like
A haltered neck, which does the hangman
    thank
For being yare about him.
    (*Re-enter* ATTENDANTS, *with* THYREUS)
               Is he whipped?   131
    FIRST ATTENDANT. Soundly, my lord.
    ANTONY.   Cried he? and begged a' pardon?
    FIRST ATTENDANT. He did ask favour.
    ANTONY. If that thy father live, let him repent
Thou wast not made his daughter; and be thou
    sorry   135
To follow Caesar in his triumph, since
Thou hast been whipped for following him:
    henceforth,
The white hand of a lady fever thee,

---

[14] reward   [15] See *Psalms* 22, verse 12   [16] the cuckold was fabled to have horns

Shake thou to look on 't. Get thee back to
    Caesar,   139
Tell him thy entertainment; look, thou say
He makes me angry with him; for he seems
Proud and disdainful, harping on what I am,
Not what he knew I was: he makes me angry;
And at this time most easy 'tis to do 't,
When my good stars, that were my former
    guides,   145
Have empty left their orbs, and shot their fires
Into the abysm of hell. If he mislike
My speech and what is done, tell him he has
Hipparchus, my enfranched [17] bondman, whom
He may at pleasure whip, or hang, or torture,
As he shall like, to quit [18] me: urge it thou: 151
Hence with thy stripes; be gone!

                        (Exit THYREUS)
    CLEOPATRA. Have you done yet?
    ANTONY.   Alack! our terrene moon
Is now eclipsed; and it portends alone
The fall of Antony.
    CLEOPATRA.   I must stay his time.   155
    ANTONY. To flatter Caesar, would you mingle
    eyes
With one that ties his points? [19]
    CLEOPATRA.   Not know me yet?
    ANTONY. Cold-hearted toward me?
    CLEOPATRA.   Ah! dear, if I be so,
From my cold heart let heaven engender hail,
And poison it in the source; and the first stone
Drop in my neck: as it determines,[20] so   161
Dissolve my life. The next Caesarion smite,
Till by degrees the memory of my womb,
Together with my brave Egyptians all,
By the discandying [21] of this pelleted storm,   165
Lie graveless, till the flies and gnats of Nile
Have buried them for prey!
    ANTONY.   I am satisfied.
Caesar sits down in Alexandria, where
I will oppose his fate. Our force by land
Hath nobly held; our severed navy too   170

Have knit again, and fleet,[22] threat'ning most
    sea-like.
Where hast thou been, my heart? Dost thou
    hear, lady?
If from the field I shall return once more
To kiss these lips, I will appear in blood;
I and my sword will earn our chronicle: 175
There's hope in 't yet.
    CLEOPATRA.   That's my brave lord!
    ANTONY. I will be treble-sinewed, hearted,
    breathed,
And fight maliciously; for when mine hours
Were nice and lucky, men did ransom lives   180
Of me for jests; but now I'll set my teeth,
And send to darkness all that stop me. Come,
Let's have one other gaudy night: call to me
All my sad captains; fill our bowls once more;
Let's mock the midnight bell.
    CLEOPATRA.   It is my birthday:
I had thought to have held it poor; but, since
    my lord   186
Is Antony again, I will be Cleopatra.
    ANTONY. We will yet do well.
    CLEOPATRA. Call all his noble captains to my
    lord.
    ANTONY. Do so, we'll speak to them; and to-
    night I'll force.   190
The wine peep through their scars. Come on,
    my queen;
There's sap in 't yet. The next time I do fight
I'll make death love me, for I will contend
Even with his pestilent scythe.
                    (Exeunt all but ENOBARBUS)
    ENOBARBUS. Now he'll outstare the lightning.
    To be furious   195
Is to be frighted out of fear, and in that mood
The dove will peck the estridge,[23] and I see still,
A diminution in our captain's brain
Restores his heart. When valour preys on reason
It eats the sword it fights with. I will seek   200
Some way to leave him.   *(Exit)*

Act IV

SCENE I. *Before Alexandria.* CAESAR's *camp.*

    (*Enter* CAESAR, *reading a letter;* AGRIPPA,
        MECAENAS, *and others*)
    CAESAR. He calls me boy, and chides as he
    had power

To beat me out of Egypt; my messenger
He hath whipped with rods; dares me to per-
    sonal combat,
Caesar to Antony. Let the old ruffian know
I have many other ways to die; meantime   5

17 freed 18 be even with me 19 laces 20 comes to an end   21 melts 22 floats 23 ostrich

Laugh at his challenge.

MECAENAS.   Caesar must think,
When one so great begins to rage, he's hunted
Even to falling. Give him no breath, but now
Make boot [1] of his distraction: never anger   9
Made good guard for itself.

CAESAR.   Let our best heads
Know that tomorrow the last of many battles
We mean to fight. Within our files there are,
Of those that served Mark Antony but late,
Enough to fetch him in. See it done;
And feast the army; we have store to do 't,   15
And they have earned the waste. Poor Antony!

(*Exeunt*)

SCENE II. *Alexandria. A room in the palace.*

(*Enter* ANTONY, CLEOPATRA, ENOBARBUS,
CHARMIAN, IRAS, ALEXAS, *and others*)

ANTONY. He will not fight with me, Domitius.

ENOBARBUS. No.

ANTONY. Why should he not?

ENOBARBUS. He thinks, being twenty times of
better fortune,
He is twenty men to one.

ANTONY.   Tomorrow, soldier,
By sea and land I'll fight: or I will live,   5
Or bathe my dying honour in the blood
Shall make it live again. Woo 't thou fight well?

ENOBARBUS. I'll strike, and cry, "Take all."

ANTONY.   Well said; come on.
Call forth my household servants; let's tonight
Be bounteous at our meal.

(*Enter three or four* SERVITORS)

Give me thy hand,
Thou hast been rightly honest; so hast thou;   11
Thou; and thou, and thou: you have served me
well,
And kings have been your fellows.

CLEOPATRA.   What means this?

ENOBARBUS (*aside to* CLEOPATRA). 'Tis one
of those odd tricks which sorrow shoots
Out of the mind.

ANTONY.   And thou art honest too.   15
I wish I could be made so many men,
And all of you clapped up together in
An Antony, that I might do you service
So good as you have done.

---

1 profit 2 termination 3 reward

SERVANTS.   The gods forbid!

ANTONY. Well, my good fellows, wait on me
tonight,   20
Scant not my cups, and make as much of me
As when mine empire was your fellow too,
And suffered my command.

CLEOPATRA (*aside to* ENOBARBUS). What does
he mean?

ENOBARBUS (*aside to* CLEOPATRA). To make
his followers weep.

ANTONY.   Tend me tonight;
May be it is the period [2] of your duty: 25
Haply, you shall not see me more; or if,
A mangled shadow: perchance tomorrow
You'll serve another master. I look on you
As one that takes his leave. Mine honest friends,
I turn you not away; but, like a master   30
Married to your good service, stay till death.
Tend me tonight two hours, I ask no more,
And the gods yield [3] you for 't!

ENOBARBUS.   What mean you, sir,
To give them this discomfort? Look, they weep;
And I, an ass, am onion-eyed: for shame,   35
Transform us not to women.

ANTONY.   Ho, ho, ho!
Now, the witch take me, if I meant it thus!
Grace grow where those drops fall! My hearty
friends,
You take me in too dolorous a sense,
For I spake to you for your comfort; did desire
you   40
To burn this night with torches. Know, my
hearts,
I hope well of tomorrow; and will lead you
Where rather I'll expect victorious life
Than death and honour. Let 's to supper, come,
And drown consideration.   (*Exeunt*) 45

SCENE III. *The same. Before the palace.*

(*Enter two* SOLDIERS *to their guard*)

FIRST SOLDIER. Brother, good night; tomorrow is the day.

SECOND SOLDIER. It will determine one way;
fare you well.
Heard you of nothing strange about the streets?

FIRST SOLDIER. Nothing. What news?

SECOND SOLDIER. Belike, 'tis but a rumour.
Good night to you.   5

FIRST SOLDIER. Well, sir, good night.
(*Enter two other* SOLDIERS)
SECOND SOLDIER. Soldiers, have careful watch.
THIRD SOLDIER. And you. Good night, good
night.
(*The first two place themselves at their
posts*)
FOURTH SOLDIER. Here we: (*They take their
posts*)
                      And if tomorrow
Our navy thrive, I have an absolute hope   10
Our landmen will stand up.
THIRD SOLDIER.   'Tis a brave army,
And full of purpose. (*Music of hautboys under
the stage*)
FOURTH SOLDIER. Peace! what noise?
FIRST SOLDIER.   List, list!
SECOND SOLDIER. Hark!
FIRST SOLDIER.   Music i' the air.
THIRD SOLDIER.   Under the earth.
FOURTH SOLDIER. It signs well, does it not?
THIRD SOLDIER.   No.
FIRST SOLDIER.   Peace, I say!
What should this mean?   15
SECOND SOLDIER. 'Tis the god Hercules, whom
Antony loved,
Now leaves him.
FIRST SOLDIER. Walk; let's see if other watch-
men
Do hear what we do. (*They advance to another
post*)
SECOND SOLDIER. How now, masters!
SOLDIERS.   How now!—
How now!—do you hear this?
FIRST SOLDIER.   Ay; is 't not strange?
THIRD SOLDIER. Do you hear, masters? do
you hear?   21
FIRST SOLDIER. Follow the noise so far as we
have quarter; [1]
Let's see how 't will give off.
SOLDIERS (*speaking together*). Content.—
'Tis strange.   (*Exeunt*)

SCENE IV. *The same. A room in the palace.*

(*Enter* ANTONY *and* CLEOPATRA; CHARMIAN,
and others, attending)
ANTONY. Eros! mine armour, Eros!
CLEOPATRA.   Sleep a little.

ANTONY. No, my chuck. Eros, come; mine
armour, Eros!
(*Enter* EROS, *with armour*)
Come, good fellow, put mine iron on:
If Fortune be not ours today, it is
Because we brave her. Come.   4
CLEOPATRA.   Nay, I'll help too.
What's this for?
ANTONY.   Ah! let be, let be; thou art
The armourer of my heart: false, false; this, this.
CLEOPATRA. Sooth, la! I'll help: thus it
must be.
ANTONY. Well, well;
We shall thrive now. Seest thou, my good
fellow?
Go put on thy defences.
EROS.   Briefly, sir.   10
CLEOPATRA. Is not this buckled well?
ANTONY.   Rarely, rarely:
He that unbuckles this, till we do please
To daff 't [1] for our repose, shall hear a storm.
Thou fumblest, Eros; and my queen's a squire
More tight [2] at this than thou: dispatch. O love!
That thou couldst see my wars today, and
knew'st   16
The royal occupation, thou shouldst see
A workman in 't.
(*Enter an armed* SOLDIER)
        Good morrow to thee; welcome;
Thou look'st like him that knows a war-like
charge:
To business that we love we rise betime, 20
And go to 't with delight.
SOLDIER.   A thousand, sir,
Early though 't be, have on their riveted trim,
And at the port [3] expect you.
(*Shout. Trumpets flourish.*)
(*Enter* CAPTAINS *and* SOLDIERS)
CAPTAIN. The morn is fair. Good morrow,
general.
ALL. Good morrow, general.
ANTONY.   'Tis well blown, lads.
This morning, like the spirit of a youth 26
That means to be of note, begins betimes.
So, so; come, give me that: this way; well said.
Fare thee well, dame, whate'er becomes of me;
This is a soldier's kiss. Rebukable (*Kisses her*) 30
And worthy shameful check it were, to stand
On more mechanic compliment; I'll leave thee

[1] occupy positions   [1] doff, put off   [2] deft   [3] gate

Now, like a man of steel. You that will fight,
Follow me close; I'll bring you to 't. Adieu.
                    (*Exeunt* ANTONY, EROS, CAPTAINS,
                                   and SOLDIERS)
CHARMIAN. Please you, retire to your chamber.
CLEOPATRA. Lead me.
He goes forth gallantly. That he and Caesar
    might   36
Determine this great war in single fight!
Then, Antony,—but now.—Well, on.   (*Exeunt*)

SCENE V. *Alexandria.* ANTONY'S *camp.*

    (*Trumpets sound. Enter* ANTONY *and*
        EROS; *a* SOLDIER *meeting them.*)

SOLDIER. The gods make this a happy day to
    Antony!
ANTONY. Would thou and those thy scars had
    once prevailed
To make me fight at land!
SOLDIER.   Hadst thou done so,
The kings that have revolted, and the soldier 4
That has this morning left thee, would have
    still
Followed thy heels.
ANTONY.   Who's gone this morning?
SOLDIER.   Who!
One ever near thee: call for Enobarbus,
He shall not hear thee; or from Caesar's camp
Say, "I am none of thine."
ANTONY.   What sayst thou?
SOLDIER.   Sir,
He is with Caesar.
· EROS.   Sir, his chests and treasure 10
He has not with him.
ANTONY.   Is he gone?
SOLDIER.   Most certain.
ANTONY. Go, Eros, send his treasure after;
    do it;
Detain no jot, I charge thee. Write to him—
I will subscribe—gentle adieus and greetings;
Say that I wish he never find more cause   15
To change a master. O! my fortunes have
Corrupted honest men. Dispatch. Enobarbus!
                                    (*Exeunt*)

SCENE VI. *Before Alexandria.* CAESAR'S *camp.*

    (*Flourish. Enter* CAESAR, *with* AGRIPPA,
        ENOBARBUS, *and others.*)

CAESAR. Go forth, Agrippa, and begin the
    fight:
Our will is Antony be took alive;
Make it so known.
AGRIPPA. Caesar, I shall.   (*Exit*)
CAESAR. The time of universal peace is near:
Prove this a prosperous day, the three-nook'd [1]
    world   6
Shall bear the olive freely.
            (*Enter a* MESSENGER)
MESSENGER.   Antony
Is come into the field.
CAESAR.   Go charge Agrippa
Plant those that have revolted in the van,
That Antony may seem to spend his fury   10
Upon himself. (*Exeunt* CAESAR *and his Train*)
    ENOBARBUS. Alexas did revolt, and went to
        Jewry on
Affairs of Antony; there did persuade
Great Herod to incline himself to Caesar,   14
And leave his master Antony: for this pains
Caesar hath hanged him. Canidius and the rest
That fell away have entertainment, but
No honourable trust. I have done ill,
Of which I do accuse myself so sorely
That I will joy no more.
            (*Enter a* SOLDIER *of* CAESAR'S)
SOLDIER.   Enobarbus, Antony
Hath after thee sent all thy treasure, with   21
His bounty overplus: the messenger
Came on my guard; and at thy tent is now
Unloading of his mules.
ENOBARBUS.   I give it you.
SOLDIER. Mock not, Enobarbus.   25
I tell you true: best you safed [2] the bringer
Out of the host; I must attend mine office
Or would have done 't myself. Your emperor
Continues still a Jove.   (*Exit*)
    ENOBARBUS. I am alone the villain of the
        earth,   30
And feel I am so most. O Antony!
Thou mine of bounty, how wouldst thou have
    paid
My better service, when my turpitude
Thou dost so crown with gold! This blows [3] my
    heart:
If swift thought break it not, a swifter mean
Shall outstrike thought; but thought will do 't,
    I feel.   36

1 three-cornered   2 conducted safely   3 swells

I fight against thee? No: I will go seek
Some ditch, wherein to die; the foul'st best fits
My latter part of life. (*Exit*)

SCENE VII. *Field of battle between the camps.*

(*Alarum. Drums and trumpets. Enter*
AGRIPPA *and others.*)

AGRIPPA. Retire, we have engaged ourselves
too far.
Caesar himself has work, and our oppression [1]
Exceeds what we expected. (*Exeunt*)
(*Alarum. Enter* ANTONY, *and* SCARUS
wounded.)

SCARUS. O my brave emperor, this is fought
indeed!
Had we done so at first, we had droven them
home   5
With clouts about their heads.

ANTONY.   Thou bleed'st apace.

SCARUS. I had a wound here that was like
a T,
But now 'tis made an H.

ANTONY.   They do retire.

SCARUS. We'll beat 'em into bench-holes: [2] I
have yet
Room for six scotches [3] more.   10
            (*Enter* EROS)

EROS. They are beaten, sir; and our advantage
serves
For a fair victory.

SCARUS.   Let us score their backs,
And snatch 'em up, as we take hares, behind:
'Tis sport to maul a runner.

ANTONY.   I will reward thee
Once for thy sprightly comfort, and ten-fold   15
For thy good valour. Come thee on.

SCARUS.   I'll halt [4] after. (*Exeunt*)

SCENE VIII. *Under the walls of Alexandria.*

(*Alarum. Enter* ANTONY, *marching;* SCARUS,
and Forces)

ANTONY. We have beat him to his camp; run
one before
And let the queen know of our gests. [1] Tomorrow,

Before the sun shall see 's, we'll spill the blood
That has today escaped. I thank you all;   4
For doughty-handed are you, and have fought
Not as you served the cause, but as 't had been
Each man's like mine; you have shown all
Hectors.
Enter the city, clip [2] your wives, your friends,
Tell them your feats; whilst they with joyful
tears
Wash the congealment from your wounds, and
kiss   10
The honoured gashes whole. (*To* SCARUS) Give
me thy hand:
            (*Enter* CLEOPATRA, *attended*)
To this great fairy [3] I'll commend thy acts,
Make her thanks bless thee. O thou day o' the
world!
Chain mine armed neck; leap thou, attire and
all,
Through proof of harness [4] to my heart, and
there   15
Ride on the pants triumphing.

CLEOPATRA.   Lord of lords!
O infinite virtue! com'st thou smiling from
The world's great snare uncaught?

ANTONY.   My nightingale,
We have beat them to their beds. What, girl!
though grey
Do something mingle with our younger brown,
yet ha' we   20
A brain that nourishes our nerves, and can
Get goal for goal of youth. Behold this man;
Commend unto his lips thy favouring hand:
Kiss it, my warrior: he hath fought today
As if a god, in hate of mankind, had   25
Destroyed in such a shape.

CLEOPATRA.   I'll give thee, friend,
An armour all of gold; it was a king's.

ANTONY. He had deserved it, were it car-
buncled
Like holy Phoebus' car. Give me thy hand:
Through Alexandria make a jolly march;   30
Bear our hacked targets like the men that owe [5]
them:
Had our great palace the capacity
To camp this host, we all would sup together
And drink carouses to the next day's fate,
Which promises royal peril. Trumpeters,   35

---

1 force opposed to us 2 privy holes 3 gashes 4 limp 1 deeds 2 embrace 3 enchantress
4 impenetrability of armour 5 own

With brazen din blast you the city's ear,
Make mingle with our rattling tabourines,
That heaven and earth may strike their sounds
   together,
Applauding our approach.   (*Exeunt*)

SCENE IX. CAESAR'S *camp*.

    (SENTINELS *on their post*)

FIRST SOLDIER. If we be not relieved within
   this hour,
We must return to the court of guard:[1] the
   night
Is shiny, and they say we shall embattle
By the second hour i' the morn.
  SECOND SOLDIER.   This last day was
A shrewd one to 's.
      (*Enter* ENOBARBUS)
ENOBARBUS.   O! bear me witness, night,— 5
THIRD SOLDIER. What man is this?
SECOND SOLDIER. Stand close and list him.
ENOBARBUS. Be witness to me, O thou blessed
   moon,
When men revolted shall upon record
Bear hateful memory, poor Enobarbus did
Before thy face repent!
  FIRST SOLDIER.   Enobarbus!
  THIRD SOLDIER.   Peace!   10
Hark further.
    ENOBARBUS. O sovereign mistress of true mel-
   ancholy,
The poisonous damp of night disponge[2] upon
   me,
That life, a very rebel to my will,   14
May hang no longer on me; throw my heart
Against the flint and hardness of my fault,
Which, being dried with grief, will break to
   powder,
And finish all foul thoughts. O Antony!
Nobler than my revolt is infamous,
Forgive me in thine own particular;[3]   20
But let the world rank me in register
A master-leaver and a fugitive.
O Antony! O Antony! (*Dies*)
  SECOND SOLDIER. Let's speak to him.
  FIRST SOLDIER. Let's hear him, for the
   things he speaks.   25
May concern Caesar.
    THIRD SOLDIER. Let's do so. But he sleeps.

FIRST SOLDIER. Swounds rather; for so bad a
   prayer as his
Was never yet for sleep.
  SECOND SOLDIER.   Go we to him.
  THIRD SOLDIER. Awake, sir, awake! speak to
   us.
  SECOND SOLDIER. Hear you, sir?
  FIRST SOLDIER. The hand of death hath
   raught[4] him.
    (*Drums afar off*)
                 Hark! the drums   30
Demurely[5] wake the sleepers. Let us bear him
To the court of guard; he is of note: our hour
Is fully out.
  THIRD SOLDIER. Come on, then;
He may recover yet. (*Exeunt with the body*)

SCENE X. *Between the two camps.*

    (*Enter* ANTONY *and* SCARUS,
      with forces, marching)

ANTONY. Their preparation is today by sea;
We please them not by land.
  SCARUS.   For both, my lord.
  ANTONY. I would they'd fight i' the fire or i'
   the air;
We'd fight there too. But this it is; our foot
Upon the hills adjoining to the city   5
Shall stay with us; order for sea is given,
They have put forth the haven,
Where their appointment we may best dis-
   cover
And look on their endeavour.   (*Exeunt*)
    (*Enter* CAESAR, *and his forces, marching*)
  CAESAR. But being charged, we will be still
   by land,   10
Which, as I take 't, we shall; for his best force
Is forth to man his galleys. To the vales,
And hold our best advantage!   (*Exeunt*)
    (*Re-enter* ANTONY *and* SCARUS)
  ANTONY. Yet they are not joined. Where
   yond pine does stand
I shall discover all; I'll bring thee word   15
Straight how 'tis like to go.   (*Exit*)
  SCARUS.   Swallows have built
In Cleopatra's sails their nests; the augurers
Say they know not, they cannot tell; look
   grimly,
And dare not speak their knowledge. Antony

---

[1] guard house   [2] squeeze out   [3] as far as you are concerned   [4] seized   [5] with subdued sound

Is valiant, and dejected; and, by starts,   20
His fretted fortunes give him hope and fear
Of what he has and has not.
     (Alarum afar off, as at a sea-fight)
     (Re-enter ANTONY)
ANTONY.   All is lost!
This foul Egyptian hath betrayed me;
My fleet hath yielded to the foe, and yonder 25
They cast their caps up and carouse together
Like friends long lost. Triple-turned whore,
    thou
Hast sold me to this novice, and my heart
Makes only wars on thee. Bid them all fly;
For when I am revenged upon my charm,[1]   30
I have done all. Bid them all fly; be gone.
                  (Exit SCARUS)
O sun! thy uprise shall I see no more;
Fortune and Antony part here; even here
Do we shake hands. All come to this? The
    hearts
That spanieled me at heels, to whom I gave 35
Their wishes, do discandy, melt their sweets
On blossoming Caesar; and this pine is barked,
That overtopped them all. Betrayed I am.
O this false soul of Egypt; this grave charm,
Whose eyes becked forth my wars, and called
    them home,   40
Whose bosom was my crownet,[2] my chief end,
Like a right[3] gipsy, hath, at fast and loose,
Beguiled me to the very heart of loss.
What, Eros! Eros!
            (Enter CLEOPATRA)
        Ah! thou spell. Avaunt!
CLEOPATRA. Why is my lord enraged against
    his love?   45
ANTONY. Vanish, or I shall give thee thy de-
    serving,
And blemish Caesar's triumph. Let him take
    thee,
And hoist thee up to the shouting plebeians;
Follow his chariot, like the greatest spot
Of all thy sex; most monster-like, be shown
For poor'st diminutives,[4] for doits; and let   51
Patient Octavia plough thy visage up
With her prepared nails.   *(Exit* CLEOPATRA)
                'Tis well thou'rt gone,
If it be well to live; but better 'twere
Thou fell'st into my fury, for one death
Might have prevented many. Eros, ho!   56

The shirt of Nessus is upon me; teach me,
Alcides, thou mine ancestor, thy rage;
Let me lodge Lichas on the horns o' the moon;
And with those hands, that grasped the heaviest
    club,   60
Subdue my worthiest self. The witch shall die:
To the young Roman boy she hath sold me, and
    I fall
Under this plot; she dies for 't. Eros, ho! *(Exit)*

SCENE XI. *Alexandria. A room in the palace.*

    (Enter CLEOPATRA, CHARMIAN, IRAS,
            and MARDIAN)
CLEOPATRA. Help me, my women! O! he is
    more mad
Than Telamon for his shield; the boar of
    Thessaly
Was never so embossed.
CHARMIAN.   To the monument!
There lock yourself, and send him word you are
    dead.
The soul and body rive[1] not more in parting
Than greatness going off.   5
CLEOPATRA.   To the monument!
Mardian, go tell him I have slain myself;
Say that the last I spoke was "Antony,"
And word it, prithee, piteously. Hence,
Mardian, and bring me how he takes my death.
To the monument!   *(Exeunt)* 10

SCENE XII. *The same. Another room.*

    (Enter ANTONY *and* EROS)
ANTONY. Eros, thou yet behold'st me?
EROS.   Ay, noble lord.
ANTONY. Sometimes we see a cloud that's
    dragonish;
A vapour sometime like a bear or lion,
A towered citadel, a pendant rock,
A forked mountain, or blue promontory   5
With trees upon 't, that nod unto the world
And mock our eyes with air: thou hast seen
    these signs;
They are black vesper's pageants.
EROS.   Ay, my lord.
ANTONY. That which is now a horse, even
    with a thought
The rack dislimns,[1] and makes it indistinct, 10

[1] charmer   [2] coronet   [3] true   [4] insignificant persons   [1] are torn   [1] cloud loses its outlines

As water is in water.

EROS.   It does, my lord.

ANTONY. My good knave, Eros, now thy captain is

Even such a body: here I am Antony;

Yet cannot hold this visible shape, my knave.

I made these wars for Egypt; and the queen,   15

Whose heart I thought I had, for she had mine,

Which whilst it was mine had annexed unto 't

A million more, now lost; she, Eros, has

Packed cards with Caesar, and false-played my
glory

Unto an enemy's triumph.   20

Nay, weep not, gentle Eros; there is left us

Ourselves to end ourselves.

            (*Enter* MARDIAN)

                         O! thy vile lady;

She has robbed me of my sword.

MARDIAN.   No, Antony;

My mistress loved thee, and her fortunes
mingled   24

With thine entirely.

ANTONY.   Hence, saucy eunuch; peace!

She hath betrayed me and shall die the death.

MARDIAN. Death of one person can be paid
but once,

And that she has discharged. What thou
wouldst do

Is done unto thy hand; the last she spake

Was, "Antony! most noble Antony!"   30

Then in the midst a tearing groan did break

The name of Antony; it was divided

Between her heart and lips. She rendered life,

Thy name so buried in her.

ANTONY.   Dead, then?

MARDIAN.   Dead.

ANTONY. Unarm, Eros; the long day's task is
done,   35

And we must sleep. (*To* MARDIAN) That thou
depart'st hence safe,

Does pay thy labour richly; go. (*Exit* MARDIAN)

                         Off, pluck off:

The seven-fold shield of Ajax cannot keep

The battery [2] from my heart. O! cleave, my sides;

Heart, once be stronger than thy continent,[3]   40

Crack thy frail case! Apace, Eros, apace.

No more a soldier; bruised pieces, go;

You have been nobly borne. From me awhile.

            (*Exit* EROS)

I will o'ertake thee, Cleopatra, and

Weep for my pardon. So it must be, for now   45

All length is torture; since the torch is out,

Lie down, and stray no further. Now all labour

Mars what it does; yea, very force entangles

Itself with strength; seal [4] then, and all is done.

Eros!—I come, my queen.—Eros!—Stay for me: 50

Where souls do couch on flowers, we'll hand in
hand,

And with our sprightly port [5] make the ghosts
gaze;

Dido and her Aeneas shall want troops,

And all the haunt be ours. Come, Eros! Eros!

            (*Re-enter* EROS)

EROS. What would my lord?

ANTONY.   Since Cleopatra died, 55

I have lived in such dishonour, that the gods

Detest my baseness. I, that with my sword

Quartered the world, and o'er green Neptune's
back

With ships made cities, condemn myself to lack

The courage of a woman; less noble mind   60

Than she, which by her death our Caesar tells

"I am conqueror of myself." Thou art sworn,
Eros,

That, when the exigent [6] should come,—which
now

Is come indeed,—when I should see behind me

The inevitable prosecution of   65

Disgrace and horror, that, on my command,

Thou then wouldst kill me: do 't; the time is
come.

Thou strik'st not me, 'tis Caesar thou defeat'st.

Put colour in thy cheek.

EROS.   The gods withhold me!

Shall I do that which all the Parthian darts, 70

Though enemy, lost aim and could not?

ANTONY.   Eros,

Wouldst thou be windowed in great Rome, and
see

Thy master thus with pleached [7] arms, bending
down

His corrigible [8] neck, his face subdued   74

To penetrative shame, whilst the wheeled seat

Of fortunate Caesar, drawn before him,
branded

His baseness that ensued?

EROS.   I would not see 't.

ANTONY. Come, then; for with a wound I

---

2 assault   3 container   4 bring to completion   5 demeanor   6 emergency

must be cured.
Draw that thy honest sword, which thou hast worn
Most useful for thy country.

EROS.   O, sir! pardon me.
ANTONY. When I did make thee free, swor'st thou not then   81
To do this when I bade thee? Do it at once,
Or thy precedent services are all
But accidents unpurposed. Draw, and come.

EROS. Turn from me then that noble countenance,   85
Wherein the worship [9] of the whole world lies.

ANTONY. Lo thee! (*Turning from him*)

EROS. My sword is drawn.

ANTONY.   Then let it do at once
The thing why thou hast drawn it.

EROS.   My dear master,
My captain, and my emperor, let me say,   90
Before I strike this bloody stroke, farewell.

ANTONY. 'Tis said, man; and farewell.

EROS. Farewell, great chief. Shall I strike now?

ANTONY. Now, Eros.

EROS. Why, there then; thus do I escape the sorrow
Of Antony's death. (*Kills himself*)

ANTONY.   Thrice-nobler than myself! 95
Thou teachest me, O valiant Eros, what
I should, and thou couldst not. My queen and Eros
Have by their brave instruction got upon me
A nobleness in record; but I will be
A bridegroom in my death, and run into 't 100
As to a lover's bed. Come, then; and, Eros,
Thy master dies thy scholar: to do thus (*Falls on his sword*)
I learned of thee. How! not dead? not dead?
The guard, ho! O! dispatch me.
       (*Enter* DERCETAS *and* GUARD)

FIRST GUARD.   What's the noise?

ANTONY. I have done my work ill, friends: O! make an end   105
Of what I have begun.

SECOND GUARD.   The star is fallen.

FIRST GUARD. And time is at his period.

ALL.   Alas, and woe!

ANTONY. Let him that loves me strike me dead.

FIRST GUARD. Not I.

SECOND GUARD. Nor I.   109

THIRD GUARD.   Nor any one.
       (*Exeunt* GUARD)

DERCETAS. Thy death and fortunes bid thy followers fly.
This sword but shown to Caesar, with this tidings,
Shall enter me with him.
       (*Enter* DIOMEDES)

DIOMEDES. Where's Antony?

DERCETAS.   There, Diomed, there.

DIOMEDES.   Lives he?
Wilt thou not answer, man?   115
       (*Exit* DERCETAS)

ANTONY. Art thou there, Diomed? Draw thy sword, and give me
Sufficing strokes for death.

DIOMEDES.   Most absolute lord,
My mistress Cleopatra sent me to thee.

ANTONY. When did she send thee?

DIOMEDES.   Now, my lord.

ANTONY.   Where is she?

DIOMEDES. Locked in her monument. She had a prophesying fear   120
Of what hath come to pass; for when she saw—
Which never shall be found—you did suspect
She had disposed [10] with Caesar, and that your rage
Would not be purged,[11] she sent you word she was dead:
But, fearing since how it might work, hath sent   125
Me to proclaim the truth; and I am come,
I dread, too late.

ANTONY. Too late, good Diomed. Call my guard, I prithee.

DIOMEDES. What, ho! the emperor's guard! The guard, what, ho!
Come, your lord calls!   130
   (*Enter four or five of the* GUARD *of* ANTONY)

ANTONY. Bear me, good friends, where Cleopatra bides;
'Tis the last service that I shall command you.

FIRST GUARD. Woe, woe are we, sir, you may not live to wear
All your true followers out.

ALL.   Most heavy day!

ANTONY. Nay, good my fellows, do not please

---

7 folded   8 submissive   9 dignity   10 come to terms   11 cleared away

sharp fate   135
To grace it with your sorrows; bid that welcome
Which comes to punish us, and we punish it
Seeming to bear it lightly. Take me up;
I have led you oft; carry me now, good friends,
And have my thanks for all.   140

(*Exeunt, bearing* ANTONY)

SCENE XIII. *The same. A monument.*

(*Enter* CLEOPATRA *and her maids aloft,
with* CHARMIAN *and* IRAS)

CLEOPATRA. O Charmian! I will never go
    from hence.
CHARMIAN. Be comforted, dear madam.
CLEOPATRA.   No, I will not.
All strange and terrible events are welcome,
But comforts we despise; our size of sorrow,
Proportioned to our cause, must be as great   5
As that which makes it.
                    (*Enter, below,* DIOMEDES)
                            How now! is he dead?
DIOMEDES. His death 's upon him, but not
    dead.
Look out o' the other side your monument;
His guard have brought him thither.

(*Enter, below,* ANTONY, *borne by the Guard*)
CLEOPATRA.   O sun!
Burn the great sphere thou mov'st in; darkling
    stand   10
The varying shore o' the world. O Antony,
Antony, Antony! Help, Charmian, help, Iras,
    help;
Help, friends below! let's draw him hither.
ANTONY.   Peace!
Not Caesar's valour hath o'erthrown Antony,
But Antony's hath triumphed on itself.   15
CLEOPATRA. So it should be, that none but
    Antony.
Should conquer Antony; but woe 'tis so!
ANTONY. I am dying, Egypt, dying; only
I here importune death awhile, until
Of many thousand kisses the poor last   20
I lay upon thy lips.
CLEOPATRA.   I dare not, dear,—
Dear my lord, pardon,—I dare not,
Lest I be taken: not the imperious show
Of the full-fortuned Caesar ever shall

Be brooched [1] with me; if knife, drugs, serpents,
    have   25
Edge, sting, or operation, I am safe:
Your wife Octavia, with her modest eyes
And still conclusion,[2] shall acquire no honour
Demuring [3] upon me. But come, come, An-
    tony,—   29
Help me, my women,—we must draw thee up.
Assist, good friends.
    ANTONY.   O! quick, or I am gone.
    CLEOPATRA. Here's sport indeed! How heavy
        weighs my lord!
Our strength is all gone into heaviness,
That makes the weight. Had I great Juno's
    power,
The strong-winged Mercury should fetch thee
    up,   35
And set thee by Jove's side. Yet come a little,
Wishers were ever fools. O! come, come, come;
        (*They heave* ANTONY *aloft to* CLEOPATRA)
And welcome, welcome! die where thou hast
    lived;
Quicken with kissing; had my lips that power,
Thus would I wear them out.
    ALL.   A heavy sight! 40
    ANTONY. I am dying, Egypt, dying:
Give me some wine, and let me speak a little.
    CLEOPATRA. No, let me speak; and let me rail
        so high,
That the false housewife [4] Fortune break her
    wheel,
Provoked by my offence.
    ANTONY.   One word, sweet queen. 45
Of Caesar seek your honour with your safety. O!
    CLEOPATRA. They do not go together.
    ANTONY.   Gentle, hear me:
None about Caesar trust, but Proculeius.
    CLEOPATRA. My resolution and my hands I'll
        trust;
None about Caesar.   50
    ANTONY. The miserable change now at my
        end
Lament nor sorrow at; but please your thoughts
In feeding them with those my former fortunes
Wherein I lived, the greatest prince o' the
    world,
The noblest; and do now not basely die,   55
Not cowardly put off my helmet to
My countryman; a Roman by a Roman

1 adorned   2 quiet inference   3 looking soberly   4 hussy, slattern

Valiantly vanquished. Now my spirit is going;
I can no more.

CLEOPATRA. Noblest of men, woo 't die?
Hast thou no care of me? shall I abide   60
In this dull world, which in thy absence is
No better than a sty? O! see my women,
   (ANTONY dies)
The crown o' the earth doth melt. My lord!
O! withered is the garland of the war,
The soldier's pole [5] is fall'n; young boys and
   girls   65
Are level now with men; the odds [6] is gone,
And there is nothing left remarkable
Beneath the visiting moon. (Swoons)
  CHARMIAN.   O, quietness, lady!
  IRAS. She is dead too, our sovereign.
  CHARMIAN.   Lady!
  IRAS.   Madam!
  CHARMIAN. O madam, madam, madam!
  IRAS.   Royal Egypt!
Empress!   71
  CHARMIAN. Peace, peace, Iras!
  CLEOPATRA. No more, but e'en a woman, and
   commanded
By such poor passion as the maid that milks   74

And does the meanest chares. [7] It were for
  me
To throw my sceptre at the injurious gods;
To tell them that this world did equal theirs
Till they had stol'n our jewel. All's but naught;
Patience is sottish, and impatience does
Become a dog that's mad; then is it sin   80
To rush into the secret house of death,
Ere death dare come to us? How do you,
  women?
What, what! good cheer! Why, how now,
  Charmian!
My noble girls! Ah, women, women, look!
Our lamp is spent, it's out. Good sirs, take
  heart;—   85
We'll bury him; and then, what's brave, what's
  noble,
Let's do it after the high Roman fashion,
And make death proud to take us. Come, away;
This case of that huge spirit now is cold;
Ah! women, women! Come; we have no friend
But resolution, and the briefest end.   91
   (Exeunt; those above bearing off
       ANTONY's body)

Act V

SCENE I. Alexandria. CAESAR's camp.

(Enter CAESAR, AGRIPPA, DOLABELLA,
MECAENAS, GALLUS, PROCULEIUS, and
       others)
CAESAR. Go to him, Dolabella, bid him yield;
Being so frustrate, tell him he mocks
The pauses that he makes.
  DOLABELLA.   Caesar, I shall. (Exit)
(Enter DERCETAS, with the sword of ANTONY)
  CAESAR. Wherefore is that? and what art
   thou that dar'st
Appear thus to us?
  DERCETAS.   I am called Dercetas;   5
Mark Antony I served, who best was worthy
Best to be served; whilst he stood up and spoke
He was my master, and I wore my life
To spend upon his haters. If thou please
To take me to thee, as I was to him   10
I'll be to Caesar; if thou pleasest not,
I yield thee up my life.

CAESAR.   What is 't thou sayst?
DERCETAS. I say, O Caesar, Antony is dead.
CAESAR. The breaking of so great a thing
  should make
A greater crack; the round world   15
Should have shook lions into civil [1] streets,
And citizens to their dens. The death of Antony
Is not a single doom; in the name lay
A moiety [2] of the world.
  DERCETAS.   He is dead, Caesar;
Not by a public minister of justice,   20
Nor by a hired knife; but that self hand,
Which writ his honour in the acts it did,
Hath, with the courage which the heart did
  lend it,
Splitted the heart. This is his sword;
I robbed his wound of it; behold it stained   25
With his most noble blood.
  CAESAR.   Look you sad, friends?
The gods rebuke me, but it is tidings
To wash the eyes of kings.

[5] polestar, guiding star   [6] superiority, gradation   [7] chores, tasks   [1] well-governed   [2] half

AGRIPPA.   And strange it is,
That nature must compel us to lament
Our most persisted deeds.
    MECAENAS.   His taints and honours
Waged equal with him.
    AGRIPPA.   A rarer spirit never 31
Did steer humanity; but you, gods, will give us
Some faults to make us men. Caesar is touched.
    MECAENAS. When such a spacious mirror's set
      before him,
He needs must see himself.
    CAESAR.   O Antony! 35
I have followed thee to this; but we do lance
Diseases in our bodies: I must perforce
Have shown to thee such a declining day,
Or look on thine; we could not stall together
In the whole world. But yet let me lament, 40
With tears as sovereign as the blood of hearts,
That thou, my brother, my competitor
In top of all design,[3] my mate in empire,
Friend and companion in the front of war,
The arm of mine own body, and the heart 45
Where mine his thoughts did kindle, that our
    stars,
Unreconciliable, should divide
Our equalness to this. Hear me, good friends,—
      (*Enter an* EGYPTIAN)
But I will tell you at some meeter season:
The business of this man looks out of him; 50
We'll hear him what he says. Whence are you?
    EGYPTIAN. A poor Egyptian yet. The queen
      my mistress,
Confined in all she has, her monument,
Of thy intents desires instruction,
That she preparedly may frame herself 55
To the way she's forced to.
    CAESAR.   Bid her have good heart;
She soon shall know of us, by some of ours,
How honourable and how kindly we
Determine for her; for Caesar cannot live
To be ungentle.
    EGYPTIAN.   So the gods preserve thee! 60
      (*Exit*)
    CAESAR. Come hither, Proculeius. Go and
    say,
We purpose her no shame; give her what com-
    forts
The quality of her passion shall require,
Lest, in her greatness, by some mortal stroke

[3] in the supreme conception of enterprise

She do defeat us; for her life in Rome 65
Would be eternal in our triumph. Go,
And with your speediest bring us what she says,
And how you find of her.
    PROCULEIUS.   Caesar, I shall.
      (*Exit*)
    CAESAR. Gallus, go you along.
      (*Exit* GALLUS)
      Where's Dolabella,
To second Proculeius?

AGRIPPA. }
MECAENAS. }   Dolabella! 70

    CAESAR. Let him alone, for I remember now
How he's employed, he shall in time be ready.
Go with me to my tent; where you shall see
How hardly I was drawn into this war;
How calm and gentle I proceeded still 75
In all my writings. Go with me, and see
What I can show in this.   (*Exeunt*)

SCENE II. *The same. The monument.*

(*Enter aloft,* CLEOPATRA, CHARMIAN, *and* IRAS)
    CLEOPATRA. My desolation does begin to make
A better life. 'Tis paltry to be Caesar;
Not being Fortune, he's but Fortune's knave,
A minister of her will; and it is great
To do that thing that ends all other deeds,
Which shackles accidents, and bolts up change,
Which sleeps, and never palates more the dung,
The beggar's nurse and Caesar's.
    (*Enter, below,* PROCULEIUS, GALLUS,
      and SOLDIERS)
    PROCULEIUS. Caesar sends greeting to the Queen
    of Egypt;
And bids thee study on what fair demands 10
Thou mean'st to have him grant thee.
    CLEOPATRA.   What's thy name?
    PROCULEIUS. My name is Proculeius.
    CLEOPATRA.   Antony
Did tell me of you, bade me trust you; but
I do not greatly care to be deceived,
That have no use for trusting. If your master
Would have a queen his beggar, you must tell
    him,
That majesty, to keep decorum, must 16
No less beg than a kingdom: if he please
To give me conquered Egypt for my son,

He gives me so much of mine own as I   20
Will kneel to him with thanks.

PROCULEIUS.   Be of good cheer;
You're fall'n into a princely hand, fear nothing.
Make your full reference [1] freely to my lord,
Who is so full of grace, that it flows over
On all that need; let me report to him   25
Your sweet dependancy, and you shall find
A conqueror that will pray in aid for kindness
Where he for grace is kneeled to.

CLEOPATRA.   Pray you, tell him
I am his fortune's vassal, and I send him
The greatness he has got. I hourly learn   30
A doctrine of obedience, and would gladly
Look him i' the face.

PROCULEIUS.   This I'll report, dear lady:
Have comfort, for I know your plight is pitied
Of him that caused it.

GALLUS. You see how easily she may be
    surprised.   35
    (PROCULEIUS *and two of the Guard ascend*
    the monument by a ladder, and come
    behind CLEOPATRA. *Some of the Guard*
    unbar and open the gates, discovering
    the lower room of the monument.)
    (*To* PROCULEIUS *and the Guard*) Guard her
    till Caesar come.   (*Exit*)

IRAS. Royal queen!

CHARMIAN. O Cleopatra! thou art taken, queen.

CLEOPATRA. Quick, quick, good hands.
    (*Drawing a dagger*)

PROCULEIUS.   Hold, worthy lady, hold!
    (*Seizes and disarms her*)
Do not yourself such wrong, who are in this   40
Relieved, but not betrayed.

CLEOPATRA.   What, of death too,
That rids our dogs of languish?

PROCULEIUS.   Cleopatra,
Do not abuse my master's bounty by
The undoing of yourself; let the world see
His nobleness well acted, which your death   45
Will never let come forth.

CLEOPATRA.   Where art thou, death?
Come hither, come! come, come, and take a
    queen
Worth many babes and beggars!

PROCULEIUS.   O! temperance, lady.

CLEOPATRA. Sir, I will eat no meat, I'll not
    drink sir;

If idle talk will once be necessary,   50
I'll not sleep neither. This mortal house I'll
    ruin,
Do Caesar what he can. Know, sir, that I
Will not wait pinioned at your master's court,
Nor once be chastised with the sober eye
Of dull Octavia. Shall they hoist me up   55
And show me to the shouting varletry
Of censuring Rome? Rather a ditch in Egypt
Be gentle grave unto me! rather on Nilus' mud
Lay me stark naked, and let the water-flies
Blow me into abhorring! rather make   60
My country's high pyramides my gibbet,
And hang me up in chains!

PROCULEIUS.   You do extend
These thoughts of horror further than you shall
Find cause in Caesar.
    (*Enter* DOLABELLA)

DOLABELLA.   Proculeius,
What thou hast done thy master Caesar knows,
And he hath sent for thee; as for the queen,   66
I'll take her to my guard.

PROCULEIUS.   So, Dolabella,
It shall content me best; be gentle to her.
    (*To* CLEOPATRA) To Caesar I will speak what
    you shall please,
If you'll employ me to him.

CLEOPATRA.   Say, I would die.
    (*Exeunt* PROCULEIUS *and* SOLDIERS)

DOLABELLA. Most noble empress, you have
    heard of me?   71

CLEOPATRA. I cannot tell.

DOLABELLA.   Assuredly you know me.

CLEOPATRA. No matter, sir, what I have heard
    or known.
You laugh when boys or women tell their
    dreams;
Is 't not your trick?

DOLABELLA.   I understand not, madam.

CLEOPATRA. I dreamed there was an Emperor
    Antony: 76
O! such another sleep, that I might see
But such another man.

DOLABELLA.   If it might please ye,—

CLEOPATRA. His face was as the heavens, and
    therein stuck
A sun and moon, which kept their course, and
    lighted,   80
The little O, the earth.

---

[1] refer the whole matter

DOLABELLA.   Most sovereign creature,—

CLEOPATRA. His legs bestrid the ocean; his
    reared arm
Crested the world; his voice was propertied
As all the tunèd spheres, and that to friends;
But when he meant to quail[2] and shake the
    orb,
He was as rattling thunder. For his bounty,   86
There was no winter in 't, an autumn 'twas
That grew the more by reaping; his delights
Were dolphin-like, they showed his back above
The element they lived in; in his livery   90
Walked crowns and crownets, realms and islands
    were
As plates[3] dropped from his pocket.

DOLABELLA.   Cleopatra,—

CLEOPATRA. Think you there was, or might
    be, such a man
As this I dreamed of?

DOLABELLA.   Gentle madam, no.

CLEOPATRA. You lie, up to the hearing of the
    gods!   95
But, if there be, or ever were, one such,
It's past the size of dreaming; nature wants stuff
To vie strange forms with fancy; yet to imagine
An Antony were nature's piece 'gainst fancy,
Condemning shadows quite.

DOLABELLA.   Hear me, good madam.   100
Your loss is as yourself, great; and you bear it
As answering to the weight: would I might
    never
O'ertake pursued success, but I do feel,
By the rebound of yours, a grief that smites
My very heart at root.

CLEOPATRA.   I thank you, sir.   105
Know you what Caesar means to do with me?

DOLABELLA. I am loath to tell you what I
    would you knew.

CLEOPATRA. Nay, pray you, sir,—

DOLABELLA.   Though he be honourable,—

CLEOPATRA. He'll lead me then in triumph?

DOLABELLA. Madam, he will; I know 't.   110
    (Within, "Make way there!—Caesar!")

(Enter CAESAR, GALLUS, PROCULEIUS, MECAENAS,
    SELEUCUS, and ATTENDANTS)

CAESAR. Which is the Queen of Egypt?

DOLABELLA. It is the emperor, madam.
    (CLEOPATRA kneels)

CAESAR. Arise, you shall not kneel.

I pray you, rise; rise, Egypt.

CLEOPATRA.   Sir, the gods   115
Will have it thus; my master and my lord
I must obey.

CAESAR.   Take to you no hard thoughts;
The record of what injuries you did us,
Though written in our flesh, we shall remember
As things but done by chance.

CLEOPATRA.   Sole sir o' the world,
I cannot project[4] mine own cause so well   121
To make it clear; but do confess I have
Been laden with like frailties which before
Have often shamed our sex.

CAESAR.   Cleopatra, know,
We will extenuate rather than enforce: 125
If you apply yourself to our intents,—
Which towards you are most gentle,—you shall
    find
A benefit in this change; but if you seek
To lay on me a cruelty, by taking   129
Antony's course, you shall bereave yourself
Of my good purposes, and put your children
To that destruction which I'll guard them from,
If thereon you rely. I'll take my leave.

CLEOPATRA. And may through all the world:
    'tis yours; and we,
Your scutcheons, and your signs of conquest,
    shall   135
Hang in what place you please. Here, my good
    lord.

CAESAR. You shall advise me in all for
    Cleopatra.

CLEOPATRA (giving a scroll). This is the brief
    of money, plate, and jewels,   139
I am possessed of: 'tis exactly valued;
Not petty things admitted. Where's Seleucus?

SELEUCUS. Here, madam.

CLEOPATRA. This is my treasurer; let him
    speak, my lord,
Upon his peril, that I have reserved
To myself nothing. Speak the truth, Seleucus.

SELEUCUS. Madam,   145
I had rather seal my lips, than, to my peril,
Speak that which is not.

CLEOPATRA.   What have I kept back?

SELEUCUS. Enough to purchase what you have
    made known.

CAESAR. Nay, blush not, Cleopatra; I approve
Your wisdom in the deed.

2 overpower   3 coins   4 put forth

CLEOPATRA.   See! Caesar! O, behold,
How pomp is followed; mine will now be
    yours;   151
And, should we shift estates, yours would be
    mine.
The ingratitude of this Seleucus does
Even make me wild. O slave! of no more trust
Than love that's hired. What! goest thou back?
    thou shalt   155
Go back, I warrant thee; but I'll catch thine
    eyes,
Though they had wings: slave, soulless villain,
    dog!
O rarely base!
    CAESAR.   Good queen, let us entreat you.
    CLEOPATRA. O Caesar! what a wounding
        shame is this,
That thou, vouchsafing here to visit me,   160
Doing the honour of thy lordliness
To one so meek, that mine own servant should
Parcel the sum [5] of my disgraces by
Addition of his envy. Say, good Caesar,
That I some lady trifles have reserved   165
Immoment toys,[6] things of such dignity
As we greet modern [7] friends withal; and say,
Some nobler token I have kept apart
For Livia and Octavia, to induce
Their mediation; must I be unfolded   170
With [8] one that I have bred? The gods! it smites
    me
Beneath the fall I have. (*To* SELEUCUS)
    Prithee, go hence;
Or I shall show the cinders of my spirits
Through the ashes of my chance.[9] Wert thou
    a man,
Thou wouldst have mercy on me.
    CAESAR.   Forbear, Seleucus.
        (*Exit* SELEUCUS)
    CLEOPATRA. Be it known that we, the greatest,
        are misthought   176
For things that others do; and, when we fall,
We answer others' merits in our name,
Are therefore to be pitied.
    CAESAR.   Cleopatra,
Not what you have reserved, nor what acknowl-
    edged,   180
Put we i' the roll of conquest: still be 't yours,
Bestow it at your pleasure; and believe,
Caesar's no merchant, to make prize [10] with you

5 sum up   6 unimportant trifles   7 ordinary   8 by   9 fortune   10 appraisal

Of things that merchants sold. Therefore be
    cheered;
Make not your thoughts your prisons: no, dear
    queen;   185
For we intend so to dispose you as
Yourself shall give us counsel. Feed, and sleep:
Our care and pity is so much upon you,
That we remain your friend; and so, adieu.   189
    CLEOPATRA. My master, and my lord!
    CAESAR.   Not so. Adieu.
        (*Flourish. Exeunt* CAESAR *and his train*)
    CLEOPATRA. He words me, girls, he words me,
        that I should not
Be noble to myself: but, hark thee, Charmian.
        (*Whispers* CHARMIAN)
    IRAS. Finish, good lady; the bright day is
        done,
And we are for the dark.
    CLEOPATRA.   Hie thee again:
I have spoke already, and it is provided;   195
Go, put it to the haste.
    CHARMIAN.   Madam, I will.
        (*Re-enter* DOLABELLA)
    DOLABELLA. Where is the queen?
    CHARMIAN.   Behold, sir.
                                            (*Exit*)
    CLEOPATRA.   Dolabella!
    DOLABELLA. Madam, as thereto sworn by
        your command.
Which my love makes religion to obey,
I tell you this: Caesar through Syria   200
Intends his journey; and within three days
You with your children will he send before.
Make your best use of this; I have performed
Your pleasure and my promise.
    CLEOPATRA.   Dolabella,
I shall remain your debtor.
    DOLABELLA.   I your servant.   205
Adieu, good queen; I must attend on Caesar.
    CLEOPATRA. Farewell, and thanks.
                            (*Exit* DOLABELLA)
            Now, Iras, what think'st thou?
Thou, an Egyptian puppet, shall be shown
In Rome, as well as I; mechanic slaves
With greasy aprons, rules and hammers, shall
Uplift us to the view; in their thick breaths,
Rank of gross diet, shall we be enclouded,   212
And forced to drink their vapour.
    IRAS.   The gods forbid!

CLEOPATRA. Nay, 'tis most certain, Iras. Saucy lictors
Will catch at us, like strumpets, and scald [11] rimers   215
Ballad us out o' tune; the quick comedians
Extemporally will stage us, and present
Our Alexandrian revels. Antony
Shall be brought drunken forth, and I shall see
Some squeaking Cleopatra boy my greatness
I' the posture of a whore.

IRAS.   O, the good gods!   221

CLEOPATRA. Nay, that's certain.

IRAS. I'll never see it; for, I am sure my nails
Are stronger than mine eyes.

CLEOPATRA.   Why, that's the way
To fool their preparation, and to conquer   225
Their most absurd intents.

(*Re-enter* CHARMIAN)

                                    Now, Charmian,
Show me, my women, like a queen; go fetch
My best attires; I am again for Cydnus,
To meet Mark Antony. Sirrah Iras, go.
Now, noble Charmian, we'll dispatch indeed;
And, when thou hast done this chare, I'll give thee leave   231
To play till doomsday. Bring our crown and all.

(*Exit* IRAS. *A noise heard*)

Wherefore's this noise?

(*Enter one of the* GUARD)

GUARD.   Here is a rural fellow
That will not be denied your highness' presence:
He brings you figs.   235

CLEOPATRA. Let him come in.   (*Exit* GUARD)
What poor an instrument
May do a noble deed! he brings me liberty.
My resolution's placed, and I have nothing
Of woman in me; now from head to foot
I am marble-constant, now the fleeting moon
No planet is of mine.

(*Re-enter* GUARD, *with a* CLOWN *bringing in a basket*)

GUARD.   This is the man.   241

CLEOPATRA. Avoid,[12] and leave him.

                                    (*Exit* GUARD)
Hast thou the pretty worm of Nilus there,
That kills and pains not?   244

CLOWN. Truly, I have him; but I would not be the party that should desire you to touch

him, for his biting is immortal; those that do die of it do seldom or never recover.

CLEOPATRA. Remember'st thou any that have died on 't?   249

CLOWN. Very many, men and women too. I heard of one of them no longer than yesterday; a very honest woman, but something given to lie, as a woman should not do but in the way of honesty, how she died of the biting of it, what pain she felt. Truly, she makes a very good report o' the worm, but he that will believe all that they say shall never be saved by half that they do. But this is most fallible, the worm's an odd worm.

CLEOPATRA. Get thee hence; farewell.   260

CLOWN. I wish you all joy of the worm.

(*Sets down the basket*)

CLEOPATRA. Farewell.

CLOWN. You must think this, look you, that the worm will do his kind.[13]

CLEOPATRA. Ay, ay; farewell   265

CLOWN. Look you, the worm is not to be trusted but in the keeping of wise people; for indeed there is no goodness in the worm.

CLEOPATRA. Take thou no care; it shall be heeded.

CLOWN. Very good. Give it nothing, I pray you, for it is not worth the feeding.   271

CLEOPATRA. Will it eat me?

CLOWN. You must not think I am so simple but I know the devil himself will not eat a woman; I know that a woman is a dish for the gods, if the devil dress her not. But, truly, these same whoreson devils do the gods great harm in their women, for in every ten that they make, the devils mar five.

CLEOPATRA. Well, get thee gone; farewell.   280

CLOWN. Yes, forsooth; I wish you joy of the worm.   (*Exit*)

(*Re-enter* IRAS, *with a robe, crown, &c.*)

CLEOPATRA. Give me my robe, put on my crown; I have
Immortal longings in me; now no more
The juice of Egypt's grape shall moist this lip.
Yare,[14] yare, good Iras; quick. Methinks I hear   285
Antony call; I see him rouse himself
To praise my noble act; I hear him mock
The luck of Caesar, which the gods give men

11 scurvy, base   12 withdraw   13 act according to his nature   14 briskly

To excuse their after wrath: husband, I
  come: 290
Now to that name my courage prove my title!
I am fire, and air; my other elements
I give to baser life. So; have you done?
Come then, and take the last warmth of my lips.
Farewell, kind Charmian; Iras, long farewell.
      (*Kisses them.* IRAS *falls and dies*)
Have I the aspic [15] in my lips? Dost fall?   296
If thou and nature can so gently part,
The stroke of death is as a lover's pinch,
Which hurts, and is, desired. Dost thou lie still?
If thus thou vanishest, thou tell'st the world
It is not worth leave-taking.   301
  CHARMIAN. Dissolve, thick cloud, and rain;
    that I may say,
The gods themselves do weep.
  CLEOPATRA.   This proves me base:
If she first meet the curled Antony,
He'll make demand of her, and spend that
  kiss   305
Which is my heaven to have. Come, thou mor-
  tal wretch,
    (*To the asp, which she applies to her
    breast*)
With thy sharp teeth this knot intrinsicate
Of life at once untie; poor venomous fool,
Be angry, and dispatch. O! couldst thou speak,
That I might hear thee call great Caesar ass
Unpolicied.
  CHARMIAN. O eastern star!
  CLEOPATRA.   Peace, peace!
Dost thou not see my baby at my breast,   312
That sucks the nurse asleep?
  CHARMIAN.   O, break! O, break!
  CLEOPATRA. As sweet as balm, as soft as air,
    as gentle,—
O Antony!—Nay, I will take thee too.   315
    (*Applying another asp to her arm*)
What should I stay— (*Dies*)
  CHARMIAN. In this vile world? So, fare thee
    well.
Now boast thee, death, in thy possession lies
A lass unparalleled. Downy windows, close;
And golden Phoebus never be beheld   320
Of eyes again so royal! Your crown's awry;
I'll mend it, and then play.
      (*Enter the* GUARD, *rushing in*)
  FIRST GUARD. Where is the queen?

  CHARMIAN.   Speak softly, wake her not.
  FIRST GUARD. Caesar hath sent—
  CHARMIAN.   Too slow a messenger.
    (*Applies an asp*)
O! come apace, dispatch; I partly feel thee.
  FIRST GUARD. Approach, ho! All's not well;
    Caesar's beguiled.   326
  SECOND GUARD. There's Dolabella sent from
    Caesar; call him.
  FIRST GUARD. What work is here! Charmian,
    is this well done?
  CHARMIAN. It is well done, and fitting for a
    princess
Descended of so many royal kings.   330
Ah! soldier. (*Dies*)
      (*Re-enter* DOLABELLA)
  DOLABELLA. How goes it here?
  SECOND GUARD.   All dead.
  DOLABELLA.   Caesar, thy thoughts
Touch their effects [16] in this; thyself art coming
To see performed the dreaded act which thou
So sought'st to hinder.   335
    (*Within.* "A way there!—a way for Caesar!")
    (*Re-enter* CAESAR *and all his train*)
  DOLABELLA. O! sir, you are too sure an
    augurer;
That you did fear is done.
  CAESAR.   Bravest at the last,
She levelled [17] at our purposes, and, being royal,
Took her own way. The manner of their
  deaths?   340
I do not see them bleed.
  DOLABELLA.   Who was last with them?
  FIRST GUARD. A simple countryman that
    brought her figs:
This was his basket.
  CAESAR.   Poisoned then.
  FIRST GUARD.   O Caesar!
This Charmian lived but now; she stood, and
  spake:
I found her trimming up the diadem   345
On her dead mistress; tremblingly she stood,
And on the sudden dropped.
  CAESAR.   O noble weakness!
If they had swallowed poison 'twould appear
By external swelling; but she looks like sleep,
As she would catch another Antony   350
In her strong toil [18] of grace.
  DOLABELLA.   Here, on her breast,

15 asp   16 fulfilment   17 guessed   18 net   19 swollen

There is a vent of blood, and something
   blown; [19]
The like is on her arm.
  FIRST GUARD. This is an aspic's trail; and
   these fig-leaves
Have slime upon them, such as the aspic
   leaves   355
Upon the caves of Nile.
   CAESAR.   Most probable
That so she died; for her physician tells me
She hath pursued conclusions [20] infinite
Of easy ways to die. Take up her bed;
And bear her women from the monument. 360
She shall be buried by her Antony:
No grave upon the earth shall clip [21] in it
A pair so famous. High events as these
Strike those that make them; and their story is
No less in pity than his glory which   365
Brought them to be lamented. Our army shall,
In solemn show, attend this funeral,
And then to Rome. Come, Dolabella, see
High order in this great solemnity.   (*Exeunt*)

DISCUSSION

The obvious conflict in this play, emphasized by all commentators, lies between love and honor, or love and ambition, between Antony's "Roman thought" and the attraction of the "Egyptian spirit." But there are other complications, an exploration of which may help to illuminate the characters of the two central figures. Antony is a man with vast natural capacities for many different activities: politics, generalship, love, friendship, pleasure. Indeed, his very versatility prevents his finding any meaningful center for his life, and his problem, in one sense, is to find some basic principle by which he may realize his essential self.

More than Antony's versatility, of course, is involved in his failure to realize his essential self. He is a man who, as the play opens, is confused and who is flagrantly derelict. Demetrius and Philo in the first scene comment upon what has happened to Antony. In their opinion he has become "a strumpet's fool." And though Antony in the same scene exclaims "Let Rome in Tiber melt . . . the nobleness of life / Is to do thus," still Antony himself has a bad conscience about his conduct. In the next scene,

[20] experiments   [21] enfold

he exclaims "I must from this enchanting queen break off" (I, ii, 137). He is ashamed of his dissipation in Egypt and sees his indulgence in it as a betrayal of his Roman character.

Cleopatra also sees Rome and Egypt as diametrically opposed. When Antony suddenly becomes serious, she remarks "A Roman thought hath struck him" (I, ii, 91). Thus, the first act shows Rome and Egypt as opposed principles competing for Antony's spirit. Our sympathies are probably—and Antony's better conscience is certainly—on the side of Rome.

Before the play is over we shall find the two principles no longer in opposition: Antony and Cleopatra unite the best that is in the Roman principle with the best in the Egyptian principle —or perhaps it would be more accurate to say that they transcend the conflict between Roman and Egyptian. But Shakespeare has not represented the process of unification as an easy one. The Antony we see early in the play is delinquent, and Cleopatra, for all her charm, is pleasure-loving and more than half interested in the love game merely as an exhibition of her own skill. Shakespeare has not simplified his characters and he has been relentlessly honest in his statement of the moral problem.

In the scenes that follow, Antony, again, for all his personal charm, displays himself as the skillful and cynical politician. He enters into marriage with Octavia, the sister of Octavius Caesar, because it is to his political advantage. In Act III, scene i, Antony's general, Ventidius, comments upon the fact that "Caesar and Antony have ever won / More in their officer than person" (ll. 16-17). He hints that Antony will jealously resent one of his subordinates winning more than moderate glory. Even Enobarbus, Antony's staunch follower, comments upon Antony's ability to make an effective display of weeping when it is to his advantage ("What willingly he did confound he wailed," III, ii, 58).

Antony, in the end, comes closest to finding a meaningful center for his life in his love for Cleopatra; but ironically enough, this discovery is in a sense forced upon him by the collapse of everything else in his life. A superficial reader might even find that his love for Cleopatra was no real center at all, since his failure as a politician and as a practical man leave only this as a meaning—a meaning upon which he seizes in desperation for want of something better.

A more careful reading of the play will, however, indicate that Antony at the end has made a discovery about himself and the world, and has thus won to something positive. But in order to see this we shall have to consider the nature of the world in which the story of Antony and Cleopatra occurs, and the nature of Octavius, Antony's great rival before whom Antony's power goes down. The world in which Antony lives is a world which has fallen into almost complete disorder. The Roman virtues and the Roman social and personal discipline have decayed. It has become a world in which the strong compete with each other for mastery without reference to any social idea—such as the Roman patriotism which had subordinated the individual for the general good. If Antony had lived in the great days of the Roman Republic, the social values dictated by the Republic might have directed his vast talents and energies according to some principle, and he would, in that case, not have been the brilliant but purposeless man who appears in the play. Indeed, it may be said that Antony epitomizes his world.

In the light of this interpretation, such an incident as that on Pompey's galley (II, vii) reveals itself as having a fundamental relationship to the central fact of the play. The scene on the galley gives us a glimpse of the condition of this world; it is a piece of exposition, but exposition which is presented in terms of action. Pompey is a pirate, a freebooter, but we see that he is in reality no different from the triumvirs. (In effect, they acknowledge this by their dealing with him. Pompey owes no obligations to anyone except himself.) Yet he cannot bring himself to become the pure opportunist, and murder the triumvirs while they are in his power. In other words, in this world in which all general values have collapsed, Pompey clings to a rag of personal honor, an ideal beyond mere practical success.

Menas, as we learn from his advice to Pompey, has thoroughly accepted his world and is a pure opportunist. When Pompey refuses his advice to cut the cable which holds the barge at

anchor and then to cut the triumvirs' throats, Menas decides at once to desert Pompey's service. We learn something further about the nature of Antony's world when we hear what price Pompey pays for his clinging to personal honor. Octavius Caesar breaks the truce and makes war on Pompey, and Pompey is murdered.

Pompey's situation thus foreshadows that of Antony and Cleopatra—the attempt to achieve some ideal interpretation of their own lives as opposed to the possession of mere power. Pompey's situation foreshadows quite literally the situation of Enobarbus, who late in the play tries to act in accord with Menas's opportunism and deserts his master, Antony, for service with Octavius, but who finds, grizzled old warrior though he is, that he cannot really follow such a course and so in remorse dies of a broken heart.

What is the character of Octavius Caesar, and what is his relation to this world in which honor has become a quixotic gesture? Octavius is all cool efficiency. He is the pure politician who is unhampered by the distractions of passion or the claims of honor. This is not to say that Octavius is the conventionally wicked man. He is "moral" as the world goes, and respectable. He is probably on the side of conventional virtue, but he is coldly and ruthlessly efficient. Doubtless he found his justification for making war on Pompey and perhaps he convinced himself quite sincerely that the inefficient Lepidus had to be crushed. But his justification that "Lepidus was grown too cruel" (III, vi, 32) is almost amusing in view of the impression of Lepidus that we get in Act II, scene vii. Perhaps Lepidus was cruel: even fatuous men can be cruel. The point is that the charge rings oddly coming from the lips of this completely ruthless and efficient organizer. Doubtless the Roman world of the time needed such efficiency, and Octavius, whom history knows as the great Roman emperor Augustus, did give the Mediterranean world efficient government and peace.

These are not matters which come directly into our play, and Shakespeare does not deny, even by implication, that Octavius was superior to Antony as a potential organizer and ruler. But if humanity is to have any meaning other than ruthless efficiency, then some of the qualities of Antony are of intrinsic value, even though they are conjoined with glaring and heinous faults and even though those very qualities fatally handicap Antony in his contest with the cold-blooded Octavius. For Cleopatra at least, Antony is the greater man, and whereas she recognizes Octavius' power, it is Antony who is godlike—not only in her personal affections but in her judgment of him as a character.

With Cleopatra, however, as with Antony, Shakespeare has been thoroughly honest. She is vain and irresponsible. She is proud and wayward. She can be almost savagely brutal. Antony himself sees her, in spite of his infatuation for her, as a destructive force. Indeed, almost to the end, he feels that she has destroyed him—though he is manly enough to put the final responsibility not upon her but upon himself. Antony's soldiers, particularly Enobarbus, certainly see her as a destructive force. It is made quite plain that in their opinion, it is she who was responsible for Antony's downfall: what happened at Actium simply represents the dramatic culmination of a long and general process of degradation under her influence.

Yet even Enobarbus testifies to something more in the relationship than mere sensuality. Qualities of mind and spirit inform it; and Shakespeare gives us some sense of these qualities early in the play—even in the scenes in which Antony thinks of his conduct as sensual dissipation and in which Cleopatra's mood is basically pride in her power for conquest. The regeneration of the pair, if one may call it that, is not an incredible transformation, totally unprepared for.

It is the defeat at Actium, moreover, which brings out the best in Antony—and, as we shall find, in Cleopatra. He advises his friends to leave him: he would not pull them down in his own ruin. He does not waste time in reproaches to Cleopatra: he takes the responsibility for his following her ship out of the engagement, and fully forgives her for her action.

He sues to Caesar for peace, asking to be allowed to live "A private man at Athens" (III, x, 15). He touches his nadir here. But when he is stung by the insolence of Caesar's emissary, he is once more aroused, and when he is convinced that Cleopatra is not selling him out to Caesar (Cf. Cleopatra's "Not know me yet?" III, xi, 157), the recovery begins. With the world well lost, he becomes the old Antony again—or rather a new Antony who is freed from politic compromises and who can live now —the short time allowed him—for honor and for love. For him, love and honor are no longer forces opposed to each other. The speeches of Cleopatra and Enobarbus in Act III, scene xi underline the situation for us: Cleopatra says: ". . . but, since my lord / Is Antony again, I will be Cleopatra" (ll. 185-186); Enobarbus remarks: "I will seek / Some way to leave him" (ll. 199-200). The return to a fine and ardent magnanimity coincides with the abandonment of "reasonable" actions calculated to gain worldly success. Caesar can refer to his opponent as "Poor Antony" (IV, i, 16); but Cleopatra sees him in these hours as at his greatest and noblest self.

This is not to say that Shakespeare has made the relationship between the lovers now calm and untroubled. Antony does not "know Cleopatra yet." There are further doubtings and recriminations. But Cleopatra speaks over the dead Antony what she truly feels about his greatness of spirit (IV, xiii, 63-67), and she plainly associates this insight into true greatness with a contempt for world success. She can say: "'Tis paltry to be Caesar" (V, ii, 2). She chooses "honor" too—not to dishonor herself or Antony by gracing Caesar's triumph, but to die instead. Cleopatra becomes "Roman": she says to her women: "Let's do it after the high Roman fashion, / And make death proud to take us" (IV, xiii, 87-88).

The uniting of the Roman and Egyptian principles or of the themes of honor and love can be suggested in still another way. Both Antony and Cleopatra have flouted the ideas of conventional wedded love. We remember Antony's marriage of convenience and Cleopatra's scornful taunt: "What says the married woman?" (I, iii, 20). But at the end of the play, Antony and Cleopatra are "wedded" and Cleopatra claims the name proudly: "husband, I come: / Now to that name my courage prove my title!" (V, ii, 289-290).

EXERCISE

1. What material does Shakespeare select from Plutarch's account? Compare Shakespeare's interpretation with that of Plutarch. (For further comparisons the student may read *All for Love* by John Dryden.)

2. Define the character of Enobarbus. What is his relation to Antony? To Cleopatra? What is his general function in the play?

3. What forces does Octavius represent in the play? How does he differ from Menas in his attitude toward the world? Why does Octavius refuse Antony's challenge to personal combat? How do you relate this refusal to the general theme of the play?

4. Note the various ways in which Cleopatra's death is led up to: the death of Enobarbus; false report of her death sent to Antony as a ruse; the death of Eros; the death of Antony himself. All of these deaths are (or purport to be) deaths for honor, and all are in some sense suicides. How do they prepare the audience for Cleopatra's death? How do they bear upon her own resolution to die?

5. Antony says (I, i, 33) "Let Rome in Tiber melt. . . ." Cleopatra says (II, v, 78) "Melt Egypt into Nile!" Discuss this echo. Is it a meaningful one? How characteristic of the speakers are these lines?

6. Antony reproaches Caesar with having waged "New wars 'gainst Pompey" (III, iv, 4). How serious is he here? If he is, why should this act affect him especially?

7. In Act V, what is the meaning of Cleopatra's speeches and messages to Caesar? Is she still playing a double game? Has she already resolved to do away with herself? Or does she still hope to escape with her life and some remnants of power? It has been argued that her attempt to withhold part of her wealth from Caesar was a ruse (perhaps entered into with Seleucus) to make Caesar think that she did not mean to kill herself. Reread Act II, scene v, and see whether you agree with this argument.

8. How important a character is Charmian? Compare her function with that of Enobarbus.

9. Cleopatra is several times compared to the goddess Venus; Antony, to Mars, and to his reputed ancestor, the demigod Hercules. What is the function of these references? Are they used to build up the suggestions of the godlike nobility of the lovers?

10. How is Cleopatra's "husband, I come" prefigured in the speeches of Antony in the latter scenes of Act IV?

11. Do the speeches of the Clown in Act V, scene ii, conflict with the mood of heroic dignity and tragic exaltation? If you feel that they do not, how would you justify them?

12. Discuss the imagery of IV, xiii, 63-68 and V, ii, 82-92.

13. Note the number of references to food in the imagery of this play (I, v, 29-31, II, i, 24-27, II, ii, 244-246, etc.). Find others. What is the function of this imagery?

14. Miss Caroline Spurgeon remarks upon "images of the world, the firmament, the ocean, and vastness generally" in this play. Locate some of the passages in which such images occur. How important is this imagery? For what specific purposes does Shakespeare use it?

15. Discuss some of the various kinds of irony to be found in this play.

16. *Hedda Gabler* contrasts with this play in theme. Hedda, surrounded by a world "ordered" to the point of dull routine, wishes for something dashing and heroic. She asks that Lövborg come from the banquet "with vine-leaves in his hair"—somewhat, perhaps, like Antony in the scene on Pompey's galley. How far may this contrast between the two plays be carried?

17. In *The Circle* two lovers "give up the world" for love. The difference between this play and *Antony and Cleopatra* is, of course, immense. How far does the resemblance in theme go? What light, if any, does one play throw upon the other?

Saint Joan

GEORGE BERNARD SHAW (1856-1950)

Characters

BERTRAND DE POULENGEY	DUNOIS' PAGE
STEWARD	RICHARD DE BEAUCHAMP, EARL OF WARWICK
JOAN	CHAPLAIN DE STOGUMBER
ROBERT DE BAUDRICOURT	PETER CAUCHON, BISHOP OF BEAUVAIS
THE ARCHBISHOP OF RHEIMS	WARWICK'S PAGE
MGR DE LA TRÉMOUILLE	THE INQUISITOR
COURT PAGE	D'ESTIVET
GILLES DE RAIS	DE COURCELLES
CAPTAIN LA HIRE	BROTHER MARTIN LADVENU
THE DAUPHIN (later CHARLES VII)	THE EXECUTIONER
DUCHESS DE LA TRÉMOUILLE	AN ENGLISH SOLDIER
DUNOIS, BASTARD OF ORLEANS	A GENTLEMAN OF 1920

Scene I

A fine spring morning on the river Meuse, between Lorraine and Champagne, in the year 1429 A.D., in the castle of Vaucouleurs.

Captain ROBERT DE BAUDRICOURT, *a military squire, handsome and physically energetic, but with no will of his own, is disguising that defect in his usual fashion by storming terribly at his* STEWARD, *a trodden worm, scanty of flesh, scanty of hair, who might be any age from 18 to 55, being the sort of man whom age cannot wither because he has never bloomed.*

The two are in a sunny stone chamber on the first floor of the castle. At a plain strong oak table, seated in chair to match, the captain presents his left profile. The STEWARD *stands facing him at the other side of the table, if so deprecatory a stance as his can be called standing. The mullioned thirteenth-century window is open behind him. Near it in the corner is a turret with a narrow arched doorway leading to a winding stair which descends to the courtyard. There is a stout fourlegged stool under the table, and a wooden chest under the window.*

ROBERT. No eggs! No eggs!! Thousand thunders, man, what do you mean by no eggs?

STEWARD. Sir: it is not my fault. It is the act of God.

ROBERT. Blasphemy. You tell me there are no eggs; and you blame your Maker for it.

STEWARD. Sir: what can I do? I cannot lay eggs.

ROBERT (*sarcastic*). Ha! You jest about it.

STEWARD. No, sir, God knows. We all have to go without eggs just as you have, sir. The hens will not lay.

ROBERT. Indeed! (*Rising*). Now listen to me, you.

STEWARD (*humbly*). Yes, sir.

ROBERT. What am I?

STEWARD. What are you, sir?

ROBERT (*coming at him*). Yes: what am I? Am I Robert, squire of Baudricourt and captain of this castle of Vaucouleurs; or am I a cowboy?

STEWARD. Oh, sir, you know you are a greater man here than the king himself.

ROBERT. Precisely. And now, do you know

what you are?

STEWARD. I am nobody, sir, except that I have the honor to be your steward.

ROBERT (*driving him to the wall, adjective by adjective*). You have not only the honor of being my steward, but the privilege of being the worst, most incompetent, drivelling snivelling jibbering jabbering idiot of a steward in France. (*He strides back to the table*)

STEWARD (*cowering on the chest*). Yes, sir: to a great man like you I must seem like that.

ROBERT (*turning*). My fault, I suppose. Eh?

STEWARD (*coming to him deprecatingly*). Oh, sir: you always give my most innocent words such a turn!

ROBERT. I will give your neck a turn if you dare tell me when I ask you how many eggs there are that you cannot lay any.

STEWARD (*protesting*). Oh sir, oh sir—

ROBERT. No: not oh sir, oh sir, but no sir, no sir. My three Barbary hens and the black are the best layers in Champagne. And you come and tell me that there are no eggs! Who stole them? Tell me that, before I kick you out through the castle gate for a liar and a seller of my goods to thieves. The milk was short yesterday, too: do not forget that.

STEWARD (*desperate*). I know, sir. I know only too well. There is no milk: there are no eggs: tomorrow there will be nothing.

ROBERT. Nothing! You will steal the lot: eh?

STEWARD. No, sir: nobody will steal anything. But there is a spell on us: we are bewitched.

ROBERT. That story is not good enough for me. Robert de Baudricourt burns witches and hangs thieves. Go. Bring me four dozen eggs and two gallons of milk here in this room before noon, or Heaven have mercy on your bones! I will teach you to make a fool of me. (*He resumes his seat with an air of finality*)

STEWARD. Sir: I tell you there are no eggs. There will be none—not if you were to kill me for it—as long as The Maid is at the door.

ROBERT. The Maid! What maid? What are you talking about?

STEWARD. The girl from Lorraine, sir. From Domrémy.

ROBERT (*rising in fearful wrath*). Thirty thousand thunders! Fifty thousand devils! Do you mean to say that that girl, who had the im-

pudence to ask to see me two days ago, and whom I told you to send back to her father with my orders that he was to give her a good hiding, is here still?

STEWARD. I have told her to go, sir. She wont.

ROBERT. I did not tell you to tell her to go: I told you to throw her out. You have fifty men-at-arms and a dozen lumps of able-bodied servants to carry out my orders. Are they afraid of her?

STEWARD. She is so positive, sir.

ROBERT (*seizing him by the scruff of the neck*). Positive! Now see here. I am going to throw you downstairs.

STEWARD. No, sir. Please.

ROBERT. Well, stop me by being positive. It's quite easy: any slut of a girl can do it.

STEWARD (*hanging limp in his hands*). Sir, sir: you cannot get rid of her by throwing me out. (ROBERT *has to let him drop. He squats on his knees on the floor, contemplating his master resignedly.*) You see, sir, you are much more positive than I am. But so is she.

ROBERT. I am stronger than you are, you fool.

STEWARD. No, sir: it isnt that: it's your strong character, sir. She is weaker than we are: she is only a slip of a girl; but we cannot make her go.

ROBERT. You parcel of curs: you are afraid of her.

STEWARD (*rising cautiously*). No sir: we are afraid of you; but she puts courage into us. She really doesnt seem to be afraid of anything. Perhaps you could frighten her, sir.

ROBERT (*grimly*). Perhaps. Where is she now?

STEWARD. Down in the courtyard, sir, talking to the soldiers as usual. She is always talking to the soldiers except when she is praying.

ROBERT. Praying! Ha! You believe she prays, you idiot. I know the sort of girl that is always talking to soldiers. She shall talk to me a bit. (*He goes to the window and shouts fiercely through it*) Hallo, you there!

A GIRL'S VOICE (*bright, strong and rough*). Is it me, sir?

ROBERT. Yes, you.

THE VOICE. Be you captain?

ROBERT. Yes, damn your impudence, I be captain. Come up here. (*To the soldiers in the yard*) Shew her the way, you. And shove her along quick. (*He leaves the window, and returns to his place at the table, where he sits magis-*

terially)

STEWARD (*whispering*). She wants to go and be a soldier herself. She wants you to give her soldier's clothes. Armor, sir! And a sword! Actually! (*He steals behind* ROBERT)

> (JOAN *appears in the turret doorway. She is an ablebodied country girl of 17 or 18, respectably dressed in red, with an uncommon face; eyes very wide apart and bulging as they often do in very imaginative people, a long well-shaped nose with wide nostrils, a short upper lip, resolute but full-lipped mouth, and handsome fighting chin. She comes eagerly to the table, delighted at having penetrated to* BAUDRI-COURT'S *presence at last, and full of hope as to the results. His scowl does not check or frighten her in the least. Her voice is normally a hearty coaxing voice, very confident, very appealing, very hard to resist.*)

JOAN (*bobbing a curtsey*). Good morning, captain squire. Captain: you are to give me a horse and armor and some soldiers, and send me to the Dauphin. Those are your orders from my Lord.

ROBERT (*outraged*). Orders from your lord! And who the devil may your lord be? Go back to him, and tell him that I am neither duke nor peer at his orders: I am squire of Baudricourt; and I take no orders except from the king.

JOAN (*reassuringly*). Yes, squire: that is all right. My Lord is the King of Heaven.

ROBERT. Why, the girl's mad. (*To the* STEW-ARD) Why didnt you tell me so, you blockhead?

STEWARD. Sir: do not anger her: give her what she wants.

JOAN (*impatient, but friendly*). They all say I am mad until I talk to them, squire. But you see that it is the will of God that you are to do what He has put into my mind.

ROBERT. It is the will of God that I shall send you back to your father with orders to put you under lock and key and thrash the madness out of you. What have you to say to that?

JOAN. You think you will, squire; but you will find it all coming quite different. You said you would not see me; but here I am.

STEWARD (*appealing*). Yes, sir. You see, sir.

ROBERT. Hold your tongue, you.

STEWARD (*abjectly*). Yes, sir.

ROBERT (*to* JOAN, *with a sour loss of confidence*). So you are presuming on my seeing you, are you?

JOAN (*sweetly*). Yes, squire.

ROBERT (*feeling that he has lost ground, brings down his two fists squarely on the table, and inflates his chest imposingly to cure the unwelcome and only too familiar sensation*). Now listen to me. I am going to assert myself.

JOAN (*busily*). Please do, squire. The horse will cost sixteen francs. It is a good deal of money: but I can save it on the armor. I can find a soldier's armor that will fit me well enough: I am very hardy; and I do not need beautiful armor made to my measure like you wear. I shall not want many soldiers: the Dauphin will give me all I need to raise the siege of Orleans.

ROBERT (*flabbergasted*). To raise the siege of Orleans!

JOAN (*simply*). Yes, squire: that is what God is sending me to do. Three men will be enough for you to send with me if they are good men and gentle to me. They have promised to come with me. Polly and Jack and—

ROBERT. Polly!! You impudent baggage, do you dare call squire Bertrand de Poulengey Polly to my face?

JOAN. His friends call him so, squire: I did not know he had any other name. Jack—

ROBERT. That is Monsieur John of Metz, I suppose?

JOAN. Yes, squire. Jack will come willingly: he is a very kind gentleman, and gives me money to give to the poor. I think John Godsave will come, and Dick the Archer, and their servants John of Honecourt and Julian. There will be no trouble for you, squire: I have arranged it all: you have only to give the order.

ROBERT (*contemplating her in a stupor of amazement*). Well, I am damned!

JOAN (*with unruffled sweetness*). No, squire: God is very merciful; and the blessed saints Catherine and Margaret, who speak to me every day (*he gapes*), will intercede for you. You will go to paradise; and your name will be remembered for ever as my first helper.

ROBERT (*to the* STEWARD, *still much bothered, but changing his tone as he pursues a new clue*).

Is this true about Monsieur de Poulengey?

STEWARD (*eagerly*). Yes, sir, and about Monsieur de Metz too. They both want to go with her.

ROBERT (*thoughtful*). Mf! (*He goes to the window, and shouts into the courtyard*) Hallo! You there: send Monsieur de Poulengey to me, will you? (*He turns to* JOAN) Get out; and wait in the yard.

JOAN (*smiling brightly at him*). Right, squire. (*She goes out*)

ROBERT (*to the* STEWARD). Go with her, you, you dithering imbecile. Stay within call; and keep your eye on her. I shall have her up here again.

STEWARD. Do so in God's name, sir. Think of those hens, the best layers in Champagne; and—

ROBERT. Think of my boot; and take your backside out of reach of it.

(*The* STEWARD *retreats hastily and finds himself confronted in the doorway by* BERTRAND DE POULENGEY, *a lymphatic French gentleman-at-arms, aged 36 or thereabout, employed in the department of the provost-marshal, dreamily absent-minded, seldom speaking unless spoken to, and then slow and obstinate in reply; altogether in contrast to the self-assertive, loud-mouthed, superficially energetic, fundamentally will-less* ROBERT. *The* STEWARD *makes way for him, and vanishes.* POULENGEY *salutes, and stands awaiting orders.*)

ROBERT (*genially*). It isnt service, Polly. A friendly talk. Sit down. (*He hooks the stool from under the table with his instep*)

(POULENGEY, *relaxing, comes into the room: places the stool between the table and the window: and sits down ruminatively.* ROBERT, *half sitting on the end of the table, begins the friendly talk.*)

ROBERT. Now listen to me, Polly. I must talk to you like a father.

(POULENGEY *looks up at him gravely for a moment, but says nothing.*)

ROBERT. It's about this girl you are interested in. Now, I have seen her. I have talked to her. First, she's mad. That doesnt matter. Second, she's not a farm wench. She's a bourgeoise. That matters a good deal. I know her class exactly. Her father came here last year to represent his village in a lawsuit: he is one of their notables. A farmer. Not a gentleman farmer: he makes money by it, and lives by it. Still, not a laborer. Not a mechanic. He might have a cousin a lawyer, or in the Church. People of this sort may be of no account socially; but they can give a lot of bother to the authorities. That is to say, to me. Now no doubt it seems to you a very simple thing to take this girl away, humbugging her into the belief that you are taking her to the Dauphin. But if you get her into trouble, you may get me into no end of a mess, as I am her father's lord, and responsible for her protection. So friends or no friends, Polly, hands off her.

POULENGEY (*with deliberate impressiveness*). I should as soon think of the Blessed Virgin herself in that way, as of this girl.

ROBERT (*coming off the table*). But she says you and Jack and Dick have offered to go with her. What for? You are not going to tell me that you take her crazy notion of going to the Dauphin seriously, are you?

POULENGEY (*slowly*). There is something about her. They are pretty foulmouthed and foul-minded down there in the guardroom, some of them. But there hasnt been a word that has anything to do with her being a woman. They have stopped swearing before her. There is something. Something. It may be worth trying.

ROBERT. Oh, come, Polly! pull yourself together. Commonsense was never your strong point; but this is a little too much. (*He retreats disgustedly*)

POULENGEY (*unmoved*). What is the good of commonsense? If we had any commonsense we should join the Duke of Burgundy and the English king. They hold half the country, right down to the Loire. They have Paris. They have this castle: you know very well that we had to surrender it to the Duke of Bedford, and that you are only holding it on parole. The Dauphin is in Chinon, like a rat in a corner, except that he wont fight. We dont even know that he is the Dauphin: his mother says he isnt; and she ought to know. Think of that! the queen denying the legitimacy of her own son!

ROBERT. Well, she married her daughter to the English king. Can you blame the woman?

POULENGEY. I blame nobody. But thanks to

her, the Dauphin is down and out; and we may as well face it. The English will take Orleans: the Bastard will not be able to stop them.

ROBERT. He beat the English the year before last at Montargis. I was with him.

POULENGEY. No matter: his men are cowed now; and he cant work miracles. And I tell you that nothing can save our side now but a miracle.

ROBERT. Miracles are all right, Polly. The only difficulty about them is that they dont happen nowadays.

POULENGEY. I used to think so. I am not so sure now. (*Rising, and moving ruminatively towards the window*) At all events this is not a time to leave any stone unturned. There is something about the girl.

ROBERT. Oh! You think the girl can work miracles, do you?

POULENGEY. I think the girl herself is a bit of a miracle. Anyhow, she is the last card left in our hand. Better play her than throw up the game. (*He wanders to the turret*)

ROBERT (*wavering*). You really think that?

POULENGEY (*turning*). Is there anything else left for us to think?

ROBERT (*going to him*). Look here, Polly. If you were in my place would you let a girl like that do you out of sixteen francs for a horse?

POULENGEY. I will pay for the horse.

ROBERT. You will!

POULENGEY. Yes: I will back my opinion.

ROBERT. You will really gamble on a forlorn hope to the tune of sixteen francs?

POULENGEY. It is not a gamble.

ROBERT. What else is it?

POULENGEY. It is a certainty. Her words and her ardent faith in God have put fire into me.

ROBERT (*giving him up*). Whew! You are as mad as she is.

POULENGEY (*obstinately*). We want a few mad people now. See where the sane ones have landed us!

ROBERT (*his irresoluteness now openly swamping his affected decisiveness*). I shall feel like a precious fool. Still, if you feel sure—?

POULENGEY. I feel sure enough to take her to Chinon—unless you stop me.

ROBERT. This is not fair. You are putting the responsibility on me.

POULENGEY. It is on you whichever way you decide.

ROBERT. Yes: thats just it. Which way am I to decide? You dont see how awkward this is for me. (*Snatching at a dilatory step with an unconscious hope that* JOAN *will make up his mind for him*) Do you think I ought to have another talk to her?

POULENGEY (*rising*). Yes. (*He goes to the window and calls*) Joan!

JOAN'S VOICE. Will he let us go, Polly?

POULENGEY. Come up. Come in. (*Turning to* Robert) Shall I leave you with her?

ROBERT. No: stay here; and back me up.

(POULENGEY *sits down on the chest.* ROBERT *goes back to his magisterial chair, but remains standing to inflate himself more imposingly.* JOAN *comes in, full of good news.*)

JOAN. Jack will go halves for the horse.

ROBERT. Well!! (*He sits, deflated*)

POULENGEY (*gravely*). Sit down, Joan.

JOAN (*checked a little, and looking to* ROBERT). May I?

ROBERT. Do what you are told.

(JOAN *curtsies and sits down on the stool between them.* ROBERT *outfaces his perplexity with his most peremptory air.*)

ROBERT. What is your name?

JOAN (*chattily*). They always call me Jenny in Lorraine. Here in France I am Joan. The soldiers call me The Maid.

ROBERT. What is your surname?

JOAN. Surname? What is that? My father sometimes calls himself d'Arc; but I know nothing about it. You met my father. He—

ROBERT. Yes, yes; I remember. You come from Domrémy in Lorraine, I think.

JOAN. Yes; but what does it matter? we all speak French.

ROBERT. Dont ask questions: answer them. How old are you?

JOAN. Seventeen: so they tell me. It might be nineteen. I dont remember.

ROBERT. What did you mean when you said that St Catherine and St Margaret talked to you every day?

JOAN. They do.

ROBERT. What are they like?

JOAN (*suddenly obstinate*). I will tell you nothing about that: they have not given me leave.

ROBERT. But you actually see them; and they talk to you just as I am talking to you?

JOAN. No: it is quite different. I cannot tell you: you must not talk to me about my voices.

ROBERT. How do you mean? voices?

JOAN. I hear voices telling me what to do. They come from God.

ROBERT. They come from your imagination.

JOAN. Of course. That is how the messages of God come to us.

POULENGEY. Checkmate.

ROBERT. No fear! (*To* JOAN) So God says you are to raise the siege of Orleans?

JOAN. And to crown the Dauphin in Rheims Cathedral.

ROBERT (*gasping*). Crown the D—! Gosh!

JOAN. And to make the English leave France.

ROBERT (*sarcastic*). Anything else?

JOAN (*charming*). Not just at present, thank you, squire.

ROBERT. I suppose you think raising a siege is as easy as chasing a cow out of a meadow. You think soldiering is anybody's job?

JOAN. I do not think it can be very difficult if God is on your side, and you are willing to put your life in His hand. But many soldiers are very simple.

ROBERT (*grimly*). Simple! Did you ever see English soldiers fighting?

JOAN. They are only men. God made them just like us; but He gave them their own country and their own language; and it is not His will that they should come into our country and try to speak our language.

ROBERT. Who has been putting such nonsense into your head? Dont you know that soldiers are subject to their feudal lord, and that it is nothing to them or to you whether he is the duke of Burgundy or the king of England or the king of France? What has their language to do with it?

JOAN. I do not understand that a bit. We are all subject to the King of Heaven; and He gave us our countries and our languages, and meant us to keep to them. If it were not so it would be murder to kill an Englishman in battle; and you, squire, would be in great danger of hell fire. You must not think about your duty to your feudal lord, but about your duty to God.

POULENGEY. It's no use, Robert: she can choke you like that every time.

ROBERT. Can she, by Saint Dennis! We shall see. (*To* JOAN) We are not talking about God: we are talking about practical affairs. I ask you again, girl, have you ever seen English soldiers fighting? Have you ever seen them plundering, burning, turning the countryside into a desert? Have you heard no tales of their Black Prince who was blacker than the devil himself, or of the English king's father?

JOAN. You must not be afraid, Robert—

ROBERT. Damn you, I am not afraid. And who gave you leave to call me Robert?

JOAN. You were called so in church in the name of our Lord. All the other names are your father's or your brother's or anybody's.

ROBERT. Tcha!

JOAN. Listen to me, squire. At Domrémy we had to fly to the next village to escape from the English soldiers. Three of them were left behind, wounded. I came to know these three poor goddams quite well. They had not half my strength.

ROBERT. Do you know why they are called goddams?

JOAN. No. Everyone calls them goddams.

ROBERT. It is because they are always calling on their God to condemn their souls to perdition. That is what goddam means in their language. How do you like it?

JOAN. God will be merciful to them; and they will act like His good children when they go back to the country He made for them, and made them for. I have heard the tales of the Black Prince. The moment he touched the soil of our country the devil entered into him, and made him a black fiend. But at home, in the place made for him by God, he was good. It is always so. If I went into England against the will of God to conquer England, and tried to live there and speak its language, the devil would enter into me; and when I was old I should shudder to remember the wickedness I did.

ROBERT. Perhaps. But the more devil you were the better you might fight. That is why the goddams will take Orleans. And you cannot stop them, nor ten thousand like you.

JOAN. One thousand like me can stop them. Ten like me can stop them with God on our side. (*She rises impetuously, and goes at him, unable to sit quiet any longer*) You do not understand, squire. Our soldiers are always beaten because they are fighting only to save their skins; and the shortest way to save your skin is to run away. Our knights are thinking only of the money they will make in ransoms: it is not kill or be killed with them, but pay or be paid. But I will teach them all to fight that the will of God may be done in France; and then they will drive the poor goddams before them like sheep. You and Polly will live to see the day when there will not be an English soldier on the soil of France; and there will be but one king there: not the feudal English king, but God's French one.

ROBERT (*to* POULENGEY). This may be all rot, Polly; but the troops might swallow it, though nothing that we can say seems able to put any fight into them. Even the Dauphin might swallow it. And if she can put fight into him, she can put it into anybody.

POULENGEY. I can see no harm in trying. Can you? And there is something about the girl—

ROBERT (*turning to* JOAN). Now listen you to me; and (*desperately*) dont cut in before I have time to think.

JOAN (*plumping down on the stool again, like an obedient schoolgirl*). Yes, squire.

ROBERT. Your orders are, that you are to go to Chinon under the escort of this gentleman and three of his friends.

JOAN (*radiant, clasping her hands*). Oh, squire! Your head is all circled with light, like a saint's.

POULENGEY. How is she to get into the royal presence?

ROBERT (*who has looked up for his halo rather apprehensively*). I dont know: how did she get into my presence? If the Dauphin can keep her out he is a better man than I take him for. (*Rising*) I will send her to Chinon; and she can say I sent her. Then let come what may: I can do no more.

JOAN. And the dress? I may have a soldier's dress, maynt I, squire?

ROBERT. Have what you please. I wash my hands of it.

JOAN (*wildly excited by her success*). Come, Polly. (*She dashes out*)

ROBERT (*shaking* POULENGEY's *hand*). Goodbye, old man, I am taking a big chance. Few other men would have done it. But as you say, there is something about her.

POULENGEY. Yes: there is something about her. Goodbye. (*He goes out*)

(ROBERT, *still very doubtful whether he has not been made a fool of by a crazy female, and a social inferior to boot, scratches his head and slowly comes back from the door.*

The STEWARD *runs in with a basket.*)

STEWARD. Sir, sir—

ROBERT. What now?

STEWARD. The hens are laying like mad, sir. Five dozen eggs!

ROBERT (*stiffens convulsively: crosses himself: and forms with his pale lips the words*). Christ in heaven! (*Aloud but breathless*) She did come from God.

Scene II

Chinon, in Touraine. An end of the throne room in the castle, curtained off to make an antechamber. The ARCHBISHOP *of Rheims, close on 50, a full-fed prelate with nothing of the ecclesiastic about him except his imposing bearing, and the Lord Chamberlain,* MONSEIGNEUR DE LA TRÉMOUILLE, *a monstrous arrogant wineskin of a man, are waiting for the* DAUPHIN. *There is a door in the wall to the right of the two men. It is late in the afternoon on the 8th of March, 1429.* THE ARCHBISHOP *stands with dignity whilst the* CHAMBERLAIN, *on his left, fumes about in the worst of tempers.*

LA TRÉMOUILLE. What the devil does the Dauphin mean by keeping us waiting like this? I dont know how you have the patience to stand there like a stone idol.

THE ARCHBISHOP. You see, I am an archbishop; and an archbishop is a sort of idol. At any rate he has to learn to keep still and suffer fools patiently. Besides, my dear Lord Chamberlain, it is the Dauphin's royal privilege to keep you waiting, is it not?

LA TRÉMOUILLE. Dauphin be damned! saving your reverence. Do you know how much money he owes me?

THE ARCHBISHOP. Much more than he owes me, I have no doubt, because you are a much richer man. But I take it he owes you all you could afford to lend him. That is what he owes me.

LA TRÉMOUILLE. Twenty-seven thousand: that was his last haul. A cool twenty-seven thousand!

THE ARCHBISHOP. What becomes of it all? He never has a suit of clothes that I would throw to a curate.

LA TRÉMOUILLE. He dines on a chicken or a scrap of mutton. He borrows my last penny; and there is nothing to shew for it. (A PAGE *appears in the doorway*) At last!

THE PAGE. No, my lord: it is not His Majesty. Monsieur de Rais is approaching.

LA TRÉMOUILLE. Young Bluebeard! Why announce him?

THE PAGE. Captain La Hire is with him. Something has happened, I think.

(GILLES DE RAIS, *a young man of 25, very smart and self-possessed, and sporting the extravagance of a little curled beard dyed blue at a clean-shaven court, comes in. He is determined to make himself agreeable, but lacks natural joyousness, and is not really pleasant. In fact when he defies the Church some eleven years later he is accused of trying to extract pleasure from horrible cruelties, and hanged. So far, however, there is no shadow of the gallows on him. He advances gaily to the* ARCHBISHOP. THE PAGE *withdraws*.)

BLUEBEARD. Your faithful lamb, Archbishop. Good day, my lord. Do you know what has happened to La Hire?

LA TRÉMOUILLE. He has sworn himself into a fit, perhaps.

BLUEBEARD. No: just the opposite. Foul Mouthed Frank, the only man in Touraine who could beat him at swearing, was told by a soldier that he shouldnt use such language when he was at the point of death.

THE ARCHBISHOP. Nor at any other point. But was Foul Mouthed Frank on the point of death?

BLUEBEARD. Yes: he has just fallen into a well and been drowned. La Hire is frightened out of his wits.

(CAPTAIN LA HIRE *comes in: a war dog with no court manners and pronounced camp ones.*)

BLUEBEARD. I have been telling the Chamberlaind and the Archbishop. The Archbishop says you are a lost man.

LA HIRE (*striding past* BLUEBEARD, *and planting himself between the* ARCHBISHOP *and* LA TRÉMOUILLE). This is nothing to joke about. It is worse than we thought. It was not a soldier, but an angel dressed as a soldier.

THE ARCHBISHOP
THE CHAMBERLAIN } (*exclaiming all together*).
BLUEBEARD   An Angel!

LA HIRE. Yes, an angel. She has made her way from Champagne with half a dozen men through the thick of everything: Burgundians, Goddams, deserters, robbers, and Lord knows who; and they never met a soul except the country folk. I know one of them: de Poulengey. He says she's an angel. If ever I utter an oath again may my soul be blasted to eternal damnation!

THE ARCHBISHOP. A very pious beginning, Captain.

(BLUEBEARD *and* LA TRÉMOUILLE *laugh at him. The* PAGE *returns.*)

THE PAGE. His Majesty.

(*They stand perfunctorily at court attention. The* DAUPHIN, *aged 26, really King Charles the Seventh since the death of his father, but as yet uncrowned, comes in through the curtains with a paper in his hands. He is a poor creature physically; and the current fashion of shaving closely, and hiding every scrap of hair under the headcovering or headdress, both by women and men, makes the worst of his appearance. He has little narrow eyes, near together, a long pendulous nose that droops over his thick short upper lip, and the expression of a young dog accustomed to be kicked, yet incorrigible and irrepressible. But he is neither vulgar nor stupid; and he has a cheeky humor which enables him to hold his own in conversation. Just at present he is excited, like a child with a new toy. He comes to* THE ARCHBISHOP's *left hand.* BLUEBEARD *and* LA HIRE *retire towards the curtains.*)

CHARLES. Oh, Archbishop, do you know what Robert de Baudricourt is sending me from

Vaucouleurs?

THE ARCHBISHOP (*contemptuously*). I am not interested in the newest toys.

CHARLES (*indignantly*). It isnt a toy. (*Sulkily*) However, I can get on very well without your interest.

THE ARCHBISHOP. Your Highness is taking offence very unnecessarily.

CHARLES. Thank you. You are always ready with a lecture, arnt you?

LA TRÉMOUILLE (*roughly*). Enough grumbling. What have you got there?

CHARLES. What is that to you?

LA TRÉMOUILLE. It is my business to know what is passing between you and the garrison at Vaucouleurs. (*He snatches the paper from the* DAUPHIN'S *hand, and begins reading it with some difficulty, following the words with his finger and spelling them out syllable by syllable*)

CHARLES (*mortified*). You all think you can treat me as you please because I owe you money, and because I am no good at fighting. But I have the blood royal in my veins.

THE ARCHBISHOP. Even that has been questioned, your Highness. One hardly recognizes in you the grandson of Charles the Wise.

CHARLES. I want to hear no more of my grandfather. He was so wise that he used up the whole family stock of wisdom for five generations, and left me the poor fool I am, bullied and insulted by all of you.

THE ARCHBISHOP. Control yourself, sir. These outbursts of petulance are not seemly.

CHARLES. Another lecture! Thank you. What a pity it is that though you are an archbishop saints and angels dont come to see you!

THE ARCHBISHOP. What do you mean?

CHARLES. Aha! Ask that bully there (*pointing to* LA TRÉMOUILLE).

LA TRÉMOUILLE (*furious*). Hold your tongue. Do you hear?

CHARLES. Oh, I hear. You neednt shout. The whole castle can hear. Why dont you go and shout at the English, and beat them for me?

LA TRÉMOUILLE (*raising his fist*). You young—

CHARLES (*running behind the* ARCHBISHOP). Dont you raise your hand to me. It's high treason.

LA HIRE. Steady, Duke! Steady!

THE ARCHBISHOP (*resolutely*). Come, come! this will not do. My Lord Chamberlain: please! we must keep some sort of order. (*To the* DAUPHIN) And you, sir: if you cannot rule your kingdom, at least try to rule yourself.

CHARLES. Another lecture! Thank you.

LA TRÉMOUILLE (*handing over the paper to the* ARCHBISHOP). Here: read the accursed thing for me. He has sent the blood boiling into my head: I cant distinguish the letters.

CHARLES (*coming back and peering round* LA TRÉMOUILLE'S *left shoulder*). I will read it for you if you like. I can read, you know.

LA TRÉMOUILLE (*with intense contempt, not at all stung by the taunt*). Yes: reading is about all you are fit for. Can you make it out, Archbishop?

THE ARCHBISHOP. I should have expected more commonsense from De Baudricourt. He is sending some cracked country lass here—

CHARLES (*interrupting*). No: he is sending a saint: an angel. And she is coming to me: to me, the king, and not to you, Archbishop, holy as you are. She knows the blood royal if you dont. (*He struts up to the curtains between* BLUEBEARD *and* LA HIRE)

THE ARCHBISHOP. You cannot be allowed to see this crazy wench.

CHARLES (*turning*). But I am the king; and I will.

LA TRÉMOUILLE (*brutally*). Then she cannot be allowed to see you. Now!

CHARLES. I tell you I will. I am going to put my foot down—

BLUEBEARD (*laughing at him*). Naughty! What would your wise grandfather say?

CHARLES. That just shews your ignorance, Bluebeard. My grandfather had a saint who used to float in the air when she was praying, and told him everything he wanted to know. My poor father had two saints, Marie de Maillé and the Gasque of Avignon. It is in our family; and I dont care what you say: I will have my saint too.

THE ARCHBISHOP. This creature is not a saint. She is not even a respectable woman. She does not wear women's clothes. She is dressed like a soldier, and rides round the country with soldiers. Do you suppose such a person can be admitted to your Highness's court?

LA HIRE. Stop. (*Going to the* ARCHBISHOP) Did you say a girl in armor, like a soldier?

THE ARCHBISHOP. So De Baudricourt describes

her.

LA HIRE. But by all the devils in hell—Oh, God forgive me, what am I saying?—by Our Lady and all the saints, this must be the angel that struck Foul Mouthed Frank dead for swearing.

CHARLES (triumphant). You see! A miracle!

LA HIRE. She may strike the lot of us dead if we cross her. For Heaven's sake, Archbishop, be careful what you are doing.

THE ARCHBISHOP (severely). Rubbish! Nobody has been struck dead. A drunken blackguard who has been rebuked a hundred times for swearing has fallen into a well, and been drowned. A mere coincidence.

LA HIRE. I do not know what a coincidence is. I do know that the man is dead, and that she told him he was going to die.

THE ARCHBISHOP. We are all going to die, Captain.

LA HIRE (crossing himself). I hope not. (He backs out of the conversation)

BLUEBEARD. We can easily find out whether she is an angel or not. Let us arrange when she comes that I shall be the Dauphin, and see whether she will find me out.

CHARLES. Yes: I agree to that. If she cannot find the blood royal I will have nothing to do with her.

THE ARCHBISHOP. It is for the Church to make saints: let De Baudricourt mind his own business, and not dare usurp the function of his priest. I say the girl shall not be admitted.

BLUEBEARD. But, Archbishop—

THE ARCHBISHOP (sternly). I speak in the Church's name. (To the DAUPHIN) Do you dare say she shall?

CHARLES (intimidated but sulky). Oh, if you make it an excommunication matter, I have nothing more to say, of course. But you havnt read the end of the letter. De Baudricourt says she will raise the siege of Orleans, and beat the English for us.

LA TRÉMOUILLE. Rot!

CHARLES. Well, will you save Orleans for us, with all your bullying?

LA TRÉMOUILLE (savagely). Do not throw that in my face again: do you hear? I have done more fighting than you ever did or ever will. But I cannot be everywhere.

THE DAUPHIN. Well, thats something.

BLUEBEARD (coming between the ARCHBISHOP and CHARLES). You have Jack Dunois at the head of your troops in Orleans: the brave Dunois, the handsome Dunois, the wonderful invincible Dunois, the darling of all the ladies, the beautiful bastard. Is it likely that the country lass can do what he cannot do?

CHARLES. Why doesnt he raise the siege, then?

LA HIRE. The wind is against him.

BLUEBEARD. How can the wind hurt him at Orleans? It is not on the Channel.

LA HIRE. It is on the river Loire; and the English hold the bridgehead. He must ship his men across the river and upstream, if he is to take them in the rear. Well, he cannot, because there is a devil of a wind blowing the other way. He is tired of paying the priests to pray for a west wind. What he needs is a miracle. You tell me that what the girl did to Foul Mouthed Frank was no miracle. No matter: it finished Frank. If she changes the wind for Dunois, that may not be a miracle either; but it may finish the English. What harm is there in trying?

THE ARCHBISHOP (who has read the end of the letter and become more thoughtful). It is true that De Baudricourt seems extraordinarily impressed.

LA HIRE. De Baudricourt is a blazing ass; but he is a soldier; and if he thinks she can beat the English, all the rest of the army will think so too.

LA TRÉMOUILLE (to the ARCHBISHOP, who is hesitating). Oh, let them have their way. Dunois' men will give up the town in spite of him if somebody does not put some fresh spunk into them.

THE ARCHBISHOP. The Church must examine the girl before anything decisive is done about her. However, since his Highness desires it, let her attend the Court.

LA HIRE. I will find her and tell her. (He goes out)

CHARLES. Come with me, Bluebeard; and let us arrange so that she will not know who I am. You will pretend to be me. (He goes out through the curtains)

BLUEBEARD. Pretend to be that thing! Holy Michael! (He follows the DAUPHIN)

LA TRÉMOUILLE. I wonder will she pick him out!

THE ARCHBISHOP. Of course she will.

LA TRÉMOUILLE. Why? How is she to know?

THE ARCHBISHOP. She will know what everybody in Chinon knows: that the Dauphin is the meanest-looking and worst-dressed figure in the Court, and that the man with the blue beard is Gilles de Rais.

LA TRÉMOUILLE. I never thought of that.

THE ARCHBISHOP. You are not so accustomed to miracles as I am. It is part of my profession.

LA TRÉMOUILLE (*puzzled and a little scandalized*). But that would not be a miracle at all.

THE ARCHBISHOP (*calmly*). Why not?

LA TRÉMOUILLE. Well, come! what is a miracle?

THE ARCHBISHOP. A miracle, my friend, is an event which creates faith. That is the purpose and nature of miracles. They may seem very wonderful to the people who witness them, and very simple to those who perform them. That does not matter: if they confirm or create faith they are true miracles.

LA TRÉMOUILLE. Even when they are frauds, do you mean?

THE ARCHBISHOP. Frauds deceive. An event which creates faith does not deceive: therefore it is not a fraud, but a miracle.

LA TRÉMOUILLE (*scratching his neck in his perplexity*). Well, I suppose as you are an archbishop you must be right. It seems a bit fishy to me. But I am no churchman, and dont understand these matters.

THE ARCHBISHOP. You are not a churchman; but you are a diplomatist and a soldier. Could you make our citizens pay war taxes, or our soldiers sacrifice their lives, if they knew what is really happening instead of what seems to them to be happening?

LA TRÉMOUILLE. No, by Saint Dennis: the fat would be in the fire before sundown.

THE ARCHBISHOP. Would it not be quite easy to tell them the truth?

LA TRÉMOUILLE. Man alive, they wouldnt believe it.

THE ARCHBISHOP. Just so. Well, the Church has to rule men for the good of their souls as you have to rule them for the good of their bodies. To do that, the Church must do as you do: nourish their faith by poetry.

LA TRÉMOUILLE. Poetry! I should call it humbug.

THE ARCHBISHOP. You would be wrong, my friend. Parables are not lies because they describe events that have never happened. Miracles are not frauds because they are often—I do not say always—very simple and innocent contrivances by which the priest fortifies the faith of his flock. When this girl picks out the Dauphin among his courtiers, it will not be a miracle for me, because I shall know how it has been done, and my faith will not be increased. But as for the others, if they feel the thrill of the supernatural, and forget their sinful clay in a sudden sense of the glory of God, it will be a miracle and a blessed one. And you will find that the girl herself will be more affected than anyone else. She will forget how she really picked him out. So, perhaps, will you,

LA TRÉMOUILLE. Well, I wish I were clever enough to know how much of you is God's archbishop and how much the most artful fox in Touraine. Come on, or we shall be late for the fun; and I want to see it, miracle or no miracle.

THE ARCHBISHOP (*detaining him a moment*). Do not think that I am a lover of crooked ways. There is a new spirit rising in men: we are at the dawning of a wider epoch. If I were a simple monk, and had not to rule men, I should seek peace for my spirit with Aristotle and Pythagoras rather than with the saints and their miracles.

LA TRÉMOUILLE. And who the deuce was Pythagoras?

THE ARCHBISHOP. A sage who held that the earth is round, and that it moves round the sun.

LA TRÉMOUILLE. What an utter fool! Couldnt he use his eyes?

(*They go out together through the curtains, which are presently withdrawn, revealing the full depth of the throne room with the Court assembled. On the right are two Chairs of State on a dais. BLUEBEARD is standing theatrically on the dais, playing the king, and, like the courtiers, enjoying the joke rather obviously. There is a curtained arch in the wall behind the dais; but the main door, guarded by men-at-arms, is at the other side of the room; and a clear path across is kept and lined by the courtiers. CHARLES is in this path in the middle of the room. LA HIRE is on his right. The ARCHBISHOP, on his left, has*)

taken his place by the dais: LA TRÉ-
MOUILLE *at the other side of it. The* DUCH-
ESS DE LA TRÉMOUILLE, *pretending to be
the Queen, sits in the Consort's chair,
with a group of ladies in waiting close by,
behind the* ARCHBISHOP.

*The chatter of the courtiers makes such a
noise that nobody notices the appearance
of the* PAGE *at the door.)*

THE PAGE. The Duke of— (*Nobody listens*).
The Duke of— (*The chatter continues. Indignant
at his failure to command a hearing, he snatches
the halberd of the nearest man-at-arms, and
thumps the floor with it. The chatter ceases; and
everybody looks at him in silence*). Attention!
(*He restores the halberd to the man-at-arms*) The
Duke of Vendôme presents Joan the Maid to
his Majesty.

CHARLES (*putting his finger on his lip*). Ssh!
(*He hides behind the nearest courtier, peering
out to see what happens*)

BLUEBEARD (*majestically*). Let her approach
the throne.

(JOAN, *dressed as a soldier, with her hair
bobbed and hanging thickly round her
face, is led in by a bashful and speechless
nobleman, from whom she detaches herself
to stop and look round eagerly for the*
DAUPHIN.)

THE DUCHESS (*to the nearest lady in waiting*).
My dear! Her hair! (*All the ladies explode in
uncontrollable laughter.*)

BLUEBEARD (*trying not to laugh, and waving
his hand in deprecation of their merriment*).
Ssh—ssh! Ladies! Ladies!

JOAN (*not at all embarrassed*). I wear it like
this because I am a soldier. Where be Dauphin?
(*A titter runs through the Court as she walks
to the dais.*)

BLUEBEARD (*condescendingly*). You are in the
presence of the Dauphin.

(JOAN *looks at him sceptically for a moment,
scanning him hard up and down to make
sure. Dead silence, all watching her. Fun
dawns in her face.*)

JOAN. Coom, Bluebeard! Thou canst not fool
me. Where be Dauphin?
(*A roar of laughter breaks out as* GILLES,
*with a gesture of surrender, joins in the
laugh, and jumps down from the dais be-*

side LA TRÉMOUILLE. JOAN, *also on the
broad grin, turns back, searching along
the row of courtiers, and presently makes
a dive, and drags out* CHARLES *by the arm.)*

JOAN (*releasing him and bobbing him a little
curtsey*). Gentle little Dauphin, I am sent to you
to drive the English away from Orleans and
from France, and to crown you king in the
cathedral at Rheims, where all true kings of
France are crowned.

CHARLES (*triumphant, to the Court*). You see,
all of you: she knew the blood royal. Who dare
say now that I am not my father's son? (*To
JOAN*) But if you want me to be crowned at
Rheims you must talk to the Archbishop, not to
me. There he is (*he is standing behind her*)!

JOAN (*turning quickly, overwhelmed with
emotion*). Oh, my lord! (*She falls on both knees
before him, with bowed head, not daring to look
up*) My lord: I am only a poor country girl; and
you are filled with the blessedness and glory of
God Himself; but you will touch me with your
hands, and give me your blessing, wont you?

BLUEBEARD (*whispering to* LA TRÉMOUILLE).
The old fox blushes.

LA TRÉMOUILLE. Another miracle!

THE ARCHBISHOP (*touched, putting his hand
on her head*). Child: you are in love with religion.

JOAN (*startled: looking up at him*). Am I? I
never thought of that. Is there any harm in it?

THE ARCHBISHOP. There is no harm in it, my
child. But there is danger.

JOAN (*rising, with a sunflush of reckless happiness irradiating her face*). There is always
danger, except in heaven. Oh, my lord, you have
given me such strength, such courage. It must
be a most wonderful thing to be Archbishop.
(*The Court smiles broadly: even titters a
little.*)

THE ARCHBISHOP (*drawing himself up sensitively*). Gentlemen: your levity is rebuked by
this maid's faith. I am, God help me, all unworthy; but your mirth is a deadly sin.
(*Their faces fall. Dead silence.*)

BLUEBEARD. My lord: we were laughing at her,
not at you.

THE ARCHBISHOP. What? Not at my unworthiness but at her faith! Gilles de Rais: this
maid prophesied that the blasphemer should be

drowned in his sin—

JOAN (*distressed*). No!

THE ARCHBISHOP (*silencing her by a gesture*). I prophesy now that you will be hanged in yours if you do not learn when to laugh and when to pray.

BLUEBEARD. My lord: I stand rebuked. I am sorry: I can say no more. But if you prophesy that I shall be hanged, I shall never be able to resist temptation, because I shall always be telling myself that I may as well be hanged for a sheep as a lamb.

(*The courtiers take heart at this. There is more tittering.*)

JOAN (*scandalized*). You are an idle fellow, Bluebeard; and you have great impudence to answer the Archbishop.

LA HIRE (*with a huge chuckle*). Well said, lass! Well said!

JOAN (*impatiently to the* ARCHBISHOP). Oh, my lord, will you send all these silly folks away so that I may speak to the Dauphin alone?

LA HIRE (*goodhumoredly*). I can take a hint. (*He salutes; turns on his heel; and goes out*)

THE ARCHBISHOP. Come, gentlemen. The Maid comes with God's blessing, and must be obeyed.

(*The courtiers withdraw, some through the arch, others at the opposite side. The* ARCHBISHOP *marches across to the door, followed by the* DUCHESS *and* LA TRÉMOUILLE. *As the* ARCHBISHOP *passes* JOAN, *she falls on her knees, and kisses the hem of his robe fervently. He shakes his head in instinctive remonstrance; gathers the robe from her; and goes out. She is left kneeling directly in the* DUCHESS's *way.*)

THE DUCHESS (*coldly*). Will you allow me to pass, please?

JOAN (*hastily rising, and standing back*). Beg pardon, maam, I am sure.

(*The* DUCHESS *passes on.* JOAN *stares after her; then whispers to the* DAUPHIN.)

JOAN. Be that Queen?

CHARLES. No. She thinks she is.

JOAN (*again staring after the* DUCHESS). Oo-oo-ooh! (*Her awestruck amazement at the figure cut by the magnificently dressed lady is not wholly complimentary*)

LA TRÉMOUILLE (*very surly*). I'll trouble your Highness not to gibe at my wife. (*He goes out.*

The others have already gone)

JOAN (*to the Dauphin*). Who be old Gruff-and-Grum?

CHARLES. He is the Duke de la Trémouille.

JOAN. What be his job?

CHARLES. He pretends to command the army. And whenever I find a friend I can care for, he kills him.

JOAN. Why dost let him?

CHARLES (*petulantly moving to the throne side of the room to escape from her magnetic field*). How can I prevent him? He bullies me. They all bully me.

JOAN. Art afraid?

CHARLES. Yes: I am afraid. It's no use preaching to me about it. It's all very well for these big men with their armor that is too heavy for me, and their swords that I can hardly lift, and their muscle and their shouting and their bad tempers. They like fighting: most of them are making fools of themselves all the time they are not fighting; but I am quiet and sensible; and I dont want to kill people: I only want to be left alone to enjoy myself in my own way. I never asked to be a king: it was pushed on me. So if you are going to say 'Son of St Louis: gird on the sword of your ancestors, and lead us to victory' you may spare your breath to cool your porridge; for I cannot do it. I am not built that way; and there is an end of it.

JOAN (*trenchant and masterful*). Blethers! We are all like that to begin with. I shall put courage into thee.

CHARLES. But I dont want to have courage put into me. I want to sleep in a comfortable bed, and not live in continual terror of being killed or wounded. Put courage into the others, and let them have their bellyful of fighting; but let me alone.

JOAN. It's no use, Charlie: thou must face what God puts on thee. If thou fail to make thyself king, thoult be a beggar: what else art fit for? Come! Let me see thee sitting on the throne. I have looked forward to that.

CHARLES. What is the good of sitting on the throne when the other fellows give all the orders? However! (*he sits enthroned, a piteous figure*) here is the king for you! Look your fill at the poor devil.

JOAN. Thourt not king yet, lad: thourt but

Dauphin. Be not led away by them around thee. Dressing up dont fill empty noddle. I know the people: the real people that make thy bread for thee; and I tell thee they count no man king of France until the holy oil has been poured on his hair, and himself consecrated and crowned in Rheims Cathedral. And thou needs new clothes, Charlie. Why does not Queen look after thee properly?

CHARLES. We're too poor. She wants all the money we can spare to put on her own back. Besides, I like to see her beautifully dressed; and I dont care what I wear myself: I should look ugly anyhow.

JOAN. There is some good in thee, Charlie; but it is not yet a king's good.

CHARLES. We shall see. I am not such a fool as I look. I have my eyes open; and I can tell you that one good treaty is worth ten good fights. These fighting fellows lose all on the treaties that they gain on the fights. If we can only have a treaty, the English are sure to have the worst of it, because they are better at fighting than at thinking.

JOAN. If the English win, it is they that will make the treaty: and then God help poor France! Thou must fight, Charlie, whether thou will or no. I will go first to hearten thee. We must take our courage in both hands: aye, and pray for it with both hands too.

CHARLES (descending from his throne and again crossing the room to escape from her dominating urgency). Oh do stop talking about God and praying. I cant bear people who are always praying. Isnt it bad enough to have to do it at the proper times?

JOAN (pitying him). Thou poor child, thou hast never prayed in thy life. I must teach thee from the beginning.

CHARLES. I am not a child: I am a grown man and a father; and I will not be taught any more.

JOAN. Aye, you have a little son. He that will be Louis the Eleventh when you die. Would you not fight for him?

CHARLES. No: a horrid boy. He hates me. He hates everybody, selfish little beast! I dont want to be bothered with children. I dont want to be a father; and I dont want to be a son: especially a son of St Louis. I dont want to be any of these fine things you all have your heads full of: I want to be just what I am. Why cant you mind your own business, and let me mind mine?

JOAN (again contemptuous). Minding your own business is like minding your own body: it's the shortest way to make yourself sick. What is my business? Helping mother at home. What is thine? Petting lapdogs and sucking sugar-sticks. I call that muck. I tell thee it is God's business we are here to do: not our own. I have a message to thee from God; and thou must listen to it, though thy heart break with the terror of it.

CHARLES. I dont want a message; but can you tell me any secrets? Can you do any cures? Can you turn lead into gold, or anything of that sort?

JOAN. I can turn thee into a king, in Rheims Cathedral; and that is a miracle that will take some doing, it seems.

CHARLES. If we go to Rheims, and have a coronation, Anne will want new dresses. We cant afford them. I am all right as I am.

JOAN. As you are! And what is that? Less than my father's poorest shepherd. Thourt not lawful owner of thy own land of France till thou be consecrated.

CHARLES. But I shall not be lawful owner of my own land anyhow. Will the consecration pay off my mortgages? I have pledged my last acre to the Archbishop and that fat bully. I owe money even to Bluebeard.

JOAN (earnestly). Charlie: I come from the land, and have gotten my strength working on the land; and I tell thee that the land is thine to rule righteously and keep God's peace in, and not to pledge at the pawnshop as a drunken woman pledges her children's clothes. And I come from God to tell thee to kneel in the cathedral and solemnly give thy kingdom to Him for ever and ever, and become the greatest king in the world as His steward and His bailiff, His soldier and His servant. The very clay of France will become holy: her soldiers will be the soldiers of God: the rebel dukes will be rebels against God: the English will fall on their knees and beg thee let them return to their lawful homes in peace. Wilt be a poor little Judas, and betray me and Him that sent me?

CHARLES (tempted at last). Oh, if I only dare!

JOAN. I shall dare, dare, and dare again, in God's name! Art for or against me?

CHARLES (*excited*). I'll risk it, I warn you I shant be able to keep it up; but I'll risk it. You shall see. (*Running to the main door and shouting*) Hallo! Come back, everybody. (*To* JOAN, *as he runs back to the arch opposite*) Mind you stand by and dont let me be bullied. (*Through the arch*) Come along, will you: the whole Court. (*He sits down in the royal chair as they all hurry in to their former places, chattering and wondering*) Now I'm in for it; but no matter: here goes! (*To the* PAGE) Call for silence, you little beast, will you?

THE PAGE (*snatching a halberd as before and thumping with it repeatedly*). Silence for His Majesty the King. The King speaks. (*Peremptorily*) Will you be silent there? (*Silence*)

CHARLES (*rising*). I have given the command of the army to The Maid. The Maid is to do as she likes with it. (*He descends from the dais*)

(*General amazement.* LA HIRE, *delighted, slaps his steel thigh-piece with his gauntlet.*)

LA TRÉMOUILLE (*turning threateningly towards Charles*). What is this? *I* command the army.

(JOAN *quickly puts her hand on* CHARLES's *shoulder as he instinctively recoils.* CHARLES, *with a grotesque effort culminating in an extravagant gesture, snaps his fingers in the* CHAMBERLAIN's *face.*)

JOAN. Thourt answered, old Gruff-and-Grum. (*Suddenly flashing out her sword as she divines that her moment has come*) Who is for God and His Maid? Who is for Orleans with me?

LA HIRE (*carried away, drawing also*). For God and His Maid. To Orleans!

ALL THE KNIGHTS (*following his lead with enthusiasm*). To Orleans!

(JOAN, *radiant, falls on her knees in thanksgiving to God. They all kneel, except the* ARCHBISHOP, *who gives his benediction with a sigh, and* LA TRÉMOUILLE, *who collapses, cursing.*)

Scene III

Orleans, April 29th, 1429. DUNOIS, *aged 26, is pacing up and down a patch of ground on the south bank of the silver Loire, commanding a long view of the river in both directions. He has had his lance stuck up with a pennon, which streams in a strong east wind. His shield with its bend sinister lies beside it. He has his commander's baton in his hand. He is well built, carrying his armor easily. His broad brow and pointed chin give him an equilaterally triangular face, already marked by active service and responsibility, with the expression of a good-natured and capable man who has no affectations and no foolish illusions. His* PAGE *is sitting on the ground, elbows on knees, cheeks on fists, idly watching the water. It is evening; and both man and boy are affected by the loveliness of the Loire.*

DUNOIS (*halting for a moment to glance up at the streaming pennon and shake his head wearily before he resumes his pacing*). West wind, west wind, west wind. Strumpet: steadfast when you should be wanton, wanton when you should be steadfast. West wind on the silver Loire: what rhymes to Loire? (*He looks again at the pennon, and shakes his fist at it*) Change, curse you, change, English harlot of a wind, change. West, west, I tell you. (*With a growl he resumes his march in silence, but soon begins again*) West wind, wanton wind, wilful wind, womanish wind, false wind from over the water, will you never blow again?

THE PAGE (*bounding to his feet*). See! There! There she goes!

DUNOIS (*startled from his reverie: eagerly*). Where? Who? The Maid?

THE PAGE. No: the kingfisher. Like blue lightning. She went into that bush.

DUNOIS (*furiously disappointed*). Is that all? You infernal young idiot: I have a mind to pitch you into the river.

THE PAGE (*not afraid, knowing his man*). It looked frightfully jolly, that flash of blue. Look! There goes the other!

DUNOIS (*running eagerly to the river brim*). Where? Where?

THE PAGE (*pointing*). Passing the reeds.

DUNOIS (*delighted*). I see.

(*They follow the flight till the bird takes cover.*)

THE PAGE. You blew me up because you were not in time to see them yesterday.

DUNOIS. You knew I was expecting The Maid when you set up your yelping. I will give you something to yelp for next time.

THE PAGE. Arnt they lovely? I wish I could catch them.

DUNOIS. Let me catch you trying to trap them, and I will put you in the iron cage for a month to teach you what a cage feels like. You are an abominable boy.

THE PAGE (*laughs, and squats down as before*)!

DUNOIS (*pacing*). Blue bird, blue bird, since I am friend to thee, change thou the wind for me. No: it does not rhyme. He who has sinned for thee: thats better. No sense in it, though. (*He finds himself close to the* PAGE) You abominable boy! (*He turns away from him*) Mary in the blue snood, kingfisher color: will you grudge me a west wind?

A SENTRY'S VOICE WESTWARD. Halt! Who goes there?

JOAN's VOICE. The Maid.

DUNOIS. Let her pass. Hither, Maid! To me!

(JOAN, *in splendid armor, rushes in in a blazing rage. The wind drops; and the pennon flaps idly down the lance; but* DUNOIS *is too much occupied with* JOAN *to notice it.*)

JOAN (*bluntly*). Be you Bastard of Orleans?

DUNOIS (*cool and stern, pointing to his shield*). You see the bend sinister. Are you Joan the Maid?

JOAN. Sure.

DUNOIS. Where are your troops?

JOAN. Miles behind. They have cheated me. They have brought me to the wrong side of the river.

DUNOIS. I told them to.

JOAN. Why did you? The English are on the other side!

DUNOIS. The English are on both sides.

JOAN. But Orleans is on the other side. We must fight the English there. How can we cross the river?

DUNOIS (*grimly*). There is a bridge.

JOAN. In God's name, then, let us cross the bridge, and fall on them.

DUNOIS. It seems simple; but it cannot be done.

JOAN. Who says so?

DUNOIS. I say so; and older and wiser heads than mine are of the same opinion.

JOAN (*roundly*). Then your older and wiser heads are fatheads: they have made a fool of you; and now they want to make a fool of me too, bringing me to the wrong side of the river. Do you not know that I bring you better help than ever came to any general or any town?

DUNOIS (*smiling patiently*). Your own?

JOAN. No: the help and counsel of the King of Heaven. Which is the way to the bridge?

DUNOIS. You are impatient, Maid.

JOAN. Is this a time for patience? Our enemy is at our gates; and here we stand doing nothing. Oh, why are you not fighting? Listen to me: I will deliver you from fear. I—

DUNOIS (*laughing heartily, and waving her off*). No, no, my girl: if you delivered me from fear I should be a good knight for a story book, but a very bad commander of the army. Come! let me begin to make a soldier of you. (*He takes her to the water's edge*). Do you see those two forts at this end of the bridge? the big ones?

JOAN. Yes. Are they ours or the goddams'?

DUNOIS. Be quiet, and listen to me. If I were in either of those forts with only ten men I could hold it against an army. The English have more than ten times ten goddams in those forts to hold them against us.

JOAN. They cannot hold them against God. God did not give them the land under those forts: they stole it from Him. He gave it to us. I will take those forts.

DUNOIS. Single-handed?

JOAN. Our men will take them. I will lead them.

DUNOIS. Not a man will follow you.

JOAN. I will not look back to see whether anyone is following me.

DUNOIS (*recognizing her mettle, and clapping her heartily on the shoulder*). Good. You have the makings of a soldier in you. You are in love with war.

JOAN (*startled*). Oh! And the Archbishop said I was in love with religion.

DUNOIS. I, God forgive me, am a little in love with war myself, the ugly devil! I am like a man with two wives. Do you want to be like a woman with two husbands?

JOAN (*matter-of-fact*). I will never take a husband. A man in Toul took an action against me for breach of promise; but I never promised him. I am a soldier: I do not want to be thought of as a woman. I will not dress as a woman. I do not care for the things women care for. They dream of lovers, and of money. I dream of leading a charge, and of placing the big guns. You soldiers do not know how to use the big guns: you think you can win battles with a great noise and smoke.

DUNOIS (*with a shrug*). True. Half the time the artillery is more trouble than it is worth.

JOAN. Aye, lad; but you cannot fight stone walls with horses: you must have guns, and much bigger guns too.

DUNOIS (*grinning at her familiarity, and echoing it*). Aye, lass; but a good heart and a stout ladder will get over the stoniest wall.

JOAN. I will be first up the ladder when we reach the fort, Bastard. I dare you to follow me.

DUNOIS. You must not dare a staff officer, Joan: only company officers are allowed to indulge in displays of personal courage. Besides, you must know that I welcome you as a saint, not as a soldier. I have daredevils enough at my call, if they could help me.

JOAN. I am not a daredevil: I am a servant of God. My sword is sacred: I found it behind the altar in the church of St Catherine, where God hid it for me; and I may not strike a blow with it. My heart is full of courage, not of anger. I will lead; and your men will follow: that is all I can do. But I must do it: you shall not stop me.

DUNOIS. All in good time. Our men cannot take those forts by a sally across the bridge. They must come by water, and take the English in the rear on this side.

JOAN (*her military sense asserting itself*). Then make rafts and put big guns on them; and let your men cross to us.

DUNOIS. The rafts are ready; and the men are embarked. But they must wait for God.

JOAN. What do you mean? God is waiting for them.

DUNOIS. Let Him send us a wind then. My boats are downstream: they cannot come up against both wind and current. We must wait until God changes the wind. Come: let me take you to the church.

JOAN. No. I love church; but the English will not yield to prayers: they understand nothing but hard knocks and slashes. I will not go to church until we have beaten them.

DUNOIS. You must: I have business for you there.

JOAN. What business?

DUNOIS. To pray for a west wind. I have prayed; and I have given two silver candlesticks; but my prayers are not answered. Yours may be: you are young and innocent.

JOAN. Oh yes: you are right. I will pray: I will tell St Catherine: she will make God give me a west wind. Quick: shew me the way to the church.

THE PAGE (*sneezes violently*). At-cha!!!

JOAN. God bless you, child! Coom, Bastard.

(*They go out. THE PAGE rises to follow. He picks up the shield, and is taking the spear as well when he notices the pennon, which is now streaming eastward.*)

THE PAGE (*dropping the shield and calling excitedly after them*). Seigneur! Seigneur! Mademoiselle!

DUNOIS (*running back*). What is it? The kingfisher? (*He looks eagerly for it up the river*)

JOAN (*joining them*). Oh, a kingfisher! Where?

THE PAGE. No: the wind, the wind, the wind (*pointing to the pennon*): that is what made me sneeze.

DUNOIS (*looking at the penon*). The wind has changed. (*He crosses himself*) God has spoken. (*Kneeling and handing his baton to* JOAN) You command the king's army. I am your soldier.

THE PAGE (*looking down the river*). The boats have put off. They are ripping upstream like anything.

DUNOIS (*rising*). Now for the forts. You dared me to follow. Dare you lead?

JOAN (*bursting into tears and flinging her arms round Dunois, kissing him on both cheeks*). Dunois, dear comrade in arms, help me. My eyes are blinded with tears. Set my foot on the ladder, and say 'Up, Joan.'

DUNOIS (*dragging her out*). Never mind the tears: make for the flash of the guns.

JOAN (*in a blaze of courage*). Ah!

DUNOIS (*dragging her along with him*). For

God and Saint Dennis!

THE PAGE (*shrilly*). The Maid! The Maid! God and The Maid! Hurray-ay-ay! (*He snatches up the shield and lance, and capers out after them, mad with excitement*)

Scene IV

A tent in the English camp. A bullnecked English chaplain of 50 is sitting on a stool at a table, hard at work writing. At the other side of the table an imposing nobleman, aged 46, is seated in a handsome chair turning over the leaves of an illuminated Book of Hours. The nobleman is enjoying himself: the chaplain is struggling with suppressed wrath. There is an unoccupied leather stool on the nobleman's left. The table is on his right.

THE NOBLEMAN. Now this is what I call workmanship. There is nothing on earth more exquisite than a bonny book, with well-placed columns of rich black writing in beautiful borders, and illuminated pictures cunningly inset. But nowadays, instead of looking at books, people read them. A book might as well be one of those orders for bacon and bran that you are scribbling.

THE CHAPLAIN. I must say, my lord, you take our situation very coolly. Very coolly indeed.

THE NOBLEMAN (*supercilious*). What is the matter?

THE CHAPLAIN. The matter, my lord, is that we English have been defeated.

THE NOBLEMAN. That happens, you know. It is only in history books and ballads that the enemy is always defeated.

THE CHAPLAIN. But we are being defeated over and over again. First, Orleans—

THE NOBLEMAN (*poohpoohing*). Oh, Orleans!

THE CHAPLAIN. I know what you are going to say, my lord: that was a clear case of witchcraft and sorcery. But we are still being defeated. Jargeau, Meung, Beaugency, just like Orleans. And now we have been butchered at Patay, and Sir John Talbot taken prisoner. (*He throws down his pen, almost in tears*) I feel it, my lord: I feel it very deeply. I cannot bear to see my countrymen defeated by a parcel of foreigners.

THE NOBLEMAN. Oh! you are an Englishman, are you?

THE CHAPLAIN. Certainly not, my lord: I am a gentleman. Still, like your lordship, I was born in England; and it makes a difference.

THE NOBLEMAN. You are attached to the soil, eh?

THE CHAPLAIN. It pleases your lordship to be satirical at my expense: your greatness privileges you to be so with impunity. But your lordship knows very well that I am not attached to the soil in a vulgar manner, like a serf. Still, I have a feeling about it; (*with growing agitation*) and I am not ashamed of it; and (*rising wildly*) by God, if this goes on any longer I will fling my cassock to the devil, and take arms myself, and strangle the accursed witch with my own hands.

THE NOBLEMAN (*laughing at him goodnaturedly*). So you shall, chaplain: so you shall, if we can do nothing better. But not yet, not quite yet.

(THE CHAPLAIN *resumes his seat very sulkily.*)

THE NOBLEMAN (*airily*). I should not care very much about the witch—you see, I have made my pilgrimage to the Holy Land; and the Heavenly Powers, for their own credit, can hardly allow me to be worsted by a village sorceress—but the Bastard of Orleans is a harder nut to crack; and as he has been to the Holy Land too, honors are easy between us as far as that goes.

THE CHAPLAIN. He is only a Frenchman, my lord.

THE NOBLEMAN. A Frenchman! Where did you pick up that expression? Are these Burgundians and Bretons and Picards and Gascons beginning to call themselves Frenchmen, just as our fellows are beginning to call themselves Englishmen? They actually talk of France and England as their countries. Theirs, if you please! What is to become of me and you if that way of thinking comes into fashion?

THE CHAPLAIN. Why, my lord? Can it hurt us?

THE NOBLEMAN. Men cannot serve two masters. If this cant of serving their country once takes hold of them, goodbye to the authority of their feudal lords, and goodbye to the authority of the Church. That is, goodbye to you and me.

THE CHAPLAIN. I hope I am a faithful servant of the Church; and there are only six cousins between me and the barony of Stogumber, which was created by the Conqueror. But is that any reason why I should stand by and see Englishmen beaten by a French bastard and a witch from Lousy Champagne?

THE NOBLEMAN. Easy, man, easy: we shall burn the witch and beat the bastard all in good time. Indeed I am waiting at present for the Bishop of Beauvais, to arrange the burning with him. He has been turned out of his diocese by her faction.

THE CHAPLAIN. You have first to catch her, my lord.

THE NOBLEMAN. Or buy her. I will offer a king's ransom.

THE CHAPLAIN. A king's ransom! For that slut!

THE NOBLEMAN. One has to leave a margin. Some of Charles's people will sell her to the Burgundians; the Burgundians will sell her to us; and there will probably be three or four middlemen who will expect their little commissions.

THE CHAPLAIN. Monstrous. It is all those scoundrels of Jews: they get in every time money changes hands. I would not leave a Jew alive in Christendom if I had my way.

THE NOBLEMAN. Why not? The Jews generally give value. They make you pay; but they deliver the goods. In my experience the men who want something for nothing are invariably Christians.

(A PAGE *appears*.)

THE PAGE. The Right Reverend the Bishop of Beauvais: Monseigneur Cauchon.

(CAUCHON, *aged about* 60, *comes in.* THE PAGE *withdraws. The two Englishmen rise.*)

THE NOBLEMAN (*with effusive courtesy*). My dear Bishop, how good of you to come! Allow me to introduce myself: Richard de Beauchamp, Earl of Warwick, at your service.

CAUCHON. Your lordship's fame is well known to me.

WARWICK. This reverend cleric is Master John de Stogumber.

THE CHAPLAIN (*glibly*). John Bowyer Spenser Neville de Stogumber, at your service, my lord: Bachelor of Theology, and Keeper of the Private Seal to His Eminence the Cardinal of Winchester.

WARWICK (*to* CAUCHON). You call him the Cardinal of England, I believe. Our king's uncle.

CAUCHON. Messire John de Stogumber: I am always the very good friend of His Eminence. (*He extends his hand to* THE CHAPLAIN, *who kisses his ring*)

WARWICK. Do me the honor to be seated. (*He gives* CAUCHON *his chair, placing it at the head of the table*)

(CAUCHON *accepts the place of honor with a grave inclination.* WARWICK *fetches the leather stool carelessly, and sits in his former place.* THE CHAPLAIN *goes back to his chair.*

Though WARWICK *has taken second place in calculated deference to the Bishop, he assumes the lead in opening the proceedings as a matter of course. He is still cordial and expansive; but there is a new note in his voice which means that he is coming to business.*)

WARWICK. Well, my Lord Bishop, you find us in one of our unlucky moments. Charles is to be crowned at Rheims, practically by the young woman from Lorraine; and—I must not deceive you, nor flatter your hopes—we cannot prevent it. I suppose it will make a great difference to Charles's position.

CAUCHON. Undoubtedly. It is a masterstroke of The Maid's.

THE CHAPLAIN (*again agitated*). We were not fairly beaten, my lord. No Englishman is ever fairly beaten.

(CAUCHON *raises his eyebrow slightly, then quickly composes his face.*)

WARWICK. Our friend here takes the view that the young woman is a sorceress. It would, I presume, be the duty of your reverend lordship to denounce her to the Inquisition, and have her burnt for that offence.

CAUCHON. If she were captured in my diocese: yes.

WARWICK (*feeling that they are getting on capitally*). Just so. Now I suppose there can be no reasonable doubt that she is a sorceress.

THE CHAPLAIN. Not the least. An arrant witch.

WARWICK (*gently reproving the interruption*). We are asking for the Bishop's opinion, Messire

John.

CAUCHON. We shall have to consider not merely our own opinions here, but the opinions —the prejudices, if you like—of a French court.

WARWICK (*correcting*). A Catholic court, my lord.

CAUCHON. Catholic courts are composed of mortal men, like other courts, however sacred their function and inspiration may be. And if the men are Frenchmen, as the modern fashion calls them, I am afraid the bare fact that an English army has been defeated by a French one will not convince them that there is any sorcery in the matter.

THE CHAPLAIN. What! Not when the famous Sir Talbot himself has been defeated and actually taken prisoner by a drab from the ditches of Lorraine!

CAUCHON. Sir John Talbot, we all know, is a fierce and formidable soldier, Messire; but I have yet to learn that he is an able general. And though it pleases you to say that he has been defeated by this girl, some of us may be disposed to give a little of the credit to Dunois.

THE CHAPLAIN (*contemptuously*). The Bastard of Orleans!

CAUCHON. Let me remind—

WARWICK (*interposing*). I know what you are going to say, my lord. Dunois defeated me at Montargis.

CAUCHON (*bowing*). I take that as evidence that the Seigneur Dunois is a very able commander indeed.

WARWICK. Your lordship is the flower of courtesy. I admit, on our side, that Talbot is a mere fighting animal, and that it probably served him right to be taken at Patay.

THE CHAPLAIN (*chafing*). My lord: at Orleans this woman had her throat pierced by an English arrow, and was seen to cry like a child from the pain of it. It was a death wound; yet she fought all day; and when our men had repulsed all her attacks like true Englishmen, she walked alone to the wall of our fort with a white banner in her hand; and our men were paralyzed, and could neither shoot nor strike whilst the French fell on them and drove them on to the bridge, which immediately burst into flames and crumbled under them, letting them down into the river, where they were drowned in heaps. Was this your bastard's generalship? or were those flames of hell, conjured up by witchcraft?

WARWICK. You will forgive Messire John's vehemence, my lord; but he has put our case. Dunois is a great captain, we admit; but why could he do nothing until the witch came?

CAUCHON. I do not say that there were no supernatural powers on her side. But the names on that white banner were not the names of Satan and Beelzebub, but the blessed names of our Lord and His holy mother. And your commander who was drowned—Clahz-da I think you call him—

WARWICK. Glasdale. Sir William Glasdale.

CAUCHON. Glass-dell, thank you. He was no saint; and many of our people think that he was drowned for his blasphemies against The Maid.

WARWICK (*beginning to look very dubious*). Well, what are we to infer from all this, my lord? Has The Maid converted you?

CAUCHON. If she had, my lord, I should have known better than to have trusted myself here within your grasp.

WARWICK (*blandly deprecating*). Oh! oh! My lord!

CAUCHON. If the devil is making use of this girl—and I believe he is—

WARWICK (*reassured*). Ah! You hear, Messire John? I knew your lordship would not fail us. Pardon my interruption. Proceed.

CAUCHON. If it be so, the devil has longer views than you give him credit for.

WARWICK. Indeed? In what way? Listen to this, Messire John.

CAUCHON. If the devil wanted to damn a country girl, do you think so easy a task would cost him the winning of half a dozen battles? No, my lord: any trumpery imp could do that much if the girl could be damned at all. The Prince of Darkness does not condescend to such cheap drudgery. When he strikes, he strikes at the Catholic Church, whose realm is the whole spiritual world. When he damns, he damns the souls of the entire human race. Against that dreadful design The Church stands ever on guard. And it is as one of the instruments of that design that I see this girl. She is inspired, but diabolically inspired.

THE CHAPLAIN. I told you she was a witch.

CAUCHON (*fiercely*). She is not a witch. She is

a heretic.

THE CHAPLAIN. What difference does that make?

CAUCHON. You, a priest, ask me that! You English are strangely blunt in the mind. All these things that you call witchcraft are capable of a natural explanation. The woman's miracles would not impose on a rabbit: she does not claim them as miracles herself. What do her victories prove but that she has a better head on her shoulders than your swearing Glass-dells and mad bull Talbots, and that the courage of faith, even though it be a false faith, will always outstay the courage of wrath?

THE CHAPLAIN (*hardly able to believe his ears*). Does your lordship compare Sir John Talbot, three times Governor of Ireland, to a mad bull?!!!

WARWICK. It would not be seemly for you to do so, Messire John, as you are still six removes from a barony. But as I am an earl, and Talbot is only a knight, I may make bold to accept the comparison. (*To the* BISHOP) My lord: I wipe the slate as far as the witchcraft goes. None the less, we must burn the woman.

CAUCHON. I cannot burn her. The Church cannot take life. And my first duty is to seek this girl's salvation.

WARWICK. No doubt. But you do burn people occasionally.

CAUCHON. No. When The Church cuts off an obstinate heretic as a dead branch from the tree of life, the heretic is handed over to the secular arm. The Church has no part in what the secular arm may see fit to do.

WARWICK. Precisely. And I shall be the secular arm in this case. Well, my lord, hand over your dead branch; and I will see that the fire is ready for it. If you will answer for The Church's part, I will answer for the secular part.

CAUCHON (*with smouldering anger*). I can answer for nothing. You great lords are too prone to treat The Church as a mere political convenience.

WARWICK (*smiling and propitiatory*). Not in England, I assure you.

CAUCHON. In England more than anywhere else. No, my lord: the soul of this village girl is of equal value with yours or your king's before the throne of God; and my first duty is to save it. I will not suffer your lordship to smile at me as if I were repeating a meaningless form of words, and it were well understood between us that I should betray the girl to you. I am no mere political bishop: my faith is to me what your honor is to you; and if there be a loophole through which this baptized child of God can creep to her salvation, I shall guide her to it.

THE CHAPLAIN (*rising in a fury*). You are a traitor.

CAUCHON (*springing up*). You lie, priest. (*Trembling with rage*) If you dare do what this woman has done—set your country above the holy Catholic Church—you shall go to the fire with her.

THE CHAPLAIN. My lord: I—I went too far. I—(*he sits down with a submissive gesture*)

WARWICK (*who has risen apprehensively*). My lord: I apologize to you for the word used by Messire John de Stogumber. It does not mean in England what it does in France. In your language traitor means betrayer: one who is perfidious, treacherous, unfaithful, disloyal. In our country it means simply one who is not wholly devoted to our English interests.

CAUCHON. I am sorry: I did not understand. (*He subsides into his chair with dignity*)

WARWICK (*resuming his seat, much relieved*). I must apologize on my own account if I have seemed to take the burning of this poor girl too lightly. When one has seen whole countrysides burnt over and over again as mere items in military routine, one has to grow a very thick skin. Otherwise one might go mad: at all events, I should. May I venture to assume that your lordship also, having to see so many heretics burned from time to time, is compelled to take—shall I say a professional view of what would otherwise be a very horrible incident?

CAUCHON. Yes: it is a painful duty: even, as you say, a horrible one. But in comparison with the horror of heresy it is less than nothing. I am not thinking of this girl's body, which will suffer for a few moments only, and which must in any event die in some more or less painful manner, but of her soul, which may suffer to all eternity.

WARWICK. Just so; and God grant that her soul may be saved! But the practical problem would seem to be how to save her soul without saving her body. For we must face it, my lord:

if this cult of The Maid goes on, our cause is lost.

THE CHAPLAIN (*his voice broken like that of a man who has been crying*). May I speak, my lord?

WARWICK. Really, Messire John, I had rather you did not, unless you can keep your temper.

THE CHAPLAIN. It is only this. I speak under correction; but The Maid is full of deceit: she pretends to be devout. Her prayers and confessions are endless. How can she be accused of heresy when she neglects no observance of a faithful daughter of The Church?

CAUCHON (*flaming up*). A faithful daughter of The Church! The Pope himself at his proudest dare not presume as this woman presumes. She acts as if she herself were The Church. She brings the message of God to Charles; and The Church must stand aside. She will crown him in the cathedral of Rheims: she, not The Church! She sends letters to the king of England giving him God's command through her to return to his island on pain of God's vengeance, which she will execute. Let me tell you that the writing of such letters was the practice of the accursed Mahomet, the anti-Christ. Has she ever in all her utterances said one word of The Church? Never. It is always God and herself.

WARWICK. What can you expect? A beggar on horseback! Her head is turned.

CAUCHON. Who has turned it? The devil. And for a mighty purpose. He is spreading this heresy everywhere. The man Hus, burnt only thirteen years ago at Constance, infected all Bohemia with it. A man named WcLeef, himself an anointed priest, spread the pestilence in England; and to your shame you let him die in his bed. We have such people here in France too: I know the breed. It is cancerous: if it be not cut out, stamped out, burnt out, it will not stop until it has brought the whole body of human society into sin and corruption, into waste and ruin. By it an Arab camel driver drove Christ and His Church out of Jerusalem, and ravaged his way west like a wild beast until at last there stood only the Pyrenees and God's mercy between France and damnation. Yet what did the camel driver do at the beginning more than this shepherd girl is doing? He had his voices from the angel Gabriel: she has her voices from St

Catherine and St Margaret and the Blessed Michael. He declared himself the messenger of God, and wrote in God's name to the kings of the earth. Her letters to them are going forth daily. It is not the Mother of God now to whom we must look for intercession, but to Joan the Maid. What will the world be like when The Church's accumulated wisdom and knowledge and experience, its councils of learned, venerable pious men, are thrust into the kennel by every ignorant laborer or dairymaid whom the devil can puff up with the monstrous self-conceit of being directly inspired from heaven? It will be a world of blood, of fury, of devastation, of each man striving for his own hand: in the end a world wrecked back into barbarism. For now you have only Mahomet and his dupes, and the Maid and her dupes; but what will it be when every girl thinks herself a Joan and every man a Mahomet? I shudder to the very marrow of my bones when I think of it. I have fought it all my life; and I will fight it to the end. Let all this woman's sins be forgiven her except only this sin; for it is the sin against the Holy Ghost; and if she does not recant in the dust before the world, and submit herself to the last inch of her soul to her Church, to the fire she shall go if she once falls into my hand.

WARWICK (*unimpressed*). You feel strongly about it, naturally.

CAUCHON. Do not you?

WARWICK. I am a soldier, not a churchman. As a pilgrim I saw something of the Mahometans. They were not so ill-bred as I had been led to believe. In some respects their conduct compared favorably with ours.

CAUCHON (*displeased*). I have noticed this before. Men go to the East to convert the infidels. And the infidels pervert them. The Crusader comes back more than half a Saracen. Not to mention that all Englishmen are born heretics.

THE CHAPLAIN. Englishmen heretics!!! (*Appealing to* WARWICK) My lord: must we endure this? His lordship is beside himself. How can what an Englishman believes be heresy? It is a contradiction in terms.

CAUCHON. I absolve you, Messire de Stogumber, on the ground of invincible ignorance. The thick air of your country does not breed theologians.

WARWICK. You would not say so if you heard us quarrelling about religion, my lord! I am sorry you think I must be either a heretic or a blockhead because, as a travelled man, I know that the followers of Mahomet profess great respect for our Lord, and are more ready to forgive St Peter for being a fisherman than your lordship is to forgive Mahomet for being a camel driver. But at least we can proceed in this matter without bigotry.

CAUCHON. When men call the zeal of the Christian Church bigotry I know what to think.

WARWICK. They are only east and west views of the same thing.

CAUCHON (bitterly ironical). Only east and west! Only!!

WARWICK. Oh, my Lord Bishop, I am not gainsaying you. You will carry The Church with you; but you have to carry the nobles also. To my mind there is a stronger case against The Maid than the one you have so forcibly put. Frankly, I am not afraid of this girl becoming another Mahomet, and superseding The Church by a great heresy. I think you exaggerate that risk. But have you noticed that in these letters of hers, she proposes to all the kings of Europe, as she has already pressed on Charles, a transaction which would wreck the whole social structure of Christendom?

CAUCHON. Wreck The Church. I tell you so.

WARWICK (whose patience is wearing out). My lord: pray get The Church out of your head for a moment; and remember that there are temporal institutions in the world as well as spiritual ones. I and my peers represent the feudal aristocracy as you represent The Church. We are the temporal power. Well, do you not see how this girl's idea strikes at us?

CAUCHON. How does her idea strike at you, except as it strikes at all of us, through The Church?

WARWICK. Her idea is that the kings should give their realms to God, and then reign as God's bailiffs.

CAUCHON (not interested). Quite sound theologically, my lord. But the king will hardly care, provided he reign. It is an abstract idea: a mere form of words.

WARWICK. By no means. It is a cunning device to supersede the aristocracy, and make the king sole and absolute autocrat. Instead of the king being merely the first among his peers, he becomes their master. That we cannot suffer: we call no man master. Nominally we hold our lands and dignities from the king, because there must be a keystone to the arch of human society; but we hold our lands in our own hands, and defend them with our own swords and those of our own tenants. Now by The Maid's doctrine the king will take our lands—our lands!—and make them a present to God; and God will then vest them wholly in the king.

CAUCHON. Need you fear that? You are the makers of kings after all. York or Lancaster in England, Lancaster or Valois in France: they reign according to your pleasure.

WARWICK. Yes; but only as long as the people follow their feudal lords, and know the king only as a travelling show, owning nothing but the highway that belongs to everybody. If the people's thoughts and hearts were turned to the king, and their lords became only the king's servants in their eyes, the king could break us across his knee one by one; and then what should we be but liveried courtiers in his halls?

CAUCHON. Still you need not fear, my lord. Some men are born kings; and some are born statesmen. The two are seldom the same. Where would the king find counsellors to plan and carry out such a policy for him?

WARWICK (with a not too friendly smile). Perhaps in the Church, my lord.

(CAUCHON, with an equally sour smile, shrugs his shoulders, and does not contradict him.)

WARWICK. Strike down the barons; and the cardinals will have it all their own way.

CAUCHON (conciliatory, dropping his polemical tone). My lord: we shall not defeat The Maid if we strive against one another. I know well that there is a Will to Power in the world. I know that while it lasts there will be a struggle between the Emperor and the Pope, between the dukes and the political cardinals, between the barons and the kings. The devil divides us and governs. I see you are no friend to The Church: you are an earl first and last, as I am a churchman first and last. But can we not sink our differences in the face of a common enemy? I see now that what is in your mind is not that this girl has never once mentioned The Church, and thinks only of God and herself, but that she has never once mentioned the peerage, and thinks only of the king and herself.

WARWICK. Quite so. These two ideas of hers are the same idea at bottom. It goes deep, my lord. It is the protest of the individual soul against the interference of priest or peer between the private man and his God. I should call it Protestantism if I had to find a name for it.

CAUCHON (*looking hard at him*). You understand it wonderfully well, my lord. Scratch an Englishman, and find a Protestant.

WARWICK (*playing the pink of courtesy*). I think you are not entirely void of sympathy with The Maid's secular heresy, my lord. I leave you to find a name for it.

CAUCHON. You mistake me, my lord. I have no sympathy with her political presumptions. But as a priest I have gained a knowledge of the minds of the common people; and there you will find yet another most dangerous idea. I can express it only by such phrases as France for the French, England for the English, Italy for the Italians, Spain for the Spanish, and so forth. It is sometimes so narrow and bitter in country folk that it surprises me that this country girl can rise above the idea of her village for its villagers. But she can. She does. When she threatens to drive the English from the soil of France she is undoubtedly thinking of the whole extent of country in which French is spoken. To her the French-speaking people are what the Holy Scriptures describe as a nation. Call this side of her heresy Nationalism if you will: I can find you no better name for it. I can only tell you that it is essentially anti-Catholic and anti-Christian; for the Catholic Church knows only one realm, and that is the realm of Christ's kingdom. Divide that kingdom into nations, and

you dethrone Christ. Dethrone Christ, and who will stand between our throats and the sword? The world will perish in a welter of war.

WARWICK. Well, if you will burn the Protestant, I will burn the Nationalist, though perhaps I shall not carry Messire John with me there. England for the English will appeal to him.

THE CHAPLAIN. Certainly England for the English goes without saying: it is the simple law of nature. But this woman denies to England her legitimate conquests, given her by God because of her peculiar fitness to rule over less civilized races for their own good. I do not understand what your lordships mean by Protestant and Nationalist: you are too learned and subtle for a poor clerk like myself. But I know as a matter of plain commonsense that the woman is a rebel; and that is enough for me. She rebels against Nature by wearing man's clothes, and fighting. She rebels against The Church by usurping the divine authority of the Pope. She rebels against God by her damnable league with Satan and his evil spirits against our army. And all these rebellions are only excuses for her great rebellion against England. That is not to be endured. Let her perish. Let her burn. Let her not infect the whole flock. It is expedient that one woman die for the people.

WARWICK (*rising*). My lord: we seem to be agreed.

CAUCHON (*rising also, but in protest*). I will not imperil my soul. I will uphold the justice of the Church. I will strive to the utmost for this woman's salvation.

WARWICK. I am sorry for the poor girl. I hate these severities. I will spare her if I can.

THE CHAPLAIN (*implacably*). I would burn her with my own hands.

CAUCHON (*blessing him*). Sancta simplicitas!

Scene V

The ambulatory in the cathedral of Rheims, near the door of the vestry. A pillar bears one of the stations of the cross. The organ is playing the people out of the nave after the coronation. JOAN is kneeling in prayer before the station. She is beautifully dressed, but still in male attire. The organ ceases as DUNOIS, also splendidly arrayed, comes into the ambulatory from the vestry.

DUNOIS. Come, Joan! you have had enough praying. After that fit of crying you will catch a chill if you stay here any longer. It is all over: the cathedral is empty; and the streets are full. They are calling for The Maid. We have told them you are staying here alone to pray; but they want to see you again.

JOAN. No: let the king have all the glory.

DUNOIS. He only spoils the show, poor devil. No, Joan: you have crowned him; and you must go through with it.

JOAN (*shakes her head reluctantly*).

DUNOIS (*raising her*). Come come! it will be over in a couple of hours. It's better than the bridge at Orleans: eh?

JOAN. Oh, dear Dunois, how I wish it were the bridge at Orleans again! We lived at that bridge.

DUNOIS. Yes, faith, and died too: some of us.

JOAN. Isnt it strange, Jack? I am such a coward: I am frightened beyond words before a battle; but it is so dull afterwards when there is no danger: oh, so dull! dull! dull!

DUNOIS. You must learn to be abstemious in war, just as you are in your food and drink, my little saint.

JOAN. Dear Jack: I think you like me as a soldier likes his comrade.

DUNOIS. You need it, poor innocent child of God. You have not many friends at court.

JOAN. Why do all these courtiers and knights and churchmen hate me? What have I done to them? I have asked nothing for myself except that my village shall not be taxed; for we cannot afford war taxes. I have brought them luck and victory: I have set them right when they were doing all sorts of stupid things: I have crowned Charles and made him a real king; and all the honors he is handing out have gone to them. Then why do they not love me?

DUNOIS (*rallying her*). Sim-ple-ton! Do you expect stupid people to love you for shewing them up? Do blundering old military dug-outs love the successful young captains who supersede them? Do ambitious politicians love the climbers who take the front seats from them? Do archbishops enjoy being played off their own altars, even by saints? Why, I should be jealous of you myself if I were ambitious enough.

JOAN. You are the pick of the basket here, Jack: the only friend I have among all these nobles. I'll wager your mother was from the country. I will go back to the farm when I have taken Paris.

DUNOIS. I am not so sure that they will let you take Paris.

JOAN (*startled*). What!

DUNOIS. I should have taken it myself before this if they had all been sound about it. Some of them would rather Paris took you, I think. So take care.

JOAN. Jack: the world is too wicked for me. If the goddams and the Burgundians do not make an end of me, the French will. Only for my voices I should lose all heart. That is why I had to steal away to pray here alone after the coronation. I'll tell you something, Jack. It is in the bells I hear my voices. Not to-day, when they all rang: that was nothing but jangling. But here in this corner, where the bells come down from heaven, and the echoes linger, or in the fields, where they come from a distance through the quiet of the countryside, my voices are in them. (*The cathedral clock chimes the quarter*) Hark! (*She becomes rapt*) Do you hear? 'Dear-child-of-God': just what you said. At the half-hour they will say 'Be-brave-go-on'. At the three-quarters they will say 'I-am-thy-Help'. But it is at the hour, when the great bell goes after 'God-will-save-France': it is then that St Margaret and St Catherine and sometimes even the blessed Michael will say things that I cannot tell beforehand. Then, oh then—

DUNOIS (*interrupting her kindly but not sympathetically*). Then, Joan, we shall hear whatever we fancy in the booming of the bell. You make me uneasy when you talk about your voices: I should think you were a bit cracked if I hadnt noticed that you give me very sensible reasons for what you do, though I hear you telling others you are only obeying Madame Saint Catherine.

JOAN (crossly). Well, I have to find reasons for you, because you do not believe in my voices. But the voices come first; and I find the reasons after: whatever you may choose to believe.

DUNOIS. Are you angry, Joan?

JOAN. Yes. (Smiling) No: not with you. I wish you were one of the village babies.

DUNOIS. Why?

JOAN. I could nurse you for awhile.

DUNOIS. You are a bit of a woman after all.

JOAN. No: not a bit: I am a soldier and nothing else. Soldiers always nurse children when they get a chance.

DUNOIS. That is true. (He laughs)

(KING CHARLES, with BLUEBEARD on his left and LA HIRE on his right, comes from the vestry, where he has been disrobing. JOAN shrinks away behind the pillar. DUNOIS is left between CHARLES and LA HIRE.)

DUNOIS. Well, your Majesty is an anointed king at last. How do you like it?

CHARLES. I would not go through it again to be emperor of the sun and moon. The weight of those robes! I thought I should have dropped when they loaded that crown on to me. And the famous holy oil they talked so much about was rancid: phew! The Archbishop must be nearly dead: his robes must have weighed a ton: they are stripping him still in the vestry.

DUNOIS (drily). Your majesty should wear armor oftener. That would accustom you to heavy dressing.

CHARLES. Yes: the old jibe! Well, I am not going to wear armor: fighting is not my job. Where is The Maid?

JOAN (coming forward between CHARLES and BLUEBEARD, and falling on her knee). Sire: I have made you king: my work is done. I am going back to my father's farm.

CHARLES (surprised, but relieved). Oh, are you? Well, that will be very nice.

(JOAN rises, deeply discouraged.)

CHARLES (continuing heedlessly). A healthy life, you know.

DUNOIS. But a dull one.

BLUEBEARD. You will find the petticoats tripping you up after leaving them off for so long.

LA HIRE. You will miss the fighting. It's a bad habit, but a grand one, and the hardest of all to break yourself of.

CHARLES (anxiously). Still, we dont want you to stay if you would really rather go home.

JOAN (bitterly). I know well that none of you will be sorry to see me go. (She turns her shoulder to CHARLES and walks past him to the more congenial neighborhood of DUNOIS and LA HIRE)

LA HIRE. Well, I shall be able to swear when I want to. But I shall miss you at times.

JOAN. La Hire: in spite of all your sins and swears we shall meet in heaven; for I love you as I love Pitou, my old sheep dog. Pitou could kill a wolf. You will kill the English wolves until they go back to their country and become good dogs of God, will you not?

LA HIRE. You and I together: yes.

JOAN. No: I shall last only a year from the beginning.

ALL THE OTHERS. What!

JOAN. I know it somehow.

DUNOIS. Nonsense!

JOAN. Jack: do you think you will be able to drive them out?

DUNOIS (with quiet conviction). Yes: I shall drive them out. They beat us because we thought battles were tournaments and ransom markets. We played the fool while the goddams took war seriously. But I have learnt my lesson, and taken their measure. They have no roots here. I have beaten them before; and I shall beat them again.

JOAN. You will not be cruel to them, Jack?

DUNOIS. The goddams will not yield to tender handling. We did not begin it.

JOAN (suddenly). Jack: before I go home, let us take Paris.

CHARLES (terrified). Oh no no. We shall lose everything we have gained. Oh dont let us have any more fighting. We can make a very good treaty with the Duke of Burgundy.

JOAN. Treaty! (She stamps with impatience)

CHARLES. Well, why not, now that I am crowned and anointed? Oh, that oil!

(THE ARCHBISHOP comes from the vestry, and joins the group between CHARLES *and* BLUEBEARD.)

CHARLES. Archbishop: The Maid wants to start fighting again.

THE ARCHBISHOP. Have we ceased fighting, then? Are we at peace?

CHARLES. No: I suppose not; but let us be content with what we have done. Let us make a treaty. Our luck is too good to last; and now is our chance to stop before it turns.

JOAN. Luck! God has fought for us; and you call it luck! And you would stop while there are still Englishmen on this holy earth of dear France!

THE ARCHBISHOP (*sternly*). Maid: the king addressed himself to me, not to you. You forget yourself. You very often forget yourself.

JOAN (*unabashed, and rather roughly*). Then speak, you; and tell him that it is not God's will that he should take his hand from the plough.

THE ARCHBISHOP. If I am not so glib with the name of God as you are, it is because I interpret His will with the authority of the Church and of my sacred office. When you first came you respected it, and would not have dared to speak as you are now speaking. You came clothed with the virtue of humility; and because God blessed your enterprises accordingly, you have stained yourself with the sin of pride. The old Greek tragedy is rising among us. It is the chastisement of hubris.

CHARLES. Yes: but she thinks she knows better than everyone else.

JOAN (*distressed, but naïvely incapable of seeing the effect she is producing*). But I do know better than any of you seem to. And I am not proud: I never speak unless I know I am right.

BLUEBEARD } (*exclaiming* { Ha ha!
CHARLES   }   *together*) { Just so.

THE ARCHBISHOP. How do you know you are right?

JOAN. I always know. My voices—

CHARLES. Oh, your voices, your voices. Why dont the voices come to me? I am king, not you.

JOAN. They do come to you; but you do not hear them. You have not sat in the field in the evening listening for them. When the angelus rings you cross yourself and have done with it; but if you prayed from your heart, and listened to the thrilling of the bells in the air after they stop ringing, you would hear the voices as well

as I do. (*Turning brusquely from him*) But what voices do you need to tell you what the blacksmith can tell you: that you must strike while the iron is hot? I tell you we must make a dash at Compiègne and relieve it as we relieved Orleans. Then Paris will open its gates; or if not, we will break through them. What is your crown worth without your capital?

LA HIRE. That is what I say too. We shall go through them like a red hot shot through a pound of butter. What do you say, Bastard?

DUNOIS. If our cannon balls were all as hot as your head, and we had enough of them, we should conquer the earth, no doubt. Pluck and impetuosity are good servants in war, but bad masters: they have delivered us into the hands of the English every time we have trusted to them. We never know when we are beaten: that is our great fault.

JOAN. You never know when you are victorious: that is a worse fault. I shall have to make you carry looking-glasses in battle to convince you that the English have not cut off all your noses. You would have been besieged in Orleans still, you and your councils of war, if I had not made you attack. You should always attack; and if you only hold on long enough the enemy will stop first. You dont know how to begin a battle; and you dont know how to use your cannons. And I do.

(*She squats down on the flags with crossed ankles, pouting.*)

DUNOIS. I know what you think of us, General Joan.

JOAN. Never mind that, Jack. Tell them what you think of me.

DUNOIS. I think that God was on your side; for I have not forgotten how the wind changed, and how our hearts changed when you came; and by my faith I shall never deny that it was in your sign that we conquered. But I tell you as a soldier that God is no man's daily drudge, and no maid's either. If you are worthy of it He will sometimes snatch you out of the jaws of death and set you on your feet again; but that is all: once on your feet you must fight with all your might and all your craft. For He has to be fair to your enemy too: dont forget that. Well, He set us on our feet through you at Orleans; and the glory of it has carried us through a few good battles here to the coronation. But if we presume on it further, and trust to God to do the work we should do ourselves, we shall be defeated; and serve us right!

JOAN. But—

DUNOIS. Sh! I have not finished. Do not think, any of you, that these victories of ours were won without generalship. King Charles: you have said no word in your proclamations of my part in this campaign; and I make no complaint of that; for the people will run after The Maid and her miracles and not after the Bastard's hard work finding troops for her and feeding them. But I know exactly how much God did for us through The Maid, and how much He left me to do by my own wits; and I tell you that your little hour of miracles is over, and that from this time on he who plays the war game best will win—if the luck is on his side.

JOAN. Ah! if, if, if, if! If ifs and ans were pots and pans there'd be no need of tinkers. (*Rising impetuously*) I tell you, Bastard, your art of war is no use, because your knights are no good for real fighting. War is only a game to them, like tennis and all their other games: they make rules as to what is fair and what is not fair, and heap armor on themselves and on their poor horses to keep out the arrows; and when they fall they cant get up, and have to wait for their squires to come and lift them to arrange about the ransom with the man that has poked them off their horse. Cant you see that all the like of that is gone by and done with? What use is armor against gunpowder? And if it was, do you think men that are fighting for France and for God will stop to bargain about ransoms, as half your knights live by doing? No: they will fight to win; and they will give up their lives out of their own hand into the hand of God when they go into battle, as I do. Common folks understand this. They cannot afford armor and cannot pay ransoms; but they followed me half naked into the moat and up the ladder and over the wall. With them it is my life or thine, and God defend the right! You may shake your head, Jack; and Bluebeard may twirl his billygoat's beard and cock his nose at me; but remember the day your knights and captains refused to follow me to attack the English at Orleans! You locked the gates to keep me in; and it was the townsfolk and the common people that followed me, and forced the gate, and shewed you the way to fight in earnest.

BLUEBEARD (*offended*). Not content with being Pope Joan, you must be Caesar and Alexander as well.

THE ARCHBISHOP. Pride will have a fall, Joan.

JOAN. Oh, never mind whether it is pride or not: is it true? is it commonsense?

LA HIRE. It is true. Half of us are afraid of having our handsome noses broken; and the other half are out for paying off their mortgages. Let her have her way, Dunois: she does not know everything; but she has got hold of the right end of the stick. Fighting is not what it was; and those who know least about it often make the best job of it.

DUNOIS. I know all that. I do not fight in the old way: I have learnt the lesson of Agincourt, of Poitiers and Crecy. I know how many lives any move of mine will cost; and if the move is worth the cost I make it and pay the cost. But Joan never counts the cost at all: she goes ahead and trusts to God: she thinks she has God in her pocket. Up to now she has had the numbers on her side; and she has won. But I know Joan; and I see that some day she will go ahead when she has only ten men to do the work of a hundred. And then she will find that God is on the side of the big battalions. She will be taken by the enemy. And the lucky man that makes the capture will receive sixteen thousand pounds from the Earl of Ouareek.

JOAN (*flattered*). Sixteen thousand pounds! Eh, laddie, have they offered that for me? There cannot be so much money in the world.

DUNOIS. There is, in England. And now tell me, all of you, which of you will lift a finger to save Joan once the English have got her? I speak first, for the army. The day after she has been dragged from her horse by a goddam or a Burgundian, and he is not struck dead: the day after she is locked in a dungeon, and the bars and bolts do not fly open at the touch of St Peter's angel: the day when the enemy finds out that she is as vulnerable as I am and not a bit more invincible, she will not be worth the life of a single soldier to us; and I will not risk that life, much as I cherish her as a companion-in-arms.

JOAN. I dont blame you, Jack: you are right.

I am not worth one soldier's life if God lets me be beaten; but France may think me worth my ransom after what God has done for her through me.

CHARLES. I tell you I have no money; and this coronation, which is all your fault, has cost me the last farthing I can borrow.

JOAN. The Church is richer than you. I put my trust in the Church.

THE ARCHBISHOP. Woman: they will drag you through the streets, and burn you as a witch.

JOAN (*running to him*). Oh, my lord, do not say that. It is impossible. I a witch!

THE ARCHBISHOP. Peter Cauchon knows his business. The University of Paris has burnt a woman for saying that what you have done was well done, and according to God.

JOAN (*bewildered*). But why? What sense is there in it? What I have done is according to God. They could not burn a woman for speaking the truth.

THE ARCHBISHOP. They did.

JOAN. But you know that she was speaking the truth. You would not let them burn me.

THE ARCHBISHOP. How could I prevent them?

JOAN. You would speak in the name of the Church. You are a great prince of the Church. I would go anywhere with your blessing to protect me.

THE ARCHBISHOP. I have no blessing for you while you are proud and disobedient.

JOAN. Oh, why will you go on saying things like that? I am not proud and disobedient. I am a poor girl, and so ignorant that I do not know A from B. How could I be proud? And how can you say that I am disobedient when I always obey my voices, because they come from God.

THE ARCHBISHOP. The voice of God on earth is the voice of the Church Militant; and all the voices that come to you are the echoes of your own wilfulness.

JOAN. It is not true.

THE ARCHBISHOP (*flushing angrily*). You tell the Archbishop in his cathedral that he lies; and yet you say you are not proud and disobedient.

JOAN. I never said you lied. It was you that as good as said my voices lied. When have they ever lied? If you will not believe in them: even if they are only the echoes of my own common-sense, are they not always right? and are not your earthly counsels always wrong?

THE ARCHBISHOP (*indignantly*). It is waste of time admonishing you.

CHARLES. It always comes back to the same thing. She is right; and everyone else is wrong.

THE ARCHBISHOP. Take this as your last warning. If you perish through setting your private judgment above the instructions of your spiritual directors, the Church disowns you, and leaves you to whatever fate your presumption may bring upon you. The Bastard has told you that if you persist in setting up your military conceit about the counsels of your commanders—

DUNOIS (*interposing*). To put it quite exactly, if you attempt to relieve the garrison in Compiègne without the same superiority in numbers you had at Orleans—

THE ARCHBISHOP. The army will disown you, and will not rescue you. And His Majesty the King has told you that the throne has not the means of ransoming you.

CHARLES. Not a penny.

THE ARCHBISHOP. You stand alone: absolutely alone, trusting to your own conceit, your own ignorance, your own headstrong presumption, your own impiety in hiding all these sins under the cloak of a trust in God. When you pass through these doors into the sunlight, the crowd will cheer you. They will bring you their little children and their invalids to heal: they will kiss your hands and feet, and do what they can, poor simple souls, to turn your head, and madden you with the self-confidence that is leading you to your destruction. But you will be none the less alone: they cannot save you. We and we only can stand between you and the stake at which our enemies have burnt that wretched woman in Paris.

JOAN (*her eyes skyward*). I have better friends and better counsel than yours.

THE ARCHBISHOP. I see that I am speaking in vain to a hardened heart. You reject our protection, and are determined to turn us all against you. In future, then, fend for yourself; and if you fail, God have mercy on your soul.

DUNOIS. That is the truth, Joan. Heed it.

JOAN. Where would you all have been now if I had heeded that sort of truth? There is no help, no counsel, in any of you. Yes: I am alone on earth: I have always been alone. My father told my brothers to drown me if I would not stay to mind his sheep while France was bleeding to death: France might perish if only our lambs were safe. I thought France would have friends at the court of the king of France; and I find only wolves fighting for pieces of her poor torn body. I thought God would have friends everywhere, because He is the friend of everyone; and in my innocence I believed that you who now cast me out would be like strong towers to keep harm from me. But I am wiser now; and nobody is any the worse for being wiser. Do not think you can frighten me by telling me that I am alone. France is alone; and God is alone; and what is my loneliness before the loneliness of my country and my God? I see now that the loneliness of God is His strength: what would He be if He listened to your jealous little counsels? Well, my loneliness shall be my strength too; it is better to be alone with God; His friendship will not fail me, nor His counsel, nor His love. In His strength I will dare, and dare, and dare, until I die. I will go out now to the common people, and let the love in their eyes comfort me for the hate in yours. You will all be glad to see me burnt; but if I go through the fire I shall go through it to their hearts for ever and ever. And so, God be with me!

(*She goes from them. They stare after her in glum silence for a moment. Then* GILLES DE RAIS *twirls his beard.*)

BLUEBEARD. You know, the woman is quite impossible. I dont dislike her, really; but what are you to do with such a character?

DUNOIS. As God is my judge, if she fell into the Loire I would jump in in full armor to fish her out. But if she plays the fool at Compiègne, and gets caught, I must leave her to her doom.

LA HIRE. Then you had better chain me up; for I could follow her to hell when the spirit rises in her like that.

THE ARCHBISHOP. She disturbs my judgment too: there is a dangerous power in her outbursts. But the pit is open at her feet; and for good or evil we cannot turn her from it.

CHARLES. If only she would keep quiet, or go home!

(*They follow her dispiritedly.*)

Scene VI

Rouen, 30th May 1431. A great stone hall in the castle, arranged for a trial-at-law, but not a trial-by-jury, the court being the Bishop's court with the Inquisition participating: hence there are two raised chairs side by side for the Bishop and the Inquisitor as judges. Rows of chairs radiating from them at an obtuse angle are for the canons, the doctors of law and theology, and the Dominican monks, who act as assessors. In the angle is a table for the scribes, with stools. There is also a heavy rough wooden stool for the prisoner. All these are at the inner end of the hall. The further end is open to the courtyard through a row of arches. The court is shielded from the weather by screens and curtains.

Looking down the great hall from the middle of the inner end, the judicial chairs and scribes' tables are to the right. The prisoner's stool is to the left. There are arched doors right and left. It is a fine sunshiny May morning.

WARWICK *comes in through the arched doorway on the judges' side, followed by his page.*

THE PAGE (*pertly*). I suppose your lordship is aware that we have no business here. This is an ecclesiastical court; and we are only the secular arm.

WARWICK. I am aware of that fact. Will it please your impudence to find the Bishop of Beauvais for me, and give him a hint that he can have a word with me here before the trial, if he wishes?

THE PAGE (*going*). Yes, my lord.

WARWICK. And mind you behave yourself. Do not address him as Pious Peter.

THE PAGE. No, my lord. I shall be kind to him, because, when The Maid is brought in, Pious Peter will have to pick a peck of pickled pepper.

(CAUCHON *enters through the same door with a Dominican monk and a canon, the latter carrying a brief.*)

THE PAGE. The Right Reverend his lordship the Bishop of Beauvais. And two other reverend gentlemen.

WARWICK. Get out; and see that we are not interrupted.

THE PAGE. Right, my lord (*he vanishes airily*).

CAUCHON. I wish your lordship good-morrow.

WARWICK. Good-morrow to your lordship. Have I had the pleasure of meeting your friends before? I think not.

CAUCHON (*introducing the monk, who is on his right*). This, my lord, is Brother John Lemaître, of the order of St Dominic. He is acting as deputy for the Chief Inquisitor into the evil of heresy in France. Brother John: the Earl of Warwick.

WARWICK. Your Reverence is most welcome. We have no Inquisitor in England, unfortunately; though we miss him greatly, especially on occassions like the present.

(*The Inquisitor smiles patiently, and bows. He is a mild elderly gentleman, but has evident reserves of authority and firmness.*)

CAUCHON (*introducing the Canon, who is on his left*). This gentleman is Canon John D'Estivet, of the Chapter of Bayeux. He is acting as Promoter.

WARWICK. Promoter?

CAUCHON. Prosecutor, you would call him in civil law.

WARWICK. Ah! prosecutor. Quite, quite. I am very glad to make your acquaintance, Canon D'Estivet.

(*D'ESTIVET bows. He is on the young side of the middle age, well mannered, but vulpine beneath his veneer.*)

WARWICK. May I ask what stage the proceedings have reached? It is now more than nine months since The Maid was captured at Compiègne by the Burgundians. It is fully four months since I bought her from the Burgundians for a very handsome sum, solely that she might be brought to justice. It is very nearly three months since I delivered her up to you, my Lord Bishop, as a person suspected of heresy. May I suggest that you are taking a rather unconscionable time to make up your minds about a very plain case? Is this trial never going to end?

THE INQUISITOR (*smiling*). It has not yet begun, my lord.

WARWICK. Not yet begun! Why, you have been at it eleven weeks!

CAUCHON. We have not been idle, my lord. We have held fifteen examinations of The Maid: six public and nine private.

THE INQUISITOR (*always patiently smiling*). You see, my lord, I have been present at only two of these examinations. They were proceedings of the Bishop's court solely, and not of the Holy Office. I have only just decided to associate myself—that is, to associate the Holy Inquisition—with the Bishop's court. I did not at first think that this was a case of heresy at all. I regarded it as a political case, and The Maid as a prisoner of war. But having now been present at two of the examinations, I must admit that this seems to be one of the gravest cases of heresy within my experience. Therefore everything is now in order, and we proceed to trial this morning. (*He moves towards the judicial chairs*)

CAUCHON. This moment, if your lordship's convenience allows.

WARWICK (*graciously*). Well, that is good news, gentlemen. I will not attempt to conceal from you that our patience was becoming strained.

CAUCHON. So I gathered from the threats of your soldiers to drown those of our people who favor The Maid.

WARWICK. Dear me! At all events their intentions were friendly to you, my lord.

CAUCHON (*sternly*). I hope not. I am determined that the woman shall have a fair hearing. The justice of the Church is not a mockery, my lord.

THE INQUISITOR (*returning*). Never has there been a fairer examination within my experience, my lord. The Maid needs no lawyers to take her part: she will be tried by her most faithful friends, all ardently desirous to save her soul from perdition.

D'ESTIVET. Sir: I am the Promoter; and it has been my painful duty to present the case against the girl; but believe me, I would throw up my case today and hasten to her defence if I did not know that men far my superiors in learning and piety, in eloquence and persuasiveness, have been sent to reason with her, to explain to her the danger she is running, and the ease with which she may avoid it. (*Suddenly bursting into forensic eloquence, to the disgust of CAUCHON and the Inquisitor, who have listened to him so far with patronizing approval*) Men have dared to say that we are acting from hate; but God is our witness that they lie. Have we tortured her? No. Have we ceased to exhort her; to implore her to have pity on herself; to come to the bosom of her Church as an erring but beloved child? Have we—

CAUCHON (*interrupting drily*). Take care, Canon. All that you say is true; but if you make his lordship believe it I will not answer for your life, and hardly for my own.

WARWICK (*deprecating, but by no means denyin*). Oh, my lord, you are very hard on us poor English. But we certainly do not share your pious desire to save The Maid: in fact I tell you now plainly that her death is a political necessity which I regret but cannot help. If the Church lets her go—

CAUCHON (*with fierce and menacing pride*). If the Church lets her go, woe to the man, were he the Emperor himself, who dares lay a finger on her! The Church is not subject to political necessity, my lord.

THE INQUISITOR (*interposing smoothly*). You need have no anxiety about the result, my lord. You have an invincible ally in the matter: one who is far more determined than you that she shall burn.

WARWICK. And who is this very convenient partisan, may I ask?

THE INQUISITOR. The Maid herself. Unless you put a gag in her mouth you cannot prevent her from convicting herself ten times over every time she opens it.

D'ESTIVET. That is perfectly true, my lord. My hair bristles on my head when I hear so young a creature utter such blasphemies.

WARWICK. Well, by all means do your best for her if you are quite sure it will be of no avail. (*Looking hard at* CAUCHON) I should be sorry to have to act without the blessing of the Church.

CAUCHON (*with a mixture of cynical admiration and contempt*). And yet they say Englishmen are hypocrites! You play for your side, my lord, even at the peril of your soul. I cannot but admire such devotion; but I dare not go so far myself. I fear damnation.

WARWICK. If we feared anything we could never govern England, my lord. Shall I send your people in to you?

CAUCHON. Yes: it will be very good of your

lordship to withdraw and allow the court to assemble.

(WARWICK *turns on his heel, and goes out through the courtyard.* CAUCHON *takes one of the judicial seats; and* D'ESTIVET *sits at the scribes' table, studying his brief.*)

CAUCHON (*casually, as he makes himself comfortable*). What scoundrels these English nobles are!

THE INQUISITOR (*taking the other judicial chair on* CAUCHON'S *left*). All secular power makes men scoundrels. They are not trained for the work; and they have not the Apostolic Succession. Our own nobles are just as bad.

(*The* BISHOP'S *assessors hurry into the hall, headed by* CHAPLAIN DE STOGUMBER *and* CANON DE COURCELLES, *a young priest of 30. The scribes sit at the table, leaving a chair vacant opposite* D'ESTIVET. *Some of the assessors take their seats: others stand chatting, waiting for the proceedings to begin formally.* DE STOGUMBER, *aggrieved and obstinate, will not take his seat: neither will the* CANON, *who stands on his right.*)

CAUCHON. Good morning, Master de Stogumber. (*To the* INQUISITOR) Chaplain to the Cardinal of England.

THE CHAPLAIN (*correcting him*). Of Winchester, my lord. I have to make a protest, my lord.

CAUCHON. You make a great many.

THE CHAPLAIN. I am not without support, my lord. Here is Master de Courcelles, Canon of Paris, who associates himself with me in my protest.

CAUCHON. Well, what is the matter?

THE CHAPLAIN (*sulkily*). Speak you, Master de Courcelles, since I do not seem to enjoy his lordship's confidence. (*He sits down in dudgeon next to* CAUCHON, *on his right*)

COURCELLES. My lord: we have been at great pains to draw up an indictment of The Maid on sixty-four counts. We are now told that they have been reduced, without consulting us.

THE INQUISITOR. Master de Courcelles: I am the culprit. I am overwhelmed with admiration for the zeal displayed in your sixty-four counts; but in accusing a heretic, as in other things, enough is enough. Also you must remember that all the members of the court are not so subtle and profound as you, and that some of your very great learning might appear to them to be very great nonsense. Therefore I have thought it well to have your sixty-four articles cut down to twelve—

COURCELLES (*thunderstruck*). Twelve!!!

THE INQUISITOR. Twelve will, believe me, be quite enough for your purpose.

THE CHAPLAIN. But some of the most important points have been reduced almost to nothing. For instance, The Maid has actually declared that the blessed saints Margaret and Catherine, and the holy Archangel Michael, spoke to her in French. That is a vital point.

THE INQUISITOR. You think, doubtless, that they should have spoken in Latin?

CAUCHON. No: he thinks they should have spoken in English.

THE CHAPLAIN. Naturally, my lord.

THE INQUISITOR. Well, as we are all here agreed, I think, that these voices of The Maid are the voices of evil spirits tempting her to her damnation, it would not be very courteous to you, Master de Stogumber, or to the King of England, to assume that English is the devil's native language. So let it pass. The matter is not wholly omitted from the twelve articles. Pray take your places, gentlemen; and let us proceed to business.

(*All who have not taken their seats, do so.*)

THE CHAPLAIN. Well, I protest. That is all.

COURCELLES. I think it hard that all our work should go for nothing. It is only another example of the diabolical influence which this woman exercises over the court. (*He takes his chair, which is on the* CHAPLAIN'S *right*)

CAUCHON. Do you suggest that I am under diabolical influence?

COURCELLES. I suggest nothing, my lord. But it seems to me that there is a conspiracy here to hush up the fact that The Maid stole the Bishop of Senlis's horse.

CAUCHON (*keeping his temper with difficulty*). This is not a police court. Are we to waste our time on such rubbish?

COURCELLES (*rising, shocked*). My lord: do you call the Bishop's horse rubbish?

THE INQUISITOR (*blandly*). Master de Cour-

celles: The Maid alleges that she paid handsomely for the Bishop's horse, and that if he did not get the money the fault was not hers. As that may be true, the point is one on which The Maid may well be acquitted.

COURCELLES. Yes, if it were an ordinary horse. But the Bishop's horse! how can she be acquitted for that? (*He sits down again, bewildered and discouraged*)

THE INQUISITOR. I submit to you, with great respect, that if we persist in trying The Maid on trumpery issues on which we may have to declare her innocent, she may escape us on the great main issue of heresy, on which she seems so far to insist on her own guilt. I will ask you, therefore, to say nothing, when The Maid is brought before us, of these stealings of horses, and dancings round fairy trees with the village children, and prayings at haunted wells, and a dozen other things which you were diligently inquiring into until my arrival. There is not a village girl in France against whom you could not prove such things: they all dance round haunted trees, and pray at magic wells. Some of them would steal the Pope's horse if they got the chance. Heresy, gentlemen, heresy is the charge we have to try. The detection and suppression of heresy is my peculiar business: I am here as an inquisitor, not as an ordinary magistrate. Stick to the heresy, gentlemen; and leave the other matters alone.

CAUCHON. I may say that we have sent to the girl's village to make inquiries about her, and there is practically nothing serious against her.

		Nothing serious,
THE CHAPLAIN	(*rising and clamoring together*).	my lord—
COURCELLES		What! The fairy tree not—

CAUCHON (*out of patience*). Be silent, gentlemen; or speak one at a time.

(COURCELLES *collapses into his chair, intimidated.*)

THE CHAPLAIN (*sulkily resuming his seat*). That is what The Maid said to us last Friday.

CAUCHON. I wish you had followed her counsel, sir. When I say nothing serious, I mean nothing that men of sufficiently large mind to conduct an inquiry like this would consider serious. I agree with my colleague the Inquisitor that it is on the count of heresy that we must proceed.

LADVENU (*a young but ascetically fine-drawn*

Dominican who is sitting next COURCELLES, *on his right*). But is there any great harm in the girl's heresy? Is it not merely her simplicity? Many saints have said as much as Joan.

THE INQUISITOR (*dropping his blandness and speaking very gravely*). Brother Martin: if you had seen what I have seen of heresy, you would not think it a light thing even in its most apparently harmless and even lovable and pious origins. Heresy begins with people who are to all appearance better than their neighbors. A gentle and pious girl, or a young man who has obeyed the command of our Lord by giving all his riches to the poor, and putting on the garb of poverty, the life of austerity, and the rule of humility and charity, may be the founder of a heresy that will wreck both Church and Empire if not ruthlessly stamped out in time. The records of the Holy Inquisition are full of histories we dare not give to the world, because they are beyond the belief of honest men and innocent women; yet they all began with saintly simpletons. I have seen this again and again. Mark what I say: the woman who quarrels with her clothes, and puts on the dress of a man, is like the man who throws off his fur gown and dresses like John the Baptist: they are followed, as surely as the night follows the day, by bands of wild women and men who refuse to wear any clothes at all. When maids will neither marry nor take regular vows, and men reject marriage and exalt their lusts into divine inspirations, then, as surely as the summer follows the spring, they begin with polygamy, and end by incest. Heresy at first seems innocent and even laudable; but it ends in such a monstrous horror of unnatural wickedness that the most tender-hearted among you, if you saw it at work as I have seen it, would clamor against the mercy of the Church in dealing with it. For two hundred years the Holy Office has striven with these diabolical madnesses; and it knows that they begin always by vain and ignorant persons setting up their own judgment against the Church, and taking it upon themselves to be the interpreters of God's will. You must not fall into the common error of mistaking these simpletons for liars and hypocrites. They believe honestly and sincerely that their diabolical inspiration is divine. Therefore you must be on your guard against your natural compassion. You are all, I hope, merciful men: how else could you have devoted your lives to the service of our gentle Savior? You are going to see before you a young girl, pious and chaste; for I must tell you, gentlemen, that the things said of her by our English friends are supported by no evidence, whilst there is abundant testimony that her excesses have been excesses of religion and charity and not of worldliness and wantonness. This girl is not one of those whose hard features are the sign of hard hearts, and whose brazen looks and lewd demeanor condemn them before they are accused. The devilish pride that has led her into her present peril has left no mark on her countenance. Strange as it may seem to you, it has even left no mark on her character outside those special matters in which she is proud; so that you will see a diabolical pride and a natural humility seated side by side in the selfsame soul. Therefore be on your guard. God forbid that I should tell you to harden your hearts; for her punishment if we condemn her will be so cruel that we should forfeit our own hope of divine mercy were there one grain of malice against her in our hearts. But if you hate cruelty—and if any man here does not hate it I command him on his soul's salvation to quit this holy court—I say, if you hate cruelty, remember that nothing is so cruel in its consequences as the toleration of heresy. Remember also that no court of law can be so cruel as the common people are to those whom they suspect of heresy. The heretic in the hands of the Holy Office is safe from violence, is assured of a fair trial, and cannot suffer death, even when guilty, if repentance follows sin. Innumerable lives of heretics have been saved because the Holy Office has taken them out of the hands of the people, and because the people have yielded them up, knowing that the Holy Office would deal with them. Before the Holy Inquisition existed, and even now when its officers are not within reach, the unfortunate wretch suspected of heresy, perhaps quite ignorantly and injustly, is stoned, torn in pieces, drowned, burned in his house with all his innocent children, without a trial, unshriven, unburied save as a dog is buried: all of them deeds hateful to God and most cruel to man. Gentlemen: I am compassionate by nature as well as by my profession; and though the work I have to do may seem cruel to those who do not know how much more cruel it would be to leave it undone, I would go to the stake myself sooner than do it if I did not know its righteousness, its necessity, its essential mercy. I ask you to address yourself to this trial in that conviction. Anger is a bad counsellor: cast out anger. Pity is sometimes worse: cast out pity. But do not cast out mercy. Remember only that justice comes first. Have you anything to say, my lord, before we proceed to trial?

CAUCHON. You have spoken for me, and spoken better than I could. I do not see how any sane man could disagree with a word that has fallen from you. But this I will add. The crude heresies of which you have told us are horrible; but their horror is like that of the black death: they rage for a while and then die out, because sound and sensible men will not under any incitement be reconciled to nakedness and incest and polygamy and the like. But we are confronted today throughout Europe with a heresy that is spreading among men not weak in mind nor diseased in brain: nay, the stronger the mind, the more obstinate the heretic. It is neither discredited by fantastic extremes nor corrupted by the common lusts of the flesh; but it, too, sets up the private judgment of the single erring mortal against the considered wisdom and experience of the Church. The mighty structure of Catholic Christendom will never be shaken by naked madmen or by the sins of Moab and Ammon. But it may be betrayed from within, and brought to barbarous ruin and desolation, by this arch heresy which the English Commander calls Protestantism.

THE ASSESSORS (whispering). Protestantism! What was that? What does the Bishop mean? Is it a new heresy? The English Commander, he said. Did you ever hear of Protestantism? etc., etc.

CAUCHON (continuing). And that reminds me. What provision has the Earl of Warwick made for the defence of the secular arm should The Maid prove obdurate, and the people be moved to pity her?

THE CHAPLAIN. Have no fear on that score, my lord. The noble earl has eight hundred men-at-arms at the gates. She will not slip through our English fingers even if the whole city be on her side.

CAUCHON (revolted). Will you not add, God grant that she repent and purge her sin?

THE CHAPLAIN. That does not seem to me to be consistent; but of course I agree with your lordship.

CAUCHON (giving him up with a shrug of contempt). The court sits.

THE INQUISITOR. Let the accused be brought in.

LADVENU (calling). The accused. Let her be brought in.

(JOAN, chained by the ankles, is brought in through the arched door behind the prisoner's stool by a guard of English soldiers. With them is the Executioner and his assistants. They lead her to the prisoner's stool, and place themselves behind it after taking off her chain. She wears a page's black suit. Her long imprisonment and the strain of the examinations which have preceded the trial have left their mark on her; but her vitality still holds; she confronts the court unabashed, without a trace of the awe which their formal solemnity seems to require for the complete success of its impressiveness.)

THE INQUISITOR (kindly). Sit down, Joan. (She sits on the prisoner's stool) You look very pale today. Are you not well?

JOAN. Thank you kindly: I am well enough. But the Bishop sent me some carp; and it made me ill.

CAUCHON. I am sorry. I told them to see that it was fresh.

JOAN. You meant to be good to me, I know; but it is a fish that does not agree with me. The English thought you were trying to poison me—

CAUCHON ⎰ (together). ⎱ What!
THE CHAPLAIN ⎱ ⎰ No, my lord.

JOAN (continuing). They are determined that I shall be burnt as a witch; and they sent their doctor to cure me; but he was forbidden to bleed me because the silly people believe that a witch's witchery leaves her if she is bled; so he only called me filthy names. Why do you leave me in the hands of the English? I should be in the hands of the Church. And why must I be chained by the feet to a log of wood? Are you afraid I will fly away?

D'ESTIVET (harshly). Woman: it is not for you to question the court: it is for us to question you.

COURCELLES. When you were left unchained,

did you not try to escape by jumping from a tower sixty feet high? If you cannot fly like a witch, how is it that you are still alive?

JOAN. I suppose because the tower was not so high then. It has grown higher every day since you began asking me questions about it.

D'ESTIVET. Why did you jump from the tower?

JOAN. How do you know that I jumped?

D'ESTIVET. You were found lying in the moat. Why did you leave the tower?

JOAN. Why would anybody leave a prison if they could get out?

D'ESTIVET. You tried to escape?

JOAN. Of course I did; and not for the first time either. If you leave the door of the cage open the bird will fly out.

D'ESTIVET (*rising*). That is a confession of heresy. I call the attention of the court to it.

JOAN. Heresy, he calls it! Am I a heretic because I try to escape from prison?

D'ESTIVET. Assuredly, if you are in the hands of the Church, and you wilfully take yourself out of its hands, you are deserting the Church; and that is heresy.

JOAN. It is great nonsense. Nobody could be such a fool as to think that.

D'ESTIVET. You hear, my lord, how I am reviled in the execution of my duty by this woman. (*He sits down indignantly*)

CAUCHON. I have warned you before, Joan, that you are doing yourself no good by these pert answers.

JOAN. But you will not talk sense to me. I am reasonable if you will be reasonable.

THE INQUISITOR (*interposing*). This is not yet in order. You forget, Master Promoter, that the proceedings have not been formally opened. The time for questions is after she has sworn on the Gospels to tell us the whole truth.

JOAN. You say this to me every time. I have said again and again that I will tell you all that concerns this trial. But I cannot tell you the whole truth: God does not allow the whole truth to be told. You do not understand it when I tell it. It is an old saying that he who tells too much truth is sure to be hanged. I am weary of this argument: we have been over it nine times already. I have sworn as much as I will swear; and I will swear no more.

COURCELLES. My lord: she should be put to the torture.

THE INQUISITOR. You hear, Joan? That is what happens to the obdurate. Think before you answer. Has she been shewn the instruments?

THE EXECUTIONER. They are ready, my lord. She has seen them.

JOAN. If you tear me limb from limb until you separate my soul from my body you will get nothing out of me beyond what I have told you. What more is there to tell that you could understand? Besides, I cannot bear to be hurt; and if you hurt me I will say anything you like to stop the pain. But I will take it all back afterwards; so what is the use of it?

LADVENU. There is much in that. We should proceed mercifully.

COURCELLES. But the torture is customary.

THE INQUISITOR. It must not be applied wantonly. If the accused will confess voluntarily, then its use cannot be justified.

COURCELLES. But this is unusual and irregular. She refuses to take the oath.

LADVENU (*disgusted*). Do you want to torture the girl for the mere pleasure of it?

COURCELLES (*bewildered*). But it is not a pleasure. It is the law. It is customary. It is always done.

THE INQUISITOR. That is not so, Master, except when the inquiries are carried on by people who do not know their legal business.

COURCELLES. But the woman is a heretic. I assure you it is always done.

CAUCHON (*decisively*). It will not be done today if it is not necessary. Let there be an end of this. I will not have it said that we proceeded on forced confessions. We have sent our best preachers and doctors to this woman to exhort and implore her to save her soul and body from the fire: we shall not now send the executioner to thrust her into it.

COURCELLES. Your lordship is merciful, of course. But it is a great responsibility to depart from the usual practice.

JOAN. Thou art a rare noodle, Master. Do what was done last time is thy rule, eh?

COURCELLES (*rising*). Thou wanton: dost thou dare call me noodle?

THE INQUISITOR. Patience, Master, patience: I fear you will soon be only too terribly avenged.

COURCELLES (*mutters*). Noodle indeed! (*He

sits down, much discontented)

THE INQUISITOR. Meanwhile, let us not be moved by the rough side of a shepherd lass's tongue.

JOAN. Nay: I am no shepherd lass, though I have helped with the sheep like anyone else. I will do a lady's work in the house—spin or weave—against any woman in Rouen.

THE INQUISITOR. This is not a time for vanity, Joan. You stand in great peril.

JOAN. I know it: have I not been punished for my vanity? If I had not worn my cloth of gold surcoat in battle like a fool, that Burgundian soldier would never have pulled me backwards off my horse; and I should not have been here.

THE CHAPLAIN. If you are so clever at woman's work why do you not stay at home and do it?

JOAN. There are plenty of other women to do it; but there is nobody to do my work.

CAUCHON. Come! we are wasting time on trifles. Joan: I am going to put a most solemn question to you. Take care how you answer; for your life and salvation are at stake on it. Will you for all you have said and done, be it good or bad, accept the judgment of God's Church on earth? More especially as to the acts and words that are imputed to you in this trial by the Promoter here, will you submit your case to the inspired interpretation of the Church Militant?

JOAN. I am faithful child of the Church. I will obey the Church—

CAUCHON (*hopefully leaning forward*). You will?

JOAN. —provided it does not command anything impossible.

(CAUCHON *sinks back in his chair with a heavy sigh. The* INQUISITOR *purses his lips and frowns.* LADVENU *shakes his head pitifully.*)

D'ESTIVET. She imputes to the Church the error and folly of commanding the impossible.

JOAN. If you command me to declare that all that I have done and said, and all the visions and revelations I have had, were not from God, then that is impossible: I will not declare it for anything in the world. What God made me do I will never go back on; and what He has commanded or shall command I will not fail to do in spite of any man alive. That is what I mean by impossible. And in case the Church should bid me do anything contrary to the command I have from God, I will not consent to it, no matter what it may be.

THE ASSESSORS (*shocked and indignant*). Oh! The Church contrary to God! What do you say now? Flat heresy. This is beyond everything, etc., etc.

D'ESTIVET (*throwing down his brief*). My lord: do you need anything more than this?

CAUCHON. Woman: you have said enough to burn ten heretics. Will you not be warned? Will you not understand?

THE INQUISITOR. If the Church Militant tells you that your revelations and visions are sent by the devil to tempt you to your damnation, will you not believe that the Church is wiser than you?

JOAN. I believe that God is wiser than I; and it is His commands that I will do. All the things that you call my crimes have come to me by the command of God. I say that I have done them by the order of God: it is impossible for me to say anything else. If any Churchman says the contrary I shall not mind him: I shall mind God alone, whose command I always follow.

LADVENU (*pleading with her urgently*). You do not know what you are saying, child. Do you want to kill yourself? Listen. Do you not believe that you are subject to the Church of God on earth?

JOAN. Yes. When have I ever denied it?

LADVENU. Good. That means, does it not, that you are subject to our Lord the Pope, to the cardinals, the archbishops, and the bishops for whom his lordship stands here today?

JOAN. God must be served first.

D'ESTIVET. Then your voices command you not to submit yourself to the Church Militant?

JOAN. My voices do not tell me to disobey the Church; but God must be served first.

CAUCHON. And you, and not the Church, are to be the judge?

JOAN. What other judgment can I judge by but my own?

THE ASSESSORS (*scandalized*). Oh! (*They cannot find words*)

CAUCHON. Out of your own mouth you have condemned yourself. We have striven for your salvation to the verge of sinning ourselves: we have opened the door to you again and again; and you have shut it in our faces and in the face of God. Dare you pretend, after what you have said, that you are in a state of grace?

JOAN. If I am not, may God bring me to it: if I am, may God keep me in it!

LADVENU. That is a very good reply, my lord.

COURCELLES. Were you in a state of grace when you stole the Bishop's horse?

CAUCHON (rising in a fury). Oh, devil take the Bishop's horse and you too! We are here to try a case of heresy; and no sooner do we come to the root of the matter than we are thrown back by idiots who understand nothing but horses. (Trembling with rage, he forces himself to sit down)

THE INQUISITOR. Gentlemen, gentlemen: in clinging to these small issues you are The Maid's best advocates. I am not surprised that his lordship has lost patience with you. What does the Promoter say? Does he press these trumpery matters?

D'ESTIVET. I am bound by my office to press everything; but when the woman confesses a heresy that must bring upon her the doom of excommunication, of what consequence is it that she has been guilty also of offences which expose her to minor penances? I share the impatience of his lordship as to these minor charges. Only, with great respect, I must emphasize the gravity of two very horrible and blasphemous crimes which she does not deny. First, she has intercourse with evil spirits, and is therefore a sorceress. Second, she wears men's clothes, which is indecent, unnatural, and abominable; and in spite of our most earnest remonstrances and entreaties, she will not change them even to receive the sacrament.

JOAN. Is the blessed St Catherine an evil spirit? Is St Margaret? Is Michael the Archangel?

COURCELLES. How do you know that the spirit which appears to you is an archangel? Does he not appear to you as a naked man?

JOAN. Do you think God cannot afford clothes for him?

(The ASSESSORS cannot help smiling, especially as the joke is against COURCELLES.)

LADVENU. Well answered, Joan.

THE INQUISITOR. It is, in effect, well answered. But no evil spirit would be so simple as to appear to a young girl in a guise that would scandalize her when he meant her to take him for a messenger from the Most High. Joan: the Church instructs you that these apparitions are demons seeking your soul's perdition. Do you accept the instruction of the Church?

JOAN. I accept the messenger of God. How could any faithful believer in the Church refuse him?

CAUCHON. Wretched woman: again I ask you, do you know what you are saying?

THE INQUISITOR. You wrestle in vain with the devil for her soul, my lord: she will not be saved. Now as to this matter of the man's dress. For the last time, will you put off that impudent attire, and dress as becomes your sex?

JOAN. I will not.

D'ESTIVET (pouncing). The sin of disobedience, my lord.

JOAN (distressed). But my voices tell me I must dress as a soldier.

LADVENU. Joan, Joan: does not that prove to you that the voices are the voices of evil spirits? Can you suggest to us one good reason why an angel of God should give you such shameless advice?

JOAN. Why, yes: what can be plainer commonsense? I was a soldier living among soldiers. I am a prisoner guarded by soldiers. If I were to dress as a woman they would think of me as a woman; and then what would become of me? If I dress as a soldier they think of me as a soldier, and I can live with them as I do at home with my brothers. That is why St Catherine tells me I must not dress as a woman until she gives me leave.

COURCELLES. When will she give you leave?

JOAN. When you take me out of the hands of the English soldiers. I have told you that I should be in the hands of the Church, and not left night and day with four soldiers of the Earl of Warwick. Do you want me to live with them in petticoats?

LADVENU. My lord: what she says is, God knows, very wrong and shocking; but there is a grain of worldly sense in it such as might impose on a simple village maiden.

JOAN. If we were as simple in the village as you are in your courts and places, there would soon be no wheat to make bread for you.

CAUCHON. That is the thanks you get for trying to save her, Brother Martin.

LADVENU. Joan: we are all trying to save you. His lordship is trying to save you. The Inquisitor could not be more just to you if you were his own daughter. But you are blinded by a terrible pride and self-sufficiency.

JOAN. Why do you say that? I have said nothing wrong. I cannot understand.

THE INQUISITOR. The blessed St Athanasius has laid it down in his creed that those who cannot understand are damned. It is not enough to be simple. It is not enough even to be what simple people call good. The simplicity of a darkened mind is no better than the simplicity of a beast.

JOAN. There is great wisdom in the simplicity of a beast, let me tell you; and sometimes great foolishness in the wisdom of scholars.

LADVENU. We know that, Joan: we are not so foolish as you think us. Try to resist the temptation to make pert replies to us. Do you see that man who stands behind you (*he indicates* THE EXECUTIONER)?

JOAN (*turning and looking at the man*). Your torturer? But the Bishop said I was not to be tortured.

LADVENU. You are not to be tortured because you have confessed everything that is necessary to your condemnation. That man is not only the torturer: he is also the Executioner. Executioner: let The Maid hear your answers to my questions. Are you prepared for the burning of a heretic this day?

THE EXECUTIONER. Yes, Master.

LADVENU. Is the stake ready?

THE EXECUTIONER. It is. In the market-place. The English have built it too high for me to get near her and make the death easier. It will be a cruel death.

JOAN (*horrified*). But you are not going to burn me now?

THE INQUISITOR. You realize it at last.

LADVENU. There are eight hundred English soldiers waiting to take you to the market-place the moment the sentence of excommunication has passed the lips of your judges. You are within a few short moments of that doom.

JOAN (*looking round desperately for rescue*). Oh God!

LADVENU. Do not despair, Joan. The Church is merciful. You can save yourself.

JOAN (*hopefully*). Yes: my voices promised me I should not be burnt. St. Catherine bade me be bold.

CAUCHON. Woman: are you quite mad? Do you not yet see that your voices have deceived you?

JOAN. Oh no: that is impossible.

CAUCHON. Impossible! They have led you straight to your excommunication, and to the stake which is there waiting for you.

LADVENU (*pressing the point hard*). Have they kept a single promise to you since you were taken at Compiègne? The devil has betrayed you. The Church holds out its arms to you.

JOAN (*despairing*). Oh, it is true: it is true: my voices have deceived me. I have been mocked by devils: my faith is broken. I have dared and dared; but only a fool will walk into a fire: God, who gave me my commonsense, cannot will me to do that.

LADVENU. Now God be praised that He has saved you at the eleventh hour! (*He hurries to the vacant seat at the scribes' table, and snatches a sheet of paper, on which he sets to work writing eagerly*)

CAUCHON. Amen!

JOAN. What must I do?

CAUCHON. You must sign a solemn recantation of your heresy.

JOAN. Sign? That means to write my name. I cannot write.

CAUCHON. You have signed many letters before.

JOAN. Yes; but someone held my hand and guided the pen. I can make my mark.

THE CHAPLAIN (*who has been listening with growing alarm and indignation*). My lord: do you mean that you are going to allow this woman to escape us?

THE INQUISITOR. The law must take its course, Master de Stogumber. And you know the law.

THE CHAPLAIN (*rising, purple with fury*). I know that there is no faith in a Frenchman. (*Tumult, which he shouts down*) I know what my lord the Cardinal of Winchester will say when he hears of this. I know what the Earl of Warwick will do when he learns that you intend to betray him. There are eight hundred men at the gate who will see that this abominable witch is burnt in spite of your teeth.

THE ASSESSORS (*meanwhile*). What is this?

What did he say? He accuses us of treachery! This is past bearing. No faith in a Frenchman! Did you hear that? This is an intolerable fellow. Who is he? Is this what English Churchmen are like? He must be mad or drunk, etc., etc.

THE INQUISITOR (*rising*). Silence, pray! Gentlemen: pray silence! Master Chaplain: bethink you a moment of your holy office: of what you are, and where you are. I direct you to sit down.

THE CHAPLAIN (*folding his arms doggedly, his face working convulsively*). I will NOT sit down.

CAUCHON. Master Inquisitor: this man has called me a traitor to my face before now.

THE CHAPLAIN. So you are a traitor. You are all traitors. You have been doing nothing but begging this damnable witch on your knees to recant all through this trial.

THE INQUISITOR (*placidly resuming his seat*). If you will not sit, you must stand: that is all.

THE CHAPLAIN. I will NOT stand (*he flings himself back into his chair*).

LADVENU (*rising with the paper in his hand*). My lord: here is the form of recantation for The Maid to sign.

CAUCHON. Read it to her.

JOAN. Do not trouble. I will sign it.

THE INQUISITOR. Woman: you must know what you are putting your hand to. Read it to her, Brother Martin. And let all be silent.

LADVENU (*reading quietly*). 'I, Joan, commonly called The Maid, a miserable sinner, do confess that I have most grievously sinned in the following articles. I have pretended to have revelations from God and the angels and the blessed saints, and perversely rejected the Church's warnings that these were temptations by demons. I have blasphemed abominably by wearing an immodest dress, contrary to the Holy Scripture and the canons of the Church. Also I have clipped my hair in the style of a man, and, against all the duties which have made my sex specially acceptable in heaven, have taken up the sword, even to the shedding of human blood, inciting men to slay each other, invoking evil spirits to delude them, and stubbornly and most blasphemously imputing these sins to Almighty God. I confess to the sin of sedition, to the sin of idolatry, to the sin of disobedience, to the sin of pride, and to the sin of heresy. All of which sins I now renounce and abjure and depart from,

humbly thanking you Doctors and Masters who have brought me back to the truth and into the grace of our Lord. And I will never return to my errors, but will remain in communion with our Holy Church and in obedience to our Holy Father the Pope of Rome. All this I swear by God Almighty and the Holy Gospels, in witness whereto I sign my name to this recantation.'

THE INQUISITOR. You understand this, Joan?

JOAN (*listless*). It is plain enough, sir.

THE INQUISITOR. And it is true?

JOAN. It may be true. If it were not true, the fire would not be ready for me in the marketplace.

LADVENU (*taking up his pen and a book, and going to her quickly lest she should compromise herself again*). Come, child: let me guide your hand. Take the pen. (*She does so; and they begin to write, using the book as a desk*) J.E.H.A.N.E. So. Now make your mark by yourself.

JOAN (*makes her mark, and gives him back the pen, tormented by the rebellion of her soul against her mind and body*). There!

LADVENU (*replacing the pen on the table, and handing the recantation to* CAUCHON *with a reverence*). Praise be to God, my brothers, the lamb has returned to the flock; and the shepherd rejoices in her more than in ninety and nine just persons. (*He returns to his seat*)

THE INQUISITOR (*taking the paper from* CAUCHON). We declare thee by this act set free from the danger of excommunication in which thou stoodest. (*He throws the paper down to the table*)

JOAN. I thank you.

THE INQUISITOR. But because thou has sinned most presumptuously against God and the Holy Church, and that thou mayst repent thy errors in solitary contemplation, and be shielded from all temptation to return to them, we, for the good of thy soul, and for a penance that may wipe out thy sins and bring thee finally unspotted to the throne of grace, do condemn thee to eat the bread of sorrow and drink the water of affliction to the end of thy earthly days in perpetual imprisonment.

JOAN (*rising in consternation and terrible anger*). Perpetual imprisonment! Am I not then to be set free?

LADVENU (*mildly shocked*). Set free, child,

after such wickedness as yours! What are you dreaming of?

JOAN. Give me that writing. (*She rushes to the table; snatches up the paper; and tears it into fragments*) Light your fire: do you think I dread it as much as the life of a rat in a hole? My voices were right.

LADVENU. Joan! Joan!

JOAN. Yes: they told me you were fools (*the word gives great offence*), and that I was not to listen to your fine words nor trust to your charity. You promised me my life; but you lied (*indignant exclamations*). You think that life is nothing but not being stone dead. It is not the bread and water I fear: I can live on bread: when have I asked for more? It is no hardship to drink water if the water be clean. Bread has no sorrow for me, and water no affliction. But to shut me from the light of the sky and the sight of the fields and flowers; to chain my feet so that I can never again ride with the soldiers nor climb the hills; to make me breathe foul damp darkness, and keep from me everything that brings me back to the love of God when your wickedness and foolishness tempt me to hate Him: all this is worse than the furnace in the Bible that was heated seven times. I could do without my warhorse; I could drag about in a skirt; I could let the banners and the trumpets and the knights and soldiers pass me and leave me behind as they leave the other women, if only I could still hear the wind in the trees, the larks in the sunshine, the young lambs crying through the healthy frost, and the blessed blessed church bells that send my angel voices floating to me on the wind. But without these things I cannot live; and by your wanting to take them away from me, or from any human creature, I know that your counsel is of the devil, and that mine is of God.

THE ASSESSORS (*in great commotion*). Blasphemy! blasphemy! She is possessed. She said our counsel was of the devil. And hers of God. Monstrous! The devil is in our midst, etc., etc.

D'ESTIVET (*shouting above the din*). She is a relapsed heretic, obstinate, incorrigible, and altogether unworthy of the mercy we have shewn her. I call for her excommunication.

THE CHAPLAIN (*to* THE EXECUTIONER). Light your fire, man. To the stake with her.

(THE EXECUTIONER *and his assistants hurry*

out through the courtyard.)

LADVENU. You wicked girl: if your counsel were of God would He not deliver you?

JOAN. His ways are not your ways. He wills that I go through the fire to His bosom; for I am His child, and you are not fit that I should live among you. That is my last word to you.

(*The soldiers seize her.*)

CAUCHON (*rising*). Not yet.

(*They wait. There is a dead silence.* CAUCHON *turns to* THE INQUISITOR *with an inquiring look.* THE INQUISITOR *nods affirmatively. They rise solemnly, and intone the sentence antiphonally.*)

CAUCHON. We decree that thou art a relapsed heretic.

THE INQUISITOR. Cast out from the unity of the Church.

CAUCHON. Sundered from her body.

THE INQUISITOR. Infected with the leprosy of heresy.

CAUCHON. A member of Satan.

THE INQUISITOR. We declare that thou must be excommunicate.

CAUCHON. And now we do cast thee out, segregate thee, and abandon thee to the secular power.

THE INQUISITOR. Admonishing the same secular power that it moderate its judgment of thee in respect of death and division of the limbs. (*He resumes his seat*)

CAUCHON. And if any true sign of penitence appear in thee, to permit our Brother Martin to administer to thee the sacrament of penance.

THE CHAPLAIN. Into the fire with the witch (*he rushes at her, and helps the soldiers to push her out*).

(JOAN *is taken away through the courtyard. The assessors rise in disorder, and follow the soldiers, except* LADVENU, *who has hidden his face in his hands.*)

CAUCHON (*rising again in the act of sitting down*). No, no: this is irregular. The representative of the secular arm should be here to receive her from us.

THE INQUISITOR (*also on his feet again*). That man is an incorrigible fool.

CAUCHON. Brother Martin: see that everything is done in order.

LADVENU. My place is at her side, my Lord.

You must exercise your own authority. (*He hurries out*)

CAUCHON. These English are impossible: they will thrust her straight into the fire. Look!

(*He points to the courtyard, in which the glow and flicker of fire can now be seen reddening the May daylight. Only the BISHOP and the INQUISITOR are left in the court.*)

CAUCHON (*turning to go*). We must stop that.

THE INQUISITOR (*calmly*). Yes; but not too fast, my lord.

CAUCHON (*halting*). But there is not a moment to lose.

THE INQUISITOR. We have proceeded in perfect order. If the English choose to put themselves in the wrong, it is not our business to put them in the right. A flaw in the procedure may be useful later on: one never knows. And the sooner it is over, the better for that poor girl.

CAUCHON (*relaxing*). That is true. But I suppose we must see this dreadful thing through.

THE INQUISITOR. One gets used to it. Habit is everything. I am accustomed to the fire: it is soon over. But it is a terrible thing to see a young and innocent creature crushed between these mighty forces, the Church and the Law.

CAUCHON. You call her innocent!

THE INQUISITOR. Oh, quite innocent. What does she know of the Church and the Law? She did not understand a word we were saying. It is the ignorant who suffer. Come, or we shall be late for the end.

CAUCHON (*going with him*). I shall not be sorry if we are: I am not so accustomed as you.

(*They are going out when WARWICK comes in, meeting them.*)

WARWICK. Oh, I am intruding. I thought it was all over. (*He makes a feint of retiring*)

CAUCHON. Do not go, my lord. It is all over.

THE INQUISITOR. The execution is not in our hands, my lord; but it is desirable that we should witness the end. So by your leave— (*He bows, and goes out through the courtyard*).

CAUCHON. There is some doubt whether your people have observed the forms of law, my lord.

WARWICK. I am told that there is some doubt whether your authority runs in this city, my lord. It is not in your diocese. However, if you will answer for that I will answer for the rest.

CAUCHON. It is to God that we both must answer. Good morning, my lord.

WARWICK. My lord: good morning.

(*They look at one another for a moment with unconcealed hostility. Then CAUCHON follows THE INQUISITOR out. WARWICK looks round. Finding himself alone, he calls for attendance.*)

WARWICK. Hallo: some attendance here! (*Silence*) Hallo, there! (*Silence*) Hallo! Brian, you young blackguard, where are you? (*Silence*) Guard! (*Silence*) They have all gone to see the burning: even that child.

(*The silence is broken by someone frantically howling and sobbing.*)

WARWICK. What in the devil's name—?

(*The CHAPLAIN staggers in from the courtyard like a demented creature, his face streaming with tears, making the piteous sounds that WARWICK has heard. He stumbles to the prisoner's stool, and throws himself upon it with heartrending sobs.*)

WARWICK (*going to him and patting him on the shoulder*). What is it, Master John? What is the matter?

THE CHAPLAIN (*clutching at his hand*). My lord, my lord: for Christ's sake pray for my wretched guilty soul.

WARWICK (*soothing him*). Yes, yes: of course I will. Calmly, gently—

THE CHAPLAIN (*blubbering miserably*). I am not a bad man, my lord.

WARWICK. No, no: not at all.

THE CHAPLAIN. I meant no harm. I did not know what it would be like.

WARWICK (*hardening*). Oh! You saw it, then?

THE CHAPLAIN. I did not know what I was doing. I am a hotheaded fool; and I shall be damned to all eternity for it.

WARWICK. Nonsense! Very distressing, no doubt; but it was not your doing.

THE CHAPLAIN (*lamentably*). I let them do it. If I had known, I would have torn her from their hands. You dont know: you havnt seen: it is so easy to talk when you dont know. You madden yourself with words: you damn yourself because it feels grand to throw oil on the flaming hell of your own temper. But when it is brought home to you; when you see the thing you have done; when it is blinding your eyes, stifling your nostrils, tearing your heart, then—then— (*Falling on his knees*). O God, take away this sight from me! O Christ, deliver me from this fire that is consuming me! She cried to Thee in the midst of it: Jesus! Jesus! Jesus! She is in Thy bosom; and I am in hell for evermore.

WARWICK (*summarily hauling him to his feet*). Come come, man! you must pull yourself together. We shall have the whole town talking of this. (*He throws him not too gently into a chair at the table*) If you have not the nerve to see these things, why do you not do as I do, and stay away?

THE CHAPLAIN (*bewildered and submissive*). She asked for a cross. A soldier gave her two sticks tied together. Thank God he was an Englishman! I might have done it; but I did not: I am a coward, a mad dog, a fool. But he was an Englishman too.

WARWICK. The fool! they will burn him too if the priests get hold of him.

THE CHAPLAIN (*shaken with a convulsion*). Some of the people laughed at her. They would have laughed at Christ. They were French people, my lord: I know they were French.

WARWICK. Hush! someone is coming. Control yourself.

(LADVENU *comes back through the courtyard to* WARWICK's *right hand, carrying a bishop's cross which he has taken from a church. He is very grave and composed.*)

WARWICK. I am informed that it is all over, Brother Martin.

LADVENU (*enigmatically*). We do not know, my lord. It may have only just begun.

WARWICK. What does that mean, exactly?

LADVENU. I took this cross from the church for her that she might see it to the last: she had only two sticks that she put into her bosom. When the fire crept round us, and she saw that if I held the cross before her I should be burnt myself, she warned me to get down and save myself. My lord: a girl who could think of another's danger in such a moment was not inspired by the devil. When I had to snatch the cross from her sight, she looked up to heaven. And I do not believe that the heavens were empty. I firmly believe that her Savior appeared to her then in His tenderest glory. She called to Him and died. This is not the end for her, but the beginning.

WARWICK. I am afraid it will have a bad effect on the people.

LADVENU. It had, my lord, on some of them. I heard laughter. Forgive me for saying that I hope and believe it was English laughter.

THE CHAPLAIN (*rising frantically*). No: it was not. There was only one Englishman there that disgraced his country; and that was the mad dog, de Stogumber. (*He rushes wildly out, shrieking*) Let them torture him. Let them burn him. I will go pray among her ashes. I am no better than Judas: I will hang myself.

WARWICK. Quick, Brother Martin: follow him: he will do himself some mischief. After him, quick.

(LADVENU *hurries out,* WARWICK *urging him.* THE EXECUTIONER *comes in by the door behind the judges' chairs; and* WARWICK, *returning, finds himself face to face with him.*)

WARWICK. Well, fellow: who are you?

THE EXECUTIONER (*with dignity*). I am not addressed as fellow, my lord. I am the Master Executioner of Rouen: it is a highly skilled mystery. I am come to tell your lordship that your orders have been obeyed.

WARWICK. I crave your pardon, Master Executioner; and I will see that you lose nothing by having no relics to sell. I have your word, have I, that nothing remains, not a bone, not a nail, not a hair?

THE EXECUTIONER. Her heart would not burn, my lord; but everything that was left is at the bottom of the river. You have heard the last of her.

WARWICK (*with a wry smile, thinking of what* LADVENU *said*). The last of her? Hm! I wonder!

Epilogue

A restless fitfully windy night in June 1456, full of summer lightning after many days of heat. King CHARLES *the Seventh of France,* formerly JOAN'S DAUPHIN, *now* CHARLES *the Victorious, aged 51, is in bed in one of his royal chateaux. The bed, raised on a dais of two steps, is towards the side of the room so as to avoid blocking a tall lancet window in the middle. Its canopy bears the royal arms in embroidery. Except for the canopy and the huge down pillows there is nothing to distinguish it from a broad settee with bed-clothes and a valance. Thus its occupant is in full view from the foot.*

CHARLES *is not asleep: he is reading in bed, or rather looking at the pictures in Fouquet's Boccaccio with his knees doubled up to make a reading-desk. Beside the bed on his left is a little table with a picture of the Virgin, lighted by candles of painted wax. The walls are hung from ceiling to floor with painted curtains which stir at times in the draughts. At first glance the prevailing yellow and red in these hanging pictures is somewhat flamelike when the folds breathe in the wind.*

The door is on CHARLES's *left, but in front of him close to the corner farthest from him. A large watchman's rattle, handsomely designed and gaily painted, is in the bed under his hand.*

CHARLES *turns a leaf. A distant clock strikes the half-hour softly.* CHARLES *shuts the book with a clap; throws it aside; snatches up the rattle; and whirls it energetically, making a deafening clatter.* LADVENU *enters, 25 years older, strange and stark in bearing, and still carrying the cross from Rouen.* CHARLES *evidently does not expect him; for he springs out of bed on the farther side from the door.*

CHARLES. Who are you? Where is my gentleman of the bedchamber? What do you want?

LADVENU (*solemnly*). I bring you glad tidings of great joy. Rejoice, O king; for the taint is removed from your blood, and the stain from your crown. Justice, long delayed, is at last triumphant.

CHARLES. What are you talking about? Who are you?

LADVENU. I am Brother Martin.

CHARLES. And who, saving your reverence, may Brother Martin be?

LADVENU. I held this cross when The Maid perished in the fire. Twenty-five years have passed since then: nearly ten thousand days. And on every one of those days I have prayed to God to justify His daughter on earth as she is justified in heaven.

CHARLES (*reassured, sitting down on the foot of the bed*). Oh, I remember now. I have heard of you. You have a bee in your bonnet about The Maid. Have you been at the inquiry?

LADVENU. I have given my testimony.

CHARLES. Is it over?

LADVENU. It is over.

CHARLES. Satisfactorily?

LADVENU. The ways of God are very strange.

CHARLES. How so?

LADVENU. At the trial which sent a saint to the stake as a heretic and a sorceress, the truth was told; the law was upheld; mercy was shewn beyond all custom; no wrong was done but the final and dreadful wrong of the lying sentence and the pitiless fire. At this inquiry from which I have just come, there was shameless perjury, courtly corruption, calumny of the dead who did their duty according to their lights, cowardly evasion of the issue, testimony made of idle tales that could not impose on a ploughboy. Yet out of this insult to justice, this defamation of the Church, this orgy of lying and foolishness, the truth is set in the noonday sun on the hilltop; the white robe of innocence is cleansed from the smirch of the burning faggots; the holy life is sanctified; the true heart that lived through the flame is consecrated; a great lie is silenced for ever; and a great wrong is set right before all men.

CHARLES. My friend: provided they can no longer say that I was crowned by a witch and a heretic, I shall not fuss about how the trick has been done. Joan would not have fussed about it if it came all right in the end: she was not that sort: I knew her. Is her rehabilitation complete? I made it pretty clear that there was to be no nonsense about it.

LADVENU. It is solemnly declared that her judges were full of corruption, cozenage, fraud, and malice. Four falsehoods.

CHARLES. Never mind the falsehoods: her judges are dead.

LADVENU. The sentence on her is broken, annulled, annihilated, set aside as non-existent, without value or effect.

CHARLES. Good. Nobody can challenge my consecration now, can they?

LADVENU. Not Charlemagne nor King David himself was more sacredly crowned.

CHARLES (*rising*). Excellent. Think of what that means to me!

LADVENU. I think of what it means to her!

CHARLES. You cannot. None of us ever knew what anything meant to her. She was like nobody else; and she must take care of herself wherever she is; for *I* cannot take care of her; and neither can you, whatever you may think: you are not big enough. But I will tell you this about her. If you could bring her back to life, they would burn her again within six months, for all their present adoration of her. And you would hold up the cross, too, just the same. So (*crossing himself*) let her rest; and let you and I mind our own business, and not meddle with hers.

LADVENU. God forbid that I should have no share in her, nor she in me! (*He turns and strides out as he came, saying*) Henceforth my path will not lie through palaces, nor my conversation be with kings.

CHARLES (*following him towards the door, and shouting after him*). Much good may it do you, holy man! (*He returns to the middle of the chamber, where he halts, and says quizzically to himself*) That was a funny chap. How did he get in? Where are my people? (*He goes impatiently to the bed, and swings the rattle. A rush of wind through the open door sets the walls swaying agitatedly. The candles go out. He calls in the darkness*) Hallo! Someone come and shut the windows: everything is being blown all over the place. (*A flash of summer lightning shews up the lancet window. A figure is seen in silhouette against it.*) Who is there? Who is that? Help! Murder! (*Thunder. He jumps into bed, and hides under the clothes*)

JOAN'S VOICE. Easy, Charlie, easy. What art making all that noise for? No one can hear thee. Thourt asleep. (*She is dimly seen in a pallid greenish light by the bedside*)

CHARLES (*peeping out*). Joan! Are you a ghost, Joan?

JOAN. Hardly even that, lad. Can a poor burnt-up lass have a ghost? I am but a dream that thourt dreaming. (*The light increases: they become plainly visible as he sits up*) Thou looks older, lad.

CHARLES. I am older. Am I really asleep?

JOAN. Fallen asleep over thy silly book.

CHARLES. That's funny.

JOAN. Not so funny as that I am dead, is it?

CHARLES. Are you really dead?

JOAN. As dead as anybody ever is, laddie. I am out of the body.

CHARLES. Just fancy! Did it hurt much?

JOAN. Did what hurt much?

CHARLES. Being burnt.

JOAN. Oh, that! I cannot remember very well. I think it did at first; but then it all got mixed up; and I was not in my right mind until I was free of the body. But do not thou go handling fire and thinking it will not hurt thee. How hast been ever since?

CHARLES. Oh, not so bad. Do you know, I actually lead my army out and win battles? Down into the moat up to my waist in mud and blood. Up the ladders with the stones and hot pitch raining down. Like you.

JOAN. No! Did I make a man of thee after all, Charlie?

CHARLES. I am Charles the Victorious now. I had to be brave because you were. Agnes put a little pluck into me too.

JOAN. Agnes! Who was Agnes?

CHARLES. Agnes Sorel. A woman I fell in love with. I dream of her often. I never dreamed of you before.

JOAN. Is she dead, like me?

CHARLES. Yes. But she was not like you. She was very beautiful.

JOAN (*laughing heartily*). Ha ha! I was no beauty: I was always a rough one: a regular soldier. I might almost as well have been a man. Pity I wasnt: I should not have bothered you all so much then. But my head was in the skies; and the glory of God was upon me; and, man or woman, I should have bothered you as long as your noses were in the mud. Now tell me what has happened since you wise men knew no better than to make a heap of cinders of me?

CHARLES. Your mother and brothers have sued the courts to have your case tried over again. And the courts have declared that your judges were full of corruption and cozenage, fraud and malice.

JOAN. Not they. They were as honest a lot of poor fools as ever burned their betters.

CHARLES. The sentence on you is broken, annihilated, annulled: null, non-existent, without value or effect.

JOAN. I was burned, all the same. Can they unburn me?

CHARLES. If they could, they would think twice before they did it. But they have decreed that a beautiful cross be placed where the stake stood, for your perpetual memory and for your salvation.

JOAN. It is the memory and the salvation that sanctify the cross, not the cross that sanctifies the memory and the salvation. (*She turns away, forgetting him*) I shall outlast that cross. I shall be remembered when men will have forgotten where Rouen stood.

CHARLES. There you go with your self-conceit, the same as ever! I think you might say a word of thanks to me for having had justice done at last.

CAUCHON (*appearing at the window between them*). Liar!

CHARLES. Thank you.

JOAN. Why, if it isnt Peter Cauchon! How are you, Peter? What luck have you had since you burned me?

CAUCHON. None. I arraign the justice of Man. It is not the justice of God.

JOAN. Still dreaming of justice, Peter? See what justice came to with me! But what has happened to thee? Art dead or alive?

CAUCHON. Dead. Dishonored. They pursued me beyond the grave. They excommunicated my dead body: they dug it up and flung it into the common sewer.

JOAN. Your dead body did not feel the spade and the sewer as my live body felt the fire.

CAUCHON. But this thing that they have done against me hurts justice; destroys faith; saps the foundation of the Church. The solid earth sways like the treacherous sea beneath the feet of men and spirits alike when the innocent are slain in the name of the law, and their wrongs are undone by slandering the pure of heart.

JOAN. Well, well, Peter, I hope men will be the better for remembering me; and they would not remember me so well if you had not burned me.

CAUCHON. They will be the worse for remembering me: they will see in me evil triumphing over good, falsehood over truth, cruelty over mercy, hell over heaven. Their courage will rise as they think of you, only to faint as they think of me. Yet God is my witness I was just: I was merciful: I was faithful to my light: I could do no other than I did.

CHARLES (*scrambling out of the sheets and enthroning himself on the side of the bed*). Yes: it is always you good men that do the big mischiefs. Look at me! I am not Charles the Good, nor Charles the Wise, nor Charles the Bold. Joan's worshippers may even call me Charles the Coward because I did not pull her out of the fire. But I have done less harm than any of you. You people with your heads in the sky spend all your time trying to turn the world upside down; but I take the world as it is, and say that topside-up is right-side-up; and I keep my nose pretty close to the ground. And I ask you, what king of France has done better, or been a better fellow in his little way?

JOAN. Art really king of France, Charlie? Be the English gone?

DUNOIS (*coming through the tapestry on* JOAN'S *left, the candles relighting themselves at the same moment, and illuminating his armor and surcoat cheerfully*). I have kept my word: the English are gone.

JOAN. Praised be God! now is fair France a province in heaven. Tell me all about the fighting, Jack. Was it thou that led them? Wert thou God's captain to thy death?

DUNOIS. I am not dead. My body is very comfortably asleep in my bed at Chateaudun; but my spirit is called here by yours.

JOAN. And you fought them my way, Jack: eh? Not the old way, chaffering for ransoms; but The Maid's way: staking life against death, with the heart high and humble and void of malice, and nothing counting under God but France free and French. Was it my way, Jack?

DUNOIS. Faith, it was any way that would win. But the way that won was always your way. I give you best, lassie. I wrote a fine letter to set you right at the new trial. Perhaps I should never have let the priests burn you; but I was busy fighting; and it was the Church's business, not mine. There was no use in both of us being burned, was there?

CAUCHON. Ay! put the blame on the priests. But I, who am beyond praise and blame, tell you that the world is saved neither by its priests nor its soldiers, but by God and His Saints. The Church Militant sent this woman to the fire; but even as she burned, the flames whitened into the radiance of the Church Triumphant.

(*The clock strikes the third quarter. A rough male voice is heard trolling an improvised tune.*)

> Rum tum trumpledum,
> Bacon fat and rumpledum,
> Old Saint mumpledum,
> Pull his tail and stumpledum
>   O my Ma—ry Ann!

(*A ruffianly English soldier comes through the curtains and marches between* DUNOIS *and* JOAN.)

DUNOIS. What villainous troubadour taught you that doggrel?

THE SOLDIER. No troubadour. We made it up ourselves as we marched. We were not gentle-folks and troubadours. Music straight out of the heart of the people, as you might say. Rum tum trumpledum, Bacon fat and rumpledum, Old Saint mumpledum, Pull his tail and stumple-dum: that dont mean anything, you know; but it keeps you marching. Your servant, ladies and gentlemen. Who asked for a saint?

JOAN. Be you a saint?

THE SOLDIER. Yes, lady, straight from hell.

DUNOIS. A saint, and from hell!

THE SOLDIER. Yes, noble captain: I have a day off. Every year, you know. Thats my allowance for my one good action.

CAUCHON. Wretch! In all the years of your life did you do only one good action?

THE SOLDIER. I never thought about it: it came natural like. But they scored it up for me.

CHARLES. What was it?

THE SOLDIER. Why, the silliest thing you ever heard of. I—

JOAN (*interrupting him by strolling across to the bed, where she sits beside* CHARLES). He tied two sticks together, and gave them to a poor lass that was going to be burned.

THE SOLDIER. Right. Who told you that?

JOAN. Never mind. Would you know her if you saw her again?

THE SOLDIER. Not I. There are so many girls! and they all expect you to remember them as if there was only one in the world. This one must have been a prime sort; for I have a day off every year for her; and, so, until twelve o'clock punctually, I am a saint, at your service, noble lords and lovely ladies.

CHARLES. And after twelve?

THE SOLDIER. After twelve, back to the only place fit for the likes of me.

JOAN (*rising*). Back there! You! that gave the lass the cross!

THE SOLDIER (*excusing his unsoldierly conduct*). Well, she asked for it; and they were going to burn her. She had as good a right to a cross as they had; and they had dozens of them. It was her funeral, not theirs. Where was the harm in it?

JOAN. Man: I am not reproaching you. But I cannot bear to think of you in torment.

THE SOLDIER (*cheerfully*). No great torment, lady. You see I was used to worse.

CHARLES. What! worse than hell?

THE SOLDIER. Fifteen years' service in the French wars. Hell was a treat after that.

(JOAN *throws up her arms, and takes refuge from despair of humanity before the picture of the Virgin.*)

THE SOLDIER (*continuing*).—Suits me some-how. The day off was dull at first, like a wet Sunday. I dont mind it so much now. They tell me I can have as many as I like as soon as I want them.

CHARLES. What is hell like?

THE SOLDIER. You wont find is so bad, sir. Jolly. Like as if you were always drunk without the trouble and expense of drinking. Tip top company too: emperors and popes and kings and all sorts. They chip me about giving that young judy the cross; but I dont care: I stand up to them proper, and tell them that if she hadnt a better right to it than they, she'd be where they are. That dumbfounds them, that does. All they can do is gnash their teeth, hell fashion; and I just laugh, and go off singing the old chanty: Rum tum trumple—Hullo! Who's that knocking at the door?

(*They listen. A long gentle knocking is heard.*)

CHARLES. Come in.

(*The door opens; and an old priest, white-haired, bent, with a silly but benevolent smile, comes in and trots over to* JOAN.)

THE NEWCOMER. Excuse me, gentle lords and ladies. Do not let me disturb you. Only a poor old harmless English rector. Formerly chaplain to the cardinal: to my lord of Winchester. John de Stogumber, at your service. (*He looks at them inquiringly*) Did you say anything? I am a little deaf, unfortunately. Also a little—well, not always in my right mind, perhaps; but still, it is a small village with a few simple people. I suffice: I suffice: they love me there; and I am able to do a little good. I am well connected, you see; and they indulge me.

JOAN. Poor old John! What brought thee to this state?

DE STOGUMBER. I tell my folks they must be very careful. I say to them, 'If you only saw what you think about you would think quite differently about it. It would give you a great shock. Oh, a great shock.' And they all say 'Yes, parson: we all know you are a kind man, and would not harm a fly.' That is a great comfort to me. For I am not cruel by nature, you know.

THE SOLDIER. Who said you were?

DE STOGUMBER. Well, you see, I did a very cruel thing once because I did not know what cruelty was like. I had not seen it, you know. That is the great thing: you must see it. And then you are redeemed and saved.

CAUCHON. Were not the sufferings of our Lord Christ enough for you?

DE STOGUMBER. No. Oh no: not at all. I had seen them in pictures, and read of them in books, and been greatly moved by them, as I thought. But it was no use: it was not our Lord that redeemed me, but a young woman whom I saw actually burned to death. It was dreadful: oh, most dreadful. But it saved me. I have been a different man ever since, though a little astray in my wits sometimes.

CAUCHON. Must then a Christ perish in torment in every age to save those that have no imagination?

JOAN. Well, if I saved all those he would have been cruel to if he had not been cruel to me, I was not burnt for nothing, was I?

DE STOGUMBER. Oh no; it was not you. My sight is bad: I cannot distinguish your features: but you are not she: oh no: she was burned to a cinder: dead and gone, dead and gone.

THE EXECUTIONER (*stepping from behind the bed curtains on* CHARLES's *right, the bed being between them*). She is more alive than you, old man. Her heart would not burn; and it would not drown. I was a master at my craft: better than the master of Paris, better than the master of Toulouse; but I could not kill The Maid. She is up and alive everywhere.

THE EARL OF WARWICK (*sallying from the bed curtains on the other side, and coming to* JOAN's *left hand*). Madam: my congratulations on your rehabilitation. I feel that I owe you an apology.

JOAN. Oh, please dont mention it.

WARWICK (*pleasantly*). The burning was purely political. There was no personal feeling against you, I assure you.

JOAN. I bear no malice, my lord.

WARWICK. Just so. Very kind of you to meet me in that way: a touch of true breeding. But I must insist on apologizing very amply. The truth is, these political necessities sometimes turn out to be political mistakes; and this one was a veritable howler; for your spirit conquered us, madam, in spite of our faggots. History will remember me for your sake, though the incidents of the connection were perhaps a little unfortunate.

JOAN. Ay, perhaps just a little, you funny man.

WARWICK. Still, when they make you a saint, you will owe your halo to me, just as this lucky monarch owes his crown to you.

JOAN (*turning from him*). I shall owe nothing to any man: I owe everything to the spirit of God that was within me. But fancy me a saint! What would St Catherine and St Margaret say if the farm girl was cocked up beside them!

(*A clerical-looking gentleman in black frockcoat and trousers, and tall hat, in the fashion of the year 1920, suddenly appears before them in the corner on their right. They all stare at him. Then they burst into uncontrollable laughter.*)

THE GENTLEMAN. Why this mirth, gentlemen?

WARWICK. I congratulate you on having invented a most extraordinarily comic dress.

THE GENTLEMAN. I do not understand. You are all in fancy dress: I am properly dressed.

DUNOIS. All dress is fancy dress, is it not, except our natural skins?

THE GENTLEMAN. Pardon me: I am here on

serious business, and cannot engage in frivolous discussions. (*He takes out a paper, and assumes a dry official manner*). I am sent to announce to you that Joan of Arc, formerly known as The Maid, having been the subject of an inquiry instituted by the Bishop of Orleans—

JOAN (*interrupting*). Ah! They remember me still in Orleans.

THE GENTLEMAN (*emphatically, to mark his indignation at the interruption*).—by the Bishop of Orleans into the claim of the said Joan of Arc to be canonized as a saint—

JOAN (*again interrupting*). But I never made any such claim.

THE GENTLEMAN (*as before*).—the Church has examined the claim exhaustively in the usual course, and, having admitted the said Joan successively to the ranks of Venerable and Blessed,—

JOAN (*chuckling*). Me venerable!

THE GENTLEMAN.—has finally declared her to have been endowed with heroic virtues and favored with private revelations, and calls the said Venerable and Blessed Joan to the communion of the Church Triumphant as Saint Joan.

JOAN (*rapt*). Saint Joan!

THE GENTLEMAN. On every thirtieth day of May, being the anniversary of the death of the said most blessed daughter of God, there shall in every Catholic church to the end of time be celebrated a special office in commemoration of her; and it shall be lawful to dedicate a special chapel to her, and to place her image on its altar in every such church. And it shall be lawful and laudable for the faithful to kneel and address their prayers through her to the Mercy Seat.

JOAN. Oh no. It is for the saint to kneel. (*She falls on her knees, still rapt*)

THE GENTLEMAN (*putting up his paper, and retiring beside* THE EXECUTIONER). In Basilica Vaticana, the sixteenth day of May, nineteen hundred and twenty.

DUNOIS (*raising* JOAN). Half an hour to burn you, dear Saint, and four centuries to find out the truth about you!

DE STOGUMBER. Sir: I was chaplain to the Cardinal of Winchester once. They always would call him the Cardinal of England. It would be a great comfort to me and to my master to see a fair statue of The Maid in Winchester Cathe-dral. Will they put one there, do you think?

THE GENTLEMAN. As the building is temporarily in the hands of the Anglican heresy, I cannot answer for that.

(*A vision of the statue in Winchester Cathedral is seen through the window.*)

DE STOGUMBER. Oh look! look! that is Winchester.

JOAN. Is that meant to be me? I was stiffer on my feet.

(*The vision fades.*)

THE GENTLEMAN. I have been requested by the temporal authorities of France to mention that the multiplication of public statues to The Maid threatens to become an obstruction to traffic. I do so as a matter of courtesy to the said authorities, but must point out on behalf of the Church that The Maid's horse is no greater obstruction to traffic than any other horse.

JOAN. Eh! I am glad they have not forgotten my horse.

(*A vision of the statue before Rheims Cathedral appears.*)

JOAN. Is that funny little thing me too?

CHARLES. That is Rheims Cathedral where you had me crowned. It must be you.

JOAN. Who has broken my sword. My sword was never broken. It is the sword of France.

DUNOIS. Never mind. Swords can be mended. Your soul is unbroken; and you are the soul of France.

(*The vision fades.* THE ARCHBISHOP *and* THE INQUISITOR *are now seen on the right and left of* CAUCHON.)

JOAN. My sword shall conquer yet: the sword that never struck a blow. Though men destroyed my body, yet in my soul I have seen God.

CAUCHON (*kneeling to her*). The girls in the field praise thee; for thou hast raised their eyes; and they see that there is nothing between them and heaven.

DUNOIS (*kneeling to her*). The dying soldiers praise thee, because thou art a shield of glory between them and the judgment.

THE ARCHBISHOP (*kneeling to her*). The princes of the Church praise thee, because thou hast redeemed the faith their worldlinesses have dragged through the mire.

WARWICK (*kneeling to her*). The cunning counsellors praise thee, because thou hast cut the knots in which they have tied their own souls.

DE STOGUMBER (*kneeling to her*). The foolish old men on their deathbeds praise thee, because their sins against thee are turned into blessings.

THE INQUISITOR (*kneeling to her*). The judges in the blindness and bondage of the law praise thee, because thou hast vindicated the vision and the freedom of the living soul.

THE SOLDIER (*kneeling to her*). The wicked out of hell praise thee, because thou hast shewn them that the fire that is not quenched is a holy fire.

THE EXECUTIONER (*kneeling to her*). The tormentors and executioners praise thee, because thou hast shewn that their hands are guiltless of the death of the soul.

CHARLES (*kneeling to her*). The unpretending praise thee, because thou hast taken upon thyself the heroic burdens that are too heavy for them.

JOAN. Woe unto me when all men praise me! I bid you remember that I am a saint, and that saints can work miracles. And now tell me: shall I rise from the dead, and come back to you a living woman?

(*A sudden darkness blots out the walls of the room as they all spring to their feet in consternation. Only the figures and the bed remain visible.*)

JOAN. What! Must I burn again? Are none of you ready to receive me?

CAUCHON. The heretic is always better dead. And mortal eyes cannot distinguish the saint from the heretic. Spare them. (*He goes out as he came*)

DUNOIS. Forgive us, Joan: we are not yet good enough for you. I shall go back to my bed. (*He also goes*)

WARWICK. We sincerely regret our little mistake; but political necessities, though occasionally erroneous, are still imperative; so if you will be good enough to excuse me— (*He steals discreetly away*)

THE ARCHBISHOP. Your return would not make me the man you once thought me. The utmost I can say is that though I dare not bless you, I hope I may one day enter into your blessedness. Meanwhile, however— (*He goes*)

THE INQUISITOR. I who am of the dead, testi-

fied that day that you were innocent. But I do not see how The Inquisition could possibly be dispensed with under existing circumstances. Therefore— (*He goes*)

DE STOGUMBER. Oh, do not come back: you must not come back. I must die in peace. Give us peace in our time, O Lord! (*He goes*)

THE GENTLEMAN. The possibility of your resurrection was not contemplated in the recent proceedings for your canonization. I must return to Rome for fresh instructions. (*He bows formally, and withdraws*)

THE EXECUTIONER. As a master in my profession I have to consider its interests. And, after all, my first duty is to my wife and children. I must have time to think over this. (*He goes*)

CHARLES. Poor old Joan! They have all run away from you except this blackguard who has to go back to hell at twelve o'clock. And what can I do but follow Jack Dunois' example, and go back to bed too? (*He does so*)

JOAN (*sadly*). Goodnight, Charlie.

CHARLES (*mumbling in his pillows*). Goo ni. (*He sleeps. The darkness envelops the bed.*)

JOAN (*to the soldier*). And you, my one faithful? What comfort have you for Saint Joan?

THE SOLDIER. Well, what do they all amount to, these kings and captains and bishops and lawyers and such like? They just leave you in the ditch to bleed to death; and the next thing is, you meet them down there, for all the airs they give themselves. What I say is, you have as good a right to your notions as they have to theirs, and perhaps better. (*Settling himself for a lecture on the subject*) You see, it's like this. If— (*the first stroke of midnight is heard softly from a distant bell*). Excuse me: a pressing appointment— (*He goes on tiptoe*).

(*The last remaining rays of light gather into a white radiance descending on JOAN. The hour continues to strike.*)

JOAN. O God that madest this beautiful earth, when will it be ready to receive Thy saints? How long, O Lord, how long?

DISCUSSION

In the long Preface to this play, Bernard Shaw says of Joan that she is "the most notable Warrior Saint in the Christian calendar, and the queerest fish among the eccentric worthies of the Middle Ages. Though a professed and most pious Catholic, and the projector of a Crusade against the Husites, she was in fact one of the first Protestant martyrs. She was also one of the first apostles of Nationalism, and the first French practitioner of Napoleonic realism in warfare as distinguished from the sporting ransom-gambling chivalry of her time." Joan, by insisting that the English should go back to England and leave France for the French, helped to undermine the old feudal system in which a man owed his primary allegiance to his liege lord, and in which nations as such did not properly exist. By heeding the divine instructions that came to her through her "voices" and not relying on the mediation of a teaching church, Joan, according to Shaw, was a kind of Protestant before Protestantism was invented.

Shaw's double thesis about Joan is interesting, and may possibly be true, but the power of his play does not depend on our believing that it is true. Many readers who would differ sharply with Shaw's interpretation of Joan find his play admirable, and proceed, at least within limits, to make their own interpretations of the character. It would be unfair to say that this play represents a narrow triumph of Shaw the artist over Shaw the propagandist, for in the play itself (as distinguished from the Preface) the artist is consistently dominant. *Saint Joan* shows that Shaw, however wedded to his thesis and however anxious to make the argument of his Preface convincing, knew his business as a playwright well enough to let the drama itself take over and qualify his thesis. The result is a play in which the heroine is no mere puppet, but has a life of her own, a life that carries conviction and which, though it may lend some support to Shaw's thesis, is much more than a mere illustration of that thesis.

The plotting of the play is interesting. It is, in some senses, a history play, and, like many history plays—for instance, those of Shakespeare —it takes in a good deal of terrain and spans a considerable period of time: two years—and if we add the epilogue, over twenty-seven years. The play does not sprawl, however, and for its own purposes, is admirably plotted.

Since Shaw is concerned not with the spectacle but with the meaning of Joan's life as it impinged upon various people, he can dispense with what might seem to be the big inevitable scenes. As he says in his Preface, he is not concerned with a theatrical presentation that would provide a river with real water and "a real bridge across it," the scene of a sham fight "for possession of it, with the victorious French led by Joan on a real horse." Nor is he interested in satisfying the taste of people who don't care "in the least why a woman is burned provided she is burned and people can see it done." We do not see Joan at the stake, for example: her ordeal is simply "reported" to us. The principle upon which Shaw has selected the scenes by which he would explore the meaning of Joan's life is clear: the incidents depicted show why she succeeded and why she failed.

The first three scenes portray Joan's rise to power. The first shows Joan's conquest of the captain, whom she persuades to send her to the Dauphin; the second, her conquest of the Dauphin, who puts her in command of the army; the third, her conquest of Dunois, the general with whom she must work if she is to capture Orleans from the English. Scene IV, by presenting the forces arrayed against Joan, foreshadows the fate that is in store for her. Scene V shows Joan at the height of her power, just after the coronation ceremony, but this scene also reveals Joan's great weakness. Because of her candor and ardor, she cannot help making her friends uncomfortable, and thus, once she has served her purpose, they wish that she would go away. Scene VI depicts Joan's trial, and here the combination of her avowed enemies and her friends—for as Shaw presents them, even some of the men who accuse her of heresy wish to reclaim her and would save her from herself if they could—ensures her conviction and death. Joan's fate is, therefore, thoroughly prepared for and can come as no shock to anyone who intelligently views the play. What happens to her in the end is not an accident or a piece of bad luck or a mere caprice of fate. The development and presentation of Joan's character makes her defeat inevitable, for her defeat grows out of her character. In some sense this is what we find true of nearly all great tragedies: a tragic flaw in the hero's character ensures his defeat and death. So it is, as we have seen, with Oedipus and with Antony. But does Joan's defeat come through *hybris,* an excess of pride? In his Preface, Shaw does speak of Joan's "overweening presumption, the superbity as they called it," that led her to the stake, but he evidently does not think that Joan was possessed by vicious pride. His phrase "as they called it" indicates his own view of the situation: human nature being what it is, a person like Joan will always prove hard to live with—a burden even to those whom she aids. Shaw's play develops this notion consistently, and his epilogue ends with Joan's cry: "Oh God that madest this beautiful earth, when will it be ready to receive Thy saints? How long, O Lord, how long?"

Joan's outcry provides a moving and climactic restatement of the thesis that runs through the play. But, as we have seen, the situation that Shaw has developed for us is too complex for Joan's cry to be taken as its summation, especially if we are tempted to regard her despairing question as a kind of moral tag.

All this has a bearing on whether or not we can regard *Saint Joan* as a tragedy. Do the traits that make Joan a "difficult" person to live with constitute a sufficient tragic flaw? And can one have an authentic tragedy unless the protagonist does have a tragic flaw? Conversely, can a saint have this kind of tragic flaw and still be a saint? Whether or not Shaw took very seriously Joan's status as a saint in the Church's sense of the term, there seems little doubt that, in his own terms, Shaw regarded Joan as saint-like—that is, as a person endowed with heroic virtues, who suffered because those very virtues were too much for frail mankind.

A revealing aspect of Shaw's treatment of the related problems of Joan's sainthood, her tragic fate, and her success as a force in history, comes out in his treatment of Joan's "miracles." (The topic of miracles recurs throughout the play, and Shaw evidently gave a good deal of attention to it.) In general, Shaw grounds the miraculous and awe-inspiring qualities of Joan firmly within her own character and personality. How did Joan, a raw country girl, persuade Captain Robert de Baudricourt to do the unheard of thing of sending her to the court of the Dauphin? This is the matter of Shaw's first scene, and it serves admirably to mirror Joan's salient traits as a person and to prepare us for the larger conquests she is to make later in the play.

Joan's talk with the captain shows why she impresses people. She is perfectly fearless, and, as the steward comments to his master, this trait tends to give people confidence in her mission and in themselves. Since she is confident that she is acting in God's behalf, she can make her requests positively, without feminine coquetry, without wheedling, and without any tinge of egotistical pride. Finally, she treats people as if they made sense, or at least were trying to make sense, in what they said. Most of us are not used to that, and may find it disconcerting, but it puts us on our mettle, too. Joan has the disarming quality of sheer integrity. The person involved with her at first refuses to believe his ears, or says that the girl is crazy, but he does not experience the normal reaction to another person's self-assertion, for Joan so clearly wants nothing for herself. People do not find such honesty easy to put up with, as Joan is later to find, but the initial effect may be tonic and bracing.

At the end of Scene I, Shaw does allow Joan a miracle, a very modest miracle, to be sure: the steward rushes in to say that the hens are laying like mad. But the author has been clever enough to have the captain make his decision in favor of Joan *before* this "miracle" occurs, and the incident is actually used primarily for a kind of comic effect. Poor Captain de Baudricourt, who has not had time to recover from Joan's ardent importunity, and who is far from sure that he was wise to give in, is surprised, but perhaps reassured by this minor manifestation of supernatural power. He says to himself with awe: "She did come from God."

Though Joan's first success is grounded on no miracle other than her own radiant integrity, Shaw, by raising the issue of miracles here, has prepared for its appearance in more important contexts. In Scene II, for example, Joan identifies the true Dauphin in spite of the attempt to deceive her, but no less a person than the archbishop plays down the miraculous aspect of the incident. This rather sceptical archbishop defines a miracle as "an event which creates faith." The archbishop is certain that this clever girl would be able to pass successfully the test of identifying the blood royal. Indeed, it is Joan's candor, integrity, and good sense that persuade the Dauphin to entrust his armies to her. Joan's only "miracle" in this scene—aside from stiffening the spine of the pusillanimous Dauphin—is one that La Trémouille slyly calls a miracle: Joan actually calls a blush to the worldly old archbishop's face by spontaneously falling at his feet and asking, with obviously intense sincerity, for his blessing, since she thinks that he is "filled with the blessedness and glory of God Himself."

This presentation of miracles which are simply events that create "faith" and which will seem miraculous only to a person insufficiently alive to Joan's sharp-eyed but passionate devotion, may represent Shaw's attempt to "secularize" Joan by deliberately playing down the supernatural and turning all miracles into mere accidents which Joan exploits through her own human powers. But whatever Shaw's purpose, the effect is to focus attention on Joan's ardent good sense. She is no vulgar magician and wields no power except that of a keen intelligence completely in the service of selfless devotion.

What are we to say, then, when the adverse wind suddenly changes at the end of Scene III, and, just as Joan comes to lead the attack on Orleans, the boats are at last able to move upstream and make the attack possible? Is this not an authentic miracle? Shaw makes no comment on it. Perhaps it was a miracle, but winds do change, and it was high time that, after blowing for weeks from the west, the wind should at last shift. The wind shift is the kind of good fortune that often attends the brave. It not only allows Joan to enter into her military career at once; it gives confidence to her soldiers that she is indeed heaven sent.

Later references to miraculous happenings are used to develop further the nature of the confidence that she begets in her friends and the fears she arouses in her enemies. In Scene V we find that Dunois, though he is very fond of Joan and has great confidence in her, cannot make very much sense of the voices that she tells him she obeys. Dunois tells her: "You make me uneasy when you talk about your voices: I should think you were a bit cracked if I hadn't noticed

that you give me very sensible reasons for what you do, though I hear you telling others that you are only obeying Madame Saint Catherine." In Scene IV Bishop Cauchon, the man who is alarmed at Joan's claims of direct divine guidance, and wants to have her tried as a heretic, scouts the notion that Joan is a sorceress or a witch. He sees Joan as a heretic, and he tells Warwick and his chaplain: "All these things that you call witchcraft are capable of a natural explanation. The woman's miracles would not impose on a rabbit: she does not claim them as miracles herself. What do her victories prove but that she has a better head on her shoulders than your swearing Glass-dells and mad bull Talbots, that the courage of faith, even though it be a false faith, will always outstay the courage of wrath?"

Shaw's conception of Joan's relation to the miraculous is thus central to his conception of the character and to his interpretation of the meaning of Joan's life and of her significance in history. Moreover, this theme of the miraculous provides for the intelligent auditor or reader of the play a kind of central spine by which he can achieve an articulation of the play. But Shaw's treatment of Joan's relation to the miraculous is only one aspect of a very rich and interesting play. Other aspects may be explored by the student as he attempts to answer the following questions.

EXERCISE

1. Why, on the basis of this play, are the voices that Joan hear important to her? Her insistence on her belief in her voices eventually takes her to the stake. As we have seen, Dunois believes in Joan, not because, but in spite, of the fact that she claims to hear her voices. Later the Dauphin petulantly remarks that the voices don't come to him even though "I am king, not you." What are these voices in Shaw's opinion?

2. Is Joan guilty of *hybris,* as the archbishop thinks she is? She tells Dunois, for example, "You may shake your head, Jack; and Bluebeard may twirl his billygoat's beard and cock his nose at me; but remember the day your knights and captains refused to follow me to attack the English at Orleans!" If Joan lacked the spirit to make these retorts, she might appear to the reader to be a doleful little plaster saint indeed, not the girl who had saved France. But what is the nature of Joan's pride? The kind that goes with a consciousness of having baked a fine cake, or

having kept a clean house? Or is it an ambitious pride? It worries the archbishop and it is deeply disturbing to Cauchon. What does a churchman like Ladvenu say of it at Joan's trial? Twenty-five years later?

3. In reading *Hedda Gabler, Antony and Cleopatra,* and *Saint Joan* we have encountered three strongminded and determined women. Do Hedda, Cleopatra, and Joan have anything else in common except their determination? Are they all willful as well?

4. What do you think of Shaw's treatment of the character of Cauchon? Questions of history and biography quite aside, does not the conception of Cauchon as an honest man actually make for the strength of Shaw's thesis about Joan and the Church? And Shaw's thesis aside, is not a Cauchon who is honest and dedicated, a more interesting character and a worthier dramatic opponent of Joan than a vicious and corrupt man would be?

5. What is Shaw's attitude toward the Dauphin? Does he make him a more sympathetic or a less sympathetic character as the play develops? What does Joan see in the Dauphin aside from the fact that he is in her opinion her true king? Is the Dauphin a stupid man? Or is he a man who is at once rather cowardly but yet knowing? Sensitive and perceptive and yet realistic—perhaps even cynical?

6. What is the value of Dunois as a character in this play? He is obviously important for the plot since he represents Joan's most direct link with the armies of France. But is he more than simply a blunt soldier? How shrewd is he in his perception of Joan's strength and weaknesses? Does his relationship to Joan reveal a side of her that we need to know in order fully to appreciate her character?

7. Is the about-face done by Warwick's chaplain, John de Stogumber, made convincing? Passionate men of the sort who become bloodthirsty over ideas are indeed sometimes the people who, when forced to realize their ideas, turn in revulsion from them and from themselves. Is his revulsion sufficiently prepared for? Or do you feel that the character is strained and unconvincing?

8. Historically, some length of time elapsed between Joan's recantation from her so-called heresies and her relapse into them. In his play, Shaw has made the recantation and the relapse occur within a few minutes' time. Why has he done so? Is the compression that he has attempted successful?

9. Consider the ending of the play proper. Scene VI ends with a conversation between the executioner and Warwick. The executioner is a competent professional who knows his job, but Joan's heart would not burn. He has disposed of that, however, by putting it at the bottom of the river, and he concludes with the statement to Warwick: "You have heard the last of her." Prophetically, Warwick remarks: "The last of her? Hm! I wonder!" Comment on this as an effective way of closing the account of Joan. Even if there were no Epilogue, would this still be an effective conclusion for the play?

10. The Epilogue is sometimes regarded as an undramatic appendage which allows the author an opportunity to chat over the meaning of the play with his audience. But what kind of curiosity is aroused by this play? Is it a curiosity that requires and justifies the kind of retrospective view which the Epilogue affords? Moreover, is the Epilogue necessarily "undramatic"? Could it not be argued that, since Joan, though burned at Rouen many years before, is still very much alive and since the last has not been heard of her, least of all by those people whose lives she had touched in her earthly career, the Epilogue is really an integral part of the drama?

11. What is the special appropriateness of Joan's appearing to King Charles on this particular night?

12. What of King Charles's attitude toward Joan, now twenty-five years after her death? Is he merely selfish? Cynical? Admiring? Perceptive?

13. When Joan appears to the king on this night, she tells him: "I am but a dream that thourt dreaming." This is perhaps Shaw's conscious rationalization of Joan's appearance after death. But if so, are the other figures who appear in the Epilogue simply more dreams in Charles's mind? What about Peter Cauchon, the English chaplain, or the "clerical-looking gentleman in black frockcoat and trousers . . . in the fashion of the year 1920"? Will Shaw's rationalization cover these? Or does it matter that we have some kind of realistic justification for the appearance of these various figures?

14. The people who appear in the Epilogue are all persons upon whom Joan has made a radiant impression. Most of them had known her in the flesh. Even those who had a part in burning Joan now state their admiration for her. The ghost of Cauchon, kneeling to her, says: "The girls in the field praise thee; for thou hast raised their eyes; and they see that there is nothing between them and heaven." But in one relation to her the ghostly spirits stand precisely where they stood when enclosed in the flesh: none of them would really like her back again. A saint in heaven is one thing, and the devotion they express to her is undoubtedly sincere; but a saint in the next room is something else again. Has Shaw been too insistent on this point? Or does the Epilogue re-emphasize it effectively?

15. What is Shaw's attitude toward Joan in the Epilogue? Does he indeed think of her as only a thought in the mind of the sleeping king, part of his dream? Do you think that he conceives of her as now a blessed spirit? Or does he count her still alive only as a force in history? Or does it matter for us, as we read the Epilogue, what answer Shaw would give to these questions?

16. Is *Saint Joan* a tragedy or is it a comedy? Or does it have aspects of both tragedy and comedy?

There is a great deal of comedy in the play; there is also the pathos of undeserved suffering; and there is some sense of exultation at heroic virtue. How are these attitudes related, if they are related?

17. Like *Antony and Cleopatra, Saint Joan* deals with historical events that occur over a period of years and scenes of action often quite far distant from one another. Shakespeare's way of handling these problems of space and time differs very much from Shaw's How successful is each dramatist in this matter? Compare and contrast the solutions of each dramatist.

18. Mr. Louis Martz has commented that we "need not be too greatly concerned with Shaw's bland assertions that he is letting us in on the truth about the Middle Ages, telling us in the play all we need to know about Joan. Books and articles have appeared —a whole cloudburst of them—devoted to proving that Shaw's methods of historical research in his play and in his preface are open to serious question." Mr. Martz goes on to say that there is, for example, "no

historical basis for [Shaw's] highly favorable characterizations of Cauchon and the Inquisitor, upon which the power and point of the trial scene are founded." If the student, by further reading, does decide that Shaw had played rather fast and loose with history, how much difference would that make with regard to the *play?* It would make a great deal of difference, obviously, wtih regard to a student's notion of the historical Joan and her contemporaries. How far and at what level would it alter his sense of the soundness of the play?

Mr. Martz's essay is to be found in *Tragic Themes in Western Literature,* Yale University Press, 1955. It is entitled "The Saint as Tragic Hero: *Saint Joan* and *Murder in the Cathedral."* His discussion will prove useful not only for *Saint Joan,* but for the play that follows, *Murder in the Cathedral,* in which T. S. Eliot also deals with an historical event and with a tragic protagonist who has been canonized by the Church.

Murder in the Cathedral

T. S. ELIOT (1888-   )

Characters

A CHORUS OF WOMEN OF CANTERBURY.
THREE PRIESTS OF THE CATHEDRAL.
A MESSENGER.

ARCHBISHOP THOMAS BECKET.
FOUR TEMPTERS.
ATTENDANTS.

The Scene is the Archbishop's Hall, on December 2nd, 1170

Part I

CHORUS. Here let us stand, close by the cathedral. Here let us wait.
Are we drawn by danger? Is it the knowledge of safety, that draws our feet
Towards the cathedral? What danger can be
For us, the poor, the poor women of Canterbury? what tribulation
With which we are not already familiar? There is no danger   5

For us, and there is no safety in the cathedral. Some presage of an act
Which our eyes are compelled to witness, has forced our feet
Towards the cathedral. We are forced to bear witness.

Since golden October declined into sombre November

And the apples were gathered and stored, and
    the land became brown sharp points of
    death in a waste of water and mud,   10

The New Year waits, breathes, waits, whispers
    in darkness.

While the labourer kicks off a muddy boot and
    stretches his hand to the fire,

The New Year waits, destiny waits for the
    coming.

Who has stretched out his hand to the fire and
    remembered the Saints at All Hallows,

Remembered the martyrs and saints who wait?
    and who shall   15

Stretch out his hand to the fire, and deny his
    master? who shall be warm

By the fire, and deny his master?

Seven years and the summer is over

Seven years since the Archbishop left us,

He who was always kind to his people.   20

But it would not be well if he should return.

King rules or barons rule;

We have suffered various oppression,

But mostly we are left to our own devices,

And we are content if we are left alone.   25

We try to keep our households in order;

The merchant, shy and cautious, tries to com-
    pile a little fortune,

And the labourer bends to his piece of earth,
    earth-colour, his own colour,

Preferring to pass unobserved.

Now I fear disturbance of the quiet seasons: 30

Winter shall come bringing death from the sea,

Ruinous spring shall beat at our doors,

Root and shoot shall eat our eyes and our ears,

Disastrous summer burn up the beds of our
    streams

And the poor shall wait for another decaying
    October.   35

Why should the summer bring consolation

For autumn fires and winter fogs?

What shall we do in the heat of summer

But wait in barren orchards for another October?

Some malady is coming upon us. We wait, we
    wait,   40

And the saints and martyrs wait, for those who
    shall be martyrs and saints.

Destiny waits in the hand of God, shaping the
    still unshapen:

I have seen these things in a shaft of sunlight.

Destiny waits in the hand of God, not in the
hands of statesmen

Who do, some well, some ill, planning and
    guessing,   45

Having their aims which turn in their hands in
    the pattern of time.

Come, happy December, who shall observe you,
    who shall preserve you?

Shall the Son of Man be born again in the litter
    of scorn?

For us, the poor, there is no action,

But only to wait and to witness.   50

(Enter PRIESTS)

    FIRST PRIEST. Seven years and the summer is
    over.

Seven years since the Archbishop left us.

    SECOND PRIEST. What does the Archbishop
    do, and our Sovereign Lord the Pope

With the stubborn King and the French King

In ceaseless intrigue, combinations,   55

In conference, meetings accepted, meetings re-
    fused,

Meetings unended or endless

At one place or another in France?

    THIRD PRIEST. I see nothing quite conclusive
    in the art of temporal government,

But violence, duplicity and frequent malversa-
    tion.   60

King rules or barons rule:

The strong man strongly and the weak man by
    caprice.

They have but one law, to seize the power and
    keep it,

And the steadfast can manipulate the greed and
    lust of others,

The feeble is devoured by his own.   65

    FIRST PRIEST. Shall these things not end

Until the poor at the gate

Have forgotten their friend, their Father in
    God, have forgotten

That they had a friend?

(Enter MESSENGER)

    MESSENGER. Servants of God, and watchers of
    the temple,   70

I am here to inform you, without circumlocu-
    tion:

The Archbishop is in England, and is close out-
    side the city.

I was sent before in haste

To give you notice of his coming, as much as
    was possible,

That you may prepare to meet him.   75
   FIRST PRIEST. What, is the exile ended, is our
     Lord Archbishop
Reunited with the King? what reconciliation
Of two proud men?
   THIRD PRIEST. What peace can be found
To grow between the hammer and the anvil?
   SECOND PRIEST. Tell us
Are the old disputes at an end, is the wall of
     pride cast down   80
That divided them? Is it peace or war?
   FIRST PRIEST. Does he come
In full assurance, or only secure
In the power of Rome, the spiritual rule,
The assurance of right, and the love of the
     people?   85
   MESSENGER. You are right to express a certain
     incredulity.
He comes in pride and sorrow, affirming all his
     claims,
Assured, beyond doubt, of the devotion of the
     people,
Who receive him with scenes of frenzied en-
     thusiasm,
Lining the road and throwing down their
     capes,   90
Strewing the way with leaves and late flowers
     of the season.
The streets of the city will be packed to suffoca-
     tion,
And I think that his horse will be deprived of
     its tail,
A single hair of which becomes a precious relic.
He is at one with the Pope, and with the King
     of France,   95
Who indeed would have liked to detain him in
     his kingdom:
But as for our King, that is another matter.
   FIRST PRIEST. But again, is it war or peace?
   MESSENGER.   Peace, but not the kiss of peace.
A patched up affair, if you ask my opinion.
And if you ask me, I think the Lord Arch-
     bishop   100
Is not the man to cherish any illusions,
Or yet to diminish the least of his pretensions.
If you ask my opinion, I think that this peace
Is nothing like an end, or like a beginning.
It is common knowledge that when the Arch-
     bishop   105
Parted from the King, he said to the King,

My Lord, he said, I leave you as a man
Whom in this life I shall not see again.
I have this, I assure you, on the highest author-
     ity;
There are several opinions as to what he
     meant   110
But no one considers it a happy prognostic.

                         (*Exit*)

   FIRST PRIEST. I fear for the Archbishop, I fear
     for the Church,
I know that the pride bred of sudden prosperity
Was but confirmed by bitter adversity.
I saw him as Chancellor, flattered by the
     King,   115
Liked or feared by courtiers, in their overbear-
     ing fashion,
Despised and despising, always isolated,
Never one among them, always insecure;
His pride always feeding upon his own virtues,
Pride drawing sustenance from impartiality,   120
Pride drawing sustenance from generosity,
Loathing power given by temporal devolution,
Wishing subjection to God alone.
Had the King been greater, or had he been
     weaker
Things had perhaps been different for
     Thomas.   125
   SECOND PRIEST. Yet our lord is returned. Our
     lord has come back to his own again.
We have had enough of waiting, from Decem-
     ber to dismal December.
The Archbishop shall be at our head, dispelling
     dismay and doubt.
He will tell us what we are to do, he will give
     us our orders, instruct us.
Our Lord is at one with the Pope, and also the
     King of France.   130
We can lean on a rock, we can feel a firm foot-
     hold
Against the perpetual wash of tides of balance
     of forces of barons and landholders.
The rock of God is beneath our feet. Let us
     meet the Archbishop with cordial thanks-
     giving:
Our lord, our Archbishop returns. And when
     the Archbishop returns
Our doubts are dispelled. Let us therefore re-
     joice,   135
I say rejoice, and show a glad face for his wel-
     come.

I am the Archbishop's man. Let us give the
    Archbishop welcome!
    THIRD PRIEST. For good or ill, let the wheel
    turn.
The wheel has been still, these seven years, and
    no good.
For ill or good, let the wheel turn. 140
For who knows the end of good or evil?
Until the grinders cease
And the door shall be shut in the street,
And all the daughters of music shall be brought
    low.
    CHORUS. Here is no continuing city, here is
    no abiding stay. 145
Ill the wind, ill the time, uncertain the profit,
    certain the danger.
O late late late, late is the time, late too late,
    and rotten the year;
Evil the wind, and bitter the sea, and grey the
    sky, grey grey grey.
O Thomas, return, Archbishop; return, return
    to France.
Return. Quickly. Quietly. Leave us to perish in
    quiet. 150
You come with applause, you come with re-
    joicing, but you come bringing death into
    Canterbury:
A doom on the house, a doom on yourself, a
    doom on the world.

We do not wish anything to happen.
Seven years we have lived quietly,
Succeeded in avoiding notice, 155
Living and partly living.
There have been oppression and luxury,
There have been poverty and licence,
There has been minor injustice.
Yet we have gone on living, 160
Living and partly living.
Sometimes the corn has failed us,
Sometimes the harvest is good,
One year is a year of rain,
Another a year of dryness, 165
One year the apples are abundant,
Another year the plums are lacking.
Yet we have gone on living,
Living and partly living.
We have kept the feasts, heard the masses, 170
We have brewed beer and cyder,
Gathered wood against the winter,
Talked at the corner of the fire,
Talked at the corners of streets,
Talked not always in whispers, 175
Living and partly living.
We have seen births, deaths and marriages,
We have had various scandals,
We have been afflicted with taxes,
We have had laughter and gossip, 180
Several girls have disappeared
Unaccountably, and some not able to.
We have all had our private terrors,
Our particular shadows, our secret fears.

But now a great fear is upon us, a fear not of
    one but of many, 185
A fear like birth and death, when we see birth
    and death alone
In a void apart. We
Are afraid in a fear which we cannot know,
    which we cannot face, which none under-
    stands,
And our hearts are torn from us, our brains un-
    skinned like the layers of an onion, our
    selves are lost lost
In a final fear which none understands. O
    Thomas Archbishop, 190
O Thomas our Lord, leave us and leave us be,
    in our humble and tarnished frame of
    existence, leave us; do not ask us
To stand to the doom on the house, the doom
    on the Archbishop, the doom on the world.
Archbishop, secure and assured of your fate,
    unaffrayed among the shades, do you realise
    what you ask, do you realise what it means
To the small folk drawn into the pattern of
    fate, the small folk who live among small
    things,
The strain on the brain of the small folk who
    stand to the doom of the house, the doom
    of their lord, the doom of the world? 195
O Thomas, Archbishop, leave us, leave us, leave
    sullen Dover, and set sail for France. Thomas
    our Archbishop still our Archbishop even
    in France. Thomas Archbishop, set the white
    sail between the grey sky and the bitter sea,
    leave us, leave us for France.
    SECOND PRIEST. What a way to talk at such a
    juncture!
You are foolish, immodest and babbling women.
Do you not know that the good Archbishop

Is likely to arrive at any moment?   200
The crowds in the streets will be cheering and
   cheering,
You go on croaking like frogs in the treetops:
But frogs at least can be cooked and eaten.
Whatever you are afraid of, in your craven ap-
   prehension,
Let me ask you at the least to put on pleasant
   faces,   205
And give a hearty welcome to our good Arch-
   bishop.

(*Enter* THOMAS)

  THOMAS. Peace. And let them be, in their
   exaltation.
They speak better than they know, and beyond
   your understanding.
They know and do not know, what it is to act
   or suffer.
They know and do not know, that acting is
   suffering   210
And suffering is action. Neither does the agent
   suffer
Nor the patient act. But both are fixed
In an eternal action, an eternal patience
To which all must consent that it may be willed
And which all must suffer that they may will
   it,   215
That the pattern may subsist, for the pattern is
   the action
And the suffering, that the wheel may turn and
   still
Be forever still.

  SECOND PRIEST. O my Lord, forgive me, I
   did not see you coming,
Engrossed by the chatter of these foolish
   women.   220
Forgive us, my Lord, you would have had a
   better welcome
If we had been sooner prepared for the event.
But your Lordship knows that seven years of
   waiting,
Seven years of prayer, seven years of emptiness,
Have better prepared our hearts for your com-
   ing,   225
Than seven days could make ready Canterbury.
However, I will have fires laid in all your rooms
To take the chill off our English December,
Your Lordship now being used to a better cli-
   mate.
Your Lordship will find your rooms in order as

you left them.   230
  THOMAS. And will try to leave them in order
   as I find them.
I am more than grateful for all your kind atten-
   tions.
These are small matters. Little rest in Canter-
   bury
With eager enemies restless about us.
Rebellious bishops, York, London, Salisbury,   235
Would have intercepted our letters,
Filled the coast with spies and sent to meet me
Some who hold me in bitterest hate.
By God's grace aware of their prevision
I sent my letters on another day,   240
Had fair crossing, found at Sandwich
Broc, Warenne, and the Sheriff of Kent,
Those who had sworn to have my head from me.
Only John, the Dean of Salisbury,
Fearing for the King's name, warning against
   treason,   245
Made them hold their hands. So for the time
We are unmolested.

  FIRST PRIEST.   But do they follow after?
  THOMAS. For a little time the hungry hawk
Will only soar and hover, circling lower,
Waiting excuse, pretence, opportunity.   250
End will be simple, sudden, God-given.
Meanwhile the substance of our first act
Will be shadows, and the strife with shadows.
Heavier the interval than the consummation.
All things prepare the event. Watch.   255

(*Enter* FIRST TEMPTER)

  FIRST TEMPTER. You see, my Lord, I do not
   wait upon ceremony:
Here I have come, forgetting all acrimony,
Hoping that your present gravity
Will find excuse for my humble levity
Remembering all the good time past.   260
Your Lordship won't despise an old friend out
   of favour?
Old Tom, gay Tom, Becket of London,
Your Lordship won't forget that evening on the
   river
When the King, and you and I were all friends
   together?
Friendship should be more than biting Time
   can sever.   265
What, my Lord, now that your recover
Favour with the King, shall we say that sum-
   mer's over

Or that the good time cannot last?
Fluting in the meadows, viols in the hall,
Laughter and apple blossom floating on the
    water,   270
Singing at nightfall, whispering in chambers,
Fires devouring the winter season,
Eating up the darkness, with wit and wine and
    wisdom!
Now that the King and you are in amity,
Clergy and laity may return to gaiety,   275
Mirth and sportfulness need not walk warily.
  THOMAS. You talk of seasons that are past. I
    remember
Not worth forgetting.
  TEMPTER.   And of the new season.
Spring has come in winter. Snow in the
    branches
Shall float as sweet as blossoms. Ice along the
    ditches   280
Mirror the sunlight. Love in the orchard
Send the sap shooting. Mirth matches melan-
    choly.
  THOMAS. We do not know very much of the
    future
Except that from generation to generation
The same things happen again and again.   285
Men learn little from others' experience.
But in the life of one man, never
The same time returns. Sever
The cord, shed the scale. Only
The fool, fixed in his folly, may think   290
He can turn the wheel on which he turns.
  TEMPTER. My Lord, a nod is as good as a
    wink.
A man will often love what he spurns.
For the good times past, that are come again
I am your man.
  THOMAS.   Not in this train.   295
Look to your behavior. You were safer
Think of penitence and follow your master.
  TEMPTER. Not at this gait!
If you go so fast, others may go faster.
Your Lordship is too proud!   300
The safest beast is not the one that roars most
    loud.
This was not the way of the King our master!
You were not used to be so hard upon sinners
When they were your friends. Be easy, man!
The easy man lives to eat the best dinners.   305
Take a friend's advice. Leave well alone,

Or your goose may be cooked and eaten to the
    bone.
  THOMAS. You come twenty years too late.
  TEMPTER. Then I leave you to your fate.
I leave you to the pleasures of your higher
    vices,   310
Which will have to be paid for at higher
    prices.
Farewell, my Lord, I do not wait upon cere-
    mony,
I leave as I came, forgetting all acrimony,
Hoping that your present gravity
Will find excuse for my humble levity.   315
If you will remember me, my Lord, at your
    prayers,
I'll remember you at kissing-time below the
    stairs.
  THOMAS.   Leave-well-alone, the springtime
    fancy,
So one thought goes whistling down the wind.
The impossible is still temptation.   320
The impossible, the undesirable,
Voices under sleep, waking a dead world,
So that the mind may not be whole in the
    present.
            (*Enter* SECOND TEMPTER)
  SECOND TEMPTER. Your Lordship has forgot-
    ten me, perhaps. I will remind you.
We met at Clarendon, at Northampton,   325
And last at Montmirail, in Maine. Now that I
    have recalled them,
Let us but set these not too pleasant memories
In balance against other, earlier
And weighter ones: those of the Chancellor-
    ship.
See how the late ones rise! You, master of
    policy   330
Whom all acknowledged, should guide the state
    again.
  THOMAS. Your meaning?
  TEMPTER. The Chancellorship that you re-
    signed
When you were made Archbishop—that was a
    mistake
On your part—still may be regained. Think, my
    Lord,
Power obtained grows to glory,   335
Life lasting, a permanent possession,
A templed tomb, monument of marble.
Rule over men reckon no madness.

THOMAS. To the man of God what gladness?
TEMPTER.   Sadness
Only to those giving love to God alone.   340
Shall he who held the solid substance
Wander waking with deceitful shadows?
Power is present. Holiness hereafter.
    THOMAS. Who then?
    TEMPTER. The Chancellor. King and Chan-
        cellor.
King commands. Chancellor richly rules.   345
This is a sentence not taught in the schools.
To set down the great, protect the poor,
Beneath the throne of God can man do more?
Disarm the ruffian, strengthen the laws,
Rule for the good of the better cause,   350
Dispensing justice make all even,
Is thrive on earth, and perhaps in heaven.
    THOMAS. What means?
    TEMPTER.   Real power
Is purchased at price of a certain submission. 355
Your spiritual power is earthly perdition.
Power is present, for him who will wield.
    THOMAS. Who shall have it?
    TEMPTER.   He who will come.
    THOMAS. What shall be the month?   360
    TEMPTER.   The last from the first.
    THOMAS. What shall we give for it?
    TEMPTER.   Pretence of priestly power.
    THOMAS. Why should we give it?
    TEMPTER.   For the power and the glory. 365
    THOMAS. No!
    TEMPTER.   Yes! Or bravery will be
        broken,
Cabined in Canterbury, realmless ruler,
Self-bound servant of a powerless Pope,
The old stag, circled with hounds.
    THOMAS. No!
    TEMPTER.   Yes! Men must manoeuvre.
        Monarchs, also,   370
Waging war abroad, need fast friends at home.
Private policy is public profit;
Dignity still shall be dressed with decorum.
    THOMAS. You forget the bishops
Whom I have laid under excommunication.   375
    TEMPTER. Hungry hatred
Will not strive against intelligent self-interest.
    THOMAS. You forget the barons. Who will
        not forget
Constant curbing of petty privilege.
    TEMPTER. Against the barons   380

Is King's cause, churl's cause, Chancellor's
    cause.
    THOMAS. No! shall I, who keep the keys
Of heaven and hell, supreme alone in England,
Who bind and loose, with power from the
        Pope,
Descend to desire a punier power?   385
Delegate to deal the doom of damnation,
To condemn kings, not serve among their serv-
        ants,
Is my open office. No! Go.
    TEMPTER. Then I leave you to your fate.
Your sin soars sunward, covering kings' fal-
        cons.   390
    THOMAS. Temporal power, to build a good
        world,
To keep order, as the world knows order.
Those who put their faith in worldly order
Not controlled by the order of God,
In confident ignorance, but arrest disorder, 395
Make it fast, breed fatal disease,
Degrade what they exalt. Power with the
        King—
I *was* the King, his arm, his better reason.
But what was once exaltation
Would now be only mean descent.   400
            (*Enter* THIRD TEMPTER)
    THIRD TEMPTER. I am an unexpected visitor.
    THOMAS.   I expected you.
    TEMPTER. But not in this guise, or for my
        present purpose.
    THOMAS. No purpose brings surprise.
    TEMPTER.   Well, my Lord,
I am no trifler, and no politician.   405
To idle or intrigue at court
I have no skill. I am no courtier.
I know a horse, a dog, a wench;
I know how to hold my estates in order,
A country-keeping lord who minds his own
        business.
It is we country lords who know the country 410
And we who know what the country needs.
It is our country. We care for the country.
We are the backbone of the nation.
We, not the plotting parasites
About the King. Excuse my bluntness: 415
I am a rough straightforward Englishman.
    THOMAS. Proceed straight forward.
    TEMPTER.   Purpose is plain.
Endurance of friendship does not depend

Upon ourselves, but upon circumstance.
But circumstance is not undetermined.   420
Unreal friendship may turn to real
But real friendship, once ended, cannot be
    mended.
Sooner shall enmity turn to alliance.
The enmity that never knew friendship
Can sooner know accord.

    THOMAS.   For a countryman 425
You wrap your meaning in as dark generality
As any courtier.

    TEMPTER.   This is the simple fact!
You have no hope of reconciliation
With Henry the King. You look only
To blind assertion in isolation.   430
That is a mistake.

    THOMAS.   O Henry, O my King!

    TEMPTER.   Other friends
May be found in the present situation.
King in England is not all-powerful;
King is in France, squabbling in Anjou;
Round him waiting hungry sons.   435
We are for England. We are in England.
You and I, my Lord, are Normans.
England is a land for Norman
Sovereignty. Let the Angevin
Destroy himself, fighting in Anjou.   440
He does not understand us, the English barons.
We are the people.

    THOMAS. To what does this lead?

    TEMPTER.   To a happy coalition
Of intelligent interests.

    THOMAS.   But what have you—
If you do speak for barons—

    TEMPTER.   For a powerful party 445
Which has turned its eyes in your direction—
To gain from you, your Lordship asks.
For us, Church favour would be an advantage,
Blessing of Pope powerful protection
In the fight for liberty. You, my Lord,   450
In being with us, would fight a good stroke
At once, for England and for Rome,
Ending the tyrannous jurisdiction
Of king's court over bishop's court,
Of king's court over baron's court.   455

    THOMAS. Which I helped to found.

    TEMPTER.   Which you helped to found.
But time past is time forgotten.
We expect the rise of a new constellation.

    THOMAS. And if the Archbishop cannot trust
    the King,   460
How can he trust those who work for King's
    undoing?

    TEMPTER. Kings will allow no power but
    their own;
Church and people have good cause against the
    throne.

    THOMAS. If the Archbishop cannot trust the
    Throne,
He has good cause to trust none but God
    alone.   465
I ruled once as Chancellor
And men like you were glad to wait at my door.
Not only in the court, but in the field
And in the tilt-yard I made many yield.
Shall I who ruled like an eagle over doves 470
Now take the shape of a wolf among wolves?
Pursue your treacheries as you have done be-
    fore:
No one shall say that I betrayed a king.

    TEMPTER. Then, my Lord, I shall not wait at
    your door;
And I well hope, before another spring   475
The King will show his regard for your loyalty.

    THOMAS. To make, then break, this thought
    has come before,
The desperate exercise of failing power.
Samson in Gaza did no more.
But if I break, I must break myself alone.   480

           (*Enter* FOURTH TEMPTER)

    FOURTH TEMPTER. Well done, Thomas, your
    will is hard to bend.
And with me beside you, you shall not lack a
    friend.

    THOMAS. Who are you? I expected
Three visitors, not four.

    TEMPTER. Do not be surprised to receive one
    more.   485
Had I been expected, I had been here before.
I always precede expectation.

    THOMAS.   Who are you?

    TEMPTER. As you do not know me, I do not
    need a name,
And, as you know me, that is why I come.   490
You know me, but have never seen my face.
To meet before was never time or place.

    THOMAS. Say what you come to say.

    TEMPTER.   It shall be said at last.
Hooks have been baited with morsels of the
    past.   495

Wantonness is weakness. As for the King,
His hardened hatred shall have no end.
You know truly, the King will never trust
Twice, the man who has been his friend.
Borrow use cautiously, employ   500
Your services as long as you have to lend.
You should wait for trap to snap
Having served your turn, broken and crushed.
As for barons, envy of lesser men
Is still more stubborn than king's anger.   505
Kings have public policy, barons private profit,
Jealousy raging possession of the fiend.
Barons are employable against each other;
Greater enemies must kings destroy.
   THOMAS. What is your counsel?
   TEMPTER.   Fare forward to the end. 510
All other ways are closed to you
Except the way already chosen.
But what is pleasure, kingly rule,
Or rule of men beneath a king,
With craft in corners, stealthy stratagem,   515
To general grasp of spiritual power?
Man oppressed by sin, since Adam fell—
You hold the keys of heaven and hell.
Power to bind and loose: bind, Thomas, bind,
King and bishop under your heel.   520
King, emperor, bishop, baron, king:
Uncertain mastery of melting armies,
War, plague, and revolution,
New conspiracies, broken pacts;
To be master or servant within an hour,   525
This is the course of temporal power.
The Old King shall know it, when at last
   breath,
No sons, no empire, he bites broken teeth.
You hold the skein: wind, Thomas, wind
The thread of eternal life and death.   530
You hold this power, hold it.
   THOMAS.   Supreme, in this land?
   TEMPTER. Supreme, but for one.
   THOMAS.   That I do not understand.
   TEMPTER. It is not for me to tell you how this
   may be so;
I am only here, Thomas, to tell you what you
   know.
   THOMAS. How long shall this be?   535
   TEMPTER. Save what you know already, ask
   nothing of me.
But think, Thomas, think of glory after death.
When king is dead, there's another king,

And one more king is another reign.
King is forgotten, when another shall come: 540
Saint and Martyr rule from the tomb.
Think, Thomas, think of enemies dismayed,
Creeping in penance, frightened of a shade;
Think of pilgrims, standing in line
Before the glittering jewelled shrine,   545
From generation to generation
Bending the knee in supplication.
Think of the miracles, by God's grace,
And think of your enemies, in another place.
   THOMAS. I have thought of these things.
   TEMPTER.   That is why I tell you. 550
Your thoughts have more power than kings to
   compel you.
You have also thought, sometimes at your
   prayers,
Sometimes hesitating at the angles of stairs,
And between sleep and waking, early in the
   morning,
When the bird cries, have thought of further
   scorning.   555
That nothing lasts, but the wheel turns,
The nest is rifled, and the bird mourns;
That the shrine shall be pillaged, and the gold
   spent,
The jewels gone for light ladies' ornament,
The sanctuary broken, and its stores   560
Swept into the laps of parasites and whores.
When miracles cease, and the faithful desert
   you,
And men shall only do their best to forget you.
And later is worse, when men will not hate
   you
Enough to defame or to execrate you,   565
But pondering the qualities that you lacked
Will only try to find the historical fact.
When men shall declare that there was no
   mystery
About this man who played a certain part in
   history.
   THOMAS. But what is there to do? what is
   left to be done?   570
Is there no enduring crown to be won?
   TEMPTER. Yes, Thomas, yes; you have
   thought of that too.
What can compare with glory of Saints
Dwelling forever in presence of God?
What earthly glory, of king or emperor,   575
What earthly pride, that is not poverty

ip on a broken step.
man may sit at meat, and feel the cold
 his groin.
RUS. We have not been happy, my Lord,
e have not been too happy.   645
e not ignorant women, we know what we
ust expect and not expect.
ow of oppression and torture,
ow of extortion and violence,
tion, disease,
d without fire in winter,   650
ild without milk in summer,
bour taken away from us,
ns made heavier upon us.
ve seen the young man mutilated,
rn girl trembling by the mill-stream.   655
eanwhile we have gone on living,
 and partly living,
 together the pieces,
ing faggots at nightfall,
g a partial shelter,   660
eping, and eating and drinking and
ghter.

ve us always some reason, some hope;
 now a new terror has soiled us, which
e can avert, none can avoid, flowing
er our feet and over the sky;
doors and down chimneys, flowing in
he ear and the mouth and the eye.
 leaving us, God is leaving us, more
g, more pain, than birth or death.
d cloying through the dark air   665
 stifling scent of despair;
ns take shape in the dark air:
 of leopard, footfall of padding

 of nodding ape, square hyaena
ing
hter, laughter, laughter. The Lords of
 are here.   670
l round you, lie at your feet, swing
wing through the dark air.
as Archbishop, save us, save us, save
self that we may be saved;
ourself and we are destroyed.
s. Now is my way clear, now is the
ing plain:
on shall not come in this kind again. 675
 temptation is the greatest treason:

To do the right deed for the wrong reason.
The natural vigour in the venial sin
Is the way in which our lives begin.
Thirty years ago, I searched all the ways   680
That lead to pleasure, advancement and praise.
Delight in sense, in learning and in thought,
Music and philosophy, curiosity,
The purple bullfinch in the lilac tree,
The tiltyard skill, the strategy of chess,   685
Love in the garden, singing to the instrument,
Were all things equally desirable.
Ambition comes when early force is spent
And when we find no longer all things possible.
Ambition comes behind and unobservable.   690
Sin grows with doing good. When I imposed
  the King's law
In England, and waged war with him against
  Toulouse,
I beat the barons at their own game. I
Could then despise the men who thought me
  most contemptible,
The raw nobility, whose manners matched
  their fingernails.   695
While I ate out of the King's dish
To become servant of God was never my wish.
Servant of God has chance of greater sin
And sorrow, than the man who serves a king.
For those who serve the greater cause may
  make the cause serve them,   700
Still doing right: and striving with political
  men
May make that cause political, not by what
  they do
But by what they are. I know
What yet remains to show you of my history
Will seem to most of you at best futility,   705
Senseless self-slaughter of a lunatic,
Arrogant passion of a fanatic.
I know that history at all times draws
The strangest consequence from remotest cause.
But for every evil, every sacrilege,   710
Crime, wrong, oppression and the axe's edge,
Indifference, exploitation, you, and you,
And you, must all be punished. So must you.
I shall no longer act or suffer, to the sword's
  end.
Now my good Angel, whom God appoints   715
To be my guardian, hover over the swords'
  points.

Compared with richness of heavenly grandeur?
Seek the way of martyrdom, make yourself the
 lowest
On earth, to be high in heaven.
And see far off below you, where the gulf is
 fixed, 580
Your persecutors, in timeless torment,
Parched passion, beyond expiation.
 Thomas.   No!
Who are you, tempting with my own desires?
Others have come, temporal tempters,
With pleasure and power at palpable price. 585
What do you offer? what do you ask?
 Tempter. I offer what you desire. I ask
What you have to give. Is it too much
For such a vision of eternal grandeur?
 Thomas. Others offered real goods, worth-
 less 590
But real. You only offer
Dreams to damnation.
 Tempter. You have often dreamt them.
 Thomas. Is there no way, in my soul's sick-
 ness,
Does not lead to damnation in pride?
I well know that these temptations 595
Mean present vanity and future torment.
Can sinful pride be driven out
Only by more sinful? Can I neither act nor
 suffer
Without perdition?
 Tempter. You know and do not know, what
 it is to act or suffer. 600
You know and do not know, that action is suffer-
 ing,
And suffering action. Neither does the agent
 suffer
Nor the patient act. But both are fixed
In an eternal action, an eternal patience
To which all must consent that it may be
 willed 605
And which all must suffer that they may will
 it,
That the pattern may subsist, that the wheel
 may turn and still
Be forever still.
 Chorus. There is no rest in the house. There
 is no rest in the street.
I hear restless movement of feet. And the air
 is heavy and thick. 610
Thick and heavy the sky. And the earth presses

up against our feet.
What is the sickly smell, t[...]
 green light from a c[...]
 tree? The earth is he[...]
 of issue of hell. Wha[...]
 that forms on the back[...]
 The Four Tempters. [...]
 and a disappointment[...]
All things are unreal,
Unreal or disappointing:
The Catherine wheel, the[...]
The prizes given at the c[...]
The prize awarded for th[...]
The scholar's degree, the[...]
All things become less rea[...]
From unreality to unreal[...]
This man is obstinate, bl[...]
On self-destruction,
Passing from deception[...]
From grandeur to grand[...]
Lost in the wonder of h[...]
The enemy of society,[...]
 The Three Priests. [...]
 not fight the intract[...]
Do not sail the irresisti[...]
Should we not wait fo[...]
 the night
Abide the coming of[...]
 may find his way,
The sailor lay course [...]
 Chorus, Priests and[...]
 C. Is it the owl t[...]
 tween the trees?
P. Is the window-bar[...]
 under lock and b[...]
T. Is it rain that taps[...]
 that pokes at the[...]
C. Does the torch flar[...]
 in the room?
P. Does the watchma[...]
T. Does the mastiff p[...]
C. Death has a hun[...]
 a thousand ways.[...]
P. He may come in[...]
 pass unseen unh[...]
T. Come whispering [...]
 shock on the sk[...]
C. A man may walk[...]
 yet be drowned[...]
P. A man may clim[...]

Interlude

'Glory to God in the highest, and on earth peace, to men of good will.' *The fourteenth verse of the second chapter of the Gospel according to Saint Luke.* In the Name of the Father, and of the Son, and of the Holy Ghost. Amen.

Dear children of God, my sermon this Christmas morning will be a very short one. I wish only that you should meditate in your hearts the deep meaning and mystery of our masses of Christmas Day. For whenever Mass is said, we re-enact the Passion and Death of Our Lord; and on this Christmas Day we do this in celebration of His Birth. So that at the same moment we rejoice in His coming for the salvation of men, and offer again to God His Body and Blood in sacrifice, oblation and satisfaction for the sins of the whole world. It was in this same night that has just passed, that a multitude of the heavenly host appeared before the shepherds at Bethlehem, saying, 'Glory to God in the highest, and on earth peace to men of good will'; at this same time of all the year that we celebrate at once the Birth of Our Lord and His Passion and Death upon the Cross. Beloved, as the World sees, this is to behave in a strange fashion. For who in the World will both mourn and rejoice at once and for the same reason? For either joy will be overborne by mourning, or mourning will be cast out by joy; so it is only in these our Christian mysteries that we can rejoice and mourn at once for the same reason. But think for a while on the meaning of this word 'peace.' Does it seem strange to you that the angels should have announced Peace, when cease-lessly the world has been stricken with War and the fear of War? Does it seem to you that the angelic voices were mistaken, and that the promise was a disappointment and a cheat?

Reflect now, how Our Lord Himself spoke of Peace. He said to His disciples 'My peace I leave with you, my peace I give unto you.' Did He mean peace as we think of it: the kingdom of England at peace with its neighbours, the barons at peace with the King, the householder counting over his peaceful gains, the swept hearth, his best wine for a friend at the table, his wife singing to the children? Those men His disciples knew no such things: they went forth to journey afar, to suffer by land and sea, to know torture, imprisonment, disappointment, to suffer death by martyrdom. What then did He mean? If you ask that, remember then that He said also, 'Not as the world gives, give I unto you.' So then, He gave to His disciples peace, but not peace as the world gives.

Consider also one thing of which you have probably never thought. Not only do we at the feast of Christmas celebrate at once Our Lord's Birth and His Death: but on the next day we celebrate the martyrdom of His first martyr, the blessed Stephen. Is it an accident, do you think, that the day of the first martyr follows immediately the day of the Birth of Christ? By no means. Just as we rejoice and mourn at once, in the Birth and in the Passion of Our Lord; so also, in a smaller figure, we both rejoice and mourn in the death of martyrs. We mourn, for the sins of the world that has martyred them; we rejoice, that another soul is numbered among the Saints in Heaven, for the glory of God and for the salvation of men.

Beloved, we do not think of a martyr simply as a good Christian who has been killed because he is a Christian: for that would be solely to mourn. We do not think of him simply as a good Christian who has been elevated to the company of the Saints: for that would be simply to rejoice: and neither our mourning nor our rejoicing is as the world's is. A Christian martyrdom is never an accident, for Saints are not made by accident. Still less is a Christian martyrdom the effect of a man's will to become a Saint, as a man by willing and contriving may become a ruler of men. A martyrdom is always the design of God, for His love of men, to warn them and to lead them, to bring them back to His ways. It is never the design of man; for the true martyr is he who has become the instrument of God, who has lost his will in the will of God, and who no longer desires anything for himself, not even the glory of being a martyr. So thus as on earth the Church mourns and rejoices at once, in a fashion that the world cannot understand; so in Heaven the Saints are most high, having made themselves most low, seeing themselves not as we see them, but in the light of the Godhead from which they draw their being.

I have spoken to you today, dear children of God, of the martyrs of the past, asking you to remember especially our martyr of Canterbury, the blessed Archbishop Elphege; because it is fitting, on Christ's birth day, to remember what is that Peace which He brought; and because, dear children, I do not think I shall ever preach to you again; and because it is possible that in a short time you may have yet another martyr, and that one perhaps not the last. I would have you keep in your hearts these words that I say, and think of them at another time. In the Name of the Father, and of the Son, and of the Holy Ghost. Amen.

Characters

THREE PRIESTS.
FOUR KNIGHTS.
ARCHBISHOP THOMAS BECKET.

CHORUS OF WOMEN OF CANTERBURY.
ATTENDANTS.

The first scene is in the Archbishop's Hall, the second scene is in the Cathedral, on December 29th, 1170

Part II

CHORUS. Does the bird sing in the South?
Only the sea-bird cries, driven inland by the storm.
What sign of the spring of the year?
Only the death of the old: not a stir, not a shoot, not a breath.
Do the days begin to lengthen?   5
Longer and darker the day, shorter and colder the night.
Still and stifling the air: but a wind is stored up in the East.
The starved crow sits in the field, attentive; and in the wood
The owl rehearses the hollow note of death.
What signs of a bitter spring?   10
The wind stored up in the East.
What, at the time of the birth of Our Lord, at Christmastide,
Is there not peace upon earth, goodwill among men?
The peace of this world is always uncertain, unless men keep the peace of God.
And war among men defiles this world, but death in the Lord renews it,   15
And the world must be cleaned in the winter, or we shall have only

A sour spring, a parched summer, an empty harvest.
Between Christmas and Easter what work shall be done?
The ploughman shall go out in March and turn the same earth
He has turned before, the bird shall sing the same song.   20
When the leaf is out on the tree, when the elder and may
Burst over the stream, and the air is clear and high,
And voices trill at windows, and children tumble in front of the door,
What work shall have been done, what wrong
Shall the bird's song cover, the green tree cover, what wrong   25
Shall the fresh earth cover? We wait, and the time is short
But waiting is long.
   (*Enter the* FIRST PRIEST *with a banner of St. Stephen borne before him. The lines sung are in italics.*)
FIRST PRIEST. Since Christmas a day: and the day of St. Stephen, First Martyr.
Princes moreover did sit, and did witness falsely

against me.
A day that was always most dear to the Archbishop Thomas.
And he kneeled down and cried with a loud voice: 30
Lord, lay not this sin to their charge.
Princes moreover did sit.
                    (*Introit of St. Stephen is heard.*)
(*Enter the* SECOND PRIEST, *with a banner of St. John the Apostle borne before him.*)
    SECOND PRIEST. Since St. Stephen a day: and the day of St. John the Apostle.
In the midst of the congregation he opened his mouth.
That which was from the beginning, which we have heard,   35
Which we have seen with our eyes, and our hands have handled
Of the word of life; that which we have seen and heard
Declare we unto you.
In the midst of the congregation.
                    (*Introit of St. John is heard.*)
(*Enter the* THIRD PRIEST, *with a banner of the Holy Innocents borne before him.*)
    THIRD PRIEST. Since St. John the Apostle a day: and the day of the Holy Innocents.   40
Out of the mouth of very babes, O God.
As the voice of many waters, of thunder, of harps,
They sung as it were a new song.
The blood of thy saints have they shed like water,
And there was no man to bury them. Avenge, O Lord,   45
The blood of thy saints. In Rama, a voice heard weeping.
Out of the mouths of very babes, O God!
                    (THE PRIESTS *stand together with the banners behind them.*)
    FIRST PRIEST. Since the Holy Innocents a day: the fourth day from Christmas.
    THE THREE PRIESTS. *Rejoice we all, keeping holy day.*
    FIRST PRIEST. As for the people, so also for himself, he offereth for sins.   50
He lays down his life for the sheep.
    THE THREE PRIESTS. *Rejoice we all, keeping holy day.*
    FIRST PRIEST. To-day?
    SECOND PRIEST. To-day, what is to-day? For the day is half gone.

    FIRST PRIEST. To-day, what is to-day? But another day, the dusk of the year.   55
    SECOND PRIEST. To-day, what is to-day? Another night and another dawn.
    THIRD PRIEST. What day is the day that we know that we hope for or fear for?
Every day is the day we should fear from or hope from. One moment
Weighs like another. Only in retrospection, selection,
We say, that was the day. The critical moment 60
That is always now, and here. Even now, in sordid particulars
The eternal design may appear.
                    (*Enter the* FOUR KNIGHTS. *The banners disappear.*)
    FIRST KNIGHT. Servants of the King.
    FIRST PRIEST.   And known to us.
You are welcome. Have you ridden far?
    FIRST KNIGHT. Not far today, but matters urgent   65
Have brought us from France. We rode hard,
Took ship yesterday, landed last night,
Having business with the Archbishop.
    SECOND KNIGHT. Urgent business.
    THIRD KNIGHT.   From the King.
    SECOND KNIGHT. By the King's order.
    FIRST KNIGHT.   Our men are outside. 70
    FIRST PRIEST. You know the Archbishop's hospitality.
We are about to go to dinner.
The good Archbishop would be vexed
If we did not offer you entertainment
Before your business. Please dine with us.   75
Your men shall be looked after also.
Dinner before business. Do you like roast pork?
    FIRST KNIGHT. Business before dinner. We will roast your pork
First, and dine upon it after.
    SECOND KNIGHT. We must see the Archbishop.   80
    THIRD KNIGHT. Go, tell the Archbishop
We have no need of his hospitality.
We will find our own dinner.
    FIRST PRIEST (*to attendant*). Go, tell His Lordship.
    FOURTH KNIGHT.   How much longer will you keep us waiting?   85
                    (*Enter* THOMAS)

THOMAS (*to* PRIESTS). However certain our
    expectation
The moment foreseen may be unexpected
When it arrives. It comes when we are
Engrossed with matters of other urgency.
On my table you will find   90
The papers in order, and the documents signed.
    (*To* KNIGHTS)
You are welcome, whatever your business may
    be.
You say, from the King?
    FIRST KNIGHT.   Most surely from the King.
We must speak with you alone.
    THOMAS (*to* PRIEST).   Leave us then alone.
Now what is the matter?
    FIRST KNIGHT.   This is the matter. 95
    THE THREE KNIGHTS. You are the Archbishop
    in revolt against the King; in rebellion to
    the King and the law of the land;
You are the Archbishop who was made by the
    King; whom he set in your place to carry
    out his command.
You are his servant, his tool, and his jack,
You wore his favours on your back,
You had your honours all from his hand; from
    him you had the power, the seal and the
    ring.   100
This is the man who was the tradesman's son:
    the backstairs brat who was born in Cheap-
    side;
This is the creature that crawled upon the
    King; swollen with blood and swollen with
    pride.
Creeping out of the London dirt,
Crawling up like a louse on your shirt,
The man who cheated, swindled, lied; broke
    his oath and betrayed his King.   105
    THOMAS. This is not true.
Both before and after I received the ring
I have been a loyal subject to the King.
Saving my order, I am at his command,
As his most faithful vassal in the land.   110
    FIRST KNIGHT. Saving your order! let your
    order save you—
As I do not think it is like to do.
Saving your ambition is what you mean,
Saving your pride, envy and spleen.
    SECOND KNIGHT. Saving your insolence and
    greed.   115

Won't you ask us to pray to God for you, in
    your need?
    THIRD KNIGHT. Yes, we'll pray for you!
    FIRST KNIGHT.   Yes, we'll pray for you!
    THE THREE KNIGHTS. Yes, we'll pray that
    God may help you!
    THOMAS. But, gentlemen, your business
Which you said so urgent, is it only   120
Scolding and blaspheming?
    FIRST KNIGHT.   That was only
Our indignation, as loyal subjects.
    THOMAS. Loyal? to whom?
    FIRST KNIGHT.   To the King!
    SECOND KNIGHT.   The King!
    THIRD KNIGHT. The King!
    THE THREE KNIGHTS.   God bless him!
    THOMAS. Then let your new coat of loyalty
    be worn
Carefully, so it get not soiled or torn.   125
Have you something to say?
    FIRST KNIGHT.   By the King's command.
Shall we say it now?
    SECOND KNIGHT.   Without delay,
Before the old fox is off and away.
    THOMAS.   What you have to say
By the King's command—if it be the King's
    command—
Should be said in public. If you make charges, 130
Then in public I will refute them.
    FIRST KNIGHT.   No! here and now!
    (*They make to attack him, but the priests
    and attendants return and quietly inter-
    pose themselves*)
    THOMAS. Now and here!
    FIRST KNIGHT. Of your earlier misdeeds I
    shall make no mention.
They are too well known. But after dissension
Had ended, in France, and you were endued 135
With your former privilege, how did you show
    your gratitude?
You had fled from England, not exiled
Or threatened, mind you; but in the hope
Of stirring up trouble in the French dominions.
You sowed strife abroad, you reviled   140
The King to the King of France, to the Pope,
Raising up against him false opinions.
    SECOND KNIGHT. Yet the King, out of his
    charity,
And urged by your friends, offered clemency,

Made a pact of peace, and all dispute ended 145
Sent you back to your See as you demanded.
   THIRD KNIGHT. And burying the memory of
      your transgressions
Restored your honours and your possessions.
All was granted for which you sued:
Yet how, I repeat, did you show your
      gratitude?   150
   FIRST KNIGHT. Suspending those who had
      crowned the young prince,
Denying the legality of his coronation;
Binding with the chains of anathema,
Using every means in your power to evince
The King's faithful servants, everyone who
      transacts   155
His business in his absence, the business of the
      nation.
   FIRST KNIGHT. These are the facts.
Say therefore if you will be content
To answer in the King's presence. Therefore
      were we sent.
   THOMAS. Never was it my wish   160
To uncrown the King's son, or to diminish
His honour and power. Why should he wish
To deprive my people of me and keep me from
      my own
And bid me sit in Canterbury, alone?
I would wish him three crowns rather than
      one,   165
And as for the bishops, it is not my yoke
That is laid upon them, or mine to revoke.
Let them go to the Pope. It was he who con-
      demned them.
   FIRST KNIGHT. Through you they were sus-
      pended.
   SECOND KNIGHT. By you be this amended. 170
   THIRD KNIGHT. Absolve them.
   FIRST KNIGHT.   Absolve them.
   THOMAS.   I do not deny
That this was done through me. But it is not I
Who can loose whom the Pope has bound.
Let them go to him, upon whom redounds
Their contempt towards me, their contempt
      towards the Church shown.
   FIRST KNIGHT. Be that as it may, here is the
      King's command: 175
That you and your servants depart from this
      land.
   THOMAS. If that *is* the King's command, I

will be bold
To say: seven years were my people without
My presence; seven years of misery and pain.
Seven years a mendicant on foreign charity 180
I lingered abroad: seven years is no brevity.
I shall not get those seven years back again.
Never again, you must make no doubt,
Shall the sea run between the shepherd and his
      fold.
   FIRST KNIGHT. The King's justice, the King's
      majesty,   185
You insult with gross indignity;
Insolent madman, whom nothing deters
From attainting his servants and ministers.
   THOMAS. It is not I who insult the King,
And there is higher than I or the King.   190
It is not I, Becket from Cheapside,
It is not against me, Becket, that you strive.
It is not Becket who pronounces doom,
But the Law of Christ's church, the judgement
      of Rome.
   FIRST KNIGHT. Priest, you have spoken in
      peril of your life.   195
   SECOND KNIGHT. Priest, you have spoken in
      danger of the knife.
   THIRD KNIGHT. Priest, you have spoken
      treachery and treason.
   THE THREE KNIGHTS. Priest! Traitor confirmed
      in malfeasance.
   THOMAS. I submit my cause to the judgement
      of Rome.
But if you kill me, I shall rise from my tomb 200
To submit my cause before God's throne.
                       (Exit)
   FOURTH KNIGHT. Priest! monk! and servant!
      take, hold, detain,
Restrain this man, in the King's name.
   FIRST KNIGHT. Or answer with your bodies.
   SECOND KNIGHT. Enough of words.
   THE FOUR KNIGHTS. We come for the King's
      justice, we come with swords.   205
                    (Exeunt.)
   CHORUS. I have smelt them, the death-
      bringers, senses are quickened
By subtile forebodings; I have heard
Fluting in the nighttime, fluting and owls, have
      seen at noon
Scaly wings slanting over, huge and ridiculous.
   I have tasted

The savour of putrid flesh in the spoon. I have
    felt   210
The heaving of earth at nightfall, restless, ab-
    surd. I have heard
Laughter in the noises of beasts that make
    strange noises: jackal, jackass, jackdaw; the
    scurrying noise of mouse and jerboa; the
    laugh of the loon, the lunatic bird. I have
    seen
Grey necks twisting, rat tails twining, in the
    thick light of dawn. I have eaten
Smooth creatures still living, with the strong salt
    taste of living things under sea; I have
    tasted
The living lobster, the crab, the oyster, the
    whelk and the prawn; and they live and
    spawn in my bowels, and my bowels dis-
    solve in the light of dawn. I have smelt 215
Death in the rose, death in the hollyhock, sweet
    pea, hyacinth, primrose and cowslip. I have
    seen
Trunk and horn, tusk and hoof, in odd places;
I have lain on the floor of the sea and breathed
    with the breathing of the sea-anemone,
    swallowed with ingurgitation of the
    sponge. I have lain in the soil and criticised
    the worm. In the air
Flirted with the passage of the kite, I have
    plunged with the kite and cowered with
    the wren. I have felt
The horn of the beetle, the scale of the viper,
    the mobile hard insensitive skin of the ele-
    phant, the evasive flank of the fish. I have
    smelt   220
Corruption in the dish, incense in the latrine,
    the sewer in the incense, the smell of sweet
    soap in the woodpath, a hellish sweet scent
    in the woodpath, while the ground heaved.
    I have seen
Rings of light coiling downwards, leading
To the horror of the ape. Have I not known,
    not known
What was coming to be? It was here, in the
    kitchen, in the passage,
In the mews in the barn in the byre in the
    market place   225
In our veins our bowels our skulls as well
As well as in the plottings of potentates
As well as in the consultations of powers.

What is woven on the loom of fate
What is woven in the councils of princes   230
Is woven also in our veins, our brains,
Is woven like a pattern of living worms
In the guts of the women of Canterbury.

I have smelt them, the death-bringers; now is
    too late
For action, too soon for contrition.   235
Nothing is possible but the shamed swoon
Of those consenting to the last humiliation.
I have consented, Lord Archbishop, have con-
    sented.
Am torn away, subdued, violated,
United to the spiritual flesh of nature,   240
Mastered by the animal powers of spirit,
Dominated by the lust of self-demolition,
By the final utter uttermost death of spirit,
By the final ecstasy of waste and shame,
O Lord Archbishop, O Thomas Archbishop, for-
    give us, forgive us, pray for us that we may
    pray for you, out of our shame.   245
            (*Enter* THOMAS.)
   THOMAS. Peace, and be at peace with your
    thoughts and visions.
These things had to come to you and you to
    accept them.
This is your share of the eternal burden,
The perpetual glory. This is one moment,
But know that another   250
Shall pierce you with a sudden painful joy
When the figure of God's purpose is made com-
    plete.
You shall forget these things, toiling in the
    household,
You shall remember them, droning by the fire,
When age and forgetfulness sweeten memory 255
Only like a dream that has often been told
And often been changed in the telling. They
    will seem unreal.
Human kind cannot bear very much reality.
   PRIESTS (*severally*). My Lord, you must not
stop here. To the minster. Through the cloister.
No time to waste. They are coming back,
armed. To the altar, to the altar.
   THOMAS. All my life they have been coming,
    these feet. All my life   260
I have waited. Death will come only when I
    am worthy,

And if I am worthy, there is no danger.
I have therefore only to make perfect my will.
   PRIESTS. My Lord, they are coming. They
     will break through presently.
You will be killed. Come to the altar. Make
     haste, my Lord. Don't stop here talking. 265
It is not right. What shall become of us, my
     Lord, if you are killed;
What shall become of us?
   THOMAS. Peace! be quiet! remember where
     you are, and what is happening;
No life here is sought for but mine,
And I am not in danger: only near to death. 270
   PRIESTS. My Lord, to vespers! You must not
     be absent from vespers. You must not be
     absent from the divine office. To vespers.
     Into the cathedral!
   THOMAS. Go to vespers, remember me at your
     prayers.
They shall find the shepherd here; the flock
     shall be spared.
I have had a tremor of bliss, a wink of heaven,
     a whisper,
And I would no longer be denied; all things 275
Proceed to a joyful consummation.
   PRIESTS. Seize him! force him! drag him!
   THOMAS. Keep your hands off!
   PRIESTS. To vespers! Hurry.
     (*They drag him off. While the* CHORUS
     speak, the scene is changed to the cathe-
     dral.)
     CHORUS (*while a* Dies Irae *is sung in Latin by*
     a choir in the distance).
Numb the hand and dry the eyelid,   280
Still the horror, but more horror
Than when tearing in the belly.

Still the horror, but more horror
Than when twisting in the fingers,
Than when splitting in the skull.   285

More than footfall in the passage,
More than shadow in the doorway,
More than fury in the hall.

The agents of hell disappear, the human, they
     shrink and dissolve
Into dust on the wind, forgotten, unmemorable;
     only is here   290

The white flat face of Death, God's silent serv-
     ant,
And behind the face of Death the Judgement
And behind the Judgement the Void, more hor-
     rid than active shapes of hell;
Emptiness, absence, separation from God;
The horror of the effortless journey, to the
     empty land   295
Which is no land, only emptiness, absence, the
     Void,
Where those who were men can no longer turn
     the mind
To distraction, delusion, escape into dream,
     pretence,
Where the soul is no longer deceived, for there
     are no objects, no tones,
No colours, no forms to distract, to divert the
     soul   300
From seeing itself, foully united forever, noth-
     ing with nothing,
Not what we call death, but what beyond death
     is not death,
We fear, we fear. Who shall then plead for me,
Who intercede for me, in my most need?

Dead upon the tree, my Saviour,   305
Let not be in vain Thy labour;
Help me, Lord, in my last fear.

Dust I am, to dust am bending,
From the final doom impending
Help me, Lord, for death is near.   310
     (*In the cathedral.* THOMAS *and* PRIESTS.)
   PRIESTS. Bar the door. Bar the door.
The door is barred.
We are safe. We are safe.
They dare not break in.
They cannot break in. They have not the
     force.   315
We are safe. We are safe.
   THOMAS. Unbar the doors! throw open the
     doors!
I will not have the house of prayer, the church
     of Christ,
The sanctuary, turned into a fortress.
The Church shall protect her own, in her own
     way, not   320
As oak and stone; stone and oak decay,
Give no stay, but the Church shall endure.

The church shall be open, even to our enemies.
Open the door!
  PRIEST. My Lord! these are not men, these
    come not as men come, but   325
Like maddened beasts. They come not like men,
who
Respect the sanctuary, who kneel to the Body of
Christ,
But like beasts. You would bar the door
Against the lion, the leopard, the wolf or the
boar,
Why not more   330
Against beasts with the souls of damned men,
against men
Who would damn themselves to beasts. My
Lord! My Lord!
  THOMAS. You think me reckless, desperate and
mad.
You argue by results, as this world does,
To settle if an act be good or bad.   335
You defer to the fact. For every life and every
act
Consequence of good and evil can be shown.
And as in time results of many deeds are blended
So good and evil in the end become con-
founded.
It is not in time that my death shall be
known;   340
It is out of time that my decision is taken
If you call that decision
To which my whole being gives entire consent.
I give my life
To the Law of God above the Law of Man.
Unbar the door! unbar the door!   345
We are not here to triumph by fighting, by
stratagem, or by resistance,
Not to fight with beasts as men. We have
fought the beast
And have conquered. We have only to
conquer
Now, by suffering. This is the easier victory.
Now is the triumph of the Cross, now   350
Open the door! I command it. OPEN THE DOOR!
    (*The door is opened. The* KNIGHTS *enter,
slightly tipsy.*)
  PRIESTS. This way, my Lord! Quick. Up the
stair. To the roof. To the crypt. Quick.
Come. Force him.
  KNIGHTS (*one line each*)
Where is Becket, the traitor to the King?

Where is Becket, the meddling priest?
Come down Daniel to the lions' den,   355
  Come down Daniel for the mark of the beast.

Are you washed in the blood of the Lamb?
  Are you marked with the mark of the beast?
Come down Daniel to the lions' den,
  Come down Daniel and join in the feast.   360

Where is Becket the Cheapside brat?
  Where is Becket the faithless priest?
Come down Daniel to the lions' den,
  Come down Daniel and join in the feast.
  THOMAS. It is the just man who   365
Like a bold lion, should be without fear.
I am here.
No traitor to the King. I am a priest
A Christian, saved by the blood of Christ,
Ready to suffer with my blood.   370
This is the sign of the Church always,
The sign of blood. Blood for blood.
His blood given to buy my life,
My blood given to pay for His death,
My death for His death.   375
  FIRST KNIGHT. Absolve all those you have ex-
communicated.
  SECOND KNIGHT. Resign the powers you have
arrogated.
  THIRD KNIGHT. Restore to the King the money
you appropriated.
  FIRST KNIGHT. Renew the obedience you have
violated.
  THOMAS. For my Lord I am now ready to
die,   380
That His Church may have peace and liberty.
Do with me as you will, to your hurt and shame;
But none of my people, in God's name,
Whether layman or clerk, shall you touch.
This I forbid.   385
  KNIGHTS. Traitor! traitor! traitor!
  THOMAS. You, Reginald, three times traitor
you:
Traitor to me as my temporal vassal,
Traitor to me as your spiritual lord,
Traitor to God in desecrating His Church.   390
  FIRST KNIGHT. No faith do I owe to a rene-
gade,
And what I owe shall now be paid.
  THOMAS. Now to Almighty God, to the
Blessed Mary ever Virgin, to the blessed John
the Baptist, the holy apostles Peter and Paul,

to the blessed martyr Denys, and to all the Saints, I commend my cause and that of the Church.

(*While the* KNIGHTS *kill him, we hear the* CHORUS)

Clear the air! clean the sky! wash the wind! take stone from stone and wash them.

The land is foul, the water is foul, our beasts and ourselves defiled with blood.   395

A rain of blood has blinded my eyes. Where is England? where is Kent? where is Canterbury?

O far far far far in the past; and I wander in a land of barren boughs: if I break them, they bleed; I wander in a land of dry stones: if I touch them they bleed.

How how can I ever return, to the soft quiet seasons?

Night stay with us, stop sun, hold season, let the day not come, let the spring not come.

Can I look again at the day and its common things, and see them all smeared with blood, through a curtain of falling blood?   400

We did not wish anything to happen.

We understood the private catastrophe,

The personal loss, the general misery,

Living and partly living;

The terror by night that ends in daily action,   405

The terror by day that ends in sleep;

But the talk in the market-place, the hand on the broom,

The nighttime heaping of the ashes,

The fuel laid on the fire at daybreak,

These acts marked a limit to our suffering.   410

Every horror had its definition,

Every sorrow had a kind of end:

In life there is not time to grieve long.

But this, this is out of life, this is out of time,

An instant eternity of evil and wrong.   415

We are soiled by a filth that we cannot clean, united to supernatural vermin,

It is not we alone, it is not the house, it is not the city that is defiled,

But the world that is wholly foul.

Clear the air! clean the sky! wash the wind! take the stone from the stone, take the skin from the arm, take the muscle from the bone, and wash them. Wash the stone, wash the bone, wash the brain, wash the soul, wash them wash them!

(*The* KNIGHTS, *having completed the murder, advance to the front of the stage and address the audience*)

FIRST KNIGHT. We beg you to give us your attention for a few moments. We know that you may be disposed to judge unfavourably of our action. You are Englishmen, and therefore you believe in fair play: and when you see one man being set upon by four, then your sympathies are all with the under dog. I respect such feelings, I share them. Nevertheless, I appeal to your sense of honour. You are Englishmen, and therefore will not judge anybody without hearing both sides of the case. That is in accordance with our long established principle of Trial by Jury. I am not myself qualified to put our case to you. I am a man of action and not of words. For that reason I shall do no more than introduce the other speakers, who, with their various abilities, and different points of view, will be able to lay before you the merits of this extremely complex problem. I shall call upon our eldest member to speak first, my neighbour in the country: Baron William de Traci.

THIRD KNIGHT. I am afraid I am not anything like such an experienced speaker as my old friend Reginald Fitz Urse would lead you to believe. But there is one thing I should like to say, and I might as well say it at once. It is this: in what we have done, and whatever you may think of it, we have been perfectly disinterested. (*The other* KNIGHTS: 'Hear! hear!') *We* are not getting anything out of this. We have much more to lose than to gain. We are four plain Englishmen who put our country first. I dare say that we didn't make a very good impression when we came in just now. The fact is that we knew we had taken on a pretty stiff job; I'll only speak for myself, but I had drunk a good deal—I am not a drinking man ordinarily—to brace myself up for it. When you come to the point, it does go against the grain to kill an Archbishop, especially when you have been brought up in good Church traditions. So if we seemed a bit rowdy, you will understand why it was; and for my part I am awfully sorry about it. We realised that this was our duty, but all the same we had to work ourselves up to it. And, as I said, *we* are not getting a penny out of this. We know perfectly well how things will turn out. King

Henry—God bless him—will have to say, for reasons of state, that he never meant this to happen; and there is going to be an awful row; and at the best we shall have to spend the rest of our lives abroad. And even when reasonable people come to see that the Archbishop *had* to be put out of the way—and personally I had a tremendous admiration for him—you must have noticed what a good show he put up at the end —they won't give *us* any glory. No, we have done for ourselves, there's no mistake about that. So, as I said at the beginning, please give us at least the credit for being completely disinterested in this business. I think that is about all I have to say.

FIRST KNIGHT. I think we will all agree that William de Traci has spoken well and has made a very important point. The gist of his argument is this: that we have been completely disinterested. But our act itself needs more justification than that; and you must hear our other speakers. I shall next call upon Hugh de Morville, who has made a special study of statecraft and constitutional law. Sir Hugh de Morville.

SECOND KNIGHT. I should like first to recur to a point that was very well put by our leader, Reginald Fitz Urse: that you are Englishmen, and therefore your sympathies are always with the under dog. It is the English spirit of fair play. Now the worthy Archbishop, whose good qualities I very much admired, has throughout been presented as the under dog. But is this really the case? I am going to appeal not to your emotions but to your reason. You are hard-headed sensible people, as I can see, and not to be taken in by emotional clap-trap. I therefore ask you to consider soberly: what were the Archbishop's aims? and what are King Henry's aims? In the answer to these questions lies the key to the problem.

The King's aim has been perfectly consistent. During the reign of the late Queen Matilda and the irruption of the unhappy usurper Stephen, the kingdom was very much divided. Our King saw that the one thing needful was to restore order: to curb the excessive powers of local government, which were usually exercised for selfish and often for seditious ends, and to reform the legal system. He therefore intended that Becket, who had proved himself an extremely able administrator—no one denies that—should unite the offices of Chancellor and Archbishop. Had Becket concurred with the King's wishes, we should have had an almost ideal State: a union of spiritual and temporal administration, under the central government. I knew Becket well, in various official relations; and I may say that I have never known a man so well qualified for the highest rank of the Civil Service. And what happened? The moment that Becket, at the King's instance, had been made Archbishop, he resigned the office of Chancellor, he became more priestly than the priests, he ostentatiously and offensively adopted an ascetic manner of life, he affirmed immediately that there was a higher order than that which our King, and he as the King's servant, had for so many years striven to establish; and that—God knows why—the two orders were incompatible.

You will agree with me that such interference by an Archbishop offends the instincts of a people like ours. So far, I know that I have your approval: I read it in your faces. It is only with the measures we have had to adopt, in order to set matters to rights, that you take issue. No one regrets the necessity for violence more than we do. Unhappily, there are times when violence is the only way in which social justice can be secured. At another time, you would condemn an Archbishop by vote of Parliament and execute him formally as a traitor, and no one would have to bear the burden of being called murderer. And at a later time still, even such temperate measures as these would become unnecessary. But, if you have now arrived at a just subordination of the pretensions of the Church to the welfare of the State, remember that it is we who took the first step. We have been instrumental in bringing about the state of affairs that you approve. We have served your interests; we merit your applause; and if there is any guilt whatever in the matter, you must share it with us.

FIRST KNIGHT. Morville has given us a great deal to think about. It seems to me that he has said almost the last word, for those who have been able to follow his very subtle reasoning. We have, however, one more speaker, who has I think another point of view to express. If there are any who are still unconvinced, I think that Richard Brito, coming as he does of a family distinguished for its loyalty to the Church, will be able to convince them. Richard Brito.

FOURTH KNIGHT. The speakers who have preceded me, to say nothing of our leader, Reginald Fitz Urse, have all spoken very much to the point. I have nothing to add along their particular lines of argument. What I have to say may be put in the form of a question: *Who killed the Archbishop?* As you have been eye-witnesses of this lamentable scene, you may feel some surprise at my putting it in this way. But consider the course of events. I am obliged, very briefly, to go over the ground traversed by the last speaker. While the late Archbishop was Chancellor, no one, under the King, did more to weld the country together, to give it the unity, the stability, order, tranquillity, and justice that it so badly needed. From the moment he became Archbishop, he completely reversed his policy; he showed himself to be utterly indifferent to the fate of the country, to be, in fact, a monster of egotism. This egotism grew upon him, until it became at last an undoubted mania. I have unimpeachable evidence to the effect that before he left France he clearly prophesied, in the presence of numerous witnesses, that he had not long to live, and that he would be killed in England. He used every means of provocation; from his conduct, step by step, there can be no inference except that he had determined upon a death by martyrdom. Even at the last, he could have given us reason: you have seen how he evaded our questions. And when he had deliberately exasperated us beyond human endurance, he could still have easily escaped; he could have kept himself from us long enough to allow our righteous anger to cool. That was just what he did not wish to happen; he insisted, while we were still inflamed with wrath, that the doors should be opened. Need I say more? I think, with these facts before you, you will unhesitatingly render a verdict of Suicide while of Unsound Mind. It is the only charitable verdict you can give, upon one who was, after all, a great man.

FIRST KNIGHT. Thank you, Brito. I think that there is no more to be said; and I suggest that you now disperse quietly to your homes. Please be careful not to loiter in groups at street corners, and do nothing that might provoke any public outbreak.

(*Exeunt* KNIGHTS)

FIRST PRIEST. O father, father, gone from us, lost to us,   420
How shall we find you, from what far place
Do you look down on us? You now in Heaven,
Who shall now guide us, protect us, direct us?
After what journey through what further dread
Shall we recover your presence? when inherit 425
Your strength? The Church lies bereft,
Alone, desecrated, desolated, and the heathen shall build on the ruins,
Their world without God. I see it. I see it.

THIRD PRIEST. No. For the Church is stronger for this action,
Triumphant in adversity. It is fortified   430
By persecution: supreme, so long as men will die for it.
Go, weak sad men, lost erring souls, homeless in earth or heaven.
Go where the sunset reddens the last grey rock
Of Brittany, or the Gates of Hercules.
Go venture shipwreck on the sullen coasts   435
Where blackamoors make captive Christian men;
Go to the northern seas confined with ice
Where the dead breath makes numb the hand, makes dull the brain;
Find an oasis in the desert sun,
Go seek alliance with the heathen Saracen,   440
To share his filthy rites, and try to snatch
Forgetfulness in his libidinous courts,
Oblivion in the fountain by the date-tree;
Or sit and bite your nails in Aquitaine.
In the small circle of pain within the skull 445
You still shall tramp and tread one endless round
Of thought, to justify your action to yourselves,
Weaving a fiction which unravels as you weave,
Pacing forever in the hell of make-believe
Which never is belief: this is your fate on earth   450
And we must think no further of you.

FIRST PRIEST.   O my lord
The glory of whose new state is hidden from us,
Pray for us of your charity.

SECOND PRIEST.   Now in the sight of God
Conjoined with all the saints and martyrs gone

before you,
Remember us.

THIRD PRIEST.   Let our thanks ascend 455
To God, who has given us another Saint in
Canterbury.

CHORUS (*while a Te Deum is sung in Latin
by a choir in the distance*).

We praise Thee, O God, for Thy glory displayed in all the creatures of the earth,

In the snow, in the rain, in the wind, in the
storm; in all of Thy creatures, both the
hunters and the hunted.

For all things exist only as seen by Thee, only
as known by Thee, all things exist

Only in Thy light, and Thy glory is declared
even in that which denies Thee; the darkness declares the glory of light.   460

Those who deny Thee could not deny, if Thou
didst not exist; and their denial is never
complete, for if it were so, they would not
exist.

They affirm Thee in living; all things affirm
Thee in living; the bird in the air, both the
hawk and the finch; the beast on the earth,
both the wolf and the lamb; the worm in
the soil and the worm in the belly.

Therefore man, whom Thou hast made to be
conscious of Thee, must consciously praise
Thee, in thought and in word and in deed.

Even with the hand to the broom, the back bent
in laying the fire, the knee bent in cleaning
the hearth, we, the scrubbers and sweepers
of Canterbury,

The back bent under toil, the knee bent under
sin, the hands to the face under fear, the
head bent under grief,   465

Even in us the voices of seasons, the snuffle of
winter, the song of spring, the drone of
summer, the voices of beasts and of birds,
praise Thee.

We thank Thee for Thy mercies of blood, for
Thy redemption by blood. For the blood
of Thy martyrs and saints

Shall enrich the earth, shall create the holy
places.

For wherever a saint has dwelt, wherever a martyr has given his blood for the blood of
Christ,

There is holy ground, and the sanctity shall not
depart from it   470

Though armies trample over it, though sight-
seers come with guide-books looking over it;

From where the western seas gnaw at the coast
of Iona,

To the death in the desert, the prayer in forgotten places by the broken imperial column,

From such ground springs that which forever
renews the earth

Though it is forever denied. Therefore, O God,
we thank Thee   475
Who hast given such blessing to Canterbury.

Forgive us, O Lord, we acknowledge ourselves
as type of the common man,

Of the men and women who shut the door and
sit by the fire;

Who fear the blessing of God, the loneliness of
the night of God, the surrender required,
the deprivation inflicted;

Who fear the injustice of men less than the
justice of God;   480

Who fear the hand at the window, the fire in
the thatch, the fist in the tavern, the push
into the canal,

Less than we fear the love of God.

We acknowledge our trespass, our weakness,
our fault; we acknowledge

That the sin of the world is upon our heads;
that the blood of the martyrs and the agony
of the saints

Is upon our heads.   485
Lord, have mercy upon us.
Christ, have mercy upon us.
Lord, have mercy upon us.
Blessed Thomas, pray for us.

DISCUSSION

This play deals with an historical event, the
murder of Thomas à Becket, Archbishop of
Canterbury in his cathedral on December 29,
1170. In earlier years, Becket had been a great
favorite of the king, Henry II, and served as his
Chancellor. In 1162 Becket was consecrated
Archbishop, and "forthwith," as one of old
chronicles puts it, "refused to deale any more
with matters of the Court, renouncing the
Chauncellorship etc." Quarrels ensued between
the king and his former favorite and in 1164,
the Archbishop fled England and went to Rome.
At the time that our play opens, he has just

returned to Canterbury after restoration to his see, though as the Messenger comments (Part I, l. 99), the restoration is merely "A patched up affair, if you ask my opinion."

But though the play deals with history and makes use of certain archaicisms in its language and sentence structure, it will quickly become obvious to the reader that the play aims at something more than the re-creation of an historical scene. It is aimed quite steadily at a modern audience. For example, the Fourth Tempter (Part I, ll. 564-569) suddenly makes a reference to the world that the modern reader knows and in which he lives:

And later is worse, when men will not hate you
Enough to defame or to execrate you,
But pondering the qualities that you lacked
Will only try to find the historical fact.
When men shall declare that there was no mystery
About this man who played a certain part in history.

This play is concerned with something more than making an "historical" interpretation. Indeed, it challenges throughout the state of mind that the Fourth Tempter describes in the passage just quoted.

Other references to the modern world and modern man occur throughout the play. Note the references made in the speech of the Four Tempters (Part I, ll. 613-27); note that Thomas's speech that closes Part I (ll. 703-16) is addressed directly to the audience; and note that the speeches of the Four Knights (pp. 825-27) are written in modern journalistic prose. The manner as well as the matter of the Knights' justification of their act thus brings us squarely up against a "modern" account of the meaning of Thomas's act: it is an account which challenges the whole religious conception of martyrdom.

The issues just raised have everything to do with the meaning of this play and with the strategies which the author has devised in order to present that meaning. Is the "martyr" a passive victim, and is martyrdom thus an accident, to be fully accounted for in historical terms? Or, if the "martyr" is not passive, but actively wills his death, is Brito not right in his charge that Thomas has really committed suicide (see p. 827)?

The author may here seem to be caught in a cleft stick: either he writes a play in which there is no essential struggle, no real conflict, since Thomas "suffers" but cannot "act," and thus he ends with a piece of pageantry which is essentially undramatic. Or else Thomas invites his own death, "acts" to get himself killed—under delusion or for hope of glory, and the note on which the play ends (see the last Chorus) is contradicted by the action of the play itself.

The editors do not seek to impose their own view here as to the success or lack of success of the play. But they do feel it important that the student should see early in his study of the play what the problem is; and they point out that the dramatist himself is certainly thoroughly aware of the problem: consider the emphasis on acting as suffering and suffering as action (Part I, ll. 210-18, ll. 600-08, and l. 714). Consider the various definitions of martyrdom (Thomas's Sermon, Brito's speech of justification, etc.). Consider most of all Thomas's own concern with his motives.

The sin that Thomas fears most is an insidious kind of pride that will constitute the wrong motive for the right action. He probably does well to fear it. From the very beginning of the play we hear constant references to Thomas's pride. The First Priest refers to Thomas's "pride always feeding upon his own virtues" (Part I, l. 119); the Second Tempter says to him "Your sin soars sunward" (Part I, l. 390); the Fourth Tempter, urging him on to martyrdom, can even quote back to him his own earlier words, not even needing to alter them in order to make them serve his argument of temptation. And the Four Tempters in the speech that they recite together condemn Thomas as a man "Lost in the wonder of his own greatness" (Part I, l. 626).

Does Thomas succeed in avoiding what he calls "the greatest treason: To do the right deed for the wrong reason" (Part I, ll. 676-77)? And if so, how has the dramatist been able to make convincing to us Thomas's growth in self-knowledge and his perfection of his own will? In this connection, a consideration of the function of the other characters is in order.

The Four Knights are given names though the dramatist has been content to leave them as rather flat types without much distinguishing personality. The Priests are not even given names. (They do, however, exhibit some differences in temperament and attitude: the Third Priest obviously is closest to Thomas in his awareness of the situation.) The women of Canterbury by the very fact that they constitute the chorus are not meant to register upon the audience as individuals. As for the Tempters, they achieve special traits of personality only in so far as they represent past or present aspects of Thomas himself.

In view of this very special focusing upon the one main character, we may be inclined to say that the other characters are of little importance, and that they contribute little to Thomas's struggle—merely witnessing it as spectators. (Even the Knights who contribute the only overt "action" to the play may seem to have little more than a physical relation to the conflict centered in Thomas.) Yet the minor characters have most important functions; and as we come to understand the essential issue of the play, those functions become easier to apprehend.

They have, in the first place, a great deal to do with defining the nature of the conflict in the play. Before the murder, the Priests, the Tempters, and the Chorus, all unite in urging Thomas to abandon his position. Their motives for urging this differ; but all are in opposition to Thomas's course of action (or "inaction"). This fact is pointed up in ll. 633-44, where the three groups speak alternately, and the voices of the Priests and the Tempters become part of the "chorus."

After the murder, the Knights in their speeches of justification restate in modern terms and in a modern idiom the case to be made against Thomas. All the speeches made before the murder oppose Thomas's taking the martyr's path; the speeches of the Knights after the murder would rob the event of its significance as a martyrdom. Even before the murder, the speeches of the Tempters challenge the conception of martyrdom, and thus look forward to what the Knights are to say later. And even the groups sympathetic to Thomas, the Priests and the Chorus, ultimately by implication deny the significance of martyrdom.

The essential conflict—external and internal—is thus sharply defined. Moreover, the external and internal conflicts are closely related. The Priests are by function and sympathy closely related to Thomas. The Tempters, as we have remarked, make appeals with which Thomas is intimately familiar. The First Tempter is almost a shade of the Thomas of the past. The Fourth Tempter is almost Thomas's present secular self. And even the Chorus has a special relation to Thomas. Like him, they are passive and condemned to "suffer." Thomas says of them "They know and do not know, what it is to act or suffer." And a little later the Fourth Tempter says to Thomas: "You know and do not know, what it is to act or suffer."

Of course the passivity of the Chorus—"the small folk drawn into the pattern of fate"—is vastly different from the passivity of Thomas; and the contrast between the members of the Chorus and Thomas is another means of defining his passivity, which is not really "passive" at all.

One further very important function of the Chorus deserves mention. The ancient Greek dramatists used the chorus to give expression to the changing emotions of the audience. The chorus voiced the growing feeling of suspense, the sense of foreboding, or the surge of joy which the audience experienced as it viewed the changing fortunes of the protagonist. But the chorus not only expressed but in a measure directed the response of the audience. Something of this function pertains to the chorus as used in this play. The Chorus of old women charges us with the peculiar horror that attends the approaching act of violence, but it also transmits the sense of cleansing and power that flows from Thomas's triumphant death, and it is a means for drawing the reader into the mood of high exaltation with which the play ends.

EXERCISE

1. How is the exposition accomplished in this play? Is it sufficient? How heavily does the play lean upon a knowledge of history?

2. Thomas says that he had expected the first three Tempters. Why had he not expected the Fourth? What does his encounter with the Fourth Tempter reveal to Thomas about himself?

3. The women of the Chorus (Part I, ll. 645-

673) express their sense of despair. Is Thomas himself at this point close to despair? Note that it is immediately after this Chorus that Thomas says, "Now is my way clear, now is the meaning plain." Why has the way suddenly become clear for him? Has the despair of the Chorus actually served to make his way clear to him?

4. Does "The Interlude," Thomas's sermon, break the dramatic pattern? If not, what does it contribute to the pattern?

5. Why do the women of the Chorus dread what they sense is about to happen? Their dread goes beyond their wish to save the Archbishop. It evidently goes beyond any concern for their own safety. It goes beyond their revulsion from mere suffering. They are used to suffering. What is the special nature of the horror and foreboding which they feel? Does the poetry which they speak in the choruses in Part I and in the first three choruses of Part II (ll. 1-27, 206-45, and 280-310) define this for you? Consider especially lines like 25 in Part I and 302 in Part II.

6. Consider carefully Thomas's speech in Part II, ll. 272-76. Does his statement "I have had a tremor of bliss" argue that Thomas is really eager for and inviting his martyrdom after all? Does it indicate that he has not yet "made perfect his will"? Or does it indicate that he has? Defend your answer.

7. How do Joan and Thomas differ in their kinds of pride? Shaw apparently does not regard Joan's pride as reprehensible. Does Eliot regard Becket's as such?

8. Eliot has remarked that in writing *Murder in the Cathedral* he might have been, for all he knows, "slightly under the influence of *Saint Joan*." Do you find any elements in *Murder in the Cathedral* which might point to that influence?

9. Through most of the play, the choruses have suggested the sense of topsy-turviness and instability in the world. How does the Chorus in Part II, ll. 394-419, sum up this sense of confusion and unreality? What is the meaning of l. 414? Is the poet saying that the women who constitute the Chorus here encounter the sense of eternity? How does this bear upon the "meaning" of Thomas's martyrdom? How does this chorus prepare for the chorus with which the play ends?

10. Eliot has been criticized for breaking so violently the mood and idiom of the play by the

speeches of justification spoken by the four Knights. Do you agree? Or can you justify the violence of the contrast as necessary to the play?

11. Discuss the use of animal imagery in the last chorus of the play. How do the animals referred to differ from the animals referred to in the earlier choruses? Note that the difference is not that the animals are all gentle (note the hawk) or attractive and beautiful (note "the worm in the belly").

12. Compare and contrast the imagery (or lack of imagery) in the Knights' speeches of justification with the imagery in ll. 394-419 and 420-89 of Part II. Is the contrast meaningful and effective? Note the tired clichés of the Knights' speeches, the sleazy political journalism, the euphemisms and circumlocutions.

13. The speech of the Third Priest (Part II, ll. 429-51) develops the theme of "homelessness." How is the theme developed in terms of imagery? Is there a dominant metaphor? What does the handling of the metrical pattern contribute? Examine with special care the system of pauses and run-on lines.

14. On closer reading, the student will discover that one of the basic themes in this play concerns the nature of reality. Certain actions seem unreal—nightmarish. But some of the things that seemed most fantastically unreal are revealed, in the developed perspective, to lie at the center of reality, and other things that had seemed most real, turn out to be illusory. (This theme engages the problem of martyrdom, of course, most importantly: Is true martyrdom possible, or are martyrs simply deluded men or else men in the grip of a perverse kind of pride?)

Note how often terms like "real," "unreal," etc., occur in this play. The Four Tempters, for example, say that "All things are unreal" (Part I, l. 614). Consider also in this connection the passage beginning "The agents of hell disappear, the human, they shrink and dissolve . . ." (Part II, ll. 289-304). Review the poetry of the play as a means for presenting this theme.

15. Is the poetry in this play "laid on from the outside," a kind of rhetorical gilding? Or is it part and parcel of the play? Try to justify your answer.

Note: A great many of Eliot's central themes are to be found in this play, themes which receive treatment in his other plays and poems. The student might consult Leonard Unger's *T. S. Eliot* for critical articles on Eliot's themes and techniques.

The Circle

W. SOMERSET MAUGHAM (1874-   )

Characters

CLIVE CHAMPION-CHENEY.
ARNOLD CHAMPION-CHENEY, M.P.
LORD PORTEOUS.
EDWARD LUTON.

LADY CATHERINE CHAMPION-CHENEY.
ELIZABETH.
MRS. SHENSTONE.
A FOOTMAN and a BUTLER

The action takes place at Aston-Adey, Arnold Champion-Cheney's house in Dorset.

Act I

SCENE: A stately drawing-room at Aston-Adey, with fine pictures on the walls and Georgian furniture. Aston-Adey has been described, with many illustrations, in Country Life. *It is not a house, but a place. Its owner takes a great pride in it, and there is nothing in the room which is not of the period. Through the French windows at the back can be seen the beautiful gardens which are one of the features. It is a fine summer morning.*

(ARNOLD comes in. He is a man of about thirty-five, tall and good-looking, fair, with a clean-cut, sensitive face. He has a look that is intellectual, but somewhat bloodless. He is very well dressed.)

ARNOLD *(calling)*. Elizabeth. *(He goes to the window and calls again)* Elizabeth! *(He rings the bell. While he is waiting he gives a look round the room. He slightly alters the position of one of the chairs. He takes an ornament from the chimney-piece and blows the dust from it. A* FOOTMAN *comes in.)* Oh, George! See if you can find Mrs. Cheney, and ask her if she'd be good enough to come here.

FOOTMAN. Very good, sir.

(The FOOTMAN *turns to go)*

ARNOLD. Who is supposed to look after this room?

FOOTMAN. I don't know, sir.

ARNOLD. I wish when they dust they'd take care to replace the things exactly as they were before.

FOOTMAN. Yes, sir.

ARNOLD *(dismissing him)*. All right.

(The FOOTMAN *goes out.* ARNOLD *goes again to the window and calls.)*

ARNOLD. Elizabeth! *(He sees* MRS. SHENSTONE*)* Oh, Anna, do you know where Elizabeth is?

(MRS. SHENSTONE comes in from the garden. She is a woman of forty, pleasant, and of elegant appearance.)

ANNA. Isn't she playing tennis?

ARNOLD. No, I've been down to the tennis court. Something very tiresome has happened.

ANNA. Oh?

ARNOLD. I wonder where the deuce she is.

ANNA. When do you expect Lord Porteous and Lady Kitty?

ARNOLD. They're motoring down in time for luncheon.

ANNA. Are you sure you want me to be here? It's not too late yet, you know. I can have my things packed and catch a train for somewhere or other.

ARNOLD. No, of course we want you. It'll make it so much easier if there are people here. It was exceedingly kind of you to come.

ANNA. Oh, nonsense!

ARNOLD. And I think it was a good thing to have Teddie Luton down.

ANNA. He is so breezy, isn't he?

ARNOLD. Yes, that's his great asset. I don't know that he's very intelligent, but, you know, there are occasions when you want a bull in a china shop. I sent one of the servants to find Elizabeth.

ANNA. I daresay she's putting on her shoes. She and Teddie were going to have a single.

ARNOLD. It can't take all this time to change one's shoes.

ANNA (with a smile). One can't change one's shoes without powdering one's nose, you know.

(ELIZABETH comes in. She is a very pretty creature in the early twenties. She wears a light summer frock.)

ARNOLD. My dear, I've been hunting for you everywhere. What *have* you been doing?

ELIZABETH. Nothing! I've been standing on my head.

ARNOLD. My father's here.

ELIZABETH (startled). Where?

ARNOLD. At the cottage. He arrived last night.

ELIZABETH. Damn!

ARNOLD (good-humoredly). I wish you wouldn't say that, Elizabeth.

ELIZABETH. If you're not going to say "Damn" when a thing's damnable, when are you going to say "Damn"?

ARNOLD. I should have thought you could say, "Oh, bother!" or something like that.

ELIZABETH. But that wouldn't express my sentiments. Besides, at that speech day when you were giving away prizes you said there were no synonyms in the English language.

ANNA (smiling). Oh, Elizabeth! It's very unfair to expect a politician to live in private up to the statements he makes in public.

ARNOLD. I'm always willing to stand by anything I've said. There *are* no synonyms in the English language.

ELIZABETH. In that case, I shall be regretfully forced to continue to say "Damn" whenever I feel like it.

(EDWARD LUTON shows himself at the window. He is an attractive youth in flannels.)

TEDDIE. I say, what about this tennis?

ELIZABETH. Come in. We're having a scene.

TEDDIE (entering). How splendid! What about?

ELIZABETH. The English language.

TEDDIE. Don't tell me you've been splitting your infinitives.

ARNOLD (with the shadow of a frown). I wish you'd be serious, Elizabeth. The situation is none too pleasant.

ANNA. I think Teddie and I had better make ourselves scarce.

ELIZABETH. Nonsense! You're both in it. If there's going to be any unpleasantness we want your moral support. That's why we asked you to come.

TEDDIE. And I thought I'd been asked for my blue eyes.

ELIZABETH. Vain beast! And they happen to be brown.

TEDDIE. Is anything up?

ELIZABETH. Arnold's father arrived last night.

TEDDIE. Did he, by Jove! I thought he was in Paris.

ARNOLD. So did we all. He told me he'd be there for the next month.

ANNA. Have you seen him?

ARNOLD. No! He rang me up. It's a mercy he had a telephone put in the cottage. It would have been a pretty kettle of fish if he'd just walked in.

ELIZABETH. Did you tell him Lady Catherine was coming?

ARNOLD. Of course not. I was flabbergasted to know he was here. And then I thought we'd better talk it over first.

ELIZABETH. Is he coming along here?

ARNOLD. Yes. He suggested it, and I couldn't think of any excuse to prevent him.

TEDDIE. Couldn't you put the other people off?

ARNOLD. They're coming by car. They may be here any minute. It's too late to do that.

ELIZABETH. Besides, it would be beastly.

ARNOLD. I knew it was silly to have them here. Elizabeth insisted.

ELIZABETH. After all, she *is* your mother, Arnold.

ARNOLD. That meant precious little to her when she—went away. You can't imagine it means very much to me now.

ELIZABETH. It's thirty years ago. It seems so

absurd to bear malice after all that time.

ARNOLD. I don't bear malice, but the fact remains that she did me the most irreparable harm. I can find no excuse for her.

ELIZABETH. Have you ever tried to?

ARNOLD. My dear Elizabeth, it's no good going over all that again. The facts are lamentably simple. She had a husband who adored her, a wonderful position, all the money she could want, and a child of five. And she ran away with a married man.

ELIZABETH. Lady Porteous is not a very attractive woman, Arnold. (*To* ANNA) Do you know her?

ANNA (*smiling*). "Forbidding" is the word, I think.

ARNOLD. If you're going to make little jokes about it, I have nothing more to say.

ANNA. I'm sorry, Arnold.

ELIZABETH. Perhaps your mother couldn't help herself—if she was in love?

ARNOLD. And had no sense of honor, duty, or decency? Oh, yes, under those circumstances you can explain a great deal.

ELIZABETH. That's not a very pretty way to speak of your mother.

ARNOLD. I can't look on her as my mother.

ELIZABETH. What you can't get over is that she didn't think of you. Some of us are more mother and some of us more woman. It gives me a little thrill when I think that she loved that man so much. She sacrificed her name, her position, and her child to him.

ARNOLD. You really can't expect the said child to have any great affection for the mother who treated him like that.

ELIZABETH. No, I don't think I do. But I think it's a pity after all these years that you shouldn't be friends.

ARNOLD. I wonder if you realize what it was to grow up under the shadow of that horrible scandal. Everywhere, at school, and at Oxford, and afterwards in London, I was always the son of Lady Kitty Cheney. Oh, it was cruel, cruel!

ELIZABETH. Yes, I know, Arnold. It was beastly for you.

ARNOLD. It would have been bad enough if it had been an ordinary case, but the position of the people made it ten times worse. My father was in the House then, and Porteous—

he hadn't succeeded to the title—was in the House too; he was Under-Secretary for Foreign Affairs, and he was very much in the public eye.

ANNA. My father always used to say he was the ablest man in the party. Everyone was expecting him to be Prime Minister.

ARNOLD. You can imagine what a boon it was to the British public. They hadn't had such a treat for a generation. The most popular song of the day was about my mother. Did you ever hear it? "Naughty Lady Kitty. Thought it such a pity . . ."

ELIZABETH (*interrupting*). Oh, Arnold, don't!

ARNOLD. And then they never let people forget them. If they'd lived quietly in Florence and not made a fuss the scandal would have died down. But those constant actions between Lord and Lady Porteous kept on reminding everyone.

TEDDIE. What were they having actions about?

ARNOLD. Of course my father divorced his wife, but Lady Porteous refused to divorce Porteous. He tried to force her by refusing to support her and turning her out of her house, and heaven knows what. They were constantly wrangling in the law courts.

ANNA. I think it was monstrous of Lady Porteous.

ARNOLD. She knew he wanted to marry my mother, and she hated my mother. You can't blame her.

ANNA. It must have been very difficult for them.

ARNOLD. That's why they've lived in Florence. Porteous has money. They found people there who were willing to accept the situation.

ELIZABETH. This is the first time they've ever come to England.

ARNOLD. My father will have to be told, Elizabeth.

ELIZABETH. Yes.

ANNA (*to* ELIZABETH). Has he ever spoken to you about Lady Kitty?

ELIZABETH. Never.

ARNOLD. I don't think her name has passed his lips since she ran away from this house thirty years ago.

TEDDIE. Oh, they lived here?

ARNOLD. Naturally. There was a house-party, and one evening neither Porteous nor my mother came down to dinner. The rest of them waited. They couldn't make it out. My father sent up to my mother's room, and a note was found on the pincushion.

ELIZABETH (*with a faint smile*). That's what they did in the Dark Ages.

ARNOLD. I think he took a dislike to this house from that horrible night. He never lived here again, and when I married he handed the place over to me. He just has a cottage now on the estate that he comes to when he feels inclined.

ELIZABETH. It's been very nice for us.

ARNOLD. I owe everything to my father. I don't think he'll ever forgive me for asking these people to come here.

ELIZABETH. I'm going to take all the blame on myself, Arnold.

ARNOLD (*irritably*). The situation was embarrassing enough anyhow. I don't know how I ought to treat them.

ELIZABETH. Don't you think that'll settle itself when you see them?

ARNOLD. After all, they're my guests. I shall try and behave like a gentleman.

ELIZABETH. I wouldn't. We haven't got central heating.

ARNOLD (*taking no notice*). Will she expect me to kiss her?

ELIZABETH (*with a smile*). Surely.

ARNOLD. It always makes me uncomfortable when people are effusive.

ANNA. But I can't understand why you never saw her before.

ARNOLD. I believe she tried to see me when I was little, but my father thought it better she shouldn't.

ANNA. Yes, but when you were grown up?

ARNOLD. She was always in Italy. I never went to Italy.

ELIZABETH. It seems to me so pathetic that if you saw one another in the street you wouldn't recognize each other.

ARNOLD. Is it my fault?

ELIZABETH. You've promised to be very gentle with her and very kind.

ARNOLD. The mistake was asking Porteous to come too. It looks as though we condoned the whole thing. And how am I to treat him? Am I to shake him by the hand and slap him on the back? He absolutely ruined my father's life.

ELIZABETH (*smiling*). How much would you give for a nice motor accident that prevented them from coming?

ARNOLD. I let you persuade me against my better judgment, and I've regretted it ever since.

ELIZABETH (*good-humoredly*). I think it's very lucky that Anna and Teddie are here. I don't foresee a very successful party.

ARNOLD. I'm going to do my best. I gave you my promise and I shall keep it. But I can't answer for my father.

ANNA. Here is your father.

(MR. CHAMPION-CHENEY *shows himself at one of the French windows*)

C.-C. May I come in through the window, or shall I have myself announced by a supercilious flunkey?

ELIZABETH. Come in. We've been expecting you.

C.-C. Impatiently, I hope, my dear child.

(MR. CHAMPION-CHENEY *is a tall man in the early sixties, spare, with a fine head of gray hair and an intelligent, somewhat ascetic face. He is very carefully dressed. He is a man who makes the most of himself. He bears his years jauntily. He kisses* ELIZABETH *and then holds out his hand to* ARNOLD.)

ELIZABETH. We thought you'd be in Paris for another month.

C.-C. How are you, Arnold? I always reserve to myself the privilege of changing my mind. It's the only one elderly gentlemen share with pretty women.

ELIZABETH. You know Anna.

C.-C. (*shaking hands with her*). Of course I do. How very nice to see you here! Are you staying long?

ANNA. As long as I'm welcome.

ELIZABETH. And this is Mr. Luton.

C.-C. How do you do? Do you play bridge?

LUTON. I do.

C.-C. Capital. Do you declare without top honors?

LUTON. Never.

C.-C. Of such is the kingdom of heaven. I see that you are a good young man.

LUTON. But, like the good in general, I am

poor.

C.-C. Never mind; if your principles are right, you can play ten shillings a hundred without danger. I never play less, and I never play more.

ARNOLD. And you—are you going to stay long, Father?

C.-C. To luncheon, if you'll have me.

(ARNOLD *gives* ELIZABETH *a harassed look*)

ELIZABETH. That'll be jolly.

ARNOLD. I didn't mean that. Of course you're going to stay for luncheon. I meant, how long are you going to stay down here?

C.-C. A week.

(*There is a moment's pause. Everyone but* CHAMPION-CHENEY *is slightly embarrassed.*)

TEDDIE. I think we'd better chuck our tennis.

ELIZABETH. Yes. I want my father-in-law to tell me what they're wearing in Paris this week.

TEDDIE. I'll go and put the rackets away.

(TEDDIE *goes out*)

ARNOLD. It's nearly one o'clock, Elizabeth.

ELIZABETH. I didn't know it was so late.

ANNA (*to* ARNOLD). I wonder if I can persuade you to take a turn in the garden before luncheon.

ARNOLD (*jumping at the idea*). I'd love it. (ANNA *goes out of the windows, and as he follows her he stops irresolutely*) I want you to look at this chair I've just got. I think it's rather good.

C.-C. Charming.

ARNOLD. About 1750, I should say. Good design, isn't it? It hasn't been restored or anything.

C.-C. Very pretty.

ARNOLD. I think it was a good buy, don't you?

C.-C. Oh, my dear boy! You know I'm entirely ignorant about these things.

ARNOLD. It's exactly my period . . . I shall see you at luncheon, then.

(*He follows* ANNA *through the window*)

C.-C. Who is that young man?

ELIZABETH. Mr. Luton. He's only just been demobilized. He's the manager of a rubber estate in the F. M. S.

C.-C. And what are the F. M. S. when they're at home?

ELIZABETH. The Federated Malay States. He joined up at the beginning of the war. He's just going back there.

C.-C. And why have we been left alone in this very marked manner?

ELIZABETH. Have we? I didn't notice it.

C.-C. I suppose it's difficult for the young to realize that one may be old without being a fool.

ELIZABETH. I never thought you that. Everyone knows you're very intelligent.

C.-C. They certainly ought to by now. I've told them often enough. Are you a little nervous?

ELIZABETH. Let me feel my pulse. (*She puts her finger on her wrist*) It's perfectly regular.

C.-C. When I suggested staying to luncheon Arnold looked exactly like a dose of castor oil.

ELIZABETH. I wish you'd sit down.

C.-C. Will it make it easier for you? (*He takes a chair*) You have evidently something very disagreeable to say to me.

ELIZABETH. You won't be cross with me?

C.-C. How old are you?

ELIZABETH. Twenty-five.

C.-C. I'm never cross with a woman under thirty.

ELIZABETH. Oh, then I've got ten years.

C.-C. Mathematics?

ELIZABETH. No. Paint.

C.-C. Well?

ELIZABETH (*reflectively*). I think it would be easier if I sat on your knees.

C.-C. That is a pleasing taste of yours, but you must take care not to put on weight.

(*She sits down on his knees*)

ELIZABETH. Am I bony?

C.-C. On the contrary. . . . I'm listening.

ELIZABETH. Lady Catherine's coming here.

C.-C. Who's Lady Catherine?

ELIZABETH. Your—Arnold's mother.

C.-C. Is she?

(*He withdraws himself a little and* ELIZABETH *gets up*)

ELIZABETH. You mustn't blame Arnold. It's my fault. I insisted. He was against it. I nagged till he gave way. And then I wrote and asked her to come.

C.-C. I didn't know you knew her.

ELIZABETH. I don't. But I heard she was in London. She's staying at Claridge's. It seemed so heartless not to take the smallest notice of her.

C.-C. When is she coming?

ELIZABETH. We're expecting her in time for

luncheon.

C.-C. As soon as that? I understand the embarrassment.

Elizabeth. You see, we never expected you to be here. You said you'd be in Paris for another month.

C.-C. My dear child, this is your house. There's no reason why you shouldn't ask whom you please to stay with you.

Elizabeth. After all, whatever her faults, she's Arnold's mother. It seemed so unnatural that they should never see one another. My heart ached for that poor lonely woman.

C.-C. I never heard that she was lonely, and she certainly isn't poor.

Elizabeth. And there's something else. I couldn't ask her by herself. It would have been so—so insulting. I asked Lord Porteous, too.

C.-C. I see.

Elizabeth. I daresay you'd rather not meet them.

C.-C. I daresay they'd rather not meet me. I shall get a capital luncheon at the cottage. I've noticed you always get the best food if you come in unexpectedly and have the same as they're having in the servants' hall.

Elizabeth. No one's ever talked to me about Lady Kitty. It's always been a subject that everyone has avoided. I've never even seen a photograph of her.

C.-C. The house was full of them when she left. I think I told the butler to throw them in the dust-bin. She was very much photographed.

Elizabeth. Won't you tell me what she was like?

C.-C. She was very like you, Elizabeth, only she had dark hair instead of red.

Elizabeth. Poor dear! It must be quite white now.

C.-C. I daresay. She was a pretty little thing.

Elizabeth. But she was one of the great beauties of her day. They say she was lovely.

C.-C. She had the most adorable little nose, like yours. . . .

Elizabeth. D'you like my nose?

C.-C. And she was very dainty, with a beautiful little figure; very light on her feet. She was like a *marquise* in an old French comedy. Yes, she was lovely.

Elizabeth. And I'm sure she's lovely still.

C.-C. She's no chicken, you know.

Elizabeth. You can't expect me to look at it as you and Arnold do. When you've loved as she's loved you may grow old, but you grow old beautifully.

C.-C. You're very romantic.

Elizabeth. If everyone hadn't made such a mystery of it I daresay I shouldn't feel as I do. I know she did a great wrong to you and a great wrong to Arnold. I'm willing to acknowledge that.

C.-C. I'm sure it's very kind of you.

Elizabeth. But she loved and she dared. Romance is such an elusive thing. You read of it in books, but it's seldom you see it face to face. I can't help it if it thrills me.

C.-C. I am painfully aware that the husband in these cases is not a romantic object.

Elizabeth. She had the world at her feet. You were rich. She was a figure in society. And she gave up everything for love.

C.-C. (*dryly*). I'm beginning to suspect it wasn't only for her sake and for Arnold's that you asked her to come here.

Elizabeth. I seem to know her already. I think her face is a little sad, for a love like that doesn't leave you gay, it leaves you grave, but I think her pale face is unlined. It's like a child's.

C.-C. My dear, how you let your imagination run away with you!

Elizabeth. I imagine her slight and frail.

C.-C. Frail, certainly.

Elizabeth. With beautiful thin hands and white hair. I've pictured her so often in that Renaissance Palace that they live in, with old Masters on the walls and lovely carved things all round, sitting in a black silk dress with old lace round her neck and old-fashioned diamonds. You see, I never knew my mother; she died when I was a baby. You can't confide in aunts with huge families of their own. I want Arnold's mother to be a mother to me. I've got so much to say to her.

C.-C. Are you happy with Arnold?

Elizabeth. Why shouldn't I be?

C.-C. Why haven't you got any babies?

Elizabeth. Give us a little time. We've only been married three years.

C.-C. I wonder what Hughie is like now!

ELIZABETH. Lord Porteous?

C.-C. He wore his clothes better than any man in London. You know he'd have been Prime Minister if he'd remained in politics.

ELIZABETH. What was he like then?

C.-C. He was a nice-looking fellow. Fine horseman. I suppose there was something very fascinating about him. Yellow hair and blue eyes, you know. He had a very good figure. I liked him. I was his parliamentary secretary. He was Arnold's godfather.

ELIZABETH. I know.

C.-C. I wonder if he ever regrets!

ELIZABETH. I wouldn't.

C.-C. Well, I must be strolling back to my cottage.

ELIZABETH. You're not angry with me?

C.-C. Not a bit.

(*She puts up her face for him to kiss. He kisses her on both cheeks and then goes out. In a moment* TEDDIE *is seen at the window.*)

TEDDIE. I saw the old blighter go.

ELIZABETH. Come in.

TEDDIE. Everything all right?

ELIZABETH. Oh, quite, as far as he's concerned. He's going to keep out of the way.

TEDDIE. Was it beastly?

ELIZABETH. No, he made it very easy for me. He's a nice old thing.

TEDDIE. You were rather scared.

ELIZABETH. A little. I am still. I don't know why.

TEDDIE. I guessed you were. I thought I'd come and give you a little moral support. It's ripping here, isn't it?

ELIZABETH. It is rather nice.

TEDDIE. It'll be jolly to think of it when I'm back in the F. M. S.

ELIZABETH. Aren't you homesick sometimes?

TEDDIE. Oh, everyone is now and then, you know.

ELIZABETH. You could have got a job in England if you'd wanted to, couldn't you?

TEDDIE. Oh, but I love it out there. England's ripping to come back to, but I couldn't live here now. It's like a woman you're desperately in love with as long as you don't see her, but when you're with her she maddens you so that you can't bear her.

ELIZABETH (*smiling*). What's wrong with England?

TEDDIE. I don't think anything's wrong with England. I expect something's wrong with me. I've been away too long. England seems to me full of people doing things they don't want to because other people expect it of them.

ELIZABETH. Isn't that what you call a high degree of civilization?

TEDDIE. People seem to me so insincere. When you go to parties in London they're all babbling about art, and you feel that in their hearts they don't care two-pence about it. They read the books that everybody is talking about because they don't want to be out of it. In the F. M. S. we don't get very many books, and we read those we have over and over again. They mean so much to us. I don't think the people over there are half so clever as the people at home, but one gets to know them better. You see, there are so few of us that we have to make the best of one another.

ELIZABETH. I imagine that frills are not much worn in the F. M. S. It must be a comfort.

TEDDIE. It's not much good being pretentious where everyone knows exactly who you are and what your income is.

ELIZABETH. I don't think you want too much sincerity in society. It would be like an iron girder in a house of cards.

TEDDIE. And then, you know, the place is ripping. You get used to a blue sky and you miss it in England.

ELIZABETH. What do you do with yourself all the time?

TEDDIE. Oh, one works like blazes. You have to be a pretty hefty fellow to be a planter. And then there's ripping bathing. You know, it's lovely, with palm trees all along the beach. And there's shooting. And now and then we have a little dance to a gramophone.

ELIZABETH (*pretending to tease him*). I think you've got a young woman out there, Teddie.

TEDDIE (*vehemently*). Oh, no!

(*She is a little taken aback by the earnestness of his disclaimer. There is a moment's silence, then she recovers herself.*)

ELIZABETH. But you'll have to marry and settle down one of these days, you know.

TEDDIE. I want to, but it's not a thing you

can do lightly.

ELIZABETH. I don't know why there more than elsewhere.

TEDDIE. In England if people don't get on they go their own ways and jog along after a fashion. In a place like that you're thrown a great deal on your own resources.

ELIZABETH. Of course.

TEDDIE. Lots of girls come out because they think they're going to have a good time. But if they're empty-headed, then they're just faced with their own emptiness and they're done. If their husbands can afford it they go home and settle down as grass-widows.

ELIZABETH. I've met them. They seem to find it a very pleasant occupation.

TEDDIE. It's rotten for their husbands, though.

ELIZABETH. And if the husbands can't afford it?

TEDDIE. Oh, then they tipple.

ELIZABETH. It's not a very alluring prospect.

TEDDIE. But if the woman's the right sort she wouldn't exchange it for any life in the world. When all's said and done it's we who've made the Empire.

ELIZABETH. What sort is the right sort?

TEDDIE. A woman of courage and endurance and sincerity. Of course, it's hopeless unless she's in love with her husband.

(*He is looking at her earnestly and she, raising her eyes, gives him a long look. There is silence between them.*)

TEDDIE. My house stands on the side of a hill, and the coconut trees wind down to the shore. Azaleas grow in my garden, and camellias, and all sorts of ripping flowers. And in front of me is the winding coast line, and then the blue sea. (*A pause*) Do you know that I'm awfully in love with you?

ELIZABETH (*gravely*). I wasn't quite sure. I wondered.

TEDDIE. And you? (*She nods slowly*) I've never kissed you.

ELIZABETH. I don't want you to.

(*They look at one another steadily. They are both grave. ARNOLD comes in hurriedly.*)

ARNOLD. They're coming, Elizabeth.

ELIZABETH (*as though returning from a distant world*). Who?

ARNOLD (*impatiently*). My dear! My mother, of course. The car is just coming up the drive.

TEDDIE. Would you like me to clear out?

ARNOLD. No, no! For goodness' sake stay.

ELIZABETH. We'd better go and meet them, Arnold.

ARNOLD. No, no; I think they'd much better be shown in. I feel simply sick with nervousness.

(*ANNA comes in from the garden*)

ANNA. Your guests have arrived.

ELIZABETH. Yes, I know.

ARNOLD. I've given orders that luncheon should be served at once.

ELIZABETH. Why? It's not half-past one already, is it?

ARNOLD. I thought it would help. When you don't know exactly what to say you can always eat.

(*The BUTLER comes in and announces*)

BUTLER. Lady Catherine Champion-Cheney! Lord Porteous!

(*LADY KITTY comes in followed by PORTEOUS, and the BUTLER goes out. LADY KITTY is a gay little lady, with dyed red hair and painted cheeks. She is somewhat outrageously dressed. She never forgets that she has been a pretty woman and she still behaves as if she were twenty-five. LORD PORTEOUS is a very bald, elderly gentleman in loose, rather eccentric clothes. He is snappy and gruff. This is not at all the couple that ELIZABETH expected, and for a moment she stares at them with round, startled eyes. LADY KITTY goes up to her with outstretched hands.*)

LADY KITTY. Elizabeth! Elizabeth! (*She kisses her effusively*) What an adorable creature. (*Turning to PORTEOUS*) Hughie, isn't she adorable?

PORTEOUS (*with a grunt*). Ugh!

(*ELIZABETH, smiling now, turns to him and gives him her hand*)

ELIZABETH. How d'you do?

PORTEOUS. Damnable road you've got down here. How d'you do, my dear? Why d'you have such damnable roads in England?

(*LADY KITTY's eyes fall on TEDDIE and goes up to him with her arms thrown back, prepared to throw them round*) *him*)

LADY KITTY. My boy, my boy! I should have known you anywhere!

ELIZABETH (*hastily*). That's Arnold.

LADY KITTY (*without a moment's hesitation*). The image of his father! I should have known him anywhere! (*She throws her arms round his neck*) My boy, my boy!

PORTEOUS (*with a grunt*). Ugh!

LADY KITTY. Tell me, would you have known me again? Have I changed?

ARNOLD. I was only five, you know, when— when you . . .

LADY KITTY (*emotionally*). I remember as if it was yesterday. I went up into your room. (*With a sudden change of manner*) By the way, I always thought that nurse drank. Did you ever find out if she really did?

PORTEOUS. How the devil can you expect him to know that, Kitty?

LADY KITTY. You've never had a child, Hughie; how can you tell what they know and what they don't?

ELIZABETH (*coming to the rescue*). This is Arnold, Lord Porteous.

PORTEOUS (*shaking hands with him*). How d'you do? I knew your father.

ARNOLD. Yes.

PORTEOUS. Alive still?

ARNOLD. Yes.

PORTEOUS. He must be getting on. Is he well?

ARNOLD. Very.

PORTEOUS. Ugh! Takes care of himself, I suppose. I'm not at all well. This damned climate doesn't agree with me.

ELIZABETH (*to* LADY KITTY). This is Mrs. Shenstone. And this is Mr. Luton. I hope you don't mind a very small party.

LADY KITTY (*shaking hands with* ANNA *and* TEDDIE). Oh, no, I shall enjoy it. I used to give enormous parties here. Political, you know. How nice you've made this room!

ELIZABETH. Oh, that's Arnold.

ARNOLD (*nervously*). D'you like this chair? I've just bought it. It's exactly my period.

PORTEOUS (*bluntly*). It's a fake.

ARNOLD (*indignantly*). I don't think it is for a minute.

PORTEOUS. The legs are not right.

ARNOLD. I don't know how you can say that.

If there is anything right about it, it's the legs.

LADY KITTY. I'm sure they're right.

PORTEOUS. You know nothing whatever about it, Kitty.

LADY KITTY. That's what you think. *I* think it's a beautiful chair. Hepplewhite?

ARNOLD. No, Sheraton.

LADY KITTY. Oh, I know. "The School for Scandal."

PORTEOUS. Sheraton, my dear. Sheraton.

LADY KITTY. Yes, that's what I say. I acted the screen scene at some amateur theatricals in Florence, and Ermeto Novelli, the great Italian tragedian, told me he'd never seen a Lady Teazle like me.

PORTEOUS. Ugh!

LADY KITTY (*to* ELIZABETH). Do you act?

ELIZABETH. Oh, I couldn't. I should be too nervous.

LADY KITTY. I'm never nervous. I'm a born actress. Of course, if I had my time over again I'd go on the stage. You know, it's extraordinary how they keep young. Actresses, I mean. I think it's because they're always playing different parts. Hughie, do you think Arnold takes after me or after his father? Of course I think he's the very image of me. Arnold, I think I ought to tell you that I was received into the Catholic Church last winter. I've been thinking about it for years, and the last time we were at Monte Carlo I met such a nice monsignore. I told him what my difficulties were and he was too wonderful. I knew Hughie wouldn't approve, so I kept it a secret. (*To* ELIZABETH) Are you interested in religion? I think it's too wonderful. We must have a long talk about it one of these days. (*Pointing to her frock*) Callot?

ELIZABETH. No, Worth.

LADY KITTY. I knew it was either Worth or Callot. Of course, it's line that's the important thing. I go to Worth myself, and I always say to him, "Line, my dear Worth, line." What *is* the matter, Hughie?"

PORTEOUS. These new teeth of mine are so damned uncomfortable.

LADY KITTY. Men are extraordinary. They can't stand the smallest discomfort. Why, a woman's life is uncomfortable from the moment she gets up in the morning till the moment she goes to bed at night. And d'you think it's comfortable to sleep with a mask on your face?

PORTEOUS. They don't seem to hold up properly.

LADY KITTY. Well, that's not the fault of your teeth. That's the fault of your gums.

PORTEOUS. Damned rotten dentist. That's what's the matter.

LADY KITTY. I thought he was a very nice dentist. He told me *my* teeth would last till I was fifty. He has a Chinese room. It's so interesting; while he scrapes your teeth he tells you all about the dear Empress Dowager. Are you interested in China? I think it's too wonderful. You know they've cut off their pigtails. I think it's such a pity. They were so picturesque.

(*The* BUTLER *comes in*)

BUTLER. Luncheon is served, sir.

ELIZABETH. Would you like to see your rooms?

PORTEOUS. We can see our rooms after luncheon.

LADY KITTY. I must powder my nose, Hughie.

PORTEOUS. Powder it down here.

LADY KITTY. I never saw anyone so inconsiderate.

PORTEOUS. You'll keep us all waiting half an hour. I know you.

LADY KITTY (*fumbling in her bag*). Oh, well, peace at any price, as Lord Beaconsfield said.[1]

PORTEOUS. He said a lot of damned silly things, Kitty, but he never said that.

(LADY KITTY'S *face changes. Perplexity is followed by dismay, and dismay by consternation.*)

LADY KITTY. Oh!

ELIZABETH. What is the matter?

LADY KITTY (*with anguish*). My lip-stick!

ELIZABETH. Can't you find it?

LADY KITTY. I had it in the car. Hughie, you remember that I had it in the car.

PORTEOUS. I don't remember anything about it.

LADY KITTY. Don't be so stupid, Hughie. Why, when we came through the gates I said: "My home, my home!" and I took it out and put some on my lips.

ELIZABETH. Perhaps you dropped it in the car.

LADY KITTY. For heaven's sake send some one to look for it.

ARNOLD. I'll ring.

LADY KITTY. I'm absolutely lost without my lip-stick. Lend me yours, darling, will you?

ELIZABETH. I'm awfully sorry. I'm afraid I haven't got one.

LADY KITTY. Do you mean to say you don't use a lip-stick?

ELIZABETH. Never.

PORTEOUS. Look at her lips. What the devil d'you think she wants muck like that for?

LADY KITTY. Oh, my dear, what a mistake you make! You *must* use a lip-stick. It's so good for the lips. Men like it, you know. I couldn't *live* without a lip-stick.

(CHAMPION-CHENEY *appears at the window holding in his upstretched hand a little gold case*)

C.-C. (*as he comes in*). Has anyone here lost a diminutive utensil containing, unless I am mistaken, a favorite preparation for the toilet?

(ARNOLD *and* ELIZABETH *are thunderstruck at his appearance and even* TEDDIE *and* ANNA *are taken aback. But* LADY KITTY *is overjoyed.*)

LADY KITTY. My lip-stick!

C.-C. I found it in the drive and I ventured to bring it in.

LADY KITTY. It's Saint Antony. I said a little prayer to him when I was hunting in my bag.

PORTEOUS. Saint Antony be blowed! It's Clive, by God!

LADY KITTY (*startled, her attention suddenly turning from the lip-stick*). Clive!

C.-C. You didn't recognize me. It's many years since we met.

LADY KITTY. My poor Clive, your hair has gone quite white!

C.-C. (*holding out his hand*). I hope you had a pleasant journey down from London.

LADY KITTY (*offering him her cheek*). You may kiss me, Clive.

C.-C. (*kissing her*). You don't mind, Hughie?

PORTEOUS (*with a grunt*). Ugh!

C.-C. (*going up to him cordially*). And how are you, my dear Hughie?

PORTEOUS. Damned rheumatic if you want to know. Filthy climate you have in this country.

C.-C. Aren't you going to shake hands with me, Hughie?

[1] Lord Beaconsfield said, on returning from the Congress of Berlin, 1878, "We have brought you peace with honor."

PORTEOUS. I have no objection to shaking hands with you.

C.-C. You've aged, my poor Hughie.

PORTEOUS. Some one was asking me how old you were the other day.

C.-C. Were they surprised when you told them?

PORTEOUS. Surprised! They wondered you weren't dead.

(*The* BUTLER *comes in*)

BUTLER. Did you ring, sir?

ARNOLD. No. Oh, yes, I did. It doesn't matter now.

C.-C. (*as the* BUTLER *is going*). One moment. My dear Elizabeth, I've come to throw myself on your mercy. My servants are busy with their own affairs. There's not a thing for me to eat in my cottage.

ELIZABETH. Oh, but we shall be delighted if you'll lunch with us.

C.-C. It either means that or my immediate death from starvation. You don't mind, Arnold?

ARNOLD. My dear father!

ELIZABETH (*to the* BUTLER). Mr. Cheney will lunch here.

BUTLER. Very good, ma'am.

C.-C. (*to* LADY KITTY). And what do you think of Arnold?

LADY KITTY. I adore him.

C.-C. He's grown, hasn't he? But then you'd expect him to do that in thirty years.

ARNOLD. For God's sake let's go in to lunch, Elizabeth!

Act II

SCENE: The same as in the preceding act.

(*It is afternoon. When the curtain rises* PORTEOUS *and* LADY KITTY, ANNA *and* TEDDIE *are playing bridge.* ELIZABETH *and* CHAMPION-CHENEY *are watching.* PORTEOUS *and* LADY KITTY *are partners.*)

C.-C. When will Arnold be back, Elizabeth?

ELIZABETH. Soon, I think.

C.-C. Is he addressing a meeting?

ELIZABETH. No, it's only a conference with his agent and one or two constituents.

PORTEOUS (*irritably*). How anyone can be expected to play bridge when people are shouting at the top of their voices all round them, I for one cannot understand.

ELIZABETH (*smiling*). I'm so sorry.

ANNA. I can see your hand, Lord Porteous.

PORTEOUS. It may help you.

LADY KITTY. I've told you over and over again to hold your cards up. It ruins one's game when one can't help seeing one's opponent's hand.

PORTEOUS. One isn't obliged to look.

LADY KITTY. What was Arnold's majority at the last election?

ELIZABETH. Seven hundred and something.

C.-C. He'll have to fight for it if he wants to keep his seat next time.

PORTEOUS Are we playing bridge, or talking politics?

LADY KITTY. I never find that conversation interferes with my game.

PORTEOUS. You certainly play no worse when you talk than when you hold your tongue.

LADY KITTY. I think that's a very offensive thing to say, Hughie. Just because I don't play the same game as you do you think I can't play.

PORTEOUS. I'm glad you acknowledge it's not the same game as I play. But why in God's name do you call it bridge?

C.-C. I agree with Kitty. I hate people who play bridge as though they were at a funeral and knew their feet were getting wet.

PORTEOUS. Of course you take Kitty's part.

LADY KITTY. That's the least he can do.

C.-C. I have a naturally cheerful disposition.

PORTEOUS. You've never had anything to sour it.

LADY KITTY. I don't know what you mean by that, Hughie.

PORTEOUS (*trying to contain himself*). Must you trump my ace?

LADY KITTY (*innocently*). Oh, was that your ace, darling?

PORTEOUS (*furiously*). Yes, it was my ace.

LADY KITTY. Oh, well, it was the only trump I had. I shouldn't have made it anyway.

PORTEOUS. You needn't have told them that.

Now she knows exactly what I've got.

Lady Kitty. She knew before.

Porteous. How could she know?

Lady Kitty. She said she'd seen your hand.

Anna. Oh, I didn't. I said I could see it.

Lady Kitty. Well, I naturally supposed that if she could see it she did.

Porteous. Really, Kitty, you have the most extraordinary ideas.

C.-C. Not at all. If anyone is such a fool as to show me his hand, of course I look at it.

Porteous (*fuming*). If you study the etiquette of bridge, you'll discover that onlookers are expected not to interfere with the game.

C.-C. My dear Hughie, this is a matter of ethics, not of bridge.

Anna. Anyhow, I get the game. And rubber.

Teddie. I claim a revoke.

Porteous. Who revoked?

Teddie. You did.

Porteous. Nonsense. I've never revoked in my life.

Teddie. I'll show you. (*He turns over the tricks to show the faces of the cards*) You threw away a club on the third heart trick and you had another heart.

Porteous. I never had more than two hearts.

Teddie. Oh, yes, you had. Look here. That's the card you played on the last trick but one.

Lady Kitty (*delighted to catch him out*). There's no doubt about it, Hughie. You revoked.

Porteous. I tell you I did not revoke. I never revoke.

C.-C. You did, Hughie. I wondered what on earth you were doing.

Porteous. I don't know how anyone can be expected not to revoke when there's this confounded chatter going on all the time.

Teddie. Well, that's another hundred to us.

Porteous (*to* Champion-Cheney). I wish you wouldn't breathe down my neck. I never can play bridge when there's somebody breathing down my neck.

(*The party have risen from the bridge-table, and they scatter about the room*)

Anna. Well, I'm going to take a book and lie down in the hammock till it's time to dress.

Teddie (*who has been adding up*). I'll put it down in the book, shall I?

Porteous (*who has not moved, setting out the cards for a patience*). Yes, yes, put it down. I never revoke. (Anna *goes out*)

Lady Kitty. Would you like to come for a little stroll, Hughie?

Porteous. What for?

Lady Kitty. Exercise.

Porteous. I hate exercise.

C.-C. (*looking at the patience*). The seven goes on the eight. (Porteous *takes no notice*)

Lady Kitty. The seven goes on the eight, Hughie.

Porteous. I don't choose to put the seven on the eight.

C.-C. That knave goes on the queen.

Porteous. I'm not blind, thank you.

Lady Kitty. The three goes on the four.

C.-C. All these go over.

Porteous (*furiously*). Am I playing this patience, or are you playing it?

Lady Kitty. But you're missing everything.

Porteous. That's my business.

C.-C. It's no good losing your temper over it, Hughie.

Porteous. Go away, both of you. You irritate me.

Lady Kitty. We were only trying to help you, Hughie.

Porteous. I don't want to be helped. I want to do it by myself.

Lady Kitty. I think your manners are perfectly deplorable, Hughie.

Porteous. It's simply maddening when you're playing patience and people won't leave you alone.

C.-C. We won't say another word.

Porteous. That three goes. I believe it's coming out. If I'd been such a fool as to put that seven up I shouldn't have been able to bring these down.

(*He puts down several cards while they watch him silently*)

Lady Kitty and C.-C. (*together*). The four goes on the five.

Porteous (*throwing down the cards violently*). Damn you! Why don't you leave me alone? It's intolerable.

C.-C. It was coming out, my dear fellow.

Porteous. I know it was coming out. Confound you!

Lady Kitty. How petty you are, Hughie!

PORTEOUS. Petty, be damned! I've told you over and over again that I will not be interfered with when I'm playing patience.

LADY KITTY. Don't talk to me like that, Hughie.

PORTEOUS. I shall talk to you as I please.

LADY KITTY (*beginning to cry*). Oh, you brute! You brute! (*She flings out of the room*)

PORTEOUS. Oh, damn! Now she's going to cry.

(*He shambles out into the garden.* CHAMPION-CHENEY, ELIZABETH *and* TEDDIE *are left alone. There is a moment's pause.* CHAMPION-CHENEY *looks from* TEDDIE *to* ELIZABETH, *with an ironical smile.*)

C.-C. Upon my soul, they might be married. They frip so much.

ELIZABETH (*frigidly*). It's been nice of you to come here so often since they arrived. It's helped to make things easy.

C.-C. Irony? It's a rhetorical form not much favored in this blessed plot, this earth, this realm, this England.

ELIZABETH. What exactly are you getting at?

C.-C. How slangy the young women of the present day are! I suppose the fact that Arnold is a purist leads you to the contrary extravagance.

ELIZABETH. Anyhow you know what I mean.

C.-C. (*with a smile*). I have a dim, groping suspicion.

ELIZABETH. You promised to keep away. Why did you come back the moment they arrived?

C.-C. Curiosity, my dear child. A surely pardonable curiosity.

ELIZABETH. And since then you've been here all the time. You don't generally favor us with so much of your company when you're down at your cottage.

C.-C. I've been excessively amused.

ELIZABETH. It has struck me that whenever they started fripping you took a malicious pleasure in goading them on.

C.-C. I don't think there's much love lost between them now, do you?

(TEDDIE *is making as though to leave the room*)

ELIZABETH. Don't go, Teddie.

C.-C. No, please don't. I'm only staying a minute. We were talking about Lady Kitty just before she arrived. (*To* ELIZABETH) Do you remember? The pale, frail lady in black satin and old lace.

ELIZABETH (*with a chuckle*). You are a devil, you know.

C.-C. Ah, well, he's always had the reputation of being a humorist and a gentleman.

ELIZABETH. Did *you* expect her to be like that, poor dear?

C.-C. My dear child, I hadn't the vaguest idea. You were asking me the other day what she was like when she ran away. I didn't tell you half. She was so gay and so natural. Who would have thought that animation would turn into such frivolity, and that charming impulsiveness lead to such a ridiculous affectation?

ELIZABETH. It rather sets my nerves on edge to hear the way you talk of her.

C.-C. It's the truth that sets your nerves on edge, not I.

ELIZABETH. You loved her once. Have you no feeling for her at all?

C.-C. None. Why should I?

ELIZABETH. She's the mother of your son.

C.-C. My dear child, you have a charming nature, as simple, frank, and artless as hers was. Don't let pure humbug obscure your common sense.

ELIZABETH. We have no right to judge. She's only been here two days. We know nothing about her.

C.-C. My dear, her soul is as thickly rouged as her face. She hasn't an emotion that's sincere. She's tinsel. You think I'm a cruel, cynical old man. Why, when I think of what she was, if I didn't laugh at what she has become I should cry.

ELIZABETH. How do you know she wouldn't be just the same now if she'd remained your wife? Do you think your influence would have had such a salutary effect on her?

C.-C. (*good-humoredly*). I like you when you're bitter and rather insolent.

ELIZABETH. D'you like me enough to answer my question?

C.-C. She was only twenty-seven when she went away. She might have become anything. She might have become the woman you expected her to be. There are very few of us who are strong enough to make circumstances serve us. We are the creatures of our environment.

She's a silly, worthless woman because she's led a silly, worthless life.

ELIZABETH (*disturbed*). You're horrible today.

C.-C. I don't say it's I who could have prevented her from becoming this ridiculous caricature of a pretty woman grown old. But life could. Here she would have had the friends fit to her station, and a decent activity, and worthy interests. Ask her what her life has been all these years among divorced women and kept women and the men who consort with them. There is no more lamentable pursuit than a life of pleasure.

ELIZABETH. At all events she loved and she loved greatly. I have only pity and affection for her.

C.-C. And if she loved what d'you think she felt when she saw that she had ruined Hughie? Look at him. He was tight last night after dinner and tight the night before.

ELIZABETH. I know.

C.-C. And she took it as a matter of course. How long do you suppose he's been getting tight every night? Do you think he was like that thirty years ago? Can you imagine that that was a brilliant young man, whom everyone expected to be Prime Minister? Look at him now. A grumpy sodden old fellow with false teeth.

ELIZABETH. You have false teeth, too.

C.-C. Yes, but damn it all, they fit. She's ruined him and she knows she's ruined him.

ELIZABETH (*looking at him suspiciously*). Why are you saying all this to me?

C.-C. Am I hurting your feelings?

ELIZABETH. I think I've had enough for the present.

C.-C. I'll go and have a look at the goldfish. I want to see Arnold when he comes in. (*Politely*) I'm afraid we've been boring Mr. Luton.

TEDDIE. Not at all.

C.-C. When are you going back to the F. M. S.?

TEDDIE. In about a month.

C.-C. I see.   (*He goes out*)

ELIZABETH. I wonder what he has at the back of his head.

TEDDIE. D'you think he was talking at you?

ELIZABETH. He's as clever as a bagful of monkeys.

(*There is a moment's pause.* TEDDIE *hesitates a little and when he speaks it is in a different tone. He is grave and somewhat nervous.*)

TEDDIE. It seems very difficult to get a few minutes alone with you. I wonder if you've been making it difficult?

ELIZABETH. I wanted to think.

TEDDIE. I've made up my mind to go away tomorrow.

ELIZABETH. Why?

TEDDIE. I want you altogether or not at all.

ELIZABETH. You're so arbitrary.

TEDDIE. You said so—you said you cared for me.

ELIZABETH. I do.

TEDDIE. Do you mind if we talk it over now?

ELIZABETH. No.

TEDDIE (*frowning*). It makes me feel rather shy and awkward. I've repeated to myself over and over again exactly what I want to say to you, and now all I'd prepared seems rather footling.

ELIZABETH. I'm so afraid I'm going to cry.

TEDDIE. I feel it's all so tremendously serious and I think we ought to keep emotion out of it. You're rather emotional, aren't you?

ELIZABETH (*half smiling and half in tears*). So are you for the matter of that.

TEDDIE. That's why I wanted to have everything I meant to say to you cut and dried. I think it would be awfully unfair if I made love to you and all that sort of thing, and you were carried away. I wrote it all down and thought I'd send it to you as a letter.

ELIZABETH. Why didn't you?

TEDDIE. I got the wind up. A letter seems so —so cold. You see, I love you so awfully.

ELIZABETH. For goodness' sake don't say that.

TEDDIE. You mustn't cry. Please don't, or I shall go all to pieces.

ELIZABETH (*trying to smile*). I'm sorry. It doesn't mean anything really. It's only tears running out of my eyes.

TEDDIE. Our only chance is to be awfully matter-of-fact.

(*He stops for a moment. He finds it quite difficult to control himself. He clears his throat. He frowns with annoyance at himself.*)

ELIZABETH. What's the matter?

TEDDIE. I've got a sort of lump in my throat.

It is idiotic. I think I'll have a cigarette. (*She watches him in silence while he lights a cigarette*) You see, I've never been in love with anyone before, not really. It's knocked me endways. I don't know how I can live without you now. . . . Does that old fool know I'm in love with you?

ELIZABETH. I think so.

TEDDIE. When he was talking about Lady Kitty smashing up Lord Porteous' career I thought there was something at the back of it.

ELIZABETH. I think he was trying to persuade me not to smash up yours.

TEDDIE. I'm sure that's very considerate of him, but I don't happen to have one to smash. I wish I had. It's the only time in my life I've wished I were a hell of a swell so that I could chuck it all and show you how much more you are to me than anything else in the world.

ELIZABETH (*affectionately*). You're a dear old thing, Teddie.

TEDDIE. You know, I don't really know how to make love, but if I did I couldn't do it now because I just want to be absolutely practical.

ELIZABETH (*chaffing him*). I'm glad you don't know how to make love. It would be almost more than I could bear.

TEDDIE. You see, I'm not at all romantic and that sort of thing. I'm just a common or garden business man. All this is so dreadfully serious and I think we ought to be sensible.

ELIZABETH (*with a break in her voice*). You owl!

TEDDIE. No, Elizabeth, don't say things like that to me. I want you to consider all the *pros* and *cons,* and my heart's thumping against my chest, and you know I love you, I love you, I love you.

ELIZABETH (*in a sigh of passion*). Oh, my precious!

TEDDIE (*impatiently, but with himself, rather than with* ELIZABETH). Don't be idiotic, Elizabeth. I'm not going to tell you that I can't live without you and a lot of muck like that. You know that you mean everything in the world to me. (*Almost giving it up as a bad job*) Oh, my God!

ELIZABETH (*her voice faltering*). D'you think there's anything you can say to me that I don't know already?

TEDDIE (*desperately*). But I haven't said a single thing I wanted to. I'm a business man and I want to put it all in a business way, if you understand what I mean.

ELIZABETH (*smiling*). I don't believe you're a very good business man.

TEDDIE (*sharply*). You don't know what you're talking about. I'm a first rate business man, but somehow this is different. (*Hopelessly*) I don't know why it won't go right.

ELIZABETH. What are we going to do about it?

TEDDIE. You see, it's not just because you're awfully pretty that I love you. I'd love you just as much if you were old and ugly. It's you I love, not what you look like. And it's not only love; love be blowed! It's that I *like* you so tremendously. I think you're such a ripping good sort. I just want to be with you. I feel so jolly and happy just to think you're there. I'm so awfully *fond* of you.

ELIZABETH (*laughing through her tears*). I don't know if this is your idea of introducing a business proposition.

TEDDIE. Damn you, you won't let me.

ELIZABETH. You said "Damn you."

TEDDIE. I meant it.

ELIZABETH. Your voice sounded as if you meant it, you perfect duck!

TEDDIE. Really, Elizabeth, you're intolerable.

ELIZABETH. I'm doing nothing.

TEDDIE. Yes, you are, you're putting me off my blow. What I want to say is perfectly simple. I'm a very ordinary business man.

ELIZABETH. You've said that before.

TEDDIE (*angrily*). Shut up. I haven't got a bob besides what I earn. I've got no position. I'm nothing. You're rich and you're a big pot and you've got everything that anyone can want. It's awful cheek my saying anything to you at all. But after all there's only one thing that really matters in the world, and that's love. I love you. Chuck all this, Elizabeth, and come to me.

ELIZABETH. Are you cross with me?

TEDDIE. Furious.

ELIZABETH. Darling!

TEDDIE. If you don't want me tell me so at once and let me get out quickly.

ELIZABETH. Teddie, nothing in the world matters anything to me but you. I'll go wherever you take me. I love you.

TEDDIE (*all to pieces*). Oh, my God!

ELIZABETH. Does it mean as much to you as that? Oh, Teddie!

TEDDIE (*trying to control himself*). Don't be a fool, Elizabeth.

ELIZABETH. It's you're the fool. You're making me cry.

TEDDIE. You're so damned emotional.

ELIZABETH. Damned emotional yourself. I'm sure you're a rotten business man.

TEDDIE. I don't care what you think. You've made me so awfully happy. I say, what a lark life's going to be!

ELIZABETH. What?

TEDDIE. Nothing. I just like to say Elizabeth.

ELIZABETH. You fool!

TEDDIE. I say, can you shoot?

ELIZABETH. No.

TEDDIE. I'll teach you. You don't know how ripping it is to start out from your camp at dawn and travel through the jungle. And you're so tired at night and the sky's all starry. It's a fair treat. Of course I didn't want to say anything about all that till you'd decided. I'd made up my mind to be absolutely practical.

ELIZABETH (*chaffing him*). The only practical thing you said was that love is the only thing that really matters.

TEDDIE (*happily*). Pull the other leg next time, will you? I should hate to have one longer than the other.

ELIZABETH. Isn't it fun being in love with some one who's in love with you?

TEDDIE. I say, I think I'd better clear out at once, don't you? It seems rather rotten to stay on in—in this house.

ELIZABETH. You can't go tonight. There's no train.

TEDDIE. I'll go tomorrow. I'll wait in London till you're ready to join me.

ELIZABETH. I'm not going to leave a note on the pincushion like Lady Kitty, you know. I'm going to tell Arnold.

TEDDIE. Are you? Don't you think there'll be an awful bother?

ELIZABETH. I must face it. I should hate to be sly and deceitful.

TEDDIE. Well, then, let's face it together.

ELIZABETH. No, I'll talk to Arnold by myself.

TEDDIE. You won't let anyone influence you?

ELIZABETH. No.

(*He holds out his hand and she takes it. They look into one another's eyes with grave, almost solemn affection. There is the sound outside of a car driving up.*)

ELIZABETH. There's the car. Arnold's come back. I must go and bathe my eyes. I don't want them to see I've been crying.

TEDDIE. All right. (*As she is going*) Elizabeth.

ELIZABETH (*stopping*). What?

TEDDIE. Bless you.

ELIZABETH (*affectionately*). Idiot!

(*She goes out of the door and TEDDIE through the French window into the garden. For an instant the room is empty. ARNOLD comes in. He sits down and takes some papers out of his despatch-case. LADY KITTY enters. He gets up.*)

LADY KITTY. I saw you come in. Oh, my dear, don't get up. There's no reason why you should be so dreadfully polite to me.

ARNOLD. I've just rung for a cup of tea.

LADY KITTY. Perhaps we shall have the chance of a little talk. We don't seem to have had five minutes by ourselves. I want to make your acquaintance, you know.

ARNOLD. I should like you to know that it's not by my wish that my father is here.

LADY KITTY. But I'm so interested to see him.

ARNOLD. I was afraid that you and Lord Porteous must find it embarrassing.

LADY KITTY. Oh, no. Hughie was his greatest friend. They were at Eton and Oxford together. I think your father has improved so much since I saw him last. He wasn't good-looking as a young man, but now he's quite handsome.

(*The FOOTMAN brings in a tray on which are tea-things*)

LADY KITTY. Shall I pour it out for you?

ARNOLD. Thank you very much.

LADY KITTY. Do you take sugar?

ARNOLD. No. I gave it up during the war.

LADY KITTY. So wise of you. It's so bad for the figure. Besides being patriotic, of course. Isn't it absurd that I should ask my son if he takes sugar or not? Life is really very quaint. Sad, of course, but oh, so quaint! Often I lie in bed at night and have a good laugh to myself as I think how quaint life is.

ARNOLD. I'm afraid I'm a very serious person.

LADY KITTY. How old are you now, Arnold?

ARNOLD. Thirty-five.

LADY KITTY. Are you really? Of course, I was a child when I married your father.

ARNOLD. Really. He always told me you were twenty-two.

LADY KITTY. Oh, what nonsense! Why, I was married out of the nursery. I put my hair up for the first time on my wedding-day.

ARNOLD. Where is Lord Porteous?

LADY KITTY. My dear, it sounds too absurd to hear you call him Lord Porteous. Why don't you call him—Uncle Hughie?

ARNOLD. He doesn't happen to be my uncle.

LADY KITTY. No, but he's your godfather. You know, I'm sure you'll like him when you know him better. I'm so hoping that you and Elizabeth will come and stay with us in Florence. I simply adore Elizabeth. She's too beautiful.

ARNOLD. Her hair is very pretty.

LADY KITTY. It's not touched up, is it?

ARNOLD. Oh, no.

LADY KITTY. I just wondered. It's rather a coincidence that her hair should be the same color as mine. I suppose it shows that your father and you are attracted by just the same thing. So interesting, heredity, isn't it?

ARNOLD. Very.

LADY KITTY. Of course, since I joined the Catholic Church I don't believe in it any more. Darwin and all that sort of thing. Too dreadful. Wicked, you know. Besides, it's not very good form, is it?

(CHAMPION-CHENEY *comes in from the garden*)

C.-C. Do I intrude?

LADY KITTY. Come in, Clive. Arnold and I have been having such a wonderful heart-to-heart talk.

C.-C. Very nice.

ARNOLD. Father, I stepped in for a moment at the Harveys' on my way back. It's simply criminal what they're doing with that house.

C.-C. What are they doing?

ARNOLD. It's an almost perfect Georgian house and they've got a lot of dreadful Victorian furniture. I gave them my ideas on the subject, but it's quite hopeless. They said they were attached to their furniture.

C.-C. Arnold should have been an interior decorator.

LADY KITTY. He has wonderful taste. He gets that from me.

ARNOLD. I suppose I have a certain *flair*. I have a passion for decorating houses.

LADY KITTY. You've made this one charming.

C.-C. D'you remember, we just had chintzes and comfortable chairs when we lived here, Kitty.

LADY KITTY. Perfectly hideous, wasn't it?

C.-C. In those days gentlemen and ladies were not expected to have taste.

ARNOLD. You know, I've been looking at this chair again. Since Lord Porteous said the legs weren't right I've been very uneasy.

LADY KITTY. He only said that because he was in a bad temper.

C.-C. His temper seems to me very short these days, Kitty.

LADY KITTY. Oh, it is.

ARNOLD. You feel he knows what he's talking about. I gave seventy-five pounds for that chair. I'm very seldom taken in. I always think if a thing's right you feel it.

C.-C. Well, don't let it disturb your night's rest.

ARNOLD. But, my dear father, that's just what it does. I had a most horrible dream about it last night.

LADY KITTY. Here is Hughie.

ARNOLD. I'm going to fetch a book I have on Old English furniture. There's an illustration of a chair which is almost identical with this one.

(PORTEOUS *comes in*)

PORTEOUS. Quite a family gathering, by George!

C.-C. I was thinking just now we'd make a very pleasing picture of a typical English home.

ARNOLD. I'll be back in five minutes. There's something I want to show you, Lord Porteous.

(*He goes out*)

C.-C. Would you like to play piquet with me, Hughie?

PORTEOUS Not particularly.

C.-C. You were never much of a piquet player, were you?

PORTEOUS. My dear Clive, you people don't know what piquet is in England.

C.-C. Let's have a game then. You may make money.

Porteous. I don't want to play with you.

Lady Kitty. I don't know why not, Hughie.

Porteous. Let me tell you that I don't like your manner.

C.-C. I'm sorry for that. I'm afraid I can't offer to change it at my age.

Porteous. I don't know what you want to be hanging around here for.

C.-C. A natural attachment to my home.

Porteous. If you'd had any tact you'd have kept out of the way while we were here.

C.-C. My dear Hughie, I don't understand your attitude at all. If I'm willing to let bygones be bygones why should you object?

Porteous. Damn it all, they're not bygones.

C.-C. After all, I am the injured party.

Porteous. How the devil are you the injured party?

C.-C. Well, you did run away with my wife, didn't you?

Lady Kitty. Now, don't let's go into ancient history. I can't see why we shouldn't all be friends.

Porteous. I beg you not to interfere, Kitty.

Lady Kitty. I'm very fond of Clive.

Porteous. You never cared two straws for Clive. You only say that to irritate me.

Lady Kitty. Not at all. I don't see why he shouldn't come and stay with us.

C.-C. I'd love to. I think Florence in springtime is delightful. Have you central heating?

Porteous. I never liked you, I don't like you now, and I never shall like you.

C.-C. How very unfortunate! Because I liked you, I like you now, and I shall continue to like you.

Lady Kitty. There's something very nice about you, Clive.

Porteous. If you think that, why the devil did you leave him?

Lady Kitty. Are you going to reproach me because I loved you? How utterly, utterly, utterly detestable you are!

C.-C. Now, now, don't quarrel with one another.

Lady Kitty. It's all his fault. I'm the easiest person in the world to live with. But really he'd try the patience of a saint.

C.-C. Come, come, don't get upset, Kitty. When two people live together there must be a certain amount of give and take.

Porteous. I don't know what the devil you're talking about.

C.-C. It hasn't escaped my observation that you are a little inclined to frip. Many couples are. I think it's a pity.

Porteous. Would you have the very great kindness to mind your own business?

Lady Kitty. It is his business. He naturally wants me to be happy.

C.-C. I have the very greatest affection for Kitty.

Porteous. Then why the devil didn't you look after her properly?

C.-C. My dear Hughie, you were my greatest friend. I trusted you. It may have been rash.

Porteous. It was inexcusable.

Lady Kitty. I don't know what you mean by that, Hughie.

Porteous. Don't, don't, don't try and bully me, Kitty.

Lady Kitty. Oh, I know what you mean.

Porteous. Then why the devil did you say you didn't?

Lady Kitty. When I think that I sacrificed everything for that man! And for thirty years I've had to live in a filthy marble palace with no sanitary conveniences.

C.-C. D'you mean to say you haven't got a bathroom?

Lady Kitty. I've had to wash in a tub.

C.-C. My poor Kitty, how you've suffered!

Porteous. Really, Kitty, I'm sick of hearing of the sacrifices you made. I suppose you think I sacrificed nothing. I should have been Prime Minister by now if it hadn't been for you.

Lady Kitty. Nonsense!

Porteous. What do you mean by that? Everyone said I should be Prime Minister. Shouldn't I have been Prime Minister, Clive?

C.-C. It was certainly the general expectation.

Porteous. I was the most promising young man of my day. I was bound to get a seat in the Cabinet at the next election.

Lady Kitty. They'd have found you out just as I've found you out. I'm sick of hearing that I ruined your career. You never had a career to ruin. Prime Minister! You haven't the brain.

You haven't the character.

C.-C. Cheek, push, and a gift of the gab will serve very well instead, you know.

LADY KITTY. Besides, in politics it's not the men that matter. It's the women at the back of them. I could have made Clive a Cabinet Minister if I'd wanted to.

PORTEOUS. Clive?

LADY KITTY. With my beauty, my charm, my force of character, my wit, I could have done anything.

PORTEOUS. Clive was nothing but my political secretary. When I was Prime Minister I might have made him Governor of some Colony or other. Western Australia, say. Out of pure kindness.

LADY KITTY (*with flashing eyes*). D'you think I would have buried myself in Western Australia? With my beauty? My charm?

PORTEOUS. Or Barbadoes, perhaps.

LADY KITTY (*furiously*). Barbadoes! Barbadoes can go to—Barbadoes.

PORTEOUS. That's all you'd have got.

LADY KITTY. Nonsense! I'd have India.

PORTEOUS. I would never have given you India.

LADY KITTY. You would have given me India.

PORTEOUS. I tell you I wouldn't.

LADY KITTY. The King would have given me India. The nation would have insisted on my having India. I would have been a vice-reine or nothing.

PORTEOUS. I tell you that as long as the interests of the British Empire—damn it all, my teeth are coming out!

(*He hurries from the room*)

LADY KITTY. It's too much. I can't bear it any more. I've put up with him for thirty years and now I'm at the end of my tether.

C.-C. Calm yourself, my dear Kitty.

LADY KITTY. I won't listen to a word. I've quite made up my mind. It's finished, finished, finished. (*With a change of tone*) I was so touched when I heard that you never lived in this house again after I left it.

C.-C. The cuckoos have always been very plentiful. Their note has a personal application which, I must say, I have found extremely offensive.

LADY KITTY. When I saw that you didn't marry again I couldn't help thinking that you still loved me.

C.-C. I am one of the few men I know who is able to profit by experience.

LADY KITTY. In the eyes of the Church I am still your wife. The Church is so wise. It knows that in the end a woman always comes back to her first love. Clive, I am willing to return to you.

C.-C. My dear Kitty, I couldn't take advantage of your momentary vexation with Hughie to let you take a step which I know you would bitterly regret.

LADY KITTY. You've waited for me a long time. For Arnold's sake.

C.-C. Do you think we really need bother about Arnold? In the last thirty years he's had time to grow used to the situation.

LADY KITTY (*with a little smile*). I think I've sown my wild oats, Clive.

C.-C.. I haven't. I was a good young man, Kitty.

LADY KITTY. I know.

C.-C. And I'm very glad, because it has enabled me to be a wicked old one.

LADY KITTY. I beg your pardon.

(ARNOLD *comes in with a large book in his hand*)

ARNOLD. I say, I've found the book I was hunting for. Oh! Isn't Lord Porteous here?

LADY KITTY. One moment, Arnold. Your father and I are busy.

ARNOLD. I'm so sorry.

(*He goes out into the garden*)

LADY KITTY. Explain yourself, Clive.

C.-C. When you ran away from me, Kitty, I was sore and angry and miserable. But above all I felt a fool.

LADY KITTY. Men are so vain.

C.-C. But I was a student of history, and presently I reflected that I shared my misfortune with very nearly all the greatest men.

LADY KITTY. I'm a great reader myself. It has always struck me as peculiar.

C.-C. The explanation is very simple. Women dislike intelligence, and when they find it in their husbands they revenge themselves on them in the only way they can, by making them—well, what you made me.

LADY KITTY. It's ingenious. It may be true.

C.-C. I felt I had done my duty by society and I determined to devote the rest of my life to my own entertainment. The House of Commons had always bored me excessively and the scandal of our divorce gave me an opportunity to resign my seat. I have been relieved to find that the country got on perfectly well without me.

Lady Kitty. But has love never entered your life?

C.-C. Tell me frankly, Kitty, don't you think people make a lot of unnecessary fuss about love?

Lady Kitty. It's the most wonderful thing in the world.

C.-C. You're incorrigible. Do you really think it was worth sacrificing so much for?

Lady Kitty. My dear Clive, I don't mind telling you that if I had my time over again I should be unfaithful to you, but I should not leave you.

C.-C. For some years I was notoriously the prey of a secret sorrow. But I found so many charming creatures who were anxious to console that in the end it grew rather fatiguing. Out of regard to my health I ceased to frequent the drawing-rooms of Mayfair.

Lady Kitty. And since then?

C.-C. Since then I have allowed myself the luxury of assisting financially a succession of dear little things, in a somewhat humble sphere, between the ages of twenty and twenty-five.

Lady Kitty. I cannot understand the infatuation of men for young girls. I think they're so dull.

C.-C. It's a matter of taste. I love old wine, old friends, and old books, but I like young women. On their twenty-fifth birthday I give them a diamond ring and tell them they must no longer waste their youth and beauty on an old fogey like me. We have a most affecting scene, my technique on these occasions is perfect, and then I start all over again.

Lady Kitty. You're a wicked old man, Clive.

C.-C. That's what I told you. But, by George! I'm a happy one.

Lady Kitty. There's only one course open to me now.

C.-C. What is that?

Lady Kitty (with a flashing smile). To go and dress for dinner.

C.-C. Capital. I will follow your example.

(As Lady Kitty goes out Elizabeth comes in)

Elizabeth. Where is Arnold?

C.-C. He's on the terrace. I'll call him.

Elizabeth. Don't bother.

C.-C. I was just strolling along to my cottage to put on a dinner jacket. (As he goes out) Arnold.   (Exit C.-C.)

Arnold. Hulloa! (He comes in) Oh, Elizabeth, I've found an illustration here of a chair which is almost identical with mine. It's dated 1750. Look!

Elizabeth. That's very interesting.

Arnold. I want to show it to Porteous. (Moving a chair which has been misplaced) You know, it does exasperate me the way people will not leave things alone. I no sooner put a thing in its place than somebody moves it.

Elizabeth. It must be maddening for you.

Arnold. It is. You are the worst offender. I can't think why you don't take the pride that I do in the house. After all, it's one of the show places in the country.

Elizabeth. I'm afraid you find me very unsatisfactory.

Arnold (good-humoredly). I don't know about that. But my two subjects are politics and decoration. I should be a perfect fool if I didn't see that you don't care two straws about either.

Elizabeth. We haven't very much in common, Arnold, have we?

Arnold. I don't think you can blame me for that.

Elizabeth. I don't. I blame you for nothing. I have no fault to find with you.

Arnold (surprised at her significant tone). Good gracious me! What's the meaning of all this?

Elizabeth. Well, I don't think there's any object in beating about the bush. I want you to let me go.

Arnold. Go where?

Elizabeth. Away. For always.

Arnold. My dear child, what are you talking about?

Elizabeth. I want to be free.

Arnold (amused rather than disconcerted). Don't be ridiculous, darling. I daresay you're run down and want a change. I'll take you over to Paris for a fortnight if you like.

ELIZABETH. I shouldn't have spoken to you if I hadn't quite made up my mind. We've been married for three years and I don't think it's been a great success. I'm frankly bored by the life you want me to lead.

ARNOLD. Well, if you'll allow me to say so, the fault is yours. We lead a very distinguished, useful life. We know a lot of extremely nice people.

ELIZABETH. I'm quite willing to allow that the fault is mine. But how does that make it any better? I'm only twenty-five. If I've made a mistake I have time to correct it.

ARNOLD. I can't bring myself to take you very seriously.

ELIZABETH. You see, I don't love you.

ARNOLD. Well, I'm awfully sorry. But you weren't obliged to marry me. You've made your bed and I'm afraid you must lie on it.

ELIZABETH. That's one of falsest proverbs in the English language. Why should you lie on the bed you've made if you don't want to? There's always the floor.

ARNOLD. For goodness' sake, don't be funny, Elizabeth.

ELIZABETH. I've quite made up my mind to leave you, Arnold.

ARNOLD. Come, come, Elizabeth, you must be sensible. You haven't any reason to leave me.

ELIZABETH. Why should you wish to keep a woman tied to you who wants to be free?

ARNOLD. I happen to be in love with you.

ELIZABETH. You might have said that before.

ARNOLD. I thought you'd take it for granted. You can't expect a man to go on making love to his wife after three years. I'm very busy. I'm awfully keen on politics and I've worked like a dog to make this house a thing of beauty. After all, a man marries to have a home, but also because he doesn't want to be bothered with sex and all that sort of thing. I fell in love with you the first time I saw you and I've been in love ever since.

ELIZABETH. I'm sorry, but if you're not in love with a man his love doesn't mean very much to you.

ARNOLD. It's so ungrateful. I've done everything in the world for you.

ELIZABETH. You've been very kind to me. But you've asked me to lead a life I don't like and that I'm not suited for. I'm awfully sorry to cause you pain, but now you must let me go.

ARNOLD. Nonsense! I'm a good deal older than you are and I think I have a little more sense. In your interests as well as in mine I'm not going to do anything of the sort.

ELIZABETH (with a smile). How can you prevent me? You can't keep me under lock and key.

ARNOLD. Please don't talk to me as if I were a foolish child. You're my wife and you're going to remain my wife.

ELIZABETH. What sort of a life do you think we should lead? Do you think there'd be any more happiness for you than for me?

ARNOLD. But what is it precisely that you suggest?

ELIZABETH. Well, I want you to let me divorce you.

ARNOLD (astounded). Me? Thank you very much. Are you under the impression I'm going to sacrifice my career for a whim of yours?

ELIZABETH. How will it do that?

ARNOLD. My seat's wobbly enough as it is. Do you think I'd be able to hold it if I were in a divorce case? Even if it were a put-up job, as most divorces are nowadays, it would damn me.

ELIZABETH. It's rather hard on a woman to be divorced.

ARNOLD (with sudden suspicion). What do you mean by that? Are you in love with some one?

ELIZABETH. Yes.

ARNOLD. Who?

ELIZABETH. Teddie Luton.

(He is astounded for a moment, then bursts into a laugh)

ARNOLD. My poor child, how can you be so ridiculous? Why, he hasn't a bob. He's a perfectly commonplace young man. It's so absurd I can't even be angry with you.

ELIZABETH. I've fallen desperately in love with him, Arnold.

ARNOLD. Well, you'd better fall desperately out.

ELIZABETH. He wants to marry me.

ARNOLD. I daresay he does. He can go to hell.

ELIZABETH. It's no good talking like that.

ARNOLD. Is he your lover?

ELIZABETH. No, certainly not.

ARNOLD. It shows that he's a mean skunk to

take advantage of my hospitality to make love to you.

ELIZABETH. He's never even kissed me.

ARNOLD. I'd try telling that to the horse marines if I were you.

ELIZABETH. It's because I wanted to do nothing shabby that I told you straight out how things were.

ARNOLD. How long have you been thinking of this?

ELIZABETH. I've been in love with Teddie ever since I knew him.

ARNOLD. And you never thought of me at all, I suppose.

ELIZABETH. Oh, yes, I did. I was miserable. But I can't help myself. I wish I loved you, but I don't.

ARNOLD. I recommend you to think very carefully before you do anything foolish.

ELIZABETH. I have thought very carefully.

ARNOLD. By God! I don't know why I don't give you a sound hiding. I'm not sure if that wouldn't be the best thing to bring you to your senses.

ELIZABETH. Oh, Arnold, don't take it like that.

ARNOLD. How do you expect me to take it? You come to me quite calmly and say: "I've had enough of you. We've been married three years and I think I'd like to marry somebody else now. Shall I break up your home? What a bore for you! Do you mind my divorcing you? It'll smash up your career, will it? What a pity!" Oh, no, my girl, I may be a fool, but I'm not a damned fool.

ELIZABETH. Teddie is leaving here by the first train tomorrow. I warn you that I mean to join him as soon as he can make the necessary arrangements.

ARNOLD. Where is he?

ELIZABETH. I don't know. I suppose he's in his room.

(ARNOLD *goes to the door and calls*)

ARNOLD. George!

(*For a moment he walks up and down the room impatiently.* ELIZABETH *watches him. The* FOOTMAN *comes in.*)

FOOTMAN. Yes, sir.

ARNOLD. Tell Mr. Luton to come here at once.

ELIZABETH. Ask Mr. Luton if he wouldn't mind coming here for a moment.

FOOTMAN. Very good, madam.

(*Exit* FOOTMAN)

ELIZABETH. What are you going to say to him?

ARNOLD. That's my business.

ELIZABETH. I wouldn't make a scene if I were you.

ARNOLD. I'm not going to make a scene. (*They wait in silence*) Why did you insist on my mother coming here?

ELIZABETH. It seemed to me rather absurd to take up the attitude that I should be contaminated by her when . . .

ARNOLD (*interrupting*). When you were proposing to do exactly the same thing. Well, now you've seen her what do you think of her? Do you think it's been a success? Is that the sort of woman a man would like his mother to be?

ELIZABETH. I've been ashamed. I've been so sorry. It all seemed dreadful and horrible. This morning I happened to notice a rose in the garden. It was all over-blown and bedraggled. It looked like a painted old woman. And I remembered that I'd looked at it a day or two ago. It was lovely then, fresh and blooming and fragrant. It may be hideous now, but that doesn't take away from the beauty it had once. That was real.

ARNOLD. Poetry, by God! As if this were the moment for poetry!

(TEDDIE *comes in. He has changed into a dinner jacket.*)

TEDDIE (*to* ELIZABETH). Did you want me?

ARNOLD. *I* sent for you. (TEDDIE *looks from* ARNOLD *to* ELIZABETH. *He sees that something has happened.*) When would it be convenient for you to leave this house?

TEDDIE. I was proposing to go tomorrow morning. But I can very well go at once if you like.

ARNOLD. I do like.

TEDDIE. Very well. Is there anything else you wish to say to me?

ARNOLD. Do you think it was a very honorable thing to come down here and make love to my wife?

TEDDIE. No, I don't. I haven't been very happy about it. That's why I wanted to go away.

ARNOLD. Upon my word, you're cool.

TEDDIE. I'm afraid it's no good saying I'm sorry and that sort of thing. You know what the situation is.

ARNOLD. Is it true that you want to marry Elizabeth?

TEDDIE. Yes. I should like to marry her as soon as ever I can.

ARNOLD. Have you thought of me at all? Has it struck you that you're destroying my home and breaking up my happiness?

TEDDIE. I don't see how there could be much happiness for you if Elizabeth doesn't care for you.

ARNOLD. Let me tell you that I refuse to have my home broken up by a twopenny-halfpenny adventurer who takes advantage of a foolish woman. I refuse to allow myself to be divorced. I can't prevent my wife from going off with you if she's determined to make a damned fool

of herself, but this I tell you: nothing will induce me to divorce her.

ELIZABETH. Arnold, that would be monstrous.

TEDDIE. We could force you.

ARNOLD. How?

TEDDIE. If we went away together openly you'd have to bring an action.

ARNOLD. Twenty-four hours after you leave this house I shall go down to Brighton with a chorus-girl. And neither you nor I will be able to get a divorce. We've had enough divorces in our family. And now get out, get out, get out!

(TEDDIE *looks uncertainly at* ELIZABETH)

ELIZABETH (*with a little smile*). Don't bother about me. I shall be all right.

ARNOLD. Get out! Get out!

Act III

SCENE: *The same as in the preceding acts. It is the night of the same day as that on which takes place the action of the second act.*

(CHAMPION-CHENEY *and* ARNOLD, *both in dinner jackets, are discovered.* CHAMPION-CHENEY *is seated.* ARNOLD *walks restlessly up and down the room.*)

C.-C. I think, if you'll follow my advice to the letter, you'll probably work the trick.

ARNOLD. I don't like it, you know. It's against all my principles.

C.-C. My dear Arnold, we all hope that you have before you a distinguished political career. You can't learn too soon that the most useful thing about a principle is that it can always be sacrificed to expediency.

ARNOLD. But supposing it doesn't come off? Women are incalculable.

C.-C. Nonsense! Men are romantic. A woman will always sacrifice herself if you give her the opportunity. It is her favorite form of self-indulgence.

ARNOLD. I never know whether you're a humorist or a cynic, Father.

C.-C. I'm neither, my dear boy; I'm merely a very truthful man. But people are so unused to the truth that they're apt to mistake it for a joke or a sneer.

ARNOLD (*irritably*). It seems so unfair that this should happen to me.

C.-C. Keep your head, my boy, and do what I tell you.

(LADY KITTY *and* ELIZABETH *come in.* LADY KITTY *is in a gorgeous evening gown.*)

ELIZABETH. Where is Lord Porteous?

C.-C. He's on the terrace. He's smoking a cigar. (*Going to window*) Hughie!

(PORTEOUS *comes in*)

PORTEOUS (*with a grunt*). Yes? Where's Mrs. Shenstone?

ELIZABETH. Oh, she had a headache. She's gone to bed.

(*When* PORTEOUS *comes in* LADY KITTY *with a very haughty air purses her lips and takes up an illustrated paper.* PORTEOUS *gives her an irritated look, takes another illustrated paper and sits himself down at the other end of the room. They are not on speaking terms.*)

C.-C. Arnold and I have just been down to my cottage.

ELIZABETH. I wondered where you'd gone.

C.-C. I came across an old photograph album this afternoon. I meant to bring it along before dinner, but I forgot, so we went and fetched it.

ELIZABETH. Oh, do let me see it! I love old photographs.

(*He gives her the album, and she, sitting*

down, puts it on her knees and begins to turn over the pages. He stands over her. LADY KITTY *and* PORTEOUS *take surreptitious glances at one another.*)

C.-C. I thought it might amuse you to see what pretty women looked like five-and-thirty years ago. That was the day of beautiful women.

ELIZABETH. Do you think they were more beautiful then than they are now?

C.-C. Oh, much. Now you see lots of pretty little things, but very few beautiful women.

ELIZABETH. Aren't their clothes funny?

C.-C. (*pointing to a photograph*). That's Mrs. Langtry.

ELIZABETH. She has a lovely nose.

C.-C. She was the most wonderful thing you ever saw. Dowagers used to jump on chairs in order to get a good look at her when she came into a drawing-room. I was riding with her once, and we had to have the gates of the livery stable closed when she was getting on her horse because the crowd was so great.

ELIZABETH. And who's that?

C.-C. Lady Lonsdale. That's Lady Dudley.

ELIZABETH. This is an actress, isn't it?

C.-C. It is, indeed. Ellen Terry: By George! How I loved that woman!

ELIZABETH (*with a smile*). Dear Ellen Terry!

C.-C. That's Bwabs. I never saw a smarter man in my life. And Oliver Montagu. Henry Manners with his eye-glass.

ELIZABETH. Nice-looking, isn't he? And this?

C.-C. That's Mary Anderson. I wish you could have seen her in "A Winter's Tale." Her beauty just took your breath away. And look! There's Lady Randolph. Bernal Osborne—the wittiest man I ever knew.

ELIZABETH. I think it's too sweet. I love their absurd bustles and those tight sleeves.

C.-C. What figures they had! In those days a woman wasn't supposed to be as thin as a rail and as flat as a pancake.

ELIZABETH. Oh, but aren't they laced in? How could they bear it?

C.-C. They didn't play golf then, and nonsense like that, you know. They hunted, in a tall hat and a long black habit, and they were very gracious and charitable to the poor in the village.

ELIZABETH. Did the poor like it?

C.-C. They had a very thin time if they didn't. When they were in London they drove in the Park every afternoon, and they went to ten-course dinners, where they never met anybody they didn't know. And they had their box at the opera when Patti was singing or Madame Albani.

ELIZABETH. Oh, what a lovely little thing! Who on earth is that?

C.-C. That?

ELIZABETH. She looks so fragile, like a piece of exquisite china, with all those furs on and her face up against her muff, and the snow falling.

C.-C. Yes, there was quite a rage at that time for being taken in an artificial snowstorm.

ELIZABETH. What a sweet smile, so roguish and frank, and debonair! Oh, I wish I looked like that! Do tell me who it is!

C.-C. Don't you know?

ELIZABETH. No.

C.-C. Why—it's Kitty.

ELIZABETH. Lady Kitty. (*To* LADY KITTY) Oh, my dear, do look! It's too ravishing. (*She takes the album over to her impulsively*) Why didn't you tell me you looked like that? Everybody must have been in love with you.

(LADY KITTY *takes the album and looks at it. Then she lets it slip from her hands and covers her face with her hands. She is crying.*)

(*In consternation*) My dear, what's the matter? Oh, what have I done? I'm so sorry.

LADY KITTY. Don't, don't talk to me. Leave me alone. It's stupid of me.

(ELIZABETH *looks at her for a moment perplexed, then, turning round, slips her arm in* CHAMPION-CHENEY'S *and leads him out on to the terrace*)

ELIZABETH (*as they are going, in a whisper*). Did you do that on purpose?

(PORTEOUS *gets up and goes over to* LADY KITTY. *He puts his hand on her shoulder. They remain thus for a little while.*)

PORTEOUS. I'm afraid I was very rude to you before dinner, Kitty.

LADY KITTY (*taking his hand which is on her shoulder*). It doesn't matter. I'm sure I was very exasperating.

PORTEOUS. I didn't mean what I said, you know.

LADY KITTY. Neither did I.

PORTEOUS. Of course I know that I'd never have been Prime Minister.

LADY KITTY. How can you talk such nonsense, Hughie? No one would have had a chance if you'd remained in politics.

PORTEOUS. I haven't the character.

LADY KITTY. You have more character than anyone I've ever met.

PORTEOUS. Besides, I don't know that I much wanted to be Prime Minister.

LADY KITTY. Oh, but I should have been so proud of you. Of course you'd have been Prime Minister.

PORTEOUS. I'd have given you India, you know. I think it would have been a very popular appointment.

LADY KITTY. I don't care twopence about India. I'd have been quite content with Western Australia.

PORTEOUS. My dear, you don't think I'd have let you bury yourself in Western Australia?

LADY KITTY. Or Barbadoes.

PORTEOUS. Never. It sounds like a cure for flat feet. I'd have kept you in London.

(*He picks up the album and is about to look at the photograph of* LADY KITTY. *She puts her hands over it.*)

LADY KITTY. No, don't look.

(*He takes her hand away*)

PORTEOUS. Don't be so silly.

LADY KITTY. Isn't it hateful to grow old?

PORTEOUS. You know, you haven't changed much.

LADY KITTY (*enchanted*). Oh, Hughie, how can you talk such nonsense?

PORTEOUS. Of course you're a little more mature, but that's all. A woman's all the better for being rather mature.

LADY KITTY. Do you really think that?

PORTEOUS. Upon my soul I do.

LADY KITTY. You're not saying it just to please me?

PORTEOUS. No, no.

LADY KITTY. Let me look at the photograph again. (*She takes the album and looks at the photograph complacently*) The fact is, if your bones are good, age doesn't really matter. You'll always be beautiful.

PORTEOUS (*with a little smile, almost as if he were talking to a child*). It was silly of you to cry.

LADY KITTY. It hasn't made my eyelashes run, has it?

PORTEOUS. Not a bit.

LADY KITTY. It's very good stuff I use now. They don't stick together either.

PORTEOUS. Look here, Kitty, how much longer do you want to stay here?

LADY KITTY. Oh, I'm quite ready to go whenever you like.

PORTEOUS. Clive gets on my nerves. I don't like the way he keeps hanging about you.

LADY KITTY (*surprised, rather amused, and delighted*). Hughie, you don't mean to say you're jealous of poor Clive?

PORTEOUS. Of course I'm not jealous of him, but he does look at you in a way that I can't help thinking rather objectionable.

LADY KITTY. Hughie, you may throw me downstairs like Amy Robsart; you may drag me about the floor by the hair of my head; I don't care, you're jealous. I shall never grow old.

PORTEOUS. Damn it all, the man was your husband.

LADY KITTY. My dear Hughie, he never had your style. Why, the moment you come into a room everyone looks and says: "Who the devil is that?"

PORTEOUS. What? You think that, do you? Well, I daresay there's something in what you say. These damned Radicals can say what they like, but, by God, Kitty! When a man's a gentleman—well, damn it all, you know what I mean.

LADY KITTY. I think Clive has degenerated dreadfully since we left him.

PORTEOUS. What do you say to making a beeline for Italy and going to San Michele?

LADY KITTY. Oh, Hughie! It's years since we were there.

PORTEOUS. Wouldn't you like to see it again—just once more?

LADY KITTY. Do you remember the first time we went? It was the most heavenly place I'd ever seen. We'd only left England a month, and I said I'd like to spend all my life there.

PORTEOUS. Of course I remember. And in a fortnight it was yours, lock, stock, and barrel.

LADY KITTY. We were very happy there,

Hughie.

PORTEOUS. Let's go back once more.

LADY KITTY. I daren't. It must be all peopled with the ghosts of our past. One should never go again to a place where one has been happy. It would break my heart.

PORTEOUS. Do you remember how we used to sit on the terrace of the old castle and look at the Adriatic? We might have been the only people in the world, you and I, Kitty.

LADY KITTY (tragically). And we thought our love would last forever.

(Enter CHAMPION-CHENEY)

PORTEOUS. Is there any chance of bridge this evening?

C.-C. I don't think we can make up a four.

PORTEOUS. What a nuisance that boy went away like that! He wasn't a bad player.

C.-C. Teddie Luton?

LADY KITTY. I think it was very funny his going away without saying good-by to anyone.

C.-C. The young men of the present day are very casual.

PORTEOUS. I thought there was no train in the evening.

C.-C. There isn't. The last train leaves at 5.45.

PORTEOUS. How did he go then?

C.-C. He went.

PORTEOUS. Damned selfish I call it.

LADY KITTY (intrigued). Why did he go, Clive?

(CHAMPION-CHENEY looks at her for a moment reflectively)

C.-C. I have something very grave to say to you. Elizabeth wants to leave Arnold.

LADY KITTY. Clive! What on earth for?

C.-C. She's in love with Teddie Luton. That's why he went. The men of my family are really very unfortunate.

PORTEOUS. Does she want to run away with him?

LADY KITTY (with consternation). My dear, what's to be done?

C.-C. I think you can do a great deal.

LADY KITTY. I? What?

C.-C. Tell her, tell her what it means.

(He looks at her fixedly. She stares at him.)

LADY KITTY. Oh, no, no!

C.-C. She's a child. Not for Arnold's sake. For her sake. You must.

LADY KITTY. You don't know what you're ask-

ing.

C.-C. Yes, I do.

LADY KITTY. Hughie, what shall I do?

PORTEOUS. Do what you like. I shall never blame you for anything.

(The FOOTMAN comes in with a letter on a salver. He hesitates on seeing that ELIZA-BETH is not in the room.)

C.-C. What is it?

FOOTMAN. I was looking for Mrs. Champion-Cheney, sir.

C.-C. She's not here. Is that a letter?

FOOTMAN. Yes, sir. It's just been sent up from The Champion Arms.

C.-C. Leave it. I'll give it to Mrs. Cheney.

FOOTMAN. Very good, sir.

(He brings the tray to CLIVE, who takes the letter. The FOOTMAN goes out.)

PORTEOUS. Is The Champion Arms the local pub?

C.-C. (looking at the letter). It's by way of being a hotel, but I never heard of anyone staying there.

LADY KITTY. If there was no train I suppose he has to go there.

C.-C. Great minds. I wonder what he has to write about! (He goes to the door leading on to the garden) Elizabeth!

ELIZABETH (outside). Yes.

C.-C. Here's a note for you.

(There is silence. They wait for ELIZABETH to come. She enters.)

ELIZABETH. It's lovely in the garden tonight.

C.-C. They've just sent this up from The Champion Arms.

ELIZABETH. Thank you.

(Without embarrassment she opens the let-ter. They watch her while she reads it. It covers three pages. She puts it away in her bag.)

LADY KITTY. Hughie, I wish you'd fetch me a cloak. I'd like to take a stroll in the garden, but after thirty years in Italy I find these Eng-lish summers rather chilly. (Without a word PORTEOUS goes out. ELIZABETH is lost in thought.) I want to talk to Elizabeth, Clive.

C.-C. I'll leave you.   (He goes out)

LADY KITTY. What does he say?

ELIZABETH. Who?

LADY KITTY. Mr. Luton.

ELIZABETH (*gives a little start. Then she looks at* LADY KITTY.) They've told you?

LADY KITTY. Yes. And now they have, I think I knew it all along.

ELIZABETH. I don't expect you to have much sympathy for me. Arnold is your son.

LADY KITTY. So pitifully little.

ELIZABETH. I'm not suited for this sort of existence. Arnold wants me to take what he calls my place in Society. Oh, I get so bored with those parties in London. All those middle-aged painted women, in beautiful clothes, lolloping round ballrooms with rather old young men. And the endless luncheons where they gossip about so-and-so's love affairs.

LADY KITTY. Are you very much in love with Mr. Luton?

ELIZABETH. I love him with all my heart.

LADY KITTY. And he?

ELIZABETH. He's never cared for anyone but me. He never will.

LADY KITTY. Will Arnold let you divorce him?

ELIZABETH. No, he won't hear of it. He refuses even to divorce me.

LADY KITTY. Why?

ELIZABETH. He thinks a scandal will revive all the old gossip.

LADY KITTY. Oh, my poor child!

ELIZABETH. It can't be helped. I'm quite willing to accept the consequences.

LADY KITTY. You don't know what it is to have a man tied to you only by his honor. When married people don't get on they can separate, but if they're not married it's impossible. It's a tie that only death can sever.

ELIZABETH. If Teddie stopped caring for me I shouldn't want him to stay with me for five minutes.

LADY KITTY. One says that when one's sure of a man's love, but when one isn't any more —oh, it's so different. In those circumstances one's got to keep a man's love. It's the only thing one has.

ELIZABETH. I'm a human being. I can stand on my own feet.

LADY KITTY. Have you any money of your own?

ELIZABETH. None.

LADY KITTY. Then how can you stand on your own feet? You think I'm a silly, frivolous woman, but I've learned something in a bitter school. They can make what laws they like, they can give us the suffrage, but when you come down to bedrock it's the man who pays the piper who calls the tune. Woman will only be the equal of man when she earns her living in the same way that he does.

ELIZABETH (*smiling*). It sounds rather funny to hear you talk like that.

LADY KITTY. A cook who marries a butler can snap her fingers in his face because she can earn just as much as he can. But a woman in your position and a woman in mine will always be dependent on the men who keep them.

ELIZABETH. I don't want luxury. You don't know how sick I am of all this beautiful furniture. These over-decorated houses are like a prison in which I can't breathe. When I drive about in a Callot frock and a Rolls-Royce I envy the shop-girl in a coat and skirt whom I see jumping on the tailboard of a bus.

LADY KITTY. You mean that if need be you could earn your own living?

ELIZABETH. Yes.

LADY KITTY. What could you be? A nurse or a typist. It's nonsense. Luxury saps a woman's nerve. And when she's known it once it becomes a necessity.

ELIZABETH. That depends on the woman.

LADY KITTY. When we're young we think we're different from everyone else, but when we grow a little older we discover we're all very much of a muchness.

ELIZABETH. You're very kind to take so much trouble about me.

LADY KITTY. It breaks my heart to think that you're going to make the same pitiful mistake that I made.

ELIZABETH. Oh, don't say it was that, don't, don't.

LADY KITTY. Look at me, Elizabeth, and look at Hughie. Do you think it's been a success? If I had my time over again do you think I'd do it again? Do you think he would?

ELIZABETH. You see, you don't know how much I love Teddie.

LADY KITTY. And do you think I didn't love Hughie? Do you think he didn't love me?

ELIZABETH. I'm sure he did.

LADY KITTY. Oh, of course in the beginning it was heavenly. We felt so brave and adventurous and we were so much in love. The first two years were wonderful. People cut me, you know, but I didn't mind. I thought love was everything. It *is* a little uncomfortable when you come upon an old friend and go towards her eagerly, so glad to see her, and are met with an icy stare.

ELIZABETH. Do you think friends like that are worth having?

LADY KITTY. Perhaps they're not very sure of themselves. Perhaps they're honestly shocked. It's a test one had better not put one's friends to if one can help it. It's rather bitter to find how few one has.

ELIZABETH. But one has some.

LADY KITTY. Yes, they ask you to come and see them when they're quite certain no one will be there who might object to meeting you. Or else they say to you: "My dear, you know I'm devoted to you, and I wouldn't mind at all, but my girl's growing up—I'm sure you understand; you won't think it unkind of me if I don't ask you to the house?"

ELIZABETH (*smiling*). That doesn't seem to me very serious.

LADY KITTY. At first I thought it rather a relief, because it threw Hughie and me together more. But you know, men are very funny. Even when they are in love they're not in love all day long. They want change and recreation.

ELIZABETH. I'm not inclined to blame them for that, poor dears.

LADY KITTY. Then we settled in Florence. And because we couldn't get the society we'd been used to we became used to the society we could get. Loose women and vicious men. Snobs who liked to patronize people with a handle to their names. Vague Italian Princes who were glad to borrow a few francs from Hughie and seedy countesses who liked to drive with me in the Cascine. And then Hughie began to hanker after his old life. He wanted to go big game shooting, but I dared not let him go. I was afraid he'd never come back.

ELIZABETH. But you knew he loved you.

LADY KITTY. Oh, my dear, what a blessed institution marriage is—for women, and what fools they are to meddle with it! The Church is so wise to take its stand on the indi—indi——

ELIZABETH. Solu——

LADY KITTY. Bility of marriage. Believe me, it's no joke when you have to rely only on yourself to keep a man. I could never afford to grow old. My dear, I'll tell you a secret that I've never told a living soul.

ELIZABETH. What is that?

LADY KITTY. My hair is not naturally this color.

ELIZABETH. Really.

LADY KITTY. I touch it up. You would never have guessed, would you?

ELIZABETH. Never.

LADY KITTY. Nobody does. My dear, it's white, premature of course, but white. I always think it's a symbol of my life. Are you interested in symbolism? I think it's too wonderful.

ELIZABETH. I don't think I know very much about it.

LADY KITTY. However tired I've been I've had to be brilliant and gay. I've never let Hughie see the aching heart behind my smiling eyes.

ELIZABETH (*amused and touched*). You poor dear.

LADY KITTY. And when I saw he was attracted by some one else the fear and the jealousy that seized me! You see, I didn't dare make a scene as I should have done if I'd been married—I had to pretend not to notice.

ELIZABETH (*taken aback*). But do you mean to say he fell in love with anyone else?

LADY KITTY. Of course he did eventually.

ELIZABETH (*hardly knowing what to say*). You must have been very unhappy.

LADY KITTY. Oh, I was, dreadfully. Night after night I sobbed my heart out when Hughie told me he was going to play cards at the club and I knew he was with that odious woman. Of course, it wasn't as if there weren't plenty of men who were only too anxious to console me. Men have always been attracted by me, you know.

ELIZABETH. Oh, of course, I can quite understand it.

LADY KITTY. But I had my self-respect to think of. I felt that whatever Hughie did I would do nothing that I should regret.

ELIZABETH. You must be very glad now.

LADY KITTY. Oh, yes. Notwithstanding all my temptations I've been absolutely faithful to

Hughie in spirit.

ELIZABETH. I don't think I quite understand what you mean.

LADY KITTY. Well, there was a poor Italian boy, young Count Castel Giovanni, who was so desperately in love with me that his mother begged me not to be too cruel. She was afraid he'd go into a consumption. What could I do? And then, oh, years later, there was Antonio Melita. He said he'd shoot himself unless I—well, you understand I couldn't let the poor boy shoot himself.

ELIZABETH. D'you think he really would have shot himself?

LADY KITTY. Oh, one never knows, you know. Those Italians are so passionate. He was really rather a lamb. He had such beautiful eyes.

(ELIZABETH *looks at her for a long time and a certain horror seizes her of this dissolute, painted old woman*)

ELIZABETH (*hoarsely*). Oh, but I think that's —dreadful.

LADY KITTY. Are you shocked? One sacrifices one's life for love and then one finds that love doesn't last. The tragedy of love isn't death or separation. One gets over them. The tragedy of love is indifference.

(ARNOLD *comes in*)

ARNOLD. Can I have a little talk with you, Elizabeth?

ELIZABETH. Of course.

ARNOLD. Shall we go for a stroll in the garden?

ELIZABETH. If you like.

LADY KITTY. No, stay here. I'm going out anyway. (*Exit* LADY KITTY)

ARNOLD. I want you to listen to me for a few minutes, Elizabeth. I was so taken aback by what you told me just now that I lost my head. I was rather absurd and I beg your pardon. I said things I regret.

ELIZABETH. Oh, don't blame yourself. I'm sorry that I should have given you occasion to say them.

ARNOLD. I want to ask you if you've quite made up your mind to go.

ELIZABETH. Quite.

ARNOLD. Just now I seem to have said all that I didn't want to say and nothing that I did. I'm stupid and tongue-tied. I never told you how deeply I loved you.

ELIZABETH. Oh, Arnold!

ARNOLD. Please let me speak now. It's so very difficult. If I seemed absorbed in politics and the house, and so on, to the exclusion of my interest in you, I'm dreadfully sorry. I suppose it was absurd of me to think you would take my great love for granted.

ELIZABETH. But, Arnold, I'm not reproaching you.

ARNOLD. I'm reproaching myself. I've been tactless and neglectful. But I do ask you to believe that it hasn't been because I didn't love you. Can you forgive me?

ELIZABETH. I don't think that there's anything to forgive.

ARNOLD. It wasn't till today when you talked of leaving me that I realized how desperately in love with you I was.

ELIZABETH. After three years?

ARNOLD. I'm so proud of you. I admire you so much. When I see you at a party, so fresh and lovely, and everybody wondering at you, I have a sort of little thrill because you're mine, and afterwards I shall take you home.

ELIZABETH. Oh, Arnold, you're exaggerating.

ARNOLD. I can't imagine this house without you. Life seems on a sudden all empty and meaningless. Oh, Elizabeth, don't you love me at all?

ELIZABETH. It's much better to be honest. No.

ARNOLD. Doesn't my love mean anything to you?

ELIZABETH. I'm very grateful to you. I'm sorry to cause you pain. What would be the good of my staying with you when I should be wretched all the time?

ARNOLD. Do you love that man as much as all that? Does my unhappiness mean nothing to you?

ELIZABETH. Of course it does. It breaks my heart. You see, I never knew I meant so much to you. I'm so touched. And I'm so sorry, Arnold, really sorry. But I can't help myself.

ARNOLD. Poor child, it's cruel of me to torture you.

ELIZABETH. Oh, Arnold, believe me, I have tried to make the best of it. I've tried to love you, but I can't. After all, one either loves or one doesn't. Trying is no help. And now I'm at the end of my tether. I can't help the consequences—I must do what my whole self yearns for.

ARNOLD. My poor child, I'm so afraid you'll be unhappy. I'm so afraid you'll regret.

ELIZABETH. You must leave me to my fate. I hope you'll forget me and all the unhappiness I've caused you.

ARNOLD (*there is a pause.* ARNOLD *walks up and down the room reflectively. He stops and faces her.*) If you love this man and want to go to him I'll do nothing to prevent you. My only wish is to do what is best for you.

ELIZABETH. Arnold, that's awfully kind of you. If I'm treating you badly at least I want you to know that I'm grateful for all your kindness to me.

ARNOLD. But there's one favor I should like you to do me. Will you?

ELIZABETH. Oh, Arnold, of course I'll do anything I can.

ARNOLD. Teddie hasn't very much money. You've been used to a certain amount of luxury, and I can't bear to think that you should do without anything you've had. It would kill me to think that you were suffering any hardship or privation.

ELIZABETH. Oh, but Teddie can earn enough for our needs. After all, we don't want much money.

ARNOLD. I'm afraid my mother's life hasn't been very easy, but it's obvious that the only thing that's made it possible is that Porteous was rich. I want you to let me make you an allowance of two thousand a year.

ELIZABETH. Oh, no, I couldn't think of it. It's absurd.

ARNOLD. I beg you to accept it. You don't know what a difference it will make.

ELIZABETH. It's awfully kind of you, Arnold. It humiliates me to speak about it. Nothing would induce me to take a penny from you.

ARNOLD. Well, you can't prevent me from opening an account at my bank in your name. The money shall be paid in every quarter whether you touch it or not, and if you happen to want it, it will be there waiting for you.

ELIZABETH. You overwhelm me, Arnold. There's only one thing I want you to do for me. I should be very grateful if you would divorce me as soon as you possibly can.

ARNOLD. No, I won't do that. But I'll give you cause to divorce me.

ELIZABETH. You!

ARNOLD. Yes. But of course you'll have to be very careful for a bit. I'll put it through as quickly as possible, but I'm afraid you can't hope to be free for over six months.

ELIZABETH. But, Arnold, your seat and your political career!

ARNOLD. Oh, well, my father gave up his seat under similar circumstances. He's got along very comfortably without politics.

ELIZABETH. But they're your whole life.

ARNOLD. After all one can't have it both ways. You can't serve God and Mammon. If you want to do the decent thing you have to be prepared to suffer for it.

ELIZABETH. But I don't want you to suffer for it.

ARNOLD. At first I rather hesitated at the scandal. But I daresay that was only weakness on my part. Under the circumstances I should have liked to keep out of the Divorce Court if I could.

ELIZABETH. Arnold, you're making me absolutely miserable.

ARNOLD. What you said before dinner was quite right. It's nothing for a man, but it makes so much difference to a woman. Naturally I must think of you first.

ELIZABETH. That's absurd. It's out of the question. Whatever there's to pay I must pay it.

ARNOLD. It's not very much I'm asking you, Elizabeth.

ELIZABETH. I'm taking everything from you.

ARNOLD. It's the only condition I make. My mind is absolutely made up. I will never divorce you, but I will enable you to divorce me.

ELIZABETH. Oh, Arnold, it's cruel to be so generous.

ARNOLD. It's not generous at all. It's the only way I have of showing you how deep and passionate and sincere my love is for you. (*There is a silence. He holds out his hand.*) Good night. I have a great deal of work to do before I go to bed.

ELIZABETH. Good night.

ARNOLD. Do you mind if I kiss you?

ELIZABETH (*with agony*). Oh, Arnold!

(*He gravely kisses her on the forehead*

and then goes out. ELIZABETH *stands lost in thought. She is shattered.* LADY KITTY *and* PORTEOUS *come in.* LADY KITTY *wears a cloak.*)

LADY KITTY. You're alone, Elizabeth?

ELIZABETH. That note you asked me about, Lady Kitty, from Teddie . . .

LADY KITTY. Yes?

ELIZABETH. He wanted to have a talk with me before he went away. He's waiting for me in the summer house by the tennis court. Would Lord Porteous mind going down and asking him to come here?

PORTEOUS. Certainly. Certainly.

ELIZABETH. Forgive me for troubling you. But it's very important.

PORTEOUS. No trouble at all.

(*He goes out*)

LADY KITTY. Hughie and I will leave you alone.

ELIZABETH. But I don't want to be left alone. I want you to stay.

LADY KITTY. What are you going to say to him?

ELIZABETH (*desperately*). Please don't ask me questions. I'm so frightfully unhappy.

LADY KITTY. My poor child!

ELIZABETH. Oh, isn't life rotten? Why can't one be happy without making other people unhappy?

LADY KITTY. I wish I knew how to help you. I'm simply devoted to you. (*She hunts about in her mind for something to do or say*) Would you like my lip-stick?

ELIZABETH (*smiling through her tears*). Thanks. I never use one.

LADY KITTY. Oh, but just try. It's such a comfort when you're in trouble.

(*Enter* PORTEOUS *and* TEDDIE)

PORTEOUS. I brought him. He said he'd be damned if he'd come.

LADY KITTY. When a lady sent for him? Are these the manners of the young men of today?

TEDDIE. When you've been solemnly kicked out of a house once I think it seems rather pushing to come back again as though nothing had happened.

ELIZABETH. Teddie, I want you to be serious.

TEDDIE. Darling, I had such a rotten dinner at that pub. If you ask me to be serious on the top of that I shall cry.

ELIZABETH. Don't be idiotic, Teddie. (*Her voice faltering*) I'm so utterly wretched.

(*He looks at her for a moment gravely*)

TEDDIE. What is it?

ELIZABETH. I can't come away with you, Teddie.

TEDDIE. Why not?

ELIZABETH (*looking away in embarrassment*). I don't love you enough.

TEDDIE. Fiddle!

ELIZABETH (*with a flash of anger*). Don't say "Fiddle" to me.

TEDDIE. I shall say exactly what I like to you.

ELIZABETH. I won't be bullied.

TEDDIE. Now look here, Elizabeth, you know perfectly well that I'm in love with you, and I know perfectly well that you're in love with me. So what are you talking nonsense for?

ELIZABETH (*her voice breaking*). I can't say it if you're cross with me.

TEDDIE (*smiling very tenderly*). I'm not cross with you, silly.

ELIZABETH. It's harder still when you're being rather an owl.

TEDDIE (*with a chuckle*). Am I mistaken in thinking you're not very easy to please?

ELIZABETH. Oh, it's monstrous. I was all wrought up and ready to do anything, and now you've thoroughly put me out. I feel like a great big fat balloon that some one has put a long pin into. (*With a sudden look at him*) Have you done it on purpose?

TEDDIE. Upon my soul I don't know what you're talking about.

ELIZABETH. I wonder if you're really much cleverer than I think you are.

TEDDIE (*taking her hands and making her sit down*). Now tell me exactly what you want to say. By the way, do you want Lady Kitty and Lord Porteous to be here?

ELIZABETH. Yes.

LADY KITTY. Elizabeth asked us to stay.

TEDDIE. Oh, I don't mind, bless you. I only thought you might feel rather in the way.

LADY KITTY (*frigidly*). A gentlewoman never feels in the way, Mr. Luton.

TEDDIE. Won't you call me Teddie? Everybody does, you know.

(LADY KITTY *tries to give him a withering*

look, but she finds it very difficult to prevent herself from smiling. TEDDIE *strokes* ELIZABETH's *hands. She draws them away.*)

ELIZABETH. No, don't do that. Teddie, it wasn't true when I said I didn't love you. Of course I love you. But Arnold loves me, too. I didn't know how much.

TEDDIE. What has he been saying to you?

ELIZABETH. He's been very good to me, and so kind. I didn't know he could be so kind. He offered to let me divorce him.

TEDDIE. That's very decent of him.

ELIZABETH. But don't you see, it ties my hands. How can I accept such a sacrifice? I should never forgive myself if I profited by his generosity.

TEDDIE. If another man and I were devilish hungry and there was only one mutton chop between us, and he said, "You eat it," I wouldn't waste a lot of time arguing. I'd wolf it before he changed his mind.

ELIZABETH. Don't talk like that. It maddens me. I'm trying to do the right thing.

TEDDIE. You're not in love with Arnold; you're in love with me. It's idiotic to sacrifice your life for a slushy sentiment.

ELIZABETH. After all, I did marry him.

TEDDIE. Well, you made a mistake. A marriage without love is no marriage at all.

ELIZABETH. *I* made the mistake. Why should he suffer for it? If anyone has to suffer it's only right that I should.

TEDDIE. What sort of a life do you think it would be with him? When two people are married it's very difficult for one of them to be unhappy without making the other unhappy too.

ELIZABETH. I can't take advantage of his generosity.

TEDDIE. I daresay he'll get a lot of satisfaction out of it.

ELIZABETH. You're being beastly, Teddie. He was simply wonderful. I never knew he had it in him. He was really noble.

TEDDIE. You are talking rot, Elizabeth.

ELIZABETH. I wonder if you'd be capable of acting like that.

TEDDIE. Acting like what?

ELIZABETH. What would you do if I were married to you and came and told you I loved somebody else and wanted to leave you?

TEDDIE. You have very pretty blue eyes, Elizabeth. I'd black first one and then the other. And after that we'd see.

ELIZABETH. You damned brute!

TEDDIE. I've often thought I wasn't quite a gentleman. Had it ever struck you?

(*They look at one another for a while*)

ELIZABETH. You know, you are taking an unfair advantage of me. I feel as if I came to you quite unsuspectingly and when I wasn't looking you kicked me on the shins.

TEDDIE. Don't you think we'd get on rather well together?

PORTEOUS. Elizabeth's a fool if she don't stick to her husband. It's bad enough for the man, but for the woman—it's damnable. I hold no brief for Arnold. He plays bridge like a foot. Saving your presence, Kitty, I think he's a prig.

LADY KITTY. Poor dear, his father was at his age. I daresay he'll grow out of it.

PORTEOUS. But you stick to him, Elizabeth, stick to him. Man is a gregarious animal. We're members of a herd. If we break the herd's laws we suffer for it. And we suffer damnably.

LADY KITTY. Oh, Elizabeth, my dear child, don't go. It's not worth it. It's not worth it. I tell you that, and I've sacrificed everything to love.   (*A pause*)

ELIZABETH. I'm afraid.

TEDDIE (*in a whisper*). Elizabeth.

ELIZABETH. I can't face it. It's asking too much of me. Let's say good-by to one another, Teddie. It's the only thing to do. And have pity on me. I'm giving up all my hope of happiness.

(*He goes up to her and looks into her eyes*)

TEDDIE. But I wasn't offering you happiness. I don't think my sort of love tends to happiness. I'm jealous. I'm not a very easy man to get on with. I'm often out of temper and irritable. I should be fed to the teeth with you sometimes, and so would you be with me. I daresay we'd fight like cat and dog, and sometimes we'd hate each other. Often you'd be wretched and bored stiff and lonely, and often you'd be frightfully homesick, and then you'd regret all you'd lost. Stupid women would be rude to you because we'd run away together. And some of them would cut you. I don't offer you peace and quietness. I offer you unrest and anxiety. I don't offer you happiness. I offer you love.

ELIZABETH (*stretching out her arms*). You hateful creature, I absolutely adore you!

(*He throws his arms round her and kisses her passionately on the lips*)

LADY KITTY. Of course the moment he said he'd give her a black eye I knew it was finished.

PORTEOUS (*good-humoredly*). You are a fool, Kitty.

LADY KITTY. I know I am, but I can't help it.

TEDDIE. Let's make a bolt for it now.

ELIZABETH. Shall we?

TEDDIE. This minute.

PORTEOUS. You're damned fools, both of you, damned fools! If you like you can have my car.

TEDDIE. That's awfully kind of you. As a matter of fact I got it out of the garage. It's just along the drive.

PORTEOUS (*indignantly*). How do you mean, you got it out of the garage?

TEDDIE. Well, I thought there'd be a lot of bother, and it seemed to me the best thing would be for Elizabeth and me not to stand upon the order of our going, you know. Do it now. An excellent motto for a business man.

PORTEOUS Do you mean to say you were going to steal my car?

TEDDIE. Not exactly. I was only going to bolshevize it, so to speak.

PORTEOUS. I'm speechless. I'm absolutely speechless.

TEDDIE. Hang it all, I couldn't carry Elizabeth all the way to London. She's so damned plump.

ELIZABETH. You dirty dog!

PORTEOUS (*sputtering*). Well, well, well! . . . (*Helplessly*) I like him, Kitty, it's no good pretending I don't. I like him.

TEDDIE. The moon's shining, Elizabeth. We'll drive all through the night.

PORTEOUS. They'd better go to San Michele. I'll wire to have it got ready for them.

LADY KITTY. That's where we went when Hughie and I . . . (*Faltering*) Oh, you dear things, how I envy you!

PORTEOUS (*mopping his eyes*). Now don't cry, Kitty. Confound you, don't cry.

TEDDIE. Come, darling.

ELIZABETH. But I can't go like this.

TEDDIE. Nonsense! Lady Kitty will lend you her cloak. Won't you?

LADY KITTY (*taking it off*). You're capable of tearing it off my back if I don't.

TEDDIE (*putting the cloak on* ELIZABETH). And we'll buy you a tooth-brush in London in the morning.

LADY KITTY. She must write a note for Arnold. I'll put it on her pincushion.

TEDDIE. Pincushion be blowed! Come, darling. We'll drive through the dawn and through the sunrise.

ELIZABETH (*kissing* LADY KITTY *and* PORTEOUS). Good-by. Good-by.

(TEDDIE *stretches out his hand and she takes it. Hand in hand they go out into the night.*)

LADY KITTY. Oh, Hughie, how it all comes back to me! Will they suffer all we suffered? And have we suffered all in vain?

PORTEOUS. My dear, I don't know that in life it matters so much what you do as what you are. No one can learn by the experience of another because no circumstances are quite the same. If we made rather a hash of things perhaps it was because we were rather trivial people. You can do anything in this world if you're prepared to take the consequences, and consequences depend on character.

(*Enter* CHAMPION-CHENEY, *rubbing his hands. He is as pleased as Punch.*)

C.-C. Well, I think I've settled the hash of that young man.

LADY KITTY. Oh!

C.-C. You have to get up very early in the morning to get the better of your humble servant.

(*There is the sound of a car starting*)

LADY KITTY. What is that?

C.-C. It sounds like a car. I expect it's your chauffeur taking one of the maids for a joy-ride.

PORTEOUS. Whose hash are you talking about?

C.-C. Mr. Edward Luton's, my dear Hughie. I told Arnold exactly what to do and he's done it. What makes a prison? Why, bars and bolts. Remove them and a prisoner won't want to escape. Clever, I flatter myself.

PORTEOUS. You were always that, Clive, but at the moment you're obscure.

C.-C. I told Arnold to go to Elizabeth and tell her she could have her freedom. I told him to sacrifice himself all along the line. I know what women are. The moment every obstacle was removed to her marriage with Teddie Luton, half the allurement was gone.

LADY KITTY. Arnold did that?

C.-C. He followed my instructions to the letter. I've just seen him. She's shaken. I'm willing to bet five hundred pounds to a penny that she won't bolt. A downy old bird, eh? Downy's the word. Downy.

(He begins to laugh. They laugh, too. Presently they are all three in fits of laughter.)

DISCUSSION

In the "Introduction to Drama" (pp. 615-16) and elsewhere we have discussed comedy. We have talked about the incongruity, and discrepancy between expectation and fulfillment, and speed of effect, and degree of sympathy or involvement. We shall come back to some of these topics in discussing this play, but for the moment let us dwell on the fact that within the general class of comedy, in whatever form, fiction or drama, there is a great range of effect, there are many kinds of comedy.

If we think back on Faulkner's story "Spotted Horses" (p. 72), we remember a kind of comedy that is violent, rambunctious, and brawling. It is the comedy of the frontier and backwoods, of the tall tale, of exaggeration. True, there is in Faulkner's story an undertone of seriousness and pathos, but the immediate effect is in the violence and hurlyburly. Let us contrast "Spotted Horses" with *The Circle*.

The most obvious difference between the two is that in *The Circle* the action is primarily in shifts of awareness, shifts of attitude. Furthermore, the whole effect of *The Circle* depends on the special world in which it is set. It is what is called a comedy of manners. Its effect depends on the relation of the action to an elaborate set of codes, conventions, and attitudes belonging to the special world of a highly organized and self-conscious society.

We can look at the play, in one perspective, as dealing with a conflict between the values of individuals and the conventions of society. For instance, Lord Porteous and Lady Kitty have defied society, and the main action of the play is the movement toward Elizabeth's decision to leave Arnold and go away with Teddie Luton. A speech by Elizabeth in Act I may almost be taken as the motto of the play: "I don't think you want too much sincerity in society. It would be like an iron girder in a house of cards." It is ironical that Elizabeth should say this, for her sincerity (and that of Teddie) is the iron girder thrust through the house of cards which is the world of the play.

Let us glance at the people of that world. Arnold himself, who is the chief antagonist of Elizabeth, is the very essence of conventionality. He is much more concerned with the forms of things, the way they appear, than with any real significance. His concern with his house and its furnishings suggests this fact (though this play, unlike *Hedda Gabler*, does not use the method of symbolism): Arnold will devote infinite time and trouble to get the furnishings of his house in the right style and period, but he is not interested in the kind of life lived in the house or in his relation with his wife, so long as there is no surface disturbance. Furthermore, he prizes his political career above his wife. That, too, belongs to his conventional picture of his life, his emphasis on the externals of position and success and propriety.

Arnold's father, Clive Champion-Cheney, is in his own way equally conventional. At first glance, he seems to be the shrewd, witty, slightly cynical old gentleman who sees through the shams of his world, and that is true. He is the "intelligence" in the play; it is he who makes the sharp repartee and utters the epigrams; it is he who seems to know the inner workings of the other characters. He plays upon Lady Kitty and Lord Porteous, having his little revenge by sharpening the irritations they feel with each other. He understands his own son completely and puts him up to the trick to win back Elizabeth. But by doing so, though he has seemed to be the one person outside conventionality, he aligns himself with the forces of conventional society, after all. He, like his son, fails to understand Elizabeth, and her sincerity.

To continue with Clive Champion-Cheney's conventionality, we can recall that Lady Kitty remembers him when young as a prig. He himself says that he was a "very good young man," then adds that he is very glad of the fact for it had enabled him to become a "very wicked old one." But this wickedness is in itself a kind of conventionality, and he is a conventional figure, the rich, witty, amiably cynical old gentleman with a taste for young girls and the habit of giving them diamond rings on the twenty-fifth birthday as a token of dismissal. His wickedness is just propriety turned upside down.

The reactions of Arnold and his father to Elizabeth's decision are fixed; they are against it, but those of Lord Porteous and Lady Kitty shift, and this shifting provides a dynamic force for the action. Before the play opens, we gradually learn, Elizabeth has already fallen in love with Teddie Luton. Her motive for inviting Lady Kitty and Lord Porteous is, presumably, to see the people who had had the courage to stand against conventional society for their love. She expects (and we are led to expect) two romantic figures about whom still clings some glow of their great adventure. But when they appear, they are anything but what Elizabeth had expected; the glow has long since died away. In fact, a considerable part of the play is now devoted to exposing the consequences of their romantic elopement. Lord Porteous is no longer handsome and brilliant, a fine horseman, the rising politician certain to be Prime Minister. He is a querulous, quarrelsome, ill-natured old man, with false teeth that don't fit; he blames Lady Kitty for his ruined career; he envies Clive Champion-Cheney his freedom, demanding, "How the devil are you the injured party?" As for Lady Kitty, she is a vain, affected, aging woman, full of sentimentality, as when she exclaims, "My home, my home," upon entering the gate, and full of triviality, as when she talks of her conversion to Catholicism.

Old Clive Champion-Cheney emphasizes to Elizabeth all these unlovely aspects of the pair, the aspects that will, presumably, deter her from her course, and that by implication align Lady Kitty and Lord Porteous on the side of conventional society in their effect, as horrible examples, upon Elizabeth. But in the early part of Act III, *not* however in the presence of Elizabeth, there is a kind of reconciliation between Lady Kitty and Lord Porteous and for a moment they recapture something of their old love. That is, they are, for the moment, no longer horrible

examples of the consequences of flouting the conventions of society. Though Elizabeth is not present, Lady Kitty and Lord Porteous are, for the audience, once more set up against the conventions: they have something of value, after all.

Now, however, another shift comes. Clive Champion-Cheney tells Lady Kitty that Elizabeth wants to leave Arnold, and persuades her, just at the moment when she is touched by the warmth of her old love, to use her influence to prevent Elizabeth's throwing her life away and, incidentally, ruining Arnold's career and comfort. Lady Kitty agrees to this, and to do it must confess to Elizabeth the disappointments in her life with Lord Porteous and her own infidelities. Elizabeth recoils in horror from "this dissolute, painted old woman," and we feel that now Lady Kitty definitely and openly supports the conventional view. This scene prepares for Elizabeth's decision to stay with Arnold.

But there is a final shift in the alignment of Lady Kitty and Lord Porteous. After Teddie has returned and has recaptured Elizabeth, not by offering happiness but by offering love, Lady Kitty and Lord Porteous swing to the support of the young lovers and lend them a car and send them off to their house in Italy. Then Lord Porteous states the point:

My dear, I don't know that in life it matters so much what you do as what you are. . . . If we made rather a hash of things perhaps it was because we were rather trivial people. You can do anything in this world if you're prepared to take the consequences, and consequences depend on character.

In other words, by offering love and not happiness to Elizabeth, Teddie has opened the eyes of Lord Porteous to the true values that are to be set off against self-indulgence as happiness on the one hand and conventionality on the other. And, of course, by the same token, Teddie has brought Elizabeth to her decision.

Elizabeth's decision is, as we have said, the issue of the play, the thing that is at stake, and as the carrier of this issue she can be regarded as the central character, even though she may not be intrinsically as interesting as Lady Kitty or Clive Champion-Cheney. But the action revolves around Elizabeth, and the other characters are grouped, as it were, in relation to her.

She is the protagonist, and here her function is to carry the value of the individual against the conventions of society.

This sort of heavy-handed discussion makes the play sound very unlike a comedy—like a serious drama instead. But, as we have said in the "Introduction to Drama," the difference between comedy and even tragedy is not absolute. It depends largely on the interpretation and treatment that the dramatist gives the situation; and behind comedy there always lurks, however far in the background, the serious issue or idea. It is a very serious idea that Lord Porteous states. How does the dramatist prevent this seriousness from killing off the comic effect?

For one thing, he does not end on this note. After Elizabeth and Teddie have left to "drive through the dawn" and after Porteous has made his solemn pronouncement, there is one more little scene before the play ends. Clive Champion-Cheney enters, very much pleased at his cleverness in having, as he thinks, prevented Elizabeth from leaving. But we know that she has gone, and Lady Kitty and Lord Porteous know that she has gone. So when Clive Champion-Cheney begins his self-congratulatory laughter, Lady Kitty and Lord Porteous burst into fits of laughter, too. But they are laughing at, not with, Clive Champion-Cheney. The joke is on him, for all his cleverness. The biter has been bit. And the cream of the jest is that the biter doesn't even know he has been bit. Not yet. We leap forward to the moment of his discovery and relish it in anticipation. At least that is what Lady Kitty and Lord Porteous are doing in their laughter, and it is on laughter and not on Lord Porteous's solemn pronouncement that the curtain comes down. We end with the comic tone.

How else has a comic tone been established in the course of the play? First, if we go back to the very beginning we see that the first little collision between Arnold and Elizabeth has a comic tone. After Arnold's fussiness about the objects in the room, and after his objection to Elizabeth's use of the word *damn,* and after his schoolmasterish talk about there being no synonyms in the English language, we are not prepared to take him very seriously. Elizabeth definitely wins the little engagement, her spirit and humor against his stuffiness, and the tone is established. Scattered throughout the play, there are other little episodes like this that in themselves have a comic effect, for instance, the quarrel in Act II between Lord Porteous and Lady Kitty.

Second, not infrequently little incongruities and juxtaposed irrelevancies help to maintain the tone. For example, when Lady Kitty is talking with Elizabeth toward the end of the first act:

I'm never nervous. I'm a born actress. Of course, if I had my time over again I'd go on the stage. You know, it's extraordinary how they keep young. Actresses, I mean. I think it's because they're always playing different parts. Hughie, do you think Arnold takes after me or after his father? Of course I think he's the very image of me. Arnold, I think I ought to tell you that I was received into the Catholic Church last winter. I've been thinking about it for years, and the last time we were at Monte Carlo I met such a nice monsignore. I told him what my difficulties were and he was too wonderful. I knew Hughie wouldn't approve, so I kept it a secret. (*To Elizabeth.*) Are you interested in religion? I think it's too wonderful. We must have a long talk about it one of these days. (*Pointing to her frock.*) Callot?

It is a comic hodgepodge, a fair sample of Lady Kitty's scatter-brained triviality—the vanity of keeping young, the notion of being an actress, religion in the temper of social chit-chat, the name of the *couturier* from whom Elizabeth has had her frock. This, and similar passages, characterize Lady Kitty, but they also help to maintain the comic flavor.

Third, there are the sharp, epigrammatic, witty (or would-be witty) turns of speech. Clive Champion-Cheney is, of course, the usual speaker for these turns. It is part of his character, the witty, amiably cynical old gentleman who sees through the world:

ARNOLD. I never know whether you're a humorist or a cynic, Father.
C.-C. I'm neither, my dear boy; I'm merely a very truthful man. But people are so unused to the truth that they're apt to mistake it for a joke or a sneer.

(Act III)

The "truth" this old gentleman tells is very well represented by the passage just preceding the lines quoted above:

ARNOLD. I don't like it, you know. It's against all my principles.

C.-C. My dear Arnold, we all hope that you have before you a distinguished political career. You can't learn too soon that the most useful thing about a principle is that it can always be sacrificed to expediency.

ARNOLD. But supposing it doesn't come off. Women are incalculable.

C.-C. Nonsense! Men are romantic. A woman will always sacrifice herself if you give her the opportunity. It is her favorite form of self-indulgence.

And so on, in a strain that defines much of the quality of the play. It even spills over now and then into other characters who themselves are not wits. For instance, Elizabeth:

TEDDIE. . . . England seems to me full of people doing things they don't want to because other people expect it of them.

ELIZABETH. Isn't that what you call a high degree of civilization?

(Act I)

And again, a few lines along:

TEDDIE. It's not much good being pretentious where everyone knows exactly who you are and what your income is.

ELIZABETH. I don't think you want too much sincerity in society. It would be like an iron girder in a house of cards.

This is scarcely Elizabeth's characteristic style, and we are tempted to conclude that Maugham saw the chance for the turns and used them, not because they are good characterization, but because they are in the temper of the play.

This remark about the temper of the play suggests a last observation. The play is not realistic. To begin with, people don't talk in this crisp epigrammatic way, and to end with, we don't expect events to balance and turn and constantly fall as pat as the events of this play balance and turn and fall. The whole effect is artificial. But is this necessarily a defect?

Perhaps we can best answer our question by thinking of the analogy of the use of verse in Shakespeare's plays. We know that the dramatist is using verse because it gives a heightening, an intensification, of effects that are, however, inherent in the situations being dealt with. When in *Antony and Cleopatra* (Act I, scene i), the queen taunts Antony with the message of his wife Fulvia, Antony replies:

Let Rome in Tiber melt, and the wide arch
Of the ranged empire fall! Here is my space.

We know that nobody ever talked like this, in iambic pentameter, but we also know that the imagery and rhythm work to give us a sense of Antony's feeling of commitment and fulfilment as he stands before Cleopatra. The words of Antony are, in a sense, artificial, but they are expressive of a real state of feeling, more expressive than plain realistic prose would be. So with the style and handling of plot in *The Circle*: there is no pretense of realism, for the world about which the play is written is here viewed as a world that is highly organized, subject to elaborate codes and conventions, and set off from the hurlyburly of common life. The artificiality of the method is an index of the artificiality of the material. If we look back at the plays of William Congreve in the seventeenth century or of Oscar Wilde in the last century, we find basically the same kind of artificiality. It is a characteristic of the type of drama we call the comedy of manners.

EXERCISE

1. A characteristic of the exposition of Act I is that Maugham both tells and doesn't tell. He builds toward the necessary revelations instead of setting forth the facts more directly and economically. What is the advantage of this?

2. We observe that there is a love scene between Elizabeth and Teddie in Act I and another in Act II. Why did Maugham not fuse the two scenes into one?

3. What comic element is in the second love scene? What is gained by the emphasis on being "businesslike"?

4. In the long passage quoted above from Lady Kitty we find the lines:

Arnold, I think I ought to tell you that I was received into the Catholic Church last winter. I've been thinking about it for years, and the last time we were at Monte Carlo I met such a nice monsignore. I told him what my difficulties were and he was too wonderful.

What comic incongruities are in this passage? Can you locate and analyze other characteristic passages from Lady Kitty?

5. What is the comic point in each of the following passages:

(a) C.-C. My dear Hughie, I don't understand your attitude at all. If I'm willing to let bygones be bygones why should you object?

PORTEOUS. Damn it all, they're not bygones.

C.-C. After all, I am the injured party.

PORTEOUS. How the devil are you the injured party?

(Act II)

(b) C.-C. It hasn't escaped my observation that you are a little inclined to frip. Many couples are. I think it's a pity.

PORTEOUS. Would you have the very great kindness to mind your own business?

LADY KITTY. It is his business. He naturally wants me to be happy.

C.-C. I have the very greatest affection for Kitty.

PORTEOUS. Then why the devil didn't you look after her properly?

C.-C. My dear Hughie, you were my greatest friend. I trusted you. It may have been rash.

PORTEOUS. It was inexcusable.

(Act II)

(c) ELIZABETH. What would you do if I were married to you and came and told you I loved somebody else and wanted to leave you?

TEDDIE. You have very pretty blue eyes, Elizabeth. I'd black first one and then the other. And after that we'd see.

ELIZABETH. You damned brute!

TEDDIE. I've often thought I wasn't quite a gentleman. Had it ever struck you?

(Act III)

6. Do you think the reconciliation between Lady Kitty and Lord Porteous early in Act III is adequately motivated?

7. Is it significant in any way that Teddie is taking Elizabeth out to the Federated Malay States and not remaining in England?

8. At the beginning of the play we are disposed to be sympathetic with Clive Champion-Cheney as the man who has been very shabbily treated and who has survived his humiliation with a great deal of decency and fortitude. At what point does our attitude toward him begin to change? Why is it important, in terms of the final effect of the play, that we feel that he has not been treated as the conventional and stock figure of the cuckolded husband but that the dramatist has been "fair" to him? Why is it important that the dramatist should have exposed, not only the stuffiness of the conventions, but also the pretences of the "romantic lovers who dare all" (Lord Porteous and Lady Kitty)? Do we feel that the dramatist has, in some sense, tried to be fair to "both sides"?

9. If the question of the morals is raised, might it be argued that, in a negative way to be sure, the play stands "for" monogamy rather than against it; that what it "attacks" is a travesty of marriage, not a true union of man and woman; and that it has few illusions about "romantic elopement" as a shortcut to happiness? In this regard, compare *The Circle* with *Antony and Cleopatra:* Cleopatra at the end of the play, though she has scoffed at Fulvia as "the married woman" (I. iii. 20), claims by implication to be Antony's true wife (V. ii. 289-290).

10. Prepare an outline of *The Circle*, indicating each scene and stating what the purpose of each scene is.

The Skin of Our Teeth

THORNTON WILDER (1897-   )

Characters

ANNOUNCER
SABINA
MR. FITZPATRICK
MRS. ANTROBUS
DINOSAUR
MAMMOTH
TELEGRAPH BOY
GLADYS
HENRY
MR. ANTROBUS
DOCTOR
PROFESSOR
JUDGE
HOMER
MISS E. MUSE
MISS T. MUSE
MISS M. MUSE
USHER

USHER
GIRL }
GIRL } *Drum Majorettes*
FORTUNE TELLER
CHAIR PUSHER
CHAIR PUSHER
CONVEENER
CONVEENER
CONVEENER
CONVEENER
CONVEENER
BROADCAST OFFICIAL
DEFEATED CANDIDATE
MR. TREMAYNE
HESTER
IVY
FRED BAILEY

Act I

SCENE: Home, Excelsior, New Jersey.

A projection screen in the middle of the curtain. The first lantern slide: the name of the theatre, and the words: NEWS EVENTS OF THE WORLD. An ANNOUNCER's voice is heard.

ANNOUNCER. The management takes pleasure in bringing to you—The News Events of the World:

(Slide of the sun appearing above the horizon.)
Freeport, Long Island.
The sun rose this morning at 6:32 A.M. This gratifying event was first reported by Mrs. Dorothy Stetson of Freeport, Long Island, who promptly telephoned the Mayor.
The Society for Affirming the End of the World at once went into a special session and postponed the arrival of that event for TWENTY-FOUR HOURS. All honor to Mrs. Stetson for her public spirit.
New York City:
(Slide of the front doors of the theatre in which this play is playing; three cleaning WOMEN with mops and pails.)
The X Theatre. During the daily cleaning of this theatre a number of lost objects were collected as usual by Mesdames Simpson, Pateslewski, and Moriarty.
Among these objects found today was a wedding ring, inscribed: To Eva from Adam. Genesis II:18. The ring will be restored to the owner or owners, if their credentials are satisfactory.
Tippehatchee, Vermont:
(Slide representing a glacier.)
The unprecedented cold weather of this summer

has produced a condition that has not yet been satisfactorily explained. There is a report that a wall of ice is moving southward across these counties. The disruption of communications by the cold wave now crossing the country has rendered exact information difficult, but little credence is given to the rumor that the ice had pushed the Cathedral of Montreal as far as St. Albans, Vermont.

For further information see your daily papers. Excelsior, New Jersey:

(*Slide of a modest suburban home.*)

The home of Mr. George Antrobus, the inventor of the wheel. The discovery of the wheel, following so closely on the discovery of the lever, has centered the attention of the country on Mr. Antrobus of this attractive suburban residence district. This is his home, a commodious seven-room house, conveniently situated near a public school, a Methodist church, and a firehouse; it is right handy to an A. and P.

(*Slide of* MR. ANTROBUS *on his front steps, smiling and lifting his straw hat. He holds a wheel.*)

Mr. Antrobus, himself. He comes of very old stock and has made his way up from next to nothing.

It is reported that he was once a gardener, but left that situation under circumstances that have been variously reported.

Mr. Antrobus is a veteran of foreign wars, and bears a number of scars, front and back.

(*Slide of* MRS. ANTROBUS, *holding some roses.*)

This is Mrs. Antrobus, the charming and gracious president of the Excelsior Mothers' Club.

Mrs. Antrobus is an excellent needlewoman; it is she who invented the apron on which so many interesting changes have been rung since.

(*Slide of the* FAMILY *and* SABINA.)

Here we see the Antrobuses with their two children, Henry and Gladys, and friend. The friend in the rear, is Lily Sabina, the maid.

I know we all want to congratulate this typical American family on its enterprise. We all wish Mr. Antrobus a successful future. Now the management takes you to the interior of this home for a brief visit.

(*Curtain rises. Living room of a commuter's home.* SABINA—*straw-blonde, over-rouged —is standing by the window back center,*

a feather duster under her elbow.)

SABINA. Oh, oh, oh! Six o'clock and the master not home yet.

Pray God nothing serious has happened to him crossing the Hudson River. If anything happened to him, we would certainly be inconsolable and have to move into a less desirable residence district.

The fact is I don't know what'll become of us. Here it is the middle of August and the coldest day of the year. It's simply freezing; the dogs are sticking to the sidewalks; can anybody explain that? No.

But I'm not surprised. The whole world's at sixes and sevens, and why the house hasn't fallen down about our ears long ago is a miracle to me.

(*A fragment of the right wall leans precariously over the stage.* SABINA *looks at it nervously and it slowly rights itself.*)

Every night this same anxiety as to whether the master will get home safely: whether he'll bring home anything to eat. In the midst of life we are in the midst of death, a truer word was never said.

(*The fragment of scenery flies up into the lofts.* SABINA *is struck dumb with surprise, shrugs her shoulders and starts dusting* MR. ANTROBUS' *chair, including the under side.*)

Of course, Mr. Antrobus is a very fine man, an excellent husband and father, a pillar of the church, and has all the best interests of the community at heart. Of course, every muscle goes tight every time he passes a policeman; but what I think is that there are certain charges that ought not to be made, and I think I may add, ought not to be allowed to be made; we're all human; who isn't?

(*She dusts* MRS. ANTROBUS' *rocking chair.*)

Mrs. Antrobus is as fine a woman as you could hope to see. She lives only for her children; and if it would be any benefit to her children she'd see the rest of us stretched out dead at her feet without turning a hair—that's the truth. If you want to know anything more about Mrs. Antrobus, just go and look at a tigress, and look hard. As to the children—

Well, Henry Antrobus is a real, clean-cut American boy. He'll graduate from High School one of these days, if they make the alphabet any easier.—Henry, when he has a stone in his hand, has a perfect aim; he can hit anything from a bird to an older brother—Oh! I didn't mean to say that!—but it certainly was an unfortunate accident, and it was very hard getting the police out of the house.

Mr. and Mrs. Antrobus' daughter is named Gladys. She'll make some good man a good wife some day, if he'll just come down off the movie screen and ask her.

So here we are!

We've managed to survive for some time now, catch as catch can, the fat and the lean, and if the dinosaurs don't trample us to death, and if the grasshoppers don't eat up our garden, we'll all live to see better days, knock on wood.

Each new child that's born to the Antrobuses seems to them to be sufficient reason for the whole universe's being set in motion; and each new child that dies seems to them to have been spared a whole world of sorrow, and what the end of it will be is still very much an open question.

We've rattled along, hot and cold, for some time now—

(*A portion of the wall above the door, right, flies up into the air and disappears.*)

—and my advice to you is not to inquire into why or whither, but just enjoy your ice cream while it's on your plate—that's my philosophy.

Don't forget that a few years ago we came through the depression by the skin of our teeth! One more tight squeeze like that and where will we be?

(*This is a cue line.* SABINA *looks angrily at the kitchen door and repeats:*)

. . . we came through the depression by the skin of our teeth; one more tight squeeze like that and where will we be?

(*Flustered, she looks through the opening in the right wall; then goes to the window and reopens the Act.*)

Oh, oh, oh! Six o'clock and the master not home yet. Pray God nothing has happened to him crossing the Hudson. Here it is the middle of August and the coldest day of the year. It's simply freezing; the dogs are sticking. One more tight squeeze like that and where will we be?

VOICE (*off-stage*). Make up something! Invent something!

SABINA. Well . . . uh . . . this certainly is a fine American home . . . and—uh . . . everybody's very happy . . . and—uh . . .

(*Suddenly flings pretense to the winds and coming downstage says with indignation:*)

I can't invent any words for this play, and I'm glad I can't. I hate this play and every word in it.

As for me, I don't understand a single word of it, anyway—all about the troubles the human race has gone through, there's a subject for you.

Besides, the author hasn't made up his silly mind as to whether we're all living back in caves or in New Jersey today, and that's the way it is all the way through.

Oh—why can't we have plays like we used to have—*Peg o' My Heart,* and *Smilin' Thru,* and *The Bat*—good entertainment with a message you can take home with you?

I took this hateful job because I had to. For two years I've sat up in my room living on a sandwich and a cup of tea a day, waiting for better times in the theatre. And look at me now: I—I who've played *Rain* and *The Barretts of Wimpole Street* and *First Lady*—God in Heaven!

(*The* STAGE MANAGER *puts his head out from the hole in the scenery.*)

MR. FITZPATRICK. Miss Somerset!! Miss Somerset!

SABINA. Oh! Anyway!—nothing matters! It'll all be the same in a hundred years.

(*Loudly.*)

We came through the depression by the skin of our teeth,—that's true!—one more tight squeeze like that and where will we be?

(*Enter* MRS. ANTROBUS, *a mother.*)

MRS. ANTROBUS. Sabina, you've let the fire go out.

SABINA (*in a lather*). One-thing-and-another; don't-know-whether-my-wits-are-upside-or-down; might-as-well-be-dead-as-alive-in-a-house-all-sixes-and-sevens.

MRS. ANTROBUS. You've let the fire go out. Here it is the coldest day of the year right in the middle of August and you've let the fire go out.

SABINA. Mrs. Antrobus, I'd like to give my two weeks' notice, Mrs. Antrobus. A girl like I can get a situation in a home where they're rich enough to have a fire in every room, Mrs. Antrobus, and a girl don't have to carry the responsibility of the whole house on her two shoulders. And a home without children, Mrs. Antrobus, because children are a thing only a parent can stand, and a truer word was never said; and a home, Mrs. Antrobus, where the master of the house don't pinch decent, self-respecting girls when he meets them in a dark corridor. I mention no names and make no charges. So you have my notice, Mrs. Antrobus. I hope that's perfectly clear.

MRS. ANTROBUS. You've let the fire go out!—Have you milked the mammoth?

SABINA. I don't understand a word of this play.—Yes, I've milked the mammoth.

MRS. ANTROBUS. Until Mr. Antrobus comes home we have no food and we have no fire. You'd better go over to the neighbors and borrow some fire.

SABINA. Mrs. Antrobus! I can't! I'd die on the way, you know I would. It's worse than January. The dogs are sticking to the sidewalks. I'd die.

MRS. ANTROBUS. Very well, I'll go.

SABINA (*even more distraught, coming forward and sinking on her knees*). You'd never come back alive; we'd all perish; if you weren't here, we'd just perish. How do we know Mr. Antrobus'll be back? We don't know. If you go out, I'll just kill myself.

MRS. ANTROBUS. Get up, Sabina.

SABINA. Every night it's the same thing. Will he come back safe, or won't he? Will we starve to death, or freeze to death, or boil to death or will we be killed by burglars? I don't know why we go on living. I don't know why we go on living at all. It's easier being dead.

(*She flings her arms on the table and buries her head in them. In each of the succeeding speeches she flings her head up—and sometimes her hands—then quickly buries her head again.*)

MRS. ANTROBUS. The same thing! Always throwing up the sponge, Sabina. Always announcing your own death. But give you a new hat—or a plate of ice cream—or a ticket to the movies, and you want to live forever.

SABINA. You don't care whether we live or die; all you care about is those children. If it would be any benefit to them you'd be glad to see us all stretched out dead.

MRS. ANTROBUS. Well, maybe I would.

SABINA. And what do they care about? Themselves—that's all they care about.

(*Shrilly.*)

They make fun of you behind your back. Don't tell me: they're ashamed of you. Half the time, they pretend they're someone else's children. Little thanks you get from them.

MRS. ANTROBUS. I'm not asking for any thanks.

SABINA. And Mr. Antrobus—you don't understand *him*. All that work he does—trying to discover the alphabet and the multiplication table. Whenever he tries to learn anything you fight against it.

MRS. ANTROBUS. Oh, Sabina, I know you.

When Mr. Antrobus raped you home from your Sabine hills, he did it to insult me.

He did it for your pretty face, and to insult me.

You were the new wife, weren't you?

For a year or two you lay on your bed all day and polished the nails on your hands and feet:

You made puff-balls of the combings of your hair and you blew them up to the ceiling.

And I washed your underclothes and I made you chicken broths.

I bore children and between my very groans I stirred the cream that you'd put on your face.

But I knew you wouldn't last.

You didn't last.

SABINA. But it was I who encouraged Mr. Antrobus to make the alphabet. I'm sorry to say it, Mrs. Antrobus, but you're not a beautiful woman, and you can never know what a man could do if he tried. It's girls like I who inspire the multiplication table.

I'm sorry to say it, but you're not a beautiful woman, Mrs. Antrobus, and that's the God's truth.

MRS. ANTROBUS. And you didn't last—you sank to the kitchen. And what do you do there? *You let the fire go out!*

No wonder to you it seems easier being dead.

Reading and writing and counting on your fingers is all very well in their way—but I keep the home going.

MRS. ANTROBUS. —There's that dinosaur on the front lawn again.—Shoo! Go away. Go away.

(*The baby DINOSAUR puts his head in the window.*)

DINOSAUR. It's cold.

MRS. ANTROBUS. You go around to the back of the house where you belong.

DINOSAUR. It's cold.

(*The* DINOSAUR *disappears.* MRS. ANTROBUS *goes calmly out.* SABINA *slowly raises her head and speaks to the audience. The central portion of the center wall rises, pauses, and disappears into the loft.*)

SABINA. Now that you audience are listening to this, too, I understand it a little better.

I wish eleven o'clock were here; I don't want to be dragged through this whole play again.

(*The* TELEGRAPH BOY *is seen entering along the back wall of the stage from the right. She catches sight of him and calls:*)

Mrs. Antrobus! Mrs. Antrobus! Help! There's a strange man coming to the house. He's coming up the walk, help!

(*Enter* MRS. ANTROBUS *in alarm, but efficient.*)

MRS. ANTROBUS. Help me quick!

(*They barricade the door by piling the furniture against it.*)

Who is it? What do you want?

TELEGRAPH BOY. A telegram for Mrs. Antrobus from Mr. Antrobus in the city.

SABINA. Are you sure, are you sure? Maybe it's just a trap!

MRS. ANTROBUS. I know his voice, Sabina. We can open the door.

(*Enter the* TELEGRAPH BOY, *12 years old, in uniform. The* DINOSAUR *and* MAMMOTH *slip by him into the room and settle down front right.*)

I'm sorry we kept you waiting. We have to be careful, you know.

(*To the* ANIMALS.)

H'm . . . Will you be quiet?

(*They nod.*)

Have you had your supper?

(*They nod.*)

Are you *ready* to come in?

(*They nod.*)

Young man, have you any fire with you? Then light the grate, will you?

(*He nods, produces something like a briquet; and kneels by the imagined fireplace, footlights center. Pause.*)

What are people saying about this cold weather?

(*He makes a doubtful shrug with his shoulders.*)

Sabina, take this stick and go and light the stove.

SABINA. Like I told you, Mrs. Antrobus; two weeks. That's the law. I hope that's perfectly clear. (*Exit.*)

MRS. ANTROBUS. What about this cold weather?

TELEGRAPH BOY (*lowered eyes*). Of course, I don't know anything . . . but they say there's a wall of ice moving down from the North, that's what they say. We can't get Boston by telegraph, and they're burning pianos in Hartford.

. . . It moves everything in front of it, churches and post offices and city halls.

I live in Brooklyn myself.

MRS. ANTROBUS. What are people doing about it?

TELEGRAPH BOY. Well . . . uh . . . Talking, mostly.

Or just what you'd do a day in February.

There are some that are trying to go South and the roads are crowded; but you can't take old people and children very far in a cold like this.

MRS. ANTROBUS. —What's this telegram you have for me?

TELEGRAPH BOY (*fingertips to his forehead*). If you wait just a minute; I've got to remember it.

(*The* ANIMALS *have left their corner and are nosing him. Presently they take places on either side of him, leaning against his hips, like heraldic beasts.*)

This telegram was flashed from Murray Hill to University Heights! And then by puffs of smoke from University Heights to Staten Island.

And then by lantern from Staten Island to Plainfield, New Jersey. What hath God wrought!

(*He clears his throat.*)

"To Mrs. Antrobus, Excelsior, New Jersey:

"My dear wife, will be an hour late. Busy day at the office. Don't worry the children about the cold just keep them warm burn everything except Shakespeare."

(*Pause.*)

MRS. ANTROBUS. Men! —He knows I'd burn ten Shakespeares to prevent a child of mine from having one cold in the head. What does it say next?

(*Enter* SABINA.)

TELEGRAPH BOY. "Have made great discoveries today have separated em from en."

SABINA. I know what that is, that's the alphabet, yes it is. Mr. Antrobus is just the cleverest man. Why, when the alphabet's finished, we'll be able to tell the future and everything.

TELEGRAPH BOY. Then listen to this: "Ten tens make a hundred semi-colon consequences far-reaching." (*Watches for effect.*)

MRS. ANTROBUS. The earth's turning to ice, and all he can do is to make up new numbers.

TELEGRAPH BOY. Well, Mrs. Antrobus, like the head man at our office said: a few more discoveries like that and we'll be worth freezing.

MRS. ANTROBUS. What does he say next?

TELEGRAPH BOY. I . . . I can't do this last part very well.

(*He clears his throat and sings.*)
"Happy w'dding ann'vers'ry to you, Happy ann'-vers'ry to you—"

(*The* ANIMALS *begin to howl soulfully;*
SABINA *screams with pleasure.*)

MRS. ANTROBUS. Dolly! Frederick! Be quiet.

TELEGRAPH BOY (*above the din*). "Happy w'dding ann'-vers'ry, dear Eva; happy w'dding ann'vers'ry to you."

MRS. ANTROBUS. Is that in the telegram? Are they singing telegrams now?

(*He nods.*)

The earth's getting so silly no wonder the sun turns cold.

SABINA. Mrs. Antrobus, I want to take back the notice I gave you. Mrs. Antrobus, I don't want to leave a house that gets such interesting telegrams and I'm sorry for anything I said. I really am.

MRS. ANTROBUS. Young man, I'd like to give you something for all this trouble; Mr. Antrobus isn't home yet and I have no money and no food in the house—

TELEGRAPH BOY. Mrs. Antrobus . . . I don't like to . . . appear to . . . ask for anything, but . . .

MRS. ANTROBUS. What is it you'd like?

TELEGRAPH BOY. Do you happen to have an old needle you could spare? My wife just sits home all day thinking about needles.

SABINA (*shrilly*). We only got two in the house. Mrs. Antrobus, you know we only got two in the house.

MRS. ANTROBUS (*after a look at* SABINA *taking a needle from her collar*). Why yes, I can spare this.

TELEGRAPH BOY (*lowered eyes*). Thank you, Mrs. Antrobus. Mrs. Antrobus, can I ask you something else? I have two sons of my own; if the cold gets worse, what should I do?

SABINA. I think we'll all perish, that's what I think. Cold like this in August is just the end of the whole world.

(*Silence.*)

MRS. ANTROBUS. I don't know. After all, what does one do about anything? Just keep as warm as you can. And don't let your wife and children see that you're worried.

TELEGRAPH BOY. Yes. . . . Thank you, Mrs. Antrobus. Well, I'd better be going.—Oh, I forgot! There's one more sentence in the telegram. "Three cheers have invented the wheel."

MRS. ANTROBUS. A wheel? What's a wheel?

TELEGRAPH BOY. I don't know. That's what it said. The sign for it is like this. Well, goodbye.

(*The* WOMEN *see him to the door, with*
goodbyes and injunctions to keep warm.)

SABINA (*apron to her eyes, wailing*). Mrs. Antrobus, it looks to me like all the nice men in the world are already married; I don't know why that is. (*Exit.*)

MRS. ANTROBUS (*thoughtful; to the* ANIMALS). Do you remember hearing tell of any cold like this in August?

(*The* ANIMALS *shake their heads.*)

From your grandmothers or anyone?

(*They shake their heads.*)

Have you any suggestions?

(*They shake their heads. She pulls her*
shawl around, goes to the front door and
opening it an inch calls:)

HENRY. GLADYS. CHILDREN. Come right in and get warm. No, no, when mama says a thing she means it.

Henry! HENRY. Put down that stone. You know what happened last time.

(*Shriek.*)

HENRY! Put down that stone!

Gladys! Put down your dress!! Try and be a lady.

(*The* CHILDREN *bound in and dash to the*
fire. They take off their winter things and
leave them in heaps on the floor.)

GLADYS. Mama, I'm hungry. Mama, why is it

so cold
HENRY (*at the same time*). Mama, why doesn't
it snow? Mama, when's supper ready? Maybe it'll
snow and we can make snowballs.

GLADYS. Mama, it's so cold that in one more
minute I just couldn't of stood it.

MRS. ANTROBUS. Settle down, both of you, I
want to talk to you.

> (*She draws up a hassock and sits front cen-
> ter over the orchestra pit before the
> imaginary fire. The* CHILDREN *stretch out
> on the floor, leaning against her lap.
> Tableau by Raphael. The* ANIMALS *edge
> up and complete the triangle.*)

It's just a cold spell of some kind. Now listen to
what I'm saying:

When your father comes home I want you to be
extra quiet.

He's had a hard day at the office and I don't
know but what he may have one of his
moods.

I just got a telegram from him very happy and
excited, and you know what that means. Your
father's temper's uneven; I guess you know that.

> (*Shriek.*)

Henry! Henry!

Why—why can't you remember to keep your
hair down over your forehead? You must keep
that scar covered up. Don't you know that when
your father sees it he loses all control over himself? He goes crazy. He wants to die.

> (*After a moment's despair she collects her-
> self decisively, wets the hem of her apron
> in her mouth and starts polishing his
> forehead vigorously.*)

Lift your head up. Stop squirming. Blessed me,
sometimes I think that it's going away—and then
there it is: just as red as ever.

HENRY. Mama, today at school two teachers
forgot and called me by my old name. They
forgot, Mama. You'd better write another letter
to the principal, so that he'll tell them I've
changed my name. Right out in class they called
me: Cain.

MRS. ANTROBUS (*putting her hand on his
mouth, too late; hoarsely*). Don't say it.

> (*Polishing feverishly.*)

If you're good they'll forget it. Henry, you didn't
hit anyone . . . today, did you?

HENRY. Oh . . . no-o-o!

MRS. ANTROBUS (*still working, not looking at
Gladys*). And, Gladys, I want you to be especially
nice to your father tonight. You know what he
calls you when you're good—his little angel, his
little star. Keep your dress down like a little
lady. And keep your voice nice and low. Gladys
Antrobus!! What's that red stuff you have on
your face?

> (*Slaps her.*)

You're a filthy detestable child!

> (*Rises in real, though temporary, repudia-
> tion and despair.*)

Get away from me, both of you! I wish I'd never
seen sight or sound of you. Let the cold come! I
can't stand it. I don't want to go on. (*She walks
away.*)

GLADYS (*weeping*). All the girls at school do,
Mama.

MRS. ANTROBUS (*shrieking*). I'm through with
you, that's all!—Sabina! Sabina!—Don't you
know your father'd go crazy if he saw that paint
on your face? Don't you know your father thinks
you're perfect? Don't you know he couldn't live
if he didn't think you were perfect?—Sabina!

> (*Enter* SABINA.)

SABINA. Yes, Mrs. Antrobus!

MRS. ANTROBUS. Take this girl out into the
kitchen and wash her face with the scrubbing
brush.

MR. ANTROBUS (*outside, roaring*). "I've been
working on the railroad, all the livelong day . . .
etc."

> (*The* ANIMALS *start running around in cir-
> cles, bellowing.* SABINA *rushes to the
> window.*)

MRS. ANTROBUS. Sabina, what's that noise
outside?

SABINA. Oh, it's a drunken tramp. It's a giant,
Mrs. Antrobus. We'll all be killed in our beds,
I know it!

MRS. ANTROBUS. Help me quick. Quick. Everybody.

> (*Again they stack all the furniture against
> the door.* MR. ANTROBUS *pounds and
> bellows.*)

Who is it? What do you want?—Sabina, have
you any boiling water ready?—Who is it?

MR. ANTROBUS. Broken-down camel of a pig's
snout, open this door.

MRS. ANTROBUS. God be praised! It's your

father.—Just a minute, George!—Sabina, clear the door, quick. Gladys, come here while I clean your nasty face!

MR. ANTROBUS. She-bitch of a goat's gizzard, I'll break every bone in your body. Let me in or I'll tear the whole house down.

MRS. ANTROBUS. Just a minute, George, something's the matter with the lock.

MR. ANTROBUS. Open the door or I'll tear your livers out. I'll smash your brains on the ceiling, and Devil take the hindmost.

MRS. ANTROBUS. Now, you can open the door, Sabina. I'm ready.

(*The door is flung open. Silence. MR. ANTROBUS—face of a Keystone Comedy Cop—stands there in fur cap and blanket. His arms are full of parcels, including a large stone wheel with a center in it. One hand carries a railroad man's lantern. Suddenly he bursts into joyous roar.*)

MR. ANTROBUS. Well, how's the whole crooked family?

(*Relief. Laughter. Tears. Jumping up and down. ANIMALS cavorting. ANTROBUS throws the parcels on the ground. Hurls his cap and blanket after them. Heroic embraces. Melee of HUMANS and ANIMALS, SABINA included.*)

I'll be scalded and tarred if a man can't get a little welcome when he comes home. Well, Maggie, you old gunny-sack, how's the broken down old weather hen?—Sabina, old fishbait, old skunkpot.—And the children—how've the little smellers been?

GLADYS. Papa, Papa, Papa, Papa, Papa.

MR. ANTROBUS. How've they been, Maggie?

MRS. ANTROBUS. Well, I must say, they've been as good as gold. I haven't had to raise my voice once. I don't know what's the matter with them.

ANTROBUS (*kneeling before GLADYS*). Papa's little weasel, eh?—Sabina, there's some food for you.—Papa's little gopher?

GLADYS (*her arm around his neck*). Papa, you're always teasing me.

ANTROBUS. And Henry? Nothing rash today, I hope. Nothing rash?

HENRY. No, Papa.

ANTROBUS (*roaring*). Well that's good, that's good—I'll bet Sabina let the fire go out.

SABINA. Mr. Antrobus, I've given my notice.

I'm leaving two weeks from today. I'm sorry, but I'm leaving.

ANTROBUS (*roar*). Well, if you leave now you'll freeze to death, so go and cook the dinner.

SABINA. Two weeks, that's the law. (*Exit.*)

ANTROBUS. Did you get my telegram?

MRS. ANTROBUS. Yes.—What's a wheel?

(*He indicates the wheel with a glance. HENRY is rolling it around the floor. Rapid, hoarse interchange: MRS. ANTROBUS: What does this cold weather mean? It's below freezing. ANTROBUS: Not before the children! MRS. ANTROBUS: Shouldn't we do something about it—start off, move? ANTROBUS: Not before the children!!! He gives HENRY a sharp slap.*)

HENRY. Papa, you hit me!

ANTROBUS. Well, remember it. That's to make you remember today. Today. The day the alphabet's finished; and the day that we *saw* the hundred—the hundred, the hundred, the hundred, the hundred, the hundred—there's no end to 'em.

I've had a day at the office!

Take a look at that wheel, Maggie—when I've got that to rights: you'll see a sight.

There's a reward there for all the walking you've done.

MRS. ANTROBUS. How do you mean?

ANTROBUS (*on the hassock looking into the fire; with awe*). Maggie, we've reached the top of the wave. There's not much more to be done. We're there!

MRS. ANTROBUS (*cutting across his mood sharply*). And the ice?

ANTROBUS. The ice!

HENRY (*playing with the wheel*). Papa, you could put a chair on this.

ANTROBUS (*broodingly*). Ye-e-s, any booby can fool with it now—but I thought of it first.

MRS. ANTROBUS. Children, go out in the kitchen. I want to talk to your father alone.

(*The CHILDREN go out. ANTROBUS has moved to his chair up left. He takes the goldfish bowl on his lap; pulls the canary cage down to the level of his face. Both the ANIMALS put their paws up on the arm of his chair. MRS. ANTROBUS faces him across the room, like a judge.*)

MRS. ANTROBUS. Well?

ANTROBUS (*shortly*). It's cold.—How things been, eh? Keck, keck, keck.—And you, Millicent?

MRS. ANTROBUS. I know it's cold.

ANTROBUS (*to the canary*). No spilling of sunflower seed, eh? No singing after lights-out, y'know what I mean?

MRS. ANTROBUS. You can try and prevent us freezing to death, can't you? You can do something? We can start moving. Or we can go on the animals' backs?

ANTROBUS. The best thing about animals is that they don't talk much.

MAMMOTH. It's cold.

ANTROBUS. Eh, eh, eh! Watch that!—

—By midnight we'd turn to ice. The roads are full of people now who can scarcely lift a foot from the ground. The grass out in front is like iron—which reminds me, I have another needle for you.—The people up north—where are they? Frozen . . . crushed. . . .

MRS. ANTROBUS. Is that what's going to happen to us?—Will you answer me?

ANTROBUS. I don't know. I don't know anything. Some say that the ice is going slower. Some say that it's stopped. The sun's growing cold. What can I do about that? Nothing we can do but burn everything in the house, and the fence-posts and the barn. Keep the fire going. When we have no more fire, we die.

MRS. ANTROBUS. Well, why didn't you say so in the first place?

(MRS. ANTROBUS *is about to march off when she catches sight of two* REFUGEES, *men, who have appeared against the back wall of the theatre and who are soon joined by others.*)

REFUGEES. Mr. Antrobus! Mr. Antrobus! Mr. An-nn-tro-bus!

MRS. ANTROBUS. Who's that? Who's that calling you?

ANTROBUS (*clearing his throat guiltily*). H'm—let me see.

(*Two* REFUGEES *come up to the window.*)

REFUGEE. Could we warm our hands for a moment, Mr. Antrobus. It's very cold, Mr. Antrobus.

ANOTHER REFUGEE. Mr. Antrobus, I wonder if you have a piece of bread or something that you could spare.

(*Silence. They wait humbly.* MRS. ANTRO-BUS *stands rooted to the spot. Suddenly a knock at the door, then another hand knocking in short rapid blows.*)

MRS. ANTROBUS. Who are these people? Why, they're all over the front yard. What have they come *here* for?

(*Enter* SABINA.)

SABINA. Mrs. Antrobus! There are some tramps knocking at the back door.

MRS. ANTROBUS. George, tell these people to go away. Tell them to move right along. I'll go and send them away from the back door. Sabina, come with me. (*She goes out energetically.*)

ANTROBUS. Sabina! Stay here! I have something to say to you.

(*He goes to the door and opens it a crack and talks through it.*)

Ladies and gentlemen! I'll have to ask you to wait a few minutes longer. It'll be all right . . . while you're waiting you might each one pull up a stake of the fence. We'll need them all for the fireplace. There'll be coffee and sandwiches in a moment.

(SABINA *looks out door over his shoulder and suddenly extends her arm pointing, with a scream.*)

SABINA. Mr. Antrobus, what's that??—that big white thing? Mr. Antrobus, it's ICE. It's ICE!!

ANTROBUS. Sabina, I want you to go in the kitchen and make a lot of coffee. Make a whole pail full.

SABINA. Pail full!!

ANTROBUS (*with gesture*). And sandwiches . . . piles of them . . . like this.

SABINA. Mr. An . . . !!

(*Suddenly she drops the play, and says in her own person as* MISS SOMERSET, *with surprise.*)

Oh, *I* see what this part of the play means now! This means refugees.

(*She starts to cross to the proscenium.*)

Oh, I don't like it. I don't like it.

(*She leans against the proscenium and bursts into tears.*)

ANTROBUS. Miss Somerset!

STAGE MANAGER (*off-stage*). Miss Somerset!

SABINA (*energetically, to the audience*). Ladies and gentlemen! Don't take this play serious. The world's not coming to an end. You know it's not. People exaggerate! Most people really have

ggie, you know . . . you know Homer?—
me right in, Judge.—

s Muse—are some of your sisters here? Come
t in. . . .

s E. Muse; Miss T. Muse, Miss M. Muse.

RS. ANTROBUS. Pleased to meet you.

. . . make yourself comfortable. Supper'll
eady in a minute. (*She goes out, abruptly.*)

NTROBUS. Make yourself at home, friends. I'll
ght back.

(*He goes out. The* REFUGEES *stare about
them in awe. Presently several voices start
whispering "Homer! Homer!" All take it
up.* HOMER *strikes a chord or two on his
guitar, then starts to speak:*)

MER.

ν ἄειδε, θεά, Πηληϊάδεω Ἀχιλῆος,
ιένην, ἣ μυρί' Ἀχαιοῖς ἄλγε' ἔθηκεν,
ἀς δ' ἰφθίμους ψυχὰς—

HOMER's *face shows he is lost in thought
and memory and the words die away on
his lips. The* REFUGEES *likewise nod in
dreamy recollection. Soon the whisper
"Moses, Moses!" goes around. An aged
Jew parts his beard and recites dramatically:*)

S.

בְּרֵאשִׁית בָּרָא אֱלֹהִים אֵת הַשָּׁמַיִם וְאֵת הָאָרֶץ׃
הָיְתָה תֹהוּ וָבֹהוּ וְחֹשֶׁךְ עַל־פְּנֵי תְהוֹם וְרוּחַ
מְרַחֶפֶת עַל־פְּנֵי הַמָּיִם׃

he same dying away of the words take
ace, and on the part of the REFUGEES
e same retreat into recollection. Some of
em murmur, "Yes, yes." The mood is
oken by the abrupt entrance of MR. and
RS. ANTROBUS *and* SABINA *bearing plat-
s of sandwiches and a pail of coffee.
BINA stops and stares at the guests.*)

TROBUS. Sabina, pass the sandwiches.

I thought I was working in a respect-
e that had respectable guests. I'm giv-
tice, Mr. Antrobus: two weeks, that's

ROBUS. Sabina! Pass the sandwiches.

Two weeks, that's the law.

ROBUS. There's the law. That's Moses.

(*stares*). The Ten Commandments—

FAUGH!!—(*To audience.*) That's the worst line
I've ever had to say on any stage.

ANTROBUS. I think the best thing to do is just
not to stand on ceremony, but pass the sandwiches around from left to right.—Judge, help
yourself to one of these.

MRS. ANTROBUS. The roads are crowded, I
hear?

THE GUESTS (*all talking at once*). Oh, ma'am,
you can't imagine. . . . You can hardly put one
foot before you . . . people are trampling one
another.

(*Sudden silence.*)

MRS. ANTROBUS. Well, you know what I think
it is—I think it's sun-spots!

THE GUESTS (*discreet hubbub*). Oh, you're
right, Mrs. Antrobus . . . that's what it is. . . .
That's what I was saying the other day.

(*Sudden silence.*)

ANTROBUS. Well, I don't believe the whole
world's going to turn to ice.

(*All eyes are fixed on him, waiting.*)

I can't believe it. Judge! Have we worked for
nothing? Professor! Have we just failed in the
whole thing?

MRS. ANTROBUS. It is certainly very strange—
well, fortunately on both sides of the family we
come of very hearty stock.—Doctor, I want you
to meet my children. They're eating their supper
now. And of course I want them to meet you.

MISS M. MUSE. How many children have you,
Mrs. Antrobus?

MRS. ANTROBUS. I have two—a boy and a girl.

MOSES (*softly*). I understood you had two sons,
Mrs. Antrobus.

(MRS. ANTROBUS *in blind suffering; she
walks toward the footlights.*)

MRS. ANTROBUS (*in a low voice*). Abel, Abel,
my son, my son, Abel, my son, Abel, Abel, my
son.

(*The* REFUGEES *move with few steps toward
her as though in comfort murmuring
words in Greek, Hebrew, German, et
cetera. A piercing shriek from the kitchen
—*SABINA's *voice. All heads turn.*)

ANTROBUS. What's that?

(SABINA *enters, bursting with indignation,
pulling on her gloves.*)

SABINA. Mr. Antrobus—that son of yours,
that boy Henry Antrobus—I don't stay in this

enough to eat and a roof over their heads. Nobody actually starves—you can always eat grass
or something. That ice business—why, it was a
long, long time ago. Besides they were only
savages. Savages don't love their families—not
like we do.

ANTROBUS *and* STAGE MANAGER. Miss Somerset!!

(*There is renewed knocking at the door.*)

SABINA. All right. I'll say the lines, but I won't
think about the play.

(*Enter* MRS. ANTROBUS.)

SABINA (*parting thrust at the audience*). And
I advise *you* not to think about the play, either.
(*Exit* SABINA.)

MRS. ANTROBUS. George, these tramps say that
you asked them to come to the house. What does
this mean?

(*Knocking at the door.*)

ANTROBUS. Just . . . uh . . . There are a few
friends, Maggie, I met on the road. Real nice,
real useful people. . . .

MRS. ANTROBUS (*back to the door*). Now, don't
you ask them in!
George Antrobus, not another soul comes in
here over my dead body.

ANTROBUS. Maggie, there's a doctor there.
Never hurts to have a good doctor in the house.
We've lost a peck of children, one way and another. You can never tell when a child's throat
will get stopped up. What you and I have
seen—!!! (*He puts his fingers on his throat, and
imitates diphtheria.*)

MRS. ANTROBUS. Well, just one person then,
the Doctor. The others can go right along the
road.

ANTROBUS. Maggie, there's an old man, particular friend of mine—

MRS. ANTROBUS. I won't listen to you—

ANTROBUS. It was he that really started off the
A.B.C.'s.

MRS. ANTROBUS. I don't care if he perishes. We
can do without reading or writing. We can't do
without food.

ANTROBUS. Then let the ice come!! Drink your
coffee!! I don't want any coffee if I can't drink
it with some good people.

MRS. ANTROBUS. Stop shouting. Who else is
there trying to push us off the cliff?

ANTROBUS. Well, there's the man . . . who

makes all the laws. Judge Mos
MRS. ANTROBUS. Judges can't
ANTROBUS. And if the ice n
we pull through? Have you ar
bring up Henry? What have v
MRS. ANTROBUS. Who are th
ANTROBUS (*coughs*). Up in t
sisters. There are three or f
They're sort of music teache
them recites and one of them
MRS. ANTROBUS. That's t
troupe! Well, take your choi
your own children before y
ANTROBUS (*gently*). Thes
much.
They're used to starving.
They'll sleep on the floor.
Besides, Maggie, listen: n
Who've we got in the hous
always afraid the worst
spirits can she keep up?
Maggie, these people ne
they'll live and work for
MRS. ANTROBUS (*wall
of the room*). All right,
You're master here.
(*Softly.*)
—But these animals m
They'll soon be big e
down, anyway. Take
ANTROBUS (*sadly*).
mammoth—! Come or
Come for a walk. Th
DINOSAUR. It's cold
ANTROBUS. Yes, ni
(*He holds the
go out. He
REFUGEES ar
from the str
MOSES wear.
beggar with
shuffles in
pectantly.
his wife w
bend of h
Make yourself a
tor . . . m . . .
ute. . . . Profes
. . . Judge . .
(*An old bl

M
C
Mi
rig
Mi
Jus
be
A
be

H

Μῆνι
οὐλο
πολλ

Mos

‏תֵּדְאֶרָץ‎ *
‏וֹהִים‎

(T
p
t
t
b
M
te
SA
MR. A
SABINA
able hous
ing my n
the law.
MR. AN
SABINA.
MR. AN
SABINA

house another moment!—He's not fit to live among respectable folks and that's a fact.

MRS. ANTROBUS. Don't say another word, Sabina. I'll be right back.

> (*Without waiting for an answer she goes past her into the kitchen.*)

SABINA. Mr. Antrobus, Henry has thrown a stone again and if he hasn't killed the boy that lives next door, I'm very much mistaken. He finished his supper and went out to play; and I heard such a fight; and then I saw it. I saw it with my own eyes. And it looked to me like stark murder.

> (MRS. ANTROBUS *appears at the kitchen door, shielding* HENRY *who follows her. When she steps aside, we see on* HENRY'S *forehead a large ochre and scarlet scar in the shape of a C.* MR. ANTROBUS *starts toward him. A pause.* HENRY *is heard saying under his breath:*)

HENRY. He was going to take the wheel away from me. He started to throw a stone at me first.

MRS. ANTROBUS. George, it was just a boyish impulse. Remember how young he is.

> (*Louder, in an urgent wail.*)

George, he's only four thousand years old.

SABINA. And everything was going along so nicely!

> (*Silence.* ANTROBUS *goes back to the fireplace.*)

ANTROBUS. Put out the fire! Put out all the fires.

> (*Violently.*)

No wonder the sun grows cold.

> (*He starts stamping on the fireplace.*)

MRS. ANTROBUS. Doctor! Judge! Help me!— George, have you lost your mind?

ANTROBUS. There is no mind. We'll not try to live.

> (*To the guests.*)

Give it up. Give up trying.

> (MRS. ANTROBUS *seizes him.*)

SABINA. Mr. Antrobus! I'm downright ashamed of you.

MRS. ANTROBUS. George, have some more coffee.—Gladys! Where's Gladys gone?

> (GLADYS *steps in, frightened.*)

GLADYS. Here I am, mama.

MRS. ANTROBUS. Go upstairs and bring your father's slippers. How could you forget a thing like that, when you know how tired he is?

> (ANTROBUS *sits in his chair. He covers his face with his hands.* MRS. ANTROBUS *turns to the* REFUGEES:)

Can't some of you sing? It's your business in life to sing, isn't it? Sabina!

> (*Several of the women clear their throats tentatively, and with frightened faces gather around* HOMER'S *guitar. He establishes a few chords. Almost inaudibly they start singing, led by* SABINA: *"Jingle Bells."* MRS. ANTROBUS *continues to* ANTROBUS *in a low voice, while taking off his shoes:*)

George, remember all the other times. When the volcanoes came right up in the front yard.

And the time the grasshhoppers ate every single leaf and blade of grass, and all the grain and spinach you'd grown with your own hands. And the summer there were earthquakes every night.

ANTROBUS. Henry! Henry!

> (*Puts his hand on his forehead.*)

Myself. All of us, we're covered with blood.

MRS. ANTROBUS. Then remember all the times you were pleased with him and when you were proud of yourself.—Henry! Henry! Come here and recite to your father the multiplication table that you do so nicely.

> (HENRY *kneels on one knee beside his father and starts whispering the multiplication table.*)

HENRY (*finally*). Two times six is twelve; three times six is eighteen—I don't think I know the sixes.

> (*Enter* GLADYS *with the slippers.* MRS. ANTROBUS *makes stern gestures to her: Go in there and do your best. The* GUESTS *are now singing "Tenting Tonight."*)

GLADYS (*putting slippers on his feet*). Papa . . . papa . . . I was very good in school today. Miss Conover said right out in class that if all the girls had as good manners as Gladys Antrobus, that the world would be a very different place to live in.

MRS. ANTROBUS. You recited a piece at assembly, didn't you? Recite it to your father.

GLADYS. Papa, do you want to hear what I recited in class?

> (*Fierce directorial glance from her mother.*)

"THE STAR" by Henry Wadsworth LONG-

FELLOW.

MRS. ANTROBUS. Wait!!! The fire's going out. There isn't enough wood! Henry, go upstairs and bring down the chairs and start breaking up the beds.

(*Exit* HENRY. *The singers return to "Jingle Bells," still very softly.*)

GLADYS. Look, Papa, here's my report card. Lookit. Conduct A! Look, Papa. Papa, do you want to hear the Star, by Henry Wadsworth Longfellow? Papa, you're not mad at me, are you?—I know it'll get warmer. Soon it'll be just like spring, and we can go to a picnic at the Hibernian Picnic Grounds like you always like to do, don't you remember? Papa, just look at me once.

(*Enter* HENRY *with some chairs.*)

ANTROBUS. You recited in assembly, did you?

(*She nods eagerly.*)

You didn't forget it?

GLADYS. No!!! I was perfect.

(*Pause. Then* ANTROBUS *rises, goes to the front door and opens it. The* REFUGEES *draw back timidly; the song stops; he peers out of the door, then closes it.*)

ANTROBUS (*with decision, suddenly*). Build up the fire. It's cold. Build up the fire. We'll do what we can. Sabina, get some more wood. Come around the fire, everybody. At least the young ones may pull through. Henry, have you eaten something?

HENRY. Yes, papa.

ANTROBUS. Gladys, have you had some supper?

GLADYS. I ate in the kitchen, papa.

ANTROBUS. If you do come through this— what'll you be able to do? What do you know? Henry, did you take a good look at that wheel?

HENRY. Yes, papa.

ANTROBUS (*sitting down in his chair*). Six

times two are—

HENRY. —twelve; six times three are eighteen: six times four are—Papa, it's hot and cold. It makes my head all funny. It makes me sleepy.

ANTROBUS (*gives him a cuff*). Wake up. I don't care if your head is sleepy. Six times four are twenty-four. Six times five are—

HENRY. Thirty. Papa!

ANTROBUS. Maggie, put something into Gladys's head on the chance she can use it.

MRS. ANTROBUS. What do you mean, George?

ANTROBUS. Six times six are thirty-six. Teach her the beginning of the Bible.

GLADYS. But, Mama, it's so cold and close.

(HENRY *has all but drowsed off. His father slaps him sharply and the lesson goes on.*)

MRS. ANTROBUS. "In the beginning God created the heavens and the earth; and the earth was waste and void; and the darkness was upon the face of the deep—"

(*The singing starts up again louder.* SABINA *has returned with wood.*)

SABINA (*after placing wood on the fireplace comes down to the footlights and addresses the audience*). Will you please start handing up your chairs? We'll need everything for this fire. Save the human race.—Ushers, will you pass the chairs up here? Thank you.

HENRY. Six times nine are fifty-four; six times ten are sixty.

(*In the back of the auditorium the sound of chairs being ripped up can be heard.* USHERS *rush down the aisles with chairs and hand them over.*)

GLADYS. "And God called the light Day and the darkness he called Night."

SABINA. Pass up your chairs, everybody. Save the human race.

Act II

SCENE: *Atlantic City Boardwalk.*

(*Toward the end of the intermission, though with the house lights still up, lantern slide projections begin to appear on the curtain. Timetables for trains leaving Pennsylvania Station for Atlantic City. Advertisements of Atlantic City hotels, drugstores, churches, rug merchants; for-*

tune tellers, Bingo parlors.

When the house lights go down, the voice of an ANNOUNCER *is heard.*)

ANNOUNCER. The Management now brings you the News Events of the World. Atlantic City, New Jersey:

(*Projection of a chrome postcard of the*

waterfront, trimmed in mica with the legend: FUN AT THE BEACH)

This great convention city is playing host this week to the anniversary convocation of that great fraternal order—the Ancient and Honorable Order of Mammals, Subdivision Humans. This great fraternal, militant and burial society is celebrating on the Boardwalk, ladies and gentlemen, its six hundred thousandth Annual Convention.

It has just elected its president for the ensuing term—

(Projection of MR. and MRS. ANTROBUS posed as they will be shown a few moments later)

Mr. George Antrobus of Excelsior, New Jersey. We show you President Antrobus and his gracious and charming wife, every inch a mammal. Mr. Antrobus has had a long and chequered career. Credit has been paid to him for many useful enterprises including the introduction of the lever, of the wheel and the brewing of beer. Credit has been also extended to President Antrobus's gracious and charming wife for many practical suggestions, including the hem, the gore, and the gusset; and the novelty of the year—frying in oil. Before we show you Mr. Antrobus accepting the nomination, we have an important announcement to make. As many of you know, this great celebration of the Order of the Mammals has received delegations from the other rival Orders—or shall we say: esteemed concurrent Orders: the WINGS, the FINS, the SHELLS, and so on. These Orders are holding their conventions also, in various parts of the world, and have sent representatives to our own, two of a kind.

Later in the day we will show you President Antrobus broadcasting his words of greeting and congratulation to the collected assemblies of the whole natural world.

Ladies and Gentlemen! We give you President Antrobus!

(The screen becomes a Transparency. MR. ANTROBUS stands beside a pedestal; MRS. ANTROBUS is seated wearing a corsage of orchids. ANTROBUS wears an untidy Prince Albert; spats; from a red rosette in his buttonhole hangs a fine long purple ribbon of honor. He wears a gay lodge hat

—something between a fez and a legionnaire's cap.)

ANTROBUS. Fellow-mammals, fellow-vertebrates, fellow-humans, I thank you. Little did my dear parents think—when they told me to stand on my own two feet—that I'd arrive at this place.

My friends, we have come a long way.

During this week of happy celebration it is perhaps not fitting that we dwell on some of the difficult times we have been through. The dinosaur is extinct—

(Applause.)

—the ice has retreated; and the common cold is being pursued by every means within our power.

(MRS. ANTROBUS sneezes, laughs prettily, and murmurs: "I beg your pardon.")

In our memorial service yesterday we did honor to all our friends and relatives who are no longer with us, by reason of cold, earthquakes, plagues and . . . and . . . (Coughs) differences of opinion.

As our Bishop so ably said . . . uh . . . so ably said. . . .

MRS. ANTROBUS *(closed lips)*. Gone, but not forgotten.

ANTROBUS. "They are gone, but not forgotten."

I think I can say, I think I can prophesy with complete . . . uh . . . with complete . . .

MRS. ANTROBUS. Confidence.

ANTROBUS. Thank you, my dear— With complete lack of confidence, that a new day of security is about to dawn.

The watchword of the closing year was: Work. I give you the watchword for the future: Enjoy Yourselves.

MRS. ANTROBUS. George, sit down!

ANTROBUS. Before I close, however, I wish to answer one of those unjust and malicious accusations that were brought against me during this last electoral campaign.

Ladies and gentlemen, the charge was made that at various points in my career I leaned toward joining some of the rival orders—that's a lie.

As I told reporters of the *Atlantic City Herald*, I do not deny that a few months before my birth I hesitated between . . . uh . . . between pin-feathers and gill-breathing—and so did many of us here—but for the last million years I have been viviparous, hairy and diaphragmatic.

(Applause. Cries of "Good old Antrobus,"
"The Prince chap!" "Georgie," etc.)

ANNOUNCER. Thank you. Thank you very
much, Mr. Antrobus.
Now I know that our visitors will wish to hear a
word from that gracious and charming mammal,
Mrs. Antrobus, wife and mother—Mrs. Antrobus!

(MRS. ANTROBUS rises, lays her program on
her chair, bows and says:)

MRS. ANTROBUS. Dear friends, I don't really
think I should say anything. After all, it was my
husband who was elected and not I.
Perhaps, as president of the Women's Auxiliary
Bed and Board Society—I had some notes here,
oh, yes, here they are—I should give a short report from some of our committees that have
been meeting in this beautiful city.
Perhaps it may interest you to know that it has
at last been decided that the tomato is edible.
Can you all hear me? The tomato *is* edible.
A delegate from across the sea reports that the
thread woven by the silkworm gives a cloth . . .
I have a sample of it here . . . can you see it?
smooth, elastic. I should say that it's rather attractive—though personally I prefer less shiny
surfaces. Should the windows of a sleeping apartment be open or shut? I know all mothers will
follow our debates on this matter with close interest. I am sorry to say that the most expert
authorities have not yet decided. It does seem
to me that the night air would be bound to be
unhealthy for our children, but there are many
distinguished authorities on both sides. Well, I
could go on talking forever—as Shakespeare says:
a woman's work is seldom done; but I think I'd
better join my husband in saying thank you, and
sit down. Thank you. *(She sits down)*

ANNOUNCER. Oh, Mrs. Antrobus!

MRS. ANTROBUS. Yes?

ANNOUNCER. We understand that you are about
to celebrate a wedding anniversary. I know our
listeners would like to extend their felicitations
and hear a few words from you on that subject.

MRS. ANTROBUS. I have been asked by this
kind gentleman . . . yes, my friends, this spring
Mr. Antrobus and I will be celebrating our five
thousandth wedding anniversary.
I don't know if I speak for my husband, but I
can say that, as for me, I regret every moment
of it.

(Laughter of confusion)

I beg your pardon. What I *mean* to say is that I
do not regret one moment of it. I hope none of
you catch my cold. We have two children. We've
always had two children, though it hasn't always
been the same two. But as I say, we have two
fine children, and we're very grateful for that.
Yes, Mr. Antrobus and I have been married five
thousand years. Each wedding anniversary reminds me of the times when there were no weddings. We had to crusade for marriage. Perhaps
there are some women within the sound of my
voice who remember that crusade and those
struggles; we fought for it, didn't we? We chained
ourselves to lampposts and we made disturbances
in the Senate—anyway, at last we women got
the ring.
A few men helped us, but I must say that most
men blocked our way at every step: they said we
were unfeminine.
I only bring up these unpleasant memories, because I see some signs of backsliding from that
great victory.
Oh, my fellow mammals, keep hold of that.
My husband says that the watchword for the year
is Enjoy Yourself. I think that's very open to misunderstanding. My watchword for the year is:
Save the Family. It's held together for over five
thousand years: Save it! Thank you.

ANNOUNCER. Thank you, Mrs. Antrobus.

(The transparency disappears)

We had hoped to show you the Beauty Contest
that took place here today.
President Antrobus, an experienced judge of
pretty girls, gave the title of Miss Atlantic City
1942, to Miss Lily-Sabina Fairweather, charming
hostess of our Boardwalk Bingo Parlor.
Unfortunately, however, our time is up, and I
must take you to some views of the Convention
City and conveeners— enjoying themselves.

(A Burst of music; the curtain rises.
The Boardwalk. The audience is sitting in
the ocean. A handrail of scarlet cord
stretches across the front of the stage. A
ramp—also with scarlet handrail—descends
to the right corner of the orchestra pit
where a great scarlet beach umbrella or
a cabana stands. Front and right stage left
are benches facing the sea; attached to
each bench is a street-lamp.

*The only scenery is two cardboard cut-outs
six feet high, representing shops at the
back of the stage. Reading from left to
right they are: SALT WATER TAFFY;
FORTUNE TELLER; then the blank
space; BINGO PARLOR; TURKISH
BATH. They have practical doors, that
of the Fortune Teller's being hung with
bright gypsy curtains.*

*By the left proscenium and rising from the
orchestra pit is the weather signal; it is
like the mast of a ship with cross bars.
From time to time black discs are hung
on it to indicate the storm and hurricane
warnings. Three roller chairs, pushed by
melancholy* NEGROES *file by empty.
Throughout the act they traverse the
stage in both directions.*

From time to time, CONVEENERS, *dressed like*
MR. ANTROBUS, *cross the stage. Some walk
sedately by; others engage in inane horse-
play. The old gypsy* FORTUNE TELLER *is
seated at the door of her shop, smoking a
corncob pipe.*

*From the Bingo Parlor comes the voice of
the* CALLER.)

BINGO CALLER. A—Nine; A—Nine. C—Twenty-
six; C—Twenty-six.

A—Four; A—Four. B—Twelve.

CHORUS (*back-stage*). Bingo!!!

(*The front of the Bingo Parlor shudders,
rises a few feet in the air and returns to
the ground trembling*)

FORTUNE TELLER (*mechanically, to the unconscious back of a passerby, pointing with her
pipe*). Bright's disease! Your partner's deceiving
you in that Kansas City deal. You'll have six
grandchildren. Avoid high places.

(*She rises and shouts after another:*)

Cirrhosis of the liver!

(SABINA *appears at the door of the Bingo
Parlor. She hugs about her a blue raincoat that almost conceals her red bathing
suit. She tries to catch the* FORTUNE
TELLER's *attention.*)

SABINA. Ssssst! Esmeralda! Sssssst!

FORTUNE TELLER. Keck!

SABINA. Has President Antrobus come along
yet?

FORTUNE TELLER. No, no, no. Get back there.

Hide yourself.

SABINA. I'm afraid I'll miss him. Oh, Esmeralda, if I fail in this, I'll die; I know I'll die.
President Antrobus!!! And I'll be his wife! If it's
the last thing I'll do, I'll be Mrs. George Antrobus.—Esmeralda, tell me my future.

FORTUNE TELLER. Keck!

SABINA. All right, I'll tell *you* my future.

(*Laughing dreamily and tracing it out with
one finger on the palm of her hand*)

I've won the Beauty Contest in Atlantic City—
well, I'll win the Beauty Contest of the whole
world. I'll take President Antrobus away from
that wife of his. Then I'll take every man away
from his wife. I'll turn the whole earth upside
down.

FORTUNE TELLER. Keck!

SABINA. When all those husbands just think
about me they'll get dizzy. They'll faint in the
streets. They'll have to lean against lampposts.—
Esmeralda, who was Helen of Troy?

FORTUNE TELLER (*furiously*). Shut your foolish
mouth. When Mr. Antrobus comes along you can
see what you can do. Until then—go away.

(SABINA *laughs. As she returns to the door
of her Bingo Parlor a group of* CON-
VEENERS *rush over and smother her with
attentions: "Oh, Miss Lily, you know me.
You've known me for years."*)

SABINA. Go away, boys, go away. I'm after
bigger fry than you are.—Why, Mr. Simpson!!
How *dare* you!! I expect that even you nobodies
must have girls to amuse you; but where you find
them and what you do with them, is of absolutely no interest to me.

(*Exit. The* CONVEENERS *squeal with pleasure
and stumble in after her. The* FORTUNE
TELLER *rises, puts her pipe down on the
stool, unfurls her voluminous skirts, gives
a sharp wrench to her bodice and strolls
towards the audience, swinging her hips
like a young woman.*)

FORTUNE TELLER. I tell the future. Keck.
Nothing easier. Everybody's future is in their
face. Nothing easier.

But who can tell your past—eh? Nobody!

Your youth—where did it go? It slipped away
while you weren't looking. While you were
asleep. While you were drunk? Puh! You're like
our friends, Mr. and Mrs. Antrobus; you lie

awake nights trying to know your past. What did it mean? What was it trying to say to you?

Think! Think! Split your heads. I can't tell the past and neither can you. If anybody tries to tell you the past, take my word for it, they're charlatans! Charlatans! But I can tell the future.

(*She suddenly barks at a passing chair-pusher*)

Apoplexy!

(*She returns to the audience*)

Nobody listens.—Keck! I see a face among you now—I won't embarrass him by pointing him out, but, listen, it may be you: Next year the watchsprings inside you will crumple up. Death by regret—Type Y. It's in the corners of your mouth. You'll decide that you should have lived for pleasure, but that you missed it. Death by regret—Type Y. . . . Avoid mirrors. You'll try to be angry—but no!—no anger.

(*Far forward, confidentially*)

And now what's the immediate future of our friends, the Antrobuses? Oh, you've seen it as well as I have, keck—that dizziness of the head; that Great Man dizziness? The inventor of beer and gunpowder. The sudden fits of temper and then the long stretches of inertia? "I'm a sultan; let my slave-girls fan me"? You know as well as I what's coming. Rain. Rain. Rain in floods. The deluge. But first you'll see shameful things— shameful things. Some of you will be saying: "Let him drown. He's not worth saving. Give the whole thing up." I can see it in your faces. But you're wrong. Keep your doubts and despairs to yourselves.

Again there'll be the narrow escape. The survival of a handful. From destruction—total destruction.

(*She points, sweeping with her hand, to the stage*)

Even of the animals, a few will be saved: two of a kind, male and female, two of a kind.

(*The heads of* CONVEENERS *appear about the stage and in the orchestra pit, jeering at her*)

CONVEENERS. Charlatan! Madam Kill-joy! Mrs. Jeremiah! Charlatan!

FORTUNE TELLER. And *you!* Mark my words before it's too late. Where'll *you* be?

CONVEENERS. The croaking raven. Old dust and ashes. Rags, bottles, sacks.

FORTUNE TELLER. Yes, stick out your tongues.

You can't stick your tongues out far enough to lick the death-sweat from your foreheads. It's too late to work now—bail out the flood with your soup spoons. You've had your chance and you've lost.

CONVEENERS. Enjoy yourselves!!!

(*They disappear. The* FORTUNE TELLER *looks off left and puts her finger on her lip.*)

FORTUNE TELLER. They're coming—the Antrobuses. Keck. Your hope. Your despair. Your selves.

(*Enter from the left,* MR. *and* MRS. ANTROBUS *and* GLADYS)

MRS. ANTROBUS. Gladys Antrobus, stick your stummick in.

GLADYS. But it's easier this way.

MRS. ANTROBUS. Well, it's too bad the new president has such a clumsy daughter, that's all I can say. Try and be a lady.

FORTUNE TELLER. Aijah! That's been said a hundred billion times.

MRS. ANTROBUS. Goodness! Where's Henry? He was here just a minute ago. Henry!

(*Sudden violent stir. A roller-chair appears from the left. About it are dancing in great excitement* HENRY *and a* NEGRO CHAIR-PUSHER.)

HENRY (*slingshot in hand*). I'll put your eye out. I'll make you yell, like you never yelled before.

NEGRO (*at the same time*). Now, I warns you. I warns you. If you make me mad, you'll get hurt.

ANTROBUS. Henry! What is this? Put down that slingshot.

MRS. ANTROBUS (*at the same time*). Henry! HENRY! Behave yourself.

FORTUNE TELLER. That's right, young man. There are too many people in the world as it is. Everybody's in the way, except one's self.

HENRY. All I wanted to do was—have some fun.

NEGRO. Nobody can't touch my chair, nobody, without I allow 'em to. You get clean away from me and you get away fast. (*He pushes his chair off, muttering*)

ANTROBUS. What were you doing, Henry?

HENRY. Everybody's always getting mad. Everybody's always trying to push you around. I'll make him sorry for this; I'll make him sorry.

ANTROBUS. Give me that slingshot.

HENRY. I won't. I'm sorry I came to this place. I wish I weren't here. I wish I weren't anywhere.

MRS. ANTROBUS. Now, Henry, don't get so excited about nothing. I declare I don't know what we're going to do with you. Put your slingshot in your pocket, and don't try to take hold of things that don't belong to you.

ANTROBUS. After this you can stay home. I wash my hands of you.

MRS. ANTROBUS. Come now, let's forget all about it. Everybody take a good breath of that sea air and calm down.

(*A passing* CONVEENER *bows to* ANTROBUS *who nods to him*)

Who was that you spoke to, George?

ANTROBUS. Nobody, Maggie. Just the candidate who ran against me in the election.

MRS. ANTROBUS. The man who ran against you in the election!!

(*She turns and waves her umbrella after the disappearing* CONVEENER)

My husband didn't speak to you and he never will speak to you.

ANTROBUS. Now, Maggie.

MRS. ANTROBUS. After those lies you told about him in your speeches! Lies, that's what they were.

GLADYS *and* HENRY. Mama, everybody's looking at you. Everybody's laughing at you.

MRS. ANTROBUS. If you must know, my husband's a SAINT, a downright SAINT, and you're not fit to speak to him on the street.

ANTROBUS. Now, Maggie, now, Maggie, that's enough of that.

MRS. ANTROBUS. George Antrobus, you're a perfect worm. If you won't stand up for yourself, I will.

GLADYS. Mama, you just act awful in public.

MRS. ANTROBUS (*laughing*). Well, I must say I enjoyed it. I feel better. Wish his wife had been there to hear it. Children, what do you want to do?

GLADYS. Papa, can we ride in one of those chairs? Mama, I want to ride in one of those chairs.

MRS. ANTROBUS. No, sir. If you're tired you just sit where you are. We have no money to spend on foolishness.

ANTROBUS. I guess we have money enough for a thing like that. It's one of the things you do at Atlantic City.

MRS. ANTROBUS. Oh, we have? I tell you it's a miracle my children have shoes to stand up in. I didn't think I'd ever live to see them pushed around in chairs.

ANTROBUS. We're on a vacation, aren't we? We have a right to some treats, I guess. Maggie, some day you're going to drive me crazy.

MRS. ANTROBUS. All right, go. I'll just sit here and laugh at you. And you can give me my dollar right in my hand. Mark my words, a rainy day is coming. There's a rainy day ahead of us. I feel it in my bones. Go on, throw your money around. I can starve. I've starved before. I know how.

(*A* CONVEENER *puts his head through Turkish Bath window, and says with raised eyebrows:*)

CONVEENER. Hello, George. How are ya? I see where you brought the WHOLE family along.

MRS. ANTROBUS. And what do you mean by that?

(CONVEENER *withdraws head and closes window*)

ANTROBUS. Maggie, I tell you there's a limit to what I can stand. God's Heaven, haven't I worked *enough?* Don't I get *any* vacation? Can't I even give my children so much as a ride in a roller-chair?

MRS. ANTROBUS (*putting out her hand for raindrops*). Anyway, it's going to rain very soon and you have your broadcast to make.

ANTROBUS. Now, Maggie, I warn you. A man can stand a family only just so long. I'm warning you.

(*Enter* SABINA *from the Bingo Parlor. She wears a flounced red silk bathing suit, 1905. Red stockings, shoes, parasol. She bows demurely to* ANTROBUS *and starts down the ramp.* ANTROBUS *and the* CHILDREN *stare at her.* ANTROBUS *bows gallantly.*)

MRS. ANTROBUS. Why, George Antrobus, how can you say such a thing! You have the best family in the world.

ANTROBUS. Good morning, Miss Fairweather.

(SABINA *finally disappears behind the beach umbrella or in a cabana in the orchestra pit*)

MRS. ANTROBUS. Who on earth was that you

spoke to, George?

ANTROBUS (*complacent; mock-modest*). Hm . . . m . . . just a . . . solambaka keray.

MRS. ANTROBUS. What? I can't understand you.

GLADYS. Mama, wasn't she beautiful?

HENRY. Papa, introduce her to me.

MRS. ANTROBUS. Children, will you be quiet while I ask your father a simple question?—Who did you say it was, George?

ANTROBUS. Why—uh . . . a friend of mine. Very nice refined girl.

MRS. ANTROBUS. I'm waiting.

ANTROBUS. Maggie, that's the girl I gave the prize to in the beauty contest—that's Miss Atlantic City 1942.

MRS. ANTROBUS. Hm! She looked like Sabina to me.

HENRY (*at the railing*). Mama, the life-guard knows her, too. Mama, he knows her well.

ANTROBUS. Henry, come here.—She's a very nice girl in every way and the sole support of her aged mother.

MRS. ANTROBUS. So was Sabina, so was Sabina; and it took a wall of ice to open your eyes about Sabina.—Henry, come over and sit down on this bench.

ANTROBUS. She's a very different matter from Sabina. Miss Fairweather is a college graduate, Phi Beta Kappa.

MRS. ANTROBUS. Henry, you sit here by mama. Gladys—

ANTROBUS (*sitting*). Reduced circumstances have required her taking a position as hostess in a Bingo Parlor; but there isn't a girl with higher principles in the country.

MRS. ANTROBUS. Well, let's not talk about it.—Henry, I haven't seen a whale yet.

ANTROBUS. She speaks seven languages and has more culture in her little finger than you've acquired in a lifetime.

MRS. ANTROBUS (*assumed amiability*). All right, all right, George. I'm glad to know there are such superior girls in the Bingo Parlors.—Henry, what's that? (*Pointing at the storm signal, which has one black disk*)

HENRY. What is it, Papa?

ANTROBUS. What? Oh, that's the storm signal. One of those black disks means bad weather; two means storm; three means hurricane; and four means the end of the world.

(*As they watch it a second black disk rolls into place*)

MRS. ANTROBUS. Goodness! I'm going this very minute to buy you all some raincoats.

GLADYS (*putting her cheek against her father's shoulder*). Mama, don't go yet. I like sitting this way. And the ocean coming in and coming in. Papa, don't you like it?

MRS. ANTROBUS. Well, there's only one thing I lack to make me a perfectly happy woman: I'd like to see a whale.

HENRY. Mama, we saw two. Right out there. They're delegates to the convention. I'll find you one.

GLADYS. Papa, ask me something. Ask me a question.

ANTROBUS. Well . . . how big's the ocean?

GLADYS. Papa, you're teasing me. It's—three-hundred and sixty million square miles—and—it—covers—three-fourths—of—the—earth's—surface—and—its—deepest-place—is—five—and—a—half—miles—deep—and—its—average—depth—is—twelve-thousand—feet. No, Papa, ask me something hard, real hard.

MRS. ANTROBUS (*rising*). Now I'm going off to buy those raincoats. I think that bad weather's going to get worse and worse. I hope it doesn't come before your broadcast. I should think we have about an hour or so.

HENRY. I hope it comes and zzzzzz everything before it. I hope it—

MRS. ANTROBUS. Henry!—George, I think . . . maybe, it's one of those storms that are just as bad on land as on the sea. When you're just as safe and safer in a good stout boat.

HENRY. There's a boat out at the end of the pier.

MRS. ANTROBUS. Well, keep your eye on it. George, you shut your eyes and get a good rest before the broadcast.

ANTROBUS. Thundering Judas, do I have to be told when to open and shut my eyes? Go and buy your raincoats.

MRS. ANTROBUS. Now, children, you have ten minutes to walk around. Ten minutes. And, Henry: control yourself. Gladys, stick by your brother and don't get lost.

(*They run off*)

MRS. ANTROBUS. Will you be all right, George?

(CONVEENERS *suddenly stick their heads out of the Bingo Parlor and Salt Water Taffy store, and voices rise from the orchestra pit*)

CONVEENERS. George. Geo-r-r-rge! George! Leave the old hen-coop at home, George. Do-mes-ticated Georgie!

MRS. ANTROBUS (*shaking her umbrella*). Low common oafs! That's what they are. Guess a man has a right to bring his wife to a convention, if he wants to.

(*She starts off*)

What's the matter with a family, I'd like to know. What else have they got to offer?

(*Exit.* ANTROBUS *has closed his eyes. The* FORTUNE TELLER *comes out of her shop and goes over to the left proscenium. She leans against it, watching* SABINA *quizzically.*)

FORTUNE TELLER. Heh! Here she comes!

SABINA (*loud whisper*). What's he doing?

FORTUNE TELLER. Oh, he's ready for you. Bite your lips, dear, take a long breath and come on up.

SABINA. I'm nervous. My whole future depends on this. I'm nervous.

FORTUNE TELLER. Don't be a fool. What more could you want? He's forty-five. His head's a little dizzy. He's just been elected president. He's never known any other woman than his wife. Whenever he looks at her he realizes that she knows every foolish thing he's ever done.

SABINA (*still whispering*). I don't know why it is, but every time I start one of these I'm nervous.

(*The* FORTUNE TELLER *stands in the center of the stage watching the following:*)

FORTUNE TELLER. You make me tired.

SABINA. First tell me my fortune.

(*The* FORTUNE TELLER *laughs drily and makes the gesture of brushing away a non-sensical question.* SABINA *coughs and says:*)

Oh, Mr. Antrobus—dare I speak to you for a moment?

ANTROBUS. What?—Oh, certainly, certainly, Miss Fairweather.

SABINA. Mr. Antrobus . . . I've been so un-happy. I've wanted . . . I've wanted to make sure that you don't think that I'm the kind of girl who goes out for beauty contests.

FORTUNE TELLER. That's the way!

ANTROBUS. Oh, I understand. I understand perfectly.

FORTUNE TELLER. Give it a little more. Lean on it.

SABINA. I knew you would. My mother said to me this morning: Lily, she said, that fine Mr. Antrobus gave you the prize because he saw at once that you weren't the kind of girl who'd go in for a thing like that. But, honestly, Mr. Antrobus, in this world, honestly, a good girl doesn't know where to turn.

FORTUNE TELLER. Now you've gone too far.

ANTROBUS. My dear Miss Fairweather!

SABINA. You wouldn't know how hard it is. With that lovely wife and daughter you have. Oh, I think Mrs. Antrobus is the finest woman I ever saw. I wish I were like her.

ANTROBUS. There, there. There's . . . uh . . . room for all kinds of people in the world, Miss Fairweather.

SABINA. How wonderful of you to say that. How generous!—Mr. Antrobus, have you a moment free? . . . I'm afraid I may be a little conspicuous here . . . could you come down, for just a moment, to my beach cabana . . . ?

ANTROBUS. Why—uh . . . yes, certainly . . . for a moment . . . just for a moment.

SABINA. There's a deck chair there. Because: you know you *do* look tired. Just this morning my mother said to me: Lily, she said, I hope Mr. Antrobus is getting a good rest. His fine strong face has deep deep lines in it. Now isn't it true, Mr. Antrobus: you work too hard?

FORTUNE TELLER. Bingo! (*She goes into her shop*)

SABINA. Now you will just stretch out. No, I shan't say a word, not a word. I shall just sit there—privileged. That's what I am.

ANTROBUS (*taking her hand*). Miss Fairweather . . . you'll . . . spoil me.

SABINA. Just a moment. I have something I wish to say to the audience.—Ladies and gentlement. I'm not going to play this particular scene tonight. It's just a short scene and we're going to skip it. But I'll tell you what takes place and then we can continue the play from there on. Now in this scene—

ANTROBUS (*between his teeth*). But, Miss Somerset!

SABINA. I'm sorry. I'm sorry. But I have to

skip it. In this scene, I talk to Mr. Antrobus, and at the end of it he decides to leave his wife, get a divorce at Reno and marry me. That's all.

ANTROBUS. Fitz!—Fitz!

SABINA. So that now I've told you we can jump to the end of it—where you say—

(*Enter in fury* MR. FITZPATRICK, *the stage manager*)

MR. FITZPATRICK. Miss Somerset, we insist on your playing this scene.

SABINA. I'm sorry, Mr. Fitzpatrick, but I can't and I won't. I've told the audience all they need to know and now we can go on.

(*Other* ACTORS *begin to appear on the stage, listening*)

MR. FITZPATRICK. And *why* can't you play it?

SABINA. Because there are some lines in that scene that would hurt some people's feelings and I don't think the theatre is a place where people's feelings ought to be hurt.

MR. FITZPATRICK. Miss Somerset, you can pack up your things and go home. I shall call the understudy and I shall report you to Equity.

SABINA. I sent the understudy up to the corner for a cup of coffee and if Equity tries to penalize me I'll drag the case right up to the Supreme Court. Now listen, everybody, there's no need to get excited.

MR. FITZPATRICK *and* ANTROBUS. Why can't you play it . . . what's the matter with the scene?

SABINA. Well, if you must know, I have a personal guest in the audience tonight. Her life hasn't been exactly a happy one. I wouldn't have my friend hear some of these lines for the whole world. I don't suppose it occurred to the author that some other women might have gone through the experience of losing their husbands like this. Wild horses wouldn't drag from me the details of my friend's life, but . . . well, they'd been married twenty years, and before he got rich, why, she'd done the washing and everything.

MR. FITZPATRICK. Miss Somerset, your friend will forgive you. We must play this scene.

SABINA. Nothing, nothing will make me say some of those lines . . . about "a man outgrows a wife every seven years" and . . . and that one about "the Mohammedans being the only people who looked the subject square in the face." Nothing.

MR. FITZPATRICK. Miss Somerset! Go to your dressing room. I'll *read* your lines.

SABINA. Now everybody's nerves are on edge.

MR. ANTROBUS. Skip the scene.

(MR. FITZPATRICK *and the other* ACTORS *go off*)

SABINA. Thank you. I knew you'd understand. We'll do just what I said. So Mr. Antrobus is going to divorce his wife and marry me. Mr. Antrobus, you say: "It won't be easy to lay all this before my wife."

(*The* ACTORS *withdraw.* ANTROBUS *walks about, his hand to his forehead muttering:*)

ANTROBUS. Wait a minute. I can't get back into it as easily as all that. "My wife is a very obstinate woman." Hm . . . then you say . . . hm . . . Miss Fairweather, I mean Lily, it won't be easy to lay all this before my wife. It'll hurt her feelings a little.

SABINA. Listen, George: *other* people haven't got feelings. Not in the same way that we have —we who are presidents like you and prize-winners like me. Listen, other people haven't got feelings; they just imagine they have. Within two weeks they go back to playing bridge and going to the movies.

Listen, dear: everybody in the world except a few people like you and me are just people of straw. Most people have no insides at all. Now that you're president you'll see that. Listen, darling, there's a kind of secret society at the top of the world—like you and me—that know this. The world was made for us. What's life anyway? Except for two things, pleasure and power, what is life? Boredom! Foolishness. You know it is. Except for those two things, life's nau-se-at-ing. So—come here!

(*She moves close. They kiss.*)

So.

Now when your wife comes, it's really very simple; just tell her.

ANTROBUS. Lily, Lily: you're a wonderful woman.

SABINA. Of course I am.

(*They enter the cabana and it hides them from view. Distant roll of thunder. A third black disk appears on the weather signal. Distant thunder is heard.* MRS. ANTROBUS *appears carrying parcels. She looks about, seats herself on the bench left, and fans herself with her handkerchief. Enter* GLADYS *right, followed by two* CONVEENERS. *She is wearing red stockings.*)

MRS. ANTROBUS. Gladys!

GLADYS. Mama, here I am.

MRS. ANTROBUS. Gladys Antrobus!!! Where did you get those dreadful things?

GLADYS. Wha-a-t? Papa liked the color.

MRS. ANTROBUS. You go back to the hotel this minute!

GLADYS. I won't. I won't. Papa liked the color.

MRS. ANTROBUS. All right. All right. You stay here. I've a good mind to let your father see you that way. You stay right here.

GLADYS. I . . . I don't want to stay if . . . if you don't think he'd like it.

MRS. ANTROBUS. Oh . . . it's all one to me. I don't care what happens. I don't care if the biggest storm in the whole world comes. Let it come.

(*She folds her hands*)

Where's your brother?

GLADYS (*in a small voice*). He'll be here.

MRS. ANTROBUS. Will he? Well, let him get into trouble. I don't care. I don't know where your father is, I'm sure.

(*Laughter from the cabana*)

GLADYS (*leaning over the rail*). I think he's . . . Mama, he's talking to the lady in the red dress.

MRS. ANTROBUS. Is that so?

(*Pause*)

We'll wait till he's through. Sit down here beside me and stop fidgeting . . . what are you crying about?

(*Distant thunder. She covers* GLADYS's *stockings with a raincoat.*)

GLADYS. You don't like my stockings.

(*Two* CONVEENERS *rush in with a microphone on a standard and various paraphernalia. The* FORTUNE TELLER *appears at the door of her shop. Other characters gradually gather.*)

BROADCAST OFFICIAL. Mrs. Antrobus! Thank God we've found you at last. Where's Mr. Antrobus? We've been hunting everywhere for him. It's about time for the broadcast to the conventions of the world.

MRS. ANTROBUS (*calm*). I expect he'll be here in a minute.

BROADCAST OFFICIAL. Mrs. Antrobus, if he doesn't show up in time, I hope you will consent to broadcast in his place. It's the most important broadcast of the year.

(SABINA *enters from cabana followed by* ANTROBUS)

MRS. ANTROBUS. No, I shan't. I haven't one single thing to say.

BROADCAST OFFICIAL. Then won't you help us find him, Mrs. Antrobus? A storm's coming up. A hurricane. A deluge!

SECOND CONVEENER (*who has sighted* ANTROBUS *over the rail*). Joe! Joe! Here he is.

BROADCAST OFFICIAL. In the name of God, Mr. Antrobus, you're on the air in five minutes. Will you kindly please come and test the instrument? That's all we ask. If you just please begin the alphabet slowly.

(ANTROBUS, *with set face, comes ponderously up the ramp. He stops at the point where his waist is level with the stage and speaks authoritatively to the* OFFICIALS.)

ANTROBUS. I'll be ready when the time comes. Until then, move away. Go away. I have something I wish to say to my wife.

BROADCAST OFFICIAL (*whimpering*). Mr. Antrobus! This is the most important broadcast of the year.

(*The* OFFICIALS *withdraw to the edge of the stage.* SABINA *glides up the ramp behind* ANTROBUS.)

SABINA (*whispering*). Don't let her argue. Remember arguments have nothing to do with it.

ANTROBUS. Maggie, I'm moving out of the hotel. In fact, I'm moving out of everything. For good. I'm going to marry Miss Fairweather. I shall provide generously for you and the children. In a few years you'll be able to see that it's all for the best. That's all I have to say.

BROADCAST OFFICIAL. Mr. Antrobus! I hope you'll be ready. This is the most important broadcast of the year.

GLADYS. What did Papa say, Mama? I didn't hear what Papa said.

BROADCAST OFFICIAL. Mr. Antrobus. All we

BINGO ANNOUNCER. A—Nine; A—Nine. D—Forty-two; D—Forty-two. C—Thirty; C—Thirty.

B—Seventeen; B. Seventeen. C—Forty; C—Forty.

CHORUS. Bingo!!

want to do is test your
voice with the alpha-
bet.

ANTROBUS. Go away.
Clear out.

MRS. ANTROBUS (*composedly with lowered eyes*). George, I can't talk to you until you wipe those silly red marks off your face.

ANTROBUS. I think there's nothing to talk about. I've said what I have to say.

SABINA. Splendid!!

ANTROBUS. You're a fine woman, Maggie, but . . . but a man has his own life to lead in the world.

MRS. ANTROBUS. Well, after living with you for five thousand years I guess I have a right to a word or two, haven't I?

ANTROBUS (*to* SABINA). What can I answer to that?

SABINA. Tell her that conversation would only hurt her feelings. It's-kinder-in-the-long-run-to-do-it-short-and-quick.

ANTROBUS. I want to spare your feelings in every way I can, Maggie.

BROADCAST OFFICIAL. Mr. Antrobus, the hurricane signal's gone up. We could begin right now.

MRS. ANTROBUS (*calmly, almost dreamily*). I didn't marry you because you were perfect. I didn't even marry you because I loved you. I married you because you gave me a promise.

(*She takes off her ring and looks at it*)

That promise made up for your faults. And the promise I gave you made up for mine. Two imperfect people got married and it was the promise that made the marriage.

ANTROBUS. Maggie . . . I was only nineteen.

MRS. ANTROBUS (*she puts her ring back on her finger*). And when our children were growing up, it wasn't a house that protected them; and it wasn't our love, that protected them—it was that promise.

And when that promise is broken—this can happen!

(*With a sweep of the hand she removes the raincoat from* GLADYS's *stockings.*)

ANTROBUS (*stretches out his arm, apoplectic*). Gladys!! Have you gone crazy? Has everyone gone crazy?

(*Turning on* SABINA)

You did this. You gave them to her.

SABINA. I never said a word to her.

ANTROBUS (*to* GLADYS). You go back to the hotel and take those horrible things off.

GLADYS (*pert*). Before I go, I've got something to tell you—it's about Henry.

MRS. ANTROUS (*claps her hands peremptorily*). Stop your noise—I'm taking her back to the hotel, George. Before I go I have a letter. . . . I have a message to throw into the ocean.

(*Fumbling in her handbag*)

Where is the plagued thing? Here it is.

(*She flings something—invisible to us—far over the heads of the audience to the back of the auditorium.*)

It's a bottle. And in the bottle's a letter. And in the letter is written all the things that a woman knows. It's never been told to any man and it's never been told to any woman, and if it finds its destination, a new time will come. We're not what books and plays say we are. We're not what advertisements say we are. We're not in the movies and we're not on the radio.

We're not what you're all told and what you think we are:

We're ourselves. And if any man can find one of us he'll learn why the whole universe was set in motion. And if any man harm any one of us, his soul—the only soul he's got—had better be at the bottom of that ocean—and that's the only way to put it. Gladys, come here. We're going back to the hotel.

(*She drags* GLADYS *firmly off by the hand, but* GLADYS *breaks away and comes down to speak to her father*)

SABINA. Such goings-on. Don't give it a minute's thought.

GLADYS. Anyway, I think you ought to know that Henry hit a man with a stone. He hit one of those colored men that push the chairs and the man's very sick. Henry ran away and hid and some policemen are looking for him very hard. And I don't care a bit if you don't want to have anything to do with Mama and me, because I'll never like you again and I hope nobody ever likes you again—so there!

(*She runs off.* ANTROBUS *starts after her.*)

ANTROBUS. I . . . I have to go and see what I can do about this.

SABINA. You stay right here. Don't you go now

while you're excited. Gracious sakes, all these things will be forgotten in a hundred years. Come, now, you're on the air. Just say anything —it doesn't matter what. Just a lot of birds and fishes and things.

BROADCAST OFFICIAL. Thank you, Miss Fairweather. Thank you very much. Ready, Mr. Antrobus.

ANTROBUS (*touching the microphone*). What is it, what is it? Who am I talking to?

BROADCAST OFFICIAL. Why, Mr. Antrobus! To our order and to all the other orders.

ANTROBUS (*raising his head*). What are all those birds doing?

BROADCAST OFFICIAL. Those are just a few of the birds. Those are the delegates to our convention—two of a kind.

ANTROBUS (*pointing into the audience*). Look at the water. Look at them all. Those fishes jumping. The children should see this!—There's Maggie's whales!! Here are your whales, Maggie!!

BROADCAST OFFICIAL. I hope you're ready, Mr. Antrobus.

ANTROBUS. And look on the beach! You didn't tell me these would be here!

SABINA. Yes, George. Those are the animals.

BROADCAST OFFICIAL (*busy with the apparatus*). Yes, Mr. Antrobus, those are the vertebrates. We hope the lion will have a word to say when you're through. Step right up, Mr. Antrobus, we're ready. We'll just have time before the storm.

(*Pause. In a hoarse whisper:*)

They're wait-ing.

(*It has grown dark. Soon after he speaks a high whistling noise begins. Strange veering lights start whirling about the stage. The other characters disappear from the stage.*)

ANTROBUS. Friends. Cousins. Four score and ten billion years ago our forefather brought forth upon this planet the spark of life,—

(*He is drowned out by thunder. When the thunder stops the* FORTUNE TELLER *is seen standing beside him.*)

FORTUNE TELLER. Antrobus, there's not a minute to be lost. Don't you see the four disks on the weather signal? Take your family into that boat at the end of the pier.

ANTROBUS. My family? I have no family. Maggie! Maggie! They won't come.

FORTUNE TELLER. They'll come.—Antrobus! Take these animals into that boat with you. All of them—two of each kind.

SABINA. George, what's the matter with you? This is just a storm like any other storm.

ANTROBUS. Maggie!

SABINA. Stay with me, we'll go . . .

(*Losing conviction*)

This is just another thunderstorm—isn't it? Isn't it?

ANTROBUS. Maggie!!!

(MRS. ANTROBUS *appears beside him with Gladys*)

MRS. ANTROBUS (*matter-of-fact*). Here I am and here's Gladys.

ANTROBUS. Where've you been? Where have you been? Quick, we're going into that boat out there.

MRS. ANTROBUS. I know we are. But I haven't found Henry.

(*She wanders off into the darkness calling "Henry!"*)

SABINA (*low urgent babbling, only occasionally raising her voice*). I don't believe it. I don't believe it's anything at all. I've seen hundreds of storms like this.

FORTUNE TELLER. There's no time to lose. Go. Push the animals along before you. Start a new world. Begin again.

SABINA. Esmeralda! George! Tell me—is it really serious?

ANTROBUS (*suddenly very busy*). Elephants first. Gently, gently.—Look where you're going.

GLADYS (*leaning over the ramp and striking an animal on the back*). Stop it or you'll be left behind!

ANTROBUS. Is the Kangaroo there? *There* you are! Take those turtles in your pouch, will you?

(*To some other animals, pointing to his shoulder*)

Here! You jump up here. You'll be trampled on.

GLADYS (*to her father, pointing below*). Papa, look—the snakes!

MRS. ANTROBUS. I can't find Henry. Hen-ry!

ANTROBUS. Go along. Go along. Climb on their backs.—Wolves! Jackals—whatever you are—tend to your own business!

GLADYS (*pointing, tenderly*). Papa—look.

SABINA. Mr. Antrobus—take me with you. Don't

leave me here. I'll work. I'll help. I'll do anything.

> (*Three* CONVEENERS *cross the stage, marching with a banner.*)

CONVEENERS. George! What are you scared of?—George! Fellas, it looks like rain.—"Maggie, where's my umbrella?"—George, setting up for Barnum and Bailey.

ANTROBUS (*again catching his wife's hand*). Come on now, Maggie—the pier's going to break any minute.

MRS. ANTROBUS. I'm not going a step without Henry. Henry!

GLADYS (*on the ramp*). Mama! Papa! Hurry. The pier's cracking, Mama. It's going to break.

MRS. ANTROBUS. Henry! Cain! CAIN!

> (HENRY *dashes onto the stage and joins his mother.*)

HENRY. Here I am, Mama.

MRS. ANTROBUS. Thank God!—now come quick.

HENRY. I didn't think you wanted me.

MRS. ANTROBUS. Quick! (*She pushes him down before her into the aisle*)

SABINA (*All the* ANTROBUSES *are now in the theatre aisle.* SABINA *stands at the top of the ramp*). Mrs. Antrobus, take me. Don't you remember me? I'll work. I'll help. Don't leave me here!

MRS. ANTROBUS (*impatiently, but as though it were of no importance*). Yes, yes. There's a lot of work to be done. Only hurry.

FORTUNE TELLER (*now dominating the stage. To* SABINA *with a grim smile*). Yes, go—back to the kitchen with you.

SABINA (*half-down the ramp. To* FORTUNE TELLER). I don't know why my life's always being interrupted—just when everything's going fine!!

> (*She dashes up the aisle. Now the* CONVEENERS *emerge doing a serpentine dance on the stage. They jeer at the* FORTUNE TELLER.)

CONVEENERS. Get a canoe—there's not a minute to be lost! Tell me my future, Mrs. Croaker.

FORTUNE TELLER. Paddle in the water, boys—enjoy yourselves.

VOICE *from the Bingo Parlor*. A—Nine; A—Nine. C—Twenty-four. C—Twenty-four.

CONVEENERS. Rags, bottles, and sacks.

FORTUNE TELLER. Go back and climb on your roofs. Put rags in the cracks under your doors.—Nothing will keep out the flood. You've had your chance. You've had your day. You've failed. You've lost.

VOICE *from the Bingo Parlor*. B—Fifteen. B—Fifteen.

FORTUNE TELLER (*shading her eyes and looking out to sea*). They're safe. George Antrobus! Think it over! A new world to make.—Think it over!

Act III

SCENE: Home, Excelsior, New Jersey.

Just before the curtain rises, two sounds are heard from the stage: a cracked bugle call.

The curtain rises on almost total darkness. Almost all the flats composing the walls of MR. ANTROBUS's *house, as of Act I, are up, but they lean helter-skelter against one another, leaving irregular gaps. Among the flats missing are two in the back wall, leaving the frames of the window and door crazily out of line.*

Off-stage, back right, some red Roman fire is burning. The bugle call is repeated. Enter SABINA *through the tilted door. She is dressed as a Napoleonic camp follower, "la fille du regiment," in begrimed reds and blues.*

SABINA. Mrs. Antrobus! Gladys! Where are you!

The war's over. The war's over. You can come out.

The peace treaty's been signed.

Where are they?—Hmpf! Are they dead, too? Mrs. Annnntrobus! Glaaaadus! Mr. Antrobus'll be here this afternoon. I just saw him downtown. Huuuurry and put things in order. He says that now that the war's over we'll all have to settle down and be perfect.

> (*Enter* MR. FITZPATRICK, *the stage manager, followed by the whole company, who stand waiting at the edges of the stage.* MR. FITZPATRICK *tries to interrupt* SABINA.)

MR. FITZPATRICK. Miss Somerset, we have to stop a moment.

SABINA. They may be hiding out in the back—

MR. FITZPATRICK. Miss Somerset! We have to stop a moment.

SABINA. What's the matter?

MR. FITZPATRICK. There's an explanation we have to make to the audience.—Lights, please.

(*To the actor who plays* MR. ANTROBUS.) Will you explain the matter to the audience?

(*The lights go up. We now see that a balcony or elevated runway has been erected at the back of the stage, back of the wall of the Antrobus house. From its extreme right and left ends ladder-like steps descend to the floor of the stage.*)

ANTROBUS. Ladies and gentlemen, an unfortunate accident has taken place back stage. Perhaps I should say *another* unfortunate accident.

SABINA. I'm sorry. I'm sorry.

ANTROBUS. The management feels, in fact, we all feel that you are due an apology. And now we have to ask your indulgence for the most serious mishap of all. Seven of our actors have . . . have been taken ill. Apparently, it was something they ate. I'm not exactly clear what happened.

(*All the* ACTORS *start to talk at once.* ANTROBUS *raises his hand.*)

Now, now—not all at once. Fitz, do you know what it was?

MR. FITZPATRICK. Why, it's perfectly clear. These seven actors had dinner together, and they ate something that disagreed with them.

SABINA. Disagreed with them!!! They have ptomaine poisoning. They're in Bellevue Hospital this very minute in agony. They're having their stomachs pumped out this very minute, in perfect agony.

ANTROBUS. Fortunately, we've just heard they'll all recover.

SABINA. It'll be a miracle if they do, a downright miracle. It was the lemon meringue pie.

ACTORS. It was the fish . . . it was the canned tomatoes . . . it was the fish.

SABINA. It was the lemon meringue pie. I saw it with my own eyes; it had blue mold all over the bottom of it.

ANTROBUS. Whatever it was, they're in no condition to take part in this performance. Naturally, we haven't enough understudies to fill all those roles; but we do have a number of splendid volunteers who have kindly consented to help us out. These friends have watched our rehearsals, and they assure me that they know the lines and the business very well. Let me introduce them to you—my dresser, Mr. Tremayne—himself a distinguished Shakespearean actor for many years; our wardrobe mistress, Hester; Miss Somerset's maid, Ivy; and Fred Bailey, captain of the ushers in this theatre.

(*These persons bow modestly.* IVY *and* HESTER *are colored girls.*)

Now this scene takes place near the end of the act. And I'm sorry to say we'll need a short rehearsal, just a short run-through. And as some of it takes place in the auditorium, we'll have to keep the curtain up. Those of you who wish can go out in the lobby and smoke some more. The rest of you can listen to us, or . . . or just talk quietly among yourselves, as you choose. Thank you. Now will you take it over, Mr. Fitzpatrick?

MR. FITZPATRICK. Thank you.—Now for those of you who are listening perhaps I should explain that at the end of this act, the men have come back from the war and the family's settled down in the house. And the author wants to show the hours of the night passing by over their heads, and the planets crossing the sky . . . uh . . . over their heads. And he says—this is hard to explain—that each of the hours of the night is a philosopher, or a great thinker. Eleven o'clock, for instance, is Aristotle. And nine o'clock is Spinoza. Like that. I don't suppose it means anything. It's just a kind of poetic effect.

SABINA. Not mean anything! Why, it certainly does. Twelve o'clock goes by saying those wonderful things. I think it means that when people are asleep they have all those lovely thoughts, much better than when they're awake.

IVY. Excuse me, I think it means—excuse me, Mr. Fitzpatrick—

SABINA. What were you going to say, Ivy?

IVY. Mr. Fitzpatrick, you let my father come to a rehearsal; and my father's a Baptist minister, and he said that the author meant that—just like the hours and stars go by over our heads at night, in the same way the ideas and thoughts of the great men are in the air around us all the time and they're working on us, even when we don't know it.

MR. FITZPATRICK. Well, well, maybe that's it. Thank you, Ivy. Anyway—the hours of the night are philosophers. My friends, are you ready? Ivy, can you be eleven o'clock? "This good estate of the mind possessing its object in energy we call divine." Aristotle.

IVY. Yes, sir. I know that and I know twelve o'clock and I know nine o'clock.

MR. FITZPATRICK. Twelve o'clock? Mr. Tremayne, the Bible.

TREMAYNE. Yes.

MR. FITZPATRICK. Ten o'clock? Hester—Plato?

(*She nods eagerly*)

Nine o'clock, Spinoza—Fred?

BAILEY. Yes, Sir.

(FRED BAILEY *picks up a great gilded cardboard numeral IX and starts up the steps to the platform.* MR. FITZPATRICK *strikes his forehead.*)

MR. FITZPATRICK. The planets!! We forgot all about the planets.

SABINA. O my God! The planets! Are they sick too?

(ACTORS *nod*)

MR. FITZPATRICK. Ladies and gentlemen, the planets are singers. Of course, we can't replace them, so you'll have to imagine them singing in this scene. Saturn sings from the orchestra pit down here. The Moon is way up there. And Mars with a red lantern in his hand, stands in the aisle over there— Tz-tz-tz. It's too bad; it all makes a very fine effect. However! Ready—nine o'clock: Spinoza.

BAILEY (*walking slowly across the balcony, left to right*). "After experience had taught me that the common occurrences of daily life are vain and futile—"

FITZPATRICK. Louder, Fred. "And I saw that all the objects of my desire and fear—"

BAILEY. "And I saw that all the objects of my desire and fear were in themselves nothing good nor bad save insofar as the mind was affected by them—"

FITZPATRICK. Do you know the rest? All right. Ten o'clock. Hester. Plato.

HESTER. "Then tell me, O Critias, how will a man choose the ruler that shall rule over him? Will he not—"

FITZPATRICK. Thank you. Skip to the end, Hester.

HESTER. ". . . can be multiplied a thousand fold in its effects among the citizens."

FITZPATRICK. Thank you.—Aristotle, Ivy?

IVY. "This good estate of the mind possessing its object in energy we call divine. This we mortals have occasionally and it is this energy which is pleasantest and best. But God has it always. It is wonderful in us; but in Him how much more wonderful."

FITZPATRICK. Midnight. Midnight, Mr. Tremayne. That's right—you've done it before.—All right, everybody. You know what you have to do.—Lower the curtain. House lights up. Act Three of THE SKIN OF OUR TEETH.

(*As the curtain descends he is heard saying:*) You volunteers, just wear what you have on. Don't try to put on the costumes today.

(*House lights go down. The Act begins again. The Bugle call. Curtain rises. Enter* SABINA.)

SABINA. Mrs. Antrobus! Gladys! Where are you?

The war's over.—You've heard all this—

(*She gabbles the main points*)

Where—are—they? Are—they—dead, too, et cetera.

I—just—saw—Mr.—Antrobus—downtown, et cetera.

(*Slowing up:*)

He says that now that the war's over we'll all have to settle down and be perfect. They may be hiding out in the back somewhere. Mrs. Antro-bus.

(*She wanders off. It has grown lighter. A trapdoor is cautiously raised and* MRS. ANTROBUS *emerges waist-high and listens. She is disheveled and worn; she wears a tattered dress and a shawl half covers her head. She talks down through the trapdoor.*)

MRS. ANTROBUS. It's getting light. There's still something burning over there—Newark, or Jersey City. What? Yes; I could swear I heard someone moving about up here. But I can't see anybody. I say: I can't see anybody.

(*She starts to move about the stage.* GLADYS's *head appears at the trapdoor. She is holding a* BABY.)

GLADYS. Oh, Mama. Be careful.

MRS. ANTROBUS. Now, Gladys, you stay out of

sight.

GLADYS. Well, let me stay here just a minute. I want the baby to get some of this fresh air.

MRS. ANTROBUS. All right, but keep your eyes open. I'll see what I can find. I'll have a good hot plate of soup for you before you can say Jack Robinson. Gladys Antrobus! Do you know what I think I see? There's old Mr. Hawkins sweeping the sidewalk in front of his A. and P. store. Sweeping it with a broom. Why, he must have gone crazy, like the others! I see some other people moving about, too.

GLADYS. Mama, come back, come back.

(MRS. ANTROBUS *returns to the trapdoor and listens*)

MRS. ANTROBUS. Gladys, there's something in the air. Everybody's movement's sort of different. I see some women walking right out in the middle of the street.

SABINA'S VOICE. Mrs. An-tro-bus!

MRS. ANTROBUS *and* GLADYS. What's that?!!

SABINA'S VOICE. Glaaaadys! Mrs. An-tro-bus!

(*Enter* SABINA)

MRS. ANTROBUS. Gladys, that's Sabina's voice as sure as I live.—Sabina! Sabina!—Are you *alive?!!*

SABINA. Of course, I'm alive. How've you girls been?—*Don't* try and kiss me. I never want to kiss another human being as long as I live. Sh-sh, there's nothing to get emotional about. Pull yourself together, the war's over. Take a deep breath—the war's over.

MRS. ANTROBUS. The war's over!! I don't believe you. I don't believe you. I can't believe you.

GLADYS. Mama!

SABINA. Who's that?

MRS. ANTROBUS. That's Gladys and her baby. I don't believe you. Gladys, Sabina says the war's over. Oh, Sabina.

SABINA (*leaning over the* BABY). Goodness! Are there any babies left in the world! Can it *see?* And can it cry and everything?

GLADYS. Yes, he can. He notices everything very well.

SABINA. Where on earth did you get it? Oh, I won't ask.—Lord, I've lived all these seven years around camp and I've forgotten how to behave. —Now we've got to think about the men coming home.—Mrs. Antrobus, go and wash your face,

I'm ashamed of you. Put your best clothes on. Mr. Antrobus'll be here this afternoon. I just saw him downtown.

MRS. ANTROBUS *and* GLADYS. He's alive!! He'll be here!! Sabina, you're not joking?

MRS. ANTROBUS. And Henry?

SABINA (*dryly*). Yes, Henry's alive, too, that's what they say. Now don't stop to talk. Get yourselves fixed up. Gladys, you look terrible. Have you any decent clothes?

(SABINA *has pushed them toward the trapdoor*)

MRS. ANTROBUS (*half down*). Yes, I've something to wear just for this very day. But, Sabina —who won the war?

SABINA. Don't stop now—just wash your face.

(*A whistle sounds in the distance*)

Oh, my God, what's that silly little noise?

MRS. ANTROBUS. Why, it sounds like . . . it sounds like what used to be the noon whistle at the shoe-polish factory. (*Exit*)

SABINA. That's what it is. Seems to me like peacetime's coming along pretty fast—shoe polish!

GLADYS (*half down*). Sabina, how soon after peacetime begins does the milkman start coming to the door?

SABINA. As soon as he catches a cow. Give him time to catch a cow, dear.

(*Exit* GLADYS. SABINA *walks about a moment, thinking.*)

Shoe polish! My, I'd forgotten what peacetime was like.

(*She shakes her head, then sits down by the trapdoor and starts talking down the hole*)

Mrs. Antrobus, guess what I saw Mr. Antrobus doing this morning at dawn. He was tacking up a piece of paper on the door of the Town Hall. You'll die when you hear: it was a recipe for grass soup, for a grass soup that doesn't give you the diarrhea. Mr. Antrobus is still thinking up new things.—He told me to give you his love. He's got all sorts of ideas for peacetime, he says. No more laziness and idiocy, he says. And oh, yes! Where are his books? What? Well, pass them up. The first thing he wants to see are his books. He says if you've burnt those books, or if the rats have eaten them, he says it isn't worthwhile starting over again. Everybody's going to be beautiful, he says, and diligent, and very intelligent.

(*A hand reaches up with two volumes*)
What language is that? Pu-u-gh—mold! And he's got such plans for you, Mrs. Antrobus. You're going to study history and algebra—and so are Gladys and I—and philosophy. You should hear him talk:

(*Taking two more volumes*)
Well, these are in English, anyway.—To hear him talk, seems like he expects you to be a combination, Mrs. Antrobus, of a saint and a college professor, and a dancehall hostess, if you know what I mean.

(*Two more volumes*)
Ugh. German!

(*She is lying on the floor; one elbow bent, her cheek on her hand, meditatively*)
Yes, peace will be here before we know it. In a week or two we'll be asking the Perkinses in for a quiet evening of bridge. We'll turn on the radio and hear how to be big successes with a new toothpaste. We'll trot down to the movies and see how girls with wax faces live—all *that* will begin again. Oh, Mrs. Antrobus, God forgive me but I enjoyed the war. Everybody's at their best in wartime. I'm sorry it's over. And, oh, I forgot! Mr. Antrobus sent you another message—can you hear me?—

(*Enter* HENRY, *blackened and sullen. He is wearing torn overalls, but has one gaudy admiral's epaulette hanging by a thread from his right shoulder, and there are vestiges of gold and scarlet braid running down his left trouser leg. He stands listening.*)
Listen! Henry's never to put foot in this house again, he says. He'll kill Henry on sight, if he sees him.

You don't know about Henry??? Well, where have you been? What? Well, Henry rose right to the top. Top of *what?* Listen, I'm telling you. Henry rose from corporal to captain, to major, to general.—I don't know how to say it, but the enemy is *Henry;* Henry is the enemy. Everybody knows that.

HENRY. He'll kill me, will he?

SABINA. Who are *you?* I'm not afraid of you. The war's over.

HENRY. I'll kill him so fast. I've spent seven years trying to find him; the others I killed were just substitutes.

SABINA. Goodness! It's Henry!—

(*He makes an angry gesture*)
Oh, I'm not afraid of you. The war's over, Henry Antrobus, and you're not any more important than any other unemployed. You go away and hide yourself, until we calm your father down.

HENRY. The first thing to do is to burn up those old books; it's the ideas he gets out of those old books that . . . that makes the whole world so you can't live in it.

(*He reels forward and starts kicking the books about, but suddenly falls down in a sitting position*)
SABINA. You leave those books alone!! Mr. Antrobus is looking forward to them a-special.—Gracious sakes, Henry, you're so tired you can't stand up. Your mother and sister'll be here in a minute and we'll think what to do about you.

HENRY. What did they ever care about me?

SABINA. There's that old whine again. All you people think you're not loved enough, nobody loves you. Well, you start being lovable and we'll love you.

HENRY (*outraged*). I don't want anybody to love me.

SABINA. Then stop talking about it all the time.

HENRY. I *never* talk about it. The last thing I want is anybody to pay any attention to me.

SABINA. I can hear it behind every word you say.

HENRY. I want everybody to hate me.

SABINA. Yes, you've decided that's second best, but it's still the same thing.—Mrs. Antrobus! Henry's here. He's so tired he can't stand up.

MRS. ANTROBUS *and* GLADYS, *with her* BABY, *emerge.*

(*They are dressed as in Act I.* MRS. ANTROBUS *carries some objects in her apron, and* GLADYS *has a blanket over her shoulder.*)
MRS. ANTROBUS *and* GLADYS. Henry! Henry! Henry!

HENRY (*glaring at them*). Have you anything to eat?

MRS. ANTROBUS. Yes, I have, Henry. I've been saving it for this very day—two good baked potatoes. No! Henry! one of them's for your father. Henry!! Give me that other potato back this minute.

(SABINA *sidles up behind him and snatches the other potato away*)

SABINA. He's so dog-tired he doesn't know what he's doing.

MRS. ANTROBUS. Now you just rest there, Henry, until I can get your room ready. Eat that potato good and slow, so you can get all the nourishment out of it.

HENRY. You all might as well know right now that I haven't come back here to live.

MRS. ANTROBUS. Sh. . . . I'll put this coat over you. Your room's hardly damaged at all. Your football trophies are a little tarnished, but Sabina and I will polish them up tomorrow.

HENRY. Did you hear me? I don't live here. I don't belong to anybody.

MRS. ANTROBUS. Why, how can you say a thing like that! You certainly do belong right here. Where else would you want to go? Your forehead's feverish, Henry, seems to me. You'd better give me that gun, Henry. You won't need that any more.

GLADYS (*whispering*). Look, he's fallen asleep already, with his potato half-chewed.

SABINA. Puh! The terror of the world.

MRS. ANTROBUS. Sabina, you mind your own business, and start putting the room to rights.

(HENRY *has turned his face to the back of the sofa.* MRS. ANTROBUS *gingerly puts the revolver in her apron pocket, then helps* SABINA. SABINA *has found a rope hanging from the ceiling. Grunting, she hangs all her weight on it, and as she pulls the walls begin to move into their right places.* MRS. ANTROBUS *brings the overturned tables, chairs and hassock into the positions of Act I.*)

SABINA. That's all we do—always beginning again! Over and over again. Always beginning again.

(*She pulls on the rope and a part of the wall moves into place. She stops. Meditatively:*)

How do we know that it'll be any better than before? Why do we go on pretending? Some day the whole earth's going to have to turn cold anyway, and until that time all these other things'll be happening again: it will be more wars and more walls of ice and floods and earthquakes.

MRS. ANTROBUS. Sabina!! Stop arguing and go on with your work.

SABINA. All right. I'll go on just out of *habit,* but I won't believe in it.

MRS. ANTROBUS (*aroused*). Now, Sabina. I've let you talk long enough. I don't want to hear any more of it. Do I have to explain to you what everybody knows—everybody who keeps a home going? Do I have to say to you what nobody should ever *have* to say, because they can read it in each other's eyes?

Now listen to me:

(MRS. ANTROBUS *takes hold of the rope*)

I could live for seventy years in a cellar and make soup out of grass and bark, without ever doubting that this world has a work to do and will do it.

Do you hear me?

SABINA (*frightened*). Yes, Mrs. Antrobus.

MRS. ANTROBUS. Sabina, do you see this house—216 Cedar Street—do you see it?

SABINA. Yes, Mrs. Antrobus.

MRS. ANTROBUS. Well, just to have known this house is to have seen the idea of what we can do someday if we keep our wits about us. Too many people have suffered and died for my children for us to start reneging now. So we'll start putting this house to rights. Now, Sabina, go and see what you can do in the kitchen.

SABINA. Kitchen! Why is it that however far I go away, I always find myself back in the kitchen? (*Exit.*)

MRS. ANTROBUS (*still thinking over her last speech, relaxes and says with a reminiscent smile*): Goodness gracious, wouldn't you know that my father was a parson? It was just like I heard his own voice speaking and he's been dead five thousand years. There! I've gone and almost waked Henry up.

HENRY (*talking in his sleep, indistinctly*). Fellows . . . what have they done for us? . . . Blocked our way at every step. Kept everything in their own hands. And you've stood it. When are you going to wake up?

MRS. ANTROBUS. Sh, Henry. Go to sleep. Go to sleep. Go to sleep.—Well, that looks better. Now let's go and help Sabina.

GLADYS. Mama, I'm going out into the backyard and hold the baby right up in the air. And show him that we don't have to be afraid any more.

(*Exit* GLADYS *to the kitchen.* MRS. ANTROBUS *glances at* HENRY, *exits into kitchen.* HENRY *thrashes about in his sleep. Enter* ANTROBUS, *his arms full of bundles, chewing the end of a carrot. He has a slight limp. Over the suit of Act I he is wearing an overcoat too long for him, its skirts trailing on the ground. He lets his bundles fall and stands looking about. Presently his attention is fixed on* HENRY, *whose words grow clearer.*)

HENRY. All right! What have you got to lose? What have they done for us? That's right—nothing. Tear everything down. I don't care what you smash. We'll begin again and we'll show 'em.

(ANTROBUS *takes out his revolver and holds it pointing downwards. With his back toward the audience he moves toward the footlights.* HENRY's *voice grows louder and he wakes with a start. They stare at one another. Then* HENRY *sits up quickly. Throughout the following scene* HENRY *is played, not as a misunderstood or misguided young man, but as a representation of strong unreconciled evil.*)

All right! Do something.

(*Pause*)

Don't think I'm afraid of you, either. All right, do what you were going to do. Do it.

(*Furiously*)

Shoot me, I tell you. You don't have to think I'm any relation of yours. I haven't got any father or any mother, or brothers or sisters. And I don't want any. And what's more I haven't got anybody over me; and I never will have. I'm alone, and that's all I want to be: alone. So you can shoot me.

ANTROBUS. You're the last person I wanted to see. The sight of you dries up all my plans and hopes. I wish I were back at war still, because it's easier to fight you than to live with you. War's a pleasure—do you hear me?—War's a pleasure compared to what faces us now: trying to build up a peacetime with you in the middle of it.

(ANTROBUS *walks up to the window*)

HENRY. I'm not going to be a part of any peacetime of yours. I'm going a long way from here and make my own world that's fit for a man to live in. Where a man can be free, and have a chance, and do what he wants to do in his own way.

ANTROBUS (*his attention arrested; thoughtfully. He throws the gun out of the window and turns with hope*). . . . Henry, let's try again.

HENRY. Try what? Living *here*?—Speaking polite downtown to all the old men like you? Standing like a sheep at the street corner until the red light turns to green? Being a good boy and a good sheep, like all the stinking ideas you get out of your books? Oh, no. I'll make a world, and I'll show you.

ANTROBUS (*hard*). How can you make a world for people to live in, unless you've first put order in yourself? Mark my words: I shall continue fighting you until my last breath as long as you mix up your idea of liberty with your idea of hogging everything for yourself. I shall have no pity on you. I shall pursue you to the far corners of the earth. You and I want the same thing; but until you think of it as something that everyone has a right to, you are my deadly enemy and I will destroy you.—I hear your mother's voice in the kitchen. Have you seen her?

HENRY. I have no mother. Get it into your head. I don't belong here. I have nothing to do here. I have no home.

ANTROBUS. Then why did you come here? With the whole world to choose from, why did you come to this one place: 216 Cedar Street, Excelsior, New Jersey. . . . Well?

HENRY. What if I did? What if I wanted to look at it once more, to see if—

ANTROBUS. Oh, you're related, all right—When your mother comes in you must behave yourself. Do you hear me?

HENRY (*wildly*). What is this?—*must behave* yourself. Don't you say *must* to me.

ANTROBUS. Quiet!

(*Enter* MRS. ANTROBUS *and* SABINA)

HENRY. Nobody can say *must* to me. All my life everybody's been crossing me—everybody, everything, all of you. I'm going to be free, even if I have to kill half the world for it. Right now, too. Let me get my hands on his throat. I'll show him.

(*He advances toward* ANTROBUS. *Suddenly,* SABINA *jumps between them and calls out in her own person:*)

SABINA. Stop! Stop! Don't play this scene. You know what happened last night. Stop the play.

(*The men fall back, panting.* HENRY *covers his face with his hands.*)

Last night you almost strangled him. You became a regular savage. Stop it!

HENRY. It's true. I'm sorry. I don't know what comes over me. I have nothing against him personally. I respect him very much . . . I . . . I admire him. But something comes over me. It's like I become fifteen years old again. I . . . I . . . listen: my own father used to whip me and lock me up every Saturday night. I never had enough to eat. He never let me have enough money to buy decent clothes. I was ashamed to go downtown. I never could go to the dances. My father and my uncle put rules in the way of everything I wanted to do. They tried to prevent my living at all.—I'm sorry. I'm sorry.

MRS. ANTROBUS (*quickly*). No, go on. Finish what you were saying. Say it all.

HENRY. In this scene it's as though I were back in High School again. It's like I had some big emptiness inside me—the emptiness of being hated and blocked at every turn. And the emptiness fills up with the one thought that you have to strike and fight and kill. Listen, it's as though you have to kill somebody else so as not to end up killing yourself.

SABINA. That's not true. I knew your father and your uncle and your mother. You imagined all that. Why, they did everything they could for you. How can you say things like that? They didn't lock you up.

HENRY. They did. They did. They wished I hadn't been born.

SABINA. That's not true.

ANTROBUS (*in his own person, with self-condemnation, but cold and proud*). Wait a minute. I have something to say, too. It's not wholly his fault that he wants to strangle me in this scene. It's my fault, too. He wouldn't feel that way unless there were something in me that reminded him of all that. He talks about an emptiness. Well, there's an emptiness in me, too. Yes—work, work, work—that's all I do. I've ceased to *live*. No wonder he feels that anger coming over him.

MRS. ANTROBUS. There! At least you've said it.

SABINA. We're all just as wicked as we can be, and that's the God's truth.

MRS. ANTROBUS (*nods a moment, then comes forward; quietly*). Come. Come and put your head under some cold water.

SABINA (*in a whisper*). I'll go with him. I've known him a long while. You have to go on with the play. Come with me.

(HENRY *starts out with* SABINA, *but turns at the exit and says to* ANTROBUS:)

HENRY. Thanks. Thanks for what you said. I'll be all right tomorrow. I won't lose control in that place. I promise.

(*Exeunt* HENRY *and* SABINA. ANTROBUS *starts toward the front door, fastens it.* MRS. ANTROBUS *goes up stage and places the chair close to table.*)

MRS. ANTROBUS. George, do I see you limping?

ANTROBUS. Yes, a little. My old wound from the other war started smarting again. I can manage.

MRS. ANTROBUS (*looking out of the window*). Some lights are coming on—the first in seven years. People are walking up and down looking at them. Over in Hawkins' open lot they've built a bonfire to celebrate the peace. They're dancing around it like scarecrows.

ANTROBUS. A bonfire! As though they hadn't seen enough things burning.—Maggie—the dog died?

MRS. ANTROBUS. Oh, yes. Long ago. There are no dogs left in Excelsior.—You're back again! All these years. I gave up counting on letters. The few that arrived were anywhere from six months to a year late.

ANTROBUS. Yes, the ocean's full of letters, along with the other things.

MRS. ANTROBUS. George, sit down, you're tired.

ANTROBUS. No, you sit down. I'm tired but I'm restless.

(*Suddenly, as she comes forward*)

Maggie! I've lost it. I've lost it.

MRS. ANTROBUS. What, George? What have you lost?

ANTROBUS. The most important thing of all: The desire to begin again, to start building.

MRS. ANTROBUS (*sitting in the chair right of the table*). Well, it will come back.

ANTROBUS (*at the window*). I've lost it. This minute I feel like all those people dancing around the bonfire—just relief. Just the desire to settle down; to slip into the old grooves and keep the neighbors from walking over my lawn. —Hm. But during the war—in the middle of all that blood and dirt and hot and cold—every day and night, I'd have moments, Maggie, when I *saw* the things that we could do when it was over. When you're at war you think about a better life; when you're at peace you think about a more comfortable one. I've lost it. I feel sick and tired.

MRS. ANTROBUS. Listen! The baby's crying. I hear Gladys talking. Probably she's quieting Henry again. George, while Gladys and I were living here—like moles, like rats, and when we were at our wits' end to save the baby's life—the only thought we clung to was that you were going to bring something good out of this suffering. In the night, in the dark, we'd whisper about it, starving and sick.—Oh, George, you'll have to get it back again. Think! What else kept us alive all these years? Even now, it's not comfort we want. We can suffer whatever's necessary; only give us back that promise.

(*Enter* SABINA *with a lighted lamp. She is dressed as in Act I.*)

SABINA. Mrs. Antrobus . . .

MRS. ANTROBUS. Yes, Sabina?

SABINA. Will you need me?

MRS. ANTROBUS. No, Sabina, you can go to bed.

SABINA. Mrs. Antrobus, if it's all right with you, I'd like to go to the bonfire and celebrate seeing the war's over. And, Mrs. Antrobus, they've opened the Gem Movie Theatre and they're giving away a hand-painted soup tureen to every lady, and I thought one of us ought to go.

ANTROBUS. Well, Sabina, I haven't any money. I haven't seen any money for quite a while.

SABINA. Oh, you don't need money. They're taking anything you can give them. And I have some . . . some . . . Mrs. Antrobus, promise you won't tell anyone. It's a little against the law. But I'll give you some, too.

ANTROBUS. What is it?

SABINA. I'll give you some, too. Yesterday I picked up a lot of . . . of beef cubes!

(MRS. ANTROBUS *turns and says calmly:*)

MRS. ANTROBUS. But, Sabina, you know you ought to give that in to the Center downtown. They know who needs them most.

SABINA (*outburst*). Mrs. Antrobus, I didn't make this war. I didn't ask for it. And, in my opinion, after anybody's gone through what we've gone through, they have a right to grab what they can find. You're a very nice man, Mr. Antrobus, but you'd have got on better in the world if you'd realized that dog-eat-dog was the rule in the beginning and always will be. And most of all now.

(*In tears*)

Oh, the world's an awful place, and you know it is. I used to think something could be done about it; but I know better now. I hate it. I hate it.

(*She comes forward slowly and brings six cubes from the bag*)

All right. All right. You can have them.

ANTROBUS. Thank you, Sabina.

SABINA. Can I have . . . can I have one to go to the movies?

(ANTROBUS *in silence gives her one*)

Thank you.

ANTROBUS. Good night, Sabina.

SABINA. Mr. Antrobus, don't mind what I say. I'm just an ordinary girl, you know what I mean, I'm just an ordinary girl. But you're a bright man, you're a very bright man, and of course you invented the alphabet and the wheel, and, my God, a lot of things . . . and if you've got any other plans, my God, don't let me upset them. Only every now and then I've got to go to the movies. I mean my nerves can't stand it. But if you have any ideas about improving the crazy old world, I'm really with you. I really am. Because it's . . . it's . . . Good night.

(*She goes out.* ANTROBUS *starts laughing softly with exhilaration.*)

ANTROBUS. Now I remember what three things always went together when I was able to see things most clearly: three things. Three things:

(*He points to where* SABINA *has gone out*)

The voice of the people in their confusion and their need. And the thought of you and the children and this house . . . And . . . Maggie! I didn't dare ask you: my books! They haven't been lost, have they?

MRS. ANTROBUS. No. There are some of them right here. Kind of tattered.

ANTROBUS. Yes.—Remember, Maggie, we almost lost them once before? And when we finally did collect a few torn copies out of old cellars they ran in everyone's head like a fever. They as good as rebuilt the world.

(*Pauses, book in hand, and looks up*)

Oh, I've never forgotten for long at a time that living is struggle. I know that every good and excellent thing in the world stands moment by moment on the razor-edge of danger and must be fought for—whether it's a field, or a home, or a country. All I ask is the chance to build new worlds and God has always given us that. And has given us (*Opening the book.*) voices to guide us; and the memory of our mistakes to warn us. Maggie, you and I will remember in peacetime all the resolves that were so clear to us in the days of war. We've come a long ways. We've learned. We're learning. And the steps of our journey are marked for us here.

(*He stands by the table turning the leaves of a book*)

Sometimes out there in the war—standing all night on a hill—I'd try and remember some of the words in these books. Parts of them and phrases would come back to me. And after a while I used to give names to the hours of the night.

(*He sits, hunting for a passage in the book*)

Nine o'clock I used to call Spinoza. Where is it: "After experience had taught me—"

(*The back wall has disappeared, revealing the platform. FRED BAILEY carrying his numeral has started from left to right. MRS. ANTROBUS sits by the table sewing.*)

BAILEY. "After experience had taught me that the common occurrences of daily life are vain and futile; and I saw that all the objects of my desire and fear were in themselves nothing good nor bad save insofar as the mind was affected by them; I at length determined to search out whether there was something truly good and communicable to man."

(*Almost without break HESTER, carrying a large Roman numeral ten, starts crossing the platform. GLADYS appears at the kitchen door and moves toward her mother's chair.*)

HESTER. "Then tell me, O Critias, how will a man choose the ruler that shall rule over him? Will he not choose a man who has first established order in himself, knowing that any deci-sion that has its spring from anger or pride or vanity can be multiplied a thousandfold in its effects upon the citizens?"

(*HESTER disappears and IVY, as eleven o'clock starts speaking.*)

IVY. "This good estate of the mind possessing its object in energy we call divine. This we mortals have occasionally and it is this energy which is pleasantest and best. But God has it always. It is wonderful in us; but in Him how much more wonderful."

(*As MR. TREMAYNE starts to speak, HENRY appears at the edge of the scene, brooding and unreconciled, but present.*)

TREMAYNE. "In the beginning, God created the Heavens and the earth; And the Earth was waste and void; And the darkness was upon the face of the deep. And the Lord said let there be light and there was light."

(*Sudden black-out and silence, except for the last strokes of the midnight bell. Then just as suddenly the lights go up, and SABINA is standing at the window, as at the opening of the play.*)

SABINA. Oh, oh, oh. Six o'clock and the master not home yet. Pray God nothing serious has happened to him crossing the Hudson River. But I wouldn't be surprised. The whole world's at sixes and sevens, and why the house hasn't fallen down about our ears long ago is a miracle to me.

(*She comes down to the footlights*)

This is where you came in. We have to go on for ages and ages yet.

You go home.

The end of this play isn't written yet.

Mr. and Mrs. Antrobus! Their heads are full of plans and they're as confident as the first day they began—and they told me to tell you: good night.

DISCUSSION

We considered *Oedipus the King* as in some senses a parable about man's yearning for, his need for, and yet his difficulty in attaining knowledge about himself and his world. *The Skin of Our Teeth* may be regarded as even more obviously a kind of parable, this one about the nature of the human endeavor. For example, the name Antrobus suggests the Greek name for man, *anthropos*, and the son of Mr. and Mrs.

Antrobus, as we find out in the play, was originally called Cain—that is, he is the eldest son
of Adam and Eve. (The word *Adam,* by the
way, is simply the Hebrew word for man.) One
of the things this play seems to be saying is that
all times are essentially alike, and that the details of the particular peril that threatens the
human race, whether of an advancing ice sheet,
or a Noah's flood, or a devastating world war,
are finally unimportant. What is important is
that man is always being challenged and that
it behooves him to make the proper response.

In a dozen different ways *The Skin of Our
Teeth* manages to suggest this unchanging character of the human situation. For example, the
play begins with a projection screen and an
announcer—presumably a radio announcer—giving the news of the world in standard twentieth-
century fashion, but the subject dominating the
news is the advancing ice sheet, the catastrophe
of 40,000 years ago. Soon a singing telegram (a
popular "gimmick" in the 1930s) arrives, but the
important information that the telegram contains is that Mr. Antrobus is making progress in
perfecting the alphabet! Thus, there is a deliberate scrambling of epochs and a series of
bewildering anachronisms. In spite of its realistic
elements, *The Skin of Our Teeth* can best be
described as an intellectual fantasy.

It may be useful at this point to sort out
several aspects of the mode of presentation used
in this play: (1) the playwright employs various
kinds of symbolic shortcuts to set forth his theme;
(2) the fantastic juxtapositions and startling
anachronisms give rise to a special kind of comedy; and (3) the playwright makes free with the
theatrical conventions as when an actor breaks
out of his or her part to criticize or comment on
the play, or when the audience is taken into
the author's confidence and let in on the workings of the play. Though the playwright may have
some very profound thoughts about mankind, he
evidently sees no need to be stuffy about them
and knows that his devices for condensing and
pointing up the essentials of the human story
will prove disastrously clumsy if they are not
handled playfully and in a spirit of comedy.

The first character to speak, Sabina, the
housemaid, provides a clue to the general tone.
Sabina's normal speech is a hash of clichés: she
tells us that "The whole world's at sixes and
sevens" and observes that "In the midst of life
we are in the midst of death, a truer word was
never said." Her comments on the members of
the Antrobus family—the announcer has called
it a "typical American family"—are in the same
vein. She remarks that if anything happened to
Mr. Antrobus "we would certainly be inconsolable"; Mr. Antrobus is "an excellent husband
and father, a pillar of the church." But Sabina
manages, perhaps unconsciously, to undercut
most of the vapidly laudatory things she is saying: after remarking that the loss of Mr. Antrobus
would leave the family "inconsolable," she adds
that they would "have to move into a less desirable residence district." That paragon, Mr.
Antrobus, "has all the best interests of the community at heart," but rather inconsequentially
Sabina notes that "Of course, every muscle [in
him] goes tight every time he passes a policeman." As for Mrs. Antrobus, although she is "as
fine a woman as you could hope to see," and lives
"only for her children," Sabina makes it plain
that, provided it benefited the children, Mrs. Antrobus would see "the rest of us stretched out
dead at her feet without turning a hair."

In addition to providing some of the comic
undercutting, Sabina is also used, and very early
in the play, to call attention to its unrealistic
character. In the first scene, she bursts out with
the remark that "the author hasn't made up his
silly mind as to whether we're all living back
in caves or in New Jersey today." She doesn't
understand the play. She says that she hates it.
She finds it a comedown to have to accept a part
in a piece of silly claptrap like this when she
has acted in celebrated "straight" plays such as
Rain and *The Barretts of Wimpole Street.*

Later on, however, Sabina suddenly catches
on, and stepping out of her role as character,
"says in her own person as Miss Somerset, with
surprise, 'Oh, *I* see what this part of the play
means now!' " When Mr. Antrobus and the
stage manager try to call her back to her proper
role, she insists on speaking directly to the audience, crying out: "Ladies and gentlemen! Don't
take this play serious. The world's not coming
to an end. You know it's not. People exaggerate!
Most people really have enough to eat and a
roof over their heads. Nobody actually starves—

you can always eat grass or something. That ice business—why, it was a long, long time ago. Besides they were only savages. Savages don't love their families—not like we do."

In the second act, Sabina refuses to play a scene because she has a friend in the audience who, thinking that her own situation was being referred to, might have her feelings hurt. At the very end of the play, Sabina speaks directly to the audience again, commenting on the fact that her last speech is identical with her first speech in the play, so that everything begins over again. The audience can go home now, but "the end of this play isn't written yet"—isn't written yet because the real play is the human endeavor in which all of us are caught up. In effect, Sabina is saying that the play is quite true and that the real play is still going on and cannot possibly end: the heads of the Antrobuses "are full of plans and they're as confident as the first day they began. . . ."

What does the playwright gain by exposing the theatrical conventions of the play in this fashion? Quite a number of things. By having Sabina express her bewilderment with the historical anachronisms, he indicates to his audience that they are deliberate and meaningful. By taking the audience from time to time *inside* the play instead of merely looking at it from across the footlights, the playwright has found a way to call our attention to the mechanism—and the meaning—of his play. By having Sabina insist that it is just a play and later that it is not just a play, the playwright suggests that the real "play" with which he is concerned is continuous with life itself. This is the sort of effect achieved by Sabina's speech at the end of the play.

One way to view Sabina is to regard her as a sort of chorus. In *Oedipus the King* we saw that the function of the chorus was to comment on the action, expressing the hopes, fears, anticipations, and anxieties of the audience as it watched the tragic spectacle. (*Murder in the Cathedral,* as we have seen, is another play with a formal chorus which has a somewhat similar, though not identical, function.) For all her goodnatured flightiness and triviality, Sabina becomes an effective means for the author's commentary on the events which the audience is witnessing.

Sabina, of course, is much more than a chorus. She is the temptress, the "other woman," the voice of banality, the flighty servant girl, the principal "comic." But she is only one of the many sources of comedy. The anachronisms, the scrambled history, the jangling of clichés, and most of all the foibles of the Antrobuses, are exploited for comic effect. At the very beginning of the play we are told that a wedding ring found in a movie house is inscribed "To Eva from Adam. Genesis II:18." The ring, of course, might have been lost by a twentieth-century Eva Smith, to whom it had been given by a certain Adam Jones, a young man who was a life-insurance agent, taught a Sunday school class, and thought it might be nice to cite the passage from Genesis in the ring. Such juxtapositions are not only amusing but, placed early in the play like this one, are hints as to what the real "time scheme" of the play is. The cleaning woman's discovery of the ring puts Adam and Eve in a new perspective, but it puts the modern inhabitants of New York City in a new perspective too.

Most of the people in the play, like Sabina, talk in platitudes and clichés. The announcer, giving his "News Events of the World," in which he features Mr. Antrobus as the discoverer of the wheel, describes Antrobus as a veteran of foreign wars, and says that he bears "a number of scars, front and back." The usual form of this oratorical phrase commends a person for having "all his scars in front," with the implication that he has never turned his back to the enemy. But the announcer, almost absent-mindedly, tell us the truth about Mr. Antrobus: he has fought some valiant battles and received honorable scars in the proper places, but like most of the rest of us, Mr. Antrobus has evidently sometimes run away in order to be able to fight another day.

The comedy characteristic of this play derives, however, from something deeper and more permanent than the mere temporary shock effect of startling juxtapositions between the life of cave men and life in suburban New Jersey of the 1940's, or the ragging and teasing of the expressions that we so constantly and thoughtlessly use. The essential comedy is based squarely upon human nature. Man remains, throughout the ages and in his various vicissitudes, much the same: amazing, cantankerous, foolish, and yet somehow a brave and admirable creature. Moreover, his folly and what, in an older America, would have been called his general "orneriness," are intimately tied up with his admirable qualities. Mr. Antrobus may occasionally break a law, but his respect for Moses the lawgiver and for law as the bedrock of civilization is genuine. He may have a foolish pride in his own accomplishments, but he is a genuine idealist, and his reverence for the great thinkers of Western civilization is profound. Mrs. Antrobus may focus her sympathies upon her own family—*her* husband and *her* son and *her* daughter. But she justifies the relative narrowness of her sympathies by her power to endure misfortune and hold the family together. Even Sabina has some admirable as well as amiable traits. One remembers her concern for the embittered Henry Antrobus at the end of Act III. In this play, human nature and the human enterprise are seen in a comic light, but it is not a withering light that dries and shrivels the heroic qualities in man.

EXERCISE

1. May it be said that playwright has divided his typical woman into two—into Mrs. Antrobus, the mother, the mate to whom her husband always finally returns, the basic prop of the family, and Sabina, the romantic attraction just across the fence from dull matrimony? Is Gladys, the daughter, to be taken as a third segment of the eternal woman? Why has the author not found it necessary to divide up his typical man in the same fashion? Or has he actually divided typical man by representing father and son in their potential rivalry?

2. Henry's past crime is obviously the principal skeleton in the Antrobus family closet. His original name, Cain, points back to the archetypal murderer, the son of Adam and Eve, who killed his brother Abel. Wilder uses the incident for various effects—the intractability of all boys and the desire of the family to conceal the blot on its good name, but Henry's Cain-like conduct evidently points to some more somber experience in the human story. Notice, for example, the effect on Mr. Antrobus when (p. 881) he hears that Henry has thrown a stone at the boy next door. Why should this boyish act have such a troubling effect on his father? Can you connect this general interpretation of Henry with the author's stage direction given on page 900: "Throughout the following scene Henry is played, not as a misunderstood or misguided young man, but as a representation of strong unreconciled evil"?

3. What is the significance of the incident in Act II when Mrs. Antrobus, in her desperate attempt to find Henry, finally calls him by his original name, Cain? Is the point that when the going gets really difficult enough, we drop our pretenses and call things by their true names? Or is the basic point that, murderer or not, the mother loves her son and means to save him even if she has to call him by the accursed name? Or do you have some other explanation for the effect and significance of the incident?

4. Is the happy ending of this play—even if it is to be regarded as only a temporary and provisional happy ending—based in good part on the fact that Henry and his father do become reconciled with each other? Notice Henry's speech to his father on page 901. What is the significance of Mr. Antrobus's speech—the one beginning "Wait a minute" (p. 901)?

5. How do the faults and virtues of Mrs. Antrobus balance those of her husband? Is she less idealistic than her husband, or more idealistic? Is she more passionate, or more reasonable, or can one state the basic difference between this husband and wife in such terms as these? In this general connection, consider the end of Act I. The refugees are invited in for coffee and warmth. It is Mr. Antrobus who has invited them in, and Mrs. Antrobus rather scolds her husband for having done so. Does this mean that Mrs. Antrobus is less kindhearted than her husband? Or what?

6. What do you think of the argument that Mrs. Antrobus makes about the nature of marriage (p. 892)? What thing or combination of things brings Mr. Antrobus back to his wife and out of the snare that Sabina has woven for him?

7. What is the justification for the way in which Act III opens? The stage manager has to call the play to a halt, explain about the illness of some of the actors, work out substitutions, and have the substitute actors recite the opening and closing lines of their speeches to make sure that they know them. The stage manager tells the audience that for Mr. Antrobus "Each of the hours of the night is a philosopher, or a great thinker. Eleven o'clock, for instance, is Aristotle. And nine o'clock is Spinoza." He goes on to apologize for this whimsy on Mr. Antrobus's part by saying: "I don't suppose it means anything. It's just a kind of poetic effect." After this little impromptu rearrangement and partial rehearsal, Act III begins again and runs on through; but surely enough, at the end of the play when Mr. Antrobus finds that his books are safe, the substitute actors come forward to recite their passages from Spinoza, Plato, Aristotle, and the book of Genesis. Does the fact that these speeches have been anticipated diminish the effect they give us now? Or enhance it? What would be the difference of effect if, without this little business at the beginning of Act III to forewarn us, the actors simply walked on at the end of the play to recite their passages? Does this use of the philosophers, by the way, mean anything? Is it just a kind of "poetic effect"?

8. If, at the end of the play, the eloquent passages spoken by the hours do come with a very different effect, what is the nature of that effect? Is it just a kind of "poetic effect" in some fancy and superficial sense? Or do these passages from Spinoza and Plato and Aristotle and the Book of Genesis come with a special power, answering to and expressing the deeper poetry of the human experience. What is their special relevance to the underlying theme of the play?

9. What is the point about the substitute actors? Do they help "universalize" the play? Make it apply to all men? Is Wilder saying that in a sense any of us can find a part in this play?

10. What is the basic view of man implied by this play? Does it resemble the view of man taken by B. F. Skinner? Or by Joseph Wood Krutch? Or by Matthew Arnold?

11. Would you say that the author of this play was optimistic about the future of mankind? Does he believe in progress? What does he seem to think is the most important thing about mankind? Does the fact that he sees the human enterprise in a comic light make his concern for the human enterprise less serious or more serious?

12. Thus far the student has been asked to look at this play as constituting a kind of parable about mankind, and to be on the alert to see symbolic meanings and connections in the various incidents. But if generalizations about civilization were the only matter of importance, Thornton Wilder need not have written a play at all. He might have given us a little sheaf of comments and observations on the nature of the human animal, or a kind of exhortation, such as William Faulkner wrote in his Nobel Prize speech, expressing his belief that man will endure and, even if this planet is blown up, will not only endure, but "prevail." What does the play "say" that could not be "said" in a speech or an editorial, or any other piece of discursive prose?

13. If *The Skin of Our Teeth* may in some sense be read as a parable about man, how has the playwright kept it from becoming a dull and rather empty parable? What is accomplished by the dramatic form? As the playwright has managed matters, the very act of dramatizing the issues involves us as readers or spectators and makes us participate imaginatively in what the dramatist has to tell us about our lives. What is the perspective in which we are asked to look at ourselves and our history? What is the tone of this play? Or, to put it in somewhat different terms, define and illustrate the precise kind of comedy which you find in *The Skin of Our Teeth*.

～GLOSSARY～

This Glossary does not attempt to give full or exhaustive definitions of the terms listed below. It does attempt to give a brief definition of the special sense or senses which the term has in literary criticism. In most cases, the term is treated rather fully in one of the "Introductions." References to these "Introductions" are abbreviated as follows: "Introduction to Poetry," as "Poetry"; "Introduction to Fiction," as "Fiction"; etc.

ABSTRACT: Abstractions are qualities and characteristics isolated as pure ideas. A piece of *sugar* is a concrete substance with its own qualities but we may *abstract* (literally *draw away*) from it *whiteness, hardness, sweetness.* Literature characteristically deals with the concrete rather than the abstract, and also the specific rather than the general. All of which is not to say that ideas, which are capable of being stated abstractly—love, courage, justice—are not involved in literature, but such ideas rarely emerge as abstractions; rather, they are incorporated in the concrete elements—in the case of fiction, in the particular characters and situations and events. The general observations that one may abstract from the particulars of a story—observations about human nature or about life—are not to be taken as the equivalent of the story. For a discussion of this point, see "Fiction," p. 15. See also CONCRETE.

ACT: In drama, a division of a play which may comprehend one or more SCENES. A scene usually represents an action occurring at a particular place and during one continuous period of time. What constitutes an *act* is more arbitrary and depends upon a unity felt by the playwright.

ACTION STORY: Fiction in which the principal element is plot suspense; *e.g.,* adventure or detective fiction. See "Fiction," p. 10.

ALEXANDRINE: A line consisting of six iambic feet. See HEXAMETER, p. 320.

ALLEGORY: An allegory is a kind of narrative in which the characters, objects, and events are to be taken not as real but as standing for some set of ideas. That is, each item in the narrative is equated with some item among the ideas. For example, in Bunyan's *Pilgrim's Progress* the character Christian, who leaves his home

to go to the Celestial City, is not to be taken as a real individual but as the type of all people who try to lead the Christian life, and each event that he encounters on his journey stands for some problem in the spiritual life. In an allegory there are frequently PERSONIFICATIONS. To personify is to give the qualities of a person to an inanimate object or to an idea. For instance, Keats in the poem "To Autumn" (p. 419) presents the season as a beautiful woman drowsing in a half-reaped field. (For another example, see pp. 381-83.) The chief danger in using allegory is that the system of equivalents may seem too complicated or too forced. See also SYMBOL. The chief distinction between allegory and symbol is this: the word *allegory* usually implies a thoroughgoing and mutually related *set* of symbols, a *system* of equivalents.

ALLITERATION: Identity of initial consonants in a group of words. See "Mechanics of Verse," p. 323.

AMBIGUITY: Multiplicity of meaning. In expository prose, ambiguity is a defect, for what is wanted is one clear, unequivocal meaning—not a doubtful or obscure statement. A more accurate term for poetic ambiguity is richness of meaning. See pp. 384-85.

ANAPAEST: A foot composed of two unaccented syllables followed by one accented syllable. See "Mechanics of Verse," p. 319.

ANECDOTE: A brief narrative usually having to do with some detached and isolated event.

ANTICLIMAX: A break in the climactic order of events or effects; a falling off from the expected intensification of effect. See CLIMAX.

ASSONANCE: Identity of vowel sounds in accented syllables without the identity of the following consonants See "Mechanics of Verse," p. 323.

ATMOSPHERE: The general pervasive feeling aroused by the various factors such as setting, character, theme, etc., in a piece of literature; the general effect on the reader of the handling of the total work. To be distinguished from SETTING. See "Fiction," pp. 24-25. Also to be distinguished from TONE (which see).

BALLAD: A ballad is a song that tells a story. A ballad such as "Sir Patrick Spens" (see p. 283) was originally sung, though now it is read like other poems. There are two general classes of ballads: (1) Popular, or Fold, Ballad and (2) Literary Ballad. "Sir Patrick Spens" is a folk ballad, for instance. Nobody knows who originally made up the poem or exactly what the original version was. But we do know how it was preserved. It was passed down by word of mouth (oral tradition), constantly being changed by the bad memory or the power of imagination of different people. A poem preserved in such a fashion would necessarily be simple in form. It would also tend to employ repetition and refrain, in part as aids to memory. There would be little or no comment or moralizing on the story, for the treatment would be objective and dramatic. The materials treated would be of a kind to appeal to a large number of rather simple people: a shipwreck in "Sir Patrick Spens," the murder of Johnny by his sweetheart in "Frankie and Johnny," etc. A literary ballad is an imitation of the method and the effect of the folk ballad by a professional poet, such as A. E. Housman, who wrote "The True Lover," (see p. 297). The literary ballad is preserved in the ordinary way, that is, by writing it down or by printing it.

BLANK VERSE: Unrimed iambic pentameter verse. See "Mechanics of Verse," p. 325.

CAESURA: The main pause within a line of verse. See "Mechanics of Verse," p. 322.

CHORUS: In ancient Greek drama, a singing and dancing group whose speeches comment upon or interpret the action. The chorus is occasionally used in later plays (see *Murder in the Cathedral,* p. 733) or a particular character may sometimes be said to have something of the interpretative function of a chorus (*e.g.,* Enobarbus in *Antony and Cleopatra:* note his speeches in Act II, Scene ii, p. 712).

CHRONICLE: An account of events arranged in the order of the time of happening; sometimes applied to a story which has relatively light emphasis on the central situation. See also EPISODE.

CLICHÉ: A phrase that has lost its force because of continued use. See the analysis of "To Ianthe," p. 331. See also for a justifiable use of the cliché the analysis of "That the Night Come," on p. 317. The cliché is one kind of appeal to a STOCK RESPONSE on the part of the reader. See SENTIMENTALITY.

CLIMAX: The highest point in an ascending series; in fiction or drama, for example, the point where the forces reach their moment of highest concentration. See "Fiction," p. 23, see also pp. 319, 356, and 619. An ANTICLIMAX is a break in the climactic order—a falling off from the expected intensification of effect.

COINCIDENCE: An accidental coming together of certain events. For the legitimate and the illegitimate use of coincidence in fiction, see "Fiction," pp. 13-14. See also pp. 47-49.

COMEDY: For discussions of this rich and complex term, and related terms such as COMIC, see pp. 87, 107-08, "Drama," 615-16, and pp. 865-68.

COMPLICATION: The interplay between character and event that builds up tension and develops a problem out of the situation given in the beginning of the story. See "Fiction," p. 23 and "Drama," pp. 618-19.

CONCRETE: Literature, especially poetry, fiction, and drama, aims, in large part, at being concrete and not abstract, particular and not general. It appeals to sensation, direct observation, perception, and experience. A novelist may wish to express an idea in his novel, but he does not give it to us in a series of general statements or in an argument; instead, he writes a novel, a long story which makes us feel the force of his idea. A poet, Robert Burns for instance, does not say merely, "I am in love." That would be a general, or an abstract, statement. Instead, he tries to convey to the reader the quality of his love by a set of particular comparisons. He says, "My love is like a red, red rose." Then he proceeds to give other comparisons, each of which adds to the concreteness of the poem. See p. 335. See also IMAGERY. Literature does treat of general ideas and abstractions, but it aims to express those ideas so that they can be felt concretely. The idea in literature is interesting just in so far as it finds an expression that will appeal to emotion.

CONFLICT: Some kind of conflict is central to any piece of fiction or drama. The conflict is involved in the original situation and is developed in the action, and the concern with the outcome generates the basic suspense. See "Fiction," pp. 11-12, and "Drama," p. 615.

CONNOTATION: See DENOTATION.

CONSONANCE: Identity of consonants of words without identity of vowels. See "Mechanics of Verse," p. 323.

CONVENTIONAL: A thing is said to be conventional when it is usual or expected: the term in particular carries the association of use in the past. For example, the fleetingness of beauty is a conventional theme in poetry, for poets in all ages have used it. So also certain forms, like the sonnet, for instance, are said to be conventional forms. To say that a theme or a form or a choice of words is conventional, however, is not necessarily to condemn it. (See p. 317.) Writers of literature have to work in terms of *conventions*, accepted ways of doing things. (See pp. 204-05). Most sound literature is to some extent conventional, but it uses its conventions for its purpose, freshening them and relating them to what is new. It does not—as in a mawkish poem, for instance—depend entirely upon them.

COUPLET: Two lines riming or unrimed. See "Mechanics of Verse," p. 324.

DACTYL: A foot composed of one accented syllable followed by two unaccented syllables. See "Mechanics of Verse," p. 320.

DENOTATION: The exact thing indicated by a word. It is opposed to CONNOTATION which means the thing or things suggested by a word, or *associated* with it. In Coleridge's lines

> In Xanadu did Kubla Khan
> A stately pleasure-dome decree

the word Xanadu *denotes* a special place on the map presumably, but it *connotes* something of remoteness, historical glamour, and Oriental splendor. The same applies to the name of the ruler, Kubla Khan. A word like *rose* carries a different connotation as well as denotation from a word like *dog fennel*. The same applies to *o'er* and *over*, *thou* and *you*, *bark* and *boat*, and numerous other pairs of words. It is a mistake to think that the word of the more remote, romantic, or fanciful connotation is better for poetry; generally it is poetical in a bad sense when used in modern poetry because it does not belong to our living language. (There are, however, no absolute rules on this point.)

DÉNOUEMENT: The untieing of the plot; the final resolution of the complications of the plot. (See pp. 23-24.) It sometimes, but not always, coincides with the climax. See CLIMAX.

DICTION: Diction is simply the choice of words in poetry or in any other form of discourse. Critics sometimes refer to POETIC DICTION as if certain words were especially poetic in themselves. But the choice of words for any given poem must be determined by the needs of that specific poem in terms of the whole context of the poem. See "Fiction," pp. 20-21. See also the analysis of "To Ianthe," p. 331, the double analysis of "His Books," and "On an Invitation to the United States," p. 337. See also DENOTATION and TONE.

DIMETER: A line consisting of two feet. See "Mechanics of Verse," p. 320.

DRAMATIC: This term is used with two meanings. The first, and more general, meaning implies the presence of a sharp struggle or conflict, or tension. (See "Drama," p. 615.) The second, and more specific, meaning refers to the way in which a scene, in a short story, for instance, is presented when action and dialogue are given without interpretation or comment by the author in a direct form. Of the short stories included in this volume, "The Killers" (p. 137) is clearly the most "dramatic" in method.

ELEGY: The term is used loosely for any poem of subjective and meditative nature, but more specially for a poem expressing grief.

END-STOPPED: A line of verse in which there is a definite pause at the end of the line. See "Mechanics of Verse," p. 321.

ENJAMBEMENT: See RUN-ON.

EPIC: A long narrative poem dealing with persons of heroic proportions and actions of great significance: for example, Homer's *Iliad* or Milton's *Paradise Lost*.

EPILOGUE: In drama, a concluding speech (or even scene), not a part of the dramatic action proper. Shaw calls the last scene of *Saint Joan*—the time is twenty-five years after Joan's death—an epilogue. The term is used more loosely to refer to a part of a story or novel that winds up matters and falls outside the action proper.

EPISODE: A separate incident in a larger piece of action. The term EPISODIC is used to describe a plot, for example, which is characterized by a rather loose linking together of separate incidents without much regard for cause and effect. In such cases one incident does not occur as a logical consequence of a previous incident, but merely follows it in time. See CHRONICLE.

EXPOSITION: The process of providing the reader with necessary information. See "Fiction," pp. 21-22; also "Drama," p. 618.

FAMILIAR ESSAY: See PERSONAL ESSAY.

FICTION: The term used to distinguish an unhistorical account from an historical; with special reference to literature, see "Fiction," pp. 9ff.

FICTIONAL POINT: The essential meaning of a piece of fiction; the basic theme brought into sharp focus. See THEME.

FEMININE ENDING: An ending in which a line closes with an extra unaccented syllable in addition to the normal accented syllable. See "Mechanics of Verse," pp. 321, 326.

FEMININE RIME: A rime of two syllables of which the second is unstressed. See "Mechanics of Verse," p. 323.

FIGURE OF SPEECH: See IMAGERY.

FIRST PERSON NARRATOR: See POINT OF VIEW.

FOCUS: The center around which the material of an imaginative work is organized. See "Fiction," pp. 18-19.

FOOT: The smallest combination of unaccented and accented syllables occurring in verse. See "Mechanics of Verse," p. 319.

FORCED PAUSE: A pause forced by the poet's handling of the various metrical elements in the line. See, for example, p. 318 and p. 319.

FORESHADOWING: The process of giving the reader an intimation of some event which is to follow later. See the analysis of "Edward," p. 291, and of *Saint Joan,* p. 802.

FORM: The arrangement of various elements in a work of literature; the organization of various materials (ideas, images, characters, setting, and the like) to give a single effect. It may be said that a story is successful—that it has achieved form—when all of the elements are functionally related to each other, when each part contributes to the intended effect. Form is not to be thought of merely as a sort of container for the story; it is, rather, the total principle of organization and affects every aspect of the composition. It is the mode in which the story exists. STRUCTURE and STYLE are also used to indicate the author's arrangement of his materials to give his effect. *Structure,* however, is usually used with more special reference to the ordering of the larger elements such as episodes, scenes, and details of action, in contrast to the arrangement of words, for which the term *style* is ordinarily employed. In the fullest sense, both the terms become synonymous with form, but in this book *style* is used merely to refer to the selection and ordering of language. See "General Introduction," p. 8. (For metrical form, see "Mechanics of Verse," pp. 319-26.)

FREE VERSE: Verse which does not conform to a fixed metrical pattern. See p. 283, and such poems as Whitman's "Come Up from the Fields, Father," p. 333, or Williams' "The Red Wheelbarrow," p. 303.

HEPTAMETER: A line consisting of seven feet. See "Mechanics of Verse," p. 320.

HERO: The word *hero,* is used to indicate the main character of a literary work. The word does not imply that the character is admirable.

HEROIC COUPLET: Two consecutive lines of iambic pentameter riming together. See "Mechanics of Verse," p. 324.

HEXAMETER: A line consisting of six feet. See "Mechanics of Verse," p. 320.

IAMB: A foot composed of an unaccented syllable followed by an accented syllable. See "Mechanics of Verse," p. 319.

IMAGERY: The calling to mind of something perceived by the senses. A poem, for example, is strong in imagery when it provokes a picture or sensation of touch, taste, sound, or odor. *Visual imagery* (picture) is most common and effective, with *aural imagery* (imagery of sound) probably next in importance. But a poet may sometimes give imagery of a sort more unusual than those mentioned above. Observe the following lines:

> The singular screech-owl's tight
> Invisible lyric . . .

The word *tight,* used to describe the sound of a screech-owl, provokes another kind of imagery, what might be called *muscular imagery. Tight* describes the way the throat would feel if one were trying to imitate the call of the screech-owl. Furthermore, a writer may sometimes use imagery belonging properly to one sense to describe something belonging to another sense. For instance, one poet, in describing a dull, rainy morning, has written:

> The morning light creaks down again.

Light, we know, does not creak, for it is soundless. But the poet is trying to convey the impression that the dawn is slow and difficult as though the light were old and worn out.

The literary artist is interested in the physical nature of the world as it appears to his senses, just as the painter or sculptor is. Poetry especially depends upon *concreteness;* it attempts to present the qualities of things. The writer, especially the poet, tries to make the reader see, feel, hear, touch, and even taste, because it is by appealing to the senses that he can

convince the reader of the reality of what he is saying. But he does not do this merely by direct description. He is constantly employing FIGURES OF SPEECH,
or figurative language as it may be called, to do this
and to express his ideas. The most common forms
of such language are called SIMILES and METAPHORS.
A SIMILE is a direct comparison of two things. For
instance: "He runs like a deer," or "Her eyes are like
stars." But a poet is always trying to make his similes
more fresh and accurate than the old comparisons
given above:

> But when he meant to quail and shake the orb,
> He was *as* rattling thunder . . .
>
> How *like* a winter hath my absence been . . .

The comparison of a simile is announced by *like* or
as. The METAPHOR, on the contrary, does not announce that comparison, but apparently declares an
identification of the two things. A plumber speaks of
the *elbow* of a pipe, not saying that the bend of the
pipe is *like* an elbow; or a carpenter speaks of the
tongue of a board. Such words represent originally
metaphorical identifications, but now *elbow* or *tongue*
has come by long use to be the actual name of the
thing. As metaphors they have been conventionalized.
The following metaphors are different in that they
have not been adopted into the language but retain
their poetic force:

> For his *bounty*
> There was no winter in it; an autumn 'twas
> That grew the more by reaping.
>
> Was it the proud full *sail* of his great *verse*.
>
> Lift up your *heads*, O ye *gates*.

In each of these instances an identification is given:
the *gates* are supposed to have *heads*, that is, to be living beings; a fine poet's *verse* is given a *sail*, that is,
is identified with a ship in motion; Antony's *bounty*,
according to Cleopatra's statement, is an *autumn*, the
season of harvest. (See p. 744.)

This kind of language is at the very center of poetry
or poetic observation; it is what people usually mean
when they say something sounds poetic.

Observe the ascending intensity, or edge, of the following expressions:

> The night is dark.
> The night is black as pitch.
> The night is black as the inside of a wolf's belly.

The first is a pure statement, the second a thoroughly
conventional comparison, the third an expression that
still retains a good deal of poetic force and violence.
The third still possesses an appeal to the imagination
and a kind of novelty, or surprise; the second does
not.

The poet is constantly regarding the items in the
world about him as related by such connections. He
gives these connections in his poetry for various purposes or combinations of various purposes:

(a) *Illustration:* This is the ordinary use of such
language in prose, but it also appears in poetry. A
writer of a handbook on physiology might say, in explaining the nervous system, that *a nerve is like a
telegraphic wire*. His only purpose is using this *simile*
is to make clear to the reader the function of the
nerve.

(b) *Ornament* or *Decoration:* This is the use that
often appears in poetry, or in the kind of prose called
"flowery." When it is used badly it distracts from
what is said: the ornament is admired because it is
pretty or interesting in itself and not because it makes
clearer the thing to which it is applied. When it is
used well, the appropriateness of the tone of the comparison, or the grandeur of the thing suggested lifts
and dignifies the original object. Such a use as (b)
generally implies also a certain illustrative aspect.
This passage from Milton shows a fine use of the
ornamental simile in describing the appearance of
Delilah:

> But who is this, what thing of Sea or Land?
> Female of sex it seems,
> That so bedeckt, ornate, and gay,
> Comes this way sailing
> Like a stately Ship
> Of Tarsus, bound for th' Isles
> Of Javan or Gadier
> With all her bravery on, and tackle trim,
> Sails filled, and streamers waving,
> Courted by all the winds that hold them play,
> An Amber scent of odorous perfume
> Her harbinger, a damsel train behind. . . .

Here the ship itself is described at length in a romantic and magnificent way from lines 6 to 11, more
emphasis being given to the ship than to the woman
to whom it is compared and who is, after all, the important object for the purpose of the action. Artis-
tically, however, the poet reintroduces the woman by
reference to a "damsel train" at the last of the passage so that the reader may not be taken too far away
from the main point. But the emphasis of the passage
is ornamental; its purpose is primarily to enrich and
ennoble the appearance of the woman, Delilah.

(c) *Necessary Communication:* This is the most important use in poetry and the most effective. By it the
poet says something that otherwise he could not say
at all or, at least, could not say with anything near
the same economy. (And poetic expression for many
poets has as its ideal economical statement.) Housman
writes about Death:

> Before this fire of sense decay,
> This smoke of thought blow clean away,

And leave with ancient night alone
The steadfast and enduring bone.

The metaphors in the first two lines (1) convey a very complicated idea (not necessarily scientific) about the relation of *sense* to *thought*—which without the metaphors would require an elaborate explanation; (2) give a feeling of the violence of physical life and appetite and the frailty or accidental quality of *thought*, which we usually regard as the directing factor in life; (3) define the pathos of the short tenure of both; (4) and by implication direct the reader to an attitude of stoicism or acceptance. This inadequate prose summary may show what a range and variety of material may be communicated by a single metaphor. This use of metaphor demands, like the *illustrative* use, a basis of comparison which holds the reader by its apparent accuracy, but unlike the accuracy of the *illustrative* use, this is a *new-discovered accuracy*. Further, unlike the *ornamental use,* this use does not demand a comparison that lifts, ennobles, or dignifies the objects. See also "Poetry," pp. 279-81. See also pp. 336-37, 362-63, and 367-68.

IMPERFECT FOOT: A metrical foot in which the unaccented syllable (or syllables) is lacking. See p. 319 and "Mechanics of Verse," p. 320.

INEVITABILITY: The sense that the result presented is the only possible result of the situation already presented. See "Fiction," p. 13.

INFORMAL ESSAY: See PERSONAL ESSAY.

INTERNAL RIME: Rime occurring within a line unit. See "Mechanics of Verse," p. 323.

IRONY: Irony always involves contrast, a discrepancy between the expected and the actual, between the apparent and the real. Such contrast may appear in many forms. A speaker uses irony, for example, when he deliberately says something which he does not mean, but indicates by his tone what he does mean. UNDERSTATEMENT—the saying of less than one feels the occasion would warrant—and PARADOX—the saying of something which is apparently untrue but which on examination proves to be true, or partially true—both of these are forms of irony. In addition to such forms of IRONY OF STATEMENT, there are also various forms of IRONY OF SITUATION. The irony of situation involves a discrepancy between what we expect the outcome of an action to be, to what would seem to be the fitting outcome, and the actual outcome. In dealing with this term, the student should always remember that there are a thousand subtle shadings of irony, and must, therefore, not take it in too restricted a sense, for example, in the sense of obvious sarcasm. Reference to, and discussion of, different kinds of ironical effect may be found on pp. 19, 48, 131, 286, 292, 341, 385, 390, 398, and 695.

ITALIAN SONNET: A sonnet composed of an octet, riming a-b-b-a-a-b-b-a, and of a sestet riming c-d-e-c-d-e (or with a variation of the c-d-e rimes). See "Mechanics of Verse," p. 325.

LENGTH VARIATION: Variation in the amount of time required to pronounce varying syllables. See "Mechanics of Verse," p. 322.

LOGIC: The relation of cause and effect which exists between character and character, or character and setting, in fiction or drama. See "Fiction," pp. 13-14.

LYRIC: The term is used in two senses: (1) A short musical poem. This use is descriptive of the technique. (2) A poem (or other literary work) directly expressing the personality of the writer; that is, SUBJECTIVE rather than OBJECTIVE in emphasis, giving the personal vision of, or reaction to, the world. This use describes the subject matter or philosophy of a literary work.

MASCULINE ENDING: An ending in which a line closes with an accented syllable. See FEMININE ENDING.

MASCULINE RIME: The common form of rime, in which the rimed syllables are the last syllables of the riming words. See "Mechanics of Verse," p. 323.

MELODRAMA: A play which depends largely on the plot suspense rather than on character. Compare the adventure story in fiction ("Fiction," p. 10). See "Drama," p. 615.

METAPHOR: See IMAGERY, and see "Poetry," pp. 279-80.

METER: The pattern on which rhythm is systematized in verse. See "Mechanics of Verse," pp. 319-22.

MONOMETER: A line consisting of one foot. See "Mechanics of Verse," p. 320.

MOTIVATION: By *motive* we understand the purpose of a person's act. Motivation, therefore, is understood in fiction or drama as the purpose, or mixture of purposes, that determines a character's behavior. See "Fiction," pp. 10-11.

NOVELETTE: Literally, a little novel. In a rough and ready way we call a piece of fiction a novelette when it runs from some 10,000 words to some 35,000. Anything longer than 35,000 words, more or less, we call a novel. But we may think of a novelette as being more than a long story. We may expect it to show something of the complication of a novel. See pp. 204-06.

OBJECTIVE: This adjective, as applied to literature, indicates an attitude of detachment on the part of the author toward the facts he is presenting. He refrains from giving his personal interpretation or commentary; therefore, the term *impersonal* in this connection is often used as synonymous with *objective*. The method of a dramatist who merely presents his characters in dialogue is an objective method. A SUBJECTIVE description, on the other hand, is one which is highly colored by the author's personal feelings. Obviously, one will not find a completely objective attitude in literature, for that attitude belongs properly to science. One does find, however, relative degrees of objectivity in literature. See the analysis of "The Eagle," p. 302. See also LYRIC.

OCTET: The first part (an eight-line unit) of an Italian sonnet. See "Mechanics of Verse," p. 325.

ODE: A rather extended poem, usually complicated in metrical and stanzaic form, dealing with a serious theme.

OMNISCIENT NARRATOR: See POINT OF VIEW.

ONOMATOPOEIA: Imitation of sense by sound. See "Mechanics of Verse," pp. 322-23.

PACE: The rate of speed with which the various parts of a story are made to move, ranging from summary to fully reported scene. See p. 158 and p. 185.

PARABLE: A parable is a short, allegorical narrative. Our most famous parables are those found in the Bible, for instance, the parable of the sower in the Gospel according to St. Mark. See also ALLEGORY.

PARADOX: A statement, apparently untrue, which on closer examination is seen to be true in reality. For example, the poet Lovelace writes:

I could not love thee dear so much
Loved I not honor more.

Keats writes:

Heard melodies are sweet, but those unheard
Are sweeter . . . (p. 416)

Paradox is often used for effects of IRONY (which see).

PERSONAL ESSAY: An essay characterized by a familiar or informal or personal tone. See pp. 432-33.

PERSONIFICATION: See ALLEGORY.

PLOT: The structure of the action in fiction or drama. See "Fiction," pp. 12-13 and p. 18.

POETIC DICTION: See DICTION.

POINT OF VIEW: The term is sometimes used, generally and loosely, to refer to the way in which a writer looks at his material. But used more strictly—as the editors will consistently use it in discussing the stories in this book—it refers to the mind through which the material of the story is presented.

Obviously a story does not exist without a point of view, for otherwise the action would have no structure or meaning; there would indeed be no story. What are some of the possible points of view that may be used? The story may be narrated in the FIRST PERSON. Thus, a writer of fiction may let a character speak in his own person to serve as the teller of the story. The character might be the hero telling his own story or he might be one of the minor characters reporting what he saw and heard.

But the writer may tell his story in the THIRD PERSON—either looking at his characters as an outside observer might do or entering into the minds and thoughts of such of them as he chooses to look at from the inside. We might call this latter point of view that of the OMNISCIENT, or all-knowing, narrator. But even the omniscient narrator does not present everything, for he selects the material for presentation in accordance with some plan in his own mind.

There are many possible variations of the point of view. In general, however, it is important to remember that by adopting a point of view the author is enabled to select and organize his material for fiction. See "Fiction," pp. 19-20, 36, 49, 71, 81 and "Drama," pp. 614-15.

PROPAGANDA: Literature which tends to state the theme abstractly, which tends to insist on the "message" at the expense of other qualities, is called propaganda literature. See "Fiction," pp. 14-15, and pp. 397-98.

PROTAGONIST: See HERO.

QUANTITATIVE VARIATION: See LENGTH VARIATION.

QUATRAIN: A stanza composed of four lines. See "Mechanics of Verse," p. 324.

REALISTIC: Having a strong sense of fact or of actuality. The term is sometimes used as the opposite of ROMANTIC. A romantic attitude may be described very summarily here as being an attitude in which the sense of fact is weakened in favor of ideality or in which the object in question is suffused with emotion, particularly with warmth of emotion. No attempt is made in this text to go into the distinction between *romantic* and *classic*.

RHETORICAL VARIATION: Variation in the movement of a line dictated by considerations of the sense of particular words. See "Mechanics of Verse," pp. 320-22.

RHYTHM: Cadenced movement in sound. All spoken language has some rhythmic quality but we tend not to notice it unless the recurrent beat is stressed. See "Poetry," pp. 282-84, and "Mechanics of Verse," pp. 319-23.

RIME: Correspondence in two or more words between the sound of their last accented syllables (and whatever syllables follow them). See "Mechanics of Verse," p. 323.

RIME SCHEME: The pattern of rime within a stanza. See "Mechanics of Verse," p. 324.

ROMANTIC: See REALISTIC.

RUN-ON: A line of verse in which there is not a definite pause at the end of the line. See "Mechanics of Verse," pp. 321-22.

SCALE: The proportion of space allotted to the treatment of events in a piece of fiction. See pp. 158, 185, and 206.

SCENE: See ACT.

SECONDARY ACCENT: Stress on a normally unaccented syllable weaker than that of a primary accent but heavier than the light stress called for by strict metrical pattern. See "Mechanics of Verse," p. 321.

SELECTIVITY: The choosing of the necessary and expressive elements and details which a writer thinks will best serve his purpose. See "Fiction," pp. 17-18.

SENTIMENTALITY: Excess of emotion or emotion which has not been adequately prepared for by the work in question. See "General Introduction," pp. 5-6. See also the analyses of "To Ianthe," p. 331, of "The Need of Being Versed in Country Things," pp. 344-45, and of "Ode on Melancholy," pp. 349-52.

SESTET: The second part (a six-line unit) of an Italian sonnet. See "Mechanics of Verse," p. 325.

SETTING: The physical background, the element of place, in literature. See "Fiction," pp. 24-25.

SHAKESPEARIAN SONNET: A sonnet composed of three quatrains and a couplet, riming a-b-a-b,c-d-c-d,e-f-e-f, g-g. See "Mechanics of Verse," p. 325.

SIMILE: See IMAGERY and "Poetry," p. 281.

SLANT RIME: An approximate rime. See "Mechanics of Verse," p. 323.

SOLILOQUY: An utterance by a character who is talking to himself.

SONNET: A stanza of fourteen lines of iambic pentam-

eter. For the common rime schemes, see "Mechanics of Verse," pp. 324-25.

SPENSERIAN STANZA: A nine-line stanza of which the first eight lines are iambic pentameter; the ninth, iambic hexameter. The rime scheme is a-b-a-b-b-c-b-c-c. See "Mechanics of Verse," p. 324.

STANZA: A pattern of lines usually repeated as a unit of composition in a poem. See "Mechanics of Verse," pp. 323-25.

STOCK RESPONSE: The automatic or conventionalized response of a reader to some word, phrase, situation, or subject in literature. See "General Introduction," pp. 6-7. See also SENTIMENTALITY.

STRUCTURE: See FORM.

STYLE: See FORM.

SUBJECTIVE: See OBJECTIVE.

SUBPLOT: A plot subordinate to the main plot. See "Drama," p. 619.

SUBSTITUTION, METRICAL: The replacing of a foot normal to the line by a foot of different character. See "Mechanics of Verse," p. 320.

SUSPENSE: Uncertainty and excitement at the outcome of a series of events. See "Fiction," pp. 10-11.

SYMBOL: An object, character, or incident that stands for something else, or suggests something else, is a *symbol* of that other thing. There are many symbols that appear in ordinary life, for the use of symbol is by no means limited to art and literature. For instance, the flag is the symbol of a country, and the cross is the symbol of the Christian religion. These are symbols adopted by a whole society and are recognized by all members of such society. There are other kinds of symbols, such as the figure *4*, which may be called *abstract symbols*. But the poetic symbol is different from either of the other types. Generally speaking, it does not have a common social acceptance, as does the flag, for instance; it is, rather, a symbol that the poet adopts for the purpose of the poem, and that is to be understood only in the context of the poem. Secondly, it differs from the kind of symbol illustrated by the figure *4* in being concrete and special. The poet uses symbols for the same reason that he uses similes and metaphors: they help him to express his meaning in a way that will appeal to the senses and to the emotions of his reader. See IMAGERY and CONCRETE. See also, for discussion of symbols and symbolism in fiction, pp. 29, 124 and 157; in poetry, pp. 290-91, 298, 301, 312, and 327; and in drama, p. 662.

TALE: A narrative, without overt complication, which gives the impression of being something "told."

TERZA RIMA: Iambic pentameter tercets in linked rime. See "Mechanics of Verse," p. 324.

TETRAMETER: A line composed of four feet. See "Mechanics of Verse," p. 320.

THEME: The special view of life or special feeling about life or special sets of values which constitute the point or basic idea of a piece of literature. See "Fiction," p. 19. See also the double analysis of "His Books" and "On an Invitation to the United States," pp. 334-38; and the analysis of "Eighth Air Force," pp. 396-98.

THIRD-PERSON NARRATOR: See POINT OF VIEW.

TONE: The attitude (or attitudes) of the author as reflected in the form and structure of his work. In conversation, we often imply our attitude by the tone of voice that we use; and the tone of our utterance may very heavily qualify our literal statements. The skilful author is able, in an analogous way, to qualify what his work "says" by the way in which he "says" it. Indeed, if we are to understand a piece of literature, even on the simplest level, we must take into account its tone. Some examples of the importance of tone are to be found in the discussion of "Wet Saturday," pp. 86-87, "Legal Aid," pp. 95-96, "Neutral Tones," pp. 327-28, "The Need of Being Versed in Country Things," pp. 344-45, and "Song," pp. 354-56. See also SENTIMENTALITY.

TRAGEDY: For discussions of this rich and complex term, and related terms such as TRAGIC, see "Drama," pp. 286, 615-17, 665, and 697-98.

TRICK ENDING: In fiction, an ending that violates the laws of probability and fictional logic. See "Fiction," pp. 13-14.

TRIMETER: A line composed of three feet. See "Mechanics of Verse," p. 320.

TROCHEE: A foot composed of one accented syllable followed by one unaccented syllable. See "Mechanics of Verse," pp. 319-20.

UNITY: The sense of oneness—of having a total and final meaning. See "Fiction," pp. 11-12.

UNDERSTATEMENT: Saying less than one might be expected to say; a sense of restraint that underplays the occasion. See analysis of "To His Coy Mistress," pp. 389-91. See also IRONY.

VARIATION, METRICAL: Departure from the strict metrical pattern. See "Mechanics of Verse," pp. 320-23.

VERS DE SOCIÉTÉ: Light verse, usually occasional and complimentary, that deals in a witty and elegant fashion with pleasantly trivial subjects. See pp. 355-56 and 390.

VERSE: Rhythm patterned and systematized. See "Poetry," pp. 282-84.

VERSE-TEXTURE: The relation of the vowel and consonant sounds in verse. For an example, see the analysis of "Neutral Tones," pp. 327-28.

~~~~INDEX~~